WITHDRAWN

THE INDIANS
OF THE
SOUTHEASTERN
UNITED STATES

by

JOHN R. SWANTON

SMITHSONIAN INSTITUTION PRESS

WASHINGTON, D. C.

1979

Originally published 1946

Reprinted 1979
Second printing, 1984

Library of Congress Cataloging in Publication Data

Swanton, John Reed, 1873–1958.
 The Indians of the southeastern United States.

 (Classics in Smithsonian anthropology; 2)
 Reprint of the 1946 ed. published by the U. S. Govt.
Print. Off., which was issued as no. 137 of Bureau of
American Ethnology bulletin.
 Bibliography: p.
 Includes index.
 1. Indians of North America—Southern States.
I. Title. II. Series. III. Series: United States.
Bureau of American Ethnology. Bulletin; 137.
[E78.S65S9 1978]   975'.004'97   78–11039

 ISBN 0–87474–895–X

Reprint of
Smithsonian Institution
Bureau of American Ethnology Bulletin 137

This volume is a photographic reprint of the original edition, which was issued in 1946 as Smithsonian Institution, Bureau of American Ethnology Bulletin 137. However, the following changes have been made:

Plate 30: new image (the original edition reproduced a later copy of this painting in the state capitol, Atlanta, Georgia). Plate 33, figures 1 and 2: images transposed to correspond with the original captions. Plate 34, figure 1: new image (the original, with the current caption, published a portrait of John Ross from McKenney and Hall). Plate 37A: caption shortened (the original read, "as it appeared in 1920," but the building had been demolished by 1880); new print is from same source as the original, but additionally cropped at top and sides. Plate 42: "Drawn by Jacques Le Moyne" deleted (the drawing is now known to be from the late eighteenth century). Plate 43, figure 2: originally appeared as Plate 45, figure 2. Plate 45, figure 1: caption corrected by transposing original with one first published under current Plate 45, figure 2. Plate 45, figure 2: originally appeared as Plate 43, figure 2; caption corrected by transposing original with one first published under Plate 45, figure 1. Plate 47, figure 2: new image (the original, with the current caption, published a portrait of the same subject taken from McKenney and Hall). Plate 51: new image (the original, with the current caption, published Plate XIX, "Ritual Observed by Mourning [Timucua] Widows," instead of Plate XXI, "[Timucua] Method of Tilling the Ground and Sowing Seed" used here, from de Bry's engravings after Le Moyne). Plate 90: reproduced as a positive, rather than the negative used in the original edition.

All illustrations designated as being "after McKenney and Hall" have been replaced with photographs of earlier, better McKenney and Hall lithographs of the same subjects—except Plate 11, figure 2, and Plate 47, figure 1, for which there are no earlier versions.

Reproductions without credit lines directly beneath them have been made from new prints from the original negatives on file in the Smithsonian Institution National Anthropological Archives, except for Plate 38, figure 2, Plate 39, figure 2, Plate 40, figure 2, and Plate 50, for which negatives could not be located. For these four plates, screened reproductions in the original edition have been photocopied. Reproductions with credit lines directly beneath them are from new photographs, of the same originals, obtained from the indicated sources (NCFA = National Collection of Fine Arts, Smithsonian Institution) ; where these contradict Swanton's original credits, the latter have been deleted.

Corresponding corrections have been made in the list of illustrations on pages IX–XIII.

SMITHSONIAN INSTITUTION
BUREAU OF AMERICAN ETHNOLOGY
BULLETIN 137

THE INDIANS OF THE SOUTHEASTERN UNITED STATES

By

JOHN R. SWANTON

CONTENTS

	PAGE
Introduction	1
Geography of the Southeast	1
Classification of the Southeastern tribes	10
Population	11
Relation of the aboriginal population to the natural areas	14
Prehistoric movements	21
History of the Southeastern Indians from the period of first white contact to the expedition of Hernando de Soto	33
The expedition of Hernando de Soto	39
The post-De Soto period	59
Sketches of the Southeastern tribes and their population	81
Abibka	81
Acolapissa	82
Acuera	83
Adai	83
Aguacaleyquen (see Utina).	
Ais	84
Akokisa	85
Alabama	86
Amacano	88
Anadarko, or, more correctly, Nadako	89
Apalachee	89
Apalachicola	92
Atakapa	93
Atasi	94
Avoyel	94
Bayogoula	95
Bidai	96
Biloxi	96
Caddo	98
Cahinnio	100
Calusa	101
Caparaz	102
Cape Fear Indians	103
Capinans	103
Catawba	104
Chakchiuma	105
Chatot	107
Chawasha	108
Cheraw, Saraw, Sara	109
Cherokee	110
Chiaha	115
Chickasaw	116
Chilucan	119
Chine	119
Chitimacha	119
Choctaw	121

Sketches of the Southeastern tribes and their population—Continued.   PAGE
    Choula _____ 123
    Chowanoc _____ 124
    Congaree _____ 124
    Coosa _____ 124
    Coree or Coranine _____ 126
    Cosapuya (see Cusabo).
    Coweta _____ 126
    Creek Confederation _____ 128
    Cusabo _____ 128
    Deadose _____ 130
    Doustioni _____ 130
    Eno _____ 130
    Eufaula or Yufala _____ 131
    Eyeish or Ha-ish _____ 132
    Fresh Water ("Agua Dulce") Indians _____ 133
    Fus-hatchee _____ 133
    Grigra, or, more often, Gris _____ 134
    Guacata _____ 134
    Guale _____ 135
    Guasco _____ 136
    Hainai _____ 136
    Hatteras _____ 137
    Hilibi _____ 137
    Hitchiti _____ 138
    Hothliwahali, or, in abbreviated form, Thliwahali (Łiwahali) _____ 139
    Houma _____ 139
    Ibitoupa _____ 140
    Icafui _____ 141
    Iroquois (see Nottoway).
    Jeaga _____ 141
    Kadohadacho _____ 141
    Kan-hatki _____ 142
    Kasihta _____ 143
    Kaskinampo _____ 143
    Kealedji _____ 144
    Keyauwee _____ 144
    Koasati _____ 145
    Kolomi or Kulumi _____ 146
    Koroa _____ 147
    Macapiras or Amacapiras _____ 148
    Machapunga _____ 148
    Manahoac _____ 148
    Meherrin _____ 149
    Michigamea _____ 149
    Mikasuki _____ 150
    Mobile _____ 150
    Mococo or Mucoço _____ 151
    Monacan _____ 152
    Moneton _____ 152
    Moratok _____ 152
    Mugulasha (see Quinipissa).
    Muklasa _____ 152
    Muskogee _____ 153
    Nabedache _____ 154

Sketches of the Southeastern tribes and their population—Continued.   PAGE
  Nacachau _____ 155
  Nacanish _____ 155
  Nacogdoche _____ 156
  Nacono _____ 156
  Nahyssan _____ 157
  Nanatsoho _____ 157
  Napochi or Nabochi _____ 157
  Nasoni _____ 158
  Natasi _____ 158
  Natchez _____ 158
  Natchitoches _____ 161
  Nechaui _____ 162
  Neche _____ 162
  Neusiok _____ 162
  Nottoway (Notowega, Nittaweega, or Nautaugue) _____ 163
  Ocale _____ 164
  Occaneechi _____ 164
  Oçita or Ucita _____ 165
  Oconee _____ 165
  Ofo, Ofogoula, or Mosopelea _____ 165
  Okchai _____ 166
  Okelousa _____ 167
  Okmulgee _____ 168
  Onatheaqua _____ 168
  Opelousa _____ 168
  Osochi _____ 169
  Pakana _____ 170
  Pamlico _____ 170
  Pascagoula _____ 170
  Pawokti _____ 171
  Patiri _____ 172
  Pedee _____ 172
  Pensacola _____ 172
  Pilthlako (Opiłłako) _____ 173
  Pohoy, Pooy, Pojoi, or Posoye _____ 173
  Potano _____ 173
  Powhatan _____ 175
  Quapaw _____ 176
  Quinipissa _____ 176
  Saluda _____ 177
  Santee _____ 177
  Saponi _____ 178
  Saturiwa _____ 179
  Sawokli _____ 179
  Seminole _____ 181
  Sewee _____ 182
  Shakori _____ 183
  Shawnee _____ 184
  Sissipahaw _____ 186
  Soacatino or Xacatin _____ 186
  Sugeree _____ 186
  Surruque, Horruque, or Surreche _____ 187

Sketches of the Southeastern tribes and their population—Continued.   **PAGE**
    Tacatacuru _____ 187
    Taensa _____ 188
    Tamathli (Tamali) _____ 189
    Tangipahoa _____ 190
    Taposa _____ 190
    Tawasa _____ 190
    Tekesta or Tequesta _____ 191
    Timucua group _____ 193
    Tiou _____ 194
    Tocobaga _____ 195
    Tohome _____ 196
    Tukabahchee _____ 197
    Tunica _____ 197
    Tuscarora _____ 199
    Tuskegee _____ 200
    Tutelo _____ 200
    Utina or Timucua _____ 201
    Waccamaw _____ 203
    Wakokai _____ 203
    Washa (French: Ouacha) _____ 204
    Washita or Ouachita _____ 204
    Wateree _____ 205
    Waxhaw _____ 206
    Weapemeoc _____ 206
    Winyaw _____ 206
    Wiwohka _____ 207
    Woccon _____ 207
    Yadkin _____ 208
    Yamasee _____ 208
    Yatasi _____ 211
    Yazoo _____ 211
    Yeopim (*see* Weapemeoc).
    Yuchi _____ 212
    Yufera _____ 215
    Yui (Spanish: Ibi) _____ 215
    Yustaga or Hostaqua _____ 216
Interpretations of tribal names _____ 216
Physical and mental characteristics _____ 219
The influence of language _____ 238
Raw materials utilized by the Southeastern Indians _____ 242
    Mineral kingdom _____ 242
    Vegetable kingdom _____ 244
    Animal kingdom _____ 249
    The distribution of raw materials _____ 253
The annual economic cycle _____ 255
Food _____ 265
    Discussion _____ 296
Horticulture _____ 304
Hunting _____ 310
    Woodcraft _____ 310
    Deer hunting _____ 312
    Bear hunting _____ 321

Hunting—Continued. PAGE
    Bison hunting_____ 324
    The hunting of other animals_____ 328
Fishing_____ 332
Domestication of animals_____ 344
    Pre-Columbian domestication_____ 344
    Horses_____ 346
    Hogs, domestic fowl, and cattle_____ 351
Preparation of vegetable foods_____ 351
Treatment of meats_____ 368
Preservation of food_____ 372
Tobacco_____ 381
Housing_____ 386
    Types of buildings_____ 386
    Materials used in buildings_____ 421
    Beds_____ 422
    Fire making_____ 422
    Smoke holes and windows_____ 427
    Doors_____ 428
    Awnings, sunshades, and flags_____ 430
    Cushions_____ 432
    Towels and soap_____ 432
    Stockades_____ 433
Clothing_____ 439
    Materials_____ 439
    Skin dressing_____ 442
    Cords, threads, and textiles_____ 448
    Featherwork_____ 454
    Clothing of men_____ 456
    Clothing of women_____ 469
    Clothing of children_____ 475
    Clothing of the medicine men_____ 477
    Bags and purses_____ 479
Ornamentation_____ 481
    Work in shell_____ 481
    Pearls_____ 488
    Porcupine-quill work_____ 489
    Work in metal_____ 490
    Manner of dressing the hair_____ 498
    Head bands_____ 508
    Ear ornaments_____ 510
    Nose ornaments_____ 514
    Labrets_____ 515
    Necklaces_____ 516
    Bracelets and arm bands_____ 521
    Finger rings_____ 522
    Leg ornaments_____ 523
    Ornamentation of belts and other articles of clothing_____ 523
    Greasing and coloring of the hair and skin_____ 526
    Body paint_____ 528
    Tattooing_____ 532
    Staining of the teeth_____ 536
    Treatment of fingernails and toenails_____ 536

Ornamentation—Continued.   PAGE
    Head deformation _____ 537
    Differences between ornaments worn by men and women _____ 541
The use of stone _____ 541
    Sources of the raw material _____ 541
    Flint implements _____ 543
    Axes _____ 544
    Stone pipes _____ 545
    Chunkey stones _____ 547
    Miscellaneous uses of stone _____ 548
Pottery _____ 549
Miscellaneous household utensils _____ 555
    Wooden stools _____ 555
    Dishes and spoons of wood and horn _____ 556
    Wooden mortars _____ 558
    Wooden chests _____ 560
    Cradles _____ 562
    Combs _____ 564
    Scratchers _____ 564
Implements used in hunting, fishing, and war _____ 564
    Knives _____ 564
    Clubs _____ 566
    Bows and arrows _____ 571
    Lances, spears, and javelins _____ 582
    Blowguns _____ 585
    Slings _____ 587
    Shields _____ 587
    Armor _____ 588
Implements serving transportation _____ 589
    Canoes and rafts _____ 589
    Litters _____ 598
    Saddles _____ 601
    Bridges _____ 601
Mats and baskets _____ 602
The coloring of manufactured articles _____ 608
Mnemonic devices _____ 610
Artistic development _____ 613
Musical instruments _____ 624
    Drums _____ 624
    Rattles _____ 626
    Flageolets _____ 628
    Rasps _____ 629
Societal and ceremonial life _____ 629
    Towns _____ 629
    Social organization _____ 641
        General features _____ 641
        Clans and gentes _____ 654
        Castes _____ 661
        Moieties _____ 663
        Terms of relationship _____ 665
        Names _____ 671
    Games _____ 674
    War _____ 686

Societal and ceremonial life—Continued.   PAGE
    Marriage customs_____ 701
    Customs relating to birth, education, and the division of labor be-
        tween the sexes_____ 709
    Burial customs_____ 718
    Crime and punishment_____ 730
    Means of communication_____ 733
    Trade_____ 736
    Religious beliefs and usages_____ 742
    Medical practices_____ 782
Conclusion_____ 799
    Common cultural characters_____ 801
    Cultural differences_____ 805
    Cultural subareas_____ 812
    Central intrusion_____ 823
    Comparison of the Southeast with corresponding areas in other parts
        of the world_____ 823
Source materials_____ 827
Bibliography_____ 832
Index_____ 857

ILLUSTRATIONS

MAPS

1. Location of Indian tribes in the Southeast about the year 1650_____ 1
2. Distribution of Earthworks in the eastern United States (reproduced
    from The Mound Builders, by Henry Clay Shetrone, fig. 8)_____ 2
3. Distribution of Indian population in the Southeast with reference to
    the physical areas_____ 4
4. Average July temperature in the Southeast_____ 6
5. Average January temperature in the Southeast_____ 6
6. Average annual rainfall in the Southeast (in inches)_____ 7
7. Drought frequencies in the Southeast_____ 8
8. Climatic regions of the world (reproduction of map by Prof. J.
    R. Smith)_____ 8
9. Biotic areas in the Southeast (from the Fourth Provisional Zone Map
    of North America of the U. S. Biological Survey, by C. Hart Mer-
    riam, Vernon Bailey, E. W. Nelson, and E. A. Preble, 1910)_____ 9
10. Tribal movements according to traditions and earliest records_____ 22
11. Locations of Indian tribes in the Southeast at different periods_____ 34
12. Route of Hernando de Soto and Luis de Moscoso through the South-
    east_____ 40
13. Map to illustrate the distribution of certain natural resources in the
    Southeast drawn upon by the Indians_____ 254

PLATES

(All plates at end of book)

1. Intertribal Indian Council called by John Ross at Tahlequah, Cherokee
    Nation, in June 1843 (after Stanley).
2. 1, Charlie Thompson in 1910, later chief of the Alabama Indians, now de-
    ceased. 2, Wife and children of Charlie Thompson.
3. Drawing by A. de Batz showing Indians of several nations— Illinois, Atakapa,
    Foxes.

4. 1, Home of Armojean Reon, one of the last speakers of the Atakapa language. 2, Home of the Catawba chief, Sam Blue.

5. 1, A group of Catawba girls, 1918. 2, Ladies' Relief Society of the Church of Jesus Christ of Latter Day Saints, Catawba Reservation.

6. 1, Old Catawba House, 1918. 2, Old Catawba House, 1918.

7. House of Worship of the Church of Jesus Christ of Latter Day Saints on the Catawba Reservation, S. C.

8. Cherokee Indians sent to England in 1730 with Sir Alexander Cuming.

9. Three Cherokee chiefs sent to England in 1762.

10. 1, Austenaco, the Great Warrior. (After a drawing by Sir Joshua Reynolds, reproduced in the Royal Magazine.) 2, The Cherokee chief Cunne Shote, in 1762 (after Parsons).

11. 1, Sequoya (after McKenney and Hall). 2, John Ross (after McKenney and Hall).

12. 1, Major Ridge (after McKenney and Hall). 2, Tahchee (Cherokee pronunciation of his English name "Dutch"). (After McKenney and Hall.)

13. 1, Tooan Tuh (Cherokee Dústú, "Spring Frog"). (After McKenney and Hall.) 2, A Chickasaw Warrior (after Romans).

14. 1, George Wilson, a Chickasaw Indian. 2, Home of a Chickasaw Indian named Mose Wolf, at Steedman, Okla.

15. The last Chickasaw Council House, at Tishomingo, Okla.

16. Benjamin Paul, last chief of the Chitimacha Indians and one of the last speakers of the Chitimacha language.

17. Registe Dardin and wife, Chitimacha Indians, Charenton, La.

18. 1, The Sacred Hill of Nanih Waiya, in the old Choctaw Nation. 2, View from the top of Nanih Waiya Hill, looking east.

19. Choctaw Indians, from the sketch by De Batz (after Bushnell).

20. 1, Pushmataha, the great Choctaw chief (after McKenney and Hall). 2, Mo-sho-la-tub-bee, another famous Choctaw chief (after Catlin).

21. 1, Home of a Choctaw Indian named John Wesley, near Philadelphia, Miss. 2, John Wesley and family.

22. 1, Thliotombi, an old Choctaw Indian living near Idabell, Okla., and his family. 2, The Old Choctaw Council House at Tuskahoma, Okla.

23. 1, Bob Verret and Baptiste Billiout, Houma Indians, Terrebonne Parish, La., 1907. 2, Houma Indians on lower Bayou Lafourche, La., 1907.

24. 1, Houma Indians on lower Bayou Lafourche, La., 1907. 2, Houma Indians on Little Barataria Bayou, La., 1907.

25. 1, Old Houma Woman, Point au Chien, La. 2, Old Houma House, at Point au Chien, La., 1907.

26. Stimafutchi, or "Good Humor" of the Coosades (Koasati) Creeks. (Sketch by Trumbull in 1790.)

27. 1, Jackson Langley, Koasati chief, living near Kinder, La. 2, Mother of Jackson Langley, Kinder, La.

28. Koasati Indian School near Kinder, La.

29. Tomo Chachi Mico (Tomochichi), or King of Yamacraw, and his nephew, Tonahowi. (From painting by Verelst.)

30. Tomochichi meeting Oglethorpe in England.

31. 1, A Creek War Chief (after Romans). 2, Mico Chlucco (Miko Thlakko), the Long Warrior, or King of the Seminoles (after William Bartram).

32. 1, Tuskatche Mico (properly Fus-hatchee Miko), or the Birdtail King of the Cusitahs (Kasihta). (After a sketch by Trumbull, 1790.) 2, Hopothle Mico (Hop-hithli Miko), or the Talasee King of the Creeks. (After a sketch by Trumbull, 1790.)

33. 1, "John—a Creek" (after a sketch by Trumbull, 1790). 2, "Hysac, or the Woman's Man," a Creek Indian. (After a sketch by Trumbull, 1790.)

34. 1, Ben Perryman, a prominent Creek Indian (after a painting by Catlin). 2, Opothleyoholo (Hopo-hithli Yoholo), the great War Speaker and leader of the Creek Indians (after McKenney and Hall).
35. 1, William McIntosh, chief of the Coweta Indians and the Lower Creeks (after McKenney and Hall). 2, William McIntosh, chief of the Coweta Indians and the Lower Creeks. (From a painting by Washington Allston.)
36. 1, Timpoochee Barnard, Chief of the Yuchi Indians among the Lower Creeks (after McKenney and Hall). 2, Yoholomicco, a Creek Indian (after McKenney and Hall).
37. 1, Tustennuggee Emathla, or Jim Boy, a leader of the Thlapthlako Creek Indians (after McKenney and Hall). 2, Menawa, a Creek Indian (after McKenney and Hall).
37A. Old Creek Council House, Okmulgee, Okla.
37B. Last Creek Council House, Okmulgee, Okla., as it appeared in 1920.
38. 1, Creek Sam, a Natchez Indian, at his home near Braggs, Okla. 2, Watt Sam in 1908, principal Natchez informant of the writer and of Dr. Haas.
39. 1, Nancy Taylor, one of the last speakers of the Natchez tongue, 1908. 2, Square Ground in the Greenleaf Mountains, Okla., where Watt Sam officiated as the Medicine Maker.
40. 1, Rosa Pierrette, last speaker of the Ofo Language, Marksville, La. 2, Ball Post and ground connected with the Square Ground shown on plate 39, figure 2.
41. The Booton portrait of Pocahontas.
42. The Timucua chief Saturiwa.
43. 1, The Seminole Head Chief, Mikonopi (after McKenney and Hall). 2, The Seminole Chief Tokos Imathla ("Tukoseemathla") (after McKenney and Hall).
44. Osceola, from the painting in the Charleston Museum by Robert John Curtis.
45. 1, Osceola (from the painting by Catlin). 2, Osceola, from the painting by King (after McKenney and Hall).
46. 1, The Seminole chief Heniha Imathla ("Ea-mat-la"), or King Philip (after Catlin). 2, The Seminole Chief Aholochi ("Ye-how-lo-gee"), or Cloud (after Catlin).
47. 1, The Seminole chief Holahta Miko ("Olactomicco"), or Billy Bowlegs (after McKenney and Hall). 2, Tenskwatawa ("Ten-squat-a-way"), the Shawnee Prophet (after Catlin).
48. Buffalo Tamer, Chief of the Tunica Indians in 1732, and the wife and child of the chief he succeeded, who was killed by the Natchez in June 1731. From the sketch by De Batz (after Bushnell).
49. 1, William Ely Johnson, Dr. A. S. Gatschet's Tunica informant, taken at Marksville, La., about 1910. 2, Volcine Chiki, Chief of the Tunica Indians in 1910.
50. Sam Young or Sesostrie Yauchicant, last speaker of the Tunica language.
51. Timucua Indians sowing their fields (after LeMoyne).
52. "Their Manner of Fishynge in Virginia" (after White).
53. Timucua Indians cooking (after Le Moyne).
54. 1, "Their Seetheynge of their Meate in Earthen Pottes" (after White). 2, "The Browyllinge of their Fishe over the Flame" (after White).
55. The Timucua Indians drying food (after Le Moyne).
56. Storehouse of the Timucua Indians (after Le Moyne).
57. A stockaded town of the Timucua Indians (after Le Moyne).
58. Creek House of the later pattern.

59. 1, Square Ground Cabin of the Alabama Indians ("Cabane du Conseil des Alibamons") in the eighteenth century, from a sketch in the French archives reproduced by Du Terrage. 2, Northern Seminole house (after MacCauley).
60. Seminole house (after MacCauley).
61. Choctaw palmetto house (after Bushnell).
62. Acolapissa Temple and Cabin of the Chief, from a sketch by De Batz (after Bushnell).
63. The Natchez Temple (after Du Pratz).
64. "A Weroan or Great Lorde of Virginia" (after White).
65. "A Cheiff Ladye of Pomeiooc" (after White).
66. "One of the Cheiff Ladyes of Secota" (after White).
67. "A Young Gentill Woeman Doughter of Secota" (after White).
68. "A Cheiff Lorde of Roanoac" (after White).
69. 1, Natives in summer, Louisiana (after Du Pratz). 2, A woman and her daughter, Louisiana (after Du Pratz).
70. 1, Natives in winter (after Du Pratz). 2, A Louisiana Indian in winter costume, from a sketch by De Batz.
71. 1, An Alabama woman dressing a skin, Polk County, Tex. 2, Alabama gourd bottle, Polk County, Tex.
72. 1, Alabama garter and hair ornament, Polk County, Tex. 2, Alabama mortar and pestle, Polk County, Tex.
73. 1, Hitchiti woman pounding corn, near Sylvian, Okla. 2, Caddo mortar and pestle, near Anadarko, Okla.
74. "The manner of makinge their boates" (after White).
75. Conveyance of the Great Sun of the Natchez (after Du Pratz).
76. 1, Chitimacha mat (now in Museum of the American Indian), from a photograph taken at Charenton, La., in 1907. 2, Ball sticks and rattle used by Watt Sam, a Natchez Indian living near Braggs, Okla.
77. "The Towne of Pomeiooc" (after White).
78. "The Towne of Secota" (after White).
79. The village of Sam Jones, or Arpeika, a Hitchiti Seminole chief in Florida (after Eastman).
80. A Choctaw ball player (after Catlin).
81. Timucua games (after Le Moyne).
82. Ceremony performed by the Timucua chief Saturiwa before going to war (after Le Moyne).
83. Plan of a fort and a prisoner in the frame prepared for execution (after Du Pratz).
84. Procession of the Peace Calumet (after Du Pratz).
85. Bringing a wife to a Timucua chief (after Le Moyne).
86. "The Tombe of their Werowans or Cheiff Lordes" (after White).
87. Burial of a Timucua chief (after Le Moyne).
88. Creek graves in Oklahoma.
89. A Choctaw burial place (after Romans).
90. Two pictographs (after Romans).
91. "The Marckes of sundrye of the cheiff mene of Virginia" (after White).
92. "The idol Kiwasa," in an Algonquian tribe of North Carolina (after White).
93. "Their Danses which they use att their Hyghe Feastes" (after White).
94. "One of the Religeous men in the town of Secota" (after White).
95. "The Coniuerer" (after White).
96. "Their manner of Prainge with Rattels abowt the Fyer" (after White).
97. Timucua sacrifice to the sun (after Le Moyne).

98. Timucua Indians taking the black drink (after Le Moyne).

99. 1, 2, Two views of the Tukabahchee Square Ground in 1912.

100. 1, The Nuyaka Square Ground in 1912. 2, The Pakan Tallahassee Square Ground in 1912.

101. 1, Part of the Eufaula Square Ground in 1912. 2, Receptacle for the ceremonial pots and other articles in the Eufaula Square Ground, 1912.

102. 1, The Alabama Square Ground west of Hanna, Okla., in 1912. 2, Receptacle for the ceremonial pots and other articles in the Alabama Square Ground, 1912.

103. 1, 2, Two views of the Square Ground of the Chiaha Seminole, Seminole County, Okla., in 1912.

104. 1, Leaders of the Chiaha Seminole Square Ground, Seminole County, Okla., in 1912. 2, The Mikasuki Square Ground, Seminole County, Okla., 1912.

105. General Dance of the Natchez Indians (after Du Pratz).

106. Treatment of the sick by Timucua Indians (after Le Moyne).

107. 1, Home of the "Knower" Yahola, near Muskogee, Okla., 1912. 2, Sweat Lodge frame at Chiaha Seminole Square Ground, Seminole County, Okla., 1912.

TEXT FIGURES

PAGE

1. Structural detail of the roof of a Creek tcokofa from beneath (after Hitchcock) _____ 390

2. Plan of Creek ceremonial ground, as given by Wm. Bartram_____ 391

3. Plan of Creek ceremonial ground and its position in a Creek town, as given by Wm. Bartram_____ 393

4. Ground plan of the house of a Seminole Indian called by the traders Bosten or Boatswain (after Bartram) _____ 397

5. Ground plan of Cherokee houses (after Bartram) _____ 404

THE INDIANS OF THE SOUTHEASTERN UNITED STATES

By John R. Swanton

INTRODUCTION

Several years ago when I was collecting materials from early writers regarding the Creek Indians and other Southeastern tribes, a quantity of notes accumulated bearing on the material culture of these people. These, augmented by a few of my own and sketches of the later history of the several tribes, I have brought together in the present work. Some material has also been included to augment earlier publications dealing with the social and ceremonial usages of the peoples in question. Although they are included in the same general area, it is not claimed that the discussion of certain of these tribes is complete, meaning particularly the Cherokee, Tuscarora, Quapaw, and Shawnee, which have been made the subject of considerable additional research and are still being studied. Indeed, no claim of a hundred-percent completion of any tribe can ever be made safely, since some manuscript may at any time be drawn from its place of concealment and modify materially everything that has been published, or even occasion a total revolution in our ideas regarding it. The present effort involves in the main a collection of source materials which it is hoped and believed will be of use to future students.

GEOGRAPHY OF THE SOUTHEAST

The Indians who are the subject of this bulletin lived between the 24th and 39th parallels of N. latitude and the 75th and 96th meridians of W. longitude on a territory now divided up among the Southern States of the American Union. It measured about a thousand miles from east to west and, including the Florida Peninsula, about the same from north to south, but omitting Florida, the north-south measurement would be little more than half as great.

Considered as an ethnological province, the Southeast includes primarily the territory now embraced in the States of Georgia, Florida, Alabama, and Mississippi, all of Louisiana except the extreme southwestern part, northeastern Texas, southern Arkansas, southern and western South Carolina, the westernmost mountain section of North Carolina, and nearly all of Tennessee. Early in the sixteenth century, it also extended over most of eastern Arkansas. As marginal districts should be added the remainder of North and South Carolina, Virginia, West Virginia, Kentucky, and some areas northward of the Ohio River itself. (See map 1.)

Considered as an archeological province, we shall have to extend not merely the marginal regions but the primary as/well over most of the Ohio Valley and as far up the Mississippi as southern Wisconsin. The difference between the two indicates plainly a later shrinkage of culture-bearing tribes toward the south and in some measure toward the east and west. (See map 2.)

The geographical conditions are shown on map 3.

EXPLANATION OF MAP 3
(Facing p. 4)

The physical areas are as given by Nevin M. Fenneman in cooperation with the Physiographic Committee of the Geological Survey, except for some changes in numbering. On Fenneman's map the areas are described as follows:

1. Coastal Plain_____	a, Embayed section_____	1a, Submaturely dissected and partly submerged, terraced coastal plain.
	b, Sea Island section_____	1b, Young to mature terraced coastal plain with submerged border.
	c, Floridian section_____	1c, Young marine plain, with sand hills, swamps, sinks, and lakes.
	d, East Gulf Coastal Plain.	1d, Young to mature belted coastal plain.
	e, Mississippi Alluvial Plain.	1e, Flood plain and delta.
	f, West Gulf Coastal Plain.	1f, Young grading inland to mature coastal plain.
2. Piedmont province.	a, Piedmont Upland_____	2a, Submaturely dissected peneplain on disordered resistant rocks; moderate relief.
	b, Piedmont Lowlands___	2b, Less uplifted peneplain on weak strata; residual ridges on strong rocks.
3. Blue Ridge province.	a, Northern section_____	3a, Maturely dissected mountains of crystalline rocks; accordant altitudes.
	b, Southern section_____	3b, Subdued mountains of disordered crystalline rocks.
4. Valley and Ridge province.	a. Tennessee section_____	4a, Second-cycle mountains of folded strong and weak strata; valley belts predominate over even-crested ridges.

4, Valley and Ridge province	b, Middle section_____	4b, The same, but even-crested ridges predominate over valleys except on east side.
	c, Hudson Valley_____	4c, Glaciated peneplain on weak folded strata.
5. Appalachian Plateaus.	a, Mohawk section_____	5a, Maturely dissected glaciated plateau; varied relief and diverse altitudes.
	b, Catskill section_____	5b, Maturely dissected plateau of mountainous relief and coarse texture (glaciated).
	c, Southern New York section.	5c, Mature glaciated plateau of moderate relief.
	d, Allegheny Mountain section.	5d, Mature plateau of strong relief; some mountains due to erosion of open folds.
	e, Kanawha section_____	5e, Mature plateau of fine texture; moderate to strong relief.
	f, Cumberland Plateau section.	5f, Submaturely dissected plateau of moderate to strong relief.
	g, Cumberland Mountain section.	5g, Higher mature plateau and mountain ridges on eroded open folds.
6. Interior Low Plateaus.	a, Highland Rim section_	6a, Young to mature plateau of moderate relief.
	b, Lexington Plain_____	6b, Mature to old plain on weak rocks; trenched by main rivers.
	c, Nashville Basin_____	6c, Mature to old plain on weak rocks; slightly uplifted and moderately dissected.
	d, Possible western section (not delimited).	6d, Low, maturely dissected plateau with silt-filled valleys.
7. Central Lowland__	a, Eastern Lake section	7a, Maturely dissected and glaciated cuestas and lowlands; moraines, lakes, and lacustrine plains.
	b, Western Lake section__	7b, Young glaciated plain; moraines, lakes, and lacustrine plains.
	c, Wisconsin Driftless section.	7c, Maturely dissected plateau and lowland invaded by glacial outwash. (Margin of old drift included.)

7. Central Lowland__ d, Till Plains_____ 7d, Young till plains; morainic topography rare; no lakes.

e, Dissected Till Plains__ 7e, Submaturely to maturely dissected till plains.

f, Osage Plains_____ 7f, Old scarped plains beveling faintly inclined strata; main streams intrenched.

8. Great Plains province. (This barely appears upon the map.)

9. Ozark Plateaus___ a, Springfield-Salem plateaus. 9a, Submature to mature plateaus.

b, Boston "Mountains"__ 9b, Submature to mature plateau of strong relief.

10. Ouachita province. a, Arkansas Valley_____ 10a, Gently folded strong and weak strata; peneplain with residual ridges.

b, Ouachita Mountains___ 10b, Second-cycle mountains of folded strong and weak strata.

Degrees of relief are herein spoken of as low, moderate, strong, and high. As used here *high* relief is measured in thousands of feet; *moderate* relief in hundreds of feet. *Strong* relief may be anything approaching 1,000 feet with a wide latitude on both sides.

Major divisions are separated by the heaviest lines. Provinces are distinguished by numbers; sections by letters. Broken lines indicate boundaries much generalized or poorly known.

More than three-fourths of the primary area is included in the Coastal Plain. Midway between the Atlantic and the Mississippi River this plain is dented by the Blue Ridge and the Appalachian Plateau with the narrow Appalachian Valley between them, and flanked by lower land masses, the Piedmont Plateau on the east of the Blue Ridge and the Interior Low Plateaus on the west side of the Appalachian Plateau. West of the Mississippi the Coastal Plain is dented slightly by the Ozark and Ouachita Plateaus, themselves separated by the narrow Arkansas Valley peneplain.

Geographers have subdivided each of these physical areas into two or more portions on account of minor characteristic differences, but most of these are without serious ethnological significance. The subdivisions of the great Coastal Plain do, however, have some importance for us. They include: (1) The Embayed section, "a submaturely dissected and partly submerged, terraced coastal plain"; (2) the Sea Island section, a "young to mature terraced coastal plain with submerged border"; (3) the Floridian section, a "young marine plain, with sand hills, swamps, sinks, and lakes"; (4) the East Gulf Coastal Plain, a "young to mature belted coastal plain"; (5) the

Mississippi Alluvial Plain, the Mississippi "flood plain and delta"; and (6) the West Gulf Coastal Plain, a "young grading inland to mature coastal plain." The first of these extends along the coast from Cape Cod to Cape Lookout; the second, from the latter point to St. Johns River; the third includes Florida south of St. Johns River and Apalachee Bay; the fourth and sixth embrace the entire coastal plain north of the Gulf of Mexico and are separated merely by the fifth area, the alluvial flood plain of the Mississippi. The Nashville Basin, a limestone island in the Interior Low Plateaus is also of ethnological significance, and the Lexington Plain, or "blue grass country," may have been of equal importance in prehistoric times, but the information that has come down to us from the tribes last in occupancy does not indicate it.

Geographically, the Southeast is one of the newest as well as one of the richest parts of North America.

It is in the warmest section of the north temperate zone, the decrease in temperature from south to north, or rather southeast to northwest, being fairly uniform except along the Appalachian Mountains, the highest land-masses east of the Rockies, which introduce a disturbing element. Throughout most of the region the average temperature during July is 80° or more, and over the rest of it not lower than 75° except in the Appalachians where it descends below 70°. The average annual maximum temperature is between 90° and 100°, somewhat exceeding the latter figure along the margin of the Western Plains. In January the difference between the southern and northern sections varies more widely, a small portion near the tip of Florida maintaining 65° or more, north of which we find successive belts of lower and lower temperatures down to 35°, and even below 30° in the high West Virginia mountains. The minimum at the tip of Florida is in the neighborhood of 40° and along the northernmost fringe somewhat under zero. (See maps 4 and 5.)

The greater part of the Southeast is in the zone where southwesterly winds prevail, but Florida and parts of the Gulf coast fall under the influence of the easterly trades, particularly in summer, and, in spite of the fact that the northern part is in the lee of the Rocky Mountains, the two work together to provide an abundant rainfall almost everywhere, the only handicap being the West India cyclones, which often come along with the trades in spring and autumn to be hurled upon the southern coast. An annual average rainfall of between 40 and 60 inches is registered everywhere and more than 60 inches in a few spots on the coast and in the Appalachians, one section of the latter even exceeding 80. In January there is less proportional precipitation on the Atlantic Coast than in

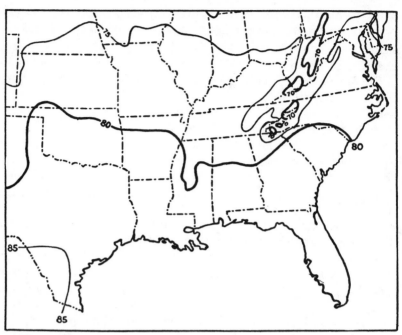

MAP 4.—Average July temperature in the Southeast.   (After Paullin and Wright.)

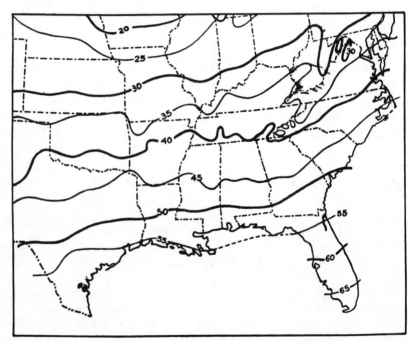

MAP. 5—Average January temperature in the Southeast.   (After Paullin and Wright.)

the central Gulf area. In July the condition is reversed. Beginning in east central Texas, the amount of precipitation falls off rapidly to less than 20 inches in the western part of that state. Naturally, droughts are most frequent there. (See maps 6 and 7.)

Climatic provinces similarly located with reference to the land masses and rainfall are found in South America, Asia, Africa, and Australia. The related South American province includes Uruguay and adjacent portions of Brazil and Argentina. The Asiatic province covers northern and central China. The analogous Australian province embraces most of New South Wales and the southeastern part of Queensland, while the African province is a very small territory in

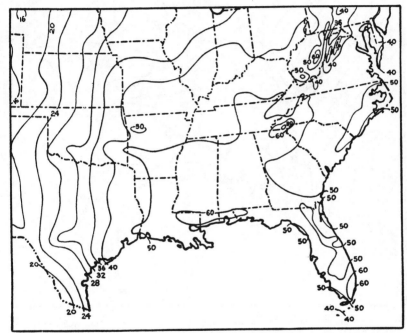

MAP 6.—Average annual rainfall in the Southeast (in inches). (After Paullin and Wright.)

the eastern part of Cape Colony and the lands adjacent toward the north. (See map 8.) Later I shall institute a comparison between the cultures of the inhabitants of these several regions.

Life zones (map 9).—Biologists have classified the territory occupied by the tribes which are the subject of the present bulletin as follows (numbers and letters refer tò those on the map (p. 9)):

Boreal Region:
    Canadian Zone: A few of the higher summits of the Allegheny Mountains (1).
Austral Region:
    Transition Zone
        The Alleghanian Faunal Area: A strip of territory along the Alleghany

Mountains in Virginia, West Virginia, Kentucky, Tennessee, North Carolina, and a bit of northern Georgia (2).

Upper Austral Zone:

The Carolinian Faunal Area: Including the Piedmont Plateau from the Potomac River through the central parts of Virginia, and North Carolina, northwestern South Carolina, northern Georgia, the northeastern corner

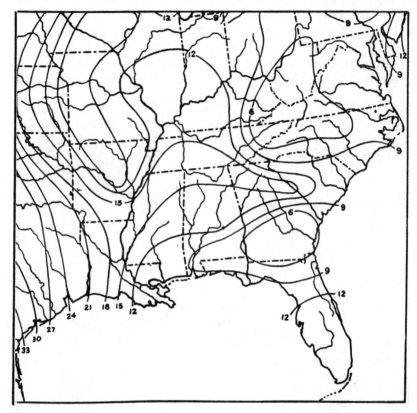

Map 7.—Drought frequencies in the Southeast. Portion of a map of the Weather Bureau, United States Department of Agriculture, showing the number of periods of 30 consecutive days or more without 0.25 inch of precipitation in 24 hours during the season March–September, inclusive, for the period 1895–1914. The smallest number is 6 or below, the highest 33 or above. (After Paullin and Wright.)

of Alabama, central Tennessee, and thence northward, including nearly all of Kentucky and western West Virginia, as also the Ozark Plateau of Arkansas (3b).

The Upper Sonoran Faunal Area: Not entering into the section under consideration, but indicated in the margin of the map toward the northwest (3a).

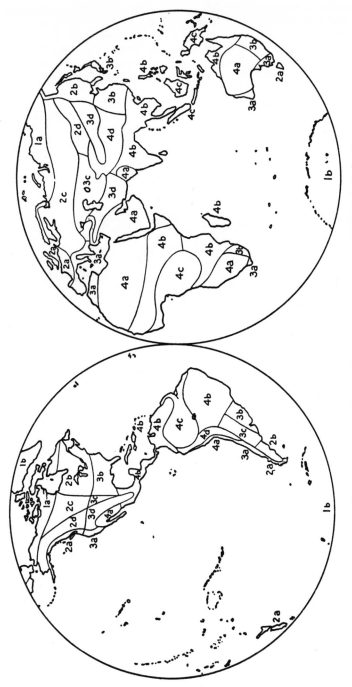

MAP 8.—Climatic regions of the world (reproduction of map by Prof. J. R. Smith in Encyclopaedia of the Social Sciences, article on Climate).

The Austroriparian Faunal Area: Occupying all of the remainder of the Gulf States and the South Atlantic States except the southernmost third of the Floridian peninsula (4b).

The Lower Sonoran Faunal Area: Not entering into the section under consideration, but indicated at the margin of the map toward the west (4a).

Tropical Region: Including merely the southernmost third of the peninsula of Florida (5).

In his bulletin on Life Zones and Crop Zones of the United States, printed in 1898, Merriam thus epitomizes the characteristic animal and plant life of the above regions, omitting those of the Canadian

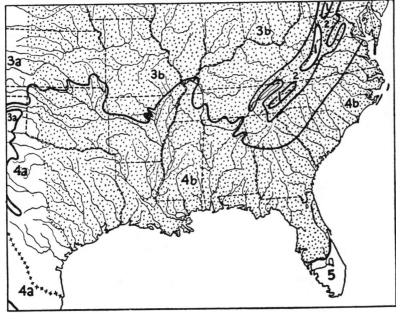

MAP 9.—Biotic areas in the Southeast (from the Fourth Provisional Zone Map of North America of the U. S. Biological Survey, by C. Hart Merriam, Vernon Bailey, E. W. Nelson, and E. A. Preble, 1910).

Zone, which is of slight importance in the Southeast, and the two Sonoran areas, which are entirely beyond it:

In the Alleghanian faunal area the chestnut, walnut, oaks, and hickories of the South meet and overlap the beech, birch, hemlock, and sugar maple of the North; the Southern mole and cottontail rabbit meet the Northern star-nosed and Brewer's moles and varying hare, and the Southern bobwhite, Baltimore oriole, bluebird, catbird, chewink, thrasher, and wood thrush live in or near the haunts of the bobolink, solitary vireo, and the hermit and Wilson's thrushes. Several native nuts, of which the beechnut, butternut, chestnut, hazelnut, hickory nut, and walnut are most important, grow wild in this belt. Of these, the chestnut, hickory nut, and walnut come in from the South (Carolinian area) and do not extend much beyond the southern or warmer parts of the Alleghanian area. (Merriam, 1898, pp. 20–21.)

Counting from the north, the Carolinian area is that in which the sassafras, tulip tree, hackberry, sycamore, sweet gum, rose magnolia, red bud, persimmon, and short-leaf pine first make their appearance, together with the opossum, gray fox, fox squirrel, cardinal bird, Carolina wren, tufted tit, gnatcatcher, summer tanager, and yellow-breasted chat. Chestnuts, hickory nuts, hazelnuts, and walnuts grow wild in abundance. (Merriam, 1898, p. 31.)

[In the Austroriparian Area] the long leaf and loblolly pines, magnolia, and live oak are common on the uplands; the bald cypress, tupelo, and cane in the swamps. Here the mocking bird, painted bunting, prothonotary warbler, red-cockaded woodpecker, chuck-wills-widow, and the swallow-tail and Mississippi kites are characteristic birds, and the southern fox squirrel, cotton rat, rice-field rat, wood rat, and free-tailed bat are common mammals. (Merriam, 1898, p. 45.)

[Tropical Area:] Among the tropical trees that grow in southern Florida are the royal palm, Jamaica dogwood, manchineel, mahogany, and mangrove; and among the birds are the caracara eagle, white-crowned pigeon, zenaida dove, a Bahama vireo, and the Bahama honey creeper. The absence of characteristic tropical mammals and the relatively small number of tropical birds in Florida is due to the lack of land connection with other tropical areas. (Merriam, 1898, p. 52.)

CLASSIFICATION OF THE SOUTHEASTERN TRIBES

A natural classification of peoples would be based upon their physical characters, but such a classification is impossible at the present time as applied to the area under consideration and would be impracticable in a treatise like the present, which deals mainly with questions of culture. Therefore, the classification which has been adopted and which is given in table 1 (opposite) is based merely upon linguistic and political considerations. In this table the Muskhogean, Tunican, and Uchean (or Yuchean) stocks are given entire, but only such tribes of the Siouan, Iroquoian, Caddoan, and Algonquian families as lived within the Southeastern province.

In its more limited sense, the Southeastern cultural province included the Muskhogean tribes with their recently annexed Natchez and Timucua divisions, the Cherokee, the Tunica and Chitimacha groups, and the Caddo. The tidewater tribes of Virginia and North Carolina, although stimulated by the culture of those just mentioned, had developed a somewhat independent pattern with an economy in which fishing, trading, and the possession of property had assumed more important positions, and the temples a different shape and character. The Siouan tribes which lay between these two areas seem to have been on a lower level (Speck, 1938) and the same may be said of the southern Florida Indians, and the Indians west of the Chitimacha and Caddo. These last, indeed, were entirely marginal to Southeastern culture and should hardly be considered as participants in it. The Siouan Quapaw and Algonquian Shawnee, although on a higher level than the central Texas tribes, were also

marginal and seem to have come within its sphere at a very recent period. The same was also true of the Biloxi and Ofo, but we know too little regarding them to make an independent category for them advisable, though Voegelin has shown that they formed one dialectic group with the Tutelo (not indicated in table 1).

POPULATION
(See map 3)

The most careful attempt to date to prepare a detailed estimate of the Indian population north of Mexico is by the late James Mooney, of the Bureau of American Ethnology, though useful modifications have been suggested by Kroeber. This gives us a total population from the Chesapeake to Texas, including the Caddo and Shawnee and excluding the Atakapa, of 171,900. The Atakapa and their relatives are placed at about 2,000. While this figure is protested by Spinden as inadequate to account for the earthworks of the region, I believe it to be rather too high than too low for the years to which it is supposed to apply, 1600–1650. At an earlier period, however, there are evidences of a great expansion of population. My own independent estimates for part of the region yield substantially the same results as Mooney reached except that I should be inclined to reduce the figures for the Creeks and Chickasaw somewhat. The figures for Florida I should also be inclined to scale down and most of those for the Siouan tribes of the east. Nevertheless, the relative strength of the tribes enumerated, I think, would be altered little if we had absolutely trustworthy figures, and those we have will give us a very good idea of the distribution of population.

It is something surprising to find that the Cherokee, the only distinctly mountain tribe in the whole area, with the possible exception of the Yuchi, were also the most numerous, the only one exceeding 20,000. Next come the Creeks of the Tallapoosa, Coosa, and Chattahoochee Valleys, and the Choctaw of southern Mississippi. If we regard density of population, we should probably find the Choctaw leading both Creeks and Cherokee. It will be noticed that these are all great corn-raising tribes and still constitute the greatest part of the remaining southern Indians. They are followed by the Powhatan Indians of Virginia, the Timucua and the Apalachee of Florida, the Chickasaw of northern Mississippi, the Catawba of the Piedmont region of South Carolina, and the Tuscarora of the Piedmont escarpment in North Carolina. Most of these are again corn-raising tribes of the interior, but Virginia and Florida now supply us with tribes which combined that industry with fishing in an eminent degree. Fourth in position, of between 2,500 and 5,000 population, come the Natchez and Quapaw, at different points along the Mississippi River; the Potano of Florida, who were inland rather than coastal, though they depended considerably on the fish found in their lakes; the Chitimacha, a nation of canoe men, but perhaps rather more lacustrine than coastal; and the Calusa of Florida, who lived almost entirely by fishing and the pursuit of marine animals. After these come a great number of small scattered tribes constituting, we may say, the fringes of the rest. The only exception to this is probably the Tunica and their allies whose cultural position with reference to their neighbors it is difficult to determine with precision. It is worth noting that the very smallest tribes seem to include a great number of eastern Siouans.

Speaking generally, we find that the horticultural tribes of the interior were the largest, but that coastal populations were dense in four places: (1) In the Sound country of Virginia and North Carolina; (2) in the similarly flooded coastland between the present Charleston, S. C., and the St. Johns River, including the course of the latter stream; (3) southwest Florida from Tampa Bay to the Keys; and (4) Grand Lake and its surrounding bayous just west of the Mississippi. The second and third were occupied by two peoples of diverse origin. When we come to southwestern Louisiana and Texas, we find a coastal population set distinctly off from the interior tribes, but in both cases they were of low culture. Rated by stocks we have the following approximate figures:

Stock	No.
Muskhogean (including Natchez and Taensa)	66, 600
Iroquoian	30, 200
Siouan	24, 000
Algonquian	16, 500
Timucua (probably related to Muskhogean)	13, 000
Caddo	8, 500
Tunican (Tunica group 2,000; Chitimacha group 4,000)	6, 000
South Florida tribes (perhaps Muskhogean)	4, 000
Uchean	3, 100

Dividing the population between the coast and the interior, we get the following result, a proportion of about 4½ to 1:

	Population
Interior	141, 500
Coast	30, 400

These data are based on Mooney's figures. My own suggested modifications appear on map 3, but practically the same proportion would be maintained whichever set we employ. If we compare the distribution of population in 1650–85 with that revealed to us by the chroniclers of De Soto a hundred years earlier, we find comparatively little change, so far as they can enlighten us on the subject, except in the region around Augusta, Ga., in the southern Appalachians, and west of the Mississippi River. In earlier as well as later times, Florida was well populated and we are reasonably certain that this was true of the Georgia coast. In the part of the Cherokee country traversed there were far fewer towns than we find later, evidently because the Cherokee had not completed their occupancy of the region. Except for the disturbance the Spaniards themselves created in the destruction of life at Mabila, Alabama and Mississippi appear to have changed little in distribution of people and their numbers. This even applied to the territory of the Natchez, if, as suspected, the province of Quigualtanqui included the Natchez tribe. In eastern and southern Arkansas, however, and in northeastern Louisiana we find a very great change. Here about 30 towns, villages, and provinces are mentioned, some of which are distinctly said to have been the most populous or the best supplied with corn of any the explorers had entered during their journey, except Coça and Apalachee. But when the French came into this country a hundred and fifty years later, what a contrast! In all Arkansas there were only four Quapaw towns, near the junction of the Arkansas with the Mississippi, which there is reason to suppose represented a later immigration, and one Caddo and one Tunica settlement on the Ouachita. In northeastern Louisiana there were only a few bands of Tunica, Yazoo, and Koroa, whose villages were usually on the other side of the Mississippi, about 800 Taensa on Lake St. Joseph, and the insignificant Avoyel tribe in the parish named after them. The rest had mysteriously disappeared.

The region about Augusta, Ga., represents a smaller area which had lost the greater part of its population between 1540 and 1670, though many tribes settled there until a late date—Yuchi, Shawnee, Apalachee, Chickasaw. In both of these cases archeology bears out history, particularly as regards the former country. The evacuation of population in this area is approached, though hardly matched, only by that in the Ohio Valley. Archeology also indicates one other displacement, the removal of a former dense population from that part of the Gulf coast between Mobile and Tampa Bays. Apart from Tampa Bay itself we have little direct information regarding the presence of Indian tribes along this part of the coast, but Pineda reported that when he skirted the north coast of the Gulf of Mexico he entered a large river, generally believed to be the Mobile, in order to careen his vessels, and claimed it was lined with 40 towns. While this may have been something of an exaggeration, he is in a measure confirmed by Iberville, who states that there were great numbers of old village sites here when he and his brother Bienville entered to make a permanent establishment in 1702. The region about the mouth of the Apalachicola was found by Moore to be rich in archeological sites from which he culled great quantities of pottery and other remains. It is important to keep this stretch of coast in mind in attempting to account for certain of the resemblances between Southeastern and Antillean cultural features.

Other centers of population in prehistoric times abandoned entirely before the dawn of the historic era were about Macon, on the Ocmulgee, the Colomokee mounds on the Chattahoochee, and Etowah on the river of that name, all in the State of Georgia, and the famous Moundville site on the Black Warrior in Alabama. In these cases, however, the principal centers of population had not removed to great distances.

RELATION OF THE ABORIGINAL POPULATION TO THE NATURAL AREAS

A single tribe, but that the largest in the entire Southeast, namely the Cherokee, was planted on the southern Appalachian highlands, mainly in the interval land of the Blue Ridge which here attains its maximum width and in the Valley and Ridge section, but extending also into the Appalachian Plateau and the Piedmont Province. The lands they held in these two latter physical areas represented for the most part late acquirements. There is evidence that the Cherokee advanced from the northeast down the great Appalachian Valley, displacing or shouldering to one side the Yuchi in eastern Tennessee, the Catawba and their allies in South Carolina, and Muskhogean people in Georgia. The advantages of this location consisted in a relative freedom from the thick forests of the low countries and a proportionately easy agricultural exploitation, the defensive possibilities of the mountains, and the control of mica mines and quarries of stone suitable for pipes. Not much profit accrued from the control of flint quarries, flint being rather too widely distributed. Upon the whole, however, these mountains seem to have been marginal areas, occupied rather through necessity than by choice.

At the end of the seventeenth century, the Ozark and Ouachita Plateaus were not permanently occupied by Indians, but in 1541 De Soto found a fairly large population there, at least in the Ouachita Province. One tribe was evidently Caddo; the others may have been Tunica, though of this we have no certain knowledge. The extent of aboriginal workings in novaculite about Hot Springs shows that the region was much resorted to, and any tribe which could control the trade would be in a position of vantage similar to that occupied by the Cherokee in the East. As a matter of fact, we have no certain knowledge that any such monopolization had taken place. We seem to have less information regarding the part played by the Ozarks in prehistoric aboriginal life than for the Ouachita Mountains, but the discovery of the Bluff Culture with its marked Southwestern affinities shows that at some time in the remote past it was of vastly more significance.

Like the main mountain masses, the low plateaus flanking the Appalachians were occupied by peoples clearly in a state of flux. This is particularly true of the low plateau on the west. The marginal portion of it along the Tennessee was occupied at various times by bands of Chickasaw, Yuchi, Muskhogeans, and, in very late times, by Cherokee. The most attractive section was the limestone-underlain Nashville Basin, but this was occupied and abandoned repeatedly. There is circumstantial evidence that the Yuchi once lived here. At a later date the Kaskinampo, probably of Muskhogean connection, supplanted them and shortly after white contact we find the Shawnee in possession. A part of these Shawnee returned at a later time. It is not a little surprising to discover that the Lexington Plain, the "blue grass country," was not occupied for any considerable period by any body of Indians in the historic era. Chartier's band of Shawnee, who lived for a few years in a town in the present Clark County, Ky., on their way to and from the Creek Nation, constitutes almost the sole exception.

The Piedmont Plateau north of Savannah River was occupied almost exclusively, in times of which we have intimate knowledge, by tribes of the Siouan linguistic stock, and it is evident that many, if not most, of these had worked their way into the territory from some section farther inland shortly before the advent of the whites. If so, they must have come in at least two distinct bodies, because the language spoken by the Siouans of Virginia was markedly distinct from that of the Siouans of the Carolinas. Between Point Lookout and Sewee Bay the latter reached the coast, but precisely here offshore bars and islands furnish less protection to shore dwellers and there is proportionately less temptation to a littoral life. Of the remaining tribes, some lived well inland on the Plateau; others at or near the fall line in order to enjoy the fish to be obtained there. Many tribes whose towns were at some distance resorted to this place when the fish were running. One section of this line, between the Cape Fear and Nottoway, had been preempted by intrusive Iroquoian tribes, the Tuscarora, Meherrin, and Nottoway, while the Coree and Neusiok possibly represented an extension of them to the coast.

The greater part of the embayed section of the Coastal Plain, from Pamlico Sound to the Potomac River, was in the hands of Algonquians, those in Virginia forming the Powhatan tribe or confederation. Here the density of population was particularly great.

Southward, beyond the Savannah, the balance between life on the coast and life in the interior again presents a problem. In the historic period the great tribes of the section, the Creeks, Choctaw, and Chickasaw, lived inland, the first mentioned along the fall line, the two others on the red lands of the Coastal Plain in the present Mississippi. Exclusive of the peninsula of Florida, the shores were but slenderly inhabited throughout most of this period, but when French and Spanish navigators first appeared upon the coast of Georgia and that part of South Carolina below Charleston there was a heavy population there consisting partly of Muskogee or Creeks and partly of tribes of the Hitchiti-speaking branch of the family afterward united with them. A rebellion against the Franciscan Spanish missionaries in the year 1597 and subsequent secessions and depletions due to the attacks of northern tribes, reduced the number of Indians here rapidly and increased those living inland. A similar shift toward the interior seems to have taken place at an earlier period along the northern shores of the Gulf, as may be inferred from the reports of Pineda and Bienville. Archeological evidence testifying to a similar movement may be adduced from the Pensacola, Choctawhatchee, and St. Andrews Bay districts. It is probable that there was at the same time a considerable inland population, but it appears likely that at the end of the sixteenth century it was not much bigger than that on the coast.

In northern Florida there is again a striking superiority of the inland tribes, the most powerful being the Apalachee of the great rise about Tallahassee and Utina and Potano of the northern lake region. The west coast north of Tampa Bay was almost devoid of population in historic times, but abundant archeological remains show that it was once thickly settled like the Gulf coast west of it. On the Atlantic side, the coast north of the St. Johns seems to have been quite well populated, while the proximity of the latter river to the seacoast gave the river tribes almost all of the advantages to be derived from the coast itself. The most exposed part of the coast of this peninsula is on the southeast upon the Atlantic. Here are narrow lagoons, protected by offshore barrier islands, which enabled a number of small tribes to maintain a precarious existence, but there were no deep bays or long rivers giving ready access to the hinterland, the principal drainage being toward the Gulf, and as the Gulf side was also better protected from the stronger waves and currents of the Atlantic, it was natural that it should be better populated than the eastern side of the peninsula and that its people should exercise a dominant influence. In fact, when the Spaniards touched upon this coast in the sixteenth century they found it occupied by a powerful tribe called the Calusa, which seems to have been under one government and to have exerted a measure of control over a number of small towns scattered about Lake Okeechobee.

At the close of the seventeenth century, the most important Mississippi River tribes were located upon the bluffs at the edge of its flood plain, like the Natchez, Tunica, and Houma, but when De Soto and his followers passed through the country in 1541–43, a number of them were on the flood plain itself. The Chitimacha, though living on alluvial soils laid down by the river, owed their prominence and permanence to the natural inland harbor furnished by Grand Lake, the food to be obtained from it and from the numerous bayous about it, and the ready access which they had to the Gulf. The Hasinai and Caddo confederations were composed of Indians who depended mainly upon their crops for sustenance, and they occupied a position west of the Mississippi similar to that of the Chickasaw and Choctaw east of it. West of the Caddo, climatic conditions prevented the same dependence on corn as was possible farther east and the cultural advantage of the interior suddenly disappears, but there continues a distinction between the coast and interior people, owing partly to the fact that the former depended mainly on fish and shellfish and the latter upon hunting, and partly to the, probably accidental, fact that they differed in language, those on the coast belonging to the Atakapa and Karankawa groups and those inland to the Tonkawa. Beyond San Antonio River the latter factor ceases to hold, and though the sea probably operated to a limited extent to bring about a change in the economic lives of the people, the culture both on the coast and inland was on an almost equally low level, and such it continued to be to the southern part of the present State of Tamaulipas in Mexico.

From the facts brought out in the foregoing discussion, and evidence drawn from other parts of the continent of North America, it seems probable that, before horticulture was introduced into the Gulf region, the most dense population was primarily along the ocean shores and secondarily along the rivers and about fresh water lakes. The shift to a farming life probably advanced the culture of all the inhabitants of our Southeast, but it evidently made more proportionate advance possible to the river and lake dwellers whose fields could lie nearer their fisheries. Along much of the Gulf, even to the present day, corn does not grow as well as farther north and the difference was probably greater in prehistoric times, before the breeder of special strains had begun his work. It is, at least, a fair inference that the population of the inland peoples increased relatively faster than the increase of those on the coast although coastal populations, as has been shown, continued large almost down to the historic period. Another noteworthy point is the effect of farming upon the growth of states. Peoples depending mainly upon fishing and hunting tend to remain divided into a great number of bands, each maintaining a high degree of local autonomy. This was true even on the north Pacific coast where food was so abundant that great numbers could maintain themselves in close contact with one another for long periods. It is still more apparent among the purely hunting, fishing, and food-gathering tribes of Texas and northeastern Mexico. Tribal solidarity and a certain measure of governmental unification begin to make their appearance, however, when we reach the coast tribes which also raised corn, but an examination of such tribes often discloses certain disturbing factors. Thus the Chitimacha were rather a lacustrine and inland people than a purely coastal tribe, and the same may be said of most of the tribes of northern Florida. Spanish records indicate that the Indians of the Georgia coast, in the province known as Guale, recognized a head chief. It is, however, doubtful how long they had been in this section and to what extent this headship was of purely native origin. The Indians of the adjoining "province" of Orista, in what is now South Carolina, seem to have been closely related in both language and culture, but to have had no supreme chief and no central organization. Exceptions also seem to confront us in the tidewater sections of North Carolina and Virginia, but the larger tribal aggregates appear to have been superficial and unstable. The most conspicuous governmental unit here was the so-called Powhatan Confederation, or "Empire of Powhatan." In 1607, when the English came to Jamestown, more than 30 tribes belonged to it, but we are informed that all but 6 of these had been brought under one government by the chief, Powhatan himself, and the others represented conquests by his father. It is likely that a state built up in such a summary manner might dissolve with equal rapidity, and this very thing probably happened in the case of the Weapemeoc, which, when the Raleigh colonists landed at Roanoke, extended over the greater part of the present North Carolina mainland north of Albemarle Sound, but by 1650 had been replaced by 4 or 5 independent bands. These "empires" were merely temporary aggregations of the small local units normally found in fishing and hunting territories. It must also be remembered that most of the coastal tribes which formed larger aggregations raised corn and pursued communal methods of agriculture of the kind in vogue among the interior nations and that this was a main factor in the evolution of their several tribal organizations. Elsewhere I have suggested that the littoral states may have represented in some measure a protective reaction against the pressure of the interior agrarian nations.

In one place, southwestern Florida, we have what appears to have been a powerful littoral community which grew up without any assistance from agriculture. This was the Calusa tribe, which, if we may trust our Spanish authorities, was under the well-nigh autocratic control of one chief. The economic life was based mainly upon fish, shellfish, and the gathering of certain roots. It seems to have owed its origin in part to the pressure of alien peoples toward the north, in part to trade, and in part probably to rather recent migration from the vicinity of the great inland nations. On other sections of the coast, such as the northern Gulf shore from the mouth of the Mississippi to the Apalachicola, in southeastern Florida, and on the coasts of South Carolina and most of North Carolina, only small tribes were to be found, often tribes confined to a single town.

Upon the whole, we may say that the tendency of the coast peoples was toward small units which only sporadically were gathered into larger bodies. Inland it was quite the other way. Along Yazoo River, and in parts of Louisiana, there were a few so-called "tribes" of insignificant proportions, but some of these, like the Taposa, Ibitoupa, and Avoyel, appear to have been temporary offshoots of the large nations; others, such as the Yazoo, Koroa, Tiou, Taensa, and Chakchiuma, vestiges of people once very much greater. In southern Georgia there were a number of small tribal groups, but they were united into the Creek Confederation at such an early period that we cannot speak with certainty regarding their original condition. The Siouan tribes of the Piedmont country were also for the most part small, but a tendency is evident among these to form larger groups or confederations such as the Manahoac and Monacan Confederacies, and the associations of tribes at Fort Christanna, and on the upper Pee Dee, while there is some reason to think that many of the southern Siouans had broken away from the Catawba at an earlier period. The greater part of the Southeastern interior, however, was occupied by large tribes or confederacies, including the Tuscarora, Catawba, Yamassee, Apalachee, Creeks, Choctaw, Chickasaw, Cherokee, Natchez, and Caddo. The Utina and Potano of Florida might also be included as well as the Quapaw and Shawnee. Four of these, together with the later-formed Seminole, were perpetuated to modern times as the Five Civilized Tribes, and existed as small republics under the suzerainty of the white man until the beginning of the twentieth century.

A word might be said regarding the position of our tribes relatively to the life zones. The Cherokee and some western Siouan tribes of Virginia were the only ones occupying the tongue of the Transitional Zone, which comprises the Alleghanian Faunal Area and the bits of the Canadian Zone. The Cherokee also extended into the Carolinian Faunal Area of the Upper Austral Zone, where lived also most of the Siouan tribes of Virginia and the Carolinas, excepting some that extended from the fall line to the coast. The Shawnee also were generally to be found in this area as well as the

Yuchi in early days and some Muskhogean tribes along the River Tennessee. The Tropical Zone of southern Florida was the home of the important Calusa tribe and a number of small, probably related, peoples on the east coast. All of the other tribes of this cultural province made their homes in the Austroriparian Faunal Area of the Lower Austral Zone. Only some of the wilder hunting peoples were found in the edges of the Upper and Lower Sonoran Faunal Areas, and these fall outside of the section under discussion.

The number and location of these various groups were evidently determined by a complex series of causes and cannot be derived immediately out of the environment. However, the adoption of a horticultural complex was without doubt one major reason behind the integration of these peoples into tribes, and the location of suitable cornland and suitable fisheries were determining factors of considerable weight. We have already noted the bearing which the position of the fall line had on the size and location of some Siouan tribes, and on the situation of the Creeks. The Apalachee were on the most important high land in Florida. The value of southern Appalachian quarries to the Cherokee and the significance of the Appalachians as means of defence have already been dwelt upon. The fertility of the old Choctaw, Chickasaw, Natchez, and Caddo territories contains a partial explanation of them, but it is probable that many important tribes formerly living along the Mississippi River had been driven out later by the chronic flooding to which the territory was subjected and, in more recent times, apparently, by wide-spread epidemics. The Natchez Bluff explains in considerable measure the prominence of the Natchez people, and the bluffs in the neighborhood of Vicksburg, the Tunica people. In the case of the Catawba, perhaps we must suppose that they were sufficiently far from the lowlands to escape the embarrassment of heavy forests to be cut down in the process of preparing fields, and were in proximity to Saluda Pass and the mountain quarries, and in a strategic position at trail crossings.

It is evident, however, that the manner in which the geographical features were utilized depended largely upon nongeographical factors such as race, language, and intertribal contacts. Nearly all of the tribes were homogeneous internally in respect to language and culture, not as much so as regards race. A few governmental organizations had reached a point of development which enabled them to take in tribes of alien speech, but in all such cases the tribes thus incorporated constituted a minority element. In the case of the Creek Confederation, it is true, the adopted elements at one time constituted nearly half of the federated body, but these were themselves diverse, and the dominant people, the Muskogee, always vastly outnumbered any one of them. The Natchez had taken under their protection two small alien tribes, and the Cherokee, Choctaw, Chickasaw, Catawba, and Caddo added foreign elements at various periods, but the incorporated peoples were insignificant in numbers and in many cases related to the dominant group.

As has been elsewhere intimated, adjustment to the environment was dependent in some measure upon the methods that had been evolved for exploiting it, notably the use of corn, beans, squashes, and a few other plants.

By comparing the location of prehistoric archeological sites with the location of tribes in historic times, we are able to form some idea of the change in adjustment that had taken place. The greatest shift of population seems to have occurred in the abandonment of the greater part of the lower Mississippi Valley above the mouth of Red River, though much of this occurred after the time of De Soto and may have been due to epidemics of European origin. Abandonment of the northwest coast of Florida appears to have taken place at a still earlier date, though the experience of Pineda suggests that it may not have antedated by many years the discovery of the New World. The abandonment of the Georgia coast and part of the Georgia hinterland was post-Columbian. If we consider marginal areas, we find that another extensive displacement of peoples of high culture had taken place along the Ohio River and the upper course of the Mississippi and its branches. This constitutes one of the great problems of eastern archeology.

PREHISTORIC MOVEMENTS

(See map 10)

Our strictly historical knowledge of these tribes is naturally confined almost entirely to the period after they came into contact with the whites, though it is hoped that a comparison of their known arts and industries with the remains in process of resurrection by archeologists will enable us to trace them back to a still more remote epoch. In Bureau of American Ethnology Bulletins 43 (Swanton, 1911), 47 (Dorsey and Swanton, 1912), and 73 (Swanton, 1922), I gave all of the information available to me at the time of writing regarding the histories of the Indians of the Muskhogean, Tunican, Timucuan, and Uchean stocks and the southern Siouans, and in Bulletin 22 (1895) Mr. Mooney performed a similar service for the Siouan tribes of the east. In the Nineteenth Annual Report of the Bureau (Mooney, 1900), he gave the history of the Cherokee. The Carolina region has recently been covered very competently by Dr. Chapman J. Milling in Red Carolinians, and the entire field in an elementary fashion in the articles in the Handbook of American Indians (Hodge, 1907, 1910). For the present undertaking it will not be necessary to go into details, but an outline of the general course of history in the section is called for.

The traditions of most Southeastern tribes indicate a belief that they had come into the section where we find them from the west or north, the region most often indicated being the northwest. This is natural when one considers that the Atlantic Ocean and Gulf of Mexico lie east and south. Still, it would have been possible for population to enter by way of the West Indies and the Florida Peninsula, or from Mexico along the Gulf shore. However, tradition is here borne out by the testimony of language because we find that relationship even in the case of the aberrant Timucua tongue of Florida is with the north and west (Swanton, 1929, pp. 450–453). This is not to deny earlier movements from the West Indies and, as we shall see later, there are clear traces of cultural contact in this quarter, but as a whole we must regard the flow of population in the Southeast as having been eastward and southward.

The only migration legends in any manner contradicting such a conclusion may readily be explained. Thus, some Hitchiti stories recorded by Gatschet gave the Gulf coast as the earlier home of that Creek subtribe, but the individuals from whom this came were probably Sawokli, and it is known historically that they had moved northward into the Creek Nation at a late period (Gatschet, 1884, pp. 77–78). Similarly, James Adair informs us that the tribes about Fort Toulouse, at the junction of the Coosa and Tallapoosa Rivers, had come "from South America" (Adair, 1930, pp. 267–268). It is not at all probable, however, that the Indians whom he interviewed had any clear conception of the southern continent or its distance, and we know that a part of the Alabama, including the Tawasa and Pawokti towns, had lived for a time near Mobile before settling among the Upper Creeks. We also know that they had come to Mobile under pressure from the Creeks and that one of them was found near the upper Alabama by De Soto, so that they appear to have moved in a circle. Finally, Du Pratz tells us that the chief of the guardians of the sacred fire, the one who related to him the Natchez origin legend, indicated the southwest as the direction from which his ancestors had come and Du Pratz believed that he meant Mexico. But the missionary De la Vente understood "northwest" instead of "southwest" and this is more in line with Muskhogean legends generally (Swanton, 1922, pp. 191–201; 1911, pp. 182–186). Evidently Du Pratz was led to tie these Indians up to Mexico on account of the relatively advanced state of Natchez culture.

Migration legends indicating a western origin include all of those, so far as I am aware, which have been collected from the Muskogee, and all of the legends preserved from the Hitchiti and Alabama with the exceptions indicated, and with the exception of a legend I obtained from an old Alabama woman in 1910, which evidently has incorporated European elements since it tells of a voyage across the Atlantic Ocean with a stop at islands on the way (Swanton, 1922, pp. 172–173, 191–192; 1928, pp. 33–75). In a moment we shall see that migration legends pointing to the west are supported by other data indicative of such a general movement. Circumstantial evidence regarding a similar origin exists also for the Timucua, though no legends whatever have been preserved from them. The migration legends of the Natchez have already been touched upon, but it is only fair to add that Du Pratz heard they had reached "Mexico" after traveling for a long time from an earlier home in the east. Remembering that they were pronounced sun worshipers, we may suspect that this is a mythological amplification. There is evidence that they had formerly extended higher up the Mississippi though hardly to the Wabash as they are said to have claimed (Swanton, 1911, pp. 182–186). Tradition would make the Avoyel a late offshoot of the Natchez (Swanton, 1911, p. 24).

Not a fragment of tradition has been preserved bearing on the past history of the Tunica or their allies except one which does not cover any time back of the historic period.

The Chitimacha held that their supreme being chose Natchez as their first place of abode, and the flood story of the Atakapa preserves a belief that the survivors of that catastrophe, their ancestors, landed upon the mountains of northwest Texas beyond San Antonio (Swanton, 1911, pp. 348, 363). However, this last may not have any special significance inasmuch as the story called for mountains and those were the nearest ones of which they had any knowledge.

It is a curious and interesting fact that the Yuchi, who are known to have moved about extensively during early historic times, retain no traditions relative to such migrations, but on the contrary used to believe that they were aborigines of the eastern part of the Gulf region (Swanton, 1922, p. 287).

It is undoubtedly significant that all traditions preserved from the eastern Siouan tribes point to the Northwest. While there are only three of these besides one or two very general statements, we shall find them backed up by more direct evidence. One Catawba legend obtained by Gregg and Schoolcraft traces their origin to Canada and dates it after the appearance of the French in that country, from which it is evident that it contains later embellishments. It also states that they lived for a while on Kentucky River, which was indeed once known by their name, and in Botetourt County, Va., where there are places named after them. These identifications are, however, rendered somewhat uncertain, one by the fact that "Catawba" was perhaps intended for Kituhwa, an old name of the Cherokee, and the other because Botetourt County lay across the war trace between their historic homes and the Iroquois, and the name may indicate merely that Catawba were to be looked for thereabout by Indians coming from the north. So far as the general direction of their movement is concerned, however, it is corroborated by all of our other evidence (Schoolcraft, 1851–57, pt. 3, pp. 293–296).

Of the eastern Carolina Indians, the surveyor John Lawson says:

When you ask them whence their forefathers came, that first inhabited the country, they will point to the westward and say, where the sun sleeps our forefathers came thence.   (Lawson, 1937, p. 279.)

This generalization might have included the Tuscarora as well as the Siouan tribes, but Lederer's testimony applies specifically to the latter:

The Indians now seated in these parts are none of those which the English removed from Virginia, but a people driven by an enemy from the Northwest, and invited to sit down here by an oracle about four hundred years since, as they pretended: for the ancient inhabitants of Virginia were far more rude and barbarous, feeding only upon raw flesh and fish, until these taught them to plant corn, and shewed them the use of it.   (Alvord, 1912, p. 142.)

Origin traditions from the coastal Algonquian tribes of North Carolina are wanting, but Strachey says of the Powhatan Indians that they "are conceived not to have inhabited here belowe [the falls] much more than three hundred years," which would actually mean less time, if there is any truth in the story at all, and, as the traditions of the Delaware and Nanticoke also pointed westward, there is no reason why those of the Powhatan may not have done the same. The possible significance of this will appear presently (Strachey, 1849, p. 33). Algonquian students have noted traces of northern dialectic influences, even of Cree, in the fragments of Powhatan speech preserved to us. (Gerard, 1904; Michelson, personal information.)

Except for some very late stories dealing with movements within the historic period, Shawnee legends point to the north (Spencer, 1908, p. 383).

Sibley speaks of a migration of the Kadohadacho, the leading Caddo tribe, down Red River from a point near the present Ogden, Ark., but this represents a relatively late movement (Sibley, 1832, p. 721). More to the point is a tradition supplied by one of Schoolcraft's contributors which traced the origin of the Caddo to the Hot Springs, for we have good evidence that the Caddo once lived about the Hot Springs and we know that they subsequently withdrew (Schoolcraft, 1851–57, pt. 5, p. 682). However, the Caddo narratives gathered by Mooney and myself suggest that these Indians spread toward the north, west, and south from the region where Louisiana, Texas, and Arkansas come together.   (Mooney, 1897, pp. 1093–1094; Swanton, 1931; 1942, pp. 25–29.)

In general, it may be said that these traditions are borne out by historical and circumstantial evidence. Were that not the case, we should be justified in maintaining a highly skeptical attitude toward them.

Reverting to the Muskogee, the tribe with which this discussion began, it is first to be noted that the longest and earliest origin myth which has survived, the legend told to Governor Oglethorpe by the Kasihta chief Chekilli, not only gives the general line of migration, but locates a number of places along the route which can be definitely placed. They came first to a muddy river and then to a red river, which cannot be identified, though some writers have seen in them the Mississippi and Red Rivers, respectively, in spite of the inverse order in which they were reached. Next they crossed a creek called Coloose-hutche, and continued east to a town named Coosaw. As Coosaw or Coosa was a well-known town located until very late times on the 'east bank of Coosa River between the mouths of Talladega and Tallaseehatchee Creeks, this point is determined with something approaching certainty. West of it lay the Black Warrior River, and beyond, the country of the Chickasaw. Hutche is simply the Creek word for "river" or "creek" and, indeed, it is so translated immediately afterward in the original story. Coloose is said to have been so named "because it was rocky there and smoked," but this is a far-fetched attempt to interpret the name in Creek, and its form along with the fact that this creek lay in the direction of the Chickasaw country indicates pretty clearly that it is intended for the Chickasaw or Choctaw name Okalusa, "Black Water." (Gatschet, 1888, pp. 41–51; Swanton, 1928, pp. 34–38.) The Ranjel narrative of the De Soto expedition tells us that, when the Spaniards reached the Chickasaw country, the Chickasaw chief gave them guides and interpreters "to go to Caluça, a place of much repute among the Indians." He goes on to say that "Caluça is a province of more than ninety villages not subject to any one, with a savage population very warlike and much dreaded, and the soil is fertile in that section." (Bourne, 1904, vol. 2, p. 132.)

They did not go there, however, unfortunately for us. A "Black Water" province is mentioned by the chroniclers Biedma and Elvas somewhere in northeastern Arkansas, apparently having nothing to do with the above, and in the early part of the eighteenth century we hear of a small Okalusa tribe on the west side of the Mississippi River below the Red (Bourne, 1904, vol. 1, p. 128; vol. 2, p. 30). As the name is fairly common, this last might or might not represent a remnant of the tribe to which Ranjel refers. Brinton suggested an identification of Chekilli's Coloose with the Black Warrior (Gatschet, 1884, p. 64) and it is possible that the Moundville people, who must have been numerous, constituted the Oka Lusa province of Ranjel, but if that had been the case the Spaniards would probably have heard of them before, while they were ascending the river Tombigbee. There is a Black Water Creek in Walker and Winston Counties, Ala., which corresponds very closely in position with the creek mentioned by Chekilli and might also have been Ranjel's province, if the name can be traced to an Indian original. There do not, however, appear to be any archeological remains of consequence in this region. But whether we are able to locate this creek definitely or not, it seems to me significant that it is placed in the direction of the Chickasaw country and the name appears to be in the Chickasaw language.

From this point on we have no difficulty in following the supposed course of the Creek migration. The position of "Coosaw" has been given. After living with the Coosa 4 years, the Creeks continued on east to "Nawphawpe" Creek, the present Naufawpi. They then reached Whooping Creek, a small northern affluent of Big Uchee. "Owatunka river" is the Wetumpka of today. The name "Aphoosa pheeskaw," which we encounter next, has been lost, but the big river that they shortly reached and followed can only have been the Chatta-hoochee, and the falls are the falls at Columbus, though they are indeed higher up than the story appears to indicate. Here the Mus-kogee formed an alliance with Apalachicola Indians who were al-ready in the country, and themselves spread out on both sides of the river, becoming divided into the Kasihta and Coweta (Gatschet, 1888, pp. 41-51).

When we encounter the Muskogee in later times, they are already settled in the country historically associated with them, part on the Coosa and Tallapoosa and part on the Chattahoochee. When De Soto crossed what is now Georgia, there is evidence that there were Creeks on Flint River, and it is pretty certain that a large body of them were about the present Augusta, while they must have consti-tuted a dominant element in the "Province of Guale" on the Atlantic seaboard of Georgia (U. S. De Soto Exped. Comm., 1939, pp. 172 et seq.). Nevertheless, the De Soto chroniclers, by the manner in which they compare them with the Indians along the lower Mississippi after they had encountered the latter, suggest that they had removed from that region at a date not very much anterior. One Muskogee tribe, the Eufaula, can be traced to Euharlee Creek near the famous Etowah works and from that place, in succession, to Eufaula Oldtown on Tal-ladega Creek, and to the lower course of the Tallapoosa, where they gave off a colony which settled on the Chattahoochee and later swarmed again to the Chukochartie, or Red House Hammock (Swanton, 1922, pp. 260-263), north of Tampa. There is also some reason to think that the Tali, who lived until a late period at the great bend of the Tennessee, were Creeks. One stage in the movement of the Tukabahchee can be traced from Tukabahchee Oldtown in the upper part of the Tallapoosa country to the great bend of the Tallapoosa River, where the site has now been provided with a marker (Swanton, 1922, pp. 277-282). The Muskogee language also shows by the breakdown of certain of its forms considerable contact with quite divergent tongues not likely to have been brought about in the midst of Muskhogean territory. That one of the languages influencing them belonged to the Algonquian stock is indicated by the fact that *pinwa*, the Creek word for "turkey", was quite certainly adopted from an Algonquian dialect. The word meaning "bear" and probably that for "raccoon" show early contacts with the Tunica, Caddo, and perhaps other western tongues. It would seem that the Muskogee must have moved from some region on or near the Mississippi not long anterior to the appearance of the Spaniards (Swanton, 1931).

Historical evidence for movements of the tribes of the Alabama group is much fuller. In 1541 De Soto found some of the Alabama themselves a few miles west of the Chickasaw town in which he had passed the winter (Bourne, 1904, vol. 1, pp. 108–109; vol. 2, pp. 24, 136). This was nearly 200 miles northwest of their later home about the present Montgomery, Ala. There is practically no doubt that the Coste, Costehe, or Acoste of De Soto's chroniclers was the Koasati town later found by English and French traders at the very same point, i. e., on Pine Island in the Tennessee River, and from them the name of the latter stream often appears as "the River of the Cussatees" (Swanton, 1922, pp. 201–207). While they were still living there, but probably late in the seventeenth century, they were joined by a tribe which there is every reason to suppose was of kindred origin and tongue, the Kaskinampo or Casquinampo. This was without any reasonable doubt the Casqui or Casquin encountered by De Soto almost immediately after he crossed the Mississippi River. They were then in what is now Arkansas not far from the site of Helena. Their affinities with the Koasati are indicated by the second component of the name, nampo, which has a plural signification in the Koasati tongue. In the references to the tribe by Ranjel, Elvas, and Biedma we find proof either that they belonged to the Muskhogean stock or that the name was obtained through Muskhogean interpreters. The final *n*, sometimes introduced and sometimes omitted, is evidently the common Muskhogean dative ending, and Icasqui, which Biedma uses, as evidently contains the possessive prefix of the third person. Finally, some later maps call both of the Pine Island towns towns of the "Cusatees," that is Koasati, and Adair informs us that the strength of the Creek Confederation had been increased by his time by the addition of "two great towns of the Koo-a-sah-te" (Swanton, 1930). As appears from the Delgado narrative, the first movement of these people preceded 1686 (Boyd, 1937). Leaving a fraction of the tribe on the Tennessee, which afterward settled near Gunter's Landing, the remainder established themselves close to the junction of the Coosa and Tallapoosa where a post village still perpetuates the name (Swanton, 1922, pp. 201–207).

The Tuskegee came from the same general region and settled near the Koasati at the very point where the Coosa and Tallapoosa come together. The "Tasqui" village which De Soto's army passed through in northern Alabama, on its way from the Tennessee to the Coosa, probably belonged to this tribe, and a few years later two soldiers sent by Juan Pardo from the Tennessee River to Coosa found near Tasqui a second settlement named "Tasquiqui." At a later date part of these Tuskegee moved up the Tennessee and made a permanent home among the Cherokee while the rest settled among the Creeks, as has just been stated (Swanton, 1922, pp. 207–211).

The Hitchiti language, while distinct from Alabama and Koasati, was nearer to them than to any other known dialects, and therefore it should not surprise us to find the Hitchiti and Alabama groups more or less associated. The Pawokti and Tawasa, though the latter did in fact speak a Timucua dialect, lived at the opening of the eighteenth century on or near the Apalachicola Indians in close contact with some tribes which afterward joined the Apalachicola, a Hitchiti group. In 1540 De Soto encountered a tribe known as Chiaha on an island in Tennessee River. They remained in this place over a quarter of a century longer, as we know from the Pardo documents, and it is probable that they moved from there to the Talladega country where a creek bears the name Chehawhaw, which Coxe extends to the Tallapoosa itself. A suggestion of Hitchiti-speaking Indians in the northwest is contained in the Louvigny map which is attributed to the year 1697. This shows a town on Yazoo River which seems to bear a variant of the name Sawokli. It has been barbarized by Coxe as "Samboukia," and has been preserved down to the present day in the designation of Sabougla Creek, a southern affluent of the Yalobusha. There is little doubt that some of the Hitchiti tribes were in southern Georgia before the Muskogee arrived, but the facts just cited point to a distribution from the west and north at a not very remote period (Swanton, 1922, pp. 137–141, 172–178; 1930; French, 1851, p. 59). We have no hint regarding an earlier home of the Apalachee other than that furnished by their language, which resembles Hitchiti and Choctaw, the latter most closely to all appearance. The Hitchiti believed the Yamasee to be related to themselves, and there are indications that the Cusabo were connected with both.

There is reason to think that some, at least, of the small Choctaw-speaking tribes of the lower Mississippi and its neighborhood were late arrivals from the north or northeast. Dumont de Montigny informs us that the symbol of the Houma Indians was a red crawfish and from this it is easy to infer that they were a branch of the Chakchiuma, or Red Crawfish, people on Yazoo River. Since De Soto in the sixteenth century found the latter about where they were still living in the eighteenth century, and since the Indians met by the survivors of his expedition on the Mississippi below the Natchez appear to have been related to the latter tribe, except those Indians living at the very mouth of the Mississippi, it seems evident that the Houma were a late offshoot of the Chakchiuma and had come from the north. (Dumont de Montigny, 1753, vol. 1, p. 184; Bourne, 1904, vol. 1, pp. 101–102; vol. 2, pp. 132–133.) There is some reason to think that the Quinipissa were an offshoot of the Acolapissa, and the Bayogoula, so conspicuous in the narratives of Iberville's expedition (1699), were not encountered by La Salle in 1682, though it must be added that Ford finds evidence of long continued occupancy of the Bayogoula site. The Chatot, whose earliest known home was on Apalachicola River, were probably a Hitchiti or Apalachee tribe. They retained their identity until dissipated in Louisiana in the early part of the nineteenth century (Swanton, 1922, pp. 134–137).

In De Soto's time the Natchez, or at least tribes with similar customs and apparently a similar language, lived on both sides of the Mississippi between the Arkansas and Red Rivers, and occupied most of the lower and middle Ouachita. The Timucua would naturally be regarded as ancient occupants of Florida were it not for the fact that the tribes south of them seem to have been more closely connected with the true Muskogee than with them and the discovery that a tribe speaking their language lived in central Alabama in 1540. These two facts indicate at least two displacements and possibly a general southeasterly drift. The Osochi I regard as a fragment of the Florida Timucua which broke away from the rest and joined the Lower Creeks after the Timucua uprising of 1656, and subsequently adopted the Hitchiti language from their friends the Chiaha (Swanton, 1929; 1922, pp. 165–167).

Archeological evidence collected by Ford and Chambers seems to show that the Natchez were preceded, in part at least of the territory later occupied by them, by Tunica people, but their earliest historic home, as indicated by the De Soto narratives and the location of the "Tunica Oldfields," would be on the Mississippi River above the St. Francis, and perhaps also in the region of the Hot Springs. They may have been driven northward by the Natchez. At a later date, however, they returned to the lower Yazoo and northeastern Louisiana, while two tribes went farther south and joined the Natchez. The others stayed on until the French began their settlements when the Tunica proper moved to the old Houma site near Red River and the others were broken up in the Natchez war and joined the Chickasaw or Choctaw (Swanton, 1911, pp. 306–336).

Just as the Tunica group appears to have been forced north, the Chitimacha seem to have been driven in the opposite direction—according to tradition, from the neighborhood of Natchez—until they reached Grand Lake and Bayou Teche, while two branches of the tribe settled on Bayou Lafourche (Swanton, 1911, pp. 337–359). Whether they displaced the related Atakapa in this region, or whether the Atakapa merely occupied the country southwest of them as in later times, we can only conjecture. There is reason to think that this entire group constituted an eastern extension of Texas peoples and were relatives of the Tonkawa, Karankawa, and Coahuilteco.

Between 1540 and 1567 part of the Yuchi were in the mountains of eastern Tennessee back from Tennessee River, but another part seems to have been on that river above Muscle Shoals. Early maps also indicate that in the late seventeenth century they had towns on the Ohio, and we know that some of them lived for a time near La Salle's fort in Illinois. When De Soto heard of them, it appears probable that they were already moving south, and where their original home lay has not yet been determined. By the latter half of the seventeeth century they had penetrated to the upper Tennessee and passed on southward as far as Augusta on Savannah River. Indeed, before 1639 they had reached the boundaries of Florida and from that time on were continually making trouble for the Spaniards. One band settled in west Florida, whence they moved later to the Tallapoosa and united with the Upper Creeks. In 1661 another band attacked the Guale Indians and before 1670 they had destroyed several Cusabo towns. From this time on Yuchi were generally established on some part of Savannah River, but in 1751 the last of them withdrew to the Lower Creeks with whom the largest single body continued, and still continues, to make its home. However, a number long remained in the Cherokee country, and one band under a chief named Uchee Billy joined the Seminole and settled near Spring Gardens (Swanton, 1922, pp. 286–312). See, however, page 213.

The De Soto and Pardo documents, particularly the latter, reveal the important fact that Siouan tribes of the Catawba division once occupied all of the present territory of South Carolina, and place names point to their occupancy of parts of North Carolina. As we have already seen, their own traditions claimed an original home much farther toward the north. Partly as a result of Cherokee pressure and partly from their desire to withdraw from the Spaniards, some Catawba-speaking tribes later moved into central North Carolina. The northern Siouan people—the Tutelo, Saponi, Monacan and their allies—were probably late comers into the Piedmont region of Virginia, which they had apparently reached from the upper Ohio. The same force that caused this migration was perhaps responsible for the movement of the Biloxi to the coast of the Gulf of Mexico, which conjecturally took place via the Tennessee, Coosa, and Alabama Rivers. Capinans, a Biloxi town or a tribe associated with the Biloxi, may have been the Capitanesses of the earlier Dutch maps, shown on the Juniata in Pennsylvania, or more probably beyond in eastern Ohio. Shortly after white contact, a Siouan tribe moved from some point on the upper Ohio River to the Cumberland, and thence successively to Arkansas River, to the Taensa at Lake St. Joseph, La., and finally to the Yazoo, where they were known as Ofogoula (Ofo) and established their settlements near the Tunica on the Yazoo. The rest of the Siouan tribes were driven, or moved, toward the west and northwest, and the linguistic test indicates that they had not been long separated from the Biloxi, Ofo, and Tutelo when the whites appeared (Swanton, 1936; Dorsey and Swanton, 1912). It was at about this time that the Quapaw must have left the Ohio, known to the Illinois as the River of the Arkansas, for their later homes at the mouth of Arkansas River (Shea, 1861, p. 120).

Traditional evidence as to Cherokee prehistoric movements is supported, it will be noticed, by that drawn from Spanish documents. Since Hiwassee is a good Cherokee word meaning "savannah," and it appears to be identical with the Guasili of the De Soto chroniclers minus a locative ending, we may infer that this town was occupied by Cherokee Indians, but "Xuala," entered just before, is Siouan, and Canasauga just beyond is probably Creek, so it would seem that the Cherokee invasion had but just begun (U. S. De Soto Exped. Comm., 1939, p. 50). Traditional and historical evidence regarding the origin of the Cherokee is here supported by circumstantial evidence, since north was the direction in which the other Iroquoian tribes lay. We must suppose that the Tuscarora, Meherrin, and Nottoway all came from the same direction, but their affinities are more nearly with the Iroquois proper than the Cherokee and we may assume that they had separated from the Susquehanna Indians.

Algonquian origin stories are reinforced similarly, for the Shawnee language is nearest Kickapoo, Fox, and Sauk, while Gerard and Michelson both find Cree resemblances in the Powhatan dialect. (Gerard, 1904; Michelson, personal information.)

A more easterly and northerly habitat for the Caddo is indicated in some measure by the distribution of Caddo pottery, by the resemblances between certain Caddo and Muskogee names and perhaps by linguistic affinities with Iroquois, though the last-mentioned evidence is tenuous (Swanton, 1931; see also writings of Sapir).

We will now attempt to put these data together in such a way as to make a coherent story. We may suppose that people with western affiliations, represented in later times by the Tunican groups, extended over much of the lower course of the Mississippi River. East of them were perhaps the Muskhogean tribes, one branch of whom, later represented by the Natchez and their allies, pushed in upon the river, forcing the Chitimacha and Atakapa south and west and the Tunica north. East of the Natchez were perhaps the Choctaw and beyond them the ancestors of the Alabama and Hitchiti. The former remained about where they were, but the latter spread east, some up the Tennessee and others down across the Coosa, Tallapoosa, and Apalachicola until they reached the Atlantic coast and pushed along it as far as the present Charleston, dividing as they went into the various tribes mentioned. Still north of this group on the Mississippi were the Muskogee, who followed their southern relatives toward the east, pushing down between tribes belonging to that group so that some were left on the Tennessee while others were forced on toward the south and east. To the east of the Muskogee were the Timucua, who shared a similar clan system. They were pushed onward into Florida, approaching it from the northeast, and extending up the St. Johns River. In the meantime some tribes of the Hitchiti or Apalachee groups had worked their way down into Florida to the very end, and they were subsequently cut off from their nearer relatives by the Timucua coming across from the east coast of the peninsula. The Muskogee, Tunica, and Caddo had been in contact with one another somewhere in Arkansas, but, after the Muskogee went east, the Tunica moved south and the Caddo southwest. In the meantime certain tribes along the northern or northeastern fringe of the Muskhogeans became specialized into the Siouan dialectic groups, that represented by the Catawba being intermediate probably and retaining contact with the Muskhogeans for a longer period. The Caddoan stock was probably spread farther east and the southern representatives of it farther north, where it is possible they were in contact with the Iroquoian tribes lying south of the Algonquians around the Great Lakes and north of the Siouans. It is possible that the Iroquois, Caddo proper, and Muskogee were once in intimate contact with one another along the Mississippi in the region of the Middle Mississippi area, from which contact they may all have derived their clan organizations with female descent. The Siouan people were perhaps split into eastern and western sections by the Algonquians moving south, but this process may have been begun by the Iroquoians at an earlier date. On the other hand, it is possible that the Iroquoian peoples entered the eastern part of the United States before any Siouans moved northwest and indeed the latter may have cut the Iroquois and Caddo apart.

Archeologists have now made it evident that all of these movements are relatively recent and superficial compared with the full extent of time during which mankind occupied the Gulf region. They find back of remains that may be attributed to the Choctaw, Natchez, Tunica, Caddo, and Muskogee the Coles Creek and Deasonville cultures, back of them Marksville, or "Southern Hopewell," back of that a culture, or cultures, represented by the Tchefuncte of Louisiana, the remains of the Green River people in Kentucky, and the shell-midden people of the Tennessee River with the Bluff Dwellers of the Ozarks occupying an ancient but uncertain position. For an interesting summary of the prehistory of this region from an archeologist's point of view, consult the paper by Ford and Willey (1941).

The forces which subsequently modified the Gulf peoples and changed their culture into its later form, if external to the region, must have come from Mexico and Central America, or the West Indies. If from the last mentioned, it would appear that they antedated the Arawakan invasion, and in any case they probably made their appearance as waves of influence rather than as masses of people or masses of cultural elements. Very recently Irving Rouse has come to the conclusion that a type of West Indian pottery, belonging to a culture which he calls Meillac, originated in North America, but this would mean, not that the culture of the Southeast was modified from this direction but that it was itself a modifying force. Influences from the west are more evident, but the most striking ones signify rather recent cultural contacts than mass migrations of people as was formerly assumed.

HISTORY OF THE SOUTHEASTERN INDIANS FROM THE PERIOD OF FIRST WHITE CONTACT TO THE EXPEDITION OF HERNANDO DE SOTO

(See map 11)

Small factors often have momentous consequences, and when Columbus, on October 7, 1492, acting on the advice of his pilot Martin Alonso Pinzon and in response to indications of land toward the southwest, altered his course in that direction, he was led on through the smaller Bahama Islands to Cuba and Haiti, and his subsequent voyages took him southward. It was only on his last voyage that he touched any part of North America, and this particular section, from the Isthmus of Panama to Honduras, happens to belong to the South American ethnological province. Since the West Indies fall into the same category, the great discoverer's journals are of interest to students working with South American Indians rather than those concerned with the northern tribes. The history of these latter, aside from the voyages of the Norsemen and possible expeditions following theirs not as yet thoroughly authenticated, begins, then, with the voyage of John Cabot in the year 1497. Cabot followed the coast south the next year, some think as far as Florida, but this is improbable, and if he did so he left no records of the Indians of that region. The alleged expedition of Vespucci in the same year, during which he is supposed to have traced the entire shore of the Gulf of Mexico and the Atlantic as far north as Virginia, is probably apochryphal. In the discussions by various writers this has been connected with a "mysterious" Portuguese expedition which has left exasperatingly inconclusive traces of itself in certain documents. The most important of these is a map prepared by some unknown cartographer in Lisbon, but bearing the name of Alberto Cantino, who was an envoy of the Duke of Ferrara at the Portuguese court and sent this map to his master from Rome about November 19, 1502. Attempts have been made to identify the land resembling Florida with Cuba or Yucatan, and Harrisse and Lowery both concurred in the opinion that it must be the Peninsula of Florida. The late Rudolf Schuller informed the writer that he believed the results of the expedition had been concealed because the lands visited belonged to that half of the world granted by Pope Alexander VI to Spain in his famous decision of 1493. This data, Schuller thought, was obtained surreptitiously by Cantino or his employee. However, Nunn seems to have disposed of the whole question as a series of cartographers' errors, and in any case the supposed discovery yields us no ethnological information. (See Harrisse, 1892, pp. 77–109; Lowery, 1901, pp. 125–130; Fiske, 1901, vol. 2, pp. 70–83; Nunn, 1924, pp. 91–141.)

In 1513 Ponce de Leon made what may be described as the official discovery of Florida, but the significance of the extant narratives of his expedition is in dispute. Although some commentators have held that the natives with whom he dealt were the Apalachee, this is improbable, for the Apalachee were mainly an inland tribe, and if De Leon was in their neighborhood at all, as some maps indicate, it is probable that he merely followed the coast without meeting the inhabitants and that his principal dealings were with the Calusa, a view championed by Lowery (1901, pp. 142, 446) and more recently by Davis (1935, p. 41). It seems likely, indeed, that the south Florida Indians were the only ones he met. This view is supported by the statement that the arrows used by these Indians were pointed with bones. The Apalachee Indians may well have used bone points also, but the greater part of their arrows were probably tipped with flint or made of cane. Furthermore, it is said that Ponce and his companions traded a little with the Indians for gold and skins. Now, there are few reports of the use of gold among the Indians

north of Mexico and the greater part of these come from Florida, particularly from the Calusa Indians living on the southwest coast. Most of their gold, however, is traceable to treasure fleets wrecked on their way from Central America and Mexico to Spain. In 1513 Mexico had not been invaded, but Enciso and Balboa landed in the Gulf of Darien in 1510 and almost immediately began to collect objects of gold from the natives of that region, so that it was soon known as Castilla del Oro. Presence in southern Florida of gold from Panama has been proved by the discovery within recent years of gold beads with ornamentation of Central American patterns. On the other hand, very little gold has been found in the archeological sites of the eastern United States north of Florida. Ponce de Leon's voyages have been given careful study by T. Frederick Davis, and he comes to practically the same conclusion as that here expressed.

At any rate the hostile reception accorded Ponce by the Indians indicates pretty certainly that they had had previous dealings with white men, and one must admit that the facts of history abundantly justify their reaction. Besides, since there was among the Indians they met one who understood Spanish, they can not have been far from the West Indies, and this may also mean that Ponce was not the first Spaniard to reach Florida, though it is inferred by Herrera that the native had come from those islands. A south Florida town is mentioned called Abaioa (Davis, 1935, pp. 18, 20).

In 1516 Diego Miruelo is said to have obtained gold from the Florida Indians during a trading expedition along the Gulf. In 1517 Francisco Hernandez de Córdova, on his way back to Santo Domingo from Yucatan, entered a harbor in Florida that had been visited by Ponce de Leon—probably Charlotte Harbor, as Lowery surmises. At any rate, while digging for water, the Spaniards were set upon in the same vigorous manner as in the case of De Leon, and there was a hard struggle before they reached their boats (Lowery, 1901, p. 149). In 1519 Alonzo Alvarez de Pineda, acting under orders from Francisco de Garay, Governor of Jamaica, visited the coast of the Gulf of Mexico, which he traced from the tip of the peninsula of Florida to Panuco, where he turned back, and presently he entered the mouth of a great river with a large town at its mouth and on both banks, within a space of 6 leagues, 40 villages. This river has generally been identified with the Mississippi, but Walter Scaife (1892, suppl.) suggested that it was Mobile Bay and River, the outlines of which are well preserved on Spanish charts from this time forward, and Hamilton (1910, p. 10) has proved it quite conclusively. It is evident from Pineda's map that he also discovered the mouth of the Mississippi at this time, but later cartographers confounded inlet and river, and made the former the outlet of the latter (De Salazar, 1914, map). At the end of the seventeenth century, the principal native tribes about Mobile Bay were the Mobile and Tohome, but they were probably not the occupants of those 40 villages seen by Pineda.

In 1521 Ponce de Leon made an attempt to further his Florida claim by establishing a settlement on the peninsula. I agree with Lowery and Davis that the place selected by him was in the Calusa country where he had had his first experiences with the natives (Lowery, 1901, pp. 158, 446; Davis, 1935, pp. 63–64). While his party were endeavoring to put up dwellings, they were attacked with the same determination as before and retired to Cuba, where Ponce soon died of wounds he had received in the encounter.

The year before this occurred, Lucas Vasquez de Ayllon, one of the auditors of the Island of Santo Domingo, sent out a caravel under the command of Francisco Gordillo with instructions to proceed northward through the Bahama Islands to the continent. On the way Gordillo fell in with another caravel commanded by a kinsman, Pedro de Quexos, sent out on a slave-hunting raid by Juan Ortiz de Matienzo, an auditor associated with Ayllon in the judiciary. The two captains continued together toward the northwest and reached the mainland at the mouth of a considerable river to which they gave the name St. John the Baptist because it was on his day that they made the landfall. This took them into the year 1521. The latitude of the place they estimated to be 30° 30′. The date when they took formal possession of the land in the name of the king and their employers was June 30. They soon opened communications with the natives, whose friendliness they rewarded by carrying off 70 to Santo Domingo. There the unfortunate Indians were officially freed and it was ordered that they should be restored to their native land at the earliest possible moment, but "meanwhile they were to remain in the hands of Ayllon and Matienzo." From what Peter Martyr tells us, it would seem that the effect of this action, so far as the Indians was concerned was exactly nothing, that some of them starved to death and that only one of them probably saw his native country again.

This exception, an Indian who came to be known as Francisco of Chicora, was noteworthy because he was afterward especially attached to Ayllon as a servant and happened to meet the historian Peter Martyr, who obtained from him an account of the Indians, the longest description of any tribe in North America which can claim such an early date of record. It is of especial value because our information regarding the Siouan tribes living near the coasts of North and South Carolina is exceedingly meager. In 1525 Ayllon sent two caravels under Pedro de Quexos to examine the newly discovered region of which he had in the meantime secured the exclusive right of settlement. They explored the coast for 250 leagues and returned to Santo Domingo in July bringing with them one or two Indians from each province to be trained as interpreters. In July 1526, Ayllon himself sailed from Santo Domingo with 3 large vessels and 600 settlers of both sexes. They landed at the mouth of a river which they named the Jordan, probably the Santee, where Francisco of Chicora and the other interpreters showed their good sense by deserting. One vessel was also lost, and, becoming dissatisfied with the place, the settlers removed to a river which they call the Gualdape, 40 or 45 leagues away. This has been variously placed, but I am inclined to think it was near the Savannah River if not that stream itself, since the country from the Savannah southward was afterward known as the Province of Guale, a name which the longer term Gualdape may contain. Here, however, many sickened and died; on October 18 Ayllon died also, dissensions arose, and in the middle of winter the survivors returned to Hispaniola. (Winsor, 1884–89, vol. 2, pp. 238–241; Anghierra, 1912, vol. 2, pp. 255–257.)

Meantime, in 1524–25, Giovanni da Verrazano explored the Atlantic coast of America from south to north. By Harrisse (1892, pp. 214–228), he is supposed to have made his first landfall as far south as Florida, but the latitude given by himself is 34°, which would indicate some point in the present North Carolina. He recorded a few interesting particulars regarding the inhabitants of the region agreeing very well with what later writers tell us.

The explorations of Estevan Gomez were well to the north.

In December, 1526, Pánfilo de Narvaez was granted title to all lands between the Rió de las Palmas and the Cape of Florida, and, after unforeseen delays, his fleet of 4 ships and a pinnace sighted the Florida coast on April 14, 1528. Two days later they anchored off the mouth of an inlet which was perhaps Johns Pass, just north of Tampa Bay. At its head was an Indian town with a large communal house, apparently one of the great town houses of the Timucua. In the deserted habitations the Spaniards found a single gold ornament and some fish nets. Later they discovered another bay, evidently Old Tampa Bay, and from there, on May 1, Narvaez started inland at the head of 300 men after having sent the 3 ships which remained to him along the coast to Panuco. The land force crossed the Withlacoochee and Suwannee and reached an Apalachee town (Ibitachuco) on June 25. There they found an abundance of corn and in the narratives of the expedition occurs what is probably the first reference to those wooden mortars used in reducing corn to flour. Twenty-five days later they set out for a town called Aute, not far from the sea, and reached it on July 28. A few days afterward they passed on to the coast of the Gulf. All of this time, and indeed until they left the country for good, they were pursued relentlessly by the Apalachee Indians. Here they determined to build boats in which to make their escape from the country, and 5 boats were finally constructed in which the 242 survivors departed, September 22, 1528. Coasting westward along the shores of the Gulf of Mexico, they presently came upon an Indian village of mat houses which "seemed to be permanent," on or near Pensacola Bay. Half an hour after sunset, although the Indians had received them at first in a friendly manner, they made a sudden onslaught and wounded Narvaez himself in the face with a stone, but were beaten off. The chief of this band was able to escape, leaving in the hands of those who had seized him a robe of "marten-ermine skin," "which," says Cabeza de Vaca (1905, p. 45), "I believe, are the finest in the world and give out an odor like amber and musk." Skins of the same kind and from the same region were particulary praised. It is probable that they were from the muskrat. The Indians made 3 furious attacks that night until they were finally ambushed from the rear by a party of 15 men, but not one white man escaped unhurt. In the morning, before leaving, the Spaniards destroyed more than 30 canoes.

After voyaging 3 days longer they entered a firth and met a canoe-load of Indians who, in reply to a request for water, promised to get some if they were given vessels in which to bring it back. A Christian Greek named Doroteo Teodoro said he would go with them and did so in spite of the attempts of his companions to dissuade him. He took a Negro along, and two Indians remained with the Spaniards as hostages. In the evening the Indians returned with the vessels but with no water in them and neither the Greek nor the Negro.

In the morning many canoes of Indians came, demanding their two companions, who had remained in the barge as hostages. The Governor answered that he would give them up, provided they returned the two Christians. With those people there came five or six chiefs, who seemed to us to be of better appearance, greater authority and manner of composure than any we had yet seen, although not as tall as those of whom we have before spoken. They wore the hair loose and very long, and were clothed in robes of marten, of the kind we had obtained previously, some of them done up in a very strange fashion, because they showed patterns of fawn-colored furs that looked very well. (Cabeza de Vaca, 1905, pp. 47–48.)

The mention of long hair shows that we are probably dealing with Indians related to the Choctaw since male Choctaw, unlike the men in surrounding tribes, did not shave any parts of their heads except in time of mourning. The most interesting point connected with these two groups of Indians is the fact that they had very few bows and arrows, but were armed mainly with slings and darts. That these events took place near Pensacola and Mobile is strongly indicated by the fact that, 12 years later, De Soto learned that the Greek and the Negro had been killed at a town called Piachi on the lower course of Alabama River. He was shown a dagger which had belonged to the former. Shortly afterward Narvaez and his companions passed the mouth of the Mississippi and, after skirting the shores of the Gulf many miles more, were finally cast ashore on Galveston Island. This location is indicated with considerable exactitude by the name of the tribe of Indians living there which they call Caoque or Cahoque, the Coço or Coaque of later writers, the easternmost tribe of the Karankawa Indians. This was on November 6, 1528. Of those whom the sea spared, only four ultimately reached their own people in Mexico, and it is from the narrative of one of these men, Cabeza de Vaca, treasurer and high sheriff of the expedition, that we derive most of our knowledge of its fortunes, or rather misfortunes. It is from that, too, that we derive one of our most important single bodies of information regarding the Indians of the Karankawan, Tonkawan, and Coahuiltecan stocks. (Cabeza de Vaca, 1905, pp. 9–54 et seq.; U. S. De Soto Exped. Comm., 1939, pp. 109–116.)

THE EXPEDITION OF HERNANDO DE SOTO [1]

(See map 12)

We now come to the most impressive of all Spanish attempts to conquer and settle the territory of our Gulf States, the expedition of Hernando de Soto. The original documents bearing on this adventure have been reviewed elsewhere and the arguments for the route accepted by the present writer. Here I will confine myself to a somewhat dogmatic review of the course of the army and brief notices of the tribes encountered by it.

De Soto was born at the little town of Xeres de los Caballeros in the Province of Estremadura, Spain, in 1500, and in 1514 he accompanied Pedro Árias de Ávila, better known by the shortened form of his name Pedrárias Dávila, when that commander accepted the government of Castilla del Oro or Darien. By the time he was 20, De Soto had become a captain, and in 10 years more of warfare with the Indians and civil broils between the Spaniards he became a seasoned commander. A trading partnership with Hernan Ponce, plus the spoils of the Indians, brought him a considerable fortune, which he risked in the most lucky gamble of his life, the Peruvian expedition of Francisco Pizarro. He took an active part in the conquest of the Inca Empire and, next to the Pizarros, benefited most largely from its plunder. In 1536 he returned to Spain to seek a government of his own, applying unsuccess-

---

[1] Authority for the material contained in this chapter will be found in the Final Report of the U. S. De Soto Expedition Commission (1939).

fully for grants of territory in Ecuador and Guatemala. On April 20, 1537, however, he received the royal permission to "conquer, pacify, and people" the territory from the Province of the Rió de las Palmas as far as Cape Fear on the Atlantic, and to this was joined the governorship of the Island of Cuba. During his sojourn in Spain he married Isabel de Bobadilla, one of the daughters of his former commander, Pedrárias. On April 7, 1538, he sailed from San Lúcar, the port of Seville, with seven large vessels and some smaller ones, touched at the Canary Islands, and reached Santiago de Cuba, then the capital of the islands, June 9 (or possibly 2 days earlier) and marched from there to Havana at the head of his cavalry, while the vessels skirted the island to the same point. During the winter of 1538–39, two caravels were sent across to Florida under Juan de Añasco and a port selected suitable as a point of debarkation for his army.

On May 18, 1539, De Soto sailed from Havana with a fleet of 9 vessels, and an army of about 600 men besides perhaps a hundred more camp followers, servants, and slaves. There were more than 200 horses, a herd of hogs, some mules, bloodhounds to track down the Indians, and a vast quantity of provisions and materials for equipping the army and founding a colony. On May 25 they came upon the Florida coast a short distance below Añasco's port. This was soon identified, however, and on May 30 most of the army was put ashore, while the vessels worked toward the Indian town which was their objective, gradually unloading with the assistance of the small boats accompanying them. The data supplied by the chroniclers and the topography of the region indicate plainly that this was the Indian town site on Terra Ceia Island, and the point where the army was landed Shaws Point. On June 3, 1539, formal possession was taken of the land of Florida, and shortly afterward they had the good fortune to be joined by a Spaniard of Seville named Juan Ortiz, formerly with Narvaez, who had lived with the Indians nearly a dozen years and spoke their language fluently. Until his death at Utiangue, west of the Mississippi, he was the chief interpreter of the expedition. The town occupied by them was called Oçita and probably belonged to one of the Timucua tribes. The country around it did not, however, appeal to De Soto as a suitable place for a permanent settlement, and on June 20 he dispatched his Chief Constable, Baltasar de Gallegos, to an inland tribe called Urriparacoxi, whose chief was said to dominate those along the coast. Although the Urriparacoxi chief proved unfriendly, Gallegos transmitted such flattering accounts of the lands farther on, that De Soto determined to move his army inland, and on July 15 began the march, leaving about a hundred men under Pedro Calderón to hold the port and form the nucleous of a colony in case he should decide to return thither. A garden was actually planted by them during their stay.

The route followed by De Soto took him across the Alafia and Hillsboro Rivers to the west bank of the Withlacoochee, near which Urriparacoxi evidently lay, and where De Soto was joined by his lieutenant. After an unsuccessful attempt to cross the river and the swampy country beyond, De Soto skirted the lowlands now occupied by Tsala Apopka Lake and crossed the river below the latter in the neighborhood of Stokes Ferry. The chief town of Ocale to which the Spaniards now came was probably not far from Silver Springs, because it is in this direction that Indian remains are most numerous.

On August 11 De Soto set out again toward the north, leaving his Master of the Camp, Luis de Moscoso, in charge of the remainder of the army. Advancing through the present Alachua County, then occupied by the powerful Potano tribe of the Timucuan connection, he came to a town called Cholupaha and nearby a river which had to be bridged. Beyond lay the capital of the Aguacaleyquen Indians, also. Timucua, and beyond that another river requiring another bridge. Finding Indians numerous, and apparently threatening, De Soto sent messengers to Moscoso from Aguacaleyquen, directing him to come on with the rest of the army and on September 4 all were reunited. The first river must have been the Santa Fe and the second in all probability Olustee Creek. Neither of these would ordinarily require bridges, but the narratives testify that the fall of 1539 was exceedingly rainy, and 3 days after leaving Aguacaleyquen they were held up for 2 days at a town, which they named Many Waters, on account of the excessive rainfall. On the way they passed through another Timucua town called Uriutina, which probably stood near Lake City. Beyond Many Waters they came to a town known as Napituca, where occurred a terrific battle with the Indians. This is sometimes called the Battle of the Two Lakes, because the Indians when defeated took refuge in two small bodies of water near by, where a part of them were forced to surrender.

One day's journey from Napetaca brought them to the River of the Deer, the Suwannee, and they were delayed another day building a bridge on which they crossed September 25 and came to another town of some importance called Uçachile, where they rested for 3 days. In 2 days more they reached Agile or Aucilla, the last town in the Timucua country; on the day following they reached the Aucilla River, where they began building another bridge; and on October 3 they got across and spent the night at the Apalachee town of Ibitachuco. The Apalachee Indians apparently retained unpleasant memories of Narvaez and opposed this new Spanish army, but on October 6 the latter reached Iniahica, which seems to have been regarded as the principal Apalachee town. This was undoubtedly on or close to the site occupied by the present capital of Florida, Tallahassee, and here the expedition spent the winter of 1539–1540.

Having determined to give up his base at Tampa Bay and march inland, De Soto now sent back 30 horsemen almost immediately with orders to Calderón to rejoin his army. These men were placed under the command of Juan de Añasco, who returned himself in the smaller boats to the Apalachee port near Shell Bay, the larger vessels having already been returned to Havana. Añasco arrived November 29 and Calderón at about the same time. Almost immediately De Soto sent another of his captains, Francisco Maldonado, westward in the pinnaces to locate a second port at which provisions and reinforcements could be delivered to his army at the end of another summer's exploration. Maldonado spent 2 months on this expedition and returned to the Apalachee port in February to announce that he had found a suitable inlet in a province called Achuse. Undoubtedly the Spaniards applied this name in later years to both Mobile Bay and Pensacola Bay, but I am inclined to favor Pensacola Bay in this instance, and it was Pensacola to which the name became ultimately affixed.

Almost immediately after his return from this mission, on February 26, 1540, to be exact, Maldonado was sent back to Havana with the pinnaces and with instructions to meet the army with supplies that fall at the port he had located.

During his fight at the Two Lakes, De Soto had captured an Indian belonging to a province in the interior of the Gulf region, probably occupied by Muskogee Indians. He is called by the chroniclers Pedro from the baptismal name afterward bestowed upon him, or by the diminutive form of it, Perico. This Indian had been telling his captors that he belonged to a great and rich province toward the northeast called Yupaha, and the Spaniards understood from him that gold was mined in that country. "He showed how the metal was taken from the earth, melted, and refined, exactly as though he had seen it all done, or else the Devil had taught him how it was," and it did not require the efforts of an expert at deception to fire the enthusiasm of the entire army to advance forthwith upon that wonderful land. On March 3, therefore, De Soto broke up his camp in the midst of the brave and persistently hostile Apalachee and set out toward the north.

Instead of moving directly northeast, however, De Soto directed his course slightly west of north to the nearest occupied territory, a province called Capachequi lying a short distance west of Flint River. During this entire expedition, but particularly after leaving Iniahica, the Spaniards were dependent upon the granaries of the unfortunate natives and consistently directed their march through the more thickly settled parts of the country. Crossing the Guacuca (Ochlockonee) River, in 3 days they came to the River of Capachequi (the Flint). The river was high and the current swift and they were obliged to construct a barge fastened at each end by a cable, in which men and equipment could be drawn across. All did not effect the passage until March 10. Next day they reached the main settlements of Capachequi, where they spent 5 days although the inhabitants were unfriendly. This province probably lay about the point where the Georgia counties Miller, Early, and Baker come together.

They left Capachequi on March 17 and spent the night at a very beautiful spring they called White Spring, probably at the head of Alligator Creek. Next day they reached the River Toa (the Ichaway-nochaway), which they also found high and running with a swift current, so that two attempts at bridge building failed until a device suggested by Nuño de Tobar was tried, after which the bridge held and by March 22 all were across. Early on the 23d they arrived at a large village called Toa, which is plausibly identified with a site around two Indian mounds on what is called Pine Island in Dougherty County, Ga.

About midnight of the same day, De Soto set forward with 40 horsemen and a large body of foot soldiers to reconnoitre a tribe farther on called Chisi or Ichisi. There is reason to think that the Toa Indians were connected with the Hitchiti, but the name of the Ichisi is similar to the word by which true Muskogee were known to the Hitchiti, and it is probable that this tribe, which they found peacefully inclined, unlike those they had been among, was related to the Muskogee or Creeks proper. De Soto first came upon a village on an island and then to other villages, to a bad passage in another stream or swamp, where a Portuguese, Benito Fernandez, was drowned, and to a town beyond that where they were met by messengers from the tribal chief. Two days more brought them to the place of residence of this chief on the opposite side of a river which they call Rió Grande. This Rió Grande can only have been the Flint, and it is surmised that the island town which they first reached was in the Kinchafoonee and that the "bad passage" was the crossing of the Muckalee.

Because this was the first chief "who came to them in peace," they "borrowed" only a few carriers from him, and they set up a wooden cross on the mound of his village. This was on April 1, and the next day they set out again, arriving on the 3d at a river which had its course eastward instead of south. There dwelt the Altamaha Indians (part of the Yamasee), who were also friendly. The chief directed them first to a town where they could obtain food and next day sent canoes to take them to his own side of the river, where they remained from April 4 until the 8th. On the 7th they set up a cross in his village also. The river turning eastward was evidently the Ocmulgee and the location of the Altamaha Indians was in Telfair County. The place where our explorers came upon this river was evidently not much if any above Abbeville, where the eastward trend of the river becomes first noticeable. Here they were met by the chief of a town higher up the river called Ocute, identified with the main settlement of the Hitchiti, and they accompanied him to his home, which was not far from the present Hawkinsville, Ga. Erecting another cross at Ocute, they passed on to two neighbor towns called Cofaqui and Patofa, 1 day's march beyond, and therefore probably near the present Westlake, or possibly as high up as the Indian site at Bullard.

At this point the army now turned directly east in search of the province of which Pedro had been telling them, between which and the settlements on the Ocmulgee lay a region at that time uninhabited. Two days' travel brought them to a river divided into two channels, which they forded with the greatest difficulty, several of their hogs being drowned in the passage. The river was, of course, the Oconee and the place where they crossed is identified by the description as Carr Shoals, 6 miles above Dublin, Ga. In 2 days more they reached the Ogeechee, but by that time they had wandered from the trail and it is impossible to know where on that stream they crossed, though it must have been not far from the present Louisville.

Another 2 days brought them to a third river, "a very large river and hard to cross which was divided into two streams." Elvas says that it was "of a more violent current [than the others], and larger, which was got over with more difficulty, the horses swimming for a lance's length at the coming out, into a pine-grove." Garcilaso identifies this river with the one on which Cofitachequi, the Yupaha capital, was located; that is, as we shall see, the Savannah. The other narratives, however, show plainly that it was distinct, and there is no other answering to the description within a day's journey of the Savannah except Brier Creek. Ordinarily Brier Creek is a rather sluggish body of water, but sometimes it rises and develops considerable current, and we know that this was a wet spring because Ranjel says, speaking of this period of their journey, that they were "drenched with continual rain, the rivers always rising and narrowing the land."

After an attempt to continue beyond this stream, De Soto deemed it best to return to it at a place where were some Indian cabins. There they camped while sending scouting parties in all directions in search of settlements. At this time the utility of their herd of swine became apparent because for many days they were reduced to an almost complete dependence on their flesh. Finally, Añasco, who had been sent down the river, returned with news of an Indian town and two Indians as guides, who took them thither.   The town was named Hymahi or Aymay, and there they found more than 30 bushels of parched corn. At the abandoned camp they left a message for the other scouting parties indicating their whereabouts and all presently came in, but one of them, Juan Rodriguez Lobillo, was sent back to bring up two companions he had left behind.   On April 30 De Soto himself went forward with an Indian woman as guide and reached "a large, deep river," the Savannah, where he camped for the night, Añasco being sent on in advance to secure interpreters and canoes in which to cross. Next morning De Soto joined him on the river bank opposite the town of Cofitachequi, and presently a kinswoman of the chieftainess came across to greet the Spanish commander, being followed shortly by the niece of that lady.   This niece is the individual usually called "the Lady of Cofitachequi."   She brought with her many presents and handed De Soto himself a necklace of pearls which she was wearing. Her people also provided canoes in which the entire army was ferried to her town, a part, however, being soon sent to another village called Ilapi where there was a plentiful supply of corn.

The traditional site of this town is Silver Bluff about 20 miles below Augusta, Ga., but on the South Carolina side of the river.   This identification rests in part on an Indian tradition coming through the trader George Galphin, who owned the bluff in the early part of the eighteenth century, but it is supported by the narratives of the Pardo expedition.   Juan Pardo was sent into the interior of what is now South Carolina by Pedro Menendez in 1566 and 1567.   He set out from the Spanish post of Santa Elena near modern Beaufort, and estimated that Cofitachequi was half way to the Appalachian Mountains.   He states also that it was the last Indian settlement with swamps in the neighborhood and that the day after leaving it on his journey toward the north they passed entirely out of the swamp country.

The chieftainess of Cofitachequi, aunt, as supposed, of the "Lady," was not seen by her European guests although they made two efforts to discover her whereabouts, and on May 13, less than 2 weeks after their arrival, they set out northward in quest of another town of which they had had previous intimation, a town called Coça.

About a league from Cofitachequi was an abandoned village called Talomeco and in it a temple or ossuary of which Garcilaso de la Vega gives an elaborate description, and where, as well as in the ossuary of Cofitachequi itself, were quantities of pearls.   In the latter they also found several articles of Spanish origin which they believed, probably correctly, to have been brought by the colonists of Lucas Vasquez de Ayllon in 1526.   The presence of an f in the name of Cofitachequi, the name of Talimeco itself, and the probable identity of the town Ilapi with the later Hilibi, all point to an identification of this province with part of the Muskogee, probably the main part of the Lower Creeks.

On leaving Cofitachequi, the Spaniards took with them many pounds of pearls from the ossuary of Cofitachequi, "presented" by the "Lady," and they carried along the "Lady" also, as was their wont in similar cases to secure subordination and service from the Indians under her influence.   The Pardo narratives help us to the conclusion that the Spaniards now kept northeast of the Savannah on a well-marked trail between that river and the Saluda.   There is no reference to a repassage of the Savannah, as some writers have assumed, and on the sixth day of their march they came to a town called Guaquili, evidently identical with the Aguaquiri of Pardo, which was clearly northeast of the Savannah.   Before reaching Guaquili, on the second day after his departure from Cofitachequi, De Soto came to a province called Chalaque.   Most writers have assumed too hastily from this reference, from an error as to distance by Elvas, and from a somewhat confusing note farther along in Ranjel's narrative, that this referred to the Cherokee country.   The location is, however, very far south of any site occupied by Cherokee in historic or traditional times.   The name is probably nothing more than a form of the Muskogee word "Chilokee," which signifies "people of a different language" and which very likely became permanently affixed to the Cherokee at a later period.   As used by the De Soto chroniclers, however, it was most likely applied to people speaking an eastern Siouan language, which would equally have been "a different speech."

On May 21 De Soto reached Xuala near the foot of the Appalachian Mountains, and there he was joined next day by Gallegos with the remainder of the army.   As Mooney pointed out many years ago, Xuala, which would be Shuala in English, was evidently a Muskogee attempt at Cheraw or Saraw, there being no *r* in the Muskogee tongue.   This town I believe to have been located on a knoll known locally as Towns Hill between Knox and Crane Creeks.   This not only corresponds to the position given by the narratives of the expedition, but is indicated by requirements laid down in the subsequent narratives.   Thus, after leaving Xuala they went over "a very high range" and in 2 days came to and "crossed the river, wading up to their shins, by which later they were to depart in the brigantines." This can only have been one of the head streams of the Tennessee, for no other waters in this section flow into the Mississippi, the river "by which they were to depart" from the country.   It has been some-times identified with the Coosa, but this is disproved by the testimony of the De Soto map and by the fact that they recognized the Coosa as one of those which flowed "into the Bay of Chuse," i. e., Mobile Bay or Pensacola. Now, the only head stream of the Tennessee which lay squarely in the path of the Spaniards was the Little Tennessee. Ranjel's language makes it clear that they crossed this at some point where it appeared to be a considerable river and this would not be the case far above Franklin, N. C. The sensible thing for them to do would have been to travel west from Towns Hill to Stekoa Creek and then north through Rabun Gap, but in that case there would have been no occasion to cross the Little Tennessee at all except near its head where they could almost have jumped it. Nor would they in passing up War Woman Creek have been obliged to cross "a very high range." It is evident, therefore, that they must have crossed to the neighborhood of Franklin by what is called the Winding Stair Trail, which crosses the Chattooga at Burrells Ford and passes through Victoria or Horse Cove and Highlands and down along Cullasaja Creek. However, it seems that there was another trail passing Chattooga River at Nicholas Ford, ascending the West Branch of that river and going down to the Little Tennessee by way of the Tessuntee.

Near the Little Tennessee their royal hostage gave them the slip, and, to their still greater regret, carried off with her a box of unbored pearls. On May 28 they left this river and spent the night in an oak wood, and the night following by "a large stream which they crossed many times." Early on the following day they reached a town of considerable importance called Guasili. Next morning, May 31, they set out from Guasili and again spent the night in an oak wood. The day after, June 1, they passed a place called Canasoga and slept in the open country beyond. The fact that for much of this time they were following a river and presently camped near a town called Canasoga gives a clue to the course they were pursuing, for the Hiwassee, flowing west into the Tennessee, lies directly west of Franklin, and just below the point where it emerges from the mountains into the Tennessee Valley it receives a stream called Cannasauga. It seems evident that the Spaniards climbed the mountains west of Franklin along the valley of Cartogechaye Creek on what was afterward known as the Macon Trail, and descended into the valley of Shooting Creek, which they followed to the Hiwassee. The well-known town site at the mouth of Peachtree Creek, where a mound of considerable size was excavated under the Civil Works Administration, between December 21, 1933, and April 1, 1934,[2] corresponds excellently with the location of Guasili. The canyon of Hiwassee River would have presented some difficulties to the progress of the army, but none greater than those they had already encountered. It is furthermore significant that there is no

---

[2] The report of the results of this work is contained in Setzler and Jennings (1941).

reference to a camp by the river for some days after they left
Canasoga and the reason is plain. At this point the great war trail
from Virginia and the New River crosses the Hiwassee and reaches
the Tennessee above Chattanooga. Evidently the Spaniards took
their line of march along this trail and that is furthermore indicated
by the fact that they indeed came out upon a great river on the second
day of their march, "the river which they had crossed in the plain
where the woman chief went off." Ranjel adds, "it was now very
large," and naturally, since this was the main channel of the Tennessee.

On June 5 the army entered Chiaha on an island in the great river
two crossbow shots from its upper end and 1 league from the lower
end. The location of this island and the description of it are perfectly
met by Burns Island in the Tennessee River just before it enters Alabama, but if it was not that island, certainly it was Williams Island
above or Long Island below. Here the explorers spent 3 weeks to re-
cuperate and rest their horses after the arduous journey from Xuala.
During that period two soldiers were sent across the mountains to the
north to visit a province called Chisca, probably occupied by Yuchi
Indians, where there was copper and where they hoped to find gold.

On June 28 the army left Chiaha and marched along the river to a
town called Coste or Costehe situated on another island almost certainly identifiable with Pine Island. The wording of Ranjel's narrative would lead us to suppose that they crossed the Tennessee twice
on the way, once to the north bank, perhaps near the foot of Long
Island, and again to the south at Bellefonte Island, and entered Coste
at the upper end of Pine Island by fording the south branch of the
river. Here they were joined by their wounded, brought from Chiaha
by canoe, and accompanying them the Chisca messengers, who had
been unable to reach their objective but brought with them a beautiful
bison skin. The reason for the detour made by the army along the
north bank of Tennessee River is to be found in a high bluff between
the mouth of Raccoon Creek and Bellefonte Island on the south shore.

Coste is identified with the Koasati town of later times which
sometimes gave its name to the river. On leaving it, we are told
specifically that the explorers crossed "the other branch of the river,"
which, if we have been correct so far, would mean the north branch.
On July 10 they entered the Tali town which is believed to have stood
on McKee Island, and next day they set out toward the great province
of Coça of which glowing accounts had reached them when they were
still in central Georgia. That night they slept in the open country,
and during the next 3 days crossed as many rivers, arriving on the
third evening at a town called Tasqui. Coça was on the Coosa River
and to reach it from the Tennessee it was necessary to cross Sand

Mountain. It is believed that the three rivers were Wills Creek, Canoe Creek, and the Coosa River, and that Tasqui was a town occupied by Tuskegee Indians, although the Tuskegee in later times were at the junction of the Coosa and Tallapoosa. Passing south along the east bank of Coosa River, they entered Coça on July 16, the chief of that town coming out to meet them in great state, borne in a litter upon the shoulders of his principal warriors.

The Spaniards remained encamped here for more than a month, and, as was usually the case, they succeeded in that time in securing the ill-will of its inhabitants. They left August 20 and encamped for the night at a place called Talimuchasy, the Creek word for "New Town," and the next day at Itaba, conjecturally located at an ancient Indian site on Hatchet Creek. On the 31st they reached Ulibahali, in which name it is not difficult to recognize the Creek war town of Hothliwa-hali. This was evidently at or near the place later occupied by it on Tallapoosa River at the junction of Chubbehatchee Creek. On September 2 they left Ulibahali and, marching west along the south side of the Tallapoosa and Alabama Rivers, camped on the 6th at Tuasi, believed to have been in the northwestern suburbs of the present Montgomery. On the 18th they reached a settlement called Talisi, where they remained until October 5. It was large and almost encircled by the Alabama River, and this fact has enabled the historians of Alabama to identify it with one of the sites on Durand's Bend. Here De Soto received a messenger from Tascalusa, a powerful chief living on the lower course of Alabama River, and he was presently followed by one of Tascalusa's own sons with whom, on his return, De Soto sent two of his companions in the capacity of spies.

On October 5 the explorers set out from Talisi, and spent the night at a town called Casiste, on the bank of Alabama River and occupied by a part of the Kasihta Indians. The following day they passed into the territory of the Mobile Indians under Tascalusa's sway, and after camping for the night at several towns along the Alabama, on October 10 they reached a new village named Athahachi, where Tascalusa had taken up his residence. This chieftain met the Spaniards in state and impressed them profoundly on account of his gigantic stature and imperial bearing. Nevertheless, they did not hesitate to make him a virtual prisoner, as was their wont, and use him as a guide in penetrating the country under his control. On the 12th they took their departure from this place and on the 13th entered Piachi, Tascalusa's capital town, which was on a high bluff overhanging the river, probably where Claiborne now stands. Here they learned that the two men sent ashore by Narvaez after water had been slain, and the inhabitants immediately showed their continued hostility by killing two of the men who had been placed as guards over their chief. They also claimed that they had no canoes and compelled the Spaniards to make cane rafts for the passage of the river. On the 15th or 16th the explorers finished crossing and camped in the forest, and in 2 or 3 days more, early on the morning of October 18, St. Luke's day, they reached a fortified town called Mabila, where Tascalusa had promised to give them carriers and supplies and to turn over to them the slayers of the two Spaniards. Except that this must have been somewhere in Clarke County, Ala., we are ignorant of its location, although from the nature of the encounter of which it was the scene, it would seem as though plenty of material for identification must have been left on the spot. Here, at any rate, the Indians of Tascalusa rose upon their European visitors and were nearly wiped out in the ensuing contest, which cost the Spaniards themselves the lives of about 20 men and a number of horses besides all the pearls they had brought from Cofitachequi and a large part of their reserve equipment. Nearly all of the remaining Spaniards bore scars upon their bodies.

This battle had a decisive influence upon the entire course of the expedition. Coming as it did just before De Soto planned to meet Maldonado at the port of Achuse, it discouraged his followers so completely that many of them fully intended to desert as soon as they reached the ships; and the loss of the pearls, the only riches they had been able to secure, deprived De Soto of the bait he counted upon to fill the files of his army. Word of the treachery contemplated, in which the treasurer of the expedition, Juan Gaytan, seems to have been the ringleader, reaching De Soto determined him to save his enterprise, one in which he had invested his entire fortune, by moving again into the interior. On November 14, therefore, after having spent nearly a month in recuperation and to allow the wounds of his followers to heal, De Soto marched directly north, and in 4 days discovered "a fine river." The trail they were pursuing was probably almost along the line of a later road which ran from Grovehill to the neighborhood of Thomasville, and then through Dixon's Mills and Linden to Old Spring Hill, where it divided, one branch going to Demopolis and the other to Greenville. The river they came upon was the Tombigbee or the Black Warrior. If the former, it must have been at the bend west of Linden; if the latter, as seems most likely, it would have been near the mouth of Prairie Creek. The next day, November 18, they passed over bad places and through swamps and reached an Indian town called Talicpacana or Taliepataua, beyond which were two others, Moçulixa and Zabusta. The location of these villages has been very satisfactorily determined by J. Y. Brame as lying along what is called Melton's Bend not far from the old town of Erie. The names are clearly in the Choctaw language and the province is called by Elvas "Pafallaya," which is undoubtedly intended for Paⁿsfalaya, "Long Hairs," an ancient name of the Choctaw Indians. In later times Choctaw were living in this neighborhood, though not on the sites mentioned.

These Choctaw, like so many other Indians, objected to being plundered, and removed their provisions to the opposite side of the river, making it necessary for the Spaniards to spend more than a week constructing a pirogue in which to effect the crossing. When it was completed, they had little difficulty in forcing the passage and confiscating the corn stored nearby. A little higher up this river was a town which seems to have been a kind of capital for the district, since it gave its name Apafalaya to the river and, as we have seen, to the province. This is believed to have occupied an old Indian town site at Stephens Bluff.

Taking the chief of this town as their "guide," in their accustomed manner, on December 9 the explorers set out once more toward the north, and on the 14th, after traversing "many bad passages and swamps and cold rivers," they came to the "River of Chicaça," which they found overflowing its bed. This was, of course, the Tombigbee, and, these Indians also being hostile, they were again obliged to take time to build a pirogue. It was probably smaller than the barge constructed to cross the Black Warrior, for they were ready to attempt the passage on December 16, the Indians having been frightened away in the meantime by a threat to their position on the part of Gallegos dispatched up river with 30 horsemen. Late that night De Soto with a body of cavalry arrived at an Indian village abandoned by its inhabitants. Next day Gallegos appeared and at the same time, presumably, the remainder of the army. It seems certain that the crossing place was either at Cotton Gin Port just below the junction of the two forks of the Tombigbee, or Morgan's Ferry just below Aberdeen, probably the latter. If the former supposition is correct, the Chickasaw town they entered may have been at or close to the Chickasaw towns of a later date close to Tupelo. If the latter theory is right, the town was evidently farther west, in the northern edge of Chickasaw County or the southern edge of Pontotoc. During the following winter De Soto was persuaded by the Indians to send a part of his force against the Sacchuma (Chakchiuma), then probably on Lines Creek, that they might divide his army and destroy it, but the ruse proved unsuccessful.

In any case, the army encamped here until March 4 following. On that date they had planned to resume their journey toward the west and had made the usual "request' of the Chickasaw chief for bearers. Early in the morning, however, the Chickasaw fell upon them, surprising the sentinels, who had been unusually remiss, and setting fire to the dwellings, which were utterly consumed. Our best authorities agree that had the Indians not been frightened away by stampeding horses, which they mistook for mustering cavalry, the entire army would have been destroyed. In this battle only about a dozen Spaniards were killed, but between 50 and 60 horses were destroyed, a loss almost as serious as that of soldiers, since the victories of the Spaniards were due largely to the greater mobility their cavalry gave them. At the same time so much clothing and equipment was consumed in the burning houses that the survivors were in a wretched condition, and they freely admitted that had the Indians attacked them again immediately afterward they would have perished to a man. Fortunately, another attack was not ventured until March 15, giving them time to retemper and rehaft their weapons and provide themselves with substitute clothing. This reconditioning took place at a second village 1 league from the one where they had passed the winter. On account of this negligence in posting sentinels on the night of the attack, Luis de Moscoso was demoted from his position as Master of the Camp and the place given to Gallegos.

The Indian attack on the 15th was easily repulsed, and on April 26 the army set out once more, first stopping at a small town belonging to the Alibamo tribe, where they sent foraging parties into the country in search of provisions, having heard that a wilderness of considerable extent lay before them. One of these parties, which was led by Juan de Añasco, discovered a stockaded fort garrisoned by a large body of Indians. Biedma affirms that this was not an occupied town, but had been erected to challenge the courage of the Europeans. De Soto ordered the place carried and this was done in short order with slight loss on both sides but no further advantage to the explorers, as it was not provisioned.

On April 30, after recuperating in some measure, they resumed their march westward, passing through unoccupied country wooded and with many swamps, and on May 8 they came to a small tribe called Quizquiz on the banks of the Mississippi, which they saw for the first time, though its mouth had been observed earlier by Pineda and Narvaez and probably others. On May 21 they established themselves near the bank and began making barges on which they crossed on June 18, spending the night at a village belonging to a tribe called Aquixo. Next day they set out toward the north, penetrated "the worst tract of swamp and water they had seen in all Florida," and came to the territory of a tribe called Casqui, a land "more high, dry, and level" than any they saw along the river. In the principal town of this tribe they set up a wooden cross and about it conducted the first Christian ceremony to take place in the State of Arkansas.

This was in answer to the prayers of the chief, whose fields were suffering from drought, and a few days afterward we learn that there were abundant rains.

At Casqui the Spaniards were told of a wealthy province toward the north called Pacaha at war with the Casqui Indians, and De Soto set out for that country on the 26th. Next day he crossed a swampy bayou which lay between the two tribes, and on the 29th entered the chief settlement of Pacaha, whose inhabitants had abandoned it and sought refuge on an island in the Mississippi higher up. Thither De Soto immediately followed them and peace was soon made, the Pacaha chief and his people returning to their town and the Spaniards establishing themselves there for a month while they sent exploring parties inland toward the west and north.

There has been much discussion over the place where De Soto crossed the Mississippi, but the strongest reasons may be adduced for locating it at Sunflower Landing below Friar Point, Miss. In the first place, we are told that, on leaving the Alibamo fort, the Spaniards went "through a wilderness, having many pondy places, with thick forests, fordable, however, on horseback, except some basins or lakes that were swum" (Elvas). Of the three routes which have been advocated by the most competent students, via Memphis, Commerce Landing, and Sunflower Landing, this description applies to only the second and third. As between these, however, it is a significant fact that Sunflower Landing is the only point south of Crowley's Ridge, and Crowley's Ridge is the only high land west of the river corresponding to that in the province of Casqui. From a lowland province, Aquixo, by the river, they passed to higher land at Casqui and again to low land by the river in the province of Pacaha. This succession would not be encountered if the Spaniards had crossed at Commerce Landing or at Memphis. There is still another argument based on the identification of Ouachita River as the River of Cayas or Anilco. Counting the number of cardinal rivers crossed back from the Ouachita, we are brought to Sunflower Landing. If we count back from the Arkansas, we are taken beyond the St. Francis. The Ouachita having been identified with the River of Cayas on independent evidence, Sunflower Landing is indicated rather than Commerce Landing or Memphis. This conclusion seems inescapable.

The affiliations of the tribes encountered by De Soto in this region are in considerable doubt. There is every reason to believe that the Casqui were the later Kaskinampo who finally united with the Muskhogean Koasati. It was formerly thought that the Pacaha were the later Quapaw and such may have been the case, though their culture, as indicated in the De Soto narratives, was quite distinct. I am rather inclined to regard them as a branch of the Tunica, as also the

Aquixo and Quizquiz Indians, since Tunica Oldfields near Friar Point marks a former location of the Tunica tribe. However, this is highly speculative. The province of Quizquiz may have been about the Alligator Mounds, Aquixo about Avenue south of Oldtown Lake, and Pacaha a short distance above the mouth of St. Francis River.

While De Soto's army was at Pacaha, one expedition penetrated the country toward the northwest but found only bands of wild huntsmen and territory difficult to pass through on account of the tall grass and underbrush. On account of this unpromising outlook and because he heard of populous towns to the south, De Soto determined to return in that direction. Taking their departure from Pacaha on July 29, the Spaniards passed through the Casqui country and August 1 came to the River of Casqui "as large as the Guadalquivir," evidently White River, and were ferried across it by the Casqui Indians. Traveling farther south they came, on the 5th, to "the largest village which they saw in that country," named Quiguate, and they remained there 20 days. The form of this name allies it with a number of other towns more to the south and suggests that it was Natchez, but the relationship is uncertain. The site corresponds very well with the Menard mound group a few miles east of Arkansas Post.

At Quiguate De Soto learned of a town "near some mountains" toward the northwest, and, thinking that silver and gold might be found there, he determined to direct his march thither. On August 26 the army set out and passing four marshes in as many days came to a river which they followed up, arriving at the town of Coligua on September 1. This was "a populous place along the gorge of a river" and is believed to have been at the present Little Rock, the river they had followed being, of course, the Arkansas. Nearby were many bison.

Although considerable plunder was secured in this town, there was no gold or silver, and on September 6 they turned toward the southwest, where they had learned of a populous province called Cayas, and next day they reached Calpista, where there was a salt spring, perhaps near the present Benton, Ark. Continuing in the same general direction by easy stages they spent one day in a province called Palisema, and on the 13th or 14th they came to a large river, the one which they afterward called the River of Cayas or Anilco. This was undoubtedly the Ouachita. On the 15th De Soto rode forward with some cavalry to a better province called Tanico, where the remainder of the army joined him next day. This is sometimes identified with the salt province and sometimes it is treated as if it were distinct. Here, in any case, they spent some time extracting salt along the banks of a rivulet which may have been Salt Creek, a stream flowing into Ouachita River near the bend above Arkadelphia. The main part of the province where they were encamped probably lay considerably farther up, about Cedarglades or Buckerville.

Hearing of Tula, a province in a southerly direction, on October 1 the Governor set out to reconnoiter it with 13 horsemen and 50 foot soldiers, but he was set upon so vigorously that he returned next day in haste. On the 5th he led the entire army thither, and they entered the town 2 days later. It was abandoned, but the next morning the inhabitants came upon them and a conflict followed so severe that, although the Indians were driven off, Ranjel calls them "the best fighting people that the Christians met with." The language of these Tula Indians was so different from the speech of those among whom the Spaniards had been traveling that they had difficulty in finding an interpreter. We know now that they were one of the Caddo tribes and feel safe in locating them about the present Caddogap and on Caddo River. There is reason to think that the Coligua, Tanico, and Palisema provinces were occupied by Tunica Indians, the first two being the tribes we later encounter under the names Koroa and Tunica, while Palisema seems to have a Tunican ending.

Acting on information obtained from the Tula Indians, De Soto now decided to turn toward the southeast where he was told of a tribe named Utiangue from which he hoped to obtain provisions for the approaching winter. In 4 days they reached a place called Quipana, which was either on the Ouachita or the Little Missouri, and, continuing on down the Ouachita came, on November 2, to the object of their search. To reach it the Spaniards may have gone down Antoine Creek to the Little Missouri River and followed that to the Ouachita, or descended to the latter by Caddo River. In any case, Utiangue was certainly upon the Ouachita and probably near Camden or Calion. At Utiangue the explorers found the provisions they were in search of and, mindful of previous experiences when in their winter quarters among the Apalachee and Chickasaw, promptly constructed a stockade about their camp. From our chroniclers it appears that the winter of 1541–42 was very cold, and they declared that there was snow during a month.

March 6, 1542, De Soto broke camp at Utiangue and descended the Ouachita in search of a province called Anilco because he heard that it was near the Rió Grande, that is, the Mississippi, and he needed to reach the sea in order to recruit his forces. During the winter Juan Ortiz had died and afterward the explorers were often in great difficulties owing to the fact that they were not able to understand their other interpreters sufficiently well. At a place called Ayays, believed to have been near Columbia, La., they crossed the Ouachita to the eastern bank and continued down it until stopped by a lake, or rather side branch, which was flowing into the main stream with great violence. After considerable delay they crossed, though whether to the east or west we are uncertain, and on March 29th entered Anilco, finding it to be in a very fertile country, with greater stores of corn than any they had visited hitherto except Apalachee and Coca.

Shortly after reaching this province, De Soto received a visit from the chief of a tribe called Guachoya, whose town was on the Mississippi and who was an enemy of the chief of Anilco. As he intended to reach the Mississippi, he determined to proceed to Guachoya with his army and led the greater part of it overland, sending 50 men in 6 canoes to the same place down the river. Upon the approach of this army, the Guachoya chief at first abandoned his town and with the rest of his Indians fled to the opposite side of the Mississippi. Presently, however, he ventured to return, peace was made, and an alliance followed resulting in a joint attack upon the Anilco settlements, the slaughter of many Anilco Indians, and the destruction of the main town. The accounts of our chroniclers render it certain that Anilco was either at the famous Indian site at Jonesville where there was formerly a mound 80 feet high or at Harrisonburg. In either case, Guachoya must have been near Ferriday or between that place and Waterproof.

On the opposite side of the Mississippi some miles lower, De Soto learned of a tribe more influential than either the Anilco or Guachoya, and called Quigualtam. Wishing to open communications with its chief, De Soto invited him to come to him, received a proud answer, and was disposed to cross the river and punish "such presumption," but was by that time very low with a fever which grew worse daily, and finally, on May 21, 1542, he passed away.

On his death bed De Soto appointed Luis de Moscoso as his successor, and this choice was ratified by the other officers. De Soto's body was first buried near one of the town gates but a few nights later, fearing that the Indians would dig it up, Moscoso had it exhumed, wrapped in a blanket weighted with sand, and dropped into the middle of the Mississippi. Immediately afterward he called together the captains and principal personages and demanded their several opinions in writing as to whether they should descend the river to the sea and follow the coast to Mexico or attempt to reach it by land. He had determined to give up the enterprise. All voted in favor of the venture by land and on June 5 they set out.

Although the province of Anilco must have lain almost directly west of Guachoya, the Spaniards did not pass through it, but mention instead another called Catalte. It is to be suspected that they avoided Anilco because of their recent attack upon it. Since we know that they crossed Ouachita River on their return from Texas and are told that they came back along the trail they had followed going out, it is suspected that Catalte lay somewhere between Columbia and the Mississippi, perhaps about Fort Necessity.

After crossing the river just mentioned, Moscoso led his troops through unoccupied country until June 20, when they reached a province called Chaguate or Chaguete. In this country salt was made and it may be identified quite certainly with the region about Drake's Salt Works, where there are quantities of Indian potsherds. Early in July they went on to another salt province, probably the area about Lake Bistineau, where are also numerous Indian remains. A journey of 4 days more brought the army to a province called. Amaye, and here we enter again into the territory of the Caddo tribes. This is evident from the names given to some of them—names which appear in later times, names of others interpretable in the Caddo language, and the associations of still others. From Amaye they went to a more important Caddo division living along a great river, and this is, of course, Red River. From the distances given and the time occupied in their travels, it is evident that this more important tribe, the Naguatex (the Namidish of later history), was living above the site of Shreveport, and the place where Moscoso crossed seems to have been near Miller's Bluff some miles higher.

Here, as we gather from Biedma and the De Soto map, a sharp turn was made to the southwest, they visited two poor tribes called Nissohone and Lacane, and a larger one called Nondacao, and reached a fourth at a considerably greater distance called Hais. These are plainly the Nasoni, Nacanish, Anadarko, and Eyeish of later history. The three first were evidently somewhat east of the locations they held at the end of the seventeenth century, but the last seems to have been at about the same spot, around the present San Augustine. Most of these tribes were unfriendly, and it may be added that the Spaniards gave them little cause to be otherwise. The Eyeish fought them from their first appearance all the way to their town.

It is difficult to trace the wanderings of the Spaniards beyond this point, the narratives of the expedition being themselves inconsistent, but it seems probable that they worked their way slowly, and doubtless circuitously, toward the southwest. First, they came to a province called Soacatino which was "in the forest," and presently to a large tribe known as the Guasco, where they obtained a quantity of much-needed corn. They visited two other tribes near the Guasco—the Naquiscoça and Naçacahoz. The missionary Casañas, writing in 1691, gives Guasco as a Hasinai tribe and the two other names are plainly Caddo. It is evident, therefore, that these were connected with the Hasinai Confederation, which lay between the Neches and the Trinity about the present Nacogdoches, a city which bears the name of a Hasinai tribe. Pushing beyond, they reached a considerable river known to the natives as Daycao, and this was undoubtedly the Trinity because the horsemen they sent beyond it returned with some Indians whose language no one could understand. This is what we should expect if the river in question was the Trinity since this was the boundary between the Caddo Indians and the Tonkawa. The identity of these strange Indians with the Tonkawa or their neighbors to the south, the Bidai, is furthermore indicated by the description of their dwellings as "very small huts" and "wretched huts."

The dryness and poverty of the country ahead determined Moscoso and his principal officers to return, to the Mississippi River and find sufficient provisions there to carry them through the winter while they built boats in which to descend to the Gulf and find their way to Mexico. As far as Ayays, they retraced their course along the same trail they had followed in coming out, but descended the Ouachita from that point with the expectation of finding the grain they wanted at Anilco. They now, however, had a sample of the evil effects of overtaxing industry, the people of Anilco having been so discouraged by previous exactions that they had not planted. Nevertheless, they presently directed these unwelcome guests to another town called Aminoya, evidently hostile to them, lying on the Mississippi but higher up than Guachoya, and Moscoso immediately dispatched a captain thither to seize this place, following shortly himself with the rest of the army.

The corn in the two villages of which Aminoya consisted proved sufficient to carry our explorers through the winter, and there they remained until the summer of 1543. During this time a plundering expedition was sent against a town called Taguanate still higher up the river, and they were also able to thwart a very natural conspiracy of the surrounding peoples to cut them off. In March the river began to rise and the spring flood of that year proved to be exceptionally high, extending clear across to Anilco and driving them off of the floors of the houses which they had occupied. In the meantime they were at work upon seven small boats, and by the end of June these were completed. Finally, on July 2, they took their departure from Aminoya, having disposed of their hogs and most of their horses and turned loose all of their Indian servants except a hundred. A few horses were carried along in a couple of dugouts lashed side by side but this makeshift conveyance moved so slowly and caused so much annoyance that they presently slaughtered some of the horses for their flesh and the few that they spared were evidently killed by the Indians. A few days after their departure, the boats were attacked by numbers of war canoes under the chief of Quigualtam, in whom it is easy to recognize the chief of the great Natchez tribe. An attempt to beat these pursuers off by Juan de Guzman and a body of Spaniards in small canoes resulted disastrously, all of the attacking party but two or three being drowned. The Indians of Quigualtam and their allies followed them until July 8, and from that time until they were almost at the Gulf they traveled in peace. Half a league above the Gulf they stopped for 2 days to rest, and there they were attacked by Indians of a different tribe having spears and atlatls. On the 18th they got under way for Mexico. They seem to have stopped the first night at the Timbalier Islands, again at a point near Galveston Harbor, and at Aransas Pass or Corpus Christi Pass. On September 10, 1543, the survivors, 311 in number according to Elvas, reached Panuco, where they were received with rejoicings and sent on in details to Mexico City. Part then returned to Spain, while others went to Peru, and a few remained in Mexico. Two or three, indeed, returned with the Luna Expedition of 1559–60 to the territory they had traversed with so much labor.

THE POST-DE SOTO PERIOD
(See map 11)

Involuntary communication was kept up between the Spaniards and the Indians of southern Florida, particularly the Calusa, through the numbers of vessels cast away upon the Florida coast. It would be interesting to know just when these disasters began because we should then be in a better position to determine the sources of the gold for which that part of Florida came to be noted. There were wrecks upon the coast in 1545, 1553, and 1554, and Narvaez in 1528 found evidences of one yet earlier, and even the discoverer of Florida is said to have found gold there. Most of those Spaniards who escaped the sea were killed by the natives, but a few survived, and the narrative of one of these, Hernando de Escalante Fontaneda, who claims to have been cast away in 1551 and to have lived many years in captivity, is a chief source of information regarding the Calusa Indians and almost our only means of knowing anything of their language (Fontaneda, 1866).

In 1558 Philip II determined to plant 2 colonies in these northern territories, one at Santa Elena and the other at an undetermined spot, and the execution of these projects was entrusted to Don Luis de Velasco, the Viceroy of Mexico. The same year Velasco sent 3 vessels under Guido de Bazares to reconnoiter the country and pick out a suitable harbor. He explored part of the coast of Texas and a section of shore east of the mouth of the Mississippi, finding what he believed to be an eligible site in a bay which he named Filipina (Mobile Bay). June 11, 1559, the prospective colonists sailed in 13 vessels under the command of Don Tristran de Luna, and settled in a bay called Polonza (Pensacola), but also established a settlement near the head of Mobile Bay. An expedition consisting of 200 men sent inland came to a large river, undoubtedly the Alabama, and found an abandoned town upon it which bore a Choctaw name, Nanipacana, "Hill Top." It had probably belonged to the Mobile Indians, as some natives whom they met farther on stated that it had been partly destroyed and its inhabitants driven away by men like them. The major at the head of De Luna's scouting party sent word back to him regarding this discovery, and De Luna presently removed there with 1,000 of his colonists, leaving a lieutenant with 50 men and some Negro slaves in charge of the port. In the spring, however, food gave out and the settlers were reduced to such straits that a detachment consisting of 50 horse soldiers and 150 foot soldiers with 5 captains under the major who had led the way to Nanipacana, and including 2 Dominican friars, was sent north in search of the reputedly rich province of Coca. These men left Nanipacana in April and must have lost their way repeatedly, as it was June before they reached Olibahali, or Hothliwahali, on Tallapoosa River.

The inhabitants of this town treated them kindly, but the burden of supporting such a horde of famished strangers was naturally not much to their taste and they soon managed to induce them to move on in search of their main objective, resorting to a simple stratagem for that purpose. A few days' march, however, brought the Spaniards at last to Coca, where they stayed for 3 months. There they learned of the death of a Levantine and a Negro, who had been left behind by De Soto and had lived 11 or 12 years among the natives.

The Coca Indians were at that time engaged in war with another tribe called Napochies, who lived west of them on a river which seems to have been the Black Warrior. The native name of this stream, as preserved by the chroniclers of the expedition, is Oquechiton, the dative form of the Choctaw words meaning "Big Water," and so it is indeed translated by Father Davila Padilla, our principal authority. Unless they had brought interpreters with them from the region of Nanipacana, this indicates that the Napochies were related to the Choctaw and Mobile Indians south and southwest of them, not to the Chickasaw, because the Chickasaw equivalent would have been Oka-ishton (in Spanish probably Oque-ixton). It could not have been in the Coca language, which was Creek.

The Coca induced their guests to take part with them in an expedition against this tribe in which they occupied and burned an abandoned town, killed one or two natives, and compelled the tribe to

make peace and pay tribute, arrangements which probably lasted
only as long as the Spaniards remained at Coça. The major sent
exploring parties throughout the surrounding country and dispatched
a dozen or more soldiers to Nanipacana to inform De Luna of his
discoveries. In the meantime, however, De Luna and his companions
had abandoned the Indian town, on or soon after June 24, 1560,
and returned to the coast leaving a message which the band of soldiers recovered. Therefore, they kept on to the port. De Luna himself wished to proceed to Coça but by this time famine and hardships had brought on a general mutiny, and the malcontents, being
in the majority, recalled the rest of the Spaniards from Coça. Dissensions continued through the winter of 1560–61 and in April, 1561,
most of the colonists left in the flotilla of Angel de Villafañe, who
had been sent to supersede Tristan de Luna and occupy Santa Elena.
De Luna and his servants sailed to Havana, and Villafañe soon followed. Many of Villafañe's men deserted there, but he reached
Santa Elena on May 27, 1561, sailed along the coast of the two Carolinas, and entered some of the rivers, returning in July to Hispaniola (Priestly, 1928).

At this point the French enter the picture. On February 16, 1562,
an expedition under Jean Ribault sailed from France for Florida
and on April 30 came in sight of its eastern coast below the mouth
of St. Johns River and skirted the shores of Florida and Georgia to a
large river which Ribault named Port Royal, probably the Broad
River of a later day. This is within the present limits of South
Carolina and here, near the present Beaufort, Ribault left a colony of
28 men. The party remained on this spot until the following spring,
being well received and entertained by the Indians around them, but,
despairing of relief from France, they finally constructed a small
vessel of 20 tons in which they made a gallant attempt to recross the
Atlantic. A number died of starvation, but finally an English vessel
picked up the survivors and they were restored to their own country.
This expedition is noteworthy for the relatively full account of the
Indians of the Cusabo and Guale provinces contained in it. In 1564
a Spanish frigate under Don Hernando de Manrique de Rojas was sent
from Havana to uproot the French settlement, the site of which he
finally located by means of a French youth who had been living among
the Indians. He burned to the ground the small structure the French
had erected and carried Ribault's monument back with him to Cuba.

On April 22, 1564, a second French expedition under René de
Laudonnière, consisting largely of Huguenots, set sail and on June
22 sighted the Florida coast. Hunting for a suitable place to settle,
they finally fixed upon a site on the east side of St. Johns River a few
miles from its mouth, where they built a fort and spent the winter.

Expeditions were sent among the surrounding tribes and quantities of corn were obtained from them, In midsummer of 1565 they were visited by Sir John Hawkins, who furnished them with provisions and some other necessities and incidentally picked up from them information regarding the customs of the Floridians. As is well known, this French colony was destroyed soon afterward by a Spanish force under Pedro Menendez de Aviles, who also continued up the coast to Port Royal rooting out all of those Frenchmen living among the Indians upon whom he could get his hands. (Laudonnière, 1586; Le Moyne, 1875; Lowery, 1901, pp. 28–207.)

St. Augustine was founded the same year and Spanish control of the Florida Peninsula and the coast to the northward as far as the lower part of South Carolina continued unchallenged, in spite of the revenge expedition of Dominique de Gourgues in 1567, until the successive settlements of South Carolina and Georgia rolled back Spain's northern possessions, and the cession of Florida to England in 1763 put a period for a time to all of her colonies in that region. To the Laudonnière expedition, however, we owe more of our knowledge of the ancient inhabitants of Florida than to the sum total of Spanish sources.

Spanish conquest of Florida extended slowly outward from St. Augustine, but control of the south Florida tribes was never much more than nominal and the missionaries made no headway among them whatever. To the north, however, the Franciscans were very successful and by the early part of the seventeenth century they had brought all the Timucua Indians under their control. Mission stations were distributed, furthermore, along the Atlantic almost to Charleston and, though native uprisings prevented complete conversion of the inhabitants, the missionaries retained a foothold there until the coming of the English. In 1633 missionary work was begun among the Apalachee and, in spite of a rebellion in 1647, the tribe was soon converted. In 1656 there came a great uprising among the Timucua which spread to the Apalachee and, although it was soon suppressed, it resulted in a considerable loss of population, not only by death but through the emigration of many Indians from the confines of Florida. In 1675 Bishop Calderón of Cuba visited the Florida missions, then under his authority, and from his report it appears that most of them were still flourishing.

About 1680, missionaries began to push northward into the country of the Lower Creeks, but two Franciscan friars sent that year (1679 according to Bolton) were ordered out of the country by the Coweta chief. In 1685 Antonio Matheos, commander of the Spanish post at Apalachee, advanced up the Chattahoochee to drive out a party of English under Henry Woodward, and was obliged to repeat the attempt the year following, when he burned the towns of Coweta, Kasihta, Tuskeegee, and Kolomi. The contest with English intruders involved several later expeditions culminating in the establishment of a stockade in 1689 at the Apalachicola village. However, the principal result of this was to induce the greater part of the Lower Creeks to quit their towns and settle upon the Ocmulgee, where they could enjoy the advantages of trade with the English and the lower rates to be obtained from them (Bolton, 1925, pp. 46–54). In 1686 Marcos Delgado had visited the country of the Upper Creeks in an abortive attempt to reach the Mississippi River (Boyd, 1937).

Meanwhile the Guale and Yamasee Indians began to suffer attacks from the Yuchi and Creeks, assisted morally, and often materially, by the English after they had settled at Charleston. Some time in the 80's part of the Guale Indians were moved to the Florida coast north of St. Johns River, but others, to avoid removal, fled to the neighborhood of the English and settled under the name Yamasee along the lower course of Savannah River. In 1704 the Apalachee were broken up by a combined English and Creek expedition under Col. James Moore, and part of the tribe were settled by the victors on Savannah River, while the rest fled to the neighborhood of Pensacola and the French post of Mobile (Swanton, 1922, pp. 89–92, 121–123; Milling, 1940, pp. 169–172). In 1706 and 1707 the Apalachicola were scattered in a second attack of northern Indians and part of them, including the Tawasa and Chatot, fled to Mobile, while another part was located on Savannah River below the Apalachee (Swanton, 1922, pp. 130–131).

In 1715 the number of Indians under Spanish control was considerably augmented by the uprising of the Yamasee against their English neighbors. They moved to Florida and settled with the Timucua and some remnants of other peoples close to St. Augustine, while the Apalachee on the Savannah reentered Florida and established themselves about St. Marks, or reunited with those of their tribe who had gone to Pensacola.

The Apalachicola Indians seem to have returned to their old country at first and to have established themselves at the junction of the Flint and Chattahoochee, but later they went north and followed the fortunes of the Lower Creeks. Meanwhile the Timucua had decreased very rapidly, partly from epidemics and partly owing to the hostilities of the northern Indians. They drew in around St. Augustine for a time, but the last of them are thought to have moved to Tomoka River, where they disappear from history. The Yamasee were likewise constantly reduced in numbers, and at the same time parties of Creek Indians began to move into the Florida Peninsula and settle near them. The last of the Yamasee are said

to have lived upon the Ocklawaha River and ultimately to have
united with the Seminole. The noted chiefs Jumper and Alligator
are supposed to have been descended from them. But there appears
to have been another body of Yamasee which gravitated westward
as far as Mobile and moved from that region successively to the
Upper Creeks, the Lower Creeks, and the western Seminole, with
whom they ultimately amalgamated.

During all this time the Indians of southern Florida seem to have
had few dealings with the Spaniards, and, as we have seen, no permanent missions were established among them. Nevertheless, they can
hardly have escaped entirely from the epidemics introduced by their
white neighbors, and we may be pretty certain that they were constantly
falling off in numbers. Romans tells us that these Indians removed
to Cuba about the time when Great Britain took possession of Florida,
but this statement probably applies more particularly to those living
along the east coast, because at least part of the Calusa, to whom the
name Muspa is frequently given, remained about Lake Okeechobee and
on the Gulf shores until the very end of the Seminole war. Part were
destroyed at that time and the rest probably retired to Cuba, where they
had been in the habit of going regularly to trade (Swanton, 1922, pp.
97–106, 124–125, 131, 339–345).

We now return to the sixteenth century to record Spain's contacts
with the native tribes farther north.

In 1566, the year after he had destroyed the French establishment in
Florida, Menendez visited Guale and Santa Elena and built a small
fort at the latter place, which he called San Felipe. Acting under his
orders, Capt. Juan Pardo left this fort on November 1 with 125 soldiers
"to discover and conquer the interior country from there to Mexico."
He traveled toward the northwest, not far probably from the Coosawhatchie River, until he reached Cofitachequi, or "Canos," as he also
calls it. From there he went toward the north until he came to
"Juada," or "Joara," the Xuala of De Soto, taking about the same
length of time, and perhaps following the same trail. His itinerary
and notes are interesting because they serve to locate Cofitachequi with
approximate accuracy, and because they show that Catawba or related
tribes of Indians were then in occupancy of all of northwestern South
Carolina. Indeed, a few days after leaving Cofitachequi, he passed
through a town called Ysa, which may have been the Issa or Iswa of a
later date, a constituent part of the Catawba tribe. However, the name
has the general signification of "River," and may have been applied to
some other tribe. He speaks of the head of this tribe as "a great chief,"
and says that there he found many chiefs and a great number of Indians. This again suggests the Catawba tribe, which was the most
populous and powerful of the group to which it gave its name. He

built a fort in the Cheraw (Joara) country and left a lieutenant named Boyano in charge. On his return from the Cheraw, he circled round toward the east and visited the Guatari Indians, the Wateree of a later date, either on the river which now bears their name or on the Broad. The Guatariatiqui, whom he met 2 days later, were evidently a branch of the same tribe, perhaps the Wateree Chickanee or Little Wateree whom Lawson came among 135 years later. Beyond them he picked up his former trail to Joara about 40 miles north of the present Augusta and returned along it. Before the end of that year Boyano sallied forth into the mountainous country to the north and destroyed a town belonging to the Chisca, i. e., the Yuchi, Indians. Shortly afterward he received word from one of the mountain chiefs, probably Yuchi also, that he was coming to attack him, whereupon Boyano decided to anticipate the visit and with a party of 20 soldiers marched to the palisaded fort of the hostiles, 4 days' journey through the mountains, stormed it, and killed by fire or sword 1,500 Indians. Unless Boyano had with him a large body of Indians whom he leaves in inglorious obscurity, this is a patent exaggeration, but the cooperation of the Cheraw is very likely since Catawba-speaking people and Yuchi were found to be hostile to each other at a later date. In the meantime Boyano had received permission from his superior, Las Alas, at Santa Elena to prosecute his first advantage, and, leaving a garrison at his fort among the Cheraw, Fort San Juan, he came in 4 days to a great stockaded town between two rivers, and in 12 days more to Chiaha, where he built a fort which he named Santa Elena, and awaited the arrival of Pardo. He began planting wheat and barley there and spent much time visiting the Indians in the neighborhood and contracting alliances with them. September 1, 1567, Pardo set out from Santa Elena on the coast, ascended into the country to Cofitachequi by the route he had previously taken and to Joara by the long loop through the country of the Wateree. The itinerary from Joara to Chiaha and beyond is given by Pardo in his own letter and by Juan de la Vandera writing from Santa Elena. In 4 days Pardo reached a "very good town consisting of wooden houses" which he calls Tocal,[3] but Vandera calls Tocar as rendered by Ruidiaz and Tocax as rendered by Buckingham Smith. This was probably the unnamed stockaded town between two rivers which Boyano had passed through in the same number of days from Joara. In 2 days more Pardo came to a town called Cauchi or Canche "on a good river," in 3 more to Tanasqui, and in one more to Chiaha, or Chihaque, also called Solameco or Lameco. In spite of rumors that the chiefs of four tribes, the "Carrosa (Okalusa), and Chisca (Yuchi) and Costehe (Koasati) and Coza (Coosa)," had

---

[3] It is printed Tocalques but the *ques* is patently no part of the name. I venture to think that the proper form was Tocare.

united against him, Pardo determined to pass on, and in 3 days spent in traversing unoccupied country he came to a town the name of which he was unable to remember when he prepared his report but which Vandera gives as Chalahume. He described the land about as very good and thought that there was gold and silver there, a rather common Spanish obsession. One day more took Pardo to Satapo, but now the Indians adopted such an unfriendly attitude that, added to renewed reports that the four tribes were united to oppose him a day's march farther on, it was decided to give up further explorations. Consequently, the Spaniards returned to Chiaha, and later reached Santa Elena by the longer route, leaving garrisons at Chiaha, Cauchi, Joara, and Guatari.

Vandera adds some interesting facts to the above narrative. He tells us that, though Pardo did not pass beyond Satapo, a soldier had gone on, probably before Pardo reached Chiaha, and he and some Indians had informed Vandera that it took 5 or 6 days to reach "Cossa" from Satapo and that there were only 3 small towns on the way, 1 of which, Tasqui, was 2 days' journey from Satapo, another called Tasquiqui a little farther on, and 1 day's journey beyond this was a destroyed town named Olitifar. The next 2 days were through deserted country, then a small town was reached and, about a league beyond, another, and then Cossa. Within the first 2 days, in going from Satapo to Tasqui, were 3 great rivers. The number of dwellings in Cossa was estimated at 150. Seven days' journey beyond lay "Trascaluza," the Tascalusa of De Soto, which they did not pretend to have visited.

Another interesting item in Vandera's narrative is the statement that the river of Guatari ran by "Sauapa and Usi, where salt is made, near the sea sixty leagues from Santa Elena." Usi may be another form of Issa or Iswa, though it is not the same province. Were it not that it is placed near the ocean, we should be tempted to see in it a synonym for the Catawba Indians, as does Mooney, and in Sauapa, which Buckingham Smith reads Sauxpa, Waxhaw, or Sissipahaw. In fact, I believe Mooney's second guess regarding Sauapa or Sauxpa is correct, though the location on the lower Santee or Pee Dee River is far from the historic seat of that tribe in central North Carolina. However, Col. Barnwell tells us that Sissipahaw was a synonym for Shakori, and it is at least probable that this tribe was a branch of the Shakori. Now, there is good reason, adduced elsewhere, for believing that the Shakori and Eno formerly lived in what is now South Carolina and moved north, partly from fear of the Spaniards and partly through pressure from the Cherokee. That being the case, the Chicora of the Ayllon documents may be identified with Shakori, another proof that the tribe was within reach of vessels on the coast—and, of course, this involves the Sissipahaw also. The form Sauxpa I accept

as probably the correct original, and this would be pronounced by a
Spaniard Sa-ushpa.   Usi may have been a synonym for "Xoxi" (pro-
nounced Shoshi) of the Ayllon narratives, and both of the coastal tribe
Sewee.   The river of Guatari was probably the Santee though the
Pee Dee and Waccamaw enter the ocean close to its mouth.   (B.
Smith, 1857; Lowery, 1901, pp. 274–298; Ruidiaz, 1894, vol. 2, pp.
465–473, 477–486; Hamilton, 1910, pp. 520–527; cf. Swanton, 1936.)

The rest of the names of tribes given in these narratives I classify
as follows, taking the list as given by Vandera, since that is the most
complete:

Uscamacu, Ahoya, and Ahoyabe we know, on independent evidence,
to have belonged to the Cusabo province or tribe, itself affiliated with
the Muskhogean stock.   Cozao represents the later Coosa of South
Carolina, distinct as a body from the Coosa Indians of Alabama and
usually classed with the Cusabo but very likely an eastern offshoot
of the Coosa River Muskogee.   Guiomaez, 40 leagues from Santa
Elena and 10 from Cofitachequi, was probably a Muskhogean town.
Ross indentifies it with the "Aymay" or "Hymahi" of the De Soto
narratives, but if she is right, there were two divisions of the tribe
or it had moved across the Savannah between 1540 and 1566.   If we
may assume a still later movement to the coast, we may also identify
it with the Wimbee.   Cofitachequi has already been discussed
at considerable length and reasons shown for regarding it as a Muskogee center, occupied by a part of the Indians later known as
Lower Creeks.

Tagaya, the place immediately north of Cofitachequi, may also have
been Muskhogean, but I am inclined to see in it the first Siouan settlement, and there is more reason to identify the next place, Gueza, with
Waxhaw than to connect Usi with it.   In that case, we must assume
a later movement toward the northeast, but I have shown that there
is evidence for such a general movement among other Siouan tribes.
The r in Aracuchi or Racuchi, which comes next, ties that town up
pretty certainly with the Catawba-speaking Siouans, and there can,
of course, be little question regarding Otariyatiqui and Guatari.
Quinahaqui, being surrounded by Catawba-Siouan places should also
be Catawba-Siouan.   This is evident if the name for the place given
by Pardo in his own communication, Quirotoqui, is accepted.   We
are informed that Issa, already identified as a synonym of Iswa,
and perhaps standing for the Catawba tribe proper, lay 12 leagues
to the "left," i.e., west of this.   Aguaquiri, which comes next, also
carries the probability of its Catawba connection with it, and in it
we recognize the Guaquili of the De Soto chronicles, except that
De Soto had a Muskhogean interpreter instead of a Siouan one.   The
next place is Joara, Juada, Xuala, etc., the Saraw or Cheraw.

As Pardo, like De Soto, was on his way from Xuala to Chiaha, it is probable that he followed the same trail, and since the time he took in reaching Tocar differed by only a fraction of a day from the time taken by De Soto in reaching Guasili the two places may be identical. The description of Tocar as a place between rivers applies very well to the site at the mouth of Peachtree Creek which has been identified as Guasili. Moreover, it took 2 days for Pardo to reach Cauchi from Tocar, the same time consumed by De Soto in passing from Guasili to Canasoga, and again the same time, 4 days, to reach Chiaha from this place, or these places. These facts suggest that Cauchi was identical with Canasoga and, remembering that Canasoga is believed to have been located near the point where the Appalachian Valley opens out, this derives some confirmation from the fact that Vandera says, "from there on I compare this country to Andalusia because this whole land is very rich." I suggest that Guasili and Canasoga may have been the names of these towns, as they were known to De Soto's Muskogee interpreters, while Tocar and Cauchi may have been used for the same by Siouans.

One notable difference between the experiences of De Soto and Pardo in this region is the discovery by the latter of a stockaded town called Tanasqui 3 days' march from Cauchi and 1 day before arriving at Chiaha. Either De Soto missed it entirely or it was not settled until after 1540. Mooney is probably correct in identifying the name with Tănăsĭ', applied to the following later Cherokee sites:

1. On Little Tennessee river, about halfway between Citico and Toco creeks, in Monroe county, Tennessee; 2. "Old Tennessee town," on Hiwassee river, a short distance above the junction of Ocoee, in Polk county, Tennessee; 3. On Tennessee creek, a head-stream of Tuckasegee river, in Jackson county, North Carolina. (Mooney, 1900, p. 534.)

As the Cherokee were late comers to the Tennessee country, the settlement of this town may have marked the beginning of their intrusion, but Guasili also appears to be a Cherokee word and on the other hand Tănăsĭ' cannot be analyzed in that tongue. Knowing that Muskhogeans preceded the Cherokee, and that Cherokee sometimes change l to n, I am inclined to trace the word to Muskogee Talasi, a contraction of Talwa ahassi, "Old Town." In any case, Tanasqui was on Tennessee River not far from the present Chattanooga. The later Tănăsĭ' towns probably represent so many sites subsequently occupied by the same people.

There is every reason to suppose that Chiaha was identical with the town of that name which appears in the De Soto narratives and that it had the same location, i.e., as identified by Brame, on Burns Island in Tennessee River. Since the Koasati (Costehe) were one of the four tribes hostile to the Spaniards, and Satapo was the first place where signs of hostility were manifested, and it took De Soto about the same length of time to come upon the first Koasati settlement from Chiaha as Pardo took to reach Satapo, we may suspect that Satapo belonged to them. Presumably Chalahume, where Pardo stopped the day before, 2 leagues from Satapo, and where the people were friendly, was in the territory of the Chiaha. De Soto's companions mention several villages passed through after leaving Chiaha, though the night before they came to Costehe they encamped in the open country.

We have some difficulty in discussing the route from Satapo to Coosa because, if we place Satapo above the main Koasati town, we must suppose that the soldier who informed Vandera regarding the route to Coosa passed inland around Costehe and Tali. It took De Soto 6 days to reach Coosa from Tali in the bend of the Tennessee and that would agree closely with the "five or six" mentioned by the soldier, but to that we should have to add 2 more days consumed in going from the supposed location of Satapo to Tali. Even without that addition, we find that the soldier reached Tasqui in 2 days, while De Soto's army required 4 or 6 from the supposed site of Satapo. The two narratives agree, however, in mentioning three big rivers between the Tennessee and Tasqui. It is possible that a white man with a few Indian companions may have covered this part of the route twice as fast as an expeditionary force composed largely of infantry and with many camp followers, particularly if he were in the neighborhood of hostile tribes.

Our soldier speaks of a town called Tasquiqui near Tasqui, and, though he does not say how long it took him to pass from one to the other, yet we are able to fix its location fairly well from the fact that, 1 day's journey beyond, they came upon the ruins of a third town called Olitifar. There is little doubt that the name of this town was preserved to later times in the form Littafutchee, probably Littaf hatchee, the Creek name of Canoe Creek. But if our soldier seems to have taken too little time to reach Tasqui from the Tennessee River, from Tasqui to Coosa he took too much, De Soto having arrived at Coosa in 2 days while our soldier required 3 and perhaps a little more. In estimating the time required to reach Tascalusa's country from Coosa he is, on the other hand, overly conservative, since he allows but 7 days, while De Soto did not come to the first village that may be supposed to have belonged to Tascalusa until the twelfth day after taking his departure from Coosa.

The affiliations of most of the towns beyond Joara can be established with high probability except for the first three. From Chiaha on, the settlements evidently belonged to Muskhogean tribes, as indicated by the names in this narrative and in the De Soto chronicles.

The Chiaha, as already stated, may have included the Chalahume village and Satapo may have belonged to the Koasati. Coosa is the well known ancient "capital" of the Upper Creeks, and Tascalusa was chief of the Mobile. Guasili may have been a Cherokee settlement and the name Tanasqui would tend toward a similar classification for that town except that we do not know that Tǎnǎsǐ' was originally a Cherokee name. In fact, I am inclined to regard it as derived from Creek or possibly Yuchi. The word Canasoga seems to be from Creek.

We have seen that there was a Spanish period in the histories of Florida, Georgia, South Carolina, and even North Carolina, and we have to add a Spanish period in the history of Virginia, though it is brief and tragic. During Angel de Villafañe's expedition to Santa Elena in 1561, he ran as far up the coast as Hatteras and sent one of his captains named Velásquez to reconnoiter to the northward. Velásquez, with whom there were some Dominican friars, entered Chesapeake Bay and discovered an Indian "province" to which the name Axacan was given, the bay being called Santa Maria de Axacan, and he brought back with him the young brother of the chief. This Indian was taken to Mexico and made such a good impression upon the Viceroy, Luis de Velasco, that the latter gave him his own name and he is always called Don Luis. In 1566, intrigued by the idea that there was a passage to the Pacific in the neighborhood of Axacan, Menendez sent a captain with 30 soldiers accompanied by two Dominican friars and the Indian Don Luis to form a settlement there. Either because they had no mind to the enterprise or on account of unfavorable weather— it is difficult to tell in such cases whether we are dealing with reasons or excuses—they proceeded to Spain. There Don Luis secured the good will and patronage of Philip II, returned to Havana with some Dominicans, and a little later joined a body of Jesuits under Father Segura who were about to proceed to his homeland. They sailed August 5, 1570, and after a stormy passage entered Chesapeake Bay, probably on September 11, ascended it, and reached the province of Axacan, where they found that a drought of 6 years' duration followed by a famine had decimated the inhabitants. All but some of the older people had left the country and there was little food to be had. The vessel that had brought the missionaries was obliged to return at once, but the latter urged the necessity of sending another not later than March of the ensuing year. During the winter, however, Don Luis abandoned them to return to his own people and in February 1571, he brought about the murder of all the whites except a little boy named Alonso, who was saved by Don Luis' brother. When the relief ship appeared, the Indians endeavored to entice some of its occupants ashore, but the meditated treachery was suspected, and after an unsuccessful attack upon the vessel, it sailed away carrying along two natives who had swum out to it. One of these, however, sprang overboard in the Bahama Channel. In the summer of 1572 Menendez proceeded to Axacan with three vessels and, although most of the Indians had fled to the mountains, he captured eight and rescued the boy Alonso, learning through him of the fate of the other whites. Since this tale implicated the Indians captured, Menendez hung them all, and, as it was now late in the season, returned immediately to Havana. No further attempts were made by Spaniards to colonize this part of the continent. The word Axacan would probably be pronounced Ashakan by a Spaniard of the period, and it is possible that it means "the land of metal," having reference to the fact that trails from the northwest brought copper into this part of the coastland (Lowery, 1901, pp. 359–366; Kenny, 1934, pp. 269–297).

Spanish contact with the Southeastern Indians was not confined to their explorations and settlements radiating from Florida, but their western sphere of influence from Mexico eastward was cut off from the other for a long period by a belt of French activity which we must first consider.

The abortive but ethnologically significant efforts of French Huguenots to establish themselves in South Carolina and Florida have already been noted. For more than a century afterward France confined herself to the colonization and exploitation of Canada, but when her explorers and missionaries had penetrated from the St. Lawrence River and Great Lakes into the basin of the Mississippi it was almost inevitable that they should be drawn on by the courses of the southward flowing streams. Moreover, it was soon evident to the government of the Bourbons, under whom France had steadily forged ahead since the coronation of Henry IV, that if she would control the Mississippi Basin at all effectively, she must establish posts all the way to the mouth of the great stream.

After the middle of the seventeenth century, her advance toward the Gulf moved steadily, though somewhat uncertainly, onward. In 1673 Jolliet and Marquette descended to the Mississippi and passed on down it to one of the Quapaw towns near the mouth of the Arkansas. In 1682, only 9 years later, La Salle passed all the way to the Gulf and took possession of the whole country in the name of his sovereign. In 1686 his faithful lieutenant, Tonti, repeated the journey intending to meet his superior, then on the way from France. La Salle and his party of colonists were, however, carried too far to the west and settled on Garcitas Creek near Lavaca Bay early in 1685. From there the French commander made two unsuccessful attempts to reach the Mississippi, and, on the second of these, he was murdered by some of his companions in March 1687. Nearly all of those who had been left at the fort were destroyed by the Indians, but a few of La Salle's immediate companions pushed on through the Caddo country to the Quapaw towns at the mouth of the Arkansas and finally reached Canada. In 1690 Tonti descended as far as the Taensa villages on Lake St. Joseph and crossed to the Natchitoches town on Red River near the present city of that name. In 1699 the priest missionaries De Montigny, La Source, Davion, and St. Cosme reached the lower course of the Mississippi, where De Montigny established himself among the Taensa and Davion among the Tunica, then on Yazoo River. De Montigny soon moved to the Natchez and not long afterward abandoned that mission also and returned to Europe, his place being taken by St. Cosme, who carried on until his murder by Chitimacha Indians in 1706. The Natchez mission was never resumed, but Davion continued with his chosen tribe with one or two interruptions until 1720 when he seems to have given up his work in despair.

In 1699 Iberville established the first permanent French settlement on Louisiana territory at Old Biloxi in Biloxi Bay and ascended the Mississippi as far as the mouth of Red River. On his second visit he reached the Taensa towns, and sent his brother Bienville overland to the Natchitoches. The same year the Jesuit Father Gravier descended the great river and his letters contain very interesting and important information regarding the Indian nations he visited. In a very short time it became evident that the permanent centers of government must be established on the Mississippi River and Mobile Bay. In consequence a small fort was erected in 1700 not many miles from the mouth of the Mississippi. In 1718 New Orleans was founded and soon became the capital of the entire colony. Four years earlier, however, an establishment had been made at Natchitoches on Red River, where the French officer St. Denis long held the frontier against Spain, enlisting the support of the Indians about him in a manner unequaled by any of the other French commanders of his time.

The first establishment in Mobile Bay was made at Twenty-seven Mile Bluff early in 1702 and named Fort Louis. Removal to the present site of Mobile was in 1710. In 1713 a trading house was established at Natchez and in 1716, as the outcome of a partial uprising of the Indians known as the First Natchez War, a fort was built on the lofty bluff by the river and called Fort Rosalie after the Duchess of Pontchartrain. A little later a small post was placed on Yazoo River. In 1717 a fort was built at the junction of the Coosa and Tallapoosa Rivers and named Fort Toulouse, but it is more often referred to as "Aux Alibamons," after the name of the tribe near by.[4] In 1735 a fort was erected on the Tombigbee at what

---

[4] The date of founding has often been given as 1714 on the authority of Pénicaut, who is clearly in error.

is now Jones' Bluff. The Chitimacha war, resulting from the murder of St. Cosme, was brought to an end in 1718 at the time when
New Orleans was founded, and not long after that event a part of
the Chitimacha and a number of small tribes gathered around the
capital for trade and protection. Among these were the Washa,
Chawasha, Bayogoula, Houma, Acolapissa, and for a time the Taensa
and Biloxi. The same thing happened in connection with the Mobile
post, where we find assembled the Taensa from the Mississippi, some
Choctaw from the neighborhood of Tombigbee River, and Apalachee, Chatot, Tawasa, and Yamasee from Florida, to say nothing
of the Mobile, Tohome, Biloxi, Pascagoula, and Pensacola, who had
been found in the neighboring country when the settlement was made.

Unhappily for the French, too, the Natchez war was succeeded
French colonization continued steadily, if somewhat slowly, until
interrupted by the great Natchez rebellion of November 28, 1729.
The leaders of this movement had planned to enlist all the surrounding Indians, but only the small Yazoo and Koroa of Yazoo River
joined them. The Ofagoula, or Ofo, left then and settled near the
Tunica, who also remained firm in their allegiance to the whites.
Yet while there were few actual defections among the tribes, the
war proved difficult and disastrous, and, although the Natchez were
driven from the colony, they long terrorized the settlements and interrupted communications between Louisiana and Canada. From
this time on the smaller tribes dropped off rapidly in numbers and
could furnish little support to the colony, although during the continuance of the Natchez struggle the Tunica and Natchitoches did
yeoman service.

Unhappily for the French, too, the Natchez war was succeeded
in 1736 by one with a much more powerful people, the Chickasaw,
who were supplied with ammunition and otherwise actively aided
by the English of Carolina. An attempt by the French officers
d'Artaguette and Bienville to crush them by simultaneous movements from the Illinois country and Mobile ended in the disastrous
rout of both parties, and a more impressive attempt in 1739–40 dissolved without permanent accomplishment. The Choctaw remained
as the one important stay of the French colony, and even of them a
part was enlisted in the interest of the English and Chickasaw, so
that a bitter civil war distracted the tribe and the colony for several
years. At a later period the French and Choctaw together were
more successful, the Chickasaw being vastly outnumbered by their
congeners to the south. In fact, plans were formulated for removing the Chickasaw to the Creek country or the immediate frontiers
of Carolina and Georgia, and there was a Chickasaw town among
the Upper Creeks for many years, while another body settled close to
Augusta under the Squirrel King. But the tide of war seems to have

turned again; French parties on the Mississippi River suffered several severe defeats, and their red foes proved veritable thorns in their flesh until at last treaties in 1762 and 1763 gave Mobile to England and Louisiana to Spain.[5]

Spanish expansion northward from Mexico had been keeping pace with that from the West Indies through Florida but had farther to go to reach the region under discussion. After the survivors of the Narvaez expedition had been cast ashore on Galveston Island in 1528, four of them, including their annalist, Cabeza de Vaca, lived for some time among the wild and wandering tribes of Texas, and finally reached Mexico City, which they entered on Sunday, July 24, 1536. Meantime, the very year in which they were cast ashore, two expeditions traced the coast northward from Panuco, advancing beyond the Rió Grande. In 1541 Francisco de Coronado, disappointed as to the gold, silver, and other treasures he had hoped to find among the Pueblos, and intrigued by the tales of a Plains Indian probably belonging to the Pawnee, crossed the northwestern part of Texas, visited the Wichita Indians then living on the Arkansas, and learned something of the tribes beyond. In 1544 Father Olmos is credited with the conversion of a south Texas tribe which came to live near Panuco and were known as Olive. In 1650 Captains Hernan Martin and Diego del Castillo reached the borders of the Hasinai country but did not enter it, and from this time on Texas was frequently entered by Spanish expeditions, particularly after the founding of Monclova, in the province of Coahuila. Coahuila has given its name to an Indian linguistic family which formerly covered parts of Coahuila, Nuevo Leon, and southwestern Texas, and may have extended more widely still.

The Spaniards were finally roused to a definite attempt to occupy Texas by the colony La Salle had inadvertently planted near Matagorda Bay, just as their final settlement of Florida had been provoked by the French Huguenot colonial efforts more than a hundred years before. In 1689 an expedition under Alonso de Leon was dispatched to uproot La Salle's colony, only to find that its work had been done for it by surrounding tribes of Indians. In 1690 De Leon, accompanied by Father Damian Massanet, traversed the entire breadth of Texas as far as the Adai beyond the Sabine, and Massanet established a mission in the Nabedache tribe under Father Jesus Maria Casañas. This prelate founded a second station during the winter and found time for an extensive report on the manners and customs of the Hasinai Indians which is one of our most valued sources of information regarding them. The missions were abandoned in 1693 but in 1716–17 five missions were begun in east Texas

---

[5] A sketch of this development is given in Swanton, 1911.

and one among the Adai Indians in the present Louisiana. These were abandoned in 1719 but reestablished 2 years later. In 1718 the mission of San Francisco Solano on the Rio Grande was moved to San Antonio and two others, San José de Aguayo and San Francisco Xavier de Nájera, were soon added. In 1731 those east Texas missions which had been under the care of the Queréteran Fathers were withdrawn to San Antonio, while the Zacatecan missions, to the Nacogdoche, Ais, and Adai, remained until 1772–73. Missions were also established among the Karankawa, Aranama, Akokisa, Tonkawa, and Lipan, but only the missions around San Antonio and Goliad lasted more than a few years. Attempts to missionize the Tonkawa, Lipan, Akokisa, and Karankawa were almost complete failures, and the only Caddo mission which had any real success was the mission to the Nacogdoches, while the temporary prosperity of the missions near Goliad is probably attributable more to the Aranama Indians than the Karankawa. The most flourishing missions were those about San Antonio and along the Rio Grande planted among Coahuiltecan tribes, but they, too, declined gradually as the number of Indians fell away, and all the Texas missions were finally secularized by an order of the Spanish Cortes promulgated September 13, 1813. It was 10 years, however, before its provisions were carried out by the Mexican authorities. Cession of Louisiana to Spain, its recession to France in 1800, and transfer to the United States in 1803 had little immediate effect upon the Indians. In 1822 Texas became part of the new independent Republic of Mexico and in 1836 established its own independence, which ended with its admission into the American Union as a State in 1845. During all of this time the Indian population was decreasing and its part in affairs political became of proportionately less importance. But a recapitulation of the fate of the Indian population is postponed until the story of European penetration has been completed by adding the history of their relations with the Anglo-Saxons. (Cf. Swanton, 1942.)

English influence on the southern Indians was of little consequence prior to the attempts at colonization made by Sir Walter Raleigh in 1584–90. Some notes regarding the Timucua are contained in the narrative of Sir John Hawkins' second expedition undertaken in the year 1565 and to which reference has already been made. On March 25, 1584, Raleigh obtained a patent empowering him to explore and settle "such remote, heathen and barbarous lands, countries, and territories, [as were] not actually possessed by any Christian prince, nor inhabited by Christian people." Later that year he fitted out two vessels, which he placed under the command of Philip Amadas and Arthur Barlowe, who explored the coasts of the present North Carolina and brought back two Indians, one named Wanchese and the other Manteo. The following year a colony was planted on Roanoke Island under Ralph Lane which endured one winter and returned to England with Sir Francis Drake in the summer of 1586. The same year a supply ship sent by Raleigh touched at Roanoke Island but, of course, found no one there, and still later Sir Charles Grenville, who had brought out the first colonists, visited the place and landed 15 men "to reteine possession of the Countrey." In 1587 another expedition was sent out in two vessels with a body of prospective colonists under the leadership of John White. They planned to relieve the 15 men and plant a new colony in Chesapeake Bay, but it was found that the men had been murdered and the ship's captain, Simon Fernandino, refused to land them in any other spot. They, therefore, attempted to renew the colony at the same place. When the vessels set out on their return to England, August 27, 1587, White was persuaded by the colonists to accompany them in order to see that they received supplies, but, due in part to the descent of the Spanish armada the year following, White was unable to return to America until 1590. On the site the colonists had occupied, he then found a message intimating that they had been obliged to move to Croatan, but bad weather, the loss of three anchors and some men, and the consequent indisposition of the captain to remain longer prevented White from visiting that place, and he was forced to return to England. Raleigh afterward sent several other vessels in search of the colonists, but they were not found and "the lost colony of Roanoke" has become something of a myth. Strachey asserts that Powhatan had had the survivors killed a short time before Jamestown was settled, but it does not seem likely that they were ever in the territories controlled by him. Lawson is on firmer ground when he suggests that the lighter color of some Hatteras Indians whom he visited in 1701 was due to members of this colony. (Burrage, 1906, pp. 225-323; Lawson, 1714, p. 108; Strachey, 1849.)

In 1607 came the first permanent English settlement in America, at Jamestown, Va. Until about the middle of the century the contacts of these colonists, except for Smith's travels, were with the Indians of the Powhatan Confederation, but in 1650 an expedition visited the Iroquoian and Algonquian tribes between Chesapeake Bay and Albemarle Sound. In 1669 and 1670 John Lederer penetrated the Appalachian Mountains, passing through the country of the Siouan tribes, of whom he gives a short but important account, and in 1671 much the same journey was undertaken by Thomas Batts and Robert Fallam. The first part of the year 1670 was devoted by John Lederer to a much longer expedition along the Occaneechi trail toward the southwest in which he visited many of the Siouan tribes in the interior of North Carolina and seems to have gone as far as the Catawba country. In

1674 came the inland journeys of James Needham and Gabriel Arthur to the more remote Siouan peoples and the Yuchi (Alvord, 1912). Unnamed traders and explorers from Virginia penetrated to the Upper Creeks at such an early date that the Creek word applied to white Americans is Watcina (Virginians). By 1700 they had gotten as far as the Quapaw country, where Gravier met one of them. As a result of the Tuscarora War of 1711–13, the most powerful tribe between Virginia and the Carolinas was removed.

In 1670 Charleston, S. C., was settled as the capital of a new colony, and new lines of influence immediately began to radiate from that point. Slight differences with the nearer tribes, particularly the Coosa, were followed by a more serious war with the Westo, believed to have been part of the Yuchi, in which the colony was rescued by a band of Shawnee, who drove this hostile tribe out of the country. In 1684 and the years immediately following, the English drew the Yamasee and some related tribes away from the Spaniards in Florida. Before the end of the century, as early as 1698 it is claimed, Englishmen had penetrated through the country of the Creeks and Chickasaw to the Mississippi, and an Englishman named Daniel Coxe projected the establishment of a colony to occupy the territory which became French Louisiana, claimed prior rights to it by virtue of exploration, and named it Carolana. A vessel sent by him, under a captain named Bond, was encountered by Bienville in 1700 at a place on the Mississippi afterward known as English Turn. In 1700–1701 John Lawson, a surveyor, traveled through the country of the Siouan Indians and left an invaluable account of them. English traders and slave hunters were circulating throughout pretty much all the country east of the Mississippi before the end of the seventeenth century. In 1700 they inspired a body of Chickasaw to fall upon the Acolapissa to obtain slaves, and in 1711, or about that time, the Chawasha were raided at British instigation by the Natchez, Yazoo, and Chickasaw. In 1704, as we have seen, they broke up the powerful Apalachee tribe and in 1706–7 treated the Apalachicola in much the same way. In 1715, however, their slave-raiding propensities brought its nemesis when they took a general census of the Indians in the neighborhood of South Carolina and were suspected of doing so with the intention of enslaving them. Milling has shown what abundant reasons existed for this suspicion.

The uprising which followed is usually known as the Yamasee War, but it was participated in more or less actively by the Apalachee, Catawba and their allies, Apalachicola, Creeks, and Cherokee. Rapid successes of the colonials, first against the Yamasee and then the Catawba, who were advancing from the north, put an end to the immediate danger, but the Yamasee, Apalachee, Apalachicola, and

Lower Creeks moved to Florida or inland to the Chattahoochee River, and it was some time before British prestige was restored among the Creeks. It was injured still further by the French when they established Fort Toulouse in 1717 in the midst of the Upper Creek country. However, the Natchez War was much more damaging to England's rivals than the Yamasee War had been to them, and it was not long before the English had enlisted the support of a considerable faction among the Choctaw. This was, indeed, suppressed by the French party and, in spite of French failures in their attacks upon the Chickasaw, British progress in this quarter was held up until the conclusion of the French and Indian war in 1763. Toward the north, also, they encountered obstinate resistance from the Cherokee, who sustained a long war against them from November 1759 to September 1761, during which Fort Loudon was captured and the so-called Fort Loudon massacre took place.

Southward, however, British influence continued to increase, especially after the founding of Georgia. As we have seen, the Indian tribes under Spanish protection were rapidly decimated and their places taken by Lower Creek Indians, who were much more favorably inclined toward the English. Finally, in 1763, Florida and all the French possessions east of the Mississippi were ceded to Great Britain, and, as we have also seen, the French possessions west of that river had passed into the hands of Spain. These cessions effectually interfered with that political trading between the British, Spaniards, and French which was a characteristic policy of the Creek Indians, particularly since the latter were usually on bad terms with the Choctaw between their territories and Louisiana or actively fighting them. In 1783 the new American republic replaced Great Britain as the dominant Anglo-Saxon power on the North American continent, but it required some time to acquire the friendships and live down the antipathies which the mother country had acquired among the various tribes, especially as Spain was in control of Florida again and the entire Gulf coast as far as the mouth of the Mississippi, besides most of the continent beyond that river. The Cherokee had already taken sides with the mother country, and after the war was officially closed they continued to maintain hostilities until 1794.

But settlers were pouring in from the Atlantic seaboard in ever increasing streams, and Spain became proportionately weaker year by year. In 1803 all of the territory to which Spain had fallen heir in 1762, except that included in the present State of Florida, was acquired by the United States, but English sympathizers, both white and Indian, were not lacking in the region of the Gulf, and they were tacitly supported by most of the Spanish officials in Florida, so that these two elements were factors in the first serious Indian war waged by the new republic in the southern part of its territory, the Creek War of 1813–14. As in most other struggles of this kind, the Indians did not fight as a unit. The Lower Creeks, Talladega Creeks, and at least one important Tallapoosa town either remained at home or sided actively with the whites. Immediately after this, difficulties developed with the Seminole Indians and, although the greater part of them lived in Spanish territory, Andrew Jackson invaded their lands and destroyed some Seminole towns. This is called the First Seminole War, and took place in 1817–18. Possibility of Spanish interference in the relations between Americans and Indians came to an end with the purchase of Florida by the United States in 1821. (Crane, 1928; Milling, 1940.)

Settlement in the territories immediately west of the Mississippi River by American colonists after these lands had been acquired presented few difficulties, partly because French and Spanish settlements had been made there and the rights of such settlers were, of course, guaranteed, partly from their relative remoteness from the populous States of the Atlantic seaboard whence most of the new colonists were coming, and partly because such tribes as had not already been rooted out were very small and occupied only small amounts of very poor land. East of the Mississippi, however, the greater part of the good land back from the coast was occupied by five tribes so large and powerful that they were usually known as nations. They represented the remnants of most of those peoples responsible for the mound-building cultures of the east-central United States, and had acquired size and stability under semicivilized economic conditions in prehistoric times, both of which were increased by the acquisition of smaller units after white contact and as a result of white pressure itself. Clashes between these nations and hordes of land-hungry and property-hungry whites from the seaboard States and from Europe were inevitable, and they became particularly frequent after American energies were released by the conclusion of the second war with Great Britain.

It was not long, indeed, before an insistent clamor arose to have the Indian occupants removed to other territories west of the Mississippi, a clamor participated in to some extent by friends of the Indians themselves who were witnesses of the debauchery and general demoralization to which the red men were exposed by proximity to frontier white settlements, often frequented by the most lawless elements.

The history of the negotiations leading up to the removal of these Indians and the story of the removal itself have been adequately told by Foreman and Milling, and all constitutes a disgusting and disgraceful chapter in our national life. Had the men in authority in the several States and in Washington been possessed of that passion for justice and that far-sighted wisdom which the situation demanded, the removal would doubtless have taken place nonetheless, but it would have been consummated in a manner satisfactory to both parties and creditable to all concerned in it. Particularly inexcusable is the callous indifference of the American chief executive, Andrew Jackson, to the sufferings of the Cherokee to whom he was more than half indebted for his brilliant victory over the Creeks at the Horseshoe Bend. Having obtained the signatures of a small number of unrepresentative Indians to a treaty of removal repugnant to nineteen-twentieths of the tribe, he insisted on its legality, and it was enforced with unspeakable brutality. During the removal of all of the five nations, the sympathy of the Chief Executive with white squatters, no matter of what character, is the most patent fact connected with it.

Intense sufferings and heavy losses were endured by all of the tribes but particularly by the Creeks and Cherokee, disturbances in the case of the Creeks reaching almost the proportions of a war. Upon the whole, however, the removal was accompanied by singularly little disturbance and surprisingly few casualties among the whites, considering the provocation, until it became the turn of the Seminole, of whose lands at that time there was so little need that this attempt to anticipate events must be regarded as a major blunder. This Seminole War lasted from 1835 to 1842, and cost the lives of nearly 1,500 American soldiers and 20 million dollars in money. The Indians were, however, gradually hunted down and the survivors shipped to Oklahoma, though with heavy losses of life in transit, until, at the conclusion of hostilities, all but about 500 had been disposed of. The bad faith displayed toward the Indians on many occasions, particularly by General Jesup in the notorious case of Osceola, rather subtracted from than added to American military glory, and the end came at last rather through the application of a milder policy than through military power. (Foreman, 1932, 1934; Milling, 1940.)

But the period of removal passed at last, and all of the Indians of the old Southeast except perhaps 1,500 Cherokee, 500 Seminole, 2,000–3,000 Choctaw, and some mixed-blood groups mainly in Virginia and the Carolinas, were gone. A few bands of Seminole, Koasati, Alabama, Biloxi, Pascagoula, and Choctaw settled in Louisiana and eastern Texas before proceeding to their ultimate destination, and there are Koasati still in Louisiana, and Alabama in Texas. The rest of the Indian population formerly resident in the area which is the subject of this study was collected in the eastern part of what was then known as Indian Territory and since 1907 has been the State of Oklahoma. Here they at first established little semiautonomous states under the patronage of the general government which were gradually extinguished, the individuals under each becoming citizens of Oklahoma and of the United States. The fragments scattered through the rest of the Southeast have for the most part declined in numbers and gradually adapted themselves to the civilization about them into which they will progressively merge both culturally and racially.

Pan-Indian movements arose from time to time, with and without the approval of the United States Government, in which the transplanted tribes took leading parts. In June 1843, a council was called at Tahlequah by John Ross to debate such a movement and the memory of this event is preserved in one of the few existing paintings by Stanley (pl. 1).

SKETCHES OF THE SOUTHEASTERN TRIBES AND THEIR POPULATION

ABIHKA

This was one of the principal divisions of the Upper Creeks and occupied what is now Talladega County, Ala. The name is one of those which appear in the Creek migration legends and it is sometimes extended to cover all of the Creeks, or at least all of the Upper Creeks. The importance of Abihka is indicated by the fact that it formed one of the four towns sometimes called the four "foundation towns" of the confederation. Hawkins was told that this tribe was "one of the oldest," and he attributed to them the introduction of some of the most ancient customs, including punishment for adultery and the regulation of marriage. The first historical appearance of the name is in the Luna narratives (1560), in the form "Apica." Stiggins says that they were possessed of a brass drum obtained, according to tradition, from a foreign people whom he identifies with the followers of De Soto, but it may well have come from the followers of Luna, or more likely from the British. The name of the principal Abihka town usually appears in the form of Abihkutci, "Little Abihka," and there was another of the same name occupied by Okfuskee Indians. Two other towns of this tribe were known respectively as Talladega (End-town) and Kan-tcati (Red-earth). This tribe welcomed part of the fugitive Natchez when they were obliged to quit the Chickasaw country, and intermarried with them extensively. They took no part in the Creek War of 1813–14. After the removal they established a Square Ground a few miles northwest of the present Eufaula, Okla., and another farther west known as "Abihka-in-the-West." The Kan-tcati and Talladega Square Grounds were reestablished, but the former was soon given up. The latter is still in existence, near Henryetta.

Gatschet enumerates two branch towns called Tcahki thlåko, or "Big Shoal," and Kayomalgi, which probably signifies "Mulberry Place." The second may have been occupied, in part at least, by Shawnee, and there was also a Chickasaw village on the creek which bore this name.

Tobias Fitch speaks of "the Lun-ham-ga Town in the Abecas," which
may have been still another out-settlement.

Abihka population.—Only one town, Abihkutci, is given in the
census lists prior to 1832, and for these only the gun-men, warriors, or
hunters are returned, as follows:

Year	Number	Year	Number
1738	30	1761	50
1750	+60	1772	45
1760	130	1792	15

The United States Census taken in 1832–33 returned 378 Indians in Abihkutci, 191 in Kan-tcati, 334 in Talladega, and 175 in
Kiamulgatown.

ACOLAPISSA

In 1699 this tribe was living on Pearl River, about 4 leagues (11
miles) from its mouth. It was said to occupy 6 villages, and the
statement is added that the Tangipahoa (q. v.) had formerly constituted a seventh. When these people were visited by Bienville in
the winter of 1699–1700, he learned that they had been attacked 2 days
before by some English slave hunters at the head of 200 Chickasaw.
In 1702 (or 1705) they moved to Bayou Castine on the north shore
of Lake Pontchartrain, and 6 months later the Natchitoches (q. v.),
whose crops had been ruined, came to St. Denis, then in command of
the Mississippi fort, and were settled by him beside the Acolapissa.
In 1714, however, when he attempted to take them back to their own
country, the Acolapissa attacked them and killed 17, besides capturing
50 women and girls, most of whom were restored later. In 1718, or
at least before 1722, the Acolapissa removed to the Mississippi River
to be near New Orleans and settled on the east side 13 leagues (about
35 miles) above it. In the year last mentioned they were visited by
Father Charlevoix, who gives a considerable description of them and
says that the house of their chief was 36 feet in diameter, 6 feet more
than that of the Natchez Great Sun. A little higher up the river
they had had a small village, then abandoned. In their old town was
a temple and this was rebuilt after they moved to the Mississippi,
as we know from the sketch of it made by A. de Batz in 1732 and
most fortunately recovered by the late D. I. Bushnell, Jr. From what
an officer with M. de Nouaille tells us 7 years later, it is evident that
this tribe and the Bayogoula and Houma, who had settled near by,
were gradually becoming amalgamated. He prefers to call them all
Acolapissa, or "Colapissas," but the name of the Houma had the
greater survival value, and the consolidated tribes appear at about
this point under that name for a considerable period. The Acolapissa
and Bayogoula seem to have combined first, and later to have united
with the Houma (q. v.).

Acolapissa population.—In 1699 Bienville gave the number of Acolapissa warriors as about 150, but La Harpe places it at 300. Iberville's census of families made in 1702 assigns 250 to this tribe, and Charlevoix in 1722 says there were 200 warriors. In 1739 the Acolapissa, Bayogoula, and Houma together were reported to have 90–100 warriors and a total population of 270–300. After that all are called Houma. Mooney's estimate of this tribe as of the year 1650 is 1,500, including the Tangipahoa, and is, if anything, somewhat too high The mixed-blood group still bearing the Houma name locally evidently formed the bulk of the 1,089 Indian population of Louisiana according to the census of 1930, whose tribal affiliations were not reported, since 899 of them were in Terrebonne Parish.

ACUERA

A Timucua tribe probably located along the upper course of Ocklawaha River, Fla. It appears first in the De Soto narratives, and Garcilaso de la Vega identifies it with the province of Ocale where the Spaniards sojourned for a month in the summer of 1539, but Ranjel, who may usually be relied upon, speaks of it as a province to which they sent for corn while they were staying at Ocale, and Gallegos reported to De Soto that Acuera and Ocale were 2 days' journey apart. After the Spaniards settled in Florida permanently, we hear of an encounter between Acuera Indians and members of an expedition sent from Havana in 1604. The Governor of Florida had some difficulty in overcoming the effects of this, but by 1655 two missions, San Luis and Santa Lucia, had been established in the Acuera country. As we do not hear of these again, it may be assumed that they were given up in consequence of the Timucua rebellion in 1656.

Acuera population.—No figures seem to have come down to us.

ADAI

A Caddo tribe living when first discovered by Europeans near the present site of Robeline, La. There were Adai Indians at the Franciscan Mission of San Francisco de los Tejas, the first in eastern Texas, founded by Capt. Alonso de Leon and Father Damian Massanet in June 1690. In 1699 Iberville seems to have been given the name of this tribe under the form Natao. In 1717 the Mission of San Miguel de Linares was established among them. Two years later it was destroyed by the French, with Natchitoches and Caddo allies, but rebuilt in 1721, and near it was located the Presidio of Nuestra Señora del Pilar de los Adaes. For 50 years this was the capital of Texas, but presidio and mission were both abandoned in 1773. In 1778 Mézières states that the tribe was almost extinct, but Sibley reported in 1805 that there was a small settlement on Lake Macdon near an affluent of Red River. The remnant probably combined with the other Caddo and followed their fortunes. The vocabulary of their language, fortunately preserved by Sibley, shows that it differed widely from the rest of the Caddo dialects.

Adai population.—Bienville reported 50 warriors in 1700, but twice as many in 1718. In 1721 the reestablished mission was said to serve 400 Indians. Sibley reported 20 men in 1805, but the proportion of women was much greater. In 1825 there were said to be 27. I estimate a maximum population of about 400.

AGUACALEYQUEN

See Utina, page 201.

AIS

A tribe located on Indian River, Fla. Pedro Menendez visited them in 1565 and before departing established 200 of his men on the lagoon three leagues from the Ais town. During the winter they got into difficulties with the Indians and moved south to the neighborhood of St. Lucie River, where lived the Guacata (q. v.), who were more friendly to them and acquired at this time the name of the mission, Santa Lucia. Fontaneda mentions the tribe in his Memoir. In 1570, or shortly before, there was war between the Spaniards and Ais, since we learn of peace being concluded that year. In 1597 Governor Mendez de Canço on his way from the head of the Florida Keys to St. Augustine, met the Ais chief, who had with him 15 canoes and more than 80 followers. At the chief's request, the Governor afterward sent an interpreter and two Indians to explain his wishes to the Ais Indians. When these emissaries were killed by the latter, Canço exacted a summary revenge which had an immediate quieting effect upon them. Later, trouble arose in consequence of the escape of two Negro slaves and their marriage with Ais women. They were finally recovered, however, and the Ais chief came to St. Augustine the same year with 24 warriors to offer his services against the French and English. Promise was extended that a young Spaniard would be sent to learn the Ais language, but it is doubtful if this was ever done. In 1609 the principal chief of the Ais visited St. Augustine, and several minor chiefs of the southeast coast were baptized. In 1703 an attempt was made to "reduce" these Indians to the Roman Catholic faith, though there is no evidence that it was carried through. In 1699 the Quaker Dickenson, who had been shipwrecked near Jupiter Inlet, passed through the Ais territory, and he gives a very good account of its inhabitants. Romans states that the last of the Calusa Indians, consisting of 80 families, crossed to Havana after the cession of Florida to Great Britain in 1763, but it is probable that these consisted largely, if not entirely, of the Indians who had lived on the east coast, and among them the Ais. Adair says that the fugitives included 30 men.

Ais population.—No figures of any kind exist other than mention of the fact, above noted, that in 1597 the chief of Ais came out to meet Governor Mendez de Canço with 15 canoes and 80 Indians, and the general statement that it was the most populous tribe on the southeast coast. For this tribe, the Tekesta, and the other small tribes of that section, Mooney made an estimate of 1,000 as of 1650. It is probable that the "Costa Indians" in the missions about St. Augustine in the first half of the eighteenth century were drawn from this and the other tribes formerly living near them. In 1726, 88 of these were reported; in 1728, 52. (See references from Romans (1775) and Adair (1775) above.)

AKOKISA

This name was given by the Spaniards to the Atakapa Indians in Texas, in particular to those about Galveston and Trinity Bays and on Trinity River. The Han, whom Cabez de Vaca placed in 1528 on the eastern end of an island believed to be Galveston Island, were probably a part of these people, the name given being perhaps a synonym of *añ*, the Atakapa and Akokisa word for "house." In 1703, according to the French traveler Pénicaut, whose dates, however, are always open to suspicion, two Frenchmen sent on an exploring expedition by Bienville returned and reported that they had reached a tribe of cannibals, and these may have been the Akokisa, though, on the other hand, they may not have gotten beyond the Atakapa proper. In 1719 a French vessel named *Maréchal-d-Estées* touched on this coast and landed five officers who had volunteered to refill the water casks. They encountered Indians, however, and only one of them, an ensign named Simars de Belle-Isle, escaped with his life. This man lived among the Akokisa for more than a year as a captive, and was reduced to the last stage of want and misery when a letter he had written fell into the hands of St. Denis, commandant at Natchitoches, who sent some Natchitoches Indians to rescue him and bring him to that post. Belle-Isle called the Akokisa "Caux," probably from Atakapa ko-i, "speech," or "language." He reached Natchitoches in February 1721, and passed from there to Biloxi, where Bienville enlisted him as interpreter on the *Subtile*, in which Bernard de la Harpe was about to set out for the Texas coast, the captain being Jean Béranger. They sailed August 17, and reached Galveston Bay 10 days later, where they opened communication with the Indians and, on their return, carried away nine of them. From these Indians Béranger took down the only vocabulary of Akokisa words now in existence. They subsequently escaped and tried to return to their homes by land. A part probably succeeded, because the French learned from other Indians to the westward of New Orleans that such a body of Indians had passed through their territories. As early as 1747 the establishment of a mission among the Akokisa was suggested by a Spanish officer, and in 1748–49 the Mission of San Ildefonso was founded 9 miles northwest of the present Rockdale, Milam County, Tex., on the San Gabriel River, to include this tribe, the Bidai, the Deadose, and the Patiri. In 1751, after an epidemic, the Indians deserted to join the Nabedache in an expedition against the Apache. On their return, 66 families encamped near San Xavier Mission, from which they were served for some time. In 1756, in consequence of the arrest of a French trader among the Akokisa 2 years before, a presidio was established 2 leagues from the mouth of the Trinity, 50 Tlascaltec families being settled about it, and it was named San Agustin de Ahumada. About the same time the Mission of Nuestra Señora de la Luz was begun some distance south of the present Liberty. In 1764 the presidio burned down and was abandoned and the mission with it. In 1805 Sibley reported that the chief town of the Akokisa was on the west side of Colorado River, which means that a removal had taken place. It is not known whether these people finally joined their relatives in Louisiana, or united with the Bidai or Karankawa, or whether they died out in their old country, but they now disappear from the records.

Akokisa population.—In 1719–21 Belle-Isle estimated a total population of 250 and La Harpe 200, figures which seem small for a people spread over so much territory. The Spanish officer Capt. Orobio y Basterra in 1747 reported that they lived in 5 villages, and he estimated that there were 300 families, but Sibley claimed that, about 1760–70, they had in the neighborhood of 80 men, a rather close agreement with the figure given by Belle-Isle.

ALABAMA

The first encounter between these Indians and the whites was at some point in the northern part of what is now Mississippi, west or northwest of the Chickasaw, but the references are a little confusing since Biedma and Garcilaso give the name to a "province," i. e., tribe, including the occupants of a barricade—thrown across the Spaniards' way, according to Biedma, simply to try their strength—while Ranjel and Elvas bestow it upon a small village where they passed the first night after leaving the Chickasaw. They do not so designate the barricade which both, none the less, mention. At any rate, there can be little doubt that at least part of the Alabama tribe were in the region in question, and that some of them were concerned in the defense of the stockade. When next we hear of them, at the end of the seventeenth century, they were living on Alabama River just below the junction of the Coosa and Tallapoosa. In 1702, when the French established themselves at Fort Louis in Mobile Bay, they found the Mobile and Tohome tribes at war with the Alabama, and they themselves became involved in the hostilities, the Alabama being abetted, and sometimes actively aided, by the English. This war lasted from 1703 to 1712. In 1715 English influence was shaken by the great Yamasee uprising and in 1717 Bienville established a post at the junction of the Coosa and Tallapoosa, which was named Fort Toulouse. It secured the tribe to the French interest until the entire territory was surrendered to England in 1763. About the time of its erection, the Tawasa, who had taken refuge near Mobile after attacks by the English and Creeks, joined the Alabama and established themselves in the towns of Tawasa and Autauga. The Pawokti seem to have accompanied them. Hawkins describes all of these towns as they existed in 1799 when the Alabama proper seem to have been confined to Red Ground (Kantcati), although we know that Alabama also occupied Okchaiutci and probably Muklasa (q. v.) and part of White Ground (Kan-hatki). Before the above movement took place, the Alabama had a town called Bear Fort (given on the maps as Nitahauritz for Nita holihta) farther down the river. After the peace concluded between England and France in 1763, the tribe began to break up. As early as 1778 some Kan-tcati and Tawasa moved to Florida to swell the numbers of the Seminole. Some Alabama of the town of Okchaiutci accompanied those Koasati who effected a temporary settlement on Tombigbee River at about this period. A considerable body went as far as the Mississippi, where they were found in August 1777 by William Bartram, 2 miles above the Manchac. This band remained here until after 1784. In the meantime other bodies of Alabama seem to have moved to Red River, and by the time Sibley made his report (1806) there was one band containing about 30 men, living near the Caddo, the greater part of a settlement that had been made 16 miles above Bayou Rapides, and another party about 30 miles northwest of Opelousas. Later some Alabama moved to the Sabine River, and the greater part of them finally drifted into Texas, where they are settled in what is now Polk County between Livingston and Woodville though a few families remained in Louisiana (pl. 2). That portion which stayed in the Creek Nation took a very active part in the Creek War of 1813–14, and after its conclusion, their old territory having been ceded to the whites, they were compelled to move north of the confluence of the Coosa and Tallapoosa. Most of them settled in a town which took the name of the Tawasa, and this may mean that the Alabama who remained in the Nation were mainly of that formerly distinct tribe. The rest are said to have gone to live on Coosa River above Wetumpka and may perhaps have constituted the settlement which appears in the census of 1932–33 as Autauga or the one occupied by the Okchaiutci Indians. As noted above, Okchaiutci, or Little Okchai, was an Alabama offshoot which seems to have owed its name to the fact that the Alabama had at one time formed one town with the Okchai Indians, or at least lived in close conjunction with them. This name appears first in 1750 and the town is said to have maintained a separate existence even after the removal to Oklahoma, but it now survives only as a ceremonial name. The Alabama Indians in Oklahoma still (1928) maintain a Square Ground in the neighborhood of Weleetka. In 1761 we hear of a branch village called Wetumpka.

The Muklasa Indians were probably a branch of the Alabama, but they have been treated separately.

Alabama population.—In 1702 Iberville estimated 400 families of Alabama in 2 villages, and a census taken by the English in 1715 gives 4 villages with a total population of 770, including 214 men. Both of these are exclusive of the Tawasa and Pawokti. A French document of the third decade of the same century gives 6 towns and 400 men, probably including the Tawasa and Pawokti. The following figures for the warriors or hunters are given for the Alabama alone, not including the Tawasa or Okchaiutci: 15 in 1750, 150 in 1760, 70 in 1761, 60 in 1792, 80 in 1799. For Okchaiutci we have: 40 in 1750, 100 in 1760, 20 in 1761, 40 in 1792. Writing in 1814, Stiggins ventures an estimate of 2,000 as the total Alabama population, but this is too high. In the census of 1832–33 they are represented only by the towns of Tawasa and Autauga with 321 Indians and 21 Negro slaves.

Sibley, writing in 1805, estimates 30 to 40 men respectively for the two towns in Louisiana. In 1817 Morse says there were 160 Alabama Indians in Texas. In 1882 the United States Indian Office estimated 290 Alabama, Koasati, and Muskogee in Texas, and it repeats these figures till 1901 when 470 are given on the authority of the census of 1900. This in turn was repeated until 1911, but in 1910 a special agent was sent to the tribe and he reported 192, a figure which was again copied in several subsequent reports. The United States Census of 1910 returned 187 Alabama in Texas and 111 in Louisiana, a total of 298. No separate enumeration of the Alabama in Oklahoma has been made, so far as I am aware.

AMACANO

A tribe associated with the Caparaz and Chine tribes in the doctrina of San Luis on the seacoast of the Apalachee country. It was established in 1674. They might have been part of the Yamasee. The three towns in which these tribes lived contained 300 persons.

ANADARKO, OR, MORE CORRECTLY, NADAKO

A tribe of the Hasinai Confederacy of the Caddo. In 1542 the Spaniards under Moscoso met them in northwestern Louisiana or northeastern Texas, probably near the site of Logansport, La. They reappear in history in the narratives of Joutel (1687), and Casañas (1691), and it is conjectured that they were then living on Shawnee Creek in the southern edge of Rusk County, Tex. A Spanish mission called San José de los Nazones was established July 10, 1716, for this tribe and the Nasoni jointly, east of Angelina River and about 20 miles northwest of Nacogdoches. It had small success and was abandoned in 1719 on account of a threatened French invasion. The same year a settlement of that tribe was visited by La Harpe. August 13, 1721, the mission was reestablished and the chief of the Nasoni reinstated as "governor." In 1729–30 it was discontinued here, withdrawn ultimately to the neighborhood of San Antonio, and rechristened San Juan Capistrano, but few if any Hasinai went with it. The tribe continued to decline in numbers during the eighteenth century but as late as 1812 a village of 200 souls, including 40 warriors, was reported on the Sabine River. Their later fortunes followed those of the other Caddo tribes.

Anadarko population.—In 1805 Sibley reported 40 men in this tribe, in 1812 we have 200 given as just noted, and in 1818–20 we have 30 given and a population of 120–130. In 1820 Padilla states that they numbered 200, and in 1828 Sanchez enumerated 29 families. In 1851 they were reported to number 202, in 1855, 205, in 1857, 210, after which date they are not given separate status. (See Caddo.)

APALACHEE

A tribe or tribal confederation living between Aucilla and Apalachicola Rivers, Fla. They were first encountered by the Spaniards under Narvaez in 1528 and to their persistent attacks the misfortunes of that expedition are mainly to be attributed. De Soto's army reached the Apalachee province October 1, 1539, crossed a swamp or river, evidently the Aucilla, and came to a town called Ivitachuco or Uitachuco, which was in flames. October 5 they came to another called Calahuchi, where they found a great quantity of dried venison, and finally they reached Iniahico or Iviahica (Iniahica), represented as the most important town of the province. They remained there until March 3, 1540, suffering constant attacks from the Indians, who preserved the character they had acquired in their dealings with Narvaez. One Relation represents the next province they traversed, one called Capachequi beyond Flint River, as subject to Apalachee. If not related to the Apalachee, the Capachequi Indians were probably connected with the Hitchiti, whom they found just beyond. In 1564–65 the French at Fort Caroline on St. Johns River heard that it was from this province that gold was to be obtained. We also get quite a description of it, albeit second-hand, from Fontaneda from information gleaned while he was held captive by the Calusa between 1551 and 1566, and incidentally we may add that he effectually disposes of the story of Apalachee gold. The Apalachee are said to have asked for missionaries as early as 1607 and Father Prieto visited them the following year, being received with great enthusiasm. The need of missionaries is repeated frequently in documents dating from 1608 to 1633, but active work was not begun until the year last mentioned when, on October 16, 2 monks set out for that tribe, and the conversion proceeded rapidly. Barcia says that it was interrupted by a native outbreak in 1638, but this notice prob-ably belongs to the year 1647 when a great revolt did take place in which 3 of the 8 missionaries were killed and the 7 churches and convents already established were destroyed, together with the sacred objects. The lieutenant of the province and his family were also slain, and the first force sent against the Indians, under Don Martin de Cuera, was compelled to retire after an all-day battle. Not long afterward, however, the uprising was put down with comparative ease, seemingly by means of friendly Apalachee. Twelve of the leaders were executed and 26 others condemned to labor on the fortifications of St. Augustine, the tribe as a whole being compelled to furnish workers annually for that purpose. The conversion of the tribe was now completed rapidly. Apalachee were involved in the Timucua rebellion of 1656, but the disturbance seems to have subsided among them without application of force though a captain and 12 soldiers were placed in San Luis, one of the head towns. Throughout the rest of the century, and indeed until 1701, the Apalachee made constant appeals for relief from the labor imposed upon them at the end of their "rebellion," but this was not finally accomplished until 1704. In the winter of 1703–4 the tribe was entirely disrupted by a South Carolina force under Col. James Moore consisting of 50 men with 1,000 Creek allies. The Apa-lachee had suffered a severe defeat the year before, but at this time Moore claims to have brought back 1,300 Apalachee with him not count-ing 100 slaves. The former he established near New Windsor below the present North Augusta, S. C. The number carried off is conceded by the Governor of Florida to have been 600, while Bienville, writing from Mobile, says the English had killed and made prisoner 6,000 or 7,000. The English estimate is probably not far wrong. Those who escaped the English went to Pensacola and most of them moved later to Mobile, probably toward the end of 1705, thinking that the French would furnish better protection. At the outbreak of the Yamasee War, the Apalachee who had been taken to the Savannah retired among the Lower Creeks, where some had already settled, and, when the English faction there acquired the ascendency, they withdraw farther south, part into their old country, part to a new settlement near San Marcos on the Gulf coast, and part to the neighborhood of Pensacola. In 1727, the Apalachee belonging to these last two groups are said to have "revolted" against Spain, but by the next year had returned to their allegiance. Later all seem to have gravitated to Pensacola, for we hear no more of the rest, but the Mobile and Pensacola bands maintained a separate existence as late as 1758, and probably until 1763, when the territories of both were ceded to Great Britain. In consequence of this political change, the Apalachee appear to have united and by about 1764 they, together with the Taensa Indians and the Pakana band of Creeks, settled on Red River. Their land and that of the Taensa adjoined, lying between Bayou d'Arro and Bayou Jean de Jean. In 1803 the Taensa sold this land to Miller and Fulton, but only a portion was allowed the purchasers by the United States commissioners in 1812 on the ground that the sale had not been agreed to by the Apalachee. The Apalachee probably lost their share before long, however, in one of those ways in which things were in the habit of taking place in bargains between whites and Indians, but the survivors remained in the region and died out or united with other tribes. A few families went to Oklahoma with the Creeks, and mention is made by Dr. Gatschet of three families of them on the North Canadian River, the following names of women being given: Simahi, Tut'hayi, and Santi.

Apalachee population.—The early population of this tribe has often been exaggerated. The most reasonable is an estimate of 5,000 made in 1676, though it is possible that a hundred years earlier there were 1,000 more, and Mooney suggests 7,000 in 1650, including a few other tribes, while Governor Salazar's mission by mission estimate made in 1675 gives a total of 6,130. The figures given by Moore (1,300 free Indians plus 100 slaves) and Bienville (400 Indians) indicate that there were about 2,000 at the time when they were destroyed (1704). The exceptionally careful Indian census taken by the English in 1715 gives 275 men and a total population of 638 in the four Apalachee villages under their control on Savannah River. The Apalachee town near Pensacola contained more than 100 in 1718. In 1725 the Mobile band had been reduced to 100, but in 1728 there were still two villages in the old Apalachee country numbering 140 and 20 persons respectively. In 1726, 87 Apalachee were enumerated in the missions about St. Augustine and 41 in 1728. In 1758 there were said to be 30 warriors in the western settlements, probably including practically all the survivors in both Spanish and French territories. In 1805 Sibley tells us there were only 14 warriors in the Apalachee tribe in Louisiana. Morse gives this band a total of 150 as of 1817, but this is probably too high. (See also Timucua.)

APALACHICOLA

This name seems to have been applied originally to a small group of tribes or towns speaking the Hitchiti language and living on the lower course of the Chattahoochee, but the Spaniards used it in a loose way for the Lower Creeks just as the French used the name of the Alabama for the Upper Creeks. However, in documents of 1675 and 1686 the word is applied to a single town, and later it is connected either with a town or a small group of towns. In 1690 two Franciscan monks were sent into the Apalachicola territory to begin missionary work, but the Coweta chief would not allow them to remain. In 1706 and 1707 Indians in alliance with the English, probably Creeks or Yuchi, attacked the Apalachicola and allied tribes which were then living on and near the Apalachicola River, scattering some and carrying off others. The narrative of these expeditions, preserved through the testimony of an Indian named Lamhatty and rescued by the late David I. Bushnell, Jr., gives the names of four towns or tribes which seem to have constituted the Apalachicola Nation at that time. These were Ephippick, Aulédly, Socsósky, and Sunepáh. They were settled cn Savannah River below the Apalachee at a place later known as the Palachocolas or Parachocolas Fort, nearly opposite Mount Pleasant. In 1716, as a consequence of the Yamasee War, they moved back to their old country in company with bands of Shawnee and Yuchi, but established their own town at the junction of the Chattahoochee and Flint Rivers, at a place long afterward known as Apalachicola Fort. Their chief at that time was named Cherokeeleechee, or "Cherokee Killer," a man who conducted many raids against the frontiers of South Carolina. Not many years later a part moved north to join the Lower Creeks and settled on the west side of the Chattahoochee just below a sharp turn which it makes to the east. Cherokeeleechee and the remainder of the people joined them a little later, and even after that the town was moved again a mile and a half higher up the river. According to Bartram, who gives us this information, the second removal would have taken place about 1757. He also tells us that fragments of the tribe moved east and south, some of them adding their strength to the nascent Seminole. According to one tradition, the Creek Confederation was initiated through a treaty of peace between the Muskogee and Apalachicola, and the importance of this town was indicated by the name Tàlwa làko, or "Big Town," which they gave to it. It seems to have been the original White town of the Lower Creeks, as stated by Hawkins, until its place was taken by Kasihta. After their removal from the country, most Apalachicola settled near the present Okmulgee, Okla.

Apalachicola population.—The Apalachicola who were placed on Savannah River numbered in 1715, just before the outbreak of the

Yamasee War, 214, including 64 warriors, in 2 villages. Later censuses give the following numbers of warriors: 105 in 1738 (in 2 villages of 60 and 45 respectively); more than 30 in 1750; 60 in 1760; 20 in 1761; 100 in 1792 (including the Chiaha); and a total population of 239 in 1832–33 (in 2 settlements). (See Timucua.)

ATAKAPA

By the French this name was applied to all of the bands of the Attacapan linguistic family of Powell except the Opelousa, Bidai, and one or two other tribes in Texas of which they had no knowledge, but as the term Akokisa, used by Spanish writers for those Atakapa on the lower Trinity River and on Trinity and Galveston Bays, has become current in Texas literature, I have considered the Texas Atakapa under that head. Besides the Opelousa, which will be considered separately, there were bands of Indians of this tribe on Vermilion Bayou, on Mermentou River, on the lakes near the mouth of the Calcasieu, and probably on the lower Sabine. Mention has been made of an exploring party sent westward by Bienville which penetrated the country for 100 leagues and finally reached a tribe of cannibals. These were undoubtedly some one of the Atakapa groups. As these Indians lay at some distance from the Mississippi and from the early European colonies, they did not suffer seriously from white intrusion until well along in the eighteenth century, though individuals frequented the French posts along with other Indians. In 1760 Skunnemoke (Skenne-mok, "Short Arrow"), often called Kinemo, sold the land on which his village stood and a strip of territory 2 leagues wide between Bayou Teche and Vermilion Bayou to a Frenchman named Fusilier de la Clair, and from this time on the lands of the tribe were steadily alienated in spite of efforts to protect them. Notwithstanding the sale above mentioned, the Vermilion village was not abandoned until early in the nineteenth century, and in 1779 it supplied 60 men to Governor Galvez to assist him in his expedition against the British forts on the Mississippi. The Mermentou band furnished 120 men to Galvez in that expedition. In 1787 the principal Atakapa village was at the "Island of Woods," later known as the "Island of Lacasine" from an Indian reputed to be its chief. It was abandoned about 1799 and the Indians moved to a village on the Mermentou. This was the last village of the Eastern Atakapa and is said to have been occupied as late as 1836, but this is not certain. Some of these Indians united with the Western Atakapa about Lake Charles, but others scattered as far afield as Oklahoma. The last village of the Western Atakapa was on Indian Lake, later called Lake Prien, which must have been occupied until after the middle of the nineteenth century. In 1885 Dr. Gatschet learned of two women living

near Lake Charles who had belonged to this town, and collected a
considerable vocabulary from them, which, along with a vocabulary
of Eastern Atakapa obtained by Martin Duralde and a list of words
from Akokisa taken down by the French captain Bérenger, has been
published in Bulletin 108 of the Bureau of American Ethnology
(Gatschet and Swanton, 1932). A sketch of a number of Louisiana
Indians belonging to several tribes made by A. de Batz at New Orleans
in 1735 includes an Atakapa in the ancient dress (pl. 3). A few of the
survivors of the old town were living in 1907 and 1908 when the writer
visited that part of the state (pl. 4, fig. 1), but all are now dead.

Atakapa population.—For the Atakapa alone the figures given
above for enlistments in Galvez' forces by the Eastern Atakapa, viz,
60+120, and the figure for all Louisiana Atakapa furnished by Sibley
in 1805, that is, 50, are all we have. My own original estimate of the
population of this linguistic group, exclusive of the Opelousa, was
3,500, which I am now inclined to regard as too high in spite of the
immense extent of country covered by them, and I even question
whether the same is not true of Mooney's more modest estimate, about
1,000 less.

ATASI

The name of an old Muskogee town historically associated with the
Tukabahchee and Kealedji and with a history paralleling the latter:
70–80 warriors in 1740–1800; 358 souls in 1832.

AVOYEL

A small tribe near the present Marksville, La., and on the lower
course of Red River below the Rapides. Their name, which probably
signifies "Stone People," or rather "Flint People," indicates that they
were active as makers of or traders in arrow points, or at least traders
in the raw material. In 1699 Iberville was given the Mobilian name
of this tribe (Tassanak Okla) as the name of Red River, and next
year he met some of the Indians themselves. They are again noted
by St. Denis in 1714 and La Harpe in 1719, and Du Pratz tells us that
they acted as middlemen in providing a market for horses and cattle
plundered by western tribes from the Spaniards. Their name appears
in 1764, in conjunction with those of the Ofo, Tunica, and Choctaw, as
participants in an attack upon a British regiment ascending Red River,
and in 1767 they were still said to have had a village near the "rapids"
of Red River. In 1805 Sibley learned of but two or three women belonging to this tribe, who made their homes in French families on the
Ouachita. Some, however, settled with the Tunica south of Marksville, and it was not until 1932 that the last individual known to have
Avoyel blood passed away.

Avoyel population.—In 1700 Iberville met 40 warriors belonging to
this nation and Bienville considered that that was their full strength.

In 1805, as we have seen, there were 2 or 3 on the Ouachita and probably there were as many more with the Tunica near Marksville.

BAYOGOULA

When the colony of Louisiana was founded in 1699, this tribe was living on the Mississippi River in one town with the Mugulasha (q. v.) near a place, Bayou Goula, which preserves their name. Since La Salle encountered no Indians along this part of the river in 1682, they may have been recent arrivals, though Ford reports that the remains on the site of their old town indicate a long period of occupancy. It is also possible that a tribe called Pischenoa (apparently a Choctaw word meaning "ours"), which Tonti encountered in 1686, 49 leagues above the Quinipissa (q. v.), may have been the tribe under consideration. In February 1699, a hunting party of Bayogoula and Mugulasha Indians discovered Iberville's colony at Biloxi and came to make an alliance with him. On March 15 Iberville visited them himself and has left a graphic description of their village. He took one of their young men back to Europe to learn the French language, but he died before returning to his people. The Bayogoula and Houma were then at war with each other, and the peace which Iberville patched up between them did not last after his return to Europe. In the spring of 1700 the Bayogoula attacked the Mugulasha, their fellow villagers, destroyed a considerable number, and drove the rest away, calling in families of Acolapissa and Tiou to take their places. This seems to have been partly because the Mugulasha had been too friendly with the Houma. In December of that year, the Bayogoula were visited by Father Gravier. In 1706, the Taensa, who had abandoned their towns on Lake St. Joseph, settled in the Bayogoula town, but presently treated the Bayogoula as they had treated the Mugulasha. The survivors were given a place to settle near the French fort on the Mississippi, and they furnished 20 warriors to St. Denis in his expedition against the Chitimacha in the year 1707. By 1725 they had removed to a point 13 leagues above New Orleans. In 1739 they were living between the Acolapissa and the Houma and had practically become fused with them. Their subsequent history is given under that of the Houma (q. v.).

Bayogoula population.—Different reports of 1699 for the Bayogoula and Mugulasha together give 400–500 population, 100 warriors, and 100 cabins. After the destruction of the Mugulasha we have in 1700 one estimate of 200 for the entire population. Iberville's estimate of Louisiana tribes, made in 1702, allows the Bayogoula 100 families. About 1725, 40 warriors are indicated (Bienville), and in 1739 this tribe, the Acolapissa, and the Houma combined were thought to number 270–300 exclusive of children. For his basal year 1650, Mooney estimated that this tribe, the Mugulasha, and the Quinipissa, assuming the last two to be distinct, included 1,500 people; my own estimate was 875.

BIDAI

A tribe living on the middle course of Trinity River, Tex., about Bedias Creek, in the country southwest of the Trinity about the Big Thicket, also toward the Neches east of the Trinity. In the narrative of Simars de Belle-Isle they are mentioned as allied with the Akokisa by whom he was held captive. In 1748-49 the Mission of San Ildefonso was established for this tribe together with the Akokisa, Deadose, and Patiri. It was on the San Xavier River, now the San Gabriel, at a place identified by Bolton as 9 miles northwest of the present Rockdale, Milam County, Tex. The medicine men of this tribe were highly esteemed by the Caddo, the exotic being assumed to be potent. In 1750 the Indians at San Ildefonso suffered from an epidemic, and next year they abandoned the mission in a body to join the Nabedache in an expedition against their common enemy, the Apache. Later the Bidai settled near the Mission of San Xavier and still later we hear of them as intermediaries between the French and Apache in supplying the latter with firearms. In 1776-77 an epidemic carried off nearly half of their number, which had been estimated as 100, but about the middle of the nineteenth century there was still one small village 12 miles from Montgomery, Tex. A diligent search for individuals of this tribe that I made in 1912 resulted in locating only one Indian of probable Bidai blood, but this person had been brought up in a white family and knew nothing of the language or customs of her people.

Bidai population.—That portion of the tribe placed in San Ildefonso mission in 1748-49, including the Akokisa, Deadose, and Patiri, was said to have numbered 176 neophytes in 1751 after having lost 40 in an epidemic. Those who located at San Xavier included 66 families. As noted above, they were supposed to have numbered about 100 in 1776-77 when they lost half their number in another epidemic, and they are now extinct.

BILOXI

A Siouan tribe located on Pascagoula River and Biloxi Bay, probably formerly residents of the Ohio Valley. The De Crenay map of 1733 shows a Biloxi site on Alabama River at the mouth of Bear Creek, which may have been occupied by them on their way south. It was possibly the Istanane mentioned in narratives of the Spanish expeditions of 1693 to survey Pensacola Bay, said to be a very numerous tribe living "along a western bayou in Mobile Bay." This was the first tribe encountered by Iberville when he brought the first permanent colonists to Louisiana in 1699. They were visited in their principal town on Pascagoula River by Bienville in June of the same year. In April 1700, Iberville found their town abandoned, and he does not state definitely where they had gone, though Sauvolle and La Harpe place them in the same settlement as the Pascagoula some miles farther up. A few years later they were induced by St. Denis to locate on a small bayou between New Orleans and Lake Pontchartrain, and while they were there 15 Biloxi warriors accompanied him in his Chitimacha expedition, March 1707. Pénicaut sets the date of their settlement near New Orleans as 1702–3 and, although his chronology is apt to be unreliable, in this case he cannot be far wrong. In 1722 they settled on Pearl River on the site formerly occupied by the Acolapissa, and between that year and 1730 they seem to have drifted back to the neighborhood of the Pascagoula on Pascagoula River. They lived near the same tribe in this general region until after 1763 when both moved across the Mississippi, the Biloxi settling first, it would seem, near the mouth of Red River where Hutchins locates them in 1784. If they actually were near the mouth of the river, they must soon have moved to the neighborhood of Marksville where later writers mention two villages, one of them on a half-section adjoining the Tunica. Soon afterward they sold or abandoned this site and moved to Bayou Rapides and thence to the mouth of the Rigolet de Bon Dieu, from whence they crossed in 1794–96 to Bayou Boeuf and established themselves on the south side below a band of Choctaw. The Pascagoula settled still farther down 2 years later. Soon after the beginning of the nineteenth century, the two tribes sold their lands to William Miller and Colonel Fulton, but though the sale was confirmed by the United States Government May 5, 1805, the Biloxi remained in the immediate neighborhood and gradually died out there or fused with the Tunica and Choctaw. A large body of these people, however, if we may trust the figures given by Morse, went to Texas and established themselves on a stream in Angelina County, still called Biloxi Bayou. Among the Alabama Indians in this neighborhood are a few descended from these; what became of the rest is unknown. In 1829, Biloxi, Pascagoula, and Caddo were said to be living near one another close to the Texas boundary. Part of one or all of these bands emigrated to Oklahoma, where some settled on Kiamichi River, a few near Atoka, and 40 years ago I discovered one representative of the tribe living on Canadian River among the Creeks, but still able to recall a few Biloxi words. In the fall of 1886 Dr. A. S. Gatschet, of the Bureau of American Ethnology, discovered a few Biloxi on Indian Creek, 5 to 6 miles west of Lecompte, La., and collected enough words to establish the Siouan connections of their tongue. January 14 to February 21, 1892, Dr. J. O. Dorsey, Siouan specialist in the same Bureau, visited this band and again in February 1893, collecting a considerable amount of material, which was published under my editorship in Bureau of American Ethnology Bulletin 47 (Dorsey and Swanton, 1912).

Biloxi population.—In 1699 the Biloxi, Pascagoula, and Moctobi together are said by La Harpe to have had 130 warriors. Iberville states that the abandoned town of the Biloxi contained 30 to 40 cabins. In 1702 Iberville allows 100 families to the united tribes, and in 1758 De Kerlérec estimated for these together and the Chatot more than 100 warriors. In 1805 Sibley sets down the number of Biloxi as 30, but Morse (1822) gives 70, and Schoolcraft sponsors 65 as of the year 1829. Mooney supplies an estimate of 1,000 for this tribe, the Pascagoula, and Moctobi, as of the year 1650; my own is a sixth smaller.

CADDO

(See Bulletin 132 (Swanton, 1942))

A division of the Caddoan linguistic family from which the family derived its name. It consisted of three lesser confederations—the Caddo proper or Kadohadacho, Hasinai, and Natchitoches, and two unattached tribes, the Adai and Eyeish, which were very likely related more closely to each other. De Soto encountered one of the tribes of this group under the name Tula in southwestern Arkansas in 1541 near the present Caddo Gap, perhaps to be identified with the later Cahinnio. While the army was encamped at Tanico somewhere to the northeast of this place, De Soto went on ahead to visit these Tula with a small body of cavalry, but met a warm reception from the inhabitants and immediately returned. October 5 the whole army left Tanico and on Friday, October 7, came to the Tula town, which they found deserted. Next morning, however, the natives returned upon them armed with long lances hardened in the fire, and they proved to be "the best fighting people that the Christians met with." In July, 1542, after De Soto's death, the Spaniards reentered Caddo territories in northwestern Louisiana, and all of the rest of their journey, until they gave up the attempt to reach Mexico by land, was among Caddo, as may readily be determined from the names. In 1650 the Spaniards in Mexico again heard of these Indians under the name Texas or Tejas, a word which signifies "friends," and made several attempts to visit their country. In 1686 and again in 1687 La Salle entered it in his quest for the Mississippi River after landing on the Texas coast. In the latter year he was killed by some of his followers near the lands of the Hasinai, and a few Frenchmen remained among the Indians while others, including the historian Joutel, passed completely through Caddo territory and came out upon the Mississippi at the mouth of the Arkansas. In 1690 Alonso de Leon, accompanied by the Missionary Damian Massanet, traversed the Caddo country from west to east as far as the Adai. A mission was established that same year in the territory of the Nabedache tribe of the Hasinai Confederation, a short distance west of Neches River, and a second not far off. These missions were abandoned in 1693, refounded in 1716–17, and abandoned again, in fear of a French invasion, in 1719. In 1721 they were once more established, but the Queréteran missions were finally withdrawn from Caddo territory in 1731 and those of the Zacatecan Fathers in 1772–73. The eastern Caddo were visited by Henry de Tonti in 1690, Iberville heard of them in 1699, and the next year his brother Bienville crossed over to the country of the Natchitoches from the Taensa villages. From 1702 (or 1705) to 1714 the Natchitoches tribe was living on the lower Mississippi, beside the Acolapissa. On being withdrawn to be returned to their own country, the Natchitoches were attacked by the Acolapissa and suffered a loss of 17 men. St. Denis established a post among them in their old country in 1714, to which a garrison was added. This became the most important guarantee of French power in this direction and a center of both open and clandestine trade. As long as St. Denis remained in charge and consistently afterward, thanks to his influence, the Indians in the neighborhood were loyal and friendly, helping to defeat in 1731 a strong body of Natchez who threatened the post. In 1803 Louisiana passed under control of the United States, and in 1835 all the Caddo in that State ceded their lands and joined their kindred in Texas, but troubles between the Texans and western Indians were reflected in harsh treatment meted out to the peaceable tribes to the east, including the Caddo. In 1855 the Federal Government secured for them a tract of land on Brazos River, but in August 1859, in order to escape massacre by the whites, they made a forced march to the Washita River in what was then Indian Territory, led by their faithful agent, Robert S. Neighbours. There a reservation was set apart for them, and during the Civil War they remained faithful to the Federal Government, most of them taking refuge in Kansas. They were returned to their former reservation in 1867–68. In 1872 the boundaries of their reservation were defined, and in 1902 they were allotted under the provisions of the severalty act of 1887.

Caddo population.—Mooney estimates that there were 8,500 Caddo in 1690, including the Hasinai and other related tribes, but I am inclined to cut this to not more than 8,000. In 1805 Sibley reported about 450 Caddo proper, but in 1849 a total of 1,200 is given, probably including the Hasinai. Subsequent figures are:

Year	No.
1851 (Not including the Anadarko and Hainai)	161
1855 (Not including the Anadarko and Hainai)	188
1857 (Not counting the Anadarko)	235
1864 In Kansas (not including the Hainai)	370
1869 ("On the reservation")	284

Year	No
1872 (Without the Hainai)	392
1873 (Without the Hainai)	401
1874 (Including the Hainai and some Delaware)	521
1875 (Including the Hainai and some Delaware)	552
1876 (Caddo alone)	467
1877–78 (Including the Hainai and some Delaware)	643
1880 (139 men, 156 women, 123 boys, 120 girls)	538
1881–82 (151 men, 151 women, 127 boys, 123 girls)	552
1883	535
1884 (271 males and 285 females)	556
1885 (278 males and 292 females)	540
1886	521
1887 (256 males and 269 females (including 121 children))	525
1888	491
1889	517
1890	538
1891	545
1892	526
1893–94	507
1895	498
1896	476
1897–1903 (Enumerated with the Wichita, Tawakoni, Waco, and some Delaware.)	
1904 (Including the Hasinai and other allies)	535
1905 (274 males and 222 females)	496
1906 (277 males and 274 females)	551
1907	555
1908–1929 (Enumerated with the Wichita, Tawakoni, Waco, and some Delaware.)	
1930 (353 males, 355 females)	708
1930 Census	625
1931 (362 males, 367 females)	729
1932 (383 males, 377 females)	760
1933 (386 males, 387 females)	773
1934 (391 males, 408 females)	799
1935 (456 males, 472 females)	928
1936 (466 males, 481 females)	947
1937 (479 males, 488 females)	967

CAHINNIO

A Caddo tribe connected with the Kadohadacho Confederacy and located in 1687 near Arkadelphia, Ark. They may have been descended from the Tula Indians encountered by De Soto in 1541 a little farther west. In the year first mentioned they were visited by some former companions of La Salle on their way to Canada after the murder of their leader. At a later date they probably moved to Red River and united with the other tribes of the group.

Cahinnio population.—The De Soto chroniclers describe the Tula Indians as numerous. Joutel, the historian of the La Salle expedition, states that they occupied 100 cabins in 1687.

CALUSA

A large tribe, or confederation of tribes, on the west coast of the Florida Peninsula south of Tampa Bay and occupying the Florida Keys and most of the interior. Knowing as we do that the Bahama Islands were being raided for slaves when Ponce de Leon landed in the Calusa country in 1513, the fact that he was met by the natives in a hostile manner and the report that he found gold among them make it highly probable that white men had touched upon the Calusa coast already. The impression these earlier navigators made can hardly have been flattering, and the subsequent landings of Miruelo in 1516 and Cordova in 1517 do not seem to have improved relations, so that the death of Ponce de Leon at the hands of the Calusa in 1521 receives sufficient explanation. Whether or not the Calusa had obtained gold as early as 1513, it is certain that soon afterward quantities of it came to them as the Spaniards conquered Darien, Mexico, and Peru, and galleons bound for Spain with the precious metal were thrown upon their coast. The Calusa in particular were noted for their ill treatment of shipwrecked sailors and passengers, some of whom were sacrificed to the native deities. From about 1551 to 1566, if we are to trust his own statements, Hernando Escalante de Fontaneda, one of these castaways, lived in this tribe and, unlike most of the other white men who had been shipwrecked there, escaped and left a memoir of his adventures and an account of the people. In 1566, the year after he drove the French from Florida, Menendez visited the Calusa country, rescued 12 men and women who had been cast away in the manner above indicated, and attempted to establish friendly relations with the Indians, going so far, indeed, as to marry the sister of the Calusa chief. The same year he sent Francisco de Reynoso with 30 soldiers to erect a fort at the main Calusa village, but in January 1567, receiving alarming reports of friction between the soldiers and natives, he went in person to that post, which had been named San Antonio, with a considerable reinforcement and accompanied by a Jesuit missionary, Father Rogel. Some time after Menendez' departure, the Calusa chief was killed on the ground that he was plotting against the Spaniards. His successor, Don Felipe, at first comported himself in a more friendly manner, but he was later detected in a similar plot and put to death along with 14 of his principal men. In consequence of this, the Calusa Indians burned their village and retreated into the forest. As the Spaniards were largely dependent upon them for supplies, the mission was withdrawn, the fort destroyed, and the garrison transferred to Havana. The date of this has been variously given as 1568, 1569, and 1571. But Father Rogel had already left for Havana in 1567 or during the first half of 1568, and he never returned. In 1612 an expedition sent from

St. Augustine reached the town of Calos, where more than 60 canoes came to meet it. In 1680 a reconnaissance of the Calusa country was undertaken preparatory to resumption of missionary work, but the emissary was turned back before he reached the town of the Calos chief and nothing seems to have resulted. About this time some of the Indians fleeing from Guale settled in Calusa territory. Another missionary effort, made in 1697, had the same fate as the others, and although in 1726 there was a mission near St. Augustine from the "Rinconada de Carlos of the Praya nation," no permanent effect seems to have been produced by it. Romans states that the last of the Calusa left the peninsula in 1763, but his remark perhaps applies rather to the Indians of the east coast. At any rate, bands of Calusa continued on the west coast until the very end of the Seminole War, and in 1839 one of them attacked the camp of Colonel Harney and killed 18 out of 30 men under him. On July 23, however, Harney attacked them in turn, killed the leader of this band, Chekika, and hanged 6 of his followers. On May 7, 1840, the same body of Indians is credited with having killed Doctor Perrine, a botanist living on Indian Key. By some early writers, these Calusa seem to have been called "Choctaw," and in 1847 we hear of a band of "Choctaw" containing 4 warriors. During a recent trip to the Florida Seminole, Miss Frances Densmore obtained a number of songs from individuals who claimed descent from this tribe. The last of them must have united with the Seminole or removed to Cuba.

Calusa population.—The tribe must have been populous at one time, since we have names of 56 towns preserved and a document of 1612 states that the chief of Calos had 70 towns under him not counting those which paid him tribute out of fear. Another informant gives them "more than 600" towns, but only the inclusion of very small fishing camps could justify that figure. The expedition sent into the Calusa country in 1680 passed through 5 villages with a total population of 960. In the band that attacked Harney there are said to have been 250 Indians, but this is a rough estimate and the band may have included Indians other than Calusa.

CAPARAZ

Indians of this tribe, numbering about 100 persons, were connected with a doctrina named San Luis established in 1674 on the seacoast of Florida near the Apalachee country. They may have been identical with the Capachequi of the De Soto narratives.

CAPE FEAR INDIANS

A body of Indians whose affiliations were probably with the Siouan peoples to the south of them. They may have been a part of the Waccamaw tribe, as no native name for them has been preserved, merely the name of a village, Necoes, and a chief, Wat Coosa. In 1661 a colony from New England settled near them, but soon provoked their enmity by seizing and sending away their children under the pretense of having them educated. In consequence, the colonists were soon driven off. In 1663 a party from Barbadoes repeated the attempt at settlement and was equally unfortunate. In 1665 a third colony settled at the mouth of Oldtown Creek, in Brunswick County on the south side of the river, but, though the Indians were friendly, the whites soon left. In 1695 these Indians rescued 52 passengers from a New England vessel wrecked on their coast, who later formed the nucleus of Christ Church Parish north of Cooper River. After the Yamasee War they were removed to South Carolina and settled inland from Charleston—as Milling thinks, somewhere in the present Williamsburg County. In 1749 the South Carolina Council made a proclamation to protect them against their white neighbors. South Carolina documents dated 1808 state that within the memory of men then living there were 30 Indians of the Pedee and Cape Fear tribes in the parishes of St. Stephens and St. Johns, under "King Johnny." There they probably died out, though some may have joined the Indians of Lumber River or the Catawba.

Cape Fear Indian Population.—The census of 1715, taken just before the Yamasee War, returned 5 towns with a population of 206. Only one mixed-blood woman survived in 1808.

CAPINANS

When Iberville and the French colonists who accompanied him reached Biloxi Bay in 1699 they learned of two tribes in the immediate neighborhood called Biloxi and Pascagoula (q.v.). Associated with their names is a third, Moctobi, which disappears soon afterward and has sometimes been regarded as the Biloxi name for the Pascagoula, or vice versa. There is, however, some reason to think that it refers to a town or tribe with the same associations later mentioned under the name Capinans. Besides being placed beside the terms Biloxi and Pascagoula in several documents, in Bienville's memoir of about 1725 the Capinans, or "Capinas," as he has it, appear in one village with the Pascagoula 12 leagues up Pascagoula River. The name of this tribe bears considerable resemblance to the "Capitanesses" laid down west of Susquehanna River on the Carte Figurative dated 1614. If they were a part of the Biloxi or related to them, this identification would not be surprising, since there is every reason to suppose that the Biloxi, as well as the related Ofo of Yazoo River, lived originally in the same general region in the upper Ohio Valley.

CATAWBA

About the beginning of the eighteenth century, the tribe later known as Catawba seems to have consisted of two bands, one called by the name generally employed and the other Iswa, the word meaning "river" in their language. Their own traditions and other evidence indicate that they had entered the country later occupied by them from the northwest. In 1566 and 1567 the Spanish captain Juan Pardo found a tribe or town known as Ysa north of the present Augusta, Ga., in western South Carolina, and another, Usi, toward the mouth of the Santee. The former, and possibly the latter, may have been the later Iswa, though neither is in the historic location of that tribe on Catawba River near the present line between the two Carolinas. They are certainly the "Ushery" visited by Lederer in 1670. In 1701 John Lawson found them divided into the two bands or subtribes mentioned above, the distinction between which was soon obliterated. They were engaged in constant wars with the Iroquois and Shawnee, but remained firm allies of the English colonists of South Carolina except for a short period at the beginning of the Yamasee uprising. Early writers concede that they were the largest of the eastern Siouan tribes, but they fell off rapidly in numbers after white contact. They aided the English colonists against the Tuscarora in 1711–13, and though they joined the conspiracy against them in 1715, peace was made in April of the following year and it was never afterward broken. In 1738 they suffered from a great epidemic of smallpox and during the middle of the century there were constant fights between them and the Iroquois and Shawnee. They took the part of the English against the French and northern Indians at Fort Duquesne. In 1759 nearly half of the tribe was destroyed by another attack of smallpox and after that time they ceased to play a prominent part in history, their last great chief, Haigler being killed August 30, 1763. The same year a reservation 15 miles square was set aside for the tribe as a permanent home. During the Revolution they took sides with the Americans against both the British and the Cherokee, served as scouts throughout the war, and assisted in the defence of Fort Moultrie June 28, 1776. When South Carolina was overrun by the enemy, they fled to Virginia. After the war, white men began to crowd into their country and lease their lands for terms of 99 years, renewable, and on March 13, 1840, a treaty was signed with the State of South Carolina by the terms of which they agreed to cede their lands in that State and remove to Haywood County, N. C. North Carolina, however, refused to sell them lands for a reservation and in 18 months they returned to their former homes, where they secured a reservation of 800 acres. During this time part of them went to live with the Cherokee, but all except a few families soon returned. Another body of Catawba settled near Sculleyville in the Choctaw Nation, Okla. Some families established themselves in other parts of Oklahoma, in Arkansas, Utah, and near Sanford, Colo., where they have gradually been absorbed by the Indian and white populations. Except for a few still among the Cherokee, the rest continue to live on the South Carolina reserve. They have lost their language, but keep up a modified pottery manufacture which adds somewhat to the income from their farms. Most of them are members of the Church of Jesus Christ of Latter Day Saints (pls. 4, fig. 2; 5; 6; 7).

Catawba population.—In 1682 their warriors were estimated at 1,500 or about 4,600 souls; in 1728 at 400 warriors and 1,400 souls. In 1743, after incorporating several small tribes, their warriors had nevertheless fallen under 400. We have estimates of 240 warriors in 1755, and 300 in 1761, with a total population the last-mentioned year of about 1,000. Subsequent figures for the entire population are: 400 in 1775; 490 in 1780; 250 in 1784; 450 in 1822; 110 in 1826; 120 on and about the reservation in 1881; about 100 in 1900. The census of 1910 returned 124, including 99 in South Carolina, 14 in Colorado, 6 in North Carolina, 4 in Virginia, and 1 in Pennsylvania. In 1930, 166 Catawba were returned, 159 of whom were in South Carolina. Mooney made an estimate of 5,000 Catawba as of the year 1600.

CHAKCHIUMA

While De Soto was among the Chickasaw in the winter of 1540–41, he was induced to send an expedition against this tribe, called in one of the narratives Sacchuma and in another Saquechuma. Their town was found abandoned and on fire, but this was interpreted as a ruse to lull the Spaniards into security so that they might be attacked with more success. In any case, the latter returned to the Chickasaw without further incident. The Chakchiuma chief at that time bore the name of Minko lusa, "Black Chief." During La Salle's journey down the Mississippi to the sea he came upon a town recently destroyed by enemies whom Tonti identifies with this tribe, though it may have been the southern branch, the Houma. In 1690, while Tonti was encamped opposite the river of the Taensa, his Shawnee companion, who had crossed the river to hunt, was attacked by 3 Chakchiuma. At this time the tribe seems to have been living near the junction of the Yazoo and Yalobusha, though Adair speaks of the country farther up as their former home. In 1700, according to Iberville, English traders induced the Quapaw to fall upon them in order to obtain slaves, but the attackers were repulsed. Shortly afterward they must have become involved in the war then going on between the Choctaw and Chickasaw, probably on the side of the former, and had descended the Yazoo to the neighborhood of the Tunica, for Iberville wrote the Tunica missionary Davion in 1702 that he had brought about peace between the 2 major tribes and that the Chakchiuma might return to their own village. In 1704, however, we are informed that members of this tribe had murdered a missionary and that, in consequence, the French let loose their allies upon them and in 2 years reduced them to one fifth of their former numbers. This event is not mentioned by La Harpe or Pénicaut, but there is little doubt of its correctness, except possibly as to the actual damage inflicted upon the tribe. Bienville, to whom we owe our knowledge of this event, says also that in 1715 the Chakchiuma had satisfaction from the Choctaw for the death of 1 of their men. In 1722 the Chakchiuma sent 2 men to inform the commandant of the Yazoo fort that the Chickasaw had started out to war against the Yazoo, Koroa, and Ofo. On the outbreak of the Natchez War, they allied themselves with the French, and a combined force of Chakchiuma and Choctaw attacked the Yazoo and Koroa, killing 18 and delivering some French women and children. In 1739 their head chief appears as leader of those Indian forces allied with the French in their intended attack upon the Chickasaw that failed to materialize. The hostilities in which they became involved at this time probably resulted in their destruction as an independent tribe and incorporation with the Chickasaw and Choctaw. Halbert places the event in 1770 and he and Cushman represent it as having been brought about by the allied Chickasaw and Choctaw. This, however, is doubtful, and the tremendous battles reported in connection with it are ridiculous in view of the insignificant size of the Chakchiuma. Traditions speak of 3 strongholds of this tribe captured by the allies—at Lyon's Bluff on the south side of Line Creek, about 8 miles northeast of Starkville; at a spot 3 miles northwest of Starkville; and on the old Grenada Road 6 miles west of Bellefontaine. These points are far east of the historic Chakchiuma country and lie exactly between the territories of the Chickasaw and Choctaw; therefore, it seems likely that, whether these places were occupied by Chakchiuma or not, their taking was incidental to the great struggle between the Chickasaw and Choctaw with the English and French backing opposite sides. But if so, it would seem that the events must have antedated the peace of 1763 by which France yielded up her American territories. From the

De Crenay map we learn that by 1733 part of the Chakchiuma were already living with the Chickasaw. It is possible that the remainder also joined that tribe, as tradition says, but it is probably not accidental that one band of Choctaw Indians bears the same name. If the latter were not connected with the historic tribe of Chakchiuma, it is probable that they represented some earlier branch of the same.

Chakchiuma population.—In 1699 De Montigny states that this tribe and the Taposa together occupied 70 cabins. Bienville claims that they had numbered 400 families in 1702 and that these had been reduced by war to 80 families in 1704. Du Pratz says they had about 50 cabins in his time, about the period of the Natchez War. In 1722 La Harpe assigns to them a total population of 150, but some may already have united with the Chickasaw. Mooney's estimate of the population of this and the other small Yazoo River tribes as of the year 1650 is 1,200. He includes the Tiou. My own estimate, exclusive of the Tiou, is 750. One thousand would certainly cover all the upper Yazoo bands.

CHATOT

A tribe which at one time gave its name to Apalachicola River and at another, apparently, to the Flint. The Choctawhatchee was probably named for them, and they ranged well westward toward Pensacola. In 1639 we get an incidental mention of them in connection with the Apalachicola Indians and Yamasee. When missions were established among them, an event which took place June 21, 1674, they were living west of the Apalachicola River, at some place near the middle course of the Chipola. There were two missions, San Nicolas de Tolentino, 9 leagues from the Sawokli mission of La Encarnacion, and San Carlos de los Chacatos, 3 leagues beyond that. During the very year in which they were established, the friars claimed to have converted the chiefs and more than 300 of the common people. Next year one of the missionaries, Fray Rodrigo de la Barreda, was driven out of the country in an uprising, almost immediately suppressed by the Apalachee commandant, Capt. Juan Fernandez de Florencia, and the Chatot soon afterward abandoned their territory and settled "in the land of San Luis," the principal Apalachee town. The mission named after them, San Carlos de los Chacatos, was plundered about 1695 by the Lower Creeks, and 42 Christians were carried away captive. One Chatot chief named Chine headed a band which occupied a village by itself in 1675 and later gave its name to the mission of San Pedro de los Chines in the Apalachee country. In 1706 or 1707 this tribe, along with the Apalachicola and several others, was attacked by a large body of Indians, probably Creeks, and the Chatot were driven out of their country. Like so many other Indians in

Spanish Florida, they took refuge in French territory and were given lands at a place on Mobile Bay, which came to be known as L'Anse des Chactas and from which they were again removed to make way for the new French settlement, destined to grow up into Mobile, and were given lands on Dog River. After this country passed into the hands of Great Britain, the Chatot moved to Louisiana and settled on Bayou Boeuf, where Sibley mentions them under the name "Chactoos," calling them "aborigines of the country," which merely means that they were among the earlier emigrants from the lands east of the Mississippi. About 1817 we hear that they were on Sabine River, but they then disappear from history, the survivors having probably moved to Oklahoma and become merged with the Choctaw or one of the other large nations.

Chatot population.—As we have seen, the Spanish missionaries claim to have baptized 300 of this tribe in 1674. Bishop Calderón gives the population of the village served by San Nicolas at this time as 30 and that of the San Carlos village as 100, but he probably means heads of families because Governor Salazar reported the very same year that there were 100 Indians at San Nicolas and 400 at San Carlos. After they settled near Mobile in 1706–7 Bienville says they could muster 250 men, but that in 1714 there were but 10 families and in 1725–26 they had become reduced to a tribe of 40 men. At about the same time Du Pratz states that they occupied in the neighborhood of 40 cabins. In 1805, after their removal to Louisiana, Sibley gives 30 men. In 1817, according to Morse, they had a total population of 240, a figure which is probably considerably too high.

CHAWASHA

A small tribe allied to the Chitimacha living in the alluvial country about the mouth of the Mississippi. It was possibly Indians of this tribe which the survivors of the De Soto expedition encountered in 1543, and who were found to be using atlatls. Their village and that of the related Washa (q. v.) was on Bayou Lafourche in 1699 when the colony of Louisiana was founded. Du Pratz says that they and the Washa attempted to attack an English vessel under Captain Bond. This had been sent to the Mississippi to uphold the claims of Daniel Coxe and ascended the Mississippi as far as English Turn, where it was turned back by Bienville September 15, 1699. The tribe furnished 40 warriors, half of the Indian contingent, to a punitive expedition sent against the Chitimacha to avenge the death of the missionary St. Cosme, and they acted as guides. In 1713 (or more likely 1715) a party of Natchez, Chickasaw, and Yazoo made a treacherous attack upon the Chawasha under guise of a peace embassy, killed the head chief, and carried off 11 prisoners, including the chief's wife. This raid was conducted in the interest of British slave traders. In 1712 Bienville states that he moved the Chawasha to the Mississippi and established them on the right bank 25 leagues from its mouth. At this point there is considerable confusion among our authorities. Charlevoix seems to speak of their old village in his time as on the west bank and a new one half a league lower down on the opposite side. Unless Bienville is speaking of the second village, we have three locations given, before Charlevoix's time, i. e., 1722. They continued to live near here until the Natchez uprising in 1729. A few months later, in 1730, in order to quiet the panic fears of the French at New Orleans, Governor Perrier was weak enough to allow a band of slaves to destroy the Chawasha town. He and most other writers represent this as a total massacre but Dumont, who is probably correct, says that the negroes had been instructed to kill adult males only and that, in fact, they murdered only seven or eight, the rest being off hunting. At any rate there are two subsequent notices of this tribe. In 1739 an officer with M. de Nouaille met them and the related Washa near the post called "Les Allemands" and on the left bank of the Mississippi. In 1758 Governor De Kerlérec states that they then formed a little village 3 or 4 leagues from New Orleans. Afterward these two tribes evidently declined steadily, and they disappear toward the close of the eighteenth century or the beginning of the nineteenth.

Chawasha population.—In 1699 La Harpe reports that there were 200 warriors in the three tribes, Chawasha, Washa, and Okelousa, and in 1702 Iberville gives that number of families in the same three. About 1725 Bienville estimates 40 warriors. In 1739 the officer with M. de Nouaille gives 30 in the two tribes together; in 1758 De Kerlérec estimates 10–12 warriors in this tribe alone. Mooney's estimate of the Chawasa population, together with that of the Washa and Opelousa, as of the year 1650, is 1,400; my own is 700 for the Washa, Chawasha, and Okelousa.

CHERAW, SARAW, SARA

(Called by the Spaniards Xuala, Xualla, Joara, Juada, *x* and *j* being equivalent to English *sh*.)

A Siouan tribe first visited by the Spaniards under De Soto when living in a town in the northwestern corner of what is now the State of South Carolina close to Chattooga Ridge and probably at Towns Hill. It was visited by the Spanish captain Juan Pardo in 1566, who built a fort there named Fort San Juan in which he left his lieutenant Boyano with some soldiers. Boyano afterward took part of his force to Chiaha on the Tennessee River, and when Pardo reached the Cheraw town in 1567 from Santa Elena, he found that the garrison Boyano had left there was besieged by the Indians. The latter submitted, however, on his arrival. Some time after

Pardo returned to Santa Elena this garrison and the others at Chiaha, Cauchi, and Guatari were destroyed by the natives, and we hear nothing more from Spanish sources regarding the people. Later they appear to have settled somewhere east of Asheville, where Swannanoa Gap preserves their name. In 1670 John Lederer seems to have found this tribe, or had it reported to him, still farther toward the east, perhaps on Yadkin River, and in 1673 they are placed by Wood between the Cape Fear and the Yadkin. They may have been pressed toward the east by the Cherokee. In 1700 they settled on the River Dan near the southern boundary of Virginia and, probably at a later date, established a second village 30 miles above on the south side of the Dan and between it and Town Fork. This was called the Upper Saura Village and the other, the Lower Saura Village. Iroquois attacks induced them, about 1710, to leave the Dan and move southeast to join the Keyauwee, and later they came to live on the Pee Dee River in what was subsequently known as the Cheraw District. Here they became involved in a war with the South Carolina settlers, who laid most of the disturbances among the Indians on this frontier to their charge. At last, between 1726 and 1739, they settled near the Catawba. In 1759 a party of Cheraw under their chief "King Johnny" joined the English in their expedition against Fort Duquesne. They are again mentioned in 1768, and ultimately part of them probably united with the Catawba and became wholly merged with them though a part are undoubtedly represented among the Siouan Indians of Lumber River.

Cheraw population.—The Indian census taken by South Carolina in 1715 returned 510 Cheraw but among them were probably included the Keyauwee tribe and perhaps some others. In 1768, 50 or 60 were living with the Catawba. The maximum number about the year 1600 would probably be 1,000.

CHEROKEE

This, the largest tribe in the Southeast, belongs to the Iroquoian family and was located in historic times in the southern Appalachians, which they had probably entered from the north. It has usually been assumed that the "province of Chalaque or Xalaque" of which the De Soto chroniclers speak was inhabited by these Indians, but the name may be the Muskogee term signifying "people of a different speech," and only one town in this region mentioned in the De Soto narratives, Guasili, near the present Murphy, N. C., may be identified as perhaps occupied by real Cherokee Indians. This is probably, as we have had occasion to note on earlier pages, the Tocar, Tocax, or Tocal(ques) of the Pardo documents. (See pp. 29, 30, 65.) There is better reason for thinking that "Tanasqui," a stockaded town on Tennessee River, which appears for the first time in these documents, was occupied by Cherokee. It is now known quite definitely that the Rechahecrians who won a battle against the allied Powhatan Indians and Virginia colonists in 1656 were not Cherokee, and there is no certainty that the Rickohokans of whom Lederer speaks were of that tribe. One of the earliest appearances of the name in English narratives is in Woodward's account of his visit to the Westo town on Savannah River in 1674 in which he states that the "Cowatoe and Chorakae Indians" lived on the head branches of the Savannah. In 1684 the South Carolina government is said to have made a treaty with the Cherokee signed by 5 chiefs of Toxawa and 3 of Keowa. In 1690 we are informed that James Moore and Col. Maurice Mathews journeyed across the Appalachian Mountains in order to discover gold, but retired on account of a difference with the Indians. In 1693 some Cherokee chiefs went to Charleston to ask protection against their enemies, the Catawba, Shawnee, and Congaree. About 1700, guns were introduced, and in 1711 traders began to arrive. Two years later, 310 Cherokee took part in Moore's expedition against the Tuscarora under Captains Harford and Thurston. Seventy Cherokee joined the Catawba and other northern Indians at the outbreak of the Yamasee War, but they soon withdrew and peace with the English followed. In the course of the negotiation, a British detachment under Colonel Chicken penetrated into the heart of the Cherokee country. About the same time they and the Chickasaw together expelled the Shawnee from the Cumberland Valley. In 1730 Sir Alexander Cuming set out on a self-constituted mission to the tribe, a peace ceremony was held, and seven Indians were taken on a visit to the English court (pl. 8). As early as 1701, a party of 5 French Canadians had penetrated the Cherokee country on their way from the Mississippi to Carolina, and the discovery of a supposed Frenchman in the tribe in 1736 frightened the English into believing that France was pushing political designs in that quarter. This man, often represented as a French Jesuit, was a Swiss named Christian Gottlieb Priber, an economic dreamer who hoped to set up an ideal state among "natural men" far from the effete conventions of Europe. He was at last captured and imprisoned in Frederica, Ga., where he died. In 1738 what appears to have been the first smallpox epidemic to visit this tribe broke out. During the very early colonial period, part of the Tuskegee and part of the Yuchi came to live among the Cherokee. In the eighteenth century the Cherokee gradually pushed their settlements down the Tennessee River until they came into direct contact with the Creeks. The contests which followed seem generally to have favored the Cherokee and are said to have culminated in the great victory of Taliwa in 1755 after which the Creeks withdrew from the Tennessee Valley. Farther east the Creeks appear to have remained undisturbed in the upper Coosa Valley until white settlers began to push the Cherokee from some of their northern towns, when the Creeks gave them permission to occupy the valley of the Coosa as far down as the mouth of Wills Creek, including the entire valley of the Coosawattee ("Old Creek Place"). At the outbreak of the French and Indian War the Cherokee assisted their English neighbors in the expedition against Fort Duquesne but in 1759 the injudicious and high-handed acts of their allies drove them into war. They destroyed Fort Loudon, which had been established in the heart of their country, after defeating a force of over 1,600 men under Colonel Montgomery near the present Franklin, N. C., June 27, 1760. Next year, however, a second expedition, led by Colonel Grant and numbering 2,600 men, burned all of the Middle Towns, the Lower Towns having been devastated by Montgomery the year before, and reduced the Indians to such straits that they were obliged to sue for peace. Immediately afterward, and at the solicitation of the chiefs, Henry Timberlake visited the Cherokee country, and later he conducted a party of chiefs to England (pls. 9, 10, fig. 1; the date and occasion of the painting shown in pl. 10, fig. 2, is unknown). Final peace between the English and the southern tribes was made in 1763, and immediately a tide of emigrants poured across the mountains into Kentucky and Tennessee, forcing the Cherokee repeatedly to cede more of their land in this direction. In 1769 they are said to have suffered a severe defeat at the hands of the Chickasaw on Chickasaw Old Fields.

At the opening of the Revolution, this tribe sided against the colonists and in consequence their lands were ravaged and their towns were repeatedly destroyed, particularly in the year 1776, when four distinct forces converged upon Cherokee territory. Although many attempts were made to restore peace, it was not finally brought about until 1794, when a conference held at Tellico blockhouse November 7 and 8 brought the long series of contests to an end. During this same year a party of Cherokee under Chief Bowl crossed the Mississippi River.

From this time until their removal, progress of the eastern Cherokee in the arts of civilization was steady, but just as steady was the flow of white population toward their borders and the demands for cessions of more and more land. The first missions among them were established by the Moravians in 1801. In the Creek War of 1813–14 they furnished decisive help, pratically in the final battle of Horseshoe Bend. Further cessions of land were made in 1817, and dissatisfaction with the terms of that treaty inspired Bowl's band to remove into the Spanish territory of Texas, where, with remnants of other tribes, they settled along Angelina, Neches, and Trinity Rivers and were joined later by Tahchee and other chiefs.

In 1820 the eastern Cherokee adopted a form of government modeled on that of the United States. In 1821 Sequoya (pl. 11, fig. 1) submitted his syllabary to the chief men of the nation; they having approved it, the nation set to work to master it with marked success. Next year Sequoya visited Arkansas in order to introduce his syllabary among the western Cherokee, and he took up a permanent abode there in 1823. Parts of the Bible were printed in this syllabary a year later, and in 1828 The Cherokee Phoenix, a weekly paper in Cherokee and English, made its appearance.

Pressure on those Cherokee remaining in the east was increased markedly by the discovery of gold near Dahlonega, Ga. The local authorities resorted to violence to bring about their removal, and they were abetted openly by the Federal Government. Finally, the Treaty of New Echota, December 29, 1835, providing for removal, was signed by an insignificant fraction of the tribe and the tribe as a whole was held to the strict observance of it by the authorities at Washington. A further movement of Cherokee to the west had, indeed, begun in 1829, and in 1838–39 the removal of the rest, the great bulk of the tribe under John Ross and the other principal chiefs, was carried out by force, involving intense suffering on the part of the Indians and the loss of nearly one-fourth of their numbers. The Cherokee who had removed to Texas had obtained a grant of land from the Mexican Government, but after Texas became an independent republic this grant was disallowed, and, in spite of the friendly attitude of Gen. Sam Houston, who had been brought up among the Indians, a contest was precipitated in 1839 in which the Cherokee chief Bowl was killed and his followers driven from the Republic. Several hundred Cherokee also remained in their old country, a fraction which escaped from the troops into the mountains. In 1842 these were given the right to remain and have a reservation in western North Carolina. The bulk of the nation reestablished their government in what is now the northeastern corner of Oklahoma. They were at first torn by internal dissentions between those who favored removal and those who had opposed it, and, during the Civil War, between factions favoring the North and South respectively. In 1867 the Delaware, and in 1870 the Shawnee were admitted into the nation. As the outcome of 15 years of effort, the lands of the tribe were finally allotted to individuals and the Cherokee Nation came to an end March 3, 1906.

John Ross (pl. 11, fig. 2) was head chief of the main body of the Cherokee nation during the troubled times before, during, and after the removal. Major Ridge (pl. 12, fig. 1) was head of the removal party and Ross' principal opponent. Tahchee (Dutch) (pl. 12, fig. 2) was carried west when a mere boy with one of the first parties to cross the Mississippi, distinguished himself in wars with the Osage, and later joined Chief Bowl's band in Texas. Another early emigrant was Tooan Tuh or Dústú, "Spring Frog" (pl. 13, fig. 1), who was a noted ball player and hunter and was prominent among the Cherokee auxiliaries in Jackson's army at the battles of Emuckfa and Horseshoe Bend.

Cherokee population.—Mooney estimates that there were 22,000 in 1650. In 1715 there were reported officially as follows: 11 Lower Towns with a population of 2,100; 30 Middle Towns with 6,350; 19 Upper Towns with 2,760; total, 60 towns with 11,210. This same year Colonel Chicken was assured that a portion, evidently the Middle and Upper Towns, had 2,370 fighting men and this agrees very well with the figures above given. In 1720 we find one estimate of 10,000 and another of 11,500. In 1721 appears a census giving 53 towns, 3,510 warriors, and a total population of 10,379. In 1729 there were said to be 20,000 Cherokee, including 6,000 warriors, distributed in 64 towns and villages, which agrees closely with the recollection of traders interviewed by Adair. They admitted at the same time that there was also a rapid decline in the next 40 years and this is borne out by the figure of 2,590 warriors given in 1755. Adair's informants agreed very nearly with this—about 2,300 warriors in 1761. A town by town census in 1808–9 gave a total population of 12,395 in the east. In 1819 it was estimated that the tribe numbered about 15,000, of whom one-third were already west of the Mississippi. A census taken in 1825 returned 13,564 in their old territories, and 10 years later, in 1835, there were 16,542, including 8,946 in Georgia, 3,644 in North Carolina, 2,528 in Tennessee, and 1,424 in Alabama. This was just before the removal and there were estimated to be 6,000 already beyond the Mississippi. As above noted, about one-fourth of the eastern Cherokee perished during the removal, and the Civil War again exacted a considerable toll. Mooney estimates that they then shrank from 21,000 to 14,000. In 1867 an enumeration of the western Cherokee showed 13,566. Meantime there was a census of the eastern Cherokee in 1848 which returned 2,133 and another in 1884 raised this to 2,956, though there was some demur among the Indians as to the legitimacy of the claims of some of those classed as Cherokee. At about the same time the western Cherokee were believed to number about 17,000. In 1902 there were officially reported 28,016 persons of Cherokee blood, but this includes several thousand individuals formerly repudiated by the tribal courts. In 1895 the eastern Cherokee were returned as 1,479, evidently a purified roll, and in 1900 the number given was 1,376. In

1907 Mooney gave an estimate of 25,000 in the entire tribe, but the census of 1910 increased this to 31,489 and that of 1930 to 45,238.

CHIAHA

A tribe associated, in its later years at least, with the Creek Confederation. These Indians probably spoke a dialect very close to Hitchiti and are said to have separated from the Yamasee, though this may imply only former geographical contiguity and of only a part of the tribe. Considerable confusion has been occasioned by the fact that there appear to have been two sections of this tribe in the sixteenth century. The name first appears in the De Soto narratives applied to a "province" on an island in Tennessee River, which Brame has identified satisfactorily with Burns Island, close to the Tennessee-Alabama line. They were said to be "subject to a chief of Coça," from which it may perhaps be inferred that the Creek Confederacy was already in existence. Early in 1567 Boyano, Pardo's lieutenant, reached this town with a small body of soldiers and constructed a fort where Pardo joined him in September. When Pardo returned to Santa Elena shortly afterward, he left a small garrison here which was later destroyed by the Indians, and that is the last we hear of this northern band of Chiaha. From Daniel Coxe, however, we learn that the Tallapoosa was sometimes called "River of the Chiaha," and an eastern affluent of the Coosa is known as Chehawhaw Creek, so named as early as the end of the eighteenth century. In the census of Creek Indians taken in 1832–33 are listed two bodies of Upper Creeks called respectively "Chehaw" and "Chearhaw," but it is more likely that they received their names from the creek above-mentioned than that they represented any survival of the northern Chiaha. In 1727 a tradition survived among the Cherokee that the Yamasee were formerly Cherokee driven out by the Tomahitans, i. e., the Yuchi., and in this there may be some reminiscence of what happened to the Chiaha.

In the Pardo narratives the name Lameco or Solameco is given as a synonym for Chiaha. This is probably intended for Tolameco, which would be the Creek equivalent for "Chief Town." It will be recalled that this was the name of a large abandoned settlement visited by De Soto and close to Cofitachequi in the middle course of the Savannah River. Since we know that Chiaha were also in this region, it is a fair supposition that the Savannah town had been occupied by people of the same connection. There is a Chehaw River on the coast of South Carolina between the Edisto and Combahee, and as Chiaha is used once as an equivalent for Kiawa, possibly the Cusabo tribe of that name on Ashley River may be brought into the picture. In 1713 we are informed that the Chiaha who were then with the Creeks on Ocmulgee River, had had their homes formerly among the Yamasee.

In 1715, they accompanied the Creek towns, which withdrew to the Chattahoochee and finally settled near the Osochi and Okmulgee inside of the great eastward bend of the river. They had several out-villages in 1797–99, one called Little Chiaha a mile and half west of the Hitchiti town, and three on Flint River, though one of these, known as Hotalgihuyana, they shared with the Osochi. After the removal to Oklahoma, they settled in the northeastern corner of the Creek reservation and maintained their Square Ground even after the Civil War, but have now practically lost their identity. Some of them, however, went to Florida and the western Seminole had a Square Ground bearing their name as late as 1929. Tradition states that the Mikasuki, who played such a part in Seminole history, branched off from these people, but final proof of this is as yet wanting.

Chiaha population.—There are no figures on the northern section of this tribe unless they were possibly represented in the two Upper Creek towns reported in 1832–33 under variations of the same name. One of these had 126 Indians, the other 306. A Spanish census of 1738 gives 120 warriors for the southern division and the Osochi and Okmulgee together. In 1750 there were reported only 20 Chiaha warriors, and in 1760 there were 160, while we have the figure 120 repeated in the roll of 1761. Marbury, in 1792, gives 100 Chiaha and Apalachicola together, and finally the census of 1832–33 returned a Chiaha population, exclusive of the northern towns above mentioned, of 381. Hawkins states that there were 20 families in Hotalgi-huyana near the end of the eighteenth century, but in 1821 Young gives a population of 210, and the rather excessive figure of 670 for the Chiaha Indians.

CHICKASAW

A tribe whose home from some time in the prehistoric past was in the northeastern part of what is now the State of Mississippi between the heads of the Tombigbee and Tallahatchie Rivers. They were found in this region by De Soto in December 1540, and his forces remained in one of their towns from about Christmas until spring. On the morning of March 4, the Chickasaw made a sudden attack upon their unwelcome guests, fired the town, and might have put an end to the expedition there and then had they not been seized with an unaccountable panic. The shattered army moved to a smaller settlement half a league to a league away and was able to put itself in sufficiently good condition to repel a second attack 8 days later. On the 25th or 26th they left the Chickasaw, and it may be said that the first experience of white men with this tribe fully justified its later reputation as a fighting nation. The Napochies with whom the Coosa were at war in 1560 were probably the Napissa mentioned by Iberville in 1699 as a tribe which had united with the one under consideration. Henry Woodward, in the account of his visit to the Westo in 1674, mentions this tribe among others, and in 1698 Colonel Welch opened communications with them and was quickly followed by many English traders through whom the tribe was enlisted in the British interest, though at an early period there was a small French faction. Shortly before 1715 this tribe and the Cherokee together drove part of the Shawnee from Cumberland Valley and in 1745 another band of Shawnee was expelled by them. We learn from French writers that the Chickasaw, under inspiration from British slave traders, were responsible for much of the disturbance along the lower Mississippi. They were charged with responsibility for raids on the Acolapissa, Chawasha, and Yazoo, and are hardly to be cleared of part responsibility for the Natchez uprising. In 1732 they cut to pieces an Iroquois war party which had invaded their country. In 1736 the French made a great effort to put an end to their capacity as trouble-makers by a concerted attack from the north and the south, but the French forces —the former consisting of 140 whites and 300 Indians from the Illinois post under Pierre d'Artaguette, and the latter of 500 French and a great number of Choctaw under the immediate command of Bienville—were attacked and defeated separately, the Illinois troops at the town of Hashuk-humma and Bienville himself in a battle before Ackia. In 1740 Bienville prepared a more formidable expedition, which came together on the Mississippi, but, as he was unable to provision it successfully, it soon dispersed. A fragment of this force under the Canadian Céloron did, however, advance into the Chickasaw country and obtain a most advantageous peace treaty from the Indians, then under the impression that it was but an advance guard of the huge force that had been assembling. Nevertheless, with the retirement of the French the treaty became practically a dead letter, and the Chickasaw continued their attacks on French voyagers along the Mississippi as before. However, they lost heavily themselves in various contests, 60 men, it is said, in the battle of Ackia alone, and at times talked of moving over into the Creek country. In fact, a Chickasaw town named Ooe-ása (probably Wiha asha, "home of emigrants") was established there on a creek called Caimulga. It was abandoned before 1772, but we learn that during the latter year an attempt was made to reestablish it, with what success is uncertain. Another band of Chickasaw settled about 1723 under a chief called the Squirrel King on the South Carolina side of Savannah River near old Fort Moore. In January, 1739, the land on which they had settled was deeded to them. In 1749 smallpox broke out among them and before 1757 white encroachments impelled most of them to move across the river to New

Savannah, though some evidently stayed on the South Carolina side. The Squirrel King was succeeded by a man named Succatabee. The Indians probably abandoned both sites just before the Revolution, and in 1783 their lands in South Carolina were confiscated by that State. In 1791 they petitioned to have them restored, but this was disallowed the year following, and although in 1795 they sent a memorial to the Congress of the United States to justify their claim, evidently nothing was done about it. From statements by Hawkins, we know that during their retreat, they first fell back to the Chattahoochee to be near their friends the Kasihta and then returned after a time to their own people in Mississippi.

In 1752 and 1753 the Chickasaw defeated Benoist and Reggio during their ascent of the Mississippi River. Shortly after this must have occurred the last war with the Cherokee, which culminated in the Chickasaw victory at Chickasaw Old Fields about the year 1769. In 1786 official relations with the United States Government began when, by the Treaty of Hopewell, their northern boundary was fixed at the Ohio. In 1793–95 there was a war with the Creeks remarkable for a signal victory won by 200 Chickasaw over 1,000 Creeks, who had invaded their country and attacked a small stockade. By this time pressure from white settlers was increasing, and the Chickasaw made successive cessions of land in 1805, 1816, and 1818. Finally, by the provisions of a treaty concluded October 20, 1832, they yielded up the rest of their territories east of the Mississippi and removed to the southern part of the then Indian Territory. The actual removal extended from 1837 to 1847. They were then placed upon the western section of the Choctaw reservation, and in 1855 this was separated and given to them and there they established a government of their own which lasted until merged into the State of Oklahoma.

The only sketch of a Chickasaw Indian that has come down to us from early times is the one here reproduced from Romans (pl. 13, fig. 2). Plate 14, figure 1, is of George Wilson, an informant of the writer and plate 14, figure 2, is the home of another informant, Mose Wolf, at Steedman. Plate 15 shows the last Chickasaw Council House, later the Court House of Johnston County at Tishomingo, Okla.

Chickasaw population.—In 1693 Tonti estimated that the Chickasaw had 2,000 warriors. In 1699 the missionary De Montigny stated that they occupied 350 cabins, a figure which another missionary, De la Vente, writing in 1704, doubles, equating them with the Choctaw. In 1702 Iberville estimates 2,000 families, but the rather careful enumeration made by the Colony of South Carolina in 1715 reported 6 villages, 700 men, and a total population of 1,900. This agrees very well with the figures given by Bienville in 1722–23, 6 or 7 villages and 800 men. A South Carolina public document of 1747 states that they had been reduced to 200–300 warriors, but the usual figure for the latter part of the eighteenth century is 500. This is given in the Georgia Colonial Records for the year 1739, and by John Stuart in 1764. Adair reports 450 for this period, an anonymous French writer 560, and Capt. Thomas Hutchins and Colonel Bouquet in 1764, 750. Lower figures are ventured by Rev. Elam Potter, 300–400 warriors in 1768, and 250 by Romans in 1771. In 1780 Purcell estimated 575 warriors and a total population of 2,290 which Schermerhorn (1814) increases to 3,500, Morse (1817) to 3,625, and Gen. Peter B. Porter (1829) to 3,600. A report reproduced by Schoolcraft, which is dated 1833, gives 4,715. In 1836 we begin to have estimates made by the United States Indian Office which indicates surprising uniformity down to the present time, allowing for intermarried whites and freedmen. They never drop as low as 4,000 nor rise much higher than 5,500. In 1919 there were reported 5,659 by blood, 645 intermarried, and 4,652 freedmen. Mooney's estimate for the Chickasaw population in the year 1650 is 8,000; my own for 1700 is 3,000–3,500.

CHILUCAN

This tribe is mentioned in an enumeration of the Indians in Florida missions made in 1726. There were then 70 individuals belonging to it at the Mission of San Buenaventura and 62 at that of Nombre de Dios. They were probably related to one of the better-known Florida groups, and it is not unlikely that the word "Chilucan" is from the Creek chiloki meaning "people of a different speech." Since San Buenaventura is said to have been occupied by Mocama Indians, "all old Christians," it is probable that these Chilucan were remnants of the old Timucua population of Cumberland Island.

CHINE

A tribe associated in 1675 with two others called Caparaz and Amacano, in a doctrina known as San Luis on the seacoast of the Apalachee country. The name seems to have been in reality that of a chief of a body of Chatot Indians (q.v.). Later they may have removed into the Apalachee country for a list of missions dated 1680 includes one called San Pedro de los Chines.

Chine population.—Their village and the villages of the other two tribes mentioned above contained 300 people in all.

CHITIMACHA

A tribe about Grand Lake, La., and between Bayou Lafourche, Bayou La Teche, and the coast of the Gulf of Mexico. They first appear as one of four tribes with which Iberville made an alliance in 1699 when the first permanent French establishment on the Gulf coast was instituted. Early references associate with their name that of a tribe called Yakna-Chitto, "Big Country," a term which may have been applied to part of the same people or to the Atakapa. In 1702 St. Denis is said to have undertaken an expedition against these Indians in order to procure slaves and, according to Pénicaut, who is our sole authority as to the identity of the tribe attacked, he brought away 20 women and children. As soon as Bienville learned of this, he ordered the captives to be restored to their people but "these orders were badly executed."

In August 1706, the Taensa invited the Chitimacha and Yakna-Chitto to come to eat the corn of the Bayogoula after they had destroyed the latter, but those who accepted the invitation were treacherously attacked and enslaved. Late the same year, a Chitimacha war party, disappointed in an attempted revenge for this outrage, discovered the missionary St. Cosme and 3 other Frenchmen encamped by the Mississippi and killed them, and on receiving word of this Bienville induced all the nations along the Mississippi to declare war on this tribe. In 1707 one of their villages was surprised and destroyed by an allied force of French and Indians. Although we hear of no other expeditions aimed directly against the Chitimacha, who retired into the remoter parts of their country behind a network of bayous, many were captured and sold among the colonists as slaves. On their side, the Chitimacha occasioned great annoyance to the settlers on the Mississippi and this induced Bienville to make peace with them. It was effected in the latter part of the year 1718 and Du Pratz supplies us with a long account of the ceremonies. In 1719 part of them removed to the banks of the Mississippi, where they continued to reside for a long period about the upper end of Bayou Lafourche and as far north as the present Plaquemine. Pénicaut speaks as if all moved there, but it is probable that only part of the nation was involved—the Mississippi band that is mentioned by a number of later writers. In 1784 Hutchins tells us that there was a village of about 27 warriors on the Lafourche and 2 others on the Teche, 1 under Fire Chief (often known as Mingo Luak), 10 leagues from the sea; the other under Red Shoes, a league and a half higher up. The last of the Mississippi band appear to have settled finally near Plaquemine, where a few years ago there was a single survivor. There seem to have been more villages among the western Chitimacha than the 2 mentioned, but all steadily declined in numbers and were as steadily encroached upon by the whites until their land was entirely occupied. The few survivors live at Charenton on Bayou Teche. In 1882 Dr. A. S. Gatschet collected a considerable vocabulary of the language at this place, and I obtained some notes regarding the customs and legends of the people in 1907, 1908, and during later visits. A much more complete study has been made since by Dr. Morris Swadesh. The old chief, Benjamin Paul, who supplied most of the information to me and also to Dr. Gatschet and Dr. Swadesh, is now dead and the language nearly extinct. Benjamin Paul is shown in plate 16 and two of the other older Chitimacha, Registe Dardin and his wife, in plate 17.

Chitimacha population.—In 1699 La Harpe estimated that there were 700–800 warriors in the tribe. In 1758 De Kerlérec reported 80 warriors in the Mississippi band, and in 1784 Hutchins reported 27 in the same. The census of 1910 returned 69, and the census of 1930, 51.

CHOCTAW

This seems to have been the largest tribe in the Southeast next to the Cherokee, although the Creek Confederation taken together may have equaled or surpassed it at times. Their first appearance in history is in the De Soto narratives, though not under the name by which we now call them. After leaving the ruins of Mabila, the Spanish army marched toward the north and came to a river and chief which, according to Ranjel, bore the name Apafalaya, while Elvas calls the province Pafallaya. These are evidently forms of the Choctaw name Pa^{n}s-falaya, meaning "Long Hair," which Adair tells us was applied to this tribe because the men, unlike those of many of the surrounding people, allowed their hair to grow at full length. From these narratives it is also evident that the tribe was already in the country with which it was later associated. In 1675 Bishop Calderón speaks of "the great and extensive province of the Chacta which includes 107 villages" (Wenhold, 1936, p. 10). Though the name appears in some later documents belonging to the seventeenth century, including Lieutenant Matheos' letter to Governor Cabrera in 1686 and Marcos Delgado's narrative of the same year, we hear little more of the tribe until 1699 when the French settled Louisiana. The Choctaw immediately became all important to this colony, since they lay like a bulwark between it and the English and their allies. It is true that Carolina and Virginia were a considerable distance off, but they had had the start of Louisiana, and traders from both colonies had pushed their way to the Mississippi. They established themselves firmly with the Chickasaw and much of the time enlisted the Creek Indians in their interest. Indeed, for a considerable period there was a strong English faction among the Choctaw themselves, including many towns in the western division of the tribe and part of the Sixtown Indians, whereas four of the Sixtowns—the Chickasawhay, Okalusa, Ayanabe, Youane—and the Coosa Indians supported the French. Among the towns in the English interest were one of the Sixtowns later known as Inkillis Tamaha (i. e., "English town"), but formerly Coussana or Toussana, another called Tala, and besides these Chanky, Ony or Oni Talimon, Oka holo, Kafitalaya, Castacha, Koe-chito, Naskobo, and West Abeka. The friction between these factions gave rise to a civil war which ended in 1750 with the defeat of the English party. War continued, however, with the Chickasaw and Creeks and came to an end only with the peace of 1763 by which France ceded all of her territories east of the Mississippi to Great Britain. Resistance to England was, of course, fomented by the Spaniards, who had fallen heir to France's trans-Mississippi territories, and relations between the Choctaw and Creeks continued hostile until American rule succeeded to that of European nations on both sides of the great river. The Choctaw as a tribe were never at war with the United States. Tecumseh endeavored to enlist it in his favor, and a few individuals did join the Creeks during their uprising, but the greater part of the nation was held out of the contest by their great chief Pushmataha. Settlers poured into the Gulf region so rapidly, however, after the Revolution that Mississippi was erected into a territory in 1798 and made a State in 1817. After the Creek War, the pressure of white immigrants increased continually, and there was constant clamor to remove the Indians to lands beyond the Mississippi. Ultimately this removal was agreed to by the Choctaw in the Treaty of Dancing Rabbit Creek, held September 27 and 28, 1830, and at the same time lands were granted them along Red River in the southeastern part of the present State of Oklahoma. To this the greater part of the tribe emigrated in 1831–33, and for a number of years that portion which had gone west was increased by additions from the old country. Nevertheless, a considerable body has remained in Mississippi down to the present day. Meantime, the emigrants established a small republic modeled somewhat on that of the United States. The independent government of the Choctaw came to an end with the organization of the State of Oklahoma, of which these Indians are now citizens.

Plate 18, figure 1, shows Nanih Waiya hill, "the hill of origins," from which the Choctaw scattered to other parts of their country and where the Chickasaw left them, or, according to others, marking the spot where they had come out from under the earth. Plate 18, figure 2, is a view from the top of this mound looking east. Plate 19 shows Choctaw warriors as sketched by the French draftsman De Batz early in the eighteenth century. Plate 20, figure 1, is Pushmataha, the great chief of the Choctaw who prevented his people from joining Tecumseh. Another likeness of this famous man is the frontispiece of Bulletin 103 (Swanton, 1931 a). Plate 20, figure 2, shows another famous chief of the emigration period, Mosholatubbee, chief of the northeastern section of the nation.   Plate 21, gives the home and family of John Wesley south of Philadelphia, Miss., and plate 22, figure 1, of a man named Thliotombi, living near Idabell, Okla., and reputed to be the oldest man in the nation at that time (1919).   Plate 22, figure 2, shows the last Council House of the Choctaw at Tuskahoma, Okla.

Choctaw population.—The numbers of Choctaw seem to have varied little from the period of first white contact, though earlier figures sometimes disagree very considerably.   Mooney and I both estimate a population of about 15,000 in 1650.   In 1702 Iberville estimated that there were 3,800–4,000 warriors and this, as well as De la Vente's guess of a total population of 7,000–8,000 in 1704, is probably much too small.   Later estimates of the number of warriors are: 8,000 in 1725–26; more than 3,000 in 1730; 1,466 (evidently a partial census) in 1732; 16,000 in 1738; 5,000 in 1739; more than 3,610, and not more than 4,500 in 1750; 3,500–4,000 in 1758; 4,500 in 1764; 5,000 in 1764; 2,600 in 1771; 4,141 in 1780; 4,500 in 1785; 4,000 in 1814.   Hutchins estimates a total population of 21,500 in 1764, Romans 9,100 in 1771, and Schermerhorn 15,000 in 1814, while Ramsey seems to supply a census of 13,423 in 1780.   In 1820 Hodgson suggests a total population of 15,000–20,000, Morse 25,000 in 1822, while a census made in 1831 gave 19,554.   The figures returned by the United States Department of Indian Affairs from this period on, fall as low as 12,760 in 1850 and rise to 22,707 in 1856.   The census of 1910 gave 14,551 in Oklahoma, 1,162 in Mississippi, 115 in Louisiana, 57 in Alabama, and 32 in other States, a total of 15,911; but the United States Department of Indian Affairs in 1916–19 gave 19,148 in Oklahoma, not including intermarried whites and freedmen, and 1,253 in Mississippi, or a total of 20,401, to which about 200 should be added to cover those in Louisiana and elsewhere.   The census of 1930 returned 17,757, of whom 16,641 were in Oklahoma, 624 in Mississippi, 190 in Louisiana, and the rest scattered over more than 12 other States.   Thus the Choctaw population seems always to have fluctuated between 15,000 and 20,000.

CHOULA

A small tribe reported in 1722 as living 25–30 leagues (about 65–85 miles) above the lower Yazoo tribes and below the Chakchiuma, near a modern town called Tchula after them.   This was probably a band of the Ibitoupa (q. v.) left behind when the main part of the latter moved higher up the Yazoo River.   Probably they reunited with the remainder of the tribe shortly afterward, as we do not hear of them again.

Choula population.—La Harpe, our only authority regarding them, gives their number in 1722 as 40.

CHOWANOC

A tribe located on Chowan River near the junction of the Meherrin and Nottoway Rivers, N. C. When the Raleigh colonists became acquainted with them in 1584–85, they were the dominant tribe in the region. They gradually dwindled away until in 1701, they had become reduced to a single village on Bennetts Creek. They made common cause with the Tuscarora Indians against the whites in 1711–13, and at the close of the conflict the remnant were assigned a small reservation on Bennetts and Catherine Creeks. In 1820 they were supposed to be extinct.

Chowanoc population.—In 1584–85 one of their villages was said to contain 700 warriors. Lawson in 1709 says they had one town on Bennetts Creek with 15 warriors but in 1713 they were estimated to have a total population of 240. In 1754 there were 2 men and 5 women belonging to the tribe living in Chowan County.

CONGAREE

A tribe living on and near the Congaree River, S. C. They do not appear, at least under that name, in the Spanish records. In 1701 Lawson found them on a small eastern affluent of the Santee below the junction of the Congaree and Wateree and under the rule of a "queen." Later we find their principal village placed on the Congaree River nearly opposite the present Columbia, and a fort called "the Congarees" was soon established near by. In 1716 war broke out between this tribe and the Santee on one side and the South Carolina colonists on the other in which the Etiwaw, a Cusabo tribe, allied themselves with the whites. The war was a short one and at its end over half of the Congaree and Santee were taken prisoner and sent as slaves to the West Indies. The survivors, as we learn from Adair, were incorporated with the Catawba and lost their identity in that tribe.

Congaree population.—In 1600 Mooney estimates that there must have been 800. In 1701 Lawson notes that there were not more than 12 houses in their town. The census taken in 1715 gives 22 men and a total population of not more than 40.

COOSA

There were two tribes of this name. One of these was on the upper courses of the Ashley, Edisto, Combahee, and Coosawhatchie Rivers and is usually reckoned a Cusabo tribe (q. v.), but its inland position and its name suggest a possible connection with the Coosa of Alabama. The second seems to have been one of the great original tribes of Muskogee and, together with the Abihka, constituted the main representative of the Muskogee in the northernmost section of the old Creek country. Old Coosa town was on Coosa River between the mouths of Talladega and Tallasseehatchee Creeks. It seems to have been there from De Soto's time, in 1540, down into the eighteenth century. In 1560 an officer under Tristan de Luna led 200 soldiers into the province of Coosa. They spent the summer there and took part in an expedition against the Napochi (q. v.), returning to the Gulf coast in November. In 1567 a soldier under Juan Pardo also visited the town, crossing from the Tennessee. In the seventeenth century, when English traders reached northern Alabama, the Coosa were still there. A part of them appear to have moved down upon Tallapoosa River before 1761, where they settled near the Creek towns of Kan-hatki and Fus-hatchee, and they may have had some connection with "Old Coosa," of which we learn about this time, a settlement between Tuskegee and Koasati. Perhaps it was a body of these Indians migrating toward Florida which occupied the "Cousah Old Fields" between the Choctawhatchee and Apalachicola Rivers some time before 1778. Besides bodies of Indians bearing the name itself, two important groups of towns are said to have descended from the Coosa. One of these included the historically important town of Otciapofa, or "Hickory Ground," sometimes called Little Tulsa, residence of Alexander McGillivray, which was on Coosa River a few miles above its junction with the Tallapoosa; and Big Tulsa, including a number of branch settlements, opposite Tukabahchee and about the great bend of the Tallapoosa. De Soto encountered a "Talisi province" on Alabama River, evidently in the point at Durand's Bend in Dallas County. It is probable that this is the earliest reference to the Tulsa people, though that is not certain. A little later, in the form Talaxe (Talashe), it appears as the name of the Altamaha River and a town on the same in the province of Guale. There was a Tulsa Old Town in the Abihka country, but it is not possible to determine whether it represents a really old settlement or one relatively late and so named because it had been abandoned. These are probably the Tulsa Indians said by Woodward to have been moved to the Tallapoosa in 1756 from the Talladega country by James McQueen. Other branches of the Tulsa were the Chowockeleehatchee, Saogahatchee, and Lutchapoga. The other group descended from Coosa is best known under the name Okfuskee, and of them there were several different settlements. There were branches bearing other names such as Tcatoksofka, Abihkutci, Tukabahchee Tallahassee or Talmutcasi, Sukaispoga, Imukfa, Tohtogagi, Ipisagi, Tukpafka (later renamed Nuyaka), Tcuthlȧko-nini, Hothli-taiga, Tcahki thlȧko, Okfuskutci, and perhaps Atcina-ulga. Most of the people of this group took part in the Creek-American war and suffered accordingly. The rest of their history is bound up in that of the Muskogee (q. v.).

Coosa population.—Garcilaso de la Vega, who is, however, given to exaggeration, cites his soldier informants to the effect that there were 500 houses in Coosa in 1540, a figure which need not be far wrong if the province of Coosa is intended since the soldier sent to Coosa by Pardo in 1567 reported 150 neighborhoods or small villages. The word "vecinos" which appears here cannot possibly mean individuals unless he is merely talking of the central town. The companions of De Luna, who visited Coosa in 1560, reported that the principal town of the province had 30 houses, and that there were seven other villages in its neighborhood, five smaller and two larger. When Coosa reappears in history at the end of the eighteenth century, it had lost the greater part of its population. In 1738 Coosa is said to have had 100 warriors and the Coosa group of towns 414; in 1750 we have figures of 30+ and 240+; an estimate of 1760 gives 430 men in the group, and one of 1761, 270 "hunters." In 1792 the "Coosa of Chickasaw Camp" were credited with 80 men, and the Coosa group of towns with 440. After this time we have figures only for the group. Hawkins (1799) estimated upward of 520 gunmen, and the census of 1832–33 a total population of 3,792. Later figures for Coosa and its towns are not available.

COREE OR CORANINE

A small tribe occupying the peninsula south of the mouth of Neuse River, N. C. It is probably the tribe intended by the name Cwarennoc of Hariot's map, for Lawson calls them in one place Connamox. Soon after first white contact, a considerable part of this tribe was destroyed by the Machapunga Indians. The survivors cast in their lot with the Tuscarora in their war with the colonists, 1711–13. In 1715 they and the Machapunga were assigned a tract of land on Mattamuskeet Lake, Hyde County, N. C., where it is probable that they remained until they became extinct. (See Machapunga.)

Coree population.—In 1709, according to Lawson, they had 25 fighting men and were living in two villages.

COSAPUYA

See Cusabo, page 128.

COWETA

One of the two great Muskogee tribes or towns among the Lower Creeks. According to tradition, they originally constituted one people with the Kasihta (q. v.) and after the separation became the head war town of the Lower Creeks, just as Kasihta became the head peace town. This town was at one time regarded by whites as the capital of the Creek Confederation, and its chief is often called "Emperor of the Creeks." There is no certain mention of it in the earlier Spanish documents. In the spring of 1540, after leaving the Apalachee country, De Soto passed through a province and towns, probably on Flint River, to which the names Chisi, Ichisi, and Achese are given. Since Otcī'si is the Hitchiti word applied particularly to the Muskogee, and the Spaniards seem to have visited a Hitchiti-speaking tribe just before, it is possible that the Creeks living here were the Coweta. Another possibility is that they were the Indians of Cofitachequi. Elsewhere (p. 143) I have identified these with the Kasihta, and there are strong arguments for doing so, but reference to a Casiste town on Alabama River, which the Spaniards passed in the fall of the same year, may mean that the Kasihta were originally west of their sister tribe instead of being east of them as represented in all later tradition. Before South Carolina was founded, the Coweta seem to have lived on Chattahoochee River and to have moved from there to the Ocmulgee in order to be nearer the English traders. After the Yamasee War in 1715 they returned to the Chattahoochee, settling first, it would seem, on the west side a little above Fort Mitchell, where in after years, was a noted branch town known as Thlikatcka, or "Broken Arrow," though Broken Arrow was at an earlier date 12 miles below Kasihta. Later they moved higher up and settled a little below the falls. In 1799 there was a branch village called Wetumka on the main fork of Uchee Creek, 12 miles northwest of the main town. The census taken in 1832–33 gives five Coweta villages besides the people of Broken Arrow, who were then divided between two settlements. The Coweta were always very friendly to the whites, sided actively with them during the Creek War of 1813–14, and agreed in 1825 to a treaty of removal. For this last act, the Coweta head man, William McIntosh, was killed on May 1, 1825, by a party of warriors sent for that purpose. After the removal, the Coweta Indians settled on the Arkansas near the present town of Coweta. For a time they also retained their premier position, but, like most of the other Lower Creeks, they gave up their ancient customs and separate existence more readily than the inhabitants of the Upper Towns.

Coweta population.—We find the following estimates of the number of Coweta warriors in eighteenth century sources: 132 in 1738, 80+ in 1750, 150 in 1760, and 130 in 1761. In 1772 Taitt gives 220 gunmen in "Coweta, Little Coweta, and Bigskin Creek," and in 1792 Marbury reports 280 in Coweta and its villages. According to Hawkins, in 1799 there were 66 gunmen in Coweta Tallahassee and its villages by actual count. The census of 1832–33 gives 896 Indians in the 5 Coweta settlements and 1,082 in those of Broken Arrow, but this last should probably be reduced to 438, giving a total Coweta population of 1,334.

CREEK CONFEDERATION

Its history is discussed under the names of the separate tribes, but particularly under the name of the dominant group, the Muskogee.

CUSABO

A tribe, or rather group of small tribes, in the southern part of South Carolina between the present site of Charleston and the Savannah River. There was an inland group called Coosa living on the upper courses of the rivers from the Ashley to the Coosawhatchie, and they gave their name to the stream last mentioned and to the Cusabo as a whole. It is possible that they were a branch of the Coosa of Coosa River, Ala., and so related to the Muskogee proper rather than to the Hitchiti, as seems to have been the case with the rest. Among the coast people there appears to have been a minor differentiation between the Indians near Charleston and those about Broad River and the Edisto. The Ayllon settlement of 1526, after removal from its first position, perhaps settled in or near the country of these last, and here, close to Beaufort, was the earliest Huguenot colony. This consisted of 28 men who were left there by Jean Ribault in 1562, survived the winter of 1562–63, and in the spring managed to build a small vessel in which a few of them finally reached France after incredible hardships. After destroying the second Huguenot colony on the St. Johns River, Fla., Menendez established a post called Santa Elena near the place where the French fort had stood. Missionary work was attempted among the neighboring Indians by the Jesuit Father Rogel in 1568–70, but it proved unproductive and was abandoned. In 1576 an uprising occurred among the neighboring Indians, two bodies of Spanish troops were cut off, and the Spanish fort abandoned, but soon restored, and in 1579 an Indian town named Cocapoy, situated in the marshes 20 leagues away, was captured and its occupants severely handled. In 1580 there was a new uprising resulting in the abandonment of the fort a second time. Late in 1582 it was reoccupied, but in 1587 the garrison was finally withdrawn. Missionary work of a somewhat sporadic nature continued, however, and one mission is mentioned called Chatuache or Satuache, 6 to 10 leagues (15.5 to 26 miles) northward from Santa Elena. We learn of wars taking place in this period between the Indians of the Cusabo province and those of Guale, and that upon one occasion part of the "vassals" of a Cusabo chief named Aluete had fled from him and gone to live on St. Simons Island.

We next get some light on these Indians from the journal of Capt. William Hilton of the English ship *Adventure*, which visited the coast in 1663, and from that of Capt. Robert Sandford, who was there 3 years later. Soon afterward they were scourged by repeated attacks

of the Westo. In 1670 the colony of South Carolina came into existence with the settlement in Charleston Harbor and from that time
on we hear considerably more of the natives. In 1671 the colonists
had a short war with the Coosa, and there were disturbances in 1674
in which the Coosa and Stono were involved. In 1675 the Coosa
ceded the land which was given the name of the Ashley Barony, and
in 1682 a more sweeping cession of territory was made by the Indians
about Broad River. In 1693 there was a short war with the Stono,
and in 1711-12 a body of Cusabo Indians joined Barnwell in his Tuscarora expedition. In 1712 the southern Cusabo were granted Palawana Island, to which most of their plantations had already been
transferred, but the Kiawa and Itwans appear to have remained in the
north until after the Yamasee War. In that contest the coast Indians
seem to have sided for the most part with the colonists and in consequence suffered little. One small body may have gone to Florida, for
in "a list of new Indian missions in the vicinity of St. Augustine"
made December 1, 1726, we find entered, "San Antonio, of the Cosapuya nation and other Indians." There is no mention of another town
occupied by these people, but 2 years later a second report on the
missions states that "the towns of the Casapullas Indians were depopulated." It is not certain that these were Cusabo, but their name
resembled in form "Cocapoy," which is given as the designation of a
Cusabo town destroyed by the Spaniards in 1579. In 1720 "King
Gilbert and ye Coosaboys" took part in Barnwell's expedition against
St. Augustine. In 1738 Palawana was granted to a band of Natchez,
from which it is to be assumed that the Cusabo had left it or died out.
In 1743 the Kiawa received a grant of land south of the Combahee
River whither it is probable that the Indians about Charleston removed. A few may have remained about their old homes, but we
hear nothing more of them after the middle of the eighteenth century.
There are still mixed-blood groups in the old Cusabo country probably
perpetuating a percentage of their blood. Some, and perhaps all, of
the Coosa, however, apparently retired inland. Adair mentions them
as one of the tribes which had united with the Catawba, but it is more
likely that they settled among the related Creeks and there are traditions suggesting such a removal. They may have numbered at most
600.

Cusabo population.—The census of 1715 gives 5 villages of southern Cusabo with 95 men and a total population of 295, while the
northern Cusabo or Itwans had 1 village, 80 men, and a total population of 240. The tribe as a whole, therefore, counted 535 in all.
The Coosa do not seem to be included in this enumeration. As these
Indians are already described as "mixed with the English settlement,"
it is fair to assume that they had already begun to decline in numbers.

DEADOSE

A tribe which seems to have been living at the end of the seventeenth century between the Trinity and Navasota Rivers, Tex. Little is known about them but the name and a statement that they had separated from the Bidai Indians. They were placed at San Ildefonso Mission in 1748–49, probably on San Gabriel River, and 9 miles northeast of the present Rockdale, Milam County, which they shared with the Akokisa, Bidai, and Patiri. With the others, they abandoned this mission in 1751, joined the Nabedache in a raid against the Apache, and then settled for a time near San Xavier Mission. They may have been swept away in the epidemic that raged among the Indians of Texas in 1777–78.

DOUSTIONI

The Doustioni appear also under the names Souchitiony, Dulchinois, and Oulchionis—a small tribe usually living near the Natchitoches in northwestern Louisiana. Joutel mentions them in 1687 as allies of the Kadohadacho. They were visited by Bienville and St. Denis in 1700. In 1702, on account of the failure of the crops, St. Denis removed the Natchitoches tribe from Red River and settled them beside the Acolapissa on Lake Pontchartrain. The Doustioni, however, remained in the country and reverted for the time being to a hunting life. In 1714, when St. Denis brought the Natchitoches back and began an establishment among them, the Doustioni accepted his invitation to settle close by. In 1719 La Harpe speaks of them as living on an island in Red River not far away. We hear nothing more about them, and they probably lost their identity in the Natchitoches tribe.

Doustioni population.—In 1701 Bienville says they occupied 15 cabins and Beaurain that they had 50 warriors. Pénicaut estimates the number of their warriors at 200 in 1714 (erroneously given as 1712 in his narrative). In 1719 La Harpe believed that the entire tribe did not embrace more than 200 persons, and Beaurain, treating of the same period, cuts this to 150.

ENO

A tribe first mentioned by Governor Yardley in 1654 under the name Haynoke and called "a great nation" by whom the northward advance of the Spaniards had been valiantly resisted. Speck has recently suggested that they may have been identical with the Weanoc or Wyanoke Indians, a Powhatan band living in 1608 in the present Charles City County, Va., on the north bank of James River, and from which they moved south during the latter part of the century as far as the borders of North Carolina. Wyanoke Creek preserves the name. I am, however, of the opinion that the two were distinct and that Yardley's remarks are based upon an actual immigration of this tribe from farther south, like several other Siouan tribes. The name of the Enoree River in South Carolina may furnish a clue as to their original habitat. In 1670 Lederer heard of them as living about the headwaters of the Tar and Neuse, where a small river preserves the name. In 1701 Lawson found their village, which he calls Adshusheer, on Eno River about 14 miles east of the site of Hillsboro, N. C. Lawson also includes Eno in his list of Tuscarora villages. In 1714, along with the other Siouan tribes, they moved toward the settlements. Two years later Governor Spotswood of Virginia proposed to place them, along with the Cheraw and Keyauwee, at Eno town on "the very frontiers" of North Carolina, but the plan was defeated by the latter colony. Afterward they moved into South Carolina and part at least ultimately united with the Catawba.

Eno population.—In 1709 this tribe and the Tutelo, Saponi, Occaneechi, and Keyauwee together were said to number only 750 souls. Mooney estimated that this tribe and the Shakori numbered 1,500 in the year 1600, a figure which I should cut to 1,000.

EUFAULA OR YUFALA

A Muskogee tribe or band which, according to Cherokee tradition, lived at a very early date upon Euharlee Creek, an affluent of Etowah River, Ga., where is a town of the same name. Whether this tradition is correct or not, we find the Eufaula in the early historic period on Talladega Creek in Talladega County, Ala., where they occupied a town later called Eufaula Hatchee or Eufaula Oldtown. Comparatively early in the eighteenth century most of these Indians seem to have left this place to settle on the middle course of Tallapoosa River, 5 miles below Okfuskee. In 1792 there were two settlements here, Big Eufaula and Little Eufaula. It was probably from this place that a colony was sent which settled Lower Eufaula on the Chattahoochee sometime before 1733. In 1752 this town was 45 miles below the main Coweta settlement, and it was reported to be made up of renegades from "all the towns of the Nation." Although the nucleus was, as we have seen, Muskogee, there was a very large Hitchiti element in it. The census of 1832–33 mentions a village belonging to these people known as "Chowokolohatches," though this may have contained Sawokli Indians. In 1767 Romans says a colony of Eufaula Indians went to Florida and established themselves in a town called Tcuko tcati, or "Red House," near a hammock north of Tampa which bears the same name. They formed the nucleus of the Muskogee element among the Seminole. The other Eufaula Indians went to Oklahoma with the Creeks, and the Tallapoosa and Chattahoochee towns maintained their distinct character for a time, but the Square Ground of Lower Eufaula has now long been given up. The other has transferred its name to a neighboring city. Early in the seventeenth century, we hear of a town in the southern part of the province of Guale called Yfulo or Ofulo which may have represented a branch of the same people, and there is another—or possibly it is the same—between the Altamaha and Cumberland Island the name of which appears in the Timucua form Yufera or Ufera.

Eufaula population.—In 1738 131 warriors were reported in the two towns (20 in Upper Eufaula and 111 in the Lower town); in 1750 there were 10 returned from the Upper and 15 from the Lower; in 1760, 100 in the Upper and 60 in the Lower; in 1761, 35 hunters in the Upper town and 90 in the Lower; in 1792, 40 men in Upper Eufaula and 40 in Eufaula Oldtown, the last possibly belonging to a different band; in 1799, Hawkins gives 70 gunmen in the Upper town; in 1822, Young estimates 670 Lower Eufaula Indians all told; and finally, in 1832–33, 459 Upper Eufaula were reported and 981 Lower Eufaula, making 1,440 in all, exclusive of 21 slaves.

EYEISH OR HA-ISH

A small Caddo tribe usually living on a creek in San Augustine County, Tex., called after them Ayish Creek. They are first mentioned in the Elvas and Biedma narratives of the De Soto expedition, from which it appears that in 1542 they were encountered by the survivors of his army in the region they later occupied. Joutel mentions them again in 1687. In 1716 the Mission of Nuestra Señora de los Dolores de los Ais was established among them, abandoned in 1719, reestablished in 1721, and finally abandoned in 1773 after more than 50 years of practically fruitless effort. In 1768 they were reported as among the "worst" Indians in Texas. In 1785 they were living on Attoyac River and in 1801 Sibley says they were almost destroyed by the smallpox. In 1828 they were between the Brazos and Colorado, and after this time they united with the other Caddo and followed their fortunes.

Eyeish population.—In 1716 their town consisted of 10 cabins and 70 families. In 1779 there were said to be 20 families. Sibley reported "not more than 25" individuals belonging to this tribe in 1805, but 15 years later there were said to be twice as many and in 1828 there were said to be 160 families, evident exaggerations, though Sibley may have underestimated them. A population in early times of perhaps 400 is indicated. (See Swanton, 1942, pp. 22–23.)

FRESH WATER ("AGUA DULCE") INDIANS

The name of "Agua Dulce" was applied by the Spaniards to the inhabitants of a group of related Timucua towns along the lagoons south of St. Augustine, Fla., the southernmost being on the upper course of the St. Johns. In 1602 the following "Christian towns" are mentioned in this province: San Sebastian, Moloa, Antonico, Tocoy, and San Julian. Later lists omit the first two, but add Filache, Equale or Toquale, Anacape, and Maiaca, though Maiaca is not always included. The native name of Antonico was perhaps Tunsa. Most of these names disappear from the mission lists after 1606, but "San Antonio de Enacape" is shown in a list made in 1616, and again in one of 1655, along with "San Salvador de Mayaca," though both vanish at that time. Ponce de Leon made his landfall on their coast in 1513 and the French captain Ribault touched upon it in 1562 and 1564, but we hear little of them until St. Augustine was founded in 1565, after which time missionary work was extended to this province, and in 1655, as above mentioned, there were two missions in the two southernmost towns, San Antonio de Anacape, and San Salvador de Maiaca (or Macaya). Maiaca is the only town mentioned very frequently. Fontaneda speaks of it along with a sister settlement Maiajuaca, which seems to have been on the coast, and Maiaca also appears in the narratives of Laudonnière and Le Moyne. By 1680 Maiaca had evidently been abandoned by its original inhabitants as it is represented as "a new conversion." This probably means that it was occupied by Yamasee or Guale Indians, and that the population of the province was already on the decline, a decline which continued, as we know, into the early part of the eighteenth century when the entire Timucua nation disappeared.

Population of the Fresh Water Province.—There are no separate figures for this province except that in the year 1602 the missionaries reported 200 Christianized Indians there and 100 more "under instruction."

FUS-HATCHEE

In the De Crenay map of 1733 this unit appears on the south side of Tallapoosa River, but it was later on the north side and the De Crenay map may be in error. It is mentioned frequently until the time of Hawkins, who has left a description of it as it existed in 1799. Some of these Indians reached Florida before 1778 and the remainder followed after the Creek War. When the Seminole were transplanted to the other side of the Mississippi, these people and the Kan-hatki formed a single settlement under their name in the southern part of the Seminole territory, but their Square Ground was known as Thliwahali because it is said that it was organized by some

Thliwahali Creeks.   However, it appears very probable that the town itself had separated from Thliwahali at a very early date.

Fus-hatchee population.—The following estimates of the effective warriors of the town are given: 20 in 1738, more than 30 in 1750, 60 (including some Tawasa) in 1760, 50 (including some Coosa Indians) in 1761, and 50 in 1792.

GRIGRA, OR, MORE OFTEN, GRIS

A small tribe probably of the Tunican stock which, previous to the arrival of the French in Louisiana, had given up its independent existence and taken a position as one of the towns of the Natchez Nation.   It was one of those towns particularly active in opposition to the French, and, in the troublous times following the Natchez uprising, lost its individuality and became merged indistinguishably with the Natchez fragments.

Grigra population.—We have but one estimate, made about 1720–25, which gives 60 warriors.

GUACATA

(A name which would probably be spelt Wacata in English)

A small tribe on the southeast coast of Florida on what are now St. Lucie Sound and St. Lucie River.   It seems to have been mentioned first by Fontaneda.   In 1565, after destroying the French colony on St. Johns River, Menendez marched to the Ais country on Indian River, left 200 men 3 leagues from the main Ais town, and returned to Havana.   Some time afterward the Ais Indians rose against his men and they moved to the neighborhood of the Guacata Indians, where they were treated in a friendly manner, and they named the place Santa Lucia.   The following year, however, the Guacata also rose against them and killed 15.   Although the Spaniards at first drove these Indians away and built a fort, natives to the number of a thousand soon assaulted the place, wounded the captain and the sub-lieutenant, and killed 8 more soldiers.   They renewed their attacks every day and it was impossible for the Spaniards to go anywhere in search of food, so that they were soon in danger of famine, and part mutinied and escaped.   The post was maintained until 1568, when the number of Spaniards was increased so much by refugees from the colony at Tekesta that they were obliged to resort to cannibalism and the place was shortly abandoned.   In 1699 we obtain an interesting view of this tribe from the narrative of the Quaker Dickenson, who was shipwrecked a short distance to the south.   It is probable that its last representatives accompanied other east coast Indians to Cuba in 1763.   (See Ais.)

Guacata population.—There are no figures available.

GUALE

(Pronounced Wali in English)

The Spaniards gave this name to a "province" extending along the present coast of Georgia from St. Andrews Sound to the Savannah River. It may be a form of Muskogee *wahali*, "the south," and the names by which it was known to the Timucua Indians—Ibaha, Ybaha, Ibaja, Iguaja, Yupaha—may have been corruptions of this. The Indians of this connection constituted a kind of confederation under one head chief and the dominant element seems to have been Muskogee, although there were probably Hitchiti-speaking Indians among them. The name itself was an extension of that given to what is now St. Catherines Island, and there was also a Guale town which seems to have been on the mainland inland from St. Catherines. It is possible that the first use of this term is in the form Gualdape in the narratives of the Ayllon colony established on the South Carolina coast in 1526. The final settlement was made on a river called Gualdape, which I regard as the Savannah or some stream in the immediate neighborhood. In 1562 the Huguenot colonists of Port Royal heard of this island under the name Ouadé and visited it several times to obtain corn. After Spain had displaced the French in 1565, Jesuit missionaries established themselves in the province and one of these, Domingo Augustin, composed a grammar of the language, but they soon abandoned the field in despair, and in about 20 years their places were taken by Franciscans whose work began in 1573 and who soon had a chain of missions along the entire coast. In 1597 all of these missions were destroyed in a general uprising and only one missionary escaped, Father Davila, of Ospo, the southernmost of the stations. A punitive expedition undertaken by the Governor of Florida reduced nearly all to submission by the spring of 1601. Later in the year the remaining hostiles were attacked by those who had returned to their former allegiance, part of them were killed, including the two leaders of the insurrection, and the rest driven into the interior. In 1604, when Governor Ibarra visited the Indians along this coast, churches had been built at St. Catherines and St. Simons (Asao), and a third was planned near Sapelo. Insurrections, which seem to have been of minor character, occurred in 1608 and 1645. In 1655 six missions are enumerated in the province, but already attacks by Indians from the north were beginning, and in 1661 there seems to have been a general assault by Yuchi, during which some of the churches were sacked. The invaders were finally beaten off by a force dispatched from St. Augustine. In 1680 there were still four missions in Guale. The same year some Yuchi, Creeks, and Cherokee, acting in the English interest, and accompanied, it appears, by several Englishmen, attacked two of these, but were forced to withdraw by the Spaniards and natives. This invasion was followed by several more in rapid succession, which occasioned some Indians to betake themselves inland, while others are said to have gone as far south as the Calusa country. In consequence of these attacks, several Guale chiefs asked that they and their people might be removed to the islands of San Pedro, Santa Maria, and San Juan, and a considerable body of them were transferred to the south in this manner except that the island of Santa Cruz, near the mouth of St. Johns River, was substituted for San Pedro. Some Indians are reported to have fled to the English rather than move into the peninsula, but there may be a confusion with the first Yamasee removal, which took place in 1685. In 1699 Dickenson gives interesting descriptions of the three Guale missions in Florida. It is uncertain whether these former Guale Indians accompanied the Yamasee to South Carolina in 1702 or not, but the remnant was evidently incorporated into the Yamasee population after they returned to the peninsula in 1715 and gradually disappeared along with the Yamasee tribe itself, though in 1726 there were two missions near St. Augustine occupied by Indians of the "Iguaja nation" and in 1728 two towns are noted served by one missionary. This mission station was said to be called commonly "Aia Chin." Fearing attack from the hostile tribes, they later moved "within the very shadow of the fort," and, as stated, they probably became fused with the Yamasee.

Guale population.—This was a populous province when the Spaniards entered it in the latter part of the sixteenth century. In 1602 the missionaries claimed there were more than 1,200 Christians there. In 1670, the English in South Carolina estimated that the Indians in the St. Catherine Mission had about 300 men, and that the Indians in all the missions, principally Guale and Yamasee, had about 700 men. In 1675 Governor Salazar stated that there were 506 Indians in the Guale missions (see also Timucua). The greater part of this nation had meanwhile evidently withdrawn among the Creeks.

GUASCO

A Hasinai tribe visited by the Spaniards in 1542, but barely mentioned afterward.

HAINAI

A Caddo tribe belonging to the Hasinai Confederation and among whom was the principal temple. It would seem that they often supplied the head chief. July 7, 1716, there was founded in this tribe the Mission of Nuestra Señora de la Purísima Concepción. It was abandoned in 1719 and reestablished in 1721 and a rudely fashioned presidio was erected nearby, but the success of the mission was so slight that in 1731 it was withdrawn from the Caddo country to San Antonio River. The tribe is mentioned again by Sibley in 1805, and it maintained a separate existence after the removal from Texas to the north side of Red River and even after the Civil War, the last reference appearing in the report of the United States Office of Indian Affairs for 1878.

Hainai population.—Late eighteenth century Spanish sources give 80 warriors, and in 1805 Sibley reported the same number, having perhaps copied the earlier figure. The United States Office of Indian Affairs returned 113 in 1851. In 1864 there were 150 refugee Hainai in Kansas. In 1872 the same source gives 85 Hainai and in 1873, the last time they were separately enumerated, 50. (See Swanton, 1942, pp. 16–25.)

HATTERAS

An Algonquian tribe reported by Lawson as living about Cape Hatteras, N. C., in 1709, and frequenting Roanoke Island. They showed traces of white blood and claimed to have had some white ancestors. Therefore, they may have been identical with the Croatan Indians with whom Raleigh's colonists are supposed to have taken refuge. Nothing further is heard regarding them.

Hatteras population.—Their single settlement, Sandbanks, is said to have had only 16 warriors, perhaps 89 inhabitants, at the date above given.

HILIBI

A Muskogee town and subtribe in the Creek Confederation. This is said to have been built up originally of outcasts from other villages. It is perhaps the Ilapi which Ranjel mentions as a town near Cofitachequi where the bulk of De Soto's army was sent for provisions in May 1540. This place was near the site of the present Augusta, Ga. In northwestern Georgia is an affluent of the Chattahoochee called Hillabeehatchee, which probably indicates the position of a former Hilibi settlement. Bishop Calderón of Cuba, in the report of his visit to Florida in 1675, lists a town called "Ilapi" among the Lower Creeks and another, "Hilapi," in the Upper division of the tribe. In or before the eighteenth century, the tribe was already located on an affluent of the Tallapoosa, with which it was afterward associated until the removal to Oklahoma. In 1799 Hawkins enumerates four branch villages belonging to Hilibi, one of which, Oktahasasi, seems to have maintained an independent existence for a considerable period. An almost equally important branch, not mentioned by him, was Kitcopataki. After the removal, the Hilibi reestablished their Square Ground near Hanna, Okla., where it was maintained until as late as 1929. Hilibi became the residence sometime in the latter part of the eighteenth century of a very intelligent Scotch trader named Robert Grierson, from whom the noted and influential Grayson family is descended.

Hilibi population.—The number of warriors in Hilibi and its branch villages is given as 80 in 1738, 20 in 1750, 80 in 1760, 40 in 1761, 100 in 1772, 150 in 1792, and 170 in 1799, while the total population, exclusive of slaves, was returned by the census of 1832–33 as 804, of whom 485 were in Hilibi itself, 131 in Oktahasasi, and 188 in Kitcopataki.

HITCHITI

This was considered the "mother town" of a considerable group known to themselves as Atcik-hata, living in what is now southern Georgia and northern Florida. It appears first in the De Soto narratives under the name Ocute, as a province and chief on the lower course of Ocmulgee River. The Spaniards set up a wooden cross in the main square of the Ocute village, and, if this is the province described by Garcilaso de la Vega under the name Cofa, it was there that the invaders left their only piece of ordnance. In 1597 it was visited again by a soldier named Gaspar de Salas and two Franciscan missionaries and seems to have been in approximately the same place. When we hear of it again, near the beginning of the eighteenth century, it is still upon the Ocmulgee, but higher up at the place known as Ocmulgee Old Fields, where is now Macon. According to a legend recorded by Wm. Bartram, this was where the Creek Confederation was founded. After the Yamasee War, they moved to a point well down the Chattahoochee but later settled farther up, below the Kasihta and on the same side of the river. Hawkins gives a description of their town as he found it in 1799 and informs us that there were also two branch villages on and near Flint River, named Little Hitchiti and Tutalosi, or the "Fowl Town." In 1820 we hear of a group of six towns known as the Fowl Towns, but some of these were probably not branches of Hitchiti. The census of 1832–33 gives a Hitchiti village named Hihaje. After removing to the west, the Hitchiti settled in the central part of the Creek Nation about the present Hichita Station and near Okmulgee. Part of these people migrated to Florida and those who subsequently moved to Oklahoma with the Seminole settled in the northern part of the Seminole territory, where they maintained a ceremonial ground of their own for a considerable period.

Hitchiti population.—The number of warriors in Hitchiti, apart from other towns speaking the language, appears as 60 in 1738, 15 in 1750, 50 in 1760, 40 in 1761, and in 1772 about 90. In 1821 Young estimates for all the Fowl Towns a population of 300. In 1832 Hitchiti and its branch village Hihaje had a population of 381, exclusive of 20 Negro slaves.

The number of warriors in the group of towns speaking the Hitchiti language, exclusive of those in Florida, is: in 1738, 403; in 1750, 205; in 1760, 620; and in 1761, 370; the total population being, in 1832, 2,036. This includes Hitchiti, Tamathli, Osochi, Chiaha, Okmulgee, Apalachicola, Sawokli, Oconee, and Okitiyakani.

HOTHLIWAHALI, OR, IN ABBREVIATED FORM, THLIWAHALI (ŁIWAHALI)

An Upper Creek town generally located on the north bank of the Tallapoosa River at the mouth of Chubbehatchee Creek. It was found in approximately the same position by De Soto, whose chroniclers call it Ulibahali or Ullibahali. It was again visited by a Spanish major with a force of 200 men sent by Tristan de Luna in 1560. It reappears in documents of the late seventeenth century when we learn that declarations of war were sent out from it after they had been determined upon by the Creek council. The towns of Atasi and Kealedji may have separated from this, but it is entirely uncertain. The only known branch of any importance was Thlapthlako, which was formed toward the end of the eighteenth century. Both mother and daughter towns preserved their separation after they went to Oklahoma, but the latter proved the more vigorous of the two and has maintained a dance ground down to the present day (1933).

Hothliwahali population.—The number of warriors or hunters in this town appears as follows in the several estimates: 10 in 1738, 15 in 1750, 70 in 1760, 35 in 1761, 110 in 1792. In 1832–33 Hothliwahali and Thlapthlako together were credited with a population of 607, of which 427 were in the former town and 180 in the latter.

HOUMA

A tribe located in 1682 on the east side of the Mississippi River opposite the mouth of Red River. They were probably a branch of the Chakchiuma (q. v.). They are first mentioned in the narratives of La Salle's descent of the Mississippi in 1682. In 1686 Tonti made an alliance with them, and in 1699 Iberville, the founder of Louisiana, renewed this and gives a considerable description of their town. In 1700 Iberville visited them again, but found that half of the tribe had been destroyed by "an abdominal flux." A Jesuit priest, Father du Rut, who accompanied him, began a mission in the Houma village and built a church. He was succeeded the same year by Father de Limoges, but the mission did not last long. In 1706 the Tunica obtained permission to settle among them, but soon rose upon their hosts and massacred a considerable number. The remainder established themselves on Bayou St. Jean near New Orleans, but soon moved higher up to the present Ascension Parish. At one time there were two settlements here known as Great Houmas and Little Houmas. In September 1739, an officer under M. de Nouaille, on his way up the Mississippi to join in the abortive attack upon the Chickasaw of the following year, found that this tribe, the Bayogoula, and Acolapissa were in process of fusion, their distinctiveness being maintained more by the chiefs than the mass of people. Governor De Kerlérec gives a brief description of the Houma in 1758, and we know that they remained in approximately the same position until 1776, when two creoles purchased 96 arpents of land from them. Either this did not include all of their territory, or they continued in the neighborhood, for we hear of them in reports by Sibley (1805) and Gallatin (1836). Both inform us that a part had intermarried with the Atakapa and were living in the territory of that tribe. Some time later, though just when is uncertain, the mixed-blood descendants of those on the Mississippi moved south and settled along the Gulf coast in the present parishes of Lafourche and Terrebonne. They have lost their language and most of their aboriginal customs but seem to be increasing in numbers.

Plates 23, 24, and 25 show some of the Houma Indians and their habitations as they appeared in 1907. Plate 23, figure 1, shows Bob Verret, the leading man in this group, and an old man called Baptiste Billiout. The originals of plate 23, figure 2, and plate 24, figure 1, were taken on lower Bayou Lafourche. Plate 24, figure 2, shows some Houma on Little Barataria Bayou, and plate 25, an ancient Houma woman and an old Houma house at Point au Chien.

Houma population.—In 1699 our authorities tell us there were 140 cabins in the tribe, 350 warriors, and a total population of between 600 and 700. In 1700 Gravier gives two estimates of the number of cabins, one of 70 and one of 80. In 1718 La Harpe reported 60 cabins and 200 warriors. In 1739 we are told that there were 90–100 warriors and 270–300 adults of both sexes among the Houma, Acolapissa, and Bayogoula. In 1758 De Kerlérec reported only 60 warriors in the united tribes, and Hutchins in 1784 but 25. In 1803 Jefferson estimated that the population of the same group was 60, but since then the mixed-blood Indian population that goes by the name has increased very markedly. In 1910, 125 Indians were returned from Terrebonne; in 1920, 639; and in 1930, 936; besides 11 in Lafourche. Speck raises this to 2,000. Mooney estimated that there were about 1,000 Houma in 1650; my own estimate was at first (1911) somewhat larger, but I am now inclined to accept Mooney's figure.

IBITOUPA

A small tribe on Yazoo River, Miss., which seems to have lived at the opening of the eighteenth century between Abyache and Chicopa Creeks. Before 1722 the greater part of them moved higher up the Yazoo, beyond the mouth of the Yalobusha and 3 leagues above the Chakchiuma town where Tippo Bayou apparently preserves the name. A small tribe known as Choula (q. v.) perhaps represented a band left behind in the removal. All of the Ibitoupa probably united with the Chakchiuma in the end and followed their fortunes. They may have been related to the Ibetap okla, who constituted two towns in the Choctaw Nation.

Ibitoupa population.—In 1722 the Ibitoupa occupied 6 cabins, but we have no other clue to their population except mention of the fact that the Choula, supposedly a part, comprised 40 persons the same year. (See Chakchiuma.)

ICAFUI

A Timucua province or tribe often called Cascangui, or confused with another province so called. It lay between the Timucua and Guale people, probably on the mainland, and consisted of seven or eight towns. It was visited by the missionary at San Pedro Tacatacuru, Cumberland Island.

IROQUOIS

See Nottoway, page 163.

JEAGA

(Probably pronounced as Hāyaga in English)

A small tribe about Jupiter Inlet on the east coast of Florida, which seems to have been mentioned first by Fontaneda. We hear little of it afterward until 1699, when the narrative of the Quaker Dickenson gives us a glimpse of the tribe under the name Hobe. Subsequently it probably united with the other east coast tribes and removed to Cuba, conjecturally in the year 1763. (See Ais.)

Jeaga population.—Beyond the fact that this tribe was very small, we have no information regarding its numbers.

KADOHADACHO

This was the leading tribe of the Kadohadacho Confederation, that which gave its name to the Caddo linguistic division and the Caddoan stock. Although the survivors of De Soto's army passed through the territory of several Caddo tribes, the name of this one does not appear among them. We learn about it first from the companions of La Salle who in 1687, after the murder of their commander, passed through the Kadohadacho town on their way to the Mississippi. The Kadohadacho were then just above the bend of Red River in the southwestern part of the present Arkansas and associated with the Nasoni, Nanatsoho, and a part of the Natchitoches. Later several French explorers reached them from Louisiana via Red River. The first was Tonti in 1690. La Harpe, however, who visited their town in 1719, has left a more complete description. It was on the north bank of Red River somewhat above the mouth of Little River. Later these Indians settled in the Nasoni town, or

else Sibley confounds them with the Nasoni, for he says they lived
on the south bank of Red River "at a beautiful prairie" which had
a clear lake of water in the middle of it and was "surrounded by a
pleasant and fertile country." Sibley adds that the Kadohadacho
believed that that country "had been the residence of their ancestors
from time immemorial," that near this lake was an eminence
upon which one family had been saved in a universal deluge, and that
from this family they themselves and a number of related tribes
were descended. But according to informants of Wm. B. Parker,
as reported to Schoolcraft, they had a tradition that they had issued
from the hot springs of Arkansas. There was at one time a French
settlement near the old Caddo town and they "erected a good flour
mill with burr stones brought from France." About 1780, however,
they abandoned the place and settled near Campti, La. A part of the
Kadohadacho settled lower down Red River on the east side, but
there their enemies, the Osages, fell upon them, slaughtered a great
many, and drove the rest away. It was then, probably, that they
moved to a point on Sodo Creek 35 miles west of the main channel of
Red River. In 1825 they agreed to share their lands with the Quapaw
Indians, and the Quapaw reached them late in the same year but
did not prosper and soon relinquished their claims in the Caddo
country for a territory in the present Oklahoma, to which they
removed in 1833. Two years later, the Caddo Indians surrendered
all of their lands within the boundaries of the United States and
removed into Texas, then a part of the Republic of Mexico. Their
subsequent history has been given under the heading Caddo.

Kadohadacho population.—It is not given separately from that of
the related bands. (See Caddo.)

KAN-HATKI

The history of this town is an almost perfect parallel of that of
Fus-hatchee, one of its nearest neighbors. It appears on the
De Crenay map of 1733 as already in existence, is noted repeatedly
from that time on, and is described by Hawkins. Swan calls it a
Shawnee town, but this was probably owing to the near neighborhood of Sawanogi and the presence of some Shawnee in the population. The census of 1832 mentions a town called "Ekun-duts-ke,"
but it probably had nothing to do with the one under discussion.
The people of this town seem to have gone to Florida in a body and
later to the Seminole Nation in Oklahoma, uniting with the Fus-
hatchee (q. v.) and following their fortunes.

Kan-hatki population.—The following figures covering the effective male population of the town are given: 12 in 1738, 15 in 1750,
40 in 1760 (including some Coosa Indians), and 30 in 1761 and in
1792.

KASIHTA

One of the two great tribes which constituted the greater part of the pure Muskogee element among the Lower Creeks. It has been supposed that these are the Cofitachequi of the De Soto narratives who were living a few miles below the site of Augusta, Ga., in 1540, but it is possible that they were Coweta and that the Kasihta are represented by a tribe which the Spaniards met on the Alabama and which appears as Casiste in the De Soto chronicles and Caxiti in the De Luna narratives. On the other hand, all of the Creek migration legends affirm that the Kasihta moved eastward in advance of the other tribes. Cofitachequi was visited by Juan Pardo in 1566 and 1567, and was perhaps the Chiquola of Laudonnière (1562). In 1628 it was visited by Pedro de Torres. In 1670 Henry Woodward visited a tribe living northwest of the South Carolina colony at Charleston which he identified with the Cofitachequi of De Soto, and there is no doubt that this at least included the Kasihta Indians. They seem to have been somewhat farther toward the north and west than the Cofitachequi of De Soto. Before 1686 we know that they were living upon Chattahoochee River because their village was burned that year by a Spanish expedition in that quarter. This and the attraction of the Charleston settlement evidently drew them to the Ocmulgee with most of the other Creek towns, where they remained until the Yamasee War, and it was on the Ocmulgee that James Moore outfitted his expedition against the Apalachee. In consequence of the Yamasee War, they returned to the Chattahoochee, where they seem to have occupied two sites successively. The second of these, on the east side of the river a little below the falls, is described at some length by Benjamin Hawkins, who mentions two settlements belonging to it in his Sketch of the Creek Country and still another in his notes taken 2 years before. In the census rolls of 1832–33 seven Kasihta settlements appear and Gatschet has recorded still another.

Kasihta population.—The number of warriors in this town is given as 111 in 1738, more than 80 in 1750, 150 in 1760, 100 in 1761 and 1772, and 375 in 1792, counting in the villages. In 1799 Hawkins says that the Indians themselves believed they had 300 gunmen, but his own estimate was 180. The census of 1832–33 returned, in all the Kasihta settlements, 1918 souls.

KASKINAMPO

A tribe which appears first in history in 1541 in the De Soto narratives under the name Casqui or Casquin. They were found near the present Helena, Ark. Before the end of the seventeenth century, they had moved to the Cumberland, from which they shifted to the Tennessee and in 1701 were on the lower end of an island in the river, probably to be identified with Pine Island, a few miles above the great bend. The Koasati were living at the upper end of this island and it seems evident from the statements of later writers that the two tribes combined soon afterward, both appearing from that time on under the name Koasati (q. v.).

Kaskinampo population.—An early French document, probably basing its information on a visit made to this tribe in 1701 by some Canadians, gives the number of warriors as 150.

KEALEDJI

Traditionally, this is said to have been a branch of the Tukabah-chee, but it is doubtful, since the early history of the two ran along different channels. The name resembles the old Creek name of St. Catherines Island. In a map dated between 1715 and 1720, it appears on Ocmulgee River, but by 1733, if we may trust the map of Baron de Crenay, it had removed to the Tallapoosa, where it seems to have occupied several different places, moving finally to a creek which came to bear the name Kowaliga. This flows into the Tallapoosa on its western side above the falls. When Hawkins described the situation of this town in 1799, there were two branch villages, one on Atcina Hatchee (Cedar Creek) and the other called Hatcheetcaba. This last appears as an independent town as far back as 1760, or even in 1675, earlier than Kealedji, if the "Archichepa" of Calderón is the same, and it retained a dance ground of its own, though no regular square, after removing to Oklahoma. The Kealedji settled in the southeastern part of the Creek reserve, where they maintained a dance ground until very recent times.

Kealedji population.—The Spanish census of 1738 gives 50 warriors in this town and the French census of 1750, more than 25, not counting a few Hatcheetcaba Indians. In 1760 the figure for Kealedji is raised to 130, but those in Hatcheetcaba are enumerated among the Indians of Wiwohka. The enumeration of 1761 gives 40 hunters here and those of Hatcheetcaba and Otciapofa together as 20. The number of gunmen reported by Taitt in 1772 was 70, and by Marbury in 1792, 100 not counting 20 in Atcina Hatchee and part of 30 credited to Hatcheetcaba and Otciapofa. The United States census of 1832 returned a total population of 591 for Kealedji, and 201 for Hatcheetcaba.

KEYAUWEE

A tribe found by Lawson in 1701 living in a palisaded village not far from the present High Point, N. C., the males said to have the pecu-liarity of wearing beards and mustaches. Their chief at that time was a Congaree, who had obtained his position by marrying the Keyauwee chieftainess. There is evidence that their former home was farther toward the southwest, and there is probably some connection between their name and that of Keowee River, S. C. Shortly after Lawson's visit, accompanied by the Saponi, Tutelo, Occaneechi, and Shakori, they moved toward the white settlements about Albemarle Sound and some time in 1733 settled farther south on Pee Dee River with the Cheraw, and probably the Eno and Shakori. At a later period they evidently united with the Catawba, and finally lost their identity in the larger tribe, though some are probably perpetuated in the so called Croatans.

Keyauwee population.—In 1701 Lawson reports that they were about equal in numbers to the Saponi, and with that tribe, the Tutelo, Occaneechi, and Shakori might number in all 750. Mooney's estimate as of 1600 is 500.

KOASATI

This tribe first appears in history in the De Soto narratives under the name Coste, Acoste, Costehe, or Acosta. They were then living on an island in Tennessee River, probably Pine Island, and the river was sometimes called after them the "River of the Cussatees." In 1567 they are enumerated among the tribes prepared to dispute Juan Pardo's advance into the interior. Before 1701 the Kaskinampo came to live at the lower end of the same island and presently united with them. They gave their name to a settlement of Creek and Cherokee Indians at Larkin's Landing, said to have been established about 1784, but, at least before 1686, part had moved into the Creek country, where they settled west of the point of junction of the Coosa and Tallapoosa Rivers, and most of the tribe soon gathered there. In 1763 a band of this tribe moved to the Tombigbee, but suffered so much from the neighboring Choctaw that they soon returned. Between 1793 and 1795 another section went to Red River, La. Those who remained behind followed the fortunes of the rest of the Creeks and formed two settlements near the Canadian River, but neither lasted many years and there is now no one belonging to that part of the tribe who speaks the old language. Those who went to Louisiana occupied several different places, the name of one of which is preserved by the present Coushatta. Some lived for a time in the Opelousas district and then went to the Sabine. Later we find Koasati on the Neches River, Tex., and others on the Trinity. Those who moved to Texas suffered severely from pestilence and the remainder collected in one village, which united with the Alabama Indians. A part, however, reunited with the Koasati still in Louisiana, and these gathered in what was then Calcasieu Parish, but is now in Allen and Jefferson Parishes between the present Elton and Kinder, where their descendants are still to be found. During the eighteenth century, there is mention of a town called Wetumpka near the Koasati settlement in Alabama, which probably branched off from it. Mention of a "Coosada Old Town" on the middle course of Choctawhatchee River in Vignoles map of Florida dated 1823, shows that a section of this tribe must have gone to Florida but, if so, its identity was soon lost.

Plate 26 is a sketch of a Koasati Indian, named Stimafutchki, or "Good Humor," presumably a chief, made by Trumbull in 1790 when a delegation of Creeks visited President George Washington in New York. Plate 27 shows the author's principal informant in 1910–14, Jackson Langley, and his mother; and plate 28, the Koasati Indian school near Kinder, La.

Koasati population.—In 1750 the first estimate of Koasati under that name gives 50 men. In 1760 there were 150 reported, and in the census of 1761 this tribe and the Tamahita (part of the Yuchi) together had 125 hunters. In 1772 Taitt reported 40 "Alibamons" in what was evidently the Koasati town. In 1792, just before the emigration to Louisiana began, they are said to have had 130 men, and in 1832 the total population of the Koasati town in the Creek Nation was 82. There is no later separate enumeration of this section of the Koasati. In 1805 Sibley states that the Louisiana Koasati supposed there were about 200 men in all their settlements. In 1814 Schermerhorn estimated a total Koasati population on Sabine River of 600, but 3 years later Morse gives 350 on Red River, 50 on the Neches, and 240 on the Trinity. In 1829 Porter gives only 180 Koasati, but Bollaert, in 1850, estimates 500 warriors in two villages on the lower Trinity, a palpable exaggeration. In 1882 the United States Indian Office estimated that there were 290 Alabama, Koasati, and Muskogee in Texas, and this figure was repeated through 1900. The census of the latter year, however, returned 470 of the allied tribes and the Indian Office repeated this until 1911. In 1910 a special agent was sent to Texas, who omitted the Koasati from his report, but the United States Census of 1910 returned 85 in Louisiana, 11 in Texas, and 2 in Nebraska, a total of 98. The census of 1920 reported 136 Indians in Allen and Jefferson Parishes, La., and in 1930, 274, the greater part of whom were undoubtedly Koasati.

KOLOMI OR KULUMI

The name of this Muskogee town or tribe appears first in Calderón's report dated 1675 when it was on the Chattahoochee River, and the maps indicate that it was located in what is now Stewart County, Ga., though Colomokee Creek in Clay County seems to indicate another site. Still later these people removed to the Tallapoosa, where they settled upon the east bank, but later crossed over.

Bartram gives an excellent description of this town as it appeared in 1777. In 1778 part of the Kolomi, along with some of the Fus-hatchee and part of the Okchai, besides an Alabama contingent from Tawasa and Kan-hatki, moved to Florida, and a tradition, which there is little reason to doubt, says that the rest of the town followed after the Creek War of 1813–14. These Indians may have constituted a large part of the population of Suwannee Oldtown, since its chief was named Kolomi Miko. A tradition preserved among the Creeks as late as 1912 asserted that the Kolomi finally united with the Fus-hatchee, Kan-hatki, and Atasi, and that is not improbable since these towns were located near one another. If so, they may have formed the Thliwahali town among the Seminole, but their ultimate fate is actually unknown.

Kolomi population.—The following estimates of the number of warriors or hunters in Kolomi have been preserved: 50 in 1738, 25 in 1750, and 50 again in 1760, 1761, and 1792.

KOROA

It is possible that this tribe appears in the De Soto narratives as the Coligua or Coligoa discovered somewhere in Arkansas, probably at Little Rock, in 1541. On Marquette's map they are called Akoroa and are placed somewhere west of the Quapaw. La Salle (1682) gave the name to two distinct bodies of Indians, one on Yazoo River, the other on the east side of the Mississippi below the Natchez. These last were probably the Tiou of later writers. There was at this time not only a settlement on Yazoo River but villages west of the Mississippi in that neighborhood mentioned by Tonti. Bienville was told of such a village but did not enter it, and we hear of a "river Coroas." The Koroa east of the Mississippi seem to have spent much of their time along the great river itself, since a part of the littoral there was known as the bank of the Koroa, mention is made of a Koroa channel, and Pénicaut speaks of a Koroa village on the Mississippi. In 1702 a French missionary named Foucault was killed among these people, but the Koroa chiefs had the murderer slain. In 1704 they are said to have suffered severely at the hands of the Quapaw and Illinois, and about this time they probably moved back to the Yazoo River, where they settled near the related Yazoo Indians. In 1729, on the outbreak of the Natchez war, the Koroa and Yazoo murdered the missionary P. Seuel and massacred the garrison of Fort St. Peter in their country, but shortly afterward they were themselves attacked by the Chakchiuma and Choctaw, who were in the French interest, and still later by the Quapaw. In 1731, when Perrier advanced against the Natchez on Tensas River, it was reported that the Koroa and Yazoo were occupying a fort by themselves. Later the same year they took part with the Natchez in an attack upon the Tunica Indians, and that is the last we hear of them. It is probable that they first retired to the Chickasaw, but since the Choctaw chief Allen Wright claimed to be descended from a Koroa, part of the tribe would appear to have reached the Choctaw.

Koroa population.—This tribe is perhaps included in the 300 families of which Iberville in 1702 estimated the Tunica, Yazoo, and Ofo to consist. In 1722 La Harpe considered that the Yazoo, Koroa, and Ofo numbered 250, all told. In 1730 Le Petit allows them 40 warriors and about the same time Du Pratz states that they had 40 cabins. (See Yazoo and Tunica.)

MACAPIRAS OR AMACAPIRAS

A tribe whose original home seems to have been near the Calusa, since from that country 24 were brought to one of the missions near St. Augustine, Fla., before 1726 along with "Posoye" (Pohoy) Indians. Some of these were destroyed in a pestilence and the remainder returned to their old homes before 1728. Their exact connection is unknown, though they may have been part of the Tocobaga (q. v.).

MACHAPUNGA

A tribe living between Albemarle and Pamlico Sounds, N. C., at the end of the seventeenth century. In 1701 they occupied a single village called Mattamuskeet. They sided with the hostiles in the Tuscarora War of 1711–13 and at its end the survivors of this tribe and the Coree were settled on a tract of land on Mattamuskeet Lake, where they gradually disappeared in the surrounding population.

Machapunga population.—In 1709 they numbered 30 warriors or perhaps 100 souls, but to these should perhaps be added the Bear River Indians with 50 fighting men, or 160–170 people.

MANAHOAC

This tribe or small confederation lived in 1607 in the Piedmont country about the upper waters of the Rappahannock River, Va. In 1654, perhaps owing to attacks by the Susquehanna Indians, they moved south along with the Tutelo and settled near the falls of James River. This movement terrified the white colonists to such an extent that they sent a body of troops, assisted by Powhatan Indians, against the intruders, but the allied force suffered a severe defeat. The Manahoac, or a part of them, seem to have settled on and given their name to Mohawk Creek, a southern affluent of the James, where they were found by John Lederer. Two of the Manahoac tribes are enumerated among those brought to Fort Christanna on Meherrin

River near the present Gholsonville, Va., in 1714. In 1728 Byrd reported that they had united with the Saponi and Occaneechi under the name of the former. The remnant evidently accompanied the Tutelo and Saponi to New York, and from this time on they disappear from history.

Manahoac population.—This is nowhere entered apart from the population of other tribes. Mooney estimated that there were 1,200 in 1600, but I would reduce this figure to 1,000.

MEHERRIN

This tribe was found by the Virginia colonists on the river of the same name. Edward Blande and his companions visited them in 1650, calling them "Maharineck." They are noted later, in 1669, as the "Menheyricks." After the disruption of the Susquehana Indians about 1675, a part of them seem to have joined this tribe, giving rise to the belief that the latter were all of Susquehanna or Conestoga descent. In April 1728, Byrd learned from three Meherrin Indians that they had deserted their ancient town near the mouth of Meherrin River for fear of the Catawba, who had killed 14 of them on the east side of Chowan. In 1761 the southern Tuscarora, Meherrin, and southern Saponi were on and near Roanoke River, and the Meherrin probably united ultimately with the first named.

Meherrin population.—In the census of Virginia Indians made in 1669, they were said to have had 50 bowmen, which would mean a total population of about 180. This figure is repeated in 1709. In 1755 there were said to be 7 or 8 fighting men. In 1761, 20 were returned, but this seems to have been owing to a confusion of notes. Mooney estimated 700 for the year 1600.

MICHIGAMEA

The "old country" of this tribe was about the headwaters of the Sangamon River in Illinois, but in 1673 Marquette found them in northeastern Arkansas on a lake, perhaps the present Big Lake, though the disturbances created by the earthquake of New Madrid may have changed considerably the topography in this section. Toward the end of the seventeenth century, they were driven out of Arkansas by the Quapaw or Chickasaw, and joined the Kaskaskia in the territory of the present Illinois. Du Pratz says that they united with the Quapaw, and a part may have done so. The name of the tribe appears as late as the year 1818, but they must have lost their identity by the middle of the nineteenth century.

Michigamea population.—Chauvignerie (1736) estimates 250 warriors, but this figure must be too high, as he gives only 508 for the entire Illinois Confederation.   In 1778 they and the Peoria together numbered 170.

MIKASUKI

A prominent Seminole tribe composed of Indians speaking the Hitchiti language but, according to their own tradition, an offshoot of the Chiaha.   Since they seem to have belonged to the Red division of Creeks and Seminole, this origin is more likely than another which traces them to the Sawokli.   They first receive historical mention toward the end of the eighteenth century.   Hawkins enters them in a list of Seminole towns made in 1799, and their first settlement seems to have been at Old Mikasuki near the lake which bears their name in Jefferson County, Fla.   In 1817 their town, consisting of 300 houses, was burned by Andrew Jackson.   They proved to be among the most bitter opponents of white intrusion in Florida, sustained more than their fair share of the brunt of the Seminole War, and a part retain their identity to the present day as the Big Cypress band.   Another part moved to the west and retained a Square Ground of their own in the Seminole Nation as late as 1912.

Mikasuki population.—The population of this tribe was estimated at 1,400 by Captain Young about the year 1817.   This figure would seem to be decidedly too high.

MOBILE

Mobile Bay was first visited, so far as we know, by Alonso Alvarez de Pineda, who found a large town near its entrance and 40 villages along the bay and river.   In 1528 Narvaez met Indians in this neighborhood, and while De Soto was in the Apalachee country, Maldonado, who was in charge of his fleet, may have visited it, though that is uncertain.   It is also somewhat uncertain whether the Indians living about the bay at that time belonged to the Mobile tribe, though they probably were related.   De Soto entered the territory of the latter on October 6, 1540, when he came to a small town known as Caxa (Kasha), on the east bank of Alabama River.   On October 10 the Spaniards reached the residence of the famous chief Tascalusa, in a "new" town called Athahachi near Alabama River.   They left this place accompanied by Tascalusa on the 12th and next day reached another town called Piachi or Piache, which Garcilaso represents as the capital, and there they crossed the river. Afterward they marched to a small fenced town on a plain which bore the name Mabila, Mauilla, or Mavila.   Here Tascalusa attempted to surprise and destroy his unwelcome guests, thereby precipitating the famous battle of Mabila, fought October 18, 1540.   At least 3,000 Indians are said to have been killed and few Spaniards escaped without wounds. Their losses were so great that they did not resume their journey until November 14. In 1559 a detachment of soldiers sent inland by Tristan de Luna from the Bay of Achuse (Pensacola) reached a town on or near Alabama River which bore a Choctaw name, Nanipacana, and evidently belonged to the Mobile Indians. The few Indians they met reported that the town had been almost destroyed by people like themselves. In 1567 Juan Pardo heard of this province, but did not visit it. In 1675 Bishop Calderón learned that the Mobile were "on the western frontier, on an island near the harbor of Spiritu Santo," meaning the mouth of the Mississippi River. In 1686 a Florida letter informs us that the Mobile were at war with the Pensacola Indians, and they are noted again in the narratives of the expeditions in 1693 undertaken to survey Pensacola Bay. When Iberville established himself in Biloxi Bay, the tribe was living on Mobile River about 2 leagues below the junction of the Alabama and Tombigbee, with the related Tohome above. In April, he visited Pascagoula River and dispatched his brother with two other men and the Pascagoula chief to visit the Mobile and Tohome. In 1702 Bienville began the construction of a fort in Mobile Bay at what is now Twenty-seven Mile Bluff, and some time later, within about 30 years, the Mobile moved to the mouth of Mobile River, where they seem to have remained until after 1763. We then lose sight of them and infer that they had become lost among the Choctaw Indians, whose language they spoke with little variation.

Mobile population.—If the lowest estimate of dead Indians in the battle of Mabila is accepted, and little allowance made for the Mobile Indians in other towns, we must suppose that they had a total population of 6,000 or 7,000 in 1540. Mooney estimates that they numbered 2,000 in 1650, including the Tohome. Bienville, however, tells us that when he first met them they counted 500 men, but that in 1725–26 the number had sunk to 60. In 1730 Regis de Rouillet gives only 30, and in 1758 De Kerlérec allows 100 warriors to the Mobile, Tohome, and Naniaba together.

MOCOCO OR MUCOCO

A province or tribe about the inner end of Hillsboro Bay, Fla., when De Soto landed in the neighboring province of Oçita in 1539. The chief of this tribe had previously saved the life of a castaway named Juan Ortiz, who afterward became De Soto's principal interpreter. The name is mentioned by Laudonnière, but it subsequently disappears from the pages of the chroniclers.

MONACAN

A tribe, or confederation of small tribes, on James River, Va., between the falls and the mouth of the Rivanna, the name being often extended to include the Saponi and Tutelo on the higher reaches of the two rivers. They were first noted by the Virginia colonists in 1607, and the following year Captain Newport visited two of their towns. The village nearest the falls was known as Mowhemcho and is the one to which the term Monacan is usually applied. By 1670 it is probable that the people of the two other settlements, Massinacack and Rassawek, had concentrated here. In 1699 part of the area was occupied by Huguenots, but a Monacan town continued in the neighborhood and is mentioned by the Swiss traveler Michel in 1702. Their name does not appear in the list of tribes stationed at Fort Christanna, but there is little reason to doubt that they joined those Indians when they moved to New York and established themselves among the Iroquois.

Monacan population.—In 1669 they had 30 bowmen, or about 100 souls. Mooney estimates 1,500 in the year 1600, including the Tutelo and Saponi.

MONETON

In 1671 Batts and Fallam came upon "oldfields" of this tribe west of the Blue Ridge in Virginia, and later met some of the Indians themselves in the Tutelo town, but the only white man to visit their village was Gabriel Arthur in 1674. Then they seem to have been living on Kanawha River, W. Va. Whether they afterward joined the Tutelo, as seems most probable, or moved farther west is unknown.

Moneton population.—Arthur speaks of the town as "great" and says that "a great number of Indians belong unto it." That is all of the information we have as to its size.

MORATOK

An Algonquian tribe called Moratok has recently been noted as located in 1585–86 on Roanoke River, N. C. (Mook, 1943 a).

MUGULASHA

See Quinipissa, page 176.

MUKLASA

This was a town affiliated probably either with the Alabama Indians or the Koasati. It makes its appearance on the lower course of the Tallapoosa in 1675, but after 1799 we lose sight of it, though it probably continued in the same region until the Creek War, when the people are reported to have removed to Florida in a body. Gatschet speaks of a town of the name in the Creek Nation in Oklahoma, but I could learn nothing about it in my several visits to the Creeks.

Muklasa population.—The following estimates of the number of warriors are given: 50 in 1760, 30 in 1761, and 30 in 1792.

MUSKOGEE

This is the name of a group of tribes speaking the language ordinarily known as Creek and constituting the dominant element in the Creek or Muskogee Confederation. It included the Kasihta and Coweta, themselves supposed, traditionally, to have resulted from the fission of a single body; the Coosa and their descendants, or supposed descendants—the Okfuskee, Otciapofa, and Tulsa; the Abihka; Hothliwahali; Hilibi; Eufaula; Wakokai; Atasi; Kolomi; Fus-hatchee; Kan-hatki; Wiwohka; Kealedji; Pakana; Okchai; and Tukabahchee. There is some reason to think that the Fus-hatchee, Kan-hatki, and perhaps the Kolomi were subdivisions of the Hothliwahali; the Wakokai and Kealedji may also have been separated from some of the larger divisions at a late period; and the Wiwohka appear to have arisen from colonists of miscellaneous origins. On the other hand, there is reason to suppose that the Tulsa may have become connected with the Coosa very recently. When we first hear of them, Muskogee tribes were the predominant, and almost the sole, people on the Coosa and Tallapoosa Rivers and about Augusta, Ga.; they were dominant apparently on the Georgia coast; and there seems to have been a tribe of this connection on Flint River, with perhaps another on the Tennessee. The Confederation evidently existed in some form at that time. Later the tribes of this group continued as the dominant element on the Coosa and Tallapoosa, while the easternmost bands concentrated on the Chattahoochee River about and below the falls. Toward the end of the eighteenth century, a large part of these last moved over to the Ocmulgee to be near English traders, but after the Yamasee War (1715), they retired to their former settlements and remained there until all emigrated to the west of the Mississippi. In Indian Territory, later Oklahoma, the Confederation took on a new form as the Creek Nation, and preserved its identity until 1907, when the Creek population was theoretically merged in the general population of Oklahoma. The rest of the history of the Muskogee is included in that of the constituent tribes.

A number of Muskogee Indians, most of them prominent men, are shown in plates 29 to 37. Plate 29 is the well-known picture of Tomochichi and his nephew Tonahowi, who played such a part in the founding of Georgia, and plate 30 is from the painting showing Tomochichi's meeting with Oglethorpe in England. The small Yamacraw tribe to which they belonged were probably connected with the

Hitchiti-speaking group rather than the true Muskogee, but we cannot well differentiate them. Plate 31, figure 1, reproduces the sketch of a Creek war chief by Romans, and plate 31, figure 2, is taken from the frontispiece to Bartram's "Travels" (1792). Plates 32 and 33 are from sketches by Trumbull showing Creek Indians who met Washington at New York in 1790. Plate 32, figure 1, shows the chief of the Kasihta band, and plate 32, figure 2, the chief of the Tulsa division. The Creeks shown in plate 33 were not particularly distinguished. Plate 34, figure 1, is from Catlin and shows an Indian of the famous Perryman family of Okmulgee. Plate 34, figure 2, is the only known picture of Opothleyoholo, the greatest man that the Creeks produced and still cherished as the national hero. Plate 35, figures 1 and 2, are from paintings of Opothleyoholo's great antagonist, William McIntosh, martyr or traitor as one may choose to regard him, the first by King in McKenney and Hall's collection and the other by Washington Allston, in the State Capitol at Montgomery, Ala. Whether he was or was not too good a friend to the white men to have been the perfect friend to his own people may still be a matter of discussion. Another friend of the whites was Timpoochee Barnard, chief of the Yuchi, shown in plate 36, figure 1. The Creeks shown in plate 36, figure 2, and plate 37 were for the most part men of mark in the troublous transition period in the first half of the nineteenth century. Plates 37$_A$ and 37$_B$ show the older and later council house of the tribe at Okmulgee, Okla.

Muskogee population.—The number of warriors and hunters in the Muskogee towns in the Creek Confederation is given as 1,660 out of 2,063 in the Spanish census of 1738; 945 out of 1,263 in the French census of 1750; 2,620 out of 3,605 in 1760; 1,385 out of 2,160 in 1761; 1,130 out of 1,185 in 1772; 2,850 out of 3,605 in 1792; and in the census of 1832–33, a total Muskogee population of 17,939 was returned out of 21,733. (See Timucua.)

NABEDACHE

This name (properly Nabahydache) in its older form seems to have referred to salt and this is also the meaning of the name Naguatex (equivalent to English Nawatesh), which appears in the De Soto chronicles as that of a tribe living on Red River near the present Shreveport. One or more towns of Nawatesh also appear in later times alongside of the Nabedache proper, and they may have had different origins, but this is not believed to have been the case. At the end of the seventeenth century, the Nabedache proper was one of the tribes of the Hasinai Confederation, and their principal village was 3 or 4 leagues west of Neches River near Arroyo San Pedro, at a site close to the old San Antonio Road. La Salle passed through this village in 1686, and the next year Joutel found another allied with it

15 leagues to the northeast.   It appears often in the journals of later
French and Spanish writers.   De Leon visited the tribe in 1690, and
Massanet and Capt. Domingo Ramon founded in the Nabedache village
the first Texas mission, San Francisco de los Texas.   A few months
later the second, Santisima Nombre de Maria, was established nearby.
In 1693 the mission was abandoned and, when it was restored in 1716,
it was placed near the Neche village on the other side of the river.   In
1751 the Nabedache took part in a gathering held for the purpose of
killing all Spaniards in eastern Texas, but the French commandant at
Natchitoches, St. Denis, prevented the execution of the design.   In
1778 or 1779 they suffered from a serious epidemic and not long afterward moved higher up Neches River.   In the nineteenth century, they
shared the fate of the other Caddo tribes and ultimately all moved to
Oklahoma, where their descendants now live.

Nabedache population.—De Mézières reported 30 men of the Nabedache in 1777–79, Morfi, about 1783, stated that there were less than
40; but Sibley's estimate in 1805 doubles this figure.   An estimate
made between 1818 and 1820 gave 30 warriors and a total population
of 130.

NACACHAU

One of the constituent tribes of the Hasinai Confederation, whose
village stood at the end of the seventeenth century just north of that
of the Neche and on the east side of Neches River.   According to
Domingo Ramon, it was in their village that the Mission of San Francisco de los Texas was placed when it was restored in the year 1716.
It soon came to be called San Francisco de los Neches, and the Nacachau
were probably absorbed in the Neche tribe.

Nacachau population.—No figures are available.

NACANISH

This tribe appears in the De Soto narratives as Lacane (Elvas),
Lacame (Biedma), and Guancane (Garcilaso).   The Spaniards under
Moscoso encountered them in 1542 in northwestern Louisiana or
northeastern Texas, southwest of the present Shreveport.   The French
and Spaniards heard of them about 1690 when they were located on
the stream now called Naconicho Bayou.   The name is also given as
Nacao.   The Mission of Nuestra Señora de Guadalupe was established
for this tribe jointly with the Nacogdoche, July 9, 1716.   Soon after
this time they may have moved farther west, since La Harpe, in
1719, reported that their villages lay north of those of the Hainai.
By 1760 they had concentrated on Trinity River, but remained near
the other Hasinai and partook of their fortunes.   The Nacono, who
were on Neches River in 1691 opposite the Nechaui, may have been
a branch of the same tribe.

Nacanish population.—No separate figures are available.

NACOGDOCHE

This tribe may possibly be the Naçacahoz or Naquiscoça, of Elvas, met by De Soto's companions in 1542. When the Spaniards entered their country in the seventeenth century, they found the tribe living approximately on the site of the present city which bears their name. They are certainly noted in 1691 by Jesus Maria under the name Nazadachotzi. In July 1716, the Franciscans of Zacatecas established their first Texas mission, Nuestra Señora de Guadalupe, in the Nacogdoche main village to serve them and the Nacanish. It was abandoned in 1719, reestablished in 1721, and finally abandoned in 1773. In 1779 some Spaniards, who had formerly been at Adaes and later on the Trinity, settled here and founded the modern town. During the middle of the eighteenth century, the tribe was under a noted chief named Chacaiauchia. By 1752 their town had been removed some 3 leagues farther north, about 1781 Morfí locates them on the Attoyac, and in 1809 Davenport placed the "Nacogdochitos" on Angelina River, 5 leagues north of Nacogdoches, while a Spanish map of 1795 to 1819 places the "Nacodoches" on the east side of the Angelina about half way between Nacogdoches and the Sabine River. Their subsequent history is that of the Caddo as a whole.

Nacogdoche population.—In 1721 Aguayo gives the total population as 390. In 1733 two chiefs belonging to the tribe went to Adaes with 60 warriors, presumably their own people. In 1752 they were reported to consist of 11 rancherias containing 52 warriors besides many youths nearly able to bear arms. In 1778 a band of "Nacogdochitos" is reported living on the Attoyac and numbering 30 families. A census taken in 1790, as reported by Gatschet, gave 34 men, 31 women, 27 boys, and 23 girls. In 1809 Davenport reported 50 men belonging to his "Nacogdochitos." An estimate printed in 1818-20 gave 50 men and a total population of 150. Later estimates are evidently exaggerated.

NACONO

A tribe of the Hasinai Confederation located in 1691 southeast of the Neche and Nabedache and, as appears from a later writer, 5 leagues from the Neche. They were one of the tribes served by the Mission of San Francisco de los Texas, founded in 1716. Only a few doubtful references are made to them after this date. Their subsequent fortunes were the same as those of the remaining Caddo.

Nacono population.—One hundred Indians from this tribe visited the Neches River in 1721. That is the only figure we have which throws any light upon their numbers.

NAHYSSAN

A Siouan tribe which appears first in history on the map of John Smith in the form Monahassanugh at a point believed by Bushnell to lie "on the left bank of the James, about 1½ miles up the stream from Wingina, in Nelson County." Edward Blande and his companions, who crossed from Virginia into eastern North Carolina in 1650, found "the old fields of Manks Nessoneicks" southwest of the present site of Petersburg, from which it would seem that part of them lived farther south at one period. In 1654–56 they and the Manahoac, who had probably been driven south by the Susquehanna Indians, settled near the falls of James River, alarming the whites to such an extent that a force of colonists was sent against them, along with some Powhatan Indians under their chief Totopotamoi. The allies were badly defeated, but there seems to have been no effort on the part of the Siouans to enter the tidewater country and, indeed, they appear to have moved farther west. In 1670 Lederer found two towns of "Nahyssan" on Staunton River, but one of these was the town of the Saponi and the Nahyssan proper must have occupied the western town, which he calls "Pintahae." In 1671 Batts and Fallam visited them also and call them "Hanathaskies" or "Hanahaskies." About 1675 they and the Saponi moved to an island below the junction of the Staunton and Dan Rivers. Their subsequent history is included in that of the Saponi (q. v.). The name was remembered by Tutelo Indians in New York State in the last century in the form "Yesaⁿ" as a native term for their own people.

NANATSOHO

An obscure tribe or subtribe of the Caddo Indians. In 1687 they are said to have had a village on Red River in Louisiana and to have been allied with the Kadohadatcho, Natchitoches, and Nasoni. In 1812 a settlement consisting of 12 families was said to exist near their former village, but it is unlikely that it consisted of Indians of this tribe. They evidently united with the tribes just mentioned and followed their fortunes.

Nanatsoho population.—Unknown.

NAPOCHI OR NABOCHI

A tribe living on the Black Warrior River, Ala., in 1560, and at war with the Coosa Indians of Coosa River. A detachment of Spaniards sent to the Coosa country that year by Tristan de Luna accompanied the Coosa in a successful expedition against them, but we do not hear of the tribe again under that name, though memory of it is preserved in certain Creek war titles. When Iberville visited the lower Mississippi in 1700 he reported that the "Napissa" had united with the Chickasaw, and it is possible that this tribe was identical with the Napochi. It is also possible that the Acolapissa and Quinipissa (q. v.) were branches of the same people. The tribe is of interest as having been one of those nearest in position to the site of the prehistoric settlement at Moundville.

Napochi population.—Unknown.

NASONI

Under the name Nissohone or Nisione, this tribe first appears in 1542 as a "province" entered by the Spaniards under Moscoso, De Soto's successor, during his attempt to reach Mexico by land. It was in northwestern Louisiana or northeastern Texas, southwest of the present Shreveport. Elvas says it was "poor" and had little corn. In 1687 Joutel, La Salle's companion, makes mention of it. There were, in fact, at that time two Nasoni towns, an upper and a lower. The latter was located 27 miles north of Nacogdoches, and it remained there until 1752 and probably longer. Upper Nasoni was near Red River, but just south of that stream. Joutel and his companions spent considerable time there, but do not call it by the name of Nasoni. However, it was so designated by La Harpe and other later explorers. In 1716 the Mission of San José de los Nazones was established in the territory of the Lower Nasoni for that tribe and the Anadarko, on a southern branch of Shawnee Creek. It was abandoned in 1719, reestablished August 13, 1721, by the Marquis de Aguayo and Father Espinoza, and suppressed in 1729–30, after the abandonment of the presidio which protected it. When again established it was outside of Caddo territory. It is not known whether the Upper Nasoni united with it or fused with the Kadohadacho. The name appears in the census of 1790, but apparently it lost its separate status before the end of the century. Its later history was identical with that of the rest of the Caddo (q. v.).

Nasoni population.—In 1778–79 the Nasoni and Anadarko together are said to have had 25 men.

NATASI

A Caddo tribe on Red River between the present Natchitoches and Shreveport mentioned by writers between 1690 and 1719. It was probably a part of the Yatasi (q. v.).

NATCHEZ

In 1542 when De Soto reached the Mississippi River at the town of Guachoya where he was soon to die, he learned of a powerful chief named Quigualtam or Quigualtanqui, living east of the river, who seemed to dominate all others in the surrounding territory. The following spring, when the survivors of his expedition were descending the Mississippi on their way to Mexico, they were followed and frequently attacked by a fleet of canoes said to be under the command of this chieftain. As the location of his province corresponds very closely to the later country of the Natchez, who also appear in history as a dominating people, the two were probably identical. March 26, 1682, La Salle came upon a crowd of Natchez Indians on the bank of the Mississippi, and he visited one of their towns. June 12, 1699, the tribe was visited by two missionary priests, De Montigny and Davion, and in the spring of 1700 the former made a more extensive examination of their towns. March 11 following, after De Montigny had returned to the Taensa, Iberville reached the landing place of the Natchez and visited the town of the Great Sun, continuing to the Taensa the following day. De Montigny returned with him to the Natchez, among whom he intended to become resident missionary, but he changed his mind later and returned to France with Iberville in May. Soon afterward, however, St. Cosme descended from the Tamaroa to take his place and continued his labors in the tribe until his death at the hands of the Chitimacha in 1706. In November 1700, the Jesuit Gravier visited the Natchez, and he has left us a valuable account of them. In 1704 Pénicaut spent part of the spring and summer among them and made some interesting notes regarding their customs. A small trading post was established among these Indians in 1713, partly to counteract English influence, which was already becoming strong. In 1714 or 1715 four Frenchmen ascending the Mississippi River were killed in the Natchez towns and this brought on a short war in 1716, resulting in the construction of a fort on the bluffs at Natchez, which was named Fort Rosalie after the Duchess of Pontchartrain. In 1718 two important concessions were established near the Natchez towns, one called St. Catherine, the other White Earth. In 1721 Father Charlevoix visited Natchez and has left a considerable description of the Indians which is almost identical with another contained in the letter of a Jesuit missionary, Father Le Petit. In 1722 a second war broke out and was followed by a third in a very brief interval of time, the latter put down with considerable severity by Bienville. Some years of peace followed in which the number of whites constantly increased, but along with them there also increased occasions of friction between whites and Indians. These an exceptionally inexperienced and unintelligent commandant named Chépart converted into a native conspiracy and an uprising on November 28, 1729, resulting in the destruction of the post and settlement, the massacre of the greater part of the white inhabitants, and the capture of the remainder.

The Yazoo post was also destroyed, but the conspiracy, which had still wider ramifications, was able to accomplish nothing more.   In January a force of French troops with Choctaw allies attacked the Natchez suddenly and rescued many prisoners, driving the Natchez into two newly constructed forts, which they also besieged, though the Natchez presently escaped across the Mississippi.   In January 1731, Governor Perrier advanced against the new fort of the Natchez on the present Sicily Island.   He induced about 400 to surrender and these were sent to the West Indies as slaves, but the remainder escaped during the night.   Part subsequently suffered a severe defeat at the hands of St. Denis and his Indian allies near Natchitoches, but the rest scattered through the low lands of the Mississippi in bands, causing the French great annoyance and considerable loss.   Gradually, however, they withdrew among the Chickasaw, who had always been in the British interest, and later separated into two main bands, one of which settled among the Upper Creeks while the other long maintained an independent existence in the territory of the Cherokee.   A third band reached South Carolina and lived at a place called Four Hole Swamp. In 1738 they were invited to occupy Palawana Island, but seem to have remained where they were until 1744 when they left in fear of the vengeance of the Catawba Indians, seven of whom they had killed. Ultimately they probably united with the Cherokee band.   This group of Natchez and those who had joined the Creeks followed the fortunes of their respective tribes when they removed to the other side of the Mississippi.   Those who went with the Creeks settled close to their particular friends, the Abihka Indians, on the Arkansas River above Eufaula, and from some of them considerable vocabularies of Natchez words were collected by early ethnologists, but the last speakers of the Natchez tongue there appear to have died before 1890.   In the Cherokee Nation, however, a few miles south of Fort Gibson, are still (1940) two individuals who are able to converse in the old language.   Otherwise the Natchez tribe may be said to be extinct, though, of course, a great deal of Natchez blood flows in the veins of both Cherokee and Creeks.

Plate 38, figure 1, shows Creek Sam, the oldest speaker of the Natchez tongue in 1907, standing at the door of his cabin; plate 38, figure 2, the home of Watt Sam (son of Creek Sam), my informant as also of all later workers on the Natchez language; plate 39, figure 1, Nancy Taylor, one of the last speakers of the Natchez language; plate 39, figure 2, Square Ground in the Greenleaf Mountains at which Watt Sam was the principal medicine maker (hilis haya); and plate 40, figure 2, a ball ground beside the Square Ground.

Natchez population.—In 1686 Henry de Tonti estimated that there were 1,500 warriors in the Natchez Nation, and in 1699 and 1700 Iberville and De Montigny found that they occupied from 300 to 400 cabins. In 1702 Iberville gives 1,500 families. In 1716 the officer De Richebourg states that they had more than 800 warriors, and Charlevoix makes estimates of 4,000 in 1715 and 2,000 in 1721, while Du Pratz a little later has 1,200. In 1730, according to Le Petit, there were left only 500, and the figures supplied by Diron d'Artaguette and Perrier in 1731 are of 200 and 300 respectively. Charlevoix, who seems to give us our maximum figure before the war, supplies us with a minimum after it by representing the tribe as reduced to 100 fighting men in 1732. However, the figure 200–300 contained in a letter dated 1735 is probably much nearer, since a French captive reported the same year that there were 180 among the Chickasaw alone. In 1764 Bouquet reported 150 among the Creeks, but in 1799 Hawkins cuts this to 50, and finally, in his paper published in 1836, Albert Gallatin represents the entire Natchez population as amounting to 300. On the basis of these figures, Mooney estimated that in 1650 there was a total Natchez population of 4,500; my estimate is 500 less.

NATCHITOCHES

When first discovered by the French under Tonti in 1690, the main tribe bearing this name, pronounced by the Indians themselves Nashitosh, was living near the city which is called after them. In 1700 Bienville crossed from the Taensa villages to renew the alliance with them. After the French had constructed their first fort on the Mississippi, representatives of the tribe came to the commander, St. Denis, reporting that their crops had been ruined, and asked that they be settled in some place where they could obtain provisions, whereupon St. Denis located them on the north side of Lake Pontchartrain near the Acolapissa. This was in 1702, and they remained there until 1714, when St. Denis took them back to their old country and established a French post close to their village. As long as he remained commandant of this post, his influence over the Indians of this tribe and other cognate tribes which came to live nearby was unbounded. It was signally exhibited in a crushing defeat which the Indians under his leadership inflicted upon a part of the Natchez in 1731. Even after his retirement, relations between the settlers and Indians continued harmonious and the latter remained in their old villages until the first part of the nineteenth century, when they joined the rest of the Caddo tribes and accompanied them successively to Texas and Oklahoma. In 1912 one of the oldest Indians of the united tribes, known as Caddo Jake, who belonged to this band, was still able to speak the Natchitoches dialect.

There was a second Natchitoches, the "upper" town, allied with the Kadohadacho. It is heard of only in earliest times and probably united with the Caddo tribe just mentioned.

Natchitoches population.—In 1700 Beaurain reports that they had 200 warriors, but by 1718 Bienville states that they and their allies had only about 80 between them. A year later French writers report a total population of only 150–200 for the group. In 1805 Sibley reported 52 for the group and a total of 32 for the entire Natchitoches population by itself. (See Swanton, 1942.)

NECHAUI

A tribe of the Hasinai Confederacy living half a league from the Nacono and southeast of the Nabedache, the Nacono being 5 leagues from the crossing of the Neches at Neche village. They do not seem to be mentioned again and must soon have been combined with some of the neighboring tribes, perhaps the Neche or Nabedache.

Nechaui population.—Unknown.

NECHE

A Hasinai tribe whose main village was a league or more east of the Neches River and almost directly west of the present city of Nacogdoches. This village was visited by La Salle and his companions in 1686–87, and this and the Nabedache were the tribes to which they applied more particularly the term Cenis. In 1716 the Queréteran friars established the Mission of San Francisco de los Neches between the Neche and Nacachau, and Ramon stationed a garrison there. In 1719 it was abandoned, reestablished by Governor Aguayo in 1721, and again abandoned, or rather withdrawn out of the Caddo country, in 1731. Shortly afterward the tribe was almost completely destroyed by the Yojuane Indians. The remnant seems to have become merged with the Nabedache and Hainai before the end of the eighteenth century and it followed their fortunes.

Neche population.—In 1721 Aguayo, while at the main Neche village, made presents to 188 men, women, and children, and this was considered an unusually "general distribution" of gifts. This and the other tribes dependent on the Neches mission, probably including the Nabedache, Nacono, Nechaui, and Nacachau, were estimated to number about 1,000.

NEUSIOK

In 1584 this tribe was found on the south side of Neuse River in the present Craven and Cartaret Counties, N. C. They decreased in numbers throughout the seventeenth century, but in 1700 still had two villages. At the time of the Tuscarora War they were probably incorporated with the Tuscarora.

Neusiok population.—In 1709 there were 15 warriors in their two settlements.

NOTTOWAY (NOTOWEGA, NITTAWEEGA, OR NAUTAUGUE)

This is a common Algonquian name for enemy tribes, particularly those of Iroquoian stock. It has received specific application to an Iroquoian tribe formerly living on the river which still bears their name in southeastern Virginia. They first appear in the narratives of the Raleigh expeditions to North Carolina under another Algonquian name, Mangoac. Edward Blande and his companions visited them in 1650. In 1728 William Byrd found them living in a stockaded town. Although not prominent in history, they maintained their identity as late as 1825, when they were living on a reservation in Southampton County and were ruled by a "queen."

The same name, in the forms "Notowega," "Nittaweega," or "Nautaugue," was given to a band of Indians which appeared on the frontiers of South Carolina in the eighteenth century. It is possible that this body of Indians is intended by the "Andasses or Iroquois" mentioned in a French document, attributed to the third decade of that century, in association with some Shawnee and Chickasaw, as living about 70 leagues below the Kaskinampo on Tennessee River. Since that would take them to the other side of the Mississippi, it is probable that we should read "above" rather than "below." The material in this particular document is unreliable in so many particulars that this single notice would deserve little credit except for later evidence. Quoting from manuscript sources, Milling tells us that in 1748 two white men named Haig and Brown were murdered in the Catawba country "by a mixed party of Indians known as Notowega or Nittaweega, who fled into the Cherokee country for protection" (Milling, 1940, p. 90). The same writer says: "The preamble to their 'talk' to Governor Glen, written soon after their arrival, suggests that they were a mixed band of Iroquois, Savannah, and Conestoga." This talk was delivered by "Asaquah, the Head beloved Man of Nautaugue, Connewawtenty of Connetstageh and about Sixty others of Different Towns of Nitiwaga Nation of Indians now in Keowee in the Cherokees" (Milling, 1940, p. 91). While a few Shawnee may have attached themselves to this band temporarily, the prevailingly Iroquoian complexion of it is evident, and this is reenforced by further information that the murderers of Haig and Brown were "a party of Warriors chiefly consisting of Seneka Indians" (Milling, 1940, p. 91). The name "Conestoga," or "Connetstageh," clearly identifies part of them as Susquehanna Indians, and Iroquois and Seneca are such general terms that we may suspect the tribe to have consisted in part of Nottoway Indians of Virginia or, more likely, of the near neighbors of the Nottoway, the Meherrin. This suspicion is founded on a record in the Colonial documents that the Meherrin consisted of fugitive Conestoga. As the name of the Meherrin appears before 1675, when the Susquehanna were broken up, it is evident that this statement is only partly correct, the truth perhaps being that the Meherrin had received a considerable influx of Conestoga Indians. Whatever their origin, we know that these "Notowega" ravaged South Carolina for 8 years, extending their depredations to within 30 miles of Charleston, until about 1754, when they seem to have retired to the Cherokee. Their subsequent history is unknown.

Nottoway population.—In 1709 Lawson reported but one town with 30 fighting men. In 1728 Byrd estimated that the Virginia Nottoway numbered 300. In 1825, 47 were reported. The "Notowega" band was said to consist of about 300 persons.

OCALE

In 1539 De Soto entered the country of this tribe, which was located northeast of Withlacoochee River, Fla., near the present Ocala. It is scarcely mentioned by later writers, but was apparently closely related to the Acuera tribe, with which it probably united. (See Acuerar.)

Ocale population.—Unknown.

OCCANEECHI

A tribe whose historic seat was on an island in Roanoke River near the present Clarksville, Va. Edward Blande and his companions learned of them in 1650, but did not visit their town. In 1670, however, Lederer reached them and found them acting as middlemen in the trade of the region. In 1676 the Saponi and Tutelo settled on islands nearby, and the same year the Conestoga sought refuge with the Occaneechi, but, attempting to dispossess them of their homes, they were driven out, and it was perhaps then that the Conestoga settled among the Meherrin. Later in the year the Occaneechi were attacked by Nathaniel Bacon and suffered a severe defeat. Under pressure from the English and Iroquois, they presently left their town and fled toward the south, where they were found in 1701 by Lawson in a village on Eno River, about the present Hillsboro, Orange County, N. C. About 1714 they were located at Fort Christanna with the Tutelo, Manahoac, and some other tribes, and when these went north, about 1740, the Occaneechi accompanied them having, according to Byrd, taken the name of the Saponi. (See Saponi and Tutelo.)

Occaneechi population.—We only know that their numbers were always small, and that the five tribes of Occaneechi, Shakori, Saponi, Tutelo, and Keyauwee were estimated to number about 750 in 1709.

OCITA OR UCITA

A tribe near the entrance to Tampa Bay in 1539, when De Soto landed in their territory. One of their principal towns was seized upon by the Spaniards as their headquarters, and it is believed that this was on Terra Ceia Island. Oçita was probably identical with the province later called Pohoy (q. v.)

OCONEE

There appear to have been at least two divisions of this tribe.   One was on or near the Georgia coast, where there was a mission in 1655 bearing their name, while another Oconee mission, possibly for the same people, makes its appearance among the Apalachee at the very same time.   It is likely that these southern Oconee were absorbed in the Apalachee.   The latter mission was named San Francisco de Oconi, and it was 1 league from Ayubale, or about 3 leagues (nearly 8 miles) west of Aucilla River.   The northern division gave its name to Oconee River and is first mentioned in 1608, unless a reference by Father Pareja 6 years earlier concerns this branch of the tribe.   In 1695 a letter of the Governor of Florida speaks of it as one of four against which an expedition had been sent.   Up to that time it was probably on Chattahoochee River, but it then moved over to the Oconee River and settled just below the Rock Landing.   The Yamasee War caused it to move back among the Lower Creeks on Chattahoochee River, where part remained until after 1799, when they were on the left bank 6 miles below the Apalachicola settlement. Part, however, had gone to Florida, probably about 1750, where they lived in the Alachua plains.   There Bartram visited them in 1774 and described their town.   Before 1832 all had probably united in Florida, where they became the nucleus of the Seminole Nation and were soon lost in the mass of the Seminole population.   A more northerly home for a part of the Oconee may be indicated in the name of the Oconee town in the Cherokee country on Seneca Creek near the present Walhalla, Oconee County, S. C.   The name bears some resemblance to the Cherokee egwâ'nĭ, "river," but it is pronounced somewhat differently, ukwû'nû.

Oconee population.—At the Mission of San Francisco de Oconi there were in 1675 about 200 persons.   Estimates of warriors in the other band were 50 men in 1738, 1760, and 1761; in 1750 the estimate was 30.

OFO, OFOGOULA, OR MOSOPELEA

This tribe first appears in history under some form of the name last given, and from the maps of Minet and Franquelin it seems that some years before 1673 they lived in 8 villages in or near southern Ohio.

They are said to have been driven from this country by the Iroquois, and in 1673 Marquette found them on the east bank of the Mississippi below the mouth of the Ohio. They were in the same neighborhood when La Salle descended the Mississippi in 1682, but when he reached the Taensa villages on Lake St. Joseph on his return, the tribe, or part of it, had sought refuge with the Taensa and had been allowed to settle among them. From Daniel Coxe's map, it would appear that on their way south they had stopped near the Quapaw village of Uzitiuhi on Arkansas River. By 1690, however, they had reached Yazoo River, where they placed themselves near the Yazoo and Tunica tribes and were there until the Natchez uprising in November 1729. The Yazoo and Koroa participated in this, but the Ofo refused to do so and went on south to the Tuniça near the mouth of Red River, allies of the French, with whom they remained until Fort Rosalie was rebuilt. By 1739 they had settled close to this latter and were there until after 1758. In 1764 they took part in an attack upon an English convoy ascending the Mississippi and were then probably about where Hutchins found them in 1784, in a small village on the west side of the Mississippi 8 miles above Point Coupée. In course of time, the few survivors joined the Tunica at Marksville, where in 1908 the writer found a single individual, a woman named Rosa Pierrette (pl. 40, fig. 1) and obtained a short vocabulary of her language. She died about 1915, and the tribe and language died with her.

Ofo population.—In 1700 Gravier reports that the Ofo occupied 10 or 12 cabins. In 1702 Iberville estimated 300 families of Tunica, Yazoo, Ofo, and (perhaps) Koroa, the last named not being actually mentioned. In 1721 Charlevoix says the Ofo, Yazoo, and Koroa together had not more than 200 men fit to bear arms. In 1722 La Harpe gives a total population of about 250 for the same three tribes. Du Pratz, about the same period, estimates the number of Ofo cabins at "about 60." In 1758 Governor De Kerlérec reports 15 warriors and in 1784 there were said to be "a dozen." (See Tunica.)

OKCHAI

The earliest known location of this Muskogee town and tribe was on the west side of Coosa River some miles above its junction with the Tallapoosa. By 1738 a part had moved to a branch of Kowaliga Creek, an affluent of the Tallapoosa, where their principal settlement seems to have been located until the removal to Oklahoma, though a part remained near their former home for a considerable period. There is a town known as Okchaiutci, or Little Okchai, formed of Alabama Indians who had formerly lived near the Okchai proper. The Okchai are often called Fish Pond Indians, and as early as 1791 there was a distinct settlement of the tribe called Thlathlogalga, or "Fish Pond," on a small affluent of Elkhatchee, a western branch of the Tallapoosa. The name was also given to a Square Ground in Oklahoma, founded in consequence of a separation brought about by the Civil War. Another Okchai branch was known as Asilanabi, or "Green Leaf." It was founded some time before 1792, and, as in the case of Fish Pond, there is a later Square Ground of this name in Oklahoma not far from the Fish Pond ground and brought into existence also by the forces to which the latter owed its origin. Hatchet Creek, or "Potcas hatchee," claimed as another branch, was in existence in Hawkins' time (1799) and maintained itself until the period of the emigration, when it probably united with the main body of Okchai. After the removal the Okchai reestablished their Square Ground near Hanna, Okla., at a site occupied down to the present day. A part of these people joined the Seminole in Florida, but we have only a bare mention of them.

Okchai population.—In 1738 the Okchai settlements proper were estimated to contain 200 men; in 1750, more than 80; in 1760, 130; in 1761, 125. In 1792 Marbury gives 200 in Okchai, 140 in Thlathlogalga, 30 in Asilanabi and a town called Pilthlako, and 15 in Potcas hatchee. The census of 1832–33 gives the total population of Okchai as 493, Thlathlogalga as 313, Asilanabi as 181, and two towns on Potcas hatchee Creek as 388, a grand total of 1,375.

OKELOUSA

(Signifying "Black Water" in Choctaw)

A small tribe living west of the lower course of the Mississippi in the early part of the eighteenth century. According to the Creek migration legend related to Oglethorpe by Chekilli, the ancestors of the Muskogee Indians stopped at one time during their movement east on a creek called "Caloose Creek," which is probably intended for Okalusa or Okeloosa Creek. In 1541 the Spaniards under De Soto, while they were in the Chickasaw country, learned of a province known as "Caluça," in which we again find Okalusa, said to contain "more than ninety villages not subject to anyone, with a savage population, very warlike and much dreaded," and occupying a fertile land. These references may be to the tribe in question before they crossed the Mississippi, but on the other hand, since we also find the name bestowed on a territory west of the Mississippi by Biedma and much farther north, it may be a general appellation for occupants of certain alluvial lands along the Mississippi or its tributaries. In 1682 the Okelousa appear as allies of the Houma in the destruction of a village of the Tangipahoa Indians on the east bank of the Mississippi, and La Harpe informs us that they were a wandering people living west of the river, but Du Pratz is the only writer to locate them definitely, on two little lakes "to the west of and above Pointe Coupée." What afterward became of the tribe we do not know, but they probably united with the Houma or some other Choctaw-speaking Indians in the vicinity.

Okelousa population.—Unless we except the sixteenth century notes, this tribe is always represented as small, but no figures are given. My own estimate of the population, together with that of the Washa and Chawasha, for the year 1650 is 700.

OKMULGEE

A branch of the Hitchiti which settled at the great bend of the Chattahoochee near the Chiaha and Osochi, probably after the Yamasee uprising. Hawkins traces their origin to the old Hitchiti town site at Macon. About 1822 they are placed east of Flint River and they retained their independence after the removal to Oklahoma, when they reestablished their Square Ground in the northeastern corner of the Creek territory, but gave it up early. Men belonging to this town, such as the Perrymans and Pleasant Porter, played a great part in the history of the Creek Nation after that date.

Okmulgee population.—In 1750 they are credited with more than 20 warriors, and the census of 1760 allows them 30. The census of 1761 gives this town, Chiaha, and Osochi together 120 hunters, and Young, quoted by Morse, estimates a total population for the Okmulgee alone of 220. They may have constituted one of the two Osochi towns included in the census of 1832, which had together a population of 539.

ONATHEAQUA

This name is given by Laudonnière and Le Moyne to one of the two principal Timucua tribes bordering upon the Apalachee in 1564–65. For lack of any suitable single term for the group, it has been adopted as a name for the Timucuans later gathered into the Missions of Santa Cruz de Tarihica, San Juan de Guacara, Santa Catalina, and Ajoica, which agree in general with the location of the Onatheaqua as shown on Le Moyne's map. Ajoica was probably a visita of Santa Catalina. Utina may also have settled in them.

Onatheaqua population.—The missions of Tarihica, Guacara, and Santa Catalina are given a total population of 230 in 1675, but may have included Indians of other tribes.

OPELOUSA

Our earliest mention of this tribe, which seems to be in a report written by Bienville about 1725, places them in the Opelousas district and near the site of the present city of Opelousas, and here they remained as long as we have any separate notice of them. In 1805 we learn that their village was 15 miles west of Opelousas. The last representatives of this tribe probably joined the Atakapa, to whom they are supposed to have been related.

Opelousa population.—About 1725 Bienville estimated that the number of Opelousa warriors might be nearly 130. In 1805 Sibley gave 40, and in 1814 their entire population was said to be reduced to 20. In his study of the aboriginal population north of Mexico, Mooney gives a figure of 1,400 for this tribe, the Chawasha, and the Washa together, but he confounds the Okelousa and Opelousa. My own estimate of Opelousa population is between 400 and 500.

OSOCHI

There is reason to think that the origin of this tribe is to be sought in Florida and that the De Soto narratives (1539) contain our first references to it under the forms Uçachile, Ossachile, etc. In 1656 a great rebellion of Timucua Indians against the Spanish government broke out. It is said that some "rebels" fled from the country, and shortly afterward we find references to a separate body of Timucua on or near Apalachicola River. The original Florida name also seems to be preserved in a Spanish official map dated 1765, which places the "Apalache ó Sachile" at the junction of the Chattahoochee and Flint. However, they were located on the Chattahoochee as early as 1675. After this time we find the Osochi laid down on maps or given in tables of population as a tribe or town between the two rivers last mentioned, but farther north, and before 1794 they were on or near the Flint, since Hawkins tells us that during that year they moved from this region to the west bank of the Chattahoochee and settled above the Chiaha in the great bend of the river. A considerable part of them continued to camp east of the river, and they and the Chiaha together founded the town of Hotalgi-huyana. After the removal to Oklahoma they first settled on the north side of Arkansas River, some distance above the present city of Muskogee. Later, in consequence of the so-called Green Peach War and in order to be near the Hitchiti, part of them went to Council Hill. They have now disappeared as a distinct element in the Creek Nation.

Osochi population.—Estimates made in 1738 and 1761 give 120 hunters or warriors in this town, Chiaha, and Okmulgee together. In 1750, 30 are given in Osochi alone, and in 1760, 50. The enumeration of 1832–33 returned a total population of 539, but one of the two towns called by the name may have been Okmulgee.

PAKANA

The earliest known home of these Indians was on Hatchet Creek in what is now Coosa County, Ala. Shortly after the foundation of Fort Toulouse at the junction of the Coosa and Tallapoosa Rivers, which happened in 1717, a part of them moved to that neighborhood to enjoy trade advantages, and they never reunited. Those who remained in their old country settled on the southern border of the Creek Nation after their removal to Oklahoma, and their Square Ground occupies the same spot today as the one then chosen. The other division of the tribe moved to Red River in 1763 or 1764, along with the Taensa and Apalachee. In 1805 Sibley found them on Calcasieu River, La., and according to Alabama tradition, they subsequently united with the Alabama in Texas, where the last of them died many years ago.

Pakana population.—The Spanish estimate of 1738 mentions only the Pakan Tallahassee Indians, whom it credits with 60 men. The French census of 1750 gives 10 men in the old town and 30 near Fort Toulouse; that of 1760 mentions only the latter, to which it assigns 50 men; and the Georgia estimates of 1761 give 45 in Pakan Tallahassee and 30 in the southern group. As has been stated above, the latter moved to Louisiana soon after this date. We have only one later figure regarding them, that by Sibley, in 1805, who says they then had about 30 men. Those who remained with the Creeks had 20 gunmen in 1772, according to Taitt; and 50 in 1792, according to Marbury; while their total population in 1832, shortly before the emigration, was 288.

PAMLICO

The earliest known home of this tribe was on the lower course of Pamlico River, N. C., and the neighboring coast, where they were discovered by the English in 1584–85. In 1696 they were nearly destroyed by smallpox and in 1710 were confined to a single village. They sided with the hostile Tuscarora in the war of 1711–13, and at its close, that part of the Tuscarora under treaty with the English agreed to exterminate them. The remnant was probably incorporated as slaves in the Tuscarora. The Pamlico are the only Algonquian people of North Carolina from whom a vocabulary has been preserved.

Pamlico population.—In 1709, after they had been reduced to a single village, they numbered 15 fighting men, or a population of perhaps 75.

PASCAGOULA

In 1699 this tribe was living 16 to 20 leagues (43 to 54 miles) up Pascagoula River. Iberville heard of them early that year very shortly after his arrival on the coast, and in the summer of 1699 Bienville visited them. Iberville also visited them in the spring of 1700 and communications continued friendly and intimate, but the attention of the French was soon drawn off in other directions. If we may trust Du Pratz, they moved to the Gulf coast some time afterward. In 1764 they crossed the Mississippi and settled for a short time on the great stream itself not far from the mouth of Red River, but in 1787 permission was granted them to locate at the confluence of the Rigolet du Bon Dieu and Red River, and they probably moved at about the same time, their territory lying between Bayou de la Coeur and Bayou Philippe. In 1795 they removed to lands granted them by a body of Choctaw Indians on Bayou Boeuf, and they continued to reside here until early in the nineteenth century when they and the neighboring Biloxi sold their lands to Miller and Fulton. Morse, writing in 1822, reports three bodies of Pascagoula, two at different points on Red River and a third on Biloxi Bayou, a branch of the Neches in Texas. Some of them probably died out here while others no doubt accompanied the Biloxi to Oklahoma. In 1908 the writer met two Indians living among the Alabama of Texas who claimed that their mother was a Pascagoula Indian.

Pascagoula population.—In 1699 the village of the Pascagoula, Biloxi, and perhaps one other tribe consisted of less than 20 cabins, and they had about 130 warriors. In 1700 Iberville reported 20 families of Pascagoula, but some years later Du Pratz said they occupied 30 cabins. In 1758 Governor De Kerlérec tells us there were more than 100 united Pascagoula, Biloxi, and Chatot. In 1805, according to Sibley, there were 25 Pascagoula warriors, but in 1822 Morse's informants estimated a total population for the tribe of 240, which another writer in 1829 reduces to 111. (See Biloxi.)

PAWOKTI

The earliest mention of this town or tribe seems to be on the Lamhatty map, where it has the form Poúhka. This applies to the year 1707 and as Pawokti afterward appears beside Tawasa as one of the Alabama towns, it seems probable that it followed the fortunes of the Tawasa, moving first to Mobile after the attack by northern Indians, which uprooted the latter, and then passing to the upper Alabama about the time when Fort Toulouse was established, which would be in 1717. Hawkins gives a description of the town as it appeared in 1799, but this is about the last separate notice we have of it, and it evidently fused with the rest of the Alabama settlements.

Pawokti population.—We have no separate figures. (See Alabama and Tawasa.)

PATIRI

This tribe lived in central Texas somewhere west of Trinity River and perhaps along Caney Creek. From the fact that it was placed in the Mission of San Ildefonso with the Akokisa, Bidai, and Deadose, and the further fact that related tribes were said to have been put under the same mission, it may be inferred that it belonged to the Atakapan group. The above-mentioned mission was founded in 1748–49, and the name of the tribe occurs again in Morfi's list applying to about 1781, but that is all we know of it though we may assume that it finally united with one of the other associated bands at San Ildefonso.

Patiri population.—There are no figures.

PEDEE

A tribe found living on the river Pee Dee in the present State of South Carolina when Charleston was founded. A map of 1715 locates the Pedee town on the east bank near the present Cheraw. In 1717 representatives of this and several other small tribes went to Charleston "to renew their old friendship." In 1744, along with some Natchez Indians, they killed seven Catawba and in consequence fled south to be near the white settlements, where some of them remained as late as 1755. In 1752, however, the Catawba asked Governor Glenn to advise the Pedee to join them and this invitation was accepted by part of the tribe, but others remained near the whites. A South Carolina document of 1808 states that within the memory of persons then living there were 30 Indians of the Pedee and Cape Fear tribes forming one settlement under a chief called "King Johnny," and that in 1808 only one half-breed woman was left. Some may be represented among the so-called Croatan Indians.

Pedee population.—Mooney estimates 600 in 1600. The census of 1715 does not list them.

PENSACOLA

Cabeza de Vaca describes at considerable length various encounters between the Spaniards who accompanied Narvaez and Indians along the coast of the Gulf of Mexico in what was afterward ascertained to be the Pensacola country. The companions of Tristan de Luna very likely met some of them in 1559–60. The first definite mention of the tribe by name occurs, however, in 1677. In 1686 they were visited by the expedition under Enríquez Barroto and we learn that they were at war with the Mobile. In 1698 the Spanish post of Pensacola was established and took the name of the tribe, but, although Indians were encountered in the vicinity, the Pensacola tribe itself was scattered and was believed to have been destroyed. This, however, was incorrect since later historians mention them among the small tribes of the region, and Bienville, in his account of the Louisiana tribes written about 1725, says that they were in a village on Pearl River not far from the Biloxi. Their language and customs seem to have been almost identical with those of the Choctaw, with whom they no doubt ultimately united.

Pensacola population.—Bienville says, in the memoir above noted, that this tribe and the Biloxi together had about 40 warriors.

PILTHLAKO (OPILŁAKO)

This was a Creek town or tribe of considerable prominence, probably a branch of some better-known Creek division. It appears on the De Crenay map of 1733 and repeatedly until 1799, when Hawkins visited it and described its location. Possibly it was one of those which removed to Florida after the Creek War, as it does not appear in the census lists of 1832. They may have split from the Okchai.

Pilthlako population.—The French census of 1750 gives 10 warriors in this town, a number which the census of 1760 raises to 40, and in 1792 Marbury enumerates 30 warriors in Pilthlako and Asilanabi together.

POHOY, POOY, POJOI, OR POSOYE

A tribe or province probably connected with the Timucua located on Tampa Bay and apparently identical with the Oçita of the De Soto chroniclers, at least in part. In 1612 it was visited by a Spanish expedition under an Ensign named Cartaya. In 1675 Bishop Calderón speaks of a "Pojoy River" which was "6 [leagues] from the beach of Pusale." In 1680 there is reference to it as "a Calusa Province" occupied by a non-Christian people, but these Indians were clearly distinct from the Calusa although bordering upon them. Some time before 1726, about 20 of these Indians were placed in a mission called Santa Fe 9 leagues south of St. Augustine, but an epidemic had destroyed most of them by that date, and before 1728 the rest had returned to their former abodes. (See Oçita.)

Pohoy population.—In 1680 there were said to be 300. The only other figures are given above.

POTANO

One of the most powerful of the Timucuan tribes, first encountered by De Soto in their historic seats in the western part of what is now Alachua County, Fla. In 1565 the French colonists on St. Johns River assisted the rival Utina Indians in a raid into the Potano country. After the Spaniards had displaced the French, this tribe caused them considerable trouble and in 1584 cut off a body of Spanish soldiers under a Captain Andrada. They were defeated later and driven from their town, or from one of them, remaining away apparently until 1601, when they asked permission to return. On September 12, 1597, 48 Potano Indians came in company with the heir to the Potano chieftainship to St. Augustine, where they remained 4 days and were given rations of 288 pounds of flour. By 1602 Potano was reported to be asking for missionaries. In "Yca Potano" (i. e., Potano Town) there were 9 Christians, and in "Potano" 10 Christians and a number of catechumens. In 1606 Father Martin Prieto with one companion entered the Potano country and founded three missions called San Francisco, San Miguel, and Santa Ana, and baptized all of the inhabitants of another place called San Buenaventura "where formerly Indians had been killed by Spanish adventurers." These adventurers were evidently the companions of De Soto, and we are told, furthermore, that the old chief of Santa Ana had been imprisoned by that Spanish explorer and had in consequence acquired such an antipathy to Spaniards in general that missionary work there would have been a failure except for the fortunate interposition of a hurricane. We are somewhat puzzled to find the towns of the Fresh Water province included at times in that of Potano. The principal Potano mission was San Francisco de Potano, except perhaps Santa Fe de Toloco, which lay between Potano and Utina and regarding the tribal affiliations of which we are left in doubt, though it was one of the most important of all missions in the Timucua country. San Miguel was perhaps the mission station afterward called Apalu, a word which means "fort" in the Timucua language. The Potano chief's name occurs among those who took part in the uprising of 1656, and Bishop Calderón reported in 1675 that the mission was deserted. Some sort of visita was perhaps kept up, however, since Governor Salazar in a letter to the king written that same year lists it among the missions and says there were about 60 persons connected with it. The name is furthermore present in a list dated 1680. After that period the Indians must have declined rapidly in numbers, since we only hear of a small town of Timucua near St. Augustine, and the rest must have scattered to other tribes.

Potano population.—Our only clue to the separate population of this tribe is contained in mission letters dated about 1602, in which it is said that there were five towns in the Potano province in which as many as 1,100 were being instructed in the Christian religion. In 1675 there were about 160 in the two Potano missions. Mooney ventures an estimate of 3,000 as the entire Potano population in 1650.

POWHATAN

This confederation of tribes was in the tidewater country of Virginia on both sides of Chesapeake Bay in 1607 when the colony of Virginia was established. Most of the tribes had been brought under one control by the chief Powhatan. No considerable number of Powhatan Indians seem ever to have removed from the locality. They gradually died out or retired into one or two reservations where a few mixed-blood descendants still live. The principal events in their early history were the unsuccessful attempt made by Spanish Jesuits in 1570 to establish a mission among them, the founding of Jamestown, the subsequent relations between the colonists and the great chief who bore the same name as the confederacy and his noted daughter Pocahontas, and the two uprisings of the Indians under Opechancanough, in 1622–36 and 1644–45, after the last of which the Indians were placed upon reservations. In 1654 the Pamunkey chief Totopotomoy and 100 of his warriors joined the Virginians in an attack on some of the Siouan tribes who were threatening the settlements, but they were defeated with great loss. In 1675 they were falsely accused of depredations actually committed by Conestoga Indians, and were attacked by a force of whites headed by Nathaniel Bacon. In August 1676, Bacon stormed a fort near Richmond into which a large number of the Indians had gathered, and massacred nearly all of its occupants of both sexes and all ages. A treaty made at Albany in 1722 put an end to attacks upon these Indians by the Iroquois, but from this time on they sink into obscurity. Most of those on the eastern shore, who had meanwhile become much mixed with negroes, were driven away in 1831 during the excitement occasioned by the slave rising under Nat Turner. There are still in existence mixed-blood descendants of the Pamunkey, Chickahominy, Powhatan, Mattapony, Werowocomoco, Nansemond, Rappahannock, Potomac, Tappahannock, Wicocomoco, and Accohanoc, though only the first two are of any considerable size. The best picture of an ancient Powhatan Indian, discounting the European dress, is that of Pocahontas (pl. 41).

Powhatan population.—In 1607, when the Virginia settlement was made, there were more than 200 villages, and in the first Powhatan uprising Governor Wyatt defeated a force of more than 1,000 Indians. Mooney estimates that there must have been a population of 9,000 at this time. In 1669 a census of the Powhatan showed 528 warriors, which perhaps indicates a population of 2,000, the Pamunkey then having 50 warriors and the Wicocomoco 70. About 1705 the historian Berkeley reported that there were 12 villages, of which 8 were on the Eastern Shore and the only one of consequence, Pamunkey, had 150 inhabitants. Jefferson, in 1785, represents them as reduced to 2 bands embracing only 15 men, but this is a distinct underestimate and today the mixed-blood descendants still number several hundred.

QUAPAW

The traditional home of this tribe was on Ohio River above the mouth of the Wabash, but by 1673, when Marquette descended the Mississippi, they were already established near the junction of the Arkansas with the great river, one town being just at the junction of the two, one considerably higher up on the west bank of the Mississippi, one on the east bank between them, and one on the Arkansas itself. They were probably distinct from the Pacaha met by De Soto, with whom they have sometimes been identified. Before 1700 the Tongigua village on the east side of the Mississippi moved across and settled with the Toriman at the junction of the Arkansas, and meanwhile the Quapaw town had moved lower down. Not many years later, all had removed to the Arkansas, and in 1805 Sibley found them in three villages on the south side of the Arkansas about 12 miles above Arkansas Post. In 1821 they ceded this territory to the United States Government and agreed to remove to the Caddo country on Red River. They were assigned a tract of land on Bayou Treache on the south side of the Red, but it was frequently overflowed and their crops were destroyed and also much sickness resulted. In consequence, they returned to their old country, but the white settlers annoyed them so much, that in 1833 the United States Government ceded to them 150 sections of land in southeastern Kansas and the northeastern part of the Indian Territory, to which they agreed to move. February 23, 1867, they ceded their lands in Kansas and the northern part of those in the Territory. In 1877 the Ponca were brought to live with them for a time, and when those Indians passed to their own reservation farther west, most of the Quapaw also went. Still later, the Quapaw lands were allotted in severalty and they are now citizens of Oklahoma.

Quapaw population.—In his memoir, Bienville states that this tribe had formerly more than 500 warriors, but was at the time of writing (about 1725) reduced to 220. Father Vivier, in 1750, estimated their warriors at 400 and the total population at 1,400. In 1829 Porter estimated that there were 500 Quapaw all told, and in 1843 the population was given as 476. In 1885 there were 120 on the Osage reservation and 54 on the Quapaw reservation; in 1890, 198 on both. The census of 1910 returned 231; the United States Indian Office Report for 1923, 347; and the census for 1930, 222. Mooney's estimate of this tribe as of the year 1650 was 2,500.

QUINIPISSA

This tribe was found by La Salle in 1682 a few miles above the present site of New Orleans, but on the opposite side of the river. The people received him with flights of arrows, and on his return used peacemaking overtures as a mask for a treacherous but futile attack upon his force. Four years later, Tonti made peace with the tribe. In 1699 Iberville hunted for them in vain, but later learned that they were identical with the Mugulasha then living with the Bayogoula (q. v.) about 20 leagues above their former settlement. According to Sauvolle, however, the Quinipissa were not identical with the Mugulasha, but had united with them. In any case, there can be no doubt that the chief of the Quinipissa in 1682 and 1686 was the same man as the chief of the Mugulasha in 1699. In May 1700, shortly after Iberville had visited them for the second time, the Mugulasha were attacked and almost completely destroyed by their fellow townsmen, the Bayogoula. The destruction was not as complete probably as the French writers would have us believe, but we do not hear of either Mugulasha or Quinipissa afterward, and the remnant must have united with the Bayogoula or Houma, the latter having been their allies.

Quinipissa population.—The Mugulasha and Bayogoula together are said to have had 100 cabins, the same number of warriors, and a total population of 400–500 in 1699. Gravier says that more than 200 were killed in the massacre the following year, but the whole tribe can hardly have numbered many more than this. (See Bayogoula.)

SALUDA

On the manuscript map of George Hunter (1730), in connection with a place name, we read "Salude town where a nation settled 35 years ago, removed 18 years to Conestogo in Pensilvania." Milling points out that this would indicate an occupancy from 1695 to 1712 (inclusive evidently). The above information also appears in the Jefferys Atlas, and the site is indicated on several other maps of the early eighteenth century. Although Siouan tribes occupied the country east of this point and Muskhogeans that to the west, it is probable that the Saluda were a band of Shawnee Indians on their way from the neighborhood of Augusta to Pennsylvania, whither so many of the Savannah River Shawnee are known to have gone.

Saluda population.—There is no clue to this.

SANTEE

The earliest mention of this tribe appears to be in the relation by the Spanish navigator Eçija of his second expedition dated 1609. They were then on the river which bears their name, where they were again found by the English at the time when they settled the province of South Carolina, 61 years later. Here they were visited by Lawson in 1701. In 1716, becoming involved along with the Congaree in hostilities with the colonists, they were defeated by the latter, assisted by the Cusabo, and most of them were sent as slaves to the West Indies. The few who escaped probably united with the Catawba.

Santee population.—In 1715 they had 2 villages with 43 warriors.

SAPONI

This is evidently a contraction of Monasukapanough, the name of a tribe located by John Smith in the Monacan country at a place identified by Bushnell as on the banks of the Rivanna, directly north of the site of the University of Virginia and about one-half mile up the river from the bridge of the Southern Railway. Some time afterward, probably due to the pressure of peoples toward the north, they left this place and settled on a creek usually identified with Otter River, a northern tributary of the Roanoke, in the present Campbell County, Va. Here they were visited by John Lederer in 1670 and Thomas Batts in 1671. From this place, they moved again to an island in Roanoke River just below the junction of the Staunton and Dan, and still later to Yadkin River, near the present Salisbury, N. C., where Lawson found them in 1701. They were accompanied during much of this time by the Tutelo and before 1711 moved in toward the Virginia settlements, uniting on the way with the Occaneechi, and crossing back over the Roanoke. Their new settlement, called Sapona Town, was a short distance east of Roanoke River and 15 miles west of the present Windsor, Bertie County, N. C. In 1714, along with other allied tribes, they were placed by Governor Spotswood close to Fort Christanna, near the present Gholsonville, Va. In 1722 peace was made at Albany between the northern and southern Indians, and about 1740 part of the Saponi and Tutelo moved north, stopping for a time at Shamokin, Pa. In 1753 this tribe and the Tutelo were formally adopted by the Cayuga, and in 1765 they were living about Sayre, Pa., where part remained until 1778, though in 1771 the principal portion had their village in the Cayuga territory about 2 miles west of the present Ithaca, N. Y. In 1789 a remnant of the tribe was still living with the Cayuga on Seneca River in Seneca County. They have presumably become incorporated with the Tutelo and are no longer distinguished as a separate tribe. One band of Saponi remained in the south, however, in Granville County, N. C., where they were reported in 1755, and are perhaps still represented by a body of "Croatan Indians" in Person County, which was cut from Granvilla. (See also Meherrin.)

Saponi population.—In 1709, according to Lawson, the Tutelo, Saponi, Occaneechi, Keyauwee, and Shakori numbered 750 souls. In 1716 a visitor, the Huguenot Fontaine, states that there were 200

Indians at Fort Christanna, including the remnants of the Saponi, Manahoac, and Tutelo. In 1765 the northern Saponi among the Cayuga had 30 warriors, and the figures given for the southern band in 1755 are 14 men and 14 women, children not being separately enumerated. (See Tutelo.)

SATURIWA

A Timucua tribe located about the mouth of St. Johns River in 1564–65 when the French Huguenot colony was established. The dealings of the colonists with them were very intimate and, after the destruction of the colony, they assisted Dominique de Gourgues in his punitive expedition of 1567. Later they became warm friends of the Spaniards and were served by the missions of San Juan del Puerto, at the mouth of the St. Johns; Nombre de Dios, close to St. Augustine; and San Diego de Salamototo, near the site of Picolata. Subject to the Mission of Nombre de Dios in 1602 were the towns of Soloy, Capuaca, and Paliaca, and to San Juan del Puerto, Vera Cruz, Arratobo, Niojo, Potaya, San Matheo, San Pablo, Hicachirico, Chinisca, and Carabay. The Mission of Nuestra Señora de Guadalupe, 3 leagues from St. Augustine, was also perhaps in their country. This appears only in the mission list of 1655 along with Nombre de Dios, San Juan del Puerto and Salamototo, the last mentioned under the name San Diego de Laca. The chief of San Juan del Puerto was among those concerned in the rising of 1656. The names of the three principal missions appear, however, in the report of Calderón and in the list of 1680, though at the latter date Nombre de Dios seems to have changed the character of its population. They are afterward lost in the rapid disintegration of all the Timucua peoples. The chief who appears so prominently in French and Spanish narratives is shown in plate 42, from a drawing by Le Moyne, rediscovered and reproduced by Bushnell.

Saturiwa population.—This province was evidently not as populous as those of Utina or Potano, but 14 towns are mentioned in which were 500 Christians. In 1675 San Juan del Puerto contained "about thirty persons" and Salamototo "about forty."

SAWOKLI [6]

When we first hear of this tribe, it was located on Apalachicola River 12 leagues (about 31 miles) from San Luis Mission (modern Tallahassee). A mission called Santa Cruz de Sabacola el Menor was established here and dedicated by Bishop Calderón February 28, 1675, under the name La Encarnación a la Santa Cruz de Sabacola. The bishop also claimed to have converted Sabacola el Grande, but no mission was begun there. Native tradition would place this tribe

---

[6] Called Sabacola by the Spaniards.

nearer the Gulf coast at some period in their past history and tradition seems to be supported by the Lamhatty map, which appears to give their name to the Choctawhatchee River and place their town nearby. The journal of Capt. Francisco Milán Tapia, who coasted the Gulf from St. Marks to Pensacola in 1693, informs us that the eastern mouth of the Apalachicola River was called "Sabacola." In Calderón's time there seems to have been another branch of the tribe living with the Lower Creeks below the falls of the Chattahoochee, and to this Fray Juan Ocon and two other missionaries were sent in 1679, but they were ordered away by the great chief of the Coweta. Two years later, Fray Francisco Gutierrez de Vera and another Franciscan were sent back with an escort of soldiers, and great expectations were entertained of the success of the mission, but within a few months the Indians became hostile and they were forced to withdraw. The Christianized Indians withdrew with them apparently to the site of the lower mission at Santa Cruz. Possibly all of the Sawokli may have moved north and returned, but our authorities do not make this point clear. In 1706 or 1707, the Sawokli were driven from this country, or rather, it seems, carried away, by hostile Indians in alliance with the English and we hear of them next among the Lower Creeks only, where all appear to have gathered for a time. Part, at least, seem to have settled upon Ocmulgee River, but after the Yamasee War (1715) we find them all on or near the Chattahoochee, lower down than all other constituent bodies of the Confederation except the Lower Eufaula. Besides a Big and Little Sawokli, there were two branch towns here called Okawaigi and Okiti-yakani. In 1832 another is recorded called Hatcheetcaba. There was yet another well up the Chattahoochee, sometimes placed between Kasihta and Coweta, its name spelt Tcawokli rather than Sawokli, and apparently called in one place New Tamathli. After removing to Oklahoma, the Sawokli settled near Okmulgee. They soon gave up their independent Square Ground and united in ceremonies with the Hitchiti.

There are indications of an offshoot of this tribe in a very unexpected place. A French map, which has been conjecturally dated in 1697, enters a tribe called "Sabougla" on Yazoo River, in the present State of Mississippi, and the name is still preserved in an affluent of the Yalobusha and a post office. This name is corrupted on Daniel Coxe's map into "Samboukia."

Sawokli population.—A mission noted by Governor Salazar, but which seems to have been confounded with another in a different section, is said to have had "about 40 people" in 1675. This certainly included only a fraction of the nation. In 1738 a Spanish report estimated 20 men in Sawokli and its villages, besides 26 in New Tamathli and 12 in Old Tamathli. In 1750 a French estimate gives

4 Sawokli settlements and more than 50 men, besides 10 in Old Tamathli (see Tamathli), but 10 years later, 190 are given in the same number of villages and 30 in Okiti-yakani. Hawkins, writing in 1799, says that Little Sawokli then contained 20 families. The total population of the Sawokli towns in 1832 was 187 exclusive of slaves, of Okawaigi 157, and of Hatcheetcaba 106.

SEMINOLE

Although now reckoned as one of the "Five Civilized Tribes," the name is applied to a body of Indians of very modern origin. The nucleus consisted of the Oconee Indians, whose home (about 1695–1715) was on Oconee River, Ga., but who moved to the Lower Creek country about 1715, and 30 or 40 years later entered Florida and established themselves on the Alachua prairie. They belonged to a non-Muskogee group of Indians of which the best known representatives were the Hitchiti, and, except for a band of Eufaula, the first tribes to join them were of this same connection, including some Sawokli, Tamathli, Apalachicola, Hitchiti, and Chiaha, a part of whom soon came to be known as Mikasuki, though under what circumstances is unknown. According to Romans, the Eufaula settlement was made in 1767, and was on a hammock north of Tampa Bay to which it gave its own name Tcuko Tcati or Red House. In 1778, a second Muskogee immigration took place, contributed by part of the people of Kolomi, Fushatchee, and Kan-tcati. Immediately after the Creek War of 1813–14, their numbers were tripled by refugee Indians, mainly from Upper Creek towns and particularly from those speaking Muskogee, so that the linguistic complexion of the entire body was changed and the language usually called Seminole is Creek. The non-Muskogees, however, still included a powerful element and supplied the head chiefs. In 1817–18 Andrew Jackson invaded Florida with a force in excess of 3,000 men and burned a large Seminole town on the Suwannee. In 1832 a treaty, promising that the Florida Indians would remove west of the Mississippi, was negotiated at Paynes Landing, but it was repudiated by the great majority of the Seminole and in 1835 the second and great Seminole War broke out, which was not terminated until August 1842, and cost the lives of nearly 1,500 American soldiers besides numerous civilians and $20,000,000 in money. Mikonopi was the titular head chief of the Seminole as chief of the Oconee element, but Osceola and Jumper, who came from the Upper Creek towns, furnished the brains of native resistance. The capture and imprisonment of the former by treachery constitutes a black passage in our military annals and particularly on the record of the perpetrator, Gen. Thomas S. Jesup, though the hysterical demand for "quick results" on the part of the white population behind him deserves equal condemnation.   The greater part of the Seminole were removed to Oklahoma, where they were given a separate strip of territory and separate government just west of the Creeks, in what is now Seminole County.   Those who remained behind consisted, and consist, of two main bands, one Muskogee (Cow Creek Indians), the other Mikasuki (Big Cypress Indians).   There were some smaller elements, but they have now lost their identity in the general body. The Seminole in Oklahoma speak Creek for the most part, but a very few also understand the Hitchiti tongue.

Mikonopi, chief of the Seminole during the first part of the Seminole War, is shown in plate 43, figure 1, from McKenny and Hall.   Three different paintings of Osceola are reproduced in plates 43, figure 2; 44; and 45, figure 1, from Catlin, Robert John Curtis (preserved in the Charleston Museum), and McKenny and Hall, respectively.   Most of the Seminole shown in plates 45, figure 2; 46; and 47, figure 1, figured prominently in that most expensive and disastrous of all southern Indian wars.

Seminole population.—In 1774 Bartram says that all of the Seminole together were probably not as numerous as the inhabitants of a single Creek town, but before the Creek War they must have numbered at least 1,500.   Estimates made after that event are of two or three thousand, but in 1823 there was an attempt at an actual census, which returned 4,883 and cannot be far wrong as it checks well with the number of Seminole afterward captured and sent west. In 1836 the United States Office of Indian Affairs reported 3,765 in the west.   In 1837 it returned 5,072, but this must be a blunder as the year following the figure had fallen to 3,565, and it fell to about 3,000 in 1845, since which time it has varied between 2,000 and 3,000 down to the present.   To these must be added the Seminole in Florida, estimated during the same period at between 350 and 550.   Exclusive of freedmen, there were in 1919, 2,141 Seminole in Oklahoma and 573 in Florida.   The census of 1930 returned 1,789 in Oklahoma, 227 in Florida, and 32 scattered in other States.

SEWEE

The first appearance of this tribe is possibly under the name Xoxi (Shoshi), given as one of the provinces on or near the coast of what is now South Carolina by Francisco of Chicora, who was taken from this region in 1521.   It is certainly mentioned by the Spanish Captain Ecija in the narrative of his voyage along the South Atlantic coast in 1609.   In 1670 the colonists who were shortly to establish themselves in Charleston met a band of Indians on Bull's Island who were probably Sewee, since the tribe is known to have occupied Bull's Bay, also called Sewee Bay, and the lower part of Santee River and inland toward the west to the vicinity of the present Monk's Corner, Berkeley County. Along with the Cusabo, they helped the South Carolina colonists repel Spanish invaders and supplied them with corn. Lawson, who visited them in 1701, found that they had been much reduced by smallpox and the use of alcoholic liquors, and, in particular, the loss of a fleet of canoes, which had attempted to sail directly to England for purposes of trade. Some of the survivors accompanied Barnwell in his expedition against the Tuscarora Indians. In 1715 they were reduced to one village and the Yamasee War probably put an end to their separate existence. It is supposed that the remnant was finally incorporated with the Catawba, though they may first have united with the Santee or Cheraw.

Sewee population.—In 1715 their single remaining village contained 57 souls.

SHAKORI

The earliest home of this tribe of which we have a hint was apparently in South Carolina. It attained early fame out of all proportion to its importance owing to the fact that an Indian brought home by the Ayllon expedition of 1521, and known as Francisco of Chicora, was probably from this tribe. Some time during the next 130 years, very likely in consequence of Juan Pardo's expeditions, 1566–67, the Shakori moved toward the north, and are next heard of in the report by Blande and his companions of the expedition into North Carolina in 1650. During their return journey, these gentlemen speak of the "Nottaway and Schockoores old fields" between Meherrin and Nottoway Rivers. Four years later, Governor Yardley was told by a Tuscarora Indian that this tribe, which he calls "Cacores," consisted of men of dwarfish stature but exceedingly brave, whom the Tuscarora had never been able to conquer. They were reported to be near neighbors of the Eno, and in 1672 Lederer found the villages of the two about 14 miles apart, that of the Shakori being farthest west. In 1701 Lawson found Eno and Shakori living in one village called Adshusheer, on Eno River about 14 miles east of the Occaneechi village, which would perhaps be a short distance northeast of the present Durham, N. C. Barnwell identified them with the Sissipahaw, but this must mean that the two were branches of one people. From then on their history is identical with that of the Eno (q. v.), both finally uniting with the Catawba. Some Shakori blood may have found its way into the Croatan.

Shakori population.—We have no figures regarding this tribe independently of the Eno (q. v.), and none for the Eno except for Lawson's statement that the Eno, Tutelo, Saponi, Occaneechi, and Keyauwee numbered 750 souls in 1709. The Shakori were perhaps included.

The Shawnee Indians were divided into the following bands: Chillicothe, Hathawekela, Kispogogi, Mequachake, and Piqua, but the constitution and history of these is not well understood, though their several towns usually bear the names of the bands. In particular there were a number of towns in Ohio known as Chillicothe and a number of others called Piqua. The most prominent band in the history of the Gulf tribes is the Hathawekela. Our earliest information regarding the Shawnee indicates that, in very early historic times, they were on the Ohio River, which they had evidently reached from some point farther north, but before the end of the seventeenth century, they were settled on the Cumberland. They may have been attracted to this spot in part by the Spanish post at St. Augustine, Fla., which they visited in order to trade. In 1674, at the Westo town near the present Augusta, Ga., Henry Woodward met two Shawnee who had recently been at St. Augustine, and it was probably owing to the representations of these men that a considerable body of Shawnee moved over to Savannah River and established themselves near the Westo. They drove these last from that region in 1681, much to the relief of the newly established colony of South Carolina. The Shawnee remained in this place long enough to give their name to Savannah River, but as early as 1707 some of them went to Pennsylvania and about 40 settled "about 40 miles from Patapsco River" in Maryland. In 1711 another band deserted South Carolina and it is thought they may have been Indians known as Saluda (q. v.). These seem to have been joined from time to time by other bands, some of whom stopped for a time on the Potomac before reaching the Quaker colony. A band numbering 30 was still on the Savannah in 1725, but may have been the Hathawekela who were reported in Pennsylvania in 1731. In 1715, however, as a result of the Yamasee War a band of these Savannah Indians had moved to the Chattahoochee and settled near the site of Fort Gaines. Later they passed over to Tallapoosa River, where they formed a town not far above its junction with the Coosa, which they occupied until the beginning of the nineteenth century. It is presumed that they reunited with their kinsmen in the north at that time, but I do not find a record of the time or the circumstances. A second body of Shawnee lived for a time among the Abihka Indians. This band, originally at least, seems to have belonged to the Piqua division. It moved into Pennsylvania in 1692 along with a Frenchman named Martin Chartier, who died there in 1718. Peter Shabonee, or Pierre Chartier, his son by a Shawnee woman, also married a Shawnee, and settled among Indians of his tribe at Allegheny some time after 1732, where Chartier's town stood, on the right bank of the Allegheny River below the mouth of the Kiskiminetas or Conemaugh. In April 1745, in consequence of a reprimand given him by Governor Gordon of Pennsylvania, he instigated 400 Shawnee to leave the government of Pennsylvania. A French document represents them as having come down from Sandusky, moved to a spot high up the Wabash, and then descended to the junction of the Wabash and Ohio, where they lived 2 years and then passed on to the Abihka country. But this statement, in a letter written by Governor Vaudreuil of Louisiana, June 24, 1750, seems to be based on misinformation, since actually Chartier appears to have descended the Ohio, capturing some English traders on the way, and to have penetrated Kentucky to a site in the present Clark County, on Lulbegrud Creek, where the Shawnee formed a town, which came to be known as Eskippakithiki. There they stayed until 1747, when they went down to the Tennessee in canoes and up the latter to Bear Creek. Ascending this stream for 30 miles and leaving their canoes there, they made an attack upon the Chickasaw, who vigorously repulsed them, and they settled in the Talladega country. In 1748 another letter by Governor Vaudreuil states that some English traders among the Creeks had endeavored to induce these Shawnee to assist in an attack upon Fort Toulouse, but they refused and wished to join the Shawnee on Tallapoosa River. It seems, however, that this intention was not carried out for they were still in the Talladega country in 1758, their settlement being at "Chatakague," which we know as Sylacauga or "Buzzard Roost." A French enumeration made in 1750 also mentions them, and some maps give the name of a second Shawnee town as Cayomulgi, signifying in the Creek language "Mulberry Place." Although, as stated, this band seems originally to have been Piqua, it is possible that it may have been the one later called Kispokotha and may have derived its name from the town of Eskippakithiki. At any rate there is evidence of a former close association between the Kispokotha and the Tukabahchee Creeks. The busk, or ceremonial name of Tukabahchee, was Ispokogi, or Spokogi, derived traditionally from certain supernatural beings who had descended from the heavens bearing the famous Tukabahchee plates, and according to one version these were entrusted first to the Shawnee. It is also of some significance that Tecumseh belonged to the Kispokotha but rather remarkable that the Tukabahchee were one of the towns which refused to ally themselves with him, retiring to the Lower Creeks to live with their friends the Coweta. I do not find any reference to the time when the Talladega Shawnee left the Creek Nation. It may have been after the treaty of 1763.

Plate 47, figure 2, shows the famous Shawnee prophet Tenskwatawa (from Catlin's painting).

Shawnee population in the southeast.—In 1708 there were three Shawnee towns on Savannah River and the number of men was estimated at 150. The census of 1715 gives in these three towns 67 men and 233 souls. In 1760 the Abihka and Tallapoosa bands together were said to number 100 warriors, but the English census of 1761 includes merely the Tallapoosa town where, it reported, were 30 hunters. In 1792 Marbury doubled this in his estimate. The Creek census of 1832–33 includes a "Kiamulgatown" with a total population of 175, but these were probably not Shawnee.

SISSIPAHAW [7]

The first mention of this tribe is probably by Vandera in recounting Juan Pardo's expedition of the year 1567, where it appears under the form Sauxpa or Sauapa. He seems to locate it near the Santee. In 1701 Lawson heard of them, but did not pay them a visit. Their principal settlement was evidently near Saxapahaw on Haw River, N. C. Barnwell identifies them with the Shakori to whom they were no doubt closely related. They are mentioned as one of those tribes which joined the confederation against the English in 1715. Afterward they probably united with the Keyauwee, Shakori, Eno, and Cheraw, and part finally fused with the Catawba, while others are no doubt represented among the Indians of Lumber River.

Sissipahaw population.—Haw Old Fields was noted as the largest body of fertile land in the region, but no figures bearing on the size of the tribe have been preserved.

SOACATINO OR XACATIN

A Caddo tribe visited by the Spaniards under Moscoso in 1542, but mentioned uncertainly, if at all, by later writers.

SUGEREE

A small tribe on Sugar Creek in the present Mecklenburg County, N. C., and York County, S. C. According to Lawson (1701), they occupied many settlements, but were probably closely related to the Catawba, with whom they ultimately united. In 1754 "Sugar Town" appears as the name of a Catawba settlement. It is not improbable that they were a branch of the Shakori.

Sugeree population.—Unknown.

---

[7] Sometimes shortened to Haw.

SURRUQUE, HORRUQUE, OR SURRECHE

A small tribe about Cape Canaveral on the east coast of Florida. This is evidently the Serropé mentioned by Laudonnière and Le Moyne, who place it on an island in a large inland lake, but the island was probably one of those in the coastal lagoons, not in Lake Okeechobee as has sometimes been assumed. In 1597 there was a short war between these people and the Spaniards, which consisted mainly in a surprise attack upon one of the Surruque towns in which 60 persons were killed and 54 captured. Nothing further is heard regarding them and they probably partook of the fortunes of the other Timucua towns and tribes.

Surruque population.—Unknown.

TACATACURU

This was the Timucua name of Cumberland Island on the Georgia coast and of the tribe occupying it. It was visited by the French under Ribault and Laudonnière and later by Menendez de Aviles. The Spaniards named the island San Pedro, and the Franciscans established there in 1587 the Mission of San Pedro Mocama on the southwest coast of the island, 2 leagues from the Barra of San Pedro. In 1597 the chief of this province, called Don Juan by the Spaniards, repulsed the Guale Indians after they had destroyed the missions in their country and were advancing south. Through an early document it is surprising to learn that this chief desired to become "mico mayor" of Guale, although the people of that province were alien in speech. He died on June 16, 1600, and was succeeded by his sister's daughter, in accordance with the custom of the country. Under the San Pedro Mission were the following stations: Santo Domingo on the island of Napoyca and Santa Maria de Sena on the same island. In 1602 Fray Baltazar Lopez was stationed at San Pedro. Pedro Ruiz seems to have been the missionary in 1604. In 1608 Governor Ibarra states that the church at San Pedro was as big as that in St. Augustine, that it had cost the Indians 300 ducats, and if they had not furnished most of the labor themselves, it would have cost them 2,000 ducats. The name of this mission is wanting in the mission list of 1655, and the chief of the Indians of San Pedro does not appear as one of those concerned in the rebellion of 1656, from which it would seem that the Mission of San Pedro was then abandoned and the population withdrawn to other Timucua towns. The later missions on Cumberland Island were occupied by Yamasee and other Indians from the north.

Tacatacuru population.—In 1602 Santo Domingo served 180 Christians and Santa Maria de Sena 112. About the same time Fray Lopez reported 8 settlements and 792 Christian Indians.

Although the people later known as Taensa were almost certainly encountered by De Soto or his followers—in particular, they may have been the people of Guachoya and Aminoya—we first learn of the tribe when they were living about the site of Newellton at the west end of Lake St. Joseph, in northeastern Louisiana. La Salle reached them in March 1682, on his way to the mouth of the Mississippi, and renewed the treaty of peace then made when he returned, spending 4 days, from April 30 to May 3, in their villages. In 1686 Tonti stopped there again, and in 1690 made their settlements his starting point on a visit to the Natchitoches and their allies. The missionaries De Montigny, La Source, Davion, and St. Cosme went to visit them in 1699, the first mentioned establishing himself among them to do missionary work, in July of that year. In March 1700, Iberville reached the Taensa, and he gives us one of our best descriptions of the tribe. While he was there, the temple was destroyed by lightning and seems never to have been rebuilt. When he left, De Montigny accompanied him to transfer his labors to the Natchez, and his place was never filled. In 1706 the tribe abandoned their old villages for fear of the Yazoo and Chickasaw, and dropped down the Mississippi to the Bayogoula village. They were well received by the Bayogoula, but soon afterward the Taensa rose upon them, destroyed a large portion, and drove the rest away. We are informed that the Taensa intended to return to their ancient villages after this event, but apparently they remained in the neighborhood of the old Bayogoula town, for they were at the Manchac in 1715. They also had a village during this period on the south side of the Mississippi, 11 leagues (about 30 miles) above New Orleans. At the date last mentioned (1715), they assisted M. de la Loire des Ursins in the apprehension of an English trader named Hughes and accompanied La Loire to Mobile, where they were assigned the village site formerly occupied by the Tawasa, 2 leagues from the French fort. Before 1744 they had moved to the Tensaw River, to which they gave their name and where they remained until the country was ceded to England in 1763. The same year, or very early in the year following, they removed to Red River and were later granted permission to settle on the Mississippi at the entrance of Bayou Lafourche. It is doubtful whether they availed themselves of the permission, as they were not there in 1784 and Sibley, writing in 1805, says that they had then been on Red River 40 years. They were living beside the Apalachee, the settlements of the two tribes extending from Bayou d'Arro to Bayou Jean de Jean and their own village standing at the head of the turn. Subsequently both tribes sold their land and moved to Bayou Boeuf. Later the Taensa parted with this land also and drifted farther south to a small bayou at the head of Grand Lake, still known on local maps as Taensa Bayou. They were known to the Chitimacha as Chosha, and intermarried with this tribe and the Alabama, becoming gradually lost as a distinct people.

Taensa population.—In 1682 Tonti estimates that they had more than 700 warriors, but in 1699 De Montigny gave this as their total population, which corresponds rather well with Iberville's figures of 120 cabins and 300 warriors. A year later St. Cosme reduces the former figure to 40 and La Harpe gives us 250 warriors in 1700. In 1702 Iberville revised his estimate to 150 families. Du Pratz, speaking of the tribe after it had removed to Mobile, estimates that they had 100 cabins. In 1764 D'Abbadie, the Louisiana Governor, states that the Taensa, Apalachee, and Pakana Creeks together totalled 200, and finally Sibley gives 25 as the number of Taensa warriors in 1805. Mooney estimated that the Taensa and some minor bodies of Indians had a combined population of 800 in 1650; my own figure for the Taensa alone is 800–900.

TAMATHLI (TAMAŁI)

It is probable that this is the Toa, Otoa, or Toalli found by De Soto near Flint River in 1540, and they may also have been connected with the Altamaha division of the Yamasee, who were then living between the Ocmulgee and Oconee and whose name appears in the form Tama in some later documents. Tomatly is given also as one of the towns of the Upper Yamasee. Possibly they were a division of the same people and if so would probably be represented in the occupants of a mission in the neighborhood of the Apalachee, which makes its appearance in a list dated 1680 under the name Nuestra Señora de la Candelaria de la Tama and is called a "new conversion." On the De Crenay map of 1733, this town is placed on the west side of Chattahoochee River below all of the other Lower Creek towns, and the same position is given it in a Spanish census of 1738, though the town here is called Old Tamathli, and "Tamaxle nuevo" is the northernmost of the Lower Creek towns. As I have indicated elsewhere (p. 180), this last may have belonged in reality to the Sawokli. The enumeration of 1750 seems to indicate a point higher up the river, but it is evident that they soon gravitated again toward Florida, and Hawkins tells us that they were one of those tribes which constituted the Seminole nation in his time (1799). There are references to the town or tribe as late as 1822, when it apears to have been on Apalachicola River, but it was probably swallowed up soon afterward in the Mikasuki band of Seminole.

It should be added that there are two occurrences of the name in the Cherokee country, one preserved in the name Tomatola, in

Cherokee County, N. C., the other about Tomotley Ford on Little Tennessee River, Monroe County, Tenn. There are so many cases of a northern and southern division of Creek tribes that it is probable we have vestiges here of still another.

Tamathli population.—The Spanish estimates of 1738 give 12 men in Old Tamathli and 26 in New Tamathli, but the French enumeration in 1750 includes only the former, supposed to have 10 men. However, in 1822 Young's census of the Seminole, contained in Morse's report to the Secretary of War, gives a total population in this town of 220.

TANGIPAHOA

A tribe probably related to the Acolapissa and perhaps originally a part of them, whose home at the end of the seventeenth century was on an affluent of Lake Pontchartrain which still bears their name. Some may at one time have moved to the Mississippi since La Salle, in 1682, found, on the east side of the river, 2 leagues below the Quinipissa settlement, a town recently destroyed and partly burned by enemies, which some said was named "Tangibao," though others called it "Maheouala" or "Mahehoualaima." The remnants of this tribe probably united, or reunited, with the Acolapissa.

Tangipahoa population.—No separate figures are known. Mooney estimates that in 1650 they and the Acolapissa together numbered 1,500; my estimate is of slightly over 1,000.

TAPOSA

A small tribe on the upper Yazoo, usually placed above the Chakchiuma, though Iberville, who has the earliest mention of them, seems to locate them below that tribe. They were evidently a part either of the Chakchiuma or the Chickasaw. The De Crenay map places them close to the Chakchiuma, and it is probable that they finally united with that tribe and shared its fortunes.

Taposa population.—They are usually enumerated with the Chakchiuma, and, in fact, the only separate figure is by Du Pratz, who estimates the number of cabins at 25 against 50 for the Chakchiuma. (See Chakchiuma.)

TAWASA

This tribe is first mentioned by the De Soto chroniclers under the names Toasi and Tuasi, and the Spaniards seem to have found it in 1540 approximately on the site of the present Montgomery, Ala. Between that date and 1693 these people seem to have moved down near the Tohome and Mobile and by 1706 had worked their way toward the Apalachicola, probably to a point between that stream

and the Choctawhatchee. In the latter year or the year following, they were driven out by northern Indians probably accompanied
by English. The greater part of them then sought refuge with the
French at Mobile though, from entrances on certain maps, it seems
possible that a small band remained in their old country a while
longer. Bienville placed his newcomers a league and a half below
the fort, the original Mobile post, and when new Mobile was founded
in 1710 located them 1 league above the Apalachee on Mobile River.
By 1715 they had left this place, because it was then given to the
Taensa, and they may have lived for a while, as Hamilton suggests, on a creek now known as Toucha, which empties into Bayou
Sara some distance east of Cleveland's Station, but on the other
hand they may have gone immediately to the upper Alabama, where
they were established in 1717 when Fort Toulouse was built. In 1760
there were two bodies of Tawasa, one with the Fus-hatchee Indians
4 leagues from Fort Toulouse on Tallapoosa River, the other an
independent body 7 leagues from that post and perhaps on the site
which they occupied in Hawkins' time (1799), at or very close to
their ancient sixteenth-century town. From information furnished
by the native chronicler, George Stiggins, it appears that the
Autauga town, lower down the Alabama in Autauga County, belonged to the same tribe. About the end of the eighteenth century
the Alabama tribe divided and the Tawasa divided also, part remaining in their old country and part moving to Louisiana, where they
followed the fortunes of the Alabama emigrants (q. v.). After the
Creek War of 1813–14, in which all of the Alabama took a conspicuous part, they were compelled to move into the district between the
Coosa and Tallapoosa Rivers, and the prominence of Tawasa among
those who had remained with the Creeks seems to be shown by the
fact that Tawasa and Autauga are the only names of Alabama towns
which appear in the census rolls of 1832. The rest of their history,
however, is bound up in that of the Alabama as a whole.

Tawasa population.—The estimates for this tribe cannot be clearly
separated from those of the Alabama. The French census of 1760,
however, returned 40 men, and the Georgia census of 1792 about 60.
If we were to suppose that only Tawasa lived in the towns called
Tawasa and Autauga in the census of 1832–33, we would be able to
give 321 as the Tawasa population at that time, but such an interpretation is of very doubtful validity.

TEKESTA OR TEQUESTA

A tribe found by the Spaniards early in the sixteenth century
living on the southeastern coast of Florida about on the site of the

present Miami. Relations between them and the much more powerful Calusa were very intimate and it had been their habit, as with the Calusa, to kill the Spaniards cast away upon their coast. But when Menendez made peace with the Calusa Tribe, the Tekesta adopted a more lenient attitude. In 1566 when a vessel filled with Spanish mutineers was forced to enter a harbor near the Tekesta town, they were well received. Later the same year, Menendez sent home some Tekesta Indians who had been held captive by the Calusa, and shortly afterward visited the town himself, where he left Fray Francisco de Villareal as missionary and received from the chief the chief's brother and two other Indians to take to Spain. During the 4 days of his stay a cross was erected, a blockhouse built, and a company of soldiers left in charge. For a time the missionary work prospered, but the new faith took no deep root in the minds of the natives and when, for some trifling offence, the soldiers killed an uncle of the chief, they tore down the crosses, burned their huts, and withdrew into the forest. They also lay in wait for the Spaniards when they went for water and killed so many of them that the survivors were driven to seek refuge at Santa Lucia in the Guacata province (q. v.). In 1569 Father Juan Bautista de Segura, accompanied by that brother of the chief whom Menendez had taken to Spain and whom the natives believed to be dead, went to Tekesta. The presence of the Indian secured a peaceful reception, and the Indians renewed their alliances with the Spaniards and restored the crosses. But the difficulties between the two peoples revived soon afterward, and in 1570 the Spanish garrison was withdrawn. In 1573 Pedro Menendez Marques, left as Lieutenant Governor of Florida, made an extended reconnaissance of the entire Atlantic coast from the head of the Florida Keys to Chesapeake Bay, and to this we probably owe the note on a Spanish map to the effect that the Indians in the neighborhood of Tekesta had been converted by him. It is very likely that this statement confuses his expedition with the earlier missionary effort. In 1597 Governor Mendez de Canço passed from the head of the Florida Keys to St. Augustine, and so directly through the Tekesta country. In 1607 we hear of a chief Don Luis who was perhaps head of this tribe, but the wording renders the matter somewhat uncertain. In a document dated 1697, it is said that the Indians of Matacumbe Island were "Catholics," and the tribe under discussion may here be indicated. It is the opinion of the writer that the 80 "Calusa" families mentioned by Romans as having gone to Cuba in 1763—including the "30 men" of Adair—were rather the inhabitants of the southeast coast than the Calusa proper. At any rate we hear nothing more regarding these Indians as a separate tribe. (See Ais.)

Tekesta population.—No early estimates seem to be preserved. For this and the other tribes of the southeast Florida coast, Mooney estimates a total population of 1,000. (See Romans and Adair above as to the number of survivors.)

TIMUCUA GROUP

Timucua was the original name of a tribe also called Utina (q. v.) living north of the Santa Fe River in Florida and extending eastward beyond the St. Johns, but it was extended by Powell, in the form Timuquanan (now usually contracted to Timucuan) to include all of the tribes of the linguistic family to which the Timucua belonged. It was given by him the status of an independent family, but was undoubtedly a branch of the great Muskhogean stock. It included the following tribes: Acuera, Fresh Water Indians, Icafui, Mocoço, Ocale (perhaps part of the Acuera), Oçita (perhaps identical with the Pohoy), Onatheaqua, Pohoy, Potano, Saturiwa, Tacatacuru, Tawasa, Tocobaga, Utina or Timucua, Yufera, Yui, and Yustaga. There is also reported a province 40 leagues or 4 days' journey inland consisting of three towns 1½ leagues apart called Abino, Tucuro, and Utiaca. This was probably connected with one of the tribes mentioned. Although most of the Timucuan divisions are being treated separately, the history of the whole may be sketched briefly. Ponce de Leon reached the country of the Fresh Water Timucua on the east coast in 1513. Some part of the Timucua coast was skirted by Miruelo in 1516, Pineda in 1519, by Ponce de Leon again in 1521, by Verrazzano (possibly) in 1524, and by Narvaez in 1528. Narvaez passed through part of the Timucua country inland, but has left scant information regarding its inhabitants. With the expedition of De Soto in 1539, we begin to get a clearer picture of these western Timucua, but the eastern tribes, except for Ponce de Leon's brief experience, are first introduced to us by Jean Ribault in 1562, and Laudonnière and Le Moyne in 1564–65, our information from these last two being the fullest on almost all aspects of Timucua life. In 1565 Sir John Hawkins touched this part of Florida. The same year the French were replaced by Spaniards, who established their capital at St. Augustine and began extending their civil and spiritual authority over the Timucua people. Both conquests proceeded rapidly and with scant resistance. In 1656, however, there was a formidable native rebellion which lasted 8 months. Moreover, the peninsula suffered from several visitations of pestilence—in 1613–17, when it is claimed that more than half of the missionized Indians died, in 1649–50, and in 1672. The decline in population seems to have begun before the great rebellion, but it was much accellerated by that outbreak and by subsequent disturbances, while toward the end of the century Indians from the north, instigated and sometimes accompanied by the English, destroyed and carried away more and more of the population. This movement was particularly accentuated after the destruction of the Apalachee in 1703–4, who had acted as a barrier. The remnants of the Timucua settled in one or two villages near St. Augustine, where they continued until after 1736. The last of these seem to have removed to the present Tomoka River in Volusia County, where we lose sight of them. The name of one town, however, Utina, may be continued in that of a Seminole settlement, Etanie, which perhaps contained some relics of the group.

Timucua population.—A Spanish document dated 1597 reports that there were then more than 1,400–1,500 Christian Indians in the Timucua territories included in the missions of Nombre de Dios (Saturiwa), San Pedro (Tacatacuru), the Fresh Water District, and San Antonio de Enacape (also of the Fresh Water District). In 1602, 792 Christians were reported under San Pedro, 500 under San Juan del Puerto, and 200 in the Fresh Water District, besides which 100 were under instruction in this last, and 1,100 in the province of Icafui (under Tacatacuru). The same manuscript states that there was a total population of 700–800 in the province of Yui, 1,500 in Utina or Timucua, and 1,000 in Potano. In 1606 the Bishop of Cuba visited Florida and confirmed 2,074 Indians, and in 1608 it was claimed that 5,000 Indians were converted or were being catechised. The writer of a letter dated February 2, 1635, claims 30,000 Christianized Indians connected with the 44 missions, but this is plainly an exaggeration. In 1675 Governor Salazar gives 1,400 in the Timucua missions, but the same year Bishop Calderón of Cuba reports that he administered the holy sacrament of confirmation to 13,152 Christianized Indians in the four provinces of "Guale, Timuqua, Apalache, and Apalachocoli." Mooney made an estimate of 13,000 Timucua for the year 1650. In 1728 the town of Nombre de Dios, or Chiquito, near St. Augustine, which seems to have contained most of the remaining Timucua, had about 15 men and 20 women. In 1736 the number of men was reported as 17.

TIOU

The earliest known home of this tribe was on Yazoo River, where they are placed by early cartographers above the Tunica, Yazoo, and Koroa, but below the Ibitoupa. Tonti says they were 25 leagues from the Mississippi. At a date not much earlier than 1682 part of them, under pressure of the Chickasaw it is claimed, moved down to the neighborhood of the Natchez. They appear to have settled first on the west bank of the Mississippi near Fort Adams, some miles below the Natchez, and were probably the Indians called Koroa by La Salle's chroniclers, who were evidently distinct from the Koroa they mention on and near Yazoo River. Afterward they moved in near the Natchez towns and remained a constituent part of the Natchez tribe during the rest of their existence. In May 1700, after the Bayogoula had destroyed their fellow townsmen, the Mugulasha, Iberville states that they called many families of Acolapissa and Tiou in to take their places. What became of these Tiou we do not know. When Fort Rosalie was built, the Tiou town was 1 league south of it and 2 leagues west of the great village of the Natchez. Later they sold their land to Sieur Roussin and went elsewhere. December 9, 1729, they were sent by the Natchez on a mission to their linguistic allies, the Tunica, to induce them to declare war against the French, but in vain. In 1731 Charlevoix says they were completely destroyed by the Quapaw and, while the completeness may well be questioned, we hear nothing of them from this time forward. The medicine men of this tribe apparently were in high repute. On the map in Charlevoix's History, the Big Black is called the "River of the Tioux," and on that of Ross their name is given to the Homochitto.

Tiou population.—Apart from the fact that this tribe was very small within the historic period, we have no figures bearing upon their numbers. Mooney includes the Tiou, Chakchiuma, Ibitoupa, and Taposa in an estimate of 1,200 for the year 1650, which I would reduce to 1,000.

TOCOBAGA

A tribe or "province" whose principal town was at the head of Old Tampa Bay, evidently the town site in Safety Harbor. The town was visited by Menendez in 1567, and he had with him the chief of the Calusa, then at war with the Indians of Tocobaga. Thirty soldiers were left there under Captain Martinez de Coz "to instruct the Indians in the faith," but the latter were so unappreciative that the following year they fell upon their guests and destroyed them all. The Tocobaga seem to have been left alone after that until the beginning of the following century, when we are informed that the chiefs of Pohoy and Tocobaga had attacked Christian Indians and, in consequence, an expedition was sent against them in 1612. After this date they again disappear from history, but it is possible that the "Tompacuas" who later appeared in the Apalachee country were a part of them. The latter were probably the "Macapiras" or "Amacapiras," who were placed in a mission near St. Augustine called San Buenaventura in 1726 and were associated later with the Pohoy in a town called Jororo. The Indians of both of these tribes are said to have been almost destroyed by pestilence in 1726, whereupon the survivors returned to their old country.

Tocobaga population.—We are told that when Menendez was visiting the Tocobaga Indians, 1,500 warriors gathered near the town to receive him, but, of course, there is no way of knowing how close an estimate Menendez's chronicler made nor how many of these Indians were bona fide members of the tribe. Mooney's estimate as of the year 1650 is 1,000. The "Macapiras" Indians brought to San Buenaventura numbered 24.

TOHOME

Indians of this tribe may possibly have been among the ones encountered on the Gulf coast by early navigators like Pineda, Narvaez, and Maldonado, but the river of the Tome which appears in the De Luna documents, and was evidently the Tombigbee, shows that by 1560 they were near, if not actually at, the spot where the French discovered them 140 years later. Their earlier home had perhaps been still farther inland, since the name of Catoma Creek, an affluent of Alabama River in Montgomery County, appears on the De Crenay map of 1733 as Auke Thome, "Thome Creek." Their name appears again associated with the Gulf locality in documents narrating the expeditions to survey Pensacola Bay in 1693. In April, 1700, when Iberville was on Pascagoula River, he learned of the Mobile and Tohome Indians, living one day's journey apart on "the river of the Mobile." He sent his brother and two other Frenchmen with the chief of the Pascagoula Indians to these tribes to establish friendly relations with them. In March 1702, while the French were engaged in erecting the first fort in Mobile Bay, Iberville paid this tribe a visit in their towns on the Tombigbee, and relations continued uninterruptedly from that time forward. The French protected them from the Alabama Indians and in 1705 prevented them from declaring war against the Mobile. In 1715 an Indian of this tribe killed the English trader Hughes, who had been apprehended by a French force on the Mississippi, but allowed to start back to South Carolina overland. From what Du Pratz tells us, it would seem that, by about 1730, the tribe had moved south to a point just above Mobile. We hear of them in various documents as late as 1771–72, but as their language and that of the Mobile differed little from Choctaw, they probably fused in time with the great Choctaw Nation. A body of Choctaw which settled on Bayou Boeuf near the Biloxi and Pascagoula Indians early in the nineteenth century may have been composed of the remnants of the Tohome and Mobile.

When the French first visited the Tohome, they were divided into two bands, called sometimes the Big Tohome and the Little Tohome, and the smaller of these was probably identical with the Naniaba Indians, since both were located near the junction of the Tombigbee and Alabama Rivers.

Tohome population.—In 1700 Iberville was given to understand by the Pascagoula Indians that there were 300 warriors in the Tohome tribe and as many more Mobile Indians but, after visiting them himself in 1702, he reduced his estimate for the two to 350. About 30 years later, Du Pratz states that they were about as numerous as the Chatot who occupied 40 cabins. In 1758 Governor De Kerlérec considered that the Mobile, Tohome, and Naniaba together had about 100 warriors. (See Mobile.)

TUKABAHCHEE

This town or tribe is supposed to have immigrated into the Gulf region from the north. Spanish letters written late in the seventeenth century speak of it in connection with the Coweta, Kasihta, and Oconee, so that it would appear to have been in some part of Georgia at that time. However, Tukabahchee Tallahassee, although the name of an Okfuskee town, probably received its designation from the fact that it had occupied a site formerly held by Tukabahchee Indians. It was on the upper course of Tallapoosa River, and in 1675 Bishop Calderón indicates that the Tukabahchee were either on the Tallapoosa or the Coosa. An early location of the tribe in Alabama is therefore to be assumed. In any case, it soon established itself in the bend of the Tallapoosa where it turns west, and it continued at this point until the Creeks removed to Oklahoma. When the Creek War broke out, these Indians refused to join the hostile party and retired to the neighborhood of their friends the Coweta until it was over. Except for a small village mentioned by Hawkins called Wī hĭli, or "Sweet Water," no branches of this town are known, though its relations with Atasi and Kealedji were very intimate. In Oklahoma, the Tukabahchee first established their Square Ground in the southeastern part of the Creek territory near Melette post office, but later they removed it to Yeager north of Holdenville, where it was maintained until a very recent date.

Tukabahchee population.—The following estimates of warriors have been made: 100 in 1738, more than 50 in 1750, 200 in 1760, 90 in 1761, including some Yuchi, 120 in 1772, and 116 in 1799, the last supposedly by actual count. The census of 1832–33 credited this town with 1,287 souls.

TUNICA

Tradition and early records point to northwestern Mississippi and the neighboring parts of Arkansas as far as the Ouachita as an early home of this tribe, but by 1682 they had concentrated upon Yazoo River a few miles above its mouth, though parties were scattered through the forests of northeastern Louisiana to boil salt with which they were in the habit of trading, and there was a village on the Ouachita as late as 1687. In 1699 a French missionary, Father Davion, established himself among them, abandoned them in 1702 after one of his confreres had been killed by the Koroa, a related tribe, but returned about 1705. In 1706, fearing that they were in imminent danger of attack by the Chickasaw and other Indians in the English interest, the Tunica abandoned their villages and moved to the Houma town opposite the mouth of Red River. They were well received, but shortly afterward they rose upon their hosts, killed more than half of them, and drove the rest away. In 1719 or 1720, Davion left his charges in despair at the meager results achieved, but his influence was sufficient to retain them definitely in the French interest during the Natchez uprising and the disturbances which followed. Some time between 1784 and 1803 they abandoned their homes on the Mississippi River and moved up the Red to Marksville Prairie, where they settled upon a strip of land they claim to have bought from the Avoyel, the earlier occupants of that section. At any rate it is a piece of land recognized as the Indian reserve, and their mixed-blood descendants have continued there down to the present day. A part of them went farther west and joined the Atakapa and still another body moved to the Chickasaw Nation in Oklahoma, where they established themselves along Red River, but these are now entirely lost sight of.

Plate 48 is one of the valuable De Batz series recovered by Bushnell and gives a sketch of the Tunica chief and the widow and child of his predecessor. Plate 49 is taken from photographs which I made of William Ely Johnson, Gatschet's Tunica informant, and Volcine Chiki, who was regarded as chief of the Tunica in 1910. Plate 50 is from a print made by Miss Caroline Dormon, of Saline, La., of Sam Young, or Sesostrie Yauchicant, last speaker of the Tunica language.

Tunica population.—In 1699 the missionary De Montigny estimated that the Tunica, Yazoo, and Ofo together numbered 2,000 souls, and La Source stated that they occupied about 260 cabins, but Gravier, in 1700, cuts this last to 50–60, while Iberville, writing in 1702, allows 300 families to these tribes, inclusion of the Ofo being somewhat uncertain. In 1719, after the Tunica had removed from the Yazoo, La Harpe estimated a total population of 460, and in 1758 Governor Kerlérec supposed that they had about 60 warriors. In 1803 Jefferson sets down 50–60 as the probable total population, and Sibley (1805) agrees quite closely, giving 25 warriors. Morse, in 1822, estimated that there were 30 Tunica altogether; and there may be about as many at the present time, racially very much mixed, but only one speaker of the Tunica language. The census of 1910 returned

43; the census of 1930 only 1. In his study of Indian population north of Mexico, Mooney allowed 2,000 to this tribe with the Yazoo, Koroa, and Ofo as of the year 1650; my estimate was 2,450.

TUSCARORA

A tribe or confederation of tribes found by white explorers on the middle courses of the Roanoke, Neuse, Tar, and Pamlico Rivers. Hewitt gives the names of three constituent bodies: Akawentcaka, Ketenuaka, and Skaruren, from the last of which the name Tuscarora comes. They are mentioned by Edward Blande and his companions in 1650 under the name Tuscarood as very powerful and addicted to trade. July 14, 1670, John Lederer, on the return journey of his second expedition, visited the town in which the Tuscarora head chief had his favorite seat, which he calls "Katearas, a place of great Indian trade and Commerce." In 1701 they were visited by Lawson, and he was later killed by them during the Tuscarora War. This war lasted from 1711 to 1713 and required two campaigns by South Carolina whites and allied Indians before the hostiles were defeated, the first headed by Colonel Barnwell, the second by Col. James Moore. As a result of their defeat, the greater portion of the tribe removed to New York where, through the intermediation of the Oneida, they were admitted into the Confederation, but not as equals until 1722. Hewitt states that the removal of the Tuscarora to the north took 90 years. Some remained for a considerable period on the Susquehanna and Juniata Rivers. Those who had remained neutral during the war in the south continued in North Carolina under the chieftainship of Tom Blunt, or Blount, and part stayed in this territory until 1802, when the last rejoined their relatives in the north. After a series of fortunes and misfortunes, the New York Tuscarora finally obtained title to a reservation of their own in the Seneca country in 1797. Those Tuscarora who took the side of Great Britain in the Revolution were given lands in severalty in Grand River reservation, Ontario.

Tuscarora population.—Lawson, whose information applies to about 1709, estimated 1,200 Tuscarora warriors and Colonel Barnwell 1,200–1,400. In 1736 Chauvignerie states there were then 250 warriors among the Tuscarora in New York. The total number in the United States in 1765 is given as 1,000, in 1778 as 2,000, in 1783 as 1,000, and in 1796 as 400. In 1885 there were 414 Tuscarora Indians in New York State and those in Canada were supposed to be about as numerous. In 1909, 364 were returned from New York and in 1910 the corresponding Canadian figure was 416, a total of 780. The United States census of 1910 returned 400.

TUSKEGEE

In 1540 De Soto passed through a town called Tasqui on or near Big Canoe Creek in northern Alabama. In 1567 a soldier under Juan Pardo visited this town again and found another nearby called Tasquiqui. The latter certainly, and the former probably, belonged to the tribe under discussion. When the English and French began to penetrate this region, they found the Tuskegee divided into two bands, one of which was said to be on an island in the Tennessee River and is evidently that which ultimately united with the Cherokee and at one time had a large town on the south side of Little Tennessee River, just above the mouth of Tellico Creek. Another settlement bearing the name was on the north bank of Tennessee River in a bend just below Chattanooga, and Mooney thought that a third existed on Tuskegee Creek, on the south bank of Little Tennessee River, north of Robbinsville, in Graham County, N. C. The other division of this tribe ultimately settled at the junction of the Coosa and Tallapoosa Rivers. From early maps it is evident that at least a part of this branch moved east to the Ocmulgee River and later on lived for a time on the Chattahoochee. Finally, however, they settled at the point above indicated and remained there, or at least in the immediate neighborhood, until the Creeks moved west of the Mississippi, when they formed a town in the southeastern part of the new Creek territories. Later a portion moved northwest and settled beyond Beggs, Okla., close to the Yuchi.

Tuskegee population.—The French estimate of 1750 returned only 10 men, meaning warriors and capable hunters, from this town, but that of 1760 gives 50, and the estimate of 1761 gives 40, including Coosa Old Town. Taitt estimated 25 in 1772 and Marbury the same number in 1792, while Hawkins in 1799 allows 35 "gunmen." The United States census of 1832–33 returned a total population of 216.

TUTELO

This name was applied by the Iroquois to the Siouan tribes of Virginia generally, and it is perhaps in this sense that we are to understand the tribe which appears under it in a map of New Netherlands dated 1614. They are located far down the Susquehanna River. It was given specifically, however, to a tribe visited by Batts and Fallam in 1671 near the site of Salem, Va., and it was from them evidently that the Big Sandy was called River of the Tutelo on eighteenth century maps. But by that time the tribe itself had removed to an island in Roanoke River near the junction of the Staunton and Dan. In 1701 Lawson learned that they were near the headwaters of the Yadkin. Sometime afterward they moved eastward, along with the Saponi, Occaneechi, Keyauwee, and Shakori, and crossed the

Roanoke, and in 1714 the Tutelo, Saponi, Occaneechi, and "Stucka-nox" or Stegaraki (which included the remains of the Manahoac) were settled at Fort Christanna on Meherrin River, the other tribes gravitating toward the south. After peace was finally made between the Iroquois and the Virginia tribes in 1722, the Saponi and the Tutelo moved northward, though not for some years, and before 1744 settled at Shamokin, Pa., under Iroquois protection. In 1748 they had moved to a town called Skogari on the north branch of the Sus-quehanna in the present Columbia County, Pa. In 1753 they were formally adopted into the League of the Iroquois. In 1771, however, they were settled on the east side of Cayuga inlet, about 3 miles from the south end of Cayuga Lake, in a town called Coreorgonel. This was destroyed by Sullivan in 1779. A part of them were located for several years near Buffalo, N. Y. Nikonha, from whom Horatio Hale collected linguistic material proving the Siouan relationship of the tribe, the last of the full-blood Tutelo, died in 1871. The last man who could speak the language fluently was John Key, of Costango, who passed away in 1898. Nevertheless, Dr. Leo J. Frachtenberg, when engaged in investigations on the Grand River Reservation, Ontario, in July 1907, for the Bureau of American Ethnology, collected a short vocabulary of Tutelo words from an old woman named Lucy Buck. (See Frachtenberg, 1913.) In August 1911, Dr. Edward Sapir collected another vocabulary from Andrew Sprague, who had been Frachtenberg's interpreter, and had been adopted into the Tutelo tribe in his early years. (See Sapir, 1913.) At the time of Frachten-berg's visit, the tribe was represented by only two families, the Buck and Williams families, and it is practically extinct as a separate entity, though Tutelo ceremonial life still persists, as reported by Speck (1942).

Tutelo population.—In 1709 the Tutelo, Saponi, Occaneechi, Keyau-wee, and Shakori numbered together 750 souls. In 1715 Governor Spotswood reports that the various tribes of Indians who were settled at Fort Christanna—the Tutelo, Saponi, Occaneechi, and Manahoac—together numbered 300. In 1673 Sir William Johnson estimated that there might be 200 fighting men in the Tutelo, Saponi, Nanticoke, and Conoy tribes, but by this time the Occaneechi and Manahoac, and probably the Monacan, had been absorbed in the two first mentioned. Mooney's estimate of the population of this tribe, the Saponi, Mana-hoac, and Monacan as of 1600 is 2,700.

UTINA OR TIMUCUA

A large tribe or confederation of tribes, between the Santa Fe and Suwannee Rivers and extending to, or in some measure controlling, the settlements on the middle course of St. Johns River, Fla. In 1528 Narvaez met a party of Indians which probably belonged to this tribe, under a chief called Dulchanchellin. They are also identified as the Indians of the towns called Aguacaleyquen, Uriutina, and Napetaca, through which De Soto passed in 1539 and who engaged him in a terrific battle near two small lakes in the same country. In 1564–65 the French belonging to the Huguenot colony came in contact with them and assisted them at one time in a war with the Potano. In 1597, after the Spaniards had expelled the French, Juan de Junco, an Indian interpreter and leader of the Timucua and Fresh Water provinces, brought the Timucua "heir apparent" and many other important Indians to St. Augustine, and Fray Baltasar López, the missionary at San Pedro Tacatacuru, spent 3 months in the Timucua province, but was recalled by the Guale revolt. In 1607 Father Prieto, during mission work among the Potano, made frequent visits to the Timucua, which he reported to contain more than 20 towns and to be ruled by a great chief "esteemed and feared through Florida." After accompanying Prieto on a visit to St. Augustine, this chief was himself converted and assisted actively in the Christianization of the rest of the tribe. The Mission of San Juan de Guacara, which dates from about the same period, also served these Indians. San Martin de Timucua was probably identical with the San Martin de Ayaocuto of later mission lists. It is believed that some at least of the missions named San Agustin de Urica, Santa Maria de los Angeles de Arapaja, Santa Cruz de Cachipile, San Ildefonso de Chamini, and San Francisco de Chuaquin also served them. In 1656, however, the chief of Ayaocuto, evidently the principal Timucua chief, led a rebellion, and the names of most of the missions just enumerated disappear from the records. In November 1659, Capt. Juan Fernandez de Florencia was sent to rebuild the towns of Ayaocuto, Chuaquin, and Toloco, but the names do not appear afterward. It is probable that many Timucua fled from the country at this time, and that the rest were represented at the missions of Santa Cruz de Tarihica, Santa Catalina, San Juan de Guacara, and perhaps San Pedro. A possible echo of the old tribal name appears in a list of Seminole towns made in 1823, one of which, located in the old Utina country "W. of St. John's, E. of Black Creek," bears the suggestive name Etanie. Otherwise the tribe disappears from the record.

Utina population.—A missionary letter dated 1602 estimates the number of Utina ("Timucua") Indians at 1,500. This account speaks of but 5 towns, but a document of 1607 states that the great chief of this tribe, as noted above, ruled over "more than twenty towns." Mooney suggests a total population of 8,000 in 1650, but includes in the figure other tribes of the linguistic division.

WACCAMAW

The name of this tribe possibly occurs in a list of "provinces" furnished by Francisco of Chicora in 1521 in the form "Guacaya." When the English established themselves in South Carolina in 1670, the Waccamaw were living along the river which bears their name and on the lower course of the Pee Dee, in close association with the Winyaw and Pedee tribes. They were somewhat remote from the white settlements, and did not play much of a part in the history of the province until the Yamasee War broke out. They joined the hostiles, but during the same year, as we learn from the South Carolina archives, "the Waccamaws and other nations bordering on the sea . . . made peace with us fearing the Cherakees." In 1717 this tribe had moved south of Black River and an alliance was feared between them and the Cheraw, who were the trouble-making tribe at the time. In fact, when they made peace in 1715, the Waccamaw admitted that the Cheraw had been supplying them with ammunition. In a letter dated June 24, 1720, we read:

We had a small war with the Vocames (Waccamaw), a nation on Winea River not above 100 men, but the gentlemen have paid for it for there is 60 men, women, and children of them taken and killed and we have not lost one white man, only a Winea Indian killed and now they petition for peace which will be granted them.

In 1755 Cherokee and Natchez were reported to have killed some Pedee and Waccamaw Indians in the white settlements. The descendants of those who were left may have joined the Catawba, though it is perhaps more likely that they are to be found among the Lumber River Indians whose homes are a little farther north. (See Woccon.)

Waccamaw population.—The census taken in 1715, just before the Yamasee War, reported 6 villages and a population of 610. As noted above, they are supposed to have had 100 warriors, perhaps 350 souls, in 1720, and 60 of the Waccamaw population were killed or captured— and presumably sent to the West Indies—the same year.

WAKOKAI

A Muskogee settlement and subdivision living in Benjamin Hawkins' time (1799) on Hatchet Creek, an eastern affluent of the Coosa. The earliest maps on which they appear show them in the same region. Their history is connected traditionally with that of the Hilibi and Eufaula Indians, from whom they perhaps separated. Tukpafka and Wiogufki were early and important branches of this tribe, and Sakapadai was probably a third, though this is uncertain. There was another Tukpafka, an Okfuskee town which later adopted the name Nuyaka. After the removal, most of these Indians settled in the extreme southwestern part of the Creek territory, where one busk ground, called Wiogufki, was kept up until very late times.

Wakokai population.—The following estimates of the number of Wakokai warriors are found: 100 in 1738, more than 60 in 1750, 100 in 1760, 60 in 1761, 100 in 1772, 300 in 1792. There are no early figures for Tukpafka, Wiogufki, or Sakapadai, and on the other hand, the census of 1832–33, which omits Wakokai entirely, returned a total population of 353 in Wiogufki, 391 in Tukpafka, and 198 in Sakapadai.

WASHA (FRENCH: OUACHA)

A small tribe living in 1699 on Bayou Lafourche, west of the present city of New Orleans, La. Indians of this tribe may have fought De Soto's Spaniards in 1543 (see Chawasha). In the year first mentioned, Iberville learned of it, and met a canoe containing people belonging to it when he was on his way up the Mississippi. In July Bienville vainly attempted to establish friendly relations with the Washa, but in 1718 they moved to the Mississippi and settled on the south side 11 leagues above New Orleans. In 1739 an officer with M. de Nouaille reported that this tribe and the related Chawasha were near the settlements called "Les Allemands," on the left bank of the river. In 1758 De Kerlérec stated that they had been practically destroyed, but as late as 1805 Sibley reported 2 men and 3 women still living but scattered in French families, and without a knowledge of their native tongue. In the French form, their name has been applied to Lake Salvador and to a small body of water on the edge of the Gulf of Mexico.

Washa population.—In 1699 La Harpe reported that the Washa, the Chawasha, and the Okelousa together had perhaps 200 warriors, but another figure for that year gives 200 warriors to the Washa alone. In 1715 Bienville estimated 50, but in 1739 there were said to be only 30 warriors of the Washa and Chawasha, and in 1805, as we have seen, there were but 5 individuals left.

WASHITA OR OUACHITA

A small Caddo tribe which has given its name to Ouachita River, La. In 1700 Bienville passed through their village located near the present site of Columbia on the Ouachita, but already by 1690 a part of them had left and settled near the Natchitoches Indians. The French governor of Louisiana, Perrier, wrote in 1730 that they had been destroyed by the Taensa, but the greater part probably withdrew to the Natchitoches or other Caddo tribes farther west.

Washita population.—Bienville reported in 1700 that there were 5 cabins and about 70 men in their town on Ouachita River.

WATEREE

The home of this tribe when the Spanish explorer Juan Pardo met them in 1566 on his return from his first expedition to the Cheraw Indians (Xoara) is in doubt. He evidently reached the tribe, which he calls Guatari, by detouring to the east, and probably found them on the Wateree River, though it may have been the Broad. Here he had a conference with more than 30 chiefs and a great number of Indians besides, and, at their request, he left them a priest and 4 soldiers. Two days later, on his way back to Santa Elena, he came to a place called Guatariatiqui, where he again held a council. On his second journey, he went sufficiently out of his way to visit Guatari-atiqui, but did not go to the main Wateree settlement. He returned through it, however, spent 16 or 17 days there, and built a fort, which he left in charge of a corporal and 17 soldiers. The Wateree were then ruled by two chieftainesses who exercised considerable authority and had both male and female servants to wait upon them. This, like the other forts established by Pardo and his lieutenant Boyano, was soon afterward destroyed by the Indians. We hear of them next through the narrative of John Lederer, who in 1670 seems to have found them a considerable distance to the north on the upper Yadkin. By 1701, however, they were on the Wateree below the present Camden and there they remained until the end of their career as an independent people. Here Lawson met them and he also met a tribe of Little Wateree, "Wateree Chickanee," who may correspond to the Guatariatiqui of Pardo. The Wateree took part in the Yamasee War in 1715, and a note in the colonial archives of South Carolina says that Wateree Jack was believed to be the author of most of the mischief done by the Catawba and the other small nations near them. Like so many other tribes, they obtained guns from the Cheraw, who very likely got them from Virginia. In 1740 they laid claim to the lands of Fredericksburg township (letter of Governor Glen). Early in 1744 Thomas Brown, a trader of the Congarees, bought from this tribe "the neck of land between the Wateree and Congaree rivers as far up as 'the Catawba fording place.'" In a letter dated September 22, 1744, we learn that certain Natchez and Wateree had killed some Catawba Indians by treachery, but that James Glen had persuaded the Natchez "king" to punish the offenders. Shortly afterward it is probable that the remainder of the Wateree settled permanently with the Catawba Indians and presently lost their identity in the larger tribe.

Wateree population.—They appear to have been more numerous than most of the other Siouan tribes of the east except the Catawba (see Rivers, 1874), and Mooney estimated their numbers at 1,000 in 1600.

WAXHAW

If this tribe is the Gueza of Vandera, it was living in 1566–67 in western South Carolina north of the present Augusta, Ga., but when the English entered this country toward the end of the seventeenth century, it was close to the Catawba Indians in what are now Lancaster County, S. C., and Union and Mecklenburg Counties, N. C. In 1670 Lederer seems to speak of these people under the name Wisacky, and they may have been the Weesock of Gabriel Arthur, reputed to be held as a subject caste by the Yuchi. In 1701 Lawson was hospitably received by them and he gives more regarding their customs than any other writer. At that time there were at least two Waxhaw villages 10 miles apart. In 1715 we learn from the South Carolina archives that when this tribe refused to make peace with the colonists, they were attacked by the Catawba and the greater part of them killed, the remainder seeking refuge with the Cheraw, along with whom they probably united with the Catawba at a later date, though some are undoubtedly now represented among the Lumber River Indians. A band of 25 Waxhaw accompanied the Yamasee to Florida in 1715 and were still there in 1720.

Waxhaw population.—Apart from the reference to two villages above, there seem to be no data on which an estimate of Waxhaw population may be based, but they were evidently a relatively small tribe.

WEAPEMEOC

A tribe or tribal confederation found by the Raleigh colonists in 1584–89 occupying the northeastern corner of North Carolina, north of Albemarle Sound. When we again get a view of the territory they occupied about a century later, we find it held by a number of independent tribes including the Yeopim, probably the principal tribe of the old confederation and the one which had given it its name, the Pasquotank, Perquiman, and Poteskeet. The names of two of these are preserved as county designations. In 1662 the Yeopim chief parted with some of his lands, and by 1701, according to Lawson, there was only a single Yeopim warrior living, though the remaining tribes of the group still counted 40.

Weapemeoc population.—Mooney estimated that there may have been 800 Weapemeoc in 1600. (See above.) In 1709 Lawson gave the number of warriors of the tribes in the former Weapemeoc territory as follows: Pasquotank, 10; Poteskeet, 30; Yeopim, 6 people.

WINYAW

Unless this tribe is the Yenyohol in the list given by Francisco of Chicora in 1521, it enters history first after the founding of South

Carolina, when it was living about Winyaw Bay and on the lower course of Pee Dee River. In 1683 the Lords Proprietors complained that their colonists had started a quarrel with these Indians in order to obtain slaves. Among Barnwell's Indian allies in his Tuscarora expedition were 24 Winyaw, but some Waccamaw may have been included with them. A trading post for the Winyaw, Waccamaw, and Pedee was established on Black River, and in 1716 removed to Saukey. According to the South Carolina archives, there were Winyaw Indians living among the Santee at that time who were to be encouraged to return to their homes. In 1720 some Winyaw allied themselves with the whites in their war upon the Waccamaw. We may suppose that the remnant finally took up their abode with the Catawba.

Winyaw population.—In 1715 they had one village with a population of 106. Mooney estimates that in 1600 the Winyaw, Waccamaw, and some other bands may have had a population of 900.

WIWOHKA

This was an old Creek town or tribe, but not a primary one. Its origin is uncertain except that it was popularly known as a "stray town," one made up of people who found it convenient to absent themselves permanently from their proper connections. It is said to have been responsible for the outbreak of the Creek War in 1813 and the Green Peach War after the removal. It appears on the De Crenay map of 1733 and is noted down to and including the census of 1832–33. For a time, after the removal, it had its own square ground, and when that was given up, the remnant associated themselves with the Okchai Indians.

Wiwohka population.—In 1738 it was reported to contain 100 warriors; in 1750, more than 40; in 1760, 100 (including Tcatoksofka and Hatcheetcaba); in 1761, 35; in 1792, 70; and in 1799 (Hawkins), 40. The census of 1832–33 credited the town with a total population of 301.

WOCCON

The history of this tribe before the eighteenth century is unknown unless, as Dr. Douglas Rights (in a personal communication) has suggested, they may have split off from the Waccamaw. Lawson reported that they were living in two villages on the lower Neuse River, or not far from it, named Yupwauremau and Tooptatmeer, perhaps about the present location of Goldsboro in Wayne County, N. C. They joined the Tuscarora in their war against the whites in 1711–13, and either remained with that tribe permanently or found a refuge among the related Catawba. This tribe is of particular interest only from the fact that it is the only one belonging to the Catawba group of Siouans besides the Catawba itself, of which a vocabulary has been preserved.

Woccon population.—The two villages mentioned by Lawson (1709) are said to have contained 120 warriors. Mooney estimates a population of 600 in 1600.

YADKIN

A tribe on the river of the same name, which first appears in history in a letter by the Indian trader, Abraham Wood, narrating the adventures of two men, James Needham and Gabriel Arthur, whom he had sent on an exploring expedition to the west. They passed through this tribe and town, which they called "Yattken," in the summer of 1674. Lawson (1709) gives the name as Reatkin, but applies it to the river, and there is no later mention of the people. They may have been identical with the Cheraw, Keyauwee, or some other Siouan tribe which appears later under another name.

Yadkin population.—Unknown.

YAMASEE

One of the provinces named by Francisco of Chicora as existing in 1521 on or near the present South Carolina coast bears the name "Yamiscaron" and is perhaps the first historical reference to this tribe. The "province of Altamaha" ("Altapaha" or "Altamaca") visited by De Soto in 1540 and then located about the eastward bend of the Ocmulgee, bears the name of a town afterward called the leading town of the Lower Yamasee, and we must suppose that the people represented a part at least of that tribe. They were then in some measure subordinate to the Hitchiti. This is the Tama province visited by a Spanish soldier named Gaspar de Salas and two Franciscan friars in 1597. Mention of them again appears in Spanish letters dated 1633 and 1639. By 1675 some of them had settled in the Apalachee country and also near the Spanish missions on the coast of Georgia. January 27, 1675, Bishop Calderón founded a mission in the Apalachee country 1 league from San Luis (modern Tallahassee), which he speaks of as "La Purificación de Tama, called Yamases." Another named Asumpción del Puerto, founded by him on February 2 following, contained Indians of the "Amacânos" tribe which may also have been Yamasee. Writing August 24, 1675, Governor Salazar gives another list of missions. He fails to enumerate "La Purificación de Tama," but substitutes "San Luís de Candelaria, a new *doctrina* established in 1675, about one and a half leagues from San Lorenzo [de Vitachuco]. . . . [with Indians drawn] from Tama and from the Yamassee county." We may infer from this that Calderón's foundation was shortly moved farther east and given a new name. He renames "Assumpción del Puerto" San Luis. At the same time he enumerates no less than three Yamasee missions on the Atlantic coast. One of these, on the "Isla de Mocama," evidently Cumberland Island, served two native villages, the first called Mocama "containing sixty persons, all Yamasee infidels," and the second "Ocotoque [there was a Lower Yamasee town named Oketee], a league away, has about forty persons, all infidels," and we may safely assume them to have been Yamasee also. The next mission, 2 leagues from Mocama, was called Tama and also consisted of "infidels." It was probably on the same island, but the third mission, Santa Maria, may have been on Amelia Island. At this period Santa Maria was occupied by "infidels," again probably Yamasee. In 1680 but one mission is entered on Cumberland Island, San Felipe de Athuluteca, but the tribe of Indians served by it is not indicated. However, it is evident that many of the Yamasee had moved nearer St. Augustine and occupied some stations formerly assigned to other Indians. Two in the Fresh Water province, San Salvador de Maiaca, and San Antonio de Anacape, are called "new conversions." That Yamasee were settled in the second of these is specifically stated. At the same time Nombre de Dios, a former Timucua mission close to St. Augustine, now appearing as "Nombre de Dios de Amacarisse," was also settled by Yamasee. In the winter of 1684–85 the Yamasee Indians became offended at some act of the Florida governor and withdrew to the frontiers of South Carolina, where the English gave them lands on the west side of Savannah River near its mouth. A town called "Amercario" makes its appearance on Savannah River and probably contained the population of the former Amacarisse mission, the name of which appears sometimes as Macarisqui and Mascarasi. It is believed that this contains the origin of the name Yamacraw. South Carolina documents inform us that the Yamasee at this time were divided into two sections of five towns each called Upper and Lower Yamasee and headed by Pocotaligo and Altamaha respectively (Pocotaligo, Huspaw, Yoa, Sadkeche, Tomatly; Altamaha, Pocasabo, Chasee, Oketee, and "probably" Tulafina). The former may have included the Indians of Amacarisse, the latter the Tama proper. In 1703 a tribe called Yoa added itself to them. The Yamasee furnished 87 warriors to the native contingent with which Barnwell attacked the Tuscarora in 1711, and proved the most reliable of his auxiliaries. In 1715, however, smarting under various outrages committed by white traders and fearing that the census taken that year meant that they were to be enslaved, the Yamasee headed an insurrection against the English colonists. They were quickly defeated by a force under Governor Craven and fled to Florida, where they were received joyfully by the people of St. Augustine and settled in villages nearby along with other Indians. In 1726 four Yamasee missions were reported in Florida with a fifth in the Apalachee country occupied jointly with Apalachee Indians. Three missions were occupied by Ybaha (Guale Indians). In 1728 one Yamasee mission was reported and another was occupied jointly with the Ybaha. Two towns were occupied entirely by Ybaha. There is also mention of a town called San Antonio de la Tama consisting of 23 persons who, we are told, had come from South Carolina. It was destroyed by the Creeks in 1725, and the Indians moved to another mission called Mose. As Nombre de Dios is called also "Macariz" it may have contained Indians of that band. In 1725 and 1728 these villages were raided by the English and their allies and in the latter year those around St. Augustine were reduced to one by order of the Spanish governor. The greater part of the Yamasee who remained in this part of Florida seem to have retired to the Oklawaha River and finally to have become incorporated into the Seminole Nations. Part of the Yamasee, as we have seen, went to the old Apalachee country from South Carolina and later on we hear of Yamasee bands near Pensacola and Mobile and along the Upper Creeks. This last was very likely composed of those who had been living near the two places mentioned. Probably, too, they were the "Emusas" enumerated by Captain Young among the Lower Creek and Seminole bands on the Chattahoochee River, where Omusee Creek perhaps preserves the name. A list of Seminole towns made in 1823 shows that these Yamasee had then moved to Florida, where they were living at the head of the Sumulga Hatchee River, 20 miles north of St. Marks. Part of these Creek Yamasee may have constituted the Yamacraw band found by Oglethorpe on the site of Savannah when he landed there in 1733 with the first Georgia colonists. It is to be suspected that it originated from the Amacarisse Yamasee which we suppose to have settled in the Upper towns. Most of the Yamacraw Indians had come from the Lower Creek towns about 1730 to the Savannah, and their chief, Tomochichi, had tarried for some time with the Apalachicola. In 1734 Tomochichi, his wife, his nephew, and a few of his warriors visited England and received much attention. (See pls. 29, 30.) He died October 5, 1739. Later his people moved to a place called New Yamacraw and finally retired to the Creek Nation.

Yamasee population.—In 1675 Governor Salazar of Florida returned a mission-by-mission estimate of the number of Indians under his jurisdiction and among these the Yamasee, including the Tama, accounted for 1,190. In 1708 the Yamasee, then living in South Carolina, were estimated to have 500 men able to bear arms. The census of 1715 returned 413 warriors and a total population of 1,215. After they removed to Florida, it was reported that the chief of the Yamasee was placed at the head of 500 Indians to be sent against the English, but only part of these were Yamasee. In 1719 a captive reported only 60 near St. Augustine, but in 1726 the Spaniards themselves give 313 in the missions there and in 1728, 144. Figures covering the Indian population about St. Augustine in 1736 indicate that there may have been about 360 so called Yamasee, though this probably included Indians of the Guale province as well. In 1761 a body of Yamasee containing 20 men was living near St. Augustine, but by that time the tribe had probably scattered widely. In 1821 the "Emusas" on Chattahoochee River numbered 20 souls. Mooney estimated that there may have been about 2,000 in all in 1650.

YATASI

This Caddo tribe was reported by Tonti in 1690 to be living on Red River northwest of the Natchitoches, and in one band with the "Natasi" and "Choye." In 1701 Bienville and St. Denis made an alliance with them. When the post of Natchitoches was established, they were being so hard pressed by the Chickasaw that a part of them sought refuge near by while another part fled to the Kadohadacho. Later they reoccupied their old country, but were very much reduced in numbers and left Louisiana for Texas along with the other Caddo of the section, whose fortunes they subsequently followed.

Yatasi population.—In 1700 the number of their warriors was said to be 200, but either this was an overestimate or they fell off very rapidly in the two decades following, since this tribe, the Natchitoches, and the Doustioni together were said to have had but 80 men in 1718. Nevertheless, a year later we get 150–200 souls reported in the group. In 1773 De Mézières reported that there were only 3 Yatasi warriors, but in 1805 Sibley found 8 men and 25 women and children. In 1825 a total of 36 was reported.

YAZOO

In 1682 these Indians were found living on the river which bears their name, and Tonti's account of the tribe here seems to indicate that they may have been in that place for a considerable time, though there is also a possibility that they had once lived higher up the Mississippi and had come down at about the same period as their congeners, the Tunica. In 1702 they were accessory to the murder of the missionary Foucault, and they and the Koroa were always decidedly anti-French in their sentiments. In 1718, if we may trust Pénicaut as to date, Fort St. Peter was established near their town, and in 1722 a plantation was laid out near it by M. de la Tour, in the interest of M. Le Blanc, but it was soon abandoned.

On the outbreak of the Natchez War, they joined the hostile Indians, murdered Father Souel, who had settled among them as missionary in 1727, and massacred the French garrison. Not long afterward, Charlevoix states that the Quapaw fell upon this tribe, the Koroa, and the Tiou, destroying all of the last mentioned and leaving only 15 men of the two others. When the Natchez were fortified on Sicily Island, it is said that the Yazoo and Koroa had a fort by themselves, and we hear that they took part in 1731 in the attack on the Tunica. Afterward they probably withdrew to the Chickasaw or Choctaw and we no longer hear of them. The two Yazoo towns among the Choctaw may have derived their name from the tribe so-called but, if so, it was in the remote prehistoric past.

Yazoo population.—In 1700 Gravier estimated that there were 30 cabins in the Yazoo village, which Du Pratz, 25 or 30 years later, increases to 100. In 1722 La Harpe estimated 250 souls in the Yazoo, Koroa, and Ofo tribes together. In 1730, according to Le Petit, there were 40 warriors in the combined Yazoo and Koroa tribes. (See Tunica.)

YEOPIM

See Weapemeoc, page 206.

YUCHI

These Indians originally consisted of a number of distinct bands, each under an independent name, and we first hear of any of them with certainty under the term Chisca. The people thus designated were living in De Soto's time in the hilly country of eastern Tennessee. De Soto sent two soldiers to the province occupied by them, lured by reports that there was "a forge there for copper, or other metal of that color," which, of course, they hoped to be gold, but, becoming discouraged at the length of the way and the roughness of the roads, these men gave up the quest. After crossing the Mississippi, De Soto was himself lured toward the north, to a province called Pacaha, because it was said to be near this Chisca. It is probable that these stories were true except for the occurrence of gold, for we find somewhat later that there were two bodies of Yuchi Indians in Tennessee, one on the western flanks of the Appalachians or the plateau country beyond, the other on Tennessee River just above Muscle Shoals. The second of these was visited by five Canadians who ascended the Tennessee in the summer of 1701 and found them between a Chickasaw town and the village of a tribe called Taly. After this date they seem to have moved up the river to the territory later comprised in Meigs County, where the "Euchee Old Fields" preserve the name, and still later to a town on Hiwassee River called Tsistuyi, by the Cherokee, but usually entered on the maps as Chestowee. Recent researches by T. M. N. Lewis and his associates render it possible, however, that the valley of the Hiwassee River had been occupied by Yuchi for a long period preceding.

In the meantime the eastern Yuchi had not remained quietly in their home territories. De Soto had merely heard of them, but in 1566 Moyano or Boyano, the lieutenant of Juan Pardo, stormed two stockades held by mountain people, one known to have been Chisca and the other probably of the same tribe. Shortly before 1639 some "Ysicas or Chiscas" had reached the frontiers of Florida, and the Governor of Florida was endeavoring to settle them at a spot where they could be watched and yet would act as protectors of the province. This is probably the band which settled in west Florida somewhat later. At least, in 1674, we learn that three Chisca Indians threatened to interfere with the labors of the missionaries among the Chatot, and it was probably they who committed depredations in and near the Apalachee province immediately after this time and against whom an expedition was undertaken by the Apalachee in 1677 which resulted in the capture of one of their stockaded towns in west Florida and the destruction of many Indians. This band of Yuchi came to be known as the Pea Creek Yuchi, and they later settled among the Upper Creeks. A second wave of Yuchi appeared on the Spanish frontiers in 1661, and it is probably these who came to live near the present Augusta, Ga., some time before 1670; are mentioned by Lederer under the name Oustack, a synonym for Westo; and were visited by Henry Woodward in 1674. War broke out between them and the English in 1680, and the year following a band of Shawnee fell upon them and drove them from the Savannah. They then retired to the Ocmulgee and still later to the Chattahoochee, where their town appears on many eighteenth century maps about the mouth of Little Uchee Creek. In 1673 still another body of Yuchi were living in a stockaded town on one of the head streams of the Tennessee, where they were visited by some white men sent out by Abraham Wood. Wood calls them Tomahittans and informs us that an indentured servant of his named Gabriel Arthur spent some time with them the following year, visiting a Siouan tribe well to the north and accompanying them on a foray against the Spaniards. Some of these were perhaps the Yuchi who were attacked by the Cherokee at Tsistuyi in 1714 and appear upon Savannah River about Uchee Island and Uchee Creek north of Augusta in 1715. In 1716 they removed to the Chattahoochee and settled well down the river not far from the Apalachicola and a band of Shawnee Indians. Later, probably

between 1733 and 1761, they accompanied the Shawnee to Tallapoosa
River, settled on the Coosa above its junction with the Tallapoosa,
and were associated with the Koasati in 1761. They seem to have
extended their settlements as far as McIntosh's Bluff on Tombigbee
River about 1763. This is the band which Hawkins found in 1796
living on Tallapoosa River, 1 league above the Shawnee, and in 1799
living with them. The Pea Creek Yuchi from west Florida had
meantime established themselves near the Tukabahchee. Both disappear from the records in the nineteenth century, and we do not know
whether they were absorbed by the Shawnee and other Upper Creek
people or rejoined their kinsmen. The last influx of Yuchi from the
north or from the Creek Nation took place some time after the Yamasee
War and resulted in the establishment of settlements of the tribe
along Savannah River from Brier Creek down to Ebenezer Creek,
and with settlements at Silver Bluff, on the Ogeechee, and—so Hawkins says—at Saltkechers and Ponpon, though these points seem
rather far east. In 1729 a Kasihta chief, who had married three Yuchi
women, was responsible for bringing part of the tribe to the Chattahoochee to a point at the mouth of Big Uchee Creek, but the rest
of the tribe did not leave the Savannah finally until 1751. Even
after the main body had gone to the Chattahoochee, they maintained
settlements to the eastward in southern Georgia, particularly Intuchculgau on Opilthlucco, a branch of the Flint, Padgeeligau on the
Flint itself, and Toccogulegau on Kinchafoonee Creek. A trader
named Timothy Barnard and his son by a Yuchi woman, Timpoochee
Barnard, played a great part in the later history of the tribe, and the
latter commanded a band of his people in aid of the whites during
the Creek War. As white settlement spread westward, the Yuchi
withdrew to their main town on Chattahoochee River, whither the
Westo had probably gone at an earlier period and possibly the Tallapoosa Yuchi. In 1832 only one main town is entered in the census
of that year, and one branch town called High Log. The Yuchi removed to Oklahoma with the Creeks and established themselves in
the northwestern part of the Creek territory, where they had as many
as three Square Grounds until a very late period and still held themselves aloof in some measure from the Creeks proper. Before the
removal, a small body went to Florida, apparently from the Chattahoochee town, since they first appear on the west side of the peninsula
near the Mikasuki. Later they moved across to Spring Garden east
of Dexters Lake in Volusia County and were under a noted chief
called Uchee Billy. In 1847 there were still some left in Florida,
since an estimate of that year mentions a band of Indians of this tribe
with four warriors. In the Seminole Nation of the west, they never
appear as a distinct element in the population, and if any did go

west they probably rejoined the Creeks. It should be added that a few Yuchi seem never to have moved out of the Appalachian region, but to have remained among the Cherokee and become gradually incorporated with them.

Yuchi population.—The census of 1715 gives two Yuchi towns with 130 men and 400 souls, but, as may be seen above, this included only a small part of the tribe. In 1725 a census taken by Captain Charlesworth Glover returned 180 men, 200 women, and 150 children in the Creek Nation. In 1730 the band still on Tennessee River was supposed to have about 150 men. In 1760, 65 warriors are reported in the Creek Nation, of whom 15 belonged to an Upper Creek town. In 1761 the Yuchi among the Lower Creeks are credited with 50 hunters. In 1774 Bartram estimated that there were 500 warriors and a population of 1,000 to 1,500. In 1792 Marbury reported that the Yuchi could muster 300 men, and in 1799 Hawkins states that they claimed 250, not including the Yuchi among the Upper Creeks. Young's list of Lower Creek and Seminole towns, dated about 1822, includes a single Yuchi settlement with a total population of 130. This was the band which united with the Seminole (see above). In 1832–33 the Creek census reported two towns among the Lower Creeks and a native population of 1,139. In 1909 Speck stated that the Yuchi population in Oklahoma could "hardly exceed 500," but the census of 1910 gives only 78, a figure probably much too low. More nearly correct is believed to be the 216 returned by the census of 1930. Mooney estimated that there may have been about the 1,500 Yuchi in 1650, a figure if anything too low, though it would be more than doubled if the Westo were included.

YUFERA

A tribe or town which seems to have been situated in the seventeenth century on the mainland northwest of the present Cumberland Island, Ga., and was probably a Timucua group, but may have been connected with the Muskogee tribe called Eufaula.

Yufera population.—Unknown.

YUI (SPANISH: IBI)

A Timucua tribe in southeastern Georgia 14 leagues (about 36.5 miles) from Cumberland Island, perhaps near the present Folkston, and containing 5 towns at the beginning of the seventeenth century. It is seldom mentioned, but probably followed the fortunes of the Timucua of Tacatacuru.

Yui population.—In 1602 it is reported to have had a population of 1,000.

YUSTAGA OR HOSTAQUA

A "province" or tribe in northwestern Florida southeast of Aucilla River. The towns of Ossachile and Asile and the Mission of San Matheo were probably within its territories. The name is first applied by Biedma to a province which De Soto traversed in 1539. It appears again in the Laudonnière and Le Moyne narratives as a consolidated tribe hostile to the Apalachee. The name appears once more in the form Ustaqua in a letter dated 1670, but mentioning operations of the year 1659. It is suspected that the Ossachile left this province about 1656 to appear in Creek history under the name Osochi. The subsequent fate of the rest of the tribe or province was probably identical with that of the remainder of the Timucua.

Yustaga population.—In 1675 there were said to be about 40 persons in Asile, about 300 in San Marcos, 300 in Machaba, and 300 in San Pedro. It is suspected that some of these were from the former Timucua province. Mooney's estimate of 1,000 as of the year 1650 would seem not to be excessive.

INTERPRETATIONS OF TRIBAL NAMES

The following tribal names are the only ones for which we are able to suggest interpretations:

Abihka. Stiggins states that they got their name from the peculiar use of an affirmative particle āw̄ instead of c̄āw̄ used by the rest of the nation. Later a folk-explanation was given referring to a supposed event in the past history of the tribe.

Acolapissa. Meaning in Choctaw "those who hear and see," and having reference perhaps to a border tribe that may have acted as scouts.

Akokisa. The terminal –isa is for ishak, "people," and the whole may mean "western people," or "river people." (Atakapa language.)

Alabama. Possibly meaning "medicine gatherers," or "thicket clearers." It may contain the word albina, "to camp." (Alabama language.)

Apalachee. Meaning "people on the other side" (of a river presumably), or "allies."

Apalachicola. From Muskhogean dialects and signifies "people of the other side," with reference probably to the Apalachicola River or some neighboring stream.

Atakapa. Meaning in Choctaw "man eaters," "cannibals."

Avoyel. Meaning "people of the rocks," or "flint people." (Avoyel or Natchez language.)

Bayogoula. Meaning in Choctaw and Chickasaw "people of the bayou," with reference either to their location or to their totem animal, the alligator.

Bidai. Perhaps from a Caddo term signifying "brushwood," and having reference to the Big Thicket about which they lived.

Biloxi. Probably a corruption of the native name of this tribe taneks aⁿya, "first people."

Caddo. A contraction of Kadohadacho, the name of a leading Caddo tribe. The term signifies "true chiefs."

Calusa. Fontaneda, who was a captive among them, says it signifies "a fierce people", but the correctness of this can neither be affirmed nor denied.

Cape Fear Indians. From the Cape and River so called; native name unknown.

Catawba. Significance unknown, but a part of the tribe was known as Iswa, "river" people. Speck has suggested derivation from native words meaning "people of the river banks," or "people of the river (Catawba) with broken banks," and I have suggested a possible derivation from a word meaning "a fork," this tribe being considered a branch of the Iswa.

Chakchiuma. From Choctaw and Chickasaw shâktci homma, "red crawfish."

Chawasha. The ending is undoubtedly the Choctaw and Chickasaw locative terminal -asha. The first part might be from shawi, "raccoon."

Cherokee. Probably from the Muskogee word tciloki, "people of a different speech."

Chiaha. Possibly has reference to mountains or highlands in some Muskhogean dialect.

Chickasaw. The ending is evidently asha, "to sit," used as a locative suffix (own language).

Chilucan. Possibly from Muskogee tciloki, "people of a different speech."

Chine. Derived from the name of a chief.

Chitimacha. The term probably means in Chitimacha "those living on Grand River," though Gatschet identified it with Choctaw words meaning "those who have pots."

Choula. Meaning "fox" in Chickasaw and Choctaw.

Chowanoc. Algonquian, signifying "people at the south."

Congaree. Speck derives this from Catawba (iswan') keran'here, "(river) deep."

Coosa. Said to have received its name from a little bird called from its cry koskosa, but it is more likely that it was connected with the Choctaw and Chickasaw word for cane, konshak, though how it came to be applied to Creek Indians remains a mystery.

Cosapuya. This may be a form of Cusabo, q. v.

Creek Confederation. The name "Creek" resulted from a shortening of "Ochesee Creek," the name by which Ocmulgee River was known to the English. Ochesee was a name of the Muskogee or true Creek Indians in the Hitchiti language.

Cusabo. Possibly signifies "Coosa River people" (own language).

Eno. Speck points to a possible connection with Catawba i'nare, "to dislike," whence "mean," "contemptible," as being enemies to the speakers.

Fus-hatchee. Said by Hawkins to signify "bird tail," but it was more likely "bird creek." (Muskogee language.)

Grigra. Said by Le Page du Pratz to be so named because of the frequent occurrence of these syllables in their language.

Guale. Possibly from the Muskogee word wahali, signifying "the south."

Hilibi. Derived by folk etymology from Muskogee hilikpi, "quick" town, and, as usual in such cases, probably erroneously.

Hitchiti. Possibly a corruption of Atcik-hata, a name given to the Hitchiti-speaking people among the Lower Creeks. It is said to have reference to the heap of white ashes piled close to the ceremonial ground.

Hothliwahali. Meaning "those who share out the war," because declarations of war were sent out from this town. (Muskogee language.)

Houma. Meaning "red" in Choctaw and Chickasaw, but probably shortened from Chakchiuma above.

Ibitoupa. Meaning in Choctaw people living "at the source" of a stream.

Kadohadacho. Meaning in their own language "true chiefs."

Kan-hatki. Meaning "white earth." (Muskogee language.)

Kaskinampo. Possibly from Koasati words meaning "many warriors."

Kealedji. With considerable probability, interpreted by Dr. Gatschet as referring in Muskogee to a warrior's headdress.

Kolomi. Meaning perhaps "where there are white oaks." (Muskogee language.)

Machapunga. Algonquian significance "bad dust" or possibly "much dust."

Manahoac. Tooker interprets it to mean "they are very merry," but this seems improbable.

Michigamea. Meaning in Algonquian "great water."

Mikasuki. This may contain the Muskogee word miko, signifying "chief."

Mobile. Possibly from the Choctaw word moeli, "to paddle."

Monacan. Possibly from an Algonquian word signifying "digging stick," or "spade" (Heckewelder), but this is doubtful. Speck suggests an origin from the Tutelo words amāñ(i) (y)ukhan, "people of the land." However, the first two syllables may be meant for mani, "water." Strachey thought that it might be from Powhatan monohacan or monowhauk, "sword."

Moneton. Meaning in their own (Siouan) language "big water."

Muklasa. Meaning "friends," or "people of one nation." (Alabama language.)

Muskogee. This is thought to have been derived from Shawnee or some other Algonquian language, and to refer to swampy ground.

Nabedache. Perhaps signifying "place of salt." (Caddo language.)

Napochi. Perhaps from a dialectic variant of the Choctaw and Chickasaw word Napissa, "those who see, or look out."

Natchitoches. Said to be from Caddo nàshitōsh, "pawpaws," but a Spanish source has it from "nascicit, a place where the soil is the color of red ochre."

Nottoway. From their Algonquian neighbors and signifying "adders."

Occaneechi. Speck suggests an origin from Tutelo yuhkañ, "man."

Ofo. Perhaps a contraction of Choctaw Ofogoula, "Dog People."

Okchai. Possibly from Okchaⁿya, "life" in Alabama.

Okelousa. Meaning "black water" in Choctaw and Chickasaw.

Okmulgee. Signifies "where water boils up," as in a spring, in Hitchiti.

Opelousa. From Choctaw and Chickasaw aba lusa, "black above," that is, "black headed," or "black haired."

Pakana. Hawkins says this means "may apple," but the word now means "peach." (Muskogee language.)

Pascagoula. Meaning "Bread People" in Choctaw and Chickasaw.

Pedee. Speck cites the following Catawba words as containing suggestions of its possible meaning: pi'ri, "something good," pīhere, "smart," "expert," "capable."

Pensacola. Choctaw word signifying "Hair People" because apparently the men wore their hair at full length.

Pilthlako. Meaning in the Creek language "big swamp."

Powhatan. Signifies in the native language "falls in a current of water."

Quapaw. Meaning "people living down stream," in their own dialect of Siouan.

Quinipissa. Meaning "those who see" in Choctaw and Chickasaw, and perhaps designating "outposts" or "scouts."

Santee. Gatschet connected this name with Catawba sa'nta or soⁿ'ta, "to run," but Speck traces it to iswaⁿ'ti, "the river," or "river is there." It sometimes appears in the form Seretee.

Sawokli. It has the ending okli which signifies "people" and the first part may mean "raccoon." (Hitchiti language.)

Seminole. People living at a distance from the settled towns and hence sometimes called "renegades" in Muskogee, but the word does not necessarily carry an opprobrious signification.

Sewee. Gatschet's derivation in this case, from sāwe[n]', "island," seems more probable than the terms adduced by Speck, ye[n] sewi'here, "playing people," and si'wi, "a flower or blossom." (Catawba language.)

Shakori. See Sugeree.

Shawnee. Meaning in Algonquian dialects "southerners."

Stegaraki. A branch of the Mannahoac; the term may, as suggested by Speck, contain the Tutelo word for "island," histēk or stēk.

Sugeree. Speck derives this name from Catawba ye[n]si'grihere, "people stingy," or "spoiled," or "of the river whose-water-cannot-be-drunk." He opens the question of a relationship between the name of this tribe and that of the Shakori which I heartily endorse.

Tacatacuru. Significance unknown, though the first element may be the Timucua word for "fire."

Tangipahoa. Meaning in Choctaw "corn gatherers," or "corncob people."

Tohome. The French commander Iberville gave the meaning of this as "Little Chief," but this is evidently an error. It is more likely to be connected with the Choctaw word meaning "white," or "shining."

Tukabahchee. The first part of the name appears to contain the Creek word tutka, "fire."

Tunica. Meaning in their own language "the people," or "those who are the people."

Tuscarora. According to Hewitt, from their native term signifying "hemp gatherers," because they made great use of *Apocynum cannabinum.*

Tuskegee. It is probable that this contains the Choctaw and Alabama word for "warrior," taska.

Tutelo. Meaning unknown, but applied by the Iroquois, who seem to have taken it from the speech of some southern tribe.

Utina. Meaning in Timucua "powerful," and containing possibly the word for "earth," uti.

Wakokai. Meaning in Muskogee "blue heron breeding place."

Washa. Perhaps from Choctaw and Chickasaw words meaning "where they hunted," or "hunting place."

Wateree. Gatschet suggests connection with the Catawba word wateran, "to float on the water," which Speck accepts but says that its full form seems to be ye[n] iswa[n]' watera'here, "people (of the) river of banks washed away."

Wiwohka. Meaning in Creek "roaring water."

Yuchi. Speck derives this from a native word signifying "far away," but it is more likely a form of the Hitchiti term Ochese, which was also applied to the Creeks and means "people of another language."

Yufera. This may be a form of Eufaula, or Yufala, in the Timucua dialect.

PHYSICAL AND MENTAL CHARACTERISTICS

No extensive review of modern studies is contemplated under this heading, but merely a record of the estimates of earlier visitors in the Southeast who received their impressions when the aborigines of the section were in a relatively primitive condition. Hrdlička has reported two physical types, one long-headed, found represented in later times on and near the Atlantic seaboard, but extending anciently as far as Louisiana; and a broad-headed type most conspicuous along the Mississippi, where it reached far enough north to include the Winnebago and comprised several other Siouan and several Caddoan tribes as well as the river tribes within the area itself. The affiliations of the Indians of the first type are with the dolichocephalic peoples in northeastern North America, while the brachycephals are believed to have had connections in the direction of Mexico. (Boas, 1895; Hrdlička, 1922; Collins, 1941.)

Krogman's summary of the results of his study of the Seminole Indians of Oklahoma probably gives us the best idea of the characteristics of these Indians in modern times, as well as of the Creeks.

The Seminole is *tall*, though not among the tallest of the American Indians. This is more true of males than of females. The *sitting height* is short relative to body and leg length. The Seminole is slightly longer-legged than Whites, especially in the proportionate length of the lower leg. His *shoulders* are relatively narrow, his *chest* is of average depth—nearer White than Negro—and his *hips* are wide. There is a pronunced tendency to take on weight during and after the fifth decade of life.

In his *head* proportions the Seminole offers an average length and breadth, a minimum frontal diameter slightly above average, and a low head, though not so low as the Sioux. The *cephalic index* is mesocephalic or sub-brachycephalic.

The *width of the face* across the zygomatic arches is typical of the American Indians, though not so pronounced as among the Plains Indians. The female possesses a relatively broader face, but in both sexes the lower face is rather broad. The *interocular breadth* is nearer White than Negro. The *facial height* is average, both total and upper, with lower face slightly below average. The *nose* is mesorrhinic, but small—smaller than the Sioux. Nasal breadth is intermediate between White and Negro. The *ear* is small and in its proportions is more White than Negro. The *mouth* is wide, typical of the American Indian, but lip height is more than among Whites and average Indians, and less than for the Negro.

The *arm* is of average length, but the forearm is relatively long, even more so than among the Negroes. The *hand* is smaller than among the Sioux and is longer and narrower than among other Indians. *Middle finger* length is intermediate between Whites and Negro.

The *leg* is relatively long, with lower leg accentuated. The *foot* is typically Indian—long and wide—but smaller than the Sioux.

The *arm-leg* proportions are nearer White than Negro. The leg is relatively long compared to arm, a bit more pronounced than among Whites.

The Seminole, then, is essentially Indian in his body proportions. As is true among American Indians in general, the majority of Seminole anthropomorphic characteristics, where not absolutely definitive for the Mongoloid type, are intermediate between White and Negro, rather nearer the former in most of the observations . . .

In all essential details the Seminole female reveals sex differences asserted by Hrdlička for the Sioux and Davenport and Steggerda for the Jamaica Negro. . . .

(Here follow tables of comparative measurements of Seminole, Sioux (Hrdlička), and Jamaica Negro (Davenport), and a comparison of Seminole, Creek, and the offspring of Seminole and Creek intermarriage. And he continues:

In practically every measurement observed differences are well within the S. D. calculated for the Seminoles and are almost certainly due to size of sample. The data corroborate an impression gained in the field; that the Seminole type and the Creek type are substantially identical. The Creek was a bit darker on the average; and we saw far more Creeks in whom Negro blood was evident, than among Seminoles. But, disregarding these more or less extraneous factors, the conclusion as to extremely close physical kinship seems warranted. . . .

In his head and face measurements the Seminole is, on the average, slightly more variable than the compared groups: "pure-blood" Sioux, W. R. U. White, W. R. U. Negro, American Negroes, Jamaica Negroes, and native Hawaiians. If this be analyzed it will be found that face is more variable than cranium, which is due, in large part, to the number of smaller measurements where variability is bound to be greater. The apparent relative nonhomogeneity is thus explained.

The Seminole cranium was basically brachycephalic, until the introduction of an oblong-headed element presumably ultimately derived from the Algonkian stock. This may have resulted in a trend toward longer-headedness, i. e., sub-brachycephaly or mesocephaly. This head type, however, was still very different from the pronounced dolichocephaly of the Negro and the long-headedness of the White (mostly Scotch) element presumed to enter in as the result of intermixture. If, then, these two differing types, i. e., round- and long-headedness, were to mix, the variability of the resultant population would be quite high. Actually, I do not consider the relative variability of the Seminole head and face measurements to be great enough to allow any pronounced impact by other groups. If there has been mixture it has been (a) comparatively slight; and (b) rather remote in time, to permit breeding out . . .

If, now, we turn to body and appendicular measurement we find the Seminole apparently even more variable. His general average variability of 6.44 is approached only by the Jamaica Negro, with an average of 5.78. The greater variability of the Seminole is rather consistent for body, arm, and leg (except that the variability of acromial and cristal breadths is probably due to individual tendencies to put on weight). I must point out that some of the variability is attributable to the so-called "compensatory variability," (operating, of course, in all the groups). Specifically, however, for the Seminoles the greater variability is attributable in a measure to the fact that all of the subjects were fully clothed and some of them rather heavily so; and that the data were collected by four different observers, so that individual error certainly is an important factor.

Insofar as the coefficient of variability can be used as a measure of homogeneity, and considering the data offered for relatively homogeneous groups, it may be concluded that the sample of male full-blood Seminole possesses a unity arguing for a minimum amount of mixture. (Krogman, 1935, pp. 101–108.)

More recently Neumann has reported two long-headed primary physical types in the Southeast which appeared early and persisted into historic times, and round-headed people who made their appearance later and became prominent only at a relatively recent date.

In the future it is to be hoped still more accurate and still more extensive data will be collected by somatologists and that their work will be supplemented by that of trained psychologists. Pending such studies, perhaps nothing more should be entered here under this heading. However, in view of the fact that aboriginal conditions have absolutely disappeared, that the remaining Indians have mixed extensively with representatives of other races, and that their mentality has been subjected to more far-reaching influences still, I believe there is a certain value in reproducing the impressions made by the relatively uncontaminated Gulf peoples on the more intelligent white men who first encountered them. The absolute value of such opinions is, of course, limited. When representatives of two different peoples meet, they waste no time in making an estimate of each other's physical, mental, and moral equipment, but if these peoples are of cultures widely diverse, one of which belongs to a disappearing culture without the means of spreading its own impressions broadcast or transmitting them to posterity, while the other is advancing and embraces all such facilities, the picture which the student receives is similar to that which a jury would have in a case in which only one side is represented. The judgments are based upon a single set of standards assumed to represent the normal, natural, and right, and this is as true of those who, like Tacitus or Rousseau, idealize the less cultured race as of downright detractors of it. In both situations the standards are the same, except that the one party attributes these to the race which it extols while the other denies that it possesses them. Obviously the standards of neither, the standards of no race, furnish a fixed basis for comparison. All we can attempt is to get the relative assumed differences between the peoples under discussion and try to allocate to them their proper positions, still relative, among the peoples of the earth taken as a whole.

First, I will insert a few quotations bearing mainly on the physical types of the Southeastern Indians.

Seeking to describe the Powhatan Indians, Strachey says:

Their haire is black, grosse, long, and thick; the men have no beardes; their noses are broad, flatt, and full at the end, great bigg lippes, and wyde mouthes, yet nothing so unsightly as the Moores; they are generally tall of stature, and streight, of comely proportion, and the women have handsome lymbes, sclender armes, and pretty hands, and when they sing they have a pleasaunt tange in their voices. (Strachey, 1849, p. 64.)

The Spanish monk, Andreas de San Miguel, gives us the following short note regarding the Indians of the Guale province about St. Simons Island, Ga., in 1595:

All commonly are very healthy, swift of foot, and have very good figures and good limbs: their color is like that of the Indians of this land [Mexico] and some are whiter, especially the Indian women; generally they are tall, equally agile and it is said that, after wounding a deer, they run after it so swiftly as not to lose sight of it. (Garcia, 1902, p. 194.)

Speaking of the related Creeks, Swan says:

The men, in general, are of a good size, stout, athletic and handsome: the women are also of good height, but coarse, thick-necked and ugly. Being condemned, by the custom of the country, to carry burdens, pound corn, and perform all the hard labor, they are universally masculine in appearance, without one soft blandishment to render them desirable or lovely. (Swan, 1855, p. 274.)

The traveler and botanist William Bartram was of a somewhat romantic type and his conclusions differ from those of Swan accordingly. In the appendix to the first London edition of his Travels he has the following general account of the southern Indians:

The males of the Cherokees, Muscogulges, Siminoles, Chickasaws, Chactaws, and confederate tribes of the Creeks, are tall, erect, and moderately robust; their limbs well shaped, so as generally to form a perfect human figure; their features regular, and countenance open, dignified and placid; yet the forehead and brow so formed, as to strike you instantly with heroism and bravery; the eye though rather small, yet active and full of fire; the iris always black, and the nose commonly inclining to the aquiline.

Their countenance and actions exhibit an air of magnanimity, superiority and independence.

Their complexion, of a reddish brown or copper colour; their hair long, lank, coarse, and black as a raven, and reflecting the like lustre at different exposures to the light.

The women of the Cherokees, are tall, slender, erect and of a delicate frame; their features formed with perfect symmetry, their countenance cheerful and friendly, and they move with a becoming grace and dignity.

The Muscogulge women, though remarkably short of stature, are well formed; their visage round, features regular and beautiful; the brow high and arched; the eye large, black and languishing, expressive of modesty, diffidence, and bashfulness; these charms are their defensive and offensive weapons, and they know very well how to play them off, and under cover of these alluring graces, are concealed the most subtile artifice; they are however loving and affectionate; they are, I believe, the smallest race of women yet known, seldom above five feet high, and I believe the greater number never arrive to that stature; their hands and feet not larger than those of Europeans of nine or ten years of age; yet the men are of gigantic stature, a full size larger than Europeans, many of them above six feet, and few under that, or five feet eight or ten inches. Their complexion much darker than any of the tribes to the North of them that I have seen. This description will I believe comprehend the Muscogulges, their confederates, the Chactaws, and I believe the Chicasaws (though I have never seen their women) excepting however some bands of the Siminoles, Uches and Savannucas, who are rather taller and slenderer, and their complexion brighter.

The Cherokees are yet taller and more robust than the Muscogulges, and by far the largest race of men I have seen; their complexions brighter and somewhat of the olive cast, especially the adults; and some of their young women are nearly as fair and blooming as European women. (Bartram, 1792, pp. 481–483.)

A more succinct statement is contained in his paper on the Creek and Cherokee Indians (1909). It is as follows:

The Cherokees are the largest race of men I ever saw. They are as comely as any, and their complexions are very bright, being of the olive cast of the Asiatics; this is the obvious reason which I suppose led the traders to give them the by-name of the Breeds, supposing them to be mixed with the white people. But though some of them are evidently adulterated by the traders, yet the natural complexion is tawny.

The women are tall, slim, and of a graceful figure, and have captivating features and manners, and I think their complexion is rather fairer than the men's.

The *Muscogulges* are in stature nearly equal to the Cherokees, have fine features, and are every way handsome men. Their noses are very often aquiline; they are well limbed, countenances upright, and their eyes brisk and fiery; but their complexions are of a dark copper color.

Their women are very small, in appearance not more than half the size of the men; but they have regular and beautiful features, the eyes large, with high-arched eyebrows, and their complexions little, if any, brighter than those of the men.

There are some tribes in the confederacy which much resemble the Cherokees, in stature and color, etc., viz.: the *Uches*, *Savannahs*, and some of the Seminoles.

I have seen Indian infants of a few weeks old; their color was like that of a healthy, male, European countryman or laborer of middle age, though inclining a little more to the red or copper tinge; but they soon become of the Indian copper. I believe this change comes naturally, as I never, from constant inquiry, could learn that the Indians had any artificial means of changing their color. . . .

I have never heard of any white, speckled, or pied people among them.

[Bartram also comments on] the lankness, extraordinary natural length, and perhaps coarseness of the hair of the head [and its] shining black or brown color, [but states that he has seen the hair of the extreme aged] as white as cotton wool. (Bartram, 1909, pp. 28–29.)

Timberlake considered the Cherokee merely "of a middle stature, and of an olive color, tho' generally painted, and their skins stained with gunpowder." (Timberlake, 1765, p. 75.)

Adair, whose knowledge of these Indians was anterior to, and much more intimate than those of Swan and Bartram, says:

As the American Indians are of a reddish or copper colour—so in general they are strong, well proportioned in body and limbs, surprisingly active and nimble, and hardy in their own way of living. . . .

It is remarkable that there are no deformed Indians—however, they are generally weaker, and smaller bodied, between the tropics, than in the higher latitudes; but not in equal proportion: for, though the Chikkasah and Choktah countries have not been long divided from each other, as appears by the similarity of their language, as well as other things, yet the Chikkasah are exceedingly taller, and stronger bodied than the latter, though their country is only two degrees farther north. Such a small difference of latitude, in so healthy a region could not make so wide a difference in the constitution of their bodies. The former are a comely, pleasant looking people; their faces are tolerably round, contrary to the visage of the others, which inclines much to flatness, as in the case of most of the other Indian Americans. The lips of the Indians, in general, are thin.

Their eyes are small, sharp, and black; and their hair is lank, coarse, and darkish. I never saw any with curled hair, but one in the Choktah country, where was also another with red hair; probably they were a mixture of the French and Indians. (Adair, 1775, pp. 4–6.)

Elsewhere this author maintains the familiar thesis that "the hotter or colder the climate is, where the Indians have long resided, the greater proportion have they either of the red, or white, color." And he adds:

I took particular notice of the Shawano Indians, as they were passing from the northward, within fifty miles of the Chikkasah country, to that of the Creeks; and by comparing them with the Indians which I accompanied to their camp, I observed the Shawano to be much fairer than the Chikkasah. [In another place we read:] The Choktah are in general more slender than any other nation of savages I have seen. They are raw-boned, and surprisingly active in ball-playing. (Adair, 1775, pp. 4, 307–308.)

It is to be noted that Speck's opinion regarding the relative physical characteristics of the Creek and Yuchi agrees with that of Bartram:

It is noticeable that there exists a slight difference in physical appearance between the two peoples. The Yuchi are a little more inclined to be tall and slender than the Creeks and their skin is a trifle lighter in tone.

He suggests that this difference may be owing to the higher percentage of Negro blood among the Creeks, but from the older writers it would seem that it represents an actual divergence of long standing (Speck, 1909, p. 12). I have not seen enough Yuchi to venture a judgment myself, but have always felt the Creeks to be intermediate in type between the Cherokee and Choctaw. If, as I suspect, the Creek and Chickasaw types agree, my judgment regarding the divergence of Choctaw would coincide with that of Adair.

Coming down to the Seminole Indians of Florida as observed by MacCauley 50 years ago, it is interesting to note the repetition of some comments made by much earlier writers, such as that referring to the small stature of Creek women:

Physically both men and women are remarkable. The men, as a rule, attract attention by their height, fullness and symmetry of development, and the regularity and agreeableness of their features. In muscular power and constitutional ability to endure they excel. While these qualities distinguish, with a few exceptions, the men of the whole tribe, they are particularly characteristic of the two most widely spread of the families of which the tribe is composed. These are the Tiger and Otter clans, which, proud of their lines of descent, have been preserved through a long and tragic past with exceptional freedom from admixture with degrading blood. To-day their men might be taken as types of physical excellence. The physique of every Tiger warrior especially I met would furnish proof of this statement. The Tigers are dark, copper-colored fellows, over six feet in height, with limbs in good proportion; their hands and feet well shaped and not very large; their stature erect; their bearing a sign of self-confident power; their movements deliberate, persistent, strong. Their heads are large, and their foreheads full and marked. An almost universal characteristic of the Tiger's face is its squareness, a widened and protruding under jawbone giving this effect to it. Of other features, I noticed that under a very large forehead are deep set, bright, black eyes, small, but expressive of inquiry and vigilance; the nose is slightly aquiline and sensitively formed about the nostrils; the lips are mobile, sensuous, and not very full, disclosing, when they smile, beautiful regular teeth; and the whole face is expressive of the man's sense of having extraordinary ability to endure and to achieve. Two of the warriors permitted me to manipulate the muscles of their bodies. Under my touch these were more like rubber than flesh. Noticeable among all are the large calves of their legs, the size of the tendons of their lower limbs, and the strength of their toes. I attribute this exceptional development to the fact that they are not what we would call "horse Indians" and that they hunt barefoot over their wide domain. The same causes, perhaps, account for the only real deformity I noticed in the Seminole physique, namely, the diminutive toe nails, and for the heavy, cracked, and seamed skin which covers the soles of their feet. The feet being otherwise well formed, the toes have only narrow shells for nails, these lying shrunken across the middles of the tough cushions of flesh, which, protuberant about them, form the toe-tips. But, regarded as a whole, in their physique the Seminole warriors, especially the men of the Tiger and Otter gentes, are admirable. Even among the children this physical superiority is seen. To illustrate, one morning Ko-i-ha-tco's son, Tin-fai-yai-kaix, a tall, slender boy, not quite twelve years old, shouldered a heavy "Kentucky" rifle, left our camp, and followed in his father's long footsteps for a day's hunt. After tramping all day, at sunset he reappeared in the camp, carrying slung across his shoulders, in addition to rifle and accouterments, a deer weighing perhaps fifty pounds, a weight he had borne for miles. The same boy, in one day, went with some older friends to his permanent home, 20 miles away, and returned. There are, as I have said, exceptions to this rule of unusual physical size and strength, but these are few; so few that, disregarding them, we may pronounce the Seminole men handsome and exceptionally powerful.

The women to a large extent share the qualities of the men. Some are proportionately tall and handsome, though, curiously enough, many, perhaps a majority, are rather under than over the average height of women. As a rule, they exhibit great bodily vigor. Large or small, they possess regular and agreeable features, shapely and well developed bodies, and they show themselves capable of long continued and severe physical exertion. Indeed, the only Indian women I have seen with attractive features and forms are among the Seminole. I would even venture to select from among these Indians three persons whom I could, without much fear of contradiction, present as types respectively of a handsome, a pretty, and a comely woman. Among American Indians, I am confident that the Seminole women are of the first rank. (MacCauley, 1887, pp. 481–482.)

Unfortunately MacCauley does not inform us as to which members of the several clans belonged to the Mikasuki division and which to the Muskogee division. It is to be suspected that the physical differences he attributes to clans belonged rather to bands.

Let us now hear Lawson's description of the Indians of North Carolina, meaning particularly the Siouan tribes and the Tuscarora:

The Indians of North Carolina are a well shaped clean made people, of different statures, as the Europeans are, yet chiefly inclined to be tall. They are very straight people, and never bend forward or stoop in the shoulders, unless much overpowered by old age. Their limbs are exceeding well shaped.

As for their legs and feet, they are generally the handsomest in the world. Their bodies are a little flat, which is occasioned by being laced hard down to a board in their infancy . . . Their eyes are black, or of a dark hazel; the white is marbled with red streaks, which is ever common to those people, unless when sprung from a white father or mother. Their color is of a tawny, which would not be so dark did they not dawb themselves with bear's oil, and a color like burnt cork. This is begun in their infancy and continued for a long time, which fills the pores and enables them better to endure the extremity of the weather. They are never bald on their heads, although never so old, which, I believe, proceeds from their heads being always uncovered, and the greasing their hair, so often as they do, with bear's fat, which is a great nourisher of the hair, and causes it to grow very fast. . . .

Their eyes are commonly full and manly, and their gate sedate and majestic. They never walk backward and forward as we do, nor contemplate on the affairs of loss and gain, the things which daily perplex us. They are dextrous and steady, both as to their hands and feet, to admiration. They will walk over deep brooks and creeks on the smallest poles, and that without any fear or concern. Nay, an Indian will walk on the ridge of a barn or house and look down the gable end, and spit upon the ground as unconcerned as if he was walking on terra firma. In running, leaping or any such other exercise, their legs seldom miscarry and give them a fall; and as for letting anything fall out of their hands, I never yet knew one example. . . . I never saw a dwarf among them, nor but one that was hump-backed. . . .

They have no hairs on their faces, except some few, and those but little, nor is there often found any hair under their arm pits. They are continually plucking it away from their faces by the roots. As for their privities, since they wore tail clouts to cover their nakedness, several of the men have a deal of hair thereon. . . . Although we reckon these a very smooth people, and free from hair; yet I once saw a middle aged man that was hairy all down his back; the hairs being above an inch long.

As there are found very few, or scarce any, deformed or cripples amongst them, so neither did I ever see but one blind man; and then they would give me no account how his blindness came. . . . No people have better eyes, or see better in the night or day than the Indians. . . .

They are not of so robust and strong bodies as to lift great burdens, and endure labor and slavish work, as the Europeans are; yet some that are slaves, prove very good and laborious; but, of themselves, they never work as the English do, taking care for no farther than what is absolutely necessary to support life. In traveling and hunting, they are very indefatigable, because that carries a pleasure along with a profit. I have known some of them very strong; and as for running and leaping, they are extraordinary fellows, and will dance for several nights together with the greatest briskness imaginable, their wind never failing them. (Lawson, 1860, pp. 280–284; cf. p. 103.)

As for the Indian women which now happen in my way, when young and at maturity, they are as fine shaped creatures, take them generally, as any in the universe. They are of a tawny complexion, their eyes very brisk and amorous, their smiles afford the finest composure a face can possess, their hands are of the finest make, with small, long fingers, and as soft as their cheeks, and their whole bodies of a smooth nature. They are not so uncouth or unlikely as we suppose them. (Lawson, 1860, p. 299.)

In spite of what he says about the keenness of vision and physical perfection of these Indians, Lawson came upon a town called "the

Lower-Quarter" where most of the inhabitants had but one eye. He could obtain no explanation of the fact. Only one case of total blindness came to his attention, "and then they would give me no account how his blindness came. They had a use for him, which was to lead him with a girl, woman or boy, by a string; so they put what burdens they pleased upon his back, and made him very serviceable upon all such occasions." He happened to see no left-handed men among them. (Lawson, 1860, pp. 99, 283, 330.)

Catesby's account is partly based on his own experience, partly derived from Lawson:

The Indians of Carolina are generally tall, and well shap'd, with well-proportioned limbs, though their wrists are small, their fingers long and slender; their faces are rather broad, yet have good features and manly aspects; their noses are not flat, nor their lips too thick; their eyes are black, and placed wide from one another; their hair is black, lank, and very coarse, approaching to the substance of horsehair; the colour of their skin is tawny, yet would not be so dark did they not daub themselves over with Bear's oyl continually from their infancy, mixing therewith some vegetable juices, particularly that of the *Sanguinaria*, figured in *Hort. Elt.* p. 334, Vol. II. The women before marriage are generally finely shaped, and many of them have pretty features. No people have stronger eyes, or see better in the night or day than *Indians*, though in their houses they live in perpetual smoke; their beards are naturally very thin of hair, which they are continually plucking away by the roots; . . . they have generally good teeth, and a sweet breath. There are few amongst these *Americans* so robust, and of so athletick a form as is amongst *Europeans*, nor are they so capable of lifting great burthens, and enduring so hard labour; but in hunting they are indefatigable, and will travel further, and endure more fatigue than a *European* is capable of. In this employment their women serve instead of pack-horses, carrying the skins of the Deer they kill, which by much practice they perform with incredible labour and patience. I have often travelled with them 15 and 20 miles a day for many days successively, each woman carrying at least 60, and some above 80 weight at their back.

Running and leaping these Savages perform with surpassing agility. They are naturally a very sweet people, their bodies emitting nothing of that rankness that is so remarkable in Negroes; and as in travelling I have been sometimes necessitated to sleep with them, I never perceived any ill smell; and though their cabbins are never paved nor swept, and kept with the utmost neglect and slovenliness, yet are void of those stinks or unsavory smells that we meet with in the dwellings of our poor and indolent. (Catesby, 1731–43, vol. 2, p. VIII.)

Du Pratz thus describes the Indians he had met along the lower course of the Mississippi River, his intimacy with the Natchez having been closest:

All the natives of America in general are very well formed. One sees few under 5½ feet, and many taller. The leg is made as if in a mold. It is sinewy and the flesh on it firm. They have long thighs, the head erect and a little flat on top. Their features are regular. They have black eyes, and hair of the same color, coarse and straight. If one never sees those who are extremely fat, no more does he see those as thin as consumptives. The men are ordinarily better formed than the women. They are more sinewy and the women more fleshy.

The men are all tall and the women of medium height, but both are well enough proportioned in figure and height, there being none, as in Europe, of gigantic stature or as short as dwarfs. I have seen a single person who was only 4½ feet high and who, although well proportioned, dared not appear among the French until three or four years after their arrival, and then he would not have done so had not some Frenchmen accidentally discovered him. (Le Page du Pratz, 1758, vol. 2, pp. 308–309; Swanton, 1911, pp. 48–49.)

Adair had also met one dwarf "in Ishtatoe (Estatoee), a northern town of the middle part of the Cheerake country,—and he was a great beloved man" (Adair, 1775, p. 213). Atakullakulla, the Little Carpenter, the most famous Cherokee chief of the eighteenth century, was also of exceptionally small stature. Possibly he was identical with "the great beloved man" just mentioned.

To the Spanish writers, the Caddo appeared tall and robust, and fairer than those they were acquainted with, but Mooney considered them "rather smaller and darker than the neighboring prairie tribes," and the Omaha called them "Black Pawnee." (Swanton, 1942, p. 122.)

When we turn to a more particular consideration of the mental and moral qualities of these Indians, we are on still more uncertain ground, the differences which appear and which are commented on by our various authorities being attributable not so much to collective variations in badness or goodness but to environment and the relative opportunities for advancement enjoyed by the peoples being compared. This the writers of that time were usually quite incapable of realizing and they classified their subjects as good or bad in proportion to the agreement between the standards extant among them and those with which they themselves were familiar.

Strachey's evaluation of the Virginia Indians was as follows:

They are inconstant in everything but what feare constraineth them to keepe; crafty, tymerous, quick of apprehension, ingenious enough in their own workes [as is testified to by their various inventions and arts]. Some of them are of disposition fearefull (as I said) and not easily wrought, therefore, to trust us or come unto our forts; others, againe, of them are so bold and audacyous, as they dare come into our forts, truck and trade with us, and looke us in the face, crying all freinds when they have but new done us a mischief, and when they intend presently againe, yf it lye in their power, to doe the like. They are generally covetous of our comodityes, as copper, white beads for their women, hatchetts, of which we make them poore ones, of iron howes to pare their corne grownd, knives, and such like.

They are soone moved to anger, and so malitious that they seldome forgett an injury; they are very thievish, and will as closely as they can convey any thing away from us; howebe yt, they seldome steale one from another, lest their connivres should revele yt, and so they be pursued and punished. That they are thus feared yt is certaine, nor lett any man doubt that the divell cannot reveile an offence actually committed. (Strachey, 1849, p. 68–69.)

Swan, the government agent, is naturally struck by those characteristics which interfered with the execution of his mission:

The Indians are credulous. Enveloped in dark ignorance, and shut out from all communion with the enlightened world, the few of them that have a desire for knowledge are deprived of the means of obtaining it. They are naturally fickle, inconstant, and excessively jealous of the encroachments of the white people. They easily become the dupes of the traders that live in their towns, who have established so complete an ascendency over them, that, whatever they tell them is implicitly believed, until contradicted by some more artful story. Thus situated, it is in the power of an ignorant vagabond trader, at anytime, over a pipe and a cup of black-drink, to persuade them that the most solemn treaty is no more than a well-covered plot, laid to deprive them of their lands, under the specious pretences of friendship and presents, and that the sooner they break it the better. This arouses their jealousy, which, with their insatiable thirst for plunder, will probably, so long as the white villains are among them, continually destroy the good effects intended by treaties. (Swan, 1855, p. 275.)

In view of the manner in which some treaties were made and their provisions executed, native distrust of them and of the government by which they were drawn up is much less difficult to understand than the subserviency of the same natives to the opinions of their nearby traders. There is still less to be said for Swan's remark regarding the "phlegmatic coldness and indifference" between the sexes made in another connection, since he proves it by citing what was really a matter of etiquette and a sign of good breeding.

The strictures of George Stiggins, himself a mixed-blood Indian, are worthier of consideration:

They in a general way appreciate a good character very little, either in themselves or anyone else in the common scenes of life as there is no perceptible difference made by them between a discreet, virtuous woman and one of ill fame and lewd practices in the common standing of society. It will equally extend to men, for thieves, murderers, and other evil practitioners are not held in disrepute nor are they subject to either scorn or reproach for they very often make head men or miccos of such men as that. Their actions are in unison with their natural inclinations and only amenable to their customary laws. So far they are the irreproachable and true sons of nature and inclination. (Stiggins, ms.)

But here again we encounter different standards. Other testimony assures us that "thieves, murderers, and other evil practictioners," as such vices were understood by the generality of the Creeks, were not held in repute. The remarks regarding feminine looseness apply, of course, to unmarried women only, since Stiggins was perfectly well aware of the punishments inflicted upon adulterers and adulteresses. Nor is it true that the moral sense of the nation failed wholly to distinguish degrees of looseness among the unmarried. Part of the immorality of which Stiggins complains was thus owing to the fact that Creeks drew moral lines in different places from Europeans, and incidentally did not regard immorality on the part of a woman as more heinous than masculine derelictions, while another part was no doubt attributable to white contact itself. It is only fair, therefore, to balance the above judgments by the somewhat too laudatory opinions of Bartram:

The Cherokees in their dispositions and manners are grave and steady; dignified and circumspect in their deportment: rather slow and reserved in conversation; yet frank, cheerful, and humane; tenacious of the liberties and natural rights of man; secret, deliberate and determined in their councils; honest, just and liberal, and ready always to sacrifice every pleasure and gratification, even their blood, and life itself, to defend their territory and maintain their rights. . . .

The national character of the Muscogulges, when considered in a political view, exhibits a portraiture of a great or illustrious heroe. A proud, haughty and arrogant race of men; they are brave and valiant in war, ambitious of conquest, restless and perpetually exercising their arms, yet magnanimous and merciful to a vanquished enemy, when he submits and seeks their friendship and protection; always uniting the vanquished tribes in confederacy with them; when they immediately enjoy, unexceptionably, every right of free citizens, and are from that moment united in one common band of brotherhood. They were never known to exterminate a tribe, except the Yamasees.[8] . . .

If we consider them with respect to their private character or in a moral view, they must, I think, claim our approbation, if we divest ourselves of prejudice and think freely. As moral men they certainly stand in no need of European civilization.

They are just, honest, liberal, and hospitable to strangers; considerate, loving and affectionate to their wives and relations; fond of their children; industrious, frugal, temperate, and persevering; charitable and forbearing. I have been weeks and months among them and in their towns, and never observed the least sign of contention and wrangling: never saw an instance of an Indian beating his wife, or even reproving her in anger. In this case they stand as examples of reproof to the most civilized nations, as not being defective in justice, gratitude and a good understanding; for indeed their wives merit their esteem and the most gentle treatment, they being industrious, frugal, careful, loving, and affectionate.

The Muscogulges are more volatile, sprightly and talkative than their Northern neighbours, the Cherokees; and, though far more distant from the white settlements than any nation east of the Mississippi or Ohio, appear evidently to have made greater advances towards the refinements of true civilization, which cannot, in the least degree, be attributed to the good examples of the white people. (Bartram, 1792, pp. 483, 487–488.)

Adair, whose experience of the Indians was earlier than that of Stiggins and longer in duration than the experiences of either Swan or Bartram, was fitted to weigh them more justly:

They are ingenious, witty, cunning, and deceitful; very faithful indeed to their own tribes, but privately dishonest, and mischievous to the Europeans and christians. Their being honest and harmless to each other, may be through fear of resentment and reprisal—which is unavoidable in case of an injury. They are very close and retentive of their secrets; never forget injuries; revengeful of blood, to a degree of distraction. They are timorous, and, conse-

---

[8] As I have pointed out elsewhere, no such wholesale destruction of Yamasee Indians actually took place.

quently, cautious; very jealous of encroachments from their christian neighbors; and, likewise, content with freedom, in every turn of fortune. They are possessed of a strong comprehensive judgment,—can form surprisingly crafty schemes, and conduct them with equal caution, silence, and address; they admit none but distinguished warriors, and old beloved men, into their councils. They are slow, but very persevering in their undertakings—commonly temperate in eating, but excessively immoderate in drinking.—They often transform themselves by liquor into the likeness of mad foaming bears. The women, in general, are of a mild, amiable, soft disposition: exceedingly modest in their behaviour, and very seldom noisy, either in the single, or married state.

The men are expert in the use of fire-arms,—in shooting the bow,—and throwing the feathered dart, and tomahawk, into the flying enemy. They resemble the lynx, with their sharp penetrating black eyes, and are exceedingly swift of foot; especially in a long chase: they will stretch away, through the rough woods, by the bare track, for two or three hundred miles, in pursuit of a flying enemy, with the continued speed, and eagerness, of a stanch pack of blood hounds, till they shed blood. When they have allayed this their burning thirst, they return home, at their leisure, unless they chance to be pursued, as is sometimes the case; whence the traders say, "that an Indian is never in a hurry, but when the devil is at his heels." . . . They seem quite easy, and indifferent, in every various scene of life, as if they were utterly divested of passions, and the sense of feeling. Martial virtue, and not riches, is their invariable standard for preferment; for they neither esteem, nor despise any of their people one jot more or less, on account of riches or dress. They compare both these, to paint on a warrior's face; because it incites others to a spirit of martial benevolence for their country, and pleases his own fancy, and the eyes of spectators, for a little time, but is sweated off, while he is performing his war-dances; or is defaced, by the change of weather. [He adds that they spoke of a deceitful person and his words as similar to a snake and to his tongue, and that the Indians viewed their white acquaintances in such an unfavorable light that] the English traders among them . . . are often very glad to be allowed to pass muster with the Indian chieftains, as fellow bretheren of the human species. [He cites in confirmation of this the fact that the Choctaw called the English, not by a term applicable to human beings, but by one resembling that of] a contemptible heterogeneous animal. (Adair, 1775, pp. 4–5, 7, 13.)

Adair's relatively unfavorable estimate of the Choctaw, as compared with the Chickasaw, which he enlarges upon elsewhere (pp. 283, 285, 304), must be counteracted by reading Romans' precisely contrary opinion and by remembering the inveterate hostility between the two tribes and the alliance of the one with the French and the other with the English.

For the rest it may be observed that the difference between intratribal and intertribal virtue was precisely that being observed by the contemporary nations of Europe and not widely different from the distinction maintained down to the present day. Adair himself witnesses to the reputation for dishonesty which the white traders had already acquired. One Indian vice, drunkenness, was of European origin. Adair justly notes that revenge was one of their besetting sins, but he admits at the same time that martial virtue was their standard of preferment instead of riches, and, in spite of the revolting manner in which martial virtue was exercised, we must admit that it was more closely bound up with individual character than wealth could have been.

Timberlake says of the Cherokee:

> They are of a very gentle and amicable disposition to those they think their friends, but as implacable in their enmity, their revenge being only compleated in the entire destruction of their enemies. They were pretty hospitable to all white strangers, till the Europeans encouraged them to scalp; but the great reward offered has led them often since to commit as great barbarities on us, as they formerly only treated their most inveterate enemies with. They are very hardy, bearing heat, cold, hunger and thirst, in a surprizing manner; and yet no people are given to more excess in eating and drinking, when it is conveniently in their power; the follies, nay mischief, they commit when inebriated, are entirely laid to the liquor; and no one will revenge an injury (murder excepted) received from one who is no more himself: they are not less addicted to gaming than drinking, and will even lose the shirt off their back, rather than give over play, when luck runs against them.
>
> They are extremely proud, despising the lower class of Europeans; and in some athletick diversions I once was present at, they refused to match or hold conference with any but officers.
>
> Here, however, the vulgar notion of the Indians uncommon activity was contradicted by three officers of the Virginia regiment, the slowest of which could outrun the swiftest of about 700 Indians that were in the place: but had the race exceeded two or three hundred yards, the Indians would then have acquired the advantage, by being able to keep the same pace a long time together; and running being likewise more general among them, a body of them would always greatly exceed an equal number of our troops.
>
> They are particularly careful of the superannuated, but are not so till of a great age. . . .
>
> They have many of them a good uncultivated genius, are fond of speaking well, as that paves the way to power in their councils; and I doubt not but the reader will find some beauties in the harangues I have given him, which I assure him are entirely genuine. . . .
>
> They seldom turn their eyes on the person they speak of, or address themselves to, and are always suspicious when people's eyes are fixed upon them. They speak so low, except in council, that they are often obliged to repeat what they are saying; yet should a person talk to any of them above their common pitch, they would immediately ask him, if he thought they were deaf. (Timberlake, Williams ed., 1927, pp. 78–81.)

Calderón describes the Indians of Florida and southern Georgia as "weak and phlegmatic as regards work, though clever and quick to learn any art they see done, and great carpenters as is evidenced in the construction of their wooden churches which are large and painstakingly wrought." (Calderón, 1936, p. 12.)

Until the recent extensive exploitation of Florida, the Seminole who remained there after their relatives had been taken to Oklahoma were held in high esteem by their white neighbors. MacCauley says of them:

I have been led to the conclusion that for Indians they have attained a relatively high degree of psychical development. They are an uncivilized, I hardly like to call them a savage, people. They are antagonistic to white men, as a race, and to the white man's culture, but they have characteristics of their own, many of which are commendable. They are decided in their enmity to any representative of the white man's government and to every thing which bears upon it the government's mark. To one, however, who is acquainted with recent history this enmity is but natural, and a confessed representative of the government need not be surprised at finding in the Seminole only forbidding and unlovely qualities. But when suspicion is disarmed, one whom they have welcomed to their confidence will find them evincing characteristics which will excite his admiration and esteem. I was fortunate enough to be introduced to the Seminole, not as a representative of our National Government, but under conditions which induced them to welcome me as a friend. In my intercourse with them, I found them to be not only the brave, self reliant, proud people who have from time to time withstood our nation's armies in defense of their rights, but also a people amiable, affectionate, truthful, and communicative. Nor are they devoid of a sense of humor. With only few exceptions, I found them genial. . . I call the Seminole communicative because most with whom I spoke were eager to talk, and, as far as they could with the imperfect means at their disposal, to give me the information I sought. 'Doctor Na-ki-ta', (Doctor What-is-it) I was playfully named at the Cat Fish Lake settlement; yet the people there were seemingly as ready to try to answer as I was to ask, "What is it?" I said they are truthful. That is their reputation with many of the white men I met, and I have reason to believe that the reputation is under ordinary circumstances well founded. They answered promptly and without equivocation "No" or "Yes" or "I don't know." And they are affectionate to one another, and so far as I saw, amiable in their domestic and social intercourse. Parental affection is characteristic of their home life, as several illustrative instances I might mention would show. . . . I have said also that the Seminole are frank. Formal or hypocritical courtesy does not characterize them. . . . They seem to be mentally active. When the full expression of any of my questions failed, a substantive or two, an adverb, and a little pantomime generally sufficed to convey the meaning to my hearers. In their intercourse with one another, they are, as a rule, voluble, vivacious, showing the possession of relatively active brains and mental fertility. Certainly, most of the Seminole I met cannot justly be called either stupid or intellectually sluggish, and I observed that, when invited to think of matters with which they are not familiar or which are beyond the verge of the domain which their intellectual faculties have mastered, they nevertheless bravely endeavored to satisfy me before they were willing to acknowledge themselves powerless. They would not at once answer a misunderstood or unintelligible question, but would return inquiry upon inquiry, before the decided "I don't know" was uttered. Those with whom I particularly dealt with were exceptionally patient under the strains to which I put their minds. (MacCauley, 1887, pp. 490–493.)

Lawson discusses the character of the Indians of his acquaintance in two places; after describing the kindness they showed to one another in time of misfortune, he continues:

They never fight with one another unless drunk, nor do you ever hear any scolding amongst them. They say the Europeans are always rangling and uneasy, and wonder they do not go out of this world, since they are so uneasy and discontented in it. All their misfortunes and losses end in laughter; for if their cabins take fire, and all their goods are burnt therein (indeed, all will strive to prevent farther damage whilst there is any possibility) yet such a misfortune ends in a hearty fitt of laughter, unless some of their kinsfolks and friends have lost their lives; but then the case is altered, and they become very pensive, and go into deep mourning, which is continued for a considerable time; sometimes longer or shorter, according to the dignity of the person, and the number of relations he had near him. . . .

On a fair scheme, we must first allow these savages what really belongs to them, that is, what good qualities and natural endowments they possess, whereby they being in their proper colors, the event may be better guessed at and fathomed.

First, they are as apt to learn any handicraft, as any people that the world affords; I will except none, as is seen by their canoes and stalking heads, which they make of themselves; but to my purpose, the Indian slaves in South Carolina and elsewhere, make my argument good.

Secondly, we have no disciplined men in Europe but what have, at one time or other been branded with mutining and murmuring against their chiefs. These savages are never found guilty of that great crime in a soldier. I challenge all mankind to tell me of one instance of it; besides, they never prove traitors to their native country, but rather chuse death than partake and side with the enemy.

They naturally possess the righteous man's gift; they are patient under all afflictions, and have a great many other natural vertues, which I have slightly touched throughout the account of these savages.

They are really better to us than we are to them, they always give us victuals at their quarters, and take care we are armed against hunger and thirst: we do not do so by them, (generally speaking) but let them walk by our doors hungry and do not often relieve them. We look upon them with scorn and disdain, and think them little better than beasts in human shape, though if well examined, we shall find that, for all our religion and education, we possess more moral deformities and evils than these savages do, or are acquainted withal.

We reckon them slaves in comparison to us, and intruders, as oft as they enter our houses, or hunt near our dwellings, but if we will admit reason to be our guide, she will inform us that these Indians are the freest people in the world, and so far from being intruders upon us that we have abandoned our own native soil, to drive them out, and possess theirs; neither have we any true balance in judging of these poor heathens, because we neither give allowance for their natural disposition, nor the sylvan education, and strange customs (uncouth to us) they lie under and have ever been trained up to. (Lawson, 1860, pp. 292–293, 384–386.)

Thus, like Bartram, Lawson plays the part of a kind of eighteenth century Tacitus. Already, early in this same century, Catesby brought up a practical objection to the education of Indians in white ways of living, which has frequently been harped upon since, but he does not, like so many, infer from it any necessary inferiority in Indian intelligence in general:

The *Indians* are generally allowed to have a good capacity, which seems adapted and even confined to their savage way of life. Reading and writing is the highest erudition that I have known or heard any of them attain to; tho' a great number of them have been, and still continue to be educated at *Williamsburg*-college in *Virginia*, by the benefaction of the great Mr. Boyle, whose pious design was that after attaining a due qualification, they should inculcate amongst their brethren true religion and virtue, yet I have never heard of an instance conformable to that worthy intention. And so innate an affection have they to their barbarous customs, that tho' from their infancy they have been bred, and fared well with the *English*, yet as they approach towards manhood, it is common for them to elope several hundred miles to their native country, and there to resume their skins, and savage way of life, making no further use of their learning so unworthily bestowed upon them. (Catesby, 1731–43, vol. 2, p. xii.)

Now the simple answer to this is that, on account of his Indian blood and ancestry, the student found that he could not function in white society, and that his white education unfitted him for Indian society. Thus he must either remain in white society but be held at arms length by it or return to his ancestral one and adopt, or re-adopt, the usages necessary to it or demanded by it. The situation is stated with remarkable clearness in the report of a committee of the board of correspondents of the Scots Society for Propagating Christian Knowledge, who visited the Oneida and Mahican Indians in 1796. This committee consisted of Jeremy Belknap and Jedidiah Morse, but which of these was responsible for the sections in quotes, or whether they were from some third person is not clear.

"An Indian youth has been taken from his friends and conducted to a new people, whose modes of thinking and living, whose pleasures and pursuits are totally dissimilar to those of his own nation. His new friends profess love to him, and a desire for his improvement in human and divine knowledge, and for his eternal salvation; but at the same time endeavour to make him sensible of his inferiority to themselves. To treat him as an equal would mortify their own pride, and degrade themselves in the view of their neighbours. He is put to school; but his fellow students look on him as being of an inferior species. He acquires some knowledge, and is taught some ornamental, and perhaps useful accomplishments; but the degrading memorials of his inferiority, which are continually before his eyes, remind him of the manners and habits of his own country, where he was once free and equal to his associates. He sighs to return to his friends; but there he meets with the most bitter mortification. He is neither a white man nor an Indian; as he had no character with us, he has none with them. If he has strength of mind sufficient to renounce all his acquirements, and resume the savage life and manners, he may possibly be again received by his countrymen: but the greater probability is, that he will take refuge from their contempt in the inebriating draught; and when this becomes habitual, he will be guarded from no vice, and secure from no crime." (Belknap, 1798, pp. 29–30.)

Estimates of the character of lower Mississippi Indians differed like those of the explorers farther east. Dumont regarded all of the Indian tribes with which the French had dealings, even those supposed to be friends, as utterly perfidious. "One is persuaded," writes the missionary St. Cosme, "that they are all thieves and try only to do harm, and that if they had no fear they would kill a man in order to get his knife." (St. Cosme, *in* Gosselin, 1907, vol. 1, pp. 45–46; Swanton, 1911, p. 49.) Advocates for these Indians are found in the missionary De la Vente and in the historian Le Page du Pratz. The former says:

> It seems to me that there remains yet among these barbarous people excellent remnants of that beautiful natural law that God engraved on the heart of men in the state of innocence.

> Union reigns to such an extent among them that not only does one see no lawsuit among them, but they even receive in common the outrages perpetrated upon a single person and the village, even if it perishes entirely, will perish rather than abandon the quarrels of one of their brothers, however unjust they may be.

> Their honesty regarding that which one sells to them is inviolable on their part, and it would be desirable that the French had as much good faith in their trading as they use themselves in what they trade to us. (De la Vente, *in* Gosselin, 1907, p. 45.)

Du Pratz:

> It is very wrong to call men savages who know how to make such very good use of their reason, who think justly, who have prudence, good faith, and generosity much more than certain civilized nations who will not suffer themselves to be placed in comparison with them for want of knowing or wishing to give things the values they deserve. (Le Page du Pratz, 1758, vol. 1, p. 88; Swanton, 1911, p. 50.)

Caddo mental and moral characteristics have been discussed in another bulletin. The general impression made by them upon the Spaniards may perhaps best be indicated by the following quotation from Morfi:

> The Texas are lively by nature, clear-sighted, sociable, proud and high minded. . . . of great heart, and very quick in military activities. With their friends they keep unchangeable peace, and with their enemies they never, or very seldom, make peace . . . With all these good qualities [particularly hospitality which he has just enlarged upon] the Texas are still not lacking in defects. In the market at Natchitoches they provide themselves with skins, tallow, and cattle, with munitions and guns, for which they have such a love that they never go out without an *escopeta* on their shoulder. They also acquire an abundance of strong liquors, and with this facility, they give themselves much to intoxication. They are lascivious and too strongly attached to their customs; but their love for the Spaniards is very peculiar, as shall be seen by some examples given in this history. (Morfi, 1932, pp. 40, 54; Swanton, 1942, p. 123.)

It is evident, of course, that virtue from the Spanish point of view was closely bound up with Spanish interest.

My own observation of the southern Indians living under varying conditions has strongly impressed me with the effect of environment on both tribal and personal character. The level of both has been seriously lowered by white contact where either less or more than justice has been done. A superfluity of possessions has been even more deadly in its effects on Indian character than white indifference and neglect, but it was perhaps inevitable that in the case of the Indians, as in our own case, we should confound well-being and wealth.

In the above quotations, attempts will have been noted to assign separate characteristics to various tribes. Without doubt there was some basis for these apparent differences, but I do not believe that one of them was attributable to anything more profound than divergence in past history, in custom, and in usage.

THE INFLUENCE OF LANGUAGE [9]

In the preceding section it was stated that most apparent differences in character were probably owing to customs and institutions, that is they were the cumulative effects of past history. The best way in which to determine what tribes have been subjected to greater environmental variations and what tribes to less is by comparing their physical types and their languages, but, as we have seen, the physical types are so much interwoven that it is doubtful whether we can gather much valuable information from a comparison of them. Upon the whole, we do appear to have indications that the tribes to the north of our particular area, those known as Algonquians, represented an aboriginal group which had a long history independent of any effective influence from the Gulf tribes, and the same may be said in general of the latter, though there are many that represent hybrids of the two and may prove to be cultural hybrids as well.

With language it should be far different, because language is the principal medium by means of which all other cultural traits are borrowed and perpetuated, and when cultural traits pass from one tribe to another, there is considerable likelihood that words or other linguistic phenomena will pass at the same time. It is probable that, in most cases, language is more conservative than other cultural characters and the borrowings are relatively less, yet we might expect to find some evidence of such borrowings. For that reason it is of primary importance to establish as accurate a linguistic classification as possible.

At the time when this section was first known to Europeans, by far the greatest part of it was occupied by tribes speaking languages belonging to what Powell designated the Muskhogean linguistic family. This embraces all but two or three of the best-known historic tribes, including the Choctaw and Chickasaw of Mississippi, the Creek Indians of Alabama and Georgia, with their later descendants the Seminole, the now extinct Apalachee of Flor-

---

[9] See discussions in Swanton, 1911, 1917, and 1922.

ida, and the extinct Yamasee, who played an important part in the early history of our Southern States. It included also the former inhabitants of that part of the South Carolina coast from Charleston to Savannah River and that part of the Georgia coast from Savannah River to St. Andrews Sound, the Coosa of inland South Carolina, a number of small tribes on the Gulf coasts of Mississippi, Alabama, and west Florida, some on the lower course of the Mississippi River itself, some on the upper Yazoo, and at an earlier period several tribes on the Tennessee and a few at least in eastern Arkansas. The Natchez of western Mississippi, and the Taensa and Avoyel, two smaller peoples in neighboring parts of Louisiana, constituted a widely varying branch of this stock which probably extended at one time over much more territory toward the north and may well have played a major role in the days when the great mound groups of the lower Mississippi Valley and the Ohio Valley were created. These Natchez seem to have originated in a fusion between Muskhogean peoples and some units from farther west, very likely belonging to the Tunican group. This is rendered all the more likely since we know that one, and perhaps two, bodies of Indians of Tunican stock were living with them when they were discovered. The Creek Confederation also consisted of a number of peoples who were originally distinct, but most of these belonged to the same stock and the exceptions, the Yuchi, a band of Shawnee, and perhaps the Tawasa and Osochi, were very late additions. The upper portion of the Florida Peninsula was occupied by a number of tribes originally classified in an independent family called Timuquanan (more recently Timucuan). This was connected with the Muskhogean stock, and discovery of a dialect formerly spoken in central Alabama in some measure intermediate between Timucua and the Muskhogean tongues proper indicates that it once had ramifications considerably farther north. (Swanton, 1929). The dialects of south Florida, those spoken by the Calusa, Tekesta, Jeaga, Guacata, and Ais, seem to have been quite different from Timucua, and, if we may judge by the few words preserved from this part of the State, they were nearer to the Muskhogean group proper. In spite of the relative nearness of south Florida to Cuba and the Bahama Islands, the connections of the Floridians appear to have been almost entirely with the north. Fontaneda speaks of a band of Cuban Indians which had crossed to the Calusa country and had been established in a town by themselves by the Calusa chief, but as yet no other evidence of their presence has been detected. (Swanton, 1922, pp. 27–81; 1929; Fontaneda (Smith trans.), 1854.)

Along the Mississippi and immediately west of it, a curious situation confronts us. The Natchez group of languages, differing wide-

ly from the other Muskhogean tongues and apparently containing
Tunica elements, has already been mentioned. The Tunica was spoken
by a tribe of some size which at one time lived as far north as the
present county in Mississippi which bears the name, but was found
by La Salle on the lower course of Yazoo River, and subsequently
moved to the mouth of the Red, near which they have continued to
reside until the present time. A few smaller tribes, including the
Yazoo, Koroa, Tiou, and Grigra, probably spoke closely related
dialects and this is distinctly stated of the Tiou. In southern
Louisiana near the coast, and including the mouth of the Mississippi, was another group of tongues embracing the Chitimacha,
Washa, and Chawasha Indians. Northwest and west of them was
still a third, the Atakapa, containing at least two dialects. The
Opelousa Indians, who gave their name to the present Opelousas,
the Indians of Vermilion Bayou, the Mermentou, Calcasieu, and
lower Sabine and Neches, the Arkokisa of Trinity Bay, and the
Bidai of Trinity River all belonged to it, as also probably the
Deadose and Patiri west of that river. These last three groups were
placed by Powell in the Tonikan, Chitimachan, and Attacapan stocks,
but the present writer believes he has demonstrated that they were
related (Swanton, 1919). In other words, a band of tribes connected linguistically formerly extended along the Gulf coast of
Texas and Louisiana from Trinity River to the mouth of the Mississippi and along the west side of the latter stream to the Yazoo,
and at an earlier period, as seems evident from certain narratives,
as far as the mouth of the Arkansas. This relationship may, also,
have extended to the Tonkawan, Karankawan, or Coahuiltecan peoples, perhaps to all of them, but it has yet to be demonstrated. In
any case, there was great linguistic diversity in the region and this
is somewhat puzzling, since there are no natural boundaries to keep
tribes apart and allow of independent development, nothing offering
a greater obstacle than a bayou or a swamp. Swamps might, of
course, have been significant barriers if they had been placed so as
to separate favorable areas from one another, but that can hardly
be said for the Mississippi marshes, nor do the boundaries between
stocks and linguistic groups follow the natural frontiers. There is
evidence that the groups known to us once had a much wider
extension, but this does not help us very much. The linguistic
diversity along the lower Mississippi is, indeed, an interesting problem in Southeastern ethnology. It remains to be seen whether
archeology can be of assistance in unraveling it. Of the stocks properly belonging to the Southeast, therefore, one lay east of the
Mississippi, except for a few minor tribes, and extended to Savannah River and the Atlantic Ocean, including probably all of Flor-

ida. The other was mainly west of the Mississippi, though it also had representatives on the east side, but its westward extension is still uncertain. The other tribes of the Southeast belonged to four different stocks, all but one of which seem to have developed outside of the area under consideration.

The possible exception is constituted by the Caddo tribes of northwestern Louisiana and northeastern Texas. They were related to the Kichai, Wichita, and a number of peoples connected with the latter, who were spread through northern Texas and most of Oklahoma, and to the Pawnee of Nebraska and northern Kansas, with the Dakota relatives of the latter, the Arikara. A tribe called Shuman or Jumano, formerly believed to have belonged to this stock, anciently lived along the middle course of the Rio Grande, in the eastern part of New Mexico and in western Texas, but Dr. Sauer, one of the more recent students of their history, believes that they belonged originally to the Uto-Aztecan family, and that part later took to the Plains and ultimately united with the Wichita (Sauer, 1934, pp. 65–74). This view has received further confirmation from the work of Scholes and Mera. (See Scholes, 1940.) Possibly the Caddo tribes may represent the original nucleus of the Caddoan peoples, and, in any case, the evidence at hand at the present time now seems to indicate an eastern rather than a western distribution point for the family.

So far as the Iroquoians are concerned, it seems pretty evident that they were invaders. Although marginal, they played an important part in the history of the entire area. The Cherokee, who are believed to have come from the northeast, speak an Iroquoian language which has undergone great modifications. It stands in one group over against all other languages of the stock. Reference has already been made to the dominant position held by the Cherokee in the Appalachian highlands and to the fact that they were the most populous tribe of the Southeast. The Tuscarora were the dominant tribe of eastern North Carolina, and two lesser Iroquoian tribes, the Nottoway and Meherrin, were of considerable significance in the aboriginal history of Virginia.

The status of the Siouans presents great difficulties. We have good evidence that many of them were late comers from some region toward the north, probably including a part of the Ohio Valley. The immigration of the Ofo, or Mosopelea, into the Yazoo territory from southern Ohio may be called historic, and late intrusions of the Biloxi and Quapaw from the same general region are clearly indicated. Finally, all traditions preserved from the eastern Siouan tribes bearing on their origin point to the same section. (Swanton, 1923; 1936.) While the main area of Siouan development is thus fairly well shown, the Siouan languages have structural resemblances to the Southeastern tongues, especially those of the Muskhogean group, and this is particularly true of the Catawba, which apparently occupied an intermediate position.   Therefore, it is probable that, though the Siouan peoples were marginal to those of the area we are discussing, they are of considerable importance in any broad study of it.

A curious people with a unique language, somewhat after the structural pattern of Muskhogean and Siouan, were the Yuchi. Only one dialect is known, but it is evident that there were once several distinct tribes with a considerable total population. Their home was also north of the Gulf area, and they, too, may have made their way down from the region of the present Middle West. When we first hear of them they were in the mountainous country of eastern Tennessee north of the river of that name, near Muscle Shoals, and on the Cumberland. It was only after the Spaniards had established themselves at St. Augustine that bands of Yuchi began to enter the Gulf region, pushed on, it would seem, by the Iroquoian tribes. (Swanton, 1922; Speck, 1909; Wagner, 1931.)   (But see remarks on p. 213.)

The Algonquians, finally, belong clearly to a different culture center. They had contacts with the Southeast at two points. One of these was through the Shawnee Indians, who probably made their presence felt at a very late date. They had evidently reached the Cumberland only a few years before Europeans came in contact with them. A part of them soon made a settlement on Savannah River, giving their name to the stream, and from this time until the opening of the nineteenth century, they had one or more settlements in the Creek Nation, where they became close friends in particular of the Tukabahchee Creeks.

The other point of contact was at the northeastern corner of the area we are considering where the southern extension of a series of Algonquian tribes which fringed the Atlantic coast came as far south as the mouth of the Neuse River. Whether this represents a late intrusion or was a condition long established we do not know, but the former opinion is the one generally held.

The distribution of the remaining cultural elements cannot be given until after a careful study and recapitulation, to which I will now address myself.

RAW MATERIALS UTILIZED BY THE SOUTHEASTERN INDIANS

The following enumeration of such materials is drawn from the printed sources mainly and does not profess to be absolutely complete. The authorities for the data here given will appear in later chapters.

MINERAL KINGDOM

The only mineral substance widely utilized as food was salt, obtained sometimes from the ocean, but oftener from salt licks. There is only one reference to the use of sea salt from the Gulf of Mexico and that is probably erroneous, but there are several regarding salt gathering on the Atlantic coast, and particularly on the coast of the present Carolinas. Dirt or clay eating is noted in Carolina and Florida.

Fish weirs in the rivers and on Tampa Bay were made out of rough stones, as were some prehistoric forts. The foundations of Timucua granaries and a few houses in Carolina are said to have been of stone, but probably the material was merely a natural tabby. The stone sweat-lodges, of which Lawson speaks, had reference merely to the stones upon which water was thrown and those used in holding down the covering (Lawson, 1860, pp. 85–86). Stone mortars were used in cracking nuts, preparing paints, and, in prehistoric times, in grinding corn. Stone projectiles were presumably used with the few slings of which we have made mention. Steatite was used in the manufacture of pipes and some vessels, but the former were made of several other kinds of stone while most of the latter belonged to a remote prehistoric period. A few catlinite pipes were imported from the northwest. Stone was used in manufacturing clubs, axes, wedges, and possibly adzes. At least stone implements were used in hollowing out canoes. Flint of various sorts was employed in the manufacture of arrow, spear, and lance heads, and for all kinds of cutting, piercing, and scraping instruments, including flint-edged clubs or swords. A smooth pebble assisted in the shaping of the insides of pots; there were stone counters and gaming stones including "chunk" stones, while stone images and banner stones are found in the section, though the use of the last mentioned belonged to a prehistoric epoch, and images were rarely made in the historic period. Some arrowheads were of quartz crystal, and crystal was used for ornaments and in religious observances. Colored stones were sometimes placed in the ears for ornaments, there is mention of stone beads in Florida, and we have one reference to importation of turquoises from the far Southwest.

Paint was made of red ocher, lampblack, black lead, cinnabar, and tobacco-pipe clay. The walls of houses, and often both walls and roofs, were made of clay mixed with grass or Spanish moss.

Artificial stone, i.e., clay hardened by means of fire, in this case pottery, was extensively employed for all purposes, including the cooking and storing of foods, as salt-boiling pans, and some drums and pipes. Pots were usually tempered with sand or shell.

Small nodules of copper big enough for manufacture into beads were obtained in certain parts of the Southeast, but most copper used in the section came from Lake Superior, and out of this they made—besides beads—gorgets, rings, bracelets, and armbands, ear and nose ornaments, decorations for the headdress, ornaments on clothing, danglers on belts, and, it is said, the points of pikes, chopping knives, sweat scrapers, and breastplates, though these last may have been in reality only large gorgets. Pieces of meteoric iron and hematite were occasionally used for ornaments or implements, and small gold and silver nuggets were hammered out into ornaments. In Florida gold beads have been found worked over from ornaments made by the Central American Indians, and cast upon the Florida coast with the vessels which were carrying them to Spain.

VEGETABLE KINGDOM

We find mention of the following cultivated food plants: Corn, beans, peas, squashes and pumpkins, orache, and sunflowers (for their seeds).

The following wild plants, shrubs, and trees were utilized in one way or another as food: Angelico, blackberries, black gum berries, blue palmetto, cane (for the seeds), cherries, chestnuts, chinquapin nuts, cockspur grass, coco berries, crabapples, *Dioscorea villosa*, gooseberries, grapes, ground nuts, hickory nuts, honeylocust, huckleberries, moss in creeks(?), mulberries, mushrooms, oak acorns, palm berries, *Panicum maximum*, wild peas, persimmons, plums, pond-lily seeds, prickly pears, raspberries, wild rice, sagittaria, sea grapes, service berries, smilax roots, strawberries, sugar from the sugar maple, wild sweetpotatoes, "tuckahoe," walnuts, zamia (in Florida), also haws.

Tobacco of the native species (*Nicotiana rustica*) was used everywhere for smoking, mixed often with sumac and sometimes with leaves of the sweetgum. Tobacco ashes mixed with wood ashes were used by women along the lower Mississippi to stain their teeth.

Corn was used for the following industrial purposes: Young Indian corn beaten to a pulp to take the place of deer brains in dressing skins; the juice of green corn to erase tattoo marks obtained under false pretenses; corncobs burned to make smoke in tanning skins and also rubbed over the outsides of pots before they were fired.

Pumpkin rind was employed in making masks, and perhaps rattles.

Grapevines were used sometimes as substitutes for cord.

There is mention of a persimmon root being worked into a comb.

Cane supplied one of the most important of all raw materials. Besides the use of its seeds, as indicated above, it was employed in making baskets and mats; as building material; in making fishing crails and traps, spears, and arrows; as backing for wattle walls; in making beds in houses and in the construction of corncribs; as a substitute for the shuttle in weaving; as knives and torches; in the "spiral fire" at Creek councils; in making boxes, cradles, sieves, fanners, hampers, blowguns, blowgun arrows, shields, stockades and fences, rafts, litters, flageolets, counters, drills, and tubes through which to blow into the medicines; as pipes to blow the fire in burning out mortars and in smoking; and sometimes a section was employed to hold braids of the hair.

Hickory was used in house frames, in backing for walls, as arrow shafts, in making fishing crails and drags, and as firewood. From it was obtained some of the punk used in kindling fires, and the bark was employed in covering houses and making fires for burning pottery. Pestles were made out of "red hickory," and the Choctaw say they used white hickory or "switch hickory," which they cut in the fall, in the manufacture of bows.

The inner bark of the mulberry was employed as thread and rope, in making textiles, nettings worn by girls, and netting for women's hair. This was one of the sources of tinder along the lower Mississippi; from the roots a yellow dye was obtained, and Lawson says that of the "white mulberry" bows were sometimes made, perhaps after the introduction of the white mulberry through Mexico.

Walnuts supplied a dye widely used in basketry and an oil with which the hair was anointed.

From the sumac, according to one informant, a black dye was made; according to another, a yellow dye; and according to a third, yellow and red dyes. It is said that berries of the common sumac were rubbed in the hair, and, according to a Natchez informant, an infusion of leaves of the *Rhus truphydon* was poured over pots to give them a bluish tint.

Cypress was the favorite wood for the manufacture of canoes. Drums were made out of cypress knees. Split shingles and bark from this tree were used as house coverings. At a place where a limb had come out, punk was obtained to be used as tinder.

We find pine employed in making house frames, canoes, frames for skin boats or rafts, and bows. It was used for torches, especially in fire-fishing, and as tinder; and houses were covered with its bark, while pitch-pine soot was used in making tattoo marks.

Bass bark was used in the manufacture of ropes and thread, sometimes including bowstrings.

The wood of the black gum or tupelo gum was employed in making drums, and gum wood was worked into dishes and spoons.

Oak trees supplied the favorite firewood, and the four logs forming the sacred fires of the Creeks were usually oak. Mortars were also made of it. White oak withes formed the backing of wattle walls, and they were employed in putting fish traps together, in the tops of beds, and in the frames of leather boats. Sticks of this wood were also used in kindling fires. White-oak bark was employed in covering houses, while red-oak bark was used as a dye, and skins undergoing tanning were soaked in an infusion of this bark. Garcilaso de la Vega is our sole authority for the employment of oak bows.

Locust wood is said to have been used sometimes in frames for houses, and black locust was the favorite bowwood east of the Mississippi.

West of the Mississippi Osage-orange, the bois d'arc, was the great bowwood.

Sassafras wood was used for house frames, fire sticks, and sometimes for bows, and from it was made a deep yellow dye.

House frames and bows were also made of cedar, while cedar bark was employed in covering houses.

House frames in Florida were made of palmetto (*Sabal palmetto*), and in the southern sections generally, palmetto leaves were widely used as roof coverings. They were also employed in baskets and panniers and even for clothing, while arrow points were made from the harder sections. Whitford has identified the material of which a Cherokee basket was made as palmetto.

The largest canoes were of poplar, and poplar was used in the manufacture of stools and the doors of houses; also fire sticks were sometimes of this wood.

Ash splints sometimes formed the tops of beds, and in Virginia there is mention of ash leaves as an extemporized towel.

Prickly ash is said to have been a favorite material for canoe poles.

Slippery-elm bark was one of the sources for cordage, and threads are said to have been obtained from it out of which textiles were woven.

Maple bark is mentioned as another source of cordage, and there are at least two notices of a dye extracted from a variety of maple, apparently the red maple, but said to be a dark purple dye. Maple was not used in the manufacture of mortars, as it gave a bad taste to the flour.

When beech trees were to be found, mortars were made from them.

Fire sticks were sometimes of willow, and the Alabama made a deer call out of the button willow.

Elm wood was made into spoons and elm bark into canoes.

Some of the bark canoes used in the northern interior of this section were probably of birch, but most of these were made outside of it.

From the box elder spoons were made.

Wood of the tulip tree was employed for the same purpose.

Another wood of which spoons were made was the sycamore.

The seat of the litter in which the Great Sun of the Natchez was carried about was covered with leaves of the "tulip laurel."

The horse chestnut or buckeye was one of the main sources of fish poison. According to some, the nuts were used; according to others, the roots; and according to still others, the small branches. Nuts of the red buckeye (*Aesculus pavia*) were used as eyes in the deer decoy.

The wild peach was one source of red dye, and skins to be tanned were sometimes soaked in an infusion of the bark of this tree.

Bows and arrow shafts in Virginia were of witch-hazel.

Dogwood was an occasional source of material for baskets and bows, and "red dogwood" was used for arrow shafts.

Arrow shafts were also made of the black haw.

Ironwood was sometimes employed for bows.

Natchez bows, according to Du Pratz, were of "acacia," but he probably means by this the black locust.

The hackberry was sometimes used in baskets.

Chinquapin nuts were occasionally strung as beads.

The material of which thread, fish nets, and fish lines were made is frequently referred to as "silkgrass," a name which probably covered several different plants, including some of the following, which have been identified in materials from the Southeast by A. C. Whitford: Indian hemp (*Apocynum cannabinum*), stingless nettle (*Boehmeria cylindrica*),, woods nettle (*Laportea canadensis*), and slender nettle (*Urtica gracilis*). Sometimes "a nettle" is definitely mentioned.

Yucca fiber was used for cord in the western part of the area and an Arkansas specimen in the Museum of the American Indian was identified by Whitford as *Yucca arkansana*.

From rushes and flags were made mats, house coverings, and bed coverings, particularly in the northeast. A mat in the United States National Museum is made of the cattail flag (*Typha latifolia*).

Spanish moss was used as clothing in the southern sections, particularly by the women and girls, and the pillow employed along the Mississippi in flattening the heads of infants was often stuffed with it. It was also employed as tinder, especially in supplying the tinder for fire arrows. Whitford has identified two cords from the Koasati Indians in the collections of the Museum of the American Indian as of this material (*Tillandsia usneoides*).

Grass was used sometimes for clothing and, mixed with clay, was commonly used in constructing the walls and roofs of houses. In the west, bundles of grass formed the sole thatch of houses.

Milkweed of the species *Asclepias syriaca*, *tuberosa*, and *pulchra* has been identified in textiles from the Southeast by Whitford, in places as wide apart as the Cherokee country, the Machapunga of eastern North Carolina, and Arkansas. Milkweed also figured extensively in remedies. It is a plant of European origin.

The devil's shoestring was employed as a fish poison.

Another fish poison was obtained from the berries of the *Cocculus carolinus*.

Thistledown was commonly used in feathering blowgun arrows. A low shrub called the "buckbush" was one source of blowgun arrow shafts.

The red root (*Sanguinaria canadensis*) was a principal source of red dyes and was the "scarlet root" imported into Virginia as a hair dye. This was known to the Indians of Virginia as "pocone" or "puccoon," often contracted to "coon," but the name covered two other plants, the *Lithospermum vulgare*, the original puccoon of Virginia, and the yellow root (*Hydrastis canadensis*), from the second of which a yellow dye was extracted.

Another plant called "yellow leaves" by the natives is mentioned as a source of yellow dye.

The "dog tail weed" is given as a source of a dark red dye.

"Achetchy" is given by Du Pratz as the native, presumably Mobilian, name of a plant yielding a red dye.

"Barks" are mentioned vaguely as employed in making fish nets, fishlines, and headdresses for the inland Siouans of Virginia, for bowstrings, wrist-guards, shields, and trumpets.

Cords from the pawpaw (*Asimina triloba*) have been identified by Whitford.

Textiles from the button-snakeroot (*Eryngium yuccaefolium*) were found in two bags obtained from Arkansas by the same investigator.

Textile material from the moosewood (*Dirca palustris*) was identified by him in a mat from the same region.

"Creepers" are mentioned employed as cords.

"Leaves" sometimes provided a makeshift clothing.

"Seeds" were used in headdresses.

"Flowers" were placed by women on their heads by way of ornament.

"An herb" is the indefinite word used in one case for a stain used in tattooing, and something equally indefinite, besides tobacco, in staining the teeth.

Implements made of "wood" of unspecified kinds were: Clubs, shields, swords, armor, carved images, paddles, counters, beads, rollers upon which to wrap the hair, points of arrows, pipe stems. To these we may add stockades and bridges.

Among Old World plants introduced at an early period may be mentioned: Peaches, apples, oranges, watermelons, muskmelons, figs, the canna, okra, passiflora, rice, and sorghum. Peanuts and potatoes were introduced from South America.

A very wide range of plants was drawn upon in medical prescriptions. In this connection, consult Plants Used as Curatives by Certain Southeastern Tribes, by Lydia Averill Taylor (1940).

ANIMAL KINGDOM

The most important food animal was the deer, and deerhide probably formed the most important single material entering into native dress. One of the bones from a deer's foot was used to remove the hair from skins. The head and neighboring parts were turned into a decoy for stalking other members of the deer tribe. The ribs were made into bracelets, part of the horn mounted on a club, and tips of the horns formed one of the commonest types of arrow points. The heads of drums were usually made by stretching a deer skin over a pot, keg, or cypress knee. Balls used in the great southern ball game were covered with deer hide, and the rattles which women wore about their ankles in dances were sometimes made of the hoofs of deer. Flutes or flageolets were sometimes made of the deer's tibia. The sinews, skin, or entrails were employed as thread or string, and bowstrings, fish nets, and the cords to fasten ballsticks together were constructed by their means. According to Strachey, bows were scraped by the use of a twisted deer hide. Parts of the horns and bones were made into needles, and the brains were employed in tanning skins. Ornaments were made from the horn, deer bones were worn stuck through the hair in Florida, and toward the north stained deer's hair was metamorphosed into crests for warriors. Deer horn was also boiled to make glue, and glue was extracted from deerskins to dilute coloring matter.

The bear was probably the next most useful animal. It was hunted for its flesh, but still more for its fat, which was preserved in skins. Heavy winter robes and bed coverings were made of the skins, and moccasins were also cut out of them. Thongs of twisted bear guts were utilized as bow strings, and bows were sometimes finished by dipping them in bear's oil. This oil was used constantly to anoint the hair and indeed the entire body. Bear claws were thrust through the ears as ornaments.

In spite of the fact that bison disappeared from the Gulf region rather rapidly in colonial times, they were formerly much relied upon as raw material for many purposes, and a knowledge of many of these has come down to us. The flesh was, of course, highly prized as food and the skins as clothing and robes to sit upon or throw over beds. Shields were also made of bison hide. The horns were used as ornaments on headdresses, and they were worked into dishes and spoons. The shoulder blade was used as a hoe and in dressing skins. Bison hair was woven into cords with which the native wooden boxes were tied together, and ribbons were made of it which the women used in tying up their hair, and out of which they made garters, belts, and other articles of adornment.

The beaver was eaten and its skin used in the manufacture of clothing, particularly pouches. The beaver tooth, usually set in the end of a stick, was an important tool, and one writer seems to imply that textiles were made of the hair, though this is doubtful.

The Indians living toward the north hunted the elk for food, and used its hide for clothing, particularly moccasins.

The otter was eaten and the skins used for clothing, though they were worn for ornamental rather than practical purposes. Pouches were, however, made of them, and since the otter was connected closely with shamanistic practices we are apt to find otter skins in the priestly costume. According to Adair, an otter-skin strap held the gorget of the Chickasaw high priest in place.

The raccoon was eaten and its skin used for clothing, including pouches. Thongs of raccoon hide were employed to form the cage of a ballstick. Raccoon claws were sometimes thrust through the ears by way of ornament. According to one writer, textiles were made of raccoon hair, though this is questionable.

Squirrels were a favorite article of food and their skins were sewed into various sorts of clothing. The claws were thrust through apertures in the ears as ornaments. A twisted skin frequently did duty as a bowstring.

We hear of the panther being eaten sometimes and the use of its skin as clothing for the person, or as bedclothes. The claws are said to have been employed as ornaments.

The muskrat was eaten and its skin formed a much prized article of clothing in early times. The companions of De Soto once found the skin or skins of muskrat made into something which they thought was a flag.

The opossum is said not to have been eaten by some tribes, but the taboo does not seem to have extended to all. The hair was woven into textiles of the same kind as those for which bison wool was employed.

Rabbits were eaten and their skins sewed into robes.

The wildcat seems to have been eaten at times and its skin was also worn.

Polecats were eaten, at least by some of the Indians, but I have no mention of the use of their skins unless this animal is meant when it is said that a badger skin was utilized as a wrist protector, or "vanbrace," to protect the wrist from the bowstring.

The skin of the fox or the skin of the wolf might also be employed for the latter purpose, and a fox skin was sometimes metamorphized into a pouch.

The manatee was hunted and eaten by the south Florida tribes, and "two large bones" taken from its head, evidently the tusks, were placed in a chief's grave.

The dog was utilized in hunting to a very limited extent. Its flesh does not seem to have been a regular article of diet anywhere, but it was consumed at certain feasts of a social or ceremonial character.

Weasel skins are mentioned as ornaments to the headdress.

There is one notice of work in porcupine quills (among the Natchez) and references to porcupine quills in use to tie up the hair (Natchez women) or to ornament the headdress (Creeks). The quills, or objects ornamented with them, were evidently imported.

The turkey seems anciently to have been the most utilized of all birds, though it was rarely tamed in this section. It was eaten, of course, and its feathers were used in making feather mantles, in the headdress (probably), as fans, and in feathering arrows; and turkey-cock spurs were turned into arrow points. They adorned the moccasins of the Chickasaw high priest.

Ducks were also used for food and clothing, particularly clothing of an ornamental character. We hear of blankets made of mallard heads, and the Caddo sprinkled reddened duck down on the hair.

Eagle feathers were employed as ornaments to the person and marks of accomplishments. Fans were made of them and they were employed frequently in ceremonies. Eagle claws were sometimes used to adorn the breechclout.

Hawk feathers were also used as ornaments, and a hawk skin was sometimes tied to the hair for this same purpose. As in the case of the eagle, hawk claws were fastened to the breechclouts as an embellishment.

Buzzard skins were used like hawk skins, and a buzzard feather was displayed by a doctor to indicate that he could cure gunshot wounds, since buzzard feathers were employed in cleansing such wounds.

Swan feathers were worked into mantles, worn as parts of the headdress by successful warriors, and on the headdress of the Chickasaw high priest. The Caddo put reddened swan's down on their heads.

Geese, partridges, and quails seem to have been valued merely as food.

Pigeons formed a considerable article of diet at certain times near the places where they were in the habit of roosting in their annual migrations.

Pheasant feathers were used as ornaments.

Flamingo feather cloaks were noted among the Indians by Bartram.

Crane or heron feathers were worn by Creek Indians as part of their headdresses, particularly by those belonging to one set of clans.

The wing of a red bird (cardinal?) was sometimes worn in the headdress.

An owl skin was often carried by the Creek medicine man or priest as a symbol of his calling.

Whales and porpoises are mentioned as food by one or two writers.

Snakes were eaten by some tribes, their fangs were employed by doctors in scarification (Lawson, 1860, p. 363), and the Virginia doctors ornamented their heads with snake skins stuffed with moss, with the rattles of rattlesnakes, and even wore live green snakes. There is a mention of the use of "vipers' teeth" as arrow points.

Turtles and terrapin were eaten and the shells of the latter were turned into rattles, which women wore at dances fastened round their calves.

Alligators were generally eaten where they were available.

There are also one or two notices regarding the eating of lizards.

We have note of the following fish used as food: Alewife, bluefish, buffalo fish, eel, herring, mullet, plaice, perch, ray, red horse, sardine, sturgeon, trout, tunny, turbot, rockfish, pickerel (Yuchi), "dog fish" (Yuchi), several kinds of bass (Yuchi), white garfish, wolf fish, trunk fish, carp, sucker, and catfish. (Names as given; the true plaice is European.) Points for fish spears were made out of the sting of the string ray.

They ate crabs, crawfish, and lobsters, and made spear points out of the tails of horseshoe crabs.

Among shell fish we have mention of clams, mussels, oysters, cockles, and "snails" as used for food, but the significance of the last term is uncertain. Some of the clams and periwinkles have particular importance because beads were made from them which not only came to be widely used as ornaments, but attained the status of media of exchange. Larger beads were made from the conch shell; a few very large ones were worn on the crown of the head, as ear pendants in the form of spikes, and as breast ornaments or gorgets. This shell was also used in serving the black drink, and it was mounted on a handle and used as a hoe. Beads were used all over the clothing as ornaments, on the headdress, to bind braids of hair, in ears and noses, wrapped around necks, and on other parts of the body. Pearls, obtained most often from fresh-water mussels, were also widely used as ornaments about neck, ears, etc., and were insignia of wealth. *Marginella* and *Olivella* shells were transformed into beads almost entire, except that the inner ends of the whorls were rubbed off in order to let a cord through for stringing.

Among other articles of diet are mentioned wasps in the comb and even honey, though the honeybee proper arrived with Europeans. We also hear of the eating of beetles, locusts, fleas, and lice.

Quivers and body armor were made of hide, but we can only guess from what animals they were taken. Animal bones were also the raw material for beads and arrow points, and powdered bone is said to have been employed as tempering for pots.

Besides the species of bird mentioned, many others were drawn upon to feather arrows, to make splints to bind arrowheads to the shaft, as wrist guards, on shields, as towels, and fans, though these last seem usually to have been made of turkey feathers. Down from bluebirds, herons, cardinals, and other birds was powdered over the body after it had been covered with oil. Feathers were worn comparatively little by women. Bird bills were sometimes utilized as arrow points, and with quills certain Indians traced designs on pottery while it was being fired. Bird claws, besides those uses of them above enumerated, were thrust through the ears by way of ornament. A much more gruesome head ornament was the head of a dead enemy.

Eggs were used as food, but there is singularly little mention of the fact. In dressing skins, they sometimes used eggs and cornmeal in a little water.

The fin bones of various fish were employed to point spears, arrows, and other weapons, and as needles. We are told several times that fish scales, particularly the scales of the great brown spotted gar, according to William Bartram, were used to point arrows; and that also fish teeth were used for such purposes. It is not surprising to find that fish were also used for glue. In Florida small fish bladders, colored red, were worn in the ears.

The shells of bivalves were employed as knives, in such occupations as the hollowing out of a canoe or scraping a bow into shape. With two such shells, the Virginians shaved off, or rather grated off, the hair of one side of the head. In North Carolina there is mention of arrow points made of shell, in one instance said to be oyster shell. A shell was constantly used in shaping up the inside of a pot, and crushed shell was a very common tempering material for pottery. The ashes of shells and hot water are mentioned as a depilatory.

THE DISTRIBUTION OF RAW MATERIALS

If all raw materials utilized by the whole of the occupants of any given territory were distributed in an absolutely even manner, there would be little seasonal migration and little trade. It would also be a matter of indifference where a family lived, and we might suppose the population to be spread evenly over the land. The contrary is, of course, the case, and this unequal distribution of materials determines in the first place the distribution of the population, and in the second place, the amount and nature of their seasonal movements and the extent and character of trade.

Of first importance, naturally, is the location of food supplies and the supplies of materials needed in clothing and for shelter, and secondly, the distribution of certain raw materials made necessary by the character of their manufactures and the demands of their social and religious life. But in so far as man has learned to control his environment by the development of agriculture and the domestication of animals both the distribution of population and its seasonal movements will be altered.

In the case of our Southeastern Indians, what we may call the natural condition with reference to their adjustment to the animal life of the section had remained unaltered, since they had practically no domestic animals, while the gathering of natural vegetable products had given way in large measure before the cultivation of corn, beans, squashes, and a few other vegetables, with consequent modification of the original natural adjustment in that direction.

On examining the distribution of food animals, we find that the ones principally depended upon, including deer, bear, and bison, were distributed quite evenly, but water mammals, mussels, aquatic birds, and fresh-water fish augmented the available supplies of food about rivers and lakes, and in the sea the quantities of fish and shellfish are enormously increased. To the attraction of food must also be added that of shells as raw material for several useful articles, but particularly ornaments and money. We should naturally not be surprised, therefore, to find great concentrations of population along the rivers and still more upon the seacoast.

Turning to vegetable production, we find that those supplied spontaneously by nature herself are also distributed with a relatively even hand in spite of certain local differences. The best corn lands, however, before fertilizer was introduced, were not on the coasts, certainly not on the southernmost coasts, nor in the strip of pine lands which extends from North Carolina semicircularly to the Mississippi, but in the interior of the country, and it is there that we encounter the great corn-raising nations, though there were sections of the coast where agriculture and fishing were combined and supported a dense population. Land animals and natural vegetable products being evenly distributed, we observe a tendency of the mass of the population to gather upon the seacoast or the corn lands, and perhaps to oscillate between the two. This had a certain effect on seasonal migration and a more pronounced effect on trade.

An even greater effect, particularly on trade, seems to have been brought about by the unequal distribution of raw materials belonging to the mineral kingdom. Flint, to be sure, was widely spread, but even here there was a constant demand for the material by tribes on the alluvial lands of the lower Mississippi and along the greater part of the coast from those living inland.   There was also a steady trade between highland and lowland sections in stone pipes or the raw material out of which they were made, and mica.   For these, shells, shell beads, and other coastal products were exchanged, and exchange had to extend outside of the section in order that the Indians might supply themselves with catlinite and copper.   Finally, the unequal distribution of salt both increased the flow of commerce from coast to interior and vice versa.   It stimulated trade, and the seasonal movements of certain tribes, about various localities where salt licks had been located, particularly in the salt-lick section of Kentucky, and in northern Louisiana and southern Arkansas and Alabama.   We shall have more to say of this elsewhere.

The location of natural productions utilized by the Indians, insofar as they had marked localization and we have record of it, including also the location of the leading fisheries and the resorts of passenger pigeons, is given in map 13.   It must be remembered that our information is very defective and the actual condition is only remotely suggested by this chart.

THE ANNUAL ECONOMIC CYCLE

Until plants have been brought into cultivation and animals under domestication, man must seek his food where nature provides it, and this ordinarily involves seasonal migrations, since it is seldom that a succession of food plants and animals sufficient to sustain life is accessible at any one spot throughout the year.

In southern Florida this condition was very nearly attained and, although horticulture was absent, at least until very late times, the population upon the whole was relatively stable.   Continued residence of the Tekesta upon the coast during winter is indicated by the fact that they then put out to sea in search of the manatee or sea cow.   The economic life of the Timucua Indians in the Fresh Water province may have resembled that of those south of them, if one informant is right in stating that they did not raise corn.   By 1699, however, Dickenson found cornfields from Cape Canaveral north (Swanton, 1922, p. 360).

The situation in the interior, about Lake Okeechobee, was similar, though from the following remarks of Fontaneda, confirmed by recent studies by Stirling, it appears that some sort of seasonal migration was made necessary by periods of high water:

This lake is situated in the midst of the country, and is surrounded by a great number of villages of from thirty to forty inhabitants each, who live on bread made from roots during most of the year.   They cannot procure it, however, when the waters of the lake rise very high.   They have roots which resemble the truffles of this country [Spain], and have besides excellent fish.   Whenever game is to be had, either deer or birds, they eat meat.   Large numbers of very fat eels are found in the rivers, some of them as large as a man's thigh, and enormous trout, almost as large as a man's body; although smaller ones are also found. The natives eat lizards, snakes, and rats, which infest the lakes, freshwater turtles, and many other animals which it would be tiresome to enumerate. They live in a country covered with swamps and cut up by high bluffs. (Swanton, 1922, p. 388.)

In central and western Texas, territories which rather frame the Southeastern cultural province than belong to it, horticulture was also absent—except it is said in the case of the Aranama and one or two related tribes—but seasonal migrations were obligatory, particularly as respects the inland Indians, who changed their abodes to conform to the movement of the herds of bison and the availability of the tuna and other food plants. Those on the coast were kept there for considerable periods by the supplies of fish, but they also hunted inland at certain seasons and collected seeds of plants out of which they made a kind of bread.

Throughout the rest of the Southeast—except perhaps for a few bands living near the larger tribes, who are said to have specialized on hunting—corn, beans, pumpkins, and a few other vegetables were raised, and the fields where these grew usually determined the sites of the towns. This was because they required labor and protection and because most of the crop was stored for later consumption. Dried meat was also stored there, but it was never possible to tell where game animals were to be found, while the location of the field was definite. This, of course, meant that the people were generally in or near their villages in summer. They had to return to them in spring to plant, and a certain amount of cultivation was also necessary during the growing season, though the Indians did not worry themselves on this point as much as our farmers. However, it was also necessary to have someone watch the fields during the sprouting season to keep the ubiquitous crow and other birds in check. Between planting and harvest they did, however, often get time for a shorter hunt. After harvest they would remain in town until well toward winter to enjoy the produce of their fields and thus place it beyond the reach of human or animal depredation. This determined the period when the greatest feasts and ceremonies were held, the people being together and the maximum amount of food being available. The time of plenty was usually inaugurated by a special ceremony known to English-speaking people popularly as "the green corn dance," though it might be more accurately defined as a feast of first fruits, the ceremony being intended to insure continued supplies of plant and animal food during the ensuing year and along with them the health and prosperity of the partakers.

As the harvest was seldom sufficient to last—nor was it expected to last—until another crop came in, the Indians were obliged to seek natural food supplies elsewhere and, since such supplies were not usually concentrated, this meant that the people themselves scattered about in camps where they remained until planting time. Along the coast food supplies were usually more plentiful, though the same scattering took place in search of favorite fishing grounds. Here the annual spring runs of herring and other fish brought about concentrations of population at fishing stations on the rivers, particularly those at the edge of the Piedmont Plateau. But as these took place near the planting season, the interruption of the winter hunt occasioned by them was relatively small. Among littoral people, however, fishing tended to take the place of the summer hunt. Nevertheless, even the inland tribes were not without opportunities to enjoy a fish diet in summer, for they had fish traps led to by converging lines of rocks, and it was then that they resorted to the poisoning of fish in pools in the shrunken streams, or dragged them for the same purpose.

We can hardly introduce specific references to the annual economic cycle better than by the following quotation from Beverley's History of Virginia, in which it is treated in connection with the general subject of standards, subdivisions of time, and methods of counting:

They make their Account by units, tens, hundreds, &c. as we do; but they reckon the Years by the Winters, or *Cohonks*, as they call them; which is a name taken from the note of the Wild Geese, intimating so many times of the Wild Geese coming to them, which is every Winter. They distinguish the several parts of the Year, by five Seasons, *viz.* The budding or blossoming of the Spring; the earing of the Corn, or roasting ear time; the Summer, or highest Sun; the Corn-gathering, or fall of the Leaf; and the Winter, or *Cohonks*. They count the Months likewise by the Moons, tho not with any relation to so many in a year, as we do: but they make them return again by the same name, as the Moon of Stags, the Corn Moon, the first and second Moon of *Cohonks*, &c. They have no distinction of the hours of the Day, but divide it only into three parts, the Rise, Power, and lowering of the Sun. And they keep their account by knots on a string, or notches on a Stick, not unlike the *Peruvian Quippoes*. (Beverley, 1705, bk. 3, pp. 43–44.)

Smith gives us the Powhatan names of the five seasons:

Their winter some call *Popanow*, the spring *Cattapeuk*, the sommer *Cohattayough*, the earing of their Corne *Nepinough*, the harvest and fall of leafe *Taquitock*. (Smith, Tyler ed., 1907, p. 95.)

It is not clear whether the Algonquian tribes of Virginia had a definite beginning of the year or distinguished a summer and a winter series of months. As we might expect, winter was the great hunting season and was spent inland. Smith tells us:

In March and Aprill they live much upon their fishing weares, and feed on fish, Turkies and squirrels. In May and June they plant their fieldes, and live most of Acornes, walnuts, and fish. But to mend their diet, some disperse themselves in small companies, and live upon fish, beasts, crabs, oysters, land

Torteyses, strawberries, mulberries, and such like. In June, Julie, and August, they feed upon the rootes of *Tocknough*, berries, fish, and greene wheat [i. e., corn]. (Smith, Tyler ed., 1907, p. 102.)

Elsewhere he amends his remarks on the planting time by saying:

In Aprill they begin to plant, but their chiefe plantation is in May, and so they continue till the midst of June. What they plant in Aprill they reape in August, for May in September, for June in October. [He says also] from September untill the midst of November are the chiefe Feasts and sacrifice. Then have they plenty of fruits as well planted as naturall, as corne greene and ripe, fish, fowle, and wild beastes exceeding fat. (Smith, Tyler ed., 1907, pp. 95, 96.)

The sturgeon season on the James lasted from the end of May until the middle of September, but until the end of June only young sturgeon were taken (Smith, Tyler ed., 1907, p. 85).

When all their fruits be gathered, little els they plant, and this is done by their women and children; neither doth this long suffice them: for neere 3 parts of the yeare, they only observe times and seasons, and live of what the Country naturally affordeth from hand to mouth, &c. (Smith, Tyler ed., 1907, p. 97.)

The winter hunting season is covered by the following remarks of Smith:

By their continuall ranging, and travel, they know all the advantages and places most frequented with Deare, Beasts, Fish, Foule, Rootes, and Berries. At their huntings they leave their habitations, and reduce themselves into companies, as the Tartars doe, and goe to the most desert places with their families, where they spend their time in hunting and fowling up towards the mountaines, by the heads of their rivers, where there is plentie of game. For betwixt the rivers, the grounds are so narrowe, that little cometh there which they devour not. It is a marvel they can so directly passe these deserts some 3 or 4 daies journey without habitation. (Smith, Tyler ed., 1907, pp. 103–104.)

Strachey covers this in the following words:

In the tyme of their huntings, they leave their habitaticns, and gather themselves into companyes, as doe the Tartars, and goe to the most desart places with their families, where they passe the tyme with hunting and fowling up towards the mountaines, by the heads of their rivers, wher in deed there is plentye of game, for betwixt the rivers the land is not so large belowe that therein breed sufficyent to give them all content. Considering especyally, how at all tymes and seasons they destroy them, yt may seeme a marveyle how they can so directly passe and wander in these desarts, sometymes three or fower dayes' journyes, meeting with no habitacions, and, by reason of the woods, not having sight of the sun, whereby to direct them how to coast yt. (Strachey, 1849, pp. 75–76.)

Hariot gives an earlier sturgeon season in North Carolina, from February to May inclusive, and Burrage asserts that there were three crops of corn in that favored land within five months.

In May they sow, in July they reape, in June they sow, in August they reape: in July they sow, in September they reape. (Hariot, 1893, p. 31; Burrage, 1906, p. 234.)

The Siouan tribes of the east and the Tuscarora seem to have kept run of the seasons in an almost identical manner:

They name the months, very agreeably, as one is the herrring month, another the strawberry month, another the mulberry month. Others name them by the trees that blossom, especially the dogwood tree; or they say, we will return when turkey cocks gobble, that is in March and April. (Lawson, 1860, p. 380.)

Lawson also gives a very good idea of the activities of the same tribes during the winter season.

When these savages go a hunting, they commonly go out in great numbers, and oftentimes a great many days' journey from home, beginning at the coming in of the winter; that is, when the leaves are fallen from the trees and are become dry. [They then fired the woods in order to kill deer and other animals.] In these hunting quarters they have their wives and ladies of the camp, where they eat all the fruits and dainties of that country, and live in all the mirth and jollity which it is possible for such people to entertain themselves withal. (Lawson, 1860, p. 336.)

There they killed deer, turkeys, ducks and smaller game, but also had corn and dried beans, peas and fruits, carried along with them from their towns, and in some places pigeon fat.

At their setting out, they have Indians to attend their hunting camp that are not good and expert hunters, therefore are employed to carry burdens, to get bark for the cabins, and other servile work; also to go backward and forward to their towns, to carry news to the old people, whom they leave behind them. The women are forced to carry their loads of grain and other provisions and get fire wood; for a good hunter or warrior in these expeditions, is employed in no other business than the affairs of game and battle. (Lawson, 1860, p. 337.)

It was during this time that the women made baskets and mats, while the men less expert in hunting made wooden bowls, dishes, and spoons and clay tobacco pipes, many of which were later traded for skins and other articles. The skins then obtained were dressed during the following summer by the slaves and poor hunters. Summer was first and foremost the time for raising corn and other vegetables, and second the great fishing season, both along the rivers, where quantities of sturgeon and herring were taken, and on the seacoast. Surplus fish and shellfish were dried over hurdles for later consumption. At that time also the coast Indians, mainly Algonquians, collected *Marginella* shells for traffic with inland peoples (Lawson, 1860, p. 339). Crawfish were caught then, and the natural vegetable foods gathered in quantities, besides plants to be used as medicines.

In summer, [says Catesby,] they feed much on vegetables, particularly *Maiz* before it is ripe, and while tender, they roast it in the fire, also pomkins, gourds, squashes, melons, cucumbers, potatoes; besides peaches, raspberries, and strawberries, which their woods abound in. *Indians* seldom plant enough corn to last them the year round, yet in some measure they supply that want by their autumn-collection of black walnuts, hiccory nuts, chinkapins and acorns, which they lay up for winter store; from these they press wholesome oil, particularly from the acorns of the live oak. The kernels also of these nuts and acorns being beat in a mortar to a paste, serve to thicken and enrich their broths. (Catesby, 1731–43, vol. 2, p. x.)

Catesby says that deer drives were in October.

Laudonnière tells us that the Timucua Indians sowed their corn twice a year, in March and June, and not in larger amounts than would last them for 6 months (pl. 51).

During the winter they retire for three or four months in the year, into the woods, where they make little cottages of palm boughs for their retreat, and live there of maste, of fish which they take, of disters [oysters], of stags, of turkey cocks, and other beasts which they take. (Laudonnière, 1586, pp. 11–12.)

Le Moyne, however, makes the strange statement that they let their seed lie in the ground over winter to come up in the spring. But he also adds that they sheltered themselves in the woods "for about three months, being from the 24th of December to the 15th of March" (Le Moyne, 1875, p. 9; illus.), rather minute dating for primitive men and explained by the fact that those happened to be the dates in the one winter when the French were able to observe them, the winter of 1564–65. It is safe to say that the Timucua ladies did not broadcast seed in the reckless manner indicated by Le Moyne.

Interesting light on the economic year along the lower Mississippi is given by Du Pratz in connection with his enumeration of the Natchez months. He says that there was a feast or ceremony on the new moon of each month showing how the economic and ceremonial cycles were intertwined.

This nation begins its year in the month of March, as was the practice for a long time in Europe, and divides it into 13 moons. This thirteenth moon is added to complete the year and to make the course of the planet [i.e., the moon] agree in the matter of time with that of the sun. At every new moon they celebrate a feast, which takes its name from the principal fruits gathered in the preceding moon, or from the animals that are usually hunted then. . . .

The first moon is that of the Deer. The renewal of the year spreads universal joy. [Du Pratz then goes on to describe a celebration consisting of the dramatic representation of an event in the past history of the Natchez.] . . . The second moon, which corresponds to our month of April, is that of the Strawberries. The women and children collect them in great quantities, and as strawberries abound in this country it may be judged whether the great Sun lacks them. . . . The warriors then make their presents of wood ducks, which they have provided by a hunt made expressly for the purpose. The third moon is that of the Little Corn. This month is often awaited with impatience, their harvest of the great corn never sufficing to nourish them from one harvest to another. The fourth is that of the Watermelons, and answers to the month of June. This month and the preceding are those in which the sardines run up against the current of the river. The fifth moon is that of the Peaches. It answers to our month of July. In this time grapes are also brought in if the birds have left any of them to ripen. The sixth moon is that of the Mulberries. It is the month of August. At this feast birds are also brought to the great Sun. The seventh moon is that of Maize or the Great Corn. [And of this feast Du Pratz also gives a lengthy description.] The eighth moon is that of the Turkeys and corresponds to our month of October. It is then that this bird comes out of the thick woods to enter the open woods in order to eat nettle seeds, of which it is very fond. The ninth moon is that of the Bison. Then they go to hunt this animal. As it always stays some leagues from the cantons inhabited by men, precaution is taken to send forward scouts to locate the animals in order to know when they have assembled. When this is known everyone sets out, young and old, girls and women, unless they have little children, for this hunt being rough there is work for everyone. Many nations wait until later before going, in order to find the bison in greater numbers and the cows fatter. . . . The tenth moon is that of the Bears. In these hunting seasons the feasts are not large, because the warriors, being all away from home, take away many of the people with them. The eleventh moon, which corresponds to our month of January, is that of the Cold Meal. At this time many bustards, geese, ducks, and other similar kinds of game are to be had. The twelfth moon is that of the Chestnuts. This fruit has indeed been collected some time before, but nevertheless this month bears that name. Finally, the thirteenth month is that of the Nuts. It is added to complete the year. It is then that the nuts are broken in order to make bread by mingling them with corn meal. (Le Page du Pratz, 1758, vol. 2, pp. 354–383.)

"Cold Meal" was parched corn meal such as men took on a war expedition or when traveling long distances. Perhaps the names Cold Meal, Chestnuts, and Nuts were given to these last three winter months because the larder was low and such foods then assumed an importance not ordinarily enjoyed by them. Surprising prominence is here given to the bison hunt, and elsewhere Du Pratz speaks of bison meat as a main reliance of the Indians and colonists, seemingly a strange statement if it is applied to lower Louisiana, but further evidence to the former greater abundance of these animals in the section is given farther on (Le Page du Pratz, 1758, vol. 2, p. 69; also see pp. 324–328, below).

Other travelers on the lower Mississippi shift the names of these months somewhat. Gravier says that the "little corn" was harvested in June and that the main harvest was not until the end of November (Gravier *in* Thwaites, 1897–1901, vol. 65, p. 145). Dumont de Montigny seems to place the harvest festival in July, and Charlevoix and Le Petit agree with him. (Dumont, 1753, vol. 1, p. 195; French, 1851, pp. 165–166; Le Petit *in* Thwaites, 1897–1901, vol. 68, p. 136.) As I have elsewhere suggested, one set of writers may be describing the feast of the "little corn" and another that which accompanied the main harvest, but we know that the dates on which these were held varied in different tribes or in different towns of the same tribe. Among the Creeks, for instance, they occurred as early as June and as late as the middle of August. For a ceremonial people like the Natchez, it seems not a little singular that every Natchez month is named for some article of food.

The names of the Tunica months have not been preserved, though we are told that the Indians lived during one of these on persimmons (Shea, 1861, p. 134).

For some reason difficult to explain, we have fewer references to the economic cycle among the great inland tribes, the Creeks, Chickasaw, and Choctaw, than for those on the margins. Swan gives us a very reliable statement regarding the Creek calendar, and we have strong evidence that the Choctaw system was practically identical in former times, though during the nineteenth century the month names, not having been corrected with reference to the natural events to which they properly applied, had gotten dislodged from their true positions. Swan distinguishes a series of winter months and a series of summer months, but the former began, not with cold weather, but apparently with the busk, or green corn ceremony, and the summer months began with February. Their year was from equinox to equinox rather than solstice to solstice. The winter months were: Much Heat, or Big Ripening (August), Little Chestnut (September), Big Chestnut (October), Iholi, probably signifying "Frost," or "Change in Weather" (November), Big Winter (December), and Little Winter (January). The summer months were: Wind Month (February), Little Spring (March), Big Spring (April), Mulberry (May), Blackberry (June), and Little Warmth, or Little Ripening (July) (Swan, 1855, p. 276). The only names which the Creeks shared with the Natchez were the names of the month of Mulberries and the month (or months) of Chestnuts, but their positions in the series differ. The Creek month names also show a striking contrast to those used by the Natchez in that relatively few of them refer to articles of food. The only ones are the Little Chestnut month, Big Chestnut month, Mulberry month, and Blackberry month, and these do not indicate foods of cardinal importance. The Chickasaw months would probably be found to agree with the Creek and Choctaw.

Speaking of all the Southeastern Indians of his acquaintance, Adair says:

They divided the year into spring—summer—autumn, or the fall of the leaf—and winter. . . . They number their years by any of those four periods, for they have no name for a year; and they subdivide these, and count the year by lunar months . . . They count the day also by the three sensible differences of the sun. . . . They subdivide the day, by any of the aforesaid three standards—as half way between the sun's coming out of the water; and in like manner by midnight, or cock-crowing, &c. . . . They begin the year, at the first appearance of the first new moon of the vernal equinox, according to the ecclesiastical year of Moses. . . . They pay a great regard to the first appearance of every new moon, and, on the occasion, always repeat some joyful sounds, and stretch out their hands towards her—but at such times they offer no public sacrifice. . . . When they lack a full moon, or when they travel, they count by sleeps. (Adair, 1775, pp. 74-77.)

The divisions of time, as remembered 30 years ago among the Yuchi, are as follows, as given by Speck:

The seasons are four in number. Spring, called *hĭnᴀ wadelé*, "when summer is near," is the time when agricultural activities are resumed after the comparative idleness of the winter. "Summer," *wädē'*, a term apparently related to *wäfá*, "south," is the long and active season. Autumn, *yacadīlé*, "when the leaves are yellow," is a period of combined rest, hunting and enjoyment. Winter was called *wĭctá*, "snow comes (?)." This season the people spent in idleness and recreation.

The year is further divided into moons or months, each of which has its name. The names of eleven of these moons with translations and the corresponding months in our calendar are as follows.

S·ä latcpī'	Ground frozen month	January
Ho'da dzó	Wind Month	February
Wäd'·á' sīnéⁿ	Little summer	March
Wäd·ä·ä'	Big summer	April
Dec·ō' nendzó	Mulberry ripening month	May
Cpáco nendzó	Blackberry ripening month	June
Wag·ä'kyä.	Middle of summer	July
Tséne agá	Dog days	August
Tsogá lĭ'ne tse·e	Hay cutting month	September
Tsot·ō' hoⁿstäné	Corn ripening month	October
Ho'ctaⁿd·ä' kyä	Middle of winter	December

The passage of time during the day time is commonly observed by glancing at the sun. During the night time the moon and stars, if the weather is clear, served the same purpose.

The day itself is divided into different periods equivalent, in our reckoning, to morning, noon, afternoon and evening. The names of these are *ägyälé*, "at dawn," "morning"; *yūbalé ⁿ*, "noon," derivative from *yū'ba*, "high," referring to the sun; *padonᴀⁿhogyé*, "afternoon," "toward the night"; *f·ä*, "evening," and lastly, *pado'*, "night." (Speck, 1909, p. 67.)

The earliest note regarding the annual movements of any of the central tribes is by Bossu. It has particular reference to the Alabama Indians, but his remarks would undoubtedly hold good for all of the tribes of the Creek Confederation.

The savages usually set out on the hunt at the end of October. The Allibamons go to a distance of 60, 80, and even 100 leagues [165–275 miles] from their village, and they carry along with them in their pirogues their entire family; they return only in March which is the season for sowing their fields. They bring back many skins and much smoked meat. When they have returned to their villages, they feast their friends, and make presents to the old people who have been unable to follow them, and who have protected the cabins of the village during the hunting period. (Bossu, 1768, vol. 2, pp. 51–52.)

Hawkins confirms these statements and adds some details:

It is usual with the old chiefs of that nation to spend the winter in the woods and they seldom return to their towns till the last of February, and I have found March, April, and May the most favourable season to gather them together. In the latter months there is grass for their horses, provisions are scarce in their towns, and they now usually return poor and hungry from their hunts. They begin their hunt late in the fall, generally in October. (Hawkins, 1916, pp. 385–386, 396.)

My own informants recalled the time as the last of October or November.

From a later note by Hawkins, dated at Kasihta, November 19, 1797, it is evident that the hunt was often prolonged much beyond February. He says,

The hunters of this nation are all gone into the woods and not expected to return till from the first of March to the beginning of September. (Hawkins, 1916, p. 241.)

During the summer, while they were in or near the town, the Creeks took part in a series of monthly ceremonies which began in April or May and culminated in July or August with the great annual busk which marked the end of the one year and the beginning of another.[9a] Food was most plentiful during the period immediately following this, and then assemblies were most in evidence. There was also a series of social feasts and dances which culminated in the Skunk Dance, or the Dance of the Ancient People, which took place in October or November (Swanton, 1928 a, pp. 546–614).

The Choctaw had few canoes and ordinarily went overland to their winter camps, but they devoted more attention to agriculture than any other Southeastern tribe and sold some of the produce to the less thrifty Chickasaw. Their hunting territories were proportionately restricted and they did not wander far from their towns. Small game, particularly squirrels, played a large part in their economy, but these were hunted mostly in summer. As in the case of the Creeks, their principal feasts and ceremonies were in the fall and anciently they seem to have had some ceremony corresponding to the busk, but next to nothing is known regarding it. An early authority tells us that

In years of scarcity when the corn crop has failed, all of the savages leave the villages and go with their families to camp in the woods at a distance of 30 or 40 leagues, in places where bison and deer are to be found, and they live there by hunting and on [wild] potatoes. (Swanton, 1918, p. 49.)

Thus even the best farmers in the Southeast were at times converted en masse into hunters, for their conquest of the vegetable world had not carried with it a similar conquest of the animal world. They must still seek flesh food where nature had placed it, and animal manure assisted wild nature alone instead of renewing the Indian farms and enabling their cultivators to continue indefinitely in one place.

[9a] From Adair's statement it seems not unlikely that there were two New Year's Days 6 months apart.

Speaking particularly of the Chickasaw, Adair says that house building was usually undertaken in fall and spring, and that little work was done in summer except, of course, the necessary care of the fields and the work of bringing in firewood for cooking. War parties started out as soon as the weather began to warm up in spring (Adair, 1775, pp. 402–403).

The seasonal movements of the eastern Caddo resembled those of the inland tribes just considered. Those of the western Caddo were determined to a great extent by the annual bison hunt.

FOOD

The chroniclers of the De Soto expedition give us our first insight into the native economy of the section, and we find the following articles of food mentioned:

Corn, kidney beans, and various sorts of pumpkins and squashes were cultivated. Among the natural productions of the vegetable kingdom they used the following: Two kinds of plums, persimmons, grapes (including muscadines), mulberries, strawberries, walnuts (including hickory nuts), chestnuts, chinquapins, acorns, and "bunches of young onions just like those of Castile, as big as the end of the thumb and larger" (Bourne, 1904, vol. 2, p. 87). The plums and persimmons were dried, and dried persimmons, made into cakes or bricks of "bread," as it is often called, were a staple throughout the section. The grapes they found growing about Hothliwahali (Ulibahali) on the Tallapoosa River were the best they tasted anywhere; they were probably muscadines (Bourne, 1904, vol. 1, p. 85; vol. 2, p. 114). A sort of bread was made out of chestnuts, and oil was extracted from walnuts (hickory nuts) and acorns (Bourne, 1904, vol. 2, pp. 15, 107; vol. 1, p. 74). Among animal foods they mention the deer, bison, bear, turkey, rabbit (often called "cony"), the last mentioned being trapped (Bourne, 1904, vol. 1, pp. 145–146). In the Appalachian country "barkless dogs" are said to have been eaten, and by some these are supposed to have been opossums, but this is probably an error, and there is also reason to believe that the one chronicler who reports Indian fondness for dog flesh was wrong or has been misinterpreted (Bourne 1904, vol. 1, p. 72; vol. 2, p. 103). Among some of the tribes it was customary for warriors about to set out upon an expedition to feast upon a dog, but this was exceptional and seems to have been accompanied by a strict taboo of dog meat at other times. However, from various parts of North America we have notices of the use of a small variety of dog as food and cannot ignore the possibility that the custom may have extended to the Southeast. Mention is made in a general way of the use of birds other than turkeys as food, and turkeys were, of course, eaten in all sections. The Gentleman of Elvas thus describes the fish taken in the Mississippi River and íts tributaries near the mouth of the Arkansas:

> There was a fish called "bagre," a third of which was head; and it had large spines like a sharp shoemaker's awl at either side of its throat and along the sides. Those of them which were in the water were as large as a "pico." In the river, there were some of one hundred and one hundred and fifty pounds. Many of them were caught with the hook. Another fish resembled the "barbell"; and others were like the "choupa," with a head like that of the "besugo" and between russet and brown. This was the one that was most relished. There was another fish called the "pexe palla." Its snout was a cubit in length and the tip of its upper lip was shaped like a shovel. There was another fish which resembled a shad. All had scales except the "bagres" and the "pexe palla." There was another fish which the Indians brought sometimes, of the size of a hog, called "pexe pereo." It had rows of teeth below and above. (Robertson, 1933, vol. 2, pp. 175–176.)

In 1933 Dr. Lewis Radcliffe, Acting Commissioner of the Bureau of Fisheries, supplied Dr. James A. Robertson with the following note regarding the fish mentioned by Elvas, to accompany the latter's translation of that work:

> The *bagre* no doubt refers to a species of catfish. Judging by the large size of the fish and its large head, as described, it was most likely the mud catfish, *Leptops olivaris*. However, there is also a possibility that the author had in mind the blue catfish, *Ictalurus furcatus*. Indeed, both species might have been seen in the vicinity, since both are of a large size and quite common in the rivers draining into the Gulf of Mexico. The word *barbo* is used in Spanish and French for several species of fresh-water fish. The British name for those species is "barbel." The species to which these names are applied are widespread throughout Europe, including Portugal. Judging from the distribution of the species and the similarity of the names in England, France, and Spain, it seems quite likely that the name *barbo* is also applied in Portugal to the same fishes. None of the species of the barbels occur in American waters, but our species of suckers resembles in general appearance the European barbels, and to a lesser extent the same may be said in regard to our buffalo fishes. There are several species of suckers and buffalo fishes in American waters; but from the author's statement it is impossible to assert which one of these he had in mind. In a list of the common fishes in Portuguese, the name *choupa* is applied to *Sargus rondeletti* and *besugo* to *Pagellus acarne*. Neither of these species, both of which are spiny-rayed fishes, occurs in the waters of the United States. The Portuguese *choupa* is shaped something like our bream and the *besugo* resembles our black bass. Since the author evidently described only the larger fishes, two possibilities suggest themselves: he had in mind either the black bass (and in some of them, especially in large specimens, the body is fairly deep) or the fresh-water drum. Since he states that it was the "most relished," he probably had in mind the large-mouthed black bass, *Micropterus salmoides*. The *pexe palla* was undoubtedly the spoonbill, *Polyodon spatula*. The description of the snout combined with the lack of scales, as stated by the author, applies to no other American species, and it fairly characterizes the spoonbill. The name *savel* (plural *savěs*) is applied to two species of European shad, *Alosa alosa* and *Alosa finta*. A species of shad, *Alosa alabama*, occurs in the Gulf drainage, although it is now quite rare. The author may have seen this or one or two other fishes, namely, the gizzard shad, *Dorosoma cepedianum*, and the menhaden, *Brevoortia patronus*.

These two latter species resemble the shad in appearance, although they usually do not grow over a foot in length. There are several other clupeoid fishes in the waters of Florida, which have some resemblance to the shad, although they are of small size. It is impossible to identify the *pexe pereo* with any exactness. The names *peixe prego* and *peixe porco* are applied to species of sharks in Portugal. Judging from the author's comparison of the fish to a hog, a fish having a deep body is suggested. The following three species, which are found in these waters, are quite common and have rather deep bodies, namely, fresh-water drum or gaspergou, *Häplodinotus grunniens*, the black drum, *Pogonias chromis*, and the jewfish, *Promicrops itaiara*. The first named is a strictly fresh-water fish, but is also common in brackish water; while the third is a salt-water species. (Robertson, 1933, vol. 2, pp. 372–374.)

When Buckingham Smith asked the opinion of Dr. Theodore Gill of the Smithsonian Institution regarding the identity of the fish described by Elvas, he got the following reply, as printed in Smith's Narratives of the Career of Hernando de Soto:

I have carefully perused the account, and although there is little on which to base the identification of the species, I am disposed to believe that the following conjectures will at least closely approximate the truth. The historian enumerates five species of which three have scales while the others are naked. The scaleless species are the "bagre" and the "peel-fish."

The "bagre" is undoubtedly the large "cat-fish" of the West, known as *Ictalurus caerulescens*, that being the only species that attains a weight of "one hundred to one hundred and fifty pounds." The head is large, as in all its congeners, but not as big as would be inferred from the text; the "great spines like very sharp awls," along the side, are the spines of the pectural fins. The species is very generally distributed in the hydrographical basin of the Mississippi. The "peel-fish," with "the snout a cubit in length, the upper lip being shaped like a shovel," is very clearly the singular fish universally known throughout the West as the "spoonbill-cat" or sturgeon, and "paddle-fish." It is related to the ordinary sturgeons, but is distinguished by the peculiar leaf-like expansion of the snout, the extension of the gill covers, and the presence of minute teeth on the jaws in the young. The species observed was the *Polyodon spatula*, occurring in the Mississippi River, and all its larger tributaries. The only other species of the genus, besides the American, inhabit the rivers of China and Japan.

The scaly fishes are not so easily determinable. The one shaped like a barbel was probably the *Cycleptus elongatus*, a member of the family of "suckers," or *Catastomidae*. That species would probably be recognized by most or all casual observers as having a greater superficial resemblance to the barbel of Europe than any other of our fishes. The fish "like a shad" was perhaps the species which has been introduced into the ichthyological system as *Pomolobus chrysochloris*, and which is very closely related to the "fall herring" or "shad" of the Eastern fishermen. The breamlike fish cannot be identified with any approach to certainty; but it is possible that it may have been the fish now known in Louisiana and Mississippi as "tarpon" or "big scale," and called by naturalists *Megalops cyprinoides*. That species more nearly fulfils the requisites as to form of head and excellence as food than any of the species known to me. The "pereo" is probably referable to the genus *Haplodinotus*, the species of which are generally called "white perch" or "drum" by the inhabitants of the west. That type, at least, is the only one that possesses the combination of scaly body, teeth in the jaws, and size, referred to in the notice. (Smith, B., 1857, pp. 223–224.)

There is also a reference to honey which has created considerable discussion, since honeybees were unknown in that part of America north of Mexico until they were introduced by the whites. Elvas represents this as one of the articles of food obtained at Chiaha near the present Chattanooga. He says:

> There was also found considerable walnut oil . . . and a pot of bee's honey; which before or after was not seen in all the land—neither honey nor bees. (Robertson, 1933, vol. 1, p. 74.)

Probably this experience was the same as one related by Ranjel, though the latter places the event at Coste, farther down the Tennessee River.

> There in Coste they found in the trunk of a tree as good honey and even better than could be had in Spain.   (Robertson, 1933, vol. 2, p. 110.)

It must be added that "honey" is mentioned by Laudonnière in 1564–65 as one of the articles of food which the Indians of Florida carried with them when they traveled some distance from home, but in this case mil, "millet" (intended to designate "corn"), has been misread "miel," for dried cornmeal was the staple provision of a warrior (Laudonnière, 1586, p. 9).

At Cofitachequi on Savannah River the Spaniards were treated to an abundance of salt; in what is now central Alabama and northern Mississippi they were taught by the Indians to burn a certain herb and mix the ashes in their food as a salt substitute; and west of the Mississippi River, in southern Arkansas and northern Louisiana, they found salt springs and salt as a staple article of trade. At some of these springs they made salt for themselves. (Bourne, 1904, vol. 2, pp. 99, 147, 148; vol. 1, p. 136; Garcilaso, 1723, pp. 175–176, 182, 189.)

So far as they can be identified, all of these foods are such as were found in use by the later comers of Spanish, English, or French extraction, except the honey, and real honeybees were soon introduced by the whites themselves.

Omitting, for the present, consideration of the foods reported in use in Florida in 1564–65 when the French and Spaniards settled there, we will turn to an excellent description by Thomas Hariot of the dietary of the Algonquian tribes in the Sound region of North Carolina, where the Raleigh Colony was settled in 1585–87:

> There are three sorts [of corn], of which two are ripe in an eleuen and twelue weekes at the most: sometimes in ten, after the time they are set, and are then of height in stalke about sixe or seuen foote. The other sort is ripe in fourteene, and is about ten foote high, of the stalkes some beare foure heads, some three, some one, and two; euery head containing fiue, sixe, or seuen hundred graines within a fewe more or lesse. (Hariot, 1893, p. 22.)

The kernels of all apparently were of mixed colors, "some white, some red, some yellow, and some blew" (Hariot, 1893, p. 21). He speaks of two kinds of native beans, called by the English, beans and peas respectively, though the latter seem to have been quite distinct from European peas.

Okindgier, called by vs *Beanes,* because in greatnesse & partly in shape they are like to the Beanes in England; sauing that they are flatter, or more diuers colours, and some pide. The leafe also of the stemme is much different. In taste they are altogether as good as our English peaze.

Wickonzówr, called by us *Peaze* in respect of the beanes for distinction sake, because they are much lesse; although in forme they little differ; but in goodnesse of tast much, & are far better than our English peaze. Both the beanes and the peaze are ripe in tenne weekes after they are set. They make them victuall either by boyling them all to pieces into a broth; or boyling them whole vntill they bee soft and beginne to breake as is vsed in England, eyther by themselues or mixtly together: Sometime they mingle of the wheate with them. Sometime also beeing whole sodden, they bruse or pound them in a morter, & thereof make loaues or lumps of dowishe bread, which they vse to eat for varietie. (Hariot, 1893, p. 22.)

His "wilde peaze" may be the marsh peas (*Lathyrus myrtifolius* or *Lathyrus venosus*).

Two varieties of pumpkins or squashes are recognized by the same writer:

Macócquwer, according to their seuerall formes called by vs, *Pompions, Mellions,* and *Gourdes,* because they are of the like formes as those kindes in England. In *Virginia* such of seuerall formes are of one taste and very good, and do also spring from one seed. These are of two sorts; one is ripe in the space of a moneth, and the other in two moneths. (Hariot, 1893, p. 22.)

There is considerable uncertainty as to the number of varieties of pumpkins and squashes known to the aborigines of North America, and our uncertainty is often increased by the fact that they are confused with melons of Old World origin or called by the same names. Watermelons in particular spread so rapidly among the aborigines that they sometimes outdistanced the explorers themselves. Thus a Spanish soldier who visited an Indian town on the Altamaha River in 1597, reports "sandias" among the vegetables being raised there (Serrano y Sanz, 1913, p. 144). Note also the name "Watermelon Month" in the calendar of the Natchez (Le Page du Pratz, 1758, pp. 354–360). However, it is rather unlikely that melons had reached the seacoast of North Carolina by 1585.

To the cultivated plants indicated by our Spanish authorities, Hariot adds two. One of these is the sunflower:

There is also another great hearbe in forme of a Marigolde, about sixe foote in height; the head with the floure is a spanne in breadth. Some take it to bee *Planta Solis:* of the seedes heereof they make both a kinde of bread and broth. (Hariot, 1893, p. 23.)

The other belongs, in part, in the category of salt substitutes like the one of which Garcilaso tells us. Hariot says of it:

There is an hearbe which in Dutch is called *Melden*. Some of those that I describe it vnto, take it to be a kinde of Orage; it groweth about foure or fiue foote high; of the seede thereof they make a thicke broth, and pottage of a very good taste: of the stalke by burning into ashes they make a kinde of salt earth, wherewithall many vse sometimes to season their brothes; other salte they knowe not. Wee our selues, vsed the leues also for pothearbes. (Hariot, 1893, pp. 22–23.)

This was perhaps the halberd-leaved orache (*Atriplex hastata*). To the "young onions" of the Spaniards, Hariot adds a considerable number of wild roots in his description of the native menu. Of one of these he says:

Openavk are a kind of roots of round forme, some of the bignes of walnuts, some far greater, which are found in moist & marish grounds growing many together one by another in ropes, or as thogh they were fastened with a string. Being boiled or sodden they are very good meate. (Hariot, 1893, p. 26.)

The late Doctor Michelson told me that "penavk," or "penauk," is a common Algonquian word meaning "root." It appears again below. The openavk were the native marsh potatoes or ground nuts of the Gulf region (*Apios tuberosa*), which were evidently used in pre-Columbian times throughout the region. To proceed:

Okeepenavk are also of round shape, found in dry grounds: some are of the bignes of a mans head. They are to be eaten as they are taken out of the ground, for by reason of their drinesse they will neither roste nor seeth. Their tast is not so good as of the former rootes, notwithstanding for want of bread & sometimes for varietie the inhabitants vse to eate them with fish or flesh, and in my iudgment they doe as well as the household bread made of rie heere in England. (Hariot, 1893, p. 26.)

It seems pretty evident that these roots were from plants of the wild sweetpotato (*Ipomoea pandurata*), although Carrier (1923, p. 32) identifies them with "a large fungus growth found in sandy soils of the Carolinas" and sometimes called tuckahoe.

Kaishcúpenauk a white kind of roots about the bignes of hen egs & nere of that forme: their tast was not so good to our seeming as of the other, and therefore their place and manner of growing not so much cared for by vs: the inhabitants notwithstanding vsed to boile & eate many. (Hariot, 1893, p. 26.)

E. P. Killip, to whom I am indebted for most of these identifications, suggests that this may be *Dioscorea villosa* (cf. Amer. Journ. Sci., vol. 25, p. 25). Generally speaking, the identity of the roots used as food is in greater doubt than any other vegetable or animal product mentioned by early writers.

There is more certainty regarding the root to be described next:

Tsinaw a kind of roote much like vnto the which in England is called the *China root* brought from the East Indies. And we know not anie thing to the contrary but that it maie be of the same kind. These roots grow manie together in great clusters and doe bring foorth a brier stalke, but the leafe in shape far vnlike; which beeing supported by the trees it groweth neerest vnto, wil reach or climbe to the top of the highest. From these roots while they be new or fresh beeing chopt into small pieces & stampt, is strained with water a iuce that maketh bread, & also being boiled, a very good spoonemeate in maner of a gelly, and is much better in tast if it bee tempered with oyle. This *Tsinaw* is not of that sort which by some was caused to be brought into England or the *China roote*, for it was discouered since, and is in vse as is afore saide: but that which was brought hither is not yet knowne neither by vs nor by the inhabitants to serue for any vse or purpose; although the rootes in shape are very like. (Hariot, 1893, pp. 25–26.)

This is the China briar of Bartram, the red kunti of the Creeks, the kantak of the Choctaw. The name seems to have been given to several species of *Smilax*, which were used everywhere in the Southeast. In southern Florida, however, it has been transferred to a *Zamia*, sometimes distinguished from the other by being called "white kunti."

Coscúshaw, some of our company tooke to bee that kinde of roote which the Spaniards in the West Indies call *Cassauy*, whereupon also many called it by that name: it groweth in very muddie pooles and moist groundes. Being dressed according to the countrey maner, it maketh a good bread, and also a good sponemeate, and is vsed very much by the inhabitants: The iuce of this root is poison, and therefore heede must be taken before any thing be made therewithal: Either the rootes must bee first sliced and dried in the Sunne, or by the fire, and then being pounded into floure will make good bread: or els while they are greene they are to bee pared, cut into pieces and stampt; loues of the same to be laid neere or ouer the fire vntill it be floure, and then being well pounded againe, bread, or spone meate very good in taste, and holsome may be made thereof. (Hariot, 1893, p. 27.)

This is the food called in Virginia tuckahoe, and in the present instance the name probably refers specifically to the goldenclub, or floating arum (*Orontium aquaticum*), though the name was also applied to the roots of the Virginia wakerobin (*Peltandra virginica*) or "poison arum," to the *apios tuberosa* (see above),[10] and to tuberlike objects due to the disintegration of the roots of certain trees (mainly coniferous). Farther south on the coast of the Carolinas, it was known as wampee, but from that region less has been preserved regarding its use (Gerard, 1907, pp. 109–110).

Habascon is a roote of hoat taste almost of the forme and bignesse of a Parseneepe, of it selfe it is no victuall, but onely a helpe beeing boiled together with other meates. (Hariot, 1893, p. 26.)

It is probably the umbelliferous plant known as angelico (*Ligusticum actaeifolium*), and popularly in the south as nondo (from Pow-

---

[10] Catesby mentions "earth-nuts which they call *Tuccaho*" (1731–1743, vol. 2, p. x.)

hatan woⁿdeu). It is boiled and used as food throughout most of the Gulf region.

Reference is also made to the use of berries found growing upon a marsh plant.

Sacqvenvmmener a kinde of berries almost like vnto capres but somewhat greater which grow together in clusters vpon a plant or herb that is found in shalow waters: being boiled eight or nine hours according to their kind are very good meate and holesome, otherwise if they be eaten they will make a man for the time franticke or extremely sicke. (Hariot, 1893, pp. 28–29.)

Beverley (1705, bk. 2, p. 14) describes this as a kind of arum, which would identify the plant as the "poison arum," or Virginia wake-robin (*Peltandra virginica*), and by inference tend to identify the "Coscúshaw" described above with *Orontium aquaticum*, unless, as is possible, the Indians gave different names to the berries and root of the former.

Hariot thus describes the persimmon:

Medlars a kind of verie good fruit, so called by vs chieflie for these respectes: first in that they are not good vntill they be rotten: then in that they open at the head as our medlars, and are about the same bignesse: otherwise in taste and colour they are farre different: for they are as red as cheries and very sweet: but whereas the cherie is sharpe sweet, they are lushious sweet. (Hariot, 1893, p. 28.)

Following is almost the only mention of the prickly pear east of the Mississippi River:

Metaqvesvnnavk, a kinde of pleasaunt fruite almost of the shape & bignes of English peares, but that they are of a perfect red colour as well within as without. They grow on a plant whose leaues are verie thicke and full of prickles as sharpe as needles. Some that haue bin in the Indies, where they haue seen that kind of red die of great price which is called Cochinile to grow, doe describe his plant right like vnto this of Metaquesunnauk but whether it be the true Cochinile or a bastard or wilde kind, it cannot yet be certified; seeing that also as I heard, Cochinile is not of the fruite but founde on the leaues of the plant; which leaues for such matter we haue not so specially obserued. (Hariot, 1893, p. 28.)

Hariot (1893, p. 28) also mentions two kinds of grapes, one evidently the famous scuppernong, besides strawberries, mulberries, huckleberries ("hurts or hurtleberies"), and crab apples ("applecrabs") *(Malus)*, also wild peas and "a kind of reed which beareth a seed almost like vnto our rie or wheat, & being boiled is good meat." This last is presumably the cane which bears seed irregularly, not every year. Whenever the "grain" from this was available, it was resorted to throughout the southern country. Another possible identification, however, is with the wild rice. He mentions chestnuts and two kinds of walnuts, the second evidently the hickory:

Chestnvts, there are in diuers places great store: some they vse to eate rawe, some they stampe and boile to make spoonemeate, and with some being sodden they make such a manner of dowe bread as they vse of their beanes before mentioned.

Walnvts: There are two kindes of Walnuts, and of them infinit store: In many places where very great woods for many miles together the third part of trees are walnuttrees. The one kind is of the same taste and forme or litle differing from ours of England, but that they are harder and thicker shelled; the other is greater and hath a verie ragged and harde shell: but the kernell great, verie oylie and sweete. Besides their eating of them after our ordinarie maner, they breake them with stones and pound them in morters with water to make a milk which they vse to put into some sorts of their spoonmeate; also among their sodde wheat, peaze, beanes and pompions which maketh them haue a farre more pleasant taste. (Hariot, 1893, pp. 27–28.)

They are noted again in the following paragraphs, along with acorns:

There is a kind of berrie or acorne, of which there are flue sorts that grow on seuerall kinds of trees; the one is called *Sagatémener*, the second *Osámener*, the third *Pummuckóner*. These kind of acorns they vse to drie vpon hurdles made of reeds with fire vnderneath almost after the maner as we dry malt in England. When they are to be vsed they first water them vntil they be soft & then being sod they make a good victuall, either to eate so simply, or els being also pounded, to make loaues or lumpes of bread. These be also the three kinds of which, I said before, the inhabitants vsed to make sweet oyle.

An other sort is called *Supúmmener* which being boiled or parched doth eate and taste like vnto chestnuts. They sometime also make bread of this sort.

The fifth sort is called *Mangúmmenauk*, and is the acorne of their kind of oake, the which beeing dried after the maner of the first sortes, and afterward watered they boile them, & their seruants or sometimes the chiefe themselues, either for variety or for want of bread, doe eate them with their fish or flesh. (Hariot, 1893, p. 29.)

The first three, as may be gathered from the concluding sentence in the paragraph describing them, were chestnuts, walnuts, and hickory nuts, the fourth probably chinquapins, and the last the acorn of one or more species of oak, probably, however, the live oak (*Quercus virginiana*). He speaks of oil extracted from nuts and also from acorns (Hariot, 1893, p. 16).

Among animals hunted for their flesh Hariot mentions several varieties of deer, rabbits ("conies"), two larger animals called "saquenúckot" and "maquówoc" (perhaps the otter and beaver), squirrels, and black bears, besides porpoises, and states that he has the names of 86 kinds of fowl (Hariot, 1893, p. 30). Among fish used as food he includes sturgeon, herring, trout, ray, alewife, mullet, and plaice, besides shellfish (Hariot, 1893, pp. 31–32).

The Virginia Algonquian menu at this time was about the same. Smith and Strachey speak of corn, beans, peas, pumpkins, and "macocks," which last appear to have been squashes (perhaps cymlings). They omit mention of the sunflower, though at a somewhat later date we find Berkeley speaking of it, as also of the plant from which a salt substitute was obtained. On the other hand we seem to hear for the first time of "maracocks," the fruit of the passion-flower (*Passiflora incarnata*), later called maypop, which they represent as native to the country, but Hariot's silence regarding it somewhat strengthens the view that it was imported from Brazil at an early period. The name maracock would then seem to be a corruption of the Brazilian Tupi word *mburucuia*. (Smith, Tyler ed., 1907, pp. 90–93; Strachey, 1849, pp. 116–121; Hodge, 1907, *art.* Maypop.)

Beverley, writing at the beginning of the eighteenth century, speaks of four varieties of corn instead of three, but whether these were all cultivated in Virginia in aboriginal times is uncertain. His description is as follows:

There are Four Sorts of *Indian* Corn, Two of which are early ripe, and Two, late ripe; all growing in the same manner; every single Grain of this when planted, produces a tall upright Stalk, which has several Ears hanging on the Sides of it, from Six to Ten Inches long. Each Ear is wrapt up in a Cover of many Folds, to protect it from the Injuries of the Weather. In every one of these Ears, are several Rows of Grain, set close to one another, with no other Partition, but of a very thin Husk. So that oftentimes the Increase of this Grain amounts to above a Thousand for one.

The Two Sorts which are early ripe, are distinguish'd only by the Size, which shows it self as well in the Grain, as in the Ear, and the Stalk. There is some Difference also in the Time of ripening.

The lesser Size of Early ripe Corn, yields an Ear not much larger than the Handle of a Case Knife, and grows upon a Stalk, between Three and Four Foot high. Of this are commonly made Two crops in a Year, and, perhaps, there might be Heat enough in England to ripen it.

The larger Sort differs from the former only in Largeness, the Ear of this being Seven or Eight Inches long, as thick as a Child's Leg, and growing upon a Stalk Nine or Ten Foot high. This is fit for eating about the latter end of *May*, whereas the smaller Sort (generally speaking) affords Ears fit to roast by the Middle of May. The Grains of both these Sorts, are as plump and swell'd, as if the Skin were ready to burst.

The late ripe Corn is diversify'd by the Shape of the Grain only, without any Respect to the accidental Differences in Colour, some being blue, some red, some yellow, some white, and some streak'd. That therefore which makes the Distinction, is the Plumpness or Shrivelling of the Grain; the one looks as smooth, and as full as the early ripe Corn, and this they call *Flint-Corn;* the other has a larger Grain, and looks shrivell'd with a Dent on the Back of the Grain, as if it had never come to Perfection; and this they call *She-Corn.* This is esteem'd by the Planters, as the best for Increase, and is universally chosen by them for planting; yet I can't see, but that this produces the Flint-Corn, accidentally among the other. (Beverley, 1705, bk. 2, pp. 28–29.)

One, and perhaps both, of the early varieties was what we know as popcorn. The smooth variety of late corn was flint corn, as Beverley himself names it, and the other what the Indians called flour corn.

Smith says that the native peas were known as Assentamens and were the same as those called in Italy Fagioli, and that their beans were identical with what "the Turkes call *Garnanses.*" Strachey apparently borrowed this statement from Smith. The only difference is that Strachey spells the native word for peas "assentemmens" and the Turkish word for beans "garvances." (Smith, Tyler ed., 1907, p. 95; Strachey, 1849, p. 117.) Beverley mentions both also, and says the native peas were "of a Kidney-Shape." (Beverley, 1705, bk. 2, p. 29; also see Spelman, *in* Smith, 1884, p. CVL.)

Like Hariot, Smith and Strachey distinguish two varieties of a pumpkin or squash, one of which they call a pumpkin ("pumpeon") and the other a macock. Smith likens this latter to a muskmelon, but says it was inferior. Strachey, however, likens it to a pumpkin and speaks of the other as a melon, treating it as if it were distinct from the pumpkin. (Smith, Tyler ed., 1907, p. 97; Strachey, 1849, p. 119.) However, it is probable that three or four varieties of plants of the squash family were known to the Virginians. Beverley enumerates, besides muskmelons and watermelons, which had by his time been introduced, "Pompions, Cushaws, Macocks, and Gourds," which he discusses as follows:

Their Pompions I need not describe, but must say they are much larger and finer, than any I ever heard of in *England*.

Their *Cushaws* are a kind of Pompion, of a bluish green Colour, streaked with White, when they are fit for Use. They are larger than the Pompions, and have a long narrow Neck: Perhaps this may be the *Ecushaw* of T. Harriot.

Their *Macocks* are a sort of *Melopepones*, or lesser sort of Pompion, of these they have great Variety, but the *Indian* name *Macock* serves for all, which Name is still retain'd among them. Yet the *Clypeateœ* are sometimes call'd *Cymmels* (as are some others also) from the *Lenten* Cake of that Name, which many of them very much resemble. *Squash*, *Squanter-Squash*, is their Name among the Northern *Indians*, and so they are call'd in *New-York*, and *New-England*. These being boil'd whole, when the Apple is young, and the Shell tender, and dished with Cream or Butter, relish very well with all sorts of Butcher's Meat, either fresh or salt. And whereas the Pompion is never eaten till it be ripe, these are never eaten after they are ripe.

The *Indians* never eat the Gourds, but plant them for other Uses. Yet the *Persians*, who likewise abound with this sort of Fruit, eat the *Cucurbita Lagenaria*, which they call *Kabach*, boiling it while it is green, before it comes to it's full Maturity; For, when it is ripe, th Rind dries, and grows as hard as the Bark of a Tree, and the Meat within is so consumed and dried away, that there is then nothing left but the Seed, which the *Indians* take clean out, and afterwards use the Shells instead of Flagons and Cups; as is done also in several other Parts of the World. (Beverley, 1705, bk. 2, p. 27.)

Cucurbita Lagenaria was the old name of the *Lagenaria*. The genus *Lagenaria* is not found in the New World and these remarks of Beverley's either apply to a period after gourds of this genus had been introduced, or to the treatment of some species of *Cucurbita*.

Another apparent omission by Smith and Strachey is the sunflower, but Beverley (1722, p. 15) tells us that "they make their Bread, of *Indian* Corn, Wild Oats, or the Seed of the Sunflower."

Beverley is the only one of the three to speak of a vegetable salt substitute, though his remarks are very general:

They have no Salt among them, but for seasoning, use the Ashes of Hiccory, Stickweed, or some other Wood or Plant, affording a Salt ash. (Beverley, 1705, bk. 3, p. 15.)

In the relation of Newport's first expedition, "hempe" and "flaxe" are listed among the productions of Powhatan's field (Smith, Arber ed., 1884, p. XLIV).

Ground nuts are not mentioned by Smith, but they appear in the narratives of Strachey (1849, p. 72) and Beverley (1705, bk. 3, p. 15), and there is no reason to doubt their identity with Hariot's Openavk.

None of the Virginia writers speaks of the "Okeepenavk" or "Kaishcúpenauk" of Hariot in such a specific manner as to enable one to identify them. It is still more surprising to find an apparently total absence of any reference to the China briar, or Kantak. Tuckahoe, the "Coscúshaw" and "Sacqvenvmmener" of Hariot, has already been discussed. Possibly the "Habascon" of the same writer may be the "small onions" to which Smith and Strachey refer, but that is quite uncertain. The former has been identified with the nondo or angelico. Beverley identifies the Sacqvenvmmener of Hariot and the Ocoughtanamnis of Smith with a food to which he gives the name "Cuttanimmons" and describes as "the Fruit of a kind of Arum, growing in the Marshes." He says: "They are like Boyl'd Peas, or Capers to look on, but of an insipid earthy taste" (Beverley, 1705, bk. 3, p. 15). As already suggested, these may be the berries of the *Peltandra virginica*.

Turning to fruits, we find the above Virginia writers mentioning strawberries, mulberries, and huckleberries. Smith and Spelman also speak of raspberries, though these could hardly have been found in the Powhatan country, while Strachey notes gooseberries and cherries. Instead of persimmons, we find Strachey including plums, and Beverley peaches. It may be assumed that both persimmons and wild plums were used, and in Beverley's time peaches had been introduced, so that his reference may be to the European fruit (Beverley, 1705, bk. 3, p. 14).

Smith (1907, p. 92) speaks of a "wild rye" and Beverley (1705, bk. 3, p. 14) of "wild oats," which respectively were probably the native wild rye and wild rice. Possibly the "reed" to which Hariot (1893, p. 28) refers, "which beareth a seed almost like unto our rie or wheat," refers to the latter instead of to cane as above suggested. We find no reference to "wild peas." Beverley adds to the above sugar from the sugar maple and, since we know it was obtained as far south as Georgia, while Byrd speaks of sugar maples along Sugartree Creek, in what is now Person County, N. C. (Bassett,

1901, p. 314), there can be no doubt that trees were tapped in the western parts of Virginia and the Carolinas. Failure of many early writers to mention this industry is probably because their acquaintance began with the tidewater people, among whom the tree was absent.

Nearly all Virginia writers speak of the use of chestnuts, walnuts, hickory nuts, chinquapins, and acorns as food. Smith says of the last-mentioned:

> The Acornes of one kind, whose barke is more white then the other, is somewhat sweetish; which being boyled halfe a day in severall waters, at last afford a sweete oyle, which they keep in goards to annoint their heads and joints. The fruit they eate, made in bread or otherwise. (Smith, Tyler ed., 1907, p. 90.)

Among animal foods, the deer and bear are constantly noted. Beverley adds the elk and bison, and it is evident that the last-mentioned animal formerly ranged well into the present State of Virginia, though its importance there can never have been very great (Beverley, 1705, bk. 2, p. 37). The rabbit, squirrel, beaver, and otter are mentioned by various writers, and it may be inferred that the last two are the two small animals noted by Hariot (1893, p. 30) under their native names.

Fowl appear collectively as part of the menu, the only bird ordinarily distinguished from the rest being the wild turkey, though Smith speaks of the partridge. (For a number of Powhatan bird names see Swanton, 1934.) Among fish we hear most of sturgeon and herring. To these must be added oysters, mussels, crabs, and tortoises, a green snake mentioned by Strachey and Beverley, and beetles and locusts, the last two noted only by Beverley. Strachey (1849, p. 127) distinguishes carefully between the common crab and the king crab and says that the latter was rarely eaten.

What Lawson has to say on the subject of Indian foods will apply to most of the Siouan tribes of the Carolinas, the Tuscarora, and one or two bands of the coastal Algonquians, though his information was derived principally from the first-mentioned:

> As to the Indians' food, it is of several sorts, which are as follows: Venison, and the fawns in the bags, cut out of the doe's belly; fish of all sorts, the lamprey eel excepted, and the sturgeon, our salt water Indians will not touch; bear, and bever, panther, polecat,[11] wild cat, possum, raccoon, hares, and squirrels, roasted with their guts in; snakes, all Indians will not eat them, though some do; all wild fruits, that are palatable, some of which they dry and keep against winter, as all sorts of fruits, and peaches, which they dry and make quiddonies and cakes, that are very pleasant, and a little tartish; young wasps, when they are white in the combs, before they can fly, this is esteemed a dainty; all sorts of tortois and

---

[11] Regarding the polecat, "The Indians love to eat their flesh which has no manner of ill smell when the bladder is out. I know no use their furs are put to." (Lawson, 1860, p. 197.)

terebins, shell fish, and stingray, or scate, dried; gourds, melons, cucumbers, squashes, pulse of all sorts; rockahomine meal, which is their maiz, made into several sorts of bread; ears of corn roasted in the summer, or preserved against winter. (Lawson, 1860, pp. 290–291.)

In the house of a Santee Indian, Lawson

found great store of Indian peas (a very good pulse), beans, oil, chinkapin nuts, corn, barbecued peaches, and peach bread, which peaches being made into a quiddony,[12] and so made up into loaves like barley cakes, these cut into thin slices, and dissolved in water, makes a very grateful acid, and extraordinary beneficial in fevers, as has often been tried and approved by our great English practitioners. (Lawson, 1860, pp. 36–37.)

One of his companions brought from the house of his Santee father-in-law "some Indian maiz and peas, which are of reddish color, and eat well, yet color the liquor they are boiled in as if it were a lixivium of red tartar" (Lawson, 1860, p. 45). He found the Congaree Indians supplied with great quantities of chinquapin and hickory nuts (Lawson, 1860, p. 53). He mentions stewed peaches again at the Waxhaw town, and found acorns in use by the Catawba, and Cape Fear Indians. Some distance beyond the Catawba town, toward the north, they came upon a pigeon roost, and he speaks of the vast numbers of birds and the quantities killed by the Indians (Lawson, 1860, p. 79). The Saponi were trapping beaver, but we are left in doubt whether this was an ancient custom among them or one stimulated by the whites. From the Tutelo, who lived then somewhere west of the Yadkin, Lawson (1860, p. 85) heard of elk and bison. Near the mouth of Cape Fear River salt was obtained (Lawson, 1860, p. 125).

Regarding peas and beans:

We have the indian rounceval, or miraculous peas, so called from their long pods, and great increase. These are later peas, and require a pretty long summer to ripen in. They are very good; and so are the bonavis, calavancies, nanticokes, and abundance of other pulse, too tedious here to name, which we found the Indians possessed of, when first we settled in America, some of which sorts afford us two crops in one year; as the bonavis and colavancies, besides several others of that kind. . . . The kidney beans were here before the English came, being very plentiful in the Indian corn fields. (Lawson, 1860, pp. 130–131.)

The "calavancies" are, of course, the "garvances" of Strachey and the "garnanses" of Smith.

In the following passage we probably have reference to the China briar or kunti:

The small bamboo . . . is a certain vine, like the rest of these species, growing in low land. They seldom, with us, grow thicker than a man's little

---

[12] A quiddony or quiddany was "a thick fruit-syrup or jelly; originally and properly, one made from quinces" (Murray).

finger, and are very tough. Their root is a round ball which the Indians boil as we do garden roots and eat them. (Lawson, 1860, p. 169.)

Service berries ("services") (*Amelanchier canadensis?*) and a kind of huckleberry growing upon trees "ten and twelve feet high," apparently the tree huckleberry (*Batodendron arboretum*), are mentioned, as also a variety of black gum which "bears a black, well tasted berry, which the Indians mix with their pulse and soups" (Lawson, 1860, p. 160). Lawson is our earliest authority to mention specificaly the use of live-oak acorns (*Quercus virginiana*). He says:

The acorns thereof are as sweet as chestnuts, and the Indians draw an oil from them, as sweet as that from the olive, though of an amber color . . . I knew two trees of this wood among the Indians, which were planted from the acorn, and grew in the freshies, and never saw anything more beautiful of that kind. (Lawson, 1860, p. 156.)

Lawson (1860, p. 174) confirms our impression regarding the extraction of maple sugar in the higher parts of Virginia and the Carolinas.

Besides describing the "common Indian plum," he gives us the following interesting information regarding peaches:

I want to be satisfied about one sort of this fruit, which the Indians claim as their own, and affirm they had it growing amongst them before any Europeans came to America. The fruit I will describe as exactly as I can. The tree grows very large, most commonly as big as a handsome apple tree; the flowers are of reddish, murrey color, the fruit is rather more downy than the yellow peach, and commonly large and soft, being very full of juice. They part freely from the stone, and the stone is much thicker than all the other peach stones we have, which seems to me that it is a spontaneous fruit of America; yet in those parts of America that we inhabit, I never could hear that any peach trees were ever found growing in the woods; neither have the foreign Indians, those that live remote from the English, any other sort. And those living amongst us have a hundred of this sort for one other. They are a hardy fruit, and are seldom damaged by the north-east blast, as others are. Of this sort we make vinegar; wherefore we call them vinegar peaches, and sometimes Indian peaches. (Lawson, 1860, p. 182.)

There can be little doubt that this "Indian peach" was a true peach, and it follows almost certainly that it was obtained from the Spaniards, probably from the Spanish colonists in Florida.

To the list of animal foods given by Lawson in his general account of Indian diet, he has little to add elsewhere except that he enumerates specifically bluefish, white guard fish [garfish], alewives, rockfish or bass, herring, and trout among the fish caught. He mentions oysters, cockles, and mussels among shellfish, and remarks tersely of the last-mentioned, that they "are eaten by the Indians, after five or six hours boiling to make them tender, and then are good for nothing." His judgment of crawfish is different and he gives an extended account of the native method of securing this crustacean. (Lawson, 1860, pp. 266, 338–339.)

The antipathy to sturgeon which coast Indians exhibited has been noted, but Lawson says elsewhere:

They that live a great way up the rivers practice striking sturgeon and rockfish, or bass, when they come up the rivers to spawn; besides the vast shoals of sturgeon which they kill and take with snares, as we do pike in Europe. (Lawson, 1860, pp. 260, 339.)

Herring were also caught upstream, principally by means of weirs.

The following comments may be made on Lawson's general statement. The panther, polecat, wildcat, and opossum seem to have been used rather rarely, and Adair (1775, p. 16) states that the Chickasaw had a distinct aversion to the flesh of the animal last mentioned, yet in one of the myths a Choctaw is represented as eating an opossum under peculiar circumstances (Swanton, 1931 a, p. 203). The melons and cucumbers noted must have been introduced, and we know independently that melons were brought to America at a very much earlier date. However, they are also noted in Barlow's narrative and we must suppose either that the Roanoke Indians had gotten them from the South by that time, which is a possibility, or that the names were given to certain varieties of squashes and pumpkins (Burrage, 1906, p. 234).

Lederer confirms Lawson regarding the consumption of wildcats by the interior Siouan tribes. (Lawson, 1860, p. 289; Lederer, 1912, p. 147.)

Lawson also mentions dirt eating.

The Indian children are much addicted to eat dirt, and so are some of the Christians, but roast a bat on a skewer, then pull the skin off, and make the child that eats dirt eat the roasted rearmouse and he will never eat dirt again. (Lawson, 1860, p. 206.)

One would hardly suppose so.

From the few notes preserved to us regarding the diet of the Cusabo Indians, it seems to have differed little from that in the regions considered except, of course, that fish and shellfish constituted a larger proportion of the food consumed, and melons, peaches, and other imported fruits and vegetables got a foothold earlier. The fig is mentioned along with these (Swanton, 1922, pp. 74–75).

In Florida we would look for greater changes and we do indeed begin to find them, but not as many as might have been expected. Fish, of course, occupy a prominent place, among the species mentioned under European names being "trout, great mullets, plaice, turbots," and crabs, lobsters, and crawfish are also mentioned. Deer, turkey, and bear appear as familiar game animals, but we read of "leopards," and "lions," presumably panthers, confirmatory of Lawson. (Laudonnière, 1586, pp. 18, 130; French, 1875, p. 178.) Calderón (1936, p. 13) includes bison among their game animals.

One of the French Huguenot colonists, Le Challeux, says that snakes were devoured, and it is implied in one of Le Moyne's illustrations showing several animals being dried over a fire, but so much imagination was used in these that the support to be derived from it is rather slight (Gaffarel, 1875, p. 462; Le Moyne, 1875, pp. 9–10, illus.). Le Challeux is our sole authority for lizard eating, but we know that alligator meat was a rather important item among flesh foods and, indeed, it constituted the main innovation encountered in the peninsula (Gaffarel, 1875, p. 462; Le Moyne, 1875, pl. 26).

In northern Florida, vegetable staples were like those found in other parts of the Gulf region. Corn was the principal food and it was cultivated along with beans and several varieties of squashes and pumpkins. It is possible that agriculture may have been restricted or even absent along the northeast coast south of St. Augustine because the monk San Miguel, who visited it in 1595, says, "these Indians neither sow nor reap, nor have other care for food and clothing than animals and birds," but he may have confused them with the Indians farther south, and Dickenson observed squashes and pumpkins growing near Cape Canaveral in 1699. (Garcia, 1902, p. 209; Lowery ms.: Dickenson, 1803, p. 66.) Ribault mentions some of these latter under the terms "citrons" and "cucumbers" (French, 1875, p. 174). The appearance of this last word serves to strengthen the theory that it was applied to some sort of pumpkin and not to the vegetables we call by that name. Gourds are noted along with these, but see comments on page 275. Laudonnière speaks of "honey" but, as explained above, French *mil* has evidently been miscopied or misspelled *miel* (see p. 268). Grapes, raspberries, and mulberries are specifically noted, the raspberries probably in reality blackberries, and there is evidence that acorns were utilized as elsewhere in the Southeast. (French, 1875, p. 173; Laudonnière *in* French, 1869, pp. 181, 182, 257). We are indebted to Ranjel for our knowledge of the use of chinquapins (Bourne, 1904, vol. 2, pp. 70–71). It appears from Pareja that Timucua taste extended at times to coal, dirt, and broken pottery, and Laudonnière confirms this, as a *forced diet*, saying, "in necessity they eat a thousand riffraffs, even to the swallowing down of coal, and putting sand into the pottage that they make with the meal." (Gatschet, 1877, vol. 16, p. 683; Laudonnière, 1586, p. 9.)

South Florida belongs to a different life zone from the rest of the Gulf territory and ought to introduce us to some innovations in diet. This expectation is in a measure realized, but the difference is rather in what was lacking than in the positive contributions. We are told that throughout this section the natives cultivated no fields, but depended mainly on fish and roots. Regarding the Calusa tribe, Fontaneda says:

Their common food consists of fish, turtles, snails, tunny fish, and whales, which they catch in their season. Some of them also eat the wolf fish, but this is not a common thing, owing to certain distinctions which they make between food proper for the chiefs and that of their subjects. On these islands is found a shell-fish known as the *langosta*, a sort of lobster, and another known in Spain as the *chapin* (trunk fish), of which they consume not less than the former. There are also on the islands a great number of animals, especially deer; and on some of them large bears are found. (Coll. Docs. Inédit., 1864–84, vol. 5, pp. 532–533.)

Regarding the "whales," see comments by Kellogg on page 329.

Around Lake Okeechobee, in the interior, was a considerable population occupying small villages. These Indians seem to have been related to the Calusa, but had a somewhat different dietary. To quote Fontaneda once more, they lived

on bread made from roots during most of the year. They cannot procure it, however when the waters of the lake rise very high. They have roots which resemble the truffles of this country [Spain], and have besides excellent fish. Whenever game is to be had, either deer or birds, they eat meat. Large numbers of very fat eels are found in the rivers, some of them as large as a man's thigh, and enormous trout, almost as large as a man's body; although smaller ones are also found. The natives eat lizards, snakes, and rats, which infest the lakes, freshwater turtles, and many other animals which it would be tiresome to enumerate. (Coll. Docs. Inédit., 1864–84, vol. 5, pp. 534–535.)

Coming over to the east coast, Dickenson—at a considerably later date, it is true—gives us some interesting notes to compare with the above. An early Spanish writer, Lopez de Velasco, describes the hunting of sea cows, which must, indeed, have been an important special industry in this region. To be sure, he is mainly interested in explaining the use the Tekesta Indians made of the tusks, which were placed with the bodies of their dead, but it would be absurd to suppose this was the only reason for hunting such animals (Swanton, 1922, p. 389). Dickenson's information regarding these people is that they had no fields, but lived mainly on fish, and secondarily on oysters and clams. The only vegetable foods mentioned by him were palm berries, coco plums (*Chrysobalanus icaco*), and seagrapes (*Coccoloba uvifera*). Dickenson adds, "The time of these fruits bearing being over they have no other till the next spring," which indicates the narrow range of their vegetable diet (Dickenson, 1803, pp. 23, 26, 51).

For the most part, therefore, the change in food which took place in this distinct economic province was omission of horticulture and greater utilization of the regional foods that nature offered. The nearest approach to a positive reaction to this environment on the part of the south Floridians was in the use of a certain root as a source of bread, one mentioned only in connection with the interior Indians. There is every reason to believe that this was what the Seminole later called kunti, or, to distinguish it from a food plant they had used before entering the peninsula, "white kunti" (kunti hâtki). This was obtained from the *Zamia integrifolia* and involved a rather elaborate process of manufacture, which might have reacted on the people to the extent of giving rise to a distinct cultural province had the supply of roots been sufficiently great or had it been possible to cultivate them (MacCauley, 1887, pp. 513–516). Rarely has a distinctive civilization of very high character arisen on the basis furnished by an uncultivated plant, though in California we have something approaching it, a distinctive culture based mainly on acorns. However, this was distinctive without being high.

Logically, the cassava culture should have been introduced into south Florida to take the place of corn, and if it had happened, that district would have been assimilated to the West Indian province. Failing that, it only presented the appearance of a marginal, aberrant cultural area of merely local importance. It occupies in Florida a position somewhat similar to that of the Chitimacha area of southern Louisiana to be considered shortly.

Something may also be learned of the earlier dietary of the original Floridians by that of their successors, the Seminole, though these last have imported some economic as well as some social customs from their old homes in Alabama, especially the cultivation of corn. MacCauley says:

Here is a list of their meats: Of flesh, at any time venison, often opossum, sometimes rabbit and squirrel, occasionally bear, and a land terrapin, called the "gopher," and pork whenever they wish it. Of wild fowl, duck, quail, and turkey in abundance. Of home reared fowl, chickens, more than they are willing to use. Of fish, they can catch myriads of the many kinds which teem in the inland waters of Florida, especially of the large bass, called "trout" by the whites of the State, while on the seashore they can get many forms of edible marine life, especially turtles and oysters. Equally well off are these Indians in respect to grains, vegetables, roots, and fruits. They grow maize in considerable quantity, and from it make hominy and flour, and all the rice they need they gather from the swamps. Their vegetables are chiefly sweet potatoes, large and much praised melons and pumpkins, and, if I may classify it with vegetables, the tender new growth of the tree called the cabbage palmetto. Among roots, there is the great dependence of these Indians, the abounding Koonti; also the wild potato, a small tuber found in black swamp land, and peanuts in great quantities. Of fruits, the Seminole family may supply itself with bananas, oranges (sour and sweet), limes, lemons, guavas, pineapples, grapes (black and red), cocoa nuts, cocoa plums, sea grapes, and wild plums. And with even this enumeration the bill of fare is not exhausted. The Seminole, living in a perennial summer, is never at a loss when he seeks something, and something good, to eat. I have omitted from the above list honey and the sugar cane juice and sirup, nor have I re-

ferred to the purchases the Indians now and then make from the white man, of
salt pork, wheat flour, coffee, and salt, and of the various canned delicacies,
whose attractive labels catch their eyes.   (MacCauley, 1887, p. 504.)

Elsewhere he says of the food from the cabbage palmetto:

> The tender new growth at the top of the tree is a very nutritious and palatable
> article of food, to be eaten either raw or baked; its taste is somewhat like that
> of the chestnut; its texture is crisp like that of our celery stalk.   (MacCauley,
> 1887, p. 517.)

Skinner, in 1910, found the Everglade bands, unlike the other
Seminoles, utilizing turtles almost entirely in lieu of the deer, turkey, and other game animals obtained by the rest (Skinner, 1913,
p. 76).

In 1761 Timberlake found that the Cherokee country was

> yielding vast quantities of pease, beans, potatoes, cabbages, Indian corn, pum-
> pions, melons, and tobacco, not to mention a number of other vegetables im-
> ported from Europe, not so generally known amongst them. . . .   Before the
> arrival of the Europeans, the natives were not so well provided, maize, melons,
> and tobacco, being the only things they bestow culture upon, and perhaps sel-
> dom on the latter.   The meadows or savannahs produce excellent grass; being
> watered by abundance of fine rivers, and brooks well stored with fish, otters and
> beavers; . . .   Of the fruits there are some of an excellent flavor, particularly
> several sorts of grapes, which, with proper culture, would probably afford
> an excellent wine.   There are likewise plums, cherries, and berries of several
> kinds, something different from those of Europe; but their peaches and pears
> grow only by culture;   add to these several kinds of roots, and medicinal
> plants. . . .   There are likewise an incredible number of buffaloes, bears,
> deer, panthers, wolves, foxes, racoons, and opossums. . . .   There are a vast
> number of lesser sort of game, such as rabbits, squirrels of several sorts, and
> many other animals, besides turkey, geese, ducks of several kinds, partridges,
> pheasants, and an infinity of other birds. . . .   The flesh of the rattle-snake
> is extremely good; being once obliged to eat one through want of provisions,
> I have eat several since thro' choice.   (Timberlake, Williams ed., 1927, pp. 68-72.)

See also what Bartram has to say below, since his statements are
partly applicable to the Cherokee.   It is remarkable that Timberlake
includes melons rather than "pumpions" in his list of plants cultivated before the arrival of Europeans, another indication of the
rapidity with which the use of this vegetable spread.   Bartram noted
the "Cassine yapon" (*Cassine vomitoria*), near the Jore village in
the Cherokee country under semicultivation:

> Here I observed a little grove of the Cassine yapon, which was the only
> place where I had seen it grow in the Cherokee country; the Indians call it
> the beloved tree, and are very careful to keep it pruned and cultivated: they
> drink a very strong infusion of the leaves, buds and tender branches of this
> plant, which is so celebrated, indeed venerated by the Creeks and all the
> Southern maritime nations of Indians.   (Bartram, 1792, p. 291.)

The only specific accounts in this region of the extraction of maple
sugar apply to the Cherokee, who may have brought the industry

with them when they came from the north. They are said to have tapped trees on a stream near Old Tellico and on Limestone Creek, while Hawkins witnessed the process at a point near the present Atlanta (Hawkins, 1916, p. 24). Mooney informed Mr. Henshaw, it is true, that before they met Europeans, the Cherokee "extracted their only saccharine from the pod of the honey locust, using the powdered pods to sweeten parched corn and to make a sweet drink," but if so they must have adopted the custom of extraction from the sugar maple at an early period and there seems to be no reason why they could not have done this before white contact as well as after it (Henshaw, 1890, p. 349).

The best accounts of Creek dietary are probably those of Romans and Bartram, though the impressions of both were recorded rather late in the eighteenth century, and Bartram's account is made to apply equally to the Cherokee. Romans (1775) says:

Their way of life is in general very abundant; they have much more of venison, bear, turkies; and small game in their country than their neighbors have, and they raise abundance of small cattle, hogs, turkeys, ducks and dunghill fowls (all of which are very good in their kind) and of these they spare not; the labour of the field is all done by the women; no savages are more proud of being counted hunters, fishermen, and warriors; were they to cultivate their plentiful country, they might raise amazing quantities of grain and pulse, as it is they have enough for their home consumption, they buy a good deal of rice, and they are the only savages that ever I saw that could bear to have some rum in store; yet they drink to excess as well as others; there are few towns in this nation where there is not some savage residing, who either trades of his own flock, or is employed as a factor. They have more variety in their diet than other savages: They make pancakes; they dry the tongues of their venison; they make a caustick salt out of a kind of moss found at the bottom of creeks and rivers, which although a vegetable salt, does not deliquiate on exposing to the air; this they dissolve in water and pound their dried venison till it looks like oakum and then eat it dipped in the above sauce; they eat much roasted and boiled venison, a great deal of milk and eggs; they dry peaches and persimmons, chestnuts and the fruit of the *chamaerops* [*Rhapidophyllum hystrix*, the "blue palmetto" or "needle palm," originally described as a *chamaerops*], they also prepare a cake of the pulp of the species of the *passi flora*, vulgarly called may apple; some kinds of acorns they also prepare into good bread; the common esculent *Convolvulus* [sweetpotato (*Ipomoea batata*)] and the sort found in the low woods [*Ipomoea pandurata*], both called potatoes, are eat in abundance among them; they have plenty of the various species of *Zea* or maize, or the *Phaseolus* [beans] and *Dolichos* [hyacinth beans], and of different kinds of *Panicum;* bears oyl, honey and hickory milk are the boast of the country; they have also many kinds of salt and fresh water turtle, and their eggs, and plenty of fish; we likewise find among them salted meats, corned venison in particular, which is very fine; they cultivate abundance of melons; in a word, they have naturally the greatest plenty imaginable; were they to cultivate the earth they would have too much. (Romans, 1775, pp. 93–94.)

Of course, this itinerary includes a great deal of European introduction and also there are some misstatements, as, for instance, that field labor was all done by the women. The planting, and at least part of the cultivation, of the town fields were carried on by men and women conjointly. The domestication of animals, of course, represents in its entirety the effects of white contact. To Europeans are also attributable the use of rice, rum, milk, eggs (except for some utilization of the eggs of wild birds and turtles), honey, melons, and probably salted meats. Mention of a vegetable salt confirms the much earlier statement of Garcilaso de la Vega's informants. From very early times persimmons were dried into cakes for later consumption here and in most other parts of the Southeast, but dried peaches represent a later innovation. When Romans visited the nation, peach trees had been introduced and planted in considerable numbers about most Indian towns. "The *passi flora*, vulgarly called may apple" is, of course, *Passiflora incarnata*, and the edible fruit of this is known as maypop and not mayapple. The variety of *Convolvulus* "found in the low woods" is evidently the wild sweetpotato (*Ipomoea pandurata*), though early writers sometimes seem to confuse this with *Apios tuberosa*. The "different kinds of *Panicum*" may include sorghum (*Sorghum drummondii*, probably), wild rice, already mentioned in use farther toward the northeast, and perhaps cockspur grass (*Echinochloa crusgalli*). These will be mentioned again when we come to speak of the Mississippi River tribes.

Bartram's information was supplied in answer to a series of queries regarding the Creek and Cherokee Indians submitted to him by Dr. B. S. Barton, at one time vice president of the American Philosophical Society. To the questions on "Food, and Means of Subsistence," he answered:

Their animal food consists chiefly of venison, bears' flesh, turkeys, hares, wild fowl, and domestic poultry; and also of domestic kine, as beeves, goats, and swine—never horses' flesh, though they have horses in great plenty; neither do they eat the flesh of dogs, cats, or any such creatures as are usually rejected by white people.

Their vegetable food consists chiefly of corn [*zea*], rice, *convolvulus batatas*, or those nourishing roots usually called sweet or Spanish potatoes (but in the Creek Confederacy they never plant or eat the Irish potato). All the species of the *phaseolus* [beans] and *dolichos* [hyacinth beans] in use among the whites, are cultivated by the Creeks, Cherokees, etc., and make up a great part of their food. All the species of *cucurbita*, as squashes, pumpkins, water-melons, etc.; but of the *cucumeres*, they cultivate none of the species as yet, neither do they cultivate our farinaceous grains, as wheat, barley, spelts, rye, buckwheat, etc. (not having got the use of the plough amongst them, though it has been introduced some years ago). The chiefs rejected it, alleging that it would starve their old people who employed themselves in planting, and selling their produce to the traders, for their support and maintenance; seeing that by permitting the traders to use the plough, one or two persons could easily raise more grain than all the old people of the town could do by using the hoe. Turnips, parsnips, salads, etc., they have no knowledge of. Rice (*oryza*) they plant in hills on high dry ground, in their gardens; by this management a few grains in a hill (the hills about four feet apart) spread every way incredibly, and seem more prolific than when cultivated in water, as in the white settlements of Carolina; the heads or *panicles* are larger and heavier, and the grain is larger, firmer, or more farinaceous; much sweeter, and more nourishing. Each family raises enough of this excellent grain for its own use.

But, besides the cultivated fruits above recited, with peaches, oranges,[13] plums [Chickasaw plums], figs, and some apples, they have in use a vast variety of wild or native vegetables, both fruits and roots, viz.: *diospyros* [persimmon], *morus rubra* [red mulberry], *gleditsia multiloba* [*meliloba* Walt.], *s. triacanthus* [honey locust or water locust]; all the species of juglans and acorns, from which they extract a very sweet oil, which enters into all their cookery, and several species of *palma*, which furnish them with a variety of agreeable and nourishing food. Grapes, too, they have in great variety and abundance, which they feed on occasionally when ripe; they also prepare them for keeping, and lay up for winter and spring time.[14] A species of smilax (*S. pseudochina*) affords them a delicious and nourishing food, which is prepared from its vast tuberous roots. . . .

I conclude these articles with mentioning a vegetable which I had but a slight opportunity of observing, just as I left the Creek country, on the waters of the Mobile river. It is a species of *palma*. It has no stalk or stem above ground; the leaves spread regularly all round, are flabelliform when fully expanded, otherwise cucullated, their slips very short, scarcely appearing at a slight view; in the centre is produced a kind of dense panicle or general receptacle of the fruit, of the form and size of a sugar-loaf. There is a vast collection of plums or drupes, of the size and figure of ordinary plums, which are covered with a fibrous, farinaceous, pulpy coating of considerable thickness; this substance, which, to the best of my remembrance, resembles manna in texture, color, and taste, is of the consistence of coarse brown sugar, mixed with particles or lumps of loaf sugar. It is a delicious and nourishing food, and diligently sought after. There were several of these clusters brought into the Ottasse town just before I left it, of which I ate freely with the Indians, and think in substance and taste it is most of anything like manna; it is a little bitterish and stinging on the palate, at first using it, but soon becomes familiar and desirable.

I own I am not able to give an accurate botanical account of this very curious and valuable vegetable, because it was disclosed to my observation just on my departure; and although I saw several of the plants on the road, yet being obliged to follow the mad career of a man travelling with pack-horses, I had left the country of its native growth before I had an opportunity or leisure to examine it,—an omission which I have severely regretted. I am convinced it is an object of itself worth a journey to these regions to examine. (Bartram, 1909, pp. 49–50.)

This *Palma* was undoubtedly the "blue palmetto," or "needle palm," mentioned by Romans above under the name *Chamaerops*. Of Old World origin were all the domesticated animals mentioned, water-

---

[13] "Oranges and figs are not much cultivated in the *Nation* or Upper Creeks; but in the Lower Creek country [i. e., Florida], near the sea-coast, they are in greater abundance, particularly the orange. Many sorts are now become wild all over East Florida."— BARTRAM.

[14] "Vitis Vinifera; I call them so because they approach, as respects the largeness of their fruit and their shape and flavor, much nearer to the grapes of Europe and Asia, of which wine is made, and are specifically different from our wild grape, and as different from the fox or bull grape of Pennsylvania and Carolina."—BARTRAM.

melons, rice, peaches, oranges, and figs. The grape Bartram extols so highly may be the scuppernong, now known as *Vitis rotundifolia*. It is rather remarkable that Romans fails to note pumpkins or squashes among the Creeks, Choctaw, or Chickasaw. Swan tells us that in his time (1791), the Creeks extracted oil from acorns, hickory nuts, and chestnuts, but that the oil from acorns was the best (Swan, 1855, p. 692).

It is Romans who gives our most complete view of Choctaw economic life:

> They cultivate for bread all the species and varieties of the *Zea*, likewise two varieties of that species of *Panicum* vulgarly called guinea corn; a greater number of different *Phaseolus* and *Dolichos* than any I have even seen elsewhere; the esculent *Convolvulus* (vulgo) sweet potatoes, and the *Helianthus giganteus;* with the seed of the last made into flour and mixed with flour of the *Zea* they make a very palatable bread; they have carried the spirit of husbandry so far as to cultivate leeks, garlic, cabbage and some other garden plants, of which they make no use, in order to make profit of them to the traders; they also used to carry poultry to market at Mobile, although it lays at the distance of an hundred and twenty miles from the nearest town; dunghill fowls, and a very few ducks, with some hogs, are the only esculent animals raised in the nation.

> They make many kinds of bread of the above grains with the help of water, eggs, or hickory milk; they boil corn and beans together, and make many other preparations of their vegetables, but fresh meat they have only at the hunting season, and then they never fail to eat while it lasts; of their fowls and hogs they seldom eat any as they keep them for profit.

> In the failure of their crops, they make bread of the different kinds of *Fagus*, of the *Diospyros*, of a species of *Convolvulus* with a tuberous root found in the low cane grounds, of the root of a species of *Smilax*, of live oak acorns, and of the young shoots of the *Canna;* in summer many wild plants chiefly of the *Drupi* and *Bacciferous* kind supply them. (Romans, 1775, pp. 84–85.)

Most of these can be identified with reasonable certitude, and this has been done for me by Paul Standley and E. P. Killip. *Zea* or corn was, of course, native. Mr. Killip suggests that the two varieties of *Panicum*, or guinea corn, were probably *Sorghum drummondii* and *Panicum maximum*, both of which represent importations from Africa. Under *Phaseolus* are probably indicated the native American kidney bean, but the *Dolichos*, or hyacinth bean, would be an Asiatic importation. *Helianthus giganteus* is the sunflower and native American. In the genus *Fagus* is now included only the beeches, but it embraced the chinquapin up to 1768 and the chestnut until 1800, when chestnuts were placed under *Castanea*. Since there are many references to bread made from chestnuts and no mention whatsoever of the use of beechnuts, unless in this instance, it seems certain that Romans had chestnuts in mind. *Diospyros* is the persimmon, the *Convolvulus* the wild sweetpotato, and the *Smilax* the China brier, or kunti. These are native to the North American continent, but the *Canna*, mentioned next, was introduced from the tropics and was probably *Canna indica*, naturalized from the West Indies. Next follow general references to *Drupi*, plums, and *Bacciferous* plants, berries.

There is good reason to believe that most of the foods which do not appear in both the Creek and Choctaw lists were, nevertheless, used by both tribes. For instance, we have found the sunflower cultivated as far east as North Carolina or Virginia, and we know that the *Smilax* root was a staple article among all the Creeks. Nor is there reason to suppose that the maypop was unknown to and unutilized by the Choctaw.

The Choctaw were less dependent on animal foods than most of their neighbors and such as they had differed little. They included the deer, bear, and, when opportunity offered, the bison and elk. They made more use than other peoples of small animals, particularly squirrels. Fish played a smaller part in their dietary. On occasion they are said to have resorted to snakes and in later times, horse meat and pork. In a Choctaw story some hunters are represented cooking a hawk (Swanton, 1931 a, pp. 208–209).

Adair gives us a fairly good idea of the Chickasaw bill of fare, and shows that it differed little from that of the neighboring Creeks and Choctaw. He says regarding corn:

Corn is their chief produce, and main dependence. Of this they have three sorts. [One of these, a small variety,] usually ripens in two months, from the time it is planted; though it is called by the English, the six weeks corn. The second sort is yellow and flinty, which they call "hommony-corn." The third is the largest, of a very white and soft grain, termed "bread-corn." (Adair, 1775, p. 407.)

Besides corn, he tells us they cultivated different sorts of peas and beans, "a sort of small tobacco, which the French and English have not," pumpkins, different kinds of melons, potatoes, watermelons, "marsh-mallows," and sunflowers, and they also utilized hickory nuts, strawberries, wild potatoes, grapes, and persimmons. Hazel nuts were eaten seldom. Among cultivated plants the corn, peas, beans, tobacco, pumpkins, and sunflowers were native; the melons, potatoes, and watermelons introduced, unless by melons he means instead of muskmelons some sort of squash (Adair, 1775, pp. 361, 408–409). By "marsh-mallows" he may intend the *Passiflora* or perhaps the okra (*Hibiscus esculentus*). In either case, we have to do with a plant foreign to the country, but if it is okra this is the first reference we seem to have noted. Another plant not certainly mentioned hitherto is the *Nelumbo lutea*. Adair says of this:

There grows a long flag, in shallow ponds, and on the edges of running waters, with an ever-green, broad, round leaf, a little indented where it joins the stalk; it bears only one leaf, that always floats on the surface of the water, and affords plenty of cooling small nuts, which make a sweet-tasted and favourite bread, when mixed with Indian corn flour. It is a sort of marsh-mallows, and reckoned a speedy cure for burning maladies, either outward or inward,—for the former, by an outward application of the leaf; and for the latter, by a decoction of it drank plentifully. The Choktah so highly esteem this vegetable, that they call one of their head-towns by its name. (Adair, 1775, p. 418.)

I have been unable as yet to identify the town thus mentioned, the only plants aside from trees that appear in Choctaw town names being the cane (used several times), blackberry, mulberry, sassafras, wild onion, and grass. We may feel sure that this was used by the Creeks also and by all other Southeastern Indians within whose borders it was found in any quantity.

They hunted the deer, bison, elk, bear, turkey, duck, goose, and pigeon, and many small animals, especially squirrels. Adair, interested in establishing a series of food restrictions which would bear out his theory of an Israelitish origin for the Indians, says that, in ancient times, they would not eat the beaver or opossum, and in later times they would not touch eagles, ravens, crows, bats, owls, flies, mosquitoes, worms, wolves, panthers, foxes, cats, mice, rats, moles, snakes, or horses, though the Choctaw ate the two last mentioned. In general the Chickasaw would touch no birds of prey or birds of night,[15] no beast of prey except the bear, and no aquatic animals including frogs. According to the same writer, they would not swallow flies, mosquitoes, or gnats lest they breed sickness or worms (Adair, 1775, p. 131).

For the tribes of the Mississippi itself, our information derived from the Natchez is most extensive. Dumont de Montigny (1753, vol. 1, pp. 32–34) speaks of two kinds of corn; but Du Pratz of several, describing three specifically:

Louisiana produces many kinds of maize, such as the flour maize which is white, flat, and corrugated, but more tender than the other kinds; and the gruel or grits maize which is round, hard, and glossy. Of this latter kind there is white, yellow, red, and blue. The maize of these two last colors is more common in the highlands than in lower Louisiana. We have besides, the little grain or little maize, so named because it is smaller than the others. (Le Page du Pratz, 1758, vol. 2, p. 3.)

The same writer tells us that beans were found in cultivation along the Mississippi, some varieties of which were red, some black, and some of other colors, and he says that they were called "forty-day beans" because they were ready to eat within 40 days from the time when the seed was planted. He mentions two kinds of pumpkins (giromons).

---

[15] An old Chickasaw woman once refused to dress a hawk Adair (1775, p. 137) had killed, but see page 289 for a reference to the eating of a hawk by the Choctaw.

The one is round and the other in the shape of a hunting horn.[16] These last are the better, having firmer flesh of a less insipid sweetness, containing fewer seeds, and keeping much better than the other. These are the ones of which they make preserves. (Le Page du Pratz, 1758, vol. 2, p. 11.)

A kind of grass yielding grain, called choupichoul in Natchez (in English shupishul) was given a kind of semicultivation by the river people, and still another known as widthloogouill (withloguithl) by the same tribe was utilized without any sort of cultivation. One of these was probably the wild rice, while the other may have been cockspur grass (*Echinochloa crusgalli*).

They also gathered the seeds from a species of wild cane which has been mentioned already. This is not produced every year, but is very abundant when it does appear.

This grain, [says Du Pratz] which rather resembles oats, except that it is three times as thick and longer, is carefully gathered by the natives, who make of it bread or porridge. This meal swells up as much as that of wheat. (Le Page du Pratz, 1758, vol. 1, pp. 316–317, vol. 2, pp. 58–59.)

Persimmons and the inevitable bread made from them are noted, along with peaches and figs introduced by the Spaniards and French. Undoubtedly pecans, hickory nuts, and acorns constituted an item in the lower Mississippi diet, but Du Pratz (1758, vol. 2, pp. 18–20, 25) speaks only of bread made from black walnuts and the occasional employment of chestnuts when other food was scanty.

Finally he mentions,

a kind of agaric or mushroom which grows at the foot of the walnut, especially when it is overthrown. The natives, who pay great attention to the choice of their nourishment, gather these with care, have them boiled in water, and eat them with their grits. I have had the curiosity to taste of these, and I have found them very delicate, but a little flat, which could be easily corrected by means of some seasoning. (Le Page du Pratz, 1758, vol. 2, p. 51.)

Among the Natchez game animals mentioned are bear, deer, and bison, besides turkeys and many other birds, and fish such as carp, sucker, catfish, and a variety of sardine. Du Pratz adds the dog, but the use of the dog was probably mainly confined to ceremonial occasions (Swanton, 1911, pp. 67–72). Absence of any mention of the alligator as a food animal is noticeable, as it was much esteemed along most of the Gulf coast.

The diet of other river tribes differed little from that of the Natchez, except that the Tunica are reported to have relied more upon corn and to have lived one entire month every year on persimmons besides putting up a great quantity of persimmon bread. Gravier mentions sunflowers growing in Tunica fields beside the corn, and they were probably grown everywhere along the river.

---

[16] *Cor de chasse*, but given by Du Pratz as "*corps de chasse*" (see Read, 1931, p. 89).

Anciently it is said that four kinds of corn were grown by the Chitimacha, one of which seems to have been the favorite flour corn. The three others differed mainly in the color of the kernels and one, a blue variety, is supposed to have been found growing wild when the Chitimacha reached their country, a bit of folklore. They were all of the kind known as "flint corn." It is evident that beans and pumpkins were also cultivated. They gathered the roots of the China brier, or *Smilax*, ground nuts (*Apios tuberosa*), the seed of the pond lily (*Nelumbo lutea*) and the palmetto, the rhizoma of the common *Sagittaria* and the *Sagittaria* with the large leaf, the fruit of the persimmon, strawberries, blackberries, mulberries, and "a white berry growing near Plaquimine Bayou," besides the seeds of a cane, evidently the one of which mention has been made already. Gatschet includes "pistaches" and "wild beans" among Chitimacha food plants, but by the former is perhaps intended peanuts or the cactus-pear. He also mentions sweetpotatoes, which may mean either wild sweetpotatoes or the varieties later imported. In Bulletin 43, on the authority of Benjamin Paul, I noted raspberries among the kinds of berries gathered by the Chitimacha, but they certainly did not know red raspberries and it is more likely that blackberries were meant. They hunted deer and bear, and ate two kinds of turtles and all sorts of fish. (Swanton, 1911, pp. 345–346; Gatschet, 1883, pp. 4–5.)

The Caddo cultivated corn, beans, pumpkins, and sunflowers, as well as tobacco, and we are told that they utilized acorns, nuts of various kinds, persimmons, plums, wild cherries, mulberries, strawberries, and blackberries, and were particularly fond of wild grapes. The gathering of grapes by the Caddo was the subject of a painting by Catlin. Among the animals they hunted are mentioned the deer, bison, bear, rabbit, "wild boars," and "dormice and other quadrupeds." These are included in a list given by Solís and he adds to it wild turkeys, geese, ducks, partridges, cranes, quail, "and other birds that are on the beach or on the banks and margins of the rivers," also "snakes and vipers," and polecats. They used fish extensively, especially the eastern Caddo. In general, their economy was in line with that of the other Southeastern tribes. The one animal which instituted an important change was the bison, their annual hunts of this animal giving them for the time being something of the cultural veneer of the Plains Indians. This tended to increase as they were pushed westward. (Swanton, 1942, pp. 127–139; Solís, 1931, p. 43.)

In 1687 Joutel found growing in the Quapaw fields corn, pumpkins (*citrouilles*), melons (*melons*), sunflowers (*soleils*), and beans (*fèvres*) (Margry, 1875–86, vol. 3, p. 462).

The usage of vegetable and animal foods in most of the main Southeastern provinces, as reported to early writers, is epitomized in tables 2 and 3. Of course, most of these were actually used throughout.

TABLE 2.—*Geographical and tribal distribution of the vegetable foods of the Southeastern Indians according to references in the literature*

Vegetable foods	Virginia	North Carolina	South Carolina	North Florida	South Florida	Creek	Choctaw	Chickasaw	Mississippi River	Caddo	Chitimacha
Bean	X	X	X	X		X	X	X	X	X	X
Corn	X	X	X	X		X	X	X	X	X	X
Gourd for vessels (*Cucurbita*)	X	X	X	X			X				
Orache	X	X									
Peas (a var. of bean)	X	X	X			X		X			
Squash, pumpkin	X	X	X	X		X	X	X	X	X	X?
Sunflower	X	X					X	X	[1] X	X	
Angelico	X?	X									
Blackberry							X				X
Black gum (berries)			X								
Blue palmetto						X					
Cane	X	X				X	X		X		X
Cherry	X										
Chestnut	X	X				X	X		X	X?	
Chinquapin	X	X	X	X			X				
Cockspur grass						X?			X?		
Coco berry					X						
Crabapple		X									
Dioscorea villosa		X									
Gooseberry	X										
Grape		X	X	X		X		X	X	X	
Groundnut	X	X	X						X		X
Hickory nut	X	X	X			X	X		X	X?	X
Honeylocust						X					
Huckleberry	X	X	X				X				
Moss (creek)						X					
Mulberry	X	X		X		X	X				X
Mushroom									X		
Oak acorn	X	X	X	X		X	X		X	X	
Palm berry					X						
Panicum maximum						X	X				
Pea, wild		X									
Persimmon		X		X		X			X	X	X
Plum	X		X	?		X	X		X	X	X
Pond lily (seeds)								X	X	X	X
Pricklypear		X									X?
Raspberry	X			X							X?
Rice, wild	X	X				X			X		X
Sagittaria											X
Seagrape					X						
Serviceberry			X								
Smilax		X	X			X	X				X
Strawberry	X	X					X	X	X		
Sugar maple	X		X								
Sweet gum							X				
Sweetpotato (wild)		X				X	X	X	X		X
Tuckahoe	X	X									
Walnut	X	X				X			X	X?	X
Zamia					X						

[1] Tunica.

TABLE 2.—*Geographical and tribal distribution of the vegetable foods of the Southeastern Indians according to references in the literature*—Continued

Vegetable foods and trees introduced by whites	Virginia	North Carolina	South Carolina	North Florida	South Florida	Creek	Choctaw	Chickasaw	Mississippi River	Caddo	Chitimacha
Apple						×					
Canna							×				
Fig			×	×	×				×		
Muskmelon	×		×			×		×			× ?
Okra								× ?			× ?
Orange				×	×						
Passiflora	×					×		×			
Peach	×		×			×			×		
Peanut											× ?
Rice					×	×					
Sorghum						×	×				
Sweetpotato						×	×	×			×
Watermelon	×		×	×		×		×	×	×	

TABLE 3.—*Geographical and tribal distribution of the animal foods of the South eastern Indians according to references in the literature*

Food animals	Virginia	North Carolina	South Carolina	North Florida	South Florida	Creek	Choctaw	Chickasaw	Mississippi River	Caddo	Chitimcha
Deer	X	X	X	X	X	X	X	X	X	X	X
Bear	X	X	X	X	X	X	X	X	X	X	X
Beaver	X	X?	X					X?			
Bison	X					X	X?	X	X	X	
Elk (properly Wapiti)	X							X?	X		
Manatee					X						
Opossum		X	X								
Otter	X	X?									
Panther		X	X	X?							
Polecat		X	X	X?							
Rabbit	X	X	X			X					
Raccoon		X	X								
Rat (muskrat)					X						
Squirrel	X	X	X				X	X			
Wildcat		X	X								
Porpoise		X									
Whale					X						
Alewife		X	X								
Bluefish			X								
Eel					X						
Herring	X	X	X								
Mullet		X		X							
Perch						X					
Plaice [1]		X		X							
Ray		X	X								
Red horse						X					
Sardine									X		
Sturgeon	X	X	X			X					
Trout		X	X	X	X	X					
Tunny					X						
Turbot				X							
Rockfish or bass			X			X					
White guard fish (garfish)			X								
Wolf fish					X						
Trunk fish					X						
Clam					X						
Crab	X		X	X							
Mussel	X		X								
Oyster	X		X		X						
Cockle			X								
Snake	X		X	X	X		X				
Tortoise and turtle	X		X		X	X					X
Lizard				X	X						
Alligator				X							
Crawfish			X	X							
Lobster				X	X						
Snail					X						
Beetle	X										
Fleas and lice					X						
Locusts	X										
Wasps in comb			X								
Partridge [2]	X		X								
Pigeon			X			X		X			
Turkey	X		X	X		X	X	X	X		
Duck and goose			X					X			
Carp									X		
Catfish									X		
Sucker									X		

[1] The true plaice is confined to Europe; the identity of this fish is unknown.   [2] Quail.

DISCUSSION

We are plainly dealing with one economic province. Several species of corn, beans, peas, and squashes or pumpkins, including gourds from the genus *Cucurbita*, were cultivated in all parts of it except in southern Florida which, as already remarked, should really have belonged to the West Indian province but was left a kind of economic no man's land by failure to introduce manioc. The result was that it had no cultivated plants at all in purely aboriginal times. The province most closely resembling it was the Chitimacha country, and it is perhaps significant that we do not seem to have a clear record of the use there, in prehistoric times, of beans, peas, and squashes, but this may be owing in part to the early displacement of these plants by rice, melons, and other food plants better suited to the country. More light upon the ancient condition of this region is urgently needed.

There were three principal varieties of corn: the little corn of the nature of popcorn, which was first to mature; the flint or hominy corn, the kernels of which were hard and smooth and were of various colors—white, yellow, red, and blue; and the flour or dent corn with corrugated kernels. Bread was made oftenest of the flour corn; it was the most valued and it seems to have been the time of its maturity which determined the occurrence of the green corn dance. I have seen some flint corn raised among the Choctaw which was mottled white and blue, and a number of years ago I remember some large ears of flour corn brought back by Mr. Mooney from the Cherokee. These were white mottled with a deep pink.

Sunflowers seem to have been cultivated generally. In the northeastern Algonquian section a kind of "orache" is said to have been raised as a salt substitute.

The wild vegetable products were also much the same. Groundnuts (*Apios tuberosa*), wild sweetpotatoes, several varieties of *Smilax* (kantak), Angelico roots, persimmons, plums, grapes, strawberries, mulberries, blackberries, some varieties of huckleberries, wild rice, the seed of a species of cane, chestnuts, walnuts, hickory nuts, acorns, particularly those of the live oak, and chinquapins must have been used in nearly all sections, though it is strange that blackberries are so seldom mentioned by name. The Virginia wakerobin (*Peltandra virginica*), floating arum, or whatever other plant was used for tuckahoe bread, seems to have been confined to the Northeast. The prickleypear, crab apple, wild pea, tree huckleberry, gooseberry, cherry, and serviceberry are mentioned only in the Algonquian or eastern Siouan sections. The blue palmetto is referred to in southern sections, as might have been expected; a pond lily, *Nelumbo lutea*, in the Southwest in the present States of Mississippi and Louisiana; and *Sagittaria* in several places. The *Zamia integrifolia*, palm berries, coco berries, and seagrapes belonged to the south Florida province, the one which lacked cultivated plants.

Raspberries were utilized in the northern highlands, but there are notes of them in Florida and Louisiana which have reference either to the blackcaps or to blackberries. The sugar maple was also exploited in highland portions of the area.

A mushroom was used by the Natchez and honey locusts by the Creeks and Cherokee.

Plants and trees introduced at a comparatively early date include the passiflora, watermelon, muskmelon, peach, peanut, canna, sorghum, the cultivated sweetpotato, rice, okra, apple, fig, and orange.

Staple animal foods in every section were provided by the deer and bear, the former being valued mainly for its flesh, the latter for its fat.   In the northern and western parts these were supplemented by the bison and elk, and the former was probably a much more important game animal in prehistoric times than it became later.   Most important of the small animals were the rabbit and the squirrel, the former mentioned oftenest in the northeastern section and the latter among the Choctaw.   In De Soto's time rabbits were eaten everywhere. Presents of rabbits were made to the Spaniards at Ocute on the east side of Ocmulgee River, and by the Chickasaw, and the explorers learned to trap them in the aboriginal manner west of the Mississippi (Bourne, 1904, vol. 1, pp. 56, 101, 145; vol. 2, p. 22).   The beaver and otter were eaten in Virginia and probably in the coast region of North Carolina.   The former was also hunted by the Siouan tribes of both Carolinas, but neither appears as a food animal elsewhere, and Adair (1775, p. 132) says that the beaver was anciently tabooed by the Chickasaw.   Lawson states that the Indians of his acquaintance, meaning the Siouan people of the Carolinas and probably the Tuscarora, ate panthers, polecats, wildcats, opossums, and raccoons, while Lederer tells us that the former consumed wildcats although their flesh was rank.   (Lawson, 1860, p. 290; Alvord, 1912, p. 147.)   "Leopards," presumably panthers, were presented to Laudonnière, by Florida Indians (1586, p. 130), but it does not appear certain that they regarded them as food, and there are no other references to suggest the eating of them in this section.   Adair (1775, pp. 16, 132) says that their flesh and the flesh of the opossum were equally taboo among the Chickasaw.   One of the smaller animals, such as the otter or muskrat, may have been intended by the "rats" which were consumed by the inhabitants of south Florida (Swanton, 1922, p. 388). They also hunted the manatee, and their successors, the Seminole, who called it the "big beaver" (Bartram, 1792), did the same.   According to Hariot, porpoises were hunted by the coast people of North Carolina, and Fontaneda mentions "whale" hunting by the south Floridians, but he probably has reference to the porpoise or perhaps the manatee, since Lawson tells a fantastic story of whale hunting which seems to be explained by south Florida usages in the chase of the manatee (but see pp. 282, 329).

Fishing was an important industry almost everywhere, but particularly on the Atlantic coast to the northeast, in Florida, and on the Mississippi and its tributaries, including the lagoon and bayou sections of Louisiana. The fish most prominent in the Northeast were the herring and sturgeon, but Lawson tells us that the coast tribes did not use the latter (see p. 277). Besides these, Hariot mentions the trout, ray, alewife, mullet, and plaice; Lawson speaks of all but the last two of these and adds the garfish, bluefish, rockfish or bass, and trout; and Florida authorities speak of the trout, turbot, mullet, and plaice (see pp. 273, 279, 280). In south Florida the trout, wolf fish, trunk fish (chapin), and tunny are mentioned (see p. 282). The carp, sucker, catfish, and sardine (herring?) are the only fish specifically named among the Natchez and other Mississippi River tribes (Swanton, 1911, p. 72). According to Bartram (1792, p. 174) the great spotted gar was sometimes eaten. Eels appear only on the menu of the southern Floridians along with oysters and clams (Swanton, 1922, pp. 388, 392). Clams, oysters, and mussels were used by practically all peoples of the Atlantic coast. Crabs, cockles, crawfish, and lobsters are mentioned by authorities on the northeastern and Floridian Indians. Land and oceanic turtles and their eggs were used as food in nearly all sections where they occurred; snakes in the Northeast, in Florida, and even by the Choctaw, though this last is on the authority of Adair, who was no friend of the Choctaw people (Adair, 1775, p. 133). However, Timberlake, while in the Cherokee country and very likely at the suggestion of Cherokee Indians, tasted rattlesnake flesh and found it so excellent that he repeated the experiment several times (Timberlake, Williams ed., 1927, p. 72). Lizards are said to have been used in both northern and southern Florida as was the alligator, which was also eaten by the coast tribes of Louisiana and probably others.

The most important game bird was the wild turkey, hunted wherever it could be found. Second in importance was the passenger pigeon, whose roosts were gathering places for Indian hunters at certain seasons. Names scattered throughout the Gulf States bear record to the places where enormous flocks of these birds used to gather. There is a Pigeon Roost Creek in northern Mississippi, a Pigeon Roost in Clay County, Ky., and the following local names have forms of the same name in the Creek language: Parchelagee

Creek in Taylor County, Ga., Patsaliga in Crenshaw County, Ala., and a creek of the same name, besides another known as Pigeon Creek, in the same part of the State. Very likely Pigeon Creek, Nassau County, Fla., and Little Pigeon Creek, Sevier County, Tenn., were pigeon resorts. Partridges were mentioned as in use in Virginia, and ducks and geese in South Carolina and the Chickasaw country, but they were undoubtedly eaten wherever they could be found. Birds' eggs were probably eaten everywhere and are specifically mentioned as an article of consumption among the Choctaw, Chickasaw, and Powhatan Indians. The remaining delicacies belonging to the animal kingdom of which we have notice are beetles and locusts in Virginia, wasps in the comb in the Piedmont Region of the Carolinas, fleas and lice in north Florida (Swanton, 1922, p. 362), and snails in south Florida.

A word might be added regarding the use of dog flesh. Ranjel, one of the De Soto chroniclers, tells us that the Indians of a town somewhere in the northwestern part of the present South Carolina gave the Spaniards "a few little dogs which are good eating," and adds: "These are dogs of a small size that do not bark; and they breed them in their homes for food" (Bourne, 1904, vol. 2, p. 103). It has been conjectured that these were opossums, but as Elvas speaks of a presentation of dogs in about the same region, but says that the Indians did not eat them, the chances are that either Ranjel or his editor has made a mistake, that the animals were dogs, and that they were not eaten by the natives. As to the absence of a bark, we may well recall what Strachey (1849, p. 124), says of the dogs of Virginia that they "cannot barke, but howle." A small variety of dog was, however, used as food in some other parts of North America.

Du Pratz includes the dog among Natchez food animals, but it is probable that he has in mind the part that it played in the feasts of which war parties partook just before starting out to engage the enemy (Swanton, 1911, p. 129). The Quapaw had the same custom, according to Romans (1775, p. 100), who speaks of it as if it did not extend farther south, but while he is, of course, in error here, we may take his remarks as an indication that the usage, like so many others, had spread south along the river and was not originally characteristic of the Gulf tribes.

An apparent exception is indicated by an anonymous French writer, who says that when the Choctaw "wish to feast their friends, they kill a dog, of which they have quantities, and serve it to them" (Swanton, 1918, p. 67). But since this statement stands entirely by itself, such feasts may have had a ceremonial significance.

Adair (1775, pp. 133–134) states that, in early times, the Indians of his acquaintance did not eat the flesh of horses, dogs, or domestic cats, though when he wrote the Choctaw had become addicted to the use of the first-mentioned.

The honeybee came into our Southern States with Europeans, but there are one or two very early references to honey which have puzzled entomologists not a little. The notices in the De Soto narratives have already been commented upon (Bourne, 1904, vol. 1, p. 74; vol. 2, p. 110) and an apparent mention of honey by Laudonnière which seems to be a translator's error (Loudonnière, 1586, p. 9; see p. 268 above).

Benjamin Hawkins, writing near the end of the eighteenth century, says:

I saw at Mr. Bailey's (in the Upper Creek country) 20 bee hives. He says they do well, and that there are wild bees in the country in every direction. They are extending themselves west, and some hunters informed him they had lately discovered some to the west of the Mississippi about 30 miles, that they had but recently arrived there, as the trees they fell had young comb only. (Hawkins, 1916, p. 40.)

Elsewhere we read:

The honey in this country is poisonous in the month of March, some negroes and Indians have been killed at that season. At that season on the small branches, there is a plant in bloom called by the whites wolf's tongue, or fire leaves, by the Indians Hochkau (oachfoe), it has a long stem with yellow blossoms, and bears around the stem, green berries, which altho' poisonous are eaten in years of scarcity by the Indians. They boil them in two or three waters, shifting them, and thus extract the poison from them. They are then pleasant to the taste, somewhat like the garden pea. The Indians are the authors of the discovery. Milk has been the only efficacious remedy discovered here for this poison. The last season a bee tree was taken in this neighborhood and all who eat of the honey sickened instantaneously. They retired to the house, except a black boy, and took some milk which restored them. The boy was unable to get to the house, and altho' aid was sent him, in 2 hours he was dead.

Those who eat of the honey are first taken with a giddiness, then blindness accompanied with great pain and uneasiness, and thirst. (Hawkins, 1916, p. 46.)

In later times the Indians secured honey by cutting down the tree in which a hive had been located. When the amount was unusually large, they would kill a small deer, make a bottle out of its skin, and put into it the honey, comb and all.

Salt was of so much importance in early trading enterprises in the Southeast that it requires rather extended notice.

When La Salle reached the lower Mississippi he heard of Indians going to the coast to make salt (La Salle, N., ms.), but in view of the extensive salt trade carried on between the river tribes and those about the Arkansas and Louisiana salt licks, and the extensive deposits of mineral salt near the shores of the Gulf, some of which are known to have been worked by Indians, it is probable that these were not going to boil down sea water.

When De Soto was at Pacaha, somewhere north of the present Helena, Ark., in 1541, Garcilaso says:

Seeing the great necessity for salt that his people were experiencing, for they were dying for lack of it, the *adelantado* made thorough inquiries of the *curacas* and their Indians in that province of Capaha in order to learn where he could get some. In the course of this questioning he found eight Indians in the hands of the Spaniards who had been captured the day they entered that pueblo, and were not natives of it, but strangers and merchants who had traversed many provinces with their goods, and among other things they were accustomed to bring salt to sell. Being brought before the governor they told him that in some mountains forty leagues away there was a great deal of very good salt, and to the repeated questions they asked them they replied that there was also in that country much of the yellow metal which they asked for. (Garcilaso, 1723, p. 187.)

Two Spaniards were sent in quest of these things with the merchants and an escort of Indians, "and at the end of the eleven days that they spent on their journey they returned with six loads of rock-salt crystals, not made artificially, but found in this state," besides some brass (evidently copper) (Garcilaso, 1723, p. 187). The copper must have gotten into that region from farther to the north but the salt may well have been a native product, though there is some doubt as to whether this episode is properly placed in the narrative. Later, the De Soto expedition encountered salt springs at places named Calpista, Cayas, Tanico, Chaguate, and Aguacay, and Garcilaso speaks of a "Province of Salt" in Arkansas, which was probably along Salt Creek, an affluent of the Ouachita. Of the salt in the "Province of Cayas," at or near this place, Elvas says:

The Indians carry it thence to other regions to exchange it for skins and blankets. They gather it along the river, which leaves it on top of the sand when the water falls. And since they can not gather it without more sand being mixed with it, they put it into certain baskets which they have for this purpose, wide at the top and narrow at the bottom. They hang the baskets to a pole in the air and put water in them, and they place a basin underneath into which the water falls. After being strained and set on the fire to boil, as the water becomes less, the salt is left on the bottom of the pot. (Robertson, 1933, pp. 192–193.)

A hundred and forty years later, the French found the Caddo, Tunica, Koroa, and Washita Indians of this section busily engaged in boiling down salt and carrying it to the Mississippi tribes in trade, the Quapaw and Taensa being particularly mentioned as customers. One of the Caddo tribes bears the name "place of salt" (Namidish) (Swanton, 1942, pp. 139–140). Du Pratz thus speaks of the salt region of Louisiana:

When one has ascended Black River for about 30 leagues, he finds on the left a stream of saline water which comes from the west. Ascending this stream about 2 leagues he comes upon a lake of salt, which is perhaps 2 leagues long by 1 wide. One league higher toward the north he comes upon another lake of salt water almost as long as the first and as wide.

This water passes without doubt through some salt mines. It has the salt taste without having the bitterness of sea water. The natives come to this place from considerable distances, to hunt during the winter and to make salt. Before the French sold them kettles they made earthen pots for this operation on the spot. When they have enough of a load, they return into their own country loaded with salt and dry meats. (Le Page du Pratz, 1758, vol. 1, pp. 307–308.)

This is a rather crude description of the salt country round Catahoula Lake. It is not the lake or communicating streams that supply the salt, but licks near by. Farther toward the northwest are the salt regions about Goldonna and Lake Bistineau, which may be identified with considerable probability with the salt provinces through which Moscoso led his Spaniards in a vain attempt to reach Mexico after De Soto's death.

From the remains of large earthen pots found around the salt deposits on Avery's Island when they were first exploited, it is known that these were utilized in prehistoric times, but there are no historic notices of such usage.

The Spaniards also found "an abundance of very good salt" at Cofitachequi on the Savannah River, which we may surmise to have come from the sea (Bourne, 1904, vol. 2, p. 99) for we are told, at a slightly later date, that the Indians near the headwaters of the Santee were in the habit of descending to the coast to obtain salt in trade. This may have been the source of the salt which Lederer observed among the Sara Indians, who are indeed mentioned in connection with the Santee trade. He says:

I did likewise, to my no small admiration, find hard cakes of white salt amongst them: but whether they were made of sea-water, or taken out of salt-pits, I know not; but am apt to believe the latter, because the sea is so remote from them. (Lawson, 1860, p. 158.)

We, too, are left in some doubt, knowing on the one hand the trade with the coast just mentioned and aware on the other of the extent to which the salt licks of Kentucky were exploited. Spanish chroniclers tell of four or five springs near the Chisca country from which salt was extracted (Serrano y Sanz, 1913, p. 151). This would be somewhere in southeastern Tennessee, and in that State a salt lick or well is reported from Roane County on the border of Anderson, a salt spring on Flynn's Creek, in Jackson County, and salt licks near Memphis and Paris. One of our earliest references to the salt regions of Kentucky is by Batts and Fallam in 1671, who were informed by a Mohetan (Moneton) Indian that the next town beyond theirs, which was somewhere in West Virginia, "lived upon a level plain, from whence came abundance of salt" (Alvord, 1912, p. 193). These were perhaps the Shawnee, who are supposed to have made use of the salt in this section.

The explorers from Barbados on the Cape Fear River report:

Some of the Indians brought very good salt aboard us, and made signs, pointing to both sides of the river's mouth, that there was great store thereabouts. (Lawson, 1860, p. 125.)

In 1650 some English explorers were told that there were "great heapes of Salt" at the mouth of Roanoke River (Alvord, 1912, p. 127). The salt trade along the Santee has already been mentioned, but it should be added that the monk San Miguel observed no salt among the Indians he visited about St. Simons Island, Ga. (Garcia, 1902, p. 198).

In the Gulf area proper between Florida and the Mississippi we know of but one source of natural salt except the sea, and that was on a small creek flowing into the lower Tombigbee River called to this day Salt Creek and in the neighboring Satilpa Creek.

As might have been anticipated, we find most of our references to salt substitutes in sections where natural supplies were wanting. Garcilaso tells us that when the Spaniards entered the province of Tascalusa, between the Alabama and Tombigbee Rivers, they lost many of their companions for want of salt, but the rest

made use of the remedy which the Indians prepared to save and help themselves in that necessity. This was that they burned a certain herb of which they knew and made lye with the ashes. They dipped what they ate in it as if it were a sauce and with this they saved themselves from rotting away and dying, like the Spaniards. (Garcilaso, 1723, pp. 175–176.)

This may have been the salt substitute mentioned by Adair:

They make salt for domestic use, out of a saltish kind of grass, which grows on rocks, by burning it to ashes, making strong lye of it, and boiling it in earthen pots to a proper consistence. (Adair, 1775, p. 116.)

Probably this "grass" was identical with the "moss" from which Bartram tells us the Creeks obtained their salt, for Catesby says that the Indians of his acquaintance used "instead of salt, wood-ashes, yet I have seen amongst the *Chigasaws* very sharp salt in christalline lumps, which they told me was made of a grass growing on rocks in fresh rivers" (Catesby, 173–43, vol. 2, p. x).

As noted above, the Algonquians of North Carolina used the stalk cf "a kinde of Orage." By burning this into ashes, Hariot (1893, pp. 21–22) tells us, "they make a kinde of salt earth, wherewithall many vse sometimes to season their brothes." He says they knew of no other salt, but this seems unlikely in view of the references made to the use of sea salt in their immediate neighborhood. Of the Virginia Indians Beverley (1705, bk. 3, p. 15) remarks: "They have no Salt among them, but for seasoning, use the Ashes of Hiccory, stickweed, or some other Wood or Plant, affording a salt ash."

And finally a word from Lawson:

The salts they mix with their bread and soup, to give them a relish, are alkalis, viz: ashes, and calcined bones of deer and other animals. Salads, they never eat any, as for pepper and mustard, they reckon us little better than madmen, to make use of it amongst our victuals. (Lawson, 1860, p. 361.)

HORTICULTURE

Farming in the Gulf province usually involved preliminary work in clearing the ground of trees and bushes. In North Carolina, Lawson (1860, p. 140) says the best lands were not used because of the size of the trees growing upon them, and Strachey (1849, p. 60) mentions one place in Virginia (Kecoughtan) in which the concentration of Indians and their greater skill as husbandmen was attributed to the fact that so much land was clear and open, about 2,000 acres being suitable for planting. Rich land adapted to cultivation and not seriously encumbered with trees would, of course, attract population as soon as agriculture was introduced in the section, and upon that would follow social and political leadership. This is perhaps an additional reason why leadership in most of the Gulf region rested with inland tribes, though the handicap was overcome in spots by abundance of sea food. The method of clearing land, where that was necessary, seems to have been the same everywhere. Adair says:

In the first clearing of their plantations, they only bark the large timber, cut down the sapplings and underwood, and burn them in heaps; as the suckers shoot up, they chop them off close to the stump, of which they make fires to deaden the roots, till in time they decay. Though, to a stranger, this may seem to be a lazy method of clearing the wood-lands; yet it is the most expeditious method they could have pitched upon, under their circumstances, as a common hoe and a small hatchet are all their implements for clearing and planting. (Adair, 1775, pp. 405–406.)

This process is practically identical with that described by Smith, Strachey, and Beverley as the one usual in Virginia.

The greatest labour they take, is in planting their corne, for the country naturally is overgrowne with wood. To prepare the ground they bruise the bark of the trees neare the roote, then do they scortch the roots with fire that they grow no more. The next yeare with a crooked peece of wood, they beat up the woodes by the rootes; and in that moulds, they plant their corne. (Smith, Tyler ed., 1907, pp. 95–96.)

Strachey's words are practically identical. It would seem that only the small saplings could have been "beat up" with the primitive instruments available, the larger trees being left to die and fall to pieces, as stated by Adair and again by Beverley. Spelman, however, affirms more robust treatment:

They take most commonly a place about their howses to sett ther corne, which if ther be much wood, in that place they cutt doune the greate trees sum half a yard aboue the ground, and y⁰ smaller they burne at the roote pullinge a good part of barke from them to make them die. (Spelman, *in* Smith, Arber ed., 1884, p. cxi.)

Byrd, indeed, intimates that the Indians of Virginia were in the habit of cutting down trees to get the nuts from them (Bassett, 1901, p. 302), but, in view of the labor necessarily entailed by pre-Columbian methods, it is evident that this can hardly have been common before the introduction of European axes, and in fact it sounds more like a jest than the sober statement of a fact.

The Barbados men who explored Cape Fear River "saw several plots of ground cleared by the Indians after their weak manner, compassed round with great timber trees, which they are no wise able to fell, and so keep the sun from corn-fields very much; yet, nevertheless, we saw as large corn-stalks, or larger, than we have seen anywhere else" (Lawson, 1860, p. 121).

Before the Spaniards came, the ancient inhabitants of southern Florida do not appear to have cultivated the ground, but their Seminole successors brought the industry with them, though it took on a particular pattern owing to the nature of the Everglade country. The villages are on hammocks, but

usually the home hammock is not big enough to accommodate both village and cornfield, hence the crops must be produced on some other island, often a day's journey or more distant. The method of cultivation followed is primitive. The trees are killed by girdling, so that the sun shines through when the leaves have fallen. Then the ground is broken with a hoe and the crops planted. These are casually tended from time to time thereafter. (Skinner, 1913, p. 76.)

The above is from notes made by Alanson Skinner in 1910. Thirty years earlier, MacCauley observed:

The ground they select is generally in the interiors of the rich hammocks which abound in the swamps and prairies of Southern Florida. There, with a soil unsurpassed in fertility and needing only to be cleared of trees, vines, underbrush, &c., one has but to plant corn, sweet potatoes, melons, or any thing else suited to the climate, and keep weeds from the growing vegetation, that he may gather a manifold return. The soil is wholly without gravel, stones, or rocks. It is soft, black, and very fertile. (MacCauley, 1887, p. 510.)

We have few detailed descriptions of the method of cultivating the ground, the principal ones being by Hariot, Spelman, Smith, and Strachey (these last two writers evidently using the same material), Le Moyne, Adair, and Du Pratz, representing the Algonquians of North Carolina and Virginia, the Timucua, the Chickasaw, and the Natchez, but notes from other tribes indicate a general uniformity throughout the region.

After describing the plants cultivated on the North Carolina coast—corn, beans, peas, pumpkins, squashes, gourds, sunflowers, and an "orage"—Hariot continues:

All the aforesaide commodities for victuall are set or sowed, sometimes in groundes apart and seuerally by themselues; but for the most part together in one ground mixtly: the manner thereof with the dressing and preparing of the ground, because I will note vnto you the fertilitie of the soile; I thinke good briefly to describe.

The ground they neuer fatten with mucke, dounge or any other thing; neither plow nor digge it as we in England, but onely prepare it in sort as followeth. A fewe daies before they sowe or set, the men with wooden instruments, made almost in forme of mattockes or hoes with long handles; the women with short peckers or parers, because they vse them sitting, of a foote long and about fiue inches in breadth: doe onely breake the vpper part of the ground to rayse vp the weedes, grasse, & old stubbes of corne stalkes with their rootes. The which after a day or twoes drying in the Sunne, being scrapte vp into many small heapes, to saue them labour for carrying them away; they burne into ashes. (And whereas some may thinke that they vse the ashes for to better the grounde; I say that then they woulde eyther disperse the ashes abroade; which wee obserued they doe not, except the heapes bee too great: or els would take speciall care to set their corne where the ashes lie, which also wee finde they are carelesse of.) And this is all the husbanding of their ground that they vse.

Then their setting or sowing is after this maner. First, for their corne, beginning in one corner of the plot, with a pecker they make a hole, wherein they put foure graines with that care they touch not one another, (about an inch asunder) and couer them with the moulde againe: and so through out the whole plot, making such holes and vsing them after such maner: but with this regard that they bee made in rankes, euery ranke differing from other halfe a fadome or a yarde, and the holes in euery ranke, as much. By this meanes there is a yarde spare ground betwene euery hole: where according to discretion here and there, they set as many Beanes and Peaze: in diuers places also among the seedes of *Macocqwer* [pumpkins], *Melden* [orache] and *Planta Solis* [sunflower].

The ground being thus set according to the rate by vs experimented, an English Acre conteining fourtie pearches in length, and foure in breadth, doeth there yeeld in croppe or of-come of corne, beanes, and peaze, at the least two hundred London bushelles: besides the *Macocqwer, Melden,* and *Planta Solis:* When as in England fourtie bushelles of our wheate yeelded out of such an acre is thought to be much. (Hariot, 1893, pp. 23-24.)

After telling how the Powhatan Indians cleared the ground for their cornfields, Spelman continues:

In this place they digg many holes which before the English brought them scauvels and spades they vsed to make with a crooked peece of woode beinge scraped on both sides in fation of a gardiners paring Iron. They put in to thes holes ordenarily 4 or 5 curnels of ther wheat [i. e., corn] and 2 beanes like french beanes, which when the wheat doe growe vp hauinge a straw as bigg as a canne reede the beanes runn vp theron like our hopps on poles, The eare of y° wheat is of great bignes in lenght and cumpace and yet for all the greatnes of it euery stalke hath most commonly sum fower or fiue eares on it. Ther corne is sett and gathered about the time we vse, but ther manner of ther gatheringe is as we doe our apells first in a hand basketts emtiinge them as they are filled into other bigger basketts wherof sum are made of the barkes of trees, sume of heampe which naturally groweth, Now after y° gatheringe, they laye it uppon matts a good thicknes in the soun to drye & euery night they make a great pile of it, coueringe it ouer with matts to defend it from the dewe, and when it is suffitiently weathered they pile it up in ther howses, dayly as occation serueth wringinge the eares in peises betwene ther hands, and so rubbinge out ther corne do put it to a great

Baskett which taketh upp the best parte of sum of ther howses, and all this is cheefly the weomens worke for the men doe only hunt to gett skinns in winter and doe tewe or dress them in summer.

But though now out of order yet let me not altogither forgett the settinge of ye Kings [i. e., Powhatan's] corne for which a day is apoynted wherin great part of ye cuntry people meete who with such diligence worketh as for the most part all ye Kinges corne is sett on a daye. After which setting the Kinge takes the croune which ye Kinge of England sent him beinge brought him by tow men, and setts it on his heade which dunn the people goeth about the corne in maner backwardes for they going before, and the king followinge ther faces are always toward the Kinge exspectinge when he should flinge sum beades amonge them which his custom is at that time to doe makinge thos which had wrought to scramble for them. But to sume he fauors he bids thos that carry his Beades to call such and such unto him unto whome he giueth beads into ther hande and this is the greatest curtesey he doth his people, when his corne is ripe the cuntry people cums to him againe and gathers drys and rubbes out all his corne for him, which is layd in howses apoynted for that purpose. (Spelman *in* Arber, 1884, pp. CXI–CXII.)

The following accounts of Smith and Strachey cover the same ground, but differ somewhat in details.

Smith:

They make a hole in the earth with a sticke, and into it they put 4 graines of wheat [i. e., corn] and 2 of beanes. These holes they make 4 foote one from another. Their women and children do continually keepe it with weeding, and when it is growne middle high, they hill it about like a hop-yard. (Smith, Tyler ed., 1907, pp. 95–96.)

Strachey:

They make a hole in the earth with a stick, and into yt they put three or five graines of wheat, and one or three of beanes: these holes they make four or five foot one from another, for the corne being set close together, one stalke would choak ells the growth of another, and so render both unprofitable. Their women and children do contynually keep the ground with weeding, and when the corne is growne middle high, they hill yt about like a hoppeyard. (Strachey, 1849, pp. 117–118.)

Beverley's contact with the Virginia Indians was also sufficiently early for him to speak from observation:

All these Sorts [of corn] are planted alike, in Rows, Three, Four or Five Grains in a Hill, the larger Sort at Four or Five Foot Distance, the lesser Sort nearer. The *Indians* used to give it One or Two Weedings, and make a Hill about it, and so the Labour was done. They likewise plant a Bean in the same Hill with the Corn, upon whose stalk it sustains itself. (Beverley, 1705, bk. 2, p. 29.)

Catesby has the following to say of corn and its cultivation, from which it appears that he either includes flint and flour corn under one head or intends to indicate but one of them:

Of this grain there are reckoned two sorts, differing in stature, largeness of the spike and grain, and different time of ripening, besides accidental variety in the colours of the grain. The largest is cultivated in *Virginia* and

Carolina. It is usually planted in *April,* and the largest ripeneth not 'till *October,* and is frequently left standing in the field 'till *December* before it is gather'd in: the smaller grain opening in half the time of the large, recommends it to the *Indians,* who according to their custom, do not provide corn for the whole winter; this by its quick ripening affords them early food, and is therefore by them most propagated: this kind is also cultivated in *New England,* where heat is deficient for ripening the larger kind. . . . The large kind grows usually nine or ten feet high, and sometimes in strong land, to the height of fourteen feet. The smaller sort grows commonly five or six feet high. In planting this corn, six or eight grains are drop'd in the circumference of about thirty inches, and covered with a hough: when it appears some inches above ground, the supernumeraries, if any, are pulled up, and three left in a triangle to grow, they are also weeded and earth raised about them with a hough, which being repeated three or four times in the summer, raises a hill about them. After the corn has come up some small height, there are drop'd into every hill two or three beans called *Bonavis,* which as they shoot up are supported by the stalks of the corn, and are ripe and gathered before the corn. These hills of corn are at the distance of about four feet or under, regularly planted in lines or quincunx order: in *June* the plants are suckered, *i. e.,* stripping off the superfluous shoots. In *August* they are topped, and their blades stripped off, and tied in small bundles for winter provender for horses and cattle. About the same time the spikes or ears of corn that grow erect naturally, are bent down to prevent wet entering the husk that covers the grain, and preserves it from rotting. In *October,* which is the usual harvest month, the spikes of corn with their husks are cut off from their stalks, and housed, and in that condition is preserved till it is wanted for use. It is then taken out of the husk, and the grain separated from the *Placenta* or Core. Then it is made saleable or fit for use. (Catesby, 1731–43, vol. 2, pp. xvi–xvii.)

This is the method of cultivation among the whites after they had had about one century of experience with this Indian product. The earlier part of the cultivation seems to follow the Indian pattern very closely; the later treatment has been added.

For Timucua agricultural methods, we have two parallel narratives, by René de Laudonnière and Jacques Le Moyne, respectively.

Laudonnière:

They sow their maize twice a year—to wit in March and in June—and all in one and the same soil. The said maize, from the time that it is sowed until the time that it be ready to be gathered, is but three months on the ground; the other six months, they let the earth rest. . . . They never dung their land, only when they would sow they set weeds on fire, which grow up the six months, and burn them all. They dig their ground with an instrument of wood, which is fashioned like a broad mattock, wherewith they dig their vines in France; they put two grains of maize together. . . At the time when the maize is gathered, it is all carried into a common house, where it is distributed to every man, according to his quality. They sow no more but that which they think will serve their turn for six months, and that very scarcely. (Laudonnière, 1856, pp. 11–12; Swanton, 1922, p. 359; French, 1869, p. 174.)

Le Moyne (pl. 51):

The Indians cultivate the earth diligently; and the men know how to make a kind of hoe from fish bones, which they fit to wooden handles, and with these they prepare the land well enough, as the soil is light. When the ground is sufficiently broken up and levelled, the women come with beans and millet, or maize. Some go first with a stick, and make holes, in which the others place the beans, or grains of maize. After planting they leave the fields alone, as the winter in that country, situated between the west and the north, is pretty cold for about three months, being from the 24th of December to the 15th of March; and during that time, as they go naked, they shelter themselves in the woods. When the winter is over, they return to their homes to wait for their crops to ripen. After gathering in their harvest, they store the whole of it for the year's use, not employing any part of it in trade, unless, perhaps some barter is made for some little household article. (Le Moyne, 1875, p. 9, illus.; Swanton, 1922, p. 359.)

From Calderón, the missionary Bishop of Cuba who visited Florida in 1675, we have the following:

During January they burn the grass and weeds from the fields preparatory to cultivation. . . . In April they commence to sow, and as the man goes along opening the trench, the woman follows sowing. All in common cultivate and sow the lands of the caciques. As alms for the missionaries and the needy widows they sow wheat [corn] in October and harvest it in June. This is a crop of excellent quality in the province of Apalache, and so abundant that it produces seventy *fanegas* from one *fanega* sown. (Wenhold, 1936, p. 13.)

Adair supplies the following notes regarding Chickasaw farming:

Every dwelling-house has a small field pretty close to it; and, as soon as the spring of the year admits, there they plant a variety of large and small beans, peas, and the smaller sort of Indian corn, which usually ripens in two months. from the time it is planted; though it is called by the English, the six weeks corn. Around this small farm, they fasten stakes in the ground, and tie a couple of long split hiccory, or white oak-sapplings, at proper distances to keep off the horses . . . . Their large fields lie quite open with regard to fencing, and they believe it to be agreeable to the best rule of economy; because, as they say, they can cultivate the best of their land here and there, as it suits their conveniency, without wasting their time in fences and childishly confining their improvements, as if the crop would eat itself. The women however tether the horses with tough young bark-ropes, and confine the swine in convenient penns, from the time the provisions are planted, till they are gathered in . . . . The chief part of the Indians begin to plant their out-fields, when the wild fruit is so ripe, as to draw off the birds from picking up the grain. This is their general rule, which is in the beginning of May, about the time the traders set off for the English settlements . . . . The women plant also pompions, and different sorts of melons, in separate fields, at a considerable distance from the town, where each owner raises an high scaffold, to over-look this favourite part of their vegetable possessions: and though the enemy sometimes kills them in this their strict watch duty, yet it is a very rare thing to pass by those fields, without seeing them there at watch. This usually is the duty of the old women, who fret at the very shadow of a crow, when he chances to pass on his wide survey of the fields; but if pinching hunger should excite him to descend, they soon frighten him away with their screeches . . . . They commonly have pretty good crops, which is owing to the richness of the soil; for they often let the weeds outgrow the corn, before they begin to be in earnest with their work, owing to their laziness and unskillfulness in planting; and this method is general through all those nations that work separately in their own fields, which in a great measure checks the growth of their crops. Besides, they are so desirous of having *multum in parvo*, without much sweating, that they plant the corn-hills so close, as to thereby choak up the field.—They plant their corn in straight rows, putting five or six grains into one hole, about two inches distance—They cover them with clay in the form of a small hill. Each row is a yard asunder, and in the vacant ground they plant pumpkins, water-melons, marsh-mallows, sun-flowers, and sundry sorts of beans and peas, the last two of which yield a large increase. (Adair, 1775, pp. 406–408.)

Du Pratz tells us that the Natchez prepared their fields for planting by means of a curved mattock made of hickory, but shoulder blades of the bison were observed among the neighboring Bayogoula employed for the same purpose, and no doubt the Natchez used them also. These mattocks were used

to weed the maize and cut down the canes in the preparation of a field. When the canes were dry they set fire to them, and to sow the maize, they made a hole with the hand in which they put some grains. These [hickory] mattocks were made like a capital L. They cut by means of the sides of the lower end, which is very flat. (La Page du Pratz, 1758, vol. 2, pp. 26, 176; Swanton, 1911, p. 75.)

Some time in 1699, the French chronicler, Pénicaut, visited the town of the Pascagoula Indians on the river which still bears their name and makes the following observations regarding their farming:

The next morning we went to walk in their fields where they sow their corn. The women were there working with their men. The savages have flat, bent sticks, which they use to hoe the ground, for they do not know how to work it as it is done in France. They scratch the soil with these crooked sticks and uproot with them the canes and weeds which they leave on the earth in the sun during fifteen days or a month. Then they set fire to them, and when they are reduced to ashes they have a stick as large as the arm, pointed at one end, with which they make holes in the earth 3 feet apart; they put into each hole seven or eight grains of corn and cover them with earth. It is thus that they sow their corn and their beans. When the corn is a foot high they take great care, as in France, to get rid of the weeds which get into it, and repeat it two or three times a year. They make use even now of their wooden hoes, because they find them lighter, although we have given them hoes of iron. (Pénicaut, *in* Margry, 1883, vol. 5, p. 304.)

Farming among the Caddo has been described in Bulletin 132 of the Bureau of American Ethnology (Swanton, 1942, pp. 127–131).

HUNTING

WOODCRAFT

Indian woodcraft has always been proverbial, and, indeed, something of mystery has often been attached to it not warranted by the facts, the skill of the Indians in this particular being a natural and inevitable outgrowth of the necessities of their economic life. Catesby has the following to say about this:

When a body of *Indians* set out on an hunting journey of five hundred miles, more or less, perhaps where none of them ever were; after the imaginary place of rendezvous is agreed on, they then consult what direction it lies in, every one pointing his finger towards the place; though but little variation appears in their pointings, the preference of judgment is given to the eldest; thus it being concluded on, they set out all singly, and different ways, except the women, who jog on a constant pace, while the men traverse a vast tract of land in hunting on each side, and meet together in small parties at night. Thus they proceed onward their journey, and though they range some hundred miles from one another, they all meet at the place appointed. And if an obstruction happens, they leave certain marks in the way, where they that come after will understand how many have passed and which way they are gone. They are never lost, though at the greatest distance from home; and where they never were before, they will find their way back by a contrary way from that they went.

An *Indian* boy that was brought up very young to school at *Williamsburgh*, at the age of 9 or 10 years, ran from school, found means (no body knew how) to pass over *James* river, and then travelled through the woods to his native home, though the nearest distance was three hundred miles, carrying no provision with him, nor having any thing to subsist on in his journey but berries, acorns, and such like as the wood afforded.

They know the north point whereever they are; one guide is by a certain moss that grows most on the north side of trees.

Their sagacity in tracing the footsteps of one another is no less wonderful: on a dry surface, where none but themselves are able to discern the least impression of any thing, they often make discoveries; but on moist land that is capable of impression, they will give a near guess, not only of the number of *Indians* that have passed, but by the make and stitching of their *Mockasins*, will know of what nation they are, and consequently whether friends or enemies. This is a piece of knowledge on which great consequences depend; therefore, they who excel in it are highly esteemed, because these discoveries enable them to ambuscade their enemies, as well as to evade surprises from them; and also to escape from a superior number by a timely discovery of their numerous tracks. (Cateby, 1731–43, vol. 2, pp. xii–xiii.)

Says Byrd:

The Indians, who have no way of travelling but on the Hoof, make nothing of going 25 miles a day, and carrying their little Necessaries at their backs, and Sometimes a Stout Pack of Skins into the Bargain. And very often they laugh at the English, who can't Stir to Next Neighbour without a Horse, and say that 2 Legs are too much for such lazy people, who cannot visit their next neighbour without six. (Bassett, 1901, p. 266.)

Lawson on the same subject:

They are expert travelers, and though they have not the use of our artificial compass, yet they understand the north-point exactly, let them be in never so great a wilderness. One guide is a short moss, that grows upon some trees, exactly on the north-side thereof.

Besides, they have names for eight of the thirty-two points, and call the winds by their several names, as we do; but indeed more properly; for the north-west wind is called the cold wind; the north-east, the wet wind; the south, the warm wind, and so agreeable of the rest. Sometimes it happens that they have a large river or lake to pass over, and the weather is very foggy, as it often happens in the spring and fall of the leaf; so that they cannot see which course to steer; in such a case, they being on one side of the river or lake, they know well enough what course such a place, (which they intend for) bears from them. Therefore, they get a great many sticks and chunks of wood in their canoe and then set off directly for their port, and now and then throw over a piece of wood, which directs them, by seeing how the stick bears from the canoe stern, which they always observe to keep right aft; and this is the Indian compass, by which they will go over a broad water ten or twenty leagues wide. They will find the head of any river, though it is five, six, or seven hundred miles off, and they never were there in their lives before, as is often proved by their appointing to meet on the head of such a river, where, perhaps, none of them ever was before, but where they shall rendezvous exactly at the prefixed time; and if they meet with any obstruction, they leave certain marks in the way where they that come after, will understand how many have passed by already, and which way they are gone. Besides, in their war-expeditions, they have very certain hieroglyphicks, whereby each party informs the other of the success or losses they have met withal; all which is so exactly performed by their sylvian marks and characters, that they are never at a loss to understand one another. . . . They will draw maps very exactly of all the rivers, towns, mountains and roads, or what you shall enquire of them, which you may draw by their directions, and come to a small matter of latitude, reckoned by their day's journeys. These maps they will draw in the ashes of the fire, and sometimes upon a mat or piece of bark. I have put a pen and ink into a savage's hand, and he has drawn me the rivers, bays, and other parts of a country, which afterwards I have found to agree with a great deal of nicety. (Lawson, 1860, pp. 331–333. See also Strachey as quoted on page 258.)

In describing the hunting customs of the Caddo, Solís says:

In securing their supplies they are very wise and cunning; when they have to cross a plain, they remain within the woods for some time, observing carefully to see if there is anything unusual, and if not, they cut a big branch from a tree in order to travel under cover so that those from a distance may not know that it is a man. In order to spy on the people who come in or go out of the woods, they climb a large tree which has a big high top and is near the road; from there they search out and see everything without being seen. (Solís, 1931, pp. 69–70; Swanton, 1942, pp. 132–138.)

DEER HUNTING

With great acuteness Indians sometimes speak of the deer as their sheep, though, outside of the bison country, the deer meant more to the ancient North Americans than did sheep to most peoples of the Old World. In that part of the continent with which we are concerned, it was the main source of animal food and the principal source of raw material for clothing, besides performing other incidental functions.

De Soto's men found deer meat and deer hides in use from one end of the Gulf region to the other. Hariot, the first writer who gives us what might fairly be called an ethnological account of any part of the section unless we except Peter Martyr, says:

In some places there are great store [of deer]: neere vnto the sea coast they are of the ordinarie bignes as ours in England, & some lesse: but further up into the countrey where there is better seed they are greater: they differ from ours onely in this, their tailes are longer and the snags of their hornes looke backward. (Hariot, 1893, p. 29.)

Strachey speaks of them thus:

> They have divers beasts fitt for provision; the chief are deare, both redd and fallow; great store in the country towards the heads of the rivers, though not so many amongst the rivers.   In our island, about James Towne, are some few nothing differing from ours in England, but that some of them the antletts of their hornes are not so manie.   Our people have seen two hundred, one hundred, and fifty in a herd.   (Strachey, 1849, p. 122.)

The early white colonists were in the habit of employing Indians to hunt for them and do other kinds of work.   This is mentioned by Lawson (1860, p. 146), and Samuel Wilson, writing of South Carolina in 1682, tells us deer were so plentiful "that an Indian hunter hath killed Nine fat Deere in a day all shot by himself, and all the considerable Planters have an Indian Hunter which they hire for less than Twenty shillings a year, and one hunter will very well find a Family of Thirty people, with as much venison and foul as they can well eat."   (Carroll, 1836, vol. 2, p. 28.)

Hunters either stalked the deer singly or killed them by means of surrounds, devices which might be called respectively the cat and dog methods of hunting.   To start up all kinds of game they fired the woods or canebrakes.

Deer stalking is described by our authorities as observed among the Powhatan Indians, the Siouan tribes, the Chickasaw and Choctaw, the Timucua, and the Natchez.   The Timucua account, given by Le Moyne in connection with one of his sketches, is the oldest of these, dating from 1565:

> The Indians have a way of hunting deer which we never saw before.   They manage to put on the skins of the largest which have been taken, in such a manner, with the heads on their own heads, so that they can see out through the eyes as through a mask.   Thus accoutered they can approach close to the deer without frightening them.   They take advantage of the time when the animals come to drink at the river, and, having their bow and arrows all ready, easily shoot them, as they are very plentiful in those regions.   (Le Moyne, 1875, p. 10 (illus.) ; Swanton, 1922, p. 357.)

This differs from most other accounts in representing use of the entire skin and in stating that the Indian clothed himself with it, his head being inserted into the deer's head.   Usually they employed only the head, but, if we may trust Smith, the Virginia Indians did make use of the entire skin:

> One Savage hunting alone, useth the skinne of a Deare slit on the one side, and so put on his arme, through the neck, so that his hand comes to the head which is stuffed, and the hornes, head, eies, eares, and every part as arteficially counterfeited as they can devise.   Thus shrowding his body in the skinne, by stalking he approacheth the Deare, creeping on the ground from one tree to another.   If the Deare chance to find fault, or stande at gaze, hee turneth the head

with his hand to his best advantage to seeme like a Deare, also gazing and licking himself. So watching his best advantage to approach, having shot him, hee chaseth him by his blood and straine till he get him. (Smith, Tyler ed., 1907, p. 105.)

A Santee Indian, from the country midway between the last two, employed the head only. He carried

an artificial head to hunt withal. They are made of the head of a buck, the back part of the horns being scraped and hollow for the lightness of carriage. The skin is left to the setting on of the shoulders, which is lined all round with small hoops, and flat sort of laths, to hold it open for the arms to go in. They have a way to preserve the eyes, as if living.[17] The hunter puts on a match coat made of deer skin, with the hair on, and a piece of the white part of the deer skin that grows on the breast, which is fastened to the neck end of this stalking head, so hangs down. In these habiliments an Indian will go as near a deer as he pleases, the exact motions and behaviour of a deer being so well counterfeited by them, that several times it hath been known for two hunters to come up with a stalking head together, and unknown to each other, so that they have killed an Indian instead of a deer, which hath happened sometimes to a brother or some dear friend ; for which reason they allow not of that sort of practice where the nation is populous. (Lawson, 1860, p. 44; Catesby, 1731–43, vol. 2, p. XII.)

The Indians of this section—and the same was true of most of those of the Southeast—carefully preserved the bones of the animals they ate and burned them "as being of opinion that if they omitted that custom the game would leave their country, and they should not be able to maintain themselves by their hunting."

A little farther south, in Georgia, is a small stream, an affluent of the Ocmulgee known as Echeconnee, but on the older maps Icho-cunno, which means, in the Muskogee language, "deer trap." It was so called because the deer used to resort to it for a certain kind of food of which they were fond and the conformity of the banks prevented them from escaping readily when pursued by hunters.

Speck's informants remembered the use of the stuffed deer head which the hunter "put over his shoulders or elevated on a stick in front of him when he was approaching the deer" (Speck, 1907, p. 22). At intervals during his approach to the intended victim the Indian sang a magic song, given by Speck (1907, p. 19).

MacCauley heard of deer stalking among the Seminole, but, curiously enough, his informants did not speak of using a decoy deer head:

The Seminole always hunt their game on foot. They can approach a deer to within sixty yards by their method of rapidly nearing him while he is feeding, and standing perfectly still when he raises his head. They say that they are able to discover by certain movements on the part of the deer when the head is about to be lifted. They stand side to the animal. They believe that they can thus deceive the deer, appearing to them as stumps of trees. (MacCauley, 1887, p. 512.)

---

[17] "The eyes are well represented by the globular shining seeds of the Pavia, or scarlet flowering horse-chestnut" (Catesby, 1731–1743, vol. 2, p. XII.)

Only Romans describes the custom in the middle Gulf region, among the Chickasaw and Choctaw:

They (the Chickasaw) hunt like all their neighbours with the skin and frontal bone of a deer's head, dried and stretched on elastic chips; the horns they scoop out very curiously, employing so much patience on this, that such a head and antlers often do not exceed ten or twelve ounces; they fix this on the left hand, and imitating the motions of the deer in sight, they decoy them within sure shot. I cannot forbear to mention a merry accident on this occasion; a Choctaw Indian, who was hunting with one of these decoys on his fist, saw a deer, and thinking to bring it to him, imitated the deer's motions of feeding and looking around in a very natural way, another savage within shot, mistaking the head for a real one, shot the ball through it, scarcely missing the fingers of the first; the affair ended in fisty cuffs, but was not is populous. (Lawson, 1860, p. 44; Catesby, 1731–43, vol. 2, p. xii.)

Historians of the Natchez furnish us with two accounts. The first is by Dumont de Montigny:

When a savage has succeeded in killing a deer he first cuts off its head as far down as the shoulders. Then he skins the neck without cutting the skin, and, having removed the bones and the flesh from it, he draws out all the brains from the head. After this operation he replaces the bones of the neck very neatly and fixes them in place with the aid of a wooden hoop and some little sticks. Then he re-covers them with their skin, and having dried this head partly in the shade and partly in the smoke, he thus has an entire deer's head, which is very light, and which with its skin preserves also its hair, its horns, and its ears. He carries it with him hung to his belt when he goes hunting, and as soon as he perceives a bison or a deer he passes his right hand into the neck of this deer, with which he conceals his face, and begins to make the same kind of movements as the living animal would make. He looks ahead, then turns the head rapidly from one side to the other. He lowers it to browse on the grass and raises it immediately afterward. In fact, always concealing his face with his head, he deceives by means of his gestures the animal which he wishes to approach, and, if during this time it happens that the animal stops to gaze at him, the savage, though he has his leg in the air to move forward, stays it there, and has enough patience to remain in this posture until the living animal, taking him for another animal of his species, begins to approach him. Then the savage, seeing him within gunshot, lets the deer head fall to the earth, passes his ready gun from his left hand to his right with admirable skill and rapidity, shoots the animal, and kills it, for he rarely misses it. (Dumont, 1753, pp. 150–151; Swanton, 1911, pp. 69–70.)

Du Pratz's parallel narrative follows:

The hunter who goes out alone provides himself for this purpose with the dried head of a deer, the brain having been removed and the skin of the neck left hanging to the head. This skin is provided with hoops made of cane splints, which are kept in place by means of other splints lengthwise of the skin so that the hand and arm can easily pass inside. Things being so arranged, the hunter goes into those parts where he thinks there are likely to be deer and takes such precautions not to be discovered as he thinks necessary. As soon as he sees one he approaches it with the step of a wolf, hiding himself behind one thicket after another until he is near enough to shoot it. But if, before that, the deer shakes its head, which is a sign that it is going to caper about and run away, the hunter, foreseeing his fancy, counterfeits this animal by making the same cry that these animals make when they call one another, which very often makes the deer come toward the hunter. Then he shows the head, which he holds in his hand, and causes it to make the movements of a deer when it browses and looks up from time to time. The hunter while waiting always keeps himself concealed behind the thicket until the deer has approached within gunshot, and although the hunter sees little of its side he shoots it in the shoulder and kills it. It is in this way that a native without hunting companions, without dogs, and without chasing, by means of a patience which we do not have, finally succeeds in killing a deer, an animal whose speed is exceeded only by the incitements which seize upon it at every instant and tend to bear it away to some place where the hunter is obliged to follow to hunt it with patience for fear lest a new fantasy will carry it away forever and its enemy lose time and trouble. (Le Page du Pratz, 1758, vol. 2, pp. 69–72; Swanton, 1911, p. 70.)

The Choctaw deer decoy and deer call were well-remembered down into the middle of the nineteenth century. Says the missionary Cushman:

They made a very ingeniously constructed instrument for calling deer to them, in the use of which they were very expert; and in connection with this, they used a decoy made by cutting the skin clear round the neck, about ten inches from the head of a slain buck having huge horns, and then stuffing the skin in one entire section up to the head and cutting off the neck where it joins the head. The skin, thus made hollow from the head back, is kept in its natural position by inserting upright sticks; the skin is then pulled upwards from the nose to the horns and all the flesh and brains removed; then the skin is repulled to its natural place and laid away to dry. In a year it has become dry; hard and inoffensive, and fit for use. All the upright sticks are then taken out except the one next to the head, which is left as a hand-hold. Thus the hunter, with his deer-caller and head decoy, easily enticed his game within the range of his deadly rifle; for, secreting himself in the woods, he commenced to imitate the bleating of a deer; if within hearing distance, one soon responds; but, perhaps, catching the scent of the hunter, stops and begins to look around. The hunter now inserts his arm into the cavity of the decoy and taking hold of the upright stick within, easily held it up to view, and attracted the attention of the doubting deer by rubbing it against the bushes or a tree; seeing which, the then no longer suspicious deer advanced, and only learned its mistake by the sharp crack of the rifle and the deadly bullet. (Cushman, 1899, p. 52.)

According to Romans, lone stalkers among the Chickasaw, and probably the Choctaw also, held the deer head in their left hands, whereas Dumont de Montigny plainly indicates that the Natchez hunters he had seen employ this method, used their right hands. This difference is probably attributable to cases of right- and left-handedness, though individual choice or possibly tribal custom might have been involved.

Speck thus describes the Yuchi deer call used in late times:

The deer call, we'ya"kané, mentioned before, which is used in calling deer within range, is a rather complex instrument and probably a borrowed one, at least in its present form. A hollow horn is fitted with a wooden mouthpiece which contains a small brass vibrating tongue. When blown this gives a rather shrill but weak sound which can be modified greatly by blowing softly or violently. A tremulous tone like the cry of a fawn is made by moving the palm of the hand over the opening of the horn. Much individual skill is shown by the hunters in using this instrument. (Speck, 1909, p. 23 and his fig. 5.)

My informants also remembered this style of hunting. They said that, as it was usually undertaken in October or November when the bucks seek the does or seek each other to fight, either the head of a buck or the head of a doe could be used. Wonderful skill was claimed for some hunters. One is said to have deceived a panther, while another very young hunter was clever enough to "take in" a man of age and experience.

A deer call was used in spring to imitate the cry of a fawn and entice does within gunshot. It was made of two pieces of button willow, round in cross section. The extreme end was covered with a piece of silver in which was a sort of pin with a knob at the end made of cane. It is claimed that, at times, a wildcat, panther, wolf, fox, or even a snake would be attracted by it.

Adair (1775, p. 402) says that in rambling through the woods in search of deer they would "frequently walk twenty-five or thirty miles through rough and smooth grounds, and fasting, before they return back to camp, loaded." But they brought back the spoils of the chase only when it was impossible to send their wives after them. When it was necessary to carry the deer some distance, they used two bison hide or rawhide straps about 2 inches wide, one of which passed over the forehead and the other around the chest.

It is rumored that deer were occasionally hunted with spears, but there is little to substantiate the claim.

For descriptions of deer stalking among the Caddo, see Swanton (1942, pp. 135–136).

The communal method of hunting, by surrounds, is described by the Virginia writers and Lawson, while Du Pratz tells us of a Natchez "sport" strongly resembling a surround. We will begin with Smith:

At their huntings in the deserts they are commonly 2 or 300 together. Having found the Deare, they environ them with many fires and betwixt the fires they place themselves. And some take their stands in the midst. The Deare being thus feared by the fires and their voices, they chace them so long within that circle, that many times they kill 6, 8, 10, or 15 at a hunting. They use also to drive them into some narrowe point of land, when they find that advantage, and so force them into the river, where with their boats they have Ambuscadoes to kill them. When they have shot a Deare by land, they follow him like blood hounds by the blood and straine, and oftentimes so take them. (Smith, Tyler ed., 1907, p. 104.)

Strachey parallel's the above, but Beverley amplifies considerably, and his remarks are probably based on information drawn from a wider geographical area:

But they had a better Way of killing the Elks, Buffaloes, Deer, and greater Game, by a Method which we call Fire-Hunting. That is, a Company of them wou'd go together back into the Woods, any time in the Winter, when the

Leaves were fallen, and so dry, that they wou'd burn; and being come to the Place design'd, they wou'd Fire the Woods, in a Circle of Five or Six Miles Compass; and when they had compleated the first Round, they retreated inward, each at his due Distance, and put Fire to the Leaves and Grass afresh, to accelerate the Work, which ought to be finished with the Day. This they repeat, till the Circle be so contracted, that they can see their Game herded all together in the Middle, panting and almost stifled with Heat and Smoak; for the poor Creatures being frighten'd at the Flame, keep running continually round, thinking to run from it, and dare not pass through the Fire; by which Means they are brought at last into a very narrow Compass. Then the *Indians* let flie their Arrows at them, and (which is very strange) tho' they stand all round quite clouded in Smoak, yet they rarely shoot each other. By this means they destroy all the Beasts, collected within that Circle. They make all this Slaughter only for the sake of the Skins, leaving the Carcases to perish in the Woods. (Beverley, 1705, bk. 2, p. 39.)

Spelman contributes the following:

Ther maner of ther Huntinge is thiss wher they meett sum 2 or 300 togither and hauinge ther bowes and arrows and euery one with a fier sticke in ther hand they besett a great thikett round about which y° Deare seinge fleeth from y° fier, and the menn comminge in by a litell and litle incloseth ther game in a narrow roome, so as with ther Bowes and arrowes they kill them at ther pleasuer takinge ther skinns which is the greatest thinge they desier, and sume flesh for their prouision. (Spelman *in* Smith, 1884, Arber ed., p. CVII.)

Possibly the slaughter of animals merely for their skins, as related by Beverley, is to be laid to the door of the white man and was one result of the stimulation of trade in furs which followed upon their advent. This seems to be confirmed by Lawson, whose account follows:

When these savages go a hunting, they commonly go out in great numbers, and oftentimes a great many days' journey from home, beginning at the coming in of the winter; that is, when the leaves are fallen from the trees and are become dry. Tis then this they burn the woods by setting fire to the leaves and withered bent and grass, which they do with a match made of the black-moss that hangs on the trees in Carolina, and is sometimes above six feet long. This, when dead, becomes black, though of an ash color before, and will then hold fire as well as the best match we have in Europe. In places where this moss is not found, as towards the mountains, they make lintels of the bark of cypress beaten, which serve as well. Thus they go and fire the woods for many miles, and drive the deer and other game into small necks of land and isthmuses where they kill and destroy what they please. . . . . Here it is that they get their compliment of deer skins and furs to trade with the English (the deer skins being in season in winter which is contrary to England). (Lawson, 1860, pp. 335-336.)

Lawson (1860, p. 25) also discovered the Sewee Indians engaged in a deer drive in January by firing the canes, and Catesby enlarges upon this as a custom presumably shared by most of the Siouan Indians at least:

Their annual custom of fire hunting is usually in *October*. At this sport associate some hundreds of *Indians*, who, spreading themselves in length through a great extent of country, set the woods on fire, which with the assistance of the wind is driven to some peninsula, or neck of land, into which deers, bears,

and other animals are drove by the raging fire and smoak, and being hemm'd in
are destroyed in great numbers by their guns. (Catesby, 1731–43, vol. 2, p. xii.)

In 1728 William Byrd's party replenished their supply of meat in
this manner:

> They fired the Dry Leaves in a Ring of five Miles' circumference, which, burn-
> ing inwards, drove all the Game to the Centre, where they were easily killed.
> It is really a pitiful Sight to see the extreme Distress the poor deer are in,
> when they find themselves Surrounded with this Circle of Fire; they weep and
> Groan like a Human Creature, yet can't move the compassion of those hard-
> hearted People, who are about to murder them. This unmerciful Sport is called
> Fire Hunting, and is much practic'd by the Indians and Frontier Inhabitants,
> who sometimes, in the Eagerness of their Diversion, are Punish't for their cruelty,
> and are hurt by one another when they Shoot across at the Deer which are in
> the Middle. (Bassett, 1901, pp. 222–223.)

According to Calderón, the Timucua distinguished two kinds of
hunting:

> During January they burn the grass and weeds from the fields preparatory to
> cultivation, surrounding them all at one time with fire so that the deer, wild
> ducks and rabbits, fleeing from it fall into their hands. This sort of hunting they
> call *hurimelas*. Then they enter the forests in pursuit of bears, bison and lions
> which they kill with bows and arrows, and this they call *ojêo*. Whatever they
> secure in either way they bring to the principal cacique, in order that he shall
> divide it, he keeping the skins which fall to his share. (Calderón, 1936, p. 13.)

The Natchez "sport" or social diversion to which reference has been
made was conducted as follows:

> When the natives wish to hold the deer dance, or to exercise themselves
> pleasantly, or even when the Great Sun takes a notion, a hundred go to hunt
> this animal [the deer] and bring it back alive. For this reason many young
> men go, who scatter about in their prairies where there are thickets to find a
> deer. As soon as they have discovered one they approach it in the form of a
> widely opened crescent. The bottom of the crescent advances until the deer
> springs up and takes to flight. Seeing a company of men in front, it very often
> flees toward one of the ends of the crescent or half circle. This point stops it,
> frightens it, and drives it back toward the other point which is a quarter of a
> league or thereabout distant from the first. This second does the same as the
> first and drives it back.
>
> The play is continued for a fairly long time, expressly to exercise the young
> men or to give pleasure to the great Sun, or to some little Sun whom he has named
> in his place. Sometimes the deer tries to escape through the opening between the
> points, but those who are at the tip ends show themselves so as to make him
> reenter and the crescent advances so as always to keep him inclosed between the
> youths. So it often happens that the men have not gone a league while the deer
> has made more than twenty with the different turns and capers which it has made
> from side to side, until at last all of the men come together a little farther and
> make a complete circle when they perceive that the animal is very much fatigued.
> Then they crouch almost to the earth when the deer comes to their side, and as
> soon as it gets near them rise with shouts and drive it from one side to the other
> so long as the deer is able to stand. But finally, not being able to do anything
> more from fatigue, its limbs fail it, it falls down and allows itself to be taken like
> a lamb. However, they take care to approach it only from behind, in order to

escape any blows of its antlers or forefeet, which however happens sometimes in spite of all their precautions.

Having seized the deer, they present it to the great Sun, if he is present, or to the one he has sent to enjoy the sport. When he sees it at his feet, and says "It is good," the hunters cut the deer open and bring it back in quarters to the cabin of the great Sun, who distributes it to the leaders of the hunting band. (Le Page du Pratz, 1758, vol. 2, pp. 71–73; Swanton, 1911, pp. 70–71.)

This last is quite different in purpose from the regular hunt and lacks certain marked elements of it such as the use of fire, so that it may have had an entirely independent origin. On the other hand, it may represent a survival or may have been suggested by the surround as observed among other tribes. The silence of our authorities regarding the use of the true surround south and west of the Algonquian and Siouan territories has been interpreted by Speck to mean that it was a northern institution which had not yet penetrated other portions of the Gulf region. This is not improbable, but it must be remembered that in some parts of this territory, notably among the Choctaw, game was so scarce that the results would probably have been scanty. However, that hardly explains its absence throughout the section. Another possibility is that it originated in connection with the bison hunt and spread from that to the pursuit of other game. While it is true that, at one time, bison ranged through most of the Southeast, it is not certain that they were ever numerous in that country and their invasions may have been sporadic.

Speck says:

The Yuchi do not seem to have used the deer fence so common in many parts of America. They have been known, however, to employ a method of driving game from its shelter to places where hunters were stationed, by means of fire. Grassy prairies were ignited and when the frightened animals fled to water they were secured by the band of hunters who were posted there. (Speck, 1909, p. 23.)

Burning of the "deserts" to rouse game is mentioned by Bartram (1940, p. 139).

None of my own informants remembered having heard of the communal hunt. An Alabama Indian said that they sometimes used dogs, but this was denied by Jackson Lewis in speaking of the Lower Creeks generally and it probably represented an innovation. True, Speck (1909, p. 22) says that among the Yuchi "dogs . . . have always been the invariable companions of the hunters, whether alone or in bands, their principal office being to track game and hold it at bay," but I think it highly improbable that any of the old Indian dogs would have been of use to a man trying to stalk deer and they were quite unnecessary in a surround. Elsewhere I have spoken of the employment of dogs in hunting turkeys and bear.

When they were getting ready to set out on a hunt, the women put up a quantity of parched meal and a quantity of bread strung together. Owing to the disappearance of game toward the east, their hunting expeditions in Oklahoma came to be directed more and more toward the west and were sometimes well rewarded, as one man is said to have killed sometimes as many as 130 deer in a single season.

BEAR HUNTING

There are incidental notes regarding the use of bearskins by Elvas and Garcilaso and mention by Elvas of "an abundance of butter in gourds [among the Chiaha Indians], in melted form like olive oil," which the inhabitants said was bear's grease (Robertson, 1933, p. 104). Later writers make incidental mention of the same uses for the bear, but it is surprising how few descriptions of bear hunting have been preserved. A short note by Hariot, and accounts by Adair, Dumont de Montigny, and Du Pratz are about all we have. Hariot says:

Beares . . . are all of black colour. The beares of this countrey are good meat: the inhabitants in time of winter do vse to take & eate manie, so also sometime did wee. They are taken commonlie in this sort. In some Ilands or places where they are, being hunted for, as soone as they haue spiall of a man they presently run awaie, & then being chased they clime and get vp the next tree, or with those wounds that they may after easily be killed; we sometime shotte them downe with our caleeuers. (Hariot, 1893, p. 30.) [18]

No one else mentions the hunting of bear except when they were in their winter quarters, and, if the account just given is correct, it may indicate a chase peculiar to the North Carolina coast. The descriptions of Dumont and Du Pratz were derived from observations of hunting customs among the tribes of the lower Mississippi. Both of these writers were particularly interested in the Natchez, but the attention of the former was focused upon them less intently than was that of Du Pratz. Dumont says:

In this province of Louisiana instead of using caverns these animals choose for their retreats hollow trees, and it may be observed that these domiciles are raised more than 30 or 40 feet above the earth and two bears never lodge there together. Towards the end of March or the first of April the females bear their young before quitting their retreat. Then, in spite of their long fast, they are not at all thin, and it is in this season that the natives pay them a visit, either to capture their cubs or make use of their fat. In order to find them, they go through the woods looking for the imprint of this animal's claws on the bark of the trees. When they have found one with these marks, they do not rest content with this indication, but in order to make the matter certain, they imitate the cry of a bear cub. The mother bear, hearing the cry at the foot of her tree and thinking it is caused by one of her little ones who has fallen to the ground, looks out of the hole and so discloses her presence. Then the savages, sure of their prey, prepare to dislodge her, but how is it to be accomplished? To uproot a big, tall tree or

---

[18] A caleeuer or caliver was "a light kind of musket or harquebus" (Murray).

cut it down with axes would take too much time. They have a more expeditious method, which is as follows:

They first choose the nearest tree they can find to that in which the animal has made its retreat, after which one of them climbs up into it and seats himself astride a branch, choosing if it is possible one of the same height as the opening of the bear's den. Then his comrades below place in his hands a big cane, 25 to 30 feet long, at the end of which is fastened a creeper or string. At the end of this creeper or string the savages tie some dry canes and set fire to them, and by swinging the cane, the man in the tree throws the fire into the hole which serves the animal as a retreat. If he cannot succeed by this means he ties a little string to the butt end of an arrow and to this string a piece of tinder, a kind of touchwood, sets fire to this and then shoots the arrow into the hole. The tinder, which is then suspended perpendicularly in the center of the hole, gradually flares up, burns through the string to which it is tied and falls upon the animal, which in moving about to shake it off sets fire to the straw, the dry grass, or the rotten wood commonly found in its habitation. Then the female bear, unable to endure the ardor of this element, decides to move, which it does back first, descending sedately, showing its teeth from time to time and its tongue, which is of a most beautiful scarlet color. It is not given time to descend far enough to place its feet on the ground but is knocked down or shot while it is on the way. Some of the little ones, wishing to imitate their mother, descend after her, but scarcely have they reached a height from the ground equal to that of a man when they are seized and cords passed around their necks. This is how they are captured and tamed. Others try to save themselves by clinging to the branches and are shot there. (Dumont, 1753, pp. 76–80; Swanton, 1911, pp. 67–68.)

Du Pratz:

After having wandered about the country for some time and found an abundance of fruits, the bears become fat, and it is then that the natives hunt them. In this state they know that the bears place themselves under cover, that is, settle in old dead trees still standing but with their hearts rotted out. There the bear makes his home. The natives make trips through the woods visiting trunks of this kind. If they notice claw marks on the bark, they feel certain that a bear is lodged within.

However, not to be mistaken in their conjectures, they strike the base of the tree a very heavy blow and run away quickly to hide behind another tree opposite the lowest of the bear's openings. If there is a bear inside, he hears the blow and feels the trembling of the trunk. Then he mounts to the opening to see what importunate persons come to trouble his repose. He looks at the foot of his fortress, and not perceiving anything there of a nature to trouble him, he returns to the bottom of his dwelling, displeased no doubt that he has been disturbed by a false alarm.

Having seen the prey which they believe cannot escape them, the natives collect dead canes and crush them with their feet so that they will burn more readily. Then they make them into a bundle which one man carries up into the nearest tree along with some fire. The others place themselves in ambush on other trees. The one with the fire lights a piece of cane and, when it is burning well, throws it dart-fashion into the bear's den. If he does not succeed [in rousing the bear] the first time, he tries again until the bear is forced out of his refuge. When enough fire is in the trunk to set fire to the rotten wood, the bear, not relishing such lively heat, comes out backward abandoning his home to the ardor of the flames. Then the hunters, who are all prepared, discharge arrows at him as rapidly as possible, and so promptly that he is often killed before he is able to reach the foot of the tree. (Le Page du Pratz, 1758, vol. 2, pp. 86–89; Swanton, 1911, pp. 68–69.)

Adair introduces some white folklore along with his narrative of Indian customs:

About Christmas, the he and she bears always separate. The former usually snaps off a great many branches of trees, with which he makes the bottom of his winter's bed, and carefully raises it to a proper height, with the green tops of large canes; he chooses such solitary thickets as are impenetrable by the sunbeams. The she bear takes an old large hollow tree for her yeaning winter-house, and chuses to have the door above, to enable her to secure her young ones from danger. When any thing disturbs them, they gallop up a tree, champing their teeth, and bristling their hair, in a frightful manner: and when they are wounded, it is surprising from what a height they will pitch on the ground, with their weighty bodies, and how soon they get up, and run off. When they take up their winter-quarters, they continue the greater part of two months, in almost an entire state of inactivity: during that time, their tracks reach no farther than to the next water, of which they seldom drink, as they frequently suck their paws in their lonely recess, and impoverish their bodies, to nourish them. While they are employed in that surprising task of nature, they cannot contain themselves in silence, but are so well pleased with their repast, that they continue singing *hum um um*: as their pipes are none of the weakest, the Indians by this means often are led to them from a considerable distance, and then shoot them down. But they are forced to cut a hole near the root of the tree, wherein the she bear and her cubs are lodged, and drive them out by the force of fire and suffocating smoke; and as the tree is partly rotten, and the inside dry, it soon takes fire. In this case, they become very fierce, and would fight any kind of enemy; but, commonly, at the first shot, they are either killed or mortally wounded. However, if the hunter chance to miss his aim, he speedily makes off to a sapling, which the bear by over-clasping cannot climb: the crafty hunting dogs then act their part, by biting behind, and gnawing its hams, till it takes up a tree. I have been often assured both by Indians and others, who get their bread by hunting in the woods, that the she-bear always endeavours to keep apart from the male during the helpless state of her young ones; otherwise he would endeavour to kill them; and that they had frequently seen the she bear kill the male on the spot, after a desperate engagement for the defence of her young ones. Of the great numbers I have seen with their young cubs, I never saw a he bear at such times, to associate with them. (Adair, 1775, pp. 309–310.)

Methods of hunting bear similar to those above described are remembered by both Creeks and Alabama Indians. Jackson Lewis described a method employed in hunting bear when they had their dens in caves among the rocks. This required skill and daring. One hunter would enter the den bearing a torch and when he saw the light reflected in the bear's eyes, he would say "Come out, sir!" and step to one side, whereupon the bear would pass right on by him and go out. Just outside a man had been stationed who was considered a sure shot, for if the animal was not fatally wounded, he would turn back and very probably kill the man who had first ventured within. Another method, involving less danger, was to have the man with the torch stand at the cave's mouth and wave his torch back and forth there until the bear was located, when his companion shot it. If the bear made a break past them, they usually succeeded in killing it outside. Sometimes a bear was shot in the open by a kind of surround, several men driving the animal toward a hunter so stationed as to have a good shot at it.

It will have been noted that, in Adair's description, mention is made of the use of dogs. My Alabama informant stated that his people sometimes chased bears with dogs until they turned to bay or climbed a tree. He also stated that dogs were employed in hunting deer and rabbits, while the Creeks used them in hunting squirrels, opossums, and raccoons. In many Southeastern myths dogs appear as the assistants of human beings in hunting wild animals, but there are few references to this in the narratives of explorers, and some writers say that dogs were not employed at all. Such uses of them may have occurred sporadically or as the result of white contact.

For Caddo bear hunting, see Swanton (1942, p. 137).

BISON HUNTING

A game animal next in importance to the deer and bear, in some places probably of more importance, was the bison. Our information regarding the economic status of this animal in the lives of the Southeastern tribes is very perplexing because the animal is often represented as if well known and commonly hunted, and indeed mention is made of herds consisting of thousands of individuals, yet few herds were actually seen by Europeans in this section and there are comparatively few notices of encounters with them. This cannot be attributed entirely to destruction occasioned by the whites, because De Soto and his followers had the same experience. Only as his army approached the Plains, some distance west of the Mississippi, did he find indications of bison in any considerable numbers. It will be of interest to note the references to this animal in various parts of the Gulf area.

Garcilaso reports that the Spaniards with De Soto found "cow horns" at a town near Savannah River, and he adds:

They were unable to learn where the Indians could have got these, because in all the places these Spaniards went in La Florida they never found cattle, and though it is true that in some places they found fresh beef they never saw the cattle, nor were they able by cajolery or threats to get the Indians to tell them where they were. (Garcilaso, 1723, p. 121.)

Ranjel saw "breastplates and head-pieces of rawhide" in the temple of Talimeco near the present Augusta, Ga. When the army was at Chiaha on the Tennessee River, two messengers sent toward the north returned with a cowskin as soft as the skin of a kid. (Bourne,

1904, vol. 2, p. 101; Robertson, 1933, p. 113.) There were heads of fierce bulls over one of the doorways at Casquin, west of the Mississippi but near the great river, and shields of raw cowhide in the neighboring town of Pacaha. Farther west, in the province of Coligua, two cowhides were presented to the Spaniards, and in the province of Tula, which seems to have been in close communication with the Plains, they found the flesh of these animals and quantities of their skins (Bourne, 1904, vol. 2, p. 139; vol. 1, pp. 122, 133, 139, 140). In the Caddo country of east Texas they found still more, a fact which caused them to give this region the name "province of herdsmen" (Garcilaso, 1723, p. 215).

The following quotation from Spark, the chronicler of Sir John Hawkins' voyage in 1565, may refer to the bison, though there is some uncertainty about it:

The Floridians haue pieces of vnicornes hornes which they weare about their necks, whereof the Frenchmen obtained many pieces (Hakluyt, 1847–89, vol. 3, p. 615).

Barlowe mentions "Buffe" skins among those taken in trade by his people from the Indians of North Carolina (Burrage, 1906, p. 232), but Hariot, Smith, and Strachey make no reference to the animal, while Beverley (1705, bk. 2, p. 39) merely mentions bison among those animals killed by "fire-hunting," i. e., in surrounds. In Dumont's account of deer stalking given above, he says that the same technique was employed with bison.

In 1673 Gabriel Arthur visited a Yuchi town on the headwaters of the Tennessee and he reports that "many hornes like bulls horns lye upon their dunghills" (Alvord, 1912, p. 213). In 1701, when Lawson was in the Saponi village near the present Salisbury, N. C., some Tutelo visited the place, and he says they were "strong and robust" on account of the abundance of bison, bear, elk, and deer in their country (Lawson, 1860, p. 85). In another place he speaks of the uses to which the skin and hair of the animal were put, but he does not localize this usage in any way (Lawson, 1860, p. 191). However, in 1728 Byrd's party, while surveying the boundary line between Virginia and North Carolina, met and killed a bull bison near Sugar Tree Creek, which runs through Person County, N. C., and Halifax County, Va., and they saw three of these animals and the tracks of many more along the Hico (Bassett, 1901, pp. 166, 286).

Somewhere in the Upper Creek country, near a big swamp, a party of Chickasaw, whom Adair was accompanying to Charleston with French prisoners, killed some bison, but Adair notes farther on that bison were then becoming scarce owing to the wasteful manner in which they were hunted (Adair, 1775, pp. 360, 445–446). And still, Romans (1775, p. 68) speaks of bison flesh among the Chickasaw in

1770–71. The anonymous French memoir which dates from about the middle of the same century, mentions a vagrant class of Indians among the Choctaw who lived almost wholly by following about the herds of bison, but the reference is not very definite.

In 1675 Bishop Calderón included bison among the animals hunted annually by the Timucua (Wenhold, 1936, p. 13). In 1739, on his way to the Lower Creek towns, Oglethorpe came upon a considerable herd of bison in central Georgia (Mereness, 1916, p. 219), but less than 40 years later Bartram wrote, speaking of the country round Augusta, Ga., "the buffalo (urus) once so very numerous, is not at this day to be seen in this part of the country" (Bartram, 1909, p. 45). One day in the spring of 1762, Lieutenant Timberlake's party was run in upon by 17 or 18 bison on or near Broad River, eastern Tennessee, and he speaks at least twice of the "incredible numbers" in that country (Timberlake, Williams ed., 1927, pp. 47, 71).

In his report on the exploration of Pensacola Bay made in 1693, Don Carlos de Sigüenza y Góngora mentions bison several times. He and his companions saw bison tracks near the western end of Santa Rosa Island, and on East Bay River, at an abandoned Indian camp, "we found a fire burning over which was a very tasteless stew of buffalo entrails in a crudely shaped earthen pan, and the flesh of the same animal roasted, or rather singed in some places and raw in others, on some spits made of sticks." They also found "in buckskin bags, the hair of buffaloes and other animals." "Small crosses made of reeds were found," which "because of the thread and bunches of buffalo hair attached to them" he concluded "served as spindles or distaffs for the women." Half a league beyond, they came upon another camp and again found bison meat cooking.

What was peculiar here was the fact that the buffalo meat was not only half-cooked as at the other camp, but it had been pounded into very fine, evil-smelling powder in wooden mortars; there was a large quantity of all this, for the reason that on this spot or near by they had killed a buffalo; this had happened only a short while before, as the exceedingly large and frightful head was still intact. Near numerous, not badly shaped pots and pans with gourd dippers and ladles of buffalo horn in them were ten or a dozen tanned hides of this animal. . . . There was considerable yarn of buffalo hair, both slender and coarse, in balls and on cross-shaped distaffs of *otate* similar to the others seen. (Leonard, 1939, pp. 157–158, 161–162.)

That very year Torres de Ayala led an expedition overland from the mission station near the present Tallahassee to the same bay, and on the banks of a river, supposed to have been the Blackwater, saw "numerous buffalo tracks" and later "found a buffalo trail leading to a ford" over a deep creek (Leonard, 1939, pp. 233–234).

In 1699, when the Frenchmen under Iberville ascended the Mississippi, they found deer, bear, and bison skins deposited in the temple of the Bayogoula Indians near the present Bayou Goula below Baton Rouge. (Margry, 1875–86, vol. 4, pp. 169–172; Swanton, 1911, pp. 274–276.) The Indians were using "bison bones" (i. e., shoulder blades of bison) as hoes in cultivating their fields, and told their visitors that they went to hunt these animals toward the mouth of the river, a direction opposite to that we would have supposed them to take. When Bienville crossed from the Mississippi to the Red in 1700 between Lake St. Joseph and Natchitoches, his party came upon bison just west of the lake and again near the site of the present Winnfield (Margry, 1875–86, vol. 4, pp. 432–439). Pénicaut, who may be called the Garcilaso of Louisiana, visited the Pascagoula on the river of that name in 1699 or 1700 and found that they had bison meat and that their beds were covered with the skins of this animal. Some time later, when he ascended the Mississippi with St. Denis, he reports that they killed 23 bison near the Manchac, and his party killed bison, deer, and other animals in considerable quantities about Bay St. Louis (Pénicaut, *in* Margry, 1875–86, vol. 5, pp. 389, 390, 497, 480). There are other references to bison hunting in the neighborhood of Mobile' and Pensacola, and Dumont and Du Pratz speak of the hunting of this animal as if in their time it were still pursued by the Natchez.

The region particularly frequented by them is perhaps indicated in another place:

Thirty leagues above the River of the Arkansas, to the north and on the same side as this river, one finds that of St. Francis; the surrounding country is always covered with herds of bison in spite of the hunting which takes place every winter in these districts; for it is to this river, that is to say the country about it, that the French and the Canadians resort to provide themselves with salted meat for the inhabitants of the capital and neighboring plantations; they are assisted by the Arkansas Indians whom they hire for this purpose. (Le Page Du Pratz, 1758, vol. 1, p. 319.)

On the other hand, Gravier tells us that they were "very scarce" in the Tunica country on Yazoo River when he visited that region in 1700 (Shea, 1861, pp. 135–136; Swanton, 1911, p. 317).

The evidence at hand seems to indicate that, while there were numerous large herds in the territory now occupied by Kentucky, northeastern Arkansas, and much of Tennessee, and, of course, in the extreme western parts of the Gulf region toward the Plains, and while bison were scattered through the remaining territory to the seaboard, except southern Florida and perhaps parts of the Atlantic coast region, the herds were relatively small in historic times and confined largely to sections remote from towns.

Aside from the meager reference by Beverley and Dumont's assertion that bison were stalked like deer, Du Pratz is the only writer to devote attention to the manner in which this animal was hunted:

This animal is hunted in winter, and at a distance from lower Louisiana and the river St. Louis [Mississippi], and besides it is fond of the tall grass found only on the high plains. A person must approach and shoot it on the lee side, aiming at the shoulder so as to knock it down at the first shot, for if it is merely wounded it runs upon the man. In this hunt the natives usually kill only the cows, having found that the flesh of the males smells bad, an inconvenience which they could easily spare themselves if they cut off the back sides as soon as the animal is dead as is done to stags and boars. That would not be the only advantage they would derive from it, because the species would not diminish, much tallow would be obtained, and the skins would be better and larger. (Le Page du Pratz, 1758, vol. 2, pp. 67–68; Swanton, 1911, p. 71.)

The quotations from Ogelthorpe, Adair, and Timberlake show that bison continued to roam well toward the Gulf until the middle of the eighteenth century. Claiborne (1880) attributes their disappearance from the region east of the Mississippi to a drought. There was anciently a bison clan among the Creeks and probably a body of lore connected with these animals, but by the time this tribe encountered them again after their removal west of the Mississippi, most of this had been forgotten. They then hunted them on foot, creeping up carefully and striving to shoot them in a vital spot said to be just below the hump, but they were scarce and hard to get.

Bison hunting was of great and, as the tribes were shoved farther westward, of increasing importance to the Caddo Indians, whose economy was markedly affected by it. (See Swanton, 1942, pp. 136–137.)

THE HUNTING OF OTHER ANIMALS

Elk are known to have come down as far as the mountain sections of Pennsylvania, West Virginia, and Ohio, the last wild elk reported in West Virginia having been seen in Pocahontas County in 1845. There seems to be no reason why they should not have extended southward over the Cherokee country. Timberlake makes no mention of them, but James Smith killed one somewhere near the lower Tennessee in 1766, and S. C. Williams, in commenting on this, states that "the names given to rivers and creeks also demonstrate their existence in early times" in that region (Williams, 1928, p. 206). On his way to Baltimore from Nashville in 1785, Lewis Brantz crossed a region known as "The Barrens," saw an elk, and "found large numbers of their horns" (Williams, 1928, p. 286). Therefore Lawson is probably right when he speaks of elk abounding in the Tutelo country northwest of Salisbury, N. C., along with bison, deer, bear, etc. (Timberlake, Williams ed., 1927, p. 85). Adair (1775, p. 446) notes the fact that elk flesh had an affinity to venison, from which it appears that he had eaten it. Beverley (1705, bk. 2, p. 39) also makes mention of elk among those animals killed in the surround. Evidently it was no great item in the Southeastern diet in historic times and was known mainly to the tribes in the northern part of the section.

One would hardly expect to find any branch of the whaling industry developed on the Florida coast, and the following mariner's tale by Lawson is not calculated to strengthen one's convictions as to its existence:

> Some Indians in America will go out to sea, and get upon a whale's back, and peg or plug up his spouts, and so kill him. (Lawson, 1860, p. 252.)

But listen to good Brother San Miguel, writing of his experiences at St. Augustine in 1595:

> In some places along this coast I saw great quantities of whale (ballenas) vertebrae, which creatures the Indians kill: they told us that they kill them with a stake and a mallet: that entire coast is of sand over which there is little depth of water and everywhere many fish: for this reason there enter upon it many whales to feed, and on seeing them the Indians go out in their little canoes and the first who arrives jumps on top of it with the stake and mallet in his hands, and although the whale wishes to dive very deep, it is not able, and touching the bottom returns to the surface, and the Indian who is alone upon it awaits his opportunity to drive the stake into his breathing-hole, which he does shortly: and so the hunter leaves it and returns to shore where the sea throws the animal suffocated to death, and there they cut it up and jerk the meat for their sustenance, and the inlanders particularly enjoy it. (Garcia, 1902, p. 209.)

With this story must be compared one told by Lopez de Velasco regarding the hunting of manatee by the Tekesta Indians of southeast Florida:

> When [the hunter] discovers a sea cow he throws his rope around its neck, and as the animal sinks under the water, the Indian drives a stake through one of its nostrils, and no matter how much it may dive, the Indian never loses it, because he goes upon its back. (Swanton, 1922, p. 389.)

Commenting upon these tales, Dr. Remington Kellogg of the United States National Museum writes me:

> It is barely possible that the . . . item [in] "Dos Antiguos Relaciones de la Florida" does relate to a kind of toothed whale. The blackfish, or pilot whale, is fairly common in those waters. Curiously enough, schools of blackfish strand rather frequently, or at least get into waters too shallow for swimming. In the Orkney Islands, for instance, the natives actually drive them ashore or into shallow water, and the early settlers along the New England coast employed the same tactics.

As Dr. Kellogg suggests, a similar method of hunting by Florida Indians is perhaps indicated, but some features of it may have been confounded with techniques employed in manatee hunting and certainly the story has not been allowed to suffer in retelling.

Fire hunting was used for small game, generally including turkeys. Speaking probably of the Siouan tribes of South Carolina, Lawson (1860, p. 337) says, "all game, as turkies, ducks and small vermine, they commonly kill with bow and arrow thinking it not worth throwing powder and shot after them." Of turkeys specifically, Adair remarks:

The wild turkeys live on the small red acorns, and grow so fat in March, that they cannot fly farther than three or four hundred yards; and not being able soon to take the wing again, we speedily run them down with our horses and hunting mastiffs. At many unfrequented places of the Mississippi, they are so tame as to be shot with a pistol, of which our troops profited, on their way to take possession of the Illinois-garrison. (Adair, 1775, p. 360.)

This would not help us much in the understanding of Indian hunting methods except that the use of dogs is again noted by Du Pratz, who professes to be describing native customs. He states that his Natchez companions told him turkeys must be taken by means of a dog which forced the birds to fly up into a tree, where they would sit still and allow themselves to be shot without attempting to escape, while if a man chased them on foot they would quickly outdistance him. (Le Page du Pratz, 1758, pp. 220–221; Swanton, 1911, p. 72.) This seems to be the best authenticated account of the use of dogs in hunting in the Southeast.

Mention has already been made of the employment of dogs in hunting bear. They are said to have been used also in the chase of rabbits, raccoons, oppossums, and squirrels, but rather in late times than in the aboriginal period. Raccoons are also said to have been caught in deadfalls of a common type, so arranged that in taking the bait the animal released a trigger and let logs down upon his back. Another sort of trap, used by De Soto's followers in the winter of 1541–42 in catching "conies," i. e., rabbits, was borrowed from Indians west of the Mississippi, probably in what is now Arkansas. They were snared "by means of stout springs which lift the feet off the ground and a noose of strong cord fastened to which is a joint of cane, which runs to the neck of the rabbit, so that it can not gnaw the cord." Elvas, who describes this, adds that many of these animals were taken in the cornfields, "especially when it froze or snowed" (Robertson, 1933, p. 205). Smith (Tyler ed., 1907, p. 94) and Strachey (1849, p. 124) say that the beaver and otter were taken with snares by the Virginians. According to MacCauley (1887, p. 513), however, the Florida Seminole usually shot otters by means of the bow and arrow or rifles, and resorted to trapping only in very late times. When Lawson visited the chief of the Saponi in 1701 he was trapping beaver, and Byrd tells us that "the Indians . . . have hardly any way to take them but by laying Snares near the place where they dam up the Water" (Lawson, 1860, p. 84; Bassett, 1901, p. 292), while Romans (1775, p. 66) asserts that the Chickasaw thought beaver hunting beneath them. The ancient Florida Indians caught partridges and other small birds and animals in snares and traps (Swanton, 1922, p. 384). Squirrels were hunted very largely by small boys armed with blowguns and bows and arrows.

I was told by the Creeks that wild turkeys were usually found in a grove of trees; after a few had been killed they would fly to another grove, and it was the native custom to follow them from grove to grove. Speck says that Yuchi hunters

are unusually proficient in calling wild turkeys by several means. One instrument made for this purpose is the hollow secondary wing bone of the turkey, about five inches in length. The hunter draws in his breath through this tube, making a noise which can best be described as a combination of smacking, squeaking and sucking. By skillfully operating the calls the birds are lured within range. Sometimes the palm of the hand is employed in making the noise. Another device is to grate a piece of stone on the top of a nail driven fast into a piece of wood. The rasping sound produced in this way will answer quite effectively as a turkey call if manipulated with skill. (Speck, 1909, pp. 22–23.)

The Florida Seminole also used turkey calls (MacCauley, 1887, p. 512).

Lawson witnessed the procedure followed in hunting passenger-pigeons, at a point not far from the boundary between the two Carolinas and near Catawba River:

We went to shoot pigeons which were so numerous in these parts that you might see many millions in a flock; they sometimes split off the limbs of stout oaks and other trees upon which they roost at nights, and making the ground as white as a sheet with their dung.[19] You may find several Indian towns of not above seventeen houses, that have more than one hundred gallons of pigeon's oil or fat; they using it with pulse or bread as we do butter. The Indians take a light and go among them in the night and bring away some thousands, killing them with long poles, as they roost in the trees. At this time of the year, the flocks as they pass by, in great measure, obstruct the light of the day. (Lawson, 1860, p. 79.)

The Alabama of later times had a trap made out of small split sticks, which they used in catching small birds. Apparently it was very much like our "figure four trap," and was probably borrowed from the whites, as they believe to have been the case.

Adair (1775, p. 30) informs us that eagle feathers were so highly valued among the Chickasaw and Creeks that "the whole town will contribute, to the value of 200 deer-skins, for killing a large eagle; and the man also gets an honorable title for the exploit," but how this hunt was pursued is not stated.

Le Moyne tells us that alligators were hunted in the following manner by the Timucua:

They put up, near a river, a little hut full of cracks and holes, and in this they station a watchman, so that they can see the crocodiles (or alligators)

---

[19] Through some confusion either in Lawson's notes or in setting the type for this particular edition, the phrase "and making the ground as white as a sheet with their dung" is displaced and put at the end of the next sentence. I have restored it to its proper position.

and hear them a good way off; for, when driven by hunger, they come out of the rivers and crawl about on the islands after prey, and, if they find none, they make such a frightful noise that it can be heard for half a mile. Then the watchman calls the rest of the watch, who are in readiness; and taking a portion, ten to twelve feet long, of the stem of a tree, they go out to find the monster, who is crawling along with his mouth wide open, ready to catch one of them if he can; and with the greatest quickness they push the pole, small end first, as deep as possible down his throat, so that the roughness and irregularity of the bark may hold it from being got out again. Then they turn the crocodile over on his back, and with clubs and arrows pound and pierce his belly, which is softer; for his back, especially if he is an old one, is impenetrable, being protected by hard scales. (Le Moyne, 1875, p. 10 (illus.) and pl. 26; Swanton, 1922, p. 358.)

The fierceness attributed to this saurian must be discounted unless Le Moyne has confused the alligator and the true Floridian crocodile, the latter being, according to all accounts, a much tougher customer. The use of the word "crocodile" has no significance, as it was employed for the alligator also at this period.

Whether gotten from Le Moyne or not, Byrd has a similar story:

As Fierce and Strong as these Monsters are, the Indians will surprise them Napping as they float upon the Surface, get astride upon their Necks, then whip a short piece of wood like a Truncheon into their Jaws, & holding the Ends with their two hands, hinder them from diving by keeping their mouths open, and when they are almost Spent, they will make to the shoar, where their riders knock them on the Head and Eat them. (Bassett, 1901, pp. 300–302.)

While Du Pratz was living on Bayou St. Jean, near New Orleans, he was surprised to see his Chitimacha slave girl kill an alligator with a stick of wood, and later he was informed by her that the Chitimacha children, when they found little alligators on the land, pursued and killed them, after which the people of the house went to skin them, carry them home, and make a good feast out of them (Le Page du Pratz, 1758, vol. 1, pp. 85–86).

This is a debunking tale to counter the "ferocious saurian" stories afloat in Europe. (See also De Villiers, 1925, pp. 122, 124.)

FISHING

There seems to have been no taboo against fish eating anywhere in the Southeast, and fish were an item in the native bill of fare in practically all sections. Methods resorted to on the coast and inland were naturally somewhat different. We know that weirs were used in both, though of distinct types on account of the divergent requirements of coast and inland fishing; that hooks and lines and nets and snares were employed; that fish were shot with arrows or speared, the fish being attracted sometimes by means of fire; that they were stupefied or "poisoned" in small pools or taken out of them with drags; and that they were "grabbled" or caught with the bare hands. Unfortunately, our data do not permit us to give the geographical distribution of these devices though some of them were, of course, dependent on the topography of specific sections. References to fish in the De Soto narratives are almost confined to the Apalachee country in northern Florida and the region of the Mississippi. In the former there is said to have been good fishing both near the sea (Bourne, 1904, vol. 2, p. 82) and in ponds (Garcilaso, 1723, p. 107), and Garcilaso tells us that they fished all the year round. Along the Mississippi, fish are often noted among presents sent in by native chiefs, but they were found in particular abundance in the canal leading from the Mississippi past a town called Pacaha. Except for a rock fishweir reported by Garcilaso's informants, used in Tampa Bay for catching rays, only two methods of fishing are given in the De Soto documents, both at Pacaha, by nets and fishhooks, though there is some doubt whether in this instance the fishhooks were of native origin (Robertson, 1933, p. 175; Garcilaso, 1723, pp. 94, 182).

One of the most complete early descriptions of fishing is by Beverley and may serve to introduce the subject:

Before the arrival of the *English* there, the Indians had Fish in such vast Plenty, that the Boys and Girls wou'd take a pointed Stick, and strike the lesser sort, as they Swam upon the Flats. The larger Fish, that kept in deeper water, they were put to a little more Difficulty to take; But for these they made Weyrs; that is, a Hedge of small riv'd Sticks, or Reeds, of the Thickness of a Man's Finger, these they wove together in a Row, with Straps of Green Oak, or other tough Wood, so close that the small Fish cou'd not pass through. Upon High-Water Mark, they pitched one End of this Hedge, and the other they extended into the River, to the Depth of Eight or Ten Foot, fastening it with Stakes, making Cods [i. e., inner pockets] out from the Hedge on one side, almost at the End, and leaving a Gap for the Fish to go into them, which were contrived so that the Fish could easily find their Passage into those Cods, when they were at the Gap, but not see their Way out again, when they were in: Thus if they offered to pass through, they were taken.

Sometimes they made such a Hedge as this, quite a-cross a Creek at High-Water, and at Low wou'd go into the Run, so contracted into a narrow Compass, and take out what Fish they pleased.

At the Falls of the Rivers, where the Water is shallow, and the Current strong, the *Indians* use another kind of Weir, thus made: They make a Dam of loose Stone, whereof there is plenty at hand, quite a-cross the River, leaving One, Two, or more Spaces or Tunnels, for the Water to pass thro'; at the Mouth of which they set a Pot of Reeds, wove in Form of a Cone, whose Base is about Three Foot, and perpendicular Ten, into which the Swiftness of the Current carries the Fish, and wedges them so fast, that they cannot possibly return.

The *Indian* Way of Catching Sturgeon, when they came into the narrow part of the Rivers, was by a Man's clapping a Noose over their Tail, and by keeping fast his hold. Thus a Fish finding it self intangled, wou'd flounce, and often pull him under Water, and then that Man was counted a *Cockarouse*, or brave Fellow, that wou'd not let go; till with Swimming, Wading, and Diving, he had tired the Sturgeon, and brought it ashore. These Sturgeon would also often leap into their Canoes, in crossing the River, as many of them do still every Year, into the Boats of the English.

They have also another Way of Fishing like those on the *Euxine Sea*, by the Help of a blazing Fire by Night. They make a Hearth in the Middle of their Canoe, raising it within Two Inches of the Edge; upon this they lay their burning Light-Wood, split into small Shivers, each Splinter whereof will blaze and burn End for End, like a Candle: 'Tis one Man's work to tend this Fire and keep it flaming. At each End of the Canoe stands an *Indian*, with a Gig, or pointed Spear, setting the Canoe forward with the Butt-end of the Spear, as gently as he can, by that Means stealing upon the Fish, without any Noise, or disturbing of the Water. Then they with great Dexterity, dart these Spears into the Fish, and so take 'em. Now there is a double Convenience in the Blaze of this Fire; for it not only dazzles the Eyes of the Fish, which will lie still, glaring upon it, but likewise discovers the Bottom of the River clearly to the Fisher-man, which the Daylight does not.

The following Print, (as all the others in this Book) was drawn by the Life, and I may justly affirm it, to be a very true Representation of the *Indian* Fishery.

Tab. I [pl. 52 which I have, however, reproduced from the original White drawing] Represents the Indians in a Canoe with a Fire in the Middle, tended by a Boy and a Girl. In one End is a Net made of Silk Grass, which they use in Fishing their Weirs. Above is the Shape of their Weirs, and the Manner of setting a Weir-Wedge, a-cross the Mouth of a Creek.

Note, That in Fishing their Weirs, they lay the Side of the Canoe to the Cods of the Weir, for the more convenient coming at them, and not with the End going into the Cods, as is set down in the Print: But we could not otherwise represent it here, lest we should confound the shape of the Weir, with the Canoe. (Beverley, 1705, bk. 2, pp. 32–34.)

Fishweirs were in use on the Atlantic coast as far south as Florida. They were extensively employed on the St. Johns River and neighboring coast according to the testimony of Laudonnière and Le Moyne, but whether this extended to the wretched bands south of Cape Canaveral is open to doubt as Dickenson (1699) makes no mention of them. The following curious note by Garcilaso seems to be the only reference to a fishweir on the Gulf side of the peninsula:

The Indians of that province (Hirrihigua) had constructed on the bay of Espíritu Santo large inclosures of rough stone in order to obtain skates and many other fish which came into them at high tide, and when it receded were trapped there almost on dry land. The Indians killed a great many fish in this manner and the Castilians who were with Captain Pedro Calderón also enjoyed them. (Garcilaso, 1723, p. 94.)

In relatively recent times the Chitimacha Indians are said to have employed a barrel-shaped fish trap, but no fishweir (Swanton. 1911, p. 346).

Aside from the above note by Garcilaso, the oldest mention of fishweirs seems to be that of Ribault in 1562, who says they were "built in the water with great reeds, so well and cunningly set to-gether after the fashion of labyrinth, with many turns and crooks, which it was impossible to construct without much skill and indus-try." (French, 1875, p. 172; Swanton, 1922, pp. 357–358.) These are noted also by Hariot, Smith, Strachey, and Lawson.

A longer description of the inland fishweir and its use is given by Adair, who says:

> The Indians have the art of catching fish in long crails, made with canes and hickory splinters, tapering to a point. They lay these at a fall of water, where stones are placed in two sloping lines from each bank, till they meet together in the middle of the rapid stream, where the intangled fish are soon drowned. Above such a place, I have known them to fasten a wreath of long grape vines together, to reach across the river, with stones fastened at proper distances to rake the bottom; they will swim a mile with it whooping, and plunging all the way, driving the fish before them into their large cane pots. With this draught, which is a very heavy one, they make a town feast, or feast of love, of which every one partakes in the most social manner, and afterward they dance together. (Adair, 1775, p. 403.)

Though he says nothing of the rock approaches, Speck has the following description of a Yuchi trap such as was used in connec-tion with them:

> These were quite large, being ordinarily about three feet or more in diameter and from six to ten feet in length. They were cylindrical in shape, with one end open and an indented funnel-shaped passageway leading to the interior. The warp splints of this indenture ended in sharp points left free. As these pointed inward they allowed the fish to pass readily in entering, but offered an obstruction to their exit. The other end of the trap was closed up, but the covering could be removed to remove the contents. Willow sticks composed the warp standards, while the wicker filling was of shaved hickory splints. The trap was weighted down in the water and chunks of meat were put in for bait. (Speck, 1909, p. 25.)

Timberlake saw such a weir in the Cherokee country.

> Building two walls obliquely down the river from either shore, just as they are near joining, a passage is left to a deep well or reservoir; the Indians then scaring the fish down the river, close to the mouth of the reservoir with a large bush, or bundle made on purpose, and it is no difficult matter to take them with baskets, when inclosed within so small a compass. (Timberlake, Williams ed., 1927, p. 69.)

My Creek informant, Jackson Lewis, said that his father once made a trap which fish would come up and fall into, and it may have been something on the order of the weir just described, although the word-ing implies rather something entered by fish ascending against the current.

Remains of rock fishweirs are widely scattered in and near the southern Appalachians. Haywood (1823, pp. 88–89) mentions one a few miles from Flat Lick, Whitley (now Knox) County, Ky. W. E. Myer (1928, p. 782) observed the vestige of such a trap on Obey River, near the mouth of Eagle Creek in the mountains of Pickett County,

Tenn. D. I. Bushnell, Jr. (1930, pl. 1) has described and figured traps of this kind at the falls of the James River, Richmond, Va., and near Fredericksburg on the Rappahannock, and Dr. Douglas L. Rights (1928, pp. 8–9, 18–19) mentions several along the headwaters of the Yadkin in North Carolina.

Lawson (1860, pp. 260, 339) observes that sturgeon were sometimes caught by means of "nets at the end of a pole," likening the method to the way in which pike were taken in Europe.

Byrd observed this method minus the pole, and wrote a description:

In the Summer time 'tis no unusual thing for Sturgeons to Sleep on the Surface of the Water and one of them having wander'd up into this Creek in the Spring, was floating in that drowsy condition.

The Indian, above mentioned, (an "Occaanechy"), ran up to the Neck into the Creek a little below the Place where he discover'd the Fish, expecting the Stream wou'd soon bring his Game down to Him. He judg'd the Matter right, and as Soon as it came within his Reach, he whip't a running Noose over his Jole. This waked the Sturgeon, which being Strong in his own Element darted immediately under Water and dragg'd the Indian after Him. The Man made it a Point of Honour to keep his Hold, which he did to the Apparent Danger of being drown'd. Sometimes both the Indian and the Fish disappear'd for a Quarter of a Minute, & then rose at some Distance from where they dived. At this rate they continued flouncing about, till at last the Hero Suffocated his Adversary, and haled his Body ashoar in Triumph. (Bassett, 1901, 248–249.)

The "net made of silk grass" recalls the nets found in use by De Soto's men on the Mississippi. Smith also speaks of fish nets, and Strachey thus describes their manufacture:

They have netts for fishing, for the quantity as formerly brayed and mashed as our's, and these are made of barkes of certaine trees, deare synewes, for a kynd of grasse, which they call pemmenaw, of which their women, betweene their hands and thighes, spin a thredd very even and redily, and this threed serveth for many uses, as about their howsing, their mantells of feathers and their trowses, and they also with yt make lynes for angles. (Strachey, 1849, p. 75.)

That the Cherokee had no nets until supplied by Europeans, as Timberlake implies (Williams ed., 1927, p. 69), seems incredible.

The net at the end of a pole used in retrieving fish from their weirs which Strachey mentions in another place is, of course, that to which Berkeley refers (Strachey, 1849, p. 68). Nets were well known to the Chitimacha Indians, at least in later times, and we may turn to Adair again for further information on this subject.

There is a favourite method among them of fishing with hand-nets. The nets are about three feet deep, and of the same diameter at the opening, made of hemp, and knotted after the usual of our nets. On each side of the mouth, they tie very securely a strong elastic green cane, to which the ends are fastened. Prepared with these, the warriors a-breast, jump in at the end of a long pond, swimming under water, with their net stretched open with both hands, and the canes in a horizontal position. In this manner, they will continue, either till their breath is expended by the want of respiration, or till the net is so ponderous as to force them to exonerate it ashore, or in a basket, fixt in a proper place for that purpose—by removing one hand, the canes instantly spring together. I have been engaged half a day at a time, with the old-friendly Chikkasah, and half drowned in the diversion—when any of us was so unfortunate as to catch water-snakes in our sweep, and emptied them ashore, we had the ranting voice of our friendly posse comitatus, whooping against us, till another party was so unlucky as to meet with the like misfortune. During this exercise, the women are fishing ashore with coarse baskets, to catch the fish that escape our nets. (Adair, 1775, pp. 432–434.)

At Key Marco, Fla., Cushing found

nets of tough fibre, both coarse and fine, knitted quite as is the common netting of our own fishermen today, in form of fine-meshed, square dip-nets, and of coarse-meshed, comparatively large and long gill-nets. To the lower edges of these, sinkers made from thick, roughly perforated umboidal bivalves, tied together in bunches, or else from chipped and notched fragments of heavy clam shells, were attached, while to the upper edges, floats made from gourds, held in place by fine net-lashings, or else from long sticks or square-ended blocks, were fastened. Around the avenues of the court I was interested to find netting of coarser cordage weighted with unusually large-sized or else heavily bunched sinkers of shell, and supplied at the upper edges with long, delicately tapered gumbo-limbo float-pegs, those of each set equal in size, each peg thereof partially split at the larger end, so as to clamp double half-turns or ingeniously knotted hitches of the neatly twisted edges-cords with which all were made fast to the nets. Now these float pegs, of which many sets were secured, varying from three and a half to eight inches in length of pegs, were so placed on the nets, that in consequence of their tapering forms they would turn against the current of the tide whichever way it flowed, and would continuously bob up and down on the ripples, however slight these were, in such manner as to frighten the fish that had been driven, or had passed over them at high tide, when, as the tide lowered, they naturally tried to follow it. In connection with these nets we found riven stays, usually of cypress or pine, such as might have been used in holding them upright. Hence I inferred that they had been stretched across the channels not only of the actual water courts of residence, like this, but, probably also, of the surrounding fish-pounds. (Cushing, 1896, pp. 366–367.)

Spearing, Hariot describes as one of the two methods of fishing in vogue among the Sound Indians of North Carolina:

They haue likewise a notable way to catche fishe in their Riuers, for whear as they lacke both yron, and steele, they fasten vnto their Reedes or longe Rodds, the hollowe tayle of a certaine fishe like to a sea crabb in steede of a poynte,[20] wherwith by nighte or day they stricke fishes, and take them opp into their boates. They also know how to vse the prickles, and pricks of other fishes. (Hariot, 1893, pl. 31.)

They also did this while wading in the shallows.

Lawson says that the Hatteras and other coast Indians would run into the sea to strike bluefish, and that the inland tribes were in the habit of "striking sturgeon and rockfish, or bass, when they come up

---

[20] The tail of the horseshoe crab. The representation of this creature in the accompanying cut is the oldest known.—D. I. Bushnell, Jr.

the rivers to spawn" (Lawson, 1860, pp. 260, 339). Presumably he is referring to the use of spears, though it might be bows and arrows or clubs. In 1699 Dickenson witnessed an Indian belonging to one of the tribes on the east coast of Florida spearing fish very dexterously from the shore as they lay in shallow water. (Dickenson, 1803, p. 19; Swanton, 1922, p. 392.) Near St. Augustine, San Miguel noted that all the skates which the Indians had killed "were wounded in [near?] the small fin in the middle of the back, and they wound them there with a little wooden point like a small harpoon a yard [vara] in length, and they are so skillful that they do not hit the little fin at [near] which they aim, because it can be seized better there than anywhere else." (Garcia, 1902, p. 208.) But strangely enough, Cushing (1896, p. 367) found no evidence of this method of fishing at Key Marco. We have from Adair the following excellent description of fish spearing in Savannah River:

Those Indians who are unacquainted with the use of barbed irons, are very expert in striking large fish out of their canoes, with long sharp pointed green canes, which are well bearded, and hardened in the fire. In Savannah River, I have often accompanied them in killing sturgeons with those green swamp harpoons, and which they did with much pleasure and ease; for, when we discovered the fish, we soon thrust into their bodies one of the harpoons. As the fish would immediately strike deep, and rush away to the bottom very rapidly, their strength was soon expended, by their violent struggles against the buoyant force of the green darts: as soon as the top end of them appeared again on the surface of the water, we made up to them, renewed the attack, and in like manner continued it, till we secured our game. (Adair, 1775, pp. 404–405.)

Bartram thus describes how "a very large salmon trout, weighing about fifteen pounds" was speared by an Indian on a branch of Broad River in Georgia:

The Indian struck this fish with a reed harpoon, pointed very sharp, barbed, and hardened by the fire. The fish lay close under the steep bank, which the Indian discovered and struck with his reed; instantly the fish darted off with it, whilst the Indian pursued, without extracting the harpoon, and with repeated thrusts drowned it, and then dragged it ashore. (Bartram, 1792, p. 44.)

Speck says of the Yuchi:

Simple harpoons of cane whittled to a sharp point are used in the killing of larger fish which swim near the surface, or wooden spears with fire-hardened points are thrown at them when found lurking near the banks. (Speck, 1909, pp. 24–25.)

There is a reference to some Natchez Indians spearing fish from a platform built for that purpose on the bank of the Mississippi. Smith and Strachey speak as if in Virginia the use of true fish spears, "staves, like unto javelins, headed with bone," were confined to the Accomac Indians of the eastern shore, and we may have a cultural difference indicated here between the Powhatan people and the Algonquians to the south and east of them. (Smith, Tyler ed., 1907, p. 103; Strachey, 1849, p. 75.)

According to these writers, Virginia Indians generally shot fish with long arrows tied to lines (idem.). Lawson again mentions this method in connection with torch or fire fishing, which he and Beverley are the only ones to note. He says:

> The youth and Indian boys go in the night, and one holding a lightwood torch, the other has a bow and arrows, and the fire directing him to see the fish, he shoots them with the arrows; and thus they kill a great many of the smaller fry, and sometimes pretty large ones. (Lawson, 1860, p. 341.)

The Maryland Indians also used bows and arrows, and Adair lets us know that in later times guns were substituted.

> If they shoot at fish not deep in the water, either with an arrow or bullet, they aim at the lower part of the belly, if they are near; and lower, in like manner, according to the distance, which seldom fails of killing. (Adair, 1775, p. 432.)

The present Alabama Indians remember that spears were once employed in this industry, and both they and the Creeks recall the use of bows and arrows.[21]

Aside from a somewhat doubtful intimation by Elvas that the Gulf Indians used fishhooks, we have the clear testimony of archeology and direct statements by Smith (Tyler ed., 1907, p. 103) and Strachey (1849, p. 75). Manufacture of bark fishing lines by the Virginians has already been described. Strachey continues:

> Theire angles are long small rodds, at the end whereof they have a clift to the which the lyne is fastened, and at the lyne they hang a hooke, made eyther of a bone grated (as they nock their arrowes) in the forme of a crooked pynne or fis-hooke, or of the splinter of a bone, and with a threed of the lyne they tye on bayte. (Strachey, 1849, p. 75.)

One probable reason for our failure to find many references to the use of hook and line is that the European colonists were so accustomed to this method of fishing that they took it for granted. On archeological sites in the section, bone fishhooks have been found in all stages of manufacture.

At Key Marco, Cushing

> found four or five fish-hooks. The shanks or stems of these were about three inches long, shaped much like those of our own, but made from the conveniently curved main branches of the foked twigs of some tough springy kind of wood. These were cut off at the forks in such manner as to leave a portion of the stems to serve as butts, which were girdled and notched in, so that the sharp, barbed points of deer bone, which were about half as long as the shanks and leaned in toward them, could be firmly attached with sinew and black rubber-gum cement.

---

[21] The Seminole preserved the custom until late times (MacCauley, 1887, p. 513) ; also see Speck, 1909, p. 24, and 1907, p. 108.

The stems were neatly tapered toward the upper ends, which terminated in slight knobs, and to these, lines—so fine that only traces of them could be recovered—were tied by half-hitches, like the turns of a bow string. Little plug-shaped floats of gumbo-limbo wood, and sinkers made from the short thick columellae of turbinella shells—not shaped and polished like the highly finished plummet-shaped pendants we secured in great numbers, but with the whorls merely battered off—seemed to have been used with these hooks and lines. That they were designed for deep-sea fishing was indicated by the occurrence of flat reels or spools shaped precisely like fine-toothed combs divested of their inner teeth. There were also shuttles or skein-holders of hard wood, six or seven inches long, with wide semicircular crotches at the ends. But these may have served in connection with a double kind of barb, made from two notched or hooked crochet-like points or prongs of deer bone, that we found attached with fibre cords to a concave round-ended plate, an inch wide and three inches long, made from the pearly nacre of a pinna shell. Since several of these shining, ovoid plates were procured, I regarded them as possibly "baiting-spoons," and this one with the barbed contrivance, as some kind of trolling gear, though it may, as the sailors thought, have been a "pair of grains," or may, like the hook proper, have been used for deep-sea fishing. (Cushing, 1902, p. 367.)

Coming to more recent times, we find the following in Speck's account of the Yuchi Indians:

Gaff-hooks for fishing do not seem to have been used, according to the older men, until they obtained pins from the whites, when the Yuchi learned how to make fish hooks of them. Prior to this, nevertheless, they had several gorge-hook devices for baiting and snagging fish. A stick with pointed reverse barbs whittled along it near the end was covered with some white meat and drawn, or trolled, rapidly through the water on a line. When a fish swallowed the bait the angler gave the line a tug and the barbs caught the fish in the stomach. Another method was to tie together the ends of a springy, sharp-pointed splinter and cover the whole with meat for bait. When this gorge device was swallowed the binding soon disintegrated, the sharp ends being released killed the fish and held it fast. Lines thus baited were set in numbers along the banks of streams and visited regularly by fishermen. (Speck, 1909, p. 25.)

Employment of what is called a trot or trat line is described by Pénicaut when he was living with the Acolapissa and Natchitoches:

After dining we went to see their fisheries. They drew from the lake their nets which were filled with fishes of all sizes. These nets are really only lines about six fathoms long. A number of small lines are fastened to these a foot apart. At the end of each line is a fish-hook where they put a little piece of hominy dough or a little piece of meat. With that they do not fail to take fishes weighing more than fifteen to twenty pounds. The end of each line is attached to a canoe. They draw them in two or three times a day, and many fish are always taken when they draw them. (Pénicaut in Margry, 1875–86, vol. 5, p. 466.)

Fish were sometimes caught with the naked hands or by "grabbling," as it is called in western North Carolina, where the practice is still found among the white population (Rights, 1928, pp. 8, 19). That it is Indian in origin is proved by Adair, who says regarding this:

They have a surprising method of fishing under the edges of rocks, that stand over deep places of a river. There, they pull off their red breeches, or their long slip of Stroud cloth, and wrapping it round their arm, so as to reach to the lower part of the palm of their right hand, they dive under the rock where the large cat-fish lie to shelter themselves from the scorching beams of the sun, and to watch for prey: as soon as those fierce aquatic animals see that tempting bait, they immediately seize it with the greatest violence, in order to swallow it. Then is the time for the diver to improve the favourable opportunity: he accordingly opens his hand, seizes the voracious fish by his tender parts, hath a sharp struggle with it against the crevices of the rock, and at last brings it safe ashore. (Adair, 1775, p. 404.)

At the falls of the Chattahoochee River near Columbus there were two fisheries, an eastern and a western, controlled respectively by the Lower Creek towns of Kasihta and Coweta.

In middle and late summer when many of the streams were partially dried up, leaving a succession of pools into which the aquatic population of the river was largely concentrated, there was opportunity for fishing on a wholesale pattern open to most of the inland people. Then it was that various devices were resorted to to stupefy the fish and harvest them while they were in that condition. As is so often the case, Adair is our best early authority:

Their method of fishing may be placed among their diversions, but this is of the profitable kind. When they see large fish near the surface of the water, they fire directly upon them, sometimes only with powder, which noise and surprise however so stupifies them, that they instantly turn up their bellies and float a top, when the fisherman secures them. . . . In a dry summer season, they gather horse chestnuts, and different sorts of roots, which having pounded pretty fine, and steeped a while in a trough, they scatter this mixture over the surface of a middle-sized pond, and stir it about with poles, till the water is sufficiently impregnated with the intoxicating bittern. The fish are soon inebriated, and make to the surface of the water, with their bellies uppermost. The fishers gather them in baskets, and barbicue the largest, covering them carefully over at night to preserve them from the supposed putrifying influence of the moon. It seems, that fish catched in this manner, are not poisoned, but only stupified; for they prove very wholesome food for us, who frequently use them. By experiments, when they are speedily moved into good water, they revive in a few minutes. (Adair, 1775, pp. 402–403.)

Speck has the following description of this custom among the Yuchi:

During the months of July and August many families gather at the banks of some convenient creek for the purpose of securing quantities of fish and, to a certain extent, of intermingling socially for a short time. A large stock of roots are thrown in and the people enter the water to stir it up. This has the effect of causing the fish, when the poison has had time to act, to rise to the surface, bellies up, seemingly dead. They are then gathered by both men and women and carried away in baskets to be dried for future use, or consumed in a feast which ends the event. The catch is equally divided among those present. Upon such an occasion, as soon as the fish appear floating on the surface of the water, the Indians leap, yell and set to dancing in exuberance. If a stranger comes along at such a time he is taken by the hand and presented with the choicest fish. . . . .

In the way of comparison, we find that the Creeks use pounded buckeye or horse chestnuts for the same purpose. Two men enter the water and strain the buckeye juice through bags. The Creeks claim that the devil's shoestring poison used by the Yuchi floats on the water, thus passing away down stream, while the buckeye sinks and does better work. It is probable, however, that neither method of poisoning the streams is used exclusively by these tribes, but that the people of certain districts favor one or the other method, according to the time of year and locality. The flesh of the fish killed in this way is perfectly palatable.

It frequently happens that the poison is not strong enough to thoroughly stupefy the fish. In such a case the men are at hand with bows and arrows, to shoot them as they flounder about trying to escape or to keep near the bottom of the pool. (Speck, 1909, p. 24.)

As will be seen below, Speck is quite right in suspecting that the uses of these poisons were not separated by tribal lines.

In describing the customs of the Taskigi Creeks, the same writer says:

They poison the streams to secure the fish by pounding up quantities of horse-chestnuts and throwing them into pools which they have dammed up at different points. Then the men go into the water to mix up the poison, beating around with their arms and stirring up the water so that the fish cannot escape by staying near the bottom. The fish are then stabbed with arrows and thrown out to the women on shore who stow them away in large splint baskets. Large quantities of catfish were procured in this way. (Speck, 1907, p. 108.)

Jackson Lewis informed me that poisoning was usually undertaken among the Creeks in July and August when the water was low. Word was sent around that on a certain date all in that neighborhood would go to a designated pool and spend the day catching fish. Each man was instructed to provide himself with a quantity of the roots of a plant popularly known as "devil's shoestring," which grows on sandy ridges in the woods. He also carried a post, about 4 inches in diameter and 4 feet long, and a wooden mallet. Arrived at the appointed place, the men ranged themselves in a row across the head of the pond and drove their posts into the stream bed until the tops of the posts were almost on a level with the water. Then they pounded up the devil's shoestring with their mallets, allowing the pieces to fall down into the water. If there were any fishes in the pool, they would begin to throw themselves out of the water before the pounding was finished, but no one tried to kill any before that time. Afterward, the men took bows and arrows, spears, and other weapons, and descending into the pool they often killed great numbers of fish, which by now would be floating about on the surface. These they roasted, baked, and fried, and they indulged in a general feast and merrymaking. Jackson Lewis claimed that the fish were stupefied by a peculiar odor. Instead of devil's shoestring, they sometimes employed the roots of the buckeye, and this was the poison best known to the Alabama Indians who called it ayoná, though I was told that it was the small branches which they mashed up. Others, like Speck's Taskigi informant, say the fruit was used.

I obtained another account of fish "poisoning" as practiced among the Creeks from Zach Cook, a Tukabahchee Indian:

When a fishing party of this kind had been decided upon, a crowd of people set out to dig roots of the devil's shoestring, and some miko hoyanīdja (red willow) was also obtained. The party was under two leaders, and a medicine maker accompanied them. After the medicines had been gathered, the managers appointed two boys to assemble them and put some of the devil's shoestring in one pot and miko hoyanīdja in the other. A cane was then given to the medicine maker, who blew through it into the medicines and repeated the usual formulae, and every man drank a little of this and rubbed a little on his face. If he did not, it was believed the fish would go down into their holes and could not be caught. An old man was appointed to watch this operation and make sure that everyone used the medicine. The object of the medicine maker in this and later activities was to make the fish drunk. If a medicine maker would not go with them, they took their chances and painted their faces in the same manner as when there had been a death. After the medicine had been taken, posts were set in the water and devil's shoestring pounded up on the tops of these by means of wooden mallets and allowed to fall into the pool. A man was appointed to watch for the fish and report when they began to float up to the surface. He took the first four fish to the medicine man, and all had a grand feast on the remainder. Later, they might move to another pond and do the same thing over again. To season their fish they used a kind of mint called kafû''tskà.

A Choctaw informant, Simpson Tubby, stated that in poisoning fish his people used buckeye and devil's shoestring, but the last in particular was very weak, and much stronger than either were the berries of a certain plant which was identified for me as probably *Cocculus carolinus*. My informant asserted that the berries of this last in places where it grows, if they happened to drop into the water, would drive fish away. He added that, when his people poisoned a pool, they cut down bushes and piled them about it to keep the stock away and cautioned their people not to drink from it.

Cook added that the Creeks sometimes dragged brush about in a pool of water until it became so muddy that the fish came to the surface for air, when they were shot with arrows or speared. Or sometimes a dozen boys in a neighborhood would go down into the water and scare the fish out of their holes so that they could be shot when they came to the surface. When De Soto was traveling through certain swamps west of the Mississippi, one chronicler reports that "the Indians whom they took along in chains roiled the water with the mud of the waters and the fish, as if stupefied would come to the surface, and they caught as many as they wished" (Robertson, 1933, p. 188).

Jackson Lewis told of another method of obtaining fish from summer pools. This was by the use of a drag constructed, something like a fence, of two long crosspieces made of medium-sized logs fastened end to end, the length being proportioned to the size of the pool, with withes of hickory or other wood filling the space between. They placed this across the pool at its lower end and dragged it upstream, the structure preserving a vertical face to the water. If it caught on the bottom someone would dive down to free it. Finally, they dragged it into the shallower water at the upper end, and sometimes they caught thousands of fish in this manner. This drag was a purely temporary affair made for the occasion only and thrown away immediately afterward.

Simpson Tubby stated that his people, the Choctaw, usually prohibited anyone from poisoning the pools, but used instead a drag which must have been similar to that employed by the Creeks. It was "made of brush fastened together with creepers." When the water was deep, ponies and oxen were secured to the drag at intervals and men sat upon it to keep it down." In this way they caught trout, jacks, perch, suckers, and sometimes catfish. Eufaubee and Nanih Waiya Creeks were particularly noted for their supplies of fish.

Lawson observed the following method in use in Carolina in securing crawfish:

Their taking of crawfish is so pleasant, that I cannot pass it by without mention; when they have a mind to get these shell fish, they take a piece of venison and half barbecue or roast it, then they cut it into thin slices, which slices they stick through with reeds about six inches asunder betwixt piece and piece; then the reeds are made sharp at one end; and so they stick a great many of them down in the bottom of the water, thus baited, in the small brooks and runs, which the crawfish frequent. Thus the Indians sit by and tend these baited sticks, every now and then taking them up to see how many are at the bait; where they generally find abundance, so take them off and put them in a basket for the purpose, and stick the reeds down again. By this method, they will, in a little time, catch several bushels, which are as good as any I ever eat. (Lawson, 1860, pp. 339–340.)

DOMESTICATION OF ANIMALS

PRE-COLUMBIAN DOMESTICATION

The only domestic animal of universal occurrence was the dog, but it was of very little economic importance. In this area there is no mention of dogs as beasts of burden, that function having been the prerogative of women until the introduction of horses, though fortunately for the women, many of the longer expeditions were made by canoe.

The employment of dogs in hunting has been touched upon. Some myths represent dogs as undertaking the hunting of game for the benefit of sick masters, but this has no reference to the hunting customs of human beings. There is one doubtful mention of the use of dogs in chasing deer, and they seem to have rendered bear hunters some assistance, as appears from a note by Adair as well as information derived from modern Indians. (See pp. 323–324.) The Alabama say that they used them in hunting rabbits and the Creeks employed them in chasing squirrels, opossums, and raccoons, but such services were evidently slight, and resort to them was probably stimulated by white example. According to Morfi, the Caddo raised to assist them in hunting "a certain kind of dog they call *Jubine*, with long, sharp-pointed snout, and as cunning as its master," but he seems to be quoting from Solís, who says nothing about the use to which these dogs were put. In the period of intertribal warfare, dogs were, of course, of some utility as sentinels, and the towns swarmed with them. In Guasili in the Cherokee mountains the Spaniards were given 300. (Robertson, 1933, p. 102; Morfi, 1932, p. 44; Solís, 1931, p. 61; Swanton, 1942, pp. 134, 137.)

Lawson (1860, p. 68) says, apropos of the treatment of dogs in advance of a feast in the Waxhaw tribe, that the dogs "are seemingly wolves made tame with starving and beating, they being the worst dog masters in the world; so that it is an infallible cure for sore eyes, ever to see an Indian's dog fat." The chances are that he has inverted cause and effect and that the dogs were made wild and wolfish by starving and beating. My Alabama informant described the old Indian dog as of medium size and with short hair. Within the remembrance of Zach Cook, a Creek informant, there were three varieties of dogs among the Indians, a short-haired, brindle dog between a bulldog and a shepherd, a spotted dog, and "a big dog." The first of these was a good hunter and had a good disposition. The second had a bad disposition and was apt to bite. The third was of small account. It is probable that only one of these was descended from the Indian dog, but mixture with European breeds began early. Bartram tells of a Seminole Indian who had trained a black dog to keep watch of his horses and drive them for him. Speck (1909, p. 22) states that the Yuchi dogs seen by him were "mongrels showing intermixture with every imaginable strain, but the wolfish appearance and habits of many of them would suggest that their semidomestic ancestors were of the wolf breed."

Byrd asserts that the Indians of Virginia, including specifically the Saponi, knew how to tame wolf puppies "and use them about their cabans instead of Dogs" (Bassett, 1901, p. 130), but this must stand by itself.

Peter Martyr reports, on the supposed authority of an Indian from the region now covered by South Carolina, that the aborigines of that country tamed deer, and kept hens, ducks, geese, and other domestic fowl, and De Soto in his letter to the civil cabildo of Santiago de Cuba informs them that the Indians of Ocale tamed deer and turkeys. (Anghierra, 1912, vol. 2, pp. 259–260; Swanton, 1922, p. 42; Bourne, 1904, vol. 2, p. 162; Robertson, 1938, p. 176.) These plainly represent misunderstandings or misrepresentations. Strachey (1849, p. 26) speaks of a people, apparently in what is now North Carolina, who bred up "tame turkeis about their howses," but as he adds that they "take apes in the mountaines," we can hardly credit this any more than the tales of Peter Martyr and De Soto's informant. A Chitimacha slave of Du Pratz told him that her people raised turkeys, but this was some time after hens had been introduced among them and they may well have been obtained from the French. (Le Page du Pratz, 1758, vol. 2, pp. 125–126; Swanton, 1911, p. 73.) The only information on this point which seems to be first hand is that of Lawson, who asserts that the Siouan Indians hatched the eggs of wild turkeys and used the young ones as decoys, though their ability to make a successful hatch of wild turkey eggs appears more than doubtful.

What the same writer says regarding tame cranes is more credible:

These Congarees have abundance of storks and cranes in their savannas. They take them before they can fly, and breed them as tame and familiar as a dunghill fowl. They had a tame crane at one of these cabins, that was scarcely less than six feet in heighth. His head being round, with a shining, natural crimson hue, which they all have. (Lawson, 1860, pp. 53–54, 245.)

In northern Florida, a Timucua chief presented one of the lieutenants of Laudonnière with two young eagles.

These notes are all that our literature affords on this subject, and it is evident that taming of animals other than the dog was sporadic and without special significance.

HORSES

The first acquaintance of the Southeastern Indians with horses was with those brought by Ayllon in 1526, Narvaez in 1528, and particularly De Soto and Moscoso, 1539–43. The Indians were terrified by them, and to his possession of these animals De Soto owed his success in penetrating the Gulf region for such long distances. Ranjel says that the people of Mabila "held horses in the greatest terror" (Bourne, 1904, vol. 2, p. 122) and promptly killed all that fell into their hands. In the surprise attack on the Chickasaw town in which

De Soto spent the winter of 1540–41, Ranjel states that the Indians "burned and captured 59 horses," and it has been supposed by some writers that the later famous Chickasaw breed originated from some of these, but both Biedma and the Fidalgo of Elvas state that the horses were killed (Bourne, 1904, vol. 1, p. 106; vol. 2, p. 23). In 1543, when they were ready to embark for Mexico, the Spaniards killed all of their remaining horses except four or five, and these terrified the Indians so much that they were probably destroyed soon afterward (Robertson, 1933, p. 283). In 1560 the Coosa Indians were evidently as unfamiliar with these animals as though they had never seen one before, since, in the war which they and the Spaniards waged jointly against the Napochies, the Spanish captain mounted the chief of the Coosa Indians on a horse, but had to detail a negro to lead it.

The cacique went or rather rode in the rear guard, not less flattered by the obsequiousness of the captain than afraid of his riding feat. (Davila Padilla, 1625, pp. 208–209; Swanton, 1922, p. 233.)

It is true that the Indians, after they had obtained horses in the eighteenth century, mounted on the opposite side from the English, but this could equally well have been learned from the Spaniards of Mexico through the western tribes from whom their horses probably did come, and none of the Spaniards belonging to De Soto's force is reported to have been taken alive by the Chickasaw or any of their immediate neighbors. Outside of the Floridian Peninsula there is no evidence of the use of horses among our Gulf Indians until the beginning of the eighteenth century. In 1674 the treatment of Gabriel Arthur's horse by the inhabitants of a Yuchi town on the headwaters of the Tennessee shows how little they understood the requirements of the animal. "A stake was sett up in ye middle of ye towne to fasten ye horse to, and aboundance of corne and all manner of pulse with fish, flesh and beares oyle for ye horse to feed upon" (Alvord, 1912, pp. 212–213). By 1700 some of the eastern Siouan tribes were getting horses from Virginia, but Lawson says, after describing the harsh treatment accorded dogs:

They are of a quite contrary disposition to horses. Some of their kings having gotten by great chance, a jade, stolen by some neighbouring Indian, and transported farther into the country and sold, or bought sometimes of a christian that trades amongst them, these creatures they continually cram and feed with maize, and what the horse will eat, till he is as fat as a hog—never making any farther use of him than to fetch a deer home, that is killed somewhere near the Indian's plantation. (Lawson, 1860, p. 68.)

In some places nearer the settlements horses were still strange animals until much later times. In April 1716, John Fontaine visited the Saponi town at Fort Christanna. On the 9th he left the fort in company with Governor Spotswood, and the party was given an escort of 12 young Indians under an old chief. Fontaine writes:

They were all afoot, so the Governor to compliment the head man of the Indians lent him his led-horse. After we had ridden about a mile, we came to a ford of Meherrin River, and being mistaken in our water-mark, we were sometimes obliged to make our horses swim, but we got over safe. The Indian Chief seeing how it was, unsaddled his horse, and stript himself all to his belt, and forded the river, leading his horse after him; the fancy of the Indian made us merry for a while. The day being warm, and he not accustomed to ride, the horse threw him before he had gone two miles, but he had courage to mount again. By the time we had got a mile further, he was so terribly galled that he was forced to dismount, and desired the Governor to take his horse, for he could not imagine what good they were for, if it was not to cripple Indians. (Maury, 1907, p. 280.)

Although St. Augustine was settled in 1565, it would seem as though the Florida Indians adopted horses from their Spanish neighbors very slowly, possibly owing to the fact that they were in the habit of traveling almost everywhere by canoe. Adoption of horses from the settlers of South Carolina also seems to have been slow.

Of the horses he saw in Florida, William Bartram says:

They are the most beautiful and sprightly species of that noble creature, perhaps any where to be seen; but are of a small breed, and as delicately formed as the American roe-buck. A horse in the Creek or Muscogulge tongue is echoclucco, that is the great deer (echo is deer, and clucco is big). The Siminole horses are said to descend originally from the Andalusian breed, brought here by the Spaniards when they first established the colony of East Florida. From the forehead to their nose is a little arched or aquiline, and so are the fine Chactaw horses among the Upper Creeks [i. e., the Creeks], which are said to have been brought thither from New-Mexico across Mississippi, by those nations of Indians who emigrated from the West, beyond the river. These horses are every where like the Siminole breed, only large, and perhaps not so lively and capricious. (Bartram, 1792, pp. 213–214.)

As the Seminole Nation did not exist until well along in the eighteenth century, this does not mean a high antiquity for the Seminole horse unless these horses had previously been used by the Timucua and Apalachee and such use does not appear to have been very extensive. At any rate, Bartram implies that the horses of the Creeks, called by him "Upper Creeks," were of Spanish Mexican origin. The idea that they had been brought along by the Indians themselves when they entered the country is, of course, quite erroneous. That the Lower Creeks had not begun using horses till after the opening of the eighteenth century is shown by the anonymous French writer, who says that about that time the chief of the Coweta Indians was mounted upon a horse by some whites who wished to honor him, but that he was in mortal terror of the animal.

About this time the French brought horses to Louisiana, but it is probable that the Chickasaw had already begun to receive them from the west. The far greater utility of this animal to the Plains Indians had already stimulated systematic plundering of the Spanish settlements in Old and New Mexico, and horses were soon passed on from tribe to tribe until they reached the Mississippi and were even transported across it toward the east. Du Pratz informs us that horses, and he adds cattle, were being brought into Louisiana via the Caddo Indians and the Avoyel tribe on Red River (Le Page du Pratz, 1758, vol. 2, pp. 241–242; Swanton, 1911, p. 273). Without much doubt these were the horses out of which came that famous Chickasaw breed, often mentioned by travelers in the Southeast.[22] The writer of the anonymous French Memoir says that in his time (the first half of the eighteenth century) the Chickasaw already had many Spanish and English horses, the latter obtained (i. e., stolen) from English traders. He adds:

> So far as the Chaquetas are concerned the greater part of those which they have come from the French. In the last war with the Natches (1729–31) they obtained a mare for each slave, French and black, which they had recaptured. In this way they provided themselves with horses, and they were soon able to sell horses to the French. They let them live in the woods whence they fetch them whenever they have need of any. I have noticed that animals accustomed to live in the woods in this manner decline visibly when one tries to keep them at home. They are not fed as in Europe and they are not curried. They would soon become expensive if one tried to keep them there the year round, owing to the insufficiency of forage. They are very lively when they are brought out of the woods and carry their riders at breakneck speed. In all the islands [i. e., all the lands of America] women and girls ride horseback like men. As horses are not numerous they make use of cattle for the cart and for plows. (Swanton, 1918, pp. 70–71.)

This last remark applies of course to the white settlers, not the Indians. By 1762, however, there were plenty of horses even among the Cherokee (Timberlake, Williams ed., 1927, p. 72).

A decade later Bernard Romans reported of the Creeks:

> Vast numbers of horses are bred here, but of an indifferent kind; and these savages are the greatest horse stealers yet known: it is impossible to be sure of a horse wherever these fellows come. (Romans, 1775, p. 94.)

The use to which Lawson's Indians put their horses, viz, to bring home deer meat, which seemed to him so trivial, was of vast consequence to that earlier beast of burden, the Indian woman, to whom it brought emancipation from much of the drudgery of existence. The place of the tough little Choctaw ponies in the life of that tribe was very important, if not as spectacular as their use on the Plains. Cushman gives us a very good picture of this:

> The famous little Choctaw pony was a veritable camel to the Choctaw hunter, as the genuine animal is to the sons of Ishmael. His unwearied patience, and

---

[22] On Chickasaw horses, see S. C. Williams, 1928, p. 340, footnote.

his seemingly untiring endurance of hardships and fatigue, were truly astonishing—surpassing, according to his inches, every other species of his race—and proving himself to be a worthy descendant of his ancient parent, the old Spanish war-horse, introduced by the early Spanish explorers of the continent. In all the Choctaws' expeditions, except those of war in which they never used horses, the chubby little pony always was considered an indispensable adjunct, therefore always occupied a conspicuous place in the cavalcade. A packsaddle which Choctaw ingenuity had invented expressly for the benefit of the worthy little fellow's back, and finely adapted in every particular for its purpose, was firmly fastened upon his back, ready to receive the burden, which was generally divided into three parts, each weighing from forty to fifty pounds. Two of these were suspended across the saddle by means of a rawhide rope one-fourth of an inch in diameter and of amazing strength, and the third securely fastened upon the top, over all of which a bear or deer skin was spread, which protected it from rain. All things being ready, the hunter, as leader and protector, took his position in front, sometimes on foot and sometimes astride a pony of such diminutive proportions, that justice and mercy would naturally have suggested a reverse in the order of things, and, with his trusty rifle in his hand, without which he never went anywhere, took up the line of march, and directly after whom, in close order, the loaded ponies followed in regular succession one behind the other, while the dutiful wife and children brought up the rear in regular, successive order, often with from three to five children on a single pony—literally hiding the submissive little fellow from view. Upon the neck of each pony a little bell was suspended, whose tinkling chimes of various tones broke the monotony of the desert air, and added cheerfulness to the novel scene.

Long accustomed to their duty, the faithful little packponies seldom gave any trouble, but in a straight line followed on after their master; sometimes, however, one here and there, unable to withstand the temptation of the luxuriant grass that offered itself so freely along the wayside, would make a momentary stop to snatch a bite or two, but the shrill, disapproving voice of the wife in close proximity behind, at once reminded him of his dereliction of order and he would hastily trot up to his position; and thus the little caravan, with the silence broken only by the tinkling pony bells, moved on amid the dense timber of their majestic forests, until the declining sun gave warning of the near approaching night. Then a halt was made, and the faithful little ponies, relieved of their wearisome loads which they had borne through the day with becoming and uncomplaining patience, were set free that they might refresh themselves upon the grass and cane—nature's bounties to the Indian—that grew and covered the forests in wild abundance. Late next morning—(for who ever knew an Indian, in the common affairs of life, to be in a hurry or to value time? Time! He sees it not; he feels it not; he regards it not. To him 'tis but a shadowy name—a succession of breathings, measured forth by the change of night and day by a shadow crossing the dial-path of life)—the rested and refreshed ponies were gathered in, and, each having received the former load, again the tinkling chimes of the pony bells alone disturbed the quiet of the then far extending wilderness, announcing in monotonous tones the onward march, as the day before, of the contented travelers; and thus was the journey continued day by day, until the desired point was reached. (Cushman, 1899, p. 54.)

HOGS, DOMESTIC FOWL, AND CATTLE

These three were introduced into the Gulf region in about the order given. As is well known, a considerable drove of swine was driven along by the Spaniards under De Soto. The Fidalgo of Elvas says that the Indians of Guachoya, a town on the west bank of the Mississippi, presented the white men, on their return from their unsuccessful attempt to reach Mexico overland, with some of these animals, descended from swine that had escaped from them the year before (Robertson, 1933, p. 269), and it would not be surprising to learn that they were already in the land when the English and French entered it at a much later date. Positive evidence of this is, however, almost lacking. In 1674, it is true, Gabriel Arthur was taken by the Yuchi Indians on a hunting expedition down Tennessee River "to kill hoggs, beares and sturgion" (Alvord, 1912, p. 223), but this stands well nigh alone, and it is possible that the stock introduced by De Soto died out. At any rate, by 1761 Timberlake found numbers of hogs among the Cherokee (Timberlake, Williams ed., 1927, p. 72).

When the French ascended the Mississippi in 1699 they found European fowl already among the Indians, said to have been obtained from some vessel cast away in the Atakapa country in southwestern Louisiana. These birds were of a small breed and came to be known as "creole hens." Much earlier than this, in 1595, San Miguel found an abundance of "Spanish fowl" among the Guale Indians on the Georgia coast (Garcia, 1902, p. 197).

According to Du Pratz cattle as well as horses were being brought into Louisiana from Mexico through the medium of the southern Plains tribes. (Le Page du Pratz, 1758, vol. 2, pp. 241–242; Swanton, 1911, p. 273.) They were adopted rather slowly by the Indians but were taken into the economy of all of the Five Civilized Tribes before their removal west.

PREPARATION OF VEGETABLE FOODS

(Plate 53)

"Roasting ears" are mentioned by nearly all of our earliest authorities. "Their corn they eat in the eares greene, roasted," says Strachey (1849, p. 73), and Smith (1907, p. 96), Beverley (1705, bk. 3, p. 15), and Lawson (1860, p. 290) refer to this use of corn, while most other writers simply take it for granted. In connection with it, Beverley notes something like an aboriginal American succession of crops.

They delight much to feed on Roasting-ears; that is, the *Indian* Corn, gathered green and milky, before it is grown to its full bigness, and roasted before the Fire, in the Ear. For the sake of this Dyet, which they love exceedingly, they are very careful to procure all the several sorts of *Indian* Corn before mentioned, by which means they contrive to prolong their Season. (Beverley, 1705, bk. 3, p. 15.)

The late varieties of corn were eaten in this way only after the annual ceremony usually called the "green corn dance," the busk of the Creeks, had been celebrated.

Catesby informs us that

Indians .... are often without corn, (and from the same negligent principle) when they have it, they are often without bread, contenting themselves with eating the grain whole, after being softened by boiling it with their meat. (Catesby, 1731–43, vol. 2, p. x.)

Ears of corn were also dried and preserved for winter use:

They also reserve that corne late planted that will not ripe, by roasting it in hot ashes, the heat thereof drying it. In winter they esteeme it being boyled with beans for a rare dish, they call Pausarowmena. (Smith, Tyler ed., 1907, p. 95).

Strachey (1849, p. 72) repeats the statement, and notes that the stalks when gathered green were sucked for the sugar they contained.

A staple dish throughout the Southeast was that known to the Creeks as sofki. It corresponded, in part at least, to the hominy of the Algonquians and the atole of the Mexicans and came to the knowledge of the French under the name sagamité, an Algonquian word but not applied by Algonquians to this food. Apparently it covered dishes made in somewhat different ways. The sofki with which I am acquainted was made either of kernels of corn deprived of their skins by means of lye and similar to what we used to call "hulled corn" or of kernels broken into coarse pieces in a wooden mortar, cleared of skins and then boiled. I do not remember to have seen any made out of finely pounded grain, but it would correspond very well with the following dish described by Smith:

The grouts and peeces of the cornes remaining, by fanning in a Platter or in the wind away the branne, they boile 3 or 4 houres with water; which is an ordinary food they call *Ustatahamen.* (Smith, Tyler ed., 1907, p. 96.)

Strachey restates this as follows:

The growtes and broken pieces of the corne remayning, they likewise preserve, and by fannying away the branne or huskes in a platter or in the wynd, they lett boyle in an earthen pott three or four howres, and thereof make a straung thick pottage, which they call Vsketehamun, and is their kind of frumentry, and indeed is like our kind of ptisane, husked barley sodden in water. (Strachey, 1849, p. 73.)

They add that some Indians went so far as to burn the corncob to powder and mix it with their meal, but remark that it never tasted well in bread or broth.   These were evidently identical with the hominy defined by Beverley as follows:

This is *Indian* corn soaked, broken in a Mortar, husked, and then boil'd in Water over a gentle Fire, for ten or twelve hours, to the consistence of Furmity: The thin of this is, what my Lord *Bacon* calls Cream of Maize, and highly commends for an excellent sort of nutriment.   (Beverley, 1705, bk. 3, p. 13.)

Catesby defines it as "grain boiled whole, with a mixture of *Bonavis* [beans], till they are tender, which requires eight or ten hours" (Catesby, 1731–43, vol. 2, p. xvii).

This hominy is of the class of food which we now called "cooked cereal."   The finer fragments were used as hominy as well as the coarser.   Du Pratz speaks of "the coarse and the fine grits (*gruau*) called in that country *sagamité*" (Le Page du Pratz, 1758, vol. 2, pp. 8–9; Swanton, 1911, p. 75), and these have continued in use down to the present day.   Hariot (1893, p. 21) perhaps refers to both when he speaks of a native dish made by "boyling the floure with water into a pappe."   Speaking of the Choctaw, Romans (1775, p. 67) says briefly: "Their common food is the *zea* or the Indian corn, of which they make meal, and boil it."   It was perhaps the "loblolly made with Indian corn" which Congaree Indians offered Lawson.   Catesby remarks that "they thicken their broths with *Roccahomony*, which is indeed, for that purpose, much preferable to oatmeal or *French* barley," [23] but this was pinole (see p. 358).   We are here speaking of atole "made of parched corn and very thick," mentioned by the monk San Miguel as a common food on the Georgia coast in 1595 (Garcia, 1902, p. 192).

There are hints of a slightly different dish, made of fine flour boiled in water and corresponding in a manner to our "corn-meal mush." This was probably the porridge (*bouillie*) of which Dumont speaks. (Dumont, 1753, vol. 1, pp. 32–34; Swanton, 1911, p. 74.)   Catesby (1731–1743, vol. 2, p. xvii) refers to it as "*Mush* . . . . . made of the meal, in the manner of hasty-pudding."

Although Byington calls them both "hominy," the distinction between hulled corn, and the dish made with broken kernels was clearly maintained by the Choctaw, who called the former tanlubo or tanlubona, which seems to mean "round corn (tanc lubo), and the latter tanfula (Anglicized as tamfula).   The following notes regarding these were given Dr. Foreman by a native Choctaw, Peter Hudson:

Tanlubo (called by him tahlobo or tash-lobona) is made by soaking the corn

long enough to loosen the hulls which are then beaten off in the mortar without breaking the grain; placed in the riddle the husks are ejected and the grain

---

[23] Catesby, 1731–1743, vol. 2, p. x; Roccahomony, or rockahominy, as spelled by Byrd, is the parched corn meal which Indians carried on their journeys (Bassett, 1901, p. 202).

then placed in a kettle with water and fresh pork and seasoned with salt. This was cooked down until it became a thick and very rich dish.

Tafala—Ta-fula (*ta^{n}fula*), was prepared in much the same way as *tashlobona*, except that the grains of corn were broken in several pieces and cooked with beans or wood ashes; but no meat was used and it was retained in a more fluid state than the latter. In making hickory *ta-fula*, hickory nuts were gathered and put in a sack over the fireplace to dry for a month or more. When ready to use the nuts were cracked and shells and kernels together were put in a sack and water poured over them; when this was drained off it was the color of milk; this fluid was then poured into the *ta-fula*, and cooked, making a rich and palatable dish. (Foreman, 1933, pp. 309–310.)

Speck identifies with Choctaw ta^{n}fula the Yuchi tsō'ci, which he describes as follows:

To make this the grains of corn, when dry, are removed from the cob and pounded in the mortar until they are broken up. These grits and the corn powder are then scooped out of the mortar and boiled in a pot with water. Wood ashes from the fire are usually added to it to give a peculiar flavor much to the native taste. Even powdered hickory nuts, or marrow, or meat may be boiled with the soup to vary its taste. It is commonly believed, as regards the origin of this favorite dish, that a woman in the mythical ages cut a rent in the sky through which a peculiar liquid flowed which was found to be good to eat. The Sun then explained its preparation and use, from which fact it was called *tsō'ci*, inferribly "sun fluid." (Speck, 1909, p. 44.)

Skinner describes Seminole usage briefly:

The meal [after having been taken from the mortar] is first sifted through an open-mesh basket and then winnowed by being tossed into the air, the breeze carrying away the chaff, while the heavier, edible portion of the corn falls back into the flat receiving basket. In this condition the meal is mixed with water and boiled to make sofki. This is the name applied primarily to this corn soup, of which, in addition to the kind mentioned, there is fermented or sour sofki, and soup made from parched corn, which is by far the most savory of the three. (Skinner, 1913, p. 77.)

The Chickasaw made a drink from corn which traders are said to have used in preference to water in spite of the fact that it was unfermented:

Though in most of the Indian nations, the water is good, because of their high situation, yet the traders very seldom drink any of it at home; for the women beat in mortars their flinty corn, till all husks are taken off, which having well sifted and fanned, they boil in large earthen pots; then straining off the thinnest part into a pot, they mix it with cold water, till it is sufficiently liquid for drinking: and when cold, it is both pleasant and very nourishing; and is much liked even by the genteel strangers. (Adair, 1775, p. 416.)

A favorite method of cooking corn meal was to wrap it in husks, which were afterwards boiled, a number at a time. Smith and Strachey mention this, and Adair tells us that chestnuts were added to the corn:

In July, when the chestnuts and corn are green and full grown, they half boil the former, and take off the rind; and having sliced the milky, swelled, long rows of the latter, the women pound it in a large wooden mortar, which is wide at the mouth, and gradually narrows to the bottom: then they knead both together, wrap them up in green corn-blades of various sizes, about an inch-thick, and boil them well, as they do every kind of seethed food. (Adair, 1775, p. 406.)

The Choctaw called this *bánaha*, and it is thus described by the Choctaw Peter Hudson, as recorded by Foreman:

To make it the Choctaw Indians soak the shelled corn in water over night; then beat it in a mortar to separate the hulls from the grain; the latter is then put in a riddle or flat basket and by manipulation the husks are expelled over the side of the riddle; the grain is then again placed in the mortar and pounded into meal, which is made into dough. The dough is rolled out into cylindrical segments of something less than a pound in weight. Each of these is encased in corn shucks and around the middle tied with shucks drawn tight so that the ends bulge somewhat larger than the middle. They are boiled until done. When ready to serve the shucks are removed. Bread so made was carried in the shuck container by hunters on their long expeditions as it would keep for weeks. After a time it became dry and hard, but the hunter placed it by his camp fire to warm and soften it. (Foreman, 1933, pp. 308–309, footnote.)

References to treatment of corn by the Caddo Indians are given in Swanton (1942, pp. 127, 131).

Percy, Smith, and Strachey give us the earliest accounts of bread making in this section. Percy says:

The manner of baking of bread is thus. After they pound their wheat into flowre, with hote water they make it into paste, and worke it into round balls and cakes, then they put it into a pot of seething water: when it is sod thoroughly, they lay it on a smooth stone, there they harden it as well as in an Oven. (Percy, *in* Smith, 1907 ed., p. 18.)

The descriptions of Smith and Strachey are, as usual, parallel. Smith tells us that

they first steep [their matured and dried corn] a night in hot water, and in the morning pounding it in a mortar, they use a small basket for their Temmes [hulls, "tamis"], then pound againe the great, and so separating by dashing their hand in the basket, receave the flower in a platter made of wood scraped to that forme with burning and shels. Tempering this flower with water, they make it either in cakes, covering them with ashes till they bee baked, and then washing them in faire water, they drie presently with their owne heat: or else boyle them in water eating the broth with the bread which they call Ponap [ponak]. (Smith, Tyler ed., 1907, pp. 95–96.)

Strachey puts this in a somewhat more intelligible form:

Their old wheat (corn) they firste steepe a night in hot water, and in the morning pounding yt in a morter, they use a small baskett for the boulter or searser, and when they have syfted fourth the finest, they pound againe the great, and so separating yt by dashing their hand in the baskett, receave the flower in a platter of wood, which, blending with water, they make into flatt, broad cakes, . . . and these they call appones, which covering with ashes till they be baked . . . , and washing them in faire water, they let dry with their own heate, or ells boyle them with water, eating the broath with the bread, which they called ponepopi. (Strachey, 1849, pp. 72–73.)

In Strachey's appones we see, of course, the modern "corn-pone" of the South.

All of the cakes or bread mentioned by early travelers in the Gulf region were baked in the manner indicated with but slight variations. Beverley (1705, bk. 3, p. 14) says:

They bake their Bread either in Cakes before the Fire, or in Loaves on a warm Hearth, covering the Loaf first with Leaves, then with Warm Ashes, and afterwards with Coals over all.

Catesby (1731–43, vol. 2, p. xvii) notes that "*pone*" was prepared by "baking in little round loaves, which is heavy, tho' very sweet and pleasant while it is new." And Newport's party was treated to "*pegatewk-Apyan* which is bread of their wheat made in Rolles and Cakes."

Beverley says nothing about the "boiled" bread referred to by Smith and Strachey in the concluding part of their descriptions, but we get this again in Adair's account:

They have another sort of boiled bread, which is mixed with beans, or potatoes; they put on the soft corn till it begins to boil, and pound it sufficiently fine;—their invention does not reach to the use of any kind of milk. When the flour is stirred, and dried by the heat of the sun or fire, they sift it with sieves of different sizes, curiously made with the coarser or finer cane-splinters. The thin cakes mixt with bear's oil, were formerly baked on thin broad stones placed over the fire, or on broad earthen bottoms fit for such a use: but now they use kettles. When they intend to bake great loaves, they make a strong blazing fire, with short dry split wood, on the hearth. When it is burnt down to coals, they carefully rake them off to each side, and sweep away the remaining ashes: then they put their well-kneeded broad loaf, first steeped in hot water, over the hearth, and an earthen bason above it, with the embers and coals a-top. This method of baking is as clean and efficacious as could possibly be done in any oven; when they take it off, they wash the loaf in warm water, and it soon becomes firm, and very white. It is likewise very wholesome, and well-tasted to any except the vitiated palate of an Epicure. (Adair, 1775, pp. 407–408.)

Here we have mention of both boiled bread and baked bread. The latter is again described by Timberlake in his treatment of Cherokee cookery:

After making a fire on the hearth-stone, about the size of a large dish, they sweep the embers off, laying a loaf smooth on it; this they cover with a sort of deep dish, and renew the fire upon the whole, under which the bread bakes to as great perfection as in any European oven. (Timberlake, Williams ed., 1927, p. 27.)

Cornbread is also mentioned in a general way by the De Soto chroniclers, by Hariot, Lawson, Romans, and the French writers. The monk Andreas de San Miguel, who was cast away upon the coast of St. Simons Island, Ga., in 1595, states that he and his companions were given "pieces of cake made of parched corn, which cakes are large and two inches in thickness" (Garcia, 1902, p. 186). Farther on we are told that

the cakes which they make of this flour are little smaller than flat earthen pans (comales) and are of the thickness of two fingers: they do not make them with salt because they have none and they cook them under the embers: it is a very palatable and sustaining sort of bread: they make little of it. (Garcia, 1902, p. 197.)

The Choctaw, and probably most of the other tribes, sometimes mixed sunflower seed with their corn meal when they made bread.

Du Pratz summarizes Natchez bread making in the statement that "they make of some of it [corn] bread cooked in a vessel, of some bread cooked in the ashes, and of some bread cooked in water," the three principal ways noted in Virginia and elsewhere.   (Le Page du Pratz, 1758, vol. 3, pp. 8–9; Swanton, 1911, p. 75.)

Here is Speck's account of bread making among the Yuchi as practiced until recent times:

A kind of flour, *tsukhá*, is made by pounding up dried corn in the mortar. At intervals the contents of the mortar are scooped up and emptied into the sieve basket. The operator holds a large basket tray in her lap and over it shakes and sifts the pounded corn until all the grits and the finer particles have fallen through. According to the desired fineness or coarseness of the flour she then jounces this tray until she has the meal as she wants it, all the chaff having blown away. The meal, being then ready to be mixed into dough, is stirred up with water in one of the pottery vessels. In the meantime a large clean flat stone has been tilted slantwise before the embers of a fire. When the dough is right it is poured out onto this stone and allowed to bake. These meal cakes constitute the native bread *kánlo*. Berries are thought to improve the flavor and are often mixed in with the dough. (Speck, 1909, p. 44.)

The method of making bread described by MacCauley is so tedious that it seems incredible any such system could have been employed unless on very special occasions.

The corn is hulled and the germ cut out, so that there is only a pure white residue. This is then reduced by mortar and pestle to an almost impalpable dust. From this flour a cake is made, which is said to be very pleasant to the taste. (MacCauley, 1887, p. 510.)

Parched corn ground into powder was extensively used because it would keep for a long time and was readily transported. We find three ways of preparing this mentioned by our authorities, and we do not know in every case to which of these a reference belongs or whether, indeed, one term may not at times have been applied to all. One of these makes its appearance only in the works of Louisiana writers, but it was probably used much more widely. It is "smoked-dried meal or meal dried in the fire and smoke, which, after being cooked, has the same taste as our small peas and is as sugary." (Dumont, 1753, pp. 32–34; Swanton, 1911, p. 74.)   Du Pratz specifically assures us that this dish originated with the Indians and he adds: "so far as smoke-dried little grain is concerned it pleases us as well as them." (Le Page du Pratz, 1758, vol. 2, pp. 3–6; Swanton, 1911, pp. 74–75.)

The other two styles are called ground meal (farine grôlée) and cold meal (farine froide) by the French, but only Romans throws any light on the distinction between them. After speaking of boiled meal as used among the Chickasaw, he continues:

. . . they also parch it, and then pound it; thus taking it on their journey, they mix it with cold water, and will travel a great way without any other food . . . they have also a way of drying and pounding their corn, before it comes to maturity; this they call *Boota Copassa* [i. e., cold flour]; this, in small quantities, thrown into cold water, boils and swells as much as common meal boiled over a fire; it is hearty food, and being sweet, they are fond of it; but as the process of making it is troublesome, their laziness seldom allows them to have it. (Romans, 1775, pp. 67–68.)

The latter is the bota kapássa of Byington. The former is probably what he calls bota laⁿshpa, meaning literally "heated corn" (Byington, 1915, p. 95). Mention of one or more of these dishes is made by the De Soto chroniclers under the term "pinole," by Hariot, San Miguel (Garcia, 1902, p. 197), Lawson, Romans, Adair, by writers on the Cusabo, by Laudonnière, by Dumont de Montigny, and by Du Pratz. The last of these gives us the best account, but before considering it it will be well to hear what Dumont de Montigny says about the use of corn in general in the Mississippi region, since Indian culture in the Southeast reached one of its highest levels there. After speaking of the three kinds of corn mentioned above he continues,

They can be prepared in 42 styles, each of which has its special name. It is useless for me to enter here in detail all the different ways in which maize may be treated. It is sufficient to inform the reader that there is made of it bread, porridge (*bouillie*), cold meal (*farine froide*), ground corn (*farine grôlée*), smoked-dried meal or meal dried in the fire and smoke, which when cooked has the same taste as our small peas and is as sugary. That is also made which is called gruel (*grut*), that is to say that having beaten and pounded it for some time in a wooden mortar, along with a little water, the skin or envelope with which it is covered is removed. The grain thus beaten and dried is transported to great distances and keeps perfectly. The finest of that left behind is used in making hominy (*sagamité*), which is a kind of porridge cooked with oil or meat. It is a very good and nourishing aliment. (Dumont, 1753, vol. 1, pp. 32–34, Swanton, 1911, pp. 74–75.)

Most of these have been discussed. It will be noticed that he calls the cold meal gruel (grut). And now for Du Pratz's description.

First, this grain is half cooked in water, then drained and well dried. When it is well dried, it is ground or scorched in a dish made expressly for the purpose, being mixed with ashes to keep it from burning, and it is moved incessantly in order to give it the red color which is proper. When it has assumed this color all the ashes are removed, it is rubbed well and placed in a mortar with ashes of dried bean plants and a little water. Then it is gently pounded, which makes the skin burst and reduces it completely to meal. This meal is crushed and dried in the sun. After this last operation this meal may be transported anywhere and kept for six months. It must be observed, however, that one ought not to forget to expose it to the sun from time to time. In order to eat it a vessel is filled with it a third full and the rest almost entirely with water, and at the end of some minutes the meal is found swollen and good to eat. It is very nourishing and is an excellent provision for travelers and for those who go trading, that is to say, to enter upon any negotiations. (Le Page du Pratz, 1758, vol. 2, pp. 5–6; Swanton, 1911, pp. 74–75.)

At the other end of the Gulf, and from a much later period, we find Skinner giving a similar description:

In parching corn, the kernels are placed in a kettle, the bottom of which is covered thickly with sand. The grains are stirred in the sand to keep them from burning. When sufficiently parched, the corn is crushed in a mortar, and, with the occasional addition of sugar, makes a delicious food. A little of the meal is sometimes added to water for use as a cooling drink. (Skinner, 1913, p. 77.)

The rest of Dumont's 42 dishes and Adair's 40 no doubt were prepared in part by mixing corn with other articles of food. A few such combinations have been mentioned already and notices of others may now be added.

According to Beverley the Virginians ate their bread by itself and not with meat, but they boiled both fish and flesh with their hominy. We have mentioned Romans' statement to the effect that the Choctaw boiled corn and beans together and mixed sunflower seed with corn meal to make bread. We have also noted the use of chestnuts with flour in the production of cakes wrapped in corn husks. This is reported by Adair and probably refers to the Chickasaw. The same Indians also cooked corn and venison in one dish.

As soon as the larger sort of corn is full-eared, they half-boil it too, and dry it either by the sun, or over a slow fire; which might be done, as well, in a moderately hot oven, if the heat was renewed as occasion required. This they boil with venison, or any other unsalted flesh. (Adair, 1775, p. 435.)

Hariot mentions the mixture of corn, beans, and peas in one dish in describing methods of treating the two former.

They make them victuall either by boyling them all to pieces into a broth; or boiling them whole vntill they bee soft and beginne to breake as is vsed in England, eyther by themselues or mixtly together: Sometime they mingle of the wheate [corn] with them. Sometime also beeing whole sodden, they bruse or pound them in a morter, & thereof make loaues or lumps of dowishe bread, which they vse to eat for varietie. (Hariot, 1893, p. 21.)

Smith and Strachey mention a dish of late unripened corn, roasted in hot ashes, and eaten boiled with beans during the ensuing winter. This dish was called pausarowmena or pausarawmena. Beverley

(1705, bk. 3, p. 14) says they ate all kinds of beans, peas, and other pulse both parched and boiled, and Lawson (1860, p. 337) that "the small red peas" were very common with the Indians of his acquaintance "and they eat a great deal of that and other sorts boiled with their meat or eaten with bear's fat." Du Pratz notes a Natchez dish called "co oëdlou" consisting of corn bread mixed with beans. Joutel found the Caddo raising many beans, but he adds that "they do not make much of a mystery in preparation of them." They placed them in a big pot without removing the strings and kept them covered with vine leaves until they were almost cooked. Before serving they poured warm water over them in which salt had been dissolved and those who partook of the meal were compelled to clean them for themselves as they ate. (Margry, 1875–86, vol. 3, pp. 394–395; Swanton, 1942, p. 132.)

References to methods of preparing pumpkins and squashes are few and short. Adair tells us that the old women raised them in their gardens at some distance from the towns along with melons, the latter of course imported, and this may mean that they were not planted in the communal fields. He adds:

When the pompions are ripe, they cut them into long circling slices, which they barbecue, or dry with a slow heat. (Adair, 1775, p. 407.)

Du Pratz describes how preserves were made out of one of the two varieties of pumpkin (giromons) cultivated by the Natchez, though the process may have been Creole rather than Indian.

For this purpose they are cut into the shapes of pears or other fruits and preserved thus with very little sugar, because they are naturally sweet. Those who are unacquainted with them are surprised to see entire fruits preserved without finding any seeds inside. The *giromons* are not only eaten preserved; they are also put into soups. Fritters (*bignets*) are made of them, they are fricasseed, they are cooked in the oven and under the embers, and in all ways they are good and pleasing. (Le Page du Pratz, 1758, vol. 2, p. 11; Swanton, 1911, p. 77.)

Strachey (1849, p. 119) tells us that the Virginia Indians "seeth a kind of *million* [presumably a pumpkin or squash], which they put into their walnut-milke, and so make a kynd of toothsome meat." Beverley is apparently speaking of the summer squash when he says of the vegetable known as macock, called squash or squanter-squash by the northern Indians,

these being boil'd whole when the Apple is young, and the Shell tender, and dished with Cream or Butter, relish very well with all sorts of Butcher's Meat, either fresh or salt. And whereas the Pompion is never eaten till it be ripe, these are never eaten after they are ripe. (Beverley, 1705, bk. 2, p. 27.)

Hariot gives the first description of the preparation of the China root or brier *Smilax* (the Choctaw kantak):

From these roots while they be new or fresh beeing chopt into small pieces & stampt, is strained with water a iuce that maketh bread, & also being boiled, a very good spoonemeate in maner of a gelly, and is much better in tast if it bee tempered with oyle. (Hariot, 1893, pp. 25–26.)

The account of Bartram is, however, fuller:

They dig up these roots, and while yet fresh and full of juice, chop them in pieces, and then macerate them well in wooden mortars; this substance they put in vessels nearly filled with clean water, when, being well mixed with paddles, whilst the finer parts are yet floating in the liquid, they decant it off into other vessels, leaving the farinaceous substance at the bottom, which, being taken out and dried, is an impalpable powder or farina, of a reddish color. This, when mixed in boiling water, becomes a beautiful jelly, which, sweetened with honey or sugar, affords a most nourishing food for children or aged people; or when mixed with fine corn flour, and fried in fresh bears grease, makes excellent *fritters*. (Bartram, 1792, p. 49.)

During a visit with some Creek Indians on St. Catherines Island, Oglethorpe and his companions were given "for Greens . . . the tops of China-Briars, which eat almost as well as asparagus." (Ga. Hist. Soc. Coll., 1840–78, vol. 4, p. 14, suppl.)

From the diary of Ethan Allen Hitchcock, Foreman quotes the following note regarding the treatment of kunti, and this is apparently the *Smilax*, and not the *Zamia*, though it occurs in the course of a discussion of the Seminole War:

They take the (kunti) root which is something like a turnip in appearance, tho' longer and larger; they scrape off the exterior, pound it, completely mashing it; put it into a bag and drain off the liquid; the liquor settling leaves a substance at the bottom which is the proper flour, the water being poured off. The flour is washed two or three times, settling each time, the water being poured off. The powder finally is then used as flour. (Foreman, 1932, p. 342.)

Almost the only description of the manner of reducing white kunti (*Zamia integrifolia*) roots to flour is given by MacCauley, who observed it among the Florida Seminole in 1880–81. The general method was probably as borrowed from the Calusa Indians and their allies:

White men call it the "Indian bread root," and lately its worth as an article of commerce has been recognized by the whites. There are now at least two factories in operation in Southern Florida in which Koonti is made into a flour for the white man's market. I was at one such factory at Miami and saw another near Orlando. I ate of a Koonti pudding at Miami, and can say that, as it was there prepared and served with milk and guava jelly, it was delicious. As might be supposed, the Koonti industry, as carried on by the whites, produces a far finer flour than that which the Indians manufacture. The Indian process, as I watched it at Horse Creek, was this: The roots were gathered, the earth was washed from them, and they were laid in heaps near the "Koonti log."

The Koonti log, so called, was the trunk of a large pine tree, in which a number of holes, about nine inches square at the top, their sides sloping downward to a point, had been cut side by side. Each of these holes was the property of some one of the squaws or of the children of the camp. For each of the holes, which were to serve as mortars, a pestle made of some hard wood had been furnished.

The first step in the process was to reduce the washed Koonti to a kind of pulp. This was done by chopping it into small pieces and filling with it one of the mortars and pounding it with a pestle. The contents of the mortar were then laid upon a small platform. Each worker had a platform. When a sufficient quantity of the root had been pounded the whole mass was taken to the creek near by and thoroughly saturated with water in a vessel made of bark.

The pulp was then washed in a straining cloth, the starch of the Koonti draining into a deer hide suspended below.

When the starch had been thoroughly washed from the mass the latter was thrown away, and the starchy sediment in the water in the deer skin left to ferment. After some days the sediment was taken from the water and spread upon palmetto leaves to dry. When dried, it was a yellowish white flour, ready for use. In the factory at Miami substantially this process is followed, the chief variation from it being that the Koonti is passed through several successive fermentations, thereby making it purer and whiter than the Indian product. Improved appliances for the manufacture are used by the white man.

The Koonti bread, as I saw it among the Indians, was of a bright orange color, and rather insipid, though not unpleasant to the taste. It was saltless. Its yellow color was owing to the fact that the flour had had but one fermentation. (MacCauley, 1887, pp. 513–516.)

Adair and Romans speak of the substitution of wild potatoes for bread, and the former adds that boiled potatoes were eaten mixed with bear's oil (Adair, 1775, p. 437). Hariot mentions a root, which seems to have been that of the wild sweetpotato, eaten raw or sometimes with fish or flesh. Groundnuts (*Apios tuberosa*) were "boiled or sodden". A plant cultivated in North Carolina and called melden, "a kind of orage," was eaten in the form of a broth or pottage besides being used as a salt. The *Dioscorea villosa* (*?*) roots and the *Ligusticum canadense* roots were boiled with other meats in the same region. The seed of a plant called Mettoume in Virginia, probably wild rice, was used for "a dainty bread buttered with deere suet." (See Hariot, 1893, p. 91.) The Creeks prepared a cake from the pulp of the passiflora or maypop (Romans, 1775, p. 94). Nelumbo seeds were made into a bread along with corn flour (Adair, 1775, p. 410), and in Louisiana at least a bread or porridge was prepared from the intermittent seed of a species of cane (Le Page du Pratz, 1758, vol. 2, pp. 58–59; Swanton, 1911, p. 76).

Tuckahoe bread appears to have been confined to the northeastern Algonquian sections and some of the adjacent Siouan territory. We have two good descriptions of the method in which it was prepared. To requote Hariot:

Being dressed according to the countrey maner, it maketh a good bread, and also a good sponemeate, and is vsed very much by the inhabitants: The iuce of this root is poison, and therefore heede must be taken before any thing be made therewithal: Either the rootes must bee first sliced and dried in the

Sunne, or by the fire, and then being pounded into floure wil make good bread; or els while they are greene they are to bee pared, cut into pieces and stampt; loues of the same to be laid neere or ouer the fire vntill it be floure, and then being well pounded againe, bread, or spone meate very good in taste, and holsome may be made thereof. (Hariot, 1893, p. 26.)

As usual Smith and Strachey nearly parallel each other, but the latter is a little fuller:

In one day a salvadge will gather sufficient for a weeke; these rootes are much of the greatness and tast of potatoes. They use to rake up a great nomber of them in old leaves and ferne, and then cover all with earth or sand, in the manner of a coal-pit; on each side they contynue a great fier a daie and a night before they dare eate yt: rawe, yt is no better than poison, and being roasted (except yt be tender and the heat abated, or sliced and dryed in the sun, mixed with sorrell and meale, or such like), yt will prickle and torment the throat extreamely, and yet in sommer they use this ordinarily for bread. (Strachey, 1849, p. 121.)

It is perhaps the berries of the same (*Peltandra virginica*) which appear under the name of Sacqvenvmmener in Hariot and Ocoughtanamnis in Smith. These were dried in summer and must be boiled a long time before being eaten, 8 or 9 hours according to Hariot (1893, pp. 27–28), half a day according to Smith (1907, p. 92), for they were poisonous otherwise.

Adair's remark that "they dry such kinds of fruit as will bear it" is applicable to the entire section, but before peaches were introduced into the country the greatest use was made of the persimmon. Dried persimmons, or persimmon bread, are constantly mentioned by the De Soto chroniclers under the name of *ameixas*. Du Pratz says regarding the use of this among the Natchez:

When [the persimmon] is well ripened the natives make bread of it, which keeps from one year to another, and the virtue of this bread, greater than that of fruit, is such that there is no diarrhea or dysentery which it does not arrest, but one ought to use it with prudence and only after being purged. In order to make this bread the natives scrape the fruit in very open sieves to separate the flesh from the skin and seeds. From this flesh, which is like thick porridge, and from the pulp they make loaves of bread 1½ feet long, 1 foot broad, and of the thickness of the finger, which they put to dry in the oven on a grill or, indeed, in the sun. In this latter fashion the bread preserves more of its taste. It is one of the merchandises which they sell to the French. (Le Page du Pratz, 1758, vol. 2, pp. 18–19; Swanton, 1911, p. 77.)

Hariot and Strachey mention persimmons but do not indicate how they were prepared for eating. Smith says that they cast the fruit "uppon hurdles on a mat, and preserve them as Pruines" (Smith, Tyler ed., 1907, pp. 90–91). Its use is mentioned among the Creeks, Chickasaw, and Choctaw.

The original "Indian peach" was probably introduced by the Spaniards, and peach trees were soon planted about most Indian towns of any consequence. Like the native plums and persimmons, the fruit was dried and seems to have supplanted all others in the estimation of the natives. The older Virginia writers are naturally silent regarding this fruit, but Beverley (1705, bk. 3, p. 15) says that peaches were dried in the sun, and Lawson mentions peaches frequently. In the Santee house he and his companions found, among other foods,

barbecued peaches, and peach bread, which peaches being made into a quiddony [see footnote 12, p. 278], and so made up into loaves like barley cakes, these cut into thin slices, and dissolved in water, makes a very grateful acid, and extraordinary beneficial in fevers, as has often been tried, and approved on by our English practitioners. (Lawson, 1860, pp. 36–37.)

Of the Saponi Indians, Lawson (1860, p. 85) purchased "a large peach loaf, made up with a pleasant sort of seed."

Catesby:

Peaches they dry in the sun for winter-use, and bake them in the form of loaves. *Phishimons*, whorts, and some other fruit and wild berries they also preserve for winter, using them in their soups and other ways. (Catesby, 1731–43, vol. 2, p. x.)

Hariot speaks of three sorts of nuts, apparently to be identified with chestnuts, walnuts, and hickory nuts, which he says

they vse to drie vpon hurdles made of reeds with fire vnderneath almost after the maner as we dry salt in England. When they are to be vsed they first water them vntil they be soft & then being sod they make a good victuall, either to eate so simply, or els being also pounded, to make loaues or lumpes of bread. (Hariot, 1893, p. 29.)

He adds that sweet oil was made from these, meaning probably the pawcohiscora, thus described by Smith.

The walnuts, Chesnuts, Acornes, and *Chechinquamens* are dryed to keepe. When they need them, they breake them betweene two stones, yet some part of the walnut shels will cleave to the fruit. Then doe they dry them againe upon a mat over a hurdle. After, they put it into a morter of wood, and beat it very small; that done, they mix it with water, that the shels may sinke to the bottome. This water will be coloured as milke; which they cal *Pawcohiscora*, and keepe it for their use. (Smith, Tyler ed., 1907, p. 90.)

Strachey (1849, p. 129) calls this pokahichory or powcohicora, but seems to indicate that it was derived from one variety of nut (perhaps *Juglans cinerea* L.) instead of many. And this seems to be confirmed by Beverley, who says:

In the woods, they gather Chincapins, Chesnuts, Hiccories, and Walnuts. The Kernels of the Hiccories they beat in a Mortar with Water, and make a White Liquor like Milk, from whence they call our Milk Hickory. (Beverley, 1705, bk. 3, p. 15.)

Probably hickory nuts, and acorns as we shall see presently, were used by preference, but the others on occasion. The usual treatment of chestnuts was to pound them into a meal and make a bread out of them, full strength or mixed with corn meal. As it happens, Hariot has more to say about the use of chestnuts as food than any subsequent writer:

Some they vse to eate rawe, some they stampe and boile to make spoone-meate, and with some being sodden they make such a manner of dowe bread as they vse of their beanes before mentioned. (Hariot, 1893, p. 26.)

Smith and Strachey tell us that of chestnuts and chinquapins boiled 4 or 5 hours the Virginia Indians made broth and bread for their chief men, or, as Strachey adds, to be used "at their greatest feasts" (Strachey, 1849, p. 118; Smith, 1907 ed., p. 90). The "Sapúmmener" of Hariot, which were boiled and parched and sometimes made into bread, were probably chinquapins (Hariot, 1893, p. 28). Ranjel mentions dried nuts, evidently chinquapins, in use among the natives of peninsula Florida (Bourne, 1904, vol. 2, pp. 70–71), and in 1701 Lawson found "good store of chinkapin nuts" among the Congaree Indians,

which they gather in winter great quantities of, drying them, so keep these nuts in great baskets for their use. Likewise hickerie nuts, which they beat betwixt two great stones, then sift them, so thicken their venison broth therewith, the small shells precipitating to the bottom of the pot, whilst the kernel, in form of flower, mixes it with the liquor, both these nuts made into meal makes a curious soup, either with clear water, or in any meat broth. (Lawson, 1860, p. 53.)

Generally speaking, chestnuts and chinquapins seem to have been used to make bread when used at all, and hickory nuts and acorns were utilized principally for their oil. Curiously enough, the French writers do not seem to mention this use of the hickory. In another place Lawson describes the various preparations made of this nut:

These nuts are gotten in great quantities, by the savages, and laid up for stores, of which they make several dishes and banquets. One of these I cannot forbear mentioning; it is this: they take these nuts, and break them very small betwixt two stones, till the shells and kernels are indifferent small; and this powder you are presented withal in their cabins, in little wooden dishes; the kernel dissolves in your mouth, and the shell is spit out. This tastes as well as any almond. Another dish is the soup which they make of these nuts, beaten, and put into venison broth, which dissolves the nut and thickens, whilst the shell precipitates, and remains at the bottom. This broth tastes very rich. (Lawson, 1860, p. 165.)

Adair also has a rather full description:

At the fall of the leaf, they gather a number of hiccory-nuts, which they pound with a round stone, upon a stone, thick and hollowed for the purpose. When they are beat fine enough, they mix them with cold water, in a clay bason, where the shells subside. The other part is an oily, tough, thick, white substance, called by the traders hiccory milk, and by the Indians the flesh, or fat of hiccory-nuts, with which they eat their bread. A hearty stranger would be apt to dip into the sediments as I did, the first time the vegetable thick milk was set before me. (Adair, 1775, p. 408.)

Hariot treats of hickory nuts and walnuts together as if both were utilized in the same way, but this may be accounted for by European ignorance of the hickory. He says:

Besides their eating of them after our ordinarie maner, they breake them with stones and pound them in morters with water to make a milk which they vse to put into some sorts of their spoonemeate; also among their sodde wheat, peaze, beanes and pompions which maketh them haue a farre more pleasant taste. (Hariot, 1893, p. 27.)

Bartram is our authority for the use of the "juglans exaltata, commonly called shell-barked hiccory," among the Creeks, remarking,

I have seen above an hundred bushels of these nuts belonging to one family. They pound them to pieces, and then cast them into boiling water, which, after passing through fine strainers, preserves the most oily part of the liquid; this they call by a name which signifies hiccory milk; it is as sweet and rich as fresh cream, and is an ingredient in most of their cookery, especially homony and corn cakes. (Bartram, 1940, p. 57.)

The Yuchi preserved hickory nuts (ya'), or rather hickory-nut oil, by pounding the nuts and boiling them in water until a milklike fluid was obtained, which was strained out and used as a beverage or a cooking ingredient (Speck, 1909, pp. 44–45).

As a source of vegetable oil, the acorn was next in importance to the hickory. Hariot (1893, p. 16) mentions "three seuerall kindes of *Berries* in the forme of Oke akornes, which also by the experience and vse of the inhabitantes, wee finde to yeelde very good and sweet oyle." One of these was called

Mangúmmenauk, and is the acorne of their kind of oake, the which being dried after the maner of the first sortes [chestnuts, walnuts, and hickories], and afterward watered they boile them & their seruants or sometime the chiefe themselues, either for variety or for want of bread, doe eate them with their fish or flesh. (Hariot, 1893, p. 29.)

Smith says:

the Acornes of one kind, whose barke is more white than the other, is somewhat sweetish; which being boyled halfe a day in seuerall waters, at last afford a sweete oyle, which they keep in goards to annoint their heads and joints. The fruit they eate, made in bread or otherwise. (Smith, Tyler ed., 1907, p. 90.)

Lawson uses similar language:

The Indians beat them [acornes] into meal and thicken their venison broth with them, and oftentimes make a palatable soup. They are used instead of bread, boiling them till the oil swims on the top of the water, which they preserve for use, eating the acorns with flesh meat. (Lawson, 1860, p. 80.)

Further on he pays particular attention to the use of live-oak acorns:

The acorns thereof are as sweet as chestnuts, and the Indians draw an oil from them, as sweet as that from the olive, though of an amber color. . . . I knew two trees of this wood among the Indians, which were planted from the acorns, and grew in the freshies, and never saw anything more beautiful of that kind. (Lawson, 1860, p. 156.)

Romans mentions their use among the Creeks, and Bartram (1909, p. 90), referring to the Southeastern Indians of his acquaintance, remarks that they "obtain from it a sweet oil, which they use in the cooking of hommony, rice, &c.; and they also roast it in hot embers, eating it as we do chestnuts."

When San Miguel and his companions were wrecked upon the Guale coast in 1595 they were given, among other things, "lumps of acorn cake, yellow and red, which are rough and bitter," and in consequence they were unable to eat them, but it appears that the Indians had more of this than of corncake (Garcia, 1902, pp. 189, 197).

There is singularly little mention of the pecan as distinguished from other nuts, though Du Pratz describes the tree with considerable care. Speaking of a point on the east bank of the Mississippi near which De Soto crossed the river, a point somewhere below Helena, Ark., Biedma says:

There we first found a little walnut of the country, which is much better than that here in Spain. (Bourne, 1904, vol. 2, p. 25.)

This is supposed to be a reference to the pecan.

Extraction of sugar from the sugar maple is mentioned by Beverley, Lawson, Adair, and Benjamin Hawkins, but the remarks of Beverley and Adair are very general and might apply to Indians inside or outside of the section. However, Adair's contacts with Indians were almost entirely with those in the South. He notes that "several of the Indians produce sugar out of the sweet maple-tree, by making an incision, draining the juice, and boiling it to a proper Consistence" (Adair, 1775, p. 414). Beverley (1705, bk. 2, p. 21) informs us that "the *Indians* make One Pound of Sugar, out of Eight Pounds of the Liquor." The section is not indicated, but the following quotations have reference to sugar making in the Southeast itself without much question. The first is from Lawson:

The Indians tap it (the sugar maple) and make gourds to receive the liquor, which operation is done at distinct and proper times, when it best yields its juice, of which, when the Indians have gotten enough, they carry it home, and boil it to a just consistency of sugar, which grains of itself, and serves for the same uses, as other sugar does. (Lawson, 1860, p. 174.)

Benjamin Hawkins was an eyewitness to the process among the Cherokee on Limestone Creek in northern Georgia:

On this creek, the sugar is made by the Indian women, they use small wooden troughs, and earthen pans to ketch the sap, and large earthen pots for boilers. (Hawkins, 1916, p. 24.)

Smith (Tyler ed., 1907, p. 95) and Strachey (1849, p. 117) tell us that the Virginia Indians of the tidewater country used to suck green cornstalks for the sweetness in them, and there is reference to a similar use of native cane before sugarcane was introduced. This is in the report of Edward Blande and his companions of their exploration of "New Brittaine," northeastern North Carolina. They state that the land composing the islands of the Occaneechi and Tutelo Indians in Roanoke River

consists all of exceeding rich Land, and cleare fields, wherein growes Canes of a foot about, and of one yeares growth Canes that a reasonable hand can hardly span; and the Indians told us they were very sweet, and that at some time of the yeare they did suck them, and eate them, and of those we brought some away with us. (Alvord, 1912, p. 124.)

At a relatively late period the Florida Seminole learned how to extract syrup and sugar from the sugarcane, and the crude method used by them in 1880–81 is described by MacCauley (1887, pp. 511–512) but need not be reproduced.

TREATMENT OF MEATS

(Plate 54)

Regarding the cookery of the native Virginians, particularly the treatment of meats, Beverley says tersely:

Their Cookery has nothing commendable in it, but that it is perform'd with little trouble. They have no other Sauce but a good Stomach, which they seldom want. They boil, broil, or tost [i. e., roast] all the Meat they eat. (Beverley, 1705, bk. 3, p. 13.)

His reference to the absence of a sauce requires modification but he is quite right in laying stress on the universality of the cooking process. They were so disinclined to raw meats that Adair (1775, p. 135) tells us the Indians of his acquaintance overdressed all of them. Du Pratz affirms:

They never eat raw meat, as so many persons have falsely imagined. Even in Europe we have entire kingdoms which do not give their meats as much time to cook as the natives of Louisiana allow to the most delicate morsels of bison, which is their principal nourishment. (Le Page du Pratz, 1758, vol. 3, p. 12; Swanton, 1911, p. 73.)

Their manner of dressing meat left much to be desired from our point of view, so far as the smaller animals were concerned. Lawson (1860, p. 92) says that the Keyauwee Indians regaled some of his companions with "one of the country hares, stewed with the guts in her belly, and her skin with the hair on," adding that "the Indians dress most things after the woodcock fashion, never taking the guts out." He seems to mention among animals treated that way the "bear and bever, panther, polecat, wild cat, possum, raccoon, hares, and squirrels," though it is somewhat uncertain whether the first mentioned belongs in this category (Lawson, 1860, p. 292). Catesby (1713–43, vol. 2, p. x) adds turkeys. However, on the same occasion, Lawson's companions were provided with "a dish in great fashion amongst the Indians, which was two young fawns taken out of the does' bellies, and boiled in the same slimy bags nature had placed them in." (Lawson, 1860, pp. 92, 292; Catesby, 1731–48, vol. 2, p. x.)

On their cookery in general, "they boil and roast their meat extraordinary much, and eat abundance of broth, except the savages whom we call the naked Indians," supposed to be the Miami and believed to owe their speed in running to their abstinence in this particular (Lawson, 1860, p. 362).

On the southeast coast of Florida the fish brought to Dickenson and his companions in 1699 were "boiled with the scales, heads, and gills, and nothing taken from them but the guts" (Dickenson, 1803, p. 36; Swanton, 1922, p. 392).

Before squirrels were cooked the Alabama Indians rolled them over and over in a bed of hot ashes to take off their hair and render them more tender.

The flesh of deer, bison, and turkeys, as well as fish and oysters, was roasted and boiled. An early Virginia document (1687) mentions "a piece of Venison barbecued, that is wrapped up in leaves and roasted in the embers" (Bushnell, 1907, p. 44).

The manner of their roasting, is by thrusting sticks through pieces of meat, sticking them around the fire, and often turning them. (Catesby, 1731–43, vol. 2, p. x.)

White illustrates the process of boiling and the broiling of fish (pl. 54, fig. 2).

By the Florida Seminole,

turtles are not infrequently roasted before the fire. The Indians seldom take the trouble to kill the unfortunate reptiles before commencing to prepare them for food—they merely cut off the plastron and butcher the animal alive and kicking, when it is set up before the fire and roasted in its own oven. (Skinner, 1913, pp. 76–77.)

The following is from Du Pratz:

When the natives wish to roast meat in order to eat it at once, which seldom happens except during the hunting season, they cut off the portion of bison which they wish to eat, which is usually the fillet. They put it on the end of a wooden spit planted in the earth and inclined toward the fire. They take care to turn this spit from time to time, which cooks the meat as well as a spit turned before the fire with much regularity. (Le Page du Pratz, 1758, vol. 3, pp. 10–12; Swanton, 1911, p. 72.)

The tongues and humps of these animals, the tongues of deer, and the tails of beaver were esteemed great delicacies.

Romans (1775, p. 94) mentions corned venison in use among the Creeks, but this device was probably introduced by white traders. The native way of preserving meats was by drying.

Speaking of the Yuchi of 30 or 40 years ago, Speck says:

The flesh of game mammals, birds, *kändī'*, fish, *cū*, were roasted or boiled on a framework of green sticks resting on cross pieces which were supported on forked uprights over the fire. The device was simply a stationary broiling frame. (Speck, 1909, p. 45.)

A favorite method of cleaning fish the instant they are caught, is to draw out the intestines with a hook through the anus, without cutting the fish open. A cottonwood stick shaved of its outer bark is then inserted in the fish from tail to head. The whole is thickly covered with mud and put in the embers of a fire. When the mud cracks off the roast is done and ready to eat. The cottonwood stick gives a much-liked flavor to the flesh. (Speck, 1909, p. 24.)

Through Bartram we hear of "a very singular dish" which the traders in his time called "tripe soup."

It is [he goes on to say] made of the belly or paunch of the beef, not over-cleansed of its contents, cut and minced pretty fine, and then made into a thin soup, seasoned well with salt and aromatic herbs; but the seasoning not quite strong enough to extinguish its original savour and scent. This dish is greatly esteemed by the Indians, but is, in my judgment, the least agreeable they have amongst them. (Bartram, 1909, p. 185.)

Catesby contributes the following:

At their festivals they make some compound dishes, which, as I have often partook of, the following may serve as a specimen of their cookery. They stew the lean of venison till little liquor remains, which is supplied with marrow out of their deer's bones; to which is added, the milky pulp of *Maiz* before it hardens. (Catesby, 1731–43, vol. 2, p. x.)

"Their meat," says Barlowe, speaking of the North Carolina coast Indians, "is very well sodden and they make broth very sweet and savorie" (Burrage, 1906, p. 236). Strachey tells us that "the broath of fish or flesh they suppe up as ordinarily as they eat the meate," and that "the salvages use to boyle oysters and mussells together, and with the broath they make a good spoonemeat, thickened with the flower of their wheat" (Strachey, 1849, pp. 72, 127). Combinations of flesh or fish with other foods were common and some of these have already been noted. Beverley (1705, bk. 3, p. 13) says: "It is very common with them to boil Fish as well as Flesh with their Homony." And Lawson (1860, p. 336): "The small red peas is very common with them, and they eat a great deal of that and other sorts boiled with their meat or eaten with bear's fat." Romans (1775, p. 92) mentions "venison and hominy cooked together" by the Creeks, and Catesby tells us that

It is common with some nations at great entertainments, to boil bear, deer, panther, or other animals, together in the same pot; they take out the bones, and serve up the meat by itself, then they stew the bones over again in the same liquor, adding thereto purslain and squashes, and thicken it with the tender grain of *Maiz*, this is a delicious soup. (Catesby, 1731–43, vol. 2, p. x.)

Nevertheless, there were taboos against certain mixtures, as Byrd was made aware of by his Saponi Indian hunter, who admonished him and his companions "with a face full of concern, that if we continued to boil Venison and Turkey together, we Shou'd for the future kill nothing, because the Spirit that presided over the Woods would drive all the Game out of our Sight," it being improper to cook "the Beasts of the Field and the Birds of the Air together in one vessel" (Bassett, 1901, pp. 178, 194).

The following experience, reported by Lawson, informs us how it was usual to treat previously dried meat on short notice. He and his companions were treated

with a fat barbecued venison, which the woman of the cabin took and tore in pieces with her teeth, so put it into a mortar, beating it to rags, afterwards stews it with water, and other ingredients, which makes a very savoury dish. (Lawson, 1860, p. 37.)

Romans (1775, pp. 68, 94) speaks of dried deer tongues among the Creeks and of dried deer and bison meat among this and neighboring tribes, but he considers them tasteless.

Strachey (1849, p. 113) mentions "deare's suet made up handsomely in cakes" to be melted later, presumably, and mixed with their other food. There is mention also of fish grease employed to take the place of butter by the Florida Indians (Gaffarel, 1875, p. 462; Swanton, 1922, p. 359), and the oil of passenger pigeons for the same purpose in Carolina (Lawson, 1860, p. 79) and probably elsewhere; it was used with breadstuffs and sometimes with meats as well.

To quote Catesby again,

The pigeons . . . afford them some years great plenty of oil, which they preserve for winter use; this and sometimes bears fat they eat with bread, with it they also supply the want of fat in wild turkeys, which in some winters become very lean by being deprived of their food, by the numerous flights of the migratory pigeons devouring the acorns, and other mast. (Catesby, 1731–43, p. x.)

The Creeks, after pounding up their dried venison, dipped it in salty "moss obtained from the stream beds in their country after the moss had been dissolved in water." (Hawkins, 1916, pp. 31, 37).

The most important "sauce," or rather gravy, was made from bear fat. Incidental mention of this has already been made. The bear was, in fact, valued for its fat rather than for its flesh. Dumont de Montigny says that a bear must be thin for the Louisiana Indians to use its flesh.

In any other condition only the four feet can be eaten. The rest is nothing but fat. (Dumont, 1753, vol. 1, p. 76; Swanton, 1911, p. 69.)

Du Pratz tells us that "the natives put the flesh and the fat of the bear to cook together so that they may detach themselves from each other." This was done either in earthen pots of their own manufacture or in kettles bought of the traders. "When this grease or oil is lukewarm they put it into a *faon* [deerskin bottle]" (Le Page du Pratz, 1758, vol. 2, pp. 86–89; Swanton, 1911, p. 69).

A little later we discover via Romans (1775, p. 68) that "the traders have learned [!] them [the Chickasaw] to make [the flesh of bears] into bacon exactly resembling that of a hog."

Adair did not observe such treatment of bear meat by this tribe in his time, remarking that,

The traders commonly make bacon of the bears in winter; but the Indians mastly flay off a thick tier of fat which lies over the flesh, and the latter they cut up into small pieces, and thrust on reeds, or suckers of sweet-tested hiccory or sassafras, which they barbecue over a slow fire. The fat they fry into clear well-tasted oil, mixing plenty of sassafras and wild cinnamon with it over the fire, which keeps sweet from one winter to another, in large earthen jars, covered in the ground. It is of a light digestion, and nutritive to hair. All who are acquainted with its qualities, prefer it to any oil, for any use whatsoever: smooth Florence is not to be compared in this respect to rough America. (Adair, 1775, p. 415.)

The salvages [of Virginia] [says Strachey] use to boyle oysters and mussells togither and with the broaths they make a good spoone meat, thickened with the flower of their wheat; and yt is a great thrift and husbandry with them to hang the oysters upon strings (being shauld and dried) in the smoake, thereby to preserve them all the yeare. (Strachey, 1849, p. 127.)

These oysters were among the articles with which these Indians traded (Smith, Tyler ed., 1907, p. 10).

Adair (1775, p. 412) notes that the Chickasaw always boiled hens' eggs very hard.

There seems to be no reference to cooking in baskets, but a farmer of Polk County, Tex., with whom I stayed during part of my work among the Alabama Indians, gave his father as authority for the assertion that, in his time, the Indians often boiled water and cooked their food in deerskins. The skin was held up at the four corners to such a height above the flames that they touched only that part of it over which there was water. In his own time the Alabama always boiled their meats in pots, or sometimes, when there was to be a feast, in a large tub.

PRESERVATION OF FOOD

(Plate 55)

Both vegetable and animal food was treated in such a manner that it could be preserved for long periods of time, usually, if sufficient forethought were exercised, until spring.

It is well known that corn was preserved in granaries by most, if not all, of the tribes in the section, and it was, in fact, these granaries or corncribs, called by the Spaniards from a Haitian Arawak word "barbacoas," which made the De Soto expedition possible. Without condoning the actions of the explorers in appropriating as of patent right the products of the Indians' labor, we may nevertheless be thankful for the knowledge of these Indians which the use of that corn has enabled us to obtain. We learn from them that corn was not only put away dried as it came from the field, but quantities were ground and preserved in that manner. The Spaniards called this pinol or pinole. As we have seen, this was the "cold meal" of later French and English settlers, and was used particularly when the Indians were on war expeditions or traveling for more peaceful purposes. Besides dried corn, the Spaniards found the well-known cakes made of dried persimmons (which the chroniclers call *ameixas*).[24] The notices are most numerous in towns along the Mississippi River. Elvas notes also dried plums in Apalachee (Bourne, 1904, vol. 1., p. 47), and Garcilaso (1902, pp. 49, 82, 221) speaks of dried plums and also of grapes and other dried fruits. In his case the plums may have been persimmons, but we know that plums were also dried. In the case of grapes, however, our evidence is not so good. Unless grapes are included in the general statements of some writers that they dried all kinds of fruits that would bear it (Lawson, 1860, p. 290; Adair, 1775, p. 439), there is no other reference to the treatment of them in this way. As soon as peaches were introduced they were dried and put away like plums and persimmons. Lawson was served dried peaches by the Congaree and bought "a large peach loaf" from the Saponi, and he says the Indians dried huckleberries on mats (Lawson, 1860, pp. 53, 85, 173). One of the De Soto chroniclers also mentions finding dried chinquapins (Bourne, 1904, vol. 2, pp. 70–71) and nuts, and the oil from them was stored throughout the region. Speaking mainly of the inland Siouan tribes, Lawson (1860, pp. 337–338) says that during their winter hunts

the wild fruits which are dried in the summer, over fires, on hurdles and in the sun, are now brought into the field; as are likewise the cakes and quiddonies of peaches, and that fruit and bilberries dried, of which they stew and make fruit bread and cakes.

The way in which persimmon bread was prepared and stored has been described above (p. 363).

Adair speaks thus regarding the artificial drying of corn, potatoes, and pumpkins:

When the pompions are ripe, they cut them into long circling slices, which they barbecue, or dry with a slow heat. And when they have half boiled the larger

---

[24] Bourne, 1904, vol. 1, pp. 47, 114, 143, 145, 149, 152; Robertson, 1933, translates the word "plums."

sort of potatoes, they likewise dry them over a moderate fire, and chiefly use them in the spring-season mixt with their favourite bear's oil. As soon as the larger sort of corn is full-eared, they half-boil it too, and dry it either by the sun, or over a slow fire; which might be done, as well, in a moderately hot oven, if the heat were renewed as occasion required. (Adair, 1775, p. 438.)

Du Pratz speaks of preserving pumpkins, but his account may refer rather to creole customs than to those of Indians (Le Page du Pratz, 1758, vol. 2, p. 11; Swanton, 1911, p. 77; see above, p. 360). Lawson appears to be the only writer to mention definitely the preservation and storage of beans or peas.

They plant a great many sorts of pulse, part of which they eat green in the summer, keeping great quantities for their winter's store, which they carry along with them into the hunting quarters and eat them. (Lawson, 1860, p. 337).

Mention is made of dried venison in the De Soto narratives (Bourne, 1904, vol. 2, pp. 79, 99) and this was a customary means of preserving the flesh of the deer, bison, and bear throughout the Gulf region. Speaking particularly of the Natchez, Du Pratz says:

That the meat may keep during the time they are hunting and that it may serve as nourishment for their families for a certain time, the men during the chase have all the flesh of the thighs, shoulders, and most fleshy parts smoked, except the hump and the tongue, which they eat on the spot. All the meat that is smoked is cut into flat pieces to cook it well. It is not cut too thin, however, for fear lest it dry up too much. The grill is on four fairly strong forked sticks and poles above a foot apart and above these canes 4 inches apart. This grill is raised about 3 feet above the earth, in order that one may be able to put a fire made of large sticks of wood underneath. They turn the meat and withdraw it only when it is cooked to such a degree that the upper side is roasted and very dry. Then they take off what is cooked and put other pieces on. Thus they smoke their meat, which can be carried everywhere and preserved as long as it is desired. (Le Page du Pratz, 1758, vol. 3, p. 11; Swanton, 1911, p. 72.)

Catesby:

Besides roasting and boiling, they *barbecue* most of the flesh of the larger animals, such as buffalo's, bear and deer; this is performed very gradually, over a slow clear fire, upon a large wooden gridiron, raised two feet above the fire. By this method of curing venison it will keep good five or six weeks, and by its being divested of the bone, and cut into portable pieces, adapts it to their use, for the more easy conveyance of it from their hunting quarters to their habitations. Fish is also thus preserved for the better conveyance of it from the maritime to the inland countries. (Catesby, 1731–43, vol. 2, p. x.)

Jackson Lewis, one of my best Creek informants, described as follows the manner in which deer meat was preserved:

They first made an incision down the middle of the deer's belly and then stripped the body meat off of the bones from front to back. The resulting piece was large and flat. It was dried in the sun, and as others were dried they were made into a pile, which was carried back to the village on the back of a pony. The thighs were treated in this way. First the long bones were removed, and then the meat was cut up into chunks somewhat larger than baseballs. Withes or sticks were passed through these and they were placed over a fire until nearly cooked, by which time the meat had shrunk to about the size of a baseball. It had also shrunk away from the stick leaving a large hole, and by means of these holes a great many such chunks of meat were strung together for transportation. The meat of 10 deer was all that could be gotten upon 1 horse. Bartram (1909, pp. 242–243) mentions meeting an Indian family having horses loaded down with meat so prepared. If a hunter had no ponies, he and his family, according to another informant, could carry home from 300 to 500 pounds of meat.

Charlie Thompson, afterward made chief of the Alabama Indians in Texas, gave a slightly different account. According to him one piece was made of the ribs and the flesh adhering to them, a thin, flat piece was stripped off of the ribs and breast, and two separate pieces were made of the loins and thighs. Sticks were run through these and they were placed on a low scaffold about 3 feet high and 3–4 feet each way, where they were roasted. Sometimes a much higher scaffold was used, depending probably upon the weather and the size of the fire. Pieces intended for immediate consumption might be impaled on a single stick over the fire, the other end of the stick being planted in the ground. The dried meat was strung together and carried home from camp packed on either side of the hunter's horse along with the deerhides, the hunter himself walking and driving the animal. Finally, the meat was stored in the corncrib, where it would usually keep for an entire year. If it had not been dried sufficiently, screwworms would breed in it. (From what I was told by some old white settlers, however, it would appear that the Indians did not have insuperable objections to wormy meat.) When dried venison was to be eaten, it was washed, pounded in a mortar, mixed with bear's grease, and partaken of with bread.

If deer were very plentiful, they sometimes threw away the ribs, shoulders, and other less desirable cuts, and occasionally are said to have hunted the deer for their hides alone, but on other occasions they might eat even the marrow and liver. When an unusually large number of deer had been killed, or there was to be a special feast at the ballground, they would sometimes string the tongues and hearts by themselves on cords of bass fiber (bàkca).

Jackson Lewis remembered that bison meat was cut into squares about a foot and a half each way and 2 inches thick, and dried on a scaffold over a fire. In preserving this meat, they sometimes made use of the salt on the salt plains (the Cimarron). The flesh of the young bison and the cows was most desired. It is claimed that a bison calf would sometimes mistake a horse for a cow and follow it all the way back to camp.

Adair is the only writer who gives us much of an idea of the way in which bear meat was preserved. His words have been quoted already (p. 372) (Adair, 1775, p. 446).

But bears were valued mainly for their fat and Adair's description of the Chickasaw treatment of this has also been given. In his time they put it "in large earthen jars, covered in the ground" (op. cit.), but it was also put away in skin receptacles and De Soto's army was treated to bear fat taken out of calabashes (Robertson, 1933, p. 104; Bourne, 1904, vol. 1, p. 74). Du Pratz describes at greatest length the method of putting up bear fat in deerskins. Having killed a deer

they begin by cutting off its head, then skin the neck, rolling the skin as one would a stocking, and cut up the flesh and bones as fast as they advance. This operation is necessarily laborious because they have to take out all the flesh and the bones through the skin of the neck in order to make a sack of its skin. They cut it as far as the hams and other places where there are outlets. When the skin is entirely empty they scrape it and clean it. Then they make a kind of cement with the fat of the same deer and a few fine ashes. They put it around the orifices which they close very tightly with the bark of the bass tree and leave only the neck through which to cask the bear's oil. It is this which the French call a *faon* of oil. The natives put the flesh and the fat to cook together so that they may detach themselves from each other. They do this cooking in earthen pots of their own manufacture, or in kettles if they have them. When this grease or oil is lukewarm they put it into the *faon*.

They come to trade this kind of oil to the French for a gun or ell of cloth or similar things. That was the price of a *faon* of oil at the time when I lived there. But the French use it only after having purified it. (Le Page du Pratz, 1758, vol. 2, pp. 88–89; Swanton, 1911, p. 69.)

Frames were set up over the fire on which the meat was dried. Le Moyne says of these:

In order to keep these animals longer they are in the habit of preparing them as follows: They set up in the earth four stout forked stakes; and on these they lay others, so as to form a sort of grating. On this they lay their game, and then build a fire underneath, so as to harden it in the smoke. In this process they use a great deal of care to have the drying perfectly performed, to prevent the meat from spoiling, as the picture shows. I suppose this stock to be laid in for their winter's supply in the woods, as at that time we could never obtain the least provision from them. (Le Moyne, 1875, pp. 9–10 (illus.); Swanton, 1922, p. 358.)

The picture in question (pl. 55) shows a scaffold with several fish on it, a deer, an alligator—or possibly a lizard, for Le Challeux tells us that lizards were eaten—a snake, and some quadruped about the size of a dog, all placed there without any previous dressing. The varieties of food placed in the granaries are indicated by the descriptions preserved to us by Le Moyne in other places. He speaks of the storage of wild vegetable products gathered "twice a year" into granaries such as are to be described presently. (Also cf. Catesby, p. 374 above.)

Here is what he says of the storage of animal food:

> At a set time every year they gather in all sorts of wild animals, fish, and
> even crocodiles; these are then put in baskets, and loaded upon a sufficient
> number of the curly-haired hermaphrodites above mentioned, who carry them
> on their shoulders to the storehouse. This supply, however, they do not resort
> to unless in case of the last necessity. (Le Moyne, 1875, p. 9 (illus.); Swan-
> ton, 1922, p. 361.)

The last were public granaries, but it seems probable that both
kinds of food were gathered into both public and family storehouses.

These statements made by Smith and Strachey lead us to think that
the Powhatan Indians had not been in the habit of providing for the
future as much as the southern tribes generally, and that influences
from farther south came to them by way of the seacoast.

Strachey:

> Powhatan and some others that are provident, roast their fish and flesh upon
> hurdells, and reserve of the same untill the scarse tymes; commonly the fish
> and flesh they boyle, either very tenderly, or broyle yt long on hurdells over
> the fier, or ells (after the Spanish fashion) putt yt on a spitt and turne first
> the one side, then the other, till yt be as dry as their jerkin beef in the West
> Indies, and so they maye keepe yt a monethe or more without putrifying.
> (Strachey, 1849, p. 73.)

Smith (1907 ed., p. 355) remarks that the people of the eastern
shore "provide Corne to serve them all the yeare, yet spare; and the
other not halfe the year, yet want." Powhatan Indians came to trade
with Newport's party, bringing "basketes full of Dryed oysters"
(Smith, Arber ed., 1884, p. xlii).

Dumont de Montigny provides us with the following descriptions
of the method by which oysters were preserved by some of the Gulf
tribes and fish by those on the Mississippi, particularly the Natchez:

> The Colapissas and Paskagoulas . . . who live near the sea have a sure
> method of preserving oysters without spoiling for a very long time, and this
> method deserves so much the more to be recorded, since they use in it neither
> pepper, nor salt, nor viniger.
>
> When the sea is low and allows these savages the liberty of laying in a
> supply of oysters, they go to fill up their dugouts, and afterwards, having
> withdrawn to the bank, they open them and put them into a bowl. While
> one part of these savages is occupied in this work, others light a fire, and place
> on opposite sides two forked sticks planted in the earth, on which there is a
> crosspiece which holds the handle of a kettle hung above the fire. Then they
> put all of their oysters into this kettle, and make them boil slightly until they
> are partly cooked, after which they remove them, and throw them into a
> basket or big sieve, in order that all of the water may drain out. During that
> time, they construct a kind of grill of four forked sticks planted in the ground
> and four sticks placed crosswise on which they place pieces of cane. After-
> ward, having spread their oysters on this grill, they make a fire underneath,
> and by this means bucan or smoke them, thus drying them and giving them a
> yellow and golden color. After having smoked them on one side in this man-
> ner, they turn them over in order to treat the other side similarly, and they

continue this operation until all that they have collected are bucanned. Then they put them in jars or in sacks which they hang from a nail after their return to their village, taking care to place them in a dry spot, and one not exposed to the heat. Seeing these oysters in this condition one would take them for the common beans on which are fed the crews of our vessels. When they wish to serve them, they begin by putting them to soak in fresh water for an hour. Afterwards the water is changed and they are cooked. After that, whether one eats them as sauce with chickens, fried, or as dough made into fritters, they are equally good and never smell of the smoke. During a long time I saw the Sieur de la Garde, director of the concession of M. de Chaumont, established on the river of the Paskagoulas, lay in a great supply of these oysters thus prepared. He bought them from the savages, and served them to his friends as a luxury. (Dumont, 1753, vol. 2, pp. 273–276.)

The savages living on the upper part of the river (Mississippi), and in districts far from the sea, not having the good fortune to be supplied with oysters, make use of the very same method to keep carps, which they do for a very long time. There is only this difference that the grill they use in bucanning this fish is raised only one foot above the earth. I saw this secret method employed by the Natchez where the carps caught are very fine and very fat. (Dumont, 1753, vol. 2, p. 276.)

Dumont further suggests that the Louisiana French might have adopted their own procedure in drying grapes, at least in part, from the Indians. From the early writers I have only one or two very general references to the drying of grapes, but if Speck's Yuchi informants who supplied the following notes regarding the preservation of food reproduced truly aboriginal customs, Dumont may be correct:

When large hauls of fish were made, by using vegetable poison in streams in the manner described, or more game was taken than was needed for immediate use, it is said that the surplus flesh was artificially dried over a slow smoky fire or in the sun, so that it could be laid away against the future. Crawfish, tcatsá, were very much liked and quantities of them were also treated for preservation in the above manner.

Wild fruits and nuts in their proper seasons added variety to the comparatively well supplied larder of the natives. Berries, yäbä', were gathered and dried to be mixed with flour or eaten alone. Wild grapes, cä, were abundant. The Indians are said to have preserved them for use out of season by drying them on frames over a bed of embers until they were like raisins, in condition to be stored away in baskets. (Speck, 1909, p. 45.)

Native storehouses were used, not only for storing corn, beans, pumpkins, and dried fruits and meats, but for less ephemeral kinds of property, and the great storehouses of Powhatan at Orapaks and of the Lady of Cofitachequi on the Savannah were assembled about temples, presumably in order that fear of sacrilege might be added to more external kinds of protection. Our first description of one of these buildings is by the Fidalgo of Elvas:

They have barbacoas in which they keep their maize. These are houses raised up on four posts, timbered like a loft, and the floor of canes. (Robertson, 1933, p. 75; Bourne, 1904, vol. 1, p. 53.)

According to Strachey, the storehouses of the Powhatan common-alty seem to have been holes in the ground:

> Their corne and (indeed) their copper, hatchetts, howses [hoes], beades, perle, and most things with them of value, according to their owne estymacion, they hide, one from the knowledge of another, in the growned within the woodes, and so keepe them all the yeare, or untill they have fitt use for them, as the Romains did their monies and treasure in certaine cellars, called, therefore, as Plinye remembers, *favissae*; and when they take them forth, they scarse make their women privie to the storehowse. (Strachey, 1849, p. 113.)

Among the Creeks and the more eastern tribes a lounging room, often on the second floor, occupied part of the storehouse.   Thus Bartram says it was

> commonly two stories high, and divided into two apartments, transversely, the lower story of one end being a potato house, for keeping such other roots and fruits as require to be kept close, or defended from cold in winter. The chamber over it is the *council*. At the other end of this building, both upper and lower stories are open on their sides: the lower story serves for a shed for their saddles, pack-saddles, and gears, and other lumber; the loft over it is a very spacious, airy, pleasant pavilion, where the chief of the family reposes in the hot seasons, and receives his guests, etc. [He adds that the Seminole had a storehouse] two stories high, of the same construction, and serving the same purpose with the granary or provision house of the Upper Creeks [i. e., the Creeks proper]. (Bartram, 1909, p. 56.)

There is a striking similarity between these private storehouses of the Creeks and Seminole and the "summer council house" of the Cherokee as described by the same writer:

> Their Summer Council House is a spacious open loft or pavilion, on the top of a very large oblong building. (Bartram, 1909, p. 57.)

The storehouse of the Chickasaw is said by Romans (1775, p. 67) to have been in the shape of "an oblong square," and was probably almost identical with that of the Creeks.

When we come to the Siouan tribes of the east we find the lounging room or "council" of Bartram in a different building from the granary. Lawson calls this condition usual among the tribes with which he was familiar. He gives the following particular description of a Santee storehouse:

> These Santee Indians . . . . . make themselves cribs after a very curious manner, wherein they secure their corn from vermin, which are more frequent in these warm climates than countries more distant from the sun. These pretty fabrics are commonly supported with eight feet or posts about seven feet high from the ground, well daubed within and without upon laths, with loam or clay, which makes them tight and fit to keep out the smallest insect, there being a small door at the gable end, which is made of the same composition, and to be removed at pleasure, being no bigger than that a slender man may creep in at, cementing the door up with the same earth when they take corn out of the crib, and are going from home, always finding their granaries in the same posture they left them—theft to each other being altogether unpracticed, never receiving spoils but from foreigners. (Lawson, 1860, p. 35.)

Of the Timucua granaries there seems to be but a single account, by Le Moyne:

There are in that region a great many islands, producing abundance of various kinds of fruits, which they gather twice a year, and carry home in canoes, and store up in roomy low granaries built of stones and earth, and roofed thickly with palm-branches and a kind of soft earth fit for the purpose. These granaries are usually erected near some mountain, or on the bank of some river, so as to be out of the sun's rays, in order that the contents may keep better. Here they also store up any other provisions which they may wish to preserve, and the remainder of their stores; and they go and get them as need may require, without any apprehensions of being defrauded. [Pl. 56.] (Le Moyne, 1875, p. 9 (illus.) ; Swanton, 1922, p. 361.)

By "mountain," forest or grove is probably intended, and by "stone" that natural cement, tapia or "tabby" into which mud made from limy soil naturally sets. Thus in Florida the earth-covered houses were used as granaries and the habitations for human beings were constructed in another manner, as elsewhere described.

A type of granary more like that of the northern Indians is, however, rather clearly implied by Bishop Calderón (1936, p. 13) in stating that the Timucua granary was supported by 12 beams.

In Virginia there appears again a combination of the lounging pavilion and storehouse, at least if we may trust Strachey, who seems to have left the sole specific description of this building:

By their howses they have sometymes a scæna, or high stage, raised like a scaffold, of small spelts, reedes, or dried oslers, covered with matts, which both gives a shadowe and is a shelter, and serves for such a covered place where men used in old tyme to sitt and talke for recreation or pleasure, which they call præstega, and where, on a loft of hurdells, they laye forth their corne and fish to dry. They eate, sleepe, and dresse theire meate all under one roofe, and in one chamber, as it were. (Strachey, 1849, p. 71.)

All of these eastern storehouses seem to have been square or at least rectangular, though we cannot be certain in all cases. The Eno storehouse, however, may have been round, for Lederer compares it to an oven. This tribe devoted itself considerably to trade and raised a large amount of corn to barter with other tribes; therefore the granary was of exceptional importance among them. Lederer says: "To each house belongs a little hovel made like an oven, where they lay up their corn and mast, and keep it dry" (Alvord, 1912, p. 157).

If this were actually round, it would seem to link the Eno in this particular with the Mississippi tribes. To be sure, the illustration accompanying Le Moyne's description of the Florida storehouse shows a round building, but we cannot trust this too far as these illustrations are faulty in many other particulars (see above).

The granaries of the Tunica were perhaps square. Gravier says that they were "made like dovecotes, built on four large posts, 15 or 16 feet high, well put together and well polished, so that the mice cannot climb up, and in this way they protect their corn and squashes." (Shea, 1861, p. 135; Swanton, 1911, p. 315.)

The private storehouses of the Natchez seem not to have been honored with a description, but Du Pratz has the following to say regarding the one in which corn was stored in preparation for the new corn ceremony:

> The granary which they construct for the storage of this grain is of round shape, raised 2 feet above the earth. It is provided inside with cane mats. The bottom is made of large entire canes; the outside is also provided with them, because the teeth of rats, however good, are unable to make an opening in them on account of the natural varnish with which they are covered. This also prevents the rats from climbing the sides of the granary to enter through the covering, which, owing to the manner in which it is made, protects this grain from the worst storms. The French call this granary "the tun," on account of its round shape. (Le Page du Pratz, 1758, vol. 2, pp. 363–370; Swanton, 1911, p. 113.)

Just below he adds that on account of the relation of its height to the diameter, it resembled a tower rather more than a tun, and Dumont's description confirms him in this and in other particulars.

Caddo houses had compartments near the entrance for the storage of food and ·other property, but they also had storehouses outside raised on posts. Joutel speaks of them as follows:

> They have a great shelf above the door, built of sticks set upright, and others laid across, and canes laid side by side and closely bound together, on which they place their corn in the ear. There is another opposite where they put the hampers and barrels they make of canes and of bark, in which they put their shelled corn, beans, nuts, acorns, and other things, and over these they store their pottery. Each family has its own private receptables. . . . They also have a large platform, ten or twelve feet high, in front of their houses, where they dry their ears of corn after gathering. (Joutel *in* Margry, 1875–86, vol. 3, pp. 393–394.)

From the drawing of a Caddo village reproduced by Bolton (1915, frontispiece), it appears that the separate storehouses were sometimes square and sometimes round. It would hence seem that round storehouses were in use in the lower Mississippi Valley and to the westward, but it is not clear that they were employed in any section to the exclusion of the square type, though we happen to have no description of a square storehouse from the Natchez or their neighbors. It is also possible that round storehouses were in use in Florida and among the Eno. Elsewhere the shape was generally square or at least quadrangular.

TOBACCO

There is no mention of tobacco in the De Soto narratives, from which it seems certain that in his time the weed had not attained the social significance it enjoyed in the seventeenth and eighteenth cen-

turies. It was undoubtedly known to the natives, for Cartier found
it among the Hurons of St. Lawrence River in 1535, and tobacco
pipes occur in deposits antedating the visit of the Spaniards by centuries. So far as the Southeast is concerned, we seem to hear of it
first in Le Moyne's narrative of the Huguenot colony in Florida and
in Spark's account of Hawkins' voyage, but it is probably significant that the historians of the French colony (1564–65) do not mention any use of it in connection with public ceremonies.[24a] Pareja
says that formulae were repeated over tobacco when a Timucua
hunting party was about to set forth, but this information applies
to a period about half a century later (Swanton, 1922, p. 384).

Following are the references by Le Moyne and Spark.

Le Moyne:

They have a certain plant, whose name has escaped me, which the Brazilians call *petum* (*petun*), and the Spaniards *tapaco*. The leaves of this,
carefully dried, they place in the wider part of a pipe; and setting them on
fire, and putting the other end in their mouths, they inhale the smoke so
strongly, that it comes out at their mouths and noses, and operates powerfully to expel the humors. (Le Moyne, 1875, pp. 8–9 (illus.); Swanton, 1922,
p. 386.)

Spark:

The Floridians when they trauell, haue a kinde of herbe dried, who with a
cane and an earthen cup in the end, with fire, and the dried herbe put together
doe sucke thorow the cane and smoke thereof, which smoke satisfieth their
hunger, and therewith they liue foure or fiue dayes without meat or drinke,
and this all the Frenchmen vsed for this purpose; yet do they hold opinion
withall, that it causeth water & fleame to void from their stomacks. (Hakluyt, 1847–89, vol. 3, p. 615; Swanton, 1922, p. 360.)

Barlowe (1584) noted tobacco growing along with corn in the fields
of the Algonquian Indians of North Carolina (Burrage, 1906, p. 292),
and Hariot describes the use of it at some length:

There is an herbe which is sowed a part of it selfe & is called by the inhabitants
Vppówoc: In the West Indies it hath diuers names, according to the seuerall
places & Countries where it groweth and is vsed: The Spaniardes generally call
it Tobacco. The leaues thereof being dried and brought into powder: they vse
to take the fume or smoke thereof by sucking it through pipes made of claie into
their stomacke and heade; from whence it purgeth superfluous fleame & other
grosse humors, openeth all the pores & passages of the body: by which meanes
the vse thereof not only preserueth the body from obstructions; but also if any
be, so that they haue not beene of too long continuance, in short time breaketh
them: whereby their bodies are notably preserued in health, & know not many
greeuous diseases wherewithall wee in England are oftentimes afflicted.

This Vppówoc is of so precious estimation amongest them, that they thinke
their gods are maruelously delighted therewith: Wherupon sometimes they make
hallowed fires & cast some of the pouder therein for a sacrifice: being in a storme
vppon the waters, to pacifie theyr gods, they cast some vp into the aire and into
the water: so a weare for fish being newly set vp, they cast some into the aire:
also after an escape of danger, they cast some into the aire likewise: but all done

---

[24a] See, however, Chicora ceremony on page 759.

with strange gestures, stamping, sometimes dauncing, clapping of hands, holding
vp of hands, & staring vp into the heauens, vttering therewithal and chattering
strange words & noises.

We our selues during the time we were there used to suck it after their
maner, as also since our returne, & haue found manie rare and wonderful experiments of the vertues thereof; of which the relation woulde require a volume
by it selfe: the vse of it by so manie of late, men & women of great calling as
else, and some learned Phisitions also, is sufficient witnes. (Hariot, 1893,
pp. 25-26.)

Thus, it was highly esteemed in connection with religious rites, but
neither Hariot nor the later Virginia writers assign it any place in
the social and political life of the tribes.

Percy (1607) was conducted by a Powhatan Indian

to the Wood side, where there was a Garden of Tobacco and other fruits and
herbes. He gathered Tobacco, and distributed to every one of us. (Percy *in*
Tyler, 1884 ed., p. 16.)

Smith (1884 ed., pp. 112–113) found that it was offered to the spirits
on altars or thrown into the water, and learned that it was supposed
to grow in the world of the dead. Strachey is our only Virginia informant who describes it at length:

There is here great store of tobacco, which the salvages call apooke; howbeit
yt is not of the best kynd, yt is but poore and weake, and of a byting tast, yt
growes not fully a yard above ground, bearing a little yellow flower, like to
hennebane, the leaves are short and thick, somewhat round at the upper end;
whereas the best tobacco of Trynidado and the Oronoque is large, sharpe, and
growing two or three yardes from the ground, bearing a flower of the bredth of
our bell-flowers in England: the salvages here dry the leaves of this apooke
over the fier, and sometymes in the sun, and crumble yt into poulder, stalks,
leaves, and all, taking the same in pipes of earth, which very ingeniously they
can make. We observe that those Indians which have one, two, or more
women, take much,—but such as yet have no appropriate woman take little or
none at all. (Strachey, 1849, pp. 121–122.)

The native tobacco was *Nicotiana rustica*, inferior to the West
Indian varieties, as Strachey states, which rapidly replaced it for all
except ceremonial use. Beverley tells us that by the end of the seventeenth century the Indians of Virginia were depending mainly upon
the English for their ordinary smoking tobacco:

How the *Indians* order'd their Tobacco, I am not certain, they now depending
chiefly upon the *English*, for what they smoak: But I am inform'd, they used to
let it all run to Seed, only succouring the Leaves, to keep the Sprouts from
growing upon, and starving them; and when it was ripe, they pull'd off the
Leaves, cured them in the Sun, and laid them up for Use. But the Planters
make a heavy Bustle with it now, and can't please the Market neither. (Beverley,
1705, bk. 2, p. 30.)

Lawson contributes the following regarding the use of tobacco
among the Indians immediately southwest of the Algonquian territories:

Their teeth are yellow with smoking tobacco, which both men and women are much addicted to. They tell us that they had tobacco amongst them before the Europeans made any discovery of that continent. It differs in the leaf from the sweet scented, and Oroonoko, which are the plants we raise and cutivate in America. Theirs differs likewise much in the smell, when green, from our tobacco before cured. They do not use the same way to cure it as we do, and therefore the difference must be very considerable in taste; for all men that know tobacco must allow that it is the ordering thereof which gives a hogoo to that weed rather than any natural relish it possesses when green. Although they are great smokers, yet they never are seen to take it in snuff or chew it. (Lawson, 1860, p. 283.)

The native tobacco (*Nicotiana rustica*) was cultivated by the Cherokee and occupied, and still occupies, an important position in the ceremonial life of the tribe and in the native pharmacopoea, but Timberlake (Williams ed., 1927, p. 69) may very well be right when he intimates that relatively little time was devoted to the care of it.

The same impression has been conveyed to the writer regarding the position of the old native tobacco among the Creeks, the hitci pàkpàgi as it is called, a shortened form of hitci atculi pàkpàgi, "blossom of the ancient people's tobacco." This was a common ingredient of their medicines. It was used as a "foundation" for their busk medicines, that is, leaves of it were put into the pot before the other medicines were added. Some of it was often laid in the post holes when new cabins were erected in a Square Ground. In particular, it was a specific against ghosts. At an earlier period it may have been the favorite smoking tobacco, but it has now been replaced so long by the superior tobaccos of the white men, that this has been forgotten, and there is no evidence that it has been used in historic times in the ceremonial smoking in connection with assemblies for religious or social purposes. The Tukabahchee believed that the first tobacco plant was found springing from the grave of one of a group of supernatural culture heroes called Ispokogi.

The position of tobacco among the Chickasaw appears to have been a replica of that it held with the Creeks. An old prophet of that nation informed Adair that the eating of green tobacco leaves, probably of the native tobacco, was among the rites he had undergone in the interest of his people (Adair, 1775, p. 93). Before the new fire was lighted at the great annual ceremony, the high priest, this writer tells us, "puts a few roots of the button-snake-root, with some green leaves of an uncommon small sort of tobacco, and a little of the new fruits, at the bottom of the fire-place" (Adair, 1775, p. 106).

Without specifying the kind of tobacco, Romans says of the Choctaw:

They raise some tobacco, and even sell some to the traders, but when they use it for smoking they mix it with the leaves of the two species of the *Car-*

iaria [*Rhus coriaria*, sumac] or of the *Liquidambar styracistua* [*Liquidambar styraciflua*, sweetgum] dried and rubbed to pieces. (Romans, 1775, p. 47.)

The use of sumac leaves was universal in the Southeast as an adulterant of tobacco, but I have usually been told that it was the leaves of the smooth sumac (*Rhus glabra*) that were thus employed, except in connection with medicine ceremonies. The above is the only notice I have come upon of the use of sweetgum leaves.

Du Pratz gives us the following account of tobacco as used by Indians along the lower Mississippi in the early years of the eighteenth century:

> The tobacco which has been found among the natives of Louisiana appears also to be native to the country, since their ancient word [tradition] teaches us that in all times they have made use of the calumet in their treaties of peace and in their embassages, the principal usage of which is that the deputies of the two nations smoke it together.
>
> The tobacco native to the country is very large. Its stalk, when it is allowed to go to seed, grows to a height of 5½ and 6 feet. The lower part of the stem is at least 18 lines in diameter and its leaves are often almost 2 feet long. Its leaf is thick and fleshy. Its sap is pungent, but it never disturb one's head.
>
> The tobacco of Virginia has a broader, but shorter leaf. Its stem is not so large and does not grow nearly as high. Its odor is not disagreeable, but it has less pungency. It requires more stems to the pound, because its leaf is thinner and not so fleshy as the native variety, a fact I proved at Natchez where I tried the two kinds. That which is cultivated in lower Louisiana is smaller and has less pungency. What is grown in the islands (the West Indies) is more slender than that of Louisiana, but it has more pungency, which gives one headache. (Le Page du Pratz, 1758, vol. 3, pp. 360–361; Swanton, 1911, p. 79.)

He has the following regarding the leaves with which this was diluted:

> The Machonctchi, or vinegar tree, is a shrub, the leaves of which somewhat resemble those of the ash, but the stem to which these leaves hang is much longer. When these leaves are dried the natives mix them with tobacco, to temper it, because in smoking they do not care to have the tobacco so strong. (Le Page du Pratz, 1758, vol. 2, p. 45.)

Machonctchi is the Mobilian and Choctaw word bashō'nkchi, the sumac which bears the purple bud, and the use of its dried leaves as tobacco is still remembered. The only other species of sumac recognized by the Choctaw is called bàti. An infusion of its roots is used as a remedy for sore mouth.

Dumont de Montigny also has a note regarding the use of the first-mentioned sumac: He says:

> They mix the tobacco with the leaves of a little shrub which is called the sumac (*vinaigrier*), whether to reduce the strength of the first or because formerly they made use of this last in lieu of tobacco. The two now mingled and chopped together are called among them *feningue*. (Dumont, 1753, vol. 1, p. 189; Swanton, 1911, p. 79.)

As to the method of smoking, Dumont remarks:

All the savages are in general very fond of tobacco smoke. They are often seen to swallow 10 or 12 mouthfuls in succession, which they keep in their stomachs without being inconvenienced after they have ceased to draw, and give up this smoke many successive times, partly through the mouth and partly through the nose. [Dumont, 1753, vol. 1, p. 189; Swanton, 1911, p. 79.]

The size attributed by Du Pratz to the native Louisiana tobacco plant occasions some doubt as to whether it was really obtained from the Indians of that section, as he supposes. The plant attributed to lower Louisiana corresponds more nearly to the *Nicotiana rustica*.

In order to induce insensibility, pellets of tobacco were swallowed by Natchez men and women about to be strangled to accompany the spirit of a dead member of the Sun caste.

From most of the other tribes along the lower Mississippi we learn little more regarding tobacco than the bare fact that it was used in connection with the calumet in the conduct of intertribal business. The Caddo offered tobacco and hominy to the scalps they had taken. In 1687 the calumet ceremony had reached the Cahinnio of southern Arkansas, but had not extended to other Caddo tribes. The brevity of time covered by tribal memory is well illustrated in the fact that there was no calumet ceremony on the lower Mississippi in 1543, while in 1725 the "ancient word" of the Natchez taught "that in all times they have made use of the calumet in their treaties of peace and in their embassages" (Le Page du Pratz, 1758, vol. 3, pp. 360–361; Swanton, 1911, p. 79).

HOUSING

(Plates 57–63)

TYPES OF BUILDINGS

Two principal types of dwelling houses were found in the Southeast, the circular house, often called by traders "hot house," which was particularly adapted to winter residence, and the less closely constructed rectangular summer house. A very good general idea of these houses is given by Elvas:

Throughout the cold lands each of the Indians has his house for the winter plastered inside and out. They shut the very small door at night and build a fire inside the house so that it gets as hot as an oven, and stays so all night long so that there is no need of clothing. Beside those houses they have others for summer with kitchens near by where they build their fires and bake their bread. . . . The difference between the houses of the lords or principal men and the others is that besides being larger they have large balconies in front and below seats resembling benches made of canes; and round about many large barbacoas in which they gather together the tribute paid them by their Indians, which consists of maize and deerskins and native blankets resembling shawls, some being made of the inner bark of trees and some from a plant like daffodils which when pounded remains like flax. (Robertson, 1933, pp. 75–76.)

Taking up the winter house first, the type which seems to have been most widely spread, we cannot do better than cite, in addition to the above, Adair's excellent description from his observations among the Chickasaw:

The clothing of the Indians being very light, they provide themselves for the winter with hot-houses, whose properties are to retain, and reflect the heat, after the manner of the Dutch stoves. To raise these, they fix deep in the ground, a sufficient number of strong forked posts, at a proportional distance, in a circular form, all of an equal height, about five or six feet above the surface of the ground: above these, they tie very securely large pieces of the heart of white oak, which are of a tough flexible nature, interweaving this orbit, from top to bottom, with pieces of the same, or the like timber. Then, in the middle of the fabric they fix very deep in the ground, four large pine posts, in a quadrangular form, notched a-top, on which they lay a number of heavy logs, let into each other, and rounding gradually to the top. Above this huge pile, to the very top, they lay a number of long dry poles, all properly notched, to keep strong hold of the under posts and wall-plate. Then they weave them thick with their split sapplings, and daub them all over about six or seven inches thick with tough clay, well mixt with withered grass; when this cement is half dried, they thatch the house with the longest sort of dry grass, that their land produces. They first lay on one round tier, placing a split sapling a-top, well tied to the different parts of the under pieces of timber, about fifteen inches below the eave: and, in this manner, they proceed circularly to the very spire, where commonly a pole is fixed, that displays on the top the figure of a large carved eagle. At a small distance below which, four heavy logs are strongly tied together across, in a quadrangular form, in order to secure the roof from the power of envious blasts. The door of this winter palace, is commonly about four feet high, and so narrow as not to admit two to enter it abreast, with a winding passage for the space of six or seven feet, to secure themselves both from the power of the bleak winds, and of an invading enemy. As they usually build on rising ground, the floor is often a yard lower than the earth, which serves them as a breast work against an enemy: and a small peeping window is level with the surface of the outside ground, to enable them to rake any lurking invaders in case of an attack. As they have no metal to reflect the heat; in the fall of the year, as soon as the sun begins to lose his warming power, some of the women make a large fire of dry wood, with which they chiefly provide themselves, but only from day to day, through their thoughtlessness of to-morrow. When the fire is a little more than half burnt down, they cover it over with ashes, and, as heat declines, they strike off some of the top embers, with a long cane, wherewith each of the couches, or broad seats, is constantly provided; and this method they pursue from time to time as need requires, till the fire is expended, which is commonly about day-light. While the new fire is burning down, the house, for want of windows and air, is full of hot smoky darkness; and all this time, a number of them lie on their broad bed places, with their heads wrapped up.

The inside of their houses is furnished with genteel couches to sit, and lie upon, raised on four forks of timber of a proper height, to give the swarming fleas some trouble in their attack, as they are not able to reach them at one spring: they tie with fine white oak splinters, a sufficient quantity of middle-sized canes of proper dimensions, to three or four bars of the same sort, which they fasten above the frame; and they put their mattresses a-top which are made of long cane splinters. Their bedding consists of the skins of wild beasts, such as of buffalo, panthers, bears, elks, and deer, which they dress with the hair on, as soft as velvet. (Adair, 1775, pp. 419–420.)

Among the Chickasaw and many other Southeastern tribes the town house or "temple" was constructed after the same pattern. To quote Adair again:

Every town has a large edifice, which with propriety may be called the mountain house, in comparison of those already described. But the only difference between it, and the winter house or stove, is in its dimensions, and application. (Adair, 1775, p. 421.)

Apparently houses of this type were used more widely than any others, but many Indians, including the Chickasaw, had a summer dwelling, as already mentioned in the quotation from Elvas. Reverting to Adair:

For their summer houses, they generally fix strong posts of pitch-pine deep in the ground, which will last for several ages. The trees of dried locust,[25] and sassafras, are likewise very durable. The posts are of an equal height; and the wall-plates are placed on top of these, in notches. Then they sink a large post in the center of each gable end, and another in the middle of the house where the partition is to be, in order to support the roof-tree; to these they tie the rafters with broad splinters of oak, or hiccory, unless they make choice of such long sapplings, as will reach from side to side over the ridge hole [pole?], which, with a proper notch in the middle of each of them, and bound as the other sort, lie very secure. Above those, they fix either split sapplings, or three large winter canes together, at proper distances, well tied. Again, they place above the wall-plates of both sides the house, a sufficient number of strong crooks to bear up the eave-boards: and they fasten each of them, both to one of the rafters and the wall-plate, with the bandages before described. As the poplar tree is very soft, they make their eave-boards of it, with their small hatchets: having placed one on each side, upon the crooks, exceeding the length of the house, and jutting a foot beyond the wall, they cover the fabric with pine, or cypress clap-boards, which they can split readily; and crown the work with the bark of the same trees, all of a proper length and breadth, which they had before provided. In order to secure this covering from the force of the high winds, they put a sufficient number of long split sapplings above the covering of each side, from end to end, and tie them fast to the end of the laths. Then they place heavy logs above, resting on the eave-boards, opposite to each crook, which overlap each other on the opposite sides, about two feet a-top, whereon they fix a convenient log, and tie them together, as well as the laths to the former, which bind it together, and thus the fabric becomes a savage philosopher's castle, the side and gables of which are bullet proof. The barrier towns cut port holes in those summer houses, daubing them over with clay, so as an enemy cannot discover them on the outside; they draw a circle round each of them in the inside of the house, and when they are attacked, they open their port holes in a trice, and fall to work. But those, that live more at ease, indulge themselves accordingly. (Adair, 1775, pp. 417–419.)

---

[25] In another place Adair says "the honeylocust."

[Elsewhere he remarks that these houses were] whitewashed within and without, either with decayed oyster-shells, coarse-chalk, or white marly clay; one or the other of which, each of our Indian nations abound with, be they ever so far distant from the sea-shore: the Indians, as well as the traders, usually, decorate their summer-houses with this favorite white-wash. The former have likewise each a corn-house, fowl-house, and a hot-house, or stove for winter. (Adair, 1775, p. 413.)

Thus each Chickasaw of consequence owned a group of dwellings, and the number seems to have been carried still further by the Creeks.

The family hot houses of the Creeks were rectangular and constituted one element in the system of buildings in the possession of each family group (Romans, 1775, p. 96), but the bad-weather ceremonial building owned by the town, the tcokofa or tcokofa-thlako, was almost identical with the Chickasaw hot house. Hawkins has left us the following account of this:

[The] Chooc-ofau thluc-co, the *rotunda* or *assembly room*, called by the traders, "hot house" . . . is near the square, and is constructed after the following manner: Eight posts are fixed in the ground, forming an octagon of thirty feet diameter. They are twelve feet high, and large enough to support the roof. On these, five or six logs are placed, of a side, drawn in as they rise. On these, long poles or rafters, to suit the height of the building, are laid, the upper ends forming a point, and the lower ends projecting out six feet from the octagon, and resting on posts five feet high, placed in a circle round the octagon, with plates on them, to which the rafters are tied with splits. The rafters are near together, and fastened with splits. These are covered with clay, and that with pine bark; the wall, six feet from the octagon, is clayed up; they have a small door into a small portico, curved round for five or six feet, then into the house.

The space between the octagon and the wall, is one entire sopha, where the visitors lie or sit at pleasure. It is covered with reed, mat or splits. (Hawkins, 1848, p. 71.)

The only differences seem to have been in the greater size of the Creek structure necessitating a main support of eight posts at the center instead of four, no mention of a carved eagle at the top, and the substitution of pine bark for grass as an outer covering.

The hot house seen by Hitchcock at the great Tukabahchee town near the Canadian River, after the removal of the Creeks to the west of the Mississippi, was still larger:

The most curious part of the preparation at the Square is at the West angle a few feet from the angle outside—the *Round House*. This is difficult to describe and considerable ingenuity has been employed in its erection. The main structure is supported upon twelve posts or pillars, one end sunk in the ground. They are disposed in a circle about 9 or 10 feet apart, making a space within of about 120 feet circumference in the centre of which, upon the ground is the sacred fire. The roof over this circle is a cone terminating in a point over the fire some 20 odd feet high. The rafters extend down from the apex of the cone beyond the twelve pillars, which are about eight feet high, to within four or five feet of the ground, which space, of four or five feet is enclosed entirely with earth—between the pillars and the extreme exterior, a space of several feet, are seats of mats, like those of the sheds. The manner of constructing the roof is very remarkable for Indian work. Upon the alternate couples of the twelve pillars are first placed horizontal pieces—then upon the ends of these are placed other horizontal pieces between the other couples of pillars then another series of horizontal pieces resting upon the second set, but drawn within towards the centre of the circle a few inches. Upon these again are other pieces still more drawn in.

There are four tiers of horizontal pieces thus placed upon each other. [Fig. 1.] *a. b. c. d.* are four of the twelve pillars; pieces are first laid upon *a. b.* and upon *c. d.* then a piece upon these and between *b. c.*, etc. These horizontal pieces are strongly bound together by leather thongs of green hide; it is evident they are of the nature of an arch. They are only carried up to the number of four sufficient for giving a direction and a foundation for the rafters, which are laid upon these extending up to a point in one direction and in the other direction over outside to near the ground. The rafters are strongly bound by thongs and covered with ordinary rived boards for shingles. There is but one small entrance to the house which is next towards the angle of the square adjacent to which the round house stands. (Hitchcock, 1930, pp. 114–115.)

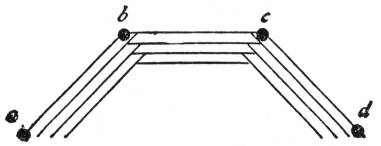

FIGURE 1.—Structural detail of the roof of a Creek tcokofa from beneath (after Hitchcock).

The hot house described by Swan, evidently that belonging to the Upper Creek town of Otciapofa, was 25 feet in diameter, and 25 in height, the outer wall being 6 feet high. There was but a single bed running round the wall inside. The house was covered with bark like the hot house described by Hawkins, and seems to have been the same as that in all other essentials.

Bartram has not left us a minute description of any of the Creek tcokofas, but he tells us that the one attached to the Upper Creek town of Atasi was identical in construction with a Cherokee council house, which he had dwelt upon earlier in his Travels, except that it was much larger—larger he seems to imply than any other known to him. That it was larger than any we have considered is indicated by the fact that the roof was supported by a central post and in addition 3 concentric rows of wooden pillars (Bartram, 1791, pp. 452–455). In the plan of a rotunda given in his Observations on the Creek and Cherokee Indians (fig. 2) (Bartram, 1909, p. 54), he evidently has this rotunda in mind. This shows 3 beds, or tiers of beds around the wall,

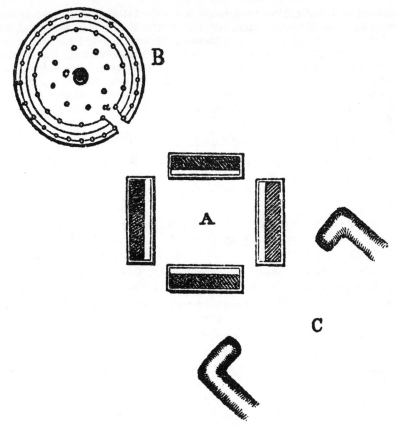

FIGURE 2.—Plan of Creek ceremonial ground as given by Wm. Bartram.   A, Square Ground ;
B, tcokofa or town "hot house" ; C, chunk yard.

a row of 25 posts flush with the front of the bed nearest the wall, a row
of 14 along the front edge of the lowest bed, the one nearest the center of the building, and a row of 8 in the open space in front of these
surrounding a central pillar.   It is not likely that Bartram counted
all of the posts in each row.   The 8 in the inner row very likely
represent the result of an exact computation, but it is quite possible
that the number in each of the other rows was also divisible by 4,
perhaps 16 in one case and 24 in the other.   But it is not necessary
that the sacred number 4 be carried into the less conspicuous details
of the structure.

In a letter written at Camp Armstrong, Chatahoocha, November
26, 1813, an officer in Floyd's army thus describes the square and hot
house of a Lower Creek town, probably Kasihta or Coweta:

These people have great ideas of grandure they have at this place a small fort
built of poles which a strong man could pull up, in this fort is their square where
they hold talks there are four houses fronting each other the front open something
like a piasar where the chiefs set agreeable to rank, in these houses are deposited

their relics, & scalps. The town house is a large building built round at the botom for three or four feet high out of sticks & mud with large post[s] of the same hight which support a plate. Inside of this wall is other large post[s] set round which support other plates on which two rest the rafters. On the last plates rest a large beam which supports another large post in the center against which rest the remainder of the rafters so as to bring the roof to a point in a conical form. On these rafters are tied small lathes which support the bark of which the roof is made. There is only one door which makes it as dark as midnight.[26]

This house is remembered by the Alabama, who called it ha′sse īca′, "grass house," because it was covered with grass, and by the Creeks of Oklahoma, who called it tcoko′fa. Jackson Lewis said that the Creek hot house was made with a circular floor-plan and a roof converging to a point at the top. It was daubed outside and in with clay and made very tight. In the center they dug a hole for the fire, but all the rest of the space inside was floored with a kind of tough clay obtained for that very purpose and patted down so that it never got dusty. They either constructed beds around the inside of the house or else lay down on skins on the floor around near the walls. For the fire they procured round pieces of wood of kinds that would make the least smoke. What smoke was produced rose to the roof, leaving the air below comparatively clear, and as the fire died down a bed of live coals was left, renewed from time to time by raking, which warmed the house up very well. The door was about 4 feet high and was either on the south or the east. This was a sort of refuge in very severe winter weather. Pumpkins, sweetpotatoes, berries, etc., were stored in these houses for fear of frost.

Plate 59, figure 1, shows the type of structure used in the Alabama ceremonial ground in the eighteenth century, no doubt typical of the Creek structures of this type during the period.

The system of dwellings used by Creek families was of a type employed elsewhere exclusively in summer, and is said to have been modeled on the plan of the Square Ground, as Bartram indicates in the following description (see fig. 3):

The dwellings of the Upper Creeks [including according to the usage of all other writers the Upper and Lower Creeks] consist of little squares, or rather of four dwelling-houses inclosing a square area, exactly on the plan of the Public Square. Every family, however, has not four of these houses; some have but three, others not more than two, and some but one, according to the circumstances of the individual, or the number of his family. Those who have four buildings have a particular use for each building. One serves as a cook-room and winter lodging-house, another as a summer lodging-house and hall for receiving visitors, and a third for a granary or provision house, etc. The last is commonly two stories high, and divided into two apartments, transversely, the lower story of one end being a potato house, for keeping such other roots and fruits as require to be kept close, or defended from cold in winter. The

[26] Copy of ms. obtained through the courtesy of Dr. Charles C. Harrold, of Macon, Ga.

chamber over it is the *council*. At the other end of the building, both upper
and lower stories are open on their sides: the lower story serves for a shed
for their saddles, pack-saddles, and gears, and other lumber; the loft over it is
a very spacious, airy, pleasant pavilion, where the chief of the family reposes
in the hot seasons, and receives his guests, etc. The fourth house (which completes the square) is a skin or ware-house, if the proprietor is a wealthy man,
and engaged in trade or traffic, where he keeps his deer-skins, furs, merchandise,
etc., and treats his customers. Smaller or less wealthy families make one, two, or
three houses serve all their purposes as well as they can. (Bartram, 1909,
pp. 55–56.)

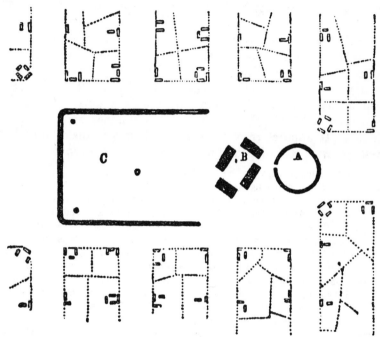

FIGURE 3.—Plan of Creek ceremonial ground and its position in a Creek town, as given by
Wm. Bartram. *A*, tcokofa or town "hot house"; *B*, Square Ground; *C*, chunk yard.

Thus the winter house of the Creeks was built like the summer house,
and these two and the corncrib or granary formed three sides of a
square to which a warehouse was sometimes added in order to complete
it. These private dwellings were patterned after the ceremonial
square, or else the ceremonial square was patterned after them. We
shall probably never know which. At any rate both conformed to a
strictly Creek pattern, the town hot house representing another type
of dwelling and either a survival from an earlier style or one adopted
from their neighbors.

In another place the same writer has the following note regarding
the houses of the Upper Creek town of Kolomi:

The plain is narrow where the town is built: their houses are neat commodious
buildings, a wooden frame with plastered walls, and roofed with Cypress bark

or shingles; every habitation consists of four oblong square houses, of one story, of the same form and dimensions, and so situated as to form an exact square, encompassing an area or court yard of about a quarter of an acre of ground, leaving an entrance into it at each corner. (Bartram, 1792, pp. 394–395.)

Of the Yuchi town on Chattahoochee River, in the Lower Creek country he remarks:

The walls of the houses are constructed of a wooden frame, then lathed and plastered inside and out with a reddish well tempered clay or mortar, which gives them the appearance of red brick walls; and these houses are neatly covered or roofed with Cypress bark or shingles of that tree. (Bartram, 1792, p. 386.)

By 1790, only a few years after the time of Bartram, some Creek houses had undergone considerable alterations which Swan illustrates for us in connection with the report of his expedition to the Creek country, the drawing itself having been made by J. C. Tidball, U. S. A. Swan describes this as "The Creek house in its best state of native improvement in 1790" (pl. 58). This has a chimney and at least one window. It appears from Swan's text, however, that most of the dwellings were still of a very much more primitive type:

The houses they occupy are but pitiful small huts, commonly from twelve to eighteen or twenty feet long, and from ten to fifteen feet wide; the floors are of earth; the walls, six, seven, and eight feet high, supported by poles driven into the ground, and lathed across with canes tied slightly on, and filled in with clay, which they always dig for, and find near the spot whereon they build. The roofs are pitched from a ridge pole near the centre, which is covered with large tufts of the bark of trees. The roofs are covered with four or five layers of rough shingles, laid upon rafters of round poles, the whole secured on the outside from being blown away, by long heavy poles laid across them, and tied with bark or withes at each end of the house. In putting on these curious roofs, they seem to observe an uniformity in all their different towns; which, upon the approach of a stranger, exhibit a grotesque appearance of rudeness, not so easily to be described with the pen, as it might be with the pencil. The chimneys are made of poles and clay, and are built up at one end, and on the outside of the houses. On each side of the fire-place, they have small cane-racks or platforms, with skins whereon they sleep; but many of them, too lazy to make these platforms, sleep on the floor, in the midst of much dirt.

They have but one door at the side and near the centre of the house; this, although nothing remains inside to be stolen, is barricaded by large heavy pieces of wood, whenever they quit the house to go out a hunting.

Their houses being but slightly made, seldom resist the weather more than one or two years, before they fall to pieces. They then erect new ones, on new plots of ground; thus, by continually shifting from one place to another, the bulk of some of their largest towns are removed three or four miles from where they stood three or four years before, and no vestiges remain of their former habitations. (Swan, 1855, pp. 692–693.)

While related to the old summer house, in certain features the house erected in modern times by the Alabama Indians is also reminiscent of the Choctaw summer dwelling to be mentioned presently. This was described to me as follows:

The ground plan was rectangular, with a door in the middle of one of the long sides and sometimes a door in the middle of the opposite side as well. The size and shape were outlined by means of seven or eight pine uprights, one at each corner, and the others in the middle of the back and at either side of the door or doors. If there was but one door, a single post was set up in the middle of the opposite side. The house is said to have faced in any direction, but this is almost certainly a modern innovation. The tops of the uprights all around were connected by means of horizontal poles tied with bàksha (bass cord), and poles of the same kind were fastened half way up, except, of course, across the doorways. Just outside of these were placed the wall planks standing on end, and they were woven together and to the horizontals by means of a pair of cords woven in and out from one end to the other. The gable ends above the eaves were closed by means of a number of boards laid horizontally and fastened at the ends and to a single upright pole at the middle. The space over the door was closed with a single horizontally placed board. The boards employed were thick, and sometimes halved logs were used instead. The skeleton of the roof consisted of about eight rafters on a side, including those at the ends. Over these were laid a number of horizontal strips, thirteen in the house my informant had in mind, and over these were laid thin slabs of pinelike shingles, their centers being laid on the horizontal strips at their centers. Nowadays such slabs are nailed in place, but anciently they were fastened by means of slender poles along the upper sides, which were tied to them and to the strips beneath and the rafters at their extremities. Between the rafters inside crosspieces are now added, but this is a modern innovation. In the roof at either end was a smoke-hole (oi′hà), one to let the fresh air in, the other to let the smoke out. The floor was the natural soil. The door was made of a single plank or of two or more fastened side by side and swung on leather hinges, sometimes inward, sometimes outward.

The later Creek house in Oklahoma was rectangular, the sides being made of split logs, and the interstices filled with clay mixed with grass. In 1819–21 the missionary Hodgson saw some "rude dwellings" among the Lower Creeks "formed of four upright saplings, and a rough covering of pine-bark, which they strip from the trees with a neatness and rapidity which we could not imitate" (Hodgson, 1823, p. 264).

As might have been anticipated, the houses of the Seminole resembled those of the Creeks, but, these Indians being scattered about in smaller bodies and moving more frequently, neither their private nor their public structures were as elaborate. Bartram says of them:

They have neither the Chunky-Yard nor Rotunda, and the Public Square is an imperfect one, having but two or three houses at furtherest . . . Their private habitations consist generally of two buildings: one a large oblong house, which serves for a cook-room, eating-house, and lodging-rooms, in three apartments under one roof; the other not quite so large, which is situated eight or ten yards distant, one end opposite the principal house. This is two stories high, of the same construction, and serving the same purpose with the granary or provision house of the Creeks. (Bartram, 1909, p. 56.)

This description is based largely on his observation of the houses composing Cuscowilla, a newly established town belonging to the Oconee and one of the oldest Seminole settlements of consequence. In his Travels he thus describes the town:

The town of Cuscowilla, which is the capital of the Alachua tribe, contains about thirty habitations, each of which consists of two houses nearly the same size, about thirty feet in length, twelve feet wide, and about the same in height. The door is placed midway on one side or in the front. This house is divided equally, across into two apartments, one of which is the cook room and common hall, and the other the lodging room.

The other house is nearly of the same dimensions, standing about twenty yards from the dwelling house, its end fronting the door. This building is two stories high, and constructed in a different manner. It is divided transversely, as the other, but the end next the dwelling house is open on three sides, supported on posts or pillars. It has an open loft or platform, the ascent to which is by a portable stair or ladder: this is a pleasant, cool, airy situation, and here the master or chief of the family retires to repose in the hot seasons, and receives his guests or visitors. The other half of this building is closed on all sides by notched logs; the lowest or ground part is a potato house, and the upper story over it a granary for corn and other provisions. Their houses are constructed of a kind of frame. In the first place, strong corner pillars are fixed in the ground, with others somewhat less, ranging on a line between; these are strengthened by cross pieces of timber, and the whole with the roof is covered close with the bark of the Cypress tree. The dwelling stands near the middle of a square yard, encompassed by a low bank, formed with the earth taken out of the yard, which is always carefully swept. Their towns are clean, the inhabitants being particular in laying their filth at a proper distance from their dwellings, which undoubtedly contributes to the healthiness of their habitations. (Bartram, 1791, pp. 189–190.)

The same writer describes the house of a Seminole chief called "the Bosten or Boatswain by the traders" as follows (fig. 4):

It was composed of three oblong uniform frame buildings [e], and a fourth, foure-square [a], fronting the principal house or common hall, after this manner, encompassing one area [A]. The hall was his lodginghouse, large and commodious; the two wings were, one a coòk-house, the other a skin or ware-house; and the large square one was a vast open *pavilion*, supporting a canopy of cedar roof by two rows of columns or pillars, one within the other. Between each range of pillars was a platform, or what the traders call cabins, a sort of sofa raised about two feet above the common ground, and ascended by two steps; this was covered with checkered mats of curious manufacture, woven of splints of canes dyed of different colors; the middle was a four-square stage or platform, raised nine inches or a foot higher than the cabins or sofas, and also covered with mats. (Bartram, 1909, pp. 37–38.)

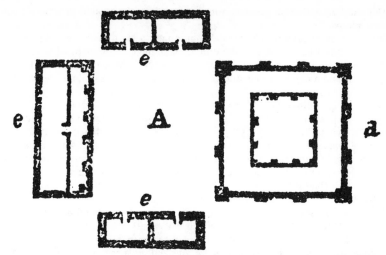

FIGURE 4.—Ground plan of the house of a Seminole Indian called by the traders Bosten or Boatswain (after Bartram).

As we follow house architecture toward the south, we observe the appearance of open pavilions or arbors possibly related to or displacing the summer house, and in southern Florida in MacCauley's time (1880) among the Seminole still left in the peninsula, they had taken the place of all other types of dwellings (pl. 60).

This house is approximately 16 by 9 feet in ground measurement, made almost altogether, if not wholly, of materials taken from the palmetto tree. It is actually but a platform elevated about three feet from the ground and covered with a palmetto thatched roof, the roof being not more than 12 feet above the ground at the ridge pole, or 7 at the eaves. Eight upright palmetto logs, unsplit and undressed, support the roof. Many rafters sustain the palmetto thatching. The platform is composed of split palmetto logs lying transversely, flat sides up, upon beams which extend the length of the building and are lashed to the uprights by palmetto ropes, thongs, or trader's ropes. This platform is peculiar, in that it fills the interior of the building like a floor and serves to furnish the family with a dry sitting or lying down place when, as often happens, the whole region is under water. The thatching of the roof is quite a work of art: inside, the regularity and compactness of the laying of the leaves display much skill and taste on the part of the builder; outside—with the outer layers there seems to have been much less care taken than with those within—the mass of leaves of which the roof is composed is held in place and made firm by heavy logs, which, bound together in pairs, are laid upon it astride the ridge. The covering is, I was informed, watertight and durable and will resist even a violent wind. Only hurricanes can tear it off, and these are so infrequent in Southern Florida that no attempt is made to provide against them.

The Seminole's house is open on all sides and without rooms. It is, in fact, only a covered platform. The single equivalent for a room in it is the space above the joists which are extended across the building at the lower edges of the roof. In this are placed surplus food and general household effects out of use from time to time. Household utensils are usually suspended from the uprights of the building and from pronged sticks driven into the ground near by at convenient places.

From this description the Seminole's house may seem a poor kind of structure to use as a dwelling; yet if we take into account the climate of Southern Florida nothing more would seem to be necessary. A shelter from the hot sun and the frequent rains and a dry floor above the damp or water covered ground are sufficient for the Florida Indian's needs.

I-ful-lo-ha-tco's three houses are placed at three corners of an oblong clearing, which is perhaps 40 by 30 feet. At the fourth corner is the entrance into the garden, which is in shape an ellipse, the longer diameter being about 25 feet. The three houses are alike, with the exception that in one of them the elevated platform is only half the size of those of the others. The difference seems to have been made on account of the camp fire. The fire usually burns in the space around which the buildings stand. During the wet season, however, it is moved into the sheltered floor in the building having the half platform. At Tus-ko-na's camp, where several families are gathered, I noticed one building without the interior platform. This was probably the wet weather kitchen.

To all appearance there is no privacy in these open houses. The only means by which it seems to be secured is by suspending, over where one sleeps, a canopy of thin cotton cloth or calico, made square or oblong in shape, and nearly three feet in height. This serves a double use, as a private room and as a protection against gnats and mosquitoes.

But while I-ful-lo-ha-tco's house is a fair example of the kind of dwelling in use throughout the tribe, I may not pass unnoticed some innovations which have lately been made upon the general style. There are, I understand, five inclosed houses, which were built and are owned by Florida Indians. Four of these are covered with split cypress planks or slabs; one is constructed of logs. (MacCauley, 1887, pp. 500–501.)

It seems that one Indian had also built a house after the white man's pattern, and in the northernmost band of Seminole, the Catfish Lake Indians, on Horse Creek, MacCauley found a somewhat different type of dwelling of a less permanent character (pl. 59, fig. 2).

In 1910 Skinner found the typical Seminole house to be of the following character:

The typical Seminole lodge is a pent roof of palmetto thatch raised over several platforms on which the occupants sit or recline. There are no sides, since the Everglades and the Big Cypress are so far below the frost-line that the atmosphere is rarely cold, and the protection from the rain afforded by the closely thatched roofs with their wide projecting eaves is all that is necessary.

The lodges average fifteen feet by twelve, but vary greatly in size. They are made of cypress logs nailed or lashed together. A few houses have a raised floor throughout, giving the appearance of a pile-dwelling. (Skinner, 1913, p. 76.)

Skinner thus describes the "cook-house" and the "eating-house" of the Seminole, the former apparently a late local institution, the latter a direct descendant of the old public house of the north though its construction has been completely altered owing to the difference in climate:

In the center of this space (on which the village was built) is the cook-house, in which a fire is constantly burning. It is kept up in a curious way. Large cypress logs are cut and laid under the cook-house, radiating from a common center like the spokes of a wheel. At the "hub" the fire is lighted, and as the wood burns it is constantly shoved inward and hence never needs to be cut into lengths. At this fire, the only one in the camp, the women cook for the entire village. . . .

One of the houses of the village (usually the largest one) is reserved for eating, and here food, generally sofki, venison, biscuits of cornbread and coffee, is always ready for the hungry. Twice a day, in the morning and evening, the Seminole have regular meals, but eating between times is a constant practice.

At meal-time the men and boys enter this common lodge. Under the pent roof of thatch are arranged several platforms, raised a few feet from the floor by means of stakes driven in the ground, and entirely independent of the supporting beams of the house. The largest of these scaffolds is the dining table, and on it squat the Indians about the sofki bowl. . . .

Every eating-house is also a guest house. Strangers or visitors arriving at a camp go directly to this lodge, and food is brought them at once by the women. When they have eaten, or while they are doing so, the men come over and question them, if they are strangers, as to their purpose in coming to the camp. If they appear to be friendly, they are allowed to remain in the eating-house as long as they stay in camp. (Skinner, 1913, pp. 70–71.)

The house covered with cypress bark which Speck's Yuchi informants remembered to have been used at an earlier period was, I think, the hot house rather than a house of Algonquian type, as he supposed. The later Yuchi house was similar to that of the Creeks generally and to that of many of the poor whites. Speck's description of the summer camps, and those put up around the ceremonial ground during the busk is exceptionally good and applies equally to the Creeks. These were open-sided structures and he says of them:

With some families this open-sided structure is merely a shade arbor, and no care seems to be given to its appearance. But with others it serves as the dwelling upon occasions and is fitted out and furnished with some semblance of permanent occupancy. During the annual tribal ceremony of the corn harvest, when the assemblage of families is largest, these structures may be best seen. The following descriptions of these temporary dwellings, in which are preserved earlier forms of architecture, are based upon observations made at such times.

To begin with, the camp shelters, as they are commonly called, are scattered irregularly about, in no wise forming a camp circle such as is found on the Plains or a camp square like that of the Chickasaw. They are left standing after they have served once, and are reoccupied by the owners when they return to the place where the ceremonial gatherings are held.

The ground space covered by a lodge of this sort varies somewhat, but may be said to be in general about sixteen feet by eighteen. The floor is simply the earth. Branches of oak with the leaves compose the roof. Eight feet above the ground is a common height for this dense screen of leaves. The branches themselves are supported by cross poles resting on stout horizontal end pieces or beams. In the support of these beams, lodge builders employ different devices. One of these, and perhaps the commonest, is the simple formed or crotched post. When trees happen to be handy, however, a modification has

been observed in the roof support which shows a rather clever adaptation of
the material at hand to suit the occasion. In such a case standing trees take the
place of sunken posts, and forked posts with the beams resting in the crotch are
leaned against them.

   . . . The general ground plan of these camp shelters is square . . . They
usually stand east of the entrance to the tent. In the center of the ground
space blankets, skins and other materials to make comfort are strewn, and
here the people eat, lounge and sleep. In one corner is a square storage scaffold or shelf elevated about five feet above the ground. This is floored with
straight sticks resting upon cross pieces which in turn are supported by uprights
in the floor. On this scaffold is a heterogeneous pile of household utensils and
property. Ball sticks, weapons, baskets, clothing, harness, blankets and in fact
nearly everything not in immediate use is all packed away here out of reach of
dogs and children. Out from under the roof to one side is the fireplace. [Accom-
panied by three illustrations in the original.] (Speck, 1909, pp. 39–40.)

By 1854 the common Chickasaw house had taken on a two-part type
common in certain sections of Oklahoma down to the present day.
W. B. Parker, who accompanied Capt. R. B. Marcy in his expedition
through the Indian country in the summer and fall of 1854, thus describes it:

   The style of building among this people is peculiar; two square pens are put
up with logs, and roofed or thatched. The space between the pens is covered
in and serves for eating place and despository of harness, saddles and bridles,
&c. A door is cut in each pen, facing the passage. They have no windows the
doors admitting all the light used. This style is *called two pens and a passage*
and is, in fact, only a shelter for the family from bad weather, for of furniture
they have but little, and that of the rudest and most uncomfortable kind.
These buildings are stuck almost invariably upon the road; no neat door yard,
with a substantial fence and neat gate encloses them; no flower or vegetable
garden is seen, but the ornamental figure of a half-starved dog, grunts lazily
on one side and a pack of miserable curs lounge on the other, the whole presenting an untidy picture of squalid discomfort, which even its temporary appearance cannot deceive. (*Quoted in* Foreman, 1934, p. 142.)

But this was not the best type of house nor was it quite fair for a
representative of the race which had uprooted the tribe unceremoni-
ously from their homes and disorganized their home lives to be so cen-
sorious regarding a condition for which his people had been largely
responsible. There were white families of the time whose houses
probably rated no higher.

Romans (1775, p. 83) mentions hot houses among the Choctaw as
well-known structures and he leads us to infer that they were made
precisely like those of the Chickasaw, but it is curious that most other
writers are silent regarding them. This is particularly surprising
in the case of the anonymous French writer so often referred to. The
omission seems, however, to be rectified by a traveler named Mease
who visited the Choctaw town of Imoklasha in 1770–71 and thus
describes the house of an Indian named Astolabe:

This house is nearly of a circular figure and built of clay mixed with haulm [straw or grass]. The top is conical and covered with a kind of thatch [the nature of] which I could not make out. The inside roof is divided into four parts and there are cane seats raised about two feet from the ground which go round the building (I mean on the inside), broad enough to lie upon, making the wall serve the purpose of a pillow. Underneath these seats or beds they keep their potatoes and pumpions, cover'd with earth, but their corn is in a building by itself raised at least eight feet from the ground. The fire place is in the middle of the floor, just as in some parts of the Highlands of Scotland only they have no aperture at top to evacuate the smoke. The door is opposite one side (for the house is round without, yet on the inside it approaches near to the figure of an octagon) and is exceedingly small both in height and breadth. (Swanton, 1931 a, p. 39.)

The anonymous relation thus describes the summer house, though without indicating that there was another type:

The house is merely a cabin made of wooden posts of the size of the leg, buried in the earth [at one end], and fastened together with *lianas*, which make very flexible bands. The rest of the wall is of mud and there are no windows; the door is only from three to four feet in height. The cabins are covered with bark of the cypress or pine. A hole is left at the top of each gable-end to let the smoke out, for they make their fires in the middle of the cabins, which are a gunshot distant from one another. The inside is surrounded with cane beds raised from three to four feet above the ground on account of the fleas which live there in quantities because of the dirt. (Swanton, 1931 a, p. 37.)

This, it will be seen, resembled the later Alabama house, and it was evidently the forerunner of the log house with which Cushman was familiar in the early part of the nineteenth century:

They lived in houses made of logs, but very comfortable; not more rude or uncouth, however, than many of the whites even of the present day [the work was published in 1899]. Their houses consisted generally of two rooms, both of which were used for every domestic purpose—cooking, eating, living and sleeping; nor was their furniture disproportionate with that of the dwelling— for the sitting room, a stool or two; for the kitchen, a pot or kettle, two or three tin cups, a large and commodious wooden bowl, and a horn spoon, constituted about the ultimatum[!] (Cushman, 1899, p. 39.)

The winter and summer house patterns seem to have been carried by the Choctaw to Louisiana, where the distinctive characters of the two were probably lost. Bushnell reports that the old people at Bayou Lacomb remembered them,

The frames were formed of small saplings; the tops and sides were constructed of palmetto thatch. According to the present inhabitants [in 1908–9], many of the circular houses were large, affording shelter for many persons. Only one door was made, this in most cases facing the south. A fire was kindled on the ground within the lodge, the smoke passing out through an opening made for the purpose at the top near the center. (Bushnell, 1909, p. 7.)

The picture of a plank house which he gives reminds one of the Alabama house. He also illustrates a palmetto thatched dwelling which stood near Mandeville on the north shore of Lake Pontchartrain in 1879 (pl. 61), and a log house and summer house or pavilion which constituted part of the Choctaw settlement at Bonfouca in 1846.

Timberlake, who passed the winter of 1761–62 in the Cherokee country, has left a description of the town house of Echota or Chota, often regarded as the capital of the Cherokee Nation:

> The town-house, in which are transacted all public business and diversions, is raised with wood, and covered over with earth, and has all the appearance of a small mountain at a little distance. It is built in the form of a sugar loaf, and large enough to contain 500 persons, but extremely dark, having, besides the door, which is so narrow that but one at a time can pass, and that after much winding and turning, but one small aperture to let the smoak out, which is so ill contrived, that most of it settles in the roof of the house. Within it has the appearance of an ancient amphitheatre, the seats being raised one above another, leaving an area in the middle, in the center of which stands the fire; the seats of the head warriors are nearest it. (Timberlake, Williams ed., 1927, p. 59.)

The Presbyterian missionary, William Richardson, visited Echota December 29, 1758, about 3 years before Timberlake, and it is the town house of Echota which he is really describing in the following words, though his remarks are intended to be of general application:

> Their Town houses are built in the Form of a Sugar Loaf & will hold 4 or 500 peo.; they are supported by ten Pillars; at the Foot of most of them are seats for the great Men among them; on ye right hand, Hop, on the 3d the Prince of ye Former Year, on the 4th The Chief Beloved Man, of ye present Year, w'm they call Prince; on the 5th the Head Warrior (Oconostata), &c., in this order I'm informed. The two seats behind y'm where the rest sit made of Canes & where some sleep all Night; they are very hot & here they sit & talk & smoke & dance sometimes all Night. (Richardson, 1931, p. 133.)

Bartram, as we have seen, emphasizes the resemblance between the enclosed ceremonial houses of the Creeks and those of the Cherokee. His period is a little later than that of the last-mentioned writers, and the particular account which he gives is based principally on his study of the town house of Cowee:

> They first fix in the ground a circular range of posts or trunks of trees, about six feet high, at equal distances, which are notched at top, to receive into them from one to another, a range of beams or wall plates; within this is another circular order of very large and strong pillars, above twelve feet high, notched in like manner at top, to receive another range of wall plates; and within this is yet another or third range of stronger and higher pillars, but fewer in number, and standing at a greater distance from each other; and lastly, in the centre stands a very strong pillar, which forms the pinnacle of the building, and to which the rafters centre at top; these rafters are strengthened and bound together by cross beams and laths, which sustain the roof or covering, which is a layer of bark neatly placed, and tight enough to exclude the rain, and sometimes they cast a thin superficies of earth over all. There is but one large door, which serves at the same time to admit light from without and the smoak to escape when a fire is kindled; but as there is but a small fire kept, sufficient to give light at night, and that fed with dry small sound wood divested of its bark, there is but little smoak. All around the inside of the building, betwixt the second range

of pillars and the wall, is a range of cabins or sophas, consisting of two or three steps, one above or behind the other, in theatrical order, where the assembly sit or lean down; these sophas are covered with mats or carpets, very curiously made of thin splints of Ash or Oak, woven or platted together; near which the musicians seat themselves, and round about this the performers exhibit their dances and other shows at public festivals, which happen almost every night throughout the year. (Bartram, 1792, pp. 366–367.)

Creek mats were usually made of cane instead of ash or oak splints. The Moravian missionary, Martin Schneider, has a few notes on the town house and the private winter house of the Cherokee as he observed them in 1783–84. He remarks of the former:

In the Midst of every Town is, as it were, a round Tower of Earth about 20 Feet high almost like a Heap where Coals are burnt, on which is a little House, but which have been mostly burnt down in the last War. (Williams, 1928, pp. 260–261.)

This impressed the Duke of Orleans, Louis Philippe, in 1797, as "a hexagonal pyramid of logs" (Williams, 1928, p. 437). It was again the town house of Echota which he had in mind.

Richardson (1931, p. 137) notes of the private hot house, having particular reference to that of Old Hop at Echota, that it "is built like a cone; this they heat as we do ovens & then cover up the ashes & in this way they live in winter wc keeps ym very warm."

Similarly Timberlake (Williams ed., 1927, p. 61) describes the hot house of Kanagatucko as "a little hut joined to the house, in which a fire is continually kept, and the heat so great, that cloaths are not to be borne the coldest day in winter." Bartram (1792, p. 366; cf. 1853 ed., p. 57) calls it "a little conical house covered with dirt" (fig. 5).

Schneider thus describes the private hot house:

Every Family has besides the Dwelling House still a smaller Hothouse. This has but a very small Opening to creep into it, & this is their Abode in cold weather; after the Fire which is made in the Middle is burnt down, the coals are covered with Ashes. Their Couches of Cane fixed round about are their Sleeping Places, which they scarce ever leave before 9 o'clock in the Morning. Then they make again Fire for the whole Day & Night they make another. The Old People having but little & the Children, till they are 10 years old, no Cloathes at all, they could not hold it out in cold Weather without such Houses. (Williams, 1928, p. 260.)

The ordinary summer house of the Cherokee was "a large oblong-square house which seems to be a cook-room, eating-house, and lodging-rooms, in three apartments under one roof" (Bartram, 1909, p. 56). (See fig. 5.) According to Timberlake it was constructed thus:

A number of thick posts is fixed in the ground, according to the plan and dimensions of the house, which rarely exceeds sixteen feet in breadth, on account of the roofing, but often extends to sixty or seventy in length, beside the little hothouse. Between each of these posts is placed a smaller one, and the whole wattled with twigs like a basket, which is then covered with clay very smooth, and sometimes white-washed. Instead of tiles, they cover them with narrow boards. Some of these houses are two-story high, tolerably pretty and capacious; but most of them very inconvenient for want of chimneys, a small hole being all the vent assigned in many for the smoak to get out at. (Timberlake, Williams ed., 1927, p. 84.)

Their summer council house corresponded to this after a fashion, being described by Bartram (1909, p. 57) as "a spacious open loft or pavilion, on the top of a very large oblong building."

The relative length of the private dwelling is somewhat suggestive of the Iroquois longhouse, but each seems to have been occupied by but one distinct family group, and it was constructed of wattle and plaster like the Gulf houses generally, though probably some-

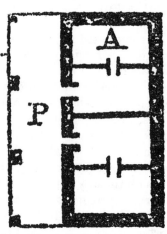

FIGURE 5.—Ground plan of Cherokee house (after Bartram). A, Summer house; P, portico of summer house; D, winter house.

times clapboarded with bark like the dwellings of their northern kinsmen.

The meager details supplied by early writers indicate that the town houses of the Muskhogeans on the coasts of South Carolina and Georgia were similar to the circular buildings we have found among the great inland nations. One of the Cusabo town houses described by Hilton and Sandford was circular in outline, at least 200 feet in circumference, the walls 12 feet high to the "wal-plate," which corresponds to our eaves, and thatched with palmetto. There appear to have been beds around the wall such as have been mentioned repeatedly, and in one place, most likely at the back, there is noted a seat raised higher than the rest, for the chief and other persons of eminence. Our best descriptions of town houses among the Guale Indians are by the Quaker Dickenson in 1699, who saw them after the Guale Indians had moved to Florida and settled on each side of the mouth of St. Johns River. The sizes and arrangements of these houses have been carefully worked out by Bushnell (1919, pp. 84–86). The town house, or "warehouse," as Dickenson calls these structures, belonging to the town of Santa Cruz, the nearest to St. Augustine, was about 50 feet in diameter, with a square smoke hole 15 feet each way, and had beds around the wall divided into 16 compartments by the wall timbers. The council house of San Juan's is not described, but it was still larger. That of Santa Maria, the largest town of all, seems to have been 81 feet in diameter, though the actual figure given is 31. It had a smoke hole 20 feet square and a bed divided into 32 sections. The words "against which the house is built" used by Dickenson of the quadrangular opening in the center suggests the same central element of 4 posts as was common in the Creek hot house.

There is relatively little information regarding the common houses. Speaking of the houses of both chiefs and commoners in Guale near St. Simons Island, San Miguel says:

All of the walls of the houses are of rough timbers and covered with palmetto . . . . . all the houses are small, because, as they have little to keep in them, they make them only for shelter, and for this reason the houses of the chiefs are also small. (Garcia, 1902, p. 195.)

The chief of one of these towns took San Miguel into his house and the visitor remarks that "he had three or four little rooms." That house in which the Spaniards were lodged is described as

a big cabin, circular in shape, made of entire pines from which the limbs and bark had been removed, set up with their lower ends in the earth and the tops all brought together above like a pavilion or like the ribs of a parasol: three hundred men might be able to live in one: it had within around the entire circumference a continuous bed or bedstead, each well fitted for the repose and sleep of many men, and because there was no bed-clothing other than some straw, the door of the cabin was so small that it was necessary for us to bend in order to enter; an arrangement due to the cold although it was spring when we arrived: and so that one may not feel the cold at night and may sweat without clothing it is sufficient to cover the doorway at night with a door made of palmetto, and to light two sticks of firewood within: with this alone we perspired at night and when we were indoors did not feel the cold during the daytime. (Garcia, 1902, p. 195.)

The cabin belonging to the Timucua chief of San Pedro on Cumberland Island "was greater than those I have described, and it was open above with a skylight such as can be made in a cabin, the cabin being round in shape and made of entire pine trees" (Garcia, 1902, p. 199).

Oviedo gives us some confusing, and possibly confused, notes regarding the public buildings and ossuaries in the province of "Gualdape," which I am inclined to identify with part of the Guale Country. He speaks of the "houses or temples" in which the dead were buried as having walls of stone about 8 or 9 feet high set in mortar made of oyster shells, the rest being constructed of pine wood. These would be public houses with walls of lime cement or tabby. The difference between the walls and roof was perhaps owing to the fact that the upper part of the cement was covered with mats or thatch to within a couple of feet of the earth. Another type of house mentioned by Oviedo reminds one of the longhouse of the Iroquois, but his description is probably based upon a somewhat distorted impression created by the rectangular town houses of the Timucua to be considered shortly:

There are several principal [i.e., big] houses all along the coast and each one of them must be considered by those people to be a village, for they are very big and they are constructed of very tall and beautiful pines, leaving the crown of leaves at the top. After having set up one row of trees to form one wall, they set up the opposite side, leaving a space between the two sides of from 15 to 30 feet, the length of the walls being 300 or more feet. As they intertwine the branches at the top and so in this manner there is no need for a tiled roof or other covering, they cover it all with matting interwoven between the logs where there may be hollows or open places. Furthermore they can cross those beams with other [pines] placed lengthwise on the inside, thus increasing the thickness of their walls. In this way the wall is thick and strong, because the beams are very close together. In each one of those houses there is easily room enough for 200 men and in Indian fashion they can live in them, placing the opening for the door where it is most convenient. (Oviedo, 1851, vol. 3, pp. 630–631; Swanton, 1922, p. 48.)

Incidental notice should perhaps be made of the "temple of Talomeco," of which a long description is given by Garcilaso de la Vega. The dimensions of this, 40 paces by 100, suggest rather the temple of the Natchez or the rectangular sacred buildings of the Virginia Indians than the hot houses we have been describing. It may have been adapted from the summer house rather than the winter dwelling, but we cannot trust to Garcilaso's descriptions in all their details (Garcilaso, 1723, pp. 129–134). Ranjel says that the house of the chief which stood opposite this

was very large, high and broad, all decorated above and below with very fine handsome mats, arranged so skillfully that all these mats appeared to be a single one; and, marvelous as it seems, there was not a cabin that was not covered with mats. (Bourne, 1904, vol. 2, pp. 101–102.)

It cannot be determined from this whether "broad" means that it was oval, or rectangular, or that it was merely large.

As has been noted in speaking of the longhouse described by Oviedo, the Timucua town house, in this case said to have been actually occupied by the chief, was oblong. At the mouth of a river believed to have been the St. Mary's, Ribault observed

one house among the rest very long and wide, with seats around about made of reeds nicely put together, which serve both for beds and seats, two feet high from the ground, set upon round pillars painted red, yellow, and blue, and neatly polished. (French, 1869, p. 180; Swanton, 1922, p. 352.)

Ucita, in Tampa Bay, where De Soto landed, had both a chief's house and a temple, situated at opposite ends of the town, an arrangement which suggests that this town may have received influences from the north.   (Robertson, 1933, p. 33; Swanton, 1922, p. 353.)   Le Moyne says that the great rectangular house (pl. 57) was "partly underground in consequence of the sun's heat" (Le Moyne, 1875, p. 12 (ill.); Swanton, 1922, p. 352); and although his remarks are general, it is this house which Spark seems to be describing in the following words:

> Their houses are not many together, for in one house an hundred of them do lodge; they being made much like a great barne, and in strength not inferiour to ours, for they haue stanchions and rafters of whole trees, and are covered with palmito-leaues, hauing no place diuided, but one small roome for their king and queene.   (Hakluyt, 1847–89, vol. 3, p. 613; Swanton, 1922, p. 353.)

This probably means that a retiring room was cut off from the town house for the particular use of the head chief and his family.

In later times the council houses seem to have been round, as indicated in the following description by Calderón:

> Each village has a council house called the great *bujio*, constructed of wood and covered with straw, round, and with a very large opening in the top. Most of them can accommodate from 2,000 to 3,000 persons. They are furnished all around the interior with niches called *barbacôas*, which serve as beds and as seats for the caciques and chiefs, and as lodgings for soldiers and transients.   Dances and festivals are held in them around a great fire in the center.   (Calderón, 1936, p. 13.)

Most of the houses of the common people were undoubtedly circular and so Le Moyne figures most of those he illustrates, but in his picture of a stockaded settlement are some square houses and two of oval pattern like many figured by White as observed in North Carolina (pl. 57).   Ribault says that most of the houses seen by him at the mouth of St. Marys River were "made of wood fitly and closely set up, and covered with reeds, after the fashion of a pavilion" (French, 1869, p. 180; Swanton, 1922, p. 352).   And so Le Challeux:

> Their dwellings are of a round shape and in style almost like the pigeon houses of this country, the foundation and main structure being of great trees, covered over with palmetto leaves, and not fearing either wind or tempest. (Gaffarel, 1875, p. 461; Swanton, 1922, p. 352.)

Bishop Calderón (1936, p. 12) describes the private house as "a hut made in round form, of straw, without a window and with a door a *vara* (2.8 feet) high and half a *vara* (1.4 feet) wide." The size of the door certainly does not seem to have been exaggerated.

Le Moyne also tells us that the common houses were roofed with palmetto.   From no less than three distinct sources we learn that the type of dwelling, at least so far as the roof was concerned, changed in what is now southern Georgia.   Thus the houses seen by

Ribault were thatched with reeds, by which he probably means cane mats, while those along the St. Johns and to the south and west were covered with palmetto. The change also seems to have been accompanied with a change in the interior structure of the roof, the roofs to the north being of mud and wattle like the walls, while those to the south were more open to the air for reasons connected with the latitude. We read in Biedma's narrative of the De Soto expedition, "there was a change in the habitations which were now in the earth, like caves: heretofore they were covered with palm leaves and with grass." (Swanton, 1922, p. 353; Bourne, 1904, vol. 2, pp. 9–10.) This was near the lower course of Flint River. The Fidalgo of Elvas places this change at approximately the same place, the houses in the province of Toalli (later Tamathli) being the first to show it. As the roofs are said to have been of "canes in the manner of tile," we seem to be confirmed in the assumption that the cane was woven into mats. Before that he says that the houses had been roofed with "hay," by which he may mean palmetto, though it is possible that grass was used in an intermediate area between the palmetto country and the region where mats prevailed (Robertson, 1933, p. 74).

The only strictly summer houses alluded to by early writers are rude arbors into which we are told the Timucua retired during 3 months of the year. They perhaps furnished the original suggestion for the open-sided Seminole houses described elsewhere.

There is no account of a Calusa house, but Dickenson has left us a brief sketch of the house of the chief of Santa Lucia on the southeast coast. This was rectangular like that of Timucua chiefs, but the main entrance was midway of one of the longer sides instead of at an end. It bears a rather striking and surprising resemblance to the Cusabo chief's house, and this might be considered of some historical significance if the details were not so meager. (Dickenson, 1803, p. 33; Swanton, 1922, pp. 64, 391; S. C. Hist. and Genealog. Mag., 1904, vol. 5, pp. 57–82.) At some earlier period it is believed that pile dwellings were in use on the southwest Florida coast, but nothing is known regarding them, except what may be inferred from the findings of Cushing at Key Marco:

None of the piles found by us exceeded six and a half feet in length. Indeed, the greater number of them were less than three and a half feet long. These shorter piles were nearly always made of palmetto wood, were not round, but broad, or somewhat flattened, although the edges were rounded. They were tapered toward the bottom and bluntly pointed, rudely squared or hollowed out at the tops as though to support round, horizontal timbers; and they were bored or notched slantingly here and there through the edges, as though for the reception of rounded braces or cross-stays of poles or saplings, abundant pieces of which were found. Some of the piles were worn at the points or lower ends, as though they had rested upon, but had not been driven into, the solid shell and clay-marl benches. They had apparently, on the contrary, been quite rigidly fastened to the horizontal timbers or frameworks of the quays or scaffolds they held up—by means of the stay-sticks—like pegs or pointed feet, so that as long as the water remained low, they would support these house scaffolds above it, as well as if driven into the benches, but when the waters rose, the entire structure would also slightly rise, or at any rate not be violently wrenched from their supports, as would inevitably have been the case had these been firmly fixed below. The longer piles were, on the contrary, round. They were somewhat smaller, quite smoothly finished, and had been, if one might judge by their more pointed and yet roughened or frayed appearance at both ends, actually driven into the bottom. It therefore appeared to me that they had been made so as to be thus driven into the edges of the benches at either side of the peg-supported platforms, in order to keep these from swerving in case an unusual rise in the waters caused them to float. There were other pieces equally long, but broken off near their points. They were slightly grooved at the upper ends and tied around with thick, well-twisted ropes or cables made of cypress bark and palmetto fibre, as though they had served as mooring-posts, probably for the further securing of the ends of the partially movable platforms— else they had not been so violently wrenched as to break them at the points— for some of them were more than four inches in diameter, and were made of tough mangrove and buttonwood or ironwood. The side-posts or stay-stakes were, on the contrary, of spruce or pine, and were, as I have said, finished to a nicety, as though to offer no resistance to the rise and fall of the big, partially floating quays between them. Around the great log or sill of cypress, mentioned as lying along the edge of the northern bench (it was uniformly nine inches in diameter, fourteen feet eleven inches in length, carefully shaved to shape and finished evidently with shark-tooth blades and shell scrapers, and was moreover, like the piles, socketed and notched or bored along its sides) were many of these piles, both short and long; and overlying the sill, as well as on either side of it, I found abundant broken timbers, poles, and traces of wattled cane matting as well as quantities of interlaced or latticed saplings—laths evidently, for they seemed to have been plastered with a clay and ash cement—and quantities also of yellow marsh-grass thatch, some of it alluringly fresh, other portions burnt to black masses of cinder. Here and elsewhere along the edges of the benches occurred fire-hardened cement or mud hearth-plastering, mingled with ashes and charcoal—which indeed occurred more or less abundantly everywhere, together with refuse, consisting not only of broken and sometimes scorched animal bones and shells, but also of the charred remains of vegetable and fruit foods. Among these remains and the more artificial objects that were associated with them we continually encountered incipient or unfinished pieces—blocked-out trays or toy canoes, untrimmed adze and axe handles, uncompleted tablets, etc., and all this evidenced to me that the place was indeed a site of former daily occupation. (Cushing, 1896, pp. 362–363.)

Returning northward to the Siouan tribes of the Carolinas, we have one very early note from Peter Martyr, who obtained his information from a native:

The natives have no temples, but use the dwellings of their sovereigns as such. As a proof of this we have said that a gigantic sovereign called Datha ruled in the province of Duhare, whose palace was built of stone, while all the other houses were built of lumber covered with thatch of grasses. (Anghierra, 1912, vol. 2, pp. 260–262; Swanton, 1922, p. 43.)

Over 150 years later the statement contained in the first sentence was repeated almost verbatim by John Lawson. By grasses we are probably to understand palmetto, where palmetto could be obtained. The reference to a stone house must also, as in cases noted already, be interpreted to mean a clay or earth house, from which it would appear that the Floridian and northern styles of building overlapped in South Carolina even at this early date. In its main outlines Datha's "stone house" was probably similar to the town house of the Waxhaw Indians described by Lawson, except that the latter was not certainly clayed over. Lawson says this was

done round with white benches of fine canes, joining along the wall; and a place for the door being left, which is so low that a man must stoop very much to enter therein. This edifice resembles a large hay rick, its top being pyramidal, and much bigger than their other dwellings, and at the building whereof, every one assists till it is finished. All their dwelling houses are covered with bark, but this differs very much; for it is very artificially thatched with sedge and rushes. As soon as finished, they place some one of their chiefest men to dwell therein, charging him with the diligent preservation thereof, as a prince commits the charge and government of a fort or castle, to some subject he thinks worthy of that trust. In these state houses is transacted all public and private business. (Lawson, 1860, p. 66.)

Lawson appends the following important note regarding the geographical distribution of these "state houses":

On our way [north from the Waxhaw town] we met with several towns of Indians, each town having its theatre, or state house; such houses being found all along the road till you come to Sapona, and then no more of those buildings, it being about one hundred and seventy miles. (Lawson, 1860, p. 72.)

Assuming Sapona to have been without one, this would suggest that the Virginia Siouans, who belonged to a distinct dialectic group, lacked such houses. It is true that Lawson does not appear to have found them in the Keyauwee, Eno, and Shakori towns, but these had probably suffered considerable displacement in the years immediately preceding Lawson's visit. The Siouan tribes using the round council house seem to have owed it to contact with the great nations to the westward, among whom it reached its highest development. Unfortunately, Lawson does not give enough of the details of the structure to enable us to tell how closely the Siouan building was connected with the others. It may also have been used by the Tuscarora.

Our only good description of the Siouan hot house used by individual families is again from Lawson:

These savages live in wigwams, or cabins, built of bark, which are made round, like an oven, to prevent any damage by hard gales of wind. They make the fire in the middle of the house, and have a hole at the top of the roof right above the fire, to let out the smoke. These dwellings are as hot as stoves, where the Indians sleep and sweat all night. The floors thereof are never paved nor swept, so that they have always a loose earth on them. (Lawson, 1860, p. 289.)

The bark they make their cabins withal, is generally cypress, or red or white cedar; and sometimes, when they are a great way from any of these woods, they make use of pine bark, which is the worser sort. In building these fabrics, they get very long poles of pine, cedar, hickory, or any other wood that will bend; these are the thickness of the small of a man's leg, at the thickest end, which they generally strip of the bark, and warm them well in the fire, which makes them tough and fit to bend. Afterwards, they stick the thickest ends of them in the ground, about two yards asunder, in a circular form, the distance they design the cabin to be (which is not always round, but sometimes oval) then they bend the tops and bring them together, and bind their ends with bark of trees, that is proper for that use, as elm is, or sometimes the moss that grows on the trees, and is a yard or two long, and never rots; then they brace them with other poles to make them strong; afterwards cover them all over with bark, so that they are very warm and tight, and will keep firm against all the weathers that blow. (Lawson, 1860, pp. 289–290.)

He has little to say regarding the houses of specific tribes except those of the Waxhaw, merely remarking of the Little Wateree dwellings and of those of a town considerably farther north that they were "dark smoky holes" (Lawson, 1860, pp. 59, 99). Of the Waxhaw cabin in which he and his party were entertained, he says, it was "a very large and lightsome cabin, the like I have not met withal" (Lawson, 1860, p. 61). The superiority of their domestic and public houses, of which a description has been given above, was very likely owing to their more intimate contact with the great nations to the west. Lederer noted in 1670 that the Eno houses differed somewhat from the dwellings of their neighbor for he says:

These and the mountain-Indians build not their houses of bark, but of watling and plaster. (Alvord, 1912, p. 157.)

These mountain Indians were probably the Cheraw, and the differences noted attributable to the fact that they had immigrated from sections farther south and west.

Catesby's notes evidently refer to the Siouan, or other northeastern, tribes. He has the following regarding their winter edifices:

The *Wigwams*, or cabbins of the *Indians* are generally either circular or oval, having but one floor, but of various dimensions, some containing a single family, others four or five families, but of the same kindred. In building their fabricks they stick into the ground at about four or five feet asunder, very long pliant poles, bending their tops, and tying them together with bark; then they brace them together with other poles to strengthen them, afterwards covering them all over, both roof and sides with bark, particularly that of sweet gum, cypress, and cedar, so that they are warm and tight, and will keep firm as against all weathers. In the top of the roof is left a hole to let out the smoak, under which, in the middle of the cabbin, is their fire; round the cabbin are fixed to the walls broad benches of split cane, laying thereon mats or skins, on which they sleep. Their state-cabbins, for the reception of ambassadors, and other publick transactions, are built with greater magnificence, being loftier, and of far larger dimensions, the inside being hung with mats of rushes or cane, as is also the *Wigwam* of the king, and some others of prime note. (Catesby, 1731–43, vol. 2, p. xi.)

In 1716, after the remnants of the Virginia Siouans had been gathered into a town near Fort Christanna on Meherrin River, it was visited by a French Huguenot, John Fontaine, who thus describes the native houses:

The houses join all the one to the other, and altogether make a circle; the walls are large pieces of timber which are squared, and being sharpened at the lower end, are put down two feet in the ground, and stand about seven feet above the ground. These posts are laid as close as possible the one to the other, and when they are all fixed after this manner, they make a roof with rafters, and cover the house with oak or hickory bark, which they strip off in great flakes, and lay it so closely that no rain can come in. Some Indian houses are covered in a circular manner, which they do by getting long saplings, sticking each end in the ground, and so covering them with bark; but there are none of the houses in this town so covered. (Bushnell, 1930, p. 29.)

As we shall see presently, these remarks are of considerable importance.

Catesby speaks as follows of the above town:

A town of *Totero Indians*, seated on *Meherin* river, is built with strong posts or trees drove into the ground close to one another, the interstices being stopt up with moss, and covered with the bark of the sweet gum-tree; from two of which trees, being bereaved of their bark, I gathered more than my hat full of the fragrant rosin that trickles from between the bark and the wood, and by the heat of the sun condenses to a resemblance of transparent amber. (Catesby, 1731–43, vol. 2, p. xi.)

In 1728, when Byrd visited the stockaded town of the Iroquoian Nottoway, he found the dwellings made like

Close Arbours made of Saplings, arched at the top; and cover'd so well with Bark as to be proof against all Weather. The fire is made in the Middle, according to the Hibernian Fashion, the Smoak whereof finds no other Vent but at the Door, and so keeps the whole family Warm, at the Expense both of their Eyes and Complexion. The Indians have no standing Furniture in their Cabanes but Hurdles to repose their Persons upon, which they cover with Mats or Deer-skins. (Bassett, 1901, p. 95.)

A hunting camp of 500 Tuscarora Indians visited by Lawson "had made themselves streets of houses built with pine-bark, not with round tops, as they commonly use, but ridge-fashion" (Lawson, 1860, p. 103).

If we may trust our few authorities, the Siouan tribes had no distinct summer house except open arbors like those in use in Florida and such as we have noticed making their appearance in Louisiana Catesby (1731–43, vol. 2, p. xi) says "they have also houses for the summer, which are built more open and airy, which in sultry weather they sleep in." Lawson speaks of these in connection with the storerooms to which special treatment has been given:

They have [he says] other sorts of cabins without windows, which are for their granaries, skins, and merchandises, and others that are covered over head; the rest left open for the air. These have reed hurdles, like tables, to lie and sit on, in summer, and serve for pleasant banqueting houses in the hot season of the year. (Lawson, 1860, p. 299.)

And of the Eno, Lederer remarks:

In summer, the heat of the weather makes them chuse to lie abroad in the night under thin arbors of wild palm. (Alvord, 1912, p. 157.)

Throughout the warmer parts of the Gulf region, it was customary to erect on short notice open-air arbors in which to hold councils when it was desirable to have these take place away from the settlements.

The eastern Siouan territory and that of the southernmost Algonquians along the coast constitute a transition area between the characteristically Gulf house patterns and the typical Algonquian wigwams. The resemblances between the town house of the Waxhaw and corresponding structures among the nations to the west has been noted and also the use of wattle walls by some of the tribes. However, Lawson's description of the common Siouan house suggests a pattern closely like the wigwam. One distinction between southern and northern houses consists in the fact that in the former the roof and walls are usually treated as distinct elements, while in the true wigwam they are not. In this transitional region, however, we shall find the two types overlapping, and this is strikingly exemplified in Fontaine's remarks on the village at Fort Christanna. It is rather surprising to find the distinction between roof and walls maintained in a house as far north as Maryland:

They Cutt downe halfe a dozen forked Poles and sett 'em up on end, then they cutt Downe some small Poles for Rafters and so Covering it with Barke. (Bushnell, 1913, pp. 535–536.)

On the other hand we have something reminiscent of the circular town house of the Gulf in the temple of Pomeioc, a town of the coastal Algonquians which was near the mouth of Gibbs Creek in what is now Hyde County, N. C.

On the one side [of the town] is their tempel separated from the other howses . . . yt is builded rownde, and couered with skynne matts, and as yt wear compassed abowt with cortynes without windowes, and hath noe lighte but by the doore. (Hariot, 1893, pl. 19.)

The distinction indicated between this building and the house of the chief is also reminiscent of the Gulf, but the houses of the common people as described by Hariot are of Algonquian pattern:

Their houses are made of small poles made fast at the tops in rounde forme after the maner as is vsed in many arbories in our gardens of England, in most townes couered with barkes, and in some with artificiall mattes made of long rushes; from the tops of the houses down to the ground. The length of them is commonly double to the breadth, in some places they are but 12 and 16 yardes long, and in other some wee haue seene of foure and twentie. (Hariot, 1893, p. 36.)

Of Pomeioc, he states:

Their dwellinges are builded with certaine potes fastened together, and couered with matts which they turne op as high as they thinke good, and soe receue in the lighte and other. (Hariot, 1893, p. 36, pl. 19.)

Barlowe and his companions were taken into a 5-room house on Roanoke Island, which may have been a longhouse with mat partitions (Burrage, 1906, p. 234). The remarks of the explorers might lead one to think, however, that it was a house belonging to one family because in an outer room their clothing was removed, washed, and dried, and their feet washed in warm water, and afterward they were taken into an inner chamber and food was served to them there as if it were a sort of dining room. Probably this dwelling was an extra large one intended for the entertainment of important visitors. In these houses the material of which the mats are made is no longer cane but rushes.

The common house of the Virginia Algonquians was like those described by Hariot, as shown by the following quotations:

Spelman:

Ther Biuldinge are made like an ouen with a litell hole to cum in at But more spatius with in hauinge a hole in the midest of ye house for smoke to goe out at. The Kinges houses are both broader and longer then ye rest hauinge many darke windinges and turnings before any cum wher the Kinge is, but in that time when they goe a Huntinge ye weomen goes to a place apoynted before, to build houses for ther husbands to lie in att night carienge matts with them to couer ther houses with all, and as the men goes furthur a huntinge the weomen goes before to make houses, always carrienge ther mattes with them. (Spelman *in* Smith, Arber ed., 1884, pp. cvi–cvii.)

Smith:

Their houses are built like our Arbors of small young springs bowed and tyed, and so close covered with mats or the barkes of trees very handsomely, that notwithstanding either winde raine or weather, they are as warme as stooves, but very smoaky, yet at the toppe of the house there is a hole made for the smoake to goe into right over the fire. (Smith, Tyler ed., 1907, p. 100.)

Strachey:

As for their howses, who knoweth one of them knoweth them all, even the chief kyng's house yt selfe, for they be all alike builded one to the other. They are like garden arbours, at best like our sheppards' cottages, made yet handsomely enough, though without strength or gaynes(s), of such yong plants as they can pluck up, bow, and make the greene toppes meete togither, in fashion of a round roofe, which they thatch with matts throwne over. The walles are made of barkes of trees, but then those be principall howses, for so many barkes which goe to the making up of a howse are long tyke of purchasing. In the midst of the howse there is a louer [chimney or vent], out of which the smoake issueth, the fier being kept right under. Every house comonly hath two dores, one before and a posterne. The doores be hung with matts, never locked nor bolted, but only those matts be to turne upp, or lett fall at pleasure; and their howses are so comonly placed under covert of trees, that the violence of fowle weather, snowe, or raine, cannot assalt them, nor the sun in

sommer annoye them; and the roofe being covered, as I say, the wynd is easily
kept out, insomuch as they are as warme as stoves, albeit very smoakye. Wyn-
dowes they have none but the light comes in at the doore and at the louer; for
should they have broad and open wydowes in the quarters of their howses,
they know not well how, upon any occasion, to make them close and let in the
light too. (Strachey, 1849, pp. 70–71.)

The description by Beverley may be included. It indicates either
that aboriginal Virginia houses did have windows or that windows
were introduced into them soon after white contact.

When they would erect a Wigwang, which is the Indian name for a House,
they stick Saplins into the ground by one end, and bend the other at the top,
fastening them together by strings made of fibrous Roots, the rind of Trees, or of
the green Wood of the white Oak, which will rive into Thongs. The smallest
sort of these Cabbins are conical like a Bee-hive; but the larger are built in an
oblong form and both are cover'd with the Bark of Trees, which will rive off
into great flakes. Their Windowes are little holes left open for the passage
of the Light, which in bad weather they stop with Shutters of the same Bark,
opening the Leeward Windows for Air and Light. Their chimney, as among
the true Born Irish, is a little hole in the top of the House, to let out the
Smoak, having no sort of Funnel, or any thing within, to confine the Smoke
from ranging through the whole Roof of the Cabbins, if the vent will not let
it out fast enough. The Fire is always made in the middle of the Cabbin.
Their Door is a Pendent Mat, when they are near home; but when they go
abroad, they barricade it with great Logs of Wood set against the Mat, which
are sufficient to keep out Wild Beasts. There's never more than one Room
in a House, except in some Houses of State, or Religion, where the Partition
is made only by Mats and loose Poles. [They also had beds along the walls
on which skins were laid as bedding, but sometimes these were placed directly
on the ground.] (Beverley, 1705, bk. 3, pp. 11–12.)

Temples, or buildings corresponding to them, existed throughout
the Powhatan territory. The temple of Pomeioc, mentioned above,
was round, it will be remembered, like the Gulf structures corresponding, but the usage to which it appears to have been put, was like that
of the sacred structures of the Powhatan Indians. These seemed to
combine the functions of true temples, i. e., sanctuaries, with mortuary
usage, as repositories of the dead, and also store houses for the property of the werowances or chiefs. Powhatan's treasure house at
Orapakes seems to have been devoted principally to the last mentioned
purpose, but, as in the case of the others, it was surrounded on the
inside with wooden images and there is little doubt that it belonged
to the same class. Naturally sacred precincts would be the safest in
which to bestow property. Smith says that this house of Powhatan's was "50 or 60 yards in length" and others are mentioned 80 to
100 feet long. Wherever anything is said of the structures we are
told specifically that they were built in the form of arbors, like the
common houses. Beverley calls these houses Quioccosans, and he
gives us an account of what he found in one of them which he examined in the absence of the Indians. There was a smaller room at one

end which reminds us somewhat of that in the temple of the Natchez. Strachey mentions this also, and he states that the door of the temple was toward the east. This was again like the Natchez temple, but the inner chamber was opposite toward the west instead of south like that of the Natchez (Beverley, 1705, bk. 3, pp. 27–30; Strachey, 1849, pp. 81–82). The sacred buildings of the Delaware, one of which still stands in Oklahoma, were probably of the same genus as these. Perhaps there was some connection with the temporary structures put up by the Chippewa for the ceremony of the Midé. Longhouses of the type mentioned were also used throughout most of New England, where their sacred character seems to have given way to some extent to their employment as council houses.

Seemingly the Algonquians of Carolina and Virginia did not have radically distinct dwellings for summer and winter, but when it was warm they raised the mats along the lower border of their wigwam and thus converted it into an open arbor (Strachey, 1849, p. 70).

Let us now turn our attention to the western margin of the Southeast, to the tribes along the lower course of the Mississippi.

A very good description of a Quapaw house is given by Joutel, who passed through their four towns in 1687, and states that their dwellings were all of one type. He was struck by the difference between them and the houses of the Caddo.

The village of the savages was built different from those we had seen hitherto, since the cabins are long and dome-shaped; they construct them of long poles the larger ends of which they plant in the earth and bring [the other ends] together so that the whole resembles an arbor, but they are very large. They cover them with pieces of bark. Each cabin contains many families, each of which has its own special fire. These cabins are much cleaner than many we had seen; but yet they were less generally so than those of the Cenis and the Assonis and others in one particular; it is that the greater part of the Akansas lie on the ground like dogs, having only some skin laid under them. (Margry, 1875–86, vol. 3, p. 442.)

In the Quapaw town first visited by Marquette, however, a town abandoned in Joutel's time, there were raised beds of the usual pattern at the ends of the structure (Thwaites, 1897–1901, vol. 59, p. 157). Joutel also tells us of scaffolds elevated to a height of 15 or 20 feet on which the Indians lay in order to be cooler and escape the mosquitoes (Margry, 1875–86, vol. 3, p. 454).

No hint is given that clay was used in these structures or that any of them were round, and therefore the house described later by Dumont de Montigny as in use in this tribe and among the Yazoo probably represents a later type unless, as is perhaps most probable, he has made a mistake in extending their range so far up the Mississippi. This description runs as follows:

[The cabins] of the Arkansas and of the Yazoos are quite round and have almost the shape of our ice houses (*glacières*). They are constructed of large, long poles planted in the earth about 2 feet apart in a great circle 40 to 50 feet in diameter which approach each other above, where they are brought together and tied, forming a kind of dome. Around these poles the savages plait pliant withes arranged horizontally at vertical distances of about a foot which they attach with cords from pole to pole. Afterward, kneading well with their feet some clay which they mix with that kind of moss of which I have spoken, commonly called "Spanish beard," they make a mud and with it they plaster their cabins, which, when this work is finished, appear as if built entirely of earth. They are then covered with the bark of the cypress or with palmetto. Such are the houses of the savages, in which one discovers neither windows nor chimneys but only a narrow door 5 feet high. (Dumont, 1753, vol. 1, pp. 142–144; Swanton, 1911, p. 59.)

The difference between this house and the dwellings of the Quapaw as revealed to us by other writers will be noted, and, on the other hand, their resemblance to the southern hot house so often mentioned. We seem to have additional testimony to the fact that this house belonged to the Yazoo River people in a statement by Gravier, who visited the Yazoo, Ofo, and Tunica in November 1700, and reports that their cabins were "round and vaulted" (Shea, 1861, p. 135). In 1721 Charlevoix visited the Tunica in a village on the east side of the Mississippi opposite the mouth of the Red of which they had dispossessed the Houma Indians. The chief was apparently living in the dwelling formerly occupied by the Houma chief and this was square, while the remaining houses of the town were partly square and partly round. It is a fair inference that the square houses were those which had formerly belonged to the Houma and the round ones the dwellings which the Tunica had themselves constructed. The only obstacle to such an identification is the fact that Charlevoix says the round houses were "like those of the Natchez," but this may be interpreted as a mistake on his part since he flatly contradicts himself elsewhere and is flatly contradicted by Du Pratz. (French, 1851, pp. 159–160, 173–174; Swanton, 1911, pp. 59, 316.)

De Montigny also describes a "fort house," which one is led to infer was also constructed by the Quapaw and Yazoo, but there is the same uncertainty here, and it is more likely to have been a southern type of house like the other since Adair tells us of Chickasaw houses provided with loopholes which appear to have been similar. (Dumont, 1753, vol. 1, pp. 142–144; Adair, 1775, p. 420.) Dumont says:

There are also some square cabins in which many holes have been pierced at regular intervals. These are something like loopholes, serving to discover the enemy and to shoot through. (Dumont, 1753, vol. 1, pp. 143–144; Swanton, 1911, p. 59.)

These were probably similar to the summer houses in general plan. The missionary Poisson mentions "an open cabin at the field where the men went to take the air" (Thwaites, 1897–1901, vol. 67, pp. 316–322). This, however, may have been one of the structures of the crop guardians.

Houses belonging to the head chiefs of both the Natchez and the Taensa about the year 1700 were square (French, 1851, pp. 159–160; Le Page du Pratz, 1758, vol. 2, pp. 172–175; Swanton, 1911, pp. 59–60), and it would seem from what has been said above that the houses of the Houma just below the Natchez were also square, so that there was a house with square foundation in use along the lower Mississippi from a point below the mouth of the Yazoo to the mouth of the Red. This is interesting and may be of some ethnological significance, though in fact this house was little more than a variation of the round winter dwelling. Du Pratz gives us an excellent description of its construction.

The cabins of the natives are all perfectly square. There is not one which measures less than 15 feet each way, but there are some more than 30. This is their method of constructing them:

The natives go into the young woods in search of poles of young walnut [hickory] trees 4 inches in diameter by 18 to 20 feet long. They plant the largest at the four corners to fix the dimensions and the size of the dome. But before planting the others they prepare the scaffold. This is composed of four poles fastened together above, the ends below resting at the four corners. On these four poles they fasten others crosswise 1 foot apart, all making a four-sided ladder or four ladders joined together.

That done they plant the other poles in the earth in straight lines between those at the corners. When they are thus planted they are bound firmly to a cross pole on the inside of each face (or side). For this purpose they use great cane splints to bind them, at the height of 5 or 6 feet, according to the size of the cabin. This forms the walls. These erect poles are not more than 15 inches apart. A young man then mounts to the top of a corner post with a cord between his teeth. He fastens the cord to the pole, and as he mounts inward the pole bends because those who are below draw the cord to make the pole curve as much as is needed. At the same time another young man does the same to the pole forming the angle opposite. Then the two poles, bent to a suitable height, are firmly and smoothly bound together. The same is done to the poles of the two remaining corners which are made to cross the first. Finally all the other poles are joined at the top, giving the whole the appearance of a bower in a greenhouse such as we have in France. After this work canes are fastened to the lower sides or walls crosswise about 8 inches apart, as high up as the pole which I have spoken of as determining the height of the walls.

These canes being fastened in this manner, they make mud walls of adobe (mortier de terre) in which they put a certain amount of Spanish beard. These walls are not more than 4 inches thick. No opening is left except the door, which is but 2 feet wide at most by 4 in height, and some are very much smaller. Finally they cover the framework I have just described with cane mats, placing the smoothest on the inside of the cabin, and they fasten them to each other carefully so that they will join well.

After this they make many bundles of grass, of the tallest they can find in the low grounds, which are 4 or 5 feet long. They are laid down in the same manner as the straw with which cottages are covered. They fasten this grass by means of large canes and splints also made of cane. After the cabin has been covered with grass they cover all with cane mats well bound together, and below they make a circle of lianas all the way around the cabin. Then the grass is clipped uniformly, and in this way, however high the wind may be, it can do nothing against the cabin. These coverings last twenty years without repairing. (Le Page du Pratz, 1758, vol. 2, pp. 172–175; Swanton, 1911, pp. 59–60.)

The houses of the Bayogoula below the Houma, are described as "round" but the walls and roof appear to have been differentiated. There is not enough detail given to enable us to classify their dwellings with accuracy and the same may be said of those of the other small tribes of this region. The Bayogoula houses as well as their temple seem, however, to have had entrance rooms or passageways like those of the Creek and Chicasaw hot houses (Margry, 1875–86, vol. 4, pp. 169–172; Swanton, 1911, p. 275). The Acolapissa temple is described as "round" by Pénicaut, and the houses in their town on the Mississippi are said to have been "in the shape of a pavilion," which ordinarily means circular, but bare references of this kind give us little satisfaction. (Margry, 1875–86, vol. 5, pp. 467–468; French, 1851, p. 177; Swanton, 1911, pp. 282, 283.) Better than any of these are the drawings and descriptions of De Batz (pl. 62). These confirm the circular character of private houses, but the temple was 22 feet by 14. De Batz's sketch of the latter seems to indicate that the ground plan was oval. The three wooden birds on the roof would, however, suggest that this temple may have been made in imitation of that of the Natchez (Bushnell, 1927, pl. 1). Thus it is probable that the small tribes of the Lower Mississippi below the Houma lived in circular dwellings like those on the Yazoo. The only puzzling point is the difference shown in the sketches between the perpendicular walls and the slope of the roof which seems to call for some corresponding differentiation in the underlying frame. Nothing of the kind is mentioned by Dumont or any other early writer so far as I am aware.

Passing to the Caddo and Hasinai Indians, we find types transitional between those of the Mississippi Valley and the Wichita grass house. All of the Hasinai houses and most of those of the eastern Caddo were of the Wichita type, but some along the Red River, particularly the temple figured in the sketch which Bolton reproduces, evidently had wattle walls. A typical grass house is thus described by Joutel. He says that some of these were 60 feet in diameter.

They are round, in the shape of beehives or rather big haystacks, being of the same material except that they are taller; they are covered with grass from bottom to top. They make the fire in the middle, the smoke escaping above through the grass. . . . They cut down tall trees as big around as the thigh, they plant them erect in a circle and bring the ends together above, after which they lath them and cover them from bottom to top.

Around the inside was a kind of shelf used for beds raised about 3 feet from the ground and they separated the different beds by means of mats (Joutel *in* Margry, 1875–86, vol. 3, p. 345; Swanton, 1942, pp. 148–154).

This was, in short, a house without eaves, resembling in that respect most of the Algonquian houses and the upper portions of the lower Mississippi houses. The walled house seems not to have been described by any early writer, but is figured in the sketch above mentioned (Bolton, 1915, frontispiece). This, as Harrington well remarks, was evidently constructed like the lower Mississippi houses, i. e., like the round houses of the Yazoo, Tunica, and Acolapissa rather than those of the Natchez. During his explorations in the Caddo country, Harrington found "fragments of these wattle-and-daub walls, accidentally preserved by burning, which turned the clay into terracotta . . . on most of the sites explored" (Harrington, 1920, p. 252).

It is also interesting to note that Harrington (1920, pp. 256–258) found in the same Caddo country numerous sites of earth lodges like those used in historic times by the Pawnee, Mandan, and other northern tribes. And just as the Wichita grass house may be described as the lower Mississippi dwelling with the roof structure carried down to the ground, so the earth lodge may be defined as the same with the wall structure carried to the top. But in the lower Mississippi structure a mud covering was generally extended over the roof under the grass and mats so that it is perhaps nearer the earth lodge than the Wichita building. However, the relation between all three seems pretty clear. Larger houses of the two first-mentioned types were employed as town houses or ceremonial houses, one of them in particular being devoted to the uses of the great chenesi or high priest of the Hasinai Confederation. Such buildings were usually placed upon mounds. In 1916 Alanson Skinner explored a square house site in southwestern Arkansas which he regarded, no doubt rightly, as the house of a chief (Harrington, 1920, pp. 291–297). Although this was in the country later occupied by the Caddo, it is highly probable that it belonged to some tribe culturally connected with the Natchez and Taensa.

Outside arbors were used by the Caddo and probably by most of the other Southeastern tribes, as we find them mentioned in Louisiana, Florida, and the Carolinas, and the descendants of many of these tribes make use of them today in Oklahoma. During summer, fires for cooking were often made out of doors (Dumont, 1753, vol. 1, p. 144; Swanton, 1911, p. 59).

Adair (1775, p. 418) mentions a partition in the summer house of the Chickasaw of his time, and this is important, for from it probably evolved the later house of both Indians and whites which was made either with a central partition or by setting two small 1-room houses end to end, usually with a platform between them. There is reason to think that this type was of purely Indian origin.

MATERIALS USED IN BUILDING

Adair indicates that the favorite wood out of which Chickasaw house frames were constructed was pine but that, at least in the summer house, locust and sassafras might be substituted if pine was not available. Pine was also a favorite material for the main structure in Carolina houses and is mentioned by Oviedo and San Miguel in their descriptions of the Guale houses. Hickory seems to have been used mainly on the lower Mississippi, and Lawson speaks of hickory, cedar, "or any other wood that would bend" as in use by the Siouan tribes as well as pine. Palmetto appears in the modern Seminole houses of south Florida, probably for lack of anything else suitable.

The backing for the wattle walls and roof was made of cane by the Natchez, while the Chickasaw employed in their summer houses withes of the white oak or hickory over which were long winter canes in bundles of three, the eave boards being of poplar because it is soft.

The clay with which houses were plastered was mixed with grass, as by the Chickasaw, or with Spanish moss, the latter particularly along the lower Mississippi as high up as the Yazoo.

Over its clay roof the Chickasaw hot house had a grass thatch, and the common houses of the Natchez were covered in the same way except that there was a layer of cane mats underneath. As we proceed westward the grass thatch becomes more prominent, being apparently the main roofing material in all Caddo houses except a few on Red River and identical with the main roofing of the Wichita grass house.

In the Creek town houses pine bark took the place of grass. Pine bark was used also as a covering for some of the common houses and was similarly employed by the Choctaw and Siouan tribes, though Lawson tells us that pine bark was the poorest sort, and that the Indians of his acquaintance used cypress bark or bark of the red or white cedar. Cedar is not mentioned by anyone else, but cypress bark seems to have been the favorite and it makes its appearance as coverings of houses among the Creeks, Chickasaw, Choctaw, Seminole, and the Indians of the Yazoo, besides the Siouans. Among the Chickasaw, Creeks, and Cherokee the bark was laid directly over split shingles, also of cypress, if that were to be had. The houses in the town at Fort Christanna were covered with bark taken from the oak or hickory tree (Fontaine *in* Maury, 1907). Catesby alone includes among the tree barks thus employed that of the sweetgum.

Toward the south, mats or palmetto leaves took the place of bark. In the Siouan and Algonquian countries we hear of rush mats; farther south the universal mat material was cane, and cane mats were employed particularly all along the lower Mississippi, cane mats being hung sometimes both on the outside and the inside. Palmetto thatch was particularly in evidence in Florida and southern Georgia, including Guale, and along the lower Mississippi.

The palmetto was "of inestimable value" to the Florida Seminole.

From the trunk of the tree the frames and platforms of their houses are made; of its leaves durable water tight roofs are made for the houses; with the leaves their lodges are covered and beds protecting the body from the dampness of the ground are made. (MacCauley, 1887, p. 517.)

BEDS

In almost all of these houses, of every type, a bench extended around the entire interior next to the wall, except at the doorway, though in a few of the longer summer houses such benches or "beds," as they were called, seem to have been confined to sections at either end, as in the late Creek house described by Swan and in some of the oval Quapaw houses. There is some indication that in Caddo houses the beds were raised somewhat higher than was usual along the Mississippi and in the territory east of it. Throughout most of the region as far as the Caddo, the material out of which they were made, except perhaps for the posts themselves, was of cane. Four or six forked posts carried long canes over which were laid crosspieces also of cane and above all were cane mats. The Waxhaw town house had benches of fine canes. Among the Cherokee, however, the more northerly Siouan tribes, and the Algonquian peoples of Carolina and Virginia other materials was used. White-oak splints are especially mentioned and Bartram says the Cherokee also employed ash splints. Rush mats take the place of cane mats. The bed clothing, such as there was, consisted of skins of bison, bear, panther, and other animals, and in Virginia rush mats sometimes served the same purpose. On the Georgia coast San Miguel says that only straw was used as bedding and that the bed was raised "more than a yard (*vara*)" above the ground. Florida Seminole beds were of palmetto (Garcia, 1902, p. 517).

FIRE MAKING

Barlowe is one of the earliest writers to describe the common method of making fire, in this case among the Algonquians of the North Carolina coast:

There is one thing to be marvelled at, for the making of their fire, and not onely they but also the Negros doe the same, which is made onely by two stickes, rubbing them one against another: and this they may doe in any place they come, where they finde sticks sufficient for the purpose.   (Salley, 1911, p. 120.)

Smith says of the Virginia Indians:

Their fire they kindle presently by chafing a dry pointed sticke in a hole of a little square peece of wood, that firing it selfe, will so fire mosse, leaves, or anie such like drie thing that will quickly burne. (Smith, Tyler ed., 1907, p. 101.)

According to Beverley (1705, bk. 3, p. 49), the punk was "a sort of soft Touchwood, cut out of the knots of Oak or Hiccory Trees, but the Hiccory affords the best."

As usual Lawson does not miss this subject:

Before the Christians came amongst them, not knowing the use of steel and flints, they got their fire with sticks, which by vehement collision or rubbing together, take fire. This method they will sometimes practice now, when it has happened through rainy weather, or some other accident, that they have wet their spunk, which is a sort of soft, corky substance, generally of a cinnamon colour, and grows in the concave part of an oak, hiccory, and several other woods, being dug out with an ax and always kept by the Indians, instead of tinder or touch-wood, both of which it exceeds. You are to understand that the two sticks they use to strike fire withal are never of one sort of wood, but always differ from each other. (Lawson, 1860, p. 331.)

Near Sugartree Creek, N. C., Byrd saw many trees of the kind used to make firesticks.

We also saw in this Place abundance of papa Trees, the Wood whereof the Indians make very dry on purpose to rub Fire out of it. Their Method of doing it is this: They hold one of these dry Sticks in each hand, and by rubbing them hard and quick together, rarify the Air in such a Manner as to fetch Fire in ten Minutes. Whenever they offer any Sacrifice to their God, they look upon it as a Profanation to make use of Fire already kindled, but produce fresh Virgin Fire for that purpose, by rubbing 2 of these Sticks together that never had been us'd before on any Occasion. (Bassett, 1901, pp. 314–315.)

This was in territory but recently vacated by the Saponi Indians, and most of Byrd's information was derived from the Saponi or some of the other Siouan remnants then settled at Fort Christanna. From Byrd's description it seems doubtful whether he had actually seen fire made.

Adair's account of fire making is among the best and it also gives some idea of the religious attitude toward the firey element, for it is in connection with the kindling of the sacred fire on the ceremonial ground. It applies to the Chickasaw or Creek custom, probably both:

The former [i.e., the fire-maker] takes a piece of dry poplar, willow, or white oak, and having cut a hole, so as not to reach through it, he then sharpens another piece, and placing that with the hole between his knees, he drills it briskly for several minutes, till it begins to smoke—or, by rubbing two pieces together, for about a quarter of an hour, by friction he collects the hidden fire; which all of them reckon to immediately issue from the holy Spirit of fire. The Muskohge call the fire their grandfather—and the supreme Father of mankind, *Eskata-Emishe*, the "breath master," as it is commonly explained. When the fire appears, the beloved waiter cherishes it with fine chips, or shaved splinters of pitch-pine, which had been deposited in the holiest; then he takes the unsullied wing of a swan, fans it gently, and cherishes it to a flame. On this, the *Archi-magus* brings it out in an old earthen vessel, whereon he had placed it, and lays it on the sacred altar, which is under an arbour, thick-weaved a-top with green boughs.   (Adair, 1775, p. 111.)

Pope says that the base stick used by the Creeks was poplar, and the upper stick sassafrass, but a missionary report dated 1852 states that they were both of ash (Pope, 1792, p. 55; Foreman, 1934, p. 18), and an old Okchai Indian told me that they were of post oak. The last-mentioned added that the true punk upon which the resulting sparks were caught was not any sort of rotten wood such as is now called by the name, but soft stuff of the kind found in hickory or cypress trees by chopping into them where a limb has come away. After the punk had caught fire, it was taken off, mixed with hay, and fanned until the whole burst into flames. Fire was transported from one place to another by means of burning oak bark. From the French they got flint and steel. Hicks (see p. 771) reports that the Cherokee used "dried grape vine" as a base stick.

By 1904 the Yuchi Indians had so far forgotten their ancient use of firesticks that they had no remembrance of them. Speck says:

The Yuchi claim that originally two pieces of stone were struck together, either two pieces of flint or a piece of flint and a piece of quartz or pyrites. In the annual tribal ceremony this method is preserved yet. Two persons are ordinarily required in producing fire, one to do the striking, the other to hold the bed of fire material into which the spark is projected when obtained. A single individual might succeed very well, but two together obtain fire much more quickly. Even then the operation often takes fifteen minutes or more. It is likely, however, that the manipulators were already out of practice when the method passed out of common use. It is nowadays admitted that the town chief who strikes the spark at the annual ceremony is greatly worried at this time over the ultimate result of his efforts. It takes him about twenty minutes to secure a flame.

The method, as observed on several ceremonial occasions, is as follows: the flint, *yätä dawoné*, is held between the thumb and forefinger of the right hand with a small piece of punk material, *tciñg ō'*, alongside of it. This punk appears to be a very close-pored fungus. In his left hand he holds the striker. The helper stands by, holding a curved tray of hickory bark heaped up with decayed wood, *sämbī'*, which has been dried and reduced to powder. The chief operator then strikes the two stones together, and when several good sparks have been seen to fly, a moment is given to watching for evidence that one has been kept alive in the punk. If the spark smoulders in this it is gently transferred to the tinder in the bark tray. From this moment the responsibility rests with the helper. He begins to sway the tinder very gradually from side to side and gauges his movements by the thin wisp of smoke that arises from the smouldering bed. After a few minutes, if things go well, the smoke increases and the helper becomes more energetic. The climax is reached when from the dried wood tinder-bed a little flame springs up. Small twigs are piled on and then larger ones until the blazing mass can be safely deposited beneath a pile of firewood. Nowadays at any rate, the fire-producing materials, flint and punk, are a part of the town chief's sacred paraphernalia and he has the prerogative of manipulating them. A piece of steel is more often used as a sparker in the modern operation, as it is more effective.

The most convenient fireplace arrangement is to have a large, not too dry backlog with the fire maintained along one side according to the number of pots to be heated. When the backlog burns away in one place the fire is moved to another, or the log itself is pushed along. (Speck, 1909, pp. 42–43.)

An ultra modern method of fire making, short of the use of matches, was thus described to MacCauley by a Florida Seminole Indian:

"Tom Tiger" showed me how he builds a fire when away from home. He held, crumpled between the thumb and forefinger of the left hand, a bit of paper. In the folds of the paper he poured from his powder horn a small quantity of gunpowder. Close beside the paper he held also a piece of flint. Striking this flint with a bit of steel and at the same time giving to the left hand a quick upward movement, he ignited the powder and paper. From this he soon made a fire among the pitch pine chippings he had previously prepared. (MacCauley, 1887, p. 518.)

In his description of the method of making fire on the lower Mississippi, Du Pratz' remarks are too general to throw much light on the subject. He says that the fire-maker selected a small limb, dead but still adhering to the tree, and about as big as one of the fingers, removed it, and twirled it violently in a cavity in a second stick until a little smoke was seen coming out.

Then, collecting in the hole the dust which this rubbing has produced, he blows upon it gently until it takes fire, after which he adds to it some very dry moss and other inflammable material. (Le Page du Pratz, 1758, vol. 2, p. 165; Swanton, 1911, p. 57.)

He also mentions the use of flints for this purpose, but it is not certain that he actually saw them in use among the Indians (Le Page du Pratz, 1758, vol. 2, p. 165; Swanton, 1711, p. 58).

An additional note relative to tinder appears in Dumont's work:

Mulberries, as I have remarked, are very common in this province, and along the trunks of the largest specimens knobs or swellings form. It is from these swellings that the savages obtain a soft, dry, and light wood, which takes fire like true touchwood, and it is this which is called tinder. (Dumont, 1753, vol. 2, pp. 203–204.)

Mention of Spanish moss for this purpose has been made already (pp. 247, 318).

According to the origin legend of the Chitimacha, the supreme being communicated to them "the art of drawing fire from two pieces of wood, the one flat and the other pointed, by turning one upon the other with force" (Swanton, 1911, pp. 356–357).

Firewood was usually of oak or hickory, and for the sacred fires, or those which it was desired to keep for a long time, the sticks were laid down flat with their ends brought together and the fire was kindled at that point. In the sacred fires four main sticks were used pointing in the direction of the four cardinal points, or sometimes the points half way between. Pine was generally used merely for kindling, but my Alabama informant stated that it made too much smoke to be employed in any other manner. A discordant note is, however, struck by Beverley in speaking of the Virginia Indians:

Their Houses or Cabbins, as we call them, are by this ill method of Building, continually Smoaky, when they have Fire in them; but to ease that inconvenience, and to make the Smoak less troublesome to their Eyes, they generally burn Pine, or Lightwood, (that is, the fat knots of dead Pine) the Smoak of which does not offend the Eyes, but smuts the Skin exceedingly, and is perhaps another occasion of the darkness of their Complexion. (Beverley, 1705, bk. 3, p. 12.)

He adds that "burning Light-Wood, split into small Shivers, each Splinter whereof will blaze and burn End for End, like a Candle" was used to attract fish (Beverley, 1722, p. 33), and the use of pine torches in fire fishing is also mentioned by Lawson (1860, p. 341).

For the illumination of their Square Grounds the Creek Indians usually depended on a single central fire and in later times the same kind of fire seems to have been kindled in the town hot house, but at an earlier day, at least when important business was being conducted, canes were arranged spirally about the central post and the fire led along this, fresh canes being added at the end before the fire reached it. From Lawson we learn that the Waxhaw, and probably other Siouan tribes of the Catawba group, had the same custom. The tribes along the lower Mississippi, however, illuminated their grounds by means of a circle of cane torches around the periphery. In one of the Natchez grounds Du Pratz asserts that more than 200 such torches were used.

While De Soto's army was occupying one of the Chickasaw towns, the Indians made a night attack, and, in apparent emulation of the tactics of Gideon, brought fire in earthen pots with which to set fire to the houses (Bourne, 1904, vol. 2, pp. 22–23). In his account of this, Garcilaso (1723, p. 166) says they employed fire-arrows, and the use of such arrows was common among the eastern Indians, being described and illustrated by Le Moyne as observed in Florida in 1564–65. But, in the same connection, Garcilaso speaks of "flambeaux" which the attackers bore in their hands, and remarks:

These torches, which seemed to be of wax because they illuminated well, were made of a certain herb which grows in that country, which, when it is twisted and lighted, preserves the fire like a wick, and shaken emits a very brilliant flame. (Garcilaso, 1723, p. 166.)

This "herb" may in reality have been nothing more than pine splinters or pieces of cane.

House fires were usually built in the middle of the cabin, and this usage was general in the winter house and in all of the others so far as we have any record. In the warmer parts of the south, however, in summer the fire was often made out of doors. This has been noted of the Florida Seminole, and Dumont observed it along the lower Mississippi. (MacCauley, 1887, p. 501; Dumont, 1753, vol. 1, p. 144; Swanton, 1911, p. 59.) As has been told me specifically of the Alabama, the fire was usually on the bare floor, but often in a depression clayed up on all sides and sometimes there was a stone hearth.

SMOKE HOLES AND WINDOWS

Apertures to allow the escape of smoke from houses are noted in Virginia Algonquian structures (Smith, Strachey, Beverley), in houses of the eastern Siouan tribes (Lawson), in the town houses of the Guale Indians (Dickenson), in the house of the Timucua chief of Cumberland Island (San Miguel), in the Bayogoula houses of the lower Mississippi (apertures 2 feet in diameter), and in the summer houses of the Cherokee, Chickasaw, and Choctaw. Choctaw houses are said to have had two smoke vents, one at each end of the gable, and, according to tradition, this type of house was also used by the Alabama. Smoke holes appear as well in Chitimacha tradition. As early as 1790, however, some Creek houses were provided with chimneys (Swan). Naturally smoke holes were less in evidence in the winter houses than in dwellings used in summer. Romans tells us that there was no opening of the kind in the Chickasaw hot house, and there seem to have been none in the corresponding structures of the Choctaw and Creeks, nor were there any in the Guale houses about St. Simons Island seen by San Miguel, though Dickenson observed them in the town houses of the expatriated Guale Indians in Florida. We do not hear of them among any of the Mississippi tribes except the Bayogoula. Apparently there were none in the houses of the Natchez, Taensa, Houma, Tunica, Yazoo, Koroa, and Quapaw. There is no mention of a smoke hole in the houses of the Timucua beyond the one given above, and we are told specifically that the Caddo allowed the smoke to filter out through the grass roofs of their dwellings. Dumont de Montigny suggests that this omission was to enable the occupants of a house to get rid of the mosquitoes, but the necessity of preserving a sufficiently high temperature throughout winter nights was an important consideration.

Both Dumont and Adair speak of "fort houses" made with loopholes, and the Spanish chroniclers state that the houses of Mabila were provided with such loopholes. According to Adair the Chickasaw had apertures in their hot houses close to the ground to enable them to detect and fire upon approaching enemies. Beverley describes small windows in the houses of the Powhatan Indians which they closed in bad weather with bark shutters, leaving those on the leeward side open, however, for the admission of air and light. As

Beverley wrote some years after white settlements had been started, this might have been an innovation.

Few Southeastern houses had more than one door except among the Powhatan tribes of Virginia, where there were usually two in the longer houses, one at the middle of each end (Strachey, 1849, p. 71). According to Garcilaso de la Vega (1723, p. 52), the house of the chief of Ochile in central Florida was very large and had doors toward the four cardinal points, but this seems to have been exceptional, though in fact our information regarding Timucua houses is very meager. Bartram (1909, p. 56) figures a Cherokee summer house with two doors, but this represents a later style and, besides, it is to be noted that the rooms to which these doors gave access did not communicate and were of the nature of two houses set side by side. Ordinarily, however, particularly in descriptions of the houses along the lower Mississippi, one door is assumed. Garcilaso (1723, p. 153) says specifically of the houses of Mabila that they had but one door. Among the Chickasaw and Caddo this door was usually turned toward the east (Adair, 1775, p. 176; Hatcher, 1928, p. 52; Swanton, 1942, p. 152), but sometimes toward the southeast or south, and this represents the commonest orientation throughout the Gulf region, the west being the bad luck quarter. Yet it is probable that circumstances altered cases, topography overriding superstition or causing a reinterpretation of it. It is not likely that houses on the east bank of a river fronted away from it, though this may well have been true of the ceremonial houses. The door of the Natchez temple was plainly east, but we are told that the door of the Head Chief's house nearby was north (Swanton, 1911, pp. 59, 162). This, however, may have been due to an unwillingness to have it open entirely away from the east and entirely away from the temple. Bushnell (1909, p. 7) was informed that, in most cases, the doors of houses occupied by the Choctaw of Bayou Lacomb in olden times faced south. The winter houses of the Chickasaw, and presumably those of the Choctaw, had short passageways before the door as a protection against drafts and enemies (Adair, 1775, p. 420). The same sort of approach was used before the tcokofa of the Creeks and the town house of the Cherokee. It was possibly an extension or modification of this sort of approach which is described as the dwelling of the keepers of the temple among the Taensa and certain other tribes (Swanton, 1911, p. 269).

No De Soto chronicler indicates the materials of which Indian doors were made except that the Fidalgo of Elvas refers to "a door with a grating" at Mabila (Robertson, 1933, p. 133). In 1595 San Miguel mentions a door made of palmetto to close the entrance of a Guale house (Garcia, 1902, p. 195). Probably the kind described by Adair was typical:

The Indians always make their doors of poplar, because the timber is large, and very light when seasoned, as well as easy to be hewed; they cut the tree to a proper length, and split it with a maul and hard wooden wedges, when they have indented it a little, in convenient places with their small hatchets. They often make a door of one plank in breadth, but, when it requires two planks, they fix two or three cross bars to the inner side, at a proper distance, and bore each of them with a piece of an old gun barrel, heated and battered for the purpose, and sew them together with straps of a shaved and wet buffalo hide, which tightens as it dries, and it is almost as strong as if it were done with long nails, riveted in the usual manner. (Adair, 1775, p. 450.)

However, the door of the Acolapissa temple figured by De Batz seems to be of a construction to which Elvas' term "grating" might be applied. This is stiffened by four crosspieces to which it is tied at intervals, apparently with withes, and withes also seem to have been used as hinges (Bushnell, 1927, pl. 1). (See pl. 62.) The Alabama house door of later times also swung on side hinges, and sometimes opened inward, sometimes outward. It was made either of a single plank or two or more fastened together.

Du Pratz gives us one truly aboriginal style of door in his description of the entrances of sacred buildings:

Many of these nations have only very simple temples, which one would often take for private cabins. However, when one comes to know, he distinguishes them by means of two wooden posts at the door made like boundary posts with a human head, which hold the swinging door with a piece of wood planted in the earth at each end, so that the children may not be able to open the door and go into the temple to play. In this way the door can be opened only by raising it above these posts, which are at least three feet long, and it requires a strong man to lift it. It is the small nations which have these temples which one would confound with private dwellings. The latter have indeed posts and a similar door, but the posts are smooth, and these doors open sideways, because there is no piece of wood at the end. A woman or a child is able to open one of these doors from the outside or inside, and at night it is closed and fastened on the inside to keep the dogs from entering. (Le Page du Pratz, 1758, vol. 3, pp. 21–23; Swanton, 1911, p. 167.)

We must suppose that these doors were hung by means of one short cord at the middle of the top, or by two or three longer ones, and that close to the outer margin of each two stakes were planted in the ground rising 3 feet out of it. Therefore the door would ordinarily be opened by shoving it, or swinging it to one side. In the case of a temple, however, a stake at each end, necessarily of the same height as the others, or thereabouts, prevented anyone from opening it in the usual manner. He must lift the door bodily and then push it over the stakes. This, of course, necessitated rather long cords at the top.

All doorways are described as very small, especially those of the hot houses, a circumstance commented upon by Elvas. Lawson (1860, p. 65) says the same of the Waxhaw town house, which was so low that one had to stoop in order to enter. The largest Natchez doors are described as 4 feet high by 2 wide, that of the Chickasaw hot house is given as 4 feet high and just wide enough for one person to enter at a time. The Choctaw door was "from three to four feet in height." (Le Page du Pratz, 1758, vol. 2, pp. 174–175; Swanton, 1911, p. 60; 1931 a, p. 37.) The entrance to the temple of the Taensa is given as 4 feet by "not more than 3," while the Quapaw and Yazoo doors are given by Dumont as 5 feet in height. This is somewhat above the average, but the recorded dimensions of the Bayogoula temple entrance, 8 by 2½ feet, on the authority of Iberville, is the maximum. (Swanton, 1911, pp. 59, 275, 269; Dumont, 1753, vol. 1, pp. 142–144.) In this case I am inclined to think that the original manuscript may have indicated 5 or 6 instead of 8.

When we come to Virginia we find that the wooden or lattice door has been replaced by a mat which one "could turn up or let fall at pleasure" (Strachey, 1849, p. 70). To protect the house against wild beasts, rather than wild men, when the occupants moved away for a time, they barricaded the entrance with great logs of wood, and similar barricades were used along the lower Mississippi.

AWNINGS, SUNSHADES, AND FLAGS

Besides the protection from the sun's rays provided by awnings in canoes and on litters, we have definite mention of a device like a parasol carried over the head of a chief or chieftainess. (See p. 599.) This was what a servant held over Tascalusa, chief of the Mobile Indians, when he gave an audience to De Soto in 1540. The memories of our several chroniclers evidently did not retain precisely the same impressions of this. Biedma describes it as "a fly-brush of plumes, so large as to afford his person shelter from the sun" (Bourne, 1904, vol. 2, pp. 17–18). Ranjel says:

Before this chief there stood always an Indian of graceful mien holding a parasol on a hurdle something like a round and very large fly fan, with a cross similar to that of the Knights of the Order of St. John of Rhodes, in the middle of a black field, and the cross was white. (Bourne, 1904, vol. 2, pp. 120–121.)

Elvas says that one of the Indians of highest rank about Tascalusa held

a sort of fan of deerskin which kept the sun from him, round and the size of a shield, quartered with black and white, with a cross made in the middle. From a distance it looked like taffeta, for the colors were very perfect. It was set on a small and very long staff. [He adds] this was the device he bore in his wars. (Robertson, 1933, p. 124.)

But the last remark represents rather Elvas' inference than his absolute knowledge. Garcilaso's informants also took this to be a standard. Garcilaso says that near the chair on which Tascalusa sat "there was an Indan with an ensign of chamois skin traversed by three azure bars of the shape of a cavalry ensign." "Our people," he continues, "were surprised at it, for they had not yet seen flags among the Indians" (Garcilaso, 1723, p. 145).

However, a little later, after the Indians of Mabila had launched an assault upon their guests and the latter had escaped from the town, the Indians closed the gates, and "beating their drums, they raised flags, with great shouting" (Bourne, 1904, vol. 2, p. 19). Reaching the "River of Chicaça" somewhere in northern Mississippi or the adjacent parts of Alabama, they found it overflowing its banks "and the Indians on the other side in arms with many white flags" (Bourne, 1904, vol. 2, p. 131). Later, when the Mississippi River Indians approached the Spaniards in their canoes to dispute the passage of that great stream, they are said to have carried "banners" (Robertson, 1933, p. 161). And, finally, when the survivors of the expedition were descending the river with the intention of abandoning the country, they made a last stop at one of the villages on its banks where they found

one piece of marten's [muskrat's] skin about eight ells long by three wide. This piece was double, alike on both sides and decorated in places with clusters of seed pearls. They believed that it was used as a standard by the Indians in their festivals; for according to appearances it could not be destined to any other use. (Garcilaso, 1723, p. 242.)

On approaching the Cherokee town of Settico, Timberlake "observed two stands of colors flying, one at the top, and the other at the door of the town-house; they were as large as a sheet, and white." He continues:

Lest therefore I should take them for French, they took great care to inform me, that their custom was to hoist red colors as an emblem of war; but white, as a token of peace. (Timberlake, Williams ed., 1927, pp. 62-63.)

On a sketch of one of the cabins forming an Alabama Square Ground, made by some French draughtsman in the eighteenth century, we find a flag over the central post, and in very recent times red and white flags have been used by the Creeks to designate the war and peace cabins (Swanton, 1930, p. 187). We may add that an American flag was presented to the Creeks of Tukabahchee town in the early days of the American Union, and since then an American flag has always been run up in the Tukabahchee square during the annual busk.

These seem to be our only references to what we should call flags, though Bartram (1792, p. 453) gave the name of "standard" to the calumet. It is possibly of some significance that most of these "flags" were reported from the western part of the Gulf area.

CUSHIONS

A pillow might readily be devised by rolling up a mat (Beverley, 1705, bk. 3, p. 12) or by throwing a mat or blanket over some soft material such as Spanish moss. When the lady of Cofitachequi crossed Savannah River to welcome De Soto, she sat on "two cushions, one on top of the other" laid upon a mat under an awning in the back part of a canoe (Robertson, 1933, p. 91). Later on, the same sort of seat was prepared for Tascalusa "on an elevated place" where he was awaiting the Spaniards (Robertson, 1933, p. 124). Ranjel not only notes the cushions, but says that when Tascalusa marched on from this town in company with the white men one of his servants carried a cushion (Bourne, 1904, vol. 2, pp. 120, 122). The chief of Coca came out to meet them seated on a cushion in a litter borne on the shoulders of his principal men (Robertson, 1933, p. 115). In an account of the "Proceedings of the English Colonies in Virginia," it is said that when the colonists visited Powhatan in 1608 he received them seated upon a bed of mats "his pillow of leather imbroydred (after their rude manner) with pearle and white beades" (Tyler, 1907, p. 134). Quite different was the pillow seen in Florida by Sir John Hawkins. "They sleepe," says his chronicler Spark, "upon certeine pieces of wood hewin in for the bowing of their backs, and another place made high for their heads" (Burrage, 1906, p. 119). Possibly this was of West Indian provenance.

TOWELS AND SOAP

Along with mention of some other refinements surrounding the principal chiefs in Virginia and Carolina, we have one or two interesting notes regarding the use of towels or towel substitutes. Smith says:

When he (Powhatan) dineth or suppeth, one of his women, before and after meat, bringeth him water in a wo[o]den platter to wash his hands. Another waiteth with a bunch of feathers to wipe them instead of a Towell, and the feathers when he hath wiped are dryed againe. (Smith, John, Tyler ed., 1907, pp. 114, 118; Strachey, 1849, p. 54.)

Similarly Strachey, in describing the state observed by the wife of a chief called Pipisco, states that her maid "brought her water for her hands, and then a braunch or twoo of fresh greene asshen leaves, as for a towell to dry them" (Strachey, 1849, p. 57).

Taking a long leap in time and place, we may add that the Creeks in relatively recent times were in the habit of making soap, hardly facial soap however, by filling a hollow section of post oak full of ashes, having first put in some straw, and then pouring water through and catching the lye at the other end.

STOCKADES

Forts are frequently mentioned by the De Soto chroniclers, and a study of their distribution affords some clue to the regions where intertribal friction was greatest and where recent or current tribal movements may be suspected. As it happens, they did not come upon a stockade in the Timucua country, or at least there is no mention of one there, but we know that Apalu, which appears as the name of a town in the northwestern part of the peninsula, means "fort" (Bourne, 1904, vol. 2, p. 78), and a little later we have a long description of Timucua forts by Le Moyne. (See pl. 57.) Garcilaso is our only early informant who speaks of stockades among the Apalachee, but most of these seem to have been temporary structures erected to oppose the Spaniards (Garcilaso, 1723, pp. 83, 99–100). Biedma and Ranjel both state that De Soto's army came upon stockaded towns at Chiaha on the Tennessee River (Bourne, 1904, vol. 2, pp. 15, 108). They were probably constructed to repel incursions of the northern tribes. They next appear on the Tallapoosa and Alabama Rivers. Elvas says that Ullibahali was fenced, Garcilaso remarks the same of Talisse, and Renjel of a town southwest of Tuasi. (Robertson, 1933, p. 120; Garcilaso, 1723, p. 144; Bourne, 1904, vol. 2, p. 115.) These were on the frontier between the Upper Creeks and the Mobile Indians, but apparently were themselves Creek towns. We know that Mabila itself was fenced and that there were other fenced towns in the country all about. (Bourne, 1904, vol. 2, pp. 18, 19; Robertson, 1933, p. 123 et seq.; Garcilaso, 1723, p. 146.) The Chakchiuma town was stockaded, and west of the Chickasaw the Spaniards (Robertson, 1933, p. 143) were confronted by a formidable stockade though, according to Biedma and Garcilaso, this was not about a town but erected merely for the purpose of opposing the advance of the Europeans. (Bourne, 1904, vol. 2, pp. 24–25, 136; Robertson, 1933, pp. 153–155; Garcilaso, 1723, pp. 172–175.) The Pacaha town in Arkansas had both a moat and a palisade (Bourne, 1904, vol. 2, pp. 28, 139; Robertson, 1933, p. 174; Garcilaso, 1723, p. 182), and its people retired before the Spaniards to a fortified island in the Mississippi higher up, where there was a triple palisade (Garcilaso, 1723, pp. 183–184). Ranjel also implies that the Aquixo and Casqui towns had stockades, but the statement is so general that little reliance may be placed upon it (Bourne, 1904, vol. 2, p. 140). Garcilaso alone of all our authorities affirms that Utiangue, where they spent the winter of 1541–42, was palisaded when the Spaniards entered it, but Elvas speaks as if the latter put up the palisade themselves

(Garcilaso, 1723, pp. 194–195; Robertson, 1933, p. 203). Both Guachoya and Aminoya were fenced (Bourne, 1904, vol. 2, p. 38; Robertson, 1933, pp. 214, 262), and the same may have been true of Anilco though it is not specifically stated. Let us now review the principal descriptions.

Speaking of the stronghold of the Apalachee chief, Garcilaso says:

The Indians had fortified it in the following manner. In the middle of a very large and very dense forest they had cleared a space where the *Curaca* and his Indians had their lodgings. As an entrance to this plaza they had opened through the same woods a narrow alley more than half a league in length. All along this alley at intervals of a hundred paces they had made strong palisades with thick logs which commanded the passage. (Garcilaso, 1723, p. 83.)

The Tennessee towns did not, apparently, excite so much interest as the stockaded settlements in central Alabama. Ranjel describes an old and abandoned town on or near Alabama River

that had two fences and good towers, and these walls are after this fashion: They drive many thick stakes tall and straight close to one another. These are then interlaced with long withes, and then overlaid with clay within and without. They make loopholes at intervals and they make their towers and turrets separated by the curtain and parts of the wall as seems best. And at a distance it looks like a fine wall or rampart and such stockades are very strong. (Bourne, 1904, vol. 2, p. 115.)

Elvas says of Ullibahali,

The enclosure, like that in other towns seen there afterward, was of thick logs, set solidly close together in the ground, and many long poles as thick as an arm placed crosswise. The height of the enclosure was that of a good lance, and it was plastered within and without and had loopholes. (Robertson, 1933, p. 120; Bourne, 1904, vol. 1, p. 85.)

According to Garcilaso, the famous town of Mabila was

on a very fine plain and had an enclosure three *estados* [about 16.5 feet] high which was made of logs as thick as oxen (*bueyes*). They were driven into the ground so close together that they touched one another. Other beams, longer and not so thick, were placed crosswise on the outside and inside and attached with split canes and strong cords. On top they were daubed with a great deal of mud packed down with long straw, which mixture filled all the cracks and open spaces between the logs and their fastenings in such manner that it really looked like a wall finished with a mason's trowel. At intervals of fifty paces around this enclosure were towers capable of holding seven or eight men, who could fight in them. The lower part of the enclosure, to the height of an *estado* [5.55 feet], was full of loopholes for shooting arrows at those on the outside. The pueblo had only two gates, one on the east and the other on the west. In the middle of the pueblo was a spacious plaza around which were the largest and most important houses. (Garcilaso, 1723, pp. 146–147.)

Garcilaso gives a very elaborate account of the Alabama fort, but it is unfortunately not checked by the other writers, though we may gather that he has exaggerated as is his wont. He says:

It was a square, with four equal curtains made of embedded logs, the curtain of each wall being four hundred paces long. Inside this square were two other curtains of wood which crossed the fort from one wall to the other. The front curtain had three small doors, so low that a mounted man could not go through them. One door was in the middle of the curtain and the other two were at the sides near the corners. In line with these three doors there were three others in each curtain, so that if the Spaniards should take the first ones, the Indians could defend themselves at those of the second curtain, and of the third and the fourth. The doors of the last curtain opened on a river which passed behind the fort. Though narrow, this river was very deep and had such steep banks that one could go up and down them only with difficulty on foot, and not at all on horseback. This was the intention of the Indians, to make a fort in which they could be sure that the Castilians would not attack them with the horses by entering through the doors or by crossing the river, but would fight on foot like themselves, for as we have said already on other occasions they had no fear whatever of the infantry, as it seemed to them that they were equal or even superior to them. They had bridges over the river made of wood, but so shaky and ruinous that they could hardly pass over them. There were no doors at all on the sides of the fort. (Garcilaso, 1723, p. 173.)

The last sentence substantiates Biedma in his assertion that this fort or stockade was built on purpose to block the passage of the Spaniards, but the force of this is weakened by mention of the "ruinous" condition of the bridges, if we are to understand that they were ruinous with age.

We learn that the principal town of the Pacaha not only had a moat and palisade, but towers like Mabila and the abandoned town Ranjel describes, as also loopholes like this latter. Thus, there is some reason for supposing Garcilaso's description is not far astray:

The pueblo had five hundred large and good houses and was on a site somewhat higher and more elevated than its surroundings. They had made it almost an island with a ditch or fosse ten or twelve fathoms deep and fifty paces wide, or forty at the narrowest parts, all made by hand. It was full of water which it received from the Rio Grande that we mentioned above, which flowed three leagues above the pueblo. The water came through an open canal, made laboriously, which went from the fosse to the Rio Grande for this purpose. The canal was three *estados* in depth and so wide that two of the large canoes could go up and down it abreast without the oars [i. e., paddles] of one touching those of the other. The fosse of water, of the width that we have said, surrounded three sides of the pueblo, the work not yet being complete. The fourth side was enclosed by a very strong palisade in the form of a wall made of thick logs set in the ground, touching one another, and other transverse logs fastened and covered with packed mud and straw such as we have described above. (Garcilaso, 1723, pp. 181–182.)

Elvas says that there were a number of towns near this one, all stockaded, and Garcilaso tells us that the island fort to which these Indians retired was protected by a triple palisade. It was here that the Spanish army came within an ace of being annihilated, if we may trust the last mentioned author, but in this he is entirely unsupported. (Robertson, 1933, p. 174; Garcilaso, 1723, pp. 183–184).

Le Moyne's description of a Timucua fort, already alluded to, follows:

A position is selected near the channel of some swift stream. They level it as even as possible, and then dig a ditch in a circle around the site, in which they set thick round pales, close together, to twice the height of a man; and they carry this paling some ways past the beginning of it, spiralwise, to make a narrow entrance admitting not more than two persons abreast. The course of the stream is also diverted to this entrance; and at each end of it they are accustomed to erect a small round building, each full of cracks and holes, and built, considering their means, with much elegance. In these they station as sentinels men who can scent the traces of an enemy at a great distance, and who, as soon as they perceive such traces, set off to discover them. As soon as they find them, they set up a cry which summons those within the town to the defense, armed with bows and arrows and clubs. The chief's dwelling stands in the middle of the town, and is partly underground, in consequence of the sun's heat. (Le-Moyne, 1875, p. 12 (illus.) ; Swanton, 1922, p. 379.)

Nothing is said of towers here, and, indeed, the forts constructed farther west appear to have been more elaborate, reaching their highest level, like so many other native productions, along the lower Mississippi. Here we have the advantage of Du Pratz's description.

When a nation is too weak to sustain a war, it endeavors to build a fort in order to protect itself. I cannot describe these forts better than by comparing them to a barrel hoop from which the withes have been cut. This circle is relaxed and the outside end is at some distance from the inside end, so that to enter the circle without passing over it it is necessary to make a turn. It is by this opening that one enters the fort, the inner side of which is protected by a half tower and the outer side in the same way. Besides, if they are in great fear, this opening or passage is filled with brambles and thorns. [See pl. 83.]

This circle is of a size proportioned to the number of warriors and the remainder of the nation which retires there when the enemy is advancing. There are, however, some cabins outside where, in moments of tranquility, are done the things most needful to life, such as cooking meat and corn. These cabins also relieve the fort, which is always very much congested when the entire nation is obliged to retire there.

The walls of these forts are composed of great posts, which are made of the trunks of trees a span in circumference, buried 5 to 6 feet in the earth and extending 10 feet above it, and pointed above. The lines of contact of these posts, however round, are covered inside with other posts a foot in diameter. This wall is provided outside with half towers 40 paces apart. They make them doubtless to prevent scaling. The lower ends of the posts are supported inside by a banquette 3 feet wide by as much in height, which is itself supported by stakes bound together with green branches in order to retain the earth which is in this banquette.

The best instructed of these people, as were the Natchez by our soldiers, make about 5 feet above this banquette a kind of penthouse (*auvent*) with fragments of trees in order to protect themselves from grenades. They also have loopholes which have only one opening outside and two within which correspond to the one. These loopholes are immediately above the banquette.

In the middle of the fort is placed a tree, the branches of which are cut to within 8 or 9 inches of the trunk to serve as a ladder. This tree serves them as a watchtower, where a young man on guard can discover the enemy at a distance. Around this ladder are some cabins to protect the women and children from falling arrows. The gate of such a fort is always on the side toward the water. If they can be prevented from getting it, one may be assured they will be reduced in a few days. (Le Page du Pratz, 1758, vol. 2, pp. 435–437; Swanton, 1911, p. 133.)

The Biloxi fort seen by Iberville on Pascagoula River in 1700 differed little from this:

The village [of from 30 to 40 cabins] was surrounded with palings eight feet in height, of about eighteen inches in diameter. There still remain three square watch towers (*guérites*) measuring ten feet on each face; they are raised to a height of eight feet on posts; the sides made of mud mixed with grass, of a thickness of eight inches, well covered. There were many loopholes through which to shoot their arrows. It appeared to me that there had been a watch-tower at each angle, and one midway of the curtains (*au milieu des courtines*); it was sufficiently strong to defend them against enemies that have only arrows. (Margry, 1875–86, vol. 4, pp. 425–426; Dorsey and Swanton, 1912, p. 6.)

Yuchi fortifications were much the same so far as we can gather from several brief notices of them. One on the headwaters of the Tennessee visited by English traders in 1674 was

seated on ye river side, haveing ye clefts of ye river on ye one side being very high for its defence, the other three sides trees of two foot over, pitched on end, twelve foot high, and on ye topps scafolds placed with parrapits to defend the walls and offend their enemies which men stand on to fight. (Alvord, 1912, p. 213.)

There is a more obscure note of a fort in west Florida captured by the Spaniards and Apalachee in 1677 which seems to have been much like the rest, and some references to Chisca forts stormed by Boyano in 1567. (Swanton, 1922, pp. 293, 303; Serrano y Sanz, 1913, pp. 214–216; Ruidiaz, 1894, vol. 2, pp. 477–480.) The very year in which the Tennessee town above mentioned was being described, Henry Woodward visited a Westo town on the Savannah River near where Augusta now stands, and it is my opinion that this was Yuchi. It was

uppon ye Westerne side soe yᵗ ye river encompasseth two-thirds thereof. . . . Ye inland side of ye towne being duble Pallisadoed, & yt part which fronts ye river haveing only a single one. (S. C. Hist. Soc. Coll., 1857–97, vol. 5, pp. 459–461; Swanton, 1922, p. 306.)

Chickasaw towns and some of the northern and eastern towns of the Choctaw were anciently protected in the same manner, but we have no good descriptions of the defenses.

As we move toward the northeast we find less pretentious structures. Barlowe describes at the north end of Roanoke Island

a village of nine houses, built of Cedar, and fortified round about with sharpe trees, to keepe out their enemies, and the entrance into it made like a turne pike very artificially. (Burrage, 1906, p. 235.)

Hariot figures a fenced town of the coast country of Carolina, and says in his text:

The townes of this contrie are in a maner like vnto those which are in Florida, yet are they not soe stronge nor yet preserued with soe great care. They are compassed abowt with poles starcke faste in the grownd, but they are not verye stronge. The entrance is verye narrowe as may be seene by this picture, which is made accordinge to the forme of the towne of Pomeiooc. Ther are but few howses therein, saue those which belonge to the kinge and his nobles. [Pl. 77.] (Hariot, 1893, pl. 19.)

We hear little about forts in the Chesapeake Bay region except the Tockwogh fort evidently built to protect that tribe from the Susquehanna. This is described as a

pallizadoed towne, mantelled with the barkes of trees, with Scaffolds like mounts, breasted about with Barks very formally. (Smith, John, 1907 ed., pp. 89, 149.)

Beverley apparently draws very largely upon Hariot:

Their fortifications consist only of a Palisado, of about ten or twelve foot high; and when they would make themselves very safe, they treble the Pale. They often encompass their whole Town: But for the most part only their Kings Houses, and as many others as they judge sufficient to harbour all their People, when an Enemy comes against them. They never fail to secure within their Palisado, all their Religious Reliques, and the Remains of their Princes. Within this Inclosure, they likewise take care to have a supply of Water, and to make a place for a Fire, which they frequently dance round with great solemnity. (Beverley, 1705, bk. 3, pp. 12–13.)

The forts which figure so prominently in the Tuscarora war seem to have been built after it began, and a runaway negro is said to have been responsible for the best features in some of them.

In his account of the first Tuscarora expedition, Barnwell says:

They have lately built small forts at about a mile distance from one another where ye men sleep all night & the women and children, mostly in the woods; I have seen 9 of these Forts and none of them a month old, & some not quite finished. [He attacked the strongest of these and on carrying the stockade found within] two Houses stronger than the fort which did puzzle us & do the most damage. (S. C. Hist. and Genealog. Mag., 1900–12, vol. 9, p. 32.)

King Hancock's fort he found

strong as well by situation on the river's bank as Workmanship, having a large Earthen Trench thrown up against the puncheons with 2 teer of port holes: the lower teer they could stop at pleasure with plugs, & large limbs of trees lay confusedly about it to make the approach intricate, and all about much with large reeds & canes to run into people's legs. The Earthen work was so high that it signified nothing to burn the puncheons, & it had 4 round Bastions or Flankers; the enemy says it was a runaway negro taught them to fortify thus, named Harry, whom Dove Williamson sold into Virginia for roguery & since fled to the Tuscaruros. (S. C. Hist. and Genealog. Mag., 1900–12, p. 43.)

This appears later as that "Fort Noo-he-roo-ka," captured by Moore in the second Tuscarora expedition, and we have an outline and description of it in Moore's report of operations (S. C. Hist. and Genealog. Mag., 1900–12, vol. 9, pp. 33–48).

The Nottoway fort visited by William Byrd in April 1728,

was a Square Piece of Ground, inclose'd with Substantial Puncheons, or Strong Palisades, about ten feet high, and leaning a little outwards, to make a Scalade more difficult. Each side of the Square might be about 100 Yards long, with Loopholes at proper Distances, through which they may fire upon the Enemy. (Bassett, 1901, p. 114.)

It would seem as if cane would not have been good material for a stockade, yet Iberville states that the Bayogoula town on the lower Mississippi "was surrounded by a palisade made entirely of canes, 1 inch apart and 10 feet in height, without a door to close it" (Margry, 1875–86, vol. 4, p. 169; Swanton, 1911, pp. 274–275). But having a *doorway*, it would seem. The stockade reminds us that, when De Soto was at Casqui near the present Helena, Ark., and had set up a cross on the summit of a mound, the Indians "brought a great quantity of cane, making a fence about it" (Bourne, 1904, vol. 2, p. 28).

CLOTHING

(Plates 64–70)

MATERIALS

Most of the garments of these Indians were made of the skins of animals, though some were woven from threads of vegetable and animal origin, some were of feathers, and a few natural vegetable productions were used without modification.

Deer hide was a major basis for clothing of all kinds and deer sinew was utilized as thread throughout the entire Southeast. Apparently the Indians least well supplied with these materials were the small tribes along the southeastern coast of Florida.

Bison robes are noted particularly among the Caddo, the Cherokee, and the Natchez, and Adair (1775, p. 7) speaks of them as winter garments of the Chickasaw women, but it is plain that they were used at a somewhat earlier period by all of the tribes even including some of those in the Florida peninsula. However, as there was greater need for them toward the north and northwest and the animals were more abundant there, it is not surprising that most of our specific references apply to those quarters. Nevertheless, Kimber (1744, p. 16) mentions both bison and deer hide as materials used by the Creeks of Georgia in the manufacture of their moccasins. Bison hair was woven into belts, garters, and other similar articles, and the Choctaw made a kind of fabric for women's clothing out of bison hair and a kind of grass (Swanton, 1918, p. 68).

Bear hides were also utilized largely in making heavy winter robes, and again we hear of them more often in the north. They were also used as bed coverings. The Chickasaw sometimes made moccasins out of them and bear-hide thongs are mentioned among the Natchez. (Adair, 1775, p. 8; Le Page du Pratz, 1758, vol. 2, p. 184; Swanton, 1911, p. 65.)

In northern sections, where elk were to be found, their skins probably took the place of deerskins, and the Chickasaw made their heavier moccasins of elk hide (Adair, 1775, p. 8).

Garcilaso de la Vega speaks of the use, among other animal pelts, of the skins of cats of different kinds, deer, bear, and lions (i.e., panthers), and according to the same writer the Indians about Tampa Bay esteemed the slaughter of a "lion" a deed of bravery (Garcilaso, 1723, p. 6, 27). Ranjel reports blankets of wildcat skins among the Indians of Cofitachequi (Bourne, 1904, vol. 2, p. 99). In the town of Pacaha on the west bank of the Mississippi, probably in the territory of the present State of Arkansas, the Spaniards found, according to Elvas, many skins of lions and cats (Robertson, 1933, p. 172). In a native house in Virginia Strachey saw the claws of a panther, while Lawson tells us that the Siouan tribes used their skins as robes (Strachey, 1849, p. 124; Lawson, 1860, p. 195).

The De Soto chroniclers are authorities for a wide use of cloaks and robes worn by the upper classes made of the skins of an animal called in the narratives of Elvas and Garcilaso "marten" and in those of Biedma and Ranjel "sable." They are always said to be "fragrant" or to have a strong odor; Garcilaso says "a very agreeable musk odor." Specific mention is made of a very fine one brought by Maldonado from the neighborhood of Pensacola or Mobile. Such a cloak was worn by the lieutenant of a chief on Ocmulgee River. They were found at Cofitachequi (S. C.), Coca (Ala.), in possession of Tascalusa, at Mabila (Ala.), and at Anilco (La.). (Garcilaso, 1723, pp. 115, 142; Bourne, 1904, vol. 2, pp. 81, 99; Robertson, 1933, pp. 115, 130–131, 210.) Mention has already been made of "a piece of marten's skin about eight ells long by three wide" found in a village near the lower Mississippi by the Spaniards in 1543. It was "double alike on both sides, and decorated in places with clusters of seed pearls," and they thought it must have been used as a standard in native festivals (Garcilaso, 1723, p. 242). These animals were probably muskrats. At any rate, later writers place considerable emphasis on the use of their skins along the lower Mississippi, and Louisiana is today famous for them.

The "conies" of Spanish writers are evidently rabbits, but it is somewhat confusing to read of "conies and hares" on the coast of North Carolina (Burrage, 1906, p. 233) and one wonders whether these names were not applied to the same animal. The De Soto chroniclers refer to "conies" only as a source of food, but Hariot informs us that in North Carolina at least clothing was made of their skins:

Those ["conies"] that we haue seen & al that we can heare of are of a grey colour like vnto hares: in some places there are such plentie that all the people of some townes make them mantles of the furre or flue of the skinnes of those they vsually take. (Hariot, 1893, p. 30.)

Later he speaks of "a shorte clocke made of fine hares skinnes quilted with the hayre outward" worn by native priests (Hariot, 1893, pl. 5). While it is probable that rabbit skins were worn much more widely, evidence of the fact seems to be lacking.

One would expect the beaver to have been an important source of clothing, and we at least learn that it was used widely. Smith and Strachey mention such use in Virginia, and Lawson in the Piedmont section of the Carolinas, and there are references to beaver-skin garments among the Chickasaw and the Indians of the lower Mississippi. There is even one reference to the employment of beaver hair in textiles. (Garcia, 1902, pp. 309–310; Swanton, 1922, p. 149; Leonard, 1939.)

Smith and Strachey refer to the use of otter skins, at least as or-naments, and Beverley states that a Virginia conjurer often hung an otter skin between his legs. As otters were connected with sha-manism in many parts of North America, this use was natural enough and may have extended widely.

Lawson mentions "match coats" of raccoon hide among the Caro-lina Indians and Catesby affirms that raccoon hair was employed in textiles, though he may have confounded this animal with the opossum (Lawson, 1860, p. 311; Catesby, 1731–43, vol. 2, p. xi). Vir-ginia Indians sometimes thrust the claws of a bear, raccoon or squirrel through their ears by way of ornament (Strachey, 1849, p. 67).

Lawson (1860, p. 311) also speaks of clothing made of squirrel skins, but though squirrels were widely hunted as accessories to the table, and their pelts were worked into bowstrings, I find no other reference to their employment in clothing. Mention of the use of their claws as ornaments has just been made.

While opossum skins do not appear to have been used at all, opos-sum hair was widely resorted to as a textile.

Virginia priests ornamented their ears with weasel skins (Smith, John, 1907 ed., p. 51; Strachey, 1849, p. 91).

Cloaks made of the feathers of various kinds of birds are con-stantly mentioned in all parts of the Southeast. Turkey feathers appear to have been used most often, but Lawson (1860, p. 311) tells of a garment composed of the heads of mallards, and Bev-erley (1705, bk. 3, p. 3) of pheasant feathers in the headdress of Vir-ginia Indians.

Use of eagle feathers was, of course, universal, and our Virginia authorities speak of the whole skin of a hawk stuffed and buzzard wings used by men in the Powhatan country as an embellishment for the headdress (Smith, John, 1907 ed., p. 99; Strachey, 1849, p. 66).

Clothing made of materials of vegetable origin had a much more restricted distribution, but skirts and cloaks were woven out of the inner fiber of the mulberry practically everywhere.

There were also substitutes for this material, among which are mentioned a native grass called usually "silk grass," a nettle, and a kind of native hemp. One of my own informants asserted that the bark of the slippery elm was used in this way.

Along the south Atlantic coast, in Florida and in Louisiana, women made clothing out of Spanish moss. (See Garcia, 1902, p. 193, for the Georgia coast.)

In southern Florida breechclouts of "a plaitwork of straws," and "braided palm leaves"—by both of which was probably meant palmetto leaves, as seems to be confirmed by San Miguel (Garcia, 1902, p. 200)—took the place of the corresponding garments of deer hide worn by men elsewhere.

In Virginia very poor Indians are said to have covered themselves with grass and leaves fastened to their belts (Strachey, 1849, p. 64; Smith, John, 1907 ed., p. 99).

SKIN DRESSING

The excellent manner in which skins were dressed by the Indians of Cofitachequi, one of the tribes later known as Creeks, is commented upon by De Soto's companions. Ranjel says:

> They make hose and moccasins and leggings with ties of white leather, although the leggings are black and with fringes or edgings of colored leather as they would have done in Spain. (Bourne, 1904, vol. 2, pp. 100–102.)

And Elvas:

> The skins are well tanned and are given the color that is desired; and so perfectly that if the color is vermillion, it seems to be very fine grained cloth, and that colored black is splendid. And of this same they make shoes. (Robertson, 1933, p. 76.)

Somewhat later Spark tells us that the Florida Indians had skins colored "yellow and red, some black and russet, and every man according to his own fancy" (Burrage, 1906, p. 120).

Very few descriptions of the process of dressing skins have been preserved. Speaking of the Guale breechclout, San Miguel remarks:

> The dress of the men of this province and of those surrounding it is nothing but a very soft deerskin, not tanned but rubbed hard between the hands and with the nails, which they never cut. (Garcia, 1902, p. 193.)

The best description seems to be that of Dumont de Montigny, who had the Natchez especially in mind:

They begin by making many holes all around [the edge of the skin] with a knife, after which they steep it in water for two or three days. Then they stretch it on a wooden frame where they fasten it with cords, binding it strongly, and they make the hair fall from it. Afterward they rub and scrape this skin, in order to soften it, with a flint which has been forced into a cleft in one end of a stick of wood, and in order to make it soft and white they make use of the cooked brain of a deer. After this operation the skin is as soft and as white as our calf or sheep skins can be made. On the skins thus dressed they daub or paint all kinds of figures, the designs for which they trace in accordance with their fancy, employing for these paintings red, yellow, black, green, blue, without making use of oil to dilute the colors, but only the glue which they extract from these same skins. The skins thus painted serve the French for gaming tables. The savages also have sufficient skill to dress and prepare bison skins in the same manner on one side only, carefully preserving the hair or wool on the other. These latter serve as bed quilts and are very warm. On the skins dressed in this manner the savages also lie, as I have said, during the winter, and I can certify that they are fully as good as a good mattress.

But though these [blankets] are well dressed and very white they cannot be wet, for as soon as they dry after being wet, they shrink so that neither leggings, nor stockings without feet, nor shoes, drawers, or other kinds of clothing can be made of them. In order to make use of them for these purposes it would be necessary to dress them with oil but the savages do not know how. They have discovered merely how to make them supple which is by the following method:

They first dig a hole in the earth about 2 feet deep, with a diameter of 6 inches at the top and a little less toward the bottom. They fill this hole with cow dung, rotted wood, and maize ears and place over it two rods in the shape of a cross, the four ends of which are planted in the earth so as to form a kind of cradle on which they stretch the skin they wish to tan. They then set fire to the combustible substances in the hole and fasten the skin down all around by means of many little pegs driven into the ground. Then they cover it with earth above and along the edges, so as to keep in the smoke. The materials in the hole becoming consumed without throwing out flame, the thick smoke that comes out of it, especially owing to the lack of any exit the cow dung fastens itself to the skin which it smoke-dries (*boucanes*) and dyes of a yellow color. After this first dressing, it is turned over on the other side and a second is given to it, and when it is thus prepared it is used for all kinds of purposes. No matter how much it is washed or lathered, provided one takes care to let it dry in the shade, it never hardens and is always as soft and supple as chamois. (Dumont, 1753, vol. 1, pp. 146–149; Swanton, 1911, pp. 64–65.)

Du Pratz has a short description of the process which is, as we should expect, very similar. Instead of a flint dressing implement, he mentions the flat bone of a bison, perhaps the shoulder blade (Le Page du Pratz, 1758, vol. 2, p. 167; Swanton, 1911, p. 65).

To Dumont we are indebted for the only description of a native manner of meeting that bane of the housewife, the moth:

The savages have another secret for the preservation of their beaver, otter, bear, or fox skins, from injurious animals, especially moths, and those Frenchmen who go to trade among them do not fail to take advantage of this in the preservation of their pelts. For this purpose they make use of the body of a certain bird which in many places is called a "fisher." After having dried it, some of them cut it into many small pieces which they put here and there on their skins. Others reduce it to fine powder, which they scatter over the skins side of the hair. In whatever way one makes use of it, it is certain that the odor of this bird drives away moths and all other destructive creatures which might be able to injure the peltries. It is asserted that the martin (martinet), a kind of bird which resembles the swallow, has the same virtue and the same properties. (Dumont, 1753, vol. 2, pp. 277–278.)

Lawson is almost the only writer among the English who has anything to say about skin dressing, and it is evident that the method he had observed differed little from the Louisiana process:

Their way of dressing their skins is, by soaking them in water, so they get the hair off with an instrument made of the bone of a deer's foot; yet some use a sort of iron drawing knife, which they purchase of the English, and after the hair is off they dissolve deer's brains, which beforehand are made in a cake and baked in the embers, in a bowl of water, so soak the skins therein till the brains have sucked up the water; then they dry [the skin] gently, and keep working it with an oyster shell, or some such thing, to scrape withal till it is dry; whereby it becomes soft and pliable. Yet these so dressed will not endure wet, but become hard thereby; which to prevent, they either cure them in the smoke or tan them with bark, as before observed [Lawson, p. 311; see p. 446 below]; not but that young Indian corn, beaten to a pulp, will effect the same as the brains. (Lawson, 1860, pp. 338–339.)

As is often the case, Catesby parallels Lawson in considerable measure:

The method of dressing their skins is by soaking them in deer's brains, tempered with water, scraping them with an oyster-shell till they become soft and pliable. *Maiz*, when young, and beat to a pulp, will effect the same as the brains; then they cure them with smoak, which is performed by digging a hole in the earth, arching it over with hoop-sticks, over which the skin is laid, and under that is kindled a slow fire, which is continued until it is smoaked enough. (Catesby, 1731–43, vol. 2, p. xi.)

Byrd, from observation of a Saponi Indian, remarks:

The Indians dress them [skins] with Deer's Brains, and so do the English here by their example. For Expedition's Sake they often Stretch their Skins over Smoak in order to dry them, which makes them smell so disagreeably that a Rat must have a good Stomach to gnaw them in that condition. (Bassett, 1901, p. 274.)

From a much later date comes Speck's account of Yuchi skin dressing:

In preparing hides and skins for use the brains of animals are employed to soften and preserve them. Hides are placed over a log, one end of which is held between the knees while the other rests on the ground, and are then scraped with a scraping implement to remove the hair. The scraper, *ts'amē'-satäné*, for this purpose is a round piece of wood about twelve inches long with a piece of metal set in edgewise on one side, leaving room for a hand grip on each end. This implement resembles the ordinary spokeshave more than anything else. A sharp edged stone is said to have taken the place of the iron blade in early times. Hides are finally thoroughly smoked until they are brown, and kneaded to make them soft and durable. (Speck, 1909, p. 35.)

Swan has the following brief statement relative to skin dressing among the Creeks:

> Smoked leather is universally used among them for moccasins, stockings, boots, and often for shirts. It is dressed with the brains of the deer, with which the skin is first impregnated, and afterwards, confined from the air, is softened and finished by the smoke of rotten wood. (Swan, 1855, p. 692.)

According to personal information, skin dressing was anciently an occupation of both men and women, though in later years it has fallen entirely upon the women. The skin was first separated from the flesh by means of sharp stones, and in later times with knives and hatchets. Then it was hung on a framework of poles to dry, and afterward taken down and soaked in water for about 2 days. Then it was put back in the frame and scraped on the outside so as to make it smooth, the implement used being either a knife or a two-handled scraper like a drawshave. I saw Celissy Henry use for this purpose a piece of iron in the shape of a grubbing hoe (pl. 71, fig. 1). Then the skin was again allowed to dry. After that, they put water and dried deer brains into a pot and heated the mixture without letting it come to a boil. The skin was immersed, the liquid allowed to soak up into it and it was then squeezed out again, the process being repeated many times, for perhaps an hour. It was again stretched on the frame to dry and was then found to be soft. Next, they scooped a hole in the ground, built a fire in it, and put corncobs upon this so that a thick smoke was produced with little flame. The hide was fastened down over this pit with the outer surface down and left until it was smoked yellow. They then procured red oak bark, boiled it for some time in water, and allowed it to cool. Into this the deerskin was plunged and allowed to remain for perhaps a day, after which it was taken out and hung up for a final drying. The moccasins, leggings, and other deerskin clothing were made of this, and, so processed, they would not get hard when wet. Sometimes bark of the red wild peach (ichoma') was used in place of oak. The red oak gives skins a yellowish red color, the wild peach a red color. When preparing a cowhide, they soaked it for 2 months in an infusion of red-oak bark. It appears that the process varied very little from that in vogue among the Natchez, and, indeed, there seems to have been little variation over most of the eastern part of North America.

Jackson Lewis stated that the Creek Indians prepared skins of deer, bison, and bear in the same way, and that those from which the hair was not removed were softened precisely like the rest. The brains of almost any animal could be used, ground up and rubbed on the skin, which was then laid out on the damp ground and allowed to remain over night. Afterward it was stretched on a frame and kneaded continually until dried.

The best modern account of skin dressing as practiced by the Choctaw is that derived by Mr. Bushnell from the band of Indians on Bayou Lacomb:

(A) Skins to be tanned soft, without the hair. A hole is dug in the ground, its size being determined by the number of skins to be prepared. The walls and bottom are made smooth and water is poured in, which, on account of the nature of the clay and sand formation, remains several hours, or sometimes during the night . . .

After the skin has become sufficiently soaked and softened, it is taken from the water and spread over the end of a beam, . . . In this position the hair is readily removed by the use of an instrument resembling a modern drawknife, and, although a piece of metal is now used in the wooden handle, it is highly probable that stone or bone was formerly employed for the same purpose.

The hair having been removed, the skin is placed in a mortar, or in a hole cut in a log which serves the purpose. Eggs and cornmeal mixed with a little water are then poured over the skin, which is thoroughly beaten with a long wooden pestle.

The skin is then taken from the mortar and wrung rather dry; a number of small holes are cut around the edge and through these cords are passed, which serve to hold the skin stretched between two upright posts. . . . While in this position it is scraped and all particles of flesh are removed. The instrument now employed consists of a piece of metal attached to a long wooden handle. A large bone probably served as the primitive implement.

The skin remains stretched until dry, when it is, of course, rather stiff. To soften it, the skin is pulled back and forth over the top of a stake driven into the ground, which has been made smooth and round to prevent tearing the skin. . . .

This process of tanning renders the skin soft and white. The Choctaw claim that it is a very ancient method of preparing skins. Eggs of various kinds they say, are used with equally good results. The method described, including the use of corn and eggs, may have been followed by all the Southern tribes. . . .

If the skins are to be smoked, a process that renders them more durable, a hole a foot or more in depth is dug in which a fire is kept until a bed of hot ashes accumulates. On this are put pieces of rotten oak, no other wood being used for this purpose; these are not permitted to blaze, as the more smoke that arises the better it is for the skins. These, already tanned soft and white and perfectly dry, are stretched over the hole and allowed to remain in the smoke an hour or more.

(B) Skins to be tanned soft, with the hair remaining. If the skin is dry and stiff it is first softened with clear water, after which it is spread over a beam and scraped on the inner surface to remove all flesh. The inside is then thoroughly rubbed with a mixture of eggs, cornmeal, and water, great care being taken not to wet the outside, or fur. When the skin is about dry it is pulled and worked back and forth over the top of a stake, as already explained, after which it remains soft. (Bushnell, 1909 a, pp. 11–12.)

From a Choctaw near Philadelphia I obtained a shorter account:

When a hide was to be dressed it was laced to a wooden frame by means of cords all around the edges. Sometimes a family had two frames, a large one for big skins such as those of the bear and deer, and a smaller one for the smaller animals such as the mink, opossum, and raccoon. Or the frame might be made so that its size could be altered. It was usually movable but in any case was ordinarily located near the spring. Assuming that the frame was movable, after a skin had been fastened in place, it was set in the sunshine and the flesh removed by means of a large scraper shaped like a knife. Then the skin was worked with a dull hardwood scraper made crescent-shaped so as not to cut the skin. This work must be done a certain length of time after the hide had been removed from the animal, not while it was still green and flabby nor after it had hardened. After it had been worked for a time in the sun, it was moved into the shade and worked as long again. This was to make it supple and bring out the grain, and the process required from three to five hours. When they were through and the skin was fairly dry they rolled it up and put it into a shed. If it got too damp, they brought it back into the sunshine and sometimes they had to work it over again. (Swanton, 1931 a, pp. 41–42.)

Still another relatively modern account is from Skinner's notes taken among the Seminole of Florida in 1910:

In preparing deerskin leather, the hide is first dried in the sun until it is stiff and hard; it is then thoroughly soaked in water and wrung out by passing it about a tree, tying the ends together, and running a stick through the knot to afford better leverage while wringing. While the skin is still damp it is thrown over the smooth upper end of an inclined log set in the ground, and the hair is scraped off with a beaming tool. While the skin is drying, it is rendered pliable by rubbing it over the edge of a spatula-like stick set up in the ground. Next deer brains are mixed with water until the liquid is thick and soapy, and the skin is then soaked therein. Great pains are taken to saturate the hide thoroughly; it is then wrung, soaked again and again, and dried. Sometimes this ends the process, when the skin is dyed a deep reddish brown by the use of oak-bark and is used without further preparation. Usually, however, the leather is finished by smoking. The skin is sewed up in bag-like form and suspended, bottom up, from an inclined stick. The edges are pegged down about a small hole in which a smouldering fire burns. The smoke and fumes are allowed to impregnate the hide thoroughly, and then the tanning is completed.

The Seminole prepare brains for preservation by smearing them over long wisps of Spanish moss and allowing them to dry. These brain-cakes which are molded in circular form, with a hole in the center, are suspended in quantities from every cook-house, and have the quaint appearance of festoons of doughnuts. Deer and pig brains are most commonly used for tanning, but bear brains are considered the most valuable. (Skinner, 1913, pp. 72–73.)

It was perhaps beaming implements rather than drawknives that Cushing found at Key Marco:

Several draw-knives made from split leg-bones of the deer sharpened to beveled edges from the inside; some ingenious shaving-knives, made from the outer marginal whorls of the true conchs—the thick indented or toothed lips of which formed their backs or handles, the thin but strong whorl-walls being sharpened to keen straight edges—completed the list of scraping and planing tools.   (Cushing, 1896, p. 370.)

CORDS, THREADS, AND TEXTILES

Textiles presuppose cords and threads which were of either animal or vegetable origin. The former were derived from sinews, skins, and hair; the latter from bark, grass, and a kind of native hemp. Of the Indians of Virginia, Smith says:

> Betwixt their hands and thighes, their women use to spin the barks of trees, deare sinews, or a kind of grasse they call *Pemmenaw;* of these they make a thred very even and readily. This thred serveth for many uses as about their housing, apparell, as also they make nets for fishing, for the quantity as formally braded as ours. They make also with it lines for angles. (Smith, John, 1907 ed., p. 103.)

Strachey (1849, p. 74) uses much the same language in describing the manufacture of fishing nets, but adds the manufacture of feather mantles and "trowsers," presumably the native leggings, to the uses enumerated by Smith.

Lederer mentions "leather thongs" among the Siouan tribes, and Lawson "the sinews of the deer divided very small" (Alvord, 1912, p. 143; Lawson, 1860, p. 312).

Leather thongs were in use throughout the region to lace up the moccasins, and mention is made of these as early as 1540, since Ranjel, one of the De Soto chroniclers, noted that the Indians of Cofitachequi (probably Creeks) made "hose and moccasins and leggings with ties of white leather" (Bourne, 1904, vol. 2, pp. 100–102). Du Pratz says that Natchez moccasins were "joined in front by means of a thong of bearskin, which extends to the ankle, and thus makes lace boots" (Le Page du Pratz, 1758, vol. 2, pp. 194–195; Swanton, 1911, p. 54). The native Indian boxes described by Adair (1775, p. 452) were held together by means of "scraped wet buffalo strings," but he speaks of deer's sinews in common use as thread. According to an Alabama informant, thongs were made by putting the point of a knife in the middle of a piece of skin and cutting round and round spirally.

Jackson Lewis described this as the way in which bowstrings were made from the thick skin on the neck of a deer, and we have abundant testimony to the employment of deer hide for this particular purpose, going back to Garcilaso de la Vega (1723, p. 7). Laudonnière says that Florida bowstrings were made of "the gut of the stag or the stag's skin." (Laudonnière, 1586, p. 7; French, 1869, pp. 170–171; Swanton, 1922, p. 356.) Of Powhatan bowstrings, Percy remarks merely that they were made of "leather," but Strachey specifies "deer's hide scraped and twisted" (Tyler, 1907, p. 17; Strachey, 1849, p. 104). Among the Natchez, Du Pratz found that steeped and twisted sinew as well as the bark of trees were employed, and Timberlake mentions "twisted bear's gut" among the Cherokee (Le Page du Pratz, 1758, vol. 2, p. 167; Swanton, 1911, p. 58). Next to deer sinew, I have been informed that the best Creek bowstrings were made of twisted squirrel skin.

The Choctaw fastened the handles of ball sticks, after they had been bent over, with strings of deer hide, but the "basket" was formed of raccoon-skin thongs (Swanton, 1931 a, p. 42).

The hair used industrially was obtained almost entirely from two animals, the bison and the opossum, and used for a limited class of productions as much ornamental as practical. Our Virginia authorities make no mention of the employment of hair by the Indians, but Byrd says of that of the bison:

> The Hair growing on his Head and Neck is long and Shagged, and so Soft that it will Spin into Thread not unlike Mohair, which might be woven into a Sort of Camlet. Some People have Stockings knit of it, that would have served an Israelite during his forty Years' march thro' the Wilderness. (Bassett, 1901, p. 288.)

Mr. Bushnell (1909, pp. 403–406) has called attention to bags made of bison hair in the Pitt-Rivers and British Museums, and the Sloane Catalogue in the British Museum refers to an object of this kind from Carolina, but only this bag is localized. However, Lawson (1860, p. 11) testifies to the use of bison hair by the Indians of his acquaintance, who spun it "into garters, girdles, sashes, and the like." We also hear of it from the interior tribes and those along the Mississippi.

> In the winter season, the women gather buffalo's hair, a sort of coarse brown curled wool; and having spun it as fine as they can, and properly doubled it, they put small beads of different colours upon the yarn, as they work it; the figures they work in these small webs, are generally uniform, but sometimes they diversify them on both sides. The Choktah weave shot-pouches, which have raised work inside and outside. (Adair, 1775, p. 454.)

According to Dumont de Montigny, the Natchez "spin without spinning wheel or distaff the hair or rather wool of the bison, of which they make garters (*jarretières*) and ribbons," and the belts worn by Natchez women were perhaps of the same material. (Dumont, 1753, vol. 1, pp. 154–155; Le Page du Pratz, 1758, vol. 2, p. 184; Swanton, 1911, p. 64.)

It was also used in the composition of straps to hold the bag, strings ornamented with beads and fastened to the hair, and in the following combined ornament and charm described by Adair:

> The Indian females continually wear a beaded string round their legs, made of buffalo hair, which is a species of coarse wool; and they reckon it a great ornament, as well as a preservative against miscarriages, hard labour, and other evils. (Adair, 1775, p. 169.)

Regarding opossum hair, we learn that the Indians observed by Lawson (1860, p. 199) spun it into girdles and garters, and Du Pratz states that, by the Natchez, it was spun and made into garters "which they afterwards dye red" (Le Page du Pratz, 1758, vol. 2, p. 94; Swanton, 1911, p. 64).

Catesby, who was familiar with the tribes earlier met by Lawson, mentions the use of raccoon hair, but the opossum may have been intended (Catesby, 1731–43, vol. 2, p. xi).

In Don Carlos de Siguenza's narrative of his reconnaisance of Pensacola Harbor, he states that, along with "bison-wool done up in balls," and "spindles," they found in a basket left by the Indians "beaver-wool or hair in bags" (Leonard, 1939, p. 162).

In later times, as Speck records of the Yuchi, horsehair probably took the place of the aboriginal materials.

The most elaborate use of animal hair, however, is recorded of the Choctaw by their anonymous chronicler, who says that the Indians of this tribe made

some articles of bison wool which the women spin, of which they make garters and tint them with various indelible colors. They also make a fabric, partly of this wool, and partly of fibre from a very strong herb which they spin. This fabric is double like two-sided handkerchiefs and thick as canvas, half an ell wide and three quarters long. That serves them as a skirt. (Swanton, 1918, pp. 67–68.)

The longer cords and ropes were made of vegetable substances, of which two are mentioned particularly by early writers, mulberry bark and a kind of native hemp. The latter was popularly called silk grass but also seems to have been known by the Powhatan Indians as pemmencaw, the spinning of which has already been described.

They make [their cordage], of their naturall hempe and flax togither with their cuning dressing of that, and preserving the whole yeare great litches or bundells of the same, to be used upon any occasyon. (Strachey, 1849, p. 68.)

I do not know whether Strachey means that two different vegetable substances were woven together or whether there was one which served the purposes of both hemp and flax.

We hear of these two materials and the textiles made from them shortly after Florida was discovered. Peter Martyr, on the authority of Francisco of Chicora, says of the aborigines of our present State of South Carolina:

Although they are partially clothed with skins of wild beasts, they use cotton such as the Milanese call bombasio, and they make nets of the fiber of certain tough grasses, just as hemp and flax are used for the same purposes in Europe. (Anghierra, 1912, p. 43.)

Cabeza de Vaca, whose observations date from the year 1528, speaks of "mantles made of thread and of poor quality, with which the women [of Apalachen] cover parts of their bodies" (Cabeza de

Vaca, 1905, p. 25). The De Soto chroniclers do not mention these until after the Spaniards had left the Apalachee, but their descriptions are intended to apply generally to the people of the entire section. The Fidalgo of Elvas notes "native blankets resembling shawls, some being made of the inner bark of trees and some from a plant like daffodils which when pounded remains like flax." He adds that the women wore two such blankets, the men only one (Robertson, 1933, pp. 75–76). Usually, however, they are spoken of as the clothing for women rather than men. A little farther on it is stated by the same writer that a considerable number of "blankets made of thread from the bark of trees" was found in the barbacoas or storehouses of the Indians of Cofitachequi (Robertson, 1933, p. 93). Ranjel is a little fuller in his description. He says that

> Indian men and women came forth [from Ichisi] to receive them, and the women were clothed in white and made a fine appearance . . . The white clothes with which the Indian women were clothed were mantles, apparently of home-spun linen and some of them were very thin. They make the thread of them from the bark of the mulberry tree, not the outside, but the intermediate layers; and they know how to make use of it and to spin it, and to dress it as well and to weave it. They make very fine mantles, and they wear one from the girdle down and another fastened on one side with the end over the shoulders like those Bohemians or gypsies, who wander sometimes through Spain; and the thread is of such a quality that one who was there assured me that he saw the women spin it from that mulberry bark and make it as good as the best thread from Portugal that women can get in Spain for their work, and finer and somewhat like it and stronger. (Bourne, 1904, vol. 2, pp. 87–88.)

The "me" referred to is not Ranjel but Oviedo, who incorporated Ranjel's narrative into his Historia. Mantles or shawls of the material just described were found throughout the Gulf area by the Spaniards, and some of them were finally used to calk the brigantines in which the Spaniards left (Robertson, 1933, p. 264). We have evidence that something besides mulberry bark, if not the "silk grass" of Virginia, was used as far west as the Mississippi, for Garcilaso de la Vega says that the blankets they obtained from the Indians there were made "of a certain herb similar to mallows, which has a fibre like linen. They make thread from it and color it beautifully in any shade they wish" (Garcilaso, 1723, pp. 726–727). This was perhaps "the bark of the nettle" which Pénicaut (in Margry, 1875–86, vol. 5, p. 465) gives as an alterative material to mulberry bark, and, with less doubt, the "wild hemp" described by Adair:

> They have a wild hemp that grows about six feet high, in open, rich, level lands, and which usually ripens in July: it is plenty on our frontier settlements. When it is fit for use, they pull, steep, peel, and beat it; and the old women spin it off the distaffs, with wooden machines, having some clay on the middle of them to hasten the motion. (Adair, 1775, p. 453.)

"A strong double thread of hemp," or the inner bark of the mulberry, was the basis for feather blankets (Adair, 1775, p. 454). Chickasaw fish nets were also made of it (Adair, 1775, p. 434).

The suggestion that Adair's "hemp" is "silk grass" is strengthened by Swan's remarks on Creek manufactures:

> Horse ropes or halters, are commonly made of twisted bark, but they have a superior kind made of silk grass, a species peculiar to the country, which, after being dried, resembles coarse flax. (Swan, 1855, p. 692.)

Byrd (1728), while engaged in running the boundary line between Virginia and North Carolina, was able to examine some of this, and he says:

> One of the men, who had been an old Indian Trader, brought me a Stem of Silk Grass, which was about as big as my little Finger. But, being so late in the Year that the Leaf was fallen off, I am not able to describe the Plant. The Indians use it in all.their little Manufactures, twisting a Thread of it that is prodigiously Strong. Of this they make their Baskets and the Aprons which their Women wear about their Middles, for Decency's Sake. These are long enough to wrap quite round them and reach down to their Knees, with a Fringe on the under part by way of Ornament. . . . As this species of Silk Grass is much Stronger than Hemp, I make no doubt but Sail Cloth and Cordage might be made of it with considerable Improvement. (Bassett, 1901, p. 75.)

Florida presents something of an exception in the source from which vegetable cords were derived, since, like so many other useful articles, they were obtained from the palmetto.

> The tough fiber which lies between the stems of the leaves and the bark furnishes them with material from which they make twine and rope of great strength and from which they could, were it necessary, weave cloth for clothing. (MacCauley, 1887, p. 517.)

From the Mississippi River region we have one reference to thread from the bark of the bass tree used as a foundation for feather mantles (Dumont, 1753, vol. 1, p. 155; Swanton, 1911, p. 63), and this is of special interest because the modern Alabama and Creek Indians remember the bass tree as the source of most of their native cordage. By some the bark of the slippery elm is also mentioned, and the Creek word for "thread," afu'swa, is closely related to, if not identical with, a word signifying "bush," "flexible branch," "switch," and it is probable that, in the first usage, it is a contraction of afus'lipa'kfa, "slippery elm." At any rate, there is said to have been a bush, or rather tree known as afu'swa with stems from 3 to 5 inches through, long strips of which were peeled off, pounded up, and plaited into ropes. According to Jackson Lewis, the bark of the maple was sometimes used for cords, and still another kind of rope was made by heating bundles of yucca blades in the lye of wood ashes until the pulp washed away. Of the stringy residue they made very nice white ropes which "looked like store ropes." The general Alabama name for rope seems to have been bâkca, apparently applicable to both the bark of the bass tree and that of the slippery elm, the latter tree being known as bâtâ'ko.

References to the use of mulberry bark appear, however, to be most numerous and most specific. The following quotation is from Catesby, whose remarks apply particularly to the Siouan tribes of the east and the Chickasaw:

> The principal of their cloth-manufacture is made of the inner bark of the wild mulberry, of which the women make for themselves petticoats and other habits. This cloth, as well as their baskets, is likewise adorned with figures of animals represented in colours; its substance and durableness recommends it for floor and table-carpets. (Catesby, 1731–43, vol. 2, p. XI.)

The only good descriptions of weaving which have come down to us are from Du Pratz, who observed the process among the Natchez, and Adair, who was particularly familiar with the Chickasaw.

Du Pratz:

> To make mulberry-bark mantles they go into the woods in search of shoots or sprouts of mulberry which come from these trees after they have been cut down. The shoots are from 4 to 5 feet tall. They cut them before the sap is gone, take off the bark, and dry it in the sun. When this bark is dry they pound it to make the gross part fall away. The interior, which is like bast, remains entire. This they pound anew, to make it finer. They then expose it to the dew, in order to bleach it.
>
> When the bark is in this state they spin it roughly, like shoemaker's thread or thread for sewing shoes. They cease to spin as soon as they have enough of it. Then they set up their frame, which consists of two stakes extending 4 feet out of the ground, between the tops of which runs a large thread on which other threads are double knotted. Finally they make a cross texture, which has a border worked in patterns extending all the way around. This stuff is at least an ell square and a line in thickness. The mantles of mulberry-bark thread are very white and very neat. They are fastened on by means of cords of the same thread, having tassels hanging at each end. (Le Page du Pratz, 1758, vol. 2, pp. 192–193; Swanton, 1911, p. 63.)

Adair:

> When the coarse thread is prepared, they put it into a frame about six feet square, and instead of a shuttle, they thrust through the thread with a long cane, having a large string through the web, which they shift at every second course of the thread. When they have thus finished their arduous labour, they paint each side of the carpet with such figures, of various colours, as their fruitful imaginations devise; particularly the images of those birds and beasts they are acquainted with; and likewise of themselves, acting in their social, and martial stations. There is that due proportion, and so much wild variety in the design, that would really strike a curious eye with pleasure and admiration. J. W. - t, Esq; a most skilful linguist in the Muskogee dialect, assures me, that time out of mind they passed the woof with a shuttle; and they have a couple of threddles, which they move with the hand so as to enable them to make good dispatch, something after our manner of weaving. This is sufficiently confirmed by their method of working broad garters, sashes, shot-pounches, broad belts, and the like, which are decorated all over with beautiful stripes and chequers. (Adair, 1775, p. 423.)

Nevertheless, a little beyond he mentions the inner bark of the mulberry tree used as an alternative to the "hemp" as a foundation for feather mantles. Possibly Adair's "hemp" is identical with Elvas' "grass resembling nettle," though the descriptions appear to indicate considerable difference in size. Moreover, there is no reason why the weaving process once understood should not have been applied to a number of different kinds of threads. Of one of these were made the "white coverings woven in panels with clever artifice and edged about with a scarlet fringe" which the French saw in the·sixteenth century upon the couch of the chief of the province of Guale on the present Georgia coast (Laudonnière, 1586, p. 48; Swanton, 1922, p. 73). If information collected by myself many years ago is correct, textile material was also obtained from the slippery elm. Jackson Lewis, through whom this comes, stated, on the authority of a very old woman who once lived at his house, that the Creeks formerly collected the small twigs of the slippery elm, tied them up in bundles, boiled them in lye of wood ashes, and then beat them until the pulp came away and a beautiful fibrous material was left, out of which they made a kind of cloth. This was woven entirely by hand and, as is usually stated of mulbery-bark clothing, clothing for the women was made out of it. Sometimes they colored these by means of certain herbs.

Mention has already been made of the Choctaw fabric woven of a mixture of bison hair and a vegetable fiber.

Needles were almost always of bone. Adair (1775, p. 6) mentions "fish-bones, or the horns and bones of deer, rubbed sharp." Early authorities have next to nothing to say regarding the Indian methods of sewing, but the following may be quoted from Speck, who is speaking of the Yuchi Indians:

Sewing is done by piercing holes in the edges to be joined with an awl. Two methods of stitching are known, the simple running stitch and the overhand. The latter, on account of its strength, is, however, more commonly used. Sinew and deerskin thongs are employed for thread.

One specimen of awl, for sewing and basket making, consists of a piece of deer antler about six inches long into which a sharp pointed piece of metal is firmly inserted. Bone is supposed to have been used for the point part before metal was obtainable. Several chevron-like scratches on the handle of this specimen [illustrated] are property marks. . . .

Softened deerskin thongs were employed for tying and binding purposes. (Speck, 1909, p. 36.)

FEATHERWORK

From Virginia to Louisiana garments and blankets were made by fastening feathers upon a kind of netting. Feather mantles were perhaps worn for ornament as much as for warmth. When the Spaniards met Tascalusa he had on "a *pelote* or mantle of feathers down to his feet" (Bourne, 1904, vol. 2, p. 120), and in the store-houses about Cofitachequi were "feather mantles (white, gray, ver-milion, and yellow), made according to their custom, elegant and suitable for winter" (Robertson, 1933, p. 93). Du Pratz thus describes the Natchez method of making these:

> The feather mantles are worked on a frame similar to that on which wig makers work hair. They lay out the feathers in the same manner and fasten them to old fish nets or old mulberry-bark mantles. They place them in the manner already outlined one over another and on both sides. For this purpose they make use of little turkey feathers. The women who can obtain feathers of the swan or Indian duck make mantles of them for the women of the Honored class. (Le Page du Pratz, 1758, vol. 2, pp. 191–192; Swanton, 1911, p. 63.)

To this we may add the words of Dumont de Montigny:

> With the thread which they obtain from the bark of the bass tree they make for themselves a kind of mantle which they cover with the finest swan feathers fastened on this cloth one by one, a long piece of work in truth, but they account their pains and time as nothing when they want to satisfy themselves. (Dumont, 1753, vol. 1, p. 155; Swanton, 1911, p. 63.)

Adair says that the Chickasaw women

> make turkey feather blankets with the long feathers of the neck and breast of that large fowl—they twist the inner end[s] of the feathers very fast into a strong double thread of hemp, or the inner bark of the mulberry tree, of the size and strength of coarse twine, as the fibres are sufficiently fine, and they work it in the manner of fine netting. As the feathers are long and glit-tering, this sort of blanket is not only very warm, but pleasing to the eye. (Adair, 1775, p. 423.)

In his description of Choctaw activities Romans (1775, p. 85) includes the manufacture of "blankets and other coverings out of the feathers of the breasts of wild turkies by a process similar to that of our wig makers, when they knit hair together for the pur-pose of making wigs."

Of the Creeks, Bartram says:

> Some have a short cloak, just large enough to cover the shoulders and breast; this is most ingeniously constructed, of feathers woven or placed in a most natural imbricated manner, usually of the scarlet feathers of the flamingo, or others of the gayest colours. (Bartram, 1792, p. 500.)

Since he does not speak of mulberry-bark textiles, it is probable that in his time the base was of European materials.

As recently as 1907, a Creek Indian remembered that an old woman—the same who recalled the use of textiles made of slippery-elm bark—remembered that these were sometimes ornamented with the iridescent feathers of the turkey gobbler arranged in designs.

Lawson informs us, regarding the Siouan tribes, that:

Their feather match coats are very pretty, especially some of them, which are made extraordinary charming, containing several pretty figures wrought in feathers, making them seem like a fine flower silk shag; and when new and fresh, they become a bed very well, instead of a quilt. . . . Others again are made of the green part of the skin of a mallard's head, which they sew perfectly well together, their thread being either the sinews of the deer divided very small, or silk grass. When they are finished, they look very fine, though they must needs be very troublesome to make. (Lawson, 1860, pp. 311–312.)

He met the chief doctor or physician of the Santee Nation "warmly and neatly clad with a match coat, made of turkies feathers" (Lawson, 1860, p. 37).

Smith says:

We have seen some [of the Virginia Indians] use mantels made of Turky feathers, so prettily wrought and woven with threads that nothing could bee discerned but the feathers, that was exceeding warme and very handsome (Smith, John, 1907 ed., p. 100.)

Strachey (1849, p. 58) refers to mantles of blue feathers.

There is much mention of feathers as ornaments in use in Florida, but little about feather mantles, though Le Moyne speaks of "many pieces of a stuff made of feathers, and most skilfully ornamented with rushes of different colors" sent in from the western Timucua by a French officer (Le Moyne, 1875, p. 8; Swanton, 1922, p. 347).

During dances some of the Creek Indian men and probably those of many other tribes carried turkey feather fans in their left hands as a sign of leadership and also to protect their eyes from the fire. They were carried about to some extent at other times. Speck says of these, with reference to the Yuchi:

The men furthermore affect the fan, *wetcá*, "turkey," of wild-turkey tail feathers. The proper possession of this, however, is with the older men and chiefs who spend much of their time in leisure. They handle the fan very gracefully in emphasizing their gestures and in keeping insects away. During ceremonies to carry the fan is a sign of leadership. It is passed to a dancer as an invitation to lead the next dance. He, when he has completed his duty, returns it to the master of ceremonies who then bestows it upon someone else. The construction of the fan is very simple, the quills being merely strung together upon a string in several places near the base. (Speck, 1909, p. 52.)

CLOTHING OF MEN

The breechclout was the one article of dress worn constantly by all males other than infants and young children. It was the first to be put on and the last to be laid aside, and when we read of an Indian stripping himself naked for war or the ball game, we may confidently assume, even when it is not specifically stated, that this particular article was excepted. Lawson says that it was not used before Europeans entered the country, but he is plainly in error since it is mentioned by the De Soto chroniclers and none of Lawson's informants could have had knowledge of a period preceding that. Thus, the Fidalgo of Elvas says that the men "have their privies covered with a truss of deerskin resembling the breechclouts formerly worn in Spain" (Robertson, 1933, p. 76). Evidently Garcilaso's informants had in mind the same article of apparel when they stated that the people of Florida "go about naked except for some garments of chamois skin of various colors almost like very short breeches, which cover them decently, as much as necessary, before and behind" (Garcilaso, 1723, p. 6). So far as our information goes, this was made in much the same manner throughout the Gulf area. Until European cloth was introduced, it was almost invariably made of skin. Deerskin is specifically mentioned as in use for that purpose by the Timucua, the Indians of Guale (Garcia, 1902, p. 189), the Algonquians of North Carolina and Virginia, the eastern Siouan tribes, and the Natchez, and implied for the Cherokee (Lawson, 1860, p. 310; Timberlake, Williams ed., 1927, p. 77).

The only references to any other material are in southern Florida which, as we have seen, constituted a somewhat distinct economic province. According to Fontaneda, the Calusa breechclout was of "braided palm leaves," and Dickenson saw some on the southeast coast composed of "a plaitwork of straws." (Fontaneda *in* Doc. Inédit., 1866, vol. 5, pp. 532–533; Dickenson, 1803, pp. 33–34; Swanton, 1922, pp. 387, 391.) San Miguel seems to carry the area over which this was spread up on the east coast as far as St. Augustine for, speaking mainly of those Indians, he says that they "wear nothing more than a breechclout woven of palmetto, four fingers wide with three ends, two passing around the waist and the other hanging down, each terminating in a tassel of the same palmetto, and all three together make a sort of broom which partly covers the buttocks." (Garcia, 1902, pp. 208–209.)

In later times English strouds, French Limbourgs, and other European materials of course took the place of everything aboriginal. The Creeks who accompanied Oglethorpe in his attack on St. Augustine in 1843 wore "flaps of red or blue Bays, hanging by a Girdle of the same" (Kimber, 1744, p. 16). Before the end of the eighteenth century Bartram could write regarding the breechclout:

It usually consists of a piece of blue cloth, about eighteen inches wide; this may pass between their thighs, and both ends being taken up and drawn through a belt round their waist, the ends fall down one before, and the other behind, not quite to the knee. [He adds that it] is usually plaited and indented at the ends, and ornamented with beads, tinsel lace, etc. (Bartram, 1792, p. 500.)

Adair (1775, p. 8) gives the dimensions as an ell and a half long by a quarter of an ell wide, i. e., about 5½ feet long by 1 foot wide.

The usual method of wearing this is as given by Bartram, but if we may trust White's drawings, it must have been usual in the Sound country of North Carolina to hang it over the belt only in front. This, however, may have been a minor local variation since Hariot seems to say that the men of Roanoke wore a skin hanging down both before and behind.   (Also Catesby, 1731–43, vol. 2, p.VIII.)   Nevertheless, breechclouts sometimes ended at the belt where they were tucked in (Speck, 1907, p. 110).   The illustrations accompanying Jacques Le Moyne's work show a single skin wrapped around the hips and apparently without any belt, but Ribault specifically mentions a belt of red leather seen by him among the same Indians, the Timucua, and it is probable that the figures do not accurately represent native usages.   (French, 1875, p. 170; Le Moyne, 1875, passim; Swanton, 1922, p. 346.)   As already noted, the Southeastern Indians also made belts out of bison and opossum hair often ornamented with beads.

Two garments were worn on the upper part of the body, a shirt and a blanket, but either they merged into each other or our descriptions lack clarity, so that it is often difficult to tell with which we have to deal.   Spanish chroniclers speak of the native garments of this class as shawls or mantles, though sometimes as blankets, but the words are loosely employed.   The shawls of native weave are usually said to have been worn by women, but Elvas tells us that the men wore "only one over the shoulder" leaving "the right arm uncovered in the manner and custom of gypsies" (Robertson, 1933, p. 76), and large white cloaks of the same material were worn by 60 old men who accompanied the Taensa chief in 1682 (French, 1846, pp. 61–62; Swanton, 1911, p. 260).   Garcilaso says of the "marten" (muskrat) garment worn "in the place of a cloak,"

they wear mantles clasped at the throat which reach half-way down the leg; they are of extremely fine marten skins which give off the odor of musk. . . . They also make them of small skins of various animals, such as several kinds of cat, fallow deer, red deer, bears, lions, and of skins of cattle [buffalo]. These hides they dress to such an extreme of perfection that the skin of a cow or a bear, with the hair on it, they prepare in a manner that leaves it so pliant and soft that it can be worn as a cloak, and it serves them for bed-covering at night.   (Bartram, 1792, p. 17.)

Shorter cloaks were also made of muskrat skin, as appears from the "robe of marten-skins, of the form and size of a woman's shawl" in which the chief of Coça came out to greet De Soto (Robertson, 1933, p. 115).   The Spanish adventurers speak of garments of this type in several places.   After Narvaez and his companions had put to sea in west Florida, they voyaged westward until they came to an Indian town in the neighborhood of what is now Pensacola Bay.   There they were at first received hospitably, but, when the Indians believed they were off their guard, they were suddenly attacked.   The Indian chief was among the white men at that time and was seized by them, but as his people were so near he escaped, leaving in our hands a robe of marten-ermine skin, which, I believe, are the finest in the world and gave out an odor like amber and musk. A single one can be smelt so far off that it seems as if there were a great many. We saw more of that kind but none like these. [Three days later they met other people, among whom were fivt or six chiefs] clothed in robes of marten, of the kind we had obtained previously, some of them done up in a very strange fashion, because they showed patterns of fawn-colored furs that looked very well. (Cabeza de Vaca, Bandelier ed., 1905, pp. 43–49; Swanton, 1922, p. 145.)

As mentioned above, this particular region seems to have been noted for its pelts because, when De Soto was among the Apalachee, Maldonado, the commander of his fleet, brought from there "a good blanket of sable fur. They had seen others in Apalache, but none like that" (Bourne, 1904, vol. 2, p. 81). Later they found the Indians of Cofitachequi clothed in "blankets of sable fur and others of the skins of wild cats which gave out a strong smell" (Bourne, 1904, vol. 2, p. 99).

When De Soto met Tascalusa, the latter was wearing a feather mantle extending to the ground, and this would be of the kind of which Timberlake (Williams ed., 1927, p. 77) speaks as a summer substitute for the native overcoat or blanket. We should perhaps class as a shirt "a shorte clocke made of fine hares skinnes quilted with the hayre out-warde" worn by the priests of Secota, but the following garment of the old men of Pomeioc should rather be regarded as a blanket or overcoat,

a large skinne which is tyed vppon their shoulders on one side and hangeth downe beneath their knees wearing their other arme naked out of the skinne, that they maye bee at more libertie. Those skynnes are Dressed with the hair on, and lyned with other furred skinnes. (Hariot, 1893, pls. 5, 9.)

These overcoats, or "match-coats," are often mentioned by writers on the Virginia and Carolina Indians, while but little is said about the more abbreviated garments that might be classed as shirts.

For their apparrell [says Strachey] they are sometimes covered with the skynnes of wyld beasts, which in winter are dressed with the haire, but in the sommer without, the better part use large mantells of deeres' skynnes, not much differing from the Irish falings [cloaks or mantels], some embroidered with white beads, some with copper, other painted after their manner, but the common sort have scarse wherewithall to cover their nakednes, but stick long blades of grasse, the leaves of trees, or such like, under broad baudricks of leather, which covers them behind and before. [Further on he continues:] We have seene some use mantells made both of Turkey feathers and other fowle, so prettily wrought and woven with threeds, that nothing could be discerned but the feathers, which were exceeding warme and very handsome. (Strachey, 1849, pp. 64–65.)

Beverley's description may be subjoined:

Their Cloaths are a large Mentle, carelessly wrapped about their Bodies, and sometimes girt close in the middle with a Girdle. The upper part of this mantle is drawn close upon the Shoulders, and the other hangs below their Knees . . . Seldom any but the Elder people wore the Winter Cloaks, (which they call Match-coats,) till they got a supply of European goods; and now most have them of one sort or other in the cold Winter Weather. Fig. 1 wears the proper Indian Match-coat, which is made of Skins, drest with the Furr on, sowed together, and worn with the Furr inwards, having the edges also gashed for beauty sake . . . Fig. 2. wears the Duffield Match-coat bought of the English. (Beverley, 1705, bk. 3, pp. 3, 5, pl. 3.)

The cloak of the Virginia priest differed somewhat, the fur being left on the outside. (See p. 477.)

Substantially the same costume was found among the Siouan people:

The Indian men have a match coat of hair, furs, feathers, or cloth, as the women have . . . Their feather match coats are very pretty, especially some of them, which are made extraordinary charming, containing several pretty figures wrought in feathers, making them seem like a fine flower silk shag;˙and when new and fresh, they become a bed very well, instead of a quilt. Some of another sort are made of hair, raccoon, bever, or squirrel skins, which are very warm. Others again are made of the green part of the skin of a mallard's head, which they sew perfectly well together, their thread being either the sinews of a deer divided very small, or silk grass. (Lawson, 1860, pp. 310–312.)

Catesby says briefly:

Their ordinary Winter dress is a loose open waistcoat without sleeves, which is usually made of a Deer skin, wearing the hairy side inwards or outwards in proportion to the cold or warmth of the season; in the coldest weather they cloath themselves with the skins of Bears, Beavers, *Rackoons*, etc. besides warm and very pretty garments made of feathers. (Catesby, 1731–43, vol. 2, p. VIII.)

In the latitude of Florida it is natural that there should have been less need for long, heavy clothing, and in fact we have only a general mention by Spark and the testimony of one illustration in Le Moyne's collection to the existence of such garments in the peninsula. (Hakluyt, 1847–89, vol. 3, p. 613; Le Moyne, 1875, pl. 39; Swanton, 1922, p. 346.) In the latter case, the chief represented as wearing the blanket is followed by another man holding up the end in a manner suggestive of sixteenth century Europe rather than America. However, Narvaez and his companions, during their march through Florida in 1528, were met by a chief borne upon the shoulders of his men and wearing a painted deerskin which may well have been of the same type (Cabeza de Vaca, Bandelier ed., 1905, p. 21).

It thus appears that, apart from certain special garments worn by the priests, there is little evidence for the use of shirts along the south Atlantic coast in ancient times, and what Timberlake says of the Cherokee seems to reinforce the idea that this garment represented a later importation.

At the time of his visit to that nation in 1761–62, they were wearing shirts of English make and large mantles or match-coats, but the old people informed him that before they had access to white men's goods they covered the upper portions of their bodies only with "a mantle of buffalo skin for the winter, and a lighter one of feathers for the summer" (Timberlake, Williams ed., 1927, p. 77).

Bartram, too, mentions a shirt of linen, and therefore of European origin, as worn by the Creeks a few years later, and, indeed, the match-coat itself seems now to have been made of imported stuff, for he says:

> Besides this attire, they have a large mantle of the finest cloth they are able to purchase, always either of a scarlet or blue colour; this mantle is fancifully decorated with rich lace or fringe round the border, and often with little round silver, or brass bells. (Bartram, 1792, p. 500.)

The Indians accompanying Oglethorpe in 1743 in his invasion of Florida wore "a Skin or Blanket tied, or loosely cast, over their Shoulders; a Shirt which they never wash, and which is consequently greasy and black to the last degree" (Kimber, 1744, p. 16).

But the feather mantles were still in use, as shown by the quotation from Bartram given on an earlier page.

Adair, whose knowledge of the Chickasaw was most intimate, mentions what seems to have been a really native shirt, but this was probably an alternative to the feather mantle.

> They formerly wore shirts, made of drest deer-skins, for their summer visiting dress; but their winter-hunting clothes were long and shaggy, made of the skins of panthers, bucks, bears, beavers, and otters; the fleshy sides outward, sometimes doubled, and always softened like velvet-cloth, though they retained their fur and hair. (Adair, 1775, p. 6.)

Yet the young Indians, male and female, of his time were wont to

> wrap a piece of cloth round them, that has a near resemblance to the old Roman toga or praetexta. 'Tis about a fathom square, bordered seven or eight quarters deep, to make a shining cavalier of the *beau monde*, and to keep out both the heat and cold. (Adair, 1775, p. 7.)

The shirt and blanket were also in use on the lower Mississippi. Du Pratz says of the Natchez:

> When it is cold the men cover themselves with a shirt made of two dressed deerskins, which resemble rather a nightgown than a shirt, the sleeves having only such a length as the breadth of the skin permits. . . . Over all of these, if the cold is a little severe, they wear a bison robe left uncolored on the side towards the [animal's] flesh, and with the hair left on, which they place against the body because it is warmer. In the country where beavers are found they make robes composed of six skins of these animals. When the days begin to grow finer and the cold is no longer so violent, the men and women cover themselves only with a deerskin dressed white, and sometimes colored black. There are some of these which have daubings in designs of different colors, as in red or in yellow with black lines. (Le Page du Pratz, 1758, vol. 2, pp. 190–197; Swanton 1911, p. 53.)

As was mentioned above (p. 458), when Tonti met the chief of the Taensa on Lake St. Joseph, he was surrounded by more than 60 old men, clothed in long white cloaks (French, 1846, pp. 61–62; Swanton, 1911, p. 260). Iberville and his companions observed that the Bayogoula men were "dressed only in a miserable deer or bear skin, which covers them from the knees to the shoulders if the skin is very large," but most were entirely naked (Margry, 1875–86, vol. 4, p. 259; Swanton, 1911, p. 276). His visit was made in the middle of March. Gravier also notes "a wretched deerskin" as the principal Houma and Tunica garment, but adds that sometimes the men, as well as the women "also have mantles of turkey feathers or of muskrat skins well woven and worked" (Shea, 1861, p. 134; Swanton, 1911, p. 317). The Koroa, too, seem to have had an upper garment consisting of a deerskin (Margry, 1875–86, vol. 1, pp. 558–559; Swanton, 1911, p. 328).

In lieu of the drawers and trousers of European peoples, most of the Gulf Indians wore at times garments sometimes called leggings or boots by the English, the latter word evidently applied in some now obsolete sense, and by the French *mitasses*. They were made in two pieces, one wrapped around each leg and brought up high enough so as to be fastened to the belt by means of leather cords, while at the lower ends they were inserted under the upper edges of the moccasins. Like the latter, they were used less about home than during excursions to some distance and they were mainly intended to protect the wearer from bushes and underbrush of various kinds. These were in use in De Soto's time, as appears from Ranjel's statement that the Indians of Cofitachequi "went clothed down to their feet with very fine skins well dressed, and blankets of the country," and that they made "hose and moccasins and leggings with ties of white leather" (Bourne, 1904, vol. 2, p. 101), although I am a little uncertain regarding the application of the three terms last employed. The first and last would both seem to apply to leggings. Elvas evidently means the same thing when he says that these same people made of colored deerskins "pantaloons, hose and shoes" (Robertson, 1933, p. 93). Hariot neither figures nor mentions this garment nor does Smith speak of it, but Strachey says:

True yt is sometymes in cold weather, or when they goe a hunting, or seeking the fruits of the woods, or gathering bents for their matts, both men and women (to defend them from the bushes and shrubs) put on a kynd of leather breeches and stockings, all fastened togither, made of deere skynns, which they type and wrappe about the loynes, after the fashion of the Turkes or Irish trouses. (Strachey, 1849, p. 65.

In his plate 3, figure 2, Beverley (1705) shows an Indian wearing breeches though they are almost covered up by his blanket. This particular figure was not from White but from a Swiss traveler, Francis Louis Michel, and is believed by Mr. Bushnell (1930, pp. 9–10) to have been intended to represent a Monacan, i. e., Siouan Indian of the interior, rather than an Algonquian.   Beverley's text describing this is as follows:

> Fig. 2 wears the Duffield Match-coat bought of the English, on his Head is a Coronet of Peak, on his Legs are Stockings made of Duffields: That is, they take a length to reach from the Ankle to the Knee, so broad as to wrap round the Leg; this they sow together, letting the edges stand out an Inch beyond the Seam.   When this is on, they Garter below Knee, and fasten the lower end in the Moccasin.   (Beverley, 1705, bk. 3, p. 5, pl. 3.)

Lawson does not seem to mention this garment, but he speaks of garters and they were almost always used in connection with the leggings, and Catesby, who covered much the same territory, says "they wear leather buskins on their legs, which they tie below the knee" (Catesby, 1731–43, vol. 2, p. VIII).   Timberlake (Williams ed., 1927, p. 76) speaks of "a sort of cloth-boots" distinct from the moccasins, worn in his time and Bartram (1792, p. 500), who essays to describe the clothing of all the principal Southeastern tribes, also refers to them, and says "they reach from the ancle to the calf, and are ornamented with lace, beads, silver bells, &c."   If he is correct, these were sometimes shorter than the one commonly described.   Adair calls them "boots."

> The men wear, for ornament, and the conveniences of hunting, thin deer-skin boots, well smoked, that reach so high up their thighs, as with their jackets to secure them from the brambles and braky thickets.   They sew them about five inches from the edges, which are formed into tossels, to which they fasten fawns trotters, and small pieces of tinkling metal, or wild turkey-cock-spurs.   (Adair, 1775, p. 7.)

The Creek women who accompanied Oglethorpe in his St. Augustine expedition of 1743 had "Boots about their Legs, of Bays" (Kimber, 1744, p. 16).   These garments were in use up to the latter half of last century and are well remembered by the Creeks of Oklahoma and the Alabama of Texas.

There is no certain reference to the employment of leggings in Florida by its ancient inhabitants.   Nearly all French writers who have undertaken to give a description of Natchez clothing mention them under the term *mitasses*.   An early writer says: "In place of stockings they envelop the leg in another piece of stuff, which they tie under the knee, and which is called *mitasse*," and Le Page du Pratz says:

> They also make a garment which the French call *mitasses*, but which ought rather to be denominated *cuissards*, since it covers the thighs and descends from the hips as far as the moccasins and enters these to the ankles.   (Swanton, 1911, pp. 52–53.)

Probably this was general in the valley, but there are no other definite references to it.

The heelless shoe for which we have adopted the eastern Algonquian term "moccasin" was universally, but not continuously, worn.   It was employed almost entirely in traveling some distance from home, on war and trading expeditions and the like, and sometimes a number of pairs were prepared to carry on an extended journey. References taken from the De Soto chroniclers have already been given in treating of the leggings. Elvas describes those skins that had been colored black specifically as the sort in use for shoes (Robertson, 1933, p. 76). Hariot, Smith, and Strachey do not describe moccasins, nor does White depict them in his drawings, but Beverley says:

> Their shoes, when they wear any, are made of an entire piece of Buck-Skin; except when they sow a piece to the bottom, to thicken the soal. They are fasten'd on with running Strings, the Skin being drawn together like a Purse on the top of the Foot, and tyed round the Ankle. The *Indian* name of this kind of Shoe is *Moccasin*. (Beverley, 1705, bk. 3, p. 5, pl. 3.)

He shows moccasins only in three illustrations, two of a man and one of a woman. One, and perhaps all of these, are believed to have been taken from the Swiss traveler, F. L. Michel (see p. 462). Of the tribes farther toward the southwest, Lawson says:

> They wear shoes of buck's and sometimes bear's skin, which they tan in an hour or two, with the bark of trees boiled, wherein they put the leather whilst hot, and let it remain a little while, whereby it becomes so qualified as to endure water and dirt, without growing hard. These have no heels, and are made as fit for the feet as a glove is for the hand, and are very easy to travel in when one is a little used to them. (Lawson, 1860, p. 311; also Catesby, 1731–43, vol. 2, pp. IX, XIII.)

Timberlake (Williams ed., 1927, pp. 76–77) speaks of moccasins as in use by the Cherokee both in his period and in times truly aboriginal, and Bartram describes the Creek footgear thus:

> The stillepica [from illin-paka, the calf of the leg] or moccasin defends and adorns the feet; it seems to be in imitation of the ancient buskin or sandal, very ingeniously made of deer skins, dressed very soft, and curiously ornamented according to fancy. (Bartram, 1792, p. 500.)

The Creeks who accompained Oglethorpe in his St. Augustine expedition of 1743 wore "Morgissons, or Pumps of Deer or Buffalo Skin" (Kimber, 1744, p. 16).

Of the Chickasaw, Adair remarks:

> They make their shoes for common use, out of the skins of the bear and elk, well dressed and smoked, to prevent hardening; and those for ornament, out of deer-skins, done in the like manner: but they chiefly go bare-footed, and always bare-headed. (Adair, 1775, p. 9.)

Both were probably made much after the manner of the Yuchi moccasin described and figured by Speck (1909, p. 48).

Du Pratz, in speaking of the Natchez shoe, takes more pains in his description than anyone else:

> The men and women seldom wear moccasins when they are not traveling. The moccasins of the natives are made of deerskins. They come together

around the foot like a sock, supposing it had the seam above. The skin is
cut three fingers longer than the foot, and the shoe is sewed only to the same
distance from the end of the foot, and all the rest is wrinkled on the foot.
The hinder part is sewed like a sock, but the flaps are from 8 to 9 inches
high. They go all the way round the leg. They are joined in front by means
of a thong of bearskin, which extends to the ankle, and thus makes lace boots.
These moccasins have neither soles nor heels.   (Le Page du Pratz, 1758, vol. 2,
pp. 194–195; Swanton, 1911, p. 54.)

After white contact, a marked modification and amplification of
native Indian costume took place, some of the effects of which have
been noted incidentally above. Its development in the northern and
central sections is best shown by Speck's description of Yuchi costume.
His account of the Yuchi man's costume in this transition era is as
follows, omitting references to the illustrations:

A bright colored calico shirt was worn by the men next to the skin. Over
this was a sleeved jacket reaching, on young men, a little below the waist, on
old men and chiefs, below the knees. The shirt hung free before and behind,
but was bound about the waist by a belt or woolen sash. The older men who
wore the long coat-like garment had another sash with tassels dangling at the
sides outside of this. These two garments, it should be remembered, were
nearly always of calico or cotton goods, while it sometimes happened that
the long coat was of deerskin. Loin coverings were of two kinds; either a
simple apron was suspended from a girdle next the skin before and behind,
or a long narrow strip of stroud passed between the legs and was tucked underneath the girdle in front and in back, where the ends were allowed to fall as
flaps. Leggings of stroud or deerskin reaching from ankle to hip were supported by thongs to the belt and bound to the leg by tasseled and beaded garter
bands below the knee. Deerskin moccasins covered the feet. Turbans of cloth,
often held in place by a metal head band in which feathers were set for ornament, covered the head. The man's outfit was then complete when he had
donned his bead-decorated side pouch, in which he kept pipe, tobacco and other
personal necessities, with its broad highly embroidered bandolier. The other
ornaments were metal breast pendants, earrings, finger rings, bracelets and
armlets, beadwork neckbands and beadwork strips which were fastened in
the hair. . . .

The bright colored calico shirt worn next to the skin was called *gōci bilané*
"what goes around the back," and was provided with buttons and often a frill
around the collar and at the wrists. The outer garment, *gōci stalé*, "over the
back," of calico also, was more characteristic. This had short sleeves with
frilled cuff bands which came just above the frills of the under shirt, thereby
adding to the frilled effect. A large turn-down collar bordered with a frill which
ran all around the lapels down the front and about the hem, added further to this
picturesque effect, and a great variety of coloring is exhibited in the specimens
which I have seen. The long skirted coat, *gocī stale'ä'*, worn by the old men,
chiefs and town officials, was usually white with, however, just as many frills.
An old specimen of Cherokee coat . . . shows very well the sort of coat
commonly worn by the men of other southeastern tribes as well as the Yuchi.
The material used is tanned buckskin with sewed-on fringe corresponding to
the calico frills in more modern specimens. It is said that as the men became
older and more venerable, they lengthened the skirts of their coats. A sash
commonly held these coats in at the waist.

The breechcloth, *gontson^{en}* . . . was a piece of stroud with decorated border, which was drawn between the legs and under the girdle before and behind. The flaps, long or short as they might be, are said to have been decorated with bead embroidery, but none of the specimens preserved show it.

Leggings, *to o'*, were originally of deerskin with the seam down the outside of the leg arranged so as to leave a flap three or four inches wide along the entire length. The stuff was usually stained in some uniform color. In the latter days, however, strouding, or some other heavy substance such as broadcloth, took the place of deerskin, and the favorite colors for this were black, red and blue. The outside edge of the broad flap invariably bore some decoration, in following out which we find quite uniformly one main idea. By means of ribbons of several colors sewed on the flap a series of long parallel lines in red, yellow, blue and green are brought out. The theme is said to represent sunrise or sunset and is one of the traditional decorations for legging flaps. . . . The legging itself reaches from the instep to the hip on the outer side where a string or thong is attached with which to fasten it to the belt for support.

The moccasin, *det ä'*, still in use . . . is made of soft smoked deerskin. It is constructed of one piece of skin. One seam runs straight up the heel. The front seam begins where the toes touch the ground and runs along the instep. At the ankle this seam ends, the uppers hanging loose. The instep seam is sometimes covered with some fancy cloth. Deerskin thongs are fastened at the instep near the bend of the ankle with which to bind the moccasin fast. The thongs are wound just above the ankle and tied in front. Sometimes a length of thong is passed once around the middle of the foot, crossing the sole underneath, when wound once around the ankle and tied in front. This extra binding going beneath the sole is employed generally by those whose feet are large, otherwise the shoe hangs too loose. The Osages, now just north of the Yuchi, employ this method of binding the moccasins quite generally, but the moccasin is quite different. The idea, however, may be a borrowed one. Yuchi moccasins have no trailers or instep flaps or lapels, the whole article being extremely plain. It seems that decoration other than the applications of red paint is quite generally lacking.

The turban, *to cĩné*, seems to have been a characteristic piece of head gear in the Southeast. The historic turban of the Yuchi was a long strip of calico or even heavier goods which was simply wound round and round the head and had the end tucked in under one of the folds to hold it. The turban cloth was of one color, or it could have some pattern according to personal fancy. Plumes of feathers were in the same way stuck in its folds for the artistic effect. That some head covering similar to the turban was known in pre-Columbian times seems probable inasmuch as a myth mentions that Rabbit, when he stole the ember of fire from its keepers, hid it in the folds of his head dress.

The sashes, *gágódī kwené*, "the two suspended from the body" . . . worn by men, are made of woolen yarn. The simplest of these consists merely of a bunch of strands twisted together and wrapped at the ends. A loose knot holds the sash about the waist. But the characteristic sash of the southeastern tribes, and one much in favor with the Yuchi, is more complex in its makeup, and quite attractive in effect, the specimens I have seen being for the most part knitted. The sashes of the Yuchi seem to be uniformly woven with yarn of a dark red color. Some specimens, however, show an intermixture of blue or yellow, or both. The main feature is a dark red ground for the white beads which are strung on the weft. Figures of triangles and lozenges or zigzags are attractively produced by the white beaded outlines and the conventional design produced is called "bull snake." The sash is tied about the waist so that the fixed tassels fall from one hip and the tassels at the knotted end depend from the other.

Customarily the tassels reach to the knee. The sash is a mark of distinction, to a certain extent, as it was only worn in former times by full-grown men. Nowadays, however, it is worn in ball games and upon ceremonial occasions by the participants in general, though only as regalia.

The woven garters, *tsē tsᴀⁿ'* . . . or *godē' kwené*, "leg suspender," should be described with the sash, as their manner of construction and their conventional decoration is the same. The garters or knee bands are several inches in width. They are commonly knitted, while the tassels are of plaited or corded lengths of yarn with tufts at the ends. Here the general form and colors of the decorative scheme are the same as those of the sash. The function of the knee band seems to be, if anything, to gather up and hold the slack of the legging so as to relieve some of the weight on the thong that fastens it to the belt. The tasseled ends fall half way down the lower leg. (Speck, 1909, pp. 46–49.)

The costume of the Seminole Indians of Florida became even more colorful and has persisted nearly to the present day. MacCauley thus describes the male costume as observed by him in the winter of 1880–1881:

The costume of the Seminole warrior at home consists of a shirt, a neckerchief, a turban, a breech cloth, and, very rarely, moccasins. On but one Indian in camp did I see more than this; on many, less. The shirt is made of some figured or striped cotton cloth, generally of quiet colors. It hangs from the neck to the knees, the narrow, rolling collar being closely buttoned about the neck, the narrow wristbands of the roomy sleeves buttoned about the wrists. The garment opens in front for a few inches, downward from the collar, and is pocketless. A belt of leather or buckskin usually engirdles the man's waist, and from it are suspended one or more pouches, in which powder, bullets, pocket knife, a piece of flint, a small quantity of paper, and like things for use in hunting are carried. From the belt hang also one or more hunting knives, each nearly ten inches in length. . . .

Having no pockets, the Seminole is obliged to submit to several inconveniences; for instance, he wears his handkerchief about his neck. I have seen as many as six, even eight, handkerchiefs tied around his throat, their knotted ends pendant over his breast; as a rule, they are bright red and yellow things, of whose possession and number he is quite proud. Having no pockets, the Seminole, only here and there one excepted, carries whatever money he obtains from time to time in a knotted corner of one or more of his handkerchiefs.

The next article of the man's ordinary costume is the turban. This is a remarkable structure and gives to its wearer much of his unique appearance. At present it is made of one or more small shawls. These shawls are generally woolen and copied in figure and color from the plaid of some Scotch clan. They are so folded that they are about 3 inches wide and as long as the diagonal of the fabric. They are then, one or more of them successively, wrapped tightly around the head, the top of the head remaining bare; the last end of the last shawl is tucked skillfully away, without the use of pins, somewhere in the many folds of the turban. The structure when finished looks like a section of a decorated cylinder crowded down upon the man's head. I examined one of these turbans and found it a rather firm piece of work, made of several shawls wound into seven concentric rings. It was over 20 inches in diameter, the shell of the cylinder being perhaps 7 inches thick and 3 in width. This headdress, at the southern settlements (Mikasuki), is regularly worn in the camps and sometimes on the hunt. While hunting, however, it seems to be the general custom for the warriors to go bareheaded. At the northern camps (Muskogee), a kerchief bound about the head frequently takes the place of the turban in everyday life, but on dress or festive occasions, at both the northern and the southern settlements, this curious turban is the customary covering for the head of the Seminole brave. Having no pockets in his dress, he has discovered that the folds of his turban may be put to a pocket's uses. Those who use tobacco (I say "those" because the tobacco habit is by no means universal among the red men of Florida) frequently carry their pipes and other articles in their turbans.

When the Seminole warrior makes his rare visits to the white man's settlements, he frequently adds to his scanty camp dress leggins and moccasins.

In the camps I saw but one Indian wearing leggins; he, however, is in every way a peculiar character among his people, and is objectionably favorable to the white man and the white man's ways. . . . The materials of which the leggins of the Seminole are usually made is buckskin. I saw, however, one pair of leggins made of a bright red flannel, and ornamented along the outer seams with a blue and white cross striped braid. The moccasins, also, are made of buckskin, of either a yellow or dark red color. They are made to lace high about the lower part of the leg, the lacing running from below the instep upward. As showing what changes are going on among the Seminole, I may mention that a few of them possess shoes, and one is even the owner of a pair of frontier store boots. The blanket is not often worn by the Florida Indians. Occasionally, in their cool weather, a small shawl, of the kind made to do service in the turban, is thrown about the shoulders. Oftener a piece of calico or white cotton cloth, gathered about the neck, becomes the extra protection against mild coolness in their winters. (MacCauley, 1887, pp. 483–485.)

Among the effects of the famous Osceola were

four black and two white ostrich feathers, large silk shawl used for head dress, a splendid belt made of ornamented beads, an Indian belt ornamented with beads, a blue guard made of beads, three silver gorgets, and a hair brush with a glass mirror on the back. (Foreman, 1932, p. 358, footnote.)

Thirty years after MacCauley, Skinner found that the costume had changed but little:

The regular everyday dress of the Seminole man consists of a bright, varicolored, calico shirt, narrow at the waist and wrists, with the expanding skirt reaching to the knees. Around the neck are usually worn a number of bandana handkerchiefs. The older men wear a shirt much more like the corresponding garment of civilization, which is not gathered at the waist. The elders also usually wear a turban made of a shawl or a series of bandanas wound together and held in place with a broad band of beaten silver. On special occasions, egrets or other plumes are thrust under the band at the sides.

The ceremonial costume consists of a turban, a shirt of the everyday sort, though silk is used for gala apparel, a calico coat with designs in appliqué, deerskin leggings dyed a rich reddish brown, and moccasins that often have a round flap at the toe, which, except that it is soft, reminds one of the protectors on Apache moccasins.

To this costume is added an array of woven bead or yarn belts. The beaded belts are woven in angular figures, in contradistinction to the otherwise similar circular designs of the Creeks, and usually symbolizing some life form.

Owing to the subtropical heat and the great moisture of their swampy habitat, the skin clothing is never worn except for some ceremony, although "Little Billy" (Billy Koniphadjo) gave assurance that in his boyhood the Seminole still wore leggings and moccasins at their daily tasks, discarding them eventually because they were "hot too much." He had no recollection of any upper garment except the calico shirt. (Skinner, 1913, pp. 65–66.)

Notes regarding Caddo clothing will be found in the Bureau of American Ethnology Bulletin 132 (Swanton, 1942, pp. 140–148).

CLOTHING OF WOMEN

This subject is well introduced by the following quotation from Adair:

Although the same things are commonly alike used or disused by males and females; yet they distinguish their sexes in as exact a manner as any civilized nation. (Adair, 1775, p. 171.)

In place of the breechclout the women wore a short skirt extending from the waist almost to the knees. This is sometimes, but improperly, called "the women's breechclout."

The Fidalgo of Elvas and Ranjel both describe the garments worn by Indian women in southern Georgia in about the same terms. The former says that they wore two garments made of native textile material, "draping one around themselves from the waist down and another over the shoulder with the right arm uncovered in the manner and customs of gypsies." (Robertson, 1933, p. 76.) Ranjel almost parallels the statement:

They [i.e., the women] make very fine mantles, and they wear one from the girdle down and another fastened on one side with the end over the shoulder like those Bohemians, or gypsies, who wander sometimes through Spain. (Bourne, 1904, vol. 2, p. 88.)

There seems to be no other mention of the female costume in these early narratives except by Garcilaso (1723, p. 18) in his general chapter on Floridian customs: "The women dress in chamois [i. e., deer] skin, having the whole body decently covered." From this it appears that even in early times the women wore clothing of skins as well as of woven materials.

The women of Secotan are described by Hariot (1893, pl. 4 [pl. 66 of this work]) as wearing "a deer skinne verye excellelye dressed, hanginge downe from their nauell vnto the mydds of their thighes, which also couereth their hynder parts," but apparently those of Pomeioc were somewhat less well protected for they tied a "deers skinne doubled about them crochinge hygher about their breasts, which hange downe before almost to their knees, and are almost altogither naked behinde" (Hariot, 1893, pl. 8 [pl. 65 of this work]). From Smith and Strachey we learn that a similar garment was worn by Virginia women.

Strachey. (1849, p. 66) says, "being once twelve yeares, they put on a kind of semicinctum lethern apron (as doe our artificers or handycrafts men) before their bellies." According to Lawson, the Indian women of the Peidmont region, except in severe weather, wore

a sort of flap or apron containing two yards in length, and better than half a yard deep. Sometimes it is a deer skin dressed white, and pointed or slit at the bottom, like fringe. . . . Others wear blue, or red flaps, made of bays and plains, which they buy of the English, of both which they tuck in the corners, to fasten the garment, and sometimes make it part with a belt. (Lawson, 1860, p. 310.)

Of approximately the same territory, Catesby says:

The women wear short petticoats of woollen, and some of moss. In summer they generally go naked from the waste upwards, but in winter they wrap themselves in a mantle of skins or woolen cloth, which they purchase of the *English*. (Catesby, 1731–43, vol. 2, p. ix.)

Byrd seems to be our only authority to mention the use of silk grass as a material in manufacturing this garment. His information is volunteered as if what he says were true for the entire Virginia-North Carolina section, but his particular informant was "an old Indian trader," and he was accompanied by a Saponi.

Of this [silk grass], [he says] they make their Baskets and Aprons which their Women wear about their Middles, for Decency's Sake. These are long enough to wrap quite round them and reach down to their Knees, with a Fringe on the under part by way of Ornament. (Bassett, 1901, p. 286.)

That this material was actually used in lieu of deerskin is indicated by the mention of "woollen" above and the well-known fact that farther south and west mulberry-bark textiles were common.

When Oglethorpe visited the Lower Creek town of Coweta in 1739 and observed the dances there, he says: "The women are mostly naked to the waist wearing only one short Peticoat w[ch] reaches to the Calves of their Legs" (Bushnell, 1908, p. 573). Bartram, having special reference to the Creeks and Cherokee, remarks of female dress, "their flap or petticoat is made after a different manner [from that of the men], is larger and longer, reaching almost to the middle of the leg, and is put on differently" (Bartram, 1792, p. 501). He mentions this in one or two other places.

The women's dress [says Adair] consists only in a broad softened skin, or several small skins sewed together, which they wrap and tye round their waist, reaching a little below their knees. (Adair, 1775, pp. 6–7.)

In his time, however, it had been largely displaced by "a fathom of the half breadth of Stroud cloth," which they wrapped around their waists and tied with a leathern belt "commonly covered with brass runners or buckles." This corresponds to the skirt, or honō', of the Alabama.

A little later Swan (1855, p. 275) stated of the Creek women in general that they "wear no clothes in summer, except one single, simple, short petticoat, of blue stroud, tied around the waist, and reaching only to the upper part of the knees."

In his description of the Choctaw, the anonymous Frenchman tells us that the women made a fabric of bison hair and the fiber from a very strong herb spun together.

> This fabric is double like the two-sided handkerchiefs and thick as canvas, half an ell wide and three quarters long. That serves them as a skirt. (Swanton, 1918, p. 68.)

It is not quite clear whether this refers only to the women but, from what we learn elsewhere, it would seem so.

In the dress of Florida women we encounter an innovation because they sometimes wore garments of the long Spanish moss instead of skins, although these were barely mentioned by Catesby in a quotation given above:

> The women also for their apparell vse painted skinnes, but most of them gownes of mosse, somewhat longer than our mosse, which they sowe together artificially, and make the same surplesse wise. (Hakluyt, 1847–89, vol. 3, p. 613; Swanton, 1922, p. 346, quoting Spark.)

The good Bishop Calderón found 400 women in the Timucua missions "naked from the waist up and from the knees down" and left them clothed from neck to feet in "a pearl-colored foliage of trees," which was evidently the tree moss (Wenhold, 1936, p. 12). Challeux is the only one of the French colonists who mentions skins along with the moss:

> The woman girds herself with a little covering of the skin of a deer or other animal, the knot saddling the left side above the thigh, in order to cover the most private parts. (Gaffarel, 1875, p. 461; Swanton, 1922, p. 346.)

The same material was used by Calusa women (Fontaneda *in* Doc. Inédit., 1866, vol. 5, pp. 532–533; Swanton, 1922, p. 387), and in 1595 San Miguel thus describes the clothing worn by Indian women about St. Simons Island on the Georgia coast:

> The dress of the women is in the style of a cloak (güeypil) and skirts of the long moss (pastle) which grows on trees, made like a fringe. The cloak hangs from the neck to a point below the waist, and the skirts from the waist to the ground. (Garcia, 1902, p. 193.)

But a chief visited by San Miguel "in place of the common clothing of moss" had his two wives wear deerskins (Garcia, 1902, p. 194).

At a considerably later date, Dickenson notes moss garments in use in the Florida towns occupied by refugee Indians from this same Georgia coast.

> The women natives of these towns clothe themselves with the moss of trees, making gowns and petticoats thereof, which at a distance, or in the night, look very neat. (Dickenson, 1803, p. 93; Swanton, 1922, p. 347.)

As far north as the Carolinas, Lawson (1860, p. 43) observed moss used as clothing when the women were mourning.

There are several brief description of the Natchez costume.

Du Pratz:

In the warm season the women wear only half an ell of Limbourg. They wind this cloth about their bodies, and are well covered from the waist to the knees. When they lack Limbourg they employ for the same purpose a deerskin.

Dumont says this was called an "alconand," from Choctaw alhkuna, "gown." Sometimes this garment was made of mulberry bark. (Dumont, 1753, vol. 1, pp. 137–139; Le Page du Pratz, 1758, vol. 2, pp. 190–197; Swanton, 1911, pp. 52–53; Read, 1931, p. 80.)

The same garment is noted among the Bayogoula and the Tunica. (Margry, 1875–86, vol. 4, pp. 169–172, 259–262; Shea, 1861, pp. 80–81, 134; Swanton, 1911, pp. 276, 316.)

As we have already seen, the women living in southern Georgia in De Soto's time sometimes wore besides a skirt a second woven garment which passed over the shoulder, the right arm being left free (Robertson, 1933, p. 76). Women's cloaks made of tree moss were worn on the Georgia coast, as may be seen by the quotation from San Miguel given above. Except for a very general statement by Garcilaso, the earliest mention of a cloak or coat of skin is by Barlowe in relating his dealings with the coast Indians of North Carolina. The wife of Granganimeo, the king's brother, "had on her backe a long cloake of leather, with the furre side next to her body, and before her a piece of the same" (Burrage, 1906, p. 232). Strachey remarks that

the better sort of [Virginia] women cover themselves (for the most part) all over with skin mantells, finely drest, shagged and fringed at the skyrt, carved and coloured with some pretty work, or the proportion of beasts, fowle, tortayses, or other such like imagry, as shall best please or expresse the fancy of the wearer. (Strachey, 1849, p. 58.)

They also wore mantles of turkey feathers and feathers of other birds, and the wife of a chief named Pipisco had a "mantell, which they call puttawus, which is like a side cloake, made of blew feathers, so arteficyally and thick sowed togither, that it seemed like a deepe purple satten, and is very smooth and sleeke" (Strachey, 1849, p. 58). The women of the Siouan tribes wore, in severe weather, a match coat, the name given in Virginia to the garment we would call an overcoat. These were made of hair, specific mention being made of opossum hair, fur, feathers, or European cloth (Lawson, 1860, pp. 43, 311). The use of opossum hair in such large quantities seems a bit doubtful. Among the Creek and Cherokee women, Bartram (1792, p. 501) noted "a little short waistcoat, usually made of calico, printed linen, or fine cloth, decorated with lace, beads, &c." This is the ilokfa of the Alabama Indians.

It will be noted that the material is largely European, and it probably took the place of the second mulberry-fiber garment mentioned by Elvas.

In cold weather, [says Adair] the Chickasaw women wrap themselves in the softened skins of buffalo calves, with the wintry shagged wool inward. (Adair, 1775, p. 8.)

It is the shawl or tàpàske' of the Alabama, except that anciently this covered one breast only, usually the left, and was fastened on the left shoulder, leaving the right arm free. There is no specific mention of a cloak or coat among the Timucua women, but Le Moyne figures some of them with a moss garment carried over one shoulder and this may correspond to the fiber cloak similarly worn farther north (Le Moyne, 1875, pls. 19, 34, 39, 40; Swanton, 1922, p. 346). Du Pratz describes the use of an upper garment in almost the same terms as Elvas about two centuries before.

When the cold makes itself felt they wear a second [mantle], the middle of which passes under the right arm, the two corners being fastened on the left shoulder. In this manner the two arms are free and only one breast is visible. (Le Page du Pratz, 1758, vol. 2, pp. 190–197; Swanton, 1911, p. 53.) [Pl. 70.]

Pénicaut notes "a garment of white cloth which extends from neck to feet, made almost like the Andriennes of our French ladies" (Pénicaut in Margry, 1875–86, vol. 5, p. 445; Swanton, 1911, p. 52). This must be the same article of clothing but with the size somewhat exaggerated. Women too poor to have this cloak protected themselves with a skin in the coldest weather. When Iberville visited the Bayogoula in the middle of March, some of them were observed wearing blankets of bearskin (Margry, 1875–86, vol. 4, p. 169; Swanton, 1911, p. 276). Robes of muskrat skins and turkey feathers are mentioned among the Houma and Tunica (Thwaites, 1897–1901, vol. 65, pp. 151–153; Shea, 1861, p. 147; Swanton, 1911, p. 289).

According to Strachey (1849, p. 66) Virginia women wore leggings as well as the men, and Beverley in one of his figures shows a woman in winter costume wearing leggings (Beverley, 1705, pl. 7, fig. 2). But this figure is probably from Michel and represents a Monacan woman at a late date. (See Bushnell, 1930, p. 9.) Elsewhere this is always mentioned as an article of male attire and Bartram specifically denies that it was used by the women.

To make up for the absence of leggings or any garments corresponding to them, the women's "breechclout" or skirt was usually made longer, as already described, and on the other hand the moccasin was sometimes brought higher up the leg. The woman figured by Beverley wearing leggings also has moccasins. Lawson (1860, p. 310) says that in the tribes with which he was acquainted the women sometimes wore "Indian shoes or moggizons, which are made after the same manner as the men's are." Bartram speaks of the woman's moccasin as carried higher up the leg, but Du Pratz tells us that those worn by the Natchez women were precisely like the moccasins of the men. (Bartram, 1792, p. 501; Le Page du Pratz, 1758, vol. 2, p. 195; Swanton, 1911, p. 54.)

Speck says of the later clothing of the Yuchi:

The women wore calico dresses often ornamented on the breast, shoulders, and about the lower part of the skirt with metal brooches. Necklaces of large round beads, metal earrings and bracelets were added for ornament, and upon festive or ceremonial occasions a large, curved, highly ornate metal comb surmounted the crown of the head. From this varicolored ribbons dangled to the ground, trailing out horizontally as the wearer moved about. The women's wardrobe also included an outside belt, decorated with bead embroidery, short leggings, and moccasins at times. . . . (Speck, 1909, p. 46.)

The belts were of leather or trade cloth and had bead embroidery decorations representing in general the same range of objects as the neckbands and hair ornaments. Such belts were usually about two inches wide. Women's dresses . . . present nothing characteristic or original. Most women are found with strings of large round blue beads about their necks. It is stated that necklaces of this sort have something to do with the fertility of women. . . .

[He also illustrates a comb and says] the narrow band of metal is decorated with punched-in circles, ovals and toothed curves. The teeth are cut off of another strip of metal which is riveted on. The upper edge of the comb is scalloped. Women's bracelets are shown [in a second figure] with similar ornamentation on the body, and grooves near the edges to render its shape firm. The rings, gōmpadī'né, and earrings need no description. Hardly any two are alike. (Speck, 1909, pp. 50–51.)

MacCauley has the following on the later costume of Seminole women:

It consists, apparently, of but two garments, one of which, for lack of a better English word, I name a short shirt, the other a long skirt. The shirt is cut quite low at the neck and is just long enough to cover the breasts. Its sleeves are buttoned close about the wrists. The garment is otherwise buttonless, being wide enough at the neck for it to be easily put on or taken off over the head. The conservatism of the Seminole Indian is shown in nothing more clearly than in the use, by the women, of this much abbreviated covering for the upper part of their bodies. The women are noticeably modest, yet it does not seem to have occurred to them that by making a slight change in their upper garment they might free themselves from frequent embarrassment . . . Gathered about the waist is the other garment, the skirt, extending to the feet and often touching the ground. This is usually made of some dark colored calico or gingham. The cord by which the petticoat is fastened is often drawn so tightly about the waist that it gives to that part of the body a rather uncomfortable appearance. This is especially noticeable because the shirt is so short that a space of two or more inches on the body is left uncovered between it and the skirt. I saw no woman wearing moccasins, and I was told that the women never wear them. For headwear the women have nothing, unless the cotton cloth, or small shawl, used about the shoulders in cool weather, and which at times is thrown or drawn over the head, may be called that. (Mac-Cauley, 1887, pp. 485–486.)

And Skinner thus reports their costume 30 years later:

The women wear a full-length skirt girt about the waist, and a cape with sleeves attached. As the waist or cape does not connect with the skirt, a broad band of coppor-colored skin is always visible between the upper and lower garments of the older women. Around their necks they carry enormous necklaces, weighing often from ten to fifteen pounds, and even more. The heavy beads are coiled about their shoulders and throats until their chins are sometimes fairly forced skyward, and causing them to look as if they were being choked.

For ceremonial purposes their garments are the same, except that then they wear capes that are bedecked with hammered silver bangles and brooches, and in the dance, knee leggings to which tortoise-shell rattles are attached, are worn. (Skinner, 1913, pp. 66–67.)

The only peculiarity we note in the costume of Caddo women seems to have been in the upper garment, a single garment which instead of being wrapped around the neck and fastened on one shoulder was provided with an opening in the center, poncho fashion. (See Swanton, 1942, pp. 140–148.) This recalls in a measure the upper garment of Seminole women as described by MacCauley.

CLOTHING OF CHILDREN

Very young children often went naked and they usually wore very simple clothing until about the age of puberty. Change in women's garments at that time was more marked than with men. Hariot says that girls of 7 or 8 in the east country of North Carolina wore about them

a girdle of skinne, which hangeth downe about their nauel with mosse of trees betwene their thighes and their skinnes to couer their priuities withall. After they be once past 10 yeares of age, they wear skinnes as the older sorte do. [Pl. 65.] (Hariot, 1893, pl. 8.)

Strachey (1849, p. 65) seems to state that girls, and presumably boys, went entirely naked until they were 11 or 12, but some rudimentary clothing may probably be assumed, of the sort described by Hariot. It may be noted that Beverley reproduces and undertakes to describe White's drawing in Hariot, except that with him the figure is that of a young boy instead of a young girl. This string clothing seems to be referred to again by Lawson (1860, p. 310), though he states that it was worn after puberty. Swan (1855, p. 275) says that Creek children went stark naked both summer and winter up to the age of 12 or 14 years, but Bartram (1792, p. 502) that Creek girls "as soon as or before they can walk" always wore the jacket, flap or skirt, and moccasins of the grown-up women, while "the male youth go perfectly naked until they are twelve or fifteen years of age." From this statement it would appear that the Creeks did not differentiate between the dress of the unmarried women and that of the married.

Along the lower Mississippi, girls seem to have worn a garment which was an amplification of that Hariot describes. Du Pratz has the fullest description:

> The boys and the young girls are not clothed at all, but when the girls are from eight to ten years of age they are covered from the belt to the ankle with a fringe of mulberry threads attached to a band which passes under the belly. There is also another band over the navel, which is joined to the first behind. The belly between the two is covered with a netting, which holds them in place, and there are behind only two large cords, each of which has a tassel. The boys begin to cover themselves only at the age of twelve or thirteen. (Le Page du Pratz, 1758, vol. 2, pp. 190–197; Swanton, 1911, p. 53.)

According to Dumont de Montigny, the girl's garment was worn by her until marriage or loss of virginity, and it consisted in

> a kind of net attached to their belt and terminating in a point just like a kind of *corps d'enfant*, the two sides of which are ornamented with ribbons of bass thread, also worked into a netting. From their belts to their knees hang many strings from the same cord, at the ends of which are attached claws of birds of prey like eagles, tiercelets, buzzards, etc., which when these girls walk make a kind of clicking which pleases them. This sort of ornament does not ill resemble those nets with which our horses are covered to protect them from the flies. (Dumont, 1753, vol. 1, pp. 137–139; Swanton, 1911, pp. 52–53.)

Pénicaut gives one more description:

> The breechclouts of the girls are ordinarily made of a fabric of white thread and cover their nakedness only in front from the belt halfway down the legs. They fasten it behind with two cords, at the end of each one of which hangs a tassel which falls behind. There are fringes sewed to the lower part of the breechclout along the front which hang down to the ankle. (Pénicaut *in* Margry, 1875–86, vol. 5, pp. 445–446; Swanton, 1911, p. 52.)

Bayogoula girls wore a garment, if it can be called that, more like the ones described by Hariot and Lawson.

> Many girls from 6 to 7 [says Iberville] have no breechclouts at all; they cover themselves with a little bunch of moss, held by a thread, which passes between their thighs and is knotted to a belt above. (Margry, 1875–86, vol. 4, pp. 171–172; Swanton, 1911, p. 275.)

The Tunica and Houma girls, if we may trust Gravier and La Source, wore thread garments like those of the Natchez. (Thwaites, 1897–1901, vol. 65, pp. 151–153; Shea, 1861, pp. 80–81, 146–147; Swanton, 1911, pp. 289, 316.)

Of Caddo girls, Morfi says, quoting Solís:

> From the time of their birth their mothers put breechclouts of grass or hay on them which modestly cover their nakedness and these they keep until death, renewing them when required to do so by necessity, without failing on this account to cover the rest of the body honestly. (Solís, 1931, p. 421; Morfi, 1932, p. 46; Swanton, 1942, p. 140.)

A note may be appended from MacCauley regarding Seminole children in Florida in 1880–81:

Girls from seven to ten years old are clothed with only a petticoat, and boys about the same age wear only a shirt. Younger children are, as a rule, entirely naked. If clothed at any time, it is only during exceptionally cool weather or when taken by their parents on a journey to the homes of the palefaces. (Mac-Cauley, 1887, p. 486.)

And Skinner says of the same tribe:

The costumes of the children are invariably the same as those of their elders, save that little girls sometimes wear a single-piece gown with an appliqué collar on festival occasions. (Skinner, 1913, p. 67.)

CLOTHING OF THE MEDICINE MEN

The clothing of the medicine men is often given separate treatment by our authorities and we will follow their example. In the first of these descriptions, by Hariot, will be included other items, though we are to consider them separately a little later.

The Priests of the aforesaid Towne of Secota are well stricken in yeers, and as yt seemeth of more experience than the comon sorte. They weare their heare cutt like a creste, on the topps of thier heades as other doe, but the rest are cutt shorte, sauings those which growe aboue their foreheads in manner of a perriwigge. They also haue somwhat hanginge in their ears. They weare a shorte clocke made of fine hares skinnes quilted with the hayre outwarde. The rest of their bodie is naked. (Hariot, 1893, pl. 5; pl. 94 of this work.)

A little farther on he speaks of the costume worn by another type of dealer in the supernatural whom he calls the "conjurer."

They shaue all their heads sauinge their crests which they weare as other doe, and fasten a small black birde aboue one of their ears as a badge of their office. They weare nothinge but a skinne which hangeth downe from their gyrdle, and couereth their priuityes. They wear a bagg by their side as is expressed in the figure. (Hariot, 1893, pl. 11; pl. 95 of this work.)

Strachey gives the following account of the costume of those priests who had charge of the principal Powhatan temple at Utamussack in the Pamunkey country:

In this place commonly are resident seven priests, the chief differing from the rest in his ornament, whilst the inferior priests can hardly be knowne from the common people, save that they had not (it maye be maye not have) so many holes in their eares to hang their jewells at. The ornaments of the chief priest were, uppon his showlders a middle-sized cloke of feathers much like the old sacrificing garment which Isodorus calls cassiola, and the burlett or attire of his head was thus made; some twelve or sixteen or more snakes' sloughes or skyns were stuffed with mosse, and of weasells or other vermyn were skynns perhapps as many; all these were tyed by the tayles, so as their tayles meet in the tope of the head like a great tassell, and round about the tassell was circled a crownett (as yt were) of feathers, the skynns hanging round about his head, neck and showlders, and in a manner covering his face. The faces of all their priests are painted so uglye as they can devise; in their hands they carry every one his rattle, for the most part as a symbole of his place and profession, some basse, some smaller. (Strachey, 1849, p. 91.)

References to certain articles of attire, or rather ornament, in other places and similar notes by Smith possibly refer to medicine men rather than common people. Beverley reproduces White's figures of priest and conjurer, and his descriptions are based upon them but he seems to have a few details from another source. He also adds an illustration of a medicine man, probably from Michel. His words are as follows:

The habit of the *Indian* priest, is a Cloak made in the form of a Woman's Petticoat; but instead of tying it about their middle, they fasten the gatherings about their Neck, and tye it upon the Right Shoulder always keeping one Arm out to use upon occasion. This Cloak hangs even at the bottom, but reaches no lower than the middle of the Thigh; but what is most particular in it, is, that it is constantly made of a skin drest soft, with the Pelt or Furr on the outside, and revers'd; insomuch, that when the Cloak has been a little worn, the hair falls down in flakes, and looks very shagged, and frightful.

The cut of their Hair is likewise peculiar to their Function; for 'tis all shaven close except a thin Crest, like a Cocks-comb which stands bristling up, and runs in a semi-circle from the Forehead up along the Crown to the nape of the Neck: They likewise have a border of Hair over the Forehead, which by its own natural strength, and by the stiffning it receives from Grease and Paint, will stand out like the peak of a Bonnet. . . .

The Conjurer shaves all his Hair off, except the Crest on the Crown, upon his Ear he wears the skin of some dark colour'd Bird; he, as well as the Priest, is commonly grim'd with Soot or the like; to save his modesty he hangs an Otter-skin at his Girdle, fastening the Tail between his Legs; upon his Thigh hangs his Pocket, which is fastn'd by tucking it under his Girdle, the bottom of this likewise is fring'd with Tassils for ornament sake. (Beverley, 1705 pls. 3, 4.)

The "chief doctor, or physician" of the Santee nation met by Lawson in 1701 "was warmly and neatly clad with a match coat, made of turkies feathers, which makes a pretty show, seeming as if it was a garment of the deepest silk shag" (Lawson, 1860, p. 37).

Turning to the Creeks we find, according to Bartram that:

The junior priests or students constantly wear the mantle or robe, which is white; and they have a great owl skin cased and stuffed very ingeniously, so well executed, as almost to represent the living bird, having large sparkling glass beads, or buttons, fixed in the head for eyes; this ensign of wisdom and divination, they wear sometimes as a crest on the top of the head, at other times the image sits on the arm, or is borne on the hand. (Bartram, 1792, p. 502.)

A very excellent description of the costume of the Chickasaw "Archi-magus," which in all probability was identical with that formerly adopted by the Creek Hilis-haya, is given by Adair:

Before the Indian *Archi-magus* officiates in making the supposed holy fire, for the yearly atonement of sin, the Sagan clothes him with a white ephod, which is a waistcoat without sleeves. When he enters on that solemn duty, a beloved attendant spreads a white-drest buck-skin on the white seat, which stands close to the supposed holiest, and then puts some white beads on it, that are given him by the people. Then the *Archi-magus* wraps around his shoulders a consecrated skin of the same sort, which reaching across under his arms, he ties behind his back, with two knots on the legs, in the form of a figure of eight. Another custom he observes on this solemn occasion, is, instead of going barefoot, he wears a new pair of buck-skin white moccasins made by himself, and stitched with the sinews of the same animal. The upper leather across the toes, he paints, for the space of three inches, with a few streaks of red—not with vermilion, for that is their continual war-emblem, but with a certain red root, its leaves and stalk resembling the ipecacuanha, which is their fixed red symbol of holy things. These shoes he never wears, but in the time of the supposed passover; for at the end of it, they are laid up in the beloved place, or holiest, where much of the like sort, quietly accompanies an heap of old, broken earthen ware, conch-shells, and other consecrated things. . . . The American *Archi-magus* wears a breast-plate, made of a white conch-shell, with two holes bored in the middle of it, through which he puts the ends of an otter-skin strap, and fastens a buckhorn white button to the outside of each. . . . . The Indian wears around his temples either a wreath of swan-feathers, or a long piece of swan-skin doubled so as only the fine snowy feathers appear on each side. . . . [and he] wears on the crown of his head, a tuft of white feathers, which they call *Yatèra*. He likewise fastens a tuft of blunted wild Turkey cock-spurs, toward the toes of the upper part of his moccasenes. (Adair, 1775, pp. 82–83.)

Strangely enough, in spite of the high development of ritualism among the Natchez, we have no good description of the priestly costume.

BAGS AND PURSES

The southern Indian male often carried a bag or pouch hung at one side in which were kept tobacco, knives, pipes, and all sorts of small personal belonging, and which the doctors used for their medicines. They were, indeed, particularly necessary to the latter, and the earliest mention is by Hariot in his description of a typical "conjurer" of the Sound region of North Carolina. The accompanying illustration by White (reproduced here as plate 95) shows it worn at the right side, fastened to the belt and ornamented with a number of strings probably of hide (Hariot, 1893, pl. 11). Beverley reproduces this figure (1705, bk. 3, p. 6, pl. 4, fig. 1), and he helps us to understand the nature of the bag a little better by introducing it also in his plate 10 (1705, bk. 3, p. 17), which in other respects is closely like one of White's drawings. Here the strings at the lower end of the bag are clearly seen to be leather ends made into a fringe. A "leather pouch," very likely similar to this, is mentioned by Lawson (1860, p. 85).

An Alabama informant stated that the bag was carried on the right side, the strap passing over the left shoulder, and this was probably the more usual way, but the illustrations of Creek and Seminole chiefs given by McKenney and Hall show that it was sometimes worn on the left side, perhaps by left-handed persons. This bag was ordinarily ornamented after the manner of the belt and garters.

Adair (1775, p. 454) tells us that "the Choktah weave shot-pouches, which have raised work inside and outside," and a Choctaw informant of the writer said that a small pouch for powder and shot was generally made of a gourd shaped like a citron upon which the skin of an otter, raccoon, or mink had been shrunk and which had afterward been hardened. Another kind was made by sewing one of these skins over a horn green, and allowing it to shrink on. The horn was taken from an adult cow or ox, not so old that the horn would be brittle or so young that it would be oversoft. It was put into water and boiled until it was soft enough to work easily. Then the inside of the horn would come out readily and they could bend the remainder, straighten it, ornament it, or spread it out by driving a stick into it, handling it like gutta percha. A large pouch corresponding to those used by the Creeks, was made of the skin of an otter, beaver, raccoon, or fox and used for grease, gun wadding, patching, and so on. The doctor carried such a pouch all of the time for his herbs and powders. The biggest pouch of all was made of the entire hide of a beaver. The mouth served as the opening and it was bent over between the rest of the pouch and the wearer's body, the tail hanging down at the side. My informant added that one could usually tell to which band of Choctaw a man belonged by his pouch (Swanton, 1931 a, pp. 42–43). A missionary report of 1852 mentions among ancient Choctaw productions "bags of the bark of trees, twisted and woven by hand" (Foreman, 1934, p. 18).

Speck has the following regarding Yuchi pouches:

Rather large pouches, *läti'*, two of which are ordinarily owned by each man as side receptacles, are made of leather, or goods obtained from the whites, and slung over the shoulder on a broad strap of the same material. It has already been said that various articles were thus carried about on the person: tobacco and pipe, tinder and flint, medicinal roots, fetishes and undoubtedly a miscellaneous lot of other things. The shoulder strap is customarily decorated with the bull snake design by attaching beads, or if the strap be woven, by beading them in. There seems to be a variety in the bead decorations on the body of the pouch. Realistic portrayals of animals, stars, crescents and other objects have been observed, but the realistic figure of the turtle is nearly always present either alone or with the others. The turtle here is used conventionally in the same way that the bull snake is used as the decorative theme on sashes and shoulder strap, that is, in imitation of the mythical being Wind who went forth with a turtle for his side pouch. (Speck, 1909, p. 49.)

ORNAMENTATION

WORK IN SHELL

The ancient bead of the interior Indians of the South is said by Adair (1775, p. 170) to have been made out of the conch shell, and it was shaped by rubbing on a hard stone, but native beads were supplanted at an early date by those of European manufacture. The former varied in their sizes and other characteristics, but we know little more than the general fact. The wampum with which those who have read about the Indians are usually familiar was made principally from the thick clam or quahog (*Venus mercenaria*), and was not introduced into the Southeast—extensively at least—until after white contact.

One reason for the profuse use of beads as ornaments was the fact that they also constituted a medium of exchange and could be made useful in that capacity at a minute's notice besides furnishing visible witness to the standing and credit of the wearer. They were strung on threads by means of a little frame and thus used in the ornamentation of hair ribbons, garters, belts, purse straps, and moccasins. In spite of a statement by Adair, to be quoted presently, one gets the impression that beads were not employed as extensively by the Southeastern Indians as by those of the northeast and the Plains, but this is probably due in large measure to an excessive expansion in the use of such ornaments after the latter had begun to import these from the whites. In the Southeast, trade in beads had not attained maximum proportions before advancing civilization seriously curtailed their use and put an end to it entirely for very many purposes.

Modification of the industry had already begun before the best notices we are able to quote regarding it had been prepared. These date from approximately the same period and are supplied by the Virginia historian Beverley and by Lawson. The former treats of beads in a special chapter devoted to The Treasure or Riches of the Indians. He says:

The *Indians* had nothing which they reckoned Riches, before the *English* went among them, except *Peak*, *Roenoke*, and such like trifles made out of the *Cunk* shell. These past with them instead of Gold and Silver, and serv'd them both for Money, and Ornament. It was the *English* alone that taught them first to put a value on their Skins and Furs, and to make a Trade of them.

Peak is of two sorts, or rather of two colours, for both are made of one Shell, tho of different parts; one is a dark Purple Cylinder, and the other a white; they are both made in size, and figure alike, and commonly much resembling the *English Buglas*, but not so transparent nor so brittle. They are wrought as smooth as Glass, being one third of an inch long, and about a quarter, diameter, strung by a hole drill'd thro the Center. The dark colour is the dearest, and distinguish'd by the name of *Wampom Peak*. The *English* men that are call'd *Indian* Traders, value the *Wampom Peak*, at eighteen pence *per* Yard, and the white *Peak* at nine pence. The *Indians* also make Pipes of this, two or three inches long, and thicker than ordinary, which are much more valuable. They also make *Runtees* of the same Shell, and grind them as smooth as *Peak*. These are either large like an Oval Bead, and drill'd the length of the Oval, or else they are circular and flat, almost an inch over, and one third of an inch thick, and drill'd edgeways. Of this Shell they also make round Tablets of about four inches diameter, which they polish as smooth as the other, and sometimes they etch or grave thereon, Circles, Stars, a Half Moon, or any other figure suitable to their fancy. These they wear instead of Medals before or behind their Neck, and use the *Peak*, *Runtees* and Pipes for Coronets, Bracelets, Belts or long Strings hanging down before the Breast, or else they lace their Garments with them, and adorn their *Tomahawks*, and every other thing that they value.

They have also another sort which is as current among them, but of far less value; and this is made of the Cockleshell, broke into small bits with rough edges, drill'd through in the same manner as Beads, and this they call *Roenoke*, and use it as the *Peak*.

These sorts of Money have their rates set upon them as unalterable, and current as the values of our Money are. (Beverley, 1705, bk. 3, pp. 58–59.)

The account of Lawson should be compared with this:

Their money is of different sorts, but all made of shells, which are found on the coast of Carolina, which are very large and hard, so that they are very difficult to cut. Some English smiths have tried to drill this sort of shell money, and thereby thought to get an advantage; but it proved so hard, that nothing could be gained. They oftentimes make, of this shell, a sort of gorge, which they wear about their neck in a string; so it hangs on their collar, whereon sometimes is engraven a cross, or some odd figure, which comes next in their fancy. There are other sorts valued at a doe skin, yet the gorges will sometimes sell for three or four buck skins ready dressed. There be others, that eight of them go readily for a doe skin; but the general and current species of all the Indians in Carolina, and, I believe, all over the continent, as far as the bay of Mexico, is that which we call Peak and Roanoak; but Peak more especially. This is that which at New York, they call wampum, and have used it as current money amongst the inhabitants for a great many years. This is what many writers call porcelan, and is made in New York in great quantities, and with us in some measure. Five cubits of this purchase a dressed doe skin, and seven or eight purchase a dressed buck skin. An Englishman could not afford to make so much of this wampum for five or ten times the value; for it is made out of a vast great shell, of which that country affords plenty; where it is ground smaller than the small end of a tobacco pipe, or a large wheat straw. Four or five of these make an inch, and every one is to be drilled through, and made as smooth as glass, and so strung, as beads are, and a cubit of the Indian measure contains as much in length, as will reach from the elbow to the end of the little finger. They never stand to question, whether it is a tall man or a short man, that measures it; but if this wampum peak be black or purple, as some part of that shell is, then it is twice the value. This the Indians grind on stones and other things, till they make it current but the drilling is the most difficult to the Englishman, which the Indians manage with a nail stuck in a cane or reed. Thus they roll it continually on their thighs, with their right hand holding the bit of shell with their left, so in time they drill a hole quite through it, which is a very tedious work; but especially in making their roanoak, four of which will scarce make one length of wampum. The Indians are a people that never value their time, so that they can afford to make them, and never need to fear the English will take the trade out of their hands. This is the money with which you may buy skins, furs, slaves, or any thing the Indians have; it being the mammon (as our money is to us) that entices and persuades them to do any thing, and part with every thing they possess, except their children for slaves. As for their wives, they are often sold, and their daughters violated for it. With this they buy off murders; and whatsoever a man can do that is ill, this wampum will quit him of, and make him in their opinion, good and virtuous, though never so black before. (Lawson, 1860, pp. 315–317.)

These writers agree with each other as to the relative value of white and purple wampum, and are supporetd by most other writers, but Beverley has strangely inverted the meaning of "wampum peak," in applying it to the black variety. There is suggested difference also regarding the relative value of peak and roanoke.

Michel has a few words to say regarding shell money in use in 1701–2 at Monacantown on the James:

They do not esteem silver or gold, and do not want to take it. Their money is like the material they hang around them, but small, of white and pearly color, like small corals, strung on a string. It is sold by the yard so to speak. They measure from the index finger to the elbow, which length costs half an English crown. (Michel, 1916, p. 134.)

We know that both Dutch and English afterward imitated wampum so successfully as to flood the greater part of the Indian country from the Atlantic to the Mississippi and far beyond and ultimately to break the market and put an end to the use of beads as media of exchange.

But if we turn back to the writings of Hariot, Smith, and Strachey we find a very limited use of shell beads, which seem to have been less in favor with the coast tribes originally than beads made of copper and bone and pearls. So far as wampum itself is concerned, we know that its manufacture and use were not native to Virginia or Carolina, but that it was introduced from New York, and the district of Long Island Sound and Narragansett Bay, the name being derived from the last-mentioned region. The Indians about Long Island Sound called it sewan. At a later time the name wampum was extended over shell beads of various descriptions, even retrospectively over beads of a type wholly distinct from that of the classical wampum of the traders.

Roanoke was the name, or a name, given to a type of bead which had attained currency in the Sound section of North Carolina and about Chesapeake Bay before white contact, but in this case also it is doubtful whether the name belonged properly to one special kind of bead or was extended over several. In the descriptions given by Beverley and Lawson it will be noted that there seems to be lack of agreement since the former says that it was lightly esteemed while

Lawson, since he states that it required much more work than wampum, would indicate that it was probably valued more highly. From these accounts and various incidental notices of roanoke in the early literature, it seems evident that the term was of general application. There is, however, one marked point of distinction between wampum and roanoke; in beads of the first type the length exceeded the diameter while the opposite was true of roanoke. The beads used in the ornamentation of a purse in the Sloan collection reproduced by Bushnell (1907, pp. 38–41, pl. 6) are probably typical roanoke. From the catalog entries of this collection, it appears that the name was applied equally to the *Marginella* shells.

Lederer gives us some inkling of the distance to which roanoke had penetrated by 1670, and contributes something regarding the money standards of the time when he says that they purchased European objects "either with their current coyn of small shells, which they call roanoak or peack, or perhaps with pearl, vermilion, pieces of christal; and towards Ushery (the Catawba country), with some odd pieces of plate or bullon, which they sometimes receive in truck from the Oestacks" (Alvord, 1912, p. 171). This shows that by the date mentioned wampum had already been introduced from the north. Before 1750 it was well known, at least by name, throughout most of the upper Gulf region as far as the Mississippi. Adair says:

Before we supplied them [the Chickasaw, Creeks, and Cherokee are particularly meant] with our European beads, they had great quantities of wampum; (the Buccinum of the ancients) made out of conch-shell, by rubbing them on hard stones, and so they form them according to their liking. With these they bought and sold at a stated current rate, without the least variation for circumstances either of time or place; and now they will hear nothing patiently of loss or gain; or allow us to heighten the price of our goods, be our reasons ever so strong, or though the exigencies and changes of time may require it. Formerly four deer-skins was the price of a large conch-shell bead, about the length and thickness of a man's fore-finger; which they fixed to the crown of their head, as an high ornament—so greatly they valued them. (Adair, 1775, p. 170.)

Adair seems to be speaking of the period immediately after white contact but before European beads had been introduced in any quantity, and it will be noticed that he applies the term wampum to conchshell beads thereby indicating that at that time neither the true wampum nor roanoke was known in the far interior.

Evidently beads made from shells had attained local use as currency before white contact in three centers: as wampumpeak, or sewan, about Manhattan Island and along Long Island Sound as far as Narragansett Bay; as roanoak in the environs of Chesapeake Bay and the sounds of North Carolina, and inland from the Gulf. In time wampum displaced the others, but native wampum was almost immediately displaced by wampum of European manufacture.

Beads were also made out of *Marginella* shells by grinding off the ends of the whorls and passing the cord through these apertures and the natural openings at the other end. The method of obtaining these is described only by Lawson, who calls the shells "Blackmoors teeth."

> At the time when they are on the salts, and sea coasts, they have another fishery, that is for a little shell fish, which those in England call Blackmoors teeth. These they catch by tying bits of oysters to a long string, which they lay in such places, as they know, those shell fish haunt. These fish get hold of the oysters, and suck them in, so that they pull up those long strings, and take great quantities of them, which they carry a great way into the main land, to trade with the remote Indians, where they are of great value; but never near the sea, by reason they are common, therefore not esteemed. (Lawson, 1860, pp. 340–341.)

In and near Virginia this was called roanoak as well as the small, wheel-shaped beads.

There is no mention of the method of securing the *Olivella* shell which was also extensively used by the inland tribes, as is proved by its occurrence in mounds and with burials.

Shell disks or gorgets are found associated with Indian remains as far west as the eastern part of Texas and also in Florida, but rather sparingly along the Gulf coast.

The surprisingly slight notice of shell beads in early Carolina and Virginia narratives is duplicated elsewhere in the section. The Florida Indians employed pearls and metal beads as did those of Carolina, but there is only a single reference to beads of any other sort, and these did not necessarily include beads of shell. This reference is by the French sailor Le Challeux, who says:

> They prize highly little beads, which they make of the bones of fishes and other animals and of green and red stones. (Gaffarel, 1875, p. 462; Swanton, 1922, p. 348.)

The monk Andreas de San Miguel states that a chief who came to meet his party off the south end of Florida in 1595 "wore more amber than all those on that coast who came to meet us," thereby implying that its use was fairly common (Garcia, 1902, p. 210).

Cushing found considerable quantities of shell beads at Key Marco in this State. It was occupied probably by the Calusa Indians (Cushing, 1896, p. 374).

Bartram makes only incidental mention of beads among the Creeks and by his time wampum had reached them.

Considering the assumed fondness of all Indians for beads, we are again surprised by the paucity of references to them on the lower Mississippi, although "beads made of sea-snails" were observed in Arkansas by De Soto (Bourne, 1904, vol. 2, p. 29). Du Pratz is the only writer to supply any description and at least some of the beads of which he speaks were introduced by the traders.

When they have beads (*rassade*) they make necklaces composed of one or many rows. They make them long enough for the head to pass through. The *rassade* is a bead of the size of the end of the finger of a small infant. Its length is greater than its diameter. Its substance is similar to porcelain. There is a smaller one, ordinarily round and white, which they value more than the other. There is a blue variety and one of another style which is banded (*bardelée*) with blue and white. The medium sized and the smallest are strung to ornament skins, garters, etc. (Le Page du Pratz, 1758, vol. 2, pp. 195–196; Swanton, 1911, p. 56.)

There is mention, however, of a conch-shell ornament not referred to, and apparently unknown, in Carolina and Virginia, but of which the mounds and cemeteries of the interior have yielded abundant samples. Du Pratz says of this:

The women ornament themselves with earrings made of the core of a great shell called "burgo," of which I have spoken already. This ear pendant is as large as the little finger and at least as long. They have a hole in the lower part of each ear large enough for the insertion of this ornament. It has a head a little larger than the rest to keep it from falling out. (Le Page du Pratz, 1758, vol. 2, pp. 195–196; Swanton, 1911, p. 55.)

Dumont de Montigny describes this ornament at greater length, and informs us that the same shell was also used in the manufacture of gorgets:

There are found besides, on the shores of the sea, beautiful shells of a spiral shape called "burgau." They are very suitable for the manufacture of pretty tobacco boxes, for they carry their mother-of-pearl with them. It is of these burgau that the Indian women make their earrings. For this purpose they rub the ends of them for a long time on hard stones and thus give them the shapes of nails with heads, in order that, when they insert them in their ears, they will be stopped by this kind of obstruction, for these Indian women have their ears laid open very much more than our French women. One might pass the thumb, however large, through [the slit]. The savages also wear on their necks plates 3 or 4 inches in diameter made of pieces of this shell, to which they give a round or oval shape by grinding them on stones in the same manner. They then pierce them near the edge by means of fire and use them as ornaments. (Dumont, 1753, vol. 1, pp. 94–95; Swanton, 1911, p. 55).

We have already noted large beads made from the columella of the conch.

The Caddo wore "little white shells they find in the fields which are shaped like beads," and the carved gorgets from their country are a glorious manifestation of their artistic ability, to be placed beside their pottery, though they are scarcely mentioned by our Spanish and French authorities. (Casañas, 1927; Swanton, 1942, p. 145; Pearce and Jackson, 1912.)

A few bead substitutes might here be referred to. The Creek Indians used the berry of a kind of bush or tree called "wild cherry" and in Creek konā hā'go ("bead-made"). The Choctaw claim that they formerly made wooden beads as big as acorns, and that they strung together chinquapin nuts, which they colored with the same dyes that they used in basketry. They also used the seeds of the red haw, but these would break up after they had been worn at one or two social gatherings. The berries of the *Cocculus carolinus* were used for a while, the same berries that were employed in poisoning fish, but they subsequently gave them up lest they poison the cattle or chickens (Swanton, 1931 a, p. 43).

Speck gives the following account of work with European beads as practiced in later times by the Yuchi:

> Like many other Indian tribes the Yuchi adopted the practice of decorating parts of their clothing with glass beads which they obtained from the whites. Beadwork, however, never reached the development with them that it did in other regions. What there was of this practice was entirely in the hands of the women. There were two ways of using the beads for decoration. One of these was to sew them onto strips of cloth or leather, making embroidered designs in outline, or filling in the space enclosed by the outline to make a solidly covered surface. The other way was to string the beads on the warp threads while weaving a fabric, so that the design produced by arranging the colors would appear on both sides of the woven piece. For the warp and woof horse hair came to be much in use. Objects decorated in the first fashion were moccasins, legging flaps, breechcloth ends, garter bands, belt sashes and girdles, tobacco pouches and shoulder straps. The more complex woven beadwork was used chiefly for hair ornaments and neckbands.
>
> The designs which appear in beadwork upon these articles of clothing are mostly conventional and some are symbolical with various traditional interpretations. . . . It should be observed here, however, that there is some reason to suspect that the beadwork of this tribe has been influenced by that of neighboring groups where beadwork is a matter of more prominence. The removal of the Yuchi and other southeastern tribes from their old homes in Georgia and Alabama to the West threw them into the range of foreign influence which must have modified some characteristics of their culture. (Speck, 1909, p. 37.)

Skinner supplies us with a short note regarding beadwork among the Seminole observed in 1910:

> Beads are woven into belts, fobs, and garters. None sewn on skin or cloth were seen. The belts are of two kinds—those worn around the waist, which are furnished with a set of long, trailing tassels at the ends and middle, and those worn over the shoulders, which have tassels only at the ends. They are woven either entirely of beads on a thread foundation, or largely of yarn with a few beads mixed in. The designs are often symbolic, but the only meanings that could be obtained were: (1) diamond-back rattlesnake, (2) "ground" rattlesnake, (3) everglade terrapin, (4) terrapin spear-point. The beads are woven on small plain heddles, made of split palmetto ribs. The beaded garters are similar to those of the more northerly tribes and are worn bound around the outside of the leggings below the knee. A photograph of one pair was seen in possession of Charlie Tigertail, but no others were heard of. (Skinner, 1913, pp. 71–72.)

Examples of modern beadwork among the Alabama Indians of Texas are shown in plate 72, figure 1.

PEARLS

Pearls were objects of such high consideration among both Indians and whites that we have frequent notices of them. Elvas speaks of some pearls of little value found in the temple of Ucita, the very first town reached by De Soto (Robertson, 1933, p. 33). When he approached Cofitachequi at the head of his army the chieftainess of that place came to meet him and, "drawing from over her head a large string of pearls"—Biedma says "a necklace of five or six strings of pearls"—threw them about his neck so that she might gain his favor. In a temple, or rather ossuary, in the same town they found many bodies, the breasts, bellies, necks, arms, and legs of which were covered with pearls, and they took away a quantity estimated by the different chroniclers to weigh from 165 to 350 pounds. Elvas adds that there were figures of babies and birds made of them, perhaps as ornaments to leather or textiles. When the chieftainess was forced to accompany the Spaniards on their journey northward, she carried along a cane box full of unbored pearls with which she subsequently escaped (Bourne, 1904, vol. 2, pp. 13, 14, 99, 100; Robertson, 1933, pp. 92, 94, 101). In narrating the fortunes of the Spaniards in the province of Iciaha (Chiaha) on the Tennessee River a little after the time when the above events took place, Garcilaso quotes the chief of that country to the effect that in his temple there were also many pearls, and he gives a description of the way in which they were extracted from the shells. To accomplish this, the Indians set fire to a quantity of wood so as to make a large bed of coals and then placed upon it the mussels, which opened in consequence of the heat revealing any pearls they might contain, though the fire deprived them of a part of their luster (Garcilaso, 1723, pp. 140–141). Practically all our authorities, from Elvas on, state that the Indians heated their pearls in the process of boring so that the bored pearls were ruined for commercial purposes. This must mean that they were bored in a different manner from the shell beads. There is no subsequent mention of pearls in the De Soto narratives, but later writers often allude to them. They were extensively used as ornaments by the Floridians, as we learn from the reports of Ribault, Le Moyne, and Laudonnière, and also by the Indians of eastern North Carolina and Virginia. Powhatan sent a chain of pearls to Smith, and pearls are mentioned among the articles of tribute which the Indian emperor received. Newport observed that a certain Pamunkey chief "had a Chaine of pearle about his neck thrice Double, the third parte of them as bygg as pease, which I could not valew lesse worth then 3 or 400 li had the pearle ben taken from the Muskle as it ought to be" (Smith, John, Arber ed., 1884, p. li).

La Salle found pearls in use among the tribes of the lower Mississippi when he descended to the sea in 1682, and Nicolas de la Salle purchased 14 of them from a Koroa Indian "for a mean little boxwood comb" (Margry, 1875–86, vol. 1, p. 328). Many were kept by the Taensa and Natchez in their temples, and infant Natchez nobles wore 2 or 3, taken from the temple, from birth until they were about 10 years old, when they were replaced (Pénicaut in Margry, 1875–86, vol. 5, p. 452; Swanton, 1911, p. 56). In spite of these facts, one gets the impression that there were more pearls among the eastern tribes, between the Chesapeake and Florida, than among those on the "Father of Waters."

Pearls were obtained from the river mussels, and from bivalves along the Atlantic coast. Mention has been made of the fishery at Chiaha on the Tennessee River, probably at Burns Island. Cofitachequi, near the present Augusta, Ga., was another pearl center, and the Suwannee in Florida was a third, though probably not superior to the St. Johns. Near the mouth of Appamattox River, Va., the Indians showed Captain Smith and his companions "the manner of their diving for Mussels, in which they finde Pearles" (Smith, John, Tyler ed., 1907, p. 34). An early chronicler says that Pearl River, Miss., received its name from the fact that the Natchez obtained pearls near its head which they "put around the necks of their idols," but there is no record of pearl hunting operations at points much nearer the mouth of this stream. Daniel Coxe speaks of two great pearl fisheries in the south, one up Red River and the other on the Tallapoosa, but his remarks are very general and no other writer refers to these (Coxe in French, 1850, pp. 227, 234). (See also Burrage, 1906, p. 127.)

PORCUPINE-QUILL WORK

Du Pratz is the only writer who describes porcupine-quill work, and, though he speaks as if he had witnessed the process, one wonders whether it was as worked by the hands of southern Indians or by some band from the north paying a visit to the French posts on the lower course of the Mississippi. If Natchez Indians actually did such work, we must suppose that they obtained their material in trade from upriver tribes. Du Pratz says:

For this purpose they take off the quills of the porcupine which are white and black. They split them fine enough to use in embroidery. They dye a part of the white red, another part yellow, while a third part remains white. Ordinarily they embroider on black skin, and then they dye the black a reddish brown. But if they embroider on the tree bark the black always remains the same.

Their designs are rather similar to some of those which one finds in Gothic architecture. They are composed of straight lines which form right angles where they meet, which a common person would call the corner of a square. They also make designs of the same style on the mantles and coverings which they fashion out of mulberry bark. (Le Page du Pratz, 1758, vol. 2, pp. 100, 184–185.)

Dumont says that porcupine quills were used by Natchez women interlaced in their hair by way of ornament (Dumont, 1753, vol. 1, p. 137; Swanton, 1911, p. 51). According to Timberlake (1927, pp. 30, 50–51), porcupine quills were employed in the ornamentation of Cherokee pipes and moccasins.

Bartram (1792, p. 499) also mentions porcupine-quill ornamentation on the headbands of Creek Indians, which at least proves that this type of decoration was known to the tribe, but it is altogether unknown whether it was a native industry.

WORK IN METAL

The principal metal used by all our Indians in pre-Columbian times was copper, and its use was very ancient, though it is probable that it was not as extensively used at the time when America was discovered as when the Southeast was thoroughly colonized in the eighteenth century. Indeed, though it must have been widely employed when De Soto entered the country, the chronicles of his expedition contain surprisingly few references to it. Elvas tells us of copper hatchets seen at Cofitachequi said to have a mixture of gold, and both he and Garcilaso report a rumor that reached the Spaniards while they were on Tennessee River, that in a province to the north named Chisca were mines of copper, or at least a highly colored yellow metal, which the explorers and the readers of their explorations back home were only too happy to think might be gold. (Robertson, 1933, p. 109; Garcilaso, 1723, p. 141.) It is quite certain that the province of Chisca was occupied by Yuchi Indians, who may have been middle men in transmitting copper from the mines about Lake Superior. That it was an article of trade is stated by Garcilaso. The Spaniards met some copper merchants at Cofitachequi, and the metal proved, to their considerable disappointment, to be nothing more valuable (Garcilaso, 1723, p. 129). We also find it an article of trade beyond the Mississippi River, for some Spaniards who accompanied native traders in an expedition westward from Capaha (Pacaha) into a sterile and poorly populated country brought back from it six loads of fossil salt and some copper (Garcilaso, 1723, p. 187).

Whatever may have been the extent to which copper was employed in 1539–43, we seemingly find an abundance of it in Florida 25 years later, though there happens to be no allusion to it in the narrative of the De Luna expedition to the Upper Creeks in 1559–60, nor in the narratives of Juan Pardo, 1566–67. In our accounts of the Huguenot colony in Florida, 1564–65, however, there is abundant evidence of the use of this metal, though perhaps fewer references than to gold and silver since the readers of these narratives were less interested in the baser metal. Besides the extensive use of metallic ornaments indicated in Le Moyne's illustrations, we read in Ribault's report of an Indian who wore about his neck "a round plate of red copper, well polished, with a small one of silver hung in the middle of it; and on his ears a small plate of copper, with which they wipe the sweat from their bodies." He also mentions copper among the metals obtained in trade. (French, 1875, p. 178; Swanton, 1922, p. 350.) Spark tells us that, while the Frenchmen had been unable to learn anything of mines of gold or silver, mines of copper had been reported to them though there is no indication where these were supposed to be located.

Copper beads seem to have been worn in considerable profusion by the Indians of the North Carolina coast, and Hariot also mentions copper gorgets, while men and women of the upper classes had pieces of this metal hanging in their ears or hair, a custom found equally in Virginia (Hariot, 1893, pl. 7; Burrage, 1906, pp. 232–233). From Lane's account it would appear that copper came principally through the Nottoway tribe from a province 20 days journey to the northwest called Chaunis Temoatan.

It is a thing most notorious to all the countrey, that there is a Province to which the said Mangoaks have recourse and trafique up that River of Moratoc, which hath a marveilous and most strange minerall. This mine is so notorious amongst them, as not onely to the Savages dwelling up the said river, and also to the Savages of Chowanook, and all them to the Westward, but also to all of them of the maine: the Countreis name is of fame, and is called Chaunis Temoatan.

The Minerall they say is Wassador, which is copper, but they call by the name of Wassador every mettall whatsoever; they say it is of the colour of our copper, but our copper is better than theirs: and the reason is for that it is redder and harder, whereas that of Chaunis Temoatan is very soft, and pale: they say that they take the saide mettall out of a river that falleth very swift from hie rockes and hils, and they take it in shallow water: the maner is this. They take a great bowle by their description as great as one of our targets, and wrappe a skinne over the hollow parte thereof, leaving one part open to receive in the minerall: that done, they watch the comming downe of the current, and the change of the colour of the water, and then suddenly chop downe the said bowle with the skinne, and receive into the same as much oare as will come in, which is ever as much as their bowle will holde, which presently they cast into a fire, and foorthwith it melteth, and doeth yeelde in five parts at the first melting, two parts of metall for three partes of oare. Of this metall the Mangoaks have so great store, by report of all the Savages adjoyning, that they beautify their houses with greate plates of the same: and this to be true, I received by report of all the countrey, and particularly by yong Skiko, the King of Chowanooks sonne of my prisoner, who also him selfe had bene prisoner with the Mangoaks, and set downe all the particularities to me before mentioned: but hee had not beene at Chawnis Temoatan himselfe: for hee said it was twentie dayes journey overland from the Mangoaks, to the said Mineral Countrey, and that they passed through certaine other territories betweene them and the Mangoaks, before they came to the said Countrey.   (Burrage, 1906, p. 255.)

This account has occasioned considerable discussion. Chaunis Temoatan means "salt-making village," and it has been suggested that the description of ore extraction was intended by Lane's informant as an account of salt boiling. However, it is quite as likely to represent a current Indian belief as to the manner in which copper was obtained since the great copper region was remote from Carolina and the Carolina Indians were probably as ignorant of the manner of its occurrence and the method of obtaining it as were the whites. Since copper was not smelted in North America, it is possible that the reference to fire may have been supplied by the imagination of Lane, or that it may have been part of an independent mention of salt boiling. But the description is so grotesque and involved that not much can be made out of it.

As the Nottoway were an Iroquoian tribe, unrelated to most of the remaining Indians of Virginia, it is possible that they kept this trade route open from the time when they themselves descended from the northwest. The salt province probably refers to the region of the salt licks in northeastern Kentucky, but that in no way interferes with the possible function of its inhabitants as intermediaries in transporting copper to the Atlantic coast. It will be remembered that the De Soto chroniclers clearly indicate that copper was a trade article, and that the only reference to a copper mine is in that passage dealing with the province of Chisca north of Tennessee River toward which two messengers were sent. The Chisca are identifiable as Yuchi, and, since there is no native copper in the part of Tennessee indicated, I interpret the episode as signifying that these Yuchi were intermediaries in the copper trade just as were those of Chaunis Temoatan. Indeed, the two provinces may have been identical, though that is extremely doubtful. The Lake Superior origin of this copper is confirmed by the fact reported by Hariot (1893, p. 18) that it was found to contain silver.

Virginia chroniclers confirm Hariot and Lane as regards the general direction from which most copper entered the country, but there was a small source nearer at hand. This was at a place called Ritanoe where the Werowance Eyanoco was said to have certain mines of copper, and where Strachey (1849, p. 25), who records the fact, believed seven of the English of the Roanoke colony had been held in confinement for the purpose of pounding out this metal. Mr. Bushnell (1907, p. 34) has identified this with a spot near Virgilina, Va., where small quantities of native float copper are to be found.   These would be big enough for the manufacture of beads but not for the gorgets and larger ornaments.   Most of the other sources of native copper south of the Ohio were probably similar and with similar limited possibilities.

It is noteworthy that Strachey, our authority for the above, also states that in the high country to the northwest lived a people called Bocootawwonaukes, said by Powhatan to "melt" copper and other metals (Strachey, 1849, p. 27), but farther on he corrects this statement:

> For copper, the hills to the northwest have that store, as the people themselves, remembered in the first chapter, called the Bocootauwanaukes, are said to part the solide mettall from the stone without fire, bellowes, or additamant, and beat it into plates, the like whereof is hardly found in any other parte of the world. (Strachey, 1849, p. 130.)

Without mentioning their connection with copper, Smith speaks of these people under a different name, Pocoughtronack:

> Hee [Powhatan] described also upon the same sea [the South Sea being assumed to lie just beyond the mountains], a mighty Nation called Pocoughtronack, a fierce Nation that did eate men, and warred with the people of Moyaoncer and Pataromerke [Potomac], Nations upon the toppe of the heade of the Bay, under his territories: where the yeare before they had slain an hundred.   He signified their crownes were shaven, long haire in the necke, tied on a knot, Swords like Pollaxes.   (Smith, John, Tyler ed., 1907, p. 49.)

The name given to them seems to signify "people of the place of fire," which Hewitt interprets, naturally enough, to mean the Potawatomi.   For the present this must be accepted as the most probable identification, but it seems strange that the Potawatomi should at that early period have made their way as far as Virginia since, in order to do so, they would have been obliged to pass through the territories of the Neutral Nation, the Erie, Black Minqua, and several Siouan tribes.   In favor of this identification is the fact that the Algonquian tribes of the coast with which they warred were those living well to the north.   In order to attack them they would seem to have descended the Potomac.   In the instructions given to Sir Thomas Gates, when he was about to sail for Virginia in 1609 as deputy governor of the colony, mention is made of a large town to the north at the head of Chesapeake Bay "where is store of Copp[er] and ffurs," the name of the town being Cataanron.   Copper collected here probably came down the Susequehanna River, which was reached, we may assume, by the Juniata trail (Bushnell, 1907, p. 35).

According to Smith, Powhatan also "described a countrie called Anone, where they have abundance of Brasse, and houses walled as ours" (Smith, John, Tyler ed., 1907, p. 49).   There is no clue to the identity of this province.

The author of the Newport relation says:

This *Wyroans Pamaunche* I holde to inhabite a Rych land of Copper and pearle. His Country lyes into the land to another Ryver, which by relatyon and Descriptyon of the Salvages comes also from the Mountaynes *Quirank*, but a shorter Iorney. The Copper he had, as also many of his people, was very flexible, I bowed a peece of the thicknes of a shilling rounde about my finger, as if it had been lead: I found them nice in parting with any; They weare it in their eares, about their neckes in long lynckes, and in broade plates on their heades: So we made no greate enquyry of it, neither seemed Desirous to have it. (Smith, Arber ed., 1884, pp. 1–li.)

Meteoric iron was used by the American aborigines just as they used copper except that there were limitations to the amount of material available and the size of the objects that could be made with it. Many objects were also worked out of hematite, a favorite material because it takes a high polish, but, of course, it could not be treated like a metal. Most of the worked meteoric iron and hematite dating from aboriginal times has been found in the Ohio valley. In later deposits there has, of course, been found a considerable amount of iron belonging to European objects introduced in trade.

A very small amount of gold was utilized by the mound-building tribes, obtained from small nuggets, and treated like copper. Some has been found in the Ohio Valley, especially at the Turner Group of mounds, and a few gold beads were discovered at Etowah, Ga. (Hodge, 1907, *art.* Gold). In Florida a considerable number of beautiful objects in gold have been obtained from the mounds, but it is believed that nearly all of these were from Spanish treasure ships bound from Panama or Mexico to Spain and cast away while passing through the Straits of Florida. This theory was held by the Spaniard Fontaneda, who was held captive by the Calusa Indians for many years, by the French commander Laudonnière, and by the Englishman Spark (Swanton, 1922, p. 349). One of Laudonnière's officers, La Roche Ferrière, believed he understood the Indians to say that they obtained gold and silver from the Appalachian Mountains, but Spark interprets this correctly in stating that the French had so far heard only of copper mines, though they had not been able to search them out. Since "gold alloyed with brass, and silver not thoroughly smelted" was sent in by the same officer from northwestern Florida, it is evident they had been able to obtain European metals. (Hakluyt, 1847–89, vol. 3, pp. 615–616; Le Moyne, 1875, p. 8.) Ribault observed a Timucua Indian with a collar of gold about his neck (French, 1875, p. 178; Swanton, 1922, p. 350). There is no reason why both gold and silver may not have reached the Gulf region from Mexico and Central America in pre-Columbian times, but we have no absolute evidence that they did so.

The case for silver is very similar to that for gold. Small bits of native silver are found sparingly, especially in association with native copper, and these are sufficient to account for the few occurrences of this metal in pre-Columbian deposits, such as the silver reported in the Turner Group, Hamilton County, Ohio, some silver nuggets in a mound in Pickaway County in the same state, and an occurrence in Warren County, Pa. (Hodge, 1910, *art.* Silver). Floridian silver may safely be attributed to the same region as Floridian gold. Besides the silver objects noted, mention may be made of "girdles of silver-colored balls, some round and some oblong," spoken of by Le Moyne, and silver chains worn by chiefs. (Le Moyne, 1875, pp. 2, 14; French, 1869, p. 350; Swanton, 1922, p. 350.) Hariot seems to supply us with one account of a silver ornament of purely native origin, and the whole paragraph in which it occurs is of special interest:

> A hundred and fiftie miles into the maine in two townes wee founde with the inhabitaunts diuerse small plates of copper, that had beene made as wee vnderstood, by the inhabitantes that dwell farther into the countrey: where as they say are mountaines and riuers that yeelde also whyte graynes of Mettall, which is to bee deemed *Siluer.* For confirmation whereof at the time of our first arriual, in the Countrey, I sawe with some others with mee, two small pieces of siluer grosly breaten about the weight of a Testrone, hangyng in the eares of a *Wiroans* or *chiefe Lorde* that dwelt about fourescore myles from vs; of whom thorowe enquiry, by the number of dayes and the way, I learned that it had come to his handes from the same place or neere, where I after vnderstood the copper was made and the white graynes of Mettall founde. The aforesaide copper wee also found by triall to holde siluer. (Hariot, 1893, pp. 17–18.)

This at once suggests that the original of this silver was a bit of native metal in association with native copper from Superior.

The avidity shown by our Indians for silver as soon as it began to reach them testifies to the slight access they had had to it. Incidentally this seems to dispose pretty effectually of the idea that there might have been any considerable trade with Middle America.

In historic times the use of silver replaced that of copper so completely that my oldest informants in the Southeast could not remember of hearing that copper ever had been employed in ornaments. Gold was worked to some extent but it was hard to obtain, gold coins not having been much in circulation in this region in early days, while it was, of course, costly. Practically all silver was from the coins of European and American countries, but, although the material itself changed, it is probable that old methods of treatment continued, being modified only by the introduction of iron and steel working tools. Silver was worked by most of the Southeastern tribes in the protohistoric period, including the Creeks, Cherokee, Seminole, Chickasaw, and Choctaw. The following notes were obtained from the Alabama Indians, who are rather closely connected by language with the Choctaw, but constituted a part of the Creek Confederation.

Men, and sometimes women, worked in silver, using little hammers, anvils, vises and other tools, obtained from the whites. They pounded out coins into round, flat, or oval pieces, cut them into smaller parts, or drew them out into wires. The Alabama made the round ornaments, for the most part, in relatively late times. According to the ornament desired they selected a silver quarter, or a 50-cent piece, or a Mexican dollar, laid it on the side of an ax, and beat it a little with a hammer. Then they took it up with a pair of pliers, held it in the fire until it was almost red hot, and dipped it in water so as to cool it a little, after which they again pounded it. The heating was to prevent it from cracking. This process was gone through with several times, considerable force being used at first which was afterward moderated as the metal got thinner so as to make it smooth. Ornamental holes and indentations were made with an awl, and a larger hole was pierced in the middle with the same implement, its size being still further increased by means of a small knife. At the side of this aperture a small hole was punched with the awl, a common brass pin inserted in this, and bent over at the end so that it would not come out. When the ornament was to be fastened upon the dress it was laid against the place to which it was to be attached, convex side out. Some of the cloth was then pulled through the central opening, the pin was run through the cloth, and when the fabric was pulled back, the ornament was held firmly in place. Pieces intended for earrings were hammered down flat, after which a portion of one edge was cut off straight, a small hole punched in the middle of this straight side, and an iron or copper wire run through this and fastened to the ear. The brother of my informant worked a Mexican silver dollar into a bracelet by beating it out long and flat, curving the ends round, and punching a hole on the edge at each end to fasten it together. To make a ring they took a silver dime, pounded it out long, cut it into an oval shape, and concaved it. A strip of tin was then taken and bent into a circle of the right size to fit about the finger. Solder and rosin were next put in the middle of the silver plate on its concave surface. The latter was afterward put over the fire, and the tin ring pressed down upon it in such a manner that the solder and rosin on melting would at the same time fasten the two ends of the tin ring to each other and to the silver plate. The resulting ring was of the type known as a marquise ring. The Alabama affirm that they did not make the crescent-shaped gorgets themselves, but bought them from the Choctaw.

A silver ornament after the manner of an elongated oval was made to wear over the braids of the hair, which were gathered together over the middle of the forehead to receive it. For this a silver quarter was selected, beaten out as already described, and concaved. Two holes were punched near the border at each end for the attachment of buckskin strings, which were then tied about the hair.

The following information is from Speck:

The manufacture of German silver ornaments, such as finger rings, earrings, bracelets, arm bands, breast pendants, head bands and brooches, seems to have been, for a long time, one of the handicrafts practiced by the Yuchi men. This art has now almost passed away among them and fallen into the hands of their Shawnee neighbors. The objects mentioned in the list were made of what appears to be copper, brass and zinc alloy. The metal was obtained from the whites, and then fashioned into desired shapes by cutting, beating, bending, and punching in the cold state. The favorite method of ornamentation was to punch stars, circles, ovals, curves, scalloped lines, and crescents in the outer surface of the objects. Sometimes the metal was punched completely through to produce an open-work effect. Several pieces of metal were sometimes fastened together by riveting. Ornamental effects were added to the edges of objects by trimming and scalloping. It is also common to see fluting near the borders of bracelets and pendants. Judging from the technique in modern specimens, metal workers have shown considerable skill in working out their patterns. It is possible, moreover, that this art was practiced in pre-historic times with sheet copper for working material, in some cases possibly sheet gold, and that some of the ornaments, such as head bands, bracelets, arm bands and breast ornaments, were of native origin. (Speck, 1909, pp. 36–37.)

On the basis of our other material, we may safely affirm such to have been the case. This use of German silver seems to be unusual in the section.

MacCauley describes a great variety of silver ornaments among the Seminole, but tells us nothing regarding the silver industry, and for that we must turn to Skinner's brief statement:

In common with all the Eastern tribes, the Seminole are very fond of silver ornaments, most of which they make for themselves. This jewelry is neither as elaborate nor as handsome as that made by more northerly tribes, nor does it have much variety in form. Head or turban bands, spangles, crescents, earrings, and fingerrings are the forms observed and collected. The process of manufacture and the tools employed are simple. To make a spangle, a coin is heated in a small fire; it is then removed with a pair of pinchers and hammered out with an ordinary commercial hammer. The poll of an axe driven into a log serves the purpose of an anvil. The process of alternate heating and pounding is repeated again and again until the coin has been flattened out considerably and the design effaced. One smith observed at work greased the coin from time to time as he heated it. After it has been heated and hammered to the satisfaction of the smith, the spangle is pared down with a butcher-knife or a razor blade until it has been reduced to the desired degree of thinness.

In this state the blank form is sometimes decorated with a design incised with a file or a knife blade. Any irregularities are filed off and the trinket is polished on a whetstone. Sometimes the designs are cut out with a cold-chisel and finished with a knife. Holes for sewing the spangle to a garment are made by driving a nail through the metal and smoothing the edges with a knife.

This process of silverworking was observed on two occasions, and there was but little difference in the tools or in the manipulation of the smiths. Antler prongs are used as punches to make raised lines and bosses, and the only other tool which was seen or collected, besides those described, was a crude blow-pipe used in the manufacture of the plain finger-rings which are much worn by the Indians. (Skinner, 1913, pp. 74–76.)

A few notes on the use of metal ornaments by the Caddo are given in Bureau of American Ethnology Bulletin 132 (Swanton, 1942, pp. 145–146).

MANNER OF DRESSING THE HAIR

By most Southeastern Indians, the hair was carefully removed from all parts of the body but the head. Exceptions are found most often in the eastern part of the territory under consideration. Garcilaso says that a place or province in southern Georgia, probably on the Ocmulgee River, was governed by "an old man, with a full beard" (Bourne, 1904, vol. 2, p. 91). Spelman (1609–10) says beards were worn by some Powhatan priests (Smith, John, Arber ed., 1884, p. cxiii). In 1650 the discoverer of New Britain (eastern North Carolina) noted "many of the people of Blandina [Roanoke] River to have beards" (Alvord, 1912, pp. 126–127), and mention is made by Lawson of mustaches and whiskers seen among the Keyauwee, which he notes as a rare custom "since the Indians are a people that commonly pull the hair of their faces and other parts, up by the roots and suffer none to grow" (Lawson, 1860, p. 91). Adair describes this process somewhat at length:

Both sexes pluck all the hair off their bodies, with a kind of tweezers, made formerly of clam-shells, now of middle-sized wire, in the shape of a gun-worm; which, being twisted round a small stick, and the ends fastened therein, after being properly tempered, keeps its form; holding this Indian razor between their fore-finger and thumb, they deplume themselves, after the manner of the Jewish novitiate priests and proselytes. (Adair, 1775, p. 6.)

But, in speaking of the customs of the Acolapissa, the French traveler Pénicaut tells us that they removed their hair "by means of the ashes of shell and hot water" (Pénicaut in Margry, 1875–86, vol. 5, pp. 468–469; Swanton, 1911, p. 282).

Women usually allowed their hair to grow long except during times of mourning, when they might cut or singe it off, though the women of certain tribes merely allowed it to remain disheveled. Barlowe says that those of the North Carolina coast, unlike the men, let their hair grow long on both sides (Burrage, 1906, p. 231). Hariot, speaking of the same region, and specifically of the Indians of Secotan, informs us that they cut their hair short in front and allowed the rest, which was "not ouer Longe," to hang down about their shoulders. Roanoke Indian girls of the upper classes wore their hair "cutt with two ridges aboue their foreheads." The rest "is trussed upp on a knott behind," as was the usage among women of another town, Pomeioc (Hariot, 1893, pls. 4, 6, 8).

According to Percy, unmarried Powhatan girls had "the fore part of their head and sides shaven close, the hinder part very long, which they tie in a pleate hanging downe to their hips." The married women, on the other hand, allowed all of their hair to grow the same length though they tied it in the same manner (Narr. Early Va., Tyler ed., 1907, p. 19). Strachey noted both feathers and flowers in the hair of Powhatan women, but the use of feathers by women was not as common as is supposed by white romancers (Strachey, 1849, p. 57).

Lawson (1860, p. 310) found that the eastern Siouan women made their hair into "a long roll like a horse's tail," which they bound with strings of roanoke, wampum, or a simple leather thong. Catesby, who had visited both the Siouan tribes and the Chickasaw, says that the women sometimes rolled it up "in a bunch to the crown of their head, others braid it, and bind it with wreaths of peak and roanoak" (Catesby 1731–43, vol. 2, p. LX). When preparing for war

they dress in their greatest gallantry, daubing their hair with bear's-fat and the juice of the *puckoon*-root, and another red root, sticking therein the wings and feathers of birds, besides rings of copper, Peak and Wampum in their ears, at the same time painting their faces in various manner, sometimes red, with a circle of black round one eye, others have one side of their face red and the other black, whilst others daub their faces with white clay, black lead, and other colours. This they do not only to terrify their enemies, but that they should not be known again; for in all their hostilities against the *English*, the savages always appeared in this disguise.   (Catesby, 1731–43, vol. 2, p. IX.)

He says elsewhere, not referring specifically to war customs, that some Indian men "strow their heads usually with the down of Swans" (Cateby, 1831–43, vol. 2, p. VIII).

Michel (1906, p. 130) observed that the Monacan women wore their hair long and that the "queen" as well as the "king, princes, and nobles," on ceremonial occasions wore "crowns" or tiaras consisting of beads strung on bark. These will be described presently. Tuscarora women and men of the better sort wore copper ornaments in their hair (Alvord, 1912, p. 162). Byrd, on his visit to the Nottoway town in 1728, found that the girls' long hair was "breeded with white and Blue Peak, and hung gracefully in a large Roll upon their sholders" (Bassett, 1901, p. 96).

Le Moyne represents Florida women with hair entirely loose and without ornament, but according to Pareja a palm leaf hat was sometimes placed on their heads (Gatschet, 1877–80, vol. 17, pp. 500–501; Swanton, 1922, p. 387). Women among the Cherokee wore their hair long "club'd, and ornamented with ribbons of various colors" (Timberlake, Williams ed., 1927, p. 77). The Creek women, so Bartram (1792, p. 501) informs us, "never cut their hair, but plait it in wreaths, which are turned up, and fastened on the crown with a silver broach, forming a wreathed top-knot, decorated with an incredible quantity of silk ribbands, of various colors, which stream down on every side, almost to the ground." He adds that these decorations were worn only on special occasions, and in fact down to the present day Creek women at the busk dances fasten numbers of ribbons to their heads and also to their shoulders. Alabama women divided their hair in the middle, carried the two parts back and tied them there by means of a string, tape, or ribbon, sometimes beaded. This style of dressing the hair was called łi'kā' bȧtcale'ñ. Bossu, who observed this tribe in the middle of the eighteenth century in its old home, said, though without confining his remarks to them, "the female savages have long hair plaited after the German fashion" (Bossu, 1768, vol. 2, pp. 7, 23). Speaking especially of the Chickasaw, Adair remarks (1775, p. 170) that they never forgot "to anoint and tie up their hair, except in their time of mourning," and that persons of both sexes tied native stones in their hair. Bushnell has illustrated one type of Choctaw feminine coiffure which seems to be the same as that described for the Yuchi (Bushnell, 1909 a, p. 10, pl. 10; Speck, 1909, p. 22).

Timberlake observed that:

the Cherokee women wear the hair of their head, which is so long that it generally reaches to the middle of their legs, and sometimes to the ground, club'd, and ornamented with ribbons of various colors; but, except their eye-brows, pluck it from all the other parts of the body, especially the looser part of the sex. (Timberlake, Williams ed., 1927, pp. 75-77.)

Of the Seminole of 30 years ago, MacCauley remarks:

The women dress their hair more simply than the men. From a line crossing the head from ear to ear the hair is gathered up and bound, just above the neck, into a knot somewhat like that often made by the civilized woman, the Indian woman's hair being wrought more into the shape of a cone, sometimes quite elongated and sharp at the apex. A piece of bright ribbon is commonly used at the end as a finish to the structure. The front hair hangs down over the forehead and along the cheeks in front of the ears, being what we call "banged." . . . Among the little Indian girls the hair is simply braided into a queue and tied with a ribbon, as we often see the hair upon the heads of our school children. (MacCauley, 1887, p. 487, and cf. Skinner, 1913, p. 67.)

According to Du Pratz, Natchez women wore their hair at full length "except that in front which is shorter. The hair behind is tied in a queue by means of a netting of mulberry threads, with tassels at the ends." (Le Page du Pratz, 1758, vol. 2, p. 195; Swanton, 1911, p. 51.) Dumont de Montigny, who was considering the Indians of the lower Mississippi more widely, states that the women wore their hair

either braided in tresses or bound into a queue with a string of . . . bison hair . . . instead of a ribbon. These tresses are usually interlaced by way of ornament with strings of blue, white, green, or black beads [made of glass], according to their taste, sometimes also with quills of the porcupine. (Dumont, 1753, vol. 1, p. 137; Swanton, 1911, p. 51.)

Iberville observes that Bayogoula women wore their hair wrapped around their heads in a queue (or bundle) (Margry, 1875–86, vol. 4, p. 275), and Gravier that Tunica women had "a great tress of hair on the back which hangs down below the waist; they also make a crown of it around the head." (Shea, 1861, p. 134; Swanton, 1911, pp. 316– 317.) Gatschet's Chitimacha informant told him that the women of that tribe used to wear their hair "in plaits or tresses ornamented with plumes" (Gatschet, 1883, p. 6; Swanton, 1911, p. 345), but the use of feathers by Indian women was certainly rare.

Of the Caddo women, Joutel tells us that they parted their hair in front and fastened it carefully behind (Joutel *in* Margry, 1875–86, vol. 3, p. 413).

Methods of wearing the hair varied more from tribe to tribe among the men than among the women, but there was a definite reason for this which Adair thus indicates:

Every different nation when at war [he says] trim their hair after a different manner, through contempt of each other; thus we can distinguish an enemy in the woods, so far off as we can see him. (Adair, 1775, p. 8.)

The main fact is confirmed by Dumont de Montigny, in its application to the Mississippi River tribes (Dumont, 1753, p. 136; Swanton, 1911, p. 51).

Hariot informs us that the men belonging to the Algonquian tribes on the North Carolina coast let their hair grow long on either side of the head and bound it up in knots under the ears or at the back of the head, but cut it short in the middle forming a roach, or "cockscomb," like some of the western tribes. It is interesting to note that the priests in this region retained the roach, but cut their hair short at the sides except that they left hair above their forehead "in manner of a perriwigge." And the conjurers wore it in the same manner (Hariot, 1893, pls. 3, 5, 7, 9, 11). This means that the priest's coiffure was like that of the ordinary Creek Indian. Barlowe, however, tells us that other Indian males wore their hair long on one side, in which case their manner of dressing the hair was identical with that of the Powhatans. He observed on the head of Granganimeo, the brother of a Carolina chief, "a broad plate of gold or copper, for being unpolished we knew not what metall it should be" (Burrage, 1906, p. 232), and other leading men had similar pieces of copper on the head. This distinction somewhat suggests Garcilaso's assertion that feathers indicated difference in rank, and, indeed, Hariot observed that the chief men of the Sound region of North Carolina had a long feather at the front of the roach and two others at each side, one above each ear (Hariot, 1893, pl. 3).

Powhatan priests, according to Spelman,

are shauen on yᵉ right side of ther head close to the scull only a little locke leaft at yᵉ eare and sum of thes haue beards. But yᵉ common people haue no beards at all for they pull away ther hares as fast as it growes. And they also cutt y⁰ heares on y⁰ right side of ther heade that it might not hinder them by flappinge about ther bow stringe, when they draw it to shoott But on y⁰ other side they lett it grow & haue a long locke hanginge doune ther shoulder. (Smith, John, Arber ed., 1884, p. cxiii.)

Percy says that the Powhatan Indians shaved the right side of the head with a shell (Narr. Early Va., Tyler ed., 1907, p. 12). Smith confirms him as to the general fact that the Virginia Indian men preserved their hair at full length on only one side, and he adds that "for Barbers they use their women, who with 2 shels grate away the haire of any fashion they please." Elsewhere he mentions reeds as well as shells used in this operation (Narr. Early Va., Tyler ed., 1907, pp. 99, 115). Strachey is somewhat more detailed:

> The men shave their haire on the right side very close, keeping a ridge commonly on the toppe or crowne like a coxcomb; for their women, with two shells, will grate away the haire into any fashion they please. On the left side they weare theire haire at full length, with a lock an ell long, which they anoint with walnut oyle, whereby it is very sleeke, and shynes like a raven's winge. Sometymes they tye up their lock with an arteficyall and well-laboured knott (just in the fashion as I have seene the Cerrazzais of Scio and Pera), stuck with many coulored gewgawes, as the cast-head or brown-antle of a deare, the hand of their enemie dryed, croisetts of bright and shyning copper, like the newe moone. Many weare the whole skyne of a hauke stuffed with the wings abroad, and buzzards' or other fowles' whole wings, and to the feathers they will fasten a little rattle, about the bignes of the chape of a rapier, which they take from the tayle of a snake, and sometymes divers kinds of shells, hanging loose by small purfleets or threeds, that, being shaken as they move, they might make a certaine murmuring or whisteling noise by gathering wynd, in which they seem to take great jollity, and hold yt a kind of bravery. (Strachey, 1849, pp. 66–67).

Smith speaks of a priest or conjurer who had "his head hung round with little Skinnes of Weasels and other vermine, with a Crownet of feathers on his head" (Smith, John, Tyler ed., 1907, p. 51). He also repeats many of the things just quoted from Strachey regarding articles of the headdress.

Percy mentions a crown of deer's hair on the head of a Rapahannock chief, and another native chief gave such a hat, "his crown which was of Deares hayre, Dyed redd," to Newport (Narr. Early Va., Tyler ed., 1907, p. 14; Smith, Arber ed., 1884, p. xliii).[27]

Beverley (1705, bk. 3, p. 2) simply says that "the Men wear their Hair cut after several fanciful Fashions, sometimes greas'd, and

---

[27] In a letter written by William Byrd, May 26, 1686, to John Clinton, the writer says: "According to your desire I have herewith sent you an Indian Habitt for your Boy, the best I could procure among our Neighbour Indians, there is a flap or Belly Clout 1 pʳ Stockings & 1 pʳ Mocosins or Indian shoes allso Some shells to put about his neck & a Cap of Wampum I could not gett any dyed Hair, wʰ would have been better & cheaper these things are put up in an Indian Basket, directed as you desired, there are a Bow and arrows tyed to itt" (Virginia Mag. Hist. and Biog., 1917, vol. 25, p. 129).

sometimes painted. The Great Men, or better sort, preserve a long lock behind for distinction." He practically repeats Hariot's (1893, pls. 3, 4) description of the method of wearing the hair in vogue among the priests and conjurers.

The Tuscarora Indians wore copper ornaments in their hair like their Algonquian neighbors (Alvord, 1912, p. 162).

Speaking of males in the Siouan tribes, Lawson says:

> Their hair is rolled up on each ear, as the women's only much shorter, and oftentimes a roll on the crown of the head, or temples, which is just as they fancy, there being no strictness in their dress. (Lawson, 1860, p. 311.)

This applies particularly to the Siouans of Carolina, and so does the following by Catesby though drawn from a somewhat wider field of experience. He says they

> wear no covering on their heads, their hair, being very long is twisted and rolled up in various manners, sometimes in a bunch on each ear, sometimes on one ear only, the hair on the other side hanging at length, or cut off. Others having their hair growing on one side of their head at full length, while the hair of the other side is cut within an inch or two of the roots, standing upright. (Catesby, 1731–43, vol. 2, p. VIII.)

Michel thus describes the usages of the Virginia Siouans in the Monacan town:

> They have . . . black hair, hanging down upon their shoulders, most of them, however, have it cut short, except the women, who wear long, black hair. When they are summoned, their king or queen, as also their princes and nobles (but with some difference) wear crowns of bark, a little more than a buckle wide, round and open above, with white and brown stripes (beads?) half an inch long, set in beautifully in spiral form, so that no bark is visible. The women, especially the queen and her three servants, were overhung with such things, strung on big and small threads or something, in place of chains. I wondered what kind of material it was. I examined, therefore, the finery of one of the maids of the queen. I cannot compare it to anything better than to strips of leather, hung over the harness of horses in this country [Switzerland]. (Michel, 1916, pp. 129–130.)

The Cusabo Indians seem to have followed the usage of the Creeks and Cherokee to be described shortly, but that of the Florida tribes was somewhat different, since they allowed most of their hair to grow long (Swanton, 1922, pp. 72, 347). Garcilaso, in the only mention made of this subject by any of the De Soto chroniclers, says of the Indians generally that they wore their hair long and tied on (i. e., close to) their heads (Garcilaso, 1723, p. 6). This corresponds to the custom in Florida and along the Gulf coast to the westward rather than to that of the interior tribes. Ribault says of the Timucua Indians, "Their hair was long and trussed up, with a lace made of herbs, to the top of their heads," and farther on that their hair "was trussed up, gathered and worked together with great cunning, and fastened after the form of a diadem," while Le Challeux has these words: "They keep their hair long, and they truss it up neatly all around their heads, and this truss of hair serves them as a quiver in which to carry their arrows when they are at war." (French, 1875, pp. 173, 178; Gaffarel, 1875, p. 461; Swanton, 1922, p. 347.) Laudonnière confirms the main fact, and in his description of scalping in Florida, Le Moyne says that they pulled the skin "off with the hair, more than a foot and a half long, still adhering, done up in a knot on the crown, and with that lower down round the forehead and back cut short into a ring about two fingers wide, like the rim of a hat." (Swanton, 1922, pp. 347, 378; Le Moyne, 1875, pp. 6–7.) His illustrations agree with this, the hair being tied in a knot at the top of the head and feathers often worked into the binding cord.

He also represents tails of animals or their entire skins fastened to the hair, and one of his subjects wears what looks like a basket hat, though it may be intended either for the "lace made of herbs," mentioned by Ribault, or a palm-leaf hat. (French, 1875, pp. 173, 178; Gaffarel, 1875, p. 461; Swanton, 1922, p. 348.)

San Miguel found that the Guale Indians of both sexes wore their hair long and cut it a little above the forehead (Garcia, 1902, p. 194).

At Key Marco in the Calusa country, though the relics there were not certainly of the Calusa people, Cushing found remains of what he

regarded as bark head-dresses quite similar to those of Northwest Coast Indians. . . . Associated with these, as well as independently, were numbers of hairpins, some made of ivory, some of bone, to which beautiful, long flexible strips of polished tortoise shell—that, alas, I could not preserve in their entirety—had been attached. One pin had been carved at the upper end with the representation of a rattlesnake's tail, precisely like those of Cheyenne warriors; another, with a long conical knob grooved or hollowed for the attachment of plume cords. (Cushing, 1896, p. 376.)

The two Hobe Indians met by Dickenson in southeastern Florida "had their hair tied in a roll behind, in which stuck two bones, shaped one like a broad arrow, the other like a spearhead." (Dickenson, 1803, pp. 9–10; Swanton, 1922, p. 391.) Calusa Indians are reported to have worn on their heads pieces of gold (Swanton, 1922, p. 388).

Near the mouth of Mobile Bay, Narvaez encountered some chiefs whose hair was "loose and very long," and this indicates a probable relationship to the Choctaw since the men of that tribe were so much addicted to the custom of allowing their hair to grow long that they were called by their neighbors as well as by themselves "Long Hairs" (Choctaw, Paⁿs falaya) (Adair, 1775, p. 192; Swanton, 1931 a, p. 4).

In the early Virginia relations, we have mentioned Indians living inland to the northwest called Pocoughtronack, who shaved their crowns and let their hair grow long on the neck. These were probably Potawatomi and therefore outside of the territory under consideration, though they might possibly have been Yuchi. From Gabriel Arthur, however, we learn of a tribe called Tamahitan, almost certainly Yuchi, who "keepe theire haire close cut to ye end an enime may not take an advantage to lay hold of them by it" (Alvord, 1912, p. 222).

Speaking of the period of 30 years ago, Speck says:

> The Yuchi men as a rule allow the hair to grow long all over the head until it reaches the neck. It is then cropped off even all around and worn parted in the middle . . . Something is usually bound about the forehead to keep the hair back from the face; either a turban, silver head band or strip of some kind. The beadwork hair ornaments used to be tied to a few locks back of the crown. Some of the older men state that a long time ago the men wore scalp locks and roached their hair, removing all but the comb of hair along the top of the crown, in the manner still practiced by the Osage. Men of taste invariably keep the mustache, beard and sometimes the eyebrows from growing by pulling them out with their finger nails. The hair was formerly trimmed by means of two stones. The tresses to be cut were laid across a flat stone and were then sawed off, by means of a sharp-edged stone, to the desired length (Speck, 1909. p. 52.)

As to hair ornaments:

> Fastened in the hair near the crown and falling toward the back, the men used to wear small strips of beadwork, *tsŭtsetsi'*, "little bead", avowedly for ornament. They were woven like the neckband on horsehair or sinew with different colored beads. One which I collected is about eight inches long and one half an inch wide, having three-fold dangling ends ornamented with yarn. The designs on these ornaments are representative of topographical and celestial features. (Speck, 1909, p .50.)

This is in line with what Timberlake tells us regarding the Cherokee:

> The hair of their head is shaved tho' many of the old people have it plucked out by the roots, except a patch on the hinder part of the head, about twice the bigness of a crown-piece, which is ornamented with beads, feathers, wampum, stained deer's hair and such like baubles. (Timberlake, Williams ed., 1927, p. 75.)

The Cherokee deer's hair "crown" is described by Grant as similar to a wig and "made of Possum's hair Dyed Red or Yellow" (Crane, 1928, p. 279).

Bartram, whose description is supposed to apply to both the Cherokee and the Creeks, says:

> The men shave their head, leaving a narrow crest or comb, beginning at the crown of the head, where it is about two inches broad and about the same height, and stands frized upright; but this crest tending backwards, gradually widens, covering the hinder part of the head and back of the neck: the lank hair behind is ornamented with pendant silver quills, and then joined or articulate silver plates; and usually the middle fascicle of hair, being by far the longest, is wrapped in a large quill of silver, or the joint of a small reed, curiously sculptured and painted, the hair continuing through it terminates in a tail or tassel. (Bartram, 1792, p. 499.)

This central lock sometimes hung forward as observed by Oglethorpe in the case of six men who danced before him at the Lower Creek town of Coweta, "their hair cut short except three locks one of wᶜʰ hangs over their Forehead like a horses fore top. They paint the short Hair and stick it full of Feathers" (Bushnell, 1908, p. 573). It is important because frequently observed on embossed copper objects and engraved shells.

According to one of my own Creek interpreters, the heads of the old time Creeks were shaved almost like the heads of monks, and the heads of the Creeks belonging to Colonel Jumper's band, which rejoined the rest of the nation after going to Mexico, were shaved exactly like those of monks. It is to be noted that Colonel Jumper was a Chiaha Indian, and that his band was from among the Lower Creeks and no doubt included many Hitchiti. The old Alabama men are said to have had their hair divided into four braids, two of which were allowed to fall down behind and two in front, and the end of each braid was fastened with a bead and called hĕ'sîs-taisîha, used, however, only on special occasions. From the Gentleman of Elvas we know that the ancient Alabama used bison horns as embellishments to their head gear, at least in war (Robertson, 1933, p. 153).

Creek customs were carried into Florida and persisted in the peninsula longer than anywhere else. MacCauley describes them as follows:

The men cut all their hair close to the head, except a strip about an inch wide, running over the front of the scalp from temple to temple, and another strip, of about the same width, perpendicular to the former, crossing the crown of the head to the nape of the neck. At each temple a heavy tuft is allowed to hang to the bottom of the lobe of the ear. The long hair of the strip crossing to the neck is generally gathered and braided into two ornamental queues. I did not learn that these Indians are in the habit of plucking the hair from their faces. I noticed, however, that the moustache is commonly worn among them and that a few of them are endowed with a rather bold looking combination of moustache and imperial . . . . For some reason there seems to be a much greater neglect of the care of the hair, and, indeed, of the whole person, in the northern (Muskogee) than in the southern camps. (MacCauley, 1887, pp. 486–487.)

But 30 years later, Skinner reports:

The men now cut their hair short after the fashion of the whites, except that they are prone to leave a lock before the ears. It is only a short time since they have ceased to wear a double scalp-lock; indeed a few conservatives still maintain the custom. (Skinner, 1913, p. 67.)

The hair on the scalp of Cooper, one of the Seminole chiefs killed in 1837, formed two braids (Foreman, 1932, p. 343).

Adair (1775, p. 8), speaking probably of the Chickasaw, says that "the men fastened several different sorts of beautiful feathers, frequently in tufts, or the wing of a red bird, or the skin of a small hawk, to a lock of hair on the crown of the heads," and he also says that they had a large conch-shell bead, about the length and thickness of a man's forefinger, which they fixed to the crown of their head, as an high ornament (Adair, 1775, p. 170). As noted above, both men and women ornamented their hair by tying on it stones picked up here and there.

Shortly after contact with the whites, some of the northern Choctaw began to imitate the Chickasaw custom of wearing the hair, and finally most of those belonging to the two northern bands adopted it.

Let us now turn to the Mississippi Valley. First may be given Du Pratz's long description of Natchez customs in this particular.

The natives cut their hair around, leaving a crown like the Capuchins, and leave only enough long hair to make a twisted tress no larger than the little finger, which hangs over the left ear. This crown is in the same place and almost as large as that of a monk. In the middle of this crown they leave about two dozen long hairs for the attachment of feathers.

Although the natives all wear this crown, yet the hair is not removed or pulled from this place, but it is cut or burned with burning coals. (Le Page du Pratz, 1758, vol. 2, p. 198; Swanton, 1911, p. 51.)

Dumont's remarks are much more general and may be supposed to apply to all the Indians from the Quapaw to the Gulf and a considerable distance east and west.

With regard to the hair of the head the men wear it differently, according to difference in nationality. Some cut it entirely, leaving only a tuft on the top of the head in the Turkish fashion. Others cut it on one side only, on the right or the left, and keep the other side very long. Many also have the head completely shaved and have only a braided tress which hangs on each side, and others are clipped like our monks, having only a crown of short hairs. (Dumont, 1753, vol. 1, pp. 136–137; Swanton, 1911, p. 51.)

The Bayogoula had their hair cut, or rather pulled out, around the forehead as well as the beard; "they leave only a little handful of hair at the top of the head, where they fasten many bird feathers of different colors" (Margry, 1875–86, vol. 4, pp. 259–260; Swanton, 1911, p. 276).

Most Tunica men are said to have worn their hair long and the same is affirmed of the Houma. (Thwaites, 1897–1901, vol. 65, pp. 150–153; Shea, 1861, pp. 134, 146–147; Swanton, 1911, pp. 289, 316.)

Gatschet was told that the Chitimacha men wore their hair long, and besides using feathers, they "fastened a piece of lead to the end of the tress behind for the purpose of keeping the head erect," a rather questionable purpose (Gatschet, 1883, p. 5; Swanton, 1911, p. 345.)

Most of the Caddo seen by Joutel had their hair cut off except for some tresses which they tied to or rolled around a small piece of wood, which they wore at one side, but all had a little tuft on top of the head behind, like the Turks. Some, however, did not cut their hair at all (Joutel *in* Margry, 1875–86, vol. 3, p. 356). Elsewhere men were said to cut their hair like the Capuchins. It appears from other narratives that roaching was common (Joutel *in* Margry, 1875–86, vol. 3, p. 413; Swanton, 1942, pp. 141–142).

HEAD BANDS

(See plates)

The nearest approach to a hat was the head band, sometimes connected with a netting so as to form a kind of cap, though in general
Adair's words regarding the Chickasaw to the effect that they always
went bareheaded were true of all the tribes of the Southeast (Adair,
1775, p. 9). Speaking of these Indians generally, Garcilaso says:

For a headdress they wear a thick skein of thread in whatever color they desire
which they wind about their heads and tie the ends over the forehead in two
half-knots, so that one end hangs down over either temple as far as the ears.
(Garcilaso, 1723, pp. 17–18.)

When Tascalusa met De Soto, Ranjel tells us that his head was "covered by a kind of coif like the almaizal, so that his headdress was
like a Moor's which gave him an aspect of authority" (Bourne, 1904,
vol. 2, p. 120). This is the first time that the headdress of an Indian of
this section was compared to an oriental turban; the resemblance became much more striking when European handkerchiefs and other
textiles took the place of the native materials.

The commonest type of head band worn in early times was ornamented with feathers. Thus Elvas tells us that the chief of Coça
came out to meet the Spaniards in 1540 wearing "a crown of feathers"
(Robertson, 1933, p. 115). Although too much reliance cannot be
placed in Le Moyne's illustrations, there seems to have been some
ground for the types of headdress depicted. We find some of his subjects with their heads covered with skins, the head of the animal being
made to fit over the head of the wearer. Others have a row of short
feathers around the entire crown of the head, and still others single
tufts of feathers in front. A ridge of hair left above the forehead
prevents us from telling whether these feathers are fastened together
by a band running all of the way around, but such was probably the
case. Finally, we observe a head band showing a succession of short
points as if it were a kind of crown. This is rather too suggestive of
European crowns, and yet in later times, at all events, bands of this
pattern, hammered out of silver, were much in use, I myself having
seen one that belonged to an Alabama Indian living in Louisiana.
It is to be observed that the illustrations indicate most of these head
bands to have been worn by leading men, the common men exhibiting
nothing of the sort.

In the Algonquian tidewater country and the Siouan hinterland,
we meet head bands of a different type. According to Hariot, the
women of Secotan wore "wreathes" about their head which were not
in vogue among the women of some other towns, such as Dasemonquepeuc. His illustration shows that he means by these articles of apparel not wreaths of flowers, as one might suppose, but head bands

seemingly twisted of cords (Hariot, 1893, pl. 4). However, in the text to the reproduction made by Beverley (1705, bk. 3, p. 7, pl. 5, fig. 2), the coronet is described as "a wreath of furs." Strachey (1849, pp. 56–57) mentions flowers along with feathers stuck in the hair of some Powhatan women.

Head bands of "coral," i. e., beads, seem to have been peculiar to this region. Barlowe notes that the wife of Granganimeo "had a bande of white Corall" about her forehead, "and so had her husband many times" (Burrage, 1906, p. 232)). Among Powhatan manufactures, Strachey (1849, pp. 68, 57) notes "their crownetts, which their weroances weare, and their queene's *fasciae crinales*, borders or frontalls of white beades, curral and copper" "A frontall of white currall" was brought to the wife of a chief named Pipisco by her maid. Crownlets of beads are represented on a few human subjects drawn by F. L. Michel and reproduced by Beverley. Bushnell (1930, pp. 9–10) thinks that they are representations of Monacan Indians but, as we have seen, bead crownlets were not confined to them.

Both Smith (Tyler ed., 1907, p. 51) and Strachey (1849, p. 91) describe headdresses of Powhatan priests consisting of a central "tassel" of the sloughed off skins of snakes, and skins of weasels "and other vermin" surrounded by a crownlet of feathers.

Lawson does not mention head bands specifically, though they may be included among some of the ornaments to which he does allude.

The feather head band seems to have reached its highest development in the crown of the Natche head chief, which is thus described by Du Pratz:

This crown is composed of a cap and a diadem, surmounted by large feathers. The cap is made of a netting which holds the diadem, a texture 2 inches broad. tied as tightly behind as is desired. The cap is of black threads, but the diadem is red and embellished with little beads or small white seeds as hard as beads. The feathers which surmount the diadem are white. Those in front may be 8 inches long and those behind 4 inches. These feathers are arranged in a curved line. At the end of each is a tuft of hair (*houpe de poil*) and above a little hairy tassel (*aigrette de crin*), all being only an inch and a half long and dyed a very beautiful red. (Le Page du Pratz, 1758, vol. 2, p. 201 (191) ; Swanton, 1911, pp. 106–107.)

Something similar was not unknown to the Creeks, as appears from the following description by Bartram. Though he makes his words of general application, the picture of "Mico Chlucco, the Long Warrior, King of the Seminoles," shows that he has the Seminole or Lower Creek Indians particularly in mind (see pl. 31, fig. 2).

A very curious diadem or band, about four inches broad, and ingeniously wrought or woven, and curiously decorated with stones, beads, wampum, porcupine quills, &c., encircles their temples ; the front peak of it being embellished with a high waving plume, of crane or heron feathers. (Bartram, 1792, pp. 499–500.)

It is curious that Adair does not furnish us with a good account of this article of dress. He merely says that "the men fasten several different sorts of beautiful feathers, frequently in tufts; or the wing of a red bird, or the skin of a small hawk, to a lock of hair on the crown of their heads" (Adair, 1775, p. 9) and swan feathers on the heads of warriors.

As already noted, the earlier forms of head band gave way in later times to a turban made of European fabrics which sometimes covered the entire head and was supplemented with skins of animals and feathers, or to head bands of silver. All of these articles were directly descended from those which our earliest records reveal, the handkerchief from the netting and skin thongs, the skins from such as are figured by Le Moyne, and the silver crowns probably from similar copper objects. The feathers underwent no change except that many or most of them were later derived from domestic fowl. It is worthy of note that the Alabama distinguish the handkerchief head band and the silver head band by different names, ĭsbă'kaicĭha' and cia'tăla, respectively. There were no restrictions regarding the wearing of these so far as the present representatives of the Alabama tribe know, except that the silver head band was used only at dances.

EAR ORNAMENTS

Barlowe observed that the wife of a North Carolina coast noble, Granganimeo, wore in her ears

bracelets [i. e., strings] of pearls hanging down to her middle. . . . and those were of the bignes of good pease. The rest of her women of the better sort had pendants of copper hanging in either eare, and some of the children of the kings brother and other noble men, have five or sixe in either eare. (Burrage, 1906, p. 232.)

In the same region Hariot reports not only seeing strings of pearls used for ear ornaments but smooth bones, claws of birds stuck through the ears, these only by the men, and in one case two small pieces of silver worn by "a Wiroans or chiefe Lorde." The priests wore earrings, but their nature was not specified (Hariot, 1893, p. 14, pls. 3, 4). Lederer found the Tuscarora women of the better sort decked with pieces of bright copper in their hair and ears (Lederer, 1912, p. 162). When Percy met the Werowance of Rapahanna, the ears of the latter were hung with strings of pearls "and in either eare a Birds Claw through it beset with fine Copper or Gold." He mentions wearing of birds' legs in the ears as a common practice (Narr. Early Va., Tyler ed., 1907, pp. 14, 12). Strachey, speaking of the Powhatan men, says:

Their eares they boare with wyde holes, comonly two or three, and in the same they doe hang chaines of stayned pearle braceletts, of white bone or shreeds of copper, beaten thinne and bright, and wound up hollowe, and with a greate pride, certaine fowles' leggs, eagles, hawkes, turkeys, etc., with beasts' clawes, beares, arrahacounes [raccoons], squirrells, etc. The clawes thrust through they let hang upon the cheeke to the full view, and some of their men there be who will weare in these holes a small greene and yellow-coloured live snake, neere half a yard in length, which crawling and lapping himself about his neck oftentymes familiarly, he suffereth to kisse his lippes. Others weare a dead ratt tyed by the tayle, and such like conundrums. (Strachey, 1849, p. 67.)

Smith covers the same ground in abbreviated fashion. He mentions only three holes in the ears. For "bracelets" we should say "strings," and the copper ornaments seem to have been beads (Smith, John, Tyler ed., 1907, p. 99). Beverley (1705, bk. 3, pls. 2, 4) makes mention of "a fine shell with pearl drops" worn at the ears by men, and the skin of some dark-colored bird worn in the ear by conjurers.

When men of the Piedmont country went to war they wore in their ears feathers, the wings of birds, rings, copper, wampum, and probably at an earlier date roanoke. Some of these Indians had in the same place "great bobs . . . and sometimes in the holes thereof they put eagles and other birds' feathers, for a trophy" (Lawson, 1860, pp. 312, 314). Catesby remarks that "some of the modish wear a large bunch of downy feathers thrust through a hole made in one and sometimes both ears." Warriors wore "rings of copper, *Peak* and *Wampum* in their ears" (Catesby, 1731–43, vol. 2, pp. VIII, IX).

Peculiar to the Timucua, or at least to the Florida Indians, was the following ear ornament:

All the men and women have the ends of their ears pierced, and pass through them small oblong fish-bladders, which when inflated shine like pearls, and which, being dyed red, look like a light-colored carbuncle. (Le Moyne, 1875, p. 14; Swanton, 1922, p. 348.)

In the drawings by Le Moyne, writer of the above words, some Indians are shown with staple-shaped earrings, one with a true ring, and one with the claws of some bird thrust through the ear, reminding us of the Virginia custom. Ribault observed small plates of copper hung to the ears of a Timucua Indian "with which they wipe the sweat from their bodies" (French, 1875, p. 178; Swanton, 1922, p. 350).

Cushing found at Key Marco

ear buttons, plates, spikes and plugs. The ear buttons were chiefly of wood, and were of special interest—the most elaborate articles of jewelry we found. They were shaped like huge cuff buttons—some, two inches in diameter, resembling the so-called spool-shaped copper bosses or ear ornaments of the mound builders. But a few of these were made in parts, so that the rear disc could be, by a partial turn, slipped off from the shank, to facilitate insertion into the slits of the ear lobe. The front discs were rimmed with white shell rings, within which were narrower circlets of tortoise shell, and within these, in turn, little round, very dark and slightly protuberant wooden bosses or plugs, covered with gum or varnish and highly polished, so that the whole front of the button exactly resembled a huge round, gleaming eyeball. Indeed, this resemblance was so striking that both

Mr. Sawyer and I independently recognized the likeness of these curious decorations to the glaring eyes of the tarpons, sharks, and other sea monsters of the surrounding waters; and as the buttons were associated with more or less warlike paraphernalia, I hazarded the opinion that they were actually designed to represent the eyes of such monsters—to be worn as the fierce, destructive, searching and terrorizing eyes, the "Seeing Ears," so to say, of the warriors. This was indicated by the eye-like forms of many of the other ear buttons we found—some having been overlaid in front with highly polished concave-convex white shell discs, perforated at the centres as if to represent eye pupils . . .

There were still other ear buttons, however, elaborately decorated with involuted figures, or circles divided equally by sinusoid lines, designs that were greatly favored by the ancient artists of these keys. The origin of these figures, both painted, as on the buttons—in contrasting blue and white—and incised, as on discs, stamps, or the ends of handles, became perfectly evident to me as derived from the "navel marks," or central involutes on the worked ends of univalvular shells; but probably here, as in the Orient, they had already acquired the significance of the human navel, and were thus mystic symbols of "the middle," to be worn by priestly Commanders of the warriors. That the ear buttons proper were badges, was indicated by the finding of larger numbers of common ear plugs; round, and slightly rounded also at either end, but grooved or rather hollowed around the middles. Although beautifully fashioned, they had been finished with shark-tooth surface-hatching, in order to facilitate coating them with brilliant varnishes or pigments. The largest of them may have been used as stretchers for ordinary wear; but the smaller and shorter of them were probably for ordinary use, or use by women, and had taken the place of like, but more primitive ornaments made from the vertebrae of sharks. Indeed a few of these earlier forms made of vertebrae, were actually found.

I could not quite determine what had been the use of certain highly ornate flat wooden discs. They were too thin to have been serviceable as ear plugs, or as labrets. But from the fact that they were so exquisitely incised with rosettes, or elaborately involuted, obliquely hatched designs, and other figures—the two faces different in each case—and that they corresponded in size to the ear buttons and plugs, I came to regard them as stamps used in impressing the gum-like pigments with which so many of these ornaments had been quite thickly coated, as also, perhaps, in the ornamentation or stamping of other articles and materials now decomposed. Very long and beautifully finished, curved plates of shell had been used probably as ear ornaments or spikes, also; since they exactly resembled those depicted as worn transversely thrust through the ears, in some of Le Moyne's drawings, of which representations I had never previously understood the nature; and many of the plummet-shaped pendants I have before referred to, must have been used after the manner remarked on in some of the old writers, as *ear weights* or stretchers, and some, being very long, not only thuswise, but also as ear spikes for wear after the manner of using the plates just described. While certain crude examples of these curious pendants had been used apparently as wattling bobbets, still others, better shaped, had as certainly served as dress or girdle pendants. (Cushing, 1896, pp. 174–175.)

In the north-central part of the Gulf region we find a remarkable ear ornament in vogue among males. Bartram, who has the Creeks primarily, and the Cherokee secondarily in mind, describes it as follows:

Their ears are lacerated, separating the border or cartilaginous limb, which at first is bound round very close and tight with leather strings or thongs, and anointed with fresh bear's oil, until healed: a piece of lead being fastened

to it, by its weight extends this cartilege an incredible length, which afterwards being craped, or bound in brass or silver wire, extends semicircularly
like a bow or crescent; and it is then very elastic, even so as to spring or
bound about with the least motion or flexure of the body: this is decorated
with soft white plumes of heron feathers.   (Bartram, 1792, p. 499; see also pl. 31,
fig. 1, herein.)

From Timberlake it is plain that the custom was shared in equal
measure by the Cherokee:

The ears are slit and stretched to an enormous size, putting the person who
undergoes the operation to incredible pain, being unable to lie on either side
for near forty days.   To remedy this, they generally slit but one at a time;
so soon as the patient can bear it, they are wound round with wire to expand
them, and are adorned with silver pendants and rings, which they likewise
wear at the nose.   This custom does not belong originally to the Cherokees,
but [was] taken by them from the Shawnese. or other northern nations.   (Timberlake, Williams ed., 1927, pp. 75–76; see also pl. 9 herein.)

Whether the custom came to this tribe through the Shawnee or
not, there are indications that it had a northern origin.   At all events,
it had extended to the Chickasaw, for Adair gives us one of our best
descriptions of it:

The young heroes cut a hole round almost the extremity of both their ears,
which till healed, they stretched out with a large tuft of buffalo's wool mixt
with bear's oil: then they twist as much small wire round as will keep them
extended in that hideous form . . .

I have been among the Indians at a drinking match, when several of their
beaus have been humbled as low as death, for the great loss of their big ears.
Being so widely extended, it is as easy for a person to take hold of, and pull
them off, as to remove a couple of small hoops were they hung within reach; but
if the ear after the pull, stick to their head by one end, when they get sober,
they pare and sew it together with a needle and deer's sinews, after sweating
him in a stove.   Thus the disconsolate warrior recovers his former cheerfulness,
and hath a lasting caution of not putting his ears a second time in danger with
bad company: however, it is not deemed a scandal to lose their ears by any
accident, because they become slender and brittle, by their virtuous compliance
with that favourite custom of their ancestors.   (Adair, 1775, p. 180.)

This type of ornamentation was "wearing off apace" in his time.
He says that the women only bored "small holes in the lobe of their
ears for their rings," and it would seem that similar borings were in
vogue with both sexes at an earlier period, for he remarks that
anciently they used native hard stones ("such coarse diamonds, as
their own hill country produced") fastened with a deer's sinew.
But when the Europeans supplied them with ornaments, they "used
brass and silver ear-rings, and finger-rings" (Adair, 1775, pp. 179–
180).

Coming down to more recent times, we find that Alabama silver-
smiths pounded silver quarters out thin to use as ear ornaments, the
ornament being tied by a piece of braid through a hole in the lobe of
the ear.   They also used 10-cent pieces.   Sometimes a small piece of
silver wire was run through the earlobe.   An earring was known as

514 BUREAU OF AMERICAN ETHNOLOGY [Bull. 137

ictå'tåkå', "something taken and hung." Alabama women used to insert silver ornaments called atcitåka sawå', "small earrings," in holes around the edges of their ears above the lobes. A long time ago a woman is said to have bought such ornaments in New York, but the actual wearing of them is one sin against good taste that cannot be charged up against the metropolis.

MacCauley says:

> Ear rings are not generally worn by the Seminole. Those worn are usually made of silver and are of home manufacture. The ears of most Indians, however, appear to be pierced, and, as a rule, the ears of the women are pierced many times; for what purpose I did not discover. Along and in the upper edges of the ears of the women from one to ten or more small holes have been made. In most of these holes I noticed bits of palmetto wood, about a fifth of an inch in length and in diameter the size of a large pin. Seemingly they were not placed there to remain only while the puncture was healing. (MacCauley, 1887, p. 489.)

The Natchez warriors, according to Du Pratz, had "the lower parts of the ears slit, in order to pass through them iron or brass wire in the form of worm screws, a full inch in diameter" (Le Page du Pratz, 1758, vol. 2, p. 200 (190); Swanton, 1911, p. 55). This custom was probably suggested by the Chickasaw and Creek ear wiring, but, since only the lower part of the ear was pierced by the Natchez, it was not developed to the same extent. On the other hand, the Natchez women appear to have had a spike-shaped ear ornament different from any reported from the tribes farther east though current enough along the Mississippi, and very far inland in archeological deposits. (See p. 486.)

Another writer speaks as if these ear bobs were sometimes replaced by beads. The Bayogoula women were observed to have wooden earrings or rather wooden plugs "of the size of the little finger," though it is possible these were the shell spikes above described and that the visitors were deceived as to the material of which they were made (Swanton, 1911, pp. 55–56, 276; Margry, 1875–86, vol. 4, pp. 259–262). Both male and female Chitimacha wore earrings, though the material of which these were made is not reported. (Gatschet, 1861, pp. 5–6; Swanton 1911, p. 345). For the Caddo, see Swanton (1942, p. 146).

NOSE ORNAMENTS

There is no evidence, either in Le Moyne's drawings or in his and other texts dealing with the Florida Indians, that they wore nose ornaments, and I find but one reference to such ornamentation among Virginia and Carolina tribes. This, curiously enough, is of relatively late date, in Francis Louis Michel's account of the Siouan Indians of Monacantown, as he observed them in 1701–2. He says: "There were also some who had a narrow spangle drawn through their nose" (Michel, 1916, p. 131). The fullest references are by Adair and so we know that the nose was a subject for ornamentation among the Chickasaw. The Creek custom was probably identical or he would have mentioned the fact. Bartram says nothing about this usage, but the Alabama, who constituted part of the Creek Confederation, continued to wear silver rings through their noses within the remembrance of people living in 1910, or at least until a time from which a clear traditional rememberance could be transmitted. After having pierced the septum, they inserted a sharp iron, sometimes an awl, in the opening until the wound was healed when they replaced it with a silver ring. It is worthy of note that the nose and ears were usually pierced in cold weather when the parts were somewhat numb, making the pain less intense. For Koasati, Creek, and Shawnee instances, see plates 26; 33; 47, fig. 2.

We also know that the northern neighbors of the Creeks, the Cherokee, were addicted to the practice:

The Indian nations are agreed in the custom of thus adorning themselves with beads of various sizes and colours; sometimes wrought in garters, sashes, necklaces, and in strings round their wrists; and so from the crown of their heads sometimes to the cartilage of the nose. [Farther on he mentions the nose as one of the places to which the old time Indians tied] such coarse diamonds as their own hill country produced. [And again] They formerly wore *nose-rings*, or jewels, both in the northern and southern regions of America. . . . and in some places they still observe it. At present, they hang a piece of battered silver or pewter, or a large bead to the nostril, like the European method of treating swine to prevent them from rooting the earth. (Adair, 1775, pp. 178–180.)

The Cherokee in Timberlake's time wore silver pendants and rings at the nose as well as the ears (Timberlake, Williams ed., 1927, p. 76). If our authorities may be relied upon, the distribution of nose ornaments on the lower Mississippi was very peculiar, since there is no mention of them among the Natchez or Tunica or any of their immediate neighbors, but only by the Bayogoula, far down the river, and the Chitimacha, their neighbors on the west. In this last case our information, too, is recent, from Dr. Gatschet's and my informants, who said that warriors used to wear these ornaments and that they were sometimes made of gold or silver (Gatschet, 1883, pp. 5–6; Swanton, 1911, p. 345). The Bayogoula reference, on the other hand, is from the records of the first visit to this tribe by Europeans. The French observed that the natives had their noses pierced "to which there hangs a piece of coral of the size of the finger" (Margry, 1875–86, vol. 4, pp. 260–261; Swanton, 1911, p. 276). The use of these seems to have been confined to the men, as was the case with the Chitimacha. The Caddo Indians were noted for this type of ornament (Swanton, 1942, pp. 146–147).

LABRETS

The only mention of lip piercing in historic times is by Cabeza de Vaca, who reports that some of the wild tribes of the section visited by him in central and southern Texas, were in the habit of boring a hole in the lower lip and inserting a piece of cane (Cabeza de Vaca, Bandelier ed., 1905, p. 65). Certain of the coastal tribes farther east were called "Bluemouths" because they tattooed the chin, and it is possible that this particular attention paid to the lower lip was connected with the lip piercing farther west (Swanton, 1931 a, p. 57).

Anciently, however, the use of labrets may have extended along the entire Gulf coast, for Cushing reported at Key Marco, Fla.,

very large labrets of wood for the lower lips, the shanks and insertions of which were small, and placed near one edge, so that the outer disc which had been coated with varnish or brilliant thin laminae of tortoise shell, would hang low over the chin. There were lip-pins too. (Cushing, 1896, p. 374.)

NECKLACES

Four sorts of neck ornaments are mentioned, necklaces proper, collars, gorgets of shell, and gorgets of metal. The distribution of the first was most general or, at least, there are more references to this type of ornament. One recalls at once the many-stringed pearl necklace which was worn by the "Lady of Cofitachequi" when she came to meet De Soto on the Savannah River. A few weeks later the Chief of Chiaha on Tennessee River presented the Spanish governor with a long string of the same precious objects and, indeed, the use of pearl and bead necklaces extended throughout the Gulf region. (See pp. 481–489; Garcilaso, 1723, p. 140.) Pénicaut tells us that there was a sacred pearl necklace kept in the Natchez temple and that two or three pearls were tied around the necks of the infant nobles when they came into the world, and that the latter wore them until they were 10, when they were replaced in the temple (Pénicaut *in* Margry, 1875–86, vol. 5, p. 452; Swanton, 1911, p. 56). Hariot describes necklaces of pearls, beads of copper, smooth bones, or shell worn by the coast Indians of Carolina, but more particularly by the women and chiefs. These are shown in White's drawings. Often several strings were worn at once, as in the case of the Lady of Cofitachequi, and different kinds were sometimes alternated, for Hariot says that Secotan girls of good parentage wore necklaces of "rownde pearles, with little beades of copper, or polished bones betweene them." However, one, at least of the chief ladies of Secotan was supplied with a false necklace in the shape of a tattooed or painted design (Hariot, 1893, pl. 6). Similar chains of beads are mentioned by Percy, Smith, and Strachey. The weroance of Rapahanna wore such a chain when he came to meet Smith, and necklaces of this character were observed about images of the supernatural beings (Narr. Early Va., Tyler ed., 1907, pp. 14, 109; Strachey, 1849, p. 83). In later times, as is well illustrated in the pages of Beverley (1705, bk. 3, p. 7), pearls are less in evidence and there is correspondingly more said of roanoke beads, a native product of the Carolina coast, and peak or wampum, the manufacture of which was introduced from New York or New England after white contact. Beverley also speaks of "runtees," round, flat beads pierced edgewise. The name is believed to be a corruption of French *arrondi* and the manufacture of them was probably post-Columbian (Beverley, 1705, bk. 3, p. 7; Hodge, 1910, *art*. Runtee).

Necklaces made of wampum were worn by Nottoway girls in 1728 (Bassett, 1901, p. 114).

Lawson merely informs us that both men and women in the interior of the Carolinas wore necklaces made of their shell money, and Beverley's illustrations, borrowed from Michel, show them to have been in use in Monacantown. (Lawson, 1860, p. 314; Catesby, 1831–43, p. ix; Beverley, 1705.)

Some of the multiple strings of beads were probably of the kind called oktcuge' by the Alabama, which consisted of three or four strings of beads hanging down in front, the strings gathered together on each shoulder and secured about the neck by a single buckskin cord.

Speck (1909, p. 50) says that 30 years ago most of the Yuchi women were "found with strings of large round blue beads about their necks" which were said to have something to do with their fertility.

Necklaces came to be developed to an excessive degree by the Seminole as early as MacCauley's time:

My attention was called to the remarkable use of beads among these Indian women, young and old. It seems to be the ambition of the Seminole squaws to gather about their necks as many strings of beads as can be hung there and as they can carry. They are particular as to the quality of the beads they wear. They are satisfied with nothing meaner than a cut glass bead, about a quarter of an inch or more in length, generally of some shade of blue, and costing (so I was told by a trader at Miami) $.75 a pound. Sometimes, but not often, one sees beads of an inferior quality worn.

These beads must be burdensome to their wearers. In the Big Cypress Swamp settlement one day, to gratify my curiosity as to how many strings of beads these women can wear, I tried to count those worn by Young Tiger Tail's wife, number one, Mo-ki, who had come through the Everglades to visit her relatives. She was the proud wearer of certainly not fewer than two hundred strings of good sized beads. She had six quarts (probably a peck of the beads) gathered about her neck, hanging down her back, down upon her breasts, filling the space under her chin, and covering her neck up to her ears. It was an effort for her to move her head. She, however, was only a little, if any, better off in her possessions than most of the others. Others were about equally burdened. Even girl babies are favored by their proud mammas with a varying quantity of the coveted neck wear. The cumbersome beads are said to be worn by night as well as by day. (MacCauley, 1887, pp. 487–488.)

In this connection may be mentioned the bead neck bands worn by Yuchi males:

These are usually an inch in width and consist of beads strung on woof of horse hair; each bead being placed between two of the warps. Beadwork of this sort is widely used by the neighboring Sauk and Fox and Osage and it may be that we are dealing here with a borrowed idea. Not only the idea of the neckband, but also many of the decorative motives brought out on it, may possibly be traceable to Sauk and Fox or other foreign sources. The religious interests of the Yuchi are largely concerned with supernatural beings residing in the sky and clouds, so we find many of the conventional designs on these neckbands interpreted as clouds, sun, sunrise, and sunset effects, and so on. Animal representations, however, are sparingly found, while on the other hand representations of rivers, mountains, land, and earth, are quite frequent. On the whole it seems that most of the expression of the art of these Indians is to be found on their neckbands and the hair ornaments. In thus bearing the burden of conventional artistic expression in a tribe, the neckband of the Yuchi is something like the moccasin of the Plains, the pottery of the Southwest and the basketry of California. (Speck, 1909, p. 50.)

Le Moyne shows many necklaces, both simple and multiple, in his figures of Florida Indians, which in a few cases are supplemented, or supplanted, by strings passing over one shoulder and under the opposite arm. The Calusa or Tekesta chief seen by San Miguel had "strings of beads of four or six fingers in breadth" hung about his neck (Garcia, 1902, p. 210). At Key Marco Cushing found

numerous objects of personal investure and adornment . . . Aside from shell beads, pendants and gorgets, of kinds found usually in other southern relic sites, there were buttons, cord-knobs of large oliva-shells, and many little conical wooden plugs that had obviously formed the cores of tassels: [and] sliding-beads of elaborately carved deer horn—for double cords. (Cushing, 1896, p. 374.)

Some of these entered into the composition of necklaces, while others were attached to the clothing. He also noted "here and there, bunches of long, delicate, semi-translucent fish-spines" which he thought "indicated use either as necklaces or wristlets" (Cushing, 1896, p. 376).

Single or multiple strings of beads were also worn on the Mississippi, but little is said of them by our principal authorities, and many of them, even in their time, were composed of trade beads.

Some neck ornaments fitted so closely that they might rather be called collars. It is not always easy to separate the collar from the necklace, as for instance when Ribault describes "a pearl hanging to a collar of gold" about the neck of a Timucua Indian (French, 1875, p. 178; Swanton, 1922, p. 350). Timberlake (Williams ed., 1927, p. 76) tells us that Cherokee who could afford it wore "a collar of wampum," and Bartram (1792, p. 501) also enumerates "a collar about the neck" among Creek ornaments, a true collar in this case, if the frontispiece of his work may be relied upon (see pl. 31, fig. 2), but nothing of the sort is to be found in the writings of Adair or those who have discussed the Mississippi tribes. By the Alabama Indians this object was called wa'tàga.

Gorgets constitute a special type of necklace. They were sometimes of shell, sometime of metal, and probably sometimes of stone or other material, but we have references in the literature to the first two only.

In describing "an Indian in his Summer Dress," Beverley (1705, bk. 3, pp. 3–4) says, "at his Breast is a Tablet or fine Shell, smooth as Polish'd Marble, which sometimes also has etched on it, a Star, Half Moon, or other Figure, according to the maker's fancy." Beverley's figure is adapted from Hariot (1893, p. 38), but the original contains no gorget nor the accompanying text mention of any.

Lawson remarks, in introducing the subject of Indian shell money:

They oftentimes make, of this shell, a sort of gorge, which they wear about their neck in a string; so it hangs on their collar, whereon sometimes is engraven a cross, or some odd sort of figure, which comes next in their fancy. There are other sorts valued at a doe skin, yet the gorges will sometimes sell for three or four buck skins ready dressed. There be others, that eight of them go readily for a doe skin. (Lawson, 1860, p. 315.)

And Catesby:

The military men especially, wear at their breasts a concave shell, cut to the form of, tho' somewhat less than a gorget; this is an universal decoration with all the *Indians* of the northern continent; and as all their mechanism, for want of good tools, is performed with great labour, so these gorgets bear a great price in proportion to their largeness and carving. (Catesby, 1731–43, vol. 2, p. IX.)

Spark speaks of "vnicornes hornes" worn by Timucua Indians about their necks, and these may have been in the nature of shell gorgets, or else were of bone, as the name would seem to indicate (Hakluyt, 1847–89, vol. 3, p. 616; Swanton, 1922, p. 351). A shell gorget was worn by the Chickasaw high priest, and shell gorgets were remembered as late as 1910 by one of my Creek informants who had lived in Alabama before the removal. At any rate the Natchez furnish us with one clear case of the use of them on the lower Mississippi in historic times.

Dumont de Montigny says,

The savages also wear on their necks plates about 3 or 4 inches in diameter, made of pieces of this shell (burgau), which they shape in the same manner on stones and to which they give a round or oval shape. They then pierce them near the edge by means of fire and use them as ornaments. (Dumont, 1753, vol. 1, p. 95; Swanton, 1911, p. 55.)

Numbers of these have been obtained in the Gulf region in the course of archeological investigation, particularly in the Caddo country and around the southern Appalachians.

Possibly metal gorgets may have displaced in part the ones made of shell. At any rate, more references to them have come down to us. In many cases, however, the reference is so general that it is impossible to tell whether we are dealing with a single metal plate or a number of them. They shade into necklaces composed of metallic beads. Hariot figures a woman of Roanoac wearing a copper gorget, and Barlowe says that one of the Indian men of that region bought a tin dish and promptly hung it before his breast as a breastplate (Hariot, 1893, pl. 7; Burrage, 1906, p. 232). Probably this was intended as an ornament rather than for defence, though Le Moyne (1875, p. 8) mentions among the Timucua "circular plates of gold and silver as large as a moderately-sized platter, such as they are accustomed to wear to protect the back and breast in war." They were usually, of course, of copper, the gold and silver having been obtained from wrecked Spanish vessels, and, moreover, it is doubtful whether they were actually used as armor though armor of another type was in use. However, both the text and the illustrations of our Florida authorities show that metal gorgets were much in vogue. They are usually represented as round, while the smaller metal ornaments are more often oval. In one plate Le Moyne represents an Indian wearing two gorgets one over the other. Occasionally several plates of a smaller size were used at the same time, and I was given to understand by an Alabama informant that these were sometimes allowed to fall in front, one from each shoulder, with cross bars between. Alabama men used to hang several around their necks by means of a silk handkerchief. References to metal gorgets farther west seem to be few except for a tradition regarding such objects reported to Gatschet by the Chitimacha (Swanton, 1911, p. 345). A modern Natchez informant affirmed that silver charms in the shape of the sun or moon were formerly worn about the neck.

One interesting type of metal breast ornament had a crescent shape. Sometimes only one was worn and sometimes several, in which case they might be of equal size or the lower ones might be successively smaller. Many Creek and Seminole chiefs and other men of note illustrated in the collection of McKenney and Hall are represented wearing them. My Alabama informants stated that they had been obtained from the Choctaw, but "silver crescents or gorgets" were observed among the Creeks and Cherokee by Bartram, and "copper crescents" are enumerated among Virginia ornaments by Strachey (1849, p. 66).

In MacCauley's time silver disks seem to have been worn more by Seminole women than by men:

Conspicuous among the other ornaments worn by women are silver disks, suspended in a curve across the shirt fronts, under and below the beads. As many as ten or more are worn by one woman. These disks are made by men, who may be called "jewelers to the tribe," from silver quarters and half dollars. The pieces of money are pounded quite thin, made concave, pierced with holes, and ornamented by a groove lying just inside the circumference. Large disks made from half dollars may be called "breast shields." They are suspended, one over each breast. Among the disks other ornaments are often suspended. One young woman I noticed gratifying her vanity with not only eight disks made of silver quarters, but also with three polished copper rifle shells, one bright brass thimble, and a buckle hanging among them. (MacCauley, 1887, p. 488.)

Metal crescents, however, were an article of male attire:

The ornaments worn by the men which are most worthy of attention, are crescents, varying in size and value. These are generally about five inches long, an inch in width at the widest part, and of the thickness of ordinary tin. These articles are also made from silver coins and are of home manufacture. They are worn suspended from the neck by cords, in the cusps of the crescents, one below another, at distances apart of perhaps two and a half inches. (MacCauley, 1887, p. 489.)

BRACELETS AND ARM BANDS

Bracelets appear in two of White's drawings, the wearers being chiefs, but the men do not have arm bands. Mention of "bracelets" in the text does not necessarily mean the use of wrist ornaments since, in the sixteenth century, the word was used for strings of beads in general. In these two cases, however, the text specifies "bracelets on their armes." In one place the writer goes on to explain that they were made "of pearles, or small beades of copper or of smoothe bone called minsal" (Beverley, 1705, pls. 5, 6; Hariot, 1893, pl. 3). In 1728 Nottoway girls were observed to wear bracelets of wampum. Beverley's references to bracelets are perhaps derived from Hariot. Lederer remarked copper ornaments on the arms of the Tuscarora women, and there is little reason to doubt that the ancient Siouans wore bracelets as well, but Lawson merely mentions "bracelets made of brass, and sometimes of iron wire," European importations, as if their use might have been recent (Alvord, 1912, p. 162; Lawson, 1860, p. 314). Le Moyne figures bracelets of beads and metal disks on certain Florida chiefs, and bead bracelets on two women of high rank. He also shows chiefs wearing arm bands of the same types just above the elbow and also above the biceps. The metal disks are fastened at intervals on leather straps encircling the limb. In his text Le Moyne notes, also, the use of "bracelets of fishes' teeth" (Le Moyne, 1875, p. 2; Swanton, 1922, p. 349).

San Miguel in 1595 saw strings of beads adorning the wrists and upper arms of Guale Indians and those of the Calusa (or Tekesta) chief (Garcia, 1902, pp. 194, 210). Among the ornamental objects found at Key Marco, Cushing noted "one superb little brooch, scarcely more than in inch in width, made of hard wood, in representation of an angle-fish, the round spots on its back inlaid with minute discs of tortoise shell, the bands of the diminutive tail delicately and realistically incised, and the mouth, and a longitudinal eyelet as delicately incut into the lower side." Also, as above, there were "bunches of long, delicate, semi-transparent fish-spines" which he thought might have been necklaces or wristlets (Cushing, 1896, pp. 374, 376).

On Savannah River, in the mortuary house of Cofitachequi, De Soto's followers found a number of dead bodies on which there were pearl bracelets (Bourne, 1904, vol. 2, p. 100). Timberlake (Williams ed., 1927, pp. 75–76) says that the Cherokee wore bracelets on their arms and wrists, which seems to indicate that they had both bracelets and armbands. Similarly Bartram (1792, p. 501) informs us that both Creeks and Cherokee arms "are ornamented with silver bands, or bracelets, and silver and gold chains." An Alabama informant seemed to think that armbands (sakbátka') were used by men and bracelets (istá'lbài'ká) by women, but my best Creek informant spoke as if they were employed by both sexes indifferently. Adair (1775, p. 170) mentions strings of beads worn around their wrists by the Chickasaw and apparently by persons of both sexes.

MacCauley says of the Seminole Indians seen by him in Florida 60 years ago:

Silver wristlets are used by the men for their adornment. They are fastened about the wrists by cords or thongs passing through holes in the ends of the metal. (MacCauley, 1887, p. 489.)

It seems probable that bead bracelets and armbands were used extensively on the lower Mississippi, yet there are very few references to them. Du Pratz, for instance, while failing to assert specifically that bead bracelets were worn, says that young men sometimes

put on bracelets made of the ribs of deer which they have worked down very thin and bent in boiling water. These bracelets are as white and smooth as polished ivory outside. (Le Page du Pratz, 1758, vol. 2, pp. 197–198; Swanton, 1911, p. 55.)

From the Journal of Le Marin, we learn that the Bayogoula wore quantities of rings (manilles) around their arms (Margry, 1875–86, vol. 4, pp. 169–170; Swanton, 1911, p. 276). Gatschet was told that the Chitimacha men and women both used bracelets and that some of these were hammered out of copper (Gatschet, 1861, pp. 5–6; Swanton, 1911, p. 345).

FINGER RINGS

Copper rings have been found on archeological sites dating from pre-Columbian times, and Adair, in commenting on the wearing of both earrings and finger rings says "they followed the like custom before they became acquainted with the English." In his time the favorite materials seem to have been brass and silver (Adair, 1775, pp. 170–171). Finger rings are mentioned by Gatschet's Chitimacha informants and by my own native informants, but are absent from the drawings of both White and Le Moyne (Gatschet, 1861, pp. 5–6; Swanton, 1911, p. 345). Creek rings consisted of a shield welded on to the ring proper. Their name for a ring was stinge wī'sakx pàdì'ka, while the Alabama called it ï'lbĭ sàwa'tàli à'lbïta. Several Yuchi rings, evidently of the same type as those of the Creek and Alabama

Indians, are illustrated by Speck (1909, p. 51). Fifty years ago MacCauley found few finger rings among the Florida Seminole. All he did see were made of silver and showed good workmanship.

Most of them were made with large elliptical tablets on them, extending from knuckle to knuckle. These also were home made. (MacCauley, 1887, p. 489.)

LEG ORNAMENTS

Most Southeastern Indians wore leggings at times, and beaded garters, made of bison hair, opossum hair, or other material, were constant accompaniments of these. Beaded strings were worn by Chickasaw women in the same place, though their functions were ornamental and magical (see p. 449).

Strings of beads seem sometimes to have been worn by men even without their leggings. The only case of the kind in Virginia and the Carolinas is the ornamentation indicated by White on the "Idol Kiwasa" (Hariot, 1893, pl. 21). (See pl. 92 herein.) Le Moyne shows strings of beads and strings of copper disks worn in this place by Floridians of both sexes, without leggings or other clothing under them. In one case he shows a string of beads worn just above the knee, and in two or three cases men and women appear wearing true anklets. These anklets never consist of metal plates, perhaps because they would have interfered too much in walking. As has always been said, we must not place too much reliance on Le Moyne's illustrations, but in the latitude of Florida, where much of the clothing could be dispensed with, there were correspondingly more opportunities for ornamentation of both arms and legs.

We may add here the testimony of San Miguel, who describes Don Luis, the Calusa—or possibly, Tekesta—chief as coming to meet his party with his body adorned with strings of beads of four or six fingers in breadth "hung about his neck, his biceps, his wrists, under his knees, above his ankle bones, and on his ankles" (Garcia, 1902, p. 210). He observed similar ornaments in use among the Guale Indians (Garcia, 1902, p. 194).

The only ornaments in any way resembling anklets described among the tribes farther west were the terrapin shells containing pebbles which Creek women and women of many other nations adopted during the dances.

ORNAMENTATION OF BELTS AND OTHER ARTICLES OF CLOTHING

The belt was very frequently made to combine decorative with utilitarian functions like the head band or necklace. Le Moyne (1875, p. 14) indicates what looks like a bead or pearl belt worn for purely ornamental purposes, and he both illustrates and mentions in his text girdles hung with little oval balls of gold, silver, and brass, which made a tinkling sound as the wearer moved. An earlier use of copper may be assumed. Such girdles were seen by Iberville worn by young Houma men and women. (Margry, 1875–86, vol. 4, pp. 175–176; Swanton, 1911, p. 286.) The Chickasaw women of Adair's time had leather belts covered with brass runners or buckles, and he mentions beaded sashes (Adair, 1775, pp. 8, 178). Gatschet was told that the Chitimacha wore copper ornaments about their waists, referring, of course, to their belts (Gatschet, 1861, pp. 5–6; Swanton, 1911, p. 345).

Le Moyne's drawings show metal danglers fastened to strings, which were tied to the lower borders of the breechclouts worn by Timucua chiefs. The breechclout of these Indians seems, however, to have been misconceived by the illustrator, and it is possible that the danglers were fastened to the belt rather than to the breechclout itself.

Mention has been made of "buttons, cord-knobs of large oliva-shells, and many little conical wooden plugs that had obviously formed the cores of tassels" found by Cushing at Key Marco. He adds the following paragraphs regarding the ornamentation of clothing:

The remains of fringes and of elaborate tassels, made from finely spun cords of the cotton-tree down—dyed, in one case green, in another yellow—betokened high skill in such decorative employment of cordage. . . . Collections of giant sea-crab claws, still mottled with the red, brown, orange, yellow and black colors of life, looked as though they had been used as fringe-rattles and ornaments combined, for the decoration of kilts. At all events their resemblance to the pendants shown as attached to the loin-cloth of a man, in one of the early paintings of Florida Indians preserved in the British Museum, was perfect. . . .

Certain delicate plates of pinna-shell, and others of tortoise-shell, square—though in some cases longer than broad—were pierced to facilitate attachment, and appeared to have been used as dress ornaments. Still other similar plates of these various materials, as well as smaller, shaped pieces of differing forms, seemed to have been inlaid, for they were worn only on one side, the outer, and a few retained traces of black gum on the backs or unworn sides. (Cushing, 1896, p. 376.)

In later times, after the introduction of European materials for clothing, silver disks were fastened to the fronts of garments which were to be worn on festive occasions, and also to the belt or sash.

The moccasins were ornamented with beads, but not to the extent common in the North and on the Plains. Before white contact, ornamentation of moccasins was probably much more restricted than in later times. The De Soto chroniclers mention no ornamentation applied here except the use of dyes. Adair (1775, p. 171) includes moccasins among those garments to which native stones were tied by way of ornament.

In describing the costume of a Virginia Indian, Beverley says:

His Apron [i. e., breechclout] is made of a Deer-skin, gashed about the edges, which hang like Tassels or Fringe; at the upper end of the Fringe is an edging of Peak, to make it finer. (Beverley, 1705, bk. 3, p. 4.)

MacCauley says of the Florida Seminole in 1880–81,

Belts, and turbans too, are often ornamented with fanciful devices wrought out of silver. It is not customary for the Indian men to wear these ornaments in every-day camp life. They appear with them on festival occasion or when they visit some trading post. (MacCauley, 1887, p. 489.)

The Yuchi sashes correspond to this. Speck describes them as

made of woolen yarn. The simplest of these consists merely of a bunch of strands twisted together and wrapped at the ends. A loose knot holds the sash about the waist. But the characteristic sash of the southeastern tribes, and one much in favor with the Yuchi, is more complex in its makeup, and quite attractive in effect, the specimens I have seen being for the most part knitted. The sashes of the Yuchi seem to be uniformly woven with yarn of a dark red color. Some specimens, however, show an admixture of blue or yellow, or both. The main feature is a dark red ground for the white beads which are strung on the weft. Figures of triangles and lozenges or zigzags are attractively produced by the white beaded outlines and the conventional design produced is called "bull snake." The sash is tied about the waist so that the fixed tassels fall from one hip and the tassels at the knotted end depend from the other. Customarily the tassels reach to the knee. The sash is a mark of distinction, to a certain extent, as it was worn in former times by full-grown men. Nowadays, however, it is worn in ball games and upon ceremonial occasions by the participants in general, though only as regalia. (Speck, 1909, pp. 48–49.)

Yuchi women's belts, however,

were made of leather or trade cloth and had bead embroidery decorations representing in general the same range of objects as the neckbands and hair ornaments. Such belts were usually about two inches wide. (Speck, 1909, p. 50.)

MacCauley thus describes the ornamentation on the later store clothing worn by the Florida Seminole:

The clothing of both men and women is ordinarily more or less ornamented. Braids and strips of cloth of various colors are used and wrought upon the garments into odd and sometimes quite tasteful shapes. The upper parts of the shirts of the women are usually embroidered with yellow, red, and brown braids. Sometimes as many as five of these braids lie side by side, parallel with the upper edge of the garment or dropping into a sharp angle between the shoulders. Occasionally a very narrow cape, attached, I think, to the shirt, and much ornamented with braids or stripes, hangs just over the shoulders and back. The same kinds of material used for ornamenting the shirt are also used in decorating the skirt above the lower edge of the petticoat. The women embroider along this edge, with their braids and the narrow colored stripes, a border of diamond and square shaped figures, which is often an elaborate decoration to the dress. In like manner many of the shirts of the men are made pleasing to the eye. I saw no ornamentation in curves: it was always in straight lines and angles. (MacCauley, 1887, p. 487.)

GREASING AND COLORING OF THE HAIR AND SKIN

In Virginia the Indians painted their heads and shoulders red "with the roote *Pocone* braied to powder mixed with oyle; this they hold in somer to preserve them from the heate, and in winter from the cold" (Smith, John, Tyler ed., 1907, p. 100). Much more complete is Strachey's description of the materials with which they anointed the body:

They are generally of a cullour browne or rather tawny, which they cast themselves into with a kind of arsenick stone, like red patise or orpement, or rather red tempered oyntments of earth, and the juyce of certaine scrused rootes, when they caome unto certaine yeares, and this they doe (keeping themselves still so smudged and besmeered) eyther for the custome of the countrye, or the better to defend them (since they goe most that naked) from the stinging of muskitoes, kinds of flies or biting gnatts, such as the Greekes called scynipes [see also Bassett, 1901, p. 276] . . . but as the men, so doe the women, dye and disguise themselves into this tawny cowler, esteeming yt the best beauty to be neerest such a kynd of murrey as a sodden quince is of (to liken yt to the neerest coulor I can), for which they daily anoint both face and bodyes all over with such a kind of fucus or unguent as can cast them into that stayne, . . . he or she that hath obteyned the perfectest art in the tempering of this collour with any better kind of earth, yearb, or root, preserves yt not yet so secrett and pretious unto her self as doe our great ladyes their oyle of talchum, or other painting white and redd, but they frindly comunicate the secret, and teach yt one another; after their anoynting (which is daylie) they dry in the sun, and thereby make their skynnes (besides the coulor) more black and spotted, which the sun kissing oft and hard, adds to their painting the more rough and rugged.

Their heads and shoulders they paint oftenest, and those red, with the roote pochone, brayed to powder, mixed with oyle of the walnutt, or bear's grease; this they hold in sommer doth check the heat, and in winter armes them in some measure against the cold. (Strachey, 1849, p. 64.)

Farther on he states of the men that they shaved the hair off on the right side of the head but "on the left side they weare theire haire at full length, with a lock of an ell long, which they annoint often with walnut oyle, whereby it is very sleeke, and shynes like a raven's winge" (Strachey, 1849, p. 66).

Beverley has a still longer account of the use of the pocone or puccoon roots:

The *Indians* also pulverize the Roots of a kind of *Anchuse* or yellow *Alkanet*, which they call *Puccoon*, and of a sort of wild *Angelica*, and mixing them together with Bears Oyl, make a yellow Ointment, with which, after they have bath'd, they anoint themselves Capapee; this supples the Skin, renders them nimble and active, and withal so closes up the Pores, that they lose but few of their Spirits by Perspiration. *Piso* relates the same of the *Brasilians*, and my Lord *Bacon* asserts, that Oyl and fat things do no less conserve the substance of the Body, than Oyl colours, and Varnish do that of the Wood.

They have also a further advantage of this Oyntment, for it keeps all Lice, Fleas, and other troublesome Vermine from coming near them; which otherwise, by reason of the nastiness of their Cabbins, they would be very much infested with.

Smith talks of this Puccoon, as if it grew on the Mountains, whereas it is common to all the Plantations of the English, except only to those situated in very low Grounds. (Beverley, 1705, bk. 3, p. 52.)

Lawson gives us a very naive account of the use of bear's grease and red hair dye among the Piedmont tribes of the Carolinas:

[The color of the Indians] is of a tawny, which would not be so dark did they not dawb themselves with bear's oil, and a color like burnt cork. This is begun in their infancy and continued for a long time, which fills the pores and enables them better to endure the extremity of the weather. They are never bald on their heads, although never so old, which, I believe, proceeds from their heads being always uncovered, and the greasing their hair so often as they do, with bear's fat, which is a great nourisher of the hair, and causes it to grow very fast. Amongst the bear's oil, when they intend to be fine, they mix a certain red powder, that comes from a scarlet root which they get in the hilly country, near the foot of the great ridge of mountains, and it is no where else to be found. They have this scarlet root in great esteem, and sell it for a very great price one to another. The reason of its value is, because they not only go a long way for it but are in great danger of the Sinnagers or Iroquois, who are mortal enemies to all our Indians, and very often take them captives or kill them before they return from this voyage. The Tuskeruros and other Indians have often brought this seed with them from the mountains; but it would never grow in our land. With this and bear's grease they anoint their heads and temples, which is esteemed as ornamental, as sweet powder to our hair. Besides, this root has the virtue of killing lice, and suffers none to abide or breed in their heads. For want of this root, they sometimes use pecoon root, which is of a crimson color, but it is apt to die the hair of an ugly hue. (Lawson, 1860, p. 281; also see Catesby, 1731–43, vol. 2, p. ix.)

In preparation for a war expedition they did their hair over very much with bear's grease and this red dye (Lawson, 1860, p. 313).

They can color their hair black, though some times it is reddish, which they do with the seed of a flower that grows commonly in their plantations. I believe this would change the reddest hair into perfect black. (Lawson, 1860, p. 358.)

The Timucua Indians of Florida kept their bodies covered with bear grease, to which Laudonnière assigns some ceremonial function and also considers a means of protection from the sun's heat (Laudonnière, 1586, p. 12; Swanton, 1922, p. 352).

In his later paper on the southern Indians, in which he has reference particularly to the Cherokee and Creeks, Bartram says:

There is one remarkable circumstance respecting the hair of the head of the Indians, which I do not know to have been observed by travellers or historians. Besides the lankness, extraordinary natural length, and perhaps coarseness of the hair of the head, it is of a shining black or brown color, showing the same splendor and changeableness at different exposures to the light. The traders informed me that they preserved its perfect blackness and splendor by the use of the red farinaceous or fursy covering of the berries of the common sumach (Rhus glabra). Over night they rub this red powder in their hair, as much as it will contain, tying it up close with a handkerchief till morning, when they carefully comb it out and dress their hair with clear bears' oil. (Bartram, 1909, pp. 29–30.)

The roots of a plant called tali'wa or tale'wa, perhaps the red root, were used for the same purpose. Gatschet says of this, it is

a plant growing 1 to 2 feet high on sandy soil, with yellow flower. When the roots are fried in oil, the color of the oil changes to a beautiful, brilliant red of the claret hue and is used among other things to make hair oil. (Gatschet, ms. Creek vocab.)

They got these roots from a place near the Natchez town among the Upper Creeks.

Adair (1775, p. 4), in treating of the customs of his savage neighbors, mainly Chickasaw, speaks of "their constant anointing themselves with bear's oil, or grease, mixt with a certain red root." And regarding bear grease, he goes into more detail:

All the Indian Americans, especially the female sex, reckon their bear's oil or grease very valuable, and use it after the same manner as the Asiatics did their fine essences and sweet perfumes; the young warriors and women are uneasy, unless their hair is always shining with it; which is probably the reason that none of their heads are bald. (Adair, 1775, p. 129.)

Mention of the use of even bear grease on the hair is conspicuously absent from accounts of the lower Mississippi Indians, and Gravier says of the Tunica:

Neither men nor women grease or oil their hair like all our Canadian Indians, but this is perhaps from lack of both, bear and deer meat being very rare in their village as well as [the flesh of] all other beasts. (Shea, 1861, p. 734; Swanton, 1911, p. 316.)

However, scarcity was not sufficiently marked to account by itself for the absence of this practice.

The Caddo greased their hair like the northern Indians and, in preparation for feasts, put reddened swans' down or ducks' down upon their heads (Joutel *in* Margry, 1875–86, vol. 3, p. 413), but there is a complete absence of references to the use of body grease as distinct from paint.

BODY PAINT

Body paint was resorted to particularly in preparing for war and ball games, but was part of a man's make-up on all official or semiofficial occasions. Red is the color mentioned most often, and red paint was quite uniformly obtained by heating ochrous earths. Red body paint was in use among the Timucua Indians about Tampa Bay when De Soto's army landed, and it is constantly mentioned by later writers. Bartram (1791, p. 501) states that the head, neck, and breast of the Indians of his acquaintance (Creeks, Seminole, and Cherokee) were painted with vermilion. Adair (1775, p. 171) speaking particularly of the Chickasaw, mentions the amount of this as one of the criteria on which the traders based their estimate of a man's wealth, thus suggesting that it had some social significance.

If we may judge by references in the literature, black was the color most in evidence after red. This was, perhaps, because of its extensive use in mourning. Elvas noted it among the colors used by Alabama warriors, Spark observed it in Florida, Hariot in Carolina, Percy and Beverley in Virginia, and the author of the Luxembourg Memoir on the lower Mississippi. (Robertson, 1933, p. 153; Hakluyt, 1847–89, vol. 3, p. 615; Hariot, 1893, pl. 21; Narr. Early Va., Tyler ed., 1907, p. 12; Beverley, 1705, bk. 2, p. 23; Swanton, 1911, p. 54.)

Yellow was noted among paints employed by the Alabama Indians, among the Florida Indians, and among those of Virginia. Spark observed a color in Florida which he calls "russet." (Robertson, 1933, p. 153; Hakluyt, 1947–89, vol. 3, p. 615; Swanton, 1922, p. 352; Beverley, 1705, bk. 3, p. 52.)

Blue is mentioned by the author of the Luxembourg Memoir among paints in use on the Mississippi, and Percy tells us that the Rappahannock chief appeared in state with his face painted blue and sprinkled with something that looked like silver ore (Swanton, 1911, p. 54; Narr. Early Va., Tyler ed., 1907, pp. 12–13). While there seems to be no reason why the Indians should not have obtained blue pigments as well as red, black, and white, the paucity of the references leads us to wonder whether there may not have been confusion here between paint and tattooing, since the soot used in tattooing always gives a dark blue color.

One of our earliest Virginia references is by Percy, who says of the Powhatan Indians which he met:

Some paint their bodies blacke, some red, with artificiall knots of sundry lively colours, very beautiful and pleasing to the eye, in a braver fashion than they in the West Indies. (Narr. Early Va., Tyler ed., 1907, p. 12.)

And Strachey remarks:

Of the men, there be some whoe will paint their bodyes black, and some yellowe, and being oyled over, they will sticke therein the soft downe of sundry couloured birdes of blew birds, white herne shewes, and the feathers of the carnation birde, which they call Ashshawcutteis [perhaps the red-start], as of so many variety of laces were stitched to their skinns, which makes a wondrous shew; then, being angry and prepared to fight, paint and crosse their foreheads, cheekes, and the right side of their heades diversly, either with terra sigillata or with their roote pochone. (Strachey, 1849, p. 66.)

Hariot observes of the North Carolina coast Indians that "They ether pownes, or paynt their forehead, cheeks, chynne, bodye, armes, and leggs, yet in another sorte then the inhabitants of Florida." But he states that the chief men of Roanoke neither painted nor tattooed (Hariot, 1893, pls. 3, 7).

In Lawson's time the Siouan Indians were accustomed to

buy vermillion of the Indian traders, wherewith they paint their faces all over red, and commonly make a circle of black about one eye and another circle of white about the other, whilst others bedawb their faces with tobacco pipe clay, lamp black, black lead, and divers other colors, which they make with the several sorts of minerals and earths that they get in different parts of the country, where they hunt and travel. (Lawson, 1860, pp. 312–313; and see above p. 527.)

The Keyauwee Indians painted their faces with lead ore obtained in "the neighboring mountains," which Rights has identified with the Carraway Mountains in central North Carolina (Lawson, 1860, p. 88; Rights, 1931, p. 415).

Lederer discovered one source of red paint in mountains near the Sara or Cheraw country close to Yadkin River, and located by Rights in Moore County.

The Indians draw great quantities of cinnabar, with which beaten to powder they colour their faces: this mineral is of a deeper purple than vermilion, and is the same which is in so much esteeme amongst physicians, being the first element of quicksilver. (Alvord, 1912, p. 158.)

Of the special patterns used at certain times or by certain persons we have some examples in the illustrations in the work of McKenney and Hall, but the significance of few of these is known.

At the town of the Occaneechi near Clarksville, Va., Lederer met "four stranger-Indians, whose bodies were painted in various colours with figures of animals whose likeness I had never seen" (Alvord, 1912, p. 154).

One is surprised to learn that, among the Indians of Virginia and Carolina, if we may trust Lawson and Beverley, women made no use of paint, and, speaking of the Creeks, Bartram tells us that the women "never paint, except those of a particular class, when disposed to grant certain favors to the other sex." (Lawson, 1860, p. 313; Beverley, 1705, bk. 3, pp. 6–7; Bartram, 1792, p. 501.) In relatively modern times, at least, Alabama women, when dressing for the dances, put small spots of red, or sometimes of yellow, on their cheeks. They are also said to have blackened the upper lip with charcoal.

What Bartram says of abstinence from paint by Creek women is confirmed by Speck for the Yuchi:

The only use ever made of paint in the case of women seems to have been to advertise the fact that they were unmarried. Women of various ages are now, however, observed with paint, and it is generally stated that no significance is attached to it. One informant gave the above information in regard to the past use of paint among women and thought that to wear it was regarded then as a sign of willingness to grant sexual privileges. The woman's pattern consists simply of a circular spot in red, about one inch across, on each cheek. (Speck, 1909, p. 53.)

On the other hand, we have positive evidence that paint was used considerably by women of the Caddo (Swanton, 1942, pp. 144-145), the lower Mississippi tribes, and those of Florida.

Speck supplies us with a little information regarding patterns used by the Yuchi men at a late period:

There are four or five patterns for men and they indicate which of two societies, namely the Chief or the Warrior society, the wearer belongs to . . . Although the privilege of wearing certain of these patterns is inherited from the father, young men are not, as a rule, entitled to use them until they have been initiated into the town and can take a wife. Face painting is an important ceremonial decoration and is scrupulously worn at ceremonies, public occasions and ball games. A man is also decorated with his society design for burial. (Speck, 1909, pp. 52-53.)

Although there exists no strictly regular design for the facial decoration of a Chief, yet the following limitations are traditionally observed. Little or no black is used, both eyes are surrounded with red, and usually on each cheek alternating bars, less than two inches long, of blue and yellow are laid horizontally. Frequently three small blue spots are placed in a line between the corner of the eye and the temple. Any of these markings may be omitted or varied to suit personal fancy, yet the characteristics are prominently retained. The young child members of the Chief society, who have not yet been formally initiated to the band, are usually decorated with red on the eyebrows, cheeks and forehead. It is asserted that this society has the privilege of exercising more freedom in the use of various colors than the Warrior society . . . The characteristic pattern [of the latter] . . . is to have one half of the face red, the other black. A variation of this pattern, said to be a simplification, is to paint only one eye socket black and the other red. Accompanying this modification the upper lip is often blackened. (Speck, 1909, p. 76.)

Red, yellow, and white earths used as body paint were obtained at the Chickasaw bluffs on the Mississippi, and red ocher was brought from the White Bluff near Natchez (Swanton, 1911, p. 62).

John Spark states of the Florida Indians that:

"In their warres they vse a sleighter colour of painting their faces [than tattooing], thereby to make themselves shew the more fierce; which after their warres ended, they wash away againe. [He adds that the colors were] red, blacke, yellow, and russet, very perfect." (Hakluyt, 1847-89, vol. 3, p. 613; Swanton, 1922, pp. 351-352.)

Laudonnière notes that these Indians put much paint upon their faces when they went to war, and this was evidently their custom when they met strangers because, when Ribault crossed the St. Johns River to revisit Indians met before, he found them "waiting for us quietly, and in good order, with new paintings upon their faces, and feathers upon their heads." (Laudonnière, 1586, p. 9; French, 1875, p. 178; Swanton, 1922, pp. 351-352.) Le Moyne observes that they were "in the habit of painting the skin around their mouths of a blue color" (Le Moyne, 1875, p. 8, 15; Swanton, 1922, p. 352).

San Miguel notes that the neighboring Indians of Guale daubed paint on their faces, breasts, biceps, and thighs (Garcia, 1902, p. 194).

TATTOOING

But if the women of aboriginal Virginia and Carolina were not much addicted to paint, the reason is perhaps to be found in a desire not to obscure the elaborate designs more permanently imprinted upon their skins by means of tattooing instruments. At all events, what they lacked in the way of paint was abundantly compensated for in tattooed designs.

Beginning with Percy, who wrote in the year when Virginia was founded, we read:

> The women kinde in this Countrey doth pounce and race their bodies, legges, thighes, armes, and faces with a sharpe Iron, which makes a stampe in curious knots, and drawes the proportion of Fowles, Fish, or Beasts; then with paintings of sundry lively colours, they rub it into the stampe which will never be taken away, because it is dried into the flesh where it is sered. (Narr. Early Va., Tyler ed., 1907, p. 19.)

Says Smith:

> Their women some have their legs, hands, breasts, and face cunningly imbroidered with diverse workes, as beasts, serpentes, artificially wrought into their flesh with blacke spots. (Narr. Early Va., Tyler ed., 1907, p. 100.)

And Strachey, as usual, elaborates the statement:

> The women have their armes, breasts, thighes, shoulders, and faces, cunningly ymbroidered with divers workes, for pouncing or searing their skyns with a kind of instrument heated in the fier. They figure therein flowers and fruits of sondry lively kinds, as also snakes, serpents, eftes, &c., and this they doe by dropping uppon the seared flesh sondry coulers, which, rub'd into the stampe, will never be taken away agayne, because yt will not only be dryed into the flesh, but growe therein. (Strachey, 1849, p. 66.)

Hariot has already been quoted regarding the paintings and tattooings of the Carolina coast Indians. Regarding Roanoke women, he says: "Their foreheads, cheeks, chynne, armes and leggs are pownced. About their necks they wear a chaine, either pricked or paynted." Below he adds that the girls also "pounce their foreheads, cheeckes, armes and legs." The "chief ladies" of the town of Pomeioc were also tattooed. The tattooings of the women of Dasemonquepeuc, a town 4 or 5 miles from Roanoke, were similar to the above except that they did not extend to the thighs (Hariot, 1893, pls. 4, 6, 8, 10).

Although Lederer mentions face paintings and Lawson describes the use of body paint at considerable length, they ignore tattooing almost entirely, but it is improbable that it was unknown to the Siouan tribes since it was so extensively developed on all sides of them.

Indeed, Catesby, who visited many of the same tribes, although he also extended his explorations to the Chickasaw, says of the Indians he met:

Their war captains and men of distinction have usually the portrait of a serpent, or other animal, on their naked bodies; this is done by puncture and a black powder conveyed under the skin. These figures are esteemed not only as ornamental, but serve to distinguish the warriors, making them more known and dreaded by their enemies. (Catesby, 1831–43, vol. 2, p. ix.)

The best descriptions of tattooing to be had in any of the early writings are those given by Bartram having special reference to the Creeks and Cherokee. In his Travels he gives the following note:

Some of the warriors have the skin of the breast, and muscular parts of the body, very curiously inscribed, or adorned, with hieroglyphick scrolls, flowers, figures of animals, stars, crescents, and the sun in the centre of the breast. This painting of the flesh, I understand, is performed in their youth, by pricking the skin with a needle, until the blood starts, and rubbing in a bluish tint which is as permanent as their life. (Bartram, 1940, p. 394.)

In the third volume of Transactions of the American Ethnological Society, he has the following:

But the most beautiful painting now to be found among the Muscogulges, is on the skin and bodies of their ancient chiefs and *micos*, which is of a bluish, lead, or indigo color. It is the breast, trunk, muscular or fleshy part of the arms and thighs, and sometimes almost every part of the surface of the body, that is thus beautifully depicted or written over with *hieroglyphics:* commonly the sun, moon, and planets occupy the breast; zones or belts, or beautiful fanciful scrolls, wind round the trunk of the body, thighs, arms, and legs, dividing the body into many fields or tablets, which are ornamented or filled up with innumerable figures, as representations of animals or battle with their enemy, or some creature of the chase,—and a thousand other fancies. These paintings are admirably well executed, and seem to be inimitable. They are performed by exceedingly fine punctures, and seem like *mezzotinto*, or very ingenious impressions from the best executed engravings. They are no doubt hieroglyphics, or mystical writings or records of their tribes or families or of memorable events, etc., etc. (Bartram, 1853, p. 19.)

Pope (1792, p. 60) informs us that tattooing was practiced on young Creek Indians of both sexes, and he cites the case of a boy of four who bore the pain with Indian stolidity and, when released, exclaimed, "Now, I'm a man, and a warrior too."

Ribault says of the Timucua Indians of Florida:

The forepart of their bodies and arms they also paint with pretty devices in azure, red, and black, so well and properly, that the best painters of Europe could not improve upon it. (French, 1875, p. 171; Swanton, 1922, p. 351.)

And this evidently refers to tattooing because Laudonnière is plainly speaking of the same designs when he remarks:

The most part of them have their bodies, arms, and thighs painted with very fair devices, the painting whereof can never be taken away, because the same is pricked into the flesh. (Laudonnière, 1586, p. 6; Swanton, 1922, p. 351.)

Le Challeux also witnesses that "for ornament they have their skin checkered (marqueté) in a strange fashion" (Gaffarel, 1875, p. 461), and John Spark, chronicler of Hawkins' second voyage had this:

They do not omit to paint their bodies also with curious knots, or antike worke, as every man in his own fancy deuiseth, which painting, to make it continue the better, they vse with a thorne to pricke their flesh, and dent in the same, whereby the painting may have better hold (Hakluyt, 1847–89, vol. 3, p. 613; Swanton, 1922, p. 351).

Le Moyne both remarks upon the custom and illustrates it in his drawings:

The reader should be informed that all these chiefs and their wives ornament their skin with punctures arranged so as to make certain designs, as the following pictures show. Doing this sometimes makes them sick for seven or eight days. They rub the punctured places with a certain herb, which leaves an indelible color. (Le Moyne, 1875, p. 15; Swanton, 1922, p. 351.)

His pictures exhibit geometrical patterns, as well as suggestions of the scroll and flower work alluded to by Bartram. One of the chiefs has straight and curving lines passing about the body with small circles between. No representations of animals or celestial objects are, however, to be detected. Women were evidently tattooed as well as men, for in his plate 37 (pl. 85 herein) Le Moyne represents a woman tattooed in bands about the neck, upper and lower arms, breasts, chest, abdomen, and upper and lower legs. The pattern is entirely different from those on men in the same series of drawings and resembles the rain pattern so common in our Southwest. The same designs appear again on a chief's wife in Le Moyne's plate 39, perhaps merely another representation of the same person.

Adair does not describe tattooing at length, but refers to the identification of captive warriors, their rank and their exploits

by the blue marks over their breasts and arms; they being as legible as our alphabetical characters are to us. Their ink is made of the soot of pitch-pine, which sticks to the inside of a greased earthern pot; then delineating the parts, like the ancient Picts of Britain, with their wild hieroglyphics, they break through the skin with gair-fish-teeth, and rub over them that dark composition, to register them among the brave; and the impression is lasting. (Adair, 1775, p. 417.)

However, erasure of falsely obtained marking was possible:

I have been told by the Chikkasah, that they formerly erazed any false marks their warriors proudly and privately gave themselves—in order to engage them to give real proofs of their martial virtue, being surrounded by the French and their red allies; and that they degraded them in a public manner, by stretching the marked parts, and rubbing them with the juice of green corn, which in a great degree took out the impression. (Adair, 1775, p. 418.)

There happens to be no good description of tattooing among the Choctaw, but what French writers tell us of the custom probably applied to them as well as to the Indians on the lower Mississippi whom the French had more immediately under their observation.

From these writers we have three excellent descriptions of tattooing among the lower Mississippi tribes, applying more particularly to the Natchez Indians. The first is from an anonymous memoir the material in which antedates the year 1718. It is as follows:

The greater part of the Indians have fantastic marks imprinted on the face, the arms, the legs, and the thighs; as to the body, this is a right which belongs only to the warriors, and one must be noted for the death of some enemy in order to merit this distinction. They imprint on the breasts of their heroes an infinity of black, red, and blue lines; which is not done without pain. They begin by tracing the design on the skin, then with a needle or a little bone well sharpened they prick until the blood comes, following the design, after which they rub the punctures with a powder of the color that the one who has himself marked demands. These colors having penetrated between the skin and flesh are never effaced.[28] (Anon., 1752, pp. 134–135.)

The next is by Dumont de Montigny:

But the greatest ornament of all these savages of both sexes consists in certain figures of suns, serpents, or other things, which they carry pictured on their bodies in the manner of the ancient Britons, of whom Cæsar tells us in his Commentaries. The warriors, as well as the wives of the chiefs and the Honored men, have these figures pictured on the face, arms, shoulders, thighs, legs, but principally on the belly and breast. It is for them not only an ornament, but also a mark of honor and distinction, which is acquired only after many brave deeds, and this is the way in which these pictures are made: First, in accordance with the color that is desired, a man makes either a black mixture of pine charcoal or, indeed, of gunpowder dissolved in water, or a red of cinnabar or vermilion. After this five medium-sized sewing needles are taken, which are arranged on a little flat, smooth piece of wood and fastened to the same depth, so that one point does not extend out beyond the others. These needles are then soaked in the color and moved quickly, being applied lightly to the design, which had before been traced on the body, and the color insinuates itself between the skin and the flesh through these needle holes. This operation never fails to give the subject a fever, and a mange rises on the skin, which afterward dries and falls into dust, but the figure imprinted on the flesh through these needle prickings, whether in red or black, is never effaced. It is carried to the tomb. (Dumont, 1753, vol. 1, pp. 139–140; Swanton, 1911, pp. 56–57.)

Finally, let us hear Du Pratz:

From youth the women have a line tattooed across the highest part of the nose, some in the middle of the chin from above downward, others in different places, especially the women of those nations which have an r in their language [i.e., the Tunica and their allies]. I have seen some of them tattooed over the entire upper part of the body. Even the breast was tattooed all over, though this part of the body is extremely sensitive. . .

The youths also have themselves tattooed on the nose, and not elsewhere until they are warriors and have performed some valorous act. But when they have killed some enemy and have brought back his scalp, they have a right to have themselves tattooed and to adopt ornaments with figures suitable to the occasion.

These tattooings are so much in vogue among the natives that there are neither

---

[28] Swanton, 1911, p. 56; gunpowder was also adopted by the Cherokee (Timberlake, Williams ed., 1927, p. 75).

men nor women who do not have them made, but the warriors especially have taken no pains to abstain from them. Those who have signalized themselves in some important feat have a war club tattooed on the right shoulder, and beneath one sees the hieroglyphic sign of the conquered nation. The others are tattooed each according to his taste. To perform this operation they attach six needles to a flat piece of wood, well fastened three by three, so that the points do not protrude more than a line [beyond the wood]. They trace the outline of the figure with charcoal or cinders. Then they prick the skin and when they have done this over a section about two fingers in length they rub the place with fine charcoal; this powder is pressed so strongly into the punctures that they never become effaced. However simple this operation is, it inflames the body considerably, sometimes gives a fever, and makes the tattooed person extremely sick if he is not very careful while the inflammation lasts to eat nothing but corn, drink nothing but water, and keep away from women. (Le Page du Pratz, 1758, vol. 2, pp. 195–196, 198–200; Swanton, 1911, p. 57.)

Pénicaut speaks as if Caddo women of the Natchitoches tribe were less addicted to tattooing than the Muskhogean Acolapissa, but Joutel tells us that Caddo of both sexes tattooed their faces and bodies and he is abundantly supported by other writers. Joutel notes specifically that some men had figures of birds and animals tattooed on their bodies, and others zigzag lines, while the women had their breasts tattooed, and great flowers (fleurons) over their shoulders. Some women had lines made in this manner from the forehead to the chin, others triangles at the corners of the eyes, and they tattooed the lips all over. (Margry, 1875–86, vol. 3, pp. 349, 353, 363, 413; Penicaut *in* Margry, vol. 5, p. 467; Swanton, 1942, pp. 142–144.)

STAINING OF THE TEETH

French writers mention the staining of the teeth by women in tribes living along the Mississippi River. The missionary Gravier says of the Natchez women:

Most have black teeth, which are considered beautiful among them. They blacken them by chewing the ashes of tobacco mixed with wood ashes and rubbing them with this every morning. (Thwaites, 1897–1901, vol. 65, p. 145; Swanton, 1911, p. 54.)

In the course of his description of the Bayogoula Indians, a Choctaw-speaking tribe below the present Baton Rouge, Iberville remarks:

It gives the women pleasure to blacken their teeth, which they do by means of an herb crushed in wax [putty]; they remain black for a time and then become white again. (Margry, 1875–86, vol. 4, pp. 171–172; Swanton, 1911, p. 276.)

This custom is also found among a number of South America tribes, and my attention was called to the coincidence some years ago by the late Baron Erland Nordenskiöld.

TREATMENT OF FINGERNAILS AND TOENAILS

The Timucua Indians allowed their fingernails and toenails to grow long. On this point Le Moyne says:

They let their nails grow long both on fingers and toes, cutting (or scraping) the former away, however, at the sides (with a certain shell), so as to leave them very sharp, the men especially; and when they take one of the enemy they sink their nails deep in his forehead, and tear down the skin, so as to wound and blind him. (Le Moyne, 1875, p. 8, 15; Swanton, 1922, p. 352.)

This custom extended to the neighboring Guale Indians and to the southern Siouans, but, speaking of the women of the North Carolina coast, particularly those of Secotan, Hariot says, "their nayles are not longe, as the women of Florida" (Garcia, 1902, p. 193; Hariot, 1893, pl. 4).

The buzzard men and women of the Choctaw and some other tribes, whose gruesome task it was to separate the bones of the dead from their flesh, also kept their fingernails long as an aid in their profession.

HEAD DEFORMATION

Accidental occipital head flattening caused by the method in which infants were tied to the cradleboard by some tribes was widespread. Intentional head deformation also existed over a very wide area, and skulls deformed in this manner have been found by archeologists in sections from which it was absent in the historic period. Our first historical reference is by Garcilaso de la Vega in his description of a province in southern Arkansas, probably south of Hot Springs:

Both men and women have ugly faces, and though they are well proportioned they deform themselves by deliberate distortion of their persons. Their heads are incredibly long and tapering on top, being made thus artificially by binding them up from birth to the age of nine or ten years. (Garcilaso, 1723, pp. 190-191.)

Skulls have since been found on Caddo sites deformed in this manner (Walker, W. M., 1935, p. 4, pls. 1-3) but it is surprising to find that when the French entered Louisiana at the end of the seventeenth century the Caddo seem to have given up the custom, and instead it was found flourishing among the tribes along the lower Mississippi. An anonymous memoir printed at Luxemburg thus describes the process of head flattening, seemingly from observation among the Natchez:

They have . . . their heads pointed and shaped almost like miters. They are not born so; this is a charm which is given them during their early years. What a mother does to the head of her infant in order to force its tender bones to assume this shape is almost beyond belief. She lays the infant on a cradle, which is nothing more than the end of a board on which is spread a piece of animal skin; one extremity of this board has a hole in which the head is put and it is lower than the rest. The infant being laid down on this entirely naked, she pushes the back of its head into this hole and applies to it on the forehead and under the head masses of clay which she binds with all her strength between two little boards. The infant cries, turns completely black, and the strain it is made to suffer is such that a white, slimy fluid is seen to come out of its nose and ears at the time when the mother presses on its forehead. It sleeps thus every night until its skull has taken on the shape prescribed by custom. Some savages near Mobile, through our example, are beginning to give up a custom which costs so much. (Swanton, 1911, pp. 54–55.)

Du Pratz, Dumont, and other writers speak of this same usage. When Iberville visited the Houma Indians opposite the mouth of Red River, in 1699 he noticed that the chief had "a very flat forehead, although the other men of his nation do not have it, at least very few of the old men. This custom is changing among them." (Margry, 1875–86, vol. 4, p. 184; Swanton, 1911, p. 286.) From what we know of the Houma tribe, we may interpret this to mean that when they were living farther north, in their old home, head deformation was not extensively practiced, but that when Iberville paid his visit, they were gradually adopting the usage from the Natchez and other neighboring Indians.

Du Pratz, in speaking of the Natchez infant, says:

The head is placed on a little pillow of skin filled with Spanish beard, which does not extend beyond the upper part of the cradle, in such a way that the head is as low as the shoulders, and is held to this pillow by thongs which are double strips of deerskin over the forehead. It is this which makes their heads flat. (Le Page du Pratz, 1758, vol. 2, pp. 309–310; Swanton, 1911, p. 86.)

Dumont remarked that:

When their children come into the world they take care to crush and flatten the upper part of the forehead with a plank, so that when they shall have grown up they may be in better condition to bear all kinds of loads. (Dumont, 1753, vol. 1, pp. 140–141; Swanton, 1911, pp. 89–90.)

Adair is one of the earliest writers to speak of head deformation among the larger tribes of the central South:

The Indians flatten their heads, in divers forms: but it is chiefly the crown of the head they depress, in order to beautify themselves, as their wild fancy terms it; for they call us *long heads*, by way of contempt. The Choktah Indians flatten their fore-heads, from the top of the head to the eye-brows with a small bag of sand; which gives them a hideous appearance; as the forehead naturally shoots upward, according as it is flattened: thus, the rising of the nose, instead of being equidistant from the beginning of the chin, to that of the hair, is, by their wild mechanism, placed a great deal nearer to the one and farther from the other. The Indian nations, round South-Carolina, and all the way to New Mexico, . . . to effect this, fix the tender infant on a kind of cradle, where his feet are tilted, above a foot higher than a horizontal position,—his head bends back into a hole, made on purpose to receive it, where he bears the chief part of his weight on the crown of the head, upon a small bag of sand, without being in the least able to move himself. The skull resembling a fine cartilaginous substance, in its infant state, is capable of taking any impression. By this pressure, and their thus flattening the crown of the head, they consequently make their heads thick, and their faces broad: for, when the smooth channel of nature is stopped in one place, if a destruction of the whole system does not thereby ensue, it breaks out in a proportional redundancy, in another. (Adair, 1775, pp. 9–10; also p. 284.)

Romans has a brief note to the effect that:

The women disfigure the heads of their male children by means of bags of sand, flattening them into different shapes, thinking it adds to their beauty. (Romans, 1775, p. 82.)

The Choctaw in particular were widely known among the traders as "Flat Heads," and it is to them again that William Bartram's description applies:

The Choctaws are called by the traders flats, or flat-heads, all the males having the fore and hind part of their skulls artificially flattened, or compressed; which is effected after the following manner. As soon as the child is born, the nurse provides a cradle or wooden case, hollowed and fashioned, to receive the infant, lying prostrate on its back, that part of the case where the head reposes, being fashioned like a brick mould. In this portable machine the little boy is fixed, a bag of sand being laid on his forehead, which by continual gentle compression, gives the head somewhat the form of a brick from the temples upwards; and by these means they have high and lofty foreheads, sloping off backwards. (Bartram, 1792, p. 515.)

The term "flat head" was also bestowed upon the Catawba Indians and their allies, but, although I am not prepared to deny that the Catawba were given to the practice, it happens that the only description that has come down to us is from the Waxhaw tribe, near neighbors of the Catawba, and it is this tribe which the writer of this description, Lawson, says were "called by their neighbors flat heads":

In their infancy, their nurses lay the back part of their children's heads on a bag of sand, (such as engravers use to rest their plates upon.) They use a roll which is placed upon the babies forehead, it being laid with its back on a flat board, and swaddled hard down thereon, from one end of this engine to the other. This method makes the child's body and limbs as straight as an arrow, there being some young Indians that are perhaps crookedly inclined, at their first coming into the world, who are made perfectly straight by this method. I never saw an Indian of mature age that was anyways crooked, except by accident, and that way seldom; for they cure and prevent deformities of the limbs and body very exactly. The instrument I spoke of before being a sort of a press, that is let out and in, more or less, according to the discretion of the nurse, in which they make the child's head flat: it makes the eyes stand a prodigious way asunder, and the hair hang over the forehead like the eves of a house, which seems very frightful. They being asked the reason why they practiced this method, replied the Indian's sight was much strengthened and quicker thereby to discern the game in hunting at larger distance, and so never missed of becoming expert hunters, the perfection of which they all aim at, as we do to become experienced soldiers, learned school-men, or artists in mechanics. (Lawson, 1860, pp. 61–62.)

Mention of the effect of this process on the stature probably serves to explain the custom reported by Peter Martyr on the authority of Ayllon and his companions and a Siouan Indian of this general region by which children of the "royal" family were given gigantic size through a kind of postnatal manipulation.

I now come to a fact which will appear incredible to your excellency. You already know that the ruler of this region is a tyrant of gigantic size. How does it happen that only he and his wife have attained this extraordinary size? No one of their subjects has explained this to me, but I have questioned the above-mentioned licentiate Ayllon, a serious and responsible man, who had his information from those who had shared with him the cost of the expedition. I likewise questioned the servant Francisco, to whom the neighbors had spoken. Neither nature nor birth has given these princes the advantage of size as an hereditary gift; they have acquired it by artifice. While they are still in their cradles and in charge of their nurses, experts in the matter are called, who by the application of certain herbs soften their young bones. During a period of several days they rub the limbs of the child with these herbs until the bones become as soft as wax. They then rapidly bend them in such wise that the infant is almost killed. Afterwards they feed the nurse on foods of a special virtue. The child is wrapped in warm covers, the nurse gives it her breast and revives it with her milk, thus gifted with strengthening properties. After some days of rest the lamentable task of stretching the bones is begun anew. Such is the explanation given by the servant Francisco Chicorana.

The Dean of La Concepcion, whom I have mentioned, received from the Indians stolen on the vessel that was saved explanations differing from those furnished to Ayllon and his associates. These explanations dealt with medicaments and other means used for increasing the size. There was no torturing of the bones, but a very stimulating diet composed of crushed herbs was used. This diet was given principally at the age of puberty, when it is nature's tendency to develop, and sustenance is converted into flesh and bones. Certainly it is an extraordinary fact, but we must remember what is told about these herbs, and if their hidden virtues could be learned I would willingly believe in their efficacy. We understand that only the kings are allowed to use them, for if anyone else dares to taste them, or to obtain the recipe of this diet, he would be guilty of treason, for he would appear to equal the king. It is considered, after a fashion, that the king should not be the size of everybody else, for he should look down and dominate those who approach him. Such is the story told to me, and I repeat it for what it is worth. Your excellency may believe it or not. (Anghierra, 1912, pp. 266–269; Swanton, 1922, p. 46.)

Very probably the ingredients of this story are: head deformation, the accompanying and synchronous effect in straightening the body, the administration of medicines to the mother, and manipulation of the head and body of the infant. The addition of medicines at puberty was in line with Indian ideas relative to the importance of that period in life and the efficacy of magical performances and magical decoctions applied then.

To sum up, we have definite statements as to the existence of the custom of head deformation among the Natchez, Taensa, Tunica, Houma (though of late introduction among these last), and probably most of the other tribes of the lower Mississippi are involved, and to these must be added the Chitimacha, and in the early historic times, the Caddo. Among the tribes farther east addicted to the practice were the Choctaw, Chickasaw (to a less extent probably), Waxhaw and perhaps Catawba and some of their neighbors, and some of the prehistoric peoples along the Gulf coast. There is, however, no historical evidence of this type of deformation among the Creeks, Cherokee, Quapaw, Shawnee, Florida tribes, the Siouan tribes of Virginia, or the Algonquian people of that State and North Carolina.

DIFFERENCES BETWEEN ORNAMENTS WORN BY MEN AND WOMEN

In general the differences between ornaments worn by men and those worn by women were confined to details. Metal and shell gorgets seem to have been worn mainly by men, as were the headdresses of dyed hair, and I have no record of a woman in this section with her nosed pierced. By the Alabama I was told that arm bands were worn only by men, but this was not universal in the Southeast. The crescent-shaped breast ornaments also seem to have been monopolized by males. Feathers were used mostly by men, and they also appear to have indulged in paints to a greater extent. For head deformation, see above.

THE USE OF STONE

SOURCES OF THE RAW MATERIAL

Having treated the manner in which the Indians of the Southeast solved the problems of food, clothing, and shelter, we now turn to consider their methods of manufacturing the implements used in these several quests, beginning with objects obtained from the mineral kingdom. The sources of supply will first be considered.

It might be supposed that the Florida Indians would have been under the necessity of importing most of their flint, and, indeed, some of the Frenchmen with Laudonnière reported that a certain stone used in northwestern Florida for arrowpoints and wedges with which to split wood was found "at the foot of the mountains," by which he meant the Appalachians (1586, p. 8). But Europeans were then unaware of the extent of country between Florida and these mountains and the quarries in between, so that little reliance can be placed upon the statement. On the other hand, we are informed that all of the arrowheads of southern Florida were made of material obtained near Ballast Point, about 5 miles below Tampa. Farther north, on a small stream known as Trouble Creek, about 5 miles south of Kootie River and 2 miles north of the mouth of Anclote River, is an outcrop of blue flint which was also worked by the aborigines (Walker, S. T., 1880, p. 394).

The French Huguenots who settled in South Carolina in 1562 were told by a chief on the Georgia coast that crystal was dug up near the foot of a high mountain in the interior, but, like the later Florida reference, this is of small value (Laudonnière, 1586, p. 52). C. C. Jones mentions quarries as existing along the Oconee, Ocmulgee, Flint,

Chattahoochee, and other southern streams, and states more specifically that there were a number of open-air workshops along the line of Savannah River and especially that portion which formed the eastern boundary of the counties of Richmond, Columbia, Lincoln, and Elbert, and in the counties of South Carolina on the opposite side (Jones, C. C., 1873). There was a flint quarry 2 miles above Columbus, Ga., in Muscogee County in the same State (Brannon, 1909, p. 194). There was certainly a great flint implement factory at Albany, Dougherty County, near Flint River. It may have been this workshop which gave its name to that stream, called in the original Creek Thlonotiska, "where flint is picked up," but it should be noted that the name Thlonoto was given specifically to the present Hogcrawl Creek between Dooly and Macon Counties.

Beverley (1705, bk. 2, p. 11) quotes Alexander Whittaker, Minister of Henrico, to the effect that "Twelve miles from the Falls [of James River], there is a Chrystal Rock, wherewith the Indians do head many of their Arrows."

In Alabama there was a quarry on the southeastern side of Story's (or Storees) Mountain, on the Western Railroad, east of Youngesboro, in the fields, in township 19, range 27 east. Another was at the eastern end of Cedar Ridge in Talladega County, in township 18, range 7 east.

West of the Mississippi about Hot Springs, Ark., were extensive novaculite quarries, and quarries were reported in sections 7 and 9, township 4 south, range 24 west, in Montgomery County, and near Magnet Cove in Hot Springs County. (Thomas, 1891, p. 15; Holmes, 1903, pp. 196–200).

An early writer speaks of flint as abounding in the country of the Avoyel Indians, La. (Dyer, 1917), and in fact there is flint near the Rapides which may have been utilized by them. It is probable, however, that they derived their name, which seems to be the Natchez equivalent of Mobilian Tasának okla, "Flint People," very largely from the fact that they acted as middle men who obtained worked or unworked flint from the Arkansas Indians about the Hot Springs, and passed it on to the Chitimacha and Atakapa on the coast, these last supplying the Karankawa farther west (Dyer, 1917, pp. 6, 7; Swanton, 1911, pp. 24–26).

At the end of the eighteenth century, the Upper Creeks obtained their pipes largely from one man who made them of a dark stone (Swan, 1855, p. 692). This may have been obtained in or near the present Talladega County, Ala., but on the other hand it may have been brought from the Cherokee country, where stone of similar color was used for this purpose. Indeed, Adair (1775, p. 423) informs us that the Cherokee made the best stone pipes and these were traded to peoples less well provided with suitable material for the manufacture. But already, in the first half of the eighteenth century, catlinite had made its way into the Gulf region.

At some time in the past steatite, or soapstone, was used considerably. This was a favorite material for pipes even in late times, and steatite pots, or fragments of pots, have been found on known Creek sites along Tallapoosa River. Bushnell has located several quarries in Virginia, and there was one near Dudleyville, Tallapoosa Co., Ala. (Tuomey, 1858, p. 46), but no tradition of its use in the manufacture of any objects except pipes has been preserved.

Muscovite mica mines were worked in Clay County, Ala., in township 19, range 7 east, section 26, and in Talladega County, township 20, range 6, section 12. A mica mine is also reported from Hall County, Ga., but the most extensive workings were in Mitchell and Yancy Counties, N. C. (Thomas, 1891, p. 15; Holmes, 1919, pp. 241–252).

FLINT IMPLEMENTS

Flint arrow points are mentioned as in use throughout almost the whole Gulf region, but flint seems to have been used nowhere to the exclusion of other material. As we have specific mention of flint, or at least "stone," arrow points in Florida and the seacoast section of Louisiana where it must have been hardest to get, we may feel sure that there was practically no exception to the universality of its employment. (Hakluyt, 1847–89, vol. 3, p. 613; Robertson, 1933, p. 37; Swanton, 1922, p. 357; 1911, p. 347.) Curiously enough, it does not appear in the rather long list of articles used by the Natchez in heading arrows, but as the Avoyel tribe, just west of the Natchez, and their near relatives, were actively engaged in trading in flints— so actively that they were known as "Flint People"—it is altogether unlikely that the Natchez never employed flints (Swanton, 1911, pp. 272–274). Timberlake does not mention flint arrow points among the Cherokee, but when he wrote that tribe had long been in contact with Europeans. Hariot does not mention stone points in North Carolina, but we have specific mention of the use of flint among the people of Florida, the Creeks about Augusta, Ga., the Virginia Indians, the Chickasaw, the Alabama Indians when they were in northern Mississippi, and all the Indians of Louisiana west of the Natchez. Mention has been made of a crystal or white stone commonly used in the Virginia section (Beverley, 1705, bk. 2, p. 11). In 1701 Lawson came upon a wretched band of Indians in North Carolina called "the lower quarter," who had already begun to take to glass bottles as a substitute for native flint (Lawson, 1860, p. 99)

Flint seems to have been employed in the manufacture of one other weapon, though there are few notices of it anywhere but in Virginia. It is described as a wooden sword the edges of which were set with sharp stones more likely to have been of flint than anything else (Smith, John, Tyler ed., 1907, p. 14). It is rather remarkable that the only description of anything similar is in Garcilaso's account of the images about the door of the temple of Talimeco. Two of these are said to have been armed with "copper axes, the edges of which are of flint" (Garcilaso, 1723, pp. 130–137). Axes and swords are not precisely the same, but the two weapons have suggestive parallels in the arming of their edges.

No early writer has left us a description of flint chipping as practiced by the Gulf tribes. Writing in the eighteenth century, Adair says:

> The Indians, by reason of our supplying them so cheap with every sort of goods, have forgotten the chief part of their ancient mechanical skill, so as not to be able now, at least for some years, to live independent of us. (Adair, 1775, p. 424.)

And the flint industry was one of the first of these to disappear, flint being unable to compete with iron for any of the uses to which it was put, except in the one particular of kindling fire and this, curiously enough, was one of the things that came in with the whites instead of giving way before them. Our lack of knowledge of flint chipping as carried on here is therefore little surprising, but there is no indication that it differed appreciably from the technique farther north, where it has been studied under better auspices.

Lance and spear points and drills were also made of flint, as well as knives. The Alabama called the old-time knife tco'kfi imā'ksàle (rabbit flint) because it was made of this stone. Knives were also made of a certain kind of cane split into sections of suitable size. Adair (1775, p. 410) states that in his time the Indians resorted to cane knives in flaying wild animals when they were out hunting and had had the misfortune to lose their steel knives.

AXES

Adair says that the stone axes of the Chickasaw

> in form commonly resembled a smith's chisel. Each weighed from one to two, or three pounds weight—They were made of a flinty kind of stone: I have seen several, which chanced to escape being buried with their owners, and were carefully preserved by the old people, as respectable remains of antiquity. They twisted two or three tough hickory slips, of about two feet long, round the notched head of the axe; and by this simple and obvious invention, they deadened the trees by cutting through the bark, and burned them, when they either fell by decay, or became thoroughly dry. (Adair, 1775, p. 405.)

To make planks they merely indented the section of a tree at one end and then split it "with a maul and hard wooden wedges" (Adair, 1775, p. 419).

A Natchez informant told me that he had seen a stone axe hafted upon a split stick which was fastened about a groove in the axe, but this must have been some attempted reconstruction by a modern red ethnologist.

Du Pratz says that the Natchez employed "deep gray stones of fine grain, almost like touchstone," ground down on pieces of sandstone, and adds,

these stone axes are fully an inch thick at the butt, and half an inch thick three quarters of the way down [to the edge]. The edge is beveled, but not sharp, and may be four inches across but the head is only three inches across. The head is pierced with a hole through which the finger may be passed which is to enable them to tie it better onto the cleft at one end of the handle, the latter being well bound so that the cleft will not split farther. (Le Page du Pratz, 1758, vol. 2, p. 166; Swanton, 1911, p. 58.)

The reliability of this description is somewhat questionable since no pierced axes of the kind described have been found. In Florida Le Moyne noted "green and blue stones, which some thought to be emeralds and saphires, in the form of wedges, which they used instead of axes, for cutting wood" (Le Moyne, 1875, p. 8; Swanton, 1922, p. 355). Beverley speaks of axes employed by the Virginia Indians as "sharp Stones bound to the end of a Stick, and glued in with Turpentine" (Beverley, 1705, bk. 3, p. 60). In the Sound country of North Carolina Hariot (1893, p. 35) speaks of a gray stone used for hatchets and Smith also of "a long stone sharpened at both ends" mounted in a wooden handle pickax-fashion and used both as a battle-ax and a hatchet. (Smith, John Tyler ed., 1907, p. 102). Catesby (1731-43, vol. 2, p. ix) also tells us that the warclubs set with celts ("stone ground to an edge") were used in hollowing out their canoes. The horn of a deer was mounted in the same way, and later the place of both was taken by iron. To the early contact between our Gulf Indians and the Spaniards we must attribute the meager notices of these stone axes and hatchets, for they were everywhere replaced by iron as soon as iron was available. It may be added that the actual splitting up of wood into planks was probably done largely by means of wedges as Adair says (above).

STONE PIPES

The stone pipes did not give way to trade objects so quickly as stone axes and flint arrow points. By the Powhatan Indians, pipes seem to have been made of pottery more often than of stone, but the words of Michel (1916, p. 130), "they also make tobacco pipes, very beautifully cut out and formed" indicate that pipes of the harder material were in use among the Indians of Monacantown. Lawson observed the women of the Congaree tribe living near the junction of the Congaree and Wateree smoking pipes of stone, and

Catesby (1731–43, vol. 2, p. xi) says that "the bowls of their tobacco-pipes are whimsically, tho' very neatly, made and polished, of black, white, green, red, and gray marble, to which they fix a reed of a convenient length." The only reference to smoking in Florida is of "earthen pipes" (Hakluyt, 1847–87, vol. 3, p. 615; Swanton, 1922, p. 360).

As usual, Adair gives us one of the longest descriptions. He says:

They make beautiful stone pipes; and the Cheerake the best of any of the Indians: for their mountainous country contains many different sorts and colours of soils proper for such uses. They easily form them with their tomo-hawks, and afterward finish them in any desired form with their knives; the pipes being of a very soft quality till they are smoked with, and used to the fire, when they become quite hard. They are often a full span long, and the bowls are about half as large again as those of our English pipes. The fore part of each commonly runs out with a sharp peak, two or three fingers broad, and a quarter of an inch thick—on both sides of the bowl, lengthwise, they cut several pictures with a great deal of skill and labour; such as a buffalo and a panther on the opposite sides of the bowl; a rabbit and a fox; and, very often, a man and a woman *puris naturalibus*. Their sculpture cannot much be commended for its modesty. The savages work so slow, that one of their artists is two months at a pipe with his knife, before he finishes it: indeed, as before observed, they are great enemies to profuse sweating, and are never in a hurry about a good thing. The stems are commonly made of soft wood about two feet long, and an inch thick, cut into four squares, each scooped till they join very near the hollow of the stem; the beaus always hollow the squares, except a little at each corner to hold them together, to which they fasten a parcel of bell-buttons, different sorts of fine feathers, and several small battered pieces of copper kettles hammered, round deer-skin thongs, and a red-painted scalp; this is a boasting, valuable, and super-lative ornament. According to their standard, such a pipe constitutes the possessor, a grand beau. They so accurately carve, or paint hieroglyphic characters on the stem, that the war-actions, and the tribe of the owner, with a great many circumstances of things, are fully delineated. (Adair, 1775, pp. 423–424.)

The skill of the Cherokee as pipe makers having been so highly commended, what Timberlake reports during his visit in the Cherokee country is of particular interest. He says that the bowl of the peace-pipe

was of red stone, curiously cut with a knife, it being very soft, tho' extremely pretty when polished. Some of these are of black stone, and some of the same earth they make their pots with, but beautifully diversified. The stem is about three feet long, finely adorned with porcupine quills, dyed feathers, deers hair, and such like gaudy trifles. (Timberlake, 1927, Williams ed., p. 39.)

The red pipes were also in use among the Choctaw, and, inasmuch as we are told that they were imported from the Illinois country (Swanton, 1918, p. 67), it is evident that we have to deal with the material from the famous red pipestone quarry of Minnesota or from one of the other similar quarries in Wisconsin. A "red pipe" in the possession of the Chickasaw and obtained by them from the Quapaw was evidently of the same material. The Quapaw had gotten this in turn from a tribe with a name which suggests that of the Lower Creek town

Osochi, but was probably intended for Osage. It may be added that a catlinite pipe was found by the workers of the Museum of the American Indian while engaged in excavating the Nacoochee mound in the old territory of the Cherokee in northern Georgia (Heye et al., 1918, p. 77, pl. 49, *a*). About the end of the eighteenth century, Swan reports that all of the pipes in the Creek nation were made by one Indian living in the Natchez town, the only one who knew where the "black marble" of which they were formed was to be obtained (Swan, 1855, p. 692). One of the few Indians now among the Cherokee who are still able to use the Natchez language is skilful in the manufacture of pipes, also from a black stone, though this is obtained somewhere in Oklahoma. In the sixteenth century, ambassadors on peace missions used flageolets, but by the time the French descended and ascended the Mississippi River late in the seventeenth century, the use of the calumet had extended over its entire course. In 1687 the Cahinnio, a Caddo tribe half way between Caddo Lake and the mouth of Arkansas River, made use of the custom, but it had not been adopted by their relatives farther west, though it had reached them a few years afterward (Joutel *in* Margry, 1875–86, vol. 3, pp. 418–419). To the east it extended to the Creeks, but seems not to have had the same significance among them as it had along the Mississippi. The calumet, it is to be remembered, was not properly the pipe but a highly ornamented and symbolic stem. The stem used in a peace-making ceremony remained with the chief who had received the embassy while the pipe bowl was taken out and carried back by the visitors. This bowl was usually, it seems, made of the red stone from the north of which we have spoken. Dumont, who probably had the Natchez chiefly in mind, says that the bowl was usually made of a red stone but sometimes of a black one (Dumont, 1753, vol. 1, pp. 190–192; Swanton, 1911, p. 139). This latter may very well have come from the Cherokee country, though it is perhaps as likely that there were several different sources of the material.

CHUNKEY STONES

Another stone object upon which great care was bestowed was the roller used in the so-called Chunkey game. Museum collections contain many specimens, which agree in general with what Adair says of these objects. He describes the ones known to him, which would be those in common use among the Chickasaw, as "about two fingers broad at the edge, and two spans round."

The hurling stones they use at present, were time immemorial rubbed smooth on the rocks, and with prodigious labour; they are kept with the strictest religious care, from one generation to another, and are exempted from being buried with the dead. They belong to the town where they are used, and are carefully preserved. (Adair, 1775, p. 402.)

This game is simply a variety of the hoop and pole game which was played over a vast extent of territory in North America. The use of a stone roller, however, seems to have been confined to two areas, one a small territory on the upper Missouri occupied by the Mandan, Hidatsa, and probably the Arikara; the other the entire Gulf region east of the Mississippi and including the tribes on both banks of the latter, except that it is not reported from Florida (Culin, 1907, pp. 420–527). There are specific notices of it among the small tribes of the Mississippi, the Choctaw, Chickasaw, Creeks, Cherokee, the smaller Muskhogean bands of eastern Georgia and southern South Carolina, and the eastern Siouan tribes as far as the Eno of central North Carolina. Hariot, Smith, and Strachey are all silent regarding the existence of any such game among the Algonquian tribes of North Carolina and Virginia, and while we may feel assured that similar games were played, it seems evident that they were not striking features of the native aboriginal life. Evidence at hand points to the probability that the chunkey game extended over the southern or Catawba group of Siouans, but not to the northern or Tutelo group or to the Algonquians. In the west evidence is wanting as to such a game among the Atakapa, or Chitimacha, though this by no means proves that some type of hoop and pole game was not played by them. They would, however, have had some difficulty in obtaining suitable stone for rollers. The Caddo apparently knew the hoop and pole game, but it is not certain that they played it with stone rollers. (See Games, pp. 674–686.)

MISCELLANEOUS USES OF STONES

Other stone objects known to have been used in the Southeast were mortars for cracking nuts and grinding paint, and, in prehistoric times in the mountain country, mortars for grinding corn. These were sometimes made of separate blocks of stone and sometimes worked in the living rock. In the Tennessee country and neighboring sections stone images have been found. We know that wooden images were in use among the Virginia and Carolina Indians and even the Creeks, but there is no certain mention of stone images in the literature. The only possible exception is the sacred stone preserved by the Natchez in their temple, though it is not positively known that this was worked. Finally, we may add two wholly different ways in which stones or rocks were utilized. One was in the formation of fishweirs. These were either inland, like the one at the falls of James River, into which fish were carried by the descending current, or coastal, like that reported by Garcilaso at Tampa Bay, which caught fish as they swam shoreward (Garcilaso, 1723, p. 94). Along most of the lower Atlantic and Gulf coasts, however, fishweirs were made of wooden piles interwoven with flexible withes. Still another use of rocks was as altars. The early writers on Virginia speak of these as if they were common in the Algonquian country, one consisting of a solid block of crystal being particularly noteworthy (Beverley, 1705, bk. 2, pp. 10–11), but fewer are mentioned in the rest of the region under discussion. It remains to be seen whether or not this omission is of cultural significance.

POTTERY

From stone we turn to artificial stone. When one considers that the Southeast was one of the great pottery-making areas of North America, it is surprising what a small amount of information early writers vouchsafe regarding it. In 1541, when the Chickasaw attacked De Soto's army, then in occupancy of their town, Biedma tells us that, after the manner of Gideon, they brought fire in little pots, presumably made of clay, with which to ignite the houses (Bourne, 1904, vol. 2, p. 23). We are also told that large pots were used in making salt in the province of Tanico, probably in southern Arkansas (Robertson, 1933, p. 193). The only mention of pottery for its own sake by these chroniclers is by the Fidalgo of Elvas who, in his description of the "province of Naguatex," occupied by Caddo people, says: "Pottery is made there of refined clay, which differs but little from that of Estremoz or Montemor" (Robertson, 1933, p. 257), and in fact, Caddo pottery has always been noted for its excellence.

Although Du Pratz's description of pottery making is thrown into a hypothetical form, it seems to represent the process as he had observed it among the Natchez. He says that the women

go in search of heavy earth, examine it in the form of dust [i.e., before it had been wet], throwing out whatever grit they find, make a sufficiently firm mortar, and then establish their workshop on a flat board, on which they shape the pottery with their fingers, smoothing it by means of a stone which is preserved with great care for this work. As fast as the earth dries they put on more, assisting with the hand on the other side. After all these operations, it is baked by means of a great fire.

These women also make pots of an extraordinary size, jugs with a medium-sized opening, bowls, two-pint bottles with long necks, pots or jugs for bear's oil, which hold as many as 40 pints, also dishes and plates like those of the French. I have had some made out of curiosity on the model of my earthenware. They were of a rather beautiful red color. (Le Page du Pratz, 1758, vol. 2, pp. 178–179; Swanton, 1911, p. 62.)

Du Pratz says also:

[Between the Tunica town opposite the mouth of Red River and the Natchez are] many bluffs which occur together: among them is the one called *Ecore Blanc*, because one finds there many veins of white earth, rich and very fine with which I have seen very beautiful pottery made. On the same bluff one sees veins of ocher which the Natchez get to daub on their pottery which was very pretty; when it was coated with ocher it became red on being baked. (Le Page du Pratz, 1758, vol. 1, p. 124.)

Quite close to Natchitoches are banks of cockle-shells like those of which is formed the Isle aux Coquilles. This neighboring nation says that their ancient word teaches them that the sea formerly came to this place; the women of this nation go there to collect them, they make of them a powder which they mix with the earth of which they make their pottery which is recognized to be of the best. (Le Page du Pratz, 1758, vol. 1, pp. 163–164.)

Dumont (1753, vol. 1, p. 154) says that the women made "all kinds of earthen vessels, dishes, plates, pots to put on the fire, with others large enough to contain 25 to 30 pots of oil." Elsewhere he continues at length thus:

Moreover, the industry of these Indian girls and women is admirable. I have already reported elsewhere with what skill, with their fingers alone and without a potter's wheel they make all sorts of pottery.

After having gathered the earth suitable for this kind of work, and having well cleansed it, they take shells which they grind and reduce to a very fine powder; they mix this very fine dust with the earth which they have provided, and, moistening the whole with a little water, they knead it with the hands and feet, forming a dough of which they make rolls 6 or 7 feet long and of whatever thickness is desired. Should they wish to fashion a dish or a vessel, they take one of these rolls and, holding down one end with the thumb of the left hand they turn it around with admirable swiftness and dexterity, describing a spiral; from time to time they dip their fingers in water, which they are always careful to have near them, and with the right hand they smooth the inside and outside of the vessel they intend to form, which, without this care, would be undulated.

In this manner they make all sorts of utensils of earth, dishes, plates, pans, pots, and pitchers, some of which contain 40 and 50 pints. The baking of this pottery does not cause them much trouble. After having dried it in the shade they build a great fire, and when they think they have enough coals they clear a place in the middle where they arrange the vessels and cover them with the coals. It is thus that they give them the baking which is necessary. After this they can be placed on the fire and have as much firmness as ours. Their strength can only be attributed to the mixture which the women make of the powdered shells with the clay.[29]

The work of the neighboring Tunica also seems to have been good. Gravier says that they "have no riches but earthenware pots, quite well made, especially little glazed pitchers, as neat as you would see in France" (Shea, 1861, p. 135; Swanton, 1911, p. 315). Pénicaut found the Pascagoula women making "large earthen pots, almost like big kettles, which hold perhaps 40 pints, and in which they have

---

[29] Dumont, 1753, vol. 2, pp. 271–273 (as translated in Holmes, 1903, p. 57).

hominy cooked enough for two or three families," the cooks taking turns providing it. He adds that "these pots are of clay and of a round shape almost like windmills" (Pénicaut *in* Margry, 1875–86, vol. 5, pp. 388–389; Swanton, 1911, p. 303).

In Florida Laudonnière saw, in the house of a native chief, "a great vessel of earth made after a strange fashion" (Laudonnière, 1586, p. 74; Swanton, 1922, p. 354), and in Le Moyne's drawings we find two or three types of pots represented, including a large cylindrical affair somewhat like the sofki pots of the Creeks, and a small round pot with a narrow mouth, to which there should perhaps be added a kind of spoon or ladle with a short handle, though this last may have been of wood or horn.

Bartram (1792, p. 325) states that the clay out of which the Creeks made pottery, as well as that which they used as plaster for their buildings, was generally obtained in a large artificial pond "just without the town," where they also cultivated, or rather kept, angelico. In 1739 Governor Oglethorpe observed the Indians of Coweta town "dress their Meat in Large pans made of Earth and not much unlike our Beehives in England" (Bushnell, 1908, p. 573), and toward the end of the same century Caleb Swan noted among the Upper Creeks

earthen pots and pans of various sizes, from one pint up to six gallons. But in these, they betray a great want of taste and invention, they have no variety of fashion; these vessels are all without handles, and are drawn so nearly to a point at the bottom, that they will not stand alone. Therefore, whenever they are set for use, they have to be propped upon three sides with sticks or stones. (Swan, 1855, p. 692.)

By this time, however, it is probable that traders' goods had caused considerable deterioration in the native arts.

Clay suitable for the manufacture of pots was obtained at some points on Oconee Creek, the modern Hatchechubbee.

Although this industry no longer exists among the Creeks, I obtained two descriptions given by old people from memory, and a third from a member of the incorporated Alabama tribe. Jackson Lewis, the Hitchiti informant, said that when a woman wanted to make a pot she hunted about until she found a clay that would not crack, and, if she could not discover such a clay, she mixed the clay she could get with the finest sand, thereby accomplishing the same result. In shaping the pot she first laid down a flat piece to form the base, and then made a ribbon of the remaining clay which she led round and round spirally, adding to her ribbon as required, until the pot was completed. Then she would take a mussel shell and smooth the pot with it both outside and inside. The inside surface, however, she made appear almost as if glazed by rubbing it with a small stone of a kind said to be found in nodules of granite. Perhaps Lewis meant limestone instead of granite, the stone being flint. She sometimes ornamented the edges of the pot by pinching it between two fingers. The pot was fired by turning it upside down upon the ground, leaning various combustibles against it all about, and setting these on fire. As fast as the fagots gave way, she replaced them until the pot became red hot, when she allowed the fire to burn out and the pot to cool. During the baking, and while the pot was still very hot, she might take the feather of a turkey and trace designs on the outside with the quill end. As she did this, the quill would burn and color the parts of the pot over which it was passing. Sometimes they got some very red stones found here and there in the hills, and perhaps the same as those out of which they made their red paint, pounded them into powder, and put some on the end of a stick with which they then made designs in the same manner as with the quill. Designs might also be made by making incisions with a pointed stick before the pot had hardened. So far as Lewis knew, they never put netting over their pots during the process of manufacture, but they took a corncob and stroked the sides of very large pots to roughen their surfaces if they were to be used in cooking.

My Upper Creek interpreter, Zach Cook, said that the potters of his acquaintance first laid down a flat piece of clay for a foundation and then coiled a thin strip round and round for the superstructure. They either used the clay, described as a blue pipe clay, plain, or else pounded up pieces of old pottery and mixed them with it. They claimed that this latter kind was the stronger. They rubbed a corncob over the outside, and then glazed it by means of a mussel shell. It was shaped up and smoothed on the inside by means of a smooth stone or a shell. Then it was placed near the fire and rotated, or moved nearer to and farther from the blaze successively, in order to make it bake properly and evenly.

According to my Alabama informant, Charlie Thompson, later chief of the Texas band, pots were made of fine white or dark blue clay mixed with a smaller quantity of burned bones and white sand to prevent them from cracking. After this had been kneaded together thoroughly, it was laid aside for a while and then kneaded again. This was repeated two or three times. Afterward a portion of the clay was worked into a ribbon and this was coiled round and round to make the pot. Then a fire was made out of small pieces of bark, the pot was turned upside down upon this, and more barks were heaped on top. Before it was cold, they rubbed it all over with a corncob to make it "smooth." Sometimes they ornamented these pots on the outside by means of lines. The greater number were made for sofki and they used to be sold for a dollar. The principal vessels used were a flat earthen skillet (i'yis patha'), an earthen pot (a'kåtce), an earthen dish (okłayåmpo), and, in more modern times, a frying pan (istapwåtle').

A few notes may be added from a Koasati informant, Jackson Langley. To make their pots they employed red clay found in certain special places. The pots were greased well before being placed over the fire, so that after they had been placed in use the spoons would not scratch through the surface and loosen the clay underneath. Old dry pieces of hickory bark were used for the fire, pine bark never, and they burned them down until there was a hot bed of coals over which the pots were placed, upside down. In that way the clay would dry slowly so as not to crack. Two or three different kinds of pots were made in this manner.

Speck says that the pots of Taskigi Creeks were made

of clean red clay coiled upon a disk-like base. To fire these they were covered with dried grass and the mass was ignited. When the combustible covering had burned off the pot was black, and so hard that it could withstand the effects of daily contact with fire. Pipes of unbaked clay are still made in some of the remote parts of the Taskigi district. (Speck, 1907, p. 109.)

The same writer's account of Yuchi pottery-making is one of the best we have (Speck, 1909, pp. 25–28).

Adair's description is presumably particularly applicable to the Chickasaw, but might also have covered the Creeks and the Cherokee:

They make earthen pots of very different sizes, so as to contain from two to ten gallons; large pitchers to carry water; bowls, dishes, platters, basons, and a prodigious number of other vessels of such antiquated forms, as would be tedious to describe, and impossible to name. Their method of glazing them, is, they place them over a large fire of smoky pitch pine, which makes them smooth, black, and firm. Their lands abound with proper clay, for that use; and even with porcelain, as has been proved by experiment. (Adair, 1775, p. 456.)

Clay suitable for pots was obtained at the Chickasaw bluffs, and a small industry was carried on there.

Timberlake (Williams ed., 1927, p. 86) noted that the Cherokee "have two sorts of clay, red and white, with both of which they make excellent vessels, some of which will stand the greatest heat."

As the Indian from whom I got the following account belonged to the Cherokee band of Natchez, it is probable that the method followed resembled that in use among the old Cherokee as much as, and perhaps more than, that of the old Natchez. He remembered having seen both pans and jars of native manufacture. He related to me the following method used by an old Natchez woman, as witnessed by himself:

The old woman first pounded up some slate which she mixed with the clay, and the material resulting was rolled into long cylindrical strips, which were coiled round and round until the pot was completed. A fresh-water mussel shell was used to shape and smooth it both on the outside and on the inside. Then it was dried in the sun for 3 or 4 days, or perhaps even longer, after which it was turned upside down and burned by means of a fire made of dry tree bark heaped all around and above it. When it was red hot, a liquid made from the leaves of the dark sumac boiled in water was poured over it. This is said to have been done in order to make it smooth. It also gave the pot a bluish tint in place of the natural red or yellow color of the clay.

Lawson, who so often illuminates ethnological problems in the Siouan area, furnishes us with little more than an archeological note on the subject of pottery, citing "the earthen pots that are often found under ground, and at the foot of the banks where the water has washed them away," as evidence for occupancy of the country earlier than by the historic tribes. These pots were, he says, "for the most part broken in pieces; but we find them of a different sort, in comparison of those the Indians use at this day [1709] who have had no other ever since the English discovered America" (Lawson, 1860, p. 279).

Michel (1916, p. 123) merely notes of the Indians of Monacan town that they had pots which they often brought to the white settlers to sell, and when it was desired they brought them full of corn.

In the text accompanying one of his plates, Hariot has this:

Their women know how to make earthen vessells with special Cunninge and that so large and fine, that our potters with lhoye (theyr) wheles can make noe better: ant then Remoue them from place to place as easelye as we can doe our brassen kettles. After they haue set them vppon an heape of erthe to stay them from fallinge, they putt wood vnder which being kyndled one of them taketh great care that the fyre burne equallye Rounde abowt. They or their women fill the vessell with water, and then putt they in fruite, flesh, and fish, and lett all boyle together like a galliemaufrye, which the Spaniarde call, olla podrida. (Hariot, 1893, pl. 15.)

In this same area, Barlowe noted that the vessels of the natives were "earthen pots, very large, white and sweete" (Burrage, 1906, p. 236). The Virginia chroniclers in general mention the use of pots without making any comment regarding them. In the Algonquian and Siouan sections, however, we have frequent mention of clay pipes (Strachey, 1849, pp. 32, 121–122; Lawson, 1860, p. 338), and they are manufactured down to the present day by the Catawba. Among the Congaree, Lawson (1860, pp. 54–55) noted stone pipes, and throughout the rest of the Gulf region as far as the Mississippi this is the only material to which reference is made.

None of our informants attempts a description of the manner in which earthenware pipes were made, and we must fall back for that on the modern process perpetuated among the Catawba Indians along with the manufacture of certain types of pottery. For a complete description of this the reader is referred to a paper by M. R. Harrington (1908, pp. 399–407). The same student has published an account of the related Cherokee pottery work (Harrington, M. R., 1922). It is to be noted that the modern Catawba potters use no tempering, and that the old Cherokee woman who described and illustrated the process to Mr. Harrington stated that it was sometimes employed, but she did not employ it herself. This seems to represent a process of degeneration.

But the study of pottery in the Southeast is mainly an archeological problem, and concerns a branch of anthropological work into which I do not propose to enter.

MISCELLANEOUS HOUSEHOLD UTENSILS

WOODEN STOOLS

In parts of the Southeast, wooden stools made in one piece were in use similar to the so-called duhos of the West Indies. If they were introduced from the islands, however, it must have been before white contact for when De Soto met Tascalusa, the great Mobile chief, according to Garcilaso (1723, p. 145), he "was seated upon a wooden chair about two feet high, without back or arms, and all of one piece." And that this was no mere inference on the Inca's part is shown by the fact that, in the early part of the eighteenth century, a stool of this kind having four legs constituted the "throne" of the Great Sun, head chief of the Natchez (Le Page du Pratz, 1758, vol. 2, pp. 360–361; Swanton, 1911, p. 112). Speaking of these stools generally as found on the lower Mississippi, Du Pratz says:

The natives have small seats or stools . . . These seats are only 6 or 7 inches high. The feet and the seat are of one piece. (Le Page du Pratz, 1758, vol. 2, p. 182; Swanton, 1911, p. 61.)

He expresses a doubt whether their use had antedated the importation of European axes considering "their small inclination to sit on them," but this is not justified in the light of the reference above given added to a note by Adair (1775, p. 421), who remarks: "Their stools they cut out of poplar wood, all of one piece, and of a convenient height and shape."

When De Gourgues visited the Timucua chief Saturiwa in 1567, the latter placed him on "a seat of wood of lentisque [gum wood] covered with moss, made of purpose like unto his own" (Laudonnière, 1586, p. 209; Swanton, 1922, p. 354). While these may have been merely parts of the bed with which every house of any size was provided, they were more probably stools. The fact that they were used by chiefs or honored men falls in line with what has already been noted, and Florida was a very probable "port of entry" for this object or the conception of it.

These stools are reported from as far west as the Caddo Indians, but not in Virginia or the Carolinas (Swanton, 1942, p. 155).

Several of these stools were found by Cushing at Key Marco, and some of them appeared to have been made especially for use in canoes (Cushing, 1896, p. 363).

DISHES AND SPOONS OF WOOD AND HORN

Their wooden dishes, and spoons made of wood and buffalo horn, [says Adair] shew something of a newer invention and date, being of nicer work‑ manship, for the sculpture of the last is plain, and represents things that are within the reach of their own ideas. (Adair, 1775, p. 421.)

By "newer" Adair can hardly mean post-Columbian, but if he does he is plainly in error, though the use of excavated wooden utensils was no doubt facilitated considerably by iron tools. On the other hand, importation of European vessels would be likely to re‑ sult in the abandonment of native artifacts. However, we have a number of notices of their use from various parts of the region under discussion. In a Timucua house visited by Laudonnière, he saw "a little vessel of wood" used as a cup, and Le Moyne, the artist, men‑ tions round bottles or wooden vessels in which they carried the black drink, though these last may in reality have been gourds. (Laudonnière, 1586, p. 74; Le Moyne, 1875, p. 12; Swanton, 1922, p. 354.) Wooden spoons were manufactured by the Creeks in Swan's time, "very large and simple in their form. One serves a whole fam‑ ily, who use it round by turns" (Swan, 1855, p. 692). The Quapaw made wooden platters which they exchanged with the Caddo and Tunica, along with other objects, for salt and bows and arrows (Joutel *in* Margry, 1875–86, vol. 3, p. 443). It is from the tribes toward the northeast, however, that we get most information regard‑ ing wooden vessels. Barlowe says that the Algonquian Indians of North Carolina had "wooden platters of sweet timber" (Burrage, 1906, p. 236). Strachey also refers to wooden pots and platters in use by the Powhatan Indians, and, from what he and Smith tell us, it is evident that the wooden food platters kept in the houses of chiefs were very large (Strachey, 1849, p. 59; Smith, John Tyler ed., 1907, pp. 45, 54). Beverley (1705, bk. 3, p. 17) makes little note of these dishes, but says that "the Spoons which they eat with, do gen‑ erally hold half a pint; and they laugh at the *English* for using small ones, which they must be forc'd to carry so often to their Mouths, that their arms are in danger of being tir'd, before their Belly." Byrd comments on the large spoons made of bison horn by Virginia Indians "which they say will Split and fall to Pieces whenever Poison is put into them" (Bassett, 1901, p. 288).

Lawson has more references to these articles than any other informant. He notes that the Congaree Indians had large wooden spoons "as big as small ladles," but showed little disposition to use them instead of their fingers. He also quotes the narrative of certain explorers who entered Cape Fear River in 1663 and broke up the "pots, platters, and spoons" found in a native house, but some of these may have been of earthenware. In his general discussion of the Indian tribes, he informs us that the Indians who were not particularly skillful as hunters made "dishes and spoons of gumwood, and the tulip tree," among other things, to trade to other Indians, and he himself met two Tuscarora who were going to the Shakori and Occaneechi to sell wooden bowls and ladles for raw skins (Lawson 1860, pp. 56, 122, 101, 337).

At least until recently, some of the Alabama knew how to make wooden spoons. They were in one piece and were of the wood of a tree called itûkàmo′, which grows near the water. These Indians also remember that in olden times spoons were made out of cow and bison horn. The horn was first immersed in hot water in order to soften it, and after that it could be cut easily.

According to a Creek informant, the best spoons were made of boxelder, but sycamore, elm, or other woods might be employed.

At Key Marco, Cushing found a great many wooden dishes:

The trays were also very numerous and exceedingly interesting; comparatively shallow, oval in outline and varying from a length of six and a half or seven inches and a width of four or five inches, to a length of not less than five feet and a width of quite two feet. The ends of these trays were narrowed and truncated to form handles, the upper faces of which were usually decorated with neatly cut-in disc-like or semilunar figures or depressions. Looking at the whole series of them secured by us—no fewer than thirty in all—I was impressed with their general resemblance to canoes, their almost obvious derivation from such, as though through a sort of technologic inheritance they had descended from the vessels which had brought not only the first food, and the first supplies of water, to these outlying keys, but also the first dwellers thereon as well. (Cushing, 1896, p. 364.)

He found also "spoons made from bivalves, ladles made from the greater halves of hollowed-out well-grown conch shells; and cups, bowls, trays, and mortars of wood" (idem).

Spoons, pot stirrers, and gourd vessels, as used by the Yuchi 30 years ago, are thus described by Speck:

Spoons, yáda ctïné, showing some variation in size and relative proportions, are found commonly in domestic service. They are all made of wood, said to be maple. The size of these varies from six or seven to fourteen inches. The bowl is usually rather deep and is widest and deepest near the handle. The latter is squared and straight with a crook near the end upon which an ownership mark consisting of a few scratches or incisions is frequently seen. . . . This type is said to represent, in the shape of the bowl, a wolf's ear and to be patterned after it.

Wooden paddle-shaped pot stirrers, *cadi'*, are nearly always to be seen where cooking is going on. They vary greatly in size and pattern. Ordinarily the top is simply disk-shaped. The use of the stirrer comes in when soup and vegetables are being boiled, to keep the mess from sticking to the pot.

Gourds, *tä'mbactŭ'*, of various shapes are made use of about the house in many different ways. They are easily obtained and require little or no labor to fit them for use. As drinking cups, general receptacles and dippers they come in very handy. (Speck, 1909, p. 42.)

Plate 71, figure 2, shows a gourd bottle seen among the Alabama Indians about 25 years ago.

Caddo spoons are shown in Bulletin 132 (Swanton, 1942, pl. 16, fig. 2).

WOODEN MORTARS

The Fidalgo of Elvas tells us that De Soto's companions were accustomed "to beat out the maize in log mortars with a one-handed pestle of wood," and there is every reason to believe that these mortars were "obtained" from the Indians, for a little farther on he refers to the "mortars, in which the natives beat maize" (Robertson, 1933, pp. 54, 74). These mortars were so much a matter of course throughout the entire area we are considering that there are relatively few references to them and scarcely any attempts to describe them. Smith and Strachey barely mention wooden mortars and pestles, and the former includes them among the articles manufactured by women, the only intimation of the kind in all our literature. (Smith, John, Tyler ed., 1907, p. 96; Strachey, 1849, p. 73.) Lawson (1860, p. 165) speaks of a tree "which we call red hickory, the heart whereof being very red, firm and durable" was used in making "walking sticks, mortars, pestles, and several other fine turnery wares."

In 1595 San Miguel reported that the Guale Indians of the neighborhood of St. Simons Island pounded their corn into flour "in deep and narrow wooden mortars: the mano is a kind of rammer more than two yards (varas) in length and the rammer widens above and is slender in the mortar" (Garcia, 1902, p. 197).

When Oglethorpe visited the Coweta Creeks in 1739, he found that "they do not make use of Mills to grind their corn in but in lieu thereof use a Mortar made out of the Stock of a Tree which they cut and burn hollow and then Pound their Corn therein" (Bushnell, 1908, pp. 573–574).

The [Florida Seminole] mortar is made [says MacCauley] from a log of live-oak (?) wood, ordinarily about two feet in length and from fifteen to twenty inches in diameter. One end of the log is hollowed out to quite a depth, and in this, by the hammering of a pestle made of mastic wood, the corn is reduced to hominy or to the impalpable flour of which I have spoken. (MacCauley, 1887, p. 517.)

The Chickasaw mortar like the others was

wide at the mouth, and gradually narrows to the bottom. The Indians always used mortars, instead of mills, and they had them, with almost every other convenience, when we first opened a trade with them—they cautiously burned a large log, to a proper level and length, placed fire a-top, and wet mortar round it, in order to give the utensil a proper form; and when the fire was extinguished, or occasion required, they chopped the inside with their stone-instruments, patiently continuing the slow process, till they finished the machine to the intended purpose. (Adair, 1775, p. 437; Swanton, 1918, p. 57.)

The anonymous relation barely mentions their use among the Choctaw but one of my informants declared that in early times mortars were made by burning holes in the side of a prostrate tree, and it was only after European axes were obtained that they excavated the ends. This seems to be an error, and it would hardly deserve serious notice except that MacCauley mentions and figures the same sort of mortar in use among the Seminole 60 years ago. The Choctaw esteemed most mortars made of hickory as conveying the best taste to the flour. The second choice was usually oak. Beech was good, but beech trees were scarce. Some woods were rejected, however, because they communicated a bad taste to anything prepared in mortars made of them, and this was particularly true of maple (Swanton, 1931 a, p. 48).

According to Du Pratz, when the Natchez made these mortars, they used

a pad of kneaded earth [which they placed] on the upper side, that which they wished to hollow. They put fire in the middle and blew it by means of a reed pipe, and if the fire consumed more rapidly on one side than on the other they immediately placed some mud there. They continued this until the mortar was sufficiently wide and deep. (Le Page du Pratz, 1758, vol. 2, p. 177; Swanton, 1911, p. 67.)

A similar method was pursued down to recent times by the Chitimacha (Swanton, 1911, p. 347) and all of the other tribal remnants of the Southeast, though steel tools facilitated the operation very considerably.

Joutel describes the use of mortars of the common type among the Caddo made in the same way (Joutel in Margry, 1875–86, vol. 3, pp. 363, 367). As many as four women might be assigned to the task of making flour in these, by which he probably means that they struck one after the other. It was common practice for two women to do this, but Joutel's reference is the only suggestion that more than that number took part.

In his discussion of the Yuchi Indians, Speck gives us an insight into the social and religious significance of the mortar:

The mortar which is simply a log several feet high with the bark removed having a cavity about eight inches deep, seems, moreover, to be an important domestic fetish. We find that it is connected in some way with the growing up and the future prospects of the children of the family. It occupies a permanent position in the door yard, or the space in front of the house. Only one mortar is owned by the family and there is a strong feeling, even today, against moving it about and particularly against selling it. We shall see later that the navel string of a female child is laid away underneath the mortar in the belief that the presiding spirit will guide the growing girl in the path of domestic efficiency.

The pestle that goes with this utensil is also of wood. Its length is usually about six feet. The lower end that goes into the cavity of the mortar and does the crushing is rounded off. The top of the pestle is left broad, to act as a weight and give force to its descent. Several forms of carving are to be observed in these clubbed pestle tops which are presumably ornamental. (Speck, 1909, p. 41.)

Mortars were found at Key Marco in the greatest profusion by Cushing, though they were evidently not used to pound corn into flour.

They ranged in size from little hemispherical bowls or cups two and a half to three inches in diameter, to great cypress tubs more than two feet in depth, tapering, flat-bottomed, and correspondingly wide at the tops. The smaller mortar-cups were marvels of beauty and finish as a rule, and lying near them and sometimes even with them, were still found their appropriate pestles or crushers. . . . The smaller mortars and pestles, like the one illustrated, seemed to have been personal property, as though they had belonged to individuals and had been used in the crushing of berries and tubers, and perhaps cunti-root; as well as in other ways, that is, in the service, rather than merely in the general preparation, of food. (Cushing, 1896, p. 364.)

Plate 72, figure 2, and plate 73 show mortars and pestles in use among the Alabama, Hitchiti, and Caddo.

Mortars made from holes cut in the sides of logs are reported from the Seminole (MacCauley, 1887, pp. 513–514), as noted above, but also from the Choctaw of Bayou Lacomb (Bushnell, 1909 a, p. 11), and the Choctaw of Mississippi (Swanton, 1931 a, p. 48).

WOODEN CHESTS

The Indians of the Southeast manufactured a wooden box or chest, and we seem to get some intimation of this even as far back as the time of De Soto. Elvas tells us of "a cane box, like a trunk, called petaca, full of unbored pearls," which was carried along by the chieftainess of Cofitachequi when she accompanied De Soto through the territories northward of her town somewhere south of the present Augusta, Ga. (Robertson, 1933, p. 101). But petacas are described by Ranjel as "baskets covered with leather and likewise ready to be so covered with their lids, for carrying clothes or whatever they want to," from which it seems that they might have been cane baskets (Bourne, 1904, vol. 2, p. 104). However, in the temple of Cofitachequi Garcilaso's informants saw "great wooden boxes without locks" containing the bones of the dead and he tells us that "they were astonished that, without tools, the Indians had been able to make them so well." He continues:

Besides these great boxes, they had smaller ones, and cane baskets very well made. These last boxes were filled with clothing of men and women, and the baskets with pearls of all sorts. (Garcilaso, 1723, p. 361.)

Mention of baskets is important as showing that by boxes something other than basket hampers is meant. Three rows of chests were seen in the temple of Talomeco, and coffins in the temples of Ucita, Pacaha, and Anilco.

Most of our later references are to the boxes or coffins constructed by Choctaw "bone-pickers" for the bones of the deceased. The anonymous Frenchman says that the bodies of common Choctaw were placed in cane hampers, only those of chiefs being put into chests, and these are said to have been "locked with keys" (Swanton, 1931 a, p. 65). This suggests an imported affair but the word "key" may not be used in the European sense, since Milfort describes the native coffin as "a kind of chest the opening of which they shut with a plank" (Milfort, 1802, pp. 293–294; Swanton, 1918, p. 174). Bartram calls this receptacle "a curiously wrought chest or coffin, fabricated of bones and splints," while Romans refer to it merely as "a neatly made chest." (Bartram, 1792, pp. 514–515; Romans, 1775, pp. 89–90; Swanton, 1931 a, pp. 173–174.) Such chests are mentioned also by Bossu and Adair, and the latter describes a native chest which was used for other purposes but may have been constructed similarly. He says it was "made of clapboards sewed to cross bars with scraped wet buffalo strings." (Bossu, 1768, vol. 2, pp. 95–96; Adair, 1775, p. 452; Swanton, 1931 a, pp. 171–172.) Thus they may have been put together like the sewed boxes of the North Pacific coast Indians. H. S. Halbert was told that the burial chest was made by the bone-picker and ornamented "to the best of his taste and ability," but perhaps certain individuals became particularly skillful coffin makers since the name of Tombigbee River is said to have been derived from a man who specialized in this work, itombi signifyng "box," or "chest," and ikbi, "maker" (Swanton, 1931 a, p. 188).

Du Pratz says that the Natchez constructed "little boxes" of cane (Le Page du Pratz, 1758, vol. 3, pp. 23-24; Swanton, 1911, p. 143). Caddo wooden receptacles are noted in Bureau of American Ethnology Bulletin 132 (Swanton, 1942, p. 155).

A box of a slightly different pattern was that which contained the medicine of a war party. Adair says of this:

It is made with pieces of wood securely fastened together in the form of a square. The middle of three of the sides extends a little out, but one side is flat, for the conveniency of the person's back who carries it. Their ark has a cover, and the whole is made impenetrably close with hiccory-splinters; it is about half the dimensions of the divine Jewish ark, and may very properly be called the red Hebrew ark of the purifier, imitated. The leader, and a beloved waiter, carry it by turns. (Adair, 1775, p. 160.)

Elsewhere he speaks as if such arks were in common use, not only by the Chickasaw but by all of the principal tribes with which they were surrounded. Although there is mention of "idols" carried by several of these tribes to war, we have no further descriptions of the containers, if such were used. Adair speaks of the Cherokee war medicine or palladium "which was covered with a drest deer-skin, and placed on a couple of short blocks" while a body of that tribe was marching to the aid of the British in 1756, but we do not know that this was in a true box. (Adair, 1775, p. 168, ftn.).

At Key Marco, Fla., Cushing found

a little jewel-box lid or bottom, of hard, dark brown wood, eight inches in length, by four in width. The ends were rabbetted and drilled for attachment (with sinew and black gum, traces of which remained), to the ends of the box, and the ends themselves were in juxtaposition. Each end was four inches long and of corresponding width, and painted lengthwise on the outside, with double mythic tie-cords and shell-clasp figures. The bottom and the other parts were missing, save for fragments. (Cushing, 1896, p. 428.)

CRADLES

Of the Indians of Virginia, Beverley (1705, bk. 3, p. 9) says that, after washing a newborn infant, they "bind it naked to a convenient Board, having a hole fitly plac'd for evacuation; but they always put Cotton, Wool, Furr, or other soft thing, for the Body to rest easy on, between the Child and the Board." Lawson's account of the Siouan cradle is much more satisfactory:

The husband takes care to provide a cradle, which is soon made, consisting of a piece of flat wood, which they hew with their hatchets to the thickness of a board; it is about two feet long, and a foot broad; to this they brace and tie the child down very close, having near the middle, a stick fastened about two inches from the board, which is for the child's breech to rest upon, under which they put a wad of moss that receives the child's excrements, by which means they can shift the moss and keep all clean and sweet. . . . These cradles are apt to make the body flat; yet they are the most portable things that can be invented, for there is a string which goes from one corner of the board to the other, whereby the mother flings her child on her back; so the infant's back is towards hers, and its face looks up towards the sky. If it rains she throws her leather or woolen matchcoat, over her head, which covers the child all over, and secures her and it from the injuries of rainy weather. (Lawson, 1860, p. 310.)

Catesby says that the native cradle

consists of a flat board about two foot long, and one broad, to which they brace the child close, cutting a hole against the child's breech for its excrements to pass through; a leather strap is tied from one corner of the board to the other, whereby the mother slings her child on her back, with the child's back towards hers; at other times they hang them against the walls of their houses, or to the boughs of trees. (Catesby, 1731–43, vol. 2, p. xv.)

In connection with head flattening, Adair remarks:

The Indian nations, round South Carolina, and all the way to New Mexico, . . . to effect this, fix the tender infant on a kind of cradle, where his feet are tilted, above a foot higher than a horizontal position,—his head bends back into a hole, made on purpose to receive it, where he bears the chief part of his weight on the crown of the head, upon a small bag of sand, without being in the least able to move himself. (Adair, 1775, p. 10.)

Bossu speaks thus of the Choctaw:

Their cradle is made of canes. The mothers lay their children in these so that their heads are three or four finger-widths lower than their bodies. (Bossu, 1768, vol. 2, p. 105; Swanton, 1931 a, p. 117.)

And, writing about a century later, Cushman discusses the subject as follows:

After a child was born, after undergoing the usual necessary preliminaries, it was placed in a curiously constructed receptacle called Ullosi afohka (infant receptacle), where it spent principally the first year of its life, only when taken out for the purpose of washing and dressing. This curiously made little cradle (for such it may truly be called) was often highly ornamented with all the paraphernalia that a mother's love and care could suggest or obtain. The little fellow's face, which was always exposed to view, was carefully protected by a piece of wood bent a few inches above and over it. . . . According to her convenience, the mother suspended her thus cradled child on her back, when walking, or the saddle when riding; or stood it up against a neighboring tree, if a pleasant day, that it might enjoy the fresh and pure air, and exhilarating sunshine; or suspended it on the projecting limb of a tree there to be rocked to sleep and pleasant dreams by the forest breeze. (Cushman, 1896, pp. 232–233; Swanton, 1931 a, p. 117.)

Du Pratz thus describes the Natchez cradle:

This cradle is about 2½ feet long by 8 to 9 inches broad. It is artistically made of straight canes running the length of the cradle, and at the end they are cut in half and bent back under to make the foot. The whole is only half a foot high. This cradle is very light, since it weighs not more than 2 pounds. (Le Page du Pratz, 1758, vol. 2, p. 309; Swanton, 1911, p. 86.)

The Luxemburg Memoir, however, describes it as "the end of a board on which is spread a piece of animal skin; one extremity of this board has a hole in which the head is put and it is lower than the rest" (Swanton, 1911, pp. 54–55).

If MacCauley's observations may be relied upon, the Florida Seminole in 1880–81 used no cradle.

The Florida Indian baby, when very young, spends his time, naked, in a hammock, or on a deer skin, or on the warm earth. (MacCauley, 1887, p. 497.)

We know that combs were used in pre-Columbian times because numerous examples of them have been found on undisturbed sites, but early writers give few notices of them. In speaking of the Choctaw, however, Romans says:

> They are very ingenious in making tools, utensils and furniture; I have seen a narrow tooth comb made by one of these savages with a knife only out of the root of the *Diospyros* [persimmon] that was as well finished as I ever saw one with all the necessary tools. (Romans, 1775, p. 83.)

SCRATCHERS

When Lawson was among the Esaw, i. e., the Catawba Indians, he observed that in treating a lame man they used a scratcher, "an instrument somewhat like a comb, which was made of a split reed, with fifteen teeth of rattlesnakes, set at much the same distance as in a large horn comb" (Lawson, 1860, p. 76). One might suspect that it was probably set with gar teeth, like most of the scratchers used in this section in aboriginal times, but the use of rattlesnake fangs is reaffirmed on a later page (Lawson, 1860, p. 363).

Swan (1855, p. 274) speaks of the scratcher used by the Creek Indians "as a jaw-bone of a gar-fish, having two teeth." Adair (1775, p. 120), however, again speaks of snakes' teeth. Its use among the Creeks was particularly widespread.

IMPLEMENTS USED IN HUNTING, FISHING, AND WAR
KNIVES

Elvas makes mention of some "copper hatchets" seen in Cofitachequi the metal of which was said to have a mixture of gold in it (Robertson, 1933, p. 109). If of pure copper, these would have been inefficient tools and the objects in question may have been ceremonial. Knives made of "the splinter of a reed" are noted by John Smith (1907, p. 101) and Strachey (1849, p. 106), and Beverley (1705, bk. 3, p. 60) says that when the English first went among the Indians of Virginia "they had no sort of Iron or Steel Instruments: but their knives were either Sharpen'd Reeds, or Shells." Foreman quotes a missionary report to the effect that the Indians anciently used the beaver tooth as a knife, and it was certainly employed as a tool though it is doubtful whether it should be classed as a knife (Foreman, 1934, p. 18). Undoubtedly knives of shell, stone, and perhaps bone were employed, but cane or reed knives are the only aboriginal instruments of this kind to be widely noted. They appear to have been in use everywhere throughout the section. Speaking of the varieties of cane in Louisiana, Du Pratz says:

The canes or reeds of which I have spoken so often may be considered of two kinds. The one grows in moist places. . . . The others, which grow in dry lands, are neither as tall nor as large, but they are so hard that these people used split portions of these canes, which they call *conshac*, with which to cut their meat before the French brought them [metal] knives. (Le Page du Pratz, 1758, vol. 2, pp. 58–59; Swanton, 1911, p. 58.)

The importance of this cane is indicated by the fact that the name is given to one great division of the Choctaw and by the Choctaw and Mobile Indians to the Creeks. The cane is said to have been split into four pieces, each of which cut very satisfactorily for a time. New ones were constantly needed but the cane was widely spread.

Lawson (1860, p. 330) notes the customary Indian mode of handling a knife, that of drawing it toward the user instead of whittling outward.

Aboriginal knives and axes were two of the implements replaced most rapidly by iron and steel after contact had been established with the whites.

Knives and related implements were found in considerable quantities at Key Marco by Cushing:

Cutting and carving knives of shark's teeth, varying in size from tiny straight points to curved blades nearly an inch in length and in width of base, were found by hundreds. Some were associated with their handles. These were of two classes. The greater number of them consisted of shafts from five to seven inches in length by not more than half or three-quarters of an inch in diameter at their thickest portions. Some were slightly curved, others straight, some pointed, others squared at the smaller ends. All were furnished with nocks at the lower ends—which were also a little tapered—for the reception of the hollow bases of the tooth-blades that had been lashed to them and cemented with black gum. Not a few of these doubly-tapered little handles were marvels of finish, highly polished, and some of them were carved or incised with involuted circlets or kwa-like decorations, or else with straight or spiral-rayed rosettes and concentric circles, at the upper ends, as though these had been used as stamps in the finishing of certain kinds of work. The other class of handles was much more various, and was designed for receiving one or more of the shark-tooth blades, not at the extremities, but at the sides of the ends, some transversely, others laterally. They were nearly all carved; a few of them most elaborately; and they ranged in length from the width of the palm of the hand to five or six inches, being adapted for use not only as carvers, but also, probably—such as had single crossblades—as finishing adzes. . . . There were also girdling tools or saws—made from the sharp, flat-toothed lower jaws of king-fishes—into the hollow ends of which curved jaw-bones, the crudest of little handles had been thrust and tied through neat lateral perforations; but these also had formed admirable tools, and I found not a few examples of work done with them, in the shape of round billets that had been severed by them and spirally haggled in such a way as to plainly illustrate the origin of one of the most frequent decorations we found on carved wood works, the spiral rosette just referred to. There were minute little bodkin-shaped chisels of bone and shell, complete in themselves; and there were, of course, numerous awls and the like, made from bone, horn and fish spines. Rasps of very small, much worn and evidently most highly prized fragments of coral sandstone, as well as a few strips of carefully rolled-up shark skin, told the story of how the harder tools had been edged, and the polished wood-, and bone-work finished, here. (Cushing, 1896, pp. 370-371.)

And besides these

. . . dirks or stilettos, made from the foreleg bones of deer, the grip ends flat, the blades conforming in curvature to the original lines of the bones from which they were made. One of them was exquisitely and conventionally carved at the hilt-end to represent the head of a buzzard or vulture, which was no doubt held to be one of the gods of death by these primitive key-dwellers. There were also striking- and thrusting-weapons of slender make and of wood, save that they were sometimes tipped with deer horn or beautifully fashioned spurs of bone, but they were so fragmentary that I have thus far been unable to determine their exact natures. (Cushing, 1896, pp. 373-374.)

CLUBS

With the exception of the throwing club, transformed into a tomahawk and purchased from complacent white traders, the war clubs passed out of use even more rapidly than the bows and arrows, and it is difficult to know how many styles were in use and their precise nature. We get incidental references to war clubs in some places in the De Soto narratives as, for instance, where we read of "clubs set with very sharp fishbones" being found in the hands of Indians at the mouth of the Mississippi (Bourne, 1904, vol. 1, p. 202; Robertson, 1933, p. 285), but nothing like a satisfactory description except in Garcilaso's account of the temple of Talomeco, and there we have to be upon our guard. As we have observed before, there were wooden giants stationed at the door of the temple of Talomeco in pairs, the first four of which were provided with as many different kinds of clubs or axes, specimens of each being preserved in the eight armories annexed to the main building.

[1] The first two [giants] on each side, which were the largest, each held a club the last quarter of which was embellished with a diamond-shaped point and bands made of that copper [already mentioned]. They were so exactly like those clubs which are described as belonging to Hercules that it seemed that either might have been copied from the other.

[2] The second on either side . . . . had broadswords made of wood in the same form that they make them in Spain of iron and steel.

[3] The third had sticks different from the clubs which resembled the swingles used to brake flax, a fathom and a half long, the first two-thirds being thick and the last gradually becoming narrower and having a shovel-shaped end.

[4] The fourth in order had large battle axes corresponding in size to the stature of the giants. One of them had a brass head, the blade being large and very well made and the other end having a four-sided point a handbreadth in length. The other axe had a head exactly like this, with its blade and point, but for greater variety and curiosity it was made of flint. . . . . . .

[5] The fifth held bows and arrows.

[6] The sixth and last figures had very large and handsome pikes with copper heads.

[The first armory they happened to investigate] was full of pikes [like those held by the last-mentioned figures], there being nothing else in it. All were very long and very well made, with heads of brass, which because it was so highly-colored looked like gold. All were adorned with rings of ordinary pearls and seed pearls having three or four turns, placed at intervals along the pikes. Many were covered in the middle (where they would rest on the shoulder and where the head joined the haft) with strips of colored deerskin and along both the upper and lower edges of this strip were borders of vari-colored threads with three, four, five, or six rows of ordinary pearls or seed pearls which embellished them greatly.

In the second room there were only clubs such as those that we said the first giant figures held, which were at the door of the temple, except that those in the room being arms which were among the lord's equipment were decorated with rings of ordinary pearls and seed pearls and borders of colored thread placed at intervals so that the colors were blended with one another and all were inter-mingled with the pearls. The other pikes [clubs?] which the giants held had no ornamentation whatever.

In another room, which was the third, there was nothing but axes like those we said the giants had who were fourth in order at the door of the temple. They had copper heads with a blade on one side and a diamond-shaped point on the other, six inches and a hand's breadth long [respectively]. Many of them had flint heads fastened solidly to the handles with copper bands. These axes also had on their handles rings of ordinary pearls and seed pearls and borders of colored thread.

In another room, which was the fourth, there were broadswords made of various kinds of hard woods such as those that the giants second in order had, all of them being decorated with pearls and seed pearls and borders on the handles and on the first third of the blades.

The fifth room contained only staffs such as those we said the giants of the third order had, but decorated with their rings of ordinary pearls and seed pearls and colored borders all along the handles to where the shovel-shaped end began.

The sixth room had [of course] bows and arrows. (Garcilaso, 1723, pp. 129–134.)

Here are clubs of four types. The first, giving the order used in describing the giants at the doorway, seem to have been like the clubs with stone or iron points let into the end used in later times by the Indians farther north and west. The second type was entirely of wood. The third was also entirely of wood, but spatula- or spoon-shaped. The fourth had edges like the edges of battle-axes or swords either made of copper or pieces of flint. Garcilaso seems to say brass instead of copper, and if they really were brass, we must suppose they had been obtained from Europeans.

We might entertain some doubts regarding the existence of such clubs if it were not for the writings of the Carolina and Virginia explorers. Barlowe say the Algonquian Indians of eastern Carolina had swords "of wood hardened," and that "they have besides a kinde of club, in the end whereof they fasten the sharpe hornes of a stagge, or other beast" (Burrage, 1906, p. 238). The first correspond either to the "swingles" or to the "battle-axes" of Talomeco, but without the metal or flint edges. Hariot (1893, p. 36) mentions "flat edged truncheons also of wood about a yard long," the "swords" of Barlowe.

The swords mentioned by Percy "beset with sharpe stones, and pieces of yron able to cleave a man in sunder" certainly recall Garcilaso's fourth type of club (Narr. Early Va., Tyler ed., 1907, pp. 14, 16). The "Swords like Pollaxes," used apparently by the Susquehanna Indians, again recall the spatula-shaped clubs (Narr. Early Va., Tyler ed., 1907, p. 49).

Their swordes be made of a kind of heavy wood which they have, much like such wooden instruments as our English women swingle their flax withall, and which they call monococks, as the salvadges in Bariena (Darien), in the West Indies, call their(s) macanas, and be alike made; but oftentymes they use for swordes the horne of a deare put through a piece of wood in forme of a pickaxe. Some use a long stone sharpened at both ends, thrust through a handle of wood in the same manner, and these last they are wont to use instead of hatchetts to fell a tree, or cut any massy thing in sonder; but now, by trucking with us, they have thowsands of our iron hatchetts, such as they be. (Strachey, 1849, p. 106.)

Smith says the same not quite so elaborately (Smith, John, Tyler ed., 1907, pp. 102–103). The first of these again seems like the truncheons. The second is like the clubs with stone or iron set into them, and is the "weapon like a hammer" of Spelman (Smith, John, Arber ed., 1884, p. cxiii). This type of club, then, must be regarded as the ancestor of the tomahawk, and the supposition is confirmed by Catesby's short description:

These [tomahawks] were of two kinds: one was a staff about three feet long, with a large knob at the end; the others were made of stone ground to an edge, of the form and size of a small hatchet, and fixed to a strong handle; these would cut, and were of most use, as well for war as for hollowing their canoes, and other mechanick uses; with these they fought and worked, but since the introduction of iron hatchets, which they still call *Tommahawks*, they have wholly laid aside their stone ones. (Catesby, 1731–43, vol. 2, p. ix; Swanton, 1911, p. 127.)

They corresponded to Garcilaso's first and second types. Du Pratz tells us of something similar on the lower Mississippi:

In order that the costume be complete, the warrior must have in his hands a war club. If it is made by the French, this will be a little ax, the edge of which is ordinarily 3 inches long. This ax is light, and is placed in the belt when one is loaded or traveling. The war clubs which the natives make for themselves are of hard wood and have the shape of a cutlass blade, 2½ inches broad and 1½ feet long. They have an edge and a back. Toward the end of the back is a ball 3 inches in diameter, which is part of the same piece. (Le Page du Pratz, 1758, vol. 2, pp. 413–414; Swanton, 1911, p. 127.)

From Stiggins' description it appears that this was the type known as atasa, and, from the fact that a similar word is applied to it by all of the principal Southeastern tribes, it would seem that it was introduced from some one tribe and spread to the rest. Stiggins says it was "shaped like a small gun about 2 feet long, and at the curve near where the lock would be is a thin square piece of iron or steel with a sharp edge drove in to leave a projection of about 2 inches" (Swanton, 1928, p. 406). This could either be retained in the hand or thrown, and was easily supplanted by the European all-metal tomahawk after white contact. The aboriginal type of club, often with the addition of an iron or steel point such as has been described, was in wide use among the Indians of the upper Mississippi after it had been abandoned in the Gulf region. The various modifications introduced into these by canny European manufacturers for the American trade are described by Timberlake as already in circulation among the Cherokee in the eighteenth century. He says that

the hammer-part of [these] being made hollow, and a small hole running from thence along the shank, terminated by a small brass-tube for the mouth, makes a compleat pipe. There are various ways of making these, according to the country or fancy of the purchaser, being all made by the Europeans; some have a long spear at top, and some different conveniences on each side. This is one of their most useful pieces of field-furniture, serving all the offices of hatchet, pipe, and sword; neither are the Indians less expert at throwing it than using it near, but will kill at a considerable distance. (Timberlake, Williams ed., 1927, pp. 77-78.)

Although the flint-edged swords find their counterpart in swords in use by the Mexicans, there seems to be a total absence of them in the intervening territory, except for Cofitachequi and the weapons discovered at Key Marco by Cushing, who describes his finds as follows:

War clubs proper, that is, of wood only, were found in considerable variety. The most common form was that of the short, knobbed bludgeon. Another was nearly three feet long, the handle rounded, tapered, and furnished at the end with an eyelet for the wrist cord. The blade was flattish, widening to about three inches at the head, and it was laterally beveled from both sides to form blunt edges and was notched or roundly serrated, precisely as are some forms of Fijian and Caroline Island clubs. The type was obviously derived from some preexisting kind of blade-set weapon. This was also true, in another way, of the most remarkable form of club we discovered. It was not quite two feet in length, and made of some dark-colored fine grained kind of hard, heavy wood, exquisitely fashioned and finished. The handle was also round and tapering, the head flattened, symmetrically flaring and sharp-edged, the end square or but slightly curved, and terminating in a groove knob or boss, to which tassel-cords had been attached. Just below the flaring head was a double blade, that is, a semilunar, sharp-edged projection on either side, giving the weapon the appearance of a double-edged battle-axe set in a broad-ended club. . . . This specimen was of especial interest, as it was the only weapon of its kind found, up to that time, in the United States; but was absolutely identical in outline with the so-called batons represented in the hands of warrior-figures delineated on the shell gorgets and copper plates found in the southern and central Mississippi mounds—as may be seen in the figure just referred to. It not only recalled these, but also typical double-bladed battle-axes or clubs of South and Central American peoples, from which type I regarded its form, although wholly of wood, as a derivative. . . .

Arrows about four feet in length, perfectly uniform, pointed with hard wood, the shafts made either of a softer and lighter kind of wood or of cane, were found. The nocks of these were relatively large. This suggested that certain curved and shapely clubs, or rather wooden sabres—for they were armed along one edge with keen shark-teeth—might have been used not only for striking, but also for flinging such nocked spears or throwing-arrows. Each of these singular and superbly finished weapons was about three feet long. The handle or grip was straight; thence the blade or shaft was gently curved downward and upward again to the end, which was obliquely truncated below, but terminated above in a creased or slightly bifurcated, spirally curved knob or volute like the end of a violin, and still more like the lower articulation of a human femur [referring at this point to his figure 5, plate 32], which the whole weapon resembled in general outline so strikingly that I was inclined to regard the type it represented as remotely derived from clubs originally made in imitation of thigh-bones. The handle was broader at the back than below, but neatly rounded, and the extreme end delicately flared to insure grasp. At both shank and butt of this grip, oblong holes had been bored obliquely through one side of the back for the attachment of a braided or twisted hand-loop or guard-cord, to still further secure hold. The back of the shaft, too, was wide, and sharp along the lateral edges, from both of which it was hollowed obliquely to the middle, the shallow V-shaped trough or groove thus formed reaching from the hilt to the turned-up end, where it terminated in a little semi-circular, sharp-edged cusp or spur in the central furrow at the base of the knob. The converging sides of the shaft were likewise evenly and sharply creased or fluted from the shank of the grip to the gracefully turned volutes at the sides of the knob. The blade proper, or lower edge, was comparatively thin, like a continuous slightly grooved tongue or an old-fashioned skate blade—save that it was obliquely square, not rounded, at the end. It was transversely pierced at regular intervals by semicircular perforations—twelve in all—beneath each of which the groove was deepened at two points to accommodate the blunt bifurcate roots of the large hooked teeth of the tiger- or "Man-Eater"—shark, with which the sabre was set; so that, like the teeth of a saw, they would all turn one way, namely, toward the handle, as can be seen by reference to the enlarged sketch of one at the end of the figure. Finely twisted cords of sinew had been threaded regularly back and forth through these perforations and alternately over the wings of the sharp teeth, so as to neatly bind each in its socket; and these lashings were reinforced with abundant black rubber-gum—to which their preservation was due.

Now the little cusp or sharp-edged spur at the end of the back-groove was so deeply placed in the crease of the knob that it could have served no practical purpose in a striking weapon. Yet, it was so shaped as to exactly fit the nock of a spear, and since by means of the guard cord, the handle could be grasped not only for striking, but, by shifting or reversing the hold, for hurling as well, I inferred that possibly the instrument had been used in part as an atlatl, in part as a kind of single-edged maquahuitl or blade-set sabre. It was, at any rate, a most formidable weapon and a superb example of primitive workmanship and ingenuity. There were other weapons somewhat like these. But they were only eight or nine inches in length, and were neither knobbed nor creased. They were, however, perforated at the backs for hand cords, and socketed below for six, instead of twelve teeth—set somewhat more closely together—and must have formed vicious slashers or rippers. Then there were certain split bear- and wolf-jaws—neatly cut off so as to leave the canines and two cuspids standing—which, from traces of cement on their bases and sides, appeared to have been similarly attached to curved clubs. (Cushing, 1896, pp. 372–373.)

BOWS AND ARROWS

Elvas describes the bows of the Floridians as "very long," but does not undertake to identify the wood of which they were made. He is more detailed regarding the arrows, however.

The arrows are made of certain reeds, like canes, very heavy, and so tough that a sharpened cane passes through a shield. Some are pointed with a fish bone, as sharp as an awl, and others with a certain stone like a diamond point. (Robertson, 1933, p. 37.)

Garcilaso thus describes the arrows belonging to a certain Cofitachequi chief:

They were all made of reeds; some had heads made of the points of deers' antlers finished to extreme perfection with four corners like the points of a diamond; others had fish-bones for heads, marvelously fashioned for use as arrows. There were others with heads of palm wood and of other strong and durable timber that grows in that country. These arrow-heads had two or three barbs as perfectly made in the wood as if they had been of iron or steel. (Garcilaso, 1723, pp. 408–409.)

One of the several pairs of human figures at the door of the temple of Talomeco held bows and arrows, and one of the latter was pointed with "the tip of a deer antler carved into four points," while "the other arrow had a flint point for a head, the same shape and size as an ordinary dagger" (Garcilaso, 1723, p. 425). In speaking of the arrows in the armory nearby, Garcilaso seems to give us a clue as to their shapes.

For arrowheads they used points of wood, of the bones of land and sea animals, and of flint, as we told in connection with the Indian noble who killed himself. Besides these kinds of arrowheads made of copper, such as those which we put on darts in Spain, there were others with harpoons, also made of copper, and in the form of small chisels, lances, and Moorish darts, which looked as if they had been made in Castile. They noted also that the arrows with flint tips had different kinds of heads; some were in the form of a harpoon, others of small chisels, others were rounded like a punch, and others had two edges like the tip of a dagger. The Spaniards examined all these curiously and wondered that they could fashion such things out of a material as resistant as flint, though in view of what Mexican history says about the broadswords and other arms which the Indians of that land made of flint, a part of this wonderment of ours will be lost. The bows were handsomely made and enameled in various colors, which they did with a certain cement that gives them such a luster that one can see himself in them. . . . Not satisfied with this lustrous finish, they put on the bows many circles of ordinary pearls and seed pearls placed at intervals, these circles or rings beginning at the handles and going in order to the tips in such manner that the first circles were of large pearls and made seven or eight turns, the second were of smaller pearls and had fewer turns, and thus they went on decreasing to the last ones, which were near the tips and were very small seed pearls. The arrows also had circles of seed pearls at intervals, but not of [the larger] pearls, there being seed pearls only. (Garcilaso, 1723, pp. 433–434.)

A little later we have information regarding Florida arrows from the French and English chroniclers. Ribault and Spark both say that the

arrow shafts were made of reeds, but the latter tells us they were
longer than the arrows of other Indians and differed also in having
nocks and feathers, which the other lacks, whereby they shoot very stedy: the
heads of the same are vipers teeth, bones of fishes, flint stones, piked points of
knives, which they hauing gotten of the French men, broke the same & put the
points of them in their arrowes heads: some of them haue their heads of siluer,
othersome that haue want of these, put in a kind of hard wood, notched, which
pierceth as farre as any of the rest. (French, 1875, p. 174; Hakluyt, 1847–89,
vol. 3, p. 613; Swanton, 1922, pp. 356–357.)

Says Laudonnière, "they head their arrows with the teeth of fish,
which they work very finely and handsomely" (Laudonnière, 1586, p.
7; Swanton, 1922, p. 356).

In Cushing's text, given above, mention is made of "arrows about
four feet in length, perfectly uniform, pointed with hard wood, or
of cane," but he immediately suggests that these may have been used
with spear throwers and not with bows.

At a later date the Cusabo Indians were found employing reed
arrows pointed with sharp stones or fishbones (Swanton, 1922, p. 74).

In eastern North Carolina, Barlowe found arrows "of small canes,
headed with a sharpe shell or tooth of a fish sufficient enough to kill a
naked man" (Burrage, 1906, p. 238). Hariot (1893, p. 36) speaks of
reed arrows, but says nothing about their points. Percy found the arrows of the Virginia Indians "of Canes or Hasell, headed with very
sharpe stones, and are made artificially like a broad Arrow: other
some of their Arrowes are headed with the ends of Deeres hornes, and
are feathered very artificially" (Percy in Narratives of Virginia,
Tyler ed., 1907, p. 17). Smith gives a more detailed account:

Their arrowes are made, some of straight young sprigs, which they head with
bone some 2 or 3 inches long. These they use to shoot at squirrles on trees. An
other sort of arrowes they use, made of reeds. These are peeced with wood, headed
with splinters of christall or some sharpe stone, the spurres of a Turkey, or the
bill of some bird. For his knife, he hath the splinter of a reed to cut his feathers
in forme. . . . To make the noch of his arrow hee hath the tooth of a Bever set
in a sticke, wherewith he grateth it by degrees. His arrow head he quickly
maketh with a little bone, which he ever weareth at his bracer, of any splint of a
stone, or glasse in the form of a hart, and these they glew to the end of their
arrowes. With the sinewes of Deare, the tops of Deares hornes boiled to a jelly,
they make a glew that will not dissolve in cold water. (Smith, John, Tyler ed.,
1907, p. 102.)

Strachey parallels this but his words are worth including:

Their arrowes are made some of streight young spriggs, which they head with
bone, two or three inches long, and these they use to shoote at squirrells and all
kind of fowle. Another sort of arrowes they use made of reedes: these are peeced
with wood, headed with splinters of cristall or some sharp stone, with the spurres
of a turkey cock, or the bill of some bird, feathered with a turkey's feather, which
with a knife (made of the splinter of a reed) which he will make as sharpe as a
surgeon's gamott [an incision knife] he cutts into forme, and with which knife,
also, he will joynt a deare, or any beast, shape his sandalls, buskins, mantell, etc.

To make the notch of his arrowe, he hath the tooth of a bever sett in a stick, wherewith he grateth yt by degrees; his arrowe hedd he quickly maketh with a litle bone (which he ever weareth at his bracer, and which bracer is commonly of some beast's skynne, eyther of the woolf, badger, or black fox, etc.) of any splint of a stone, or peece of a deare's bone, of an oyster shell, or of a cristall, in the form of a heart, barb'd and jagged, and these they glue to the end of their arrowes with the synewes of deare and the topps of deare's horne boyled into a jelly, of which they make a glue that will not dissolve in cold water. (Strachey, 1849, p. 106.)

And now Beverley:

They made their Arrows of Reeds or small Wands, which needed no other cutting, but in the length, being otherwise ready for Notching, Feathering and Heading. They fledged their Arrows with Turkey Feathers, which they fastened with Glue made of the Velvet Horns of a Deer, but it has not that quality it's said to have, of holding against all Weathers; they arm'd the Heads with a white transparent Stone, like that of Mexico mentioned by Peter Martyr, of which they have many Rocks; they also headed them with the Spurs of the Wild Turkey Cock. (Beverley, 1705, bk. 3, p. 60)

Writing in 1728, Byrd states that the Indians of his acquaintance, meaning probably the Nottoway, used formerly to point their arrows with the spurs of turkey cocks, "tho' now they point them with a Sharp Stone" (Bassett, 1909, p. 150), which looks like a reversion, but may probably be explained by the decrease in wild turkeys.

Lawson:

Arrowwood growing on the [sand] banks is used by the Indians [of the Piedmont tribes] for arrows and gun stocks. It grows as straight as if plained, and is of all sizes. This is as tough and pliable as the smallest canes. (Lawson 1860, p. 167.)

Catesby:

Their arrows were reeds headed with pieces of stone, spurs of turkey-cocks, and the bones of fish. (Catesby, 1731–43, vol. 2, p. ix.)

Cherokee arrows were pointed as follows:

Cutting a bit of thin brass, copper, bone, or scales of a particular fish, into a point with two beards, or some into an acute triangle, they split a little of their arrow, which is generally of reeds; into this they put the point, winding some deers sinew round the arrow, and through a little hole they make in the head; then they moisten the sinew with their spittle, which, when dry, remains fast glewed, or ever untwists. (Timberlake, Williams ed., 1927, p. 85.)

Adair:

They make perhaps the finest bows, and the smoothest barbed arrows, of all mankind. On the point of them is fixed either a scooped point of buck-horn, or turkey-cock spurs, pieces of brass, or flint-stone. (Adair, 1775, p. 456–457.)

Speck has a rather detailed account of Yuchi arrows which adds important details:

Arrows, *la cū'*, for hunting are made of the straight twigs of arrow-wood or of cane stalks of the proper thickness. In the former case it was only necessary to scrape off the bark and season the twigs. The Yuchi do not seem to have had the idea of the foreshaft. The point, *lacipá*, which was formerly of stone is nowadays made of iron and is bound by means of sinew into a split in the shaft. The arrows are feathered preferably with hawk feathers, as the Indians believe the hawk to be swift and sure in its flight. Turkey tail feathers are much used also. The split plumes, two in number, are bound to the shaft at both ends with sinew. One side of the feather is shaved clean of ribs up to within an inch of the outer end. The lower or base end of the quill is then lashed on flat. The outer end is turned down and the turned down length is lashed on. In this way an ingenious twist is given to the feather, which causes the arrow to revolve in its flight, acting on the principle of the rifled bullet. There is some diversity in the length of the arrow shaft and in the size of the arrow head. For killing large game and in warfare the shafts used are almost three feet long with iron triangular arrow heads. But in hunting small game they have simple round sharpened shafts which are seasoned in heat to make them stiff. The arrows used for shooting fish are somewhat different from the ones described above. . . . [They are generally unfeathered shafts with charred points, but the better ones are provided with points like cones made by pounding a piece of some flat metal over the end of the shaft. (Speck, 1909, p. 24.)] Blunt wooden-headed arrows, so common everywhere, were also used for stunning small animals and birds.

The arrow shaft in all cases is cylindrical, and of the same width throughout. In some cases, however, there is a slight widening at the notch to give a better grip. Several instances were also noticed where there were two notches at right angles to each other. This feature, according to the native idea, makes it possible for the shooter to send his arrow so that the iron point is either vertical or horizontal. In the former case the point passes more readily between the ribs of deer, bison and other animals, while in the latter case it is designed to pass between the ribs of man. The double notching also facilitates adjustment in rapid shooting. An old arrow, one that has seen use, is thought to shoot better and to be more effective in general than a new one. (Speck, 1909, pp. 21–22.)

According to the same writer, arrows of the Taskigi Creeks were of the same materials but feathered on three sides instead of two (Speck, 1907, p. 110).

The Seminole arrows described by MacCauley seem to be of the type used in shooting fish:

The arrows are of cane and of hard wood and vary in length from two to four feet; they are, as a rule, tipped with a sharp conical roll of sheet iron. (MacCauley, 1887, p. 517.)

One of the oldest and best Creek informants of the writer, a man who was born in Alabama before the removal of his people west and who had spent a large part of his life hunting, when the bow was the principal hunting weapon, gave me the following items regarding arrows:

In hunting birds, squirrels, and other small animals cane arrows were used, but for larger game such as bear and deer they resorted to arrows with iron points, though he was aware that they pointed their arrows anciently with fish bones and flint. He thought that the ends of the cane arrows might sometimes have been hardened by putting them in the fire, but he did not know personally of its having been done. For shafts they sometimes used hickory and sometimes young shoots of the red dogwood obtained in the bottoms in Oklahoma. Two or three feathers, most often those of young turkeys, though the kind mattered little, were fastened to the shaft by means of a glue obtained from deer antlers.

An Alabama informant said that his people made arrow shafts of cane or of wood from several different kinds of bushes and trees, one of which was the black haw. The points were sometimes hardened in the fire and sometimes made of pieces of iron or tin. He did not know what arrow points were made of before they had metals of European origin. The shafts were feathered either in two places, on opposite sides of the shaft, or else in three places, at equal intervals around its circumference. No poison was used (author's notes).

William Bartram noted that the Florida Creeks pointed their arrows with the scales of the "great brown spotted gar" (Bartram, 1792, p. 174), perhaps the sharp fish bones which Elvas and Spark had noted so many years before. Use of shell in the manufacture of arrow points has been assumed by some writers, but I find no reference in the literature as applying to Florida.

Our descriptions of the arrows in use on the lower Mississippi are not very good. Du Pratz states that the Natchez made them of the wood from a tree called by the name of the arrow "which is very hard." He adds, "The points are put into the fire to harden," but this was not the only type of arrow point in use, for those intended for bison or deer were provided with great splinters of bone adjusted in the split end of the arrow shaft, the cleft and the casing being bound with splints of feathers and the whole soaked in fish glue. War arrows were ordinarily armed with the scales of the garfish fixed in place in the same manner, while arrows intended for large fish such as the carp, sucker, or catfish, were merely provided with a bone pointed at both ends "so that the first pierces and makes an entrance for the arrow, and the other end, which stands out from the wood, prevents the arrow from falling out of the fish's body." This arrow was also attached by a cord to a wooden float which prevented the fish from diving to the bottom or becoming lost. Besides the use or arrowwood, shafts were made of cane (Le Page du Pratz, 1758, vol. 2, pp. 167–168; Swanton, 1911, pp. 58–59). The feathers were fastened in place by fish glue, or as noted above, of a glue made from deer horn. Glue was also obtained from bison hoofs (Morfi, 1935, p. 67).

There are some few suggestions that arrows may occasionally have been poisoned. Du Pratz states that a certain creeper was known to native doctors as "the medicine for poisoned arrows" (Le Page du Pratz, 1758, vol. 2, p. 56; Swanton, 1911, p. 84), though it is not clear whether he means that poison was obtained from it to use on arrows or whether it was an antidote for such poison. But Du Pratz himself makes no positive affirmation that poisoned arrows were employed. Father Padilla, in his narrative of the De Luna expedition, mentions the practice, but in a very incidental way, and the reference by itself is worth little (Padilla, 1919, pp. 205–217; Swanton, 1922, p. 233). Garcilaso (1723, p. 189) tells us that De Soto's Spaniards were told that the Indians of a province called Colima, which must have been in central Arkansas, used poison in this way, but on entering that province they found the accusation to be false. Finally Ranjel makes a sweeping statement to the effect that none of the Indians in the region traversed by De Soto employed poison (Bourne, 1904, vol. 2, p. 69), and no one has even suggested that their blowgun arrows were poisoned. In Virginia, however, a certain plant was used to poison individuals and there seems to be some ground for supposing that poisoned arrows were used, for one of Newport's party (1607) says: "One gaue me a Roote wherewith they poison their arrows" (Smith, John, Arber ed., 1884, xlviii).

They used arrows often in setting fire to enemy houses or other buildings. Garcilaso (1723, p. 166) says that the Chickasaw fastened a certain inflammable herb to their arrows and with these set fire to the houses in a village where the Spaniards spent the winter of 1540–41. Le Moyne describes and illustrates the same custom as common in the Florida peninsula, except that they utilized some of the long Spanish moss common in the country instead of the herb reported by Garcilaso (Le Moyne, 1875, p. 12; Swanton, 1922, pp. 379–380).

Elvas and Garcilaso both state that the Indian bow was "very long," and the latter is somewhat detailed regarding the construction and use of it:

The arms which these Indians carry are bows and arrows, and although it is true that they are skillful in the use of the other weapons which they have . . . they do not [ordinarily] use any other arms except the bow and arrow, because for those who carry them they are the greatest embellishment and ornament. . . . For all these reasons, and because of the effectiveness of these arms which are superior to all others at both short and long range, in re- treating or attacking, in fighting in battle or in the recreation of the chase, these Indians carry them, and these arms are much used throughout the New World.

The bows are of the same height as he who carries them, and as the Indians of La Florida are generally of tall stature, their bows are more than two varas in length and thick in proportion. They make them of oak and of various other hard and very heavy woods which they have. They are so hard to bend that no Spaniard, however much he might try, was able to pull the cord back so that his hand touched his face, but the Indians through their long experience and skill drew back the cord with the greatest ease to a point behind the ear and made such terrible and wonderful shots as we shall see presently.

They make the cords of the bows from deerskin, taking a strip two finger-breadths in width from the hide, running from the tip of the tail to the head. After removing the hair they dampen and twist it tightly; one end they tie to the branch of a tree and from the other they hang a weight of four or five *arrobas*, and they leave it thus until it becomes about the thickness of the larger strings of a bass-viol. These cords are extremely strong. In order to shoot safely in such a manner that when the cord springs back it may not injure the left arm, they wear as a protection on the inner side a half-bracer, which covers them from the wrist to the part of the arm that is usually bled (sangradura). It is made of thick feathers and attached to the arm with a deerskin cord which they give seven or eight turns at the place where the cord springs back most strongly. (Garcilaso, 1723, pp. 6–7; Robertson, 1933, pp. 18–19.)

The adornments lavished upon the bows at Talomeco have been described already.

Elvas extols the efficiency of Floridian bows to an almost equal degree. It is unlikely that any of the bows were made of oak as Garcilaso (1723, p. 7) supposes. At least there is no other reference to the use of that kind of wood.

Spark is on the right track when, in speaking of the Indians of Florida, he says:

Their bowes are made of a kind of Yew, but blacker than ours [probably the black locust], and for the most part passing the strength of the Negros or Indians, for it is not greatly inferior to ours. (Hakluyt, 1847–89, vol. 3, p. 613; Swanton, 1922, p. 356.)

Laudonnière agrees with Garcilaso as to the string:

They make the string of their bow of the gut of the stag, or of a stag's skin, which they know how to dress as well as any man in France, and with as different sorts of colors. (Laudonnière, 1586, p. 7; Swanton, 1922, p. 356.)

Hariot states that the bows of the coast people of Carolina were of "Witch hazle," which Percy confirms, adding that their strings were of leather (Smith, John, Tyler ed., 1907, p. 17; Hariot, 1893, p. 34). Smith tells us that "they bring their bowes to the forme of ours by the scraping of a shell," but Strachey who is apt to parallel Smith, here diverges.

The bowes are of some young plant, eyther of the locust-tree or of weech [witch hazel], which they bring to the forme of ours by the scraping of a deare's hide twisted. (Smith, John, Tyler ed., 1907, p. 105.)

Beverley gives us another item bearing on the manufacture:

They made their Bows of the Locust Treet, an excessive hard Wood when it is dry, but much more easily cut when it is green, of which they always took the advantage. (Beverley, 1705, bk. 3, p. 60.)

Lawson speaking for the Carolina area, remarks: "Of this [locust] the Indians made their choicest bows, it being very tough and flexible," and that, when they could not get that material, they used white [red?] mulberry (Lawson, 1860, p. 163, 172). Catesby (1731–43, vol. 2, p. ix) also mentions the use of wood of "the locust-tree, i. e., *pseudo-acacia*, it being when old a very tough and pliant wood."

Timberlake says of the Cherokee:

Their bows are of several sorts of wood, dipped in bears oil, and seasoned before the fire, and a twisted bear's gut for the string. (Timberlake, Williams ed., 1927, pp. 85–86.)

The [Yuchi] bow, [according to Speck], is a single almost straight stave of bois d'arc (*Toxylon pomiferum*) or Osage Orange, about five feet in length. Sassafras and hickory bows were sometimes made. No backing of sinew is known to have been used. The stave is broadest in the middle, where it is about one and one-half inches in width, tapering to one inch at the ends. The thickness of the stave is about three-quarters of an inch. The rich dark color of the wood is brought out by greasing. In section the bow is almost rectangular. The ends are cut into little knobs of several shapes to hold the string. The bow string is made of deer sinew, or strips of rawhide twisted tightly. Squirrel skins are much in use for bowstrings. The skin is cut around the edge spirally toward the center, thus giving a single long strip. As extra strength is desired, four such strips are twisted together, forming quite a thick cord. (Speck, 1909, p. 20.)

The Taskigi Creek Indians mentioned, like the Yuchi, used the Osage Orange and hickory (Speck, 1907, p. 110). Adair (1775, p. 355) observed the Choctaw using hickory bows in their civil war.

The bow seen in use by the Florida Seminole in 1880–81 by Mac-Cauley was of "a single piece of mulberry or other elastic wood" and "from four to six feet in length," the bowstring being "of twisted deer rawhide" (MacCauley, 1887, p. 517).

A reliable Creek informant already quoted gave me the following information regarding the bows of his people:

In their homes west of the Mississippi they used Osage orange, or bois d'arc, called by them "yellow wood" (ito la' ni), but this was not to be had in Alabama, where they employed black locust, sassafras, or cedar, the woods being rated in about that order. The best bowstring was of deer sinews or the sinews of other large animals, which they tore apart and softened in water, after which two or three strands were twisted together to make the cord. Strings made of squirrel skin were excellent but not as good as the last. The squirrel skin was cut very carefully to the desired length, evidently by running the point of a knife round upon it in spiral fashion, then softened in warm water, after which two or three strands were twisted together, as in the case of the string first-mentioned. Sometimes bowstrings were made out of the entrails of a bear, but they were not as good as those already described. Still another kind was cut from the thick skin on a deer's neck by running the point of a knife round on it spirally, the piece thus obtained being twisted carefully. They never made bowstrings out of bark.

According to my Alabama informant, bows were made of cedar, ironwood, pine, dogwood, and still other woods, but he regarded cedar bows as the best. Bowstrings were of cowhide, skin from the loins of a deer, and buckskin and were cut out by the usual spiral process. He thought that in former times they had probably been made of bákca, bass, or slippery elm bark. He had never seen a bow with sharply bent ends, and my Creek informant stated that his people did not make these, though he had seen them in use by the Indians on the Plains. For the manufacture of bow strings, see also pages 448–449.

The Natchez bows, according to Du Pratz, were made of "acacia wood [evidently the black locust] which is hard and easy to split." Cords were of the bark of trees or steeped and twisted sinew (Le Page du Pratz, 1758, vol. 2, p. 167; Swanton, 1911, p. 58).

West of the Mississippi, the one great source of bow material was the Osage orange, which also bears the significant name of bois d'arc. This was especially abundant in the country of the Caddo Indians who trafficked with it as far as the Quapaw Indians at the mouth of Arkansas River and westward to the Pueblos of New Mexico (Margry, 1875–86, vol. 3, p. 412; Harrington, J. P., 1916, p. 68).

Wrist guards were probably in general use. Garcilaso has already been quoted.

A bark wrist guard is mentioned and figured by Le Moyne, Smith speaks of "shooting gloves and bracers", and Strachey says that this bracer was "commonly of some beast's skynne, eyther of the woolf, badger, or black fox, etc." (Le Moyne, 1875, p. 10, pl. 14; Swanton, 1922, p. 357; Narr. Early Va., Tyler ed., 1907, pp. 66, 69, 172; Strachey, 1849, p. 106; and pl. 67 herein). This is not mentioned farther west, the use of the bow having passed out rapidly for the heavier sort of work, but my Creek and Alabama informants both remembered that a cowhide guard was used for this purpose, probably like the one figured by Speck (1909, fig. 3). The Creek name for this was kápálká. A type of bow in use by the Chitimacha had such sharply bent ends that a wrist guard would seem to have been superfluous (Swanton, 1911, p. 347).

Quivers are seldom mentioned. They were usually made of skin. (Swanton, 1922, p. 357; Smith, John, Tyler ed., 1907, p. 45; Adair, 1775, p. 457.) Le Challeux states that the Timucua ordinarily kept their arrows in their hair, from which they could withdraw them to discharge with great rapidity (Gaffarel, 1875, p. 461; Swanton, 1922, p. 347).

So rapidly did guns replace bows and arrows as the offensive weapon of major importance to be used in war, and to a less degree in hunting, that our best accounts of the bow technique come from the earliest narratives. In the narrative of the Fidalgo of Elvas, we read:

Those people are so warlike and so quick that they make no account of foot-soldiers; for if these go for them, they flee, and when their adversaries turn their backs they are immediately on them. The farthest they flee is the distance of an arrow shot. They are never quiet but always running and crossing from one side to another so that the crossbows or the arquebuses can not be aimed at them; and before a crossbowman can fire a shot, an Indian can shoot three or four arrows, and very seldom does he miss what he shoots at. If the arrow does not find armor, it penetrates as deeply as a crossbow . . . generally when [the stone-pointed arrows] strike against armor, they break off at the place where they [i. e., the points] are fastened on. Those of cane split and enter through the links of mail and are more hurtful.   (Robertson, 1933, p. 37.)

However, in describing the fight about the Alibamo fort, Garcilaso (1723, p. 174) states that the flint-pointed arrows did more harm than the rest because, besides their piercing qualities, the sides cut any surface that they grazed. Yet he also testifies that at one point west of the Mississippi River, a cane arrow "with the point of the same material cut obliquely and hardened in the fire" penetrated the leg armor of a horseman, "went through the right thigh, and after going through the tree and pad of the saddle, two or three inches of the arrow passed on and wounded the horse" (Garcilaso, 1723, p. 217). Ranjel relates how a stout ash lance, borne by one of the Spanish cavaliers at the battle of Mabila, was pierced by an arrow as by an auger, and in the battle with the Chickasaw three horses were shot through both shoulders (Bourne, 1904, vol. 2, pp. 127, 134). Garcilaso affirms of the Apalachee Indians that

while a Spaniard was firing one shot and making ready for another, an Indian would shoot six or seven arrows. They are so skillful and ready that they scarcely have discharged one before they have another in the bow.   (Garcilaso, 1723, p. 73.)

The force of Indian arrows seems to have become the occasion for some "tall" stories, Garcilaso supplying the following:

In one of the first skirmishes which the Spaniards had with the Indians of Apalache the *maese de campo* Luis de Moscoso received an arrow wound in the right side [the arrow] passing through a buckskin jacket and a coat of mail that he wore beneath it, which because it was so highly burnished had cost a hundred and fifty ducats in Spain. The rich men had brought many of these, because they were very highly regarded. The arrow also passed through a quilted doublet and wounded him in such a manner that, entering obliquely, it did not kill him. Amazed at such an unusual shot the Spaniards wished to see just what their highly burnished coats of mail upon which they had depended so much could withstand. On arriving at the pueblo they set up in the plaza one of the baskets which the Indians make of reeds, resembling vintage-baskets, and having chosen the best coat of mail that they had they put it over the basket, which was very firmly woven. Taking off the chains of one of the Apalache Indians they gave him a bow and arrow and ordered him to shoot at the coat of mail, which was fifty paces away.

The Indian, having shaken his arms with his fists closed in order to call up his strength, shot the arrow, which passed through the coat of mail and the basket so clean and with such force that if a man had been on the other side it would have transfixed him also. Seeing the little or no protection that one coat of mail gave against an arrow, the Spaniards wished to see what two would do. Thus they ordered another very fine one to be put on over the one on the basket, and giving the Indian another arrow they told him to shoot it as he had the first one, to see if he were man enough to shoot through both of them.

The Indian, again shaking his arms as if he were gathering new strength, for the defense against him was now doubled, discharged the arrow. He struck the coats of mail and the basket through the center and the arrow passed through the four thicknesses of steel and lodged there, half-way through. When the Indian saw that it had not come out clean on the other side he showed great annoyance, and said to the Spaniards: "Let me shoot another, and if it does not pass clear through both sides as the first one did, hang me here and now. The second arrow did not leave the bow as I wished it to and therefore did not pass through the coats of mail like the first one."

The Spaniards were unwilling to grant the Indian's request because they did not want their coats of mail further maltreated, and thenceforth they were undeceived with regard to the little defense that their much esteemed coats of mail afforded against arrows. Thus the owners themselves made fun of them, calling them linen from Flanders, and in place of them they made loose quilted jackets three or four finger-breadths in thickness with long skirts which would cover the breasts and haunches of the horses. These jackets made from blankets would resist the arrows better than any other defensive armament, and the thick and unpolished coats of mail which were not much valued, with some other protection which they put under them, were a better defense against arrows than the very elegant and highly burnished ones. Thus the cheaper ones came to be more valued and the expensive ones laid aside. (Garcilaso, 1723, pp. 96–97.)

This idea of quilted armor may have been borrowed from the Mexican Indians.

Percy gives us the results of a similar test of native American archery:

One of our Gentlemen having a Target which hee trusted in, thinking it would beare out a slight shot, hee set it up against a tree, willing one of the Savages to shoot; who tooke from his backe an Arrow of an elle long, drew it strongly in his Bowe, shoots the Target a foote thorow, or better: which was strange, being that a Pistoll could not pierce it. Wee seeing the force of his Bowe, afterwards set him up a steele Target; he shot again, and burst his arrow all to pieces. (Narr. Early Va., Tyler ed., 1907, p. 17.)

Smith and Strachey say:

Forty yards will they shoot levell, or very neare the mark, and 120 is their best at Random. (Smith, John, Tyler ed., 1907, p. 104; Strachey, 1849, p. 106.)

The great bane of the American archer, as of his European brother, seems to have been rain. Alonso de Carmona related that the Chickasaw were foiled by a heavy fall of rain in an attempted attack upon De Soto's troops while they were recovering from the disaster at the Chickasaw town (Garcilaso, 1723, p. 170).

In spite of the efficiency of their major weapon, the Gulf Indians took readily to firearms so that Adair, writing in the middle of the eigtheenth century, is able to assert:

No people are more expert than the Indians in the use of fire-arms, and the bow and quiver: they can fresh stock their guns, only with a small hatchet and knife, and straighten the barrels, so as to shoot with proper direction. They likewise alter, and fix all the springs of the lock, with others of the sort they may have out of use; but such a job costs .the red artist about two months work. (Adair, 1775, p. 425.)

As to their skill with this imported weapon, Lawson (1860, p. 51) tells us that his Indian guide in South Carolina "always shot with a single ball, missing but two shots in about forty; they being curious artists in managing a gun to make it carry either ball or shot, true."

LANCES, SPEARS, AND JAVELINS

Fish spears were in use throughout the region under discussion, and Hariot describes those of the coast Indians of North Carolina as follows:

They fasten vnto their Reedes or longe Rodds, the hollowe tayle of a certaine fishe like to a sea crabb in steede of a poynte, wherewith by nighte or day they stricke fishes, and take them opp into their boates. They also know how to vse the prickles, and pricks of other fishes. [Hariot, 1893, pl. 14.]

According to Smith and Strachey, in the Virginia tidewater country fish were generally shot with arrows, but the Accomack Indians of the eastern shore used "staves like unto Javelins headed with bone" (Smith, John, Tyler ed., 1907, p. 103; Strachey, 1849, p. 75). A very primitive kind of fish spear is indicated by Beverley (1705, bk. 2, p. 32) in the following words:

Before the Arrival of the *English* there, the *Indians* had Fish in such vast Plenty, that the Boys and Girls wou'd take a pointed Stick, and strike the lesser sort, as they Swam upon the Flats.

He also mentions "a gig, or pointed spear" in use during the night in "fire-fishing" (Beverley, 1705, bk. 2, p. 34). On a branch of Broad River, an Indian in Bartram's party (1773) caught a fish by means of "a reed harpoon, pointed very sharp, barbed, and hardened by the fire" (Bartram, 1792, p. 44). Adair mentions this type of spear and the use to which it was put, and so does Speck in his account of the Yuchi, the material being cane whittled to a sharp point, or a wooden spear with the point hardened in the fire (Speck, 1909, pp. 24–25).

There are also references to the use of pikes, lances, javelins, and similar weapons in war. In 1528 the Indians near Mobile Bay attacked Narvaez and his companions with "slings and darts" though possibly we have to deal here with spear-throwers (Cabeza de Vaca, Bandelier ed., 1905, p. 49; Swanton, 1922, p. 146). The sixth and last pair of human figures at the door of the temple of Talomeco held in their hands "very large and handsome pikes with copper heads" (Garcilaso, 1723, p. 131). Similar pikes were found in one of the storehouses nearby although Garcilaso seems to say here that they were pointed with brass instead of copper. However, if they were of native manufacture they could only have been of copper. These were ornamented with rings of pearls (Garcilaso, 1723, p. 133). Nothing is said, however, about the use of such implements in war until we come to the province of Tula in southwestern Arkansas. The people there, who were quite different from all their neighbors to the eastward and almost certainly belonged to the Caddoan stock, resisted the Spaniards savagely and used "large, long poles, like lances, the ends hardened by "fire" (Bourne, 1904, vol. 2, p. 148). Elvas calls them "long poles resembling pikes" (Robertson, 1933, p. 196). Garcilaso (1723, p. 191) describes these as "clubs two or three *varas* long," which would mean a different sort of weapon. Garcilaso's words might also lead one to suppose that this was a temporary device adopted for the occasion, but such was evidently not the case. It is plain from Ranjel's narrative that the lance was already well known to them. We are here approaching the Plains and along with the Plains evidences of bison hunting on a large scale in which lances were usefully employed. Garcilaso tells us several times that the Indians on and near the lower Mississippi were in the habit of putting the heads of their enemies on the heads of lances stuck up at the entrances of their temples, but these may have been on "pickets" instead of "lances" for the French a century and a half later found these Indians using pickets in this way.

At a later period Ribault observed "short lances" among the Timucua (French, 1875, p. 174; Swanton, 1922, p. 356). Most of these seem to have been kept in the hand, but Adair (1775, p. 415) speaks of the "sure-shafted javelin" as one of the weapons of a Chickasaw warrior and Timberlake (Williams ed., 1927, p. 77) probably has the same weapon in mind when he mentions "darts" in the war equipment of a Cherokee. These are distinguished from tomahawks, and we seem to have no description of them and no indication of their exact character.

One of my own Alabama informants had heard of spears thrown from the hand, and a Natchez Indian stated that they anciently had cane spears 6 or 7 feet long headed with long, barbed points of flint, later replaced by iron. The latter claimed that these were used in hunting large animals like bison, deer, and bear. They were thrown at the animal or else stuck into the ground with the point protruding, when the hunter would sing a song which caused animals to run upon them. This introduces a magical element, but the story indicates a belief that such weapons were used in former times.

Spear throwers have been found in the deposits at Key Marco, Fla., among the remains of the Bluff Dwellers of Arkansas, and along the Tennessee, but there is, to my knowledge, only one certain historical reference to their employment in this section, though spear throwers may have figured in the attack upon Narvaez near modern Pensacola. The special reference is by Garcilaso, the weapon in question being observed among Indians at the mouth of the Mississippi, and is as follows:

One Spaniard was wounded by a weapon that the Castilians in the Indies call a *tiradera* (javelin), which we shall call more accurately a *bohordo* because it is shot with a stock (*amiento*) of wood or a cord. The Spaniards had not seen this weapon in all the places they had visited in Florida until that day. In Peru the Indians use it a great deal. It is a weapon a fathom long made of a firm rush, though spongy in the center, of which they also make arrows. They make heads for them of deer horn, fashioned in all perfection with four points or harpoons of palm or other wood that they have, as strong and heavy as iron. So that the part of the arrow or dart made of the rush will not split by the barb when it hits its mark, they make a knot where the head or harpoon joins it and another one at the other end, which the crossbowmen call *batalla* on their darts, where it receives the cord of the bow or the stock with which they shoot it. The stock is of wood two *tercias* long, and they shoot the dart with it with extreme force, so that it has been known to pass through a man armed with a coat of mail. The Spaniards in Peru feared this weapon more than any other the Indians had, for their arrows are not so terrible as those of Florida.

The dart or long arrow with which they wounded our Spaniard of whom we were speaking had three barbs in the place of one, similar to the three longest fingers of the hand. The barb in the center was a hand-breadth longer than the two on the sides, and thus it went through the thigh from one side to the other. (Garcilaso, 1723, pp. 249–250.)

Cushing describes the atlatls found at Key Marco as follows:

It was significant that no bows were discovered in any portion of the court, but of atlatls or throwing sticks, both fragmentary and entire, four or five examples were found. Two of the most perfect of these were also the most characteristic, since one was double-holed, the other single-holed. The first . . . was some eighteen inches in length, delicate, slender, slightly curved and originally, quite springy. It was fitted with a short spur at the smaller end and was unequally spread or flanged at the larger or grasping end. The shaft-groove terminated in an ornamental device, whence a slighter crease led quite to the end of the handle, and the whole implement was delicately carved and engraved with edge-lines and when first taken from the muck exhibited a high polish and beautiful rosewood color. The other . . . was somewhat longer, slightly thicker, wider shafted, more curved, and, as I have said before, furnished with only a single finger-hole. At the smaller end was a diminutive but very perfect carving of a rabbit, in the act of thumping, so placed that his erect tail formed the propelling spur. This instrument also was fitted with a short shaft-groove and was carved and decorated with edge and side lines, and the handle-end was beautifully curved down and rounded so as to form a volute or rolled knob, giving it a striking resemblance to the ornate forms of the atlatl of Central America; a resemblance that also applied somewhat to the double-holed specimen, and to various of the fragmentary spear-throwers. (Cushing, 1896, p. 371.)

BLOWGUNS

Speaking of the Choctaw, Bossu says that the boys

are very skilful in the use of the blowgun. It is made of a cane about seven feet long, into which they put a little arrow provided with thistle-down, and when they see something [which they want to hit] they blow into it, and they often kill small birds. (Bossu, 1768, vol. 2, p. 103.)

Romans, who visited the Choctaw a few years later, describes the use of the blowgun as follows:

The young savages also use a very strait cane, eight or nine feet long, cleared of its inward divisions of the joints; in this they put a small arrow, whose one end is covered one third of the whole length with cotton or something similar to it: this they hold nearest their mouth and blow it so expertly as seldom to miss a mark fifteen or twenty yards off and that so violently as to kill squirrils and birds therewith; with this instrument they often plague dogs and other animals according to the innate disposition to cruelty of all savages, being encouraged to take a delight in torturing any poor animal that has the misfortune to fall into their hands. (Romans, 1775, p. 77.)

In 1761 Timberlake observed that the Cherokee children

at eight or ten years old, are very expert at killing [small animals and birds] with a sarbacan, or hollow cane, through which they blow a small dart, whose weakness obliges them to shoot at the eye of the larger sort of prey, which they seldom miss. (Timberlake, Williams ed., 1927, p. 72.)

Bushnell found a single blowgun in use among the Choctaw of Bayou Lacomb, La.:

The blowgun (kaklu'mpa) is about 7 feet in length; it is made of a single piece of cane (*Arundinaria macrosperma;* Choctaw uske), formed into a tube by perforation of the joints, which was given a smooth bore of uniform diameter throughout. The darts (*shumä'nte*) are made of either small, slender canes or pieces of hard yellow pine, sharpened at one end; they are from 15 to 18 inches in length. The lower end is wrapped for a distance of 4 or 5 inches with a narrow band of cloth having a frayed edge, or a piece of soft tanned skin is used. The effect of this band is to expand and fill the bore of the gun, a result that could not possibly be secured by the use of feathers, as in the case of ordinary arrows. (Bushnell, 1909 a, p. 18.)[30]

Among the mixed-blood Houma Indians near the mouth of the Mississippi a compound, two-piece blowgun is in use, and a specimen is in the collection of the Museum of the American Indian. It is suspected that these were owing to late West Indian or South American influence. (But cf. statement by Speck's Taskigi informant, p. 586.)

Instead of thistledown, the Chitimacha sometimes "feathered" their blowgun arrows with the down of a plant called locally "fireweed," and they were twisted like those of the Houma, presenting an analogy to rifling in firearms.

---

[30] Byington, 1915, has uski łumpa instead of kaklu'mpa.

Speck had the following from his Yuchi informants:

One form of the blowgun, which is obsolete now, was, according to memory, made of a cane stalk with the pith removed. It was between five and a half and six feet long. The darts were made of hard wood, the points being charred and sharpened. A tuft of cotton wrapped about the end of the dart like a wad formed the piston. This was almost exclusively used for bringing down small animals, squirrels and birds. (Speck, 1909, p. 22.)

His Taskigi Creek Indian stated that the blowgun (*wókko*) was made of a cane stalk about as long as a man is tall. To remove the pith it was sometimes necessary to section the cane, then bind it together again. The darts were made of sharpened stems wound about one end with some soft material, such as cotton, which acted as a piston. (Speck, 1907, p. 110.)

Jackson Lewis described the Creek blowgun as having a length of 8 to 10 feet. The sections were cleared out by putting a slender rod of iron inside and shaking it up and down. When it was in use, the smaller end was thrown forward, the taper serving the purpose of a chokebore. Blowgun arrows were made of slivers of cane or of the "buckbush," which is said to be very much like Scotch heather, and it was feathered with down from the bull thistle (Creek àgā'djo). In later times it was feathered with cotton. The bull thistles, after they had been collected, at the proper time of the year, were stuck together in large circular masses, or, as I observed in another case, were placed in a double row between two slender strips of wood. When needed they were taken out, the seeds and dried flower ends removed, and the down tied along the arrow shaft with the original outer ends still outward. The cane shaft was made square, and then wet in the mouth and heated over a candle flame, after which it was twisted. This twist prevented the animal into which it was shot from shaking it out. At least in later times, blowguns were ornamented on the outside by wrapping a strip of cloth spirally about them and putting them over the fire long enough to char the exposed portion. When the cloth was removed the whole would be ornamented with black and white spirals. My Alabama informant said that his people treated the arrows in this manner instead of the blowguns themselves.

Speck (1938 a) has published a lengthy account of the method of manufacture of the Catawba blowgun and the uses to which it was put. He states that the ones seen by him ordinarily had a length of 5 or 6 feet though some were as long as 8 feet and that, while they could send darts 100 feet, they were not effective beyond 25 or 30. The Cherokee blowgun, on the other hand, was 9 or 10 feet long and was effective at between 40 and 60 feet. The arrows were also longer than those of the Catawba, and the all around workmanship much better. Catawba blowgun darts were made of "oak, pine, or cedar slivers," usually 8 to 10 inches long. W. J. Fewkes reported locust, mulberry, and white oak among Cherokee materials.

SLINGS

When Cabeza de Vaca and his companions of the Narvaez expedition were passing along the Gulf coast near Pensacola and Mobile Bays, they were attacked by Indians carrying slings and darts, but with few bows. Although several distinct attacks were made by at least two different bodies of Indians, slings and darts are mentioned only in connection with the last of these. Nevertheless, it seems evident that all of these Indians were mainly armed with these unusual weapons since the very first Indians they met are described as "tall and well built," but carrying "neither bows nor arrows," and we are told that they wounded Narvaez in the face with a stone (Cabeza de Vaca, Bandelier ed., 1905, pp. 43–49; Swanton, 1922, pp. 144–146). These people had abundance of fish, but little if any corn. One wonders whether the "darts" mentioned may not have been of the kind used with spear throwers.

The only other reference to a sling that has been brought to my attention is by Hawkins, who cites the case of an unintentional murder committed by a Creek boy upon his companion when they were out "playing and slinging stones. One of them let slip his sling, the stone flew back and killed his companion" (Hawkins, 1848, p. 342). This happened, however, toward the close of the eighteenth century, and the sling used might have been of white origin.

SHIELDS

Shields seem to have been known throughout most of the territory under consideration, though we have no record regarding them from all of the tribes. Ranjel reports shields found in the temple of Talomeco, and it may be inferred from the context that these were of bison hide (Bourne, 1904, vol. 2, pp. 100–102). Garcilaso (1723, p. 132) was informed that on the walls of this temple there hung "round and oblong shields, large and small, made of cane so strongly woven that they could turn a dart shot from a cross-bow, though an harquebuce-shot penetrated more than did the dart." In one of the eight rooms around this temple "were large numbers of round shields made of wood and of cow-hide, both brought from distant countries," and in another "a great many oblong shields, all made of cane very skillfully woven and so strong that the Spaniards had very few cross-bows that could send a dart clear through them, as was experienced in other places outside of Cof[it]achiqui" (Garcilaso, 1723, p. 134). We come upon cane shields again on the banks of the Mississippi. The Indians who assembled in canoes to dispute De Soto's passage of that river all "had shields made of canes joined, so strong and so closely interwoven with such thread that a cross-bow could hardly pierce them" (Bourne, 1904, vol. 2, pp. 137–138). Biedma mentions these shields, and Elvas also, though neither states of what they were constructed (Bourne, 1904, vol. 2, p. 26; Robertson, 1933, p. 159). A little later we learn that "shields made of raw cowhide" were found in the town of Pacaha (Robertson, 1933, p. 173).

Byington says that the most ancient name for this implement in Choctaw was tilikpi and that it was later called telihpa. It "was made of stiff hide of a cow, or of an alligator" (Byington, 1915, p. 350). In the northeastern part of our chosen territory we hear of another kind of shield made of bark. Hariot (1893, p. 36) mentions this. Smith says, "For their wars also they use Targets that are round and made of the barkes of trees" (Smith, John, Tyler ed., 1907, p. 112), and Strachey:

Targetts they have, though not many, nor every where; but those they have are made of the barkes of trees, rownd and thicke ynough to keepe out an arrowe. (Strachey, 1849, p. 106.)

Spelman, curiously enough, extends the term "tomahawk" to them:

Ther Tomahaucks for defence which are shields made of the barke of a tree and hanged on ther leaft shoulder to couer that side as they stand forth to shoote. (Smith, John, Arber ed., 1884, p. cxvii.)

We are also told that the "Massawomeckes" and "Sasquesahanocks" had shields but are not informed as to the material (Smith, John, Tyler ed., 1907, pp. 148–149). Leathern targets were in the possession of the "Oustack Indians" (Alvord, 1912, p. 160). Du Pratz includes the buckler in an Indian's war equipment. He says it was "made of two round pieces of bison leather bound together, of a diameter of a foot and a half." He adds, however, that it was almost confined to the northern Indians and that "one does not see it among those of the south" (Le Page du Pratz, 1758, vol. 2, pp. 420–425; Swanton, 1911, p. 129). For Hasinai shields, after the Hasinai had become horse Indians, see Margry (1875–86, vol. 5, p. 502) and Swanton (1942, p. 147).

ARMOR

References to body armor are so scanty that one wonders whether the few we seem to have are to be relied upon. The most important of these is from Ranjel, who tells us that, besides shields, the Spaniards saw in the temple of Talimeco "breastplates like corselets and head-pieces made of rawhide, the hair stripped off" (Bourne, 1904, vol. 2, p. 101). After speaking of the bark shields of the Carolina Indians, Hariot (1893, p. 36) adds that they were also possessed of "some armours made of stickes wickered together with thread." This construction recalls the cane shields so vividly that one wonders, in the absence of any later evidence regarding this armor, whether the objects he saw were not really shields.

Le Moyne mentions circular metal plates which Timucua Indians "were accustomed to wear to protect the back and breast in war," but it is somewhat questionable whether the service they rendered in this way was intentional or accidental (Le Moyne, 1723, p. 8; Swanton, 1922, p. 350). Similarly, Barlowe tells us that a Carolina Indian bought a bright tin dish and hung it in front of his breast as a breastplate (Burrage, 1906, p. 232).

From the foregoing data it may be inferred that the use of armor was rare. There is also some reason to think that the hide shields represented a later intrusion from the north upon an area in which cane shields were usually employed. The "Oustack" or Westo, for instance, are known to have moved south in late times, the Pacaha may very well have been farther northwest at a not remote period, and there is reason to believe that the Cofitachequi Indians had come from the middle Mississippi region not long before De Soto met them.

IMPLEMENTS SERVING TRANSPORTATION

CANOES AND RAFTS

The use of dugout canoes was almost universal in the Southeast, though parts of the Choctaw and Chickasaw Nations had little occasion to resort to them in their immediate territories. Bark canoes were employed as supplementary means of conveyance, especially along the northern borders of the section in the interior. The De Soto chroniclers mention dugouts in Florida, on the Ocmulgee, Savannah, Tennessee, Alabama, Tombigbee, and Mississippi Rivers and their principal branches, and along the coast. They were brought most closely in contact with canoes along the Mississippi, where it is natural to suppose that the canoe technique was highly developed. White and Le Moyne attempted to depict dugouts, and we can get some idea of them from specimens which have been found buried in muck as described by Jones (1873, pp. 53–54); as preserved in the Valentine Museum, at Richmond; from a specimen in the National Museum; from several at the museum of the University of Florida; and from models rescued by Cushing from the muck of Key Marco.

In 1528 Narvaez and his followers destroyed over 30 dugout canoes in front of a village in the neighborhood of modern Pensacola (Cabeza de Vaca, Bandelier ed., 1905, pp. 42–44; Swanton 1922, p. 145), and Cabeza de Vaca, in his account of the expedition, mentions them all along the Gulf shore as far as the mouth of the Mississippi. Two hundred canoes filled with warriors prepared to dispute the passage of the latter river with De Soto's army, and 100 or more pursued them toward the sea when they finally left that country (Robertson, 1933, pp. 159, 276).

San Miguel (1595) says that the Florida canoes were hollowed out of "sauinas," which would indicate the red cedar, but he probably means the cypress, as that was almost universally employed in the section. It is interesting to find that although the earlier method of manufacture was well known, he notes that the Indians around St. Augustine already had iron from the Spaniards and that most of the canoes he saw seemed to have been worked out by means of it (Garcia, 1902, p. 206).

Cushing's finds cast a great deal of light upon the types of canoes used in Florida and their appurtenances. He discovered several toy canoes shown to be such

from the fact that some were not only well finished, but considerably worn by use. There were six or seven of these, and while they generally conformed to a single type, that is the dugout, they differed very materially in detail. Three of them were comparatively flat-bottomed. One, about five inches in length by two in breadth of beam and an inch in depth, was shaped precisely like a neat punt or flat-bottomed row boat. . . . Both ends were somewhat squared, but the stern was wider than the prow, and above the stern was a little protuberance, indicating that such had been used in guiding, and perhaps as well in sculling, little light draught vessels like this, obviously designed, my sailors thought, for the navigation of shallow streams, inlets, bayous, and the canals. Another of these flat-bottomed little toy boats was much sharper and higher at the stem and stern, had very low gunwales, and was generally narrower in proportion to its length, and enlarged would have been admirably adapted to swift tidal currents, or to the running of low breakers. Yet another looked like a clumsy craft for the bearing over shoals of heavy loads or burdens. It was comparatively wide, and its ends also quite broad. All except one of these, I observed, were decorated at one end or both, with the same sort of semilunar or disc-like devices, that were observable on the trays. . . . Two others of the toy canoes . . . were not more than three inches broad by nearly two feet in length, gracefully and slenderly formed, tapered cleanly toward the forward ends, which were high and very narrow, yet square at the sterns, which were also high. We found them almost in juxtaposition near the midmost of the western benches. Little sticks and slight shreds of twisted bark were lying across them and indicated to me that they had once been lashed together, and, as a more finished and broken spar-like shaft lay near by, I was inclined to believe that they represented the sea-going craft of the ancient people here; that the vessels in which these people had navigated the high seas had been made double—of canoes lashed together, catamaran fashion—and propelled not only with paddles, but also, perhaps, by means of sails, made probably from the thin two-ply kind of bark matting I have before described, of which there were abundant traces near the mid-channel, associated with cordage and with a beautifully regular, much worn and polished spar. At any rate, the natives of these South Florida seas and of the West Indies are mentioned by early writers as having navigated fearlessly in their cypress canoes; as having sometimes crossed the Gulf itself, and as having used in these long cruises sails of some simple sort. (Cushing, 1896, pp. 364–365.)

Cushing then cites Dickenson's description of the return to his home of the Ais chief seated on a platform constructed between two canoes.

He continues his discussion of apparatus connected with Floridian canoe culture as follows:

Two tackle-blocks, real prehistoric pulleys, that we found, may have pertained to such canoes as these. Each was three inches long, oval, one side rounded, the other cut in at the edges, or rabbetted so to say. The tenon-like portion was gouged out midway, transversely pierced, and furnished with a smooth peg or pivot over which the cordage turned. I have already mentioned the finding of a paddle near the mouth of the inlet canal . . . It was neatly shaped, the handle round and lengthy, although burned off at the end, and the blade also long, leaf-shaped, and tapered to a sharp point, convex or beveled on one side, flat or slightly spooned or concave on the other. The splintered gunwales and a portion of the prow of a long, light cypress-wood canoe, and various fragments of a large but clumsier boat of some soft spongy kind of wood—gumbo-limbo, probably— were found down toward the middle of the court. Not far from the remains of these I came across an ingenious anchor. It consisted of a bunch of large triton-shells roughly pierced and lashed together with tightly twisted cords of bark and fibre so that the long, spike-like ends stood out radiatingly, like the points of a star. They had all been packed full of sand and cement, so as to render them, thus bunched, sufficiently heavy to hold a good-sized boat. Near the lower edge of the eastern bench lay another anchor. It was made of flat, heart-shaped stones, similarly perforated and so tied and cemented together with fibre and a kind of vegetable gum and sand, that the points stood out radiatingly in precisely the same manner. Yet another anchor was formed from a single boulder of coraline limestone a foot in diameter. Partly by nature, more by art, it was shaped to resemble the head of a porpoise perforated for attachment at the eye-sockets. Balers made from large conch shells crushed in at one side, or of wood, shovel shaped, or else scoop shaped, with handles turned in, were abundant. (Cushing, 1896, pp. 365–366.)

One of the earliest descriptions of the manufacture of dugout canoes, that by Hariot, is also one of the best:

The manner of makinge their boates in Virginia is verye wonderfull. For whereas they want Instruments of yron, or other like vnto ours, yet they knowe howe to make them as handsomelye, to saile with whear they liste in their Riuers, and to fishe withall, as ours. First, they choose some longe, and thicke tree, accordinge to the bignes of the boate which they would frame, and make a fyre on the grownd abowt the Roote thereof, kindlinge the same by little, and little with drie mosse of trees, and chipps of woode that the flame should not mounte opp to highe, and burne to muche of the lengthe of the tree. When yt is almost burnt through, and readye to fall they make a new fyre, which they suffer to burne vntill the tree fall of yts owne accord. Then burninge of the topp, and bowghs of the tree in suche wyse that the bodie of the same may Retayne his iust lengthe, they raise yt vppon poles laid ouer cross wise vppon forked posts, at suche a reasonable heighte as they may handsomlye worke vppon yt. Then take they of the barke with certayne shells: they reserue the innermost parte of the lennke [bark?], for the nethermost parte of the boate. On the other side they make a fyre according to the lengthe of the bodye of the tree, sauinge at both the endes. That which they thinke is sufficientlye burned they quenche and scrape away the shells, and makinge a new fyre they burne yt agayne, and so they continue sometymes burninge and sometymes scrapinge, vntill the boate haue sufficient bothowmes. [Pl. 74.]   (Hariot, 1893, pl. 12.)

Barlowe tells us that native canoes were "made either of Pine or of Pitch trees," and gives us the following short description:

They burne downe some great tree, or take such as are winde fallen, and putting gumme and rosen upon one side thereof, they set fire into it, and when it hath burnt it hollow, they cut out the coale with their shels, and ever where they would burne it deeper or wider they lay on gummes, which burne away the timber, and by this meanes they fashion very fine boates, and such as will transport twentie men. Their oares are like scoopes, and many times they set with long poles, as the depth serveth. (Burrage, 1906, p. 234.)

Moving to the Chesapeake we find the following account by Strachey, closely paralleling that of Smith:

These [boats] they call quintans, as the West Indians call their canoes. They make them with one tree, by burning and scraping awaye the coales with stones and shells, tyll they have made them in forme of a trough. Some of them are an ell deepe, and forty or fifty foote in length, and some will transport forty men; but the most ordinary are smaller, and will ferry ten or twenty, with some luggage, over their broadest rivers. Instead of oares, they use paddles and sticks, which they will rowe faster then we in our barges. (Strachey, 1849, p. 75; Smith, John, Tyler ed., 1907, p. 102.)

Beverley, while following the other Virginia writers, speaks also from personal experience:

They bring down a great Tree, by making a small Fire round the Root, and keeping the Flame from running upward, until they burn away so much of the basis, that the least puff of Wind throws it down. When it is prostrate, they burn it off to what length they would have it, and with their Stone *Tomahawks* break off all the Barke, which when the Sap runs, will easily strip, and at other times also, if it be well warm'd with Fire. When it is brought to a due length, they raise it upon a Bed to a convenient height for their working, and then begin by gentle Fires to hollow it, and with scrapers rake the Trunk, and turn away the Fire from one place to another, till they have deepen'd the Belly of it to their desire: Thus also they shape the ends, till they have made it a fit Vessel for crossing the Water, and this they call a Canoe, one of which I have seen thirty foot long. (Beverley, 1705, bk. 3, p. 61.)

Moving to the Siouan country we read, in Lawson's History:

Of these great trees [cypresses] the pereaugus and canes [canoes?] are scooped and made, which sort of vessels are chiefly to pass over the rivers, creeks, and bays, and to transport goods and lumber from one river to another. Some are so large as to carry thirty barrels, though of one entire piece of timber. Others that are split down the bottom and a piece added thereto, will carry eighty or an hundred. Several have gone out of our inlets on the ocean to Virginia, laden with pork and other produce of the country. (Lawson, 1860, p. 162.)

He adds that "a canoe will outlast four boats, and seldom wants repair" (Lawson, 1860, p. 163).

Their canoes, [says Catesby] are made of pine or tulip trees, which (before they had the use of English tools), they burned hollow, scraping and chipping them with oyster-shells and stone-hatchets. (Catesby, 1731–43, vol. 2, p. XI.)

We now come to the Cherokee.

Their canoes are generally made of a large pine or poplar, from thirty to forty feet long, and about two broad, with flat bottoms and sides, and both ends alike; the Indians hollow them now with the tools they get from the Europeans, but formerly did it by fire: they are capable of carrying about fifteen or twenty men, are very light, and can by the Indians, so great is their skill in managing them, be forced up a strong current, particularly the bark canoes; but these are seldom used but by the northern Indians. (Timberlake, Williams ed., 1927, pp. 84–85.)

Du Pratz is the only French writer who devotes much attention to this subject. After describing the method in which trees were felled, a method almost identical with that employed in Virginia and Carolina, he goes on:

This occasions them an infinite amount of labor, since they have no utensils for this work other than wood for making fire and wood for scraping, and only small pieces of wood must be used in burning. In order to set fire to this tree destined for a pirogue, a pad of clay, which is found everywhere, has to be made for the two sides and each end. These pads prevent the fire from passing beyond and burning the sides of the boat. A great fire is made above, and when the wood is consumed it is scraped so that the insides may catch fire better and may be hallowed out more easily, and they continue thus until the fire has consumed all of the wood in the inside of the tree. And if the fire burns into the sides they put mud there which prevents it from working farther than is demanded. This precaution is taken until the pirogue is deep enough, The outside is made in the same manner and with the same attention.

The bow of this pirogue is made sloping, like those of the boats which one sees on French rivers. This bow is as broad as the body of the pirogue. I have seen some 40 feet long by 3 broad. They are about 3 inches thick which makes them very heavy. These pirogues can carry 12 persons and are all of buoyant wood. Those of the Arkansas are of black walnut.

To guide these pirogues the natives make little oars, which are not fastened to that boat. They are called paddles (*pagaies*). They are similar to those given in illustrations, where they are placed in the hands of river gods when they are depicted. They are only 6 feet long. The French make them only an inch thick, and they are infinitely lighter. (Le Page du Pratz, 1728, vol. 2, pp. 188–189; Swanton, 1911, pp. 66–67.)

It is not surprising that we get a considerable diversity of opinion as to the carrying capacity of these canoes. Garcilaso de la Vega says that the largest had 25 "oars" to the bench and the smallest 14, and that the former carried from 75 to 80 warriors. We look for exaggeration in the figures he gives, but Biedma states that some of those canoes assembled to attack De Soto's men during their descent of the Mississippi held 80 men, and Elvas gives the number as 60 to 70. In Virginia Percy saw a canoe about 45 feet long, Beverley one of 30 feet. (Garcilaso, 1723, p. 240; Bourne, 1904, vol. 2, p. 39; Robertson, 1933, p. 276; Narr. Early Va., Tyler ed., 1907, pp. 10–11; Beverley, 1705, bk. 3, p. 61.) As noted already, Strachey (1849, p. 74) gives the length of some canoes as 40 to 50 feet and their capacity as 40 men, but he adds that the commoner type accommodated only 10 to 20. Barlowe also confines himself to the modest figure of 20, while Timberlake and Ribault, although one was writing of the Cherokee country and the other of Florida, agree on 15 to 20. (Burrage, 1906, p. 233; Timberlake, Williams ed., 1927, p. 85; French, 1875, p. 178; Swanton, 1922, p. 355.) At the Tamahita (Yuchi) town on the upper Tennessee, Gabriel Arthur saw 150 canoes, the least of which would carry 20 men. He adds that they were "made sharp at both ends," which would indicate that they were of a somewhat different type from the coast canoes (Alvord, 1912, p. 213). On the Georgia coast, San Miguel's party (in 1595) was accommodated with 2 canoes of 6 and 8 paddlers, respectively, but their total capacity was greater. The south Florida canoe which later came out to meet them had 16 paddlers, but this canoe had been made "in the Spanish manner" (Garcia, 1902, pp. 198, 210). William Bartram speaks thus of the Seminole and Lower Creek canoes:

These Indians have large canoes, which they form out of the trunks of cypress trees (*Cupressus disticha*), some of them commodious enough to accommodate twenty or thirty warriors. In these large canoes they descend the river [Apalachicola] on trading and hunting expeditions to the sea coast, neighboring islands and keys, quite to the point of Florida, and sometimes across the gulph, extending their navigation to the Bahama islands and even to Cuba: a crew of these adventurers had just arrived, having returned from Cuba but a few days before our arrival, with a cargo of spirituous liquors, Coffee, Sugar, and Tobacco. (Bartram, 1792, p. 225.)

Du Pratz, as we have just noted, though he claims to have seen some Mississippi River canoes 40 feet long by 3 broad, places their capacity at the modest figure of 12. Indeed, in one place he says that they held only from 2 to 10, though he cites the case of a dugout made by the French which carried 50 Negroes for 30 leagues, packed rather closely (Le Page du Pratz, 1758, vol. 1, p. 107; vol. 2, pp. 188–189; Swanton, 1911, p. 67).

If we could be sure that the device of enlarging a canoe by splitting it lengthwise and making an addition to the breadth of the bottom was aboriginal, it would prove that some Gulf Indians had taken the first step from a canoe to a boat. Just how the 80 to 100 barrels of which Lawson (1860, p. 162) speaks in this connection compare with human freight is a question I am not able to answer.

The favorite material for canoes was cypress wherever suitable timber of that kind was to be had. We are informed, however, that the largest canoes on the lower Mississippi were of poplar, which was also employed sometimes by the Cherokee; that those of the Quapaw were of black walnut; and Adair mentions the "light poplar canoes of the Indians of Koosah town," the most ancient Creek town in the Talladega country, and on Coosa River. (Le Page du Pratz, 1758, vol. 2, pp. 188–189; Swanton, 1911, pp. 66–67; Adair, 1775, p. 395.) Pine was used by the coast Indians of North Carolina, and Timberlake implies that it was the principal canoe wood of the Cherokee (Timberlake, Williams ed., 1927, p. 84; Burrage, 1906, p. 232).

The ornamentation of canoes is scarcely touched upon by any of our authorities, and therefore Garcilaso's statement is of some interest to the effect that "the boats of the [Indian] fleet were painted within and without, yellow, blue, white, green, red, or some other color, according to the fancy of him to whom the vessel belonged" (Garcilaso, 1723, p. 240). Without doubt, then, there was a certain amount of decoration, though one may question whether decoration was carried anywhere near as far as on the North Pacific coast. But when Garsilaso goes on to say that the clothing of the occupants of each canoe was colored to match the canoe itself, one is inclined to be skeptical.

Du Pratz's mention of 6 feet as the length of paddles is about all the information vouchsafed us regarding these necessary articles (Le Page du Pratz, 1758, vol. 2, p. 189; Swanton, 1911, p. 67). The paddle found by Cushing was burned off, and he does not even tell us the length of the portion preserved. Two Cape Fear River Indians came off to visit the Barbadoes explorers in a canoe, "one paddling with a great cane, the other with his hands" (Lawson, 1860, p. 122).

It will be remembered that Barlowe speaks of the use of canoe poles "as the depth serveth," and Lawson tells us that both the Indians and the English were in the habit of making poles out of prickly ash "to set their canoes along in shoal water" because it "grows up like a pole" (Burrage, 1906, p. 233; Lawson, 1860, p. 168). Dickenson mentions poling as a common means of progression along the shallow lagoons on the east coast of Florida (Dickenson, 1803, p. 48; Swanton, 1922, p. 392).

Along the coast of Georgia the Indian paddlers employed a peculiar method which came to be known as "Yamasee stroke" (Hodge, 1910, *art.* Yamasee). In Virginia, Byrd tells us that the Indian swimmers used their hands alternately instead of synchronously, and he regarded the method as superior (Bassett, 1901, p. 305).

Our only authority who discusses the manufacture and employment of bark canoes at length is Beverley:

When in their Travels, they meet with any Waters, which are not fordable, they make Canoes of Birch Bark, by slipping it whole off the Tree, in this manner. First, they gash the Bark quite round the Tree, at the length they wou'd have the Canoe of, then slit down the length from end to end; when that is done, they with their *Tomahawks* easily open the Bark, and strip it whole off. Then they force it open with Sticks in the middle, slope the underside of the ends, and sow them up, which helps to keep the Belly open; or if the Birch Trees happen to be small, they sow the Bark of two together; The Seams they dawb with Clay or Mud, and then pass over in these Canoes, by two, three, or more at a time, according as they are in bigness. By reason of the lightness of these Boats, they can easily carry them overland, if they foresee that they are like to meet with any more Waters, that may impede their March; or else they leave them at the Water-side, making no farther account of them; except it be to repass the same Waters in their return. (Beverley, 1705, bk. 3, p. 19.)

In other words, in the Southeast bark canoes were not the primary means of transportation by water they had become in the Northeast, that function having been taken over by dugouts, but they were still employed as ferries or, as we shall see, in long-distance one-way transportation down rivers, another kind of ferryage in which men and goods could be rapidly borne toward points nearer the sea for trade or war. Their occupants could then abandon them and return on foot. That bark canoes made of various materials, birch and other, were well known in interior sections of the Southeast, can be proved from a number of sources. Beginning at the margin of the area, and, in fact, a bit outside of it, we recall Smith's mention of the Susquehanna canoes made of "the barkes of trees, sewed with barke and well luted with gumme," and canoes, or the material for them, was disseminated thence toward the south (Smith, John, Tyler ed., 1907, p. 106).

During the early spring of one year, it was reported that some of the Nanticoke Indians had gone north to the vicinity of the Susquehanna River, where it was thought they would remain 'till the Barque will peal soe they can make Canooes (Semmes, 1937, p. 80).

When Henry Fleet was visiting the Nacotchtank Indians the Piscattaways came to him in "their birchen canoes" (Semmes, 1937, p. 90). Timberlake (Williams ed., 1927, p. 88) speaks of bark canoes as known to the Cherokee yet "seldom used but by the northern Indians." However, Yuchi Indians in this same region carried Gabriel Arthur on a lengthy expedition to the south in one of them:

There [at the head of Port Royal River, evidently the Savannah] they made perriaugers of bark and soe past down ye streame with much swiftness. (Alvord, 1912, p. 220.)

La Salle's famous voyage to the mouth of the Mississippi in 1682 was made in canoes of elm bark, but these were manufactured outside of the Gulf area. At the same time Adair (1775, p. 381) relates how the Chickasaw used to embark in "large cypress-bark canoes" to apprehend French convoys on the Mississippi. A Chitimacha informant had heard his father speak of "elm bark" canoes, but it is doubtful whether this was anything more than a temporary device since it crops up in a territory far removed from the bark-canoe country (Swanton, 1911, p. 347).

Where birchbark canoes were not used as ferries, their place was taken by rafts. The raft (cajeu) is described by Du Pratz as a float composed of bundles of canes bound side by side and then crossed double [a second tier being placed at right angles crosswise]. Travelers employ these vessels in crossing rivers. They are made on the spot when one encounters a river. This happens only to those who travel far away from the habitations of the natives, and when one does not go by water. In all Louisiana one is always assured of having continually at hand something with which to cross a river because canes are found very near the water. (Le Page du Pratz, 1758, vol. 2, pp. 186–187; Swanton, 1911, p. 67.)

At a place called Piachi on the lower Alabama, De Soto was informed that the inhabitants had no canoes, and so they were given rafts of cane and dry wood with which to make the passage (Robertson, 1933, p. 126). According to the modern form of the flood stories of the Alabama, Natchez, and other tribes, the Indian Noah was borne up on a raft, and the raft seems to be aboriginal no matter what we may think of the rest of the story (Swanton, 1929 a, pp. 121, 214; Mooney, 1900, p. 261).

For the Spanish Commander Aguayo, the Hasinai constructed "a raft after their own fashion of dry wood and canes" (Morfi, 1935, p. 236).

Adair favors us with a description of another type of raft which is of particular interest as recalling the bull boat of the Missouri, though there can have been no direct connection between the two.

It may not be improper here to mention the method we commonly use in crossing deep rivers—When we expect high rivers, each company of traders carry a canoe, made of tanned leather, the sides over-lapped about three fingers breadth, and well sewed with three seams. Around the gunnels, which are made of saplings, are strong loop-holes, for large deer-skin strings to hang down both the sides: with two of these, is securely tied to the stem and stern, a well-shaped sappling, for a keel, and in like manner the ribs. Thus, they usually rig out a canoe, fit to carry over ten horse loads at once, in the space of half an hour: the apparatus is afterwards commonly hidden with great care, on the opposite shore. Few take the trouble to paddle the canoe; for, as they are commonly hardy, and also of an amphibious nature, they usually jump into the river, with their leathern barge ahead of them, and thrust it through the deep part of the water, to the opposite shore. When we ride only with a few luggage horses, as was our case at *Sip-se*, or "Poplar," the above-mentioned high-swelling river, we make a frame of dry pines, which we tie together with strong vines, well twisted; when we have raised it to be sufficiently buoyant, we load and paddle it across the stillest part of the water we can conveniently find, and afterward swim our horses together, we keeping at a little distance below them. (Adair, 1775, p. 272.)

Bartram tells us something about this:

[In order to cross the Ocmulgee River] we immediately sat about rigging our portable leather boat, about eight feet long, which was of thick soal leather, folded up and carried on the top of a pack of deer-skins. The people soon got her rigged, which was effected after the following manner. We, in the first place, cut down a White-Oak sapling, and by notching this at each end, bent it up, which formed the keel, stem and stern post of one piece; this was placed in the bottom of the boat, and pretty strong hoop-poles being fixed in the bottom across the keel, turning up their ends, expanded the hull of the boat, which being fastened by thongs to two other poles bent round, the outside of the rim formed the gunwhales: thus in an hour's time our bark was rigged, to which afterwards we added two little oars or sculls. (Bartram, 1792, p. 457.)

Later they crossed the Oconee in the same manner (Bartram, 1792, p. 458).

This is represented as a device of white traders, but the following experience of Swan shows that something similar was also used by Indians, whether or not it was of Indian origin:

The Indians killed a stray cow in the woods, and stretched her skin over hoops, into the shape of a bowl, with which to make the experiment of getting over the [Alapaha] river . . . Early in the morning the Indians commenced the business by swimming and towing the skin boat by a string, which they held in their teeth, getting up a general war-hoop, to frighten away the voracious alligators that inhabit this river in vast numbers. (Swan, 1855, p. 253.)

LITTERS

There is no evidence in the Southeast of any device similar to a travois, but chiefs were carried about on occasions of political, social, or ceremonial importance in litters borne on the shoulders of a number of their most distinguished subjects. The De Soto chroniclers tell us that the Lady of Cofitachequi, the chief of Coça, the Chickasaw chief, and seemingly the Apalachee chief, were carried about in this way. In all cases except the last, the notables concerned were being brought to meet the Spaniards. Garcilaso tells us that Capasi, the Apalachee chief, was so fat that his subjects had to carry him everywhere on a litter. (Bourne, 1904, vol. 2, pp. 16, 22, 98–99; Robertson, 1933, pp. 91, 115; Garcilaso, 1723, p. 316.) When the people of Pacaha were trying to escape from their town in anticipation of the arrival of the Spaniards, Elvas speaks of "the abundance of clothing which the Indians had in hurdles and on wooden rafts in order to take it across from the other side" (Robertson, 1933, p. 177). This suggests the possibility that such litters may in the Gulf region have taken the place of the travois. Two of the principal descriptions of the use of this litter are appended.

Ranjel thus describes the approach of the Coça chief:

The chief came out to receive the Governor in a litter covered with the white mantles of the country, and the litter was borne on the shoulders of sixty or seventy of his principal subjects, with no plebeian or common Indian among them; and those that bore him took turns by relays with great ceremonies after their manner. (Bourne, 1904, vol. 2, p. 112.)

Elvas adds that he was sitting on a cushion (Robertson, 1933, p. 115). The latter also speaks thus of the approach of the "Lady of Cofitachequi":

Shortly thereafter, the cacica came from the town in a carrying chair in which certain principal Indians carried her to the river. (Robertson, 1933, p. 91.)

It is to be noted that the chiefs of the Naguatex (Namidish) and Nondacao (Anadarko) tribes visited strangers on foot, which may indicate a difference in custom among the Caddo. In 1687, when Joutel and his companions reached the Caddo proper during their journey from the Texas coast to the Mississippi, the Caddo brought them into their town on their backs "it being the custom of the country" (Margry, 1875–86, vol. 3, p. 405). This might suggest that at an earlier date the Caddo used litters, but Joutel seems to imply that the Caddo tribes to the west did not have this custom and it might very well have been adopted from the river people, just as the calumet rite had reached only to the Cahinnio.

Le Moyne, whose date, 1564–65, is only slightly later than that of De Soto, gives a short account of the litter in which the prospective wife of a Florida chief was brought to him.

When a king chooses to take a wife, he directs the tallest and handsomest of the daughters of the chief men to be selected. Then a seat is made on two stout poles and covered with the skin of some rare sort of animal, while it is set off with a structure of boughs, bending over forward so as to shade the head of the sitter. The queen elect having been placed on this, four strong men take up the poles and support them on their shoulders, each carrying in one hand a forked wooden stick to support the pole at halting. Two more walk at the sides, each carrying on a staff a round screen elegantly made, to protect the queen from the sun's rays. Others go before, blowing upon trumpets made of bark, which are smaller above and larger at the farther end and having only the two orifices, one at each end. They are hung with small oval balls of gold, silver and brass, for the sake of a finer combination of sounds. Behind follow the most beautiful girls that can be found, elegantly decorated with necklaces and armlets of pearls, each carrying in her hand a basket full of choice fruits and belted below the navel and down to the thighs with the moss of certain trees, to cover their nakedness. After them come the bodyguards. (Le Moyne, 1875, p. 13; Swanton, 1922, p. 372.)

The introduction of horses probably put an end to this custom for we rarely hear of it after this time, the only mention in point of fact, being in connection with the harvest, or rather first fruits, festival of the Natchez, for it was in such a litter that the Great Sun or his representative was brought to the ground where that ceremony took place (pl. 75). Du Pratz says:

This litter is composed of four red bars crossing each other at the four corners of the seat, which has a depth of about 1½ feet. The entire seat is garnished inside with common deerskins, because unseen. Those which hang outside are painted with designs according to the taste and of different colors. They conceal the seat so well that the substance of which it is composed cannot be seen. The back part of this seat is covered like the equipages we call chaises (soufflets). It is covered outside and in with leaves of the tulip laurel. The outside border is garnished with three strings (cordons) of flowers.

That which extends outside is red. It is accompanied on each side with a string of white flowers.

Those who prepare this conveyance are the first and the oldest warriors of the nation. They place it on the shoulders of the 8 who are the only ones to take it out of the village. In this way there remain only 16 of them there, because all the others have gone, a little after sunrise, with their great chief [of war] and those who command the warriors under his orders. He disperses them a hundred paces apart and places 8 in each relay. For this purpose he chooses those of his warriors who are the strongest and the most vigorous. The others wait at the open space with him to receive the Great Sun.

These dispositions made and the warriors' post having been reddened and planted by itself in the middle of the space, with ceremony (for the great war chief has to hold it while the warriors make it firm), the Great Sun, when the sun is a quarter of the way up, goes forth from his cabin adorned with his diadem and the other ornaments which indicate his dignity. On the instant, the warriors who have remained to carry him utter many redoubled cries and with so much strength that those who hear them may be assured that these men are not consumptives. As the warriors of the relays are not more than a hundred paces apart, they hear the first cries and repeat them on the spot, so that in a minute they are informed at the square, although it is half a league distant.

The Great Sun seats himself in the litter, adorned with the ornaments suitable to the supreme rank, for good sense alone has enabled these people to know that these ornaments are the marks of sovereignty, and in the ceremonies their princes always wear them, if not all, at least a part. Then the 8 oldest warriors place him in this state on the shoulders of those who are going to carry him. The cries are continued from the time of his departure from his cabin until he is beyond the village. At most this is a matter of two minutes. Those who carry him and those who receive him do it with so much quickness and skill that a good horse would be able to follow them only at a canter, for those who await him at each relay lift him from the shoulders of those who arrive with so much agility that he does not stop at all and does not cease to go with the same rapidity, so that that journey, I believe, lasts only six or seven minutes at most. (Le Page du Pratz, 1758, vol 2, pp. 363-381; Swanton, 1911, p. 114.)

Dumont de Montigny says that the road over which the Sun was to be carried was cleaned of grass 8 days before the ceremony which he was to attend.

The day of this feast having arrived the savages stretched a beautiful bison skin, daubed and painted with different colors, on a kind of litter, covered with a fine cloth in the manner of a cradle, and on this litter they laid their great chief who on that day was dressed in the French manner but without shoes. This ceremony was gone through to the noise of many guns which the savages discharged from time to time. Afterward all being ranged in a column of a width of four or five men they raised the cradle in which was their chief upon their heads and passing him from hand to hand from the great village to the place where the tun ["tun"=granary] was, they made him cover this entire route in the air much more quickly than our Frenchmen could do it, although they were very well mounted, since he was more than a quarter of an hour before them at this rustic camp where he had himself held in the air until they arrived. If by mischance in its course the litter had fallen to the earth it would have cost his subjects more than a hundred heads. (Dumont, 1753, vol. 1, pp. 195–200; Swanton, 1911, p. 118.)

And so the last use of the litter was ceremonial, as might have been anticipated, and with the uprooting of the Natchez, it disappeared.

SADDLES

Saddles were, of course, a post-Columbian device, but the Indians were not wholly dependent upon traders for them. At least that was true of the Chickasaw and their neighbors, according to Adair:

They are good saddlers, for they can finish a saddle with their usual instruments, without any kind of iron to bind the work; but the shape of it is so antiquated and mean, and so much like those of the Dutch West-Indians, that a person would be led to imagine they had formerly met, and been taught the art in the same school. The Indians provide themselves with a quantity of white oak boards, and notch them, so as to fit the saddle-trees; which consist of two pieces before, and two behind, crossing each other in notches, about 3 inches below the top ends of the frame. Then they take a buffalo green hide, covered with its winter curls, and having properly shaped it to the frame, they sew it with large thongs of the same skin, as tight and secure as need be; when it is thoroughly dried, it appears to have all the properties of a cuirass saddle. A trimmed bearskin serves for a pad; and formerly their bridle was only a rope around the horse's neck, with which they guided him at pleasure. (Adair 1775, pp. 425–426.)

He adds that the Choctaw were using that method in his own time, and also the universal observation that the Indians mounted from what we should consider the "off side." Some Choctaw, with whom he discussed this point, "urged it was most natural, and commodious, to put the right foot into the stirrup, and at the same time lay hold of the mane with the strongest hand, instead of using either of the farthermost or opposite ones, as they term the left" (Adair, 1775, p. 426).

BRIDGES

In the low, marshy country along the coast the Indians had learned to construct rude bridges or causeways. Garcilaso (1723, p. 42) mentions "a wretched bridge of two large trees felled in the water, supported by some stakes fixed in the ground, and some crosspieces of wood, after the fashion of a hand-rail," over the deepest part of a marsh which the Spaniards were obliged to cross in the neighborhood of the Withlacoochee. A still more primitive causeway is mentioned just before they came to a town which seems to have been in the province of Capachequi, though Garcilaso (1723, p. 340) does not give the name. Garcilaso, Ranjel, and Elvas all describe a native bridge or system of bridges west of the Mississippi, on a marsh or estuary near the great river and between the provinces of Casqui and Pacaha. Garcilaso (1723, p. 181) refers to these as "wretched wooden bridges," but Ranjel speaks of "a well-constructed bridge, broad and very cleverly built" (Bourne, 1904, vol. 2, p. 139). This was made especially for the Spaniards.

Elvas says:

The bridge was constructed of wood, in the manner of beams extending from tree to tree, and at one of the sides a line of wood higher than the bridge in order to support those who should cross. (Robertson, 1933, p. 171.)

Later references to bridges are scanty except in the Chesapeake region. Smith says that on the way to Powhatan's house "in the mid way I was intercepted by a great creek over which they had made a bridge of grained stakes and railes" (Smith, John, Tyler ed., 1907, p. 53). In documents bearing upon this region, Wm. B. Marye has collected notices of a very great number of structures of this kind.

MATS AND BASKETS

Skins of animals, more particularly of the bear, bison, and deer, often performed the functions of mats, but more elaborate mats were made of various vegetable materials, principally rushes and cane. "Their mats," says Catesby (1731–43, vol. 2, p. xi), "are neatly made of rushes, and serve them to lie on and hang their cabins with," but Lawson goes into the matter more extensively:

The mats the Indian women make, are of rushes, and about five feet high, and two fathoms long, and sewed double, that is, two together; whereby they become very commodious to lay under our beds, or to sleep on in the summer season in the day time, and for our slaves in the night.

There are other mats made of flags, which the Tuskeruro Indians make, and sell to the inhabitants . . .

A great way up in the country, both baskets and mats are made of the split reeds, which are only the outward shining part of the cane. Of these I have seen mats, baskets, and dressing boxes, very artificially done. (Lawson, 1860, p. 308.)

In fact, cane mats were very extensively used throughout the Southeast as coverings for private houses and the temples. On the lower Misssissippi the walls and roofs of the temples both outside and in were covered with them. Ranjel tells us that all of the houses of Talimeco (on Savannah River), as well as the great temple, were covered with mats (Bourne, 1904, vol. 2, pp. 101–102), and Garcilaso represents the latter as presenting a most magnificent appearance. The roof, he says,

is of canes, very thin, split in two, of which the Indians make mats which resemble the rush carpets of the Moors, which are very beautiful to view. Five or six of these mats, placed one upon the other, serve to prevent the rain from penetrating and the sun from entering the temple; which the private people of the country and their neighbors imitate in their houses. (Garcilaso, 1723, p. 131.)

At Key Marco, according to Cushing,

portions of mats, some thick, as though for use as rugs, others enveloping various objects, and others still of shredded bark in strips so thin and flat and closely platted that they might well have served as sails, were frequently discovered. (Cushing, 1896, p. 363.)

The Frenchmen who visited the Guale (Ouade) chief in 1562 reported that "upon the place where the king slept were white coverings woven in panels with clever artifice and edged about with a scarlet fringe" (Laudonnière, 1586, p. 48; Swanton, 1922, p. 73). The description suggests cane mats, though the "coverings" might have been made of native textiles.

When La Salle reached Lake St. Joseph in northeastern Louisiana, the chief of the Taensa came to visit him, a servant bringing a beautifully woven mat for him to sit upon during the interview (Margry, 1875-86, vol. 2, pp. 209-210; Swanton, 1911, p. 262). This would have been like the Natchez mats which Du Pratz describes,

ordinarily 6 feet long by 4 broad and . . . worked in designs. The gloss of the cane, yellows in aging. Some of them, besides having designs indicated by different weaves, have variously colored splints, some red, some black, making [with the natural shade of the cane] three different kinds of colors. (Le Page du Pratz, 1758, vol. 2, pp. 182-183; Swanton, 1911, p. 61.)

To this day the mats of the Chitimacha are made similarly (pl. 76, fig. 1).

References to baskets in the De Soto documents have been mentioned in connection with boxes. Whether the "petaca" was or was not a basket, at least Garcilaso (1723, pp. 132-133) clearly refers to both baskets and boxes.

There is a singular paucity of references to baskets in Virginia and North Carolina, but in "The proceedings of the English Colonies in Virginia" there is mention of "many women loaded with great painted baskets," meaning, of course, carrying baskets, in the train of Opechancanough, and Beverley (1705, bk. 3, p. 62) refers to baskets made of silk grass (Smith, John, Tyler ed., 1907, p. 175).

In 1701-2 Michel observed that the Indians of Monacantown were bringing in in trade, among other things,

a large number of baskets, carried on the arms, of different colors, made very artistically. The material is a kind of root. They weave into them all kinds of animals, flowers and other strange things, very beautifully. (Michel, 1916, p. 130.)

About the same time Lawson wrote:

The baskets our neighboring Indians make are all made of a very fine sort of bulrushes, and sometimes of silk grass, which they work with figures of beasts, birds, fishes, &c. (Lawson, 1860, p. 307.)

Catesby almost parallels Lawson here:

They also make very pretty baskets of rushes and silk-grass, dyed of various colours and figures, which are made by the *Indians* of *Virginia*, and those inhabiting further north. (Catesby, 1731–43, vol. 2, p. XI.)

In Florida, judging by Le Moyne's illustrations, there was as great a variety of baskets as anywhere else in the Gulf province, and they added to these receptacles of palmetto leaves. In 1562 a Timucua chief presented Ribault with "a basket made of palm boughs, after the Indian fashion, and wrought very artificially," while 3 years later one of his lieutenants received "little panniers skilfully made of palm leaves, full of gourds, red and blue." (Laudonnière, 1586, p. 17; French, 1869, p. 180; Swanton, 1922, p. 355.) Cushing, on the basis of his finds at Key Marco, declared it "obvious" that the former occupants "understood well, not only platting, but weaving and basketry-making too" (Cushing, 1896, p. 363).

For the Indians of the interior, Adair's general account is the best early statement we have:

They make the handsomest baskets I ever saw, considering their materials. They divide large swamp canes, into long, thin, narrow splinters, which they dye of several colours, and manage the workmanship so well, that both the inside and outside are covered with a beautiful variety of pleasing figures; and, though for the space of two inches below the upper edge of each basket, it is worked into one, through the other parts they are worked asunder, as if they were two joined a-top by some strong cement. A large nest consists of eight or ten baskets, contained within each other. Their dimensions are different, but they usually make the outside basket about a foot deep, a foot and a half broad, and almost a yard long . . . Formerly, those baskets which the Cheerake made, were so highly esteemed even in South Carolina, the politest of our colonies, for domestic usefulness, beauty, and skilful variety, that a large nest of them cost upwards of a moidore. (Adair, 1775, p. 424.)

Catesby:

The baskets made by the more southern *Indians*, particularly the *Choctaugns* and *Chigasaws*, are exceeding neat and strong, and is one of their masterpieces in mechanicks. These are made of cane in different forms and sizes, and beautifully dyed black and red with various figures; many of them are so close wrought that they will hold water, and are frequently used by the *Indians* for the purposes that bowls and dishes are put to. But that which they are more especially useful for to the *English* inhabitants is for portmantuas, which being made in that form are commodious, and will keep out wet as well as any made of leather. (Catesby, 1731–43, vol. 2, p. XI.)

In 1739 Oglethorpe mentions the use of "a Sieve made of Reed or Cane" in the preparation of corn meal by the Creek Indians of Coweta town (Bushnell, 1908, p. 574), and Swan includes the following note in his description of the industries of the Creeks at the end of the same century:

Baskets for gathering, and fanners for cleaning corn, and other uses, are made of cane splinters of various sizes, but all of one shape. The workmanship of these is neat and well executed, except that they have neither covers nor handles. (Swan, 1855, p. 692.)

Speck has the following from the Creek Indians of Taskigi town:

Baskets of various shapes were made of cane and hickory splints for household use. The favorite technique in basketry was the twilled. The weaving showed some diversity in details, produced by allowing the woof strands to pass over one, two, three, and frequently four warp strands at a time. Decoration on baskets, so they say, was rare, but when desired was obtained by manipulating varicolored splints in the woof. The splints were shaved from the rind of the cane. This gave a smooth glossy surface on one side which was turned outward in weaving. The commonest basket shape had the bottom quite flat and wide with the wall tapering slightly inward toward the top. Sieves of open twilled work were made for sifting pounded corn. Twilled mats of cane were formerly made, but are not now to be seen. (Speck, 1907, p. 109.)

Basket making among the Yuchi is treated at length by the same writer in his report on that tribe (Speck, 1909, pp. 31–34).

Sixty years ago the Florida Seminole made "from the swamp cane, and sometimes from the covering of the stalk of the fan palmetto. . . . flat baskets and sieves for domestic service" (MacCauley, 1887, p. 517).

Jackson Lewis, my oldest and in many respects my best Creek informant, who belonged originally to the Hitchiti town among the Lower Creeks and was born before the removal of his family to the West, gave me the following description of the manufacture of cane baskets as observed by him:

They first selected canes about as large as one's finger or perhaps a bit larger and split them up into several pieces, after which they stripped the outside bark from each. This was known as "stripping the cane" and it was usually done in the canebrake itself, the stripped cane being afterward made into bundles and carried home. Before using they were soaked in warm water. The big hampers were generally made with a simpler weave, but with heavier borders.

When colors were to be used, they dyed the requisite number of strips in advance. The bark of the black walnut was used when they wanted a black dye. A color between red and brown was furnished by boiling the roots of a plant called tále'wa or táli'wa, perhaps the celandine poppy. (It has small yellow flowers and grows on sandy ridges.) To get the most beautiful red dye, they boiled these roots in "hair oil." A plant growing about yards and along fences, which I was not able to identify, made a still deeper red.

Sometimes, especially when cane was scarce, or when they had moved out of the region where it was to be found, they had recourse to the hackberry. Pieces of this of considerable size were pounded up, whereupon layers would strip off of it. After being immersed for a time in warm water, these would become pliant and work very well. The dogwood was employed by the Koasati weavers of Oklahoma.

From the Alabama Indians now living in Texas I obtained the following notes. They used the outside bark of a cane known as iłåne', which was stripped off, split into pieces of suitable width, and cut into lengths measuring perhaps 1½ or 2 feet, which were then woven into baskets.

The dyes were red, yellow, black, and in later times blue, the last probably a store dye. Black was made from the leaves of the dark sumac, which were boiled in water all day, after which the dye was allowed to cool and the cane placed in it and allowed to remain all night. Black was also made from the black walnut. There were two kinds of red, one obtained from the bark of the wild peach (ichoma') and the other from the red oak. The outside bark of these trees having been removed, the inside bark was scraped off and put into some water along with the canes to be dyed, after which all was boiled for 2 to 3 hours, when the canes would be colored red. Dye was made from the black walnut in a similar manner. Yellow was made from the leaves and limbs of bushes called å'ci lä'na (yellow leaves) in a similar manner. The strips of cane were added just as boiling began and they were found to be colored when the time was over.

Among the dyes used by southern Indians, Bartram mentions two of those cited by my informants, i. e., if the bloodroot (*Sanguinaria canadensis*) is identical with the tåle'wa, but this is doubtful. He also speaks of the use of the low sumac (*Rhus truphydon*). He adds to these the red or soft maple (*Acer rubrum*), and the poison ivy (*Rhus radicans*).

My principal Alabama informant, Charlie Thompson, did not know that his people had woven double baskets, but this fact was clearly remembered by a very old woman Celissy Henry. She added that, if cane were lacking, they sometimes resorted to the outer skin or stalks of the palmetto split lengthwise. She asserted that the designs on baskets were not named.

Charlie Thompson gave me the names of the following types of baskets:

tɑlqō' caîmeca', "knife basket," for the purpose indicated.

tcū'mîtcofa', "sharp bottom," used for needles and thread, and other things.

tcū'mî tok'lo', "blunt point," also used for needles and thread.

îñkåwä'så, "elbow basket," used for knives and articles such as spoons and forks.

kōbi't'a, the carrying-basket used for carrying potatoes, corn, etc. A rope or cowhide string was passed over the forehead, and another one around the waist.

kolbe', a flat close-woven basket for fanning corn.

sak'la', a flat basket sieve used for sifting corn the first time.

sak'lɑ tîcawa', a sieve with smaller holes for the second sifting.

sa'k'la pa'ta, a still smaller sifter used in making bread before the whites came.

There is no early account of Choctaw basket-making. The anonymous French writer merely says that they made "cane hampers of different colors, very pretty" (Swanton, 1918, p. 68). A native informant, however, gave me the following particulars regarding this industry which I quote:

They collected the canes and made baskets from them in winter because cane is said to be too brittle in summer. The outside skins of the canes which were to be used were split off by means of a knife made especially for the purpose, and usually by the silversmith. Before the whites came it is claimed that they skinned the cane "with a whetstone made of a piece of hickory which had turned to rock." Canes were kept in stacks covered an inch or two with water. After the skins had been removed they were made into rolls of different sizes, selling about fifty years ago for 25 cents to a dollar. A 25-cent roll would make about three baskets, each holding four quarts of meal. A basket of meal packed in this way was formerly sold for 25 cents, but now it brings from 50 cents to a dollar. They had both single-woven baskets and double-woven baskets. The following names of baskets were given me:

Nanàskàta tapushik, "a scrap basket."

Bàshpo apita, "knife basket."

Shapo tapushik, the hamper carrying-basket, "load basket."

Hàlat nōwa tapushik, dinner basket, "to walk holding basket," hand basket.

Okhiⁿsh apita tapushik, "medicine basket," a basket with a division in it, two lids and two handles.

Okhiⁿsh ahoyo tapushik, "medicine gathering basket."

Ufko tapushik, fanner, a basket for sifting corn, etc.

The word for a plait or weave is pana. A single weave, skipping one, is pana chafa, a double weave, skipping two, is pana tukalo, a triple weave, skipping three, pana tuchina. A double basket is called tapushik pothoma.

A yellowish dye for baskets was obtained from puccoon or "coon" roots, walnut was employed rather rarely to give a brownish color, and maple yielded a dark purple. Roots were gathered in the fall when all the substance was in them. They were boiled until the infusion was thick, when it was strained and put into bottles. . . . Cane was wound into a coil and boiled in a round pot containing the dye. It was turned over once unless the dye had taken hold rapidly. Then it was removed, and hung up after the liquid had been carefully shaken back into the pot. Sometimes they had pots of each of the three dyes in use at the same time. (Swanton, 1931 a, pp. 40–41.)

One of the surviving speakers of the Natchez language gave me some notes on basketry which may, however, be equally applicable to the Cherokee, among whom these people are living. He remembered that they made a large conical carrying basket, a winnowing basket, a sifter for flour, a sifter for grits, and trinket baskets. Some baskets were made out of the roots of the buck bush which run along the top of the ground. The root of the "dog-tail weed" (wà'cgup i'ci) was employed in the concoction of a dark red, almost black, dye. A black dye was also made out of the black walnut. Other dyes were prepared by burning various fruits and roots, among them a bright red dye, but the plant supplying it was scarce. My informant did not know the name of it.

Du Pratz describes two varieties of cane, the shorter and harder of which was used to make knives. The other grows in moist places, to a height of 18 to 20 feet and is as large in diameter as the fist. The natives make of it mats, sieves, little boxes, and many other articles. (Le Page du Pratz, 1758, vol. 2, pp. 58–59; Swanton, 1911, p. 58.)

But he has preserved nothing of the technique, nor has Dumont de Montigny, though the latter has considerable to say regarding the articles manufactured of cane:

With the skin which they take from the outer part of the canes they make very fine sifters (*tamis*). They also make some with larger openings which serve as sieves (*cribles*), and they work others without openings which take the place of winnowing baskets (*van*). They sell these little pieces of work to the French, who obtain them for trifles. They also make hampers (*paniers*) worked very neatly, and baskets for corn. (Dumont, 1753, vol. 1, p. 154; Swanton, 1911, p. 62.)

Du Pratz also mentions these sifters, sieves, and winnowing baskets as well as

burden baskets for carrying grain, meat, fish, or other provisions which they have to transport from one place to another . . . They are round, with a depth greater than the diameter, and as large below as above. They make them of all sizes. The medium sized are for the young girls. There are very little ones for gathering strawberries. [He adds the interesting information, interesting in view of the modern work of the Chitimacha Indians, that] they make double baskets, or those which have no reverse (one basket fitting into another). The cover is large enough to enclose all the lower part, and it is into these that they put their earrings, bracelets, garters, beads, hair ribbons, and vermilion (or ochre) with which to paint themselves. (Le Page du Pratz, 1758, vol. 2, p. 179, 183–184; Swanton, 1911, p. 62.)

Among the Chitimacha, thanks to the intelligent and sympathetic interest of Mrs. Sidney Bradford and her sister, Miss McIlhenny, the basketry of the lower Mississippi type has been preserved down to modern times, modified considerably, of course, but still remarkably pure. (See Swanton, 1911, pp. 347–353, and a few scanty notices of Caddo mats and baskets in Swanton, 1942, pp. 156–157.)

THE COLORING OF MANUFACTURED ARTICLES

Considerable has already been said regarding the use of dyes in making mats and baskets, particularly by the Creeks, Alabama, and Choctaw.

In the De Soto narratives we find many references to the use of various colors, plain or in designs, on deerskins, woven cloaks, wood, and feather garments. At Cofitachequi Ranjel observed moccasins and leggings with ties of white leather though the leggings were black, and with fringes or edging of colored leather (Bourne, 1904, vol. 2, p. 100). Mention is made of skins colored red and black (Robertson, 1933, p. 76). The sunshade carried by an attendant of chief Tascalusa attracted particular attention. Ranjel tells us it was ornamented with a white cross on a black ground, and Elvas confirms this, though Buckingham Smith has mistranslated "black" as "red." The memories of Garcilaso's informants were probably at fault, though part of the ornamentation may have been of the character they indicate. Garcilaso calls the shade "a banner" and says it was traversed by three blue bars (Bourne, 1904, vol. 2, p. 121; vol. 1, pp. 87–88; Robertson, 1933, p. 124). According to the same writer, the canoes which came out against the Spaniards during their descent of the Mississippi were painted "even to the oars" in different colors, though each of a single color, as blue, yellow, white, red, green, rose, violet, or black (Garcilaso, 1723, p. 240).

Hariot has the following to say of dyes used on the North Carolina coast:

There is Shoemake well knowen, and vsed in England for blacke; the seede of an hearbe called Wasewówr: little small rootes called Cháppacor; and the barke of the tree called by the inhabitants Tangomóckonomindge: which Dies are for diuers sortes of red: their goodnesse for our English clothes remaynes yet to be proued. The inhabitants vse them onely for the dying of hayre; and colouring of their faces, and Mantles made of Deare skinnes; and also for the dying of Rushes to make artificiall workes withall in their Mattes and Baskettes; hauing no other thing besides that they account of, apt to vse them for. (Hariot, 1893, p. 19.)

Smith speaks of roots called "pocones," the well-known roots now called coon roots, which the Virginia Indians employed as a medicine and to paint their heads and garments (Smith, John, Tyler ed., 1907, p. 93). He also refers to the "musquaspenne, . . . a roote of the bigness of a finger, and as red as bloud. In drying, it will wither almost to nothing. This they use to paint their Mattes, Targets, and such like" (idem). Beverley (1705, bk. 2, p. 23) speaks of "the Shumack and Sassafras, which make a deep yellow." Romans (1775, p. 85) found that the Choctaw dyed their mulberry-bark textiles yellow with the roots of the same tree (or shrub?), and notes that they used other roots which he was unable to identify with which to "dye most substances of a bright lasting scarlet." Bartram gives us the origins of four dyes used by the Creeks.

The *poccoon* or *Sanguinaria Gallium*, bark of the *Acer rubrum*, *Toxcodendron radicans*, *Rhus truphydon*, and some other vegetable pigments are yet in use by the women, who still amuse themselves in manufacturing some few things, as belts and coronets for their husbands, *feather cloaks*, moccasons, etc. (Bartram, 1909, p. 29.)

Catesby tells us that both textiles and baskets were ornamented with animal designs in colors.

Of the hair of buffalo's, and sometimes that of *Rackoons*, they make garters and sashes, which they dye black and red; the fleshy sides of the deer-skins and other skins which they wear, are painted black, red and yellow, which in winter they wear on the outside, the hairy side being next their skins. (Catesby, 1731–43, vol. 2, p. xi.)

464735—46——40

Iberville notes that the girls belonging to the Houma tribe on the lower Mississippi wore clothing colored red, yellow, and white (Margry, 1875–86, vol. 4, p. 285).

Du Pratz has the following items regarding Natchez dyes:

The *bois-ayac* is a tree which is ordinarily small and does not grow larger than the leg, perhaps because it is cut very often. . . . The natives use it in making [yellow] dyes. They cut it into little bits, crush it, and then boil it in water, after which they drain off this water and put the feathers and hair, which they customarily dye yellow before dyeing them red, into this to steep. In performing this operation they take care to cut the wood in winter, but when they wish to give only a slight color to their hides, for they are not very fond of yellow, they pay no attention to the season and cut the wood at all times. . . .

It is of the root of this plant (*achetchy*) that the natives make their red dyes. After having dyed an object yellow or a beautiful citron color with *bois-ayac*, as I have described before, they boil the roots of the *achetchy* in water and squeeze them with all their strength. Then they steep what they wish to dye in this boiling water. What was naturally white before having been dyed yellow takes on a beautiful poppy color, and what was brown, as bison hair, which is chestnut colored, becomes red-brown. (Le Page du Pratz, 1758, vol. 2, p. 63; Swanton, 1911, p. 66.)

When red was used on pottery, red ocher was the source of the color (Swanton, 1911, p. 62). (See also De Villiers, 1925, p. 123.)

The Chitimacha color their baskets down to the present day by means of a dock (*Rhus*) treated with lime to produce red, untreated for yellow; and black walnut for black (Swanton, 1911, p. 348).

MNEMONIC DEVICES

Speaking of the eastern Siouan Indians, Lederer says:

Three ways they supply their want of letters: first by counters, secondly by emblems or hieroglyphicks, thirdly by tradition delivered in long tales from father to son, which being children they are made to learn by rote.

For counters, they use either pebbles, or short scantlings of straw or reeds. Where a battle has been fought, or a colony seated, they raise a small pyramid of these stones, consisting of the number slain or transplanted. . . .

An account of time, and other things, they keep on a string or leather thong tied in knots of several colours. I took particular notice of small wheels serving for this purpose amongst the Oenocks, because I have heard that the Mexicans use the same. (Alvord, 1912, pp. 142–143.)

Beverley also refers to the use of "knots on a string" and notes their resemblance to Peruvian quipus, and he mentions reckoning by means of "notches on a stick" (Beverley, 1705, bk. 3, p. 44).

The following episode in the story of Newport's first exploratory trip from Jamestown belongs in this place:

There was an olde man with King *Pamaunche* (which I omitted in place to specify) who wee understood to be. 110. yere olde; for *Nauiraus* (their guide) with being with vs in our boate had learned me so much of the Languadge, and was so excellently ingenious in signing out his meaning, that I could make him vnderstand me, and perceive him also wellny in any thing. But this knowledge our Captaine gatt by taking a bough and singling of the leaues, let one drop after another, saying *caische* which is. 10. so first *Nauiraus* tooke. 11. beanes and tolde them to vs, pointing to this olde fellow, then 110. beanes; by which he awnswered to our Demand for. 10. yeares a beane, and also euery yere by it selfe. This was a lustye olde man, of a sterne Countenance, tall and streight, had a thinne white beard, his armes overgrowne with white haires, and he went as strongly as any of the rest. (Smith, John, Arber ed., 1884, pp. li–lii.)

Lawson contributes the following:

[In connection with his funeral oration a speaker] diverts the people with some of their traditions, as when there was a violent hot summer, or very hard winter; when any notable distempers raged amongst them; when they were at war with such and such nations; how victorious they were; and what were the names of their war-captains. To prove the times more exactly, he produces the records of the country, which are a parcel of reeds of different lengths, with several distinct marks, known to none but themselves, by which they seem to guess very exactly at accidents that happened many years ago; nay, two or three ages or more. The reason I have to believe what they tell me on this account, is, because I have been at the meetings of several Indian Nations, and they agreed, in relating the same circumstances as to time, very exactly; as for example, they say there was so hard a winter in Carolina 105 years ago, that the great sound was frozen over, and the wild geese came into the woods to eat acorns, and that they were so tame, (I suppose through want) that they killed abundance in the woods by knocking them on the head with sticks. (Lawson, 1860, p. 295; see also pp. 311–312 under Woodcraft.)

The use of bundles of small sticks to mark the passage of time or keep appointments was general throughout the section. The Creeks called them the "broken days," and used them when they assembled for their annual ceremonies. The rising of the Natchez Indians against the French was timed by means of such sticks, and its miscarriage attributed to the accidental destruction of some of these (Swanton, 1911, pp. 223–224). Adair speaks of both quipu and notched sticks:

They count certain remarkable things, by knots of various colors and make, after the manner of the South-American Aborigines; or by notched square sticks, which are likewise distributed among the head warriors, and other chieftains of different towns, in order to number the winters, &c.—the moons also—their sleeps—and the days when they travel; and especially certain secret intended acts of hostility. Under such a circumstance, if one day elapses, each of them loosens a knot, or cuts off a notch, or else makes one, according to previous agreement; which those who are in the trading way among them, call broken days. Thus they proceed day by day, till the whole time is expired, which was marked out, or agreed upon; and they know with certainty, the exact time of any of the aforesaid periods, when they are to execute their secret purposes, be they ever so various. (Adair, 1775, p. 79.)

Milfort indicates that there were also mnemonic belts made of beads:

Since my arrival among the Creeks the old chiefs had often spoken to me of their ancestors, and they had shown me the belts (banderoles), or varieties of chaplets, which contained their histories. These chaplets were their archives;

they are of little seeds like those which are called Cayenne pearls; they are of different colors and strung in rows; and it is on their arrangement and their pattern that their meaning depends. As only the principal events are preserved on these belts and without any details, it sometimes happens that a single chaplet contains the history of twenty to twenty-five years. These pearls are placed in such a manner as to preserve the various periods exactly; and each year is easily distinguished by those who know the arrangement. (Milfort, 1802, pp. 47–48.)

Devices of this kind may help to explain how the Natchez could have preserved knowledge of 45 or 50 successive Great Suns, and how the migration of a part of the Creeks could be recorded in such a topographically exact manner (De la Vente quoted by Swanton, 1911, p. 185; Swanton, 1928, pp. 34–35).

During the ball games, scores were kept by setting up sticks in the ground and then removing them, the number of points in the game being twice as many as the number of sticks. Adair (1775, p. 77) tells us that the Chickasaw figured out mercantile transactions on the ground in accordance with a system which they called "scoring on the ground" (yakni tapa, "ground—spread out on"), in which they made a single short line for each unit and a cross to mark off the tens. Eakins says that this system was also in vogue among the Creeks (Eakins *in* Schoolcraft, 1851–57, vol. 1, p. 273). Though Adair believed that the cross was a device borrowed from whites, it is a rather natural secondary symbol and may have been purely aboriginal. The fingers were used in counting as is true the world around, and throughout the Southeast the decimal system was in vogue. Measures of length were provided by the parts of the human body; long distances were measured in "sleeps." Standards of exchange, or money, have been treated in considering "Work in Shell," pp. 481–488.

The following device was one used by the Choctaw when they began to assemble at certain rendezvous in 1831 preparatory to removal west of the Mississippi. They made

a stick about the size of a quill to represent the man heading the family, a smaller stick tied to it with a string to signify each son over ten years of age; and notches in the middle of the large stick to represent females over ten years of age, and other notches cut near the end of the large stick indicated all younger children, boys and girls. The leader of each band collected these sticks, tied them together and gave the bundle to the agent from which he made up his roll of the party. (Foreman, 1932, p. 48, ftn.)

Commenting upon the influence which St. Denis exercised over the Indians, Du Pratz says:

It was not necessary for him to go for them himself to have them come to him, it was sufficient for M. de S. Denis to mark on paper a well formed leg and hieroglyphic figures indicating the war: the well formed leg indicated himself, because they called him the Chief with the big leg. To indicate war the picture of a club was made; to indicate the time when help was needed the months were indicated by moons, and the days in addition by I's of this kind, if help is urgently needed, only as many I's were marked as days were needed to make the journey; the nation to be attacked was indicated by the figure proper to it. The number of warriors is not indicated, the chiefs of the nations send their warriors; it is known what each nation is able to furnish, and so one makes his intention known to as many chiefs as are necessary to furnish the number of men desired. Arrows also indicate war but only in declaring it, there are then two arrows in the form of a St. Andrews cross broken. (Le Page du Pratz, 1758, vol. 1, pp. 300–301.)

ARTISTIC DEVELOPMENT

If we may trust early writers, artistic development in the Southeast turned in the direction of ornamentation of the human body by means of tattooings and paintings. There were also paintings on hides, designs on basketry and mats, modeling and painting of pots, beadwork,—and possibly some work in imported porcupine quills. Along the Mississippi and as far east as Florida, it was customary to place carved images of birds, usually three, on the roofs of the temples. In the town of Ucita in Tampa Bay, where De Soto landed, was a temple upon which was a wooden bird with its eyes "gilded" (Robertson, 1933, p. 33). In the Choctaw country, Adair observed on each of the mortuary houses in a certain town "the carved image of a dove, with its wings stretched out, and its head inclining down, as if earnestly viewing or watching over the bones of the dead" (Adair, 1775, p. 193). The three wooden images of birds on the roof of the Taensa temple are said to have been intended for eagles, and sometimes the same thing is stated of the wooden birds on the roof of the Natchez temple. (Margry, 1875–86, vol. 1, p. 602; Thwaites, 1897–1901, vol. 68, pp. 122–123; Swanton, 1911, pp. 260, 269.) Du Pratz, however, is noncommittal. He merely says that they were

representations of three great birds [carved] on flat pieces of wood. They are twice as large as a goose. They have no feet. The neck is not as long as that of a goose, and the head does not resemble one. The wing feathers are large and very distinct. The ground color is white and they are mingled with feathers of a beautiful red color. (Le Page du Pratz, 1758, vol. 3, pp. 17–18; Swanton, 1911, p. 162.)

Of the Acolapissa temple we should know nothing apart from the bare fact of its existence except for the fortunate recovery of the De Batz drawing of the temple by Mr. Bushnell. The wooden figures on the temple, the artist explains, had bodies and tails representing turkeys, and the head that of an eagle. Possibly all of the other figures were really of the same composite nature (Bushnell, 1927, p. 3, pl. 1).

A series of images which seem to be related to each other, but are distinct from those just given, appear among the tribes toward the Atlantic. First we have noted the wooden images about the temple of

Talomeco. At the doorway, Garcilaso's informants stated, there were 12 statues of giants made of wood arranged in pairs, one on each side, and diminishing in size inward so as to create an apparent perspective. Each pair held a different type of weapon all of which have been discussed elsewhere. Around the four sides of the temple inside were two rows of statues, one of men and one of women. These were life-size. The coffins of the dead were placed below on a raised platform and above each was a wooden image of the deceased said to have been very lifelike (Garcilaso, 1723, pp. 132–133).

In Virginia and North Carolina we encounter similar images in the sacred buildings. Strachey says:

Their principall temple, or place of superstition, is at Vtamussack, at Pamunky. Neere unto the towne, with in the woods, is a chief holie howse, proper to Powhatan, upon the top of certaine red sandy hills, and it is accompanied with two other sixty feet in length, filled with images of their kings and devills, and tombes of the predicessors. This place they count so holy as that none but the priests and kings dare come therein. (Strachey, 1849, p. 90.)

Smith has a parallel account (Smith, John, Tyler ed., 1907, p. 109). Beverley (1705, p. 31) notes it also, but represents the images as being those of the gods only.

Unlike the former inhabitants of Talomeco, these Indians thus had images of their supernatural beings in their temples. Barlowe heard of an "idol" at Roanoke, but it is uncertain whether this was really in a temple or a private house (Burrage, 1906, p. 236). There can be no doubt, however, of the place of installation of the idols of which Hariot speaks:

They thinke that all the gods are of human shape, & therefore they represent them by images in the formes of men, which they call *Kewasowok*, one alone is called *Kewás;* Them they place in houses appropriate or temples which they call *Mathicómuck;* Where they woorship, praie, sing, and make manie times offerings vnto them. In some *Machicomuck* we haue seene but one *Kewas*, in some two, and in other some three; The common sort thinke them to be also gods. (Hariot, 1893, p. 38.)

Hariot repeats the same facts, with some amplifications, in his description of his plate 21:

The people of this contrie haue an Idol, which they call Kiwasa: yt is carued of woode in lengthe 4. foote whose heade is like the heades of the people of Florida, the face is of a flesh colour, the brest white, the rest is all blacke, the thighes are also spottet with whitte. He hath a chayne abowt his necke of white beades, betweene which are other Rownde beades of copper which they esteeme more then golde or siluer. This Idol is placed in the temple of the town of Secotan, as the keper of the kings dead corpses. Somtyme they haue two of thes idoles in theyr churches, and sometine 3. but neuer aboue, which they place in a darke corner wher they shew terrible. (Hariot, 1893, pl. 21.)

And similar are the accounts we get of the Chesapeake Bay tribes:

In their temples, they have his image [the image of Oke] evill favouredly carved, and then painted and adorned with chaines, copper, and beades, and covered with a skin, in such manner as the deformity may well suit with such a God. (Smith, John, Tyler ed., 1907, p. 109.)

At the 4 corners [of Powhatan's treasure house at Orapakes] stand 4 Images as Sentinels, one of a Dragon, another of a Beare, the 3 like a Leopard, and the fourth like a giantlike man: all made evill favordly, according to their best workmanship. (Smith, John, Tyler ed., 1907, p. 114.)

In his general description of Virginia temples, Strachey states they had:

At the west end a spence or chauncell from the body of the temple, with hollow wyndings and pillers, whereon stand divers black imagies, fashioned to the shoulders, with their faces looking downe the church, and where within their wero-ances, upon a kind of beere of reedes, lye buryed; and under them, apart, in a vault low in the ground (as a more secrett thing), vailed with a matt, sitts their Okeus, an image ill-favouredly carved, all black dressed, with chaynes of perle, the presentment and figure of that god (say the priests unto the laity). (Strachey, 1849, p. 83.)

Later Beverley entered clandestinely into one of the Powhatan temples and discovered a wooden image made in sections, supposed by him to be an "idol."

Round about the House, at some distance from it, were set up Posts, with Faces carved on them, and painted. (Beverley, 1705, bk. 3, pp. 28–31.)

These posts belong to a somewhat different type set up outside of or away from the buildings. Elsewhere he speaks of these more at length:

The *Indians* have Posts fix'd round their *Quioccasan*, which have Mens Faces carved upon them, and are painted. They are likewise set up round some of their other celebrated places, and make a Circle for them to dance about, on certain solemn occasions. (Beverley, 1705, bk. 3, p. 46.)

Hariot is the earliest writer to mention them:

The place where they meet (from all about) is a broade playne, abowt the which are planted in the grownde certayne posts carued with heads like to the faces of Nonnes couered with theyr vayles. (Hariot, 1893, pl. 18.)

Lawson (1860, pp. 285–286) says that the Indians of the Piedmont country set up "idols" in their fields to encourage the young men in their work, and we have references to such images from a much earlier date, the period of the Ayllon settlement in South Carolina. According to Peter Martyr, the Spaniards found, in the courtyard of a gigantic chief called Datha, "two idols as large as a three-year-old child, one male and one female." He adds: "These idols are both called Inamahari, and had their residence in the palace." They were connected also with the horticultural activities of the people. Farther on the same chronicler says:

Another feast is celebrated every year when a roughly carved wooden statute is carried into the country and fixed upon a high pole planted in the ground. This first pole is surrounded by similar ones, upon which people hang gifts for the gods.

each one according to his means. (Anghierra, 1912, vol. 2, pp. 261–263; Swanton, 1922, pp. 43–44.)

Some Creek towns also possessed carved figures.   The earliest mention of one of these seems to be by Adair:

There is a carved human statue of wood, to which, however, they pay no religious homage: It belongs to the head war-town of the upper Muskohge country, and seems to have been originally designed to perpetuate the memory of some distinguished hero, who deserved well of his country; for, when their *cusseena*, or bitter, black drink is about to be drank in the synhedrion, they frequently, on common occasions, will bring it there, and honour it with the first conch-shell-full, by the hand of the chief religious attendant: and then they return it to its former place.   It is observable, that the same beloved waiter, or holy attendant, and his co-adjutant, equally observe the same ceremony to every person of reputed merit, in that quadrangular place.   When I past that way, circumstances did not allow me to view this singular figure; but I am assured by several of the traders, who have frequently seen it, that the carving is modest, and very neatly finished, not unworthy of a modern civilized artist. (Adair, 1775, p. 25.)

Again:

I have seen in several of the Indian synhedria, two white painted eagles carved out of poplar wood, with their wings stretched out, and raised five feet off the ground, standing at the corner, close to their red and white imperial seats: and, on the inner side of each of the deep-notched pieces of wood, where the eagles stand, the Indians frequently paint, with a chalky clay, the figure of a man, with buffalo horns—and that of a panther with the same colour.

Near to the red and white imperial seats, they have the representation of a full moon, and either a half moon, or a breastplate, raised five or six feet high at the front of the broad seats, and painted with chalky clay; sometimes black paintings are intermixed. (Adair, 1775, pp. 30–31.)

Mention of carved eagles recalls a statement made by one of my own informants to the effect that the Coweta Indians used to have a wooden figure resembling a spotted eagle represented with blood dripping from its mouth, and that whenever an important council was to be held it was brought out and set up in the ground in front of the miko's seat facing east.

The front posts in some of the Square Grounds were carved. Speaking of Atasi, Bartram says:

The pillars and walls of the houses of the square are decorated with various paintings and sculptures; which I suppose to be hieroglyphic, and as a historic legendary of political and sacerdotal affairs: but they are extremely picturesque or caricature, as men in a variety of attitudes, some ludicrous enough, others having the head of some kind of animal, as those of a duck, turkey, bear, fox, wolf, buck, &c. and again those kind of creatures are represented having the human head.   These designs are not ill executed; the outlines bold, free and well proportioned   The pillars supporting the front or piazza of the councilhouse of the square, are ingeniously formed in the likeness of vast speckled serpents, ascending upwards; the Ottasses being of the snake family or tribe. (Bartram, 1791, p. 454.)

My above-mentioned informant asserted that the front pillars in the Square Ground of Tukabahchee were carved like alligators, and those of the Koasati square like garfishes. He showed me a stone pipe made by an old Tukabahchee Indian on which was the carving of an alligator. It is evident that the gar was held in considerable reverence by the Koasati Indians, and we have the testimony of Swan as eyewitness that participants in the garfish dance in this town bore carved images of the gar in their hands. Mention may also be made of the notched posts set up in front of the pillars in old Creek grounds which were intended to represent war clubs. Before leaving the Creeks we must note the representations of fish surmounting ball posts in the Fish Pond towns, and a carved wooden eagle on the top of the ball post at Eufaula. In 1820 Hodgson noted a carved wooden bird on the Kasihta ball post. Adair tells us that a wooden eagle was usually put at the very summit of the center post of the tcokofa of the Chickasaw and Creeks (Adair, 1775, p. 419), but these recall rather the temple figures alluded to already.

In the house of the head chief of Asao (St. Simons Island) on the Georgia coast, San Miguel saw "near the door, the face directed toward it, a little idol or human figure badly fashioned: its ears were made of those of a coyote and its tail was from the same coyote, the rest of the body being painted red" (Garcia, 1902, p. 196).

For coyote we should evidently substitute timber wolf.

Later, a soldier told him that this image was made in contempt in imitation of a sailor whom they had killed when he was attempting to pass through their country (Garcia, 1902, p. 205).

Aside from the wooden birds, there is one interesting mention of a carving or group of carvings in the Mississippi towns. This was at the entrance of the Houma temple and has a distant analogy to the carved gaints about the temple of Talomeco, though the subject seems to have been different. Gravier first described this:

There is nothing fine about the temple except the vestibule, which is embellished with the most pleasing and best executed grotesque figures that one can see. These are four satyrs, two of which are in relief, all four standing out from the wall, and having on their heads, their hands, and their legs—for fillets, bracelets, garters, baldrics, and belts—snakes, mice, and dogs. The colors are black, white, red, and yellow, and are applied so well and with such absence of confusion that they constitute an agreeably surprising spectacle.

At a later date the Tunica Indians expelled the Houma from this village and occupied it, but the ornamentation about the Tunica chief's house which Charlevoix notes in 1721 was probably identical with that just described: "The cabin of the chief is much adorned on the outside for the cabin of a savage. We see on it some figures *in relievo*, which are not so ill done as one expects to find them."

(Thwaites, 1897–1901, vol. 65, pp. 145–149; Shea, 1861, pp. 143–144; French, 1851, pp. 173–174; Swanton, 1911, pp. 288, 312.)

Mention must, besides, be made of certain small objects carved to represent animals. Pénicaut states that there was a figure of a rattlesnake in the Natchez temple and also "a quantity of little stone figures inclosed in a coffer" (Margry, 1875–86, vol. 5, p. 159). Charlevoix mentions "some wooden heads, a little better wrought than the two [properly three] eagles on the roof," seen by himself, but he was told "that there are marmosets of wood, and a figure of a rattlesnake likewise of wood, which they set upon the altar, and to which they pay great honors" (French, 1851, pp. 160–161; Swanton, 1911, p. 160). In the smaller compartment of this temple, Du Pratz observed "two hand-worked planks on which are many minute carvings (*plusieurs minuties*) which one is unable to identify, owing to the insufficient light" (Le Page du Pratz, 1758, vol. 3, pp. 17–18; Swanton, 1911, p. 162). The missionary La Source says there were in the Taensa temple "serpents and other like superstitions" (Shea, 1861, pp. 62–63; Swanton, 1911, p. 264). Reverence for the serpent was also noted by De Montigny (Shea, 1861, pp. 76–78; Swanton, 1911, p. 265). In describing what he supposed was the Natchez temple but was evidently that of the Taensa and on another's authority, Le Petit says: "They have a temple filled with idols, which are different figures of men and of animals, and for which they have the most profound veneration." Whoever reported this would seem to have had better eyesight than the others who described it. These "idols" were supposed to be inside of "many flat baskets very gorgeously painted." "These," he goes on to say, "are figures of men and women made of stone or baked clay, the heads and the tails of extraordinary serpents, some stuffed owls, some pieces of crystal, and some jawbones of large fish. In the year 1699 they had there a bottle and the foot of a glass, which they guarded as very precious" (Thwaites, 1897–1901, vol. 68, pp. 122–125; Swanton, 1911, p. 269). La Source notes that in the Tunica temple were "earthen figures which are their manitous," and La Harpe is possibly describing some of these when he states that "their household gods are a frog and a figure of a woman which they worship, thinking that they represent the sun," though we cannot be sure that these were temple images or household gods. (Shea, 1861, p. 81; Margry, 1875–86, vol. 6, p. 247; Swanton, 1911, p. 318.)

On the Bayogoula temple "there were figures of animals, like cocks, painted red. . . . At the side of the temple door were many figures of animals, such as bears, wolves, birds; on this side, that of one which they call choucoüacha (opossum), which is an animal with a head shaped like a sucking pig and as large, hair like a badger, gray and white, the tail like a rat, the feet like a monkey, which has a pouch under the belly in which it brings forth its young and nourishes them." This opossum was painted in many places in red and black so that Iberville inferred it was a form of their deity, but in view of the general repugnance to this animal in the Southeast this seems unlikely. (Margry, 1875–86, vol 4, pp. 169–172; Swanton, 1911, p. 275.)

Pénicaut, our only authority on the Acolapissa temple aside from De Batz, notes:

> There are at the door of the temple wooden figures of birds; there are in the temple a quantity of little idols, as well of wood as of stone, which represent dragons, serpents, and varieties of frogs, which they keep inclosed in three coffers which are in the temple, and of which the great chief has the key. (Margry, 1875–86, vol. 5, pp. 467–469; Swanton, 1911, p. 282.)

There are said to have been no carved or painted objects in the Chitimacha house (or houses) of worship (Gatschet, 1883, pp. 6–7; Swanton, 1911, p. 352), but Gatschet was informed by one of the women from whom he obtained his vocabulary of the Atakapa language that there was a dance house in the village of the head chief Lo surrounded by a picket fence, and containing statues, stuffed animals, and other objects (Gatschet, 1932, p. 24).

Elvas mentions "figures of babies and birds" made of pearls found in the temple of Cofitachcqui (Robertson, 1933, p. 94).

In the "Province of Guacane," by which we may understand the Caddo tribe Nacanish, Garcilaso's informants told him the Spaniards found that the houses were ornamented with wooden crosses, and he attributed this device to what the people had heard of Narvaez, but this tribe was too far inland to render the suggestion plausible (Garcilaso, 1723, pp. 200–201).

A considerable number of wooden tablets carved in low relief and sometimes painted have been exhumed in Florida by Cushing and Stirling. The former describes as follows the best specimen of this class of objects which he found at Key Marco:

> The most elaborate of them all was the one already referred to . . . for it, like the first specimen found, had been decorated with paint (as at one time probably had been all of the others). Upon the head or shovel-shaped portion were two eye-like circles surrounding central dots. At the extreme end was a rectangular line enclosing lesser marginal lines, as though to represent conventionally a mouth enclosing nostrils or teeth or other details. The body or lower and flatter portion was painted from the shoulders downward toward the taillike tenon with a double-lined triangular figure, and there were three broad transverse black bands leading out from this toward either edge. On the obverse or flat under surface of the tablet were painted equidistantly, in a line, four black circles enclosing white centers, exactly corresponding to other figures of the sort found on various objects in the collection, and from their connection, regarded by me as word-signs, or symbols of the four regions. (Cushing, 1896, p. 382.)

Other decorated objects from the same site are described as follows with typically Cushingesque interpretations of the significance of certain of them:

That these curious tablets (as above) were symbolical—even if designed for attachment to other more utilitarian things—was indicated by the fact that various similar objects, too small for use otherwise than as batons or amulets, were found. Several of these were of wood, but one of them was of fine-grained stone . . . and all were exquisitely finished. Those of wood were not more than eight inches in length by three inches in width; and they were most elaborately decorated by incised circles or lenticular designs on the upper convex sides—still more clearly representing eyes—and by zigzag lines around the upper margins as clearly representing mouths, teeth, etc., and on the same side of the lower portions or bodies, by either triangular or concentric circular figures; while on the obverse or flat side of one of them was beautifully incised and painted the figure of a Wheeling Dolphin or Porpoise, one of the most perfect drawings in the collection. The little object in stone . . . was only two inches in length by a little more than an inch in width. It was wrought from very fine dioritic stone, and as may be seen by the illustration was so decorated with incised lines as to generally resemble the comparatively gigantic wooden object of the same general kind shown above it. The very slight tenon-like projection at the lower end of it was, however, grooved, as if for attachment by a cord. Plainly, therefore, it was designed for suspension, and no doubt constituted an amulet representative of the larger kind of object. The moderately small, highly finished wooden figures of this kind, seemed also to have been used more as portable paraphernalia—as batons or badges in dramatic or dance ceremonies perhaps—than for permanent setting up or attachment. That this may have been the case was indicated by the finding of a "head-tablet" of the kind. It was fifteen inches in length by about eight inches in width, although wider at the somewhat rounded top than at the bottom. On the flatter, or what I have called the under, side of the lower portion or end, this tablet was hollowed to exactly fit the forehead, or back of the head, while on the more convex side, it was figured by means of painted lines, almost precisely as were the upper surfaces of the small wooden batons or miniature carved tablets. My conclusion relative to its character as a "head-tablet" was based, not only upon the fact that it was thus hollowed as though to fit the head, but also upon the comparison of its general outlines and those represented on its painted surface, with the outlines and delineations on certain objects represented on the head-dresses of human figures etched on shell gorgets found in the ancient mounds of the Mississippi Valley. . . .

In addition to the head tablet I have spoken of, various thin, painted slats of wood were found in two or three places. They were so related to one another in each case, that it was evident they had also formed portions of ceremonial head-dresses, for they had been arranged fan-wise as shown by cordage, traces of which could still be seen at their bases. Besides these, other slats and parts of other kinds of head-dresses, bark tassels, wands—one in the form of a beautifully shaped spear, and others in the form of staffs—were found; many of them plainly indicating the practice of mimetically reproducing useful forms, and especially weapons, for ceremonial appliance.

Perhaps the most significant object of a sacred or ceremonial nature, however, was a thin board of yellowish wood, a little more than sixteen inches in length by eight and a half inches in width, which I found slantingly upward near the central western shell-bench (Section 22). On slowly removing the peaty muck from its surface, I discovered that an elaborate figure of a crested bird was painted upon one side of it, in black, white, and blue pigments, . . . Although conventionally treated, this figure was at once recognizable as representing either the jay or the king-fisher, or perhaps a mythologic bird-being designed to typify both.   There were certain nice touches of an especially symbolic nature in portions of this pictorial figure (and the same may also be said of various other figures illustrated in the plates), the nicety of which is not sufficiently shown in the drawings, that were unfortunately made from very imperfect prints of our photographs.   It will be observed, however, not only that considerable knowledge of perspective was possessed by the primitive artist who made this painting, but also that he attempted to show the deific character of the bird he here represented by placing upon the broad black paint-band beneath his talons (probably symbolic of a key), the characteristic animal of the keys, the raccoon; by placing the symbol or insignia of his dominion over the water—in form of a double-bladed paddle—upright under his dextral wing; and to show his dominion over the four quarters of the sea and island world thus typified, by placing the four circles or word-signs, as if issuing from his mouth,—for in the original, a fine line connects this series of circlets with his throat, and is further continued downward from his mouth toward the heart,—as is so often the case with similar representations of mythologic beings in the art of correspondingly developed primitive peoples. . . .

Upon one side of [a box lid] was drawn, in even, fine lines of black . . . the representation of a horned crocodile.   Again, in this as in the painted tablet, may be seen a clear indication of a knowledge of perspective in drawing, on the part of the primitive artists who designed it.   This is apparent in the treatment of the legs, of the serrated tail, and of the vanishing scales both at the back and under the belly of the figure. . . . Upon another box-lid or tablet was painted in outline, a graceful and realistic figure of a doe, and along the middles of the ingeniously rabbeted sides and ends of these boxes—whether large or small—were invariably painted double lines, represented as tied with figure-of-eight knots, midway, or else fastened with clasps of oliva shell—as though to mythically join these parts of the boxes and secure their contents.

The painted shells I have referred to as contained in the pack just described, were those of a species of Solenidae, or the radiatingly bandied bivalves that are locally known in that portion of Florida as "sun-shells."   Each pair of them was closed and neatly wrapped about with strips of palmetto leaves that were still green in color, but which of course immediately decomposed on exposure to the air.   On opening this pair of them, I found that in one of the lids or valves, the left one, was a bold, conventional painting, in black lines, of an outspread hand.   The central creases of the palm were represented as descending divergingly from between the first and middle fingers, to the base. This was also characteristic of the hands in another much more elaborately painted shell of the kind, that was found by Mr. George Gause within four or five feet of the bird-painting or altar-table . . . this painting represented a man, nearly nude, with outspread hands, masked (as indicated by the pointed, mouthless face), and wearing a head-dress consisting of a frontlet with four radiating lines—presumably symbolic of the four quarters—represented thereon, and with three banded plumes or hair-pins divergingly standing up from it.   The palm-lines in the open hands of this figure were drawn in precisely the same manner as were those in the hand painting of the pair of shells found with the ceremonial pack, and the thumbs were similarly crooked down.   Upon the wrist, and also just below the knees, were reticulate lines, evidently designed to represent plaited wristlets and leg-bands.   Otherwise, as I have said, the figure was nude. . . .

As evidenced by the exquisite finish and ornamental designs of so many of the implements, weapons, and utensils I have described, the ancient key dwellers excelled especially in the art of wood-carving. While their arts in painting were also of an unusually highly developed character—as the work of a primitive people—their artistic ability in relief-work was preëminently so. This was further illustrated in a little wooden doll, representing a round-faced woman wearing a sort of cloak or square tunic, that was found near the southernmost shell-bench along the western side of the court, in Section 15. Near this little figure was a superbly carved and finished statuette in dark-colored, close-grained wood, of a mountain-lion or panther-god. . . . Nothing thus far found in America so vividly calls to mind the best art of the ancient Egyptians or Assyrians. as does this little statuette of the Lion-God, in which it was evidently intended to represent a manlike being in the guise of a panther. Alhough it is barely six inches in height, its dignity of pose may fairly be termed "heroic," and its conventional lines are to the last degree masterly. While the head and features—ears, eyes, nostrils and mouth—are most real-istically treated, it is observable that not only the legs and feet, but also even the paws, which rest so stoutly upon the thighs or knees of the sitting or squatting figure, are cut off, unfinished; bereft, as it were, of their talons. . . .

To me the remains that were most significant of all discovered by us in the depths of the muck, were the carved and painted wooden masks and animal figureheads. The masks were exceptionally well modeled, usually in realistic representation of human features, and were life-size; hollowed to fit the face, and provided at either side, both above and below, with string-holes for at-tachment thereto. Some of them were also bored at intervals along the top, for the insertion of feathers or other ornaments, and others were accom-panied by thick, gleaming white conch-shell eyes . . . that could be inserted or removed at will, and which were concave—like the hollowed and polished eye-pupils in the carving of the mountain-lion god—to increase their gleam. Of these masks we found fourteen or fifteen fairly well-preserved specimens, be-sides numerous others which were so decayed that, although not lost to study, they could not be recovered. The animal figureheads, as I have called them, were somewhat smaller than the heads of the creatures they represented. Nearly all of them were formed in parts; that is, the head and face of each was carved from a single block; while the ears and other accessory parts, and, in case of the representation of birds, the wings, were formed from separate pieces. Among these animal figureheads were those of the snouted leather-back turtle, the alligator, the pelican, the fish-hawk and the owl; the wolf, the wild-cat, the bear and the deer. But curiously enough, the human masks and these animal figureheads were associated in the finds, and by a study of the conventional decorations or painted designs upon them, they were found to be very closely related symbolically, as though for use together in dramaturgic dances or ceremonials. On one or two occasions I found the masks and figureheads actually bunched, just as they would have been had they thus pertained to a single ceremonial and had been put away when not in use, tied or suspended together. In case of the animal figureheads the movable parts, such as the ears, wings, legs, etc., had in some instances been laid be-side the representations of the faces and heads and wrapped up with them. We found two of these figureheads—those of the wolf and deer—thus care-fully wrapped in bark matting, but we could neither preserve this wrapping, nor the strips of palmetto leaves or flags that formed an inner swathing around them. The occurrence of these animal figureheads in juxtaposition to the human masks which had so evidently been used ceremonially in connection with them, was most fortunate; for it enabled me to recognize, in several instances, the true meaning of the *face-paint* designs on the human masks thus associated with these animal figures. I cannot attempt to fully describe the entire series, but must content myself with reference only to a few of the more typical of them.

Near the nothernmost shell beach, . . . was found, carefully bundled up, as I have said, the remarkable figurehead of a wolf with the jaws distended, separate ears, and conventional, flat, scroll-shaped shoulder- or leg-pieces, designed for attachment thereto with cordage. . . . A short distance from this specimen was found the beautifully featured man-mask sketched in Fig. 2 of the same plate. Now both of these specimens had been painted with black, white, and blue designs, which unfortunately cannot be shown with sufficient clearness in the uncolored sketches. When I observed that the designs on the human mask represented, albeit conventionally, the general features and lines of the wolf figurehead associated with it, I was no longer at loss to understand the connection of the two. It will be observed that on the ear-pieces of the wolf figurehead, are two well-defined and sharp-pointed dark areas representing the openings of the erect ears, and that correspondingly, above the eyebrows of the mask itself, similarly pointed black areas are painted, while the tusked open mouth of the wolf figurehead is also represented by jagged or zigzag lines on the mask, extending across the cheeks upward to the corners of the mouth, apparently to symbolize the gnashing teeth of the wolf; and even the conventionally represented shoulders and feet of the springing wolf figurehead are drawn in clean white lines over the entire middle of the face of this mask. It was therefore evident to me, that these painted lines upon the human mask were designed, really, to represent the aspect and features and even the characteristic action or spring, of the wolf. Hence I looked upon these two painted carvings as having been used in a dramaturgic- or dance-ceremonial of these ancient people, in which it was sought to symbolize successively the different aspects or incarnations of the same animal-god, namely the wolf-god,—that is, his animal aspect, and his human aspect.

Now, this association of the animal figureheads with the masks presenting their human counterparts was not exceptional. In another portion of the court the rather diminutive but exquisitely carved head, breast and shoulders (with separate parts representative of the outspread wings, near by) of a pelican, was found, and in connection with this, a full-sized human mask of wood, also. Upon the forehead, cheeks, and lower portion of the face of the mask, was painted in white over the general black background, the full outline (observed from above) of a flying pelican, . . . the under lip and chin of this man-pelican mask was quaintly pouted and protruded to represent the pouch of the pelican—in a manner that does not show in the full-face drawing.

The remarkable and elaborately carved and painted figurehead of the leather-back turtle; the large figurehead or mask-like carving representative of a bear—its face also elaborately painted—and others of the animal figureheads which we found, were likewise paired or associated with their human presentmentations or counterparts—that is, human masks painted with practically the same face-designs as occurred on these animal figures. (Cushing, 1896, pp. 382–389, pls. 33, 34.)

Speck (1909, pp. 54–60) has given us by far the longest account of the artistic development of a southern tribe which is in existence, though it applies to a decadent period.

Cosmic designs are remarkable for their abundance as well as the absence of those of animal and plant origin. Indeed, among these latter, almost exclusive attention is devoted to the snake. It is noteworthy that Skinner found the same thing true of the Florida Seminole. The only meanings he could obtain for any of the designs in beadwork were "(1) diamond-back rattlesnake, (2) 'ground' rattlesnake, (3) everglade terrapin, (4) terrapin spear-point" (Skinner, 1913, p. 71). We also find, as appears, terrapin, bull snake, and centipede designs among the Yuchi (Speck, 1909, pp. 54–60).

The Florida Seminole seem to have derived nothing from the art of the wood-carving tribes which preceded them in the peninsula, and to have taken little into it. MacCauley says:

I saw but few attempts at ornamentation beyond those made on the person and on clothing. Houses, canoes, utensils, implements, weapons, were almost all without carving or painting. In fact, the only carving I noticed in the Indian country was on a pine tree near Myers. It was a rude outline of the head of a bull. The local report is that when the white men began to send their cattle south of the Caloosahatchie River the Indians marked this tree with this sign. The only painting I saw was the rude representation of a man, upon the shaft of one of the pestles used at the Koonti log at Horse Creek. It was made by one of the girls for her own amusement. (MacCauley, 1887, p. 519.)

MUSICAL INSTRUMENTS

DRUMS

Drums were known to these Indians from the earliest times of which we have any record. Garcilaso (1723, p. 45) reports that drums were used by the Indians about the marshy country along what we now know as the Withlacoochee River. Biedma mentions drums at Mabila, and Elvas says that, as soon as the Alabama Indians "saw the Christians approach with loud cries and beating two drums, they came out in great fury to meet them" (Bourne, 1904, vol. 2, p. 19; Robertson, 1933, p. 153). In all these cases, except perhaps the first, the drum is represented as an instrument used in war. The same is equally noteworthy in the descriptions which we have of the Chickasaw attack upon De Soto's men. This impressed them so much that all chroniclers except Biedma allude to it. Ranjel says that "the Indians . . . entered the camp in many detachments, beating drums as if had been in Italy." Elvas mentions but one drum, but Garcilaso says they attacked to the accompaniment of "fifes, horns, and drums." (Bourne, 1904, vol. 2, p. 134; Robertson, 1933, p. 147; Garcilaso, 1723, p. 166.) This military use of the drum is repeated by Smith, speaking of the Powhatan Indians:

For their warres, they have a great deepe platter of wood. They cover the mouth thereof with a skin, at each corner they tie a walnut, which meeting on the backside neere the bottome, with a small rope they twitch them togither till it be so tought and stiffe, that they may beat upon it as upon a drumme. (Smith, John, Tyler ed., 1907, p. 107.)

This Strachey rewords:

For their drums they have a great deepe platter of wood, the mouth whereof covering with a skyn, at each corner they ty a walnutt, which meeting on the back side neere the bottome, with a small cord they twitch them together untill they be so tough and stiffe, that they maye beat upon them as doe wee upon a drum, and they yield a reasonable rattling sownde. (Strachey, 1849, p. 107.)

However, Beverley (1705, bk. 3, p. 55) says "Their Drums are made of a Skin, stretched over an Earthen Pot half full of water." In the Nottoway town Byrd saw a drum made of "a large Gourd with a Skin bract tort over the Mouth of it" (Bassett, 1901, p. 114).

The drum used by the Waxhaw is described by Lawson (1860, p. 67) as "made of a dressed deer's skin, tied hard upon an earthen porridge pot." For mention of the Ais drum, see page 765.

The music observed by Adair at Chickasaw festivals consisted "of two clay-pot drums covered on the top with thin wet deer-skins, drawn very tight, on which each of the noisy musicians beats with a stick, accompanying the noise with their voices" (Adair, 1775, p. 116). Bartram praises Creek and Seminole songs as accompanied by the drum and rattle, but has nothing to say regarding the construction of the instruments (Bartram, 1792, pp. 243, 503). Timberlake, Iberville, and Pénicaut barely mention their use by the Cherokee, Houma, and Pascagoula, respectively. Pénicaut says they were small. Timberlake observed that the Cherokee he encountered used not only their home-made drums but some drums they had captured from the English after the massacre at Fort Loudon. (Timberlake, Williams ed., 1927; p. 63; Margry, 1875-86, vol. 4, pp. 174-176; vol. 5, pp. 388-390; Swanton, 1911, p. 285, 303.) For use of a stone as a drum, see page 693.

The following description of a Choctaw drum was obtained by Mr. Bushnell from the band of that tribe living at Bayou Lacomb, Louisiana, in 1908-9:

This is 30 inches in height and 15 inches in diameter. It is made of a section of a black gum tree; the cylinder wall is less than 2 inches in thickness. The head consists of a piece of untanned goat skin. The skin is stretched over the open end, while wet and pliable, and is passed around a hoop made of hickory about half an inch thick. A similar hoop is placed above the first. To the second hoop are attached four narrow strips of rawhide, each of which is fastened to a peg passing diagonally through the wall of the drum. To tighten the head of the drum it is necessary merely to drive the peg farther in. In this respect, as well as in general form, the drum resembles a specimen from Virginia in the British Museum, as well as the drum even now used on the west coast of Africa. It is not possible to say whether this instrument is a purely American form or whether it shows the influence of the negro. (Bushnell, 1909 a, p. 22.)

The "Virginia" drum just mentioned was described and figured by Bushnell (1906, pp. 676–678). As Bushnell himself concludes, it was evidently from the west coast of Africa, or at least in imitation of a drum from that region. Although the Bayou Lacomb specimen was certainly of American manufacture, one is led to suspect that the inspiration was originally from the same part of the Old World.

A Choctaw living near Philadelphia, Miss., gave me a description of the drum he was familiar with among his people, which I have printed elsewhere. The construction suggests that from Bayou Lacomb and is under the same suspicion.

It was made of a section of black gum or tupelo gum, hollowed out and 12 or 16 inches across, and of about the same length. Over the ends of this deerskins were fitted, each skin being first brought over the outside of a hoop or "cuff" and fastened tight, the cuff being just large enough to fit over the end of the body. After these had been put in place, a larger cuff was made and fitted tight over each and the two outside cuffs were fastened together by means of diagonal cords. Midway of the drum were two other cuffs or hoops fastened to the diagonal cords in such a way that when they were pushed in opposite directions they tightened the heads of the drum. The cuffs were made of white switch hickory, the cords anciently of deer hide, but later of store leather. Two deer-hide strings were allowed to lie across the end of the drum opposite that which was struck. One of these was looser than the other, so that two distinct notes resulted.

Drum sticks were made principally of maple, poplar, or ash. Each had a knob at the end, one made smaller to "beat the seconds," while most of the noise was made with the other. They beat on the end of the drum opposite that across which the strings lay but most of the noise is supposed to have been made by the other end, the compressed air transferring the vibrations across. If they wish to protect the drumhead they wrapped the knobs of the drumsticks with cloth. (Swanton, 1931 a, p. 224.)

There are references to Caddo drums in Bureau of American Ethnology Bulletin 132 (Swanton, 1942, p. 156).

RATTLES

Rattles accompanied songs and dances throughout the Southeast. Hariot says of the Carolina Indians that

when they haue escaped any great danger by sea or lande, or be returned from the warr in token of Ioye they make a great fyer abowt which the men, and woemen sitt together, holdinge a certaine fruite in their hands like vnto a rownde pompion or a gourde, which after they haue taken out the fruits, and the seedes, then fill with small stons or certayne bigg kernells to make the more noise, and fasten that vppon a sticke, and singinge after their manner, they make merrie: as my selfe obserued and noted downe at my beinge amonge them (Hariot, 1893, pl. 17.)

Smith gives some details regarding the varieties of rattles:

But the chiefe instruments are Rattels made of small gourds or Pumpion shels. Of these they have Base, Tenor, Countertenor, Meane and Trible. These mingled with their voices sometimes 20 or 30 togither, make such a terrible noise as would rather affright then delight any man. (Smith, John, Tyler ed., 1907, p. 107.)

Strachey (1849, p. 79) uses almost identical words. Beverley (1705, bk. 3, p. 55) tells us that "their Rattles are the Shell of a small Gourd, or Macock of the creeping kind, and not of those call'd Callibaches, which grow upon Trees."

Lawson observed among the Waxhaw a rattle consisting of a gourd with corn in it. He mentions the use of rattles at Adshusheer, the Eno and Shakori town. When he comes to discuss the culture of the Piedmont tribes in general, he speaks of "a rattle, made of a gourd, with some beans in it" (Lawson, 1860, pp. 98, 286). Adair, Bartram, Pénicaut, and Du Pratz mention gourd rattles in use among the Chickasaw, Creeks, Pascagoula, and Chitimacha, but Bushnell did not find this implement among the Bayou Lacomb Choctaw, nor did I learn of it among those about Philadelphia. In a certain dance they stated that two sticks were struck together but that was all. (Adair, 1775, p. 116; Bartram, 1792, pp. 243, 502; Margry, 1875–86, vol. 5, pp. 388–390; Le Page du Pratz, 1758, vol. 1, pp. 106–110; Swanton, 1911, pp. 303, 340; 1931 a, p. 224.)

On the Mississippi rattles were particularly in evidence in the peace-making ceremonies. Dumont describes them as "empty calabashes, in which are some beads or little stones to make a noise." Du Pratz calls the rattle by a common trader's name, the "chichicois," and describes it as "a gourd pierced at both ends for the insertion of a little stick one end of which is longer to serve as a handle; within are placed large bits of gravel to make the noise; in the absence of gravel they put in beans or dried kidney beans; it is with this instrument that they beat time while singing." (Dumont, 1753, vol. 1, pp. 193–195; Swanton, 1911, p. 137; Le Page du Pratz, 1758, vol. 1, p. 108.)

The terrapin shell rattles worn by Creek women about their ankles during the annual dances in the Square Grounds represent another type, but there is little mention of this outside of the Creek Nation. The following description by Romans may apply to a substitute or to an earlier form:

I observed the women dressed their legs in a kind of leather stockings, hung full of the hoofs of the roe deer in form of bells, in so much as to make a sound exactly like that of the Castagnettes: I was very desirous of examining these stockings and had an opportunity of satisfying my curiosity on those of my landlady at her return home. I counted in one of her stockings four hundred and ninety-three of these claws; there were nine of the women at the dance with this kind of ornament, so that allowing each of them to have had the same number of hoofs, and eight hoofs to a deer, there must have been killed eleven hundred and ten deer to furnish this small assembly of ladies with their ornaments. (Romans, 1775, p. 95.)

Thus terrapin shells may have taken the place of deer hoofs after the deer became scarce. Farther east we find European bells used as rattles on the clothing of some of the Siouan Indians (Lawson, 1860, pp. 68–69).

My Natchez informant, Watt Sam, used a rattle made out of a coconut (pl. 76, fig. 2).

FLAGEOLETS

Over much of the Gulf area, when it was first visited by Europeans, it was customary to welcome strangers of quality coming in peace by sending men forward, usually including the chief himself, blowing upon flutes, or rather flageolets. This custom is first alluded to by Cabeza de Vaca in his account of the Narvaez expedition to Florida. After Narvaez and his companions had left the coast and advanced inland, on June 17, 1528, they were met by a chief "whom an Indian carried on his shoulders. He wore a painted deerskin, and many people followed him, and he was preceded by many players on flutes made of reeds" (Cabeza de Vaca, Bandelier ed., 1905, p. 21). This was in the Timucua territory.

The custom was again observed by the followers of De Soto among the same people. Flageolets are probably to be understood by the "trumpets" in the hands of Indians near the Withlacoochee River, since conch-shell horns are mentioned separately (Garcilaso, 1723, p. 45). When the army left Aguacaleyquen, Ranjel states that "messengers were coming and going from Uçachile, a great chief, playing upon a flute for ceremony," and Elvas, who also notes the circumstance, says it was "their sign by which they make known that they come in peace." (Bourne, 1904, vol. 2, pp. 72–73; Robertson, 1933, p. 58.) Flageolets were probably among the instruments in the train of the great Coca chief and in that of Tascalusa on similar occasions, although the instrument is not specifically mentioned (Robertson, 1933, pp. 115, 128). They were evidently the "fifes" to the sound of which, along with other instruments, the Chicksaw launched their attack some months later (Garcilaso, 1723, p. 166). On another occasion, the Casqui Indians, west of the Mississippi, came to De Soto "singing" but nothing is said regarding instruments.

A little later the French also note wind instruments in the Florida peninsula. Le Moyne describes how the chief Saturiwa once came to visit him accompanied by a considerable military force, and

next to himself were twenty pipers, who produced a wild noise without musical harmony or regularity, but only blowing away with all their might, each trying to be the loudest. Their instruments were nothing but a thick sort of reed or cane, with two openings, one at the top to blow into and the other end for the wind to come out of, like organ pipes or whistles. (Le Moyne, 1875, p. 3; Swanton, 1922, p. 375.)

When the chief took a wife, Le Moyne tells us, she was brought in a litter preceded by men

blowing upon trumpets made of bark, which are smaller above and larger at the farther end and having only the two orifices, one at each end. They are hung with small oval balls of gold, silver and brass, for the sake of a finer combination of sounds. (Le Moyne, 1875, p. 13; Swanton, 1922, p. 372.)

In 1607, Percy observed that the werowance of Rapahannock in Virginia came to his party "playing on a Flute made of a Reed" (Narr. Early Va., Tyler ed., 1907, p. 14), and Smith and Strachey give short descriptions of the instrument. Smith says:

For their musicke they use a thicke cane, on which they pipe as on a Recorder. (Smith, John, Tyler ed., p. 107.)

And Strachey:

They have a kynd of cane on which they pipe as on a recorder, and are like the Greeke pipes, which they called *bombyces*, being hardly to be sounded without great strayning of the breath, upon which they observe certain rude times. (Strachey, 1849, p. 79.)

Romans (1775, p. 62) says that in his time the Chickasaw played "on an aukward kind of flute made of a cane." Bartram describes the flutes seen by him belonging to the Creek (or rather Seminole) and perhaps the Cherokee tribes, as

made of a joint of reed or the tibia of the deer's leg: on this instrument they perform badly, and at best it is rather a hideous melancholy discord, than harmony. It is only young fellows who amuse themselves on this howling instrument. (Bartram, 1792, p. 503.)

A Caddo flageolet is illustrated in Bureau of American Ethnology Bulletin 132 (Swanton, 1942, pl. 17, fig. 1).

RASPS

A rasp is shown in Catlin's painting of the Choctaw eagle dance. The Chitimacha say that they formerly used a dried alligator skin for that purpose (Swanton, 1931 a, pl. 6, p. 222; 1911, p. 350). The Hasinai missionary Espinosa saw the Indians make "a noise nothing less than infernal" by rubbing "little polished sticks with slits like a snake's rattles" on a hollow skin (Espinosa, 1927, p. 165).

SOCIETAL AND CEREMONIAL LIFE

TOWNS

Strachey thus describes the towns of the Powhatan Indians:

Theire habitations or townes are for the most part by the rivers, or not far distant from fresh springs, comonly upon a rice of a hill, that they may overlooke the river, and take every small thing into view which sturrs upon the same.

Their howses are not many in one towne, and those that are stand dissite and
scattered without forme of a street, farr and wyde asunder . . . About their
howses they have commonly square plotts of cleered grownd, which serve them
for gardens, some one hundred, some two hundred foote square. (Strachey,
1849, p. 72.)

Every werowance or chief had certain well-understood fishing territories. It is difficult to determine whether these corresponded to the
hunting territories of the northern Algonquians or the town lands
of the southern Indians in general. Very likely they formed a transition type, an adaptation of the former custom to southern conditions.
Strachey says of these:

Every weroance knoweth his owne meeres and lymitts to fish, fowle, or hunt
in (as before said), but they hold all of their great weroance Powhatan.
(Strachey, 1849, p. 81.)

Smith thus describes a small town called Kegquouhtan:

The Towne conteineth eighteene houses, pleasantly seated upon three acres
of ground, uppon a plaine, halfe invironed with a great Baye, with a little Ile
fit for a Castle in the mouth thereof, the Towne adjoyning to the maine by a
necke of Land of sixtie yardes. (Smith, John, Tyler ed., 1907, p. 38.)

In another place he thus indicates the nature of Indian neighborhood
villages:

Their houses are in the midst of their fields or gardens; which are smal plots
of ground, some 20 [acres], some 40, some 100, some 200, some more, some lesse.
Some times from 2 to 100 of these houses togither, or but a little separated by
groves of trees. Neare their habitations is little small wood, or old trees on the
ground, by reason of their burning of them for fire. So that a man may gallop
a horse amongst these woods any waie, but the creekes or Rivers shall hinder . . .
(Smith, John, Tyler ed., 1907, p. 101.)

In the Proceedings of the English Colonies in Virginia we read:

These wilde named natives live not in great numbers together; but dispersed,
commonly in thirtie, fortie, fiftie, or sixtie in a company. Some places have two
hundred, few places more, but many lesse. (Narr. Early Va., Tyler ed., 1907, p.
363.)

As might have been expected, the same situation occurs in the coastal
sections of North Carolina. According to Hariot:

Their townes are but small, & neere the sea coast but few, some containing but
10 or 12 houses; some 20. the greatest that we haue seene haue bene but of 30
houses; if they be walled it is only done with barks of trees made fast to stakes,
or els with poles onely fixed vpright and close one by another. (Hariot, 1893,
p. 36.)

The following descriptions of a fenced and an unfenced town are
among the best our literature affords:

The townes of this contrie are in a maner like vnto those which are in
Florida, yet are they not soe strong nor yet preserued with soe great care.
They are compassed abowt with poles starcke faste in the grownd, but they
are not verye stronge. The entrance is verye narrowe as may be seene by this
picture, which is made accordinge to the forme of the towne of Pomeiooc.

Ther are but few howses therin, saue those which belonge to the kinge and his nobles. On the one side is their tempel separated from the other howses, and marked with the letter A. Yt is builded rownde, and covered with skynne matts, and as it wear compassed abowt with cortynes without windowes, and hath noe lighte but by the doore. On the other side is the kings lodginge marked with the letter B. Their dwellinges are builded with certaine poles fastened together, and couered with matts which they turne op as high as they thinke good, and soe receue in the lighte and other. Some are also couered with boughes of trees, as euery man lusteth or liketh best. They keepe their feasts and make good cheer together in the midds of the towne as yt is described in the 17. Figure. When the towne standeth fare from the water they digg a great ponde noted with the letter C wherhence they fetche as muche water as they neede. [Pl. 77.]

Their townes that are not inclosed with poles are commonlye fayrer then suche as are inclosed, as appereth in this figure which liuelye expresseth the towne of Secotam. For the howses are Scattered heer and ther, and they haue a gardein expressed by the letter E. wherin groweth Tobacco which the inhabitants call Vppowoc. They hauve also groaues wherein thei take deer, and fields wherin they sowe their corne. In their corne fields they builde as yt weare a scaffolde wher on they sett a cottage like to a rownde chaire, signiffied by F. wherin they place one to watche, for there are suche a nomber of fowles, and beasts, that vnless they keepe the better watche, they would soone deuoure all their corne. For which cause the watcheman maketh continual cryes and noyse. They sowe their corne with a certaine distance noted by H. other wise one stalke would choke the growthe of another and the corne would not come vnto his rypenes G. For the leaves therof are large, like vnto the leaues of great reedes. They haue also a seuerall broade plotte C. whear after they haue ended their feaste they make merrie togither. Ouer against this place they haue a rownd plott B. wher they assemble themselues to make their solemne prayers. Not far from which place ther is a lardge buildinge A. wherin are the tombes of their kings and princes, as will appere by the 22. figure likewise they haue garden notted bey the letter I. wherin they vse to sowe pompions. Also a place marked with K. wherin they make a fayre att their solemne feasts, and hard without the towne a riuer L. from whence they fetche their water. [Pl. 78.]   (Hariot, 1893, pls. 19, 21.)

Narhantes, the Coree town attacked by Barnwell in his expedition against the Tuscarora in 1711, is thus described in one of his letters:

Tho' this be called a town, it is only a plantation here and there scattered about the Country, no where 5 houses together, and then ¼ a mile such another and so on for several miles, so it is impossible to surprize many before the alarm takes.

Shortly before his arrival they had built nine small forts, one of which he stormed. Afterward he

marched thro' the 5 Towns of the Enemy whose Country is almost as fine . . . as Appalatcha. I ordered that Fruit trees w'ch are plenty both of apples & peeches & Quinces to be preserved but destroyed all the rest, being about 374 houses, wherein there could not be less than 2000 bushells of corn. (South Carolina Hist. and Genealog. Mag., 1908, vol. 9, No. 1, pp. 32–34.)

The Tuscarora village of Tasqui to which Graffenried was taken was palisaded, the cabins being arranged in a circle inside with a great open space in the center (De Graffenried, 1886, p. 937).

In 1701 Lawson came upon "a settlement of Santee Indians, there being plantations lying scattering here and there, for a great many miles." He found that the Congaree towns consisted of not "above a dozen houses, they having other straggling plantations up and down the country" (Lawson, 1860, pp. 37, 52).

The town at Fort Christanna which was built by the Tutelo, Saponi, and their allies about 1714 and was therefore relatively late, is thus described by Fontaine:

It lieth in a plain by the riverside, the houses join all the one to the other, and altogether make a circle . . . There are three ways for entering into this town or circle of houses, which are passages of about six feet wide, between two of the houses. All the doors are on the inside of the ring, and the ground is very level withinside, which is in common between all the people to divert themselves. There is in the centre of the circle a great stump of a tree; I asked the reason they left that standing, and they informed me it was for one of their head men to stand upon when he had anything of consequence to relate to them, so that being raised, he might the better be heard. (Maury, 1907, p. 276.)

Florida towns having been mentioned, two short notices of these towns are now in order. The first is Elvas' description of Ucita on Tampa Bay already quoted in part:

The town consisted of seven or eight houses. The chief's house stood near the beach on a very high hill which had been artificially built as a fortress. At the other side of the town was the temple and on top of it a wooden bird with its eyes gilded. (Robertson, 1933, p. 33.)

In his description of a stockaded town Le Moyne says:

The chief's dwelling stands in the middle of the town, and is partly underground in consequence of the sun's heat. Around this are the houses of the principal men, all lightly roofed with palm branches, as they are occupied only nine months in the year; the other three, as has been related, being spent in the woods. (Le Moyne, 1875, p. 12; Swanton, 1922, pp. 352–353.)

Capt. Sandford thus describes the town of the Edisto in the Cusabo country which he visited in 1666:

The Towne is scituate on the side or rather in the skirts of a faire forest in wch at severall distances are diverse feilds of Maiz with many little houses straglingly amongst them for the habitations of the particular families. On the East side and part of the South It hath a large prospect over meadows very spatious and delightful, before the Doore of their Statehouse is a spatious walke rowed wth trees on both sides tall & full branched, not much unlike to Elms wch serves for the Exercise and recreation of the men [in the chunkey game]. (South Carolina Hist. Soc. Colls., 1897, vol. 5, pp. 60-82; Swanton, 1922, p. 64.)

He found the principal Indian town at Santa Elena (Port Royal) very much like it.

In the De Soto narratives we get many important details regarding Gulf towns but there are few attempts at description other than the very brief one above given. It would seem, however, that they found most of these grouped around a mound or mounds on which were the

ceremonial buildings and nearby a plaza or square. The same arrangement was observed in later times except that the mound was
generally wanting. This was included partly for defense no doubt
and also to enhance the respect due to the sacred edifices. Garcilaso
indicates several towns, particularly those along the Mississippi in
which there were two mounds with an intervening plaza.

Cabeza de Vaca, in his account of the entrance of Narvaez into an
Apalachee town, probably Ibitachuco, says:

> The village contained forty small and low houses, reared in sheltered places,
> out of fear of the great storms that continually occur in the country. The
> buildings are of straw, and they are surrounded by dense timber, tall trees and
> numerous water-pools, where there were so many fallen trees and of such size
> as to greatly obstruct and impede circulation. (Cabeza de Vaca, Bandelier ed.,
> 1905, p. 113.)

Let us turn to the Creek towns. Hawkins says of Tuskegee:

> This little town is in the fork of the two rivers, Coo-sau and Tal-la-poo-sa,
> where formerly stood the French fort Toulouse. The town is on a bluff on
> the Coo-sau, forty-six feet above low-water mark; the rivers here approach
> each other within a quarter of a mile, then curve out, making a flat of low
> land of three thousand acres, which has been rich canebrake; and one-third
> under cultivation in times past; the center of this flat is rich oak and hickory,
> margined on both sides with rich cane swamp; the land back of the town,
> for a mile, is flat, a whitish clay; small pine, oak, and dwarf hickory, then
> high pine forest. There are thirty buildings in the town compactly situated,
> and from the bluff a fine view of the flat lands in the fork, and on the right
> bank of Coo-sau, which river is here two hundred yards wide. (Hawkins, 1848,
> pp. 37–39; Swanton, 1922, pp. 209–210.)

A rather late view of Kasihta is given by the missionary Hodgson
in 1820:

> It appeared to consist of about 100 houses, many of them elevated on poles
> from two to six feet high, and built of unhewn logs, with roofs of bark, and
> little patches of Indian corn before the doors. . . . In the center of the town
> we passed a large building, with a conical roof, supported by a circular wall
> about three feet high; close to it was a quadrangular space, enclosed by four
> open buildings, with rows of benches rising above one another; the whole was
> appropriated, we were informed, to the Great Council of the town, who meet
> under shelter or in the open air, according to the weather. Near the spot
> was a high pole, like our may-poles, with a bird at the top, round which the
> Indians celebrate their Green-Corn Dance. (Hodgson, 1823, pp. 265–266; Swan
> ton, 1922, p. 224.)

Here is Coweta, the sister town, in 1799:

> Cow-e-tuh, on the right bank of Chat-to-ho-che, three miles below the falls,
> on a flat extending back one mile. The land is fine for corn; the settlements
> extend up the river for two miles on the river flats. These are bordered with
> broken pine land; the fields of the settlers who reside in the town, are on a
> point of land formed by a bend of the river, a part of them adjoining the point,
> are low, then a rise of fifteen feet, spreading back for half a mile, then an
> other rise of fifteen feet, and flat a half mile to a swamp adjoining the high-

lands; the fields are below the town.   (Hawkins, 1848, pp. 52–55; Swanton, 1922, p. 227.)

In 1739 Oglethorpe found that the houses of this town were "built with Stakes and Plaistered wth clay Mixed with Moss which makes them very warm and Tite," not yet having given way to logs (Bushnell, 1908, p. 573).

Coosa was described by the chroniclers of De Soto's expedition as a large and prosperous place, but when the Spanish officer under De Luna reached it in 1560

it did not have above thirty houses, or a few more. There were seven little hamlets in its district, five of them smaller and two larger than Coza itself, which name prevailed for the fame it had enjoyed in its antiquity. (Padilla, 1919, p. 205; Swanton, 1922, p. 231.)

Garcilaso, who usually exaggerates, states that in 1540 there were 500 houses in Coosa, but a soldier sent there by Juan Pardo in 1567 reported 150 "vecinos" (Garcilaso, 1723, p. 142; Ruidiaz, 1894, vol. 2, pp. 485–486).   The latter should evidently be taken to mean neighborhoods or villages, or possibly families.

Hawkins' numerous descriptions of Creek settlements say more about the topography than about the towns themselves, but Bartram gives us a worthwhile picture of Kolomi as he saw it in 1774, which I append entire:

Here are very extensive old fields, the abandoned plantations and commons of the old town, on the east side of the river; but the settlement is removed, and the new town now stands on the opposite shore, in a charming fruitful plain, under an elevated ridge of hills, the swelling beds or bases of which are covered with a pleasing verdure of grass; but the last ascent is steeper, and towards the summit discovers shelving rocky cliffs, which appear to be continually splitting and bursting to pieces, scattering their thin exfoliations over the tops of the grassy knolls beneath. The plain is narrow where the town is built; their houses are neat commodious buildings, a wooden frame with plastered walls, and roofed with Cypress bark or shingles; every habitation consists of four oblong square houses, of one story, of the same form and dimensions, and so situated as to form an exact square, encompassing an area or courtyard of about a quarter of an acre of ground, leaving an entrance into it at each corner. Here is a beautiful new square or areopagus, in the centre of the new town; but the stores of the principal trader, and two or three Indian habitations, stand near the banks of the opposite shore on the site of the old Coolome town. The Tallapoose River is here three hundred yards over, and about fifteen or twenty feet deep; the water is very clear, agreeable to the taste, esteemed salubrious, and runs with a steady, active current. (Bartram, 1792, p. 267.) [But compare text fig. 3, p. 393.]

His impressions of a Seminole town are equally captivating:

As I continued coasting the Indian shore of this bay (an expansion of the St. Johns River), on doubling a promontory, I suddenly saw before me an Indian settlement, or village. It was a fine situation, the bank rising gradually from the water. There were eight or ten habitations, in a row or street fronting the water, and about fifty yards distant from it. Some of the youth were naked, up to their hips in the water, fishing with rods and lines; whilst others, younger, were diverting themselves in shooting frogs with bows and arrows. On my near approach, the little children took to their heels, and ran to some women who were hoeing corn; but the stouter youth stood their ground, and, smiling, called to me. As I passed along, I observed some elderly people reclined on skins spread on the ground, under the cool shade of spreading Oaks and Palms, that were ranged in front of their houses: they arose, and eyed me as I passed, but perceiving that I kept on without stopping, they resumed their former position. They were civil, and appeared happy in their situation.

There was a large Orange grove at the upper end of their village; the trees were large, carefully pruned, and the ground under them clean, open, and airy. There seemed to be several hundred acres of cleared land about the village; a considerable portion of which was planted, chiefly with corn (Zea), Batatas, Beans, Pompions, Squashes (Cucurbita verrucosa), Melons (Cucurbita citrullus) Tobacco (Nicotiana), &c. abundantly sufficient for the inhabitants of the village. (Bartram, 1792, pp. 90–91.)

With this may be compared the Seminole village in the Everglades visited in 1913 by Skinner and thus pleasantly described:

On a little "hammock," or meadow island, surrounded by dark cypress trees that stood in the glass-clear water, were clustered eight or ten Seminole lodges. The palmetto fans with which they were thatched had faded from green to old gold in color, and above them the sky formed a soft background. Some naked Indian children, who had been playing and bathing in the water near the trail, saw us and splashed screaming into the camp at our approach. One little girl carried on her brown back a baby brother nearly as large as herself. Several gaunt dogs came bounding to the water's edge to greet us with their hoarse barking . . .

This village (like all the others that we saw during our sojourn in the Big Cypress and the Everglades) is situated on a hammock, or meadow island. As the hammocks are never very large, the village is of no great size. The houses are built around the edge of the land, not far from the water, with an open area, in this case roughly rectangular in shape, in the middle. In the center of this space is the cook-house, in which a fire is constantly burning. (Skinner, 1913, pp. 69–70.)

Plate 79 reproduces Eastman's sketch of an earlier Seminole settlement.

Henry Woodward has the following short sketch of the Westo town on Savannah River somewhere near the site of the present Augusta. He says that it

. . . stands uppon a poynt of ye river . . . uppon ye Westerne side soe yt ye river encompasseth two-thirds thereof . . . ye Towne . . . is built in a confused manner, consisting of many long houses whose sides and tops are both artifitially done with barke uppon ye tops of most whereof fastened to ye ends of long poles hang ye locks of haire of Indians that they have slaine. Ye inland side of ye towne being duble Pallisadoed, & yt part which fronts ye river haveing only a single one, under whose steep banks seldom ly less then one hundred faire canoes ready uppon all occasions. (South Carolina Hist. Soc. Colls., 1897, vol. 5, pp. 459–461.)

This reminds us very much of the Tamahita town, also Yuchi, visited by Gabriel Arthur and situated on one of the headstreams of the Tennessee.

This towne is seated on ye river side, haveing ye clefts of ye river on ye one side being very high for its defence, the other three sides trees of two foot over, pitched on end, twelve foot high, and on ye topps scafolds placed with parrapits to defend the walls and offend theire enemies which men stand on to fight, . . . this forte is foure square; 300 paces over and ye houses sett in streets, many hornes like bulls hornes lye upon theire dunghills. (Alvord, 1912, p. 185.)

And at a considerable distance from both of these was the Chattahoochee River town mentioned by Bartram:

The Uche town is situated in a low ground immediately bordering on the river; it is the largest, most compact, and best situated Indian town I ever saw; the habitations are large and neatly built; the walls of the houses are constructed of a wooden frame, then lathed and plastered inside and out with a reddish well-tempered clay or mortar, which gives them the appearance of red brick walls; and these houses are neatly covered or roofed with Cypress bark or shingles of that tree. The town appeared to be populous and thriving, full of youth and young children. I suppose the number of inhabitants, men, women and children, might amount to one thousand or fifteen hundred, as it is said they are able to muster five hundred gunmen or warriors. (Bartram, 1940, p. 309.)

A few notes on Cherokee towns also appear in Bartram's Travels:

The Cherokee town of Sinica is a very respectable settlement, situated on the East bank of the Keowe river, though the greatest number of Indian habitations are on the opposite shore, where likewise stands the council-house, in a level plain betwixt the river and the range of beautiful lofty hills, which rise magnificently, and seem to bend over the green plains and the river: but the chief's house, with those of the traders, and some Indian dwellings, are seated on the ascent of the heights on the opposite shore. (Bartram, 1792, pp. 327–328.)

Later he states:

After riding about four miles (on the way to Cowe), mostly through fields and plantations, the soil incredibly fertile, arrived at the town of Echoe, consisting of many good houses, well inhabited. I passed through and continued three miles farther to Nucasse, and three miles more brought me to Whatoga. Riding through this large town, the road carried me winding about through their little plantations of Corn, Beans, &c. up to the council-house, which was a very large dome or rotunda, situated on the top of an ancient mount, and here my road terminated. All before me and on every side, appeared little plantations of young Corn, Beans, &c. divided from each other by narrow strips or borders of grass, which marked the bounds of each one's property, their habitation standing in the midst. (Bartram, 1792, p. 348.)

Brother Martin Schneider, a Moravian missionary, in the journal describing his visit to the Cherokee country in 1784–1785, states that

In the Midst of Every Town is, as it were, a round Tower of Earth about 20 Feet high almost like a Heap where Coals are burnt, on which is a little House.

but which have been mostly burnt down in the last War. Here the first Chief climbs up every Morning at the Time of the Work in the Field, & calls the People with a loud voice together. (Williams, 1928, p. 260.)

The only descriptions of Chickasaw towns include an account of the location of the entire nation and its subdivisions (Adair, 1775, pp. 252-253; Swanton, 1922, p. 417). Romans thus speaks of them:

They live near the center of a very large and somewhat uneven savannah, of a diameter of above three miles; this savannah at all times has but a barren look, the earth is very Nitrous, and the savages get their water out of holes or wells dug near the town; in any drought the ground will gape in fissures of about six or seven inches wide, and again, two or three days rain will cause an inundation; the water is always nitrous, and this field abounds, with flint, marl, and those kinds of anomalous fossils mistaken for oyster shells, which cannot be burnt into lime; yet this produces a grass of which cattle are so fond as to leave the richest cane brakes for it; and notwithstanding the soil appears barren and burnt up, they thrive to admiration; it also affords a vast, or even immense store of the salubrious *Fragaria*, vulgarly known by the name of wood strawberry.

They have in this field what might be called one town, or rather an assemblage of huts, of the length of about one mile and a half, and very narrow and irregular; this however they divide into seven . . .

The nearest running water, is about one mile and a half off, to the south of the town, in the edge of the field, but it is of no note; the next is four miles off; and at high times, canoes might come up here out of the river *Tombechbé*; this place is a ford, which often proves difficult, and on this account is called *Nahoola Inalchubba* (i. e.) the white mens hard labour. (Romans, 1775, pp. 62–63.)

From Du Roullet's journal we can perhaps get our best idea of ancient Choctaw towns. It will be seen that they were groups of villages and single houses with farms surrounding them. There were undoubtedly buildings used for general gatherings, ceremonials, etc. but these were not as conspicuous as the corresponding ones among the Creeks.

The village of Boukfouka is one of those of the Choctaw Nation the Huts of which are the most widely separated from one another; this village is divided into three hamlets, each hamlet a quarter of a league from the others, and all three surrounded by Bayous: lastly this village is at least twenty leagues in circumference . . . [an incredible figure it would seem even granting the conditions].

The village of Castachas is one of the finest of the nation; it is situated in a large plain, in the middle of which there is a small hill and from its top one can see all the Indian huts placed on the plain and the (gardens?) around the Huts of each savage. . . .

The village of Jachou (Yazoo) is situated in a great plain which lies on a height; the savages have their fields in this plain and a large part of their huts are around the plain. The plain of Jachou is not so vast as that of Castachas, but it is of about two leagues circumference at the least. . . .

The village of Jachene atchoukima (Yakni achukma) is situated on a little elevation or height. The huts are well separated from one another.

The village of Crouetchitou (Kowi chito) or the Great Village is situated on a small plain surrounded by very high hills, where nearly all the huts of the savages are built and their fields are in the plain. . . .

Sapatchitou (Sapa chito) . . . is a small hamlet of the village of Boukfouka, which lies in a small plain where the savages have built a little stockaded fort, into which they retreat with their families every night on account of the frequent incursions of the Chikachas (Chickasaw) who cross the river near this hamlet when they come in a band upon the Choctaws. (De Villiers, 1923, pp. 239–241; Swanton, 1931 a, p. 76.)

Bushnell (1919, pl. 11) shows a later Louisiana settlement of the Choctaw at Bonfouca.

We get our views of the Natchez villages only in snatches for, like Southeastern towns generally, they consisted mainly of neighborhoods scattered through the woods and interspersed with fields. Iberville has this note:

We repaired to [the cabin of the Great Chief], which is raised to a height of 10 feet on earth brought thither, and is 25 feet wide and 45 feet long. Near by are eight cabins. Before that of the chief is the temple mound, which has a circular shape, a little oval, and bounds an open space about 250 paces wide and 300 long. A stream passes near, from which they draw their water. . . . From the landing place on the [Mississippi] river one ascends a very steep hillside about 150 fathoms high covered completely with woods. Being on top of the hill one finds a country of plains and prairies filled with little hills, in some places groves of trees, many oaks, and many roads cut through, going from one hamlet to another or to cabins. Those who traveled 3 or 4 leagues about say they found everywhere the same country, from the edge of the hill to the village of the chief. (Margry, 1875–86, vol. 4, pp. 410–412; Swanton, 1911, p. 191.)

Nicolas de la Salle says that the village of the Taensa Indians

extends along the lake (Lake St. Joseph) for 1 league. The temple, the cabin [of the chief], and seven or eight cabins of the old men are surrounded by stakes and make a kind of fort; on the stakes human heads are placed; the temple is dome-shaped, the door painted red, guarded day and night by two men. (Margry, 1875–86, vol. 1, pp. 566–567; Swanton, 1911, p. 263.)

Iberville visited it in 1700:

There may be in this nation 150 cabins in the space of 2 leagues along the edge of the lake. There is in this place a fairly handsome temple. The nation was numerous formerly, but at present there are not more than 300 men. They have very large fields (deserts) and a very fine country which is never inundated along the borders of this lake, [a body of water] perhaps a fourth of a league broad and 4½ leagues long, coming from the northeast and making a turn to the west. The main part of this village is about 2 leagues from the end, coming from the Mississippi river and opposite a little [inlet] or stream about a hundred paces wide, on the banks of which are some native cabins. (Margry, 1875–86, vol. 4, pp. 412–414; Swanton, 1911, p. 266.)

Iberville's journal and that of the commandant of his second ship, *Le Marin*, contain the following items regarding the Bayogoula town:

I found this village a quarter of a league from the river, and near it there passes a little stream from which they get their drinking water. It was surrounded by a palisade made entirely of canes, 1 inch apart and 10 feet in height, without a gate to close the gateway.

I saw in the middle of the village, [a space] which is like a great parade ground, two large posts, 40 feet in height, before their temple, on which two scalps were elevated. There is a chief who takes care of the fire in the temple. The village is composed of from 400 to 500 persons of both sexes, great and small, with large huts made dome shaped. The fields where they raise their corn are near their villages and are cultivated by means of bison bones. They pass the greater part of their time playing there with great sticks, which they throw after a little stone made almost round like a cannon ball. When any of their people dies they carry the body 50 paces off from the village and put it on 4 posts, covered above and below with mats by way of coffin, raised 4 feet above the ground and thither they carry food. [Iberville says that on the walls of the temple were figures of animals painted red and that] at the entrance was a shed 8 feet wide and 12 feet long, held up by two great pillars, with a crosspiece which served as a girder. (Margry, 1875–86, vol. 4, pp. 169–172, 259–262; Swanton, 1911, pp. 275–276.)

The same year Iberville visited the Houma village and states that:

This village is on a hill, where there are 140 cabins; there may be 350 men there at most, and many children. All the cabins are on the edge of the hill, in a double row in places, and ranged in a circle. There is a very neat square 200 paces across. The cornfields are in the valleys and on the other hills in the neighborhood.

They elevated the bodies of the dead upon posts like the Bayogoula. Late the same year Father Gravier passed:

The village is on the crest of a steep mountain, precipitous on all sides. There are 80 cabins in it, and in the middle of the village is a fine and very level space, where, from morning to night, young men exercise themselves. (Margry, 1875–86, vol. 4, pp. 176–177, 265–271; Swanton, 1911, pp. 286, 288; Thwaites, 1896–1901, vol. 65, pp. 145–150; Shea, 1861, pp. 143–147.)

In 1699 Fathers De Montigny and La Source visited the Tunica villages on Yazoo River, and the latter says:

The first village is 4 leagues from the Mississippi inland, on the bank of a fairly pretty river; they are dispersed in little villages; they cover in all 4 leagues of country. . . . The village of the great chief is in a beautiful prairie. (Shea, 1861, pp. 80–81; Swanton, 1911, p. 308.)

In 1700 Gravier stopped there, ascending the Yazoo from the Mississippi, and left his canoe 4 leagues from the latter,

at the foot of a hill, where there are five or six cabins. The road, which is 2 leagues by land, is quite pretty. I found persimmon trees loaded with fruit and many copal trees exuding gum. We passed in the roads canes 40 feet high and as thick as your arm. The stalk of the corn, which we call Indian corn, is over 15 to 20 feet high, and so are the sunflowers and thick in proportion. We saw five or six hamlets of a few cabins, and I was surprised that the Indians, who rarely see Frenchmen, showed so little curiosity. (Shea, 1861, pp. 132–134; Swanton, 1911, pp. 308–309.)

Charlevoix visited the Tunica after they had removed to the former Houma village, and therefore it is not surprising that he describes their town as "built in a circle, round a very large open space, without any inclosure, and moderately peopled." He adds:

The other cabins of the village are partly square, like that of the chief, and partly round, like those of the Natchez. The open space round which they all stand is about 100 paces in diameter. (French, 1851, p. 174; Swanton, 1911, p. 313.)

A Koroa village, which La Salle visited in his descent of the Mississippi in 1682 and on his return, was on the bluffs, reached by a well beaten path, and had a square "as large as the square in front of the Palais Royal at Paris" (Margry, 1875–86, vol. 1, p. 565; Swanton, 1911, p. 328). Probably this was really the village of the Tiou.

The Caddo towns, like most of those we have been considering, were generally scattered about "in hamlets and cantons," but our authority for this general statement makes an exception in the case of the Cahinnio who appear to have lived on or near the Ouachita River in southern Arkansas in 1687 for these, he says, had about 100 cabins collected in one place. A plan reproduced by Bolton and Harrington gives a general view of Caddo settlements. (Margry, 1875–86, vol. 3, pp. 387, 416; Bolton, 1915, frontispiece; Swanton, 1942, pl. 1.)

Probably the best descriptions of the Quapaw villages are given by Joutel, who passed through them in 1687 after the death of La Salle. There were four of these, two on the Arkansas, one on the east side of the Mississippi above the mouth of the Arkansas, and one on the west side still higher up. Joutel and his party came first to the village highest up the Arkansas, which he calls Otsoté or Otsotchavé. It was

on a slight elevation which the said river never overflows. . . . [and] built differently from those [of the Caddo] we had seen before, since the cabins were long and dome-shaped. They make them out of long poles placed upright with the larger ends buried in the earth, and they bring them together like arbors, but they are very large. They cover them with pieces of bark. Each cabin contains many families, each with its own fire. These cabins are much cleaner than many we have seen, but they were inferior in general to those of the Cenis and the Assonis and others on one point, in that most of the Arkansas lie down on the earth like dogs, with only a skin under them. (Margry, 1875–86, vol. 3, p. 442.)

The cabins of the next village, Toriman, which was on the Arkansas close to its junction with the Mississippi, were like the cabins of Otsoté. Joutel adds that the people of that village made structures like scaffolds raised to a height of 15 to 20 feet.

on which they lie to take advantage of the wind and to protect themselves from the mosquitoes (*maringouins*), the most uncomfortable creatures I have found in America, although little, in that they prevent one from sleeping. But thanks to these scaffolds, when there is a little wind, the said creatures are carried away. (Margry, 1875–86, vol. 3, p. 454.)

Tongigua, the third village, differed from the others only in size, being much smaller. The last one, Kappa, was the largest and was situated on the left of the river [Mississippi] as one went up, on a bluff or elevation about thirty feet high. . . . They have their cleared lands or fields behind the village, which are about a league wide by a league and a half long, in which they harvest a quantity of corn, pumpkins, melons, sunflower seeds, beans, and other similar things, as also a great quantity of peaches and plums. They have the same advantages in hunting as the others, but they are not as favorably situated for fishing, since the water of this great river is almost always disturbed and muddy. According to what I was able to learn, four hundred warriors might be drawn from this village and three hundred from the others. (Margry, 1875–86, vol. 3, p. 462.)

Le Sueur describes the same dome-shaped structures, but he says there was but a single fire in each. La Harpe, in 1722, counted 41 cabins in the village of Zautoouys (Otsoté) and estimated that it contained 330 persons. He tells us that the bank of the river here had an elevation of about 2 feet. Ougapa was at an isolated spot on the west bank of the Mississippi, and its lands might "have a front of a quarter of a league on the river and a depth of three leagues, very good land all cleared." Tourima and Tongigua stood at distances of a league, and the three together La Harpe estimated to have population of 400 (Margry, 1875–86, vol. 6, p. 365).

SOCIAL ORGANIZATION

GENERAL FEATURES

Professor Speck has made known to anthropologists the hunting territory system of the Algonquian Indians of the far north, and he and his pupils have traced this down into New England and Pennsylvania. In the Gulf region generally, as we shall see, each town controlled the land immediately about it, but there is no evidence that the more distant territories of the tribe were parceled up in this way, though the data are so scanty that such a possibility cannot be ignored. The following quotation from Strachey, which has already been given but may here be repeated, comes nearest to giving us information as to the condition of affairs in the tidewater region of Virginia:

Every weroance knoweth his owne meeres and lymitts to fish, fowle, or hunt in (as before said), but they hold all of their great weroance Powhatan, unto whome they pay eight parts of ten tribute of all the comodities which their country yeldeth, as of wheat, pease, beanes, eight measures of ten of all sorts of skyns, and furrs eight of ten; and so he robbes the people, in effect, of all they have, even to the deare's skyn wherewith they cover them from cold, in so much as they dare not dresse yt and put yt on untill he have seene yt and refused yt, for which he commaundeth they dare not disobey in the least thinge. (Strachey, 1849, p. 81.) [See also p. 644 herein.]

We also know from the marriage customs as described by Spelman that residence was patrilocal, a decidedly Algonquian feature. Of course, the absolutism of Powhatan was something almost unknown in the north, but his empire was of very recent growth, and although similar dictatorships probably preceded it, there is no evidence that any great continuity existed among any of them.   Otherwise the power itself reminds one of parts of the Gulf region, particularly Florida and the lower Mississippi, though the closest analogy is furnished by some eastern Siouan tribes.   Stripping away this overgrowth, we probably have in the strictly bounded dominion of the werowance a lineal descendant of the hunting territory, perhaps a transition from the hunting territory of the band to the town land of the Gulf region.

The common Virginian word for "chief" was, as just given, "werowance," which Strachey defines as follows:

> The word weroance, which we call and conster for a king, is a common word, whereby they call all comaunders, for they have but fewe words in their language, and but few occasions to use any officers more than one comaunder, which comonly they call weroance.   (Strachey, 1849, p. 51.)

Strachey and Smith both expatiate at length on the power and absolute authority of Powhatan.

> In all his ancyent inheritances [says the former] he hath howses built after their manner, and at every howse provision for his entertainment according to the tyme.   About his person ordinarily attendeth a guard of forty or fifty of the tallest men his country doe affourd.   Every night, upon the four quarters of his howse, are four centinells drawen forth, each standing from other a flight shott; and at every half houre, one from the *corps du guard* doth hallowe, unto whome every sentinell returnes answere round from his stand; yf any fayle, an officer is presentlye sent forth that beateth him extreamlye. . . .   According to the order and custome of sensuall heathenisme, in the allowance of poligamie, he may have as many women as he will, and hath (as is supposed) many more then one hundred, all which he doth not keepe, yet as the Turk, is one seragalia or howse, but hath an appointed number, which reside still in every their severall places, amongst whome, when he lyeth on his bedd, one sitteth at his head and another at his feet; but when he sitteth at meat, or in presenting himself to any straungers, one sitteth on his right hand, and another on his leaft. . . .   It is strange to see with what great feare and adoration all this people doe obey this Powhatan, for at his feete they present whatsoever he comaundeth, and at the least frowne of his brow the greatest will tremble, yt may be, because he is very terrible, and inexorable in punishing such as offend him.   (Strachey, 1849, pp. 51–53.)

Yet most of the chiefs or "kings" do not seem to have gone about ordinarily in much state for Spelman says:

> The King is not know by any difference from other of y⁰ better chefe sort in y⁰ cuntry but only when he cums to any of ther howses they present him with copper Beads or Vitall, and shew much reuerence to him.   (Smith, John, Arber ed., 1884, p. cxiii.)

They were, however, greeted on their arrival and dismissed with a general shout several times repeated (Smith, John, Arber ed., 1884, pp. xliii, xlvii).

On the return from their first expedition, Newport's party had the following encounter with a Virginia chieftainess:

Assending a pretty Hill, we sawe the Queene of the Country comminge in selfe same fashion of state as *Pawatah* or *Arahatec;* yea rather with more maiesty: she had an vsher before her who brought her to the matt prepared vnder a faire mulbery tree, where she satt her Downe by her selfe with a stayed Countenance. She would permitt none to stand or sitt neere her: she is a fatt lustie manly woman: she had much Copper about her neck, a Crownet of Copper upon her hed: she had long black haire, which hanged loose downe her back to her myddle, which only part was Covered with a Deares skyn, and ells all naked. She had her woemen attending on her adorned much like her selfe (save they wanted y⁰ Copper). (Smith, John, Arber ed., 1884, pp. xlix–l.)

The power of Powhatan is witnessed in a number of ways. On one occasion he showed Smith his canoes and "described unto me how hee sent them over the Baye, for tribute Beades: and also what Countries paid him Beads, Copper, or Skins" (Smith, John, Tyler ed., 1907, p. 56). It is shown also by his depositaries of goods scattered in various places. (See quotations from Strachey above and Smith below.)

To one accustomed to think of absolutism in government as something quite foreign to the American Indians, much of the above and what Smith says about Powhatan and his subject werowances will come as a shock:

Although the countrie people be very barbarous; yet have they amongst them such governement, as that their Magistrats for good commanding, and their people for du[e] subiection and obeying, excell many places that would be counted very civill.

The forme of their Common wealth is a monarchicall governement. One as Emperour ruleth over many kings or governours. Their chiefe ruler is called Powhatan, and taketh his name of the principall place of dwelling called Powhatan. But his proper name is Wahunsonacock. Some countries he hath, which have been his ancestors, and came unto him by inheritance, as the countrie called Powhatan, Arrohateck, Appamatuke, Pamaunke, Youghtanud, and Mattapanient. All the rest of his Territories expressed in the Map, they report have beene his severall conquests. In all his ancient inheritances, hee hath houses built after their manner like arbours, some 30, some 40 yardes long, and at every house, provision for his entertainement, according to the time. At Werowocomoco, he was seated upon the North side of the river Pamaunke, some 14 miles from James Towne, where for the most part, hee was resident, but he tooke so little pleasure in our neare neighbourhood, that were able to visit him against his will in 6 or 7 houres, that he retired himself to a place in the deserts at the top of the river Chickahamania betweene Youghtanund and Powhatan. His habitation there is called Orapacks, where he ordinarily now resideth. He is of parsonage a tall well proportioned man, with a sower looke, his head somwhat gray, his beard so thinne that it seemeth none at al. His age neare 60; of a very able and hardy body to endure any labour. About his person ordinarily attendeth a guard of 40 or 50 of the tallest men his Country doth afford. Every night upon the 4 quarters of his house are 4 Sentinels, each standing from other a flight shoot: and at every halfe houre, one from the Corps du guard doth hollowe, unto whom every Sentinell doth answer round from his stand. If any faile, they presently send forth an officer that beateth him extremely. (Smith, John, Tyler ed., 1907, pp. 113–114.)

Now follows a description of his treasure-temple a mile from Orapaks, after which Smith continues:

He hath as many women as he will: whereof when hee lieth on his bed, one sitteth at his head, and another at his feet, but when he sitteth, one sitteth on his right hand, and another on his left. As he is wearie of his women, hee bestoweth them on those that best deserve them at his hands. When he dineth or suppeth, one of his women, before and after meat, bringeth him water in a wo[o]den platter to wash his hands. Another waiteth with a bunch of feathers to wipe them instead of a Towell, and the feathers when he hath wiped are dryed againe. His kingdome descendeth not to his sonnes nor children: but first to his brethren, whereof he hath 3, namely Opitchapan, Opechancanough, and Catataugh, and after their decease to his sisters. First to the eldest sister, then to the rest: and after them to the heires male and female of the eldest sister, but never to the heires of the males.

He nor any of his people understand any letters wherby to write or read, only the lawes whereby he ruleth is custome. Yet when he listeth, his will is a law and must bee obeyed: not only as a king, but as halfe a God they esteeme him. His inferiour kings whom they cal werowances are tyed to rule by customes, and have power of life and death as their command in that nature. But this word Werowance which we call and conster (construe) for a king, is a common worde whereby they call all commanders: for they have but fewe words in their language and but few occasions to use anie officers more then one commander, which commonly they call werowances. They all knowe their severall landes, and habitations, and limits to fish, fowle, or hunt in, but they hold all of their great Werowances Powhatan, unto whome they pay tribute of skinnes, beades, copper, pearle, deare, turkies, wild beasts, and corne. What he commandeth they dare not disobey in the least thing. It is strange to see with what great feare and adoration all these people doe obay this Powhatan. For at his feet, they present whatsoever he commandeth, and at the least frowne of his browe, their greatest spirits will tremble with feare: and no marvell, for he is very terrible and tyrannous in punishing such as offend him. For example, hee caused certaine malefactors to be bound hand and foot, then having of many fires gathered great store of burning coles, they rake these coles round in the forme of a cockpit, and in the midst they cast the offenders to broyle to death. Sometimes he causeth the heads of them that offend him, to be laid upon the altar or sacrificing stone, and one with clubbes beates out their braines. When he would punish any notorious enimie or malefactor, he causeth him to be tied to a tree, and, with muscle shels or reeds, the executioner cutteth of[f] his joints one after another, ever casting what they cut of[f] into the fire; then doth he proceed with shels and reeds to case the skinne from his head and face; then doe they rip his belly, and so burne him with the tree and all. Thus themselves reported they executed George Cassen. Their ordinary correction is to beate them with cudgels. Wee have seene a man kneeling on his knees, and at Powhatans command, two men have beat him on the bare skin, till he hath fallen senseless in a s[w]ound, and yet never cry nor complained.

In the yeare 1608, hee surprised the people of Payankatank, his neare neighbours and subjects. The occasion was to us unknowne, but the manner was thus. First he sent diverse of his men as to lodge amongst them that night, then the Ambuscadoes invironed al their houses, and at the houre appointed, they all fell to the spoile; 24 men they slewe, the long haire of the one side of their heades with the skinne cased off with shels or reed, they brought away. They surprised also the women and the children and the Werowance. All these they present to Powhatan. The Werowance, women and children became his prisoners, and doe him service. The locks of haire with their skinnes he hanged on a line unto two trees. And thus he made ostentation as of a great triumph at Werowocomoco, shewing them to the English men that then came unto him, at his appointment: they expecting provision; he, to betray them, supposed to halfe conquer them, by this spectacle of his terrible crueltie. (Smith, John, Tyler ed., 1907, pp. 114–116.)

In the report on the Proceedings of the English Colonies in Virginia, we learn that Powhatan was found in the following state by his English visitors:

Sitting upon his bed of mats, his pillow of leather imbroydred (after their rude manner) with pearle and white beades, his attire a faire Robe of skins as large as an Irish mantle, at his head and feet a handsome young woman: on each side his house sate 20 of his concubines, their heads and shoulders painted red, with a great chaine of white beades about their necks; before those sate his chiefest men, in like order, in his arbor-like house. (Narr. Early Va., Tyler ed., 1907, p. 134.)

Such honors were also paid to the wives of chiefs, as appears from what Strachey tells us of the entourage of the wife of a native chief named Pipisco already alluded to. She lay

upon a pallett of osiers, spred over with four or five fyne grey matts, herself covered with a faire white drest deare skynne or two; and when she rose, she had a mayd who fetcht her a frontall of white currall, and pendants of great but imperfect coloured and worse drilled pearles, which she put into her eares, and a chayne, with long lyncks of copper, which they call Tapoantaminais, and which came twice or thrice about her neck, and they accompt a jolly ornament; and sure thus attired, with some variety of feathers and flowers stuck in their haires, they seems as *debonaire*, quaynt, and well pleased as (I wis) a daughter of the howse of Austria behune with all her jewells; likewise her mayd fetcht her a mantell, which they call puttawus, which is like a side cloake, made of blew feathers, so arteficyally and thick sowed togither, that it seemed like a deepe purple satten, and is very smooth and sleeke; and after she brought her water for her hands, and then a braunch or twoo of fresh greene asshen leaves, as for a towell to dry them. I offend in this digression the willinger, since these were ceremonyes which I did little look for, carrying so much presentment of civility, and which are not ordinarily perfourmed to any other amongst them. (Strachey, 1849, pp. 57–58.)

Beverley generalizes from the example of Powhatan to what he assumes to have been customary in the Tidewater region, and he is probably right:

The method of the *Indian* Settlements is altogether by Cohabitation, in Towneships, from fifty to five hundred Families in a Town, and each of these Towns is commonly a Kingdom. Sometimes one King has the command of several of these Towns, when they happen to be united in his Hands, by Descent or Conquest; but in such cases there is always a Viceregent appointed in the dependent Town, who is at once Governour, Judge, Chancellour, and has the same Power and Authority which thê King himself has in the Town where he resides. This Viceroy is oblig'd to pay to his Principal some small Tribute, as an acknowledgment of his submission, as likewise to follow him to his Wars, whenever he is requir'd. (Beverley, 1705, bk. 3, pp. 10–11.)

However, we are told that the Chickahominy tribe was ruled by their priests, and that the Chesapeake remained unconquered.

There are passages in the narratives of the Raleigh colony that confirm the Virginia narratives. The general situation is thus dealt with by Hariot:

In some places of the countrey one onely towne belongeth to the gouernment of a *Wiróans* or chiefe Lorde; in other some two or three, in some sixe, eight, & more; the greatest *Wiróans* that yet we had dealing with had but eighteene townes in his gouernment, and able to make not aboue seuen or eight hundred figthing men at the most: The language of euery gouernment is different from any other, and the farther they are distant the greater is the difference. (Hariot, 1893, p. 36.)

And we have further confirmation of the state observed by chiefs and their wives from Barlowe:

There came downe from all parts great store of people, bringing with them leather, corall, divers kindes of dies, very excellent, and exchanged with us: but when Granganimeo the kings brother was present, none durst trade but himselfe: except such as weare red pieces of copper on their heads like himselfe: for that is the difference betweene the noble men, and the governours of countreys, and the meaner sort. And we both noted there, and you have understood since by these men, which we brought home, that no people in the worlde cary more respect to their King, Nobilitie, and Governours, then these doe. The Kings brothers wife, when she came to us (as she did many times) was followed with forty or fifty women alwayes: and when she came into the shippe, she left them all on land, saving her two daughters, her nurse and one or two more. The Kings brother alwayes kept this order, as many boates as he would come withall to the shippes, so many fires would hee make on the shore a farre off, to the end we might understand with what strength and company he approached. (Burrage, 1906, p. 233.)

The chieftainess of a town at the northern end of Roanoke Island who entertained them, had the bows and arrows of some returning hunters broken and the men themselves beaten in order to reassure her guests (Burrage, 1906, p. 236).

The Siouan tribes were in general small in numbers, yet in some of them the chief was as absolute as Powhatan. Of their government in general Lawson says:

The king is the ruler of the nation, and has others under him, as his war captains, and counsellors, who are picked out and chosen from among the ancientest men of the nation he is king of. These meet him in all general councils and debates, concerning war, peace, trade, hunting, and all the adventures and accidents of human affairs, which appear within their verge; where all affairs are discoursed of and argued pro and con, very deliberately (without making any manner of parties or divisions) for the good of the public;

for, as they meet there to treat, they discharge their duty with all the integrity imaginable, never looking towards their own interest, before the public good. After every man has given his opinion, that which has most voices, or, in summing up, is found the most reasonable, that they make use of without any jars and wrangling, and put it in execution, the first opportunity that offers.

The succession falls not to the king's son, but to his sister's son, which is a sure way to prevent imposters in the succession. Sometimes they poison the heir to make way for another, which is not seldom done, when they do not approve of the youth that is to succeed them. The king himself is commonly chief Dr. in that cure. (Lawson, 1860, pp. 317–318.) [31]

The power he attributes to the Santee chief was greater:

The Santee King . . . is the most absolute Indian ruler in these parts, although he is head but of a small people, in respect to some other nations of Indians, that I have seen. He can put any of his people to death that hath committed any fault which he judges worthy of so great a punishment. This authority is rarely found among these savages, for they act not (commonly) by a determinative voice in their laws towards any one that hath committed murder, or such other great crime. (Lawson, 1860, pp. 40–41.)

Lederer, writing a little earlier, tells us that the Wateree Indians "differ in government from all the other Indians of these parts: for they are slaves, rather than subjects to their king." The chief ruling in his time hired three youths and sent them forth "to kill as many young women of their enemies as they could light on, to serve his son, then newly dead, in the other world" (Alvord, 1912, pp. 157–158).

The prerogatives of the Wateree chief seem to have been of long standing since Juan Pardo, who visited them in 1566, reports that they were governed by two chieftainesses who were waited upon by pages and female servants (Ruidiaz, 1894, vol. 2, pp. 482–484).

In spite of a natural tendency to exaggerate the power and state of Indian chiefs in agreement with ideas of the kingship prevailing in contemporary Europe, there must be some basis for the lofty position assigned them in the information Peter Martyr gives, derived from Francisco of Chicora. He not only describes the chiefs and chief women of Duhare (some region in South Carolina), as persons of gigantic size, which he affirms to have been produced artificially—treason in that biologically regulated land consisting in any attempt to imitate the process—but says that the reigning chief, Datha, lived in a palace built of stone while all the other houses were of wood covered with thatch or grass (Anghierra, 1912, pp. 259–265; Swanton, 1922, p. 43).

The tribe was possessed of twin idols which, on a certain occasion, the chief brought forth and exhibited to the people. Then "he and they are saluted with respect and fear by the people, who fall upon their knees or throw themselves on the ground with loud shouts"

---

[31] For descent, consult also Lawson, 1860, p. 89.

(Anghierra, 1912, pp. 259–265; Swanton, 1922, pp. 43–44). Farther on we read: "Their kings are of gigantic size, as we have already mentioned. All the provinces we have named pay them tributes and these tributes are paid in kind" (Anghierra, 1912, pp. 265–267; Swanton, 1922, p. 45). Finally, the ceremonialism used toward the chief is suggestive of that employed before the chiefs of the Natchez and Taensa:

It is quite laughable to hear how the people salute the lords and how the king responds, especially to his nobles. As a sign of respect the one who salutes puts his hands to his nostrils and gives a bellow like a bull, after which he extends his hands toward the forehead and in front of the face. The king does not bother to return the salutes of his people, and responds to the nobles by half bending his head toward the left shoulder without saying anything. (Anghierra, 1912, pp. 266–267; Swanton, 1922, p. 46.)

The aristocratic nature of Timucua society and the great power of Timucua chiefs is evident from information contained in both French and Spanish documents. Pareja gives a description of several lineages which is somewhat obscure but seems to indicate a sort of caste system resembling that of the Natchez (Pareja, 1612, pp. 130–133; Swanton, 1922, p. 370).

From Pareja's catechism it also appears that chiefs were allowed to exact tribute from their subjects, and that they sometimes punished those who were disobedient by having their arms broken. Moreover, the French witnessed the punishment of two men, for negligence when on watch, who were beaten on the head with a club made of very hard wood (Le Moyne, 1875, p. 12; Swanton, 1922, p. 380). A chief sometimes wore a long, painted skin the ends of which were held up by another Indian in a manner rather suspiciously suggestive of European courts, but this custom is directly attested by Laudonnière as an eyewitness. When the chief married, his bride was brought to him in great state seated on a litter, and when he died he was buried with ceremony, friendly chiefs participating in the mourning, and special female mourners assisting. When councils were held, the chief's seat was raised to a greater height than those of the others, or at least was distinguished from theirs. Thither came his "nobles" and saluted him in turn,

the oldest first, by lifting both hands twice to the height of the head and saying, "Ha, he, ya, ha, ha." To this the rest answer, "Ha, ha." Each as he completes his salutation, takes his seat on the bench.

When they were to hold a council with the French or some tribe away from home, men were sent on ahead to erect an arbor. The state observed by chiefs in conducting a war expedition also testifies to their power, and this was particularly in evidence in that observed by the Timucua or Utina chief (Laudonnière, 1586, p. 9; Le Moyne, 1785, pp. 6–7, 11–12; Swanton, 1922, pp. 374–375, 377–378). Each greater chief had a number of smaller, local chiefs under him upon whom he probably drew heavily at times, though the things obtained in this manner were no doubt rather of the nature of "friendly" forced loans than tribute. The Calusa chief in southwest Florida, however, is said to have taken tribute from the Indians around Lake Okeechobee, tribute consisting of "fish, game, roots, deer skins, etc." (Colección de Documentos Inéditos, 1864–1884, vol. 5, p. 535; Swanton, 1922, p. 388). The chief contemporary with Laudonnière had combined the priestly power with the civil and military authority and Lopez de Velasco states that every time the son of a cacique died "each neighbor sacrifices his sons or daughters who have accompanied the dead body" and that "when the cacique himself dies, or the caciqua, every servant of his or hers, as the case may be, is put to death." The same writer tells us that the Indians of Tekesta, near the present Miami, had the custom

when the cacique dies, of disjointing his body and taking out the largest bones. These are placed in a large box and carried to the house of the cacique, where every Indian from the town goes to see and adore them, believing them to be their gods. (Swanton, 1922, p. 389.)

The chief of Ais was, however, treated with more veneration than the chiefs of the other towns on the eastern coast and appears to have dominated them. On his return from Hobe, whither he had gone for some European wreckage, Dickenson says, speaking of the chief ruling in 1699,

he was received by his people with great homage, holding out his hands, as their custom is, to be kissed, having his chest carried before him to his house. (Dickenson, 1803, p. 48; Swanton, 1922, p. 396.)

Absolutism reached its height, as is well known, among the Natchez and Taensa Indians of the lower Mississippi. Speaking of the tribes from the Taensa southward, but more particularly of the latter, the missionary Membré writes to his superior:

They have temples where they preserve the bones of their dead chiefs, and what is noteworthy is that the chiefs have much more power and authority than among all our savages [to the northward]. They command and are obeyed. A person does not pass between them and the reed torch which burns in their houses, but makes a circuit with some ceremony. They have their servants (valets), who wait upon them at table. People bring them food from outside. They serve them with drink in their cup after having rinsed it, and no one drinks before they [do]. Their wives and children are treated in the same manner. They distribute presents according to their will, to whomsoever among them it seems good. It is sufficient to tell you that the chief of the Taënsa coming to see M. de la Salle, a master of ceremonies came two hours before with five or six flunkeys whom he made sweep with their hands the road over which he must pass, prepare a place for him, and spread out a rug, which consisted of a cane mat very delicately and artistically made. The chief who was coming was clothed in a very beautiful white cloth. Two men preceded him, in state, with fans of white feathers, as if to chase away the evil spirits;

a third was loaded with a sheet of copper and a circular plaque of the same material. (Margry, 1875–1886, vol. 2, pp. 209–210; Swanton, 1911, p. 262.)

Du Pratz has this to tell us regarding the power of the Natchez Great Sun:

> In fact these people are reared in such perfect submission to their sovereign that the authority which he exerts over them is a veritable despotism, which can be compared only with that of the first Ottoman emperors. He is, like them, absolute master of the goods and life of his subjects, he disposes of them according to his pleasure, his will is his reason, and, an advantage which the Ottomans have never had, there is neither any attempt on his person nor seditious movements to fear. When he orders one who has merited it to be put to death, the unhappy condemned man neither begs nor makes intercession for his life, nor seeks to escape. The order of the sovereign is executed on the spot and no one murmurs. The relatives of the great chief share more or less of his authority in proportion to nearness in blood, and the Tattooed Serpent has been seen to have three men put to death who had arrested and bound a Frenchman whom he loved much, in order to kill him, although we were then at war with the Natchez. (Du Pratz, 1758, vol. 2, pp. 352–353; Swanton, 1911, p. 106.)

Nevertheless, it is plain that in practice the absolutism of the Great Sun depended upon his age and personal abilities, and that his power was considerably curtailed by the other members of the Sun caste, particularly the other town chiefs, back of whom again lay that great body of usage and prejudice which no sovereign can indefinitely override.

The influence of Natchez culture upon the other tribes along the lower Mississippi is apparent and no doubt tended to augment the power of the chiefs, but we find singularly few traces of marked regard paid to them. Apparently the prerogatives of the Tunica chiefs were somewhat above those enjoyed by the chiefs of the Choctaw-speaking tribes, but even they must have lacked most of the pomp and circumstance of the Natchez or we should hear more about it. We are told that shortly before 1700 there was a chieftainess among the Houma who lead many war parties and that "when she walked about she was always preceded by four young men who sang and danced the calumet to her." But we are distinctly told at the same time that she was not the head chief of the tribe and it is evident that her peculiar privileges were immediately connected with her personal abilities. (Thwaites, 1897–1901, vol. 65, pp. 147–151; Shea, 1861, pp. 144–145; Swanton, 1911, p. 288.) This was something wholly unlike the situation among the Natchez and Taensa. When we come to the Chitimachan tribes, however, we encounter something reminiscent of the Natchez, a fact which tends to confirm early traditions linking the two groups of people together. Even in the case of the insignificant Chawasha tribe of Chitimachan lineage, we find Charlevoix writing:

The chief is very absolute, as are all those of Florida. He never hunts or shoots but for his diversion, for his subjects are obliged to give him part of their game. (French, 1851, p. 182; Swanton, 1911, p. 300.)

In the Chitimacha tribe proper there is evidence of a caste system which seems to have been a true one, the castes being endogamous, unlike the castes among the Natchez. There was a chief in each town and a head chief under whom were a number of officers called netekmesh (netē′xmēc) (Swanton, 1911, pp. 348–349).

Dr. Gatschet's Atakapa informants told of certain chiefs whose authority extended over a number of towns,[32] but any tendencies of this kind are probably to be attributed to influences emanating from the Chitimacha and other peoples farther east.

The Caddo chiefs apparently occupied an intermediate position, by no means on a level with the chiefs of the Natchez nor yet on the plane of the Wichita or Tonkawa, but they were under a sort of priest king, called *xinesi*, whose powers were very great.

We have now completed a circuit of the Gulf region from Chesapeake Bay along the coasts and nearer hinterlands of the Atlantic and Gulf to the mouth of the Mississippi and up that river and the Red to the borders of the Plains. It remains to consider the territory inland, the region of the great corn-raising nations. If we compare the position of chiefs indicated in the narratives of De Soto, who, as we know, cut through the very heart of this territory in the early part of the sixteenth century, with the descriptions of later writers, we appear to get very different ideas of the status of chiefs in the region covered. No doubt much of this difference is attributable to the tendency of the Spaniards to identify American institutions with European ones, but their representations as to the status of some of these chiefs are so completely borne out by certain later writers, French and English, that we cannot discard their testimony altogether. Thus the inhabitants of the provinces of Anilco, Guachoya, Aminoya, Teguanate, and as far north as Quiguate were in all probability related to, or ancestors of, the later Taensa and Natchez, and from certain statements in the De Soto narratives we may be assured that their customs were similar. Nor is it strange that we should find absolutism or caste tendency in Florida similar to that noted in later times.

Our main difficulties are with what we read regarding the chieftainess of Cofitachequi, undoubtedly closely related to the Lower Creeks of the historic period, the chief of Coça, and the chief of the Mobile, the famed Tascalusa. So far as the two former are concerned, there is evidence of very considerable changes in some of the institutions of the two people between the early sixteenth century and the late seventeenth century. A certain amount of democratization seems

---

[32] Notes in Gatschet and Swanton, 1932, p. 11.

to have accompanied these changes. Possibly this was due to the entrance of a new element from the north such as is represented by the Cherokee and Yuchi among whom there is little evidence of a developed aristocracy, or it may be attributable to a late wave of Muskogee. Although the Abihka Creeks are mentioned in the De Luna documents dating from 1560 to 1561, they were probably late comers, and, since Hawkins notes that the later form of the punishment meted out to adulterers originated with them, they may have brought about other changes. Yet, after all, the Choctaw seem to have been among the most democratic of all southern tribes, and they were planted in the heart of the south as far back as our records go. Probably the impressions of chieftainship imbibed by the Spaniards were in part due to their European prepossessions and in part based on actual conditions which later events modified.

Tascalusa presents us with a somewhat different problem. In the first place it is evident that he owed much of his authority to physical strength and force of character. His state, however, was not remarkable, certainly not on a par with that which surrounded the Great Sun. Ranjel says that

he was seated on some high cushions and many of the principal men among his Indians were with him. . . . Before this chief there stood always an Indian of graceful mien holding a parasol on a handle something like a round and very large fly fan . . .

ornamented in a manner already described. When they left that place to go to Mobile, two Indians always remained in attendance upon him, one with the sunshade and one with a cushion (Bourne, 1904, vol. 2, pp. 151–152). Elvas also mentions the sunshade, if such it really was, and cushions (Robertson, 1933, p. 124). There is nothing in all this to indicate that the power of the Mobile chief was exceptional, but even if it was, the terrible losses his tribe suffered in the battle with the Spaniards would have served to reduce not only the tribe but the state of its head for all future time. In any case there is no evidence that it was founded on a long-descended body of custom, a caste system, or religious sanctions. The "state" of the chief of Coça, the Chickasaw chief, and the chieftainess of Cofitachequi was expressed mainly by the fact that they were borne about in litters.

While some of the later Creek chiefs attained great authority, they owed little of this to inheritance, theocratic institutions, or caste. There seems to have been a special thread of authority resident in the Coweta chief, possibly descended from the days of old Cofitachequi, but it carried little with it beyond a certain amount of prestige. As the Lower Creek chief William McIntosh favored the claims of the white inhabitants of Georgia, he and his supporters made an effort to show that the authority of Coweta was paramount over that of all the other towns, but when he signed a treaty surrendering the lands of the confederacy, a body of Indians from the Upper Creeks attacked him in his home and killed him. Hobo-hithli Yahola, who exerted the most powerful influence in the Nation, was not a chief and owed his pre-eminence very largely to oratorical gifts. There was a rough division between the chiefs and higher officials and the mass of the people which was exploited in later times in order to secure to the former a greater proportion of the annuities from the United States Government, but this never exceeded the limits of a tenuous and nebulous aristocracy.

Among the Chickasaw each totemic division or iksa had its own chief and the head of one of these, according to Schoolcraft's informant, was automatically chief of the nation. Cushman calls him "king" but says that his power was strictly circumscribed. If what Romans remarks of the head chief in his time is correct, it is evident that inheritance was a minor qualification for leadership. He states that the grand chief, Opaya Mataha

has killed his man upwards of forty times, for which great feats he has been raised to this nominal dignity, which by all savages is as much regarded, as among us a titular nobleman would be if he should be obliged to be a journeyman taylor for his maintenance. (Romans, 1775, p. 64.)

The following note by Adair who knew the people intimately shows that Chickasaw headship was far removed from that of Powhatan, Utina, or the Great Sun:

When any national affair is in debate, you may hear every father of a family speaking in his house on the subject, with rapid, bold language, and the utmost freedom that a people can use. Their voices, to a man, have due weight in every public affair, as it concerns their welfare alike. (Adair, 775, pp. 215–216.)

And when we get to the Choctaw we find a still further devolution of chiefly authority. Each of the three or four main Choctaw divisions seems to have had a head chief from early times but the missionary Beaudoin affirms that the head chieftainship of the nation was a very late institution, brought on by white contact. Though the towns, cantons, and families had their separate heads, there was nothing absolute in the authority of any of them. Inheritance counted even less than among the Creeks, and the greatest of all Choctaw chiefs, Pushmataha, was of such obscure origin that it was a matter of comment.

We know so little about the structure of the old Cherokee state or confederacy that it is impossible for us to tell whether inheritance played any part in the attainment of power, but such incidental evidence as we have is quite to the contrary. The Cherokee chiefs seem for the most part to have been self-made men like those of the Choctaw. Charles Hicks, a prominent chief living in the early part of the last century, says of the government under the head chief:

The national council is composed of chiefs from each clan, some sending more some less, regard being had to the population of each—though the number is not very definitely fixed. Each clan has its separate portion of land, which it holds in common right—the poorest men having the same right as the greatest. (See Raleigh Register, 1818.) [But see Gilbert, 1943.]

Sometimes the activities of Spanish, French, and English colonial officials tended to undermine the central authority in a tribe as when Americans backed McIntosh and Ridge in order to secure the removal of the Creeks and Cherokee from their territories. But, on the other hand, they not infrequently sought to subsidize the regular rulers so as to accomplish similar ends; they augmented the power of several of the larger nations by destroying some of their rivals such as the Timucua, Apalachee, Yamasee, Mobile, and Natchez; and their influence was sufficient at times, as in the case of Alexander McGillivray, to centralize authority to an unprecedented extent.

CLANS AND GENTES

Throughout most of the Gulf area descent was matrilineal, but we can no longer assume, as was often done by earlier writers, that this fact involves the existence of clans or gentes. The only noteworthy exceptions to matrilineal descent were among the Quapaw and Shawnee whose entry into the region was probably very late, and we note a partial exception in the case of the Yuchi, also latecomers. In a recent article Speck has taken up "The Question of Matrilineal Descent in the Southeastern Siouan Area," and comes to a negative conclusion. He argues, however, rather against the existence of a matrilineal totemic clan system than against matrilineal descent apart from clans. So limited, I think he makes an excellent case; the only early evidence for clans throughout this area is a single reference by Lederer, and we do not know that the four supposedly clan names he cites were actually totemic in significance. But matrilineal descent independent of clans is affirmed so frequently by Lawson that we can hardly deny it unless it can be shown that his knowledge of Tuscarora had affected his views regarding all the other tribes. Nevertheless, he states distinctly that this type of descent prevailed among the Keyauwee (Lawson, 1860, p. 89).

Among the Creeks we find the greatest profusion of totemic clans. The Timucua of northern Florida and the eastern Caddo stood next. The Chickasaw had a smaller number and the Cherokee in historic times only seven. Seven or eight clans have been reported from the Tuscarora but it is possible that some of these have arisen since their removal north and contact with the other Iroquois tribes. The names of a few supposedly totemic clans have been obtained from the Chitimacha but the status of these, though strengthened by a statement of Martin Duralde, is rather doubtful. The Choctaw had small divisions similar to clans but without totemic names, and such cantons or house groups were found among the Chickasaw alongside of their totemic subdivisions. As has been said, one eastern Siouan tribe, apparently one of those in Virginia, may have had clans but they appear to have been nontotemic. It may be assumed that the Nottoway and Meherrin had clans like their relatives the Tuscarora but the fact cannot be established. Bare statements by Smith as well as Lawson inform us that the coastal Algonquians and the Piedmont tribes reckoned descent in the female line, but we have no further information on the subject except from the Tutelo after they had been living many years with the Iroquois, whose institutions they may have adopted. J. O. Dorsey was told of four Tutelo clans, Bear, Deer, Wolf, and Turtle (Dorsey, J. O., 1897, p. 244). A document dated 1789 unearthed by Schaeffer lists part of the Tutelo in two clans, the Snipe and Wolf, but it looks as if these totemic names had been superposed upon as many originally distinct tribes (Speck and Herzog, 1942). The surviving Natchez have totemic clans and matrilineal descent, and descent was prevailingly matrilineal among the Natchez in the early eighteenth century, before they were broken up and dispersed, but there is no proof that they then had totemic clans. We may infer that the internal organization of the Taensa and Avoyel was like that of the Natchez. There is no further information regarding the tribes along the lower Mississippi or anywhere adjacent to it.

In 1763 there were four clans among the Kadohadacho called Beaver, Otter, Wolf, and Panther but it is not known whether they were exogamic groups, and in later times five clans were reported among the western Caddo called Bison, Bear, Panther, Wolf, and Beaver, which were not exogamous. They were arranged in a sort of caste system in the order of strength as given and when a marriage occurred between them and the mother belonged to a "stronger" animal, the children all belonged to her clan whereas when the mother belonged to a weaker animal only the girls followed her. The Louisiana Caddo are said to have had a true clan system with exogamous animal-named divisions (Swanton, 1942, pp. 163–166).

Table 4 (pp. 658–660) contains a list of totemic clans and gentes in all parts of the area under discussion and in the Northeast as well. The Choctaw and eastern Siouan clans are omitted because the former were nontotemic and the status of clans among the latter is unknown.

A fairly complete study of the distribution of clan names in the eastern part of North America brings out the following facts. The Bear, Wolf, Deer, and Beaver were widely, and rather uniformly, distributed and were represented respectively in 33, 31, 24, and 19 tribes. The Bear, Deer, and Beaver were prominent among the

Muskhogeans, though the Beaver was of consequence only in one group of Creek towns, those belonging to the Otciapofa and Tulsa Indians. The Wolf clan was prominent among the Cherokee but among the Creeks was regarded as a minor clan affiliated with the Bear. The Eagle, Snake, and Fish were represented among southern tribes, Siouans, and Algonquians but almost wanting among the Iroquois and Huron. Hawk clans scarcely appear among southern tribes. Clans found mainly among southern tribes and Algonquians were the Fox, Turkey, Potato, Raven, Rabbit, Squirrel, Blackbird, and Corn, though only the first three were of much consequence in the former area. The Bird and Wind clans appear among southern tribes and Siouans and so does the Paint clan, though it is very slenderly represented. The Turtle clan is of little consequence in the south and among the Siouans, but of major importance among the Iroquoian and Algonquian people. The Elk, Bison, Crane, Grouse, Sun, Moon, Thunder, Stone, Tree, Swan, and Big Fire were shared principally by the Algonquians and Siouans. The Snipe and Eel were almost confined to the Iroquoians of the north. Found mainly among Siouans were the Pigeon, Earth, Night, Star, and Owl. Found mainly among the Muskhogeans and their neighbors were the Panther, Raccoon, Wildcat, Skunk, Alligator, Otter, Buzzard, and Spanish clans. Found mainly among the Algonquians were the Dog, Muskrat, Sturgeon, Water, Loon, Great Sea, Moose, Lynx, Bass, Carp, Sea Gull, Man, and Marten.

This distribution may be explained in part by the environment. It was natural that the Elk and Bison should be utilized most by tribes to the north and west, the Moose, Reindeer, Lynx, Marten, and Snow by tribes to the north, and the Alligator by tribes to the south, while a Spanish clan would naturally be looked for only in the south near Spanish-occupied territories. The openness of their country and the prominence of physical phenomena as opposed to animal life may very well account for the Night, Star, Sun, Moon, Thunder, Big Fire, Stone, Earth, and even the Tree clan among the Siouan tribes and some of the Algonquian tribes toward the west. The environment of the Great Lakes is also clearly reflected in the number of clan names taken from fish, waterfowl, or names associated with water found among the Algonquian tribes which centered there. Thus we have a Water clan among the Shawnee, Miami, and Kickapoo; Great Sea among the Potawatomi, Sauk, and Fox; and also such clans as Sturgeon, Bass, Carp, Trout, Bullhead, Pickerel, Catfish, Whitefish, Sucker, Water Snake, Swan, Loon, Sea Gull, Duck, Shagpoke, Coot, Goose, Cormorant, Muskrat, Fisher, and Merman in the general area. On the other hand, there seems to be no particular reason why hawks should not have been used by the southern tribes as clan animals; why the fox, turkey, potato, and raven should not have been popular with Iroquoians and Siouans; and why the turtle should not have had as great a vogue in the South and among Siouans as among the Iroquoian and Algonquian peoples, although in this latter case the position of the turtle in mythology may account for it. As much can hardly be said, however, for the failure of the panther, wildcat, raccoon, skunk, wind, and otter to take hold upon the imaginations of the northern and western Indians as they did those of the southern Indians. As in so many other cases involving human institutions, obvious, or at least plausible, explanations will carry us part of the way and yet leave a substantial residuum.

In table 4, showing the distribution of clans in the area under discussion, the Muskogee or Creeks proper and the Hitchiti have not been kept apart because the two peoples were living in intimate contact in the historic period. The only differentiation seems to have been in the greater development of the Snake, Otter, Mole, Toad, and Tcikote clans among the latter. The Alabama data are drawn from the Alabama living in Texas, who seem to have preserved more of the distinctive traits of the tribe. Perhaps the most important Alabama peculiarities consisted in the development of Daddy-long-legs and Salt clans. The names of the clans attributed to the Natchez were learned from modern informants and may have been borrowed entirely from the Creeks and Cherokee. It is again doubtful how many clans attributed to the Yuchi antedate Creek contact. For the Timucua we are entirely dependent upon information from the missionary Pareja, which may be incomplete. When we are able to translate all of the names he gives us, a few more totem animals may be discovered. The Chickasaw clans were probably borrowed in the main from the Creeks. Mooney is our principal authority for the Cherokee and Caddo, Hewitt for the Tuscarora, and J. O. Dorsey for the Quapaw and Tutelo, while the only notes we have on Chitimacha are from Duralde or were obtained by me from Benjamin Paul, the late Chitimacha chief (Swanton, 1928, pp. 114–120; 1911, p. 349).

TABLE 4.—*Distribution of totemic clans among the Indian tribes*

Clan	Freq. of occur.	Western Siouan tribes									Algonquians										Iroquois and Tutelo								Southern tribes								
		Winnebago	Quapaw	Ponca	Oto	Osage	Omaha	Missouri	Kansa	Iowa	Shawnee	Sauk	Potawatomi	Ottawa	Miami	Menomini	Kickapoo	Fox	Delaware	Chippewa	Tutelo	Tuscarora	Seneca	Onondaga	Oneida	Mohawk	Huron	Cayuga	Yuchi	Timucua	Natchez	Creek	Chitimacha	Chickasaw	Cherokee	Caddo	Alabama
Alligator	4																															X		X		X	X
Arrow	1																																			X	
Bass	2													X						X																	
Bear	33	X	X	X	X	X	X	X	X	X	X	X	X	X	X	X	X	X		X	X	X	X	X			X	X	X	X	X	X	X	X	X	X	X
Beaver	19		X			X					X	X	X	X	X	X	X	X	X	X		X	X	X			X	X				X				X	
Berry	1																			X																	
Big Fire	2	X														X																					
Bird	10	X	X	X	X	X	X	X	X	X																						X					
Bison	15		X	X	X	X	X	X	X	X	X	X	X	X		X	X	X																			
Blackbird	2					X	X																														
Bullhead	1																			X																	
Buzzard	3																															X		X	X		
Cane	1					X																															
Carp	3		X													X				X																	
Catfish	1		X																																		
Chief	1																															X					
Cloud	1						X																														
Coot	1															X																					
Cormorant	1																			X																	
Corn	2																						X				X										
Crane	7										X	X	X	X		X				X							X										
Crawfish	1																			X																	
Daddy-long-legs	1																															X					
Deer	24	X	X	X	X	X	X	X	X	X	X	X	X		X	X		X		X		X	X	X				X				X		X		X	X
Dog	6		X			X										X							X									X	X				
Duck	3		X													X																X					
Eagle	20	X	X	X	X	X	X	X	X	X	X	X	X		X	X		X		X		X	X									X			X		
Earth	5						X																X	X			X			X							
Eel	4																			X			X	X				X									
Elk	15	X	X	X		X	X			X	X	X	X			X		X		X												X		X			X
Fish	10	X	X			X	X		X			X				X				X												X					X
Fisher	1																			X																	
Forked Tree	2	X																														X					
Fox	10	X									X	X	X			X	X	X		X			X									X					
Goose	1																			X																	
Great Sea	3																						X	X				X									
Grizzly Bear	2		X			X																															
Grouse	2		X							X																											

For footnotes, see p. 660.

Hair
Hawk
Hickory Nut
Horse
House
Long Dew
Loon
Lye Drip
Lynx
Man
Marten
Medicine
Merman
Mole
Moon
Moose
Muskrat
Night
Opossum
Otter
Owl
Panther
Partridge
Pheasant
Pickerel
Pigeon or Dove
Porcupine
Potato
Rabbit
Raccoon
Raven and Crow
(Red) Paint
Reindeer
Salt
Sea Gull
Shagpoke
Skunk
Snake
Snipe
Snow
Spanish
Spanish Moss
Squirrel
Star
Stone
Sturgeon
Sucker
Sun
Swan
Thunder
Toad

TABLE 4.—Distribution of totemic clans among the Indian tribes—Continued

Clan	Southern tribes									Iroquois and Tutelo								Algonquians										Western Siouan tribes									Frequency of occurrence
	Alabama	Caddo	Cherokee	Chickasaw	Chitimacha	Creek	Natchez	Timucua	Yuchi	Cayuga	Huron	Mohawk	Oneida	Onondaga	Seneca	Tuscarora	Tutelo	Chippewa	Delaware	Fox	Kickapoo	Menomini	Miami	Ottawa	Potawatomi	Sauk	Shawnee	Iowa	Kansa	Missouri	Omaha	Osage	Oto	Ponca	Quapaw	Winnebago	
Tree																					×					×	×					×[12]					3
Trout																										×	×										1
Turkey						×			×	×	×	×	×	×	×	×	×	×	×		×	×	×		×		×				×	×			×		9
Turtle	×					×			×	×	×	×	×	×	×	×	×	×	×		×		×		×	×	×										19
Warrior						×															×		×														1
Water						×												×									×									×	3
Water Moccasin																																					1
Water Monster																																					1
Water Snake						×																															1
Weevil																																					1
Whitefish					(×?)													×																			1
Wildcat			×[13]	×					×																						×				×(?)		8
Wind	×		×[14]	×(?)		×	×		×									×									×	×	×		×	×		×		×	10
Wolf	×	×	×	×(?)	×	×			×	×	×	×	×	×	×	×	×	×	×	×	×	×	×		×	×	×	×	×		×	×	×	×	×(?)	×	31

[1] Hawk sometimes so called.
[2] Or Star.
[3] Sahâni.
[4] Said to be equated with Snipe.
[5] Gatâgewi.
[6] Crow.
[7] Paint.
[8] Red Earth.
[9] Paint.
[10] Plover, Sandpiper, Killdee.
[11] Or Night.
[12] Cotton Tree.
[13] Under Panther.
[14] Long Hair.

Association of clans with linguistic groups

Clans found in all sections_____	Bear, Beaver, Deer, Wolf.
Clans found mainly among Southern Indians, Siouans, and Algonquians___	Eagle, Fish, Snake.
Clans found mainly among Iroquoians, Algonquians, and Siouans_____	Hawk.
Clans found mainly among Algonquians and Siouans_____	Big Fire, Bison, Crane, Elk, Grouse, Moon, Stone, Sun, Swan, Thunder, Tree.
Clans found mainly among Southern Indians and Algonquians_____	Blackbird, Corn, Fox, Potato, Rabbit, Raven, Squirrel, Turkey.
Clans found mainly among Southern Indians and Siouans_____	Bird, Wind.
Clans found mainly among Iroquoians and Algonquians_____	Porcupine, Turtle.
Clans found mainly among Southern Indians_____	Alligator, Arrow, Buzzard, Cane, Chief, Daddy-long-legs, Hair, Hickory Nut, Long Dew, Lye Drip, Medicine, Mole, Opossum, Otter, Panther, Raccoon, Salt, Skunk, Partridge, Spanish, Spanish Moss, Toad, Water Moccasin, Weevil, Wildcat.
Clans found mainly among Iroquoians_	Eel, Snipe.
Clans found mainly among Algonquians_	Bass, Berry, Bullhead, Carp, Catfish, Cloud, Coot, Cormorant, Dog, Duck, Fisher, Forked Tree, Goose, Great Sea, Grizzly Bear, Horse, House, Loon, Lynx, Man, Marten, Merman, Moose, Muskrat, Pheasant, Reindeer, Sea Gull, Shagpoke, Snow, Sturgeon, Sucker, Trout, Warrior, Water, Water Snake, Whitefish.
Clans found mainly among Siouans___	Crawfish, Earth, Night, Owl, Pigeon, Star, Water-monster.

CASTES

A true caste system is reported only from the Chitimacha of southern Louisiana, where the nobility is said to have been endogamous (Swanton, 1911, pp. 348–349). We seem to infer from Pareja that some sort of pyramiding of privileged groups existed in northern Florida (Pareja, 1612, pp. 130–133; Swanton, 1922, p. 370), and the general machinery of the Natchez caste system is fairly well understood. The last was not, indeed, a true cast system at all since, instead of being forbidden, alliances were imperative between members of the highest or governing caste and the common people. The reason for this is said to have been that on the death of anyone of the Sun family or caste it was necessary that the wife or husband be killed in order to accompany the deceased. The Sun caste was perpetuated in the female line, but children and grandchildren of male Suns enjoyed certain prerogatives in descending order, though by the time great-grandchildren were reached the dilution of low caste blood was supposed to have been sufficient to reduce one to the "Stinkard" category. (Dumont, 1753, vol. 1, pp. 175–181; Du Pratz, 1758, vol. 2, pp. 393–397; Swanton, 1911, pp. 100–108.) Elsewhere in the Southeast we get fewer indications of social stratification. Among the Creeks we learn that the Wind clan enjoyed a privileged position and that the Bear clan possessed minor privileges, also that some clans, particularly the smaller ones, were looked down upon (Swanton, 1928, pp. 114 et seq.). The non-Muskogee towns are said to have been looked down upon similarly by those belonging to the dominant tribe, and Dr. Haas seems to have found preferential ratings among the latter (Haas, 1940). According to an informant of Schoolcraft, the totemic clans of the Chickasaw were ranged in a scale as follows, beginning with that of the chief which, of course, stood at the top: Minko (Chief), Shawi (Raccoon), Ko ishto (Panther), Spani (Spanish), Nani (Fish), Hâskona (Skunk). This is confirmed in the main by Gibbs who, however, gives more clans and arranges them somewhat differently. He begins with the Spanish and follows with the Raccoon, Panther, Wildcat, Fish, Deer, Haloba, Bird, and Skunk. Speck was told of a gradation among the house groups of which the clans consisted but there is some confusion in his material between clans and house groups, and his informant may actually have had the clans in mind (Schoolcraft, 1851–1857, vol. 1, p. 311; Swanton, 1928 c, p. 191). We should expect equality among the Choctaw if anywhere. One of our earliest authorities says that one of the two moieties into which the house groups were divided was called "captives," or "slaves," and was less regarded than the other, but it is questionable whether this may not have had rather a ceremonial than a social significance (Swanton, 1931 a, pp. 76–79; Swanton, 1932). Nothing of a caste nature has been reported from the Cherokee and nothing from the eastern Caddo. By an old man belonging to the western Caddo, I was told that their clans were ranged into a kind of caste pattern, in accordance with the relative "strength" of the totemic animals. This has been described above. Needless to say marriages took place within the clan more often than outside or some clans would have disappeared (Swanton, 1931, p. 204).

Chiefs and their families certainly occupied a privileged position among the coastal Algonquians and the Piedmont Siouans, but we do not know how definitely the distinctions were established. Barlowe says that those Indians who had pieces of copper in their hair were the only ones among the Algonquians he met in the Sound country of

North Carolina allowed to trade with the whites at the same time as the chiefs (Burrage, 1906, p. 231).

Michelson was told that there was gradation of the Shawnee bands.[33] However, this probably had very little practical effect in the tribe as a whole.

MOIETIES

Many tribes of North America, and indeed in all parts of the world, are, or were, divided socially into two major sections which generally determined marriage relationships and usually added certain other functions, such as partnership in ball games, the ordering of mortuary ceremonies, and so on.

In the Southeast, a dichotomous division of this sort existed among the Choctaw. One moiety was called Imoklasha, "their own people," or "friends," Kashapa okla, "divided people," or, according to one early writer, Yuka-tathlapi, "the five slave [groups];" and the other, Iⁿholahta, which probably signifies "chiefs." We know that these moieties were strictly exogamous, and indeed exogamy went somewhat farther since Halbert heard of two minor groups on opposite sides which could not intermarry. Funeral obsequies for a person of one moiety were conducted by those of the other side, and we seem to have clear intimations that one moiety, the one first mentioned, presided over ceremonial matters concerned with peace, the other being the war division. The writer who calls the former Yuka-tathlapi says that it was in fact considered less noble than the other, but we have no supporting evidence. (Swanton, 1931 a, pp. 76–79; Swanton, 1932).

We know that the Chickasaw also had moieties but our information regarding them is so confusing that we are not sure whether they ere exogamous or endogamous. Possibly they may have had two kinds of dual divisons, one of clans or minor local groups and one of towns, the former analogous to the Choctaw, the latter to the Creeks. The association of one of these (the Tcuka falaha) was said to have been with war and they were said to have lived in a flat or prairie country, while the other (the Tcukilissa) was the peace side, and they lived in the timber. This recalls the Choctaw divisions. Clans and house groups were separated in general by moiety lines, but the Raccoon clan is reported to have married indifferently into either, and there was a house name (possibly a house group) used on both sides. Speck learned that malevolent conjuration resulting in sickness was "believed, with a certain degree of hostility, to come from the opposite group," and "it is considered a grave offense, frequently punishable by death, for a member of one group to be present at

---

[33] Michelson, personal information.

the *Picófa* of the other group, as his presence would nullify the good effect of the ceremony." It is also reported that one of these moieties, the Tcuka falaha, was superior to the other (Speck, 1907 a, p. 54; Swanton, 1928 c, p. 195).

The Creek Nation had a dual division of clans into the Hathagálgi, "Whites," and the Tcilokogálgi, "People of a different speech." The colors white and red were associated with these respectively and they were associated in the same way with peace and war, but in this warlike body, strange to say, the peace clans seem to have stood higher, judging by the fact that the Wind and Bear clans, both White, possessed prerogatives above all others. The towns and subtribes were also divided into two, headed by Kasihta and Coweta respectively, and these also had to do with war and peace. The great games always occurred between towns on opposite sides, and the players who took part in practice games within the several towns divided along lines determined by the two moieties. In matrimonial affairs, however, the influence of the dual divisions of towns and clans was quite distinct, for the town moieties had a strong tendency toward endogamy, marriage between opposing towns being discouraged, while it is commonly reported that the clan moieties were exogamous. However, exceptions to clan exogamy were quite numerous and it will always be doubtful whether it was ever the absolute institution some informants contend. Members of the two clan moieties at Tukabahchee used different feathers in the feather dance, feathers of the white crane and those of the eagle (Swanton, 1928, pp. 156–165).

In northern Florida the clans were grouped into several phratries, but it is not apparent that these were ranged into moieties, nor is there a trace of either moieties or phratries among the Cherokee. It is, indeed, rumored that the 7 clans of the last-mentioned tribe were originally 14 and that they had been reduced to the historic number by combination in twos. But no assertion has ever been made that the original 14 were divided into moieties, and effacement of moieties instead of clans in this manner is entirely without precedent (Mooney, 1900, pp. 212–213).

In more recent times, the Yuchi adopted the dual division of clans of the Creeks, but they had an older dual division, into what Speck calls the "Chiefs' Society" and the "Warriors' Society (Speck, 1909, pp. 70–78). These suggest in some measure the Choctaw and Chickasaw moiety systems, but differed from them in being perpetuated in the male line.

Duality among the Natchez and Chitimacha took the form of castes and it has been described. This should not be regarded as a true moiety system. In 1882 John Key, a Tutelo living on Grand River reservation with the Iroquois, told Dr. J. O. Dorsey that his people formerly had four clans, the Bear, Deer, Wolf, and Turtle, and that the first two were on one side of the fire, the last two on the other, but this dichotomy may have been brought about by association with the Iroquois (Dorsey, J. O., 1897, p. 244).

The Quapaw also seem to have had a moiety system similar to that of most of the other tribes of the Dhegiha group of the Siouan stock. Dr. Dorsey was able to learn of the following groupings:

Hañka Moiety: Large Hañka or Crawfish People (called by another informant Ancestral People), two gentes called Small Bird, Bison or Small Hañka, Elk, Eagle, Reddish-yellow Bison, Dog (or Wolf?); of an unnamed moiety: Fish People, Ni'kia'la, Turtle People; not of Hañka but not certainly classed with the last three: Lion People, Tiju (the Tciju of other tribes).

Another informant added these gentile names, which may as well be inserted here: Deer, Black-bear, Grizzly-bear (?), Beaver, Star, Crane, Thunder-being, Serpent, Sun. He also mentioned the Panther or Mountain Lion, evidently identical with the Lion of the first list (Dorsey, J. O., 1897, pp. 229-230).

TERMS OF RELATIONSHIP

Our knowledge of the terms of relationship of the Cherokee, Creeks, Chickasaw, Choctaw, and Timucua is fairly adequate, as also of the marginal Shawnee. Data from the Caddo and Yuchi leave something to be desired, but we have only fragmentary information regarding the systems of the Natchez, Tunica, Chitimacha, Tutelo, and Quapaw. The tribes, or rather tribal remnants speaking these tongues have been subjected to outside influences for such a long period that it is not likely that they retain the old system in a very pure form. Except for a few Catawba terms, we have practically nothing from the Siouan tribes of the east and the Algonquian tribes of Virginia and Carolina, nor do the remaining tribes yield any information of consequence.

In spite of slight minor variations, the systems of the Cherokee, Creeks, Chickasaw, Choctaw, Koasati, and Timucua are very much alike and are classed by Spier with what he calls the Crow type. Recent researches by Gilbert, Eggan, and Spoehr seem to show that the divergencies from the Crow system which my own data and those of Morgan present are relatively recent in origin and attributable to white contact. To this type the Yuchi are added somewhat doubtfully.

Nearly all of the tribes which exhibit this type possess clans having matrilineal descent, the only exceptions in fact being the Southern Pomo and the Wappo of California, and the Pawnee. It is in many ways the converse of the Omaha Type, which takes in mainly tribes having subdivisions with patrilineal descent, the principal exceptions being again in California. To this last type belonged the Shawnee, and in all probability the Quapaw which were marginal to the Gulf region. The only Southeastern tribe belonging in any other class is the Caddo, which Spier has himself studied and which he places in the Mackenzie Basin Type.

In the Crow system, Spier says

the father's sister is an "aunt" and her female descendants through females are "aunts." The sons of these "aunts" are "fathers," whose children are "brothers" (or "fathers") and "sisters." The mother's brother is an "uncle," whose children are "son" and "daughter" (less commonly for a female speaker) and their children "grandchildren." The children of a man's brother and a woman's sister are "son" and "daughter": the children of their other siblings are usually called by nepotic terms. (Spier, 1925, pp. 73–74.)

In Creek, Koasati, Chickasaw, Yuchi, Timucua, Sixtown Choctaw, and by all female Choctaw the same term is used for grandmother and father's sister. It is somewhat uncertain which is the original term and which the derivative one, since in Koasati the term for father's sister seems to be secondary while in Timucua it is the other way about. In Creek, Koasati, Chickasaw, and Choctaw a woman called her brother's child "grandchild." This evidently is directly connected with the fact that the grandchild called her "grandmother." Inasmuch as a man did not use the term "grandchild" for his nephew or niece, we can understand why among most of the Choctaw he employed another term than "grandmother" for his father's sister, though she did in fact call him "grandson." In a two-moiety society like that of the Choctaw, the Chickasaw, and perhaps that of the Creeks in ancient times, the children of the father, and his brothers and, in fact, all males belonging to his moiety would also be the children of the mother, mother's sister, and women of the same moiety as self, therefore it is not surprising that they should be called brothers and sisters. On the other hand, we do not find that the terminology used toward members of the opposite moiety conforms to the expectable. In such a system, of course, all of the women one calls paternal aunts, and all of the men one calls maternal uncles, will have children who belong to the opposite moiety. There seems to be no reason why these men and women should not have married, but there are separate terms provided for children of mother's brothers and children of the father's sisters. In Creek, children of the latter receive the same title as do father's brother and father's sister and this to the most remote generations. This is said to have been true of the Choctaw by one informant, at least as it applies to the female line, but according to others the father's sister's daughter was sometimes called "mother" and the father's sister's granddaughter "sister." In Chickasaw the father's sister's daughter and her daughter were known as "aunt" or "grandmother" and male descendants on both sides were known as "father," but the father's sister's son's daughter was called "sister." One can easily see why there should be more stability in the female line than in the male line because in the former case the moiety remained unchanged while in the other cases it would alter with every generation. Choctaw shows less stability than Creek or Chickasaw in this respect, and Muskogee the most. In Cherokee the descendants of father's sister are usually "father's sister" and "father," but there are some exceptions for the father's sister's son's daughter is called "sister." The children of the mother's brother, on the other hand, in Choctaw, Chickasaw, Creek, Timucua, and Cherokee all receive the same terms as those applied to one's own children, and the next generation are grandchildren. And, of course, one's own children—I am now speaking of a man as "self"—belong to the opposite moiety. Following down the various lines of descent of self and relatives, we find that all start with two terms of relationship applied to grandparents, "grandfather" and "grandmother," that two streams pass down through father and father's brothers and mother and mother's sisters, respectively meeting in self, my brothers and sisters, my father's brothers' children, and my mother's sisters' children, to my own children, the children of my brothers, the children of the brothers of my father, and the sisters of my mother, where they are met by a stream of blood passing from my maternal grandparents through my mother's brothers. These all have the same name, son and daughter, and their children I call grandchildren. The stream passing through my father's sister divides repeatedly. Her direct female descendants are all called "paternal aunt," or among most of the tribes "grandmother," and their brothers "fathers," and this goes on indefinitely. This appears to be the only line of descent which does not end with the term "grandchild." My father's sister's son's children, however, appear usually to have been called "brother," or "sister" and, although it is not quite certain, their children probably fell into the class of grandchildren. My sister's children I call by distinct terms, "nephew," and "niece," but their children also fall into the class of grandchildren. This is the system in Choctaw and Chickasaw in the main though there are some few variations, whether due to errors in recording or to actual changes in nomenclature is uncertain. In Creek all descendants of the father's sister are said to have been called by the same terms as father's brother and father's sister but it would now be difficult to be certain as to the ancient custom. So far as it has been preserved, the Timucua system is substantially the same as those above described. Cherokee agrees in the main with Creek and Chickasaw. From the fact that the father's sister's son's daughter has the same term as own sister and father's sister's son's son the same term as the father, the discrepancies I noted in Choctaw and Chickasaw may not be mistakes. The terms which a woman uses are very much like those used by a man except that she distinguishes her elder sister and younger sister instead of her elder brother from her younger brother, there being but one term for her brothers ordinarily, as a man has one term for his sisters, and except, of course, that she calls her sister's children by the same terms as her own and speaks of her brother's children as grandchildren. In Cherokee, however, a woman uses for her brother's children the same words that her brother applies to her own, ones which are about equivalent to our "nephew" and "niece."

The terms for father-in-law and mother-in-law vary in the several languages. In Creek each has a separate term and they are used both by the son-in-law and the daughter-in-law. In Cherokee one word is used for both father-in-law and mother-in-law by individuals of both sexes, but there is an independent term employed only by women. In Choctaw and Chickasaw, as has been already pointed out, a woman calls her father-in-law and mother-in-law "grandfather" and "grandmother" respectively. There is one independent term employed by a man but it appears to be related to the words for grandmother and grandchild. In Koasati only one stem is used for both relations by persons of both sexes. In Timucua the father-in-law sometimes had the same term as the grandfather, but both parents-in-law also were known by a term based upon that for son-in-law and daughter-in-law. In Cherokee, Chickasaw, Choctaw, Koasati, and Timucua there is one term each for son-in-law and daughter-in-law and these are extended to the husbands and wives of brothers' and sisters' children. Muskogee is peculiar in having one term covering both these relations. "Mihaiwa" is given by Loughridge and Hodge as a term meaning daughter-in-law, but I have no further information regarding it. I also have the word, "tcukowāki" applied to the sister's daughter's husband, the same term as that used for sister's husband and sometimes for the brother's wife (m. sp.) The exact significance of this term is in doubt. In Chickasaw and Choctaw three principal terms are used to cover relations by marriage. Brother's wife has a term to itself no matter whether a man is speaking or a woman. The term for sister's husband, on the other hand, is extended by the use of the diminutive suffix, to the wife's brother and sister, and in Chickasaw to the husband's brother and sister. Choctaw is exceptional in that two distinct terms are used for these relatives by a woman. The third general term is applied to a connection by marriage such as the wife's brother's wife and wife's sister's husband. In Muskogee there is some uncertainty. A single term is employed for the wife's sister, the wife's brother's wife, and perhaps the brother's wife, and by a woman for the spouse of her husband's brother or sister, the husband's brother or sister, the sister's husband, and probably the brother's wife, though Morgan gives a distinct term for this last. It is also used for the mother's brother's wife. A second term is used for the wife's sister's husband and the wife's brother, and a third for the sister's husband (m. sp.), and perhaps the brother's wife, also the sister's daughter's husband, as noted above. According to Morgan, a woman calls her brother's wife by a term similar to the term for wife. In general, however, in each of these languages the terms for husband and wife are distinct and not given to anyone else. In Cherokee all of these relations of brother-in-law and sister-in-law are covered by one term except those for wife's sister's husband and wife's brother's wife, each of which has one to itself.

In Timucua a man uses one term, sometimes modified, for his sister's husband, brother's wife, and wife's sister, and a woman employs the same for her sister's husband. A man has a distinct term for his wife's sister's husband, and a woman a distinct term for her husband's brother and another term for her brother's wife and husband's sister.

Yuchi, as already stated, agrees with Creek, Chickasaw, and Timucua in having one term for grandmother and father's sister. It differs from all these considered in having one term for the father's brother and the mother's brother, and in having a word applied to the mother's sister's son distinct from that given to one's brother, though the terms for mother's sister's daughter and own sister are the same.

As it has come down to us, Chitimacha has terms for mother's sister and father's brother distinct from those for mother and father, and a single term for brother's and sister's child distinct from those for own child. The other terms are in considerable doubt. As recorded, Tunica has one stem for grandfather, grandmother, and grandchild differentiated by means of the sex and diminutive suffix.

Dr. Spier thinks that Biloxi should possibly be classed with the Yuman Type because the terms of relationship collected by Dorsey suggested a considerable development of age distinctions, but I am of the opinion that most of these distinctions are recent, due to the break down of the language and the native customs, and that it probably belongs in the Crow group.[34]

The record of Quapaw terms is poor but it probably belonged to the same system as Shawnee, that is, the Omaha Type. This agrees with the systems we have been considering in having one term for grandfather, one term for grandmother, and one term for grandchild. The father's brother is also called by the same term as the father

---

[34] Consult Spier (1924, 1925) for preceding data.

and the mother's sister by the same term as the mother. The mother's sister's husband is called by the same term as the father, and the father's brother's wife by the same term as the mother, as in Chickasaw, for instance. There is a distinct term for mother's brother as in all the systems we have been discussing, and a distinct term for father's sister as in Cherokee and northern Choctaw. The mother's brother's wife, however, is called by the same term as the father's sister, and the father's sister's husband by the same term as uncle. The father's sister's sons and daughters are classed with the sister's sons and daughters because, descent being male, their mothers belong to the same clan. In both cases those in the next generation are grandchildren. Conversely to the case in the Crow system, the male descendants of mother's brothers are all called mother's brothers. The daughters are classed with the mother, their children with sons and daughters, the children of these with uncles and nieces depending on the sex, and the children of all with uncles and grandchildren. This appears somewhat confusing, and it is to be suspected that descendants of uncles falling outside of the clan were reckoned in the categories. There are distinct terms for father-in-law and mother-in-law, and as in most of the systems already considered except Creek, son-in-law and daughter-in-law relations are covered by a single male and a single female term. A man employs one term for his sister's husband and his wife's brother, and a woman uses the same for her brother's wife. The man has another for his brother's wife and his wife's sister, and the woman uses the same for her husband's brother and her sister's husband.

Of all the Southeastern systems of which we have information in any way satisfactory, Caddo is the most divergent. Like those we have been considering, it has one term for grandfather, one for grandmother, and one for grandchild, except that each sex uses a different expression for the last-mentioned relation. The father's brothers and the mother's sisters are also classed with the father and mother respectively though older and younger individuals of these groups are discriminated. As in the systems considered, there is also one term each for the son-in-law and daughter-in-law. Differences appear, however, in the fact that a reciprocal term is employed between father-in-law and son-in-law, and that the same term is used for mother's brother's wife as for son's wife. The most striking difference is in the extension of the terms for elder brother, younger brother, and sister over the children of both the father's brothers and sisters and the mother's brothers and sisters (Swanton, 1942, pp. 166–170).

NAMES

Spelman furnishes us with the following note regarding the naming customs of the Powhatan Indians:

After the mother is deliuered of hir child with in sum feaw dayes after the kinsfolke and neyburs beinge intreated ther unto, cums unto yᵉ house: wher beinge assembled the father, takes the child in his armes: and declares that his name shall be, as he then calls him, so his name is, which dunn yᵉ rest of yᵉ day is spent in feastinge and dauncinge. (Smith, John, Arber ed., 1884, p. cix.)

Strachey has more to say on this subject:

Both men, women, and childrene have their severall names; at first according to the severall humour of their parents; and for the men children, at first, when they are young, their mothers give them a name, calling them by some affectionate title, or, perhapps observing their promising inclination give yt accordingly; and so the great King Powhatan called a young daughter of his, whome he loved well, Pochahuntas, which may signifie little wanton; howbeyt she was rightly called Amonate at more ripe yeares. When they become able to travel into the woods, and to goe forth a hunting, fowling, and fishing with their fathers, the fathers give him another name as he finds him apt and of spiritt to prove toward and valiant, or otherwise changing the mother's which yet in the family is not so soone forgotten; and if soe be yt be by agility, strength, or any extraordinary straine of witt he performes any remarkeable or valerous exploite in open act of armes, or by stratagem, especyally in the time of extreamity in the warrs for the publique and common state, upon the enemie, the king, taking notice of the same, doth then not only in open view and solemnely reward him with some present of copper, or chaine of perle, and bedes, but doth then likewise (and which they take for the most emynent and supreme favour) give him a name answearable to the attempt, not much different herein from the auncyent warlike encouragement and order of the Romans to a well deserving and gallant young spirit. (Strachey, 1849, p. 111.)

Lawson speaks as follows of the Piedmont tribes of Carolina:

All the Indians give a name to their children, which is not the same as the father or mother, but what they fancy. This name they keep, (if boys) till they arrive at the age of a warrior, which is sixteen or seventeen years; then they take a name to themselves, sometimes, eagle, panther, allegator, or some such wild creature, esteeming nothing on earth worthy to give them a name, but these wild fowl, and beasts. Some again take the name of a fish, which they keep as long as they live. (Lawson, 1860, p. 317.)

The general implications of this paragraph, that women generally kept one name through life while men had at least two, a boyhood name and at least one adult name or title bestowed in consequence of some warlike exploit, seems to have been true of the entire section. Further on Lawson says:

They have no different titles for man, only king, war captain, old man, or young man, which respect the stations and circumstances men are employed in, and arrive to, and not ceremony. (Lawson, 1860, p. 327.)

However, the number of war names, and indeed nicknames, might be considerable. This appears from Timberlake's account of Cherokee naming, but it was general:

There common names are given them by their parents; but this they can either change, or take another when they think proper; so that some of them have near half a dozen, which the English generally increase, by giving an English one, from some circumstance in their lives or disposition, as the Little Carpenter to Attakulla, from his excelling in building houses; Judd's friend, or corruptly the Judge, to Ostenaco, for saving a man of that name from the fury of his countrymen; or sometimes a translation of his Cherokee name, as pigeon to Woey that being the signification of the word. (Timberlake, Williams ed., 1927, p. 95.)

Olbrechts says, however, that in modern times a child is named by one of the prominent old women of the settlement, but thinks that in former days it may have been by the chief woman of the clan. It is sometimes bestowed before birth so as to establish a kind of material hold upon it if parturition is difficult, but formerly it was given either 4 or 7 days after birth in a special ceremony. Later, names were bestowed descriptive of physical or moral qualities or commemorative of some feat in war. The ending "killer" was common in these last as was the case with war names among the Chickasaw and Choctaw (Mooney and Olbrechts, 1932, pp. 127–128).

Creek children received their first names from those previously used in the family, or else names were made up on the spot and were frequently connected with some warlike exploit, often one that occurred when the child was born. Again, the name of the clan totem might be bestowed upon a male child, or he was familiarly known as tcibā'ni, "Little Boy." The greater number of war names among the Creeks were formed of two words, of which the second was hadjo, "mad," "desperately brave"; fiksiko, "no heart"; yaholo, "cryer," referring to the cry uttered by bearers of the black drink when they were serving it. The first word might be that of a town or clan in its regular or its diminutive form, i. e., with the diminutive suffix. Common names of ancestors or names of events were also used. A few names, such as Katcili, "Panther Foot," Kotcugani, "Short," and Tàskona, had no second element. The words īmathla, tàstanàgi, hĕniha, and miko, which take the place of the second word in the combinations given above, very frequently, are really titles carrying a certain status with them. In later life many parents adopted the names of their children, sometimes in succession as the older children died (Swanton, 1928, pp. 97–106).

The stratification of Timucua society indicates that there must have been graduation in names, and as elements entering into Creek war names were borrowed from the Timucua, the customs of the latter in conferring war titles may be assumed to have been similar, but definite data are lacking.

Adair furnishes us with a considerable description of the Chickasaw naming system. He says that they named their children on account of "their tempers, outward appearances, and other various circumstances," but before such a name was bestowed we learn that there was one general name given to a boy and another general name given to a girl. Besides the names directly significant, however, there was a stock of names belonging to each clan from which the child's name might be selected, and the selection was probably made by the men of the father's clan as was customary among the Creeks. Parents also carried the names of their children, being known as "the father (or mother) of so-and-so." If this child died, they allowed a certain time to elapse and then called themselves after the name of the next. The dead were not called by name but only faintly alluded to. Chickasaw men were also given one or more war names after they came of age and had performed exploits considered worthy of note, and most of these were combinations of two elements, the second signifying "to kill," as "He counted and killed." "He shook hands and killed," "He came and killed," and so on. Women's names appear to have had the same origin as men's names among the Creeks, but their signification has in most cases been lost (Swanton, 1928 c, pp. 187–190; Adair, 1775, pp. 191–193).

Cushman thought that the Choctaw names had a totemic significance, but he is followed by no one else and the Choctaw had no totems; therefore Claiborne is probably correct when he says that a child was named after some incident which happened at the moment of birth. Adult males received names from circumstances connected with war. As in the case of the Chickasaw, most of these ended in -àbi, "to kill," but some consisted of two words of which the second resembled similar words used by the Creeks. Among these we find hacho, mi^{n}ko, holahta (a certain kind of chief), hopai, "leader," or "prophet," imataha, probably related to Creek īmathla, iskitini, "little," and humma, "red." This last is said to have been used of a special class of warriors, the na humma, desperate fighters who were never supposed to turn their backs in combat. They may have constituted one of the four grades of warriors of which an anonymous French writer speaks (Cushman, 1899, p. 98; Swanton, 1931 a, pp. 119–124). Among Creeks, Chickasaw, and Choctaw alike an individual was averse to telling his own name or mentioning those of the dead, and the terms of relationship show that this must have been true of the Timucua.

We have little information regarding Natchez common names. War titles were given out by the old war chiefs, and these are said to have indicated all of his exploits, the name telling how many enemies he had slain. To deserve the name of a great man-killer, it was necessary to take 10 slaves or 20 scalps. We are also told that there were 3 classes of warriors, "true warriors," "common warriors," and "apprentice warriors" (Du Pratz, 1758, vol. 2, pp. 415–425; Swanton, 1911, p. 129).

A few Chitimacha personal names have been preserved, but none of these appear to be war names. Some are derived from animals but there is no suggestion of totemism, since certain of the animals were of kinds not likely to become totem animals. Like the Creeks, Choctaw, Chickasaw, and the neighboring Atakapa, a man dropped his own name as soon as a child was born and became known by the name of the child (Swanton, 1911, p. 353).

Caddo naming customs are described by Espinosa and Morfi. (Espinosa, 1921, p. 164; Morfi, 1932, pp. 36–37; Swanton, 1942, p. 160.)

GAMES

The principal game played in the area under consideration was a variety of that which has been borrowed by whites in a modified form and goes by the name of lacrosse. Lacrosse, however, was adopted from the Algonquian Indians about the Great Lakes, who used but a single stick, whereas the southern Indians used two sticks. These were similar in general pattern to our lacrosse sticks, each being bent over at one end to form a loop which, with the addition of crossed cords, formed a cage in which the ball could be caught and held (see pl. 76, fig. 2). The game was between two parties, usually representing distinct moieties, towns, or occasionally tribes, and each had a goal to which it was the object of the side to bring home the ball.

Apparently it was not a prominent element in the culture of the Algonquian tribes of the seaboard, but Strachey (1849, p. 77) has the following brief reference to it:

A kynd of exercise they have often amongst them much like that which boyes call bandy [the name of a bat with which the ball was struck] in English.

Except for the Caddo, the game appears to have been played by all the southern Indians, and it was very likely known to the Caddo, although we have no description of it. We cannot, indeed, speak with assurance regarding the Florida Indians nor many smaller groups from which there is little information of any kind. Even in the case of the eastern Siouan tribes, our references are confined to Peter Martyr's statement, based on conversation with the Indian, Francisco of Chicora, that the latter's people played "tennis," and Lawson's mention of a game "with a batoon and ball" like "our trap ball." (Anghierra, 1912, vol. 2, pp. 263–265; Swanton, 1922, p. 45; Lawson, 1860, p. 289.) The latter may be intended as a description of the single-pole ball game, but, if the Spaniard understood his Indian correctly, the southern type of lacrosse must have been known.

Football was more in evidence in the Powhatan country. According to Strachey,

they have the exercise of football, in which they only forceable encounter with the foot to carry the ball the one from the other, and spurned yt to the goale with a kind of dexterity and swift footmanship, which is the honor of yt; but they never strike up one another's heeles, as we doe, not accompting that praiseworthie to purchase a goale by such an advantage.   (Strachey, 1849, p. 78.)

From Spelman it seems that there was a men's and a women's football game:

They vse beside football play which wemen and young boyes doe much play at. The men neuer. They make ther Gooles as ours only they neuer fight nor pull one another doune.

The men play with a litel balle lettinge it fall out of ther hand and striketh it with the tope of his foot, and he that can strike the ball furthest winns that they play for.   (Smith, John, Arber ed., 1884, p. cxiv.)

The common type of ball game was well known to Cherokee, Creeks, Chickasaw, and Choctaw, and, of course, to the Seminole. It had an important place in the social and ceremonial life of each of these tribes. The Cherokee sticks were somewhat less than 2 feet in length and the netting was of twisted squirrel skin or Indian hemp. The ball was made of deerhide and covered with the skin of the same animal. As known to Mooney's informants, each of the goals was made by driving a pair of sticks into the ground, but an early writer, Rev. George White, describes the goals as 100 yards long and marked out by 2 parallel lines of poles, the lines being also separated by a distance of 100 feet. A goal was counted when the ball was driven between the 2 posts in the former case or carried across either line in the latter. Mooney says that the common number of players on a side was 9 to 12 and that 22 was the most anyone had ever heard of, but White affirms there were 50 on a side. Mooney says that they played for 12 points.

There was a vast amount of ceremonial preceding and accompanying a Cherokee game. For at least 7 days preceding and usually for 28 (4×7) no player must touch a woman, and a man whose wife was pregnant was not allowed to play. Several doctors were employed by each side. Before the game the players were taken to running water, where certain rites were performed over them including scratching. The ball dance was held the night before, but the place kept a profound secret lest the magic of the opposite side be exerted against the participants. There was a harangue after which seven women, representing the seven Cherokee clans, danced. According to Cherokee myth, a game between the birds and animals was won by the latter through the help of the bat and the flying squirrel. For that reason pieces of a bat were tied to the poles on which the rackets were hung before the game and to the rattle. Symbolic objects were also worn on the head and the breechclout, and paintings were employed which had symbolic meanings. Skins of the players were made slippery with the slippery elm or sassafras. The doctors employed various devices to bewitch the opposing team and increase the strength of their own. The players were raised symbolically to each of the seven heavens in succession, and the doctors carried on their incantations throughout the game. Before the game began extensive wagers were made on both sides. Then an old man advanced at one end of the field and, after a short harangue, threw up the ball so that it would fall in the middle. The game was exceedingly rough and deliberate efforts were made to put good players out of the game. After each goal, the chief of the side which had made it threw up the ball to put it in play again, the other chief facing him. White states that it not only counted one to carry the ball across the goal line but as well when the chief opposing the one who threw it up made a catch. Before leaving, the defeated party challenged the other to play again (Mooney, 1890, pp. 105–132).

William Bartram has the following description of a ball-play dance he witnessed in the Cherokee town of Cowe:

The people being assembled and seated in order, and the musicians having taken their station, the ball opens, first with a long harangue or oration, spoken by an aged chief, in commendation of the manly exercise of the ball-play, recounting the many and brilliant victories which the town of Cowe had gained over the other towns in the nation, not forgetting or neglecting to recite his own exploits, together with those of other aged men now present, coadjutors in the performance of these athletic games in their youthful days.

This oration was delivered with great spirit and eloquence, and was meant to influence the passions of the young men present, excite them to emulation, and inspire them with ambition.

This prologue being at an end, the musicians began, both vocal and instrumental; when presently a company of girls, hand in hand, dressed in clean white robes and ornamented with beads, bracelets and a profusion of gay ribbands, entering the door, immediately began to sing their responses in a gentle, low, and sweet voice, and formed themselves in a semicircular file or line, in two ranks, back to back, facing the spectators and musicians, moving slowly round and round. This continued about a quarter of an hour, when we were surprised by a sudden very loud and shrill whoop, uttered at once by a company of young fellows, who came in briskly after one another, with rackets or hurls in one hand. These champions likewise were well dressed, painted, and ornamented with moccasins and high waving plumes in their diadems: they immediately formed themselves in a semicircular rank also, in front of the girls, when these changed their order, and formed a single rank parallel to the men, raising their voices in responses to the tunes of the young champions, the semicircles continually moving round. There was something singular and diverting in their step and motions, and I imagine not to be learned to exactness but with great attention and perseverance. The step, if it can be so termed, was performed after the following manner; first, the motion began at one end of the semicircle, gently rising up and down upon their toes and heels alternately, when the first was up on tip-toe, the next began to raise the heel, and by the time the first rested again on the heel, the second was on tip-toe, thus from one end of the rank to the other, so that some were always up and some down, alternately and regularly, without the least baulk or confusion; and they at the same time, and in the same motion, moved on obliquely or sideways, so that the circle performed a double or complex motion in its progression, and at stated times exhibited a grand or universal movement, instantly and unexpectedly to the spectators, by each rank turning to right and left, taking each others places: the movements were managed with inconceivable alertness and address, and accompanied with an instantaneous and universal elevation of the voice, and shrill whoop. (Bartram, 1940, pp. 298–299.)

The great or "regular" Creek game was played between 2 or more towns of opposite town moieties. Practice games within a town were usually between the 2 clan moieties, though the Yuchi are said to have divided up by placing men with children on one side and men without children on the other. As many as 62 are mentioned on a side in the great games. Right to use men married into the town or sons married out of it was a great subject of discussion and was determined at the preliminary conferences. After these matters had been settled, and when the day for the game approached, the players of each town and their friends started at such a time as to arrive on the ground the night before the game, advancing as if they were going to war. They danced 4 times the night before and took medicine, the women dancing first to be followed by the men brandishing their ball sticks. Each side employed a medicine man who brewed and administered the medicines and scratched all the players, making 4 parallel scratches on their calves about deep enough to draw the blood. He also put medicine on their ball sticks. Next day a great quantity of property was wagered. The ball sticks were usually made of hickory tapered and turned in opposite directions, depending on whether the owner were right-handed or left-handed, and the cage was of deer- or raccoon-skin thongs. Each hoop was also bent sidewise a little so that the ball could be held in the cage between them. The ball was of deer hair covered with deerhide, and sewed with deer sinews, and each side had the privilege of making a "medicine ball" which they could use to make their fourth goal. This had some magical object, like a measuring worm, in the center which the doctor sitting behind the goal post of his side was believed able to draw to himself. The players wore only their flaps, but with the tail of a fleet or masterful animal behind. They were usually brilliantly painted, however, with designs of a kind likely to bring good luck, though little is remembered regarding this. In games between the clan moieties, crane feathers were worn by the Whites and eagle feathers by the Tcilokis. The goals formerly are said to have been as much as a quarter of a mile apart and consisted of 2 saplings with a space of about 10 feet between them and without a crossbar, but in later years, when there were usually fewer players, they were not more than 150 to 200 yards from each other, the uprights 3 to 3½ feet apart and with crossbars placed pretty well up. Bartram speaks of but one "pillar" used for a goal at each end and this was at all events the customary goal among the Choctaw down to modern times. As a hit on the crossbar or the posts, no matter from which side thrown, counted as a goal, the goal might be thought of as actually a solid object, the space between the uprights and crossbar not having been filled in. Midway of the field on one side sat 2 scorers, 1 for each party. They usually played for 20 points, sticking in 10 sticks in a row in succession and then pulling them out. The Texas Alabama, however, made marks on opposite sides of a long straight line, the points for one side being on one side of the line and those for the opponents on the other. The balls were thrown up in the middle of the field, the first by the best speaker they could find, who made a few appropriate remarks before putting the ball in play. After a goal was made, the ball was again put in play by one of 2 old men, 1 from each side, who also acted as referees. There was a man at each goal to see that the goals were made fairly and 2 or more men on each side to umpire and keep order.

Before starting play the participants threw down their sticks on opposite sides of a line extending down the center of the ground so that the ends of opponents' sticks would be opposite and there would be assurance that the number of players on each side was the same. Then each party divided up into five squads, one in the middle of the ground, one at each goal, and two half way. The rules of the game allowed extreme roughness, limbs were frequently broken and lives occasionally sacrificed. During the entire period of play, the doctors continued their conjurations. When it was over, the victorious side ran to their ball post and danced about it before leaving the ground while their friends possessed themselves of the property that had been wagered (Swanton, 1928, pp. 456–466).

The game as played by the Chickasaw was practically identical with the Creek game. Adair says that the goals were about 500 yards from each other, each made of two long limber poles, set up 3 yards apart but slanting outward. If the ball were thrown over or between these it counted a point, but if it went under it counted nothing. He says that, after fasting and taking medicine all of the preceding night, the players turned out next morning covered with white paint. He mentions button snakeroot among the medicines taken by them (Swanton, 1928 c, pp. 242–244).

The Choctaw game seems to present some minor peculiarities. The great games were between different towns or cantons, but it is impossible to determine whether the Choctaw anciently had town moieties similar to those of the Creeks. It was usual for the women to play after the men were through, something that seems not to have been customary elsewhere. One of our earliest authorities says that 20 played on a side, another, somewhat later, gives 40, and a recent writer saw 30 used on a side, but the missionary Cushman raises the number to from 75 to 100 per side, and Catlin speaks of several hundred. The night before the game each party danced as did the Cherokee and Creeks. A chief seated himself back of the ball post of his side but facing it, two rows of women ranged themselves between him and the post facing each other, and the players themselves formed a circle near the post. The men danced about the post, then the women danced, and these dances were repeated 12 times according to Halbert, while Catlin merely states that they danced every half hour all night. That night they put on their paint, rubbed their limbs, and took medicines. As in the case of the other tribes, a doctor was employed by each party, but we hear of his activities less in connection with the preliminaries than during the game itself when each engaged in various conjuring practices such as throwing the rays of the sun on the players of their sides by means of a mirror to increase their strength. The ball sticks were made of hickory usually, but Bossu adds chestnut. The lengths given, 2½ to 3 feet, would seem to belie assertions that their sticks were shorter than those used by the Creeks. The ball appears to have been identical with the ball of the Creeks and Chickasaw, except that one later writer mentions rags used in stuffing instead of deer hair. Starr asserts that one party sometimes tied a long tail to a ball to impede it when their opponents had to throw against the wind, and this must mean that the device of the medicine ball was in force among the Choctaw. Their dress consisted of the usual breechclout and belt with a horsetail or tail of some other animal, the raccoon being the only one mentioned, fastened behind, and at times a mane made of horsehair fastened around the neck (pl. 80). They were also brilliantly painted. The goals are given by two early writers as about 150 feet apart, but the later ones all make it between 600 and 1,200. Romans (1775) states that the goals were in the shape of St. Andrew's crosses and that the ball had to be driven between them under the point where they crossed. In the game Catlin witnessed there were two posts about 25 feet high and 6 feet apart with a crossbar. Later writers, however, all tell us that each goal was made of two flat pieces of board 15 to 20 feet high and lashed side by side so as to present a single solid surface. To count as a goal, a ball must go between the posts when there was space or strike the goal and fall back within the line of the goal posts. The central point, midway of the goals, was indicated by a short stake and directly opposite this on one side of the ground was a scaffold for the property wagered, this under the charge of a stakeholder. The number of points for which they played evidently varied, and Romans is undoubtedly correct in saying that they agreed in advance what it was to be. Thus Bossu mentions 16 points, Cushman 10 to 20, Halbert and Starr 12, and Catlin 100. We are also informed that they sometimes played all day without reaching the number agreed upon, when the side which had scored the most points would be adjudged the winner. However, Halbert stated that a game sometimes lasted 2 days. Some of the old men superintended the preparations, and Catlin tells us that, in the game he witnessed, four medicine men acted as judges. A medicine man, probably one of these, threw the ball up at the center to start the game, after which the side which made a goal had the privilege of putting the ball in play again. Nothing more is said regarding the officials. There are said to have been three principal squads formed by the men on each side, one at either goal, and one in the center, the other players being scattered about. Players could run with the ball held between their sticks or throw it. As among the other tribes, the play was violent and many injuries resulted. The wagers were made on the morning of the game and all weapons had to be left in the respective encampments. According to one informant almost any sort of action on the part of the players was permitted except butting with the head, which cost the party of the offender five goals. During the progress of the game, the women ran about serving the men of their side with coffee or whipping up those that seemed slothful.

Bossu says that when the women played this game they used rackets with curved handles. The women's game of which Halbert speaks, played with sticks and balls like the game of battledore and shuttlecock, may have been descended from that (Swanton, 1931 a, pp. 140–151).

There was a variety of this game in which only the hands were employed, the ball being larger, and it was connected apparently with football. Thus, among the Creeks we hear of a game in which the men and women played against one another, the men being obliged to kick the ball while the women could use both hands and feet (Swanton, 1928, p. 468). The Chickasaw called this towācto-cōli and seem to have played it in the same manner. The games were for 12 points and continued for 4 days, after which a feast was held. The Chickasaw also had a game called akabàtle in which they used a ball as big as a baseball propelled along the ground by means of bent sticks. The goal was made of 3-foot posts placed 2 feet apart, and the bent sticks recall the Choctaw game mentioned by Bossu, except that the latter was played by women against women, whereas in the former men and women were opponents. As in the other, they played for 12 points (Swanton, 1928 c, p. 244). Romans tells us of a game played promiscuously by men and women in which they used a ball made of woolen rags which they beat about with their hands (Romans, 1775, p. 79; Swanton, 1931 a, p. 141). This was perhaps related to the game remembered by the Choctaw of Bayou Lacombe in which they used merely their hands and the goals were formed of stakes 10 feet high, a few inches in diameter and 200 feet apart, though the goals remind us of the regular Choctaw game (Bushnell, 1909 a, p. 20).

This hand-ball game seems to have been the only one of this type known to the Natchez.

We have descriptions of it by Du Pratz and Dumont de Montigny, as it was played during the great First Fruits Ceremony corresponding to the Creek busk. Du Pratz places this in September, but Dumont in July. Presumably it was played at other times, and indeed Dumont implies as much, but we have no other records. On these two occasions numbers of men took part, Dumont stating that there were 800 on each side, and this would facilitate the carrying out of one great object of the game, which was to prevent the ball from falling to the ground. According to Du Pratz, it must not be retained in the hand of any player, and if one attempted to hold it, it would be instantly snatched from him. Dumont, on the other hand, makes the ultimate victory depend on the retention of the ball by someone. Du Pratz tells us that the players were divided into two parties, under the Great Sun and the Great War Chief, respectively, the heads of the former being decorated with white feathers and those of the latter with red ones. It began about 9 o'clock in the morning, when the two leaders made their appearance and summoned their followers by sounding upon a drum. First the chiefs threw the ball back and forth for a while, until suddenly the Great Sun sent it among the massed participants and the game was on in earnest. The ball was of the size of the fist, and consisted of a piece of deer hide stuffed, according to Du Pratz, with Spanish moss, and according to Dumont with sawdust. Du Pratz states that the object of each party was to make it touch the cabin of its leader. A single tally ended the game but it usually lasted 2 hours, and Dumont says it sometimes extended for more than 3 hours. Du Pratz adds that the chief of the losing side made the winners a considerable present and the latter were permitted "to wear distinguishing plumes until the following year or until the next time they play ball." The war dance followed this and afterward all went to bathe. (Du Pratz, 1758, vol. 2, pp. 379–381; Dumont, 1753, pp. 197–205; Swanton, 1911, pp. 117, 119–120.)

There is reason to think that the single-pole ball game was older than the other, partly because the ground on which this was played constituted one element in each of the old Creek ceremonial areas.

Sometimes, it is true, the games were not actually played in this ground but about a second pole outside. Curiously enough, this particular game is almost the only one among the Timucua of which we have any account. We are told that they set up a tree 8 or 9 fathoms high in the midst of an open space, at the top of which was a mat of reeds, or bull rushes, or a frame of twigs, and that the object of the game was to hit this last with a ball (pl. 81). Apparently, as in the case of the Natchez ball game, one tally settled the contest. (Laudonnière, 1586, p. 7; Le Moyne, 1875, p. 13; Swanton, 1922, p. 381.) In 1560 the De Luna colonists mention ball-posts in the squares of the towns they visited, from which it would seem that the game was already in existence among the Upper Creeks and the Mobile Indians (Priestly, 1928, vol. 1, pp. 238–241). The single-post ball game among the Creeks was always between the men and women though sometimes the women's side was reenforced by two good male players. The men used their regular ballsticks, the women their hands. Part way up the pole was a mark and whichever side made a hit upon the pole above this mark scored one point. On top there was a wooden image, or in modern times a cow skull or a horse skull, and if a player hit this his or her side scored an extra number of points, usually five (Swanton, 1928, pp. 467–468). Adair makes mention of this game as known to the old people of the Chickasaw "time out of mind." They used a pole with a bush tied at the top (Adair, 1775, pp. 113–114). I find no specific reference to this game among the Choctaw, but they certainly knew it.

Probably the most frequently mentioned Southeastern game is the one called chunkey. There were evidently several different varieties, but all made use of a smooth stone roller and two long slender poles, often supplied with short crosspieces midway of their length. While there were usually only two active participants, numbers of onlookers wagered quantities of property on the outcome. The essence of the game was to start the roller along a smooth piece of ground with which every town was supplied, after which the two players threw their poles after it with the idea of hitting the stone, coming as near it as possible when the stone came to rest, or preventing the opponent's stick from accomplishing either of these results. Lederer and Lawson both observed the Eno Siouans playing chunkey in their town. It is not surprising to find the Cusabo towns provided with chunk yards since they belonged to the Muskhogean stock (Alvord, 1912, p. 157; Lawson, 1860, p. 98).

There is no mention of the game in Florida but in this case, on account of the paucity of our material, silence signifies little, and a form of the game is described in 1595 as observed by Brother San Miguel among the Guale Indians. Immediately after the priest and his companions had been escorted to the town of the head chief of the province of Asao, about the present St. Simons Island,

they began to entertain us with a certain game, in order to begin which they put all the players together with their chief at one side of the square (plaza), each one with a staff or piece of sharp-pointed horn of the form and shape of a dart, but one of them did not resemble it(?) : the chief held a stone in his hand of the shape and size of a five cent loaf of bread (una torta de pan de a medio real), and to begin the game he who held it set it rolling with his whole strength, and all at one time and without order threw their staffs after the stone and at the same time started after them on the run : I did not understand the game very well, but it appeared to me that he who ran fastest and arrived first took his staff and the stone and without stopping a moment returned to dart it at the place which they had left, and in the same manner the others took theirs and returned to dart them: at this exercise they spent a considerable period of time and they were so much engaged in running that sweat poured down all over their bodies. (Garcia, 1902, pp. 195–196.)

William Bartram observed chunk yards in the Cherokee country, and Timberlake mentions the game specifically, stating that the count was in accordance with the nearness of the bowl to marks upon the poles (Timberlake, Williams ed., 1927, pp. 99–100). Adair's description is probably applicable to both the Creeks and Chickasaw and is the only one that has come down to us from either tribe. He says that not more than one or two played on a side, that the sticks were 8 feet long and the stone rollers, measuring about 2 fingers in breadth and 2 spans around, were the property of towns, which preserved them carefully from one generation to another. After the stone and sticks had come to rest, he whose pole lay nearest to the roller scored one point, and if it was in contact with it two. If both sticks were equally near, neither side scored. The poles were anointed with bear grease (Adair, 1775, pp. 401–402; Swanton, 1928 c, p. 244).

Romans says that the Choctaw used poles 15 feet long, that one threw the stone, his antagonist tried to hit it by throwing his pole after it, and the first player attempted to throw his own in such a way as to intercept the pole of the second. The winner threw the stone for the next play (Romans, 1775, pp. 79–80). Cushman's account is similar to that of Romans except that he shortens the poles from 15 feet to 8 or 10, and states that one point was scored by the man who hit the stone and one by the man who hit the pole of his antagonist (Cushman, 1899, p. 190). Halbert tells us that this ancient game, called achahpi, was revived in 1876 and played for the last time by an aged Choctaw named Mehubbee and some younger men whom he instructed. From one of these Halbert learned that the yard was about 100 feet by 12, that the poles were hickory saplings with rounded ends, which had been barked, scraped, and seasoned over the fire.

Four notches were cut near the head, one in the middle, and two halfway between the above points. The score depended on the nearness of the notches to the roller when they came to rest, and 12 points constituted a game (Swanton, 1931 a, p. 156). Dumont de Montigny says that the Natchez used poles 15 to 16 feet long, that he whose pole lay nearest to the stone won, and that the game was for 10 points. Du Pratz reduces the length of the poles to 8 feet and adds that they were shaped like a capital **F**. The stone roller was 3 inches in diameter and 1 inch thick. The object was as stated by Dumont, the winner of each throw having the right to hurl the roller next time. After making a throw the players kept on running beside their poles, evidently with the thought that they might exert upon them some psychic influence. Both Dumont and Du Pratz comment on the amount of property which changed hands during the course of these games (Dumont, 1753, vol. 1, pp. 140–141; Du Pratz, 1758, vol. 3, pp. 2–4). The Chitimacha and various tribes along the Mississippi River played it, and G. A. Dorsey has recorded a Caddo myth in which it is plainly mentioned, though in this the Plains type of ring appears, made out of elm bark (Dorsey, G. A., 1905, p. 34; Swanton, 1942, p. 175). From the description of the game which Gravier witnessed among the Houma, it is possible that, instead of throwing two sticks at a stone roller, they threw a stone roller at a wooden one. However, it is more likely that there has been an error in his notes. (Thwaites, 1897–1901, vol. 65, pp. 145–148; Shea, 1861, 143–145; Swanton, 1911, p. 288.)

The Creeks played a game which was possibly descended from the one last described. They pitched arrows in succession and if the point of one player's arrow touched the feather of another's, the second player kept the arrow of the first.

The Creeks also had another game distantly resembling chunkey. This was called "rolling the stone," or "rolling the bullet," and was played by rolling a large marble or bullet along a trench with the object of making it come to rest in certain hollows which counted differently depending on the difficulty of reaching them.

The moccasin game, usually called by the Creeks "hiding the bullet," was played by two sides each of which in turn strove to conceal a bullet or some similar object so skillfully under one of a number of moccasins, hats, socks, or gloves that the opponents could not guess its location. We have mention of this among the Creeks, Chickasaw, and Choctaw. It seems to have been played by men only, and at least this is specifically stated of the Chickasaw. The four socks or gloves they used were the kind they were accustomed to weave at home. One on each side took turns in doing the hiding. If the bullet was disclosed on the first guess, it counted four; if on the second, two. Cane slivers were employed as counters. Among the Choctaw the game is said to have been played with six on a side and seven hats under which a small stone or bullet was concealed.   The players guessed in turn (Swanton, 1928, p. 469; 1928 c, p. 244; 1931 a, pp. 158–159; 1942, p. 175).

This introduces us to stick and dice games.   Beverley says of the Virginia Algonquians

> They have also one great diversion, to the practising of which are requisite whole handfuls of little sticks or hard straws, which they know how to count as fast as they can cast their eyes upon them, and can handle with a surprising dexterity.

We may also quote Strachey:

> Dice play, or cardes, or lotts they knowe not, how be it they use a game upon russhes much like primero (an ancient English card game), wherein they card and discard, and lay a stake too, and so win and loose.   They will play at this for their bowes and arrowes, their copper beads, hatchets, and their leather coats.   (Strachey, 1849, p. 78.)

Lawson describes the same, or a similar, game among the eastern Siouans and perhaps Tuscarora:

> Their chiefest game is a sort of arithmetic, which is managed by a parcel of small, split reeds, the thickness of a small bent; these are made very nicely, so that they part and are tractable in their hands.   They are 51 in number; their length about 7 inches.   When they play, they throw part of them to their antagonist.   The art is, to discover upon sight, how many you have, and what you throw to him that plays with you.   Some are so expert at their numbers that they will tell ten times together, what they throw out of their hands.   Although the whole play is carried on with the quickest motion it is possible to use, yet some are so expert at this game, as to win great Indian estates by this play.   A good set of these reeds, fit to play withal, are valued and sold for a dressed doe skin.   (Lawson, 1860, p. 288.)

Romans observed the Choctaw women playing a game that reminds us strongly of jackstones:

> The women also have a game where they take a small stick, or something else off the ground after having thrown up a small ball which they are to catch again, having picked up the other; they are fond of it, but ashamed to be seen at it.   (Romans, 1775, p. 81.)

Games in which objects like dice were used were of two kinds, one in which the "dice" were small bits of cane or slivers of wood; the other in which fruit stones, beans, grains of corn, or similar objects were employed.

To one of these types probably belonged the game which Lawson observed among some Congaree women.   He says:

> The name or grounds of it I could not learn, though I looked on above two hours.   Their arithmetic was kept with a heap of Indian grain.   (Lawson, 1860, p. 52.)

The Creek women, and occasionally the men, played a game in which four sections of cane were used split in half.   These were thrown into the air and the count depended on the relative number of convex and concave surfaces presented after they had come to rest (Swanton, 1928, pp. 468–469). Our anonymous French writer mentions a Choctaw game played with four canes which was probably identical with this (Swanton, 1918, p. 68), and Du Pratz describes at considerable length a related game among the Natchez:

> The pieces with which they play are three bits of cane, 8 to 9 inches long, split in two equal parts, and pointed at the ends. Each piece is distinguished by designs cut into the convex side. Three play together and each has her bit. In playing they hold two of these pieces of cane on the open left hand and the third in the right hand, the rounded side above, with which they strike on the two others, taking care to touch only the ends. The three pieces fall, and when two of them have the convex side up the one who has played scores a point. If there is only one she scores nothing. After the first the two others play in their turn. (Le Page du Pratz, 1758, vol. 3, pp. 4–6.)

They are said not to have used this in gambling (Du Pratz, 1758, vol. 3, pp. 4–6; Swanton, 1911, p. 91).

According to Benjamin Paul, Chitimacha women also played a game in which bits of cane were used (Swanton, 1911, p. 350), and so did the Caddo (Swanton, 1942, p. 175).

Among the Siouans Lawson noted a game played with dice made of persimmon stones (Lawson, 1860, p. 288). The Cherokee played a game in which 6 beans, made dark on one side and white on the other, were put into a shallow basket, shaken and tossed into the air, the score depending, of course, upon the number of black or white sides shown when they came to rest. Twelve beans were kept as counters, from which it appears that the game was for 12 points (Culin, 1907, p. 105). This must have been almost identical with the Creek game in which grains of corn were used which had been blackened on one side. According to Culin, the Choctaw played this with 8 grains of corn, but Bushnell was told by the Choctaw of Bayou Lacomb that they used 5 or 7 (Swanton, 1928, p. 469; Culin, 1907, p. 146).

Footraces are noted in some places, in Florida in the very earliest accounts, and among the Caddo in particular. The Chitimacha are said to have played a game in which a ball was thrown through a ring, but it is by no means certain that this was pre-Columbian, and the Alabama once had a bearskin marked off into compartments which reminds one very much of the familiar parchesi board. The game itself was similar (Swanton, 1928, pp. 468–469). A considerable number of children's games were in imitation of those of their elders.

WAR

Offensive and defensive weapons have already been described as well as stockades, but the following notes may be added bearing more particularly on customs observed during hostilities between tribes.

The Powhatan Indians used bows and arrows, clubs, and shields in warfare, but according to Strachey they did not have very many of these last (Strachey, 1849, p. 106).

Barlowe states that the Algonquians of the North Carolina coast,

when they goe to warres . . . cary about with them their idol, of whom they aske counsel, as the Romans were woont of the Oracle of Apollo. They sing songs as they march towardes the battell in stead of drummes and trumpets: their warres are very cruell and bloody, by reason whereof, and of their civil dissentions which have happened of late yeers amongst them, the people are marvelously wasted, and in some places the countrey left desolate. (Burrage, 1906, p. 238.)

Beverley says:

When they fear being discover'd, or follow'd by an Enemy in their Marches they, every morning, having first agreed where they shall rendezvouse at night, disperse themselves into the Woods, and each takes a several way, that so, the Grass or Leaves being but singly prest, may rise again, and not betray them. For the *Indians* are very artful in following a track, even where the Impressions are not visible to other People, especially if they have any advantage from the looseness of the Earth, from the stiffness of the Grass, or the stirring of the Leaves, which in the Winter Season lye very thick upon the ground, and likewise afterwards, if they do not happen to be burned. (Beverley, 1705, bk. 3, pp. 18–19.)

It would appear that they did not invariably make their attacks early in the morning, for when a reconnoitering party from the vessels which established the colony of Virginia was returning to the ships, Percy says:

At night, when wee were going aboard, there came the Savages creeping upon all foure, from the Hills, like Beares, with their Bowes in their mouthes, charged us very desperately in the faces. (Narr. Early Va., Tyler ed., 1907, p. 10.)

Wars were conducted as follows by the Powhatan according to Strachey:

When they intend any warrs, the weroances usually advise with their priests or conjurers, their allies and best trusted chauncellors and freinds; but comonly the priests have the resulting voice, and determyne therefore their resolutions. Eyther a weroance or some lustie fellowe is appointed captaine over a nation or regiment to be led forth; and when they would presse a number of soldiers to be ready by a day, an officer is dispacht awaye, who comyng into the townes, or otherwise meeting such whome he hath order to warne, to strike them over the back a sound blow with a bastinado, and bidds them be ready to serve the great king, and tells them the rendevous, from whence they dare not at any tyme appointed be absent. They seldome make warrs for lands or goods, but for women and children, and principally for revenge, so vindicative and jealous they to be made a dirision of, and to be insulted upon by an enemy. (Strachey, 1849, pp. 100–101.)

He adds that because some of his priests had prophesied that a nation should arise from the Chesapeake Bay region destined to overthrow his empire, Powhatan had decimated the tribes formerly in occupancy there.

Farther on we read:

Their chief attempts are by stratagems, surprizes, and trecheries, yet the weroances, women, or children, they put not to death, but keep them captives. They have a method in warre, and for a pleasure Powhatan would needs have yt shewed once to our people, and yt was in this manner performed at Matta panient.

Having painted and disguised themselves in the fairest manner they could devise, they devided themselves into two companies, well neere one hundred in a company; the one company they called Monacan's, the other Powhatan's, eyther army had their captaine. These (as enemies) took their stand a muskett shott one from another, ranckng themselves fifteen abreast, and each ranck from other four or five yardes, not in file, but in the opening betwixt their files, so as the reare could shoot as convenyently as the front. Having thus pitched the field, from eyther part went a messenger with condicions that whosoever were vanquished, such as escaped, upon their submission or comying in, though two daies after, should live, but their wives and childrene should be prize for the conquerors. The messengers were no soner returned, but they approached in their orders, on each flank a serjeant, and in the reare an officer for lieutenant, all duly keeping their rancks, yet leaping and singing after their accustomed tune, which they use only in warrs. Upon the first flight of arrowes, they gave such horrible showts and scritches as so many infernall helhounds; when they had spent their arrowes they joyned togither prettily, charging and retiring, every ranck seconding other. As they gett advantage, they catch their enemies by the haire of their head, and downe he came that was taken; his enemy, with a woodden sword, seemed to beat out his braines, and still they crept to the reare to mayntayne the skyrmish. The Monocans decreasing, the Powhatans charged them in forme of a halfe moone; they, unwilling to be inclosed, fled all in a troupe to their ambuscadoes, on whome they led them very cunningly. The Monocans disperst themselves among the freshmen, whereupon the Powhatans retired themselves with all speed to their seconds, which the Monocans seeing, tooke that advantage to retire againe to theire owne battaile, and each returned to theire owne quarter. All their accion, voices, and gestures, both in chardging and retiring, were so strayned to the height of their quality and nature, that the strangness thereof made yt seeme very delightfull. (Strachey, 1849, pp. 107–108.)

Spelman supplies us with a picture of warfare among the Chesapeake Bay tribes from direct observation:

They neuer fight in open fields but always ether amonge reede or behind trees takinge ther oportunitie to shoot at ther enimies and till they can nocke another arrow they make the trees ther defence.

In y⁰ time that I was ther I sawe a Battell fought betwene the Patomeck and the Masomeck, ther place where they fought was a marish ground full of Reede. Beinge in the cuntry of the Patomecke the peopel of Masomeck weare brought thether in Canoes which is a kind of Boate they haue made in the forme of an Hoggs trowgh But sumwhat more hollowed in, On Both sids they scatter them selues sum litle distant one from the other, then take they ther bowes and arrows and hauinge made ridie to shoot they softly steale toward ther enimies, Sumtime squattinge doune and priinge if they can spie any to shoot at whom if at any time he so Hurteth that he can not flee they make hast to him to knock him on the heade, And they that kill most of ther enimies are heald the cheafest men amonge them; Drums and Trumpetts they haue none, but when they will gather themselues togither they haue a kind of Howlinge or Howbabub so differinge in sounde one from the other as both part may uery aesely be distinguished. Ther was no greater slawter of nether side but yᵉ massomecks hauing shott away most of ther arrows and wantinge Vital weare glad to retier. (Smith, John, Arber ed., 1884, pp. cxiii–cxiv.)

The Virginia chiefs were particularly well guarded. Powhatan had a bodyguard about himself continually, and four sentinels kept watch around him at night. At the time when Smith was taken captive by Opechancanough, the latter was

well guarded with 20 bowmen 5 flanck and rear, and each flanck before him a sword and a peece, and after him the like, then a bowman, then I on each hand a boweman, the rest in file in the reare, which reare led foorth amongst the trees in a bishion, eache his bowe and a handfull of arrowes, a quiver at his back grimly painted: on eache flanck a sargeant, the one running alwaies towards the front, the other towards the reare, each a true pace and in exceeding good order. (Smith, John, Tyler ed., 1907, p. 45.)

Lawson says that the hair of warriors about to set forth on an expedition was combed out and much ornamented by the women with paint, bear's grease, feathers, copper, and beads. They often painted their faces red and daubed circles about their eyes. A council always preceded an expedition, and during the latter they left "hieroglyphic" signs of their tribe scattered about so that the enemy would know by whom the blow was struck.

Their cruelty to their prisoners of war is what they are seemingly guilty of an error in, I mean as to a natural failing, because they strive to invent the most inhuman butcheries for them that the devils themselves could invent or hammer out of hell; they esteeming death no punishment, but rather an advantage to him, that is exported out of this into another world.

Therefore, they inflict on them torments, wherein they prolong life in that miserable state as long as they can, and never miss skulping of them as they call it, which is, to cut off the skin from the temples and taking the whole head of hair along with it, as if it was a night-cap. Sometimes they take the top of the skull along with it; all which they carefully preserve and keep by them, for a trophy of their conquest over their enemies. Others keep their enemies teeth which are taken in war, whilst others split the pitch pine into splinters, and stick them into the prisoner's body yet alive. Thus they light them which burn like so many torches; and in this manner they make him dance round a great fire, every one buffeting and deriding him, till he expires, when every one strives to get a bone or some relic of this unfortunate captive. One of the young fellows that has been at the wars, and has had the fortune to take a captive, returns the proudest creature on earth, and sets such a value on himself, that he knows not how to contain himself in his senses. . . . When they take a slave and intend to keep him to work in their fields, they flea the skin from the setting on of his toes to the middle of his foot, so cut off one half of his feet, wrapping the skin over the wounds, and healing them.[35] By this cruel method, the Indian captive is hindered from making his escape, for he can neither run fast or go anywhere, but his feet are more easily traced and

---

[35] Also Lawson, 1860, p. 93; Catesby states that this was done only after a prisoner had attempted to escape (1731–43, vol. 2, p. XIII).

discovered. Yet I know one man who made his escape from them, though they had thus disabled him, as you may see in my journal.

The Indians ground their wars on enmity, not on interest, as the Europeans generally do; for the loss of the meanest person in the nation, they will go to war and lay all at stake, and prosecute their designs to the utmost, till the nation they were injured by, be wholly destroyed, or make them that satisfaction which they demand. They are very politic in waging and carrying on their war: first, by advising with all the ancient men of conduct and reason, that belong to their nation; such as superannuated war captains, and those that have been counsellors for many years, and whose advice has commonly succeeded very well. They have likewise their field counsellors, who are accustomed to ambuscades and surprises, which methods are constantly used by the savages, for I scarce ever heard of a field battle fought amongst them. (Lawson, 1860, pp. 321–323; copied by Catesby, 1731–43, vol. 2, p. XIII.)

He then gives an account of a stratagem by means of which a relatively weak war party overcame a stronger body, namely, by lighting a great fire and laying logs of wood about it wrapped up in such a way as to resemble men asleep. Thinking to surprise them, the attacking party was itself surprised and killed or captured. As the same device is said to have been used by the Creek Indians in overcoming a large Apalachee war party, it is possibly a war legend. Lawson also cites the treacherous manner in which the Machapunga destroyed the Coranine Indians of Point Lookout with whom they had just made peace (Lawson, 1860, p. 325). This seems to have been one of those disturbances in the interest of British slave trade which too often accompanied the advance of white civilization.

Catesby adds:

A body of *Indians* will travel four or five hundred miles to surprise a town of their enemies, travelling by night only, for some days before they approach the town. Their usual time of attack is at break of day, when, if they are not discovered, they fall on with dreadful slaughter, and scalping, which is to cut off the skins of the crown from the temples, and taking the whole head of hair along with it as if it was a night cap: sometimes they take the top of the scull with it; all which they preserve, and carefully keep by them for a trophy of their conquest. Their caution and temerity is such, that at the least noise, or suspicion of being discovered, though at the point of execution, they will give over the attack, and retreat back again with precipitation. (Catesby, 1731–43, vol. 2, p. XIII.)

He illustrates this by referring to a personal experience when a party of 60 Cherokee descended the Savannah River to Augusta to cut off the small Chickasaw settlement there but were moved to turn back by some trifling incident. He continues:

It is the custom of *Indians*, when they go on these bloody designs, to colour the paddles of their canoes, and sometimes the canoes, red. No people can set a higher esteem on themselves, than those who excel in martial deeds, yet their principles of honour, and what they deem glorious, would in other parts of the world be esteemed most base and dishonourable: they never face their enemies in open field (which they say is great folly in the *English*) but skulk from one covert to another in the most cowardly manner; yet their confidence in, and the opinion they have of the prowess of white men is such, that a party of them being led on by an *European* or two, have been frequently known to behave with great bravery.

Their savage nature appears in nothing more than their barbarity to their captives, whom they murder gradually with the most exquisite tortures they can invent. At these diabolical ceremonies attend both sexes, old and young, all of them with great glee and merriment assisting to torture the unhappy wretch, till his death finishes their .diversion. However timorous these savages behave in battle, they are quite otherwise when they know they must die, shewing then an uncommon fortitude and resolution, and in the height of their misery will sing, dance, revile, and despise their tormentors till their strength and spirits fail. (Catesby, 1731–43, vol. 2, p. xiv.)

To warfare he attributed the relatively small population of North America at the arrival of Europeans, who also contributed to a further decline:

The *Indians* (as to this life) seem to be a very happy people, tho' that happiness is much eclipsed by the intestine feuds and continual wars one nation maintains against another, which sometimes continue some ages, killing and making captive, till they become so weak, that they are forced to make peace for want of recruits to supply their wars. This probably has occasioned the depopulated state of north *America* at the arival of *Europeans*, who by introducing the vices and the distempers of the old world, have greatly contributed even to extinguish the race of these savages, who it is generally believed were at first four, if not six times as numerous as they now are. (Catesby, 1731–43, vol. 2, pp. xv–xvi.)

In Timberlake's time the Cherokee warriors were provided with bows and arrows, darts, scalping knives, and tomahawks, but had also obtained guns, and trade tomahawks with a pipe opposite the blade were already common. Like the other Indians of the section, they went on these war expeditions wearing little besides their breechclouts, but elaborately painted. Again, like the other Indians, they were in the habit of leaving a club "something of the form of a cricket-bat, but with their warlike exploits engraved on it, in their enemy's country." Timberlake adds that "the enemy accepts the defiance, by bringing this back to their country." In case they won a victory it was their custom "to engrave their victory on some neighboring tree, or set up some token of it near the field of battle" (Timberlake, Williams ed., 1927, pp. 82–83). Warriors were not compelled to take part in an expedition or to support their leader once they had set out, except apparently in the action itself. Timberlake also tells us that there were two grades of warriors under the chiefs, and that many women were famous both in war and in council. In 1762 this explorer witnessed the return of a war party which had been out against the northern Indians:

On the 10th of March, while we were again preparing for our departure, the *Death Hallow* was heard from the top of Tommotly town-house. This was to give notice of the return of a party commanded by Willinawaw, who went to war towards the Shawnese country some time after my arrival . . . About eleven o'clock the Indians, about forty in number, appeared within sight of the town; as they approached, I observed four scalps, painted red on the flesh-side, hanging on a pole, and carried in front of the line, by the second in command, while Willinawaw brought up the rear. When near the town-house, the whole marched round it three times, singing the war-song, and at intervals giving the *Death Hallow;* after which, sticking the pole just by the door, for the crowd to gaze on, they went in to relate in what manner they had gained them. (Timberlake, Williams ed., 1927, pp. 112–113.)

Timberlake has also provided us with the translation of a war song into which he has, unfortunately, thought it necessary to introduce English rhythms. Elsewhere he adds:

The prisoners of war are generally tortured by the women, at the party's return, to revenge the death of those that have perished by the wretch's countrymen. This savage custom has been so much mitigated of late, that the prisoners were only compelled to marry, and then generally allowed all the privileges of the natives. This lenity, however, has been a detriment to the nation; for many of these returning to their countrymen, have made them acquainted with the country-passes, weakness, and haunts of the Cherokees; besides that it gave the enemy greater courage to fight against them. (Timberlake, Williams ed., 1927, p. 82.)

Timberlake's judgment cannot, however, be trusted here. This very custom of adoption was in large measure responsible for the rise to power of the great Iroquois Confederation.

Though it is not mentioned by Timberlake, a war medicine or "ark," similar to those used by other Southeastern tribes was carried by a Cherokee war party. Mooney, and Washburn whom Mooney cites, regarded this as a tribal palladium, and the latter says that it was captured by the Delaware Indians and that the old priests of the Cherokee ascribed to this circumstance the later degeneracy of their people (Washburn, 1869, pp. 191, 221; Mooney, 1900, p. 503). Whether there was one or several, however, they were treated in much the same manner. When the Overhill Cherokee under Ostenaco (or Outasite) were on a campaign in 1756 in aid of the British and colonial forces, Adair was informed by a white man who accompanied it that

he saw a stranger there very importunate to view the inside of the Cheerake ark, which was covered with a drest deer-skin, and placed on a couple of short blocks. An Indian centinel watched it, armed with a hiccory bow, and brass-pointed barbed arrows, and he was faithful to his trust; for finding the stranger obtruding to pollute the supposed sacred vehicle, he drew an arrow to the head, and would have shot him through the body, had he not suddenly withdrawn; the interpreter when asked by the gentleman (Adair's informant) what it contained, told him there was nothing in it but a bundle of conjuring traps. (Adair, 1775, p. 161, footnote.)

Timucua weapons consisted of bows and arrows, darts, and clubs, the last-mentioned differing from those used by the Creeks. War was declared against an enemy by sticking up arrows with hair on the ends along the trail. Towns were sometimes surrounded with stockades, the stockade overlapping at the entrance, where there was also a small house to accommodate two sentinels. Men out fishing were protected by means of a watchman, and a sentinel who failed in his duty was cruelly punished by being beaten on the head with a heavy club. If it was necessary, we are informed that the course of a stream might be diverted so that it passed near the gate of the fort. Information was conveyed by means of smoke signals, and fire arrows were used to ignite the roofs of enemy dwellings. Before setting out on an expedition, warriors bathed in an infusion of certain herbs. Saturiwa, on such an occasion, sprinkled water over his chiefs and poured more over the fire so as to extinguish it, these acts having symbolical significance (pl. 82). Provisions were carried along by women, boys, and male concubines. Saturiwa's men preserved no order on the march, but those of Utina went in regular ranks and encamped in parties of tens ranged in concentric circles about their chief. On the wings of the army were scouts. Adult male enemies were killed and their heads carried off to be scalped later if there was no time to do this at once, reed knives being used for this purpose. From the experience of Juan Ortiz it is evident that male prisoners were sometimes taken to be tortured to death later. The women and children were also brought home alive. We are told that the side which was first to kill a man of the enemy claimed the victory though it might have lost more in actual numbers. If there was time, they dried the scalps they had taken before their return and cut off parts of the bodies of their enemies, which they also brought home and dried. For some religious reason they shot arrows as deeply as possible into the arms of each enemy corpse.[35a] After their return, they hung the scalps and other fragments of human flesh on a row of poles and a sorcerer cursed these, holding an image in his hand which was possibly the one that had been taken on the expedition. He was accompanied by three musicians, one of whom beat on a flat stone, while the others used rattles. We are informed that this sort of celebration was held every time they returned from the war. Saturiwa shared his scalps with his subchiefs and hung the one he had taken before his door crowned with branches of laurel. In the afternoon they mourned for the dead, but at night this gave place to singing and dancing (Swanton, 1922, pp. 377–381).

Among the Creeks and Chickasaw, war parties were organized and war expeditions carried on in about the same manner. A warrior wore his breechclout and belt, and moccasins, and was painted red and black. He carried a blanket, cords, and leather with which to repair his

---

[35a] An expurgation is suspected here.

moccasins, and some parched corn for his sustenance. His weapons consisted of a bow and arrows or a gun, a knife, a tomahawk, a war club, and a javelin. By 1743 some Creek warriors are said to have carried pistols (Kimber, 1744, p. 16). Anciently shields were used. After horses had been introduced, ropes with which to lead away stolen horses were part of his equipment. War expeditions usually set out in the spring. Sometimes only 2 or 3 persons formed such a party, but there might be very many, and Adair says that the common number was 20 or 30. A town was seldom unanimous on the subject of war and not more than half of the nation was engaged at any one time. After war had been determined upon at a council, the war leader went 3 times round his winter house, a drum was beaten, red colors hung out, and all who wished to take part in the enterprise repaired to that place with their parched corn and took medicine together for 3 days and nights (Kimber, 1744, p. 17).[36] A fast was carefully observed and the young warriors were watched closely so as to be certain that they broke none of the taboos. Cushman says that a retired warrior made an address at that time, the war pipe was lighted and passed around, the war dance was held lasting 2 or 3 days, followed by a feast, and the relatives fasted. An inexperienced leader would go off at midnight in a modest manner, but a veteran started at daybreak, the party whooping and discharging their guns. They marched in single file headed by the Hobai or war chief, who is said to have had the training of a priest. He was followed by an official usually called Waiter who distributed food and drink to the men and carried along the sacred medicine bundle or "ark" (Swanton, 1928, pp. 405–443). Adair tells us that this ark

contains several consecrated vessels, made by beloved superannuated women, and of such various antiquated forms, as would have puzzled Adam to have given significant names to each. The leader and his attendant, are purified longer than the rest of the company that the first may be fit to act in the religious office of a priest of war, and the other to carry the awful sacred ark. (Adair, 1775, pp. 168–169; Swanton, 1928, p. 411.)

Again

The Indian ark is deemed so sacred and dangerous to be touched either by their own sanctified warriors, or the spoiling enemy, that they durst not touch it upon any account. It is not to be meddled with by any, except the war chieftain and his waiter, under the penalty of incurring great evil. Nor would the most inveterate enemy touch it in the woods for the very same reason. (Adair, 1775, pp. 170–171; Swanton, 1928, p. 412.)

In one place he seems to say that the war chief carried the ark rather than his waiter, but probably both shared the duty (Adair, 1775, p. 409).

---

[36] The medicine observed by him in use among the Creek warriors in 1743 was "a kind of red Paste" (p. 18).

Memory of such an ark was preserved until recently by the Alabama Indians, who seemed to think there was but one in the tribe (Swanton, 1928, p. 425). As a whole the Creeks appear to have had two principal war medicines, the horn of a horned snake, and bones of another mythic creature called "man-eater," but later, after white contact, "lion" (Hawkins, 1848, pp. 79–80; Swanton, 1928, p. 429). Milfort tells us that each minor band chief heading a large force carried along "a little sack in which there are certain stones and some pieces of cloth which he has taken from the clothing of the head chief" (Swanton, 1928, p. 432). The ark was set down on stones or pieces of wood, never on the ground.

When the party entered the woods all were silent. While they were away they must not lean against a tree and they must sit on rocks. A bad dream might cause a warrior to return home at any time, and the note of a certain bird would disband them. Captive women and children of both sexes were usually saved unless they had been "devoted" in advance, "devoted" meaning that all captives were to be killed indiscriminately for a certain period. Speaking of the Creek warriors that he observed in 1743, Kimber says:

If none of their own Party is kill'd, they take Prisoners all they can lay Hands on; but if on the contrary, they give no Quarter. (Kimber, 1744, p. 17.)

They had no compunction regarding the taking of scalps from women and children, however, the Creeks saying that it indicated more valor since they had to go into their enemies' territory to get them. In later times, as we have seen, one of the main objects was to capture horses. Youths were in a kind of disgrace until they had secured "hair or horses," after which they obtained war honors and were given new names. After they had killed an enemy they tied firebrands to grapevines about the place and marked hieroglyphic signs upon the trees to indicate what tribe had committed the deed. No matter how successful he might be otherwise, a leader who had lost several men was degraded. The bodies of dead enemies, besides being scalped, were cut up and the various parts were borne along homeward as was done by the Timucua. Scalps placated the spirits of the dead besides advancing the social position of the man who took them. When they got near home, the women paid in tobacco to enjoy the honor of whipping the captives. In later times (Swan) grown men as well as women might be saved if the ransom price were sufficient. Otherwise their only chance of survival was to escape to the house of the high priest or a white town. Bearskin moccasins were tied to the feet of one who had been condemned to torture and a firebrand was fastened above his head. It was not usual to kill a man who had been given food. Scalps were not of equal value in distributing war honors. When this distribution took place, the recipients wore deerskin moccasins painted red, had their bodies anointed with bear's oil, an otter skin tied to each leg, and a collar made of swan feathers about the neck. A white wand and white crown was given to each, feathers of the swan being used in the case of ordinary warriors and feathers of the war eagle for the war leaders. War honors were usually tattooed on the arm of him who had won them, but there was a way to remove such marks if it was discovered that the wearer's claim was false. Milfort states that when an army of the Creek Confederation went out, each group participating was sent a club partly colored red and a bunch of sticks to indicate when they were to meet. The number of warriors needed is also said to have been indicated in this manner but such a requisition appears to be un-Indian. He adds that the Great War chief sometimes started out with but one or two warriors and was joined by the rest at some appointed place. He also says that the war camp was circular, the chief facing the opening, and the clans camping in a circle. There was a great war bundle and a little one. War pipes were in use but they were of relatively late introduction (Swanton, 1928, pp. 405–443).

Adair had an exceptional opportunity to observe the ceremonies of a Chickasaw party after their return. While they were away, the house of the war leader was kept swept and the sweepings were left behind the door until he appeared. Every utensil that had been used by the women was carried outside. The party was painted red and black and wore swan feathers on their heads. They carried the scalps on a pine branch. First the war leader walked round his house singing. The ark was placed upon two blocks of wood near the war pole and opposite the fire in the middle of the house. The party first walked around this war pole and then went into the house where they remained 3 days purifying themselves internally and externally with an infusion of the button snakeroot. All this took place in the daytime. That night their wives and female relations formed two lines at the door of the hothouse facing each other and stood that way till day, absenting themselves from their husbands and from salt and some other articles of food. At intervals the warriors came out and circled about the war pole singing. Later they bathed and then went in procession to affix a bit of scalp attached to a piece of pine on the houses of those relations who had lost kindred as yet unavenged. The holy men and priests were forbidden to shed blood. Cushman says that the war songs and dances of the Choctaw and Chickasaw were entirely different (Adair, 1775, pp. 164–167; Swanton, 1928, pp. 421–423; 1928 c, p. 238).

The Choctaw weapons and equipment were similar to those of the Chickasaw and Creeks. War, in the usual limited sense the term had among our Indians, was declared at a council after which those who were to form the party assembled, painted in black and red and with swan wings tied to their arms, and danced the war dance (hoyopa hithla) for 8 days, fasting and rubbing themselves with herbs prescribed by the doctor, who also performed certain conjuring rites to insure them success. They usually traveled at night and resorted to all sorts of ruses to escape detection. Adair says that the Choctaw were especially clever in imitating the movements of animals. Like Indians generally, they launched their attacks most often in the early morning, but as a people they were more inclined to await attacks in their own territories than to invade the territories of their neighbors. In this way, they informed Romans, they were assured of getting only the scalps of warriors, whereas, if they went abroad to fight, they would have to be content mainly with the scalps of women and children. This justification of their conduct may be set over against that of the Creeks and Chickasaw given above. Victory with the loss of many men was not esteemed, and lack of success as the Choctaw understood it might bring demotion to the war leader, who in fact ruled by prestige and never ventured to deliver orders. Romans says that he often saw armed women in the parties which set out to pursue invaders, and we are told that some wives were so fond of their husbands that they went with them on the regular parties, though it does not appear that they underwent the same ceremonies (Swanton, 1931 a, pp. 162–170).

What Bossu calls a "manitou," adopting an Algonquian word, and at any rate a war medicine of some kind equivalent to the Creek and Chickasaw "ark," was carried by each war party (Bossu, 1768, vol. 2, pp. 89–90; Swanton, 1931 a, p. 163). Romans gives the best description of this:

Their addictedness to pretended witchcraft leads them into a very superstitious behaviour when on an expedition which is remarkable. They carry with them a certain thing which they look on as the genius of the party; it is most commonly the stuffed skin of an owl of a large kind; they are very careful of him, keep a guard over him, and offer him a part of their meat; should he fall, or any other ways be disordered in position, the expedition is frustrated; they always set him with his head towards the place of destination, and if he should prove to be turned directly contrary, they consider this as portending some very bad omen, and an absolute order to return; should therefore any one's heart fail him, he needs only watch his opportunity to do this to save his character of a brave or true man. (Romans, 1775, pp. 76–77; Swanton, 1931 a, p. 165.)

A bad dream while en route toward the enemy would usually occasion the return home of the dreamer, and if the leader had such a dream, the whole party might turn back. Romans says that the chirp of a species of *Motacilla* near the camp would have the same effect (Romans, 1775, pp. 76–77; Swanton, 1931 a, p. 165).

The Choctaw war camp was circular, with the fire in the center, and each man had a forked stick planted at his head on which to hang the bag containing his powder and shot. Adair considered the Choctaw the swiftest of foot of all Indians. When a successful party came within sight of their own town, they uttered a cry to indicate victory and a dance of rejoicing followed. The chief divided such property as had been captured among the relatives of those killed in combat, retaining nothing for himself. Romans says that they were not as cruel as other tribes, since they dispatched those captives who had been devoted to death with bullets or blows of hatchets, but our earliest authority states that the adult captives were burned, while the women, girls, and young boys were enslaved. Romans adds that the bodies of slain enemies were afterward cut up, scalps being made of the hairy portions and the rest buried, but those killed at a distance were simply scalped. After the women had danced about them, the red-painted scalps were exposed upon the roofs of the hot houses until they were destroyed. Sometimes, however, they were taken down and carried about on pine boughs. A man who had taken a scalp was in the habit of sharing it with a child or nephew who had not yet accomplished such a feat, so that the latter might be accepted as a warrior; but he was compelled to submit to 200 blows of a neck band, singing meanwhile and showing no signs of flinching. Each of the seasoned warriors wore at this time a piece of otter skin tied to his head and having white feathers stuck into it equal to the number of enemies he had killed. Records of their war feats were also tattooed on their bodies and arms, and afterward the successful warrior must not comb his hair for a month and must scratch his head only with a stick employed for that particular purpose. The quarterings of a family obtained in this way were also painted on the handles of war clubs and on trees as guides in bringing them together. During the Choctaw civil war, the two parties took each other's scalps as though they had been hostile people, and the head of one of their own men was thrown down to be mourned over by the Indians and French. A war calumet was presented by one tribe to another when they wanted their alliance against a third. An informant of the writer claimed that they used formerly to poison springs belonging to the enemy and any meat that might be hung up near them, but I am uncertain whether this represents a historic fact or should be classed as folklore (Swanton, 1931 a, pp. 162–170).

Turning our attention to the lower Mississippi country, we find little information regarding the war customs of any tribe except the Natchez. Natchez warriors were divided into three classes. Most of our authorities describe the raising of a war party which was to be under the direct command of the national war chief, but there is one account of a party organized under more plebeian auspices. The warriors were clothed with breechclouts and belts, wearing ear pendants and carrying rattles and war clubs. The rattles were probably for use merely in the preliminary ceremonies. They carried along provisions, mainly consisting, it would seem, of the "cold meal" to which reference has been made elsewhere. They had axes, guns, war clubs, and sometimes shields, the guns having taken the place of the bows and arrows of an earlier period. A man who desired to lead what may be denominated a private war party, planted at a certain spot two posts ornamented with feathers, arrows, and war clubs painted red. Volunteers repaired to this spot evening and morning to take a war medicine which acted as an emetic, to dance, and tell their military feats.

If the Natchez nation deemed that it had received an injury from some other tribe calling for collective action, a council was held and the calumet of war was hung on a pole at the door of the house where the matter was under deliberation. The occasion for war was presented by the head war chief, but the decision rested with the council. In order to avert hostilities a peace calumet might be sent to the offending nation accompanied by a strong party, to attempt a reconciliation. When war was determined upon, a war feast and dance were held at the house of the war chief, though one writer asserts that the rallying ground was before the temple. The war calumet was placed upon a pole in the middle of the ground, and this was surrounded by various articles of food, principally made of corn and venison, placed in wooden dishes, in the very center of which was a wooden dish containing a dog roasted whole. A speech was made by a retired warrior who lighted the calumet and put it in circulation beginning with the war chief, after which he put it back upon the pole. After that they feasted on the dog meat, and drank the war drink (*Ilex vomitoria*), the ceremony being punctuated at intervals with war cries raised by the younger warriors. One writer states that each volunteer harangued the war chief at this time. At any rate the use of the emetic was followed by the ceremony of striking the post on which hung the calumet, each warrior as he did so recounting his notable exploits. This was followed by the war dance, the old men meanwhile coloring the war clubs red and making the incised wooden objects which were to be left in the enemy's territory. Three days later they set out, traveling in single file, though, if the party were a large one, they might move in five or six columns. If they found they had been discovered, they might return, leaving 10 or 20 warriors behind them to surprise stray hunters and isolated families. Before they retired for the night a war party sent out scouts to considerable distances but they never posted sentinels all night. Fires were extinguished, however, so that they might not be detected. As in the case of the other tribes, a bad omen or dream might send some or all of them back home. They also carried a fetish or war medicine (Swanton, 1911, pp. 123–134). Charlevoix says of this:

> Their idols were exposed on a long pole leaning toward the enemy, and all the warriors, before they lie down, pass one after another, with their war clubs in their hands, before their pretended deities; then they turn toward the enemies' country, and make great threatenings, which the wind often carries another way. (French, 1851, p. 167; Swanton, 1911, p. 123.)

Le Petit's version of this, from the same original document, runs thus:

> As the war chiefs always carry with them their idols, or what they call their spirits, well secured in some skins, at night they suspend them from a small pole painted red, which they erect in a slanting position, so that it may be bent to the side of the enemy. The warriors, before they go to sleep, with war club in hand, pass one after the other in a dance before these pretended spirits, at the same time uttering the fiercest threats toward the side on which are their enemies. (Thwaites, 1897–1901, vol. 68, pp. 145–149; Swanton, 1911, p. 125.)

Attacks were usually made at daybreak, and there was the same sensitiveness to losses of men that we have noted elsewhere. If the Great Sun accompanied a war expedition and should happen to be killed, the chiefs of the party and other leading warriors would be put to death. If two war parties happened to meet, both would turn back. In order to keep it from falling into the hands of the enemy, the friends of a man who had fallen far from home would remove his scalp and bring it back.

The engraved or painted sticks in the shape of war clubs which have already been mentioned were left about the place where a successful blow had been struck, bearing upon them the mark of the town from which they came or the war leader. If no damage had been done, they carved such designs on trees instead, and a small tree was split in two and the ends bent over into half circles, one of which was painted red and one black. If a cabin had been attacked, besides leaving the clubs, they set up two arrows in the manner of a St. Andrew's cross.

Captives were made to sing and dance for several days before the temple and then they were delivered to the relatives of persons who had been killed, from whom the warriors received some recompense. The hair of female captives was cut short and they were kept as slaves. The men were stunned with blows of a club and scalped, unless a woman redeemed such a captive to marry him. Afterward they were fastened to a square frame of sticks, scorched in several places with canes, and finally burned to death (pl. 83). One who had taken a scalp for the first time must remain away from his wife and eat no meat for the space of 6 months, living mainly on fish and broth.

Otherwise it was thought that his destruction would be effected by the soul or souls of those killed. After a new exploit a warrior changed his name (Swanton, 1911, pp. 124–125). The following description of the engraved wooden tablets left in an enemy's country is given by Du Pratz:

At the very top of the tablet on the right side is the hieroglyphic sign which designates the nation declaring war; then a naked man, easy to recognize, with a war club in his hand; then an arrow placed as if about to pierce a woman who flees, her hair disheveled and floating in the air. Immediately in front of this woman is the proper sign of the nation on which war is declared. All this is on the same line and the meaning is evident. What is below is not so clear, and besides it does not count for much. This line begins with the figure of a month which is soon to come. The days which follow are the I marks, and the moon is indicated by a face without rays. A man is to be seen, before whom are many arrows, which appear to be about to strike a fleeing woman. All this means that when such a month shall be so many days old they will come in great numbers to attack such a nation. (Le Page du Pratz, 1758, vol. 2, pp. 430–435; Swanton, 1911, pp. 132–133.)

This is to be regarded as a specimen tablet rather than a standard form invariably employed.

Caddo war customs are treated in Bureau of American Ethnology Bulletin 132 (Swanton, 1942, pp. 184–192).

Forts were made in the general shape of hoops with the ends overlapping to form the gate and towers at intervals along the walls. There was generally a tree in the centre used as a watchtower, and a banquette around the inside, while in late times they had learned to protect their fighters by means of a penthouse. The gate was always on the side toward the water supply (Le Page du Pratz, 1758, vol. 2, pp. 430–435; Swanton, 1911, pp. 132–133). (See pl. 83.)

By the end of the seventeenth century the calumet ceremony used in making peace had extended down the Mississippi to its mouth. Plate 84 is supposed to illustrate the peace ceremony as performed by the Chitimacha when they made peace with the French.

MARRIAGE CUSTOMS

Very little has been preserved regarding the marriage customs of the Algonquian tribes of Virginia and North Carolina except the following from Spelman, which applies particularly to the Powhatan tribes along the James and to the Potomac band:

The custom of yᵉ cuntry is to haue many wiues and to buye them, so that he which haue most copper and Beads may haue most wiues, for if he taketh likinge of any woman he makes loue to hir, and seeketh to hir father or kindsfolke to sett what price he must paye for hir, which beinge once agreed on the kindred meett and make good cheere, and when the sume agreed on be payd she shall be deliuered to him for his wife. The cerimony is thus The parents bringes ther daughter betwene them (if hir parents be deade then sume of hir kinsfolke, or whom it pleaseth y⁰ king to apoynt (for y⁰ man goes not unto any place to be maried But y⁰ woman is brought to him wher he dwelleth). At hir cumminge to him, hir father or cheefe frends ioynes the hands togither and then y⁰ father or cheef frend of y⁰ man Bringeth a longe stringe of Beades and measuring his armes leangth therof doth breake it ouer y⁰ hands of thos that are to be married while ther handes be ioyned together, and giues it unto y⁰ womans father or him that brings hir, And so with much mirth and feastinge they goe togither, When y⁰ Kinge of y⁰ cuntry will haue any wiues he acquaintes his cheef men with his purpose, who sends into all parties of y⁰ cuntry for y⁰ fayrest and cumliest mayds out of which y⁰ Kinge taketh his choyse giuen to ther parents what he pleaseth. If any of y⁰ Kings wiues haue once a child by him, he neuer lieth with hir more but puts hir from him giuinge hir suffitient Copper and beads to maytayne hir and the child while it is younge and then [it] is taken from hir and mayntayned by y⁰ Kings charge, it now beinge lawfull for hir beinge put away to marry with any other, The Kinge Poetan hauinge many wiues when he goeth a Huntinge or to visitt another Kinge vnder him (for he goeth not out of his owne cuntry), He leaueth them with tow ould men who haue the charge on them till his returne. (Smith, John, Arber ed., 1884, pp. cvii–cviii.)

According to Strachey, Powhatan had more than a hundred wives and he supplies us with the names of twelve of the most favored. Of marriages in general he says:

They expresse their loves to such women as they would make choise to live withall, by presenting them with the fruicts of their labours, as by fowle, fish, or wild beasts, which by their huntings, their bowes and arrowes, by weeres, or otherwise, they obteyne, which they bring unto the young women, as also of such somer fruicts and berries which their travells abroad hath made them knowe readely where to gather, and those of the best kind in their season. Yf the young mayden become once to be *sororians virgo*, (i.e. arrived at puberty), and live under parents, the parents must allow of the sutor; and for their good wills, the woer promiseth that the daughter shall not want of such provisions, nor of deare skynns fitly drest for to weare; besides he promiseth to doe his endeavour to procure her beades, perle, and copper, and for handsell gives her before them something as a kind of *arrasponsalitia* (earnest money in ratification of the espousal), token of betroathing or contract of a further amity and acquaintance to be contynued betweene them, as so after as the likeing growes; and as soone as he hath provided her a house (if he have none before) and some platters, morters, and matts, he takes her home; and the weroances after this manner maye have as many as they can obteyne, howbeyt all the rest whome they take after their first choise are (as yt were) mercynary, hired but by covenant and condicion, for a tyme, a yeare or soe, after which they may putt them awaye; but if they keepe them longer then the tyme appointed, they must ever keepe them, how deformed, diseased, or unaccompaniable soever they may prove. (Strachey, 1849, pp. 109–110.)

He gives as "the reason whie each chief patron of a familie, especially weroances, are desirous, and indeed strive for manie wives, is, because they would have manie children, who maie, if chaunce be, fight for them when they are old, as also then feed and mayntein them" (p. 114), but from observed conditions in Virginia he doubts the success of polygyny in furthering this object.

In succession to the chieftainship Algonquians preferred the female side to the male side though there is no evidence of a totemic system, and from the above it appears that the residence was patrilocal.

Lawson, whose information was drawn particularly from the Siouan peoples, states that unmarried girls were free to bestow their favors on whomsoever they chose and he adds that they generally chose to exact payment for the same. There was also a regular class of prostitutes, distinguished by the cut of their hair, whose activities were a matter of concern to their families or, in case of relations with men of other tribes or white traders, to the chief of the town himself. This commercialization of sex was of a piece with the general commercial tendencies in the region. Marriages, like temporary relations, were debated by the kindred on both sides and sometimes by the head men and chiefs, but the woman's consent was necessary. Property was paid for the wife as well as for the temporary companion, and wives were passed from hand to hand freely on payment of the original purchase price. In cases of adultery the man alone was punished and the second husband or lover of a widow might be called upon to pay all of her first husband's debts. A man might marry two sisters, and he was expected to espouse the widow of his brother, but incest was punished severely, and sodomy is said to have been unknown. Divorce appears to have been fairly common, the children going with the mother. Among the northern Siouan tribes at least there were tribal subdivisions similar to clans (Lawson, 1860, pp. 299–307).

Creek girls had the same freedom to dispose of their bodies as they saw fit, previous to marriage, as did those of the Siouan tribes, and they usually did so to their pecuniary advantage. There was also a class of prostitutes consisting of adulteresses repudiated by their husbands or of outcasts who indicated their calling by a peculiar manner of painting the face. Temporary alliances were often contracted with such women by the men. Marriage itself, however, was a very serious affair, in which the woman was "bound" to her husband by a payment to the relatives of the bride and also by presents to her and by assistance given her in taking care of her cornfields. According to some this had to be done annually, especially where a man had taken a number of wives who were living in different places and whom he did not visit often. An offer of marriage seems to have emanated sometimes from a youth, sometimes from the people of the youth's clan, and sometimes from the people of the girl's clan. The father and his people had nothing to do with it. Certain writers inform us that the couple themselves were not consulted, but opportunities for vetoing the arrangements of the elders were probably not wanting. In fact Hitchcock states that at an appointed time a bowl of sofki was placed under the projecting eaves of the corncrib and that if the youth was allowed to steal up and take a spoonful of this it was a sign that he was accepted, whereas the girl might not permit it. Bartram mentions the exchange of reeds such as they used in the corn hills as symbols of marriage, and we also hear of an ear of corn being divided by the two and of venison being given to the woman by her intended husband and an ear of corn to him by his intended wife. Hawkins says that

when a man has built a house, made his crop, and gathered it in, then made his hunt and brought home the meat, and put all this in the possession of his wife, the ceremony ends, and they are married; or as they express it, the woman is bound. (Hawkins, 1848, p. 73.)

The youth made his first visit to his wife late at night, left very early, and spoke little to any of his wife's family for a month. After the succeeding busk their union was considered established. Claiborne says that either of them could leave the other at that time. Having passed it, according to Stiggins, the woman is regarded by her husband's family as bound to him "for life or his pleasure." This would appear at variance with what has been said regarding the necessity for repeated presents, but these last seem to have been made most often to retain the later and subordinate wives, testifying that their husband still retained an interest in and authority over them. These wives could be added only with the consent of the first wife, and if he married another without her consent she and the people of her family had the right to fall upon him and his new wife, beat them unmercifully and cut off their ears, in other words treat them as adulterers. Except by consent of the first wife, none of the others might stay in her house. Punishment for adultery was very severe and will be treated when we come to consider crime and punishment. As has been said, divorce might take place at the time of the first busk after marriage, but it was unusual if there were children, and presumably if there were immediate prospects of any. It might also occur in consequence of the husband having taken a second wife without his first wife's consent, in the manner above indicated. Under such circumstances husband and wife separated, the former being compelled to live with his new wife, while the latter had to remain single for 4 years under penalty of being treated as an adulteress. There was the same prescription regarding a widow, who was forced to remain in the house most of the time in unkempt clothing and with dissheveled hair and to avoid festivities of any kind until the 4 years were past. She was, indeed, under suspicion all that time unless she was very careful, and it is said that a man who should wade into water upstream from her or ask her for a drink of water from a pitcher might be accused of adultery. She was under the particular surveillance of her deceased husband's sister and the latter might take pity on her by giving her in marriage to another brother. Probably the Creek and Chickasaw customs were the same in this particular, and Adair avers that if the deceased husband's elder brother took the widow or even lay with her one night, she was freed from the penalty of her widowhood. Stiggins says that any of the brothers could relieve her by taking her in marriage, or the clan of her husband might shorten the period voluntarily. At the end of the 4 years, in any case, she was formally released. Sometimes a man was offered her from the clan of her former husband and she was at liberty to accept or refuse him. In either case the claims of her husband's clan were satisfied and they had no more control of her. The regulations governing the behavior of a widower were almost the same except that he was allowed to remarry in 4 months time. In all this the clan claim to the woman or the man is apparent but the right was evidently based on a thought of the woman or man as property which the clan had acquired. No idea of collective marriage is involved. Prohibition of speech between mother-in-law and son-in-law, "mother-in-law avoidance," was well developed. A man and woman guilty of adultery who could elude pursuit until after the next succeeding busk were free from punishment. Complaints of indolence, a quarrelsome disposition, inattention, and disobedience on the part of a wife are given by Stiggins as additional grounds for divorce. Bossu says that in cases of adultery, the man was free to remarry immediately but the woman only after the expiration of a year. However, elopement and escape until the next busk would shorten this term. On separation of a couple with children, the mother took the children but the father contributed to their support. Child betrothal existed, at least in the case of a man who already had adult wives (Swanton, 1928, pp. 368–384).

We have no account of marriage customs among the Timucua, except in the ceremonial by which a woman was united to a chief (pl. 85), but we know that certain ceremonies were undergone by widows, and they are represented by Le Moyne as coming to the chief weeping to induce him to revenge their loss (Le Moyne, 1875, pp. 13–14, 37–38; Swanton, 1922, p. 372).

Chickasaw customs seem to have resembled those of the Creeks very closely. Child betrothals and temporary unions are noted. The prospective groom sent a bundle of clothing to the parents of his intended. If they accepted the offer, they handed it to the girl herself, and her acceptance paved the way for the final ceremonies. Adair mentions a more direct address on the part of a would-be husband.

When an Indian makes his first address to the young woman he intends to marry, she is obliged by ancient custom to sit by him until he is done eating and drinking, whether she likes or dislikes him; but afterward, she is at her own choice whether to stay or retire.

He says that the groom might divide two ears of corn before witnesses and give the girl one, retaining the other himself, or give her a deer's foot for which she returns some cakes of bread. Another writer notes that the groom gave venison and received corn or potatoes. Immediately before the consummation of the marriage the youth and the girl's father took a meal together with no one else present. A deer was also killed and laid at the woman's door, and when she had dressed and cooked this and given the youth some to eat, they were regarded as husband and wife. Chiefs commonly celebrated their marriages with a feast, being assisted by the husband's kinsmen in slaughtering deer and bison for the occasion. As with the Creeks, they brought meat to the houses of their several subordinate wives in order to keep them bound (Swanton, 1928 c, pp. 225–228).

Choctaw customs in general differed considerably from both those of the Creeks and those of the Chickasaw and it may be assumed that their marriage rites also embraced certain peculiarities, but our information regarding Choctaw customs of the earlier period is unfortunately scanty. Romans merely remarks that

they take wives without much ceremony, and live together during pleasure, and after separation, which is not very frequent, they often leave the second to retake the first wife.

A somewhat earlier French writer states that the prospective husband made presents to the father and mother of his intended, led the latter home, and afterward must be careful to avoid meeting or having anything to do with his mother-in-law. He says that divorce was easy and polygyny in vogue, but it is evident that they usually married in the same family group whether several wives were espoused or a wife was to replace one who was deceased. He had direct knowledge of a case where a man had married three sisters. But even at that time it is evident that the actual procedure was much more complicated, and we learn something of this from writers in the early part of the nineteenth century. According to these, the youth first established an affirmative standing in the eyes of his intended bride, but Claiborne was told that the woman often made the first approach, especially a widow whose property frequently proved attractive to young men with more looks than energy. After satisfying himself that he might take up the question of marriage formally, the prospective husband or his mother or some other near relative approached the uncle, mother, or other responsible guardian of the girl. A present of cloth was made to the girl's mother which she divided up and distributed among her female relatives, at the same time suggesting what part of the marriage feast she expected each to provide. Just before the marriage ritual the girl was pursued and caught in a ceremonial race by her intended, each assisted by the respective relatives, and this gave the woman an opportunity to change her mind if she so desired. Usually, however, she allowed herself to be caught after an exhibition of formal reluctance, and was seated on the ground with her intended groom near at hand. The friends of the latter now brought property and laid it upon the girl's head, from which it was immediately snatched by her over-eager female relatives. According to one informant, there was a property contest between the families, one placing property on the head of the girl, the other on that of the man. Symbolic acts consisting in the deposit of a bag of bread near the girl and a bag of meat near the man were also performed. The male, and sometimes female, relatives of the bride now approached the groom and called him by the new term of relationship created between them, after which they did the same to his male relatives. Now followed the wedding feast in which it is sometimes said that each side feasted the other. At this time the chief formerly made a long speech in which he instructed the young people regarding their duties and managed to admonish the youths of the tribe generally on the side. Anciently, weddings were arranged in the afternoon, so that the feast would follow and all be concluded by an all-night dance. It was customary for a man, on the death of his first wife, to espouse one of her sisters, or he might espouse one or more of them at the same time. Polygynous marriages, either with several sisters, or with unrelated women, were fairly common. We are told that several wives who were sisters might live in the same yard but not in the same house, but those who were not sisters would not live even in the same yard. Divorce was easy, the children going with the mother. Marriage with too close relatives was opposed and it was claimed as a reason that if they married persons already connected by blood, they would not know how to name their relatives. Mother-in-law avoidance was practiced to the same extent as by the Creeks and Chickasaw, and a woman would not mention her husband by name but would designate him by the name of their child or as the father of their son or daughter. As we have seen, there were two exogamous moieties in the Choctaw nation and in general within those moieties residence was matrilocal (Swanton, 1931 a, pp. 127-138).

If we may trust our authorities, Natchez girls were not only allowed sexual freedom before marriage but encouraged in the exercise of it. On the other hand, it is said that infidelity after marriage was uncommon, divorce rare and repudiation of the wife not allowed after a child was born. Wives were, however, often lent to friends by their husbands. As elsewhere, the sororate was in vogue and polygamy fairly widespread, being apparently especially common among the chiefs. Chiefs married with less ceremony than commoners, but this was because the peculiar Natchez social system compelled the chiefs, and the women of the nobility as well, to take their spouses from the common people, in considerable measure because wives and husbands of the upper class were killed on the death of those to whom they had been united. One of our authorities states that when there were several wives, the one who bore a child first took precedence over the others. In marriages among commoners, Le Petit tells us that the prospective groom first approached the father or brother of his intended. Du Pratz states that marriages were arranged by the chiefs of the two families, who were sometimes old enough to be great-grandparents, and that during the ceremony the groom held a bow and arrows in his hand and the bride held a laurel branch and an ear of corn. Le Petit states that there was a marriage feast at which the pair ate out of the same dish, and they lived with the parents of the groom until a new house could be built. Cohabitation did not take place during certain phases of the moon. In the material available there is no reference to mother-in-law avoidance, but, as in so many other tribes, there was a class of male prostitutes or berdaches (Swanton, 1911, pp. 94–100).

Caddo girls enjoyed the same premarital freedom we have noted elsewhere, and after marriage we are told that they frequently abandoned one husband for another, if they thought he would give them more advantages. Some Caddo tribes are said to have been polygamous, while in others the wife would not knowingly tolerate a rival, and if she discovered that her husband had taken up with a woman living at some distance, she would abandon him.

If a man fancied a woman whom he knew to be a maiden, he would take to her some of the best things he had. If her parents allowed her to accept the gift, this was an assent to the marriage, but he could not take her along with him until the caddi (chief) was first informed. If the woman was not a maiden, all that was necessary was for the man to say, "Will you be my friend? I will give you ——;" whatever he desired to offer. If his offer pleased her, she went with him. Sometimes the offer was made only for a few days, sometimes it was stated it was to last forever. "But they never kept their word," nor were there any penalties attached to unfaithfulness.

However,

in the xinesi (priestly) and caddi families and those of the officers there was seldom anything of this, because no one dared to give the two first named an affront, as it was punishable with death, and the officers, who were accounted nobles, tried to imitate their superiors, and so set a good example to the rest of the tribe. The wives of the xinesi and caddis were called by one common name—Aquidau. That marked their station immediately, for all the other women had each her individual name.

Like the women of the Timucua, Caddo women were accustomed to weep before the chief in order to get him to avenge them on enemies of the tribe (Margry, 1875–86, vol. 3, p. 363; Swanton 1942, pp. 160–162).

CUSTOMS RELATING TO BIRTH, EDUCATION, AND THE DIVISION OF LABOR BETWEEN THE SEXES

Strachey supplies us the following regarding Powhatan customs:

The women are said to be easily delivered of child; yet do they love childrene very dearly. To make the children hardye, in the coldest mornings they wash them in the rivers, and by paintings and oyntements so tanne their skynns that, after a yeare or twoo no weather will hurt them; as also, to practize their children in the use of ther bowes and arrowes, the mothers doe not give them their breakfast in the morning before they have hitt a marke which she appoints them to shoot at: and comonly so cunning they will have them, as throwing up in the ayre a piece of mosse, or some such light thinge, the boy must with his arrowe meete yt in the fall, and hit it, or ells he shall not have his breckfast. (Strachey, 1849, pp. 110–111.)

Later in life some children were subjected to a strange hardening ceremony called by Beverley and Lawson the huskanaw. Strachey's description of this parallels Smith's but seems to be somewhat more intimate:

In some part of the country they have yerely a sacrifice of children; such a one was at Quiyoughcohanock, some ten miles from James Towne, as also at Kecoughtan, which Capt. Georg Percy was at, and observed. The manner of it was, fifteene of the properest yonge boyes, betweene ten and fifteene yeares of age, they paynted white; having brought them forth, the people spent the forenone in dauncing and singing about them with rattles. In the afternoone they solemly led those childrene to a certayne tree appointed for the same purpose; at the roote whereof, round about, they made the childrene to sitt downe, and by them stood the most and ablest of the men, and some of them the fathers of the childrene, as a watchfull guard, every one having a bastinado in his hand of reedes, and these opened a lane betweene all along, through which were appointed five young men to fetch those childrene; and accordingly every one of the five tooke his turne and passed through the guard to fetch a child, the guard fiercely beating them the while with their bastinadoes, and shewing much anger and displeasure to have the children so ravisht from them; all which the young men pacyently endured, receaving the blowes and defending the children, with their naked bodies, from the unmersifull stroakes, that paid them soundly, though the children escaped. All the while sate the mothers and kinswomen afar off, looking on, weeping and crying out very passionately, and some, in pretty waymenting tunes, singing (as yt were) their dirge or funeral song, provided with matts, skynnes, mosse, and dry wood by them, as things fitting their children's funeralls. After the childrene were thus forceably taken from the guard, the guard possessed (as yt were) with a vyolent fury, entred uppon the tree and tore yt downe, bowes and braunches, with such a terrible fierceness and strength, that they rent the very body of yt, and shivered yt in a hundred peeces, whereof some of them made them garlandes for their heads, and some stuck of the braunches and leaves in their haire, wreathinge them in the same, and so went up and downe as mourners, with heavy and sad downcast lookes. What ells was done with the childrene might not be seene by our people, further then that they were all cast on a heape in a valleye, where was made a great and solemne feast for all the companye; at the going whereunto, the night now approaching, the Indians desired our people that they would withdraw themselves and leave them to their further proceedings, the which they did: only some of the weroances being demanded the meaning of this sacrifice, made answeare, that the childrene did not all of them suffer death, but that the okeus did suck the blood from the leaft breast of the child whose chaunce it was to be his by lott, till he was dead, and the remaine were kept in the wilderness by the said young men till nine moones were expired, during which tyme they must not converse with any; and of these were made the priests and conjurers, to be instructed by tradition from the elder priests. These sacrifices, or catharmata, they hold to be so necessary, that if they should omitt them they suppose this okeus, and all the other quioughcosughes, which are their other gods, would let them no deare, turkies, corne, nor fish, and yet besides he would make a great slaughter amongst them. (Strachey, 1849, pp. 94–96.)

Powhatan women, except those of the upper class who were treated with much ceremony and waited upon by servants, did pretty much all the work except hunting, fishing, conducting ceremonies, and going to war. Women prepared food and cooked; planted and gathered in the corn; dressed skins; made mats, baskets, pots, and mortars; and bore all kind of burdens. Though no exception is made by our authorities, and Spelman is quite emphatic on this point, it is probable that some of the care of the fields was performed by men, at least the older ones, and by slaves, and it is possible that a mistake has been made in including the manufacture of mortars among feminine industries since it was elsewhere a male occupation. To male occupations should almost certainly be added the manufacture of all implements of war, the chase, fishing, and participation in ball games though we have no mention of these, and such heavy work as the erection of houses, the felling of trees, and the hollowing out of canoes (Smith, John, Tyler ed., 1907, pp. 111–112; Arber ed., 1884, p. cxii).

The following paragraphs are again from Strachey:

The men fish, hunt, fowle, goe to the warrs, make the weeres, botes, and such like manly exercises and all laboures abroad. The women, as the weaker sort, be put to the easier workes, to sow their corne, to weed and cleanse the same of the orabauke, dodder, and choak weed, and such like, which ells would wynd about the corne and hinder the growth of yt; for, by reason of the rankness and lustines of the grownd, such weedes spring up very easely and thick, and if not pluckt awaie, the corn would prosper so much the worse; for which they keepe the hillocks of theire corne, and the passadg between (for they sett their wheat as we doe our hoppes, an equal distance one hill from another) as neat and cleane as we doe our gardein bedds: likewise the women plant and attend the gardeins, dresse the meate brought home, make their broaths and pockerchicory drinckes, make matts and basketts, pownd their wheat, make their bread, prepare their vessels, beare all kindes of burthens, and such like, and to which the children sett their handes, helping their mothers.

There are notes to be taken by which may be discerned a marryed woman from a mayd: the maydes have the forepart of their heads and sides shaven close, the hinder part very long, which they wynd very prettely and ymbroyder in playtes, letting yt hang so to the full length: the marryed women weare their haire all of a length, shaven as the Irish by a dish.

The women have a great care to maynteyne and keepe fier light still within their howses, and at any time it go out, they take yt for an evil sign, but if yt be out they kindle yt againe presently. (Strachey, 1849, pp. 111–112.)

Spelman says:

They sett on matts round about yᵉ howse yᵉ men by them selues and yᵉ weomen by ther selues yᵉ weomen brings to euery one a dish of meat for the better sort neuer eates togither in one dish, when he hath eaten what he will, or that which was giuen him, for he looks for no second corse he setts doune his dish by him and mumbleth ceartayne words to himself in maner of giuinge thankes, if any leaft yᵉ weomen gather it up & ether keeps it till yᵉ next meall, or gives it to yᵉ porer sort, if any be ther. (Smith, John, Arber ed., 1884, p. cxiii.)

One of White's noted drawings entitled "their sitting at meate" would thus be erroneous unless we suppose, as is probably the case, that it represents an Indian in the inner privacy of his family life.

Lawson states of the Siouan Indians and their neighbors that he never heard of a barren woman among them, that childbirth was easy, and that women sometimes brought their children into the world alone, though it is evident that that was unusual, there being a class of midwives among them. As soon as the child was born, its mother washed it in a stream and daubed it with bear grease from which it appears not to have escaped during its natural life. The mother remained away from men for 40 days and, unless she became pregnant again, nursed her child until it was well grown. The husband made a cradle out of a single piece of board on which the child was tied flat, and the deformation of the head was produced at that time. Children were rarely corrected, and Lawson tells us that he knew of but one exception to this rule. In cases of divorce, the custodianship of the children devolved entirely upon their mother. During menstrual periods women quit all company and did not even dress their own food. Women beat corn in mortars, cooked, made mats, baskets, girdles of opossum hair, and pots, and carried along grain and other provisions on a hunt besides providing firewood. They evidently did most of the cultivation of the soil, but Lawson says that they never planted corn "like the Iroquois women." Men pursued about the same occupations as they did among the Algonquians and other tribes. The poorer hunters among them made wooden bowls, dishes, spoons and clay pipes, and they and the slaves dressed skins in summer (Lawson, 1860, pp. 308–310, 326).

Lawson notes two, Machapunga families which had the custom of circumcision (Lawson, 1860, p. 341).

Here is his account of the huskanaw:

There is one most abominable custom amongst them, which they call husque-nawing their young men, which I have not made any mention of as yet, so will give you an account of it here. You must know, that most commonly, once a year, at farthest, once in two years, these people take up so many of their young men, as they think are able to undergo it, and husquenaugh them, which is to make them obedient and respective to their superiors, and, as they say, is the same to them as it is to us to send our children to school, to be taught good breed-ing and letters. This house of correction is a large, strong cabin, made on purpose for the reception of the young men and boys, that have not passed the graduation already; and it is always at christmas that they husquenaugh their youth, which is by bringing them into this house and keeping them dark all the time, where they more than half starve them. Besides, they give the pellitory bark, and several intoxicating plants, that make them go raving mad as ever were any people in the world; and you may hear them make the most dismal and hellish cries and howlings that ever human creatures expressed; all which continues about five or six weeks, and the little meat they eat, is the nastiest, loathsome stuff, and mixt with all manner of filth it is possible to get. After the time is expired, they are brought out of the cabin, which never is in the town, but always a distance off, and guarded by a jailor or two, who watch by turn. Now when they first come out, they are as poor as ever any creatures were; for you must know several die under the diabolical purgation. Moreover, they either really are, or pretend to be dumb, and do not speak for several days; I think, twenty or thirty, and look so ghastly, and are so changed, that it is next to an impossibility to know them again, although you were never so well acquainted with them before. I would fain have gone into the mad house, and have seen them in their time of purgatory, but the king would not suffer it, because, he told me they would do me or any other white man an injury, that ventured in amongst them, so I desisted. They play this prank with girls as well as boys, and I believe it a miserable life they endure, because I have known several of them run away at that time to avoid it. Now the savages say if it were not for this, they could never keep their youth in subjection, besides that it hardens them ever after to the fatigues of war, hunting, and all manner of hardship, which their way of living exposes them to. Beside, they add, that it carries off those infirm weak bodies, that would have been only a burden and disgrace to their nation, and saves the victuals and clothing for better people that would have been ex-pended on such useless creatures. (Lawson, 1860, pp. 380–382.)

But alas for this aboriginal experiment in eugenics! The Algon-quian and Siouan tribes who attempted it are extinct or carry on in small mixed-blood fragments and the Tuscarora are by no means distinguished above the descendants of the non-huskanawing tribes.

Catesby has the following on childbirth including an account of the native cradle, which has been quoted (p. 562):

Indian women by their field as well as by domestick imployment, acquire a healthy constitution, which contributes no doubt to their easy travail in child-bearing, which is often alone in the woods; after two or three days have con-firmed their recovery, they follow their usual affairs, as well without as within doors: the first thing they do after the birth of a child, is to dip, and wash it in the nearest spring of cold water, and then daub it all over with bear's oil; the father then prepares a singular kind of cradle, which consists of a flat board about two foot long, and one broad, to which they brace the child close, cutting a hole against the child's breech for its excrements to pass through; a leather strap is tied from one corner of the board to the other, whereby the mother flings her child on her back, with the child's back towards hers; at other times they hang them against the walls of their houses, or to the boughs of trees; by these, and other conveniences, these portable cradles are adapted to the use of *Indians;* and I can't tell why they may not as well to us, if they were introduced here. They cause a singular erectness in the *Indians,* nor did I ever see a crooked *Indian* in my life. (Catesby, 1731–43, vol. 2, p. xv.)

White's drawing of a "ladye" of the town of Dasemonquepeuc in the Algonquian country of North Carolina carrying a child represents evidently the method in use after the child had been released from the cradle (pl. 10 in De Bry).

Little is known specifically regarding Timucua customs. We are merely told that women did all the work about the house, and planted the fields. Preparation of the ground, however, was a male duty. The male concubines or berdaches relieved women of much of their labor. They carried provisions for a war party, undertook the burial of the dead, and removed those who had contagious diseases to special places where they could be taken care of. The Guale Indians of St. Simons Island were probably related to the Muskogee and Hitchiti, but they were near neighbors of the Timucua, and the following incident may here be inserted. After the monk San Miguel and his companions had reached a town belonging to these people, they spent the night under a tree, and

the day following, as soon as it was day many Indian boys came to the sloop, and all, though they were very small, had bows and arrows proportioned to their size and stature, and all these began shooting into the top of the tree where we had slept, chattering merrily to one another, without our understanding them or understanding why they were shooting there, when we saw falling from the tree a little snake, its small head pierced by an arrow, and one of those boys came proudly and lifting on his arrow the pierced snake, showed it to us joyfully as the conqueror and more skilful than the rest. (Swanton, 1922, p. 373; Garcia, 1902, p. 193.)

During the menstrual periods and for some time after the birth of her child, a woman did not eat fish or venison. It was also considered wrong for her to anoint herself with bear grease or to eat fish for a number of moons after having given birth. Both at that time and at the menstrual period she must not make a new fire or approach one.

Timberlake says that a Cherokee child was usually born without extraneous help and forthwith dipped into water, the dipping being repeated every morning for 2 years. Probably by the absence of help he means absence of a doctor, for Olbrechts reports that in modern times there must be four women present at a birth and that a doctor was summoned only when some difficulty was anticipated.

He says that as soon as a woman discovered she was pregnant she informed her husband and the news was quickly communicated to the whole settlement. She was subjected to many taboos, the most important of which was that she was taken to water to pray and bathe every new moon, for at least 3 months before the delivery. A priest and her husband, mother, or some other near relative accompanied her, and the priest dipped some water out and placed it upon the crown of her head, her breast, and sometimes her face, and prognosticated the future fate of the child by conjuring with certain white and red beads. Anciently, a separate house was built for the woman during that period. The placenta was buried on the farther side of two ridges of mountains by the father or nearest relative. There is now no cradle, but when the child is 3 or 4 weeks old it is carried about astride of its mother's back. At the age of 4 or 5, boys come under the supervision of their fathers or elder brothers and learn to handle bows and arrows, while girls help their mothers and older sisters. They learn their own culture rapidly and play games in which the activities of their elders are imitated. A child may be raised to become a wizard and such a career is particularly marked out for twins. Such a child is kept secluded during the first 24 days of its life something after the manner of the seclusion of the Iroquois child. Meanwhile it is not allowed to taste its mother's milk but given instead the liquid portion of corn hominy. While such children are growing up they are often supposed to go away and talk with the "Little People," a race of dwarfs believed in by nearly all southern Indians (Timberlake, Williams ed., 1927, p. 90; Mooney, 1932, pp. 116–130).

At the time of her monthly periods and after the birth of a child a Creek woman lived in a house by herself for 4 days. She had separate dishes and other utensils which were kept for these occasions. Afterward she must bathe and change her clothes. Speck was told that she could not prepare her husband's meals for a month. Swan says that the woman was entirely alone at childbirth, but this was certainly unusual. She was generally assisted by her mother or some other old woman or women. The newborn child was immediately plunged into cold water, and thereafter every morning during the rest of its life it was supposed to take a bath in running water before eating, though in cold weather women and children were let off with a slight sprinkling. Infants of unmarried mothers were sometimes killed, and a woman is known to have killed her child for spite, but generally speaking children were desired by both sexes. A child was sometimes kept from nursing for 4 days and not taken out of the house for 4 months, so that it might live long. It was believed that the younger of twin brothers would probably become a great prophet. Certain small roots were also given to it. There were cradle songs in use. In its early years the principal care of the child fell naturally upon its mother, who never struck it, particularly if it was a male, but scratched it with a pin, a needle, or gar teeth to deter it from wrong doing and also to harden it. If scratching was resorted to as a punishment, the skin was scratched dry, otherwise only after it had been soaked in water. The girls remained under the tutelage of their mother and her clan sisters, but the boys were taken in hand by the oldest uncle of the clan or clan group, who maintained a general oversight of the education of all the young men. He admonished them, lectured them at the time of the busk or other gatherings, and at times resorted to flagellation, in which Bossu says that a carrying-strap was used, but canes were also employed. Menial offices were exacted of those who had not taken part in a war expedition and thereby acquired war honors and a war name. War honors were also bestowed upon one who performed the hazardous task of securing eagle feathers, and in later times on one who killed many deer. There were regular courses of instruction for prospective medicine men under the supervision of old doctors experienced in the science and practice of the profession. These men were also keepers of the sacred lore of the tribe and war leaders are said to have been chosen from among them, for all do not seem to have confined their attention to medical practice as we understand the term. A careful separation of men from women was maintained in the houses and at ceremonials. Women made pottery, baskets, mats, spun and wove mulberry bark, grasses, bison and opossum hair, dried and cooked food, did most of the work of preparing skins and making clothing, pounded corn, gathered nuts and acorns and extracted oil from them, shared with the men the cultivation of the town fields and did all of the work on the individual house lots, cut and brought in firewood, sometimes from long distances, though they were often helped in this by the old men, and Romans says that they had most to do with the preparation of the black drink, though this seems doubtful. Besides contributing to the care of the town fields, men hunted, fished, warred, played in the great ball games, led in the ceremonies, built houses, corncribs, and Square Ground structures, felled trees, hollowed out canoes and mortars, made drums, pipes, calumets, ball sticks, axes, arrows, bows, and war clubs, and cut up and brought back meat when game had been killed at a distance from home (Swanton, 1928, pp. 358–367, 384–387).

Chickasaw customs were very similar to those of the Creeks. They also had menstrual huts into which the women retired every month and when they were about to be delivered. Before returning to the house they always bathed. A prospective mother could not leave this hut until after her child was born, and while she was pregnant her husband remained aloof from all gatherings. She remained away from the rest of the family for some time after delivery—Speck says 2 months—and ate no fresh meat, while her husband abstained from work for about a month and was avoided by other men. Twins were considered supernatural, though favorable, manifestations of the higher powers, but children were allowed to eat nothing of a double nature. Children were nursed for a long time, and boys were laid upon panther skins while girls were laid down upon skins of fawns or bison calves. They were not allowed to sleep with old people, and boys were never whipped by their own parents but corrected by an old man, probably the oldest uncle of the clan or family group, who, as with the Creeks, was much venerated. Adair reports one such case of whipping from personal observation. Besides being forced to plunge into water at the coldest season, boys were given herbs to make them strong. Children were often affianced in childhood but were not married till they were fairly mature. In infancy the head of a Chickasaw child was flattened by means of a block of wood covered with buckskin or a bag of sand fastened tight over the forehead. Labor was divided between the sexes almost exactly as among the Creeks. To cultivate the corn and gather nuts, they frequently had to go 2 or 3 miles from home (Swanton, 1928 c, pp. 220–221, 228).

The women of the Choctaw, like those of the Creeks and Chickasaw, retired to a small cabin apart every month and when they were about to give birth to a child. While his wife was in travail a man took food only after sunset, and if a girl was born, he continued this 8 days longer. He also abstained from pork and salt. The woman herself also had to submit to many taboos. One of our early informants states that the woman in childbed had no assistance, but in later times at least there was an old woman to help her. An eelskin was tied about her belly to keep it from protruding. Right after birth the child was washed, and it was placed in the cradle with a bag of earth or sand tied over the forehead to flatten it. Weaning is said to have taken place at the pleasure of the child, and after it was removed from the cradle it was made to sleep straight out with its head to the east. Very young children were not allowed to carry anything heavy. Adoption of children was common. The mother was not permitted to strike her boys but they were sometimes scratched with nettles, presumably by the oldest, or rather the ablest, maternal uncle who was their teacher. They were assembled morning and evening to listen to the legends of their people, learned to handle the bow and arrow early in life, and engaged in archery contests in which the best shot was suitably rewarded. They often roamed through the woods shooting birds and squirrels, and we are told that they used to test one another's endurance by stirring up yellow jackets and seeing who could withstand their stings longest. They were allowed to torture dogs and wild animals with their blowguns. Later they learned to wrestle, run, throw and lift weights, and play ball, and the chunkey game. We are told specifically that the men hunted, warred, engaged in official tasks, in games, in races, in jumping and wrestling, built houses, made wooden and stone implements, and helped their women in the fields. Women did most of the farm work and went for water and firewood. The other tasks of both sexes were probably much like those of the Chickasaw, but they remained at home a longer time during the year and it is probable that men did more of the farming proportionately. (Swanton, 1931 a, pp. 115–126, 139.)

Immediately after birth a Natchez infant was washed and laid in a cradle made of cane softened with Spanish moss. A pillow of Spanish moss or a plank was placed immediately over the forehead to flatten it. The child is said to have been rocked lengthwise on two pieces of cane. When it was a month old threads of bison hair were tied about the calves and they were worn until the fourteenth or fifteenth year. The child's body was rubbed with bear oil for the express purpose of rendering the sinews supple and keeping off flies. When the child was a little over a year old, it learned to walk, a young girl going along with it and holding it under the armpits. Children could suckle as long as they wanted to unless the mother was again pregnant. They bathed every morning after they had reached the age of three and soon learned to swim. Boys were never beaten it is said, yet this statement may require some revision since they were put under the special charge of an old family patriarch who supervised their education. They were disciplined by means of jests, but this treatment was never pursued so far as to occasion a quarrel, and the boys did not fight one another. At 10 to 12 years of age they carried small burdens. About 12 they were given bows and arrows and practiced shooting at a bunch of grass, receiving praise according to their markmanship, and they engaged in foot races. Later they were allowed to accompany the men on hunts to learn the rules. Those old men who were the custodians of the tribal lore taught it to selected youths. We are told that the men hunted, fished, cut down trees and cut them into firewood, cultivated the sacred fields, went to war, played the major part in games, dressed skins, aided one another in building cabins, made bows and arrows, canoes, mattocks, and paddles. The women pounded corn into flour and cooked, brought in the firewood and fed the fires, made pottery, baskets, mats, and clothes, and undertook all the beadwork, besides assuming the major burden in caring for the crops. Men always had precedence over women and were fed first (Swanton, 1911, pp. 86–90).

Dumont de Montigny ridicules the formality ascribed to Indian education by Du Pratz. He says:

I will merely state here in passing that no trust must be given in what that author (Le Page du Pratz) has written regarding the education which the natives of Louisiana give their children, and that what he says is false to the effect that in each village there is an old man whose duty it is to educate the boys and an old woman who takes care of the girls. As long as I have lived among these savage nations, I avow that I have never seen anything like it. Each Indian woman brings up her children as she desires, and as she considers right. Or rather, they are not given any education. And one sees children six to seven years old who are still nursed by their mothers. They always go with bare heads in spite of the most intense heat, and although they bathe very often in the midst of the roughest winter as well as in summer, they are not thereby neater or less full of vermin. The manner in which the mothers clean themselves is more disgusting still than the filth itself. When one says that among these savages the young people are only given the occupation of drawing the bow, and that they are never assigned any painful work for fear of wearying them, he is doubtless less concerned with the instruction of the public than recounting marvels and following in the footsteps of Xenophon in his imaginary relations of the advantageous education given young people among the Persians. As for me who have never known how to varnish the truth, I can inform my readers that from the time the Indian boys are nine or ten, their commonest occupation is to accompany their fathers to the hunt or in fishing, and to bring back afterward burdens I could carry with difficulty myself. Nor are the girls spared any more. From this age onward they are employed in crushing grain, in carrying hampers of grain or fruit, and in many other painful duties proper to their sex.

Moreover, the industry of these Indian girls and women is admirable. I have noted elsewhere with what skill, with their fingers only and without a wheel, they make all kinds of pottery. (Dumont, 1753, vol. 1, pp. 269–271.)

We know, however, that the young people of every Creek clan or clan association were disciplined by the most respected male member of it, and Adair tells us the same of the Chickasaw. That there was a corresponding old woman to instruct the girls is not so certain but Du Pratz says little about this personage. For the most part the differences between Dumont and Du Pratz are differences in points of view.

Caddo usages are described in Bureau of American Ethnology Bulletin 132 (Swanton, 1942, pp. 159–160 and 162–163).

BURIAL CUSTOMS

Among the Powhatan Indians, says Smith,

for their ordinary burials, they digge a deep hole in the earth with sharpe stakes, and the corp[s]es being lapped in skins and mats with their jewels, they lay them upon sticks in the ground, and so cover them with earth. The burial ended, the women being painted all their faces with black cole and oile, doe sit 24 howers in the houses mourning and lamenting by turnes, with such yelling and howling as may expresse their great passions.

But the bodies of chiefs were placed upon a raised platform in the temple or ossuary (Smith, John, Tyler ed., 1907, p. 109). The custom was very similar among the Algonquians of Virginia and Carolina. Our earliest account, that by Hariot, is the best:

They builde a Scaffolde 9. or 10. foote highe as is expressed in this figure vnder the tombs of their Weroans, or cheefe lordes which they couer with matts, and lai the dead corpses of their weroans theruppon in manner followinge. First the bowells are taken forthe. Then layinge downe the skinne, they cutt all the flesh cleane from the bones, which they drye in the sonne, and well dryed they inclose in Matts, and place at their feete. Then their bones (remaininge still fastened together with the ligaments whole and vncorrupted) are couered agayne with leather, and their carcase fashioned as yf their flesh wear not taken away. They lapp eache corps in his owne skinne after the same is thus handled, and lay yt in his order by the corpses of the other cheef lordes. By the dead bodies they sett their Idol Kiwasa, whereof we spake in the former chapter: For they are persuaded that the same doth kepe the dead bodyes of their cheefe lordes that nothinge may hurt them. Moreouer vnder the foresaid scaffolde some one of their preists hath his lodginge, which Mumbleth his prayers nighte and day, and hath charge of the corpses. For his bedd he hath two deares skinnes spredd on the grownde, yf the wether bee cold hee maketh a fyre to warme by withall. [pl. 86.] (Hariot, 1893, pl. 22.)

Turning back to the Powhatan Indians, we find the following description by Spelman:

Ther is a scaffould built about 3 or 4 yards hye from the ground and the deade bodye wraped in a matt is brought to the place, wher when he is layd ther on, the kinsfolke falles a weopinge and make great sorrow, and instead of a dole for him, (the poorer people beinge gott togither) sum of his kinsfolke flinges Beades amonge them makinge them to scramble for them, so that many times diuers doe breake their armes and legges beinge pressed by the cumpany, this finished they goe to yᵉ parties house wher they haue meat giuen them which beinge Æten all yᵉ rest of the day they spend in singinge and dauncinge vsinge then as much mirth as before sorrow more ouer if any of yᵉ kindreds bodies which haue bin layd on yᵉ scaffould should be consumed as nothing is leaft but bonns they take thos bonns from yᵉ scaffould and puttinge them into a new matt, hangs them in ther howses, wher they continew while ther house falleth and then they are buried in the ruinges of yᵉ house. What goods the partye leaueth is deuided amonge his wiues and children. But his house he giueth to the wife he liketh best for life: after her death, unto what child be most loueth. (Smith, John, Arber ed., 1884, p. cx.)

Smith says that the bodies of chiefs were buried between mats, and both he and Strachey indicate that the corpses were put upon a raised platform in temples or ossuaries which also contained the images of their deities, to which is added by both Smith and Strachey "images of their kings." Strachey says that a chief's body was hung about with chains of copper, beads, and pearls and that baskets were laid at his feet containing tobacco, his pipe, and any valued things; while the body itself was stuffed with pearls, copper, beads, etc. (Strachey, 1849, p. 89).

As to the burial of the dead among the Siouan tribes, we are wellnigh confined to what Lawson has to tell us, and his remarks may also apply to the Tuscarora:

The burial of their dead is performed with a great deal of ceremony, in which one nation differs in some few circumstances from another, yet not so much but we may, by a general relation, pretty nearly account for them all.

When an Indian is dead the greater person he was, the more expensive is his funeral. The first thing which is done, is to place the nearest relations near the corpse, who mourn and weep very much, having their hair hanging down their shoulders in a very forlorn manner. After the dead person has lain a day and a night in one of their hurdles of canes, commonly in some out house made for that purpose, those that officiate about the funeral go into the town, and the first young men they meet withal, that have blankets or match coats on, whom they think fit for their turn, they strip them from their backs, who suffer them so to do without any resistance. In these they wrap the dead bodies, and cover them with two or three mats which the Indians make of rushes or cane; and, last of all, they have a long robe of woven reeds or hollow canes, which is the coffin of the Indians, and is brought round several times and tied fast at both ends, which, indeed, looks very decent and well. Then the corps is brought out of the house into the orchard of peach trees, where another hurdle is made to receive it, about which comes all the relations and nation that the dead person belonged to, besides several from other nations in alliance with them; all which sit down on the ground upon mats spread there for that purpose; where the doctor or conjurer appears; and, after some time, makes a sort of o-yes [oyez], at which all are very silent, then he begins to give an account who the dead person was, and how stout a man be approved himself; how many enemies and captives he had killed and taken; how strong, tall, and nimble he was; that he was a great hunter; a lover of his country, and possessed of a great many beautiful wives and children, esteemed the greatest of blessings among these savages, in which they have a true notion. Thus this orator runs on, highly extoling the dead man for his valor, conduct, strength, riches, and good humor; and enumerating his guns, slaves, and almost everything he was possessed of when living . . . [after which he turns to the assembly and adjures them to follow in the footsteps of their dead friend and so be assured of the happy land of the dead which he describes and escape the Indian inferno.] . . . After all this harangue he diverts the people with some of their traditions [including their victories in war and so forth]. . . . When this long tale is ended, by him that spoke first; perhaps a second begins another long story; and so a third, and fourth, if there be so many doctors present; which all tell one and the same thing. At last the corps is brought away from that hurdle to the grave by four young men, attended by the relations, the king, old men, and all the nation. When they come to the sepulchre, which is about six feet deep and eight feet long, having at each end, that is, at the head and feet, a lightwood or pitch pine fork driven close down the sides of the grave firmly into the ground; these two forks are to contain a ridge pole, as you shall understand presently, before they lay the corps into the grave, they cover the bottom two or three times over with bark of trees, then they let down the corps with two belts, that the Indians carry their burden withal, very leisurely upon the said bark; then they lay over a pole of the same wood in the two forks, and having a great many pieces of pitch pine logs, about two feet and a half long, they stick them in the sides of the grave down each end and near the top thereof, where the other ends lie on the ridge pole, so that they are declining like the roof of a house. These being very thick placed, they cover them many times double with bark, then they throw the earth thereon that came out of the grave and beat it down very firm; by this means the dead body lies in a vault, nothing touching him; so that when I saw this way of burial I was mightily pleased with it, esteeming it very decent and pretty, as having seen a great many christians buried without the tenth part of that ceremony and decency.   Now when the flesh is rotted and moulded from the bone, they take up the carcass and clean the bones and joint them together; afterwards they dress them up in pure white dressed deer skins, and lay them amongst their grandees and kings in the quiogozon, which is their royal tomb or burial place of their kings and war captains.   This is a very large magnificent cabin, according to their building, which is raised at the public charge of the nation, and maintained in a great deal of form and neatness.   About seven feet high is a floor or loft made, on which lie all their princes and great men that have died for several hundred years, all attired in the dress I before told you of.   No person is to have his bones lie here, and to be thus dressed, unless he gives a round sum of their money to the rulers for admittance.   If they remove never so far, to live in a foreign country, they never fail to take all these dead bones along with them, though the tediousness of their short daily marches keeps them never so long on their journey.   They reverence and adore this quiogozon with all the veneration and respect that is possible for such a people to discharge, and had rather lose all than any violence or injury offered thereto.

These savages differ some small matter in their burials; some burying right upwards, and otherwise, as you are acquainted withal in my journal from South to North Carolina; yet they all agree in their mourning, which is, to appear every night at the sepulchre, and howl and weep in a very dismal manner, having their faces dawbed over with lightwood soot, (which is the same as lampblack) and bear's oil.   This renders them as black as it is possible to make themselves, so that theirs very much resemble the faces of executed men boiled in tar.   If the dead person was a grandee, to carry on the funeral ceremonies, they hire people to cry and lament over the dead man.   Of this sort there are several who practice it for a livelihood, and are very expert at shedding abundance of tears, and howling like wolves, and so discharging their office with abundance of hypocrisy and art.   The women are never accompanied with these ceremonies after death, and to what world they allot that sex, I never understood, unless to wait on their dead husbands: but they have more wit than some of the other eastern nations, who sacrifice themselves to accompany their husbands into the next world.   It is the dead man's relations by blood, as his uncles, brothers, sisters, cousins, sons and daughters, that mourn in good earnest, the wives thinking their duty is discharged, and that they are become free, when their husband is dead; so as fast as they can look out for another to supply his place.   (Lawson, 1860, pp. 293–299.)

He states specifically of the Santee that they "put up a mound for the dead," embalmed the body "with a small root beaten to powder, which looks as red as vermillion," and clothed themselves with moss while mourning (Lawson, 1860, pp. 42–43).   Later he notes a Tuscarora burial conducted like that of the Santee (Lawson, 1860, p. 104).   One case of suicide is alluded to but no hint of the native attitude toward it is given (Lawson, 1860, p. 328).

What appears to have been a reburial custom is mentioned by Peter Martyr in his account of usages in the Duhare province in the present South Carolina (Anghierra, 1912, pp. 260–267; Swanton, 1922, p. 44).

Laudonnière and Le Moyne give almost identical accounts of burial and mourning customs among the Timucua, and I will quote from the former while reproducing Le Moyne's illustration (pl. 87):

When a king dieth, they bury him very solemnly, and, upon his grave they set the cup wherein he was wont to drink; and round about the said grave, they stick many arrows, and weep and fast three days together, without ceasing. All the kings which were his friends make the like mourning; and, in token of the love which they bear him, they cut off more than the one-half of their hair, as well men as women. During the space of six moons (so they reckon their months), there are certain women appointed which bewail the death of this king, crying, with a loud voice, thrice a day—to wit, in the morning, at noon, and at evening. All the goods of this king are put into his house, and, afterwards they set it on fire, so that nothing is ever more after to be seen. The like is done with the goods of the priests; and, besides, they bury the bodies of their priests in their houses, and then set them on fire. (Laudonnière, 1586, pp. 10–11; Swanton, 1922, p. 373; Le Moyne, 1875, p. 15.)

The Tocobaga, a Timucua tribe living about Tampa Bay, had a method of treating the bodies of the dead reminiscent of the Powhatan, Choctaw, and many other tribes:

When one of the principal caciques dies, they cut him to pieces and cook him in large pots during two days, when the flesh has entirely separated from the bones, and adjust one to another until they have formed the skeleton of the man, as he was in life. Then they carry it to a house which they call their temple. This operation lasts four days and during all this time they fast. At the end of the four days, when everything is ready, all the Indians of the town get together and come out with the skeleton in procession, and they bury it with the greatest show and reverence. Then they say that all those who have participated in the ceremonies gain indulgences. (Swanton, 1922, p. 374.)

Of the Calusa we only know that "when the son of a chief dies, each neighbor sacrifices his sons or daughters who have accompanied the dead body," and "when the cacique, or the caciqua, dies, every servant of his or hers, as the case may be, is put to death" (Swanton, 1922, p. 389). The Tekesta had a usage similar to the Tocobaga Indians. When the chief died they disjointed his body and took out the largest bones.

These are placed in a large box and carried to the house of the cacique, where every Indian from the town goes to see and adore them, believing them to be their gods.

They were also in the habit of putting the two large tusks from the head of a manatee in the coffin with the bones of their dead (Swanton, 1922, p. 389).

The place occupied by wailing in the mortuary rites of many of the people of the Southeast has been dwelt upon and is well known, and it is also well known that, in the case of certain tribes such as the

Caddo, wailing had become part of the ritual of greeting. Probably the two were connected, since Mooney was told by Kiowa Indians that they greeted a friend in this manner after a long absence because his coming reminded them of those who had died since his last appearance. A somewhat similar thought was probably behind the wailing observed by San Miguel among both the Muskhogean and the Timucuan Indians of Georgia and Florida. Speaking of the return home of the chief of Asao (St. Simons Island) on the Georgia coast, San Miguel says:

When we [the Spaniards] knew he was approaching the bank, we all went to bid him welcome: the same reception was accorded him by all of his vassals who knew of his coming, and these were many: having sprung ashore and spoken to us, he directed his course to the cabin, all of our people accompanying him: moreover the Indian men and women, little and big, began with loud voices as great a wailing as if they had him dead before them: thus they went along following him wailing to the cabin, where he seated himself on the long bed, when all the Indians, continuously weeping, knelt before him, while he listened to them with much tranquillity and gravity until, from weariness, he rose and went away: ceasing to weep, the Indians rose and went off drying their tears: those who were not at the reception on account of absence from home, and the people of distant towns, came afterward, and, many being gathered together, the chief came and seated himself on a bedstead, and the Indians knelt in front of him and wept until he rose and left, when they returned to their houses: they continued to come and weep in this manner for many days: they told us that his vassals had to do the same to our chiefs when they came to their land: afterwards, while I was in St. Augustine, I went out on the river every day to fish and heard from thence each afternoon one person begin weeping in a loud voice, whereupon the whole followed at once in the same tone: on asking the cause, I learned that their chief had died, and that they had to weep in this manner for an entire year: so do all of these people weep for their chiefs, alive or dead. (Garcia, 1902, p. 200.)

Timberlake has the following paragraph on mortuary ceremonies among the Cherokee:

They seldom bury their dead, but throw them into the river; yet if any white man will bury them, he is generally rewarded with a blanket, besides what he takes from the corpse, the dead having commonly their guns, tomahawkes, powder, lead, silver ware, wampum, and a little tobacco, buried with them; and as the persons who bring the corpse to the place of burial, immediately leave it, he is at liberty to dispose of all as he pleases, but must take care never to be found out, as nothing belonging to the dead is to be kept, but everything at his decease destroyed, except those articles, which are destined to accompany him to the other world. It is reckoned, therefore, the worst of thefts. (Timberlake, Williams ed., 1927, pp. 90–91.)

The abundance of burials in the Cherokee country sufficiently refutes the idea that there was any such extensive water burial as Timberlake claims. Perhaps he got the idea from the widely spread river ceremonials peculiar to this tribe. Adair says they sometimes covered the dead with piles of stones (Adair, 1775, p. 184).

In recent times bodies of Cherokee were buried on the slope of a hill. The corpse was laid out in the best clothes worn by the deceased and property was placed by it, especially, in the case of a woman, a cup or saucer, the latter not being "killed." A little vessel of salt was added. The body was not put into the coffin for 2 or 3 days and meanwhile the neighbors came to watch and sometimes sing over it, probably to keep witches from stealing the liver. The women did not mourn out loud. The coffin-makers and grave diggers are now elected for a year, and a medicine man cannot assist. Immediately after the inhumation the near relatives bathed in the river, but if they had to postpone their ablutions, they bathed four times. The old ashes were scattered about the yard of the house in which the deceased had lived and the whole interior was fumigated by means of burning pine boughs. Anciently, a dance was held 7 days after the burial to speed the ghost on its way and comfort the relatives. The grave itself was not visited for fear bad luck would follow (Mooney, 1932, pp. 131–137).

The customs of the Creeks and Chickasaw appear, as we find in other instances, much the same. This is no doubt due in part to the fact that one of our principal authorities, James Adair, was familiar with both tribes and tends to mix their customs in his exposition, and in part to the adoption of Creek usages by the Chickasaw. In old times the body of a Creek is said to have been flexed and wrapped in a blanket and buried in a sitting position. In later times they were laid out straight, head to the west, and the seated corpses are said to have faced the sunrise, but I was told by the Alabama that they formerly placed bodies of the dead in the ground with their heads toward the east, a practice reversed after the introduction of Christianity. Explorations in the territory of these tribes indicate that orientation was not as uniform as has commonly been supposed. A large part of the movable property of the deceased was placed about the corpse. Some say that this was the fate of all their property in ancient times. Coffee was poured into a cup at the left shoulder, and a knife is said to have been put into the hand of an Alabama Indian with which to fight an eagle supposed to beset the spirit trail. The face of the corpse was painted red and black. Only relatives might bury the body but a handful of earth was thrown upon it by each of those present. The grave was covered over with canes and clay and it was very often inside of the house and used as a bed, but sometimes the family moved out and put up another dwelling. Anyhow, medicine was blown about the house, the fire was allowed to go out and a new fire lighted, and guns were discharged to drive away the ghost. In the case of a warrior, a pole was set up and notches cut into it in accordance with the number of his deeds. At least in the case of a prominent man, green boughs were hung in the town square. After all was over, those who had attended the ceremony bathed in the creek, but for 4 days a fire was kept up at the grave. As has been stated elsewhere, the widower mourned and remained strictly continent for 4 months, and a widow for 4 years (Swanton, 1928, pp. 388–397). Plate 88 shows a latter day Creek burial ground in Oklahoma. The orientation, head to the west, is apparently due to Christian influence.

Most of our data regarding Chickasaw customs are from Adair, which may be supplemented by some notes from Romans. Adair says that as soon as a death occurred a firebrand was dropped into the water, and Romans states that the house fire was extinguished and a new fire started. Guns were discharged and howls raised to drive away ghosts or as a signal to the relatives (Foreman, 1934, p. 103). A frame of white sticks was placed over the doorway where a household was mourning, and the mourners had a lock of hair clipped off from the deceased's body and refrained from salt food. When a warrior died a natural death, drums and musical instruments were laid aside for 3 days, while the body was washed, anointed, dressed in the best clothes the deceased had possessed, and seated outside facing the door of the winter house. It was borne around the winter house three times and afterward seated in the grave facing east with the arms and other movable property the departed had possessed in life ranged around it. Thick logs were then laid over the tomb covered in turn with cypress bark and clay, and the living often slept on top, particularly the widow or widower of the deceased. Those who performed the last rites must be cleansed, button snakeroot being used as a medicine, and they went about their usual tasks in 3 days while the relations mourned for a long time and cried at the grave like the Choctaw. In rocky country it was common for passersby to throw stones on the grave of one who had died far from home (Swanton, 1928 c, pp. 229–234).

The ancient Choctaw mortuary customs were quite different and of such a striking character that they have been often described, though these descriptions do not agree in all details. We are fortunate, however, in having an early drawing of a burial place from Romans (pl. 89). We are told that if a doctor declared the patient could not recover, he was killed without more ado. The house of the deceased was burned along with the provisions it contained or the latter were sold at a low price. The corpse was first laid on a scaffold near the house along with food and property, the skull being painted red. The bier was made of cypress bark and the body covered with bear or bison skins or a woolen blanket. The scaffold was decorated and the poles painted red if the deceased were a man of note. A small bark fire was lighted under the scaffold 4 days in succession. The mourners anciently had their hair entirely cut off but later on a single lock was treated in this manner. At any rate the women left their hair disheveled, paid mourners were utilized, and there were wailings three times a day—at sunrise, at noon, and at sunset. Benches were made near the scaffold for the mourners, and there was a fence or mud wall about the scaffold itself. After the flesh was thought to be sufficiently decayed, the bone picker or "buzzard man" of that particular canton appointed a day, and in the presence of the mourners, who meanwhile sang lugubrious songs, he removed the flesh from the bones and restored the latter to the family, who put them into a chest made of bones and splints or a hamper and took it in procession to the cantonal mortuary house. If the bones belonged to a chief, they were placed in a separate charnel house. Adair says that the bones were laid in this chest in their natural order, but this would seem to imply a longer chest than is commonly indicated. Some writers say the flesh was buried and some that it was burned—according to one, along with the scaffold on which it rested. Immediately before this there was a feast. Adair states that there was a wooden ladder at each burial house and on top of the house itself a dove carved in wood. At both the burial house and the private tomb there hung a chain, the links made of grapevines, and this is said by some writers to have been intended as a ladder by which the spirit of the dead might ascend to the world above, but Halbert scouts the idea, and rings used in connection with Natchez burial ceremonies indicated the war honors of the deceased. After the charnel house had become pretty well filled with boxes of bones, a final disposition was made of them. The bone pickers of the various cantons agreed upon a day when the grave boxes should be moved, and they were carried to one place in solemn procession, piled up into a pyramid there and covered with earth. According to some, the burial mound might be added to on several different occasions, and according to one informant, the bone house was covered over in situ after it had become full. Early in November there was a great feast to the dead when the cantonal ossuary was visited by the relatives of those whose bones had been laid away there. Halbert says there were two such gatherings annually, in spring and fall. At these each moiety cried and danced alternately for the deceased belonging to the other, and each piled up and buried the bones of the "opposites."

In the early part of the nineteenth century, under the influence of the missionaries, a change was introduced into the burial customs. A death was first announced by the discharge of guns. The corpse was buried in the ground immediately and seven poles were set up around it, three on each side and one at the head, on which was hung a string of grapevine hoops and a flag. According to Claiborne, mourning at the grave was continued for 13 months, and a hoop was taken from the grapevine chain each time, but Halbert denies that the number of hoops was specified or that one was removed each month. He states that there were only six poles, three at each side, and that on the central pole on each side was fastened a string of hoops and streamers. Each set, he says, was set up by members of one of the moieties who had formerly been bone pickers. The pole planting was the occasion for the entrance of the family into mourning, when they discarded all their ornaments and good clothing and left their hair unshorn. Every morning and evening thereafter they went to the grave to weep and a visitor was supposed to do the same, while a stranger passing by the place was supposed to stop for a few minutes to wail. After some time what is called "the little cry" was held at the grave, and then the family agreed on a time for "the big cry," which might take place several months later and was participated in by the whole community. A cry at the grave was followed by a feast, the two moieties eating apart, preceded by long orations by the headman of each moiety. Later came a dance continuing until almost daylight when, after an interval of quietness of about 15 minutes, all were summoned to the last cry, there was a brief speech by the headman of the opposite moiety, and after four repetitions of "the warrior's call" on the part of the headmen and reply by the pole pullers, the latter took the poles and carried them off into the woods. A man and a woman of the opposite moiety cut off a lock of hair from the heads of each member of the same sex in the mourning moiety, the period of mourning was over, and all returned to their homes. Relatives living at a distance were allowed to set up a pole in their own neighborhood about which to carry on their lamentations (Swanton, 1931 a, pp. 170–193).

The corpse of a Biloxi or Pascagoula chief was dried by the fire immediately after death and then fastened on a kind of table near the door of the temple, whither the people came every day to address it and offer it food. Later it was placed with the bodies of the preceding chiefs, which had been similarly treated, around the interior of the temple (Dumont, 1753, vol. 1, pp. 240–243; Dorsey and Swanton, 1912, p. 7).

Along the lower Mississippi the symbols of grief were much the same as those exhibited farther east. The hair was singed or cut off, the face was left unpainted, and the mourner stayed away from all dances and assemblies. The corpse was laid out in the best clothing with arms and such other articles as a kettle and provisions by its side. After burial the relatives repaired to the grave morning and evening to bring food and to weep, mentioning as they did so their degree of relationship. The food was placed at the feet of the corpse.

Cremation and embalming are said to have been unknown. When the Tattooed-serpent, the Great War Chief of the Natchez, died in 1725, guns were discharged to warn his people of the portentous event, and the death cry was raised and repeated from town to town. Water was thrown upon the fire in his dwelling as a signal that all fires were to be extinguished throughout the nation, but this was, in part at least, because the Great Sun himself, the civil head of the nation, had expressed a determination to end his own life at the same time. After the latter had been induced to change his mind, they were relighted. The chiefs and relatives all cut their hair in accordance with the common custom and all the property of the deceased was thrown out of his cabin, perhaps in preparation for its destruction by fire, for this custom was usual among the nobility. From this treatment of property must be excluded the guns, bow and arrows, and war club of the deceased, which were tied to his bed. Calumets he had received were placed ceremonially around his bed, and from a pole nearby hung 46 rings of reddened cane splints indicating the number of men and women he had killed. The fire burning in his house had been brought from the temple and could not be used for ordinary purposes such as the lighting of a pipe. The master of ceremonies for this occasion held a baton ornamented with red and black feathers. Between the dead man's house and the temple were a number of persons who were to be killed to accompany him to the spirit world, each standing upon a platform with his or her executioners. Among these were his wives, some of his officers, and some persons who desired to obtain honor for their children or children of persons who wished to obtain honor for themselves. They had their hair daubed red and each held the shell of a river mussel in the right hand and a calumet in the left hand. Six pills of tobacco, previously blessed by a doctor, were swallowed by each of the victims, so that they might lose consciousness, after which they were strangled by means of cords. The body was borne on a litter on the shoulders of a number of leading men, who approached the temple in spirals, now nearer now farther off. The Tattooed-serpent, his wives, and two leading men were buried in or near the temple, but the bones of the Tattooed-serpent, at least, were subsequently removed and placed in a hamper in the temple beside the hampers holding the bones of other Suns. It is said that the bodies of some of the victims were first placed on scaffolds and shut in until the flesh could be removed from the bones, which, after a prescribed interval of time, were placed in hampers, like the bones of the Tattooed-serpent himself. It is said to have been customary in the Natchez nation to weep for 3 days after the death of a leading man, but probably this was really considered as 4 days (Swanton, 1911, pp. 138–157).

We are told by Dumont that the corpse of a Yazoo or Chakchiuma Indian was carried into the woods for burial by relations on each side, each bearing a lighted pine torch which they threw into the grave before it was covered with earth. Afterward the relations and friends went to the grave to cry there "almost every night," for the space of 6 months. At the head of a chief's grave they also set up a post on which had been cut with the point of a knife the figure he had worn painted on the body during life (Dumont, 1753, vol. 1, pp. 246–247; Swanton, 1911, p. 334).

From the fact that the Bayogoula and Houma Indians placed their dead on scaffolds, as well as from the general location of those tribes, it may be inferred that their burial customs were similar to those of the Choctaw, and this derives support from the usages of the Chitimacha, which were similar. Gatschet was told that

One year after the death of a [Chitimacha] head chief, or of any of the village war chiefs, of whom there were four or five, their bones were dug up by a certain class of ministrants called "turkey-buzzard men" (ōsh hä'tchna), the remaining flesh separated, the bones wrapped in a new and checkered mat, and brought to [a "bone house"]. Inhumation of these bones took place just before the beginning of the Kut-nähä [properly Kut-nahīn] worshipping ceremony or dance. The people assembled there, walked six times around a blazing fire, after which the bones were placed in a mound. The widow and the male orphans of the deceased chief had to take part in the ceremonial dance. The burial of the common people was effected in the same way, one year after death; but the inhumation of the bones took place at the villages where they had died. (Gatschet, 1883, p. 8; Swanton, 1911, p. 350.)

I was told that, instead of being wrapped in the mat entire, the bones were burned by the buzzard man and the ashes put into a little basket and then put into the mound (Swanton, 1911, p. 350).

Our knowledge of Tunica customs belongs to very recent times. It is said that the corpse was buried with its head to the east, and that a fire was lighted at the head on 4 successive nights while the people watched at the grave and fasted. Just before daybreak, after the expiration of the 4 nights, all went down to the water and plunged in. They breakfasted, and the principal speaker delivered an address, after which all put on mourning, the speaker and his relations wearing it during 6 months. A second or corn fast was held for the dead when the little corn was just right to eat. It lasted for 4 days, and was concluded by another plunge into the water followed by a speech, and a dinner ending in an all-night dance. Each cemetery was located on a hill and was under the care of a guardian. Each new year he called the people to throw corn and beans upon the ground there, and they cut the cemetery grass annually (Swanton, 1911, pp. 325–326).

For the elaborate Caddo burial customs, see Bureau of American Ethnology Bulletin 132 (Swanton, 1942, pp. 203-210).

CRIME AND PUNISHMENT

Chiefs among the Virginia Algonquians were so powerful that they were able to inflict corporal punishment on guards who failed in their duty, and they did not hesitate to use poison in disposing of rivals. The Powhatan Indians stole freely from the English but very much less from one another. A considerable item on this head is added by Spelman:

Concerninge ther lawes my years and understandinge, made me the less to looke after bycause I thought that Infidels wear lawless yet when I saw sum put to death I asked the cause of ther offence, for in the time that I was with y° Patomecke I saw 5 executed 4 for murther of a child (id est) y° mother, and tow other that did the fact with hir and a 4 for consealing it as he passed by, beinge bribed to hould his pease, and one for robbinge a traueler of coper and beades for to steale ther neyburs corne or copper is death, or to lye one with anothers wife is death if he be taken in the manner.

Thos that be conuicted of capitall offences are brought into a playne place before y° Kinges house when then he laye, which was at Pomunkeye the chefest house he hath wher one or tow apoynted by the Kinge did bind them hand and foote, which being dunn a great fier was made. Then cam the officer to thos that should dye, and with a shell cutt off ther long locke, which they weare on the leaft side of ther heade, and hangeth that on a bowe before the Kings house. Then thos for murther wear Beaten with staues till ther bonns weare broken and beinge aliue weare flounge into the fier, the other for robbinge was knockt on y° heade and beinge deade his bodye was burnt. (Smith, John, Arber ed., 1884, pp. cx–cxi.)

Individuals who had excited Powhatan's wrath were treated as follows:

He caused certaine malefactors, at what tyme Captain Smith was with him, (and to the sight whereof Captain Smith, for some purpose, was brought,) to be bound hand and foote, when certaine officers appointed thereunto, having from many fiers gathered great store of burning coales, raked the coales rounde in forme of a cockpitt, and in the midst they cast the offenders to broyle to death. Some tymes he causeth the headds of them that offend to be layd upon the aulter or sacrificing stone, and one or two, with clubbs, beat out their braynes. When he would punish any notorious enemye or trespasser, he causeth him to be tyed to a tree, and with muscle-shells or reedes the executioner cutteth off his joints one after another, ever casting what is cutt off into the fier; then doth he proceede with shells and reedes to case the skyn from his head and face; after which they rip up his belly, teare out his bowells, and so burne him with the tree and all . . . Howbeit, his ordinary correction is to have an offender, whome he will only punish and not put to death, to be beatten with cudgells as the Turks doe. We have seen a man kneeling on his knees, and, at Powhatan's command, two men have beaten him on the bare skyn till the skyn have ben all bollen and blistered, and all on a goare blood, and till he hath fallen senceles in a swound, and yet never cryed, complayned, nor seemed to ask pardon, for that they seldom doe. (Strachey, 1849, p. 52.)

Such tortures, when inflicted by an arbitrary potentate of whatever color, may only euphemistically be called punishments.

Among Siouan tribes retaliation was the common method of treating murder. Poison was resorted to in getting unwanted persons out of the way, but when they discovered a man who habitually used poison, they killed him and cut his body to pieces. If a man committed incest, his body was burned and the ashes thrown into the river. Sodomy was said to be unknown. According to the earliest account of the eastern Siouans we have, widows were forbidden to marry again if their husbands had died a natural death, but permitted if they had been executed, but Lawson contradicts the prohibition absolutely. Perhaps the meaning is that they could not marry until after a certain period of time (Lawson, 1860, pp. 318–319, 299, 326–337).[37]

The following excerpt from Catesby bears on the problem of theft:

They have no fence to part one another's lots in their corn fields, every man knows his own, and it scarce ever happens that they rob one another of so much as an ear of corn, which if any is found to do, the thief is sentenced by the elders to work or plant for him that was robbed, till he is recompensed for all the damage he has suffered in his corn-fields: yet they make no scruple to rob the *English*, having been taught this lesson by the latter. (Catesby, 1731–43, vol. 2, p. x.)

Reminiscent of the Algonquians is the Timucua usage in accordance with which a negligent watchman was punished by being beaten on the head with a club having sharp sides. Chiefs could exact tribute and labor from their subjects and could punish them for negligence by breaking their arms. We are told that marriage was protected "very rigorously," something we can readily credit, as their customs in many particulars were much like those of the Creeks (Swanton, 1922, p. 380).

We are told that Cherokee chiefs could inflict no punishment, but that a man who committed a crime in violation of a treaty might be delivered over to the enemy. Charles Hicks, a Cherokee chief, stated in 1818,

Murder committed by a person of one clan on one of another is always punished with death; but if both belong to the same clan, it frequently happens that the clan intercedes with the chief head of the nation, and obtains a pardon, which pardon is published in the national council when convened. (Hicks, *in* Raleigh Register, 1818.)

Cases of murder or serious injury—sometimes of trivial injury—were handled in the Creek Nation by the tribe, clan, or subdivision in accordance with the old "law" of retaliation, and in many cases lack of intention was not admitted as a valid excuse though Bossu states that it was at times. An adult captive was killed by his captor in revenge for former injuries or the right could be transferred to

---

[37] Lawson also adds: "Another destroyer of them, is, the art they have and often practice, of poisoning one another; which is done by a large white spongy root, that grows in the fresh-marshes, which is one of their poisons, not but that they have many other drugs, which they poison one another withal" (p. 365).

another. According to one writer, rape and a third conviction of theft were also punished with death. The aged were killed only at their own desire, and infanticide was optional with the mother for only a month after the birth of her child. A witch or wizard was treated like a murderer and suffered the same punishment. Adultery was punished by beating and the cropping of the ears and hair, and, in the prehistoric period, adulterers were shot to death with arrows. A widow or widower marrying too soon was treated in the same manner. In this type of punishment the Wind and Bear clans enjoyed certain immunities. Ordinary fornication was not regarded as a crime, but incest, if between near relatives, brought down the death penalty, and, if between relatives more remote, the long scratch, a deep incision from neck to foot. Stealing was punished with whipping, loss of ears, or death, depending upon the number of offences. Minor lapses from the code were punished, in such cases as failure to take the morning bath, especially in the case of children, with dry scratching. In later times, theft of horses and nonattendance at the busk were occasions for levying fines. McGillivray punished some recalcitrant towns by removing the white traders from them. Oaths and epithets were used, but much more sparingly than with us, and there was no special punishment in such cases except such as might be exacted by the object of wrath. It may be added that individuals who had escaped punishment or who had fled from home in order to escape it are reputed to have founded a number of towns, many of them towns of prominence (Swanton, 1928, pp. 338–357).

Again, Chickasaw customs were similar to those of the Creeks. Retaliation was the one way of treating murder and a wizard or witch was also regarded as a murderer. A detected adulteress was punished by beating, and by cropping the ears, nose, and so forth, but male offenders in this particular went free. Sodomy is said to have been common and apparently it went unpunished. Whipping was resorted to in minor offenses, but it may not have been extended to adults until later years. The failure of a woman to separate herself from the household every month was as much of a crime as murder and adultery. Epithets were employed as by the Creeks. Oaths were used in attesting the truth of a proposition (Swanton, 1928 c, pp. 216–219).

Retaliation again lay at the base of the composition in all cases of murder among the Choctaw, but executions in later times were placed in the hands of the light horsemen instead of those of the murdered man's kin. Witchcraft was also punished with death. One who received a personal affront might challenge the other to mutual suicide. Sodomy and male concubinage were said to be common and unpunished. A woman accused of adultery was exposed to the lust of as many men as chose to have intercourse with her and then cast off to become a temporary wife or prostitute. If, however, she belonged to a higher family than her husband, she might escape this fate. Theft within the tribe was punished in later times by whipping and the imposition of fines. The Choctaw swore by the sun, but there is a difference of opinion regarding their general veracity. They are said to have been exceedingly clever beggars (Swanton, 1931 a, pp. 104–114).

Du Pratz affirms that the Natchez parents did not beat their children and that the old man who trained them stopped short with threatenings of various kinds, among which he mentions threats of banishment. It is evident that the tooth-for-tooth philosophy also obtained among these people, but it is equally evident that a crime committed by one of the Sun caste was lightly regarded as compared with one committed against the Sun caste. Upon commoners the death penalty was inflicted by the Great Sun ad libitum (Le Page du Pratz, 1758, vol. 2, pp. 319–321; Swanton, 1911, p. 88).

For Caddo usages, see Bureau of American Ethnology Bulletin 132 (Swanton, 1942, pp. 183–184).

MEANS OF COMMUNICATION

Some of these, particularly communication by mnemonic devices (see pp. 610–613) have been treated already. Such an incredibly small number of explorers were sufficiently interested in Indian usages to set down their impressions that customs and devices which must have been matters of everyday knowledge to them are mentioned only occasionally. Among these we may refer to fire or smoke signaling, which is apparently noted in Carolina and along the Chesapeake in Virginia, by De Soto's followers when they came to land at Tampa Bay, by the western Seminole and Creeks, and by the Chickasaw (Swanton, 1928, p. 446; 1928 c, p. 246; Percy *in* Tyler, 1907, pp. 10–11).

Adair notes the transmission of news by means of intoned whoops, and he is the only one to speak of a sign language:

The present American aborigines seem to be as skillful pantomimi as ever were those of ancient Greece or Rome or the modern Turkish mutes, who describe the meanest things spoken by gestures, action, and the passions of the face. Two far-distant Indian nations, who understand not a word of each other's language, will intelligibly converse together and contract engagements without an interpreter in such a surprising manner as is scarcely credible. (Adair, 1775, p. 79.)

From what we are told of the representation of the Creek migration legend on a bison skin which Chekilli gave to Governor Oglethorpe, it is evident that a pictographic system was in use similar probably to that employed in the Walam Olum (Gatschet, 1883, vol. 1, p. 236; Swanton, 1928, p. 34).

In their war-expeditions [says Catesby] they have certain hieroglyphicks, whereby each party informs the other of the successes or losses they have met with; all which is so exactly performed by their *Sylvan* marks and characters, that they are never at a loss to understand one another. (Catesby, 1731–43, vol. 2, p. XIII.)

Bernard Romans is almost the only writer who seems to have preserved any samples of this (pl. 90). One of these was made by the Choctaw and was found by Romans near Pascagoula River in the Choctaw country. He says it

means that an expedition by seventy men, led by seven principal warriors, and eight of inferior rank, had in an action killed nine of their enemies, of which they brought the scalps, and that the place where it was marked was the first publick place in their territories where they arrived with the scalps.

The second was "found at a Choctaw place called 'Hoopah Ullah (i. e.) the noisy owl'," but was made by a Creek war party.

It means that ten of that nation of the Stag family came in three canoes into their enemies country, that six of the party near this place, which was at *Oopah Ullah*, a brook so called on the road to the Choctaws, had met two men, and two women with a dog, that they lay in ambush for them, killed them, and that they all went home with the four scalps; the scalp in the stag's foot implies the honour of the action to the whole family. (Romans, 1775, p. 102.)

It was customary for many of these tribes, at least those along the Mississippi and those near Virginia, to use tribal marks. The former generally employed them in war. After committing some depredation upon an enemy, instead of concealing the authors of the mischief, they left about the spot wooden tablets bearing the tribal sign. That of the Natchez was, naturally enough, the sun. That of the Houma was the red crawfish, from which, in fact, the tribe derived its name. That of the Bayogoula was the alligator, also possibly reflected in the tribal designation "bayou people" (Dumont, 1753, vol. 1, p. 184).

Catesby says:

In their hunting marches, at the entrance of the territories, or hunting grounds of an enemy, the captain, or leader of them chips off the bark from one side of a tree, on which he delineates his own person, with the dreadful hieroglyphick figure before-mentioned, which is sometimes a rattle-snake open mouth'd, at a corner of his mouth, twisting in spiral meanders round his neck and body, the hero also holding in his hand a bloody *Tommahawk*. By this menace or challenge is signified, that he whose pourtrait is there displayed, hunts in these grounds, where if any of his enemies dare intrude, they shall feel the force of his *Tommahawk*. (Catesby, 1731–43, vol. 2, p. IX.)

The symbols on a typical war tablet are given on page 701.

Among the Algonquians of Virginia and Carolina it was usual to make tribal marks upon the shoulders of individuals. Hariot, who is the first to speak of these, says:

The inhabitants of all the cuntrie for the most parte haue marks rased on their backs, whereby yt may be knowen what Princes subiects they bee, or of what place they haue their originall. For which cause we haue set downe those marks in this figure, and haue annexed the names of the places, that they might more easelye be discerned. Which industrie hath god indued them withal although they be verye simple, and rude. And to confesse a truthe, I cannot remember that euer I saw a better or quietter people then they.

The marks which I obserued amonge them, are heere put downe in order folowinge.

The marke which is expressed by A. belongeth to Wingino, the cheefe lorde of Roanoac.

That which hath B. is the marke of Wingino his sisters husbande.

Those which be noted with the letters, of C. and D. belong vnto diverse chefe lordes in Secotam.

Those which haue the letters E. F. G. are certaine cheefe men of Pomeiooc, and Aquascogoc. [Pl. 91.] (Hariot, 1893, pl. 23.)

Beverley reproduces Hariot's figure as usual, though in a slightly altered form, and notes his statement very briefly (Beverley, bk. 3, 1705, p. 4).

Lederer reports that

every nation gives his particular ensigne or arms: The Sasquesahanaugh a Tarapine, or small tortoise; the Akenatzy's a serpent; the Nahyssanes three arrows, etc. (Alvord, 1912, p. 143.)

Lederer also gives some interesting information regarding a form of symbolism by which abstract qualities were, as he claims, represented by animals:

The faculties of the minde and body they commonly express by emblems. By the figure of a stag, they imply swiftness; by that of a serpent, wrath; of a lion, courage; of a dog, fidelity; by a swan they signifie the English, alluding to their complexion, and flight over the sea. (Alvord, 1912, p. 143.)

The symbols applied to some of the Creek towns have already been indicated, as the eagle for Coweta, alligator for Tukabahchee, garfish for Koasati and possibly Alabama, snake for Atasi (Swanton, 1928, pp. 243–246).

These devices represent the nearest approach to a written language to be found in this region until Sequoya the Cherokee, adapted into a syllabary for his people some of the phonetic symbols he had seen in European books. Of course, missionaries have also attempted the representation of Indian sounds and words, usually in roman letters or some modifications of these, and more recently special students of language have attempted to represent them still more accurately for purely scientific purposes.

Lawson has a little information regarding the ability of the Indians in drawing maps.

They will draw maps very exactly of all the rivers, towns, mountains and roads, or what you shall enquire of them, which you may draw by their directions, and come to a small matter of latitude, reckoned by their day's journeys. These maps they will draw in the ashes of the fire, and sometimes upon a mat or piece of bark. I have put a pen and ink into a savage's hand, and he has drawn me the rivers, bays, and other parts of country, which afterwards I have found to agree with a great deal of nicety. But you must be very much in their favor, otherwise they will never make these discoveries to you, especially if it be in their own quarters. (Lawson, 1860, p. 333.)

We have in the map of Lamhatty (Bushnell, 1908, pl. 35) an example of native map drawing which is far from indicating exceeding accuracy, but in this case the territory represented includes regions remote from the cartographer's native land, and through most of which he was carried rapidly as a captive.

TRADE

In pre-Columbian times few Indians of the Southeastern tribes traveled very far from home, but there were some exceptions, native traders or individuals of a curious or vagrant type of mind such as are to be found in all classes of society, civilized as well as savage. Du Pratz speaks of a Yazoo who asserted he had been as far west as the shores of the Pacific (Le Page du Pratz, 1758, vol. 3, pp. 89–128), some Chickasaw are said to have reached Mexico, and we know that they constantly crossed the Mississippi to make war on the Caddo. General Milfort claims to have taken a band of Creeks far up Red River to a place where they believed their ancestors formerly lived (Milfort, 1802, pp. 86–111), but in his time the western emigration of the southern Indians due to the pressure of the whites and the attractiveness of western hunting fields had already begun. In late colonial times there appears to have been a Chickasaw settlement in Pennsylvania, and in the early part of the eighteenth century the Iroquois on one side and the Cherokee and Siouan Indians on the other maintained a bitter war. Most of this, however, was at a relatively late period.

Trade is determined to a considerable extent by the distribution of raw materials which have a demand value at a given place and time. This distribution has already been discussed, and we have also noted two general drifts of trade, from the coast inland and vice versa, and between the mountains or uplands and the plains, of which the intercourse between the tribes of the lower Mississippi and the Caddo may be regarded as a special case.

Cabeza de Vaca gives some interesting information relative to the trade carried on by coast and interior peoples of Texas between the Brazos and Guadalupe Rivers, a trade in which he himself took part (Cabeza de Vaca, Bandelier ed., 1905, pp. 74–75). In the territory now embraced in the State of Louisiana there was regular traffic between the Chitimacha and Atakapa Indians and the Avoyel, the Opelousa tribe acting as middlemen. The last named obtained fish from the Chitimacha and Atakapa, which they exchanged with the Avoyel for flints. Although it is said that flint was abundant in the Avoyel country, it seems probable that they got much of it still farther inland, at the novaculite quarries about Hot Springs, Ark. Some of the flints which the Atakapa obtained in this manner were passed on to the Karankawa, and the Karankawa supplied them with globular or conical oil jugs. It is also said, though this may apply to a later period, that the Atakapa carried moss and dried smoked fish to Galveston Island. It would hardly seem as though the last-mentioned article would be in demand with a people such as the Karankawa, themselves coastal. The Atakapa are also said to have gotten most of their pots either from the Karankawa, as just mentioned, or from the inland tribes, and they probably obtained skins from the inland tribes as well. To the latter they gave in exchange sharks' teeth, "marine curios," dried or smoked fish, and feathers of birds (Dyer, 1917, pp. 6–7). We may suspect that they got this pottery not only from the Avoyel but from the Caddo tribes, who were noted pottery makers, but it may have come from sources as distant as the Quapaw, who are said to have traded in pots (Margry, 1875–86, pp. 412, 424, 442–443). The Chitimacha claim that they formerly got stone beads as well as arrow points from the inland tribes (Swanton, 1911, pp. 345, 347). We may suspect that the coast Indians also got bowwood from the Caddo in the same way, since tribes came to the Caddo from long distances to secure it (Margry, 1875–86, vol. 3, p. 412). There are records that the Tewa obtained bows from this section through the medium of the Comanche (Harrington, J. P., 1916, p. 68). The Quapaw exchanged earthern vessels, canoes, and wooden platters with the Caddo for bows and arrows and for salt (Margry, 1875–86, vol. 3, pp. 442–443). When De Soto was at Pacaha in 1541, "he met with eight Indian merchants who traded it (salt) through the provinces" and said that it was to be found in the mountains 40 leagues from Pacaha. Some of the Spaniards set out with them to purchase salt, and to get specimens of a yellow metal which they supposed to be gold but actually proved to be copper, and the Pacaha chief supplied them with pearls, deerskins, and beans with which to make the trade. They returned in 11 days with six loads of "fossil salt" and some copper (Garcilaso, 1723, pp. 187–188). Later on they themselves found salt in the provinces of Colima and Cayas. These places were in what is now Arkansas, but other salt provinces, Chaguete and

Aguacay, were evidently in Louisiana. (Garcilaso, 1723, p. 189; Bourne, 1904, vol. 2., pp. 147–148; Robertson, 1933, pp. 192–193, 237–238.) When the French entered the country, trade in salt was still active but most salt seems to have been extracted in northern Louisiana. The Tunica Indians are particularly mentioned in connection with it, but the Koroa, Washita, and Natchitoches were also concerned in it, and the Cahinnio were active as middle men. The principal outlets on the Mississippi appear to have been the Taensa and Quapaw towns (Margry, 1875–86, vol. 3. pp. 442–443; vol. 4, pp. 432, 435; Cox, 1905, vol. 1., p. 45). Smaller centers of trade were the town of the Namidish and the Chitimacha country. The Natchez are said to have obtained pearls for their Sun caste from the upper course of Pearl River (Hennepin, 1698, p. 177; Jones, C. C., 1873, p. 470). Still farther east, on the lower Tombigbee, we find the Tohome tribe exploiting a small salt lick.[38] Some of this salt may have found its way to the Mississippi, since it appears from an early French narrative that the Yazoo sometimes went as far as the River of Mobile for shells.

These items, which thus bring the region of Mobile Bay into the picture, constitute almost all the information supplied us in the literature regarding trade in the midgulf section though there must have been considerable, this being the territory of the great southern nations.

Although, as already noted, the inhabitants of Florida obtained much of their flint without going outside of the peninsula, the early French and Spanish narratives give evidence that stone for various purposes was obtained from Flint River and in the Appalachian Mountains, and that copper was imported from this latter country (Le Moyne, 1875, p. 7; Fontaneda, 1854, p. 20). When De Soto was in the Apalachee country, Garcilaso tells us that a youth was brought to him who had traveled far inland in Florida, meaning the North American continent in general, with traders. He said that they obtained at Cofitachequi a yellow metal, evdently copper, which they carried long distances in trade. In southern Florida we are told that the natives traded in fruit and the kunti flour obtained from a Zamia. Later they bartered "skins, mocking birds, and pet squirrels" at Havana for guns, ammunition, and clothing (Garcilaso, 1723, p. 104; Swanton, 1922, p. 344). About 1774 Bartram tells us the coast Indians of Florida would give two or three buckskins for a single root of Angelica (Bartram, 1792, p. 325; 1909, pp. 46–67). And Catesby says regarding the *Ilex vomitoria*:

This medicinal shrub, so universally esteem'd by the *Indians* of north *America*, is produced but in a small part of the continent, confined by northern

---

[38] See De Crenay map in Swanton, 1922, pl. 5.

and western limits, *viz.* North to lat. 37, and west to the distance of about fifty miles from the ocean: yet the *Indian* inhabitants of the north and west are supplied with it by the maritime *Indians* in exchange for other commodities. By the sour faces the *Indians* make in drinking this salubrious liquor, it seems as little agreeable to an *Indian* as to an *European* palate, and consequently that the pains and expences they are at in procuring it from remote distances, does not proceed from luxury (as tea with us from *China*) but from its virtue, and the benefit they receive by it. (Catesby, 1731–43, vol. 2, p. xv.)

According to the same writer Indians as far away as Canada were supplied with bills taken from the ivory-billed woodpecker (Catesby, 1731–43, vol. 2, p. xv).

As we pass northeast along the Atlantic coast, we seem to discover more evidence of trade. It is several times intimated that Cofitachequi was a considerable mart, and this was in the neighborhood of Augusta, Ga. About 60 years after the time of De Soto, the Spanish explorer Eçija reports that Indians were in the habit of descending the Santee River with cloaks "and many other things" and also copper and "plata blanca," probably mica, which they exchanged with the coast Indians for fish and salt (Lowery ms.).

In the region about Chesapeake Bay, the sounds of North Carolina, and among the Tuscarora and the Siouan tribes in their vicinity, references to native trade become more numerous. Lederer speaks of Katearas, chief residence of the Tuscarora head chief, as "a place of great Indian trade and commerce" (Alvord, 1912, p. 162). The Occaneechi devoted themselves very largely to trade, as is testified by the fact that their language had become the trade jargon over a considerable extent of territory. It is not surprising, therefore, to learn that they had been built up largely of outcasts from other people (Alvord, 1912, p. 225). Of the Eno tribe somewhat farther south, Lederer says,

They are of mean stature and courage, couvetous and thievish, industrious to earn a peny; and therefore hire themselves out to their neighbours, who employ them as carryers or porters. They plant abundance of grain, reap three crops in a summer, and out of their granary supply all the adjacent parts. (Alvord, 1912, p. 156.)

Farther on he met some Cheraw Indians who had gone to trade with the Ushery (probably the Catawba). As media of exchange he mentions "small shells, which they call roanoack or peack," and also pearls, vermilion, and pieces of crystal. Toward the south the Indians used "some odde pieces of plate or bullon" which evidently came from the Spaniards (Alvord, 1912, p. 170). The peack or peak had been introduced into the south from New Netherlands and New England, but the roanoke was a truly local and aboriginal medium of exchange and was used for all purposes, as Lawson states at considerable length (Lawson, 1860, pp. 314–317; see pp. 482–483 above.)

Michel says that the Indians of Monacantown often brought pottery in to trade "and when desired fill it with corn" (Michel, 1916, p. 123). The Powhatan Indians brought corn in baskets to sell to the Virginia colonists. We read that when Capt. Ratclyffe visited Powhatan in November 1609, the Indians

carried our English to their storehouse where their corne was to traffique with them, giueing them pieces of copper and beades and other things. According to y⁸ proportions of y⁸ basketts of corne which they brought but the Indians dealing deceitfully by pulling or beareing vpp the bottom of their baskets with their hands soe that y⁸ lesse corne might serue to fill them. (Smith, John, Arber ed., 1884, p. civ.)

Strachey says of the Powhatan Indians:

They are much desirous of our comodityes, and therefore when any of our boates arrive before their townes, they will come downe unto us, or suffer us to come up into their howses, and demaund after copper, white beades, howes to pare their corne feilds, and hatchetts, for which they will give us of such things as they have in exchaung, as deere skins, furrs of the wild catt, black fox, beaver, otter, arachoune, fowle, fish, deare, or beare's flesh dried, or deare's suet made up handsomely in cakes, their country corne, peas, beanes, and such like; and indeed (to say truith) their victuall is their chief riches. (Strachey, 1849, p. 113.)

We also find here the tribal desire to control trade so characteristic of peoples in all parts of the world. The Wainoakes were said to slander the English to the Tuscarora and vice versa for this purpose, and the Occaneechi used every effort to prevent English traders from passing beyond them (Alvord, 1912, p. 119). The traders also had to suffer at times from the cupidity of the tribes they visited. Upon one occasion three Indians from the Chesapeake Bay section were killed by the Hocomawananck [Roanoke River] Indians "for lucre of the Roanoke they brought with them to trade for Otterskins" (Alvord, 1912, p. 122). Lawson met two Tuscarora Indians going to the Shakori and Occaneechi to barter some wooden bowls and ladles for raw skins, "which," Lawson adds, "they [the Occaneechi] make great advantage of, hating that any of these westward Indians should have any commerce with the English which would prove a hindrance to their gains" (Lawson, 1860, p. 101).

As is common the world over, feasts and ceremonies were made occasions for trading. "They meet," says Lawson, "from all the towns within fifty or sixty miles round, where they buy and sell several commodities, as we do at fairs and markets" (Lawson, 1860, p. 288). In this region the poorer hunters made bowls, dishes, and spoons of gumwood and the tulip tree, "others, where they find a vein of white clay, fit for their purpose, make tobacco pipes, all which are often transported to other Indians," including seemingly baskets and mats made by the women (Lawson, 1860, p. 338; also see p. 364).

Catesby is repeating Lawson in part but in part adding to him when he says:

Those who are not good hunters dress skins, make bowls, dishes, spoons, tobacco-pipes, with other domestick implements. . . . These manufactures are usually transported to some remote nations, who having plenty of deer and other game, our neighbouring *Indians* barter these commodities for their raw hides with the hair on, which are brought home and dressed by the sorry hunters. (Catesby, 1731–43, vol. 2, p. XI.)

Marginella shells were also obtained in the Sound country to trade with the interior Indians, and the effects of this trade are noted when archeologists lay open mounds and burials along the Mississippi and Ohio Rivers.

From beyond the limits of this area catlinite pipes were obtained as already noted, along with much of their copper. In later times, gold and silver were picked up on the Florida coast from wrecked Spanish treasure ships, and the Choctaw got silver by raiding the Caddo Indians after they had taken it from the Spaniards. By this Red River route the famous Chickasaw horses were also brought into the country (see p. 348). But trade across the southern Plains had been established before white contact, for De Soto's party found blue stones, evidently turquoises, and shawls in a province called Guasco west of the Mississippi, and the trade in Caddo bows seems to have extended to the Pueblo country in prehistoric times (Robertson, 1933, p. 256). A European product much more serious for the Indians was rum, which also was distributed in part through native channels.

The following interesting view of the changes introduced by white contact is given by Catesby:

Before the introduction of fire-arms amongst the *American Indians*, (though hunting was their principal employment) they made no other use of the skins of deer, and other beasts, than to cloath themselves, their carcasses for food, probably, then being of as much value to them as the skins; but as they now barter the skins to the *Europeans* for other cloathing and utensils they were before unacquainted with, so the use of guns has enabled them to slaughter far greater number of deer and other animals than they did with their primitive bows and arrows. This destruction of deer and other animals being chiefly for the sake of their skins, a small part of the venison they kill suffices them; the remainder is left to rot; or becomes a prey to the wolves, panthers, and other voracious beasts. With these skins they purchase of the *English*, guns, powder and shot, woollen cloth, hatchets, kettles, porridge-pots, knives, vermilion, beads, rum, &c. (Catesby, 1731–43, vol. 2, pp. XI–XII.)

By 1728, when William Byrd visited the Nottoway town in southern Virginia, he found that the Indians used in hunting and war nothing but firearms which they purchased from the English in exchange for skins.

Bows and Arrows are grown into disuse, except only amongst their Boys. Nor is it ill Policy, [he adds shrewdly] but on the contrary very prudent, thus to furnish the Indians with Fire-Arms, because it makes them depend entirely upon the English, not only for their Trade, but even for their subsistence. Besides, they were really able to do more mischief, while they made use of Arrows, of which they wou'd let Silently fly Several in a Minute with Wonderful Dexterity, whereas now they hardly ever discharge their Firelocks more than once, which they insidiously do from behind a Tree, and then retire as nimbly as the Dutch Horse us'd to do now and then formerly in Flanders. (Bassett, 1901, p. 116.)

Caddo trade has been discussed more at length in Bureau of American Ethnology Bulletin 132 (Swanton, 1942, pp. 192–203).

RELIGIOUS BELIEFS AND USAGES

In an inner room of the house at Roanoke where Granganimeo's wife entertained Amadas and Barlowe was "their Idoll, which they worship, of whome they speake incredible things" (Burrage, 1906, p. 236). This is represented as if it were the chief's own dwelling, but images of the gods were generally kept in ossuaries or temples apart and such may really have been the case in the present instance. Quoting Hariot:

They thinke that all the gods are of human shape, & therefore they represent them by images in the formes of men, which they call *Kewasowok*, one alone is called *Kewás;* Them they place in houses appropriate or temples which they call *Machicómuck;* Where they woorship, praie, sing, and make manie times offerings vnto them. In some *Machicómuck* we haue seene but one *Kewas*, in some two, and in other some three; The common sort thinke them to to be also gods. (Hariot, 1893, p. 38.)

Farther on he gives an illustration and description of an image of one of these beings and the house in which it was installed:

The people of this cuntrie haue an Idol, which they call Kiwasa: yt is carued of woode in lengthe 4. foote whose heade is like the heades of the people of Florida, the face is of a flesh colour, the brest whitte. He hath a chayne abowt his necke of white beades, betweene which are other Rownde beades of copper which they esteeme more then golde or siluer. This Idol is placed in the temple of the towne of Secotam, as the keper of the kings dead corpses. Somtyme they haue two of these idoles in theyr churches, and somtime 3. but neuer aboue, which they place in a darke corner wher they shew terrible. [Pl. 92.] (Hariot, 1893, pl. 21.)

It may be assumed that minor deities of some kind were represented on the carved posts which he describes elsewhere:

The place where they meet (from all about) is a broade playne, abowt the which are planted in the grownde certayne posts carued with heads like to the faces of Nonnes couered with their vayles. [Pl. 93.] (Hariot, 1893, pl. 18.)

From what Hariot says farther on, when he comes to describe "the tombe of their werowans or cheiff lordes," it is evident that the royal ossuary and the temple were one and the same thing. In the town of Pomeioc at any rate the temple was of a general circular outline, but farther north was more nearly rectangular.

There seems to have been a distinction between the priests and conjurers or wonder workers. Hariot says that "the Priests of the aforesaid Towne of Secota are well stricken in yeers, and as yt seemeth of more experience then the comon sorte" (pl. 94.) (Hariot, 1893, pl. 5). He remarks of the "coniurers or iuglers" that they

vse strange gestures, and often contrarie to nature in their enchantments: For they be verye familiar with deuils, of whome they enquier what their enemys doe, or other such thinges. [Pl. 95.]   (Hariot, 1893, pl. 11.)

The costumes of these learned gentlemen have been described elsewhere (pp. 477–479).

Public expressions of religion were much the same among the Virginia Algonquians.

Henry Spelman has the following naive account of the religious beliefs of the Powhatan and Potomac Indians among whom he was a captive:

You must understand that for ye most part they worship ye diuell, which yᵉ coniuerers who are ther preests, can make apeare unto them at ther pleasuer, yet neuer ye less in euery cuntry they haue a seuerall Image whom they call ther god. As with the great Pawetan he hath an Image called Cakeres which most commonly standeth at Yaughtawnoone (in one of ye Kinges houses) or at Oropikes in a house for that purpose and with him are sett all the Kings goods and presents that are sent him as ye Cornne. But ye beades or Crowne or Bedd which ye Kinge of England sent him are in ye gods house at Oropikes, and in their houses are all ye Kinge ancesters and kindred commonly buried. In ye Patomecks cuntry they haue an other god whom they call Quioquascacke, and unto ther Images they offer Beades and Copper if at any time they want Rayne or haue to much, and though they obserue no day to worshipe ther god: but vppon necessitye, yet once in the yeare, ther preests which are ther coniuerers with yᵉ men, weomen, and children doe goe into the woods, wher ther preests makes a great cirkell of fier in ye which after many obseruanses in ther coniurations they make offer of 2 or 3 children to be giuen to ther god if he will apeare unto them and shew his mind whome he will haue. Vppon which offringe they heare a noyse out of ye Cirkell Nominatinge such as he will haue, whome presently they take bindinge them hand and footte and cast them into ye circle of the fier, for be it the Kinges sonne he must be giuen if once named by ther god. After yᵉ bodies which are offered are consumed in the fier and ther cerimonees performed the men depart merily, the weomen weaping. (Smith, John, Arber ed., 1884, pp. cv–cvi.)

Powhatan is said, upon one occasion, to have "vowed revenge" against his enemies, "after their manner, pointing to the Sunne" (Smith, John, Arber ed., p. xliv).

In their temples [notes Smith] they have his image [i. e. the image of Oke] evill favouredly carved, and then painted and adorned with chaines, copper, and beades, and covered with a skin, in such manner as the deformity may well suit with such a God.   (Smith, John, Tyler ed., 1907, p. 109.)

Elsewhere he speaks of Oke as their chief god and says that they called the others "quiyoughcosughes." Strachey, however, applies this term to the priests, and very likely with some slight modification it was used for both god or spirit and priest. Strachey's account of Powhatan beliefs is probably the best:

> In every territory of a weroance is a temple and a priest, peradventure two or three; yet happy doth that weroance accompt himself who can detayne with him a Quiyoughquisock, of the best, grave, lucky, well instructed in their misteryes, and beloved of their god; and such a one is noe lesse honoured than was Dianae's priest at Ephesus, for whome they have their more private temples, with oratories and chauncells therein, according as is the dignity and reverence of the Quiyoughquisock, which the weroance wilbe at charge to build upon purpose, sometyme twenty foote broad and a hundred in length, fashioned arbour wyse after their buylding, having comonly the dore opening into the east, and at the west end a spence or chauncell from the body of the temple, with hollow wyndings and pillers, whereon stand divers black imagies, fashioned to the shoulders, with their faces looking downe the church, and where within their weroances, upon a kind of beere of reedes, lye buryed; and under them, apart, in a vault low in the ground (as a more secrett thing), vailed with a matt, sitts their Okeus, an image ill-favouredly carved, all black dressed, with chaynes of perle, the presentment and figure of that god (say the priests unto the laity, and who religiously believe what the priests saie) which doth them all the harme they suffer, be yt in their bodies or goods, within doores or abroad. (Strachey, 1849, p. 83.)

He gives the name of the good deity as Ahone. The great temple of Powhatan at Utamussack was of this same general type, where were two supplementary buildings "filled with images of their kings and devills, and tombes of the predicessors" (Strachey, 1849, p. 90). These buildings were known as quioccosan, evidently another form of quiyoughquisock. Beverley has left us a considerable account of one of these buildings of which he had made a clandestine examination.

> Having removed about fourteen Loggs from the Door, with which it was barricado'd, we went in, and at first found nothing but naked Walls, and a Fire place in the middle. This House was about eighteen foot wide, and thirty foot long, built after the manner of their other Cabbins, but larger, with a Hole in the middle of the Roof, to vent the Smoke, the Door being at one end: Round about the House, at some distance from it, were set up Posts, with Faces carved on them, and painted. We did not observe any Window, or passage for the Light, except the Door, and the vent of the Chimney. At last, we observ'd, that at the farther end, about ten foot of the Room, was cut off by a Partition of very close Mats; and it was dismal dark behind that Partition. We were at first scrupulous to enter this obscure place, but at last we ventur'd, and groping about, we felt some Posts in the middle; then reaching our hands up those Posts, we found large Shelves, and upon these Shelves three Mats, each of which was roll'd up, and sow'd fast. These we handed down to the light, and to save time in unlacing the Seams, we made use of a Knife, and ripp'd them, without doing any damage to the Mats. In one of these we found some vast Bones, which we judg'd to be the Bones of Men, particularly we measured one Thigh-bone, and found it two foot nine inches long: In another Mat, we found some *Indian Tomahawks* finely grav'd, and painted. These resembl'd the wooden Faulchion use'd by the Prize-fighters in *England*, except that they have no guard to save the Fingers. They were made of a rough heavy Wood. . . . . Among these *Toma-*

hawks was the largest that ever I saw; there was fasten'd to it a Wild Turky's Beard painted red, and two of the longest Feathers of his Wings hung dangling at it, by a string of about 6 Inches long, ty'd to the end of the *Tomahawk*. In the third Mat there was something, which we took to be their Idol, tho of an underling sort, and wanted putting together. The pieces were these, first a Board three foot and a half long, with one indenture at the upper end, like a Fork, to fasten the Head upon, from thence half way down, were Half hoops nail'd to the Edges of the Board, at about four Inches distance, which was bow'd out, to represent the Breast and Belly; on the lower half was another Board of half the length of the other, fasten'd to it by Joynts or pieces of Wood, which being set on each side, stood out about 14 inches from the Body, and half as high; we suppos'd the use of these to be for the bowing out of the Knees, when the Image was set up. There were packt up with these things, red and blue pieces of Cotton Cloath, and Rolls made up for Arms, Thighs and Legs, bent to at the Knees, as is represented in the Figure of their Idol, which was taken by an exact Drawer in the Country. It wou'd be difficult to see one of these Images at this day, because the *Indians* are extreme shy of exposing them. We put the Cloaths upon the Hoops for the Body, and fasten'd on the Arms and Legs, to have a view of the representation: But the Head and rich Bracelets, which it is usually adorn'd with, were not there, or at least we did not find them. . . . This Image when drest up, might look very venerable in that dark place; where 'tis not possible to see it, but by the glimmering light, that is let in, by lifting up a piece of the Matting, which we observ'd to be conveniently hung for that purpose; for when the light of the Door and Chimney, glance in several directions, upon the Image thro that little passage, it must needs make a strange representation, which those poor people are taught to worship with a devout Ignorance. There are other things that contribute towards carrying on this Imposture; first the chief Conjurer enters within the Partition in the dark, and may undiscern'd move the Image as he pleases: Secondly, a Priest of Authority stands in the room with the people, to keep them from being too inquisitive, under the penalty of the Deity's displeasure, and his own censure. (Beverley, 1705, bk. 3, pp. 28–30.)

Beverley's illustration of the idol is a mere adaptation of that of White in Hariot, but the text represents apparently direct observation:

The Dark edging shews the Sides and Roof (of) the House, which consist of Saplins and Bark. The paler Edging shews the Mats, by which they make a Partition, of about ten foot, at the end of the House, for the Idols abode. The Idol is set upon his Seat of Mats, within his dark recess, above the peoples heads, and the Curtain is drawn up before him. (Beverley, 1705, bk. 3, p. 31.)

Altars made of unworked stones and out under the open sky were common in the Algonquian territories. Whether this is accidental or not, the fact remains that we find very few notices of them elsewhere. Smith:

They have also certaine Altar stones they call *Pawcorances*: but these stand from their Temples, some by their houses, other in the woodes and wildernesses. Upon these, they offer blood, deare suet, and Tobacco. These they doe when they returne from the warres, from hunting, and upon many other occasions. (Smith, John, Tyler ed., 1907, p. 111; cf. Strachey, 1849, p. 93.)

The most lengthy notices of these sacred places are by Beverley:

There also [i. e., at Uttamussack] was their great *Pawcorance*, or Altar-Stone, which, the *Indians* tell us, was a solid Chrystal, of between Three and Four Foot

Cube, upon which, in their greatest Solemnities, they used to sacrifice. This, they would make us believe, was so clear, that the Grain of a Man's Skin might be seen through it; and was so heavy too, that when they remov'd their Gods and Kings, not being able to carry it away, they buried it thereabouts: But the Place has never been yet discover'd. (Beverley, 1705, bk. 2, pp. 10–11.)

They erect Altars where-ever they have any remarkable occasion; and because their principal Devotion consists in Sacrifice, they have a profound respect for these Altars. They have one particular Altar, to which, for some mystical reason, many of their Nations pay an extraordinary Veneration; of this sort was the Crystal Cube, mention'd Book II. Chap. 3 (art. 8.) The *Indians* call this by the name of *Pawcorance*, from whence proceeds the great Reverence they have for a small Bird that uses the Woods, and in their note continually sounds that name. This Bird flys alone, and is only heard in the twilight. They say this is the Soul of one of their Princes; and on that score, they wou'd not hurt it for the World. But there was once a profane *Indian* in the upper parts of *James* River, who, after abundance of fears and scruples, was at last brib'd to kill one of them with his Gun; but the *Indians* say he paid dear for his presumption, for in a few days after he was taken away, and never more heard of.

When they travel by any of these Altars, they take great care to instruct their Children and Young people in the particular occasion and time of their erection, and recommend the respect which they ought to have for them; so that their careful observance of these Traditions proves as good a Memorial of such Antiquities, as any Written Records; especially for so long as the same people continue to inhabit in, or near the same place. (Beverley, 1705, bk. 3, pp. 46–47.)

As regards the Indians' conception of the After Life:

Concerning the ymmortality of the sowle [says Strachey] they suppose that the common people shall not live after death; but they thinck that their weroances and priests, indeed whom they esteeme half quioughcosughes, when their bodyes are laied in the earth, that that which is within shall goe beyond the mountaynes, and travell as farr as where the sun setts into most pleasant fields, growndes, and pastures, where yt shall doe no labour; but, stuck finely with feathers, and painted with oyle and pocones, rest in all quiet and peace, and eat delicious fruicts, and have store of copper, beades, and hatchetts; sing, daunce, and have all variety of delights and merryments till that waxe old there, as the body did on earth, and then yt shall dissolve and die, and come into a woman's womb againe, and so be a new borne unto the world. (Strachey, 1849, p. 96; see also p. 749 below.)

Smith and Strachey do not differentiate between the priest and the conjurer as does Hariot, but Beverley is probably right in what he has to say regarding the separate functions of the two though he chooses to illustrate his account of them by patent reproductions of the White drawings. Strachey says that at Uttamussack, the principal temple,

commonly are resident seven priests, the chief differing from the rest in his ornament, whilst the inferior priests can hardly be knowne from the common people, save that they had not (it may be may not have) so many holes in their eares to hang their jewells at . . . . . In their hands they carry every one his rattle, for the most part as a symbole of his place and profession, some basse, some smaller. (Strachey, 1849, p. 91.)

Beverley's description of the costumes of these men has been quoted elsewhere (p. 478). He says of their function:

The Conjurer is a Partner with the Priests, not only in the Cheat, but in the advantages of it, and sometimes they officiate for one another. When this Artist is in the Act of Conjuration, or of Pauwawing, as they term it, he always appears with an air of Haste, or else in some Convulsive posture, that seems to strain all the faculties, like the *Sybils*, when they pretended to be under the Power of Inspiration. (Beverley, 1705, bk. 2, p. 45.)

Turning to ceremonials, we may quote the following from Smith:

Their devotion was most in songs which the chiefe Priest beginneth and the rest followed him: sometimes he maketh invocations with broken sentences, by starts and strange passions, and at every pause, the rest give a short groane.

It could not bee perceived that they keepe any day as more holy than other: but only in some distresse, of want, feare of enimies, times of triumph and gathering together their fruits, the whole country of men, women and children come togither to solemnities. The manner of their devotion is sometimes to make a great fire in the house or fields, and all to sing and dance about it, with rattles and shouts togither, 4 or 5 houres. Sometimes they set a man in the midst, and about him they dance and sing, he all the while clapping his hands as if he would keepe time. And after their songs and dauncings ended, they goe ot their feasts. [This is the sort of performance illustrated by Hariot and described as "their manner of prainge with rattels abowt the fyer" (pl. 96).]

They have also divers conjurations. One they made when Captaine Smith was their prisoner (as they reported) to know if any more of his countrymen would arrive there, and what he there intended. The manner of it was thus. First they made a faire fire in a house. About this fire set 7 Priests setting him by them, and about the fire, they made a circle of meale. That done, the chiefe Priest attired as is expressed, began to shake his rattle, and the rest followed him in his song. At the end of the song, he laid downe 5 or 3 graines of wheat, and so continued counting his songs by the graines, till 3 times they incirculed the fire. Then they divide the graines by certaine numbers with little stickes, laying downe at the ende of every song a little sticke. In this manner, they sat 8, 10, or 12 houres without cease, with such strange stretching of their armes, and violent passions and gestures as might well seeme strange to him they so conjured, who but every houre expected his end. Not any meat they did eat till, late in the evening, they had finished this worke: and then they feasted him and themselves with much mirth. But 3 or 4 daies they continued this ceremony. (Smith, John, Tyler ed., 1907, pp. 110–111.)

Spelman says regarding the social gatherings and dances:

When they meet at feasts or otherwise they vse sprorts much like to ours heare in England as ther daunsinge, which is like our darbysher Hornepipe a man first and then a woman, and so through them all, hanging all in a round, ther is one which stand in the midest with a pipe and a rattell with which when he begins to make a noyes all the rest Gigetts about wriinge ther neckes and stampinge on yᵉ ground. (Smith, John, Arber ed., 1884, p. cxiv.)

Beverley:

Their Singing is not the most charming that I have heard, it consists much in exalting the voice, and is full of slow melancholy accents. However, I must allow even this Musick to contain some wild Notes that are agreeable.

Their Dancing is perform'd either by few or a great Company, but without much regard either to Time or Figure. The first of these is by one or two persons, or at most three. In the mean while, the Company sit about them in a Ring upon the Ground, singing outrageously and shaking their Rattles. The Dancers sometimes Sing, and sometimes look menacing and terrible, beating their Feet furiously against the Ground, and showing ten thousand Grimaces and Distortions. The other is perform'd by a great number of people, the Dancers themselves forming a Ring, and moving round a Circle of carv'd Posts, that are set up for that purpose; or else round a Fire, made in a convenient part of the Town; and then each has his Rattle in his hand, or what other thing he fancies most, as his Bow and Arrows, or his Tomahawk. They also dress themselves up with Branches of Trees, or some other strange accoutrements. Thus they proceed, Dancing and Singing, with all the antick postures they can invent; and he's the bravest Fellow that has the most prodigious gestures. Sometimes they place three young Women in the middle of the Circle, as you may see in the Figure. [See pl. 93.] (Beverley, 1705, bk. 3, pp. 53–54.)

And Strachey:

As for their dauncyng, the sport seemes unto them, and the use almost as frequent and necessary as their meat and drynck, in which they consume much tyme, and for which they appoint many and often meetings, and have therefore, as yt were, set orgies or festivalls for the same pastyme, as have yet at this daye the merry Greekes within the Arches. At our colonies first sitting downe amongst them, when any of our people repaired to their townes, the Indians would not thinck they had expressed their welcome sufficyentlie enough untill they had shewed them a daunce, the manner of which is thus: One of them standeth by, with some furre or leather thing in his leaft hand, upon which he beats with his right hand, and sings with all as if he began the quier, and kept unto the rest their just tyme, when upon a certaine stroke or more (as upon his cue or tyme to come in) one riseth up and begynns to dawnce; after he hath daunced a while stepps forth another, as if he came in just upon his rest; and in this order all of them, so many as there be, one after another, who then daunce an equall distaunce from each other in ring, showting, howling, and stamping their feete against the ground with such force and paine that they sweat agayne, and with all variety of strang mymick tricks and distorted faces, making so confused a yell and noyse as so many frantique and disquieted bachanalls, and sure they will keepe stroak just with their feete to the tyme he gives, and just one with another, but with the hands, head, face, and body, every one hath a severall gesture; and who have seene the darvises, in their holy daunces, in their mosces, upon Wednesdayes and Frydayes in Turkey, maye resemble these unto them. Strachey, 1849, pp. 80–81.)

Beverley has the following fragment of myth:

They have likewise in other cases many fond and idle Superstititions, as for the purpose, by the falls of *James* River upon Collonel *Byrd's* Land, there lies a Rock which I have seen, about a mile from the River, wherein is fairly imprest several marks like the footsteps of a Gigantick Man, each step being about five foot asunder: These they aver to be the track of their God. (Beverley, 1705, bk. 3, p. 44.)

But the longest myth recorded among these Indians is contained in the following quotation from Strachey, which also gives an idea

of their beliefs in general.   It was obtained from Jopassus, brother
of the great chief of the Potomac tribe:

We have (said he) five gods in all; our chief god appeares often unto us
in the likenes of a mighty great hare; the other four have noe visible shape,
but are indeed the four wynds which keepe the four corners of the earth
(and then, with his hand, he seemed to quarter out the scytuations of the
world).   Our god, who takes upon him this shape of a hare, conceaved with
himself how to people this great world, and with what kinde of creatures,
and yt is true (said he) that at length he devised and made divers men and
women, and made provision for them, to be kept up yet a while in a great
bag.   Nowe there were certayne spiritts, which he described to be like great
giants, which came to the hare's dwelling-place (being towards the rising of
the sun), and had perseveraunce of the men and women which he had put
into that great bagg, and they would have had them to eat, but the godlye
hare reproved those canniball spiritts, and drove them awaye. . . . The old
man went on, and said how that godlike hare made the water, and the fish
therein, and the land, and a great deare, which should feed upon the land;
at which assembled the other four gods, envyous hereat, from the east, the
west, from the north and south, and with hunting pooles kild this great deare,
dreast him, and, after they had feasted with him, departed againe, east, west,
north, and south; at which the other god, in despight for this their mallice
to him, tooke all the haires of the slaine deare, and spred them upon the
earth, with many powerfull words and charmes, whereby every haire became
a deare; and then he opened the great bag, wherein the men and the women
were, and placed them upon the earth, a man and a woman in one country,
and a man and a woman in another country, and so the world tooke his first
begynning of mankind.   The captaine bad the boy ask him what he thought
became of them after their death, to which he answered somewhat like as is
expressed before of the inhabitaunts about us, how that after they are dead
here, they goe up to a top of a high tree, and there they espie a faire plaine
broad path waye, on both sides whereof doth grow all manner of pleasant
fruicts, as mulberies, straberries, plombes, etc.   In this pleasant path they
rune toward the rising of the sun, where the godly hare's howse is, and in the
midway they come to a house where a woman goddesse doth dwell, whoe hath
alwaies her doares open for hospitality, and hath at all tymes ready drest greene
vskatahomen and pokahichory, (which is greene corne brused and boyled, and
walnutts beaten small, then washed from the shells with a quantity of water,
which makes a kind of milke, and which they esteeme an extraordinary dish,)
togither with all manner of pleasant fruicts, in a readiness to entertayne all such
as doe travell to the great hare's howse; and when they are well refreshed, they
run in this pleasant path to the rising of the sun, where they fynd their forefathers lyving in great pleasure, in a goodly field, where they doe nothing but
dawnce and sing, and feed on delitious fruicts with that great hare, who is their
great god; and when they have lyved there untill they be starke old men, they
saie they dye there likewise by turnes, and come into the world againe.
(Strachey, 1849, pp. 98–100; see p. 746 above).

Our knowledge of the religion of the Virginia Siouans, as distinguished from that of the Carolinian tribes of this stock, is nearly
confined to the information which William Byrd extracted from his
guide Bearskin, a Saponi, who, says Byrd, explained his views "without any of that Reserve to which his Nation is Subject."

He told us he believed that there was one Supreme God, who had Several Subaltern Deities under Him. And that this Master-God made the World a long time ago. That he told the Sun, the Moon, and Stars, their Business in the Beginning, which they, with good looking after, have faithfully perform'd ever Since.

That the same Power that made all things at first has taken care to keep them in the same Method and Motion ever since.

He believ'd God had form'd many Worlds before he form'd this, that those Worlds either grew old and ruinous, or were destroyed for the Dishonesty of the Inhabitants.

That God is very just and very good—ever well pleas'd with those men who possess those God-like Qualities. That he takes good People into his safe Protection, makes them very rich, fills their Bellies plentifully, preserves them from sickness, and from being surpriz'd or Overcome by their Enemies.

But all such as tell Lies, and Cheat those they have Dealings with, he never fails to punish with Sickness, Poverty and Hunger, and after all that, Suffers them to be knockt on the Head and scalpt by those that fight against them.

He believ'd that after Death both good and bad People are conducted by a strong Guard into a great Road, in which departed Souls travel together for some time, till at a certain Distance this Road forks into two Parts, the one extremely Levil, and the other Stony and Mountainous.

Here the good are parted from the bad by a flash of Lightening, the first being hurry'd away to the Right, the other to the Left. The Right hand Road leads to a charming warm Country, where the Spring is everlasting, and every Month is May; and as the year is always in its Youth, so are the People, and particularly the Women are bright as Stars, and never Scold.

That in this happy Climate there are Deer, Turkeys, Elks, and Buffaloes innumerable, perpetually fat and gentle, while the Trees are loaded with delicious Fruit quite throughout the four Seasons.

That the Soil brings forth Corn Spontaneously, without the Curse of Labour, and so very wholesome, that None who have the hapiness to eat of it are ever Sick, grow old, or dy.

Near the Entrance into this Blessed Land Sits a Venerable Old Man on a Mat richly woven, who examines Strictly all that are brought before Him, and if they have behav'd well, the Guards are order'd to open the Crystal Gate, and let them enter into the Land of Delights.

The left Hand Path is very rugged and uneven, leading to a dark and barren County, where it is always Winter. The Ground is the whole year round cover'd with Snow, and nothing is to be seen upon the Trees but Icicles.

All the People are hungry, yet have not a Morsel of any thing to eat, except a bitter kind of Potato, that gives them the Dry-Gripes, and fills their whole Body with loathsome Ulcers, that Stink, and are unsupportably painfull.

Here all the Women are old and ugly, having Claws like a Panther, with which they fly upon the Men that Slight their Passion. For it seems these haggard old Furies are intolerably fond, and expect a vast deal of Cherishing. They talk much and exceedingly Shrill, giving exquisite Pain to the Drum of the Ear, which in that Place of the Torment is so tender, that every Sharp Note wounds it to the Quick.

At the End of this Path sits a dreadful old Woman on a monstrous Toad-Stool, whose head is cover'd with Rattle-Snakes instead of Tresses, with glaring white Eyes, that strike a Terror unspeakable into all that behold her.

This Hag pronounces Sentence of Woe upon all the miserable Wretches that hold up their hands at her Tribunal. After this they are deliver'd over to huge Turkey-Buzzards, like harpys, that fly away with them to the Place above mentioned.

Here, after they have been tormented a certain Number of years, according to their several Degrees of Guilt, they are again driven back into this World, to try if they will mend their Manners, and merit a place the next time in the Regions of Bliss. (Bassett, 1901, pp. 140–143.)

In his Secret History of the Line, there is little variation from the published narrative except for certain omissions. However, he there adds that the Supreme Being "protects and prospers good People in this World, & punishes the bad with Sickness & Poverty," and in the Saponi hell

all the People are old, have no teeth, & yet are very hungry. Only those who labour very hard make the Ground Produce a Sort of Potato pleasant to the Tast, but gives them the dry Gripes, & fills them full of Sores, which stink and are very painfull.

There is some amplification also in treating of the activities of the female custodian of the nether world:

On the Borders sits a hideous Old Woman whose Head is cover'd with Rattle-Snakes instead of Tresses, with glaring white Eyes, sunk very deep in her Head. Her Tongue is 20 Cubits long arm'd with sharp Thorns as strong as Iron. This Tongue besides the dreadfull Sound it makes in pronouncing sentence, serves the purpose of an Elephant's Trunk, with which the Old Gentlewoman takes up those she has convicted of Wickedness & throws them over a vast high wall hewn out of one Solid Rock, that Surrounds this Region of Misery, to prevent Escapes. They are receiv'd on the inside by another Hideous Old Woman who consigns them over to Punishments proper for their Crimes. When they have been chastiz'd here a certain Number of Years according to their degrees of Guilt, they are thrown over the Wall again, & drawn once more back into this World of Trial, where if they mend their Manners they are conducted into the abovemention'd fine Country after their Death. (Bassett, 1901, p. 201.)

It would seem either that Bearskin had considerable decorative imagination or that Byrd exercised much of that which we know him to have possessed, while the teachers nad missionaries which the former had encountered at Fort Christanna may have had some influence. The substructure is no doubt Indian nonetheless.

Byrd provides us with the following Messianic story concerning the Tuscarora Indians:

The Indians have a very odd Tradition amongst them, that many years ago, their Nation was grown so dishonest, that no man cou'd keep any Goods, or so much as his loving Wife to himself. That, however, their God, being unwilling to root them out for their crimes, did them the honour to send a Messenger from Heaven to instruct them, and set Them a perfect Example of Integrity and kind Behavior towards one another.

But this holy Person, with all his Eloquence and Sanctity of Life, was able to make very little Reformation amongst them. Some few Old Men did listen a little to his Wholesome Advice, but all the Young fellows were quite incorrigible. They not only Neglected his Precepts, but derided and Evil Entreated his Person. At last, taking upon Him to reprove some Young Rakes of the Conechta Clan very sharply for their impiety, they were so provok'd at the Freedom of his Rebukes, that they tied him to a Tree, and shot him with Arrows through the Heart. But their God took instant Vengeance on all who had a hand in that Monstrous Act, by Lightning from Heaven, & has ever since visited their Nation with a continued Train of Calamities, nor will he ever leave off punishing, and wasting their People, till he shall have blotted every living Soul, of them out of the World. (Bassett, 1901, pp. 290–292.)

Lawson informs us that the Indians of his acquaintance were great believers in spirits and witches but were not afraid of them at night, something of an exaggeration one would think:

Not but that the Indians have as many lying stories of spirits and conjurers, as any people in the world; but they tell it with no disadvantage to themselves; for the great esteem which the old men bring themselves to, is by making the others believe their familiarity with devils and spirits, and how great a correspondence they have therewith, which if it once gains credit, they ever after are held in the greatest veneration imaginable, and whatever they after impose upon the people, is received as infallible. They are so little startled at the thoughts of another world, that they not seldom murder themselves. (Lawson, 1860, pp. 327–328.)

In another place:

They all believe, that this world is round, and that there are two spirits; the one good, the other bad. The good one they reckon to be the author and maker of everything, and say, that it is he, that gives them the fruits of the earth, and has taught them to hunt, fish, and be wise enough to overpower the beasts of the wilderness, and all other creatures, that they may be assistants, and beneficial to man; to which they add, that the quera, or good spirit, has been very kind to the Englishmen, to teach them to make guns, and ammunition, besides a great many other necessaries, that are helpful to man, all which, they say will be delivered to them, when that good spirit sees fit. They do not believe that God punishes any man either in this life, or that to come; but that he delights in doing good, and in giving the fruits of the earth, and instructing us in making several useful and ornamental things. They say, it is a bad spirit, who lives separate from the good one, that torments us with sicknesses, disappointments, losses, hunger, travel, and all the misfortunes, that human life is incident to. (Lawson, 1860, pp. 342–343.)

The misfortunes of the wicked after death alluded to elsewhere must have been attributed to the bad spirit.

They think [he says] that the country of souls lies a great way off in this world which the sun visits in his ordinary course, and that [the good soul] will have the enjoyment of handsome young women, great stores of deer to hunt, never meet with hunger, cold or fatigue, but every thing to answer his expectation and desire. This is the heaven they propose to themselves; but, on the contrary, for those Indians that are lazy, thievish amongst themselves, bad hunters, and no warriors, nor of much use to the nation, to such they allot, in the next world, hunger, cold, troubles, old ugly women for their companions, with snakes, and all sorts of nasty victuals to feed on. (Lawson, 1860, p. 295.)

The Siouan tribes had temples (quiozogon) similar to those of the Algonquians. Lawson describes the quiozogon as

a very large magnificent cabin, according to their building, which is raised at the public charge of the nation, and maintained in a great deal of form and neatness. About seven feet high is a floor or loft made, on which lie all their princes and great men that have died for several hundred years, all attired in the dress I before told you of.

He adds that when forced to migrate, they always took the bones in this temple with them.

They reverence and adore this quiozogon with all the veneration and respect that is possible for such a people to discharge, and had rather lose all than have any violence or injury offered thereto. (Lawson, 1860, p. 298.)

The Waxhaw ceremonial house, which he describes in another place was similar to the town house of the Creeks (see pp. 410–411 above).

He found such "state houses," as he calls them all along the road to Sapona and then no more of them.

Near Adshusheer, the town of the Eno and Shakori, he noted a stone to which the Indians made sacrifices (Lawson, 1860, p. 99).

As related elsewhere, priests or conjurers officiated at every funeral and it was mainly they who acted as custodians of the sacred lore of the tribe. Some notes regarding their costumes have been detailed elsewhere. Lawson has the following on the practices of these men in addition to what is given below in the section on medicine. After a discussion of their method of treating disease, he cites the following instances of seeming clairvoyance:

One rainy night a certain Indian undermined a house made of logs, such as the Swedes in America very often made, and are very strong, which belonged to Seth Southwell, Esq., governor of North Carolina, and one of the proprietors. There was but one place the Indian could get in at, which was very narrow; the rest was secured, by having barrels of pork and other provisions set against the side of the house, so that if this Indian had not exactly hit the very place he undermined, it had been impossible for him to have got therein, because of the full barrels that stood round the house, and barricaded it within. The Indian stole sixty or eighty dressed deer skins, besides blankets, powder, shot and rum, this being the Indian store house, where the trading goods were kept. Now, the Indian had made his escape, but dropped some of the skins by the way and they tracked his footsteps, and found him to be an Indian; then they guessed who it was, because none but that Indian had lately been near the house. Thereupon, the governor sent to the Indian town that he belonged to, which was the Tuskeruros, and acquainted them that if they did not deliver up the Indian, who had committed the robbery, he would take a course with them, that would not be very agreeable. Upon this, the Indians of the town he belonged to, brought him in bound, and delivered him up to the governor, who laid him in irons. At the same time, it happened that a robbery was committed amongst themselves, at the

Indian town, and this prisoner was one of their conjurers; so the Indians came down to the governor's house, and acquainted him with what had happened amongst them, and that a great quantity of peak was stolen away out of one of their cabins, and no one could find out the thief, unless he would let the prisoner conjure for it, who was the only man they had at making such discoveries. The governor was content he should try his skill for them, but not to have the prisoner's irons taken off, which was very well approved of. The Indian was brought out in his fetters where were the governor's family and several others of the neighborhood, now living, to see this experiment; which he performed thus.

The conjurer ordered three fires to be made in a triangular form, which was accordingly done; then he was hoodwinked very securely, with a dressed deer skin, two or three doubles, over his face. After he had made some motions, as they always do, he went directly out of one of the three gaps, as exactly as if he had not been blindfolded, and kept muttering to himself, having a stick in his hand, with which, after some time, he struck two strokes very hard, upon the ground, and made thereon a cross, after which he told the Indian's name that had stolen the goods, and said, that he would have a cross on his back; which proved true; for when they took and searched him, there appeared two great wheals, on his back, one cross the other; for the thief was at governor Southwell's house, and was under no apprehension of being discovered. The Indians proffered to sell him as a slave to the governor, but he refused to buy him; so they took him bound away. . . .

There are a great many other stories of this nature, which are seemingly true, being told by persons that afirm they were eye witnesses thereof; as, that they have seen one Roncommock, a Chuwou [Chowan] Indian, and a great conjurer, take a reed about two feet long in his mouth, and stand by a creek side, where he called twice or thrice with the reed in his mouth, and, at last, has opened his arms and fled over the creek, which might be near a quarter of a mile wide or more; but I shall urge no man's belief, but tell my own; which is, that I believe the two first accounts which were acted at Mr. Southwell's plantation, as firmly as any man can believe any thing of that which is told him by honest men, and he has not seen; not at all doubting the credit of my authors. (Lawson, 1860, pp. 347–353.)

The rest of Lawson's account concerns the treatment of disease by conjurers and will be given under the heading of medicine.

Peter Martyr was informed of a province in what is now South Carolina called Tihe where

the inhabitants wear a distinctive priestly costume, and they are regarded as priests and venerated as such by their neighbors. They cut their hair leaving only two locks growing on their temples, which are bound under the chin. When the natives make war against their neighbors, according to the regrettable custom of mankind, these priests are invited by both sides to be present, not as actors, but as witnesses of the conflict. When the battle is about to open, they circulate among the warriors who are seated or lying on the ground, and sprinkle them with the juice of certain herbs they have chewed with their teeth; just as our priests at the beginning of the Mass sprinkle the worshipers with a branch dipped in holy water. When this ceremony is finished, the opposing sides fall upon one another. While the battle rages, the priests are left in charge of the camp, and when it is finished they look after the wounded, making no distinction between friends and enemies, and busy themselves in burying the dead. (Anghierra, 1912, 259–262; Swanton, 1922, pp. 42–43.)

It is probable that Peter Martyr's informants were actually describing the activities of a class of doctors within a tribe or tribes, not a tribe consisting of doctors.   We should also be skeptical of the neutral position they are alleged to have taken, since no such thing was found in this part of North America.   Anointing with medicine before battle was, however, common.   Mention is made elsewhere of the oration performed by a medicine man over the deceased about as described nearly two centuries later by Lawson.   Perhaps the following is an example of native jugglery:

> Another fraud of the priests is as follows: When the chief is at death's door and about to give up his soul they send away all witnesses, and then surrounding his bed they perform some secret jugglery which makes him appear to vomit sparks and ashes.   It looks like sparks jumping from a bright fire, or those sulphured papers which people throw into the air to amuse themselves.   These sparks, rushing through the air and quickly disappearing, look like those shooting stars which people call leaping wild goats.   The moment the dying man expires a cloud of those sparks shoots up 3 cubits high with a noise and quickly vanishes.   They hail this flame as the dead man's soul, bidding it a last farewell and accompanying its flight with their wailings, tears, and funeral cries, absolutely convinced that it has taken its flight to heaven.   Lamenting and weeping they escort the body to the tomb.   (Anghierra, 1912, pp. 263–266.)

Naturally, a tale recorded early in the sixteenth century by superstitious Spaniards from superstitious Indians would be dismissed as a mere creation of the undisciplined imagination.   But in 1711, nearly two hundred years later, De Graffenried, leader of the Swiss colony at Newbern, thus describes an occurrence of which he was an eyewitness during a Tuscarora burial:

> After the tomb was covered, I noticed something which passes imagination, and which I should not believe had I not seen it with my own eyes.   From the tomb arose a little flaming fire, like a big candle-light, which went up straight in the air, and noiselessly—went straight over the cabin of the deceased's widow, and thence further across a big swamp above 1½ mile broad until it finally vanished from sight in the woods.   At that sight, I gave way to my surprise, and asked what it meant, but the Indians laughed at me, as if I ought to have known that this was no rarity among them, they refused however, to tell me what it was.   All that I could ascertain, was that they thought a great deal of it,—that this light is a favourable omen, which makes them think the deceased a happy soul,—during [the burial rites] they deem it a most unpropitious sign when a black smoke ascends from the tomb.   This flying flame, yet, could not be artificial, on account of the great distance; it could be some physical phenomenon, like sulphurous vapors,—but this great uniformity in its appearance surpasses nature.   (De Graffenried, 1886, p. 984.)

Although De Graffenried was not devoid himself of what we should now call superstition, it seems quite certain from his experience that a conjuring trick is involved known to the medicine men of that particular section.   It may be added that the   Spanish explorers of Chicora were informed of magical means used in forcing the growth of bodies of princes of the family of the chief Datha to huge proportions (Anghierra, 1912, vol. 2, pp. 267–269; Swanton 1922, p. 46). This, however, contains some distorted record of head deformation.

The ceremonial life, was, as usual, tied up with the social life and social gatherings. Lawson gives about all that we know regarding the latter:

Their dances are of different natures; and for every sort of dance they have a tune, which is allotted for that dance; as, if it be a war dance, they have a war-like song, wherein they express, with all the passion and vehemence imagineable, what they intend to do with their enemies; how they will kill, roast, scalp, beat, and make captive, such and such numbers of them; and how many they have destroyed before. All these songs are made new for every feast; nor is one and the same song sung at two several festivals. Some one of the nation, which has the best gift of expressing their designs, is appointed by their king and war captains to make these songs.

Others are made for feasts of another nature; as, when several towns, or sometimes different nations have made peace with one another; then the song suits both nations, and relates how the bad spirit made them go to war and destroy one another; but it shall never be so again; but that their sons and daughters shall marry together, and the two nations love one another, and become as one people.

They have a third sort of feasts and dances, which are always when the harvest of corn is ended and in the spring. The one to return thanks to the good spirit for the fruits of the earth; the other, to beg the same blessings for the succeeding year. And to encourage the young men to labor stoutly in planting their maiz and pulse, they set a sort of an idol in the field, which is dressed up exactly like an Indian, having all the Indians habit, besides abundance of wampum and their money, made of shells, that hangs about his neck. The image none of the young men dare approach; for the old ones will not suffer them to come near him, but tell them that he is some famous Indian warrior that died a great while ago, and now is come amongst them to see if they work well, which if they do, he will go to the good spirit and speak to him to send them plenty of corn, and to make the young men all expert hunters and mighty warriors. All this while, the king and old men sit round the image and seemingly pay a profound respect to the same. One great help to these Indians in carrying on these cheats, and inducing youth to do what they please, is, the uninterrupted silence which is ever kept and observed with all the respect and veneration imaginable.

At these feasts which are set out with all the magnificence their fare allows of, the masquerades begin at night and not before. There is commonly a fire made in the middle of the house, which is the largest in the town, and is very often the dwelling of their king or war captain; where sit two men on the ground upon a mat; one with a rattle, made of a gourd, with some beans in it; the other with a drum made of an earthern pot, covered with a dressed deer skin, and one stick in his hand to beat thereon; and so they both begin the song appointed. At the same time one drums and the other rattles, which is all the artificial music of their own making I ever saw amongst them. To these two instruments they sing, which carries no air with it, but is a sort of unsavory jargon; yet their cadences and raising of their voices are formed with that equality and exactness that, to us Europeans, it seems admirable how they should continue these songs without once missing to agree, each with the others note and tune.

As for their dancing, were there masters of that profession amongst them as there are with us, they would dearly earn their money; for these creatures take the most pains at it that men are able to endure. I have seen thirty odd together a dancing, and every one dropped down with sweat, as if water had been poured down their backs. They use those hard labors to make them able to endure fatigue and improve their wind, which indeed is very long and durable, it being a hard matter in any exercise to dispossess them of it.

At these feasts, they meet from all the towns within fifty or sixty miles round, where they buy and sell several commodities, as we do at fairs and markets. (Lawson, 1860, pp. 285–287.)

This account covers the Tuscarora as well as the Siouan tribes, but the following description of a Waxhaw festivity is from direct observation of a ceremony among the latter:

[The dogs having been ejected from the "state house" of the tribe] the company was summoned by beat of drum; the music being made of a dressed deer's skin, tied hard upon an earthern porridge pot. Presently in came five men dressed up with feathers, their faces being covered with vizards made of gourds; round their ancles and knees were hung bells of several sorts; having wooden falchions in their hands, (such as stage fencers commonly use); in this dress they danced about an hour, showing many strange gestures, and brandishing their wooden weapons as if they were going to fight each other; oftentimes walking very nimbly round the room, without making the least noise with their bells, a thing I much admired at; again turning their bodies, arms and legs, into such frightful postures, that you would have guessed they had been quite raving mad: at last, they cut two or three high capers and left the room. In their stead came in a parcel of women and girls, to the number of thirty odd, every one taking place according to her degree of stature— the tallest leading the dance and the least of all being placed last; with these they made a circular dance, like a ring representing the shape of the fire they danced about. Many of these had great horse bells about their necks.—They had musicians, who were two old men, one of whom beat a drum, while the other rattled with a gourd that had corn in it to make a noise withal. To these instruments they both sang a mournful ditty; the burthen of their song was, in remembrance of their former greatness, and numbers of their nation, the famous exploits of their renowned ancestors, and all actions of moment that had, in former days, been performed by their forefathers.

At these festivals it is, that they give a traditional relation of what hath passed amongst them, to the younger fry, these verbal deliveries being always published in their most public assemblies, serve instead of our traditional notes by the use of letters. Some Indians, that I have met withal, have given me a very curious description of the great deluge, the immortality of the soul, with a pithy account of the reward of good and wicked deeds in the life to come; having found amongst some of them, great observers of moral rules, and the law of nature; indeed, a worthy foundation to build christianity upon, were a true method found out and practiced for the performance thereof.

Their way of dancing is nothing but a sort of stamping motion, much like the treading upon founder's bellows. This female gang held their dance for above six hours, being all of them of a white lather, like a running horse, that has just come in from his race. My landlady was the ringleader of the Amazons, who when in her own house, behaved herself very discreetly and warily in her domestic affairs; yet, custom had so infatuated her, as to almost break her heart with dancing amongst such a confused rabble. During this dancing, the spectators do not neglect their business in working the loblolly-pots, and the other meat that was brought thither; more or less of them being continually eating, whilst the others were dancing. When the dancing was ended, every youth that was so disposed catched hold of the girl he liked best, and took her that night for his bed fellow, making as short courtship and expeditious weddings, as the foot guards used to do with the trulls in Salisbury court. (Lawson, 1860, pp. 68–71.)

Short descriptions of some ceremonies which seem to have been performed by the Siouan Indians of South Carolina are supplied by Peter Martyr on the authority of an Indian of that region, and they are of particular interest owing to the early date of the information, 1520–30. Speaking of the palace of a gigantic chief called Datha who ruled in a province known as Duhare, he says:

In the courtyard of this palace, the Spaniards found two idols as large as a three-year-old child, one male and one female. These idols are both called Inamah'ari, and had their residence in the palace. Twice each year they are exhibited, the first time at the sowing season, when they are invoked to obtain successful results for their labors. We will speak later of the harvest. Thanksgivings are offered to them if the crops are good; in the contrary case they are implored to show themselves more favorable the following year.

The idols are carried in procession amidst much pomp, accompanied by the entire people. It will not be useless to describe this ceremony. On the eve of the festival the king has his bed made in the room where the idols stand, and sleeps in their presence. At daybreak the people assemble, and the king himself carries these idols, hugging them to his breast, to the top of his palace, where he exhibits them to the people. He and they are saluted with respect and fear by the people, who fall upon their knees or throw themselves on the ground with loud shouts. The king then descends and hangs the idols, draped in artistically worked cotton stuffs, upon the breasts of two venerable men of authority. They are, moreover, adorned with feather mantles of various colors, and are thus carried escorted with hymns and songs into the country, while the girls and young men dance and leap. Anyone who stopped in his house or absented himself during the procession would be suspected of heresy; and not only the absent, but likewise any who took part in the ceremony carelessly and without observing the ritual. The men escort the idols during the day, while during the night the women watch over them, lavishing upon them demonstrations of joy and respect. The next day they are carried back to the palace with the same ceremonies with which they were taken out. If the sacrifice is accomplished with devotion and in conformity with the ritual, the Indians believe they will obtain rich crops, bodily health, peace, or if they are about to fight, victory, from these idols. Thick cakes, similar to those the ancients made from flour, are offered to them. The natives are convinced that their prayers for harvests will be heard, especially if the cakes are mixed with tears.

Another feast is celebrated every year when a roughly carved wooden statue is carried into the country and fixed upon a high pole planted in the ground. This first pole is surrounded by similar ones, upon which people hang gifts for the gods, each one according to his means. At nightfall the principal citizens divide these offerings among themselves, just as the priests do with the cakes and other offerings given them by the women. Whoever offers the divinity the most valuable presents is the most honored. Witnesses are present when the gifts are offered, who announce after the ceremony what every one has given, just as notaries might do in Europe. Each one is thus stimulated by a spirit of rivalry to outdo his neighbor. From sunrise till evening the people dance round this statue, clapping their hands, and when nightfall has barely set in, the image and the pole on which it was fixed are carried away and thrown into the sea, if the country is on the coast, or into the river, if it is along a river's bank. Nothing more is seen of it, and each year a new statue is made.

The natives celebrate a third festival, during which, after exhuming a long-buried skeleton, they erect a black tent out in the country, leaving one end open so that the sky is visible; upon a blanket placed in the center of the tent they then spread out the bones. Only women surround the tent, all of them weeping, and each of them offers such gifts as she can afford. The following day the bones are carried to the tomb and are henceforth considered sacred. As soon as they are buried, or everything is ready for the burial, the chief priest addresses the surrounding people from the summit of a mound, upon which he fulfills the function of orator. Ordinarily he pronounces a eulogy on the deceased, or on the immortality of the soul, or the future life. He says that souls originally came from the icy regions of the north, where perpetual snow prevails. They therefore expiate their sins under the master of that region who is called Mateczungua, but they return to the southern regions, where another great sovereign, Quexuga, governs. Quexuga is lame and is of a sweet and generous disposition. He surrounds the newly arrived souls with numberless attentions, and with him they enjoy a thousand delights; young girls sing and dance, parents are reunited to children, and everything one formerly loved is enjoyed. The old grow young and everybody is of the same age, occupied only in giving himself up to joy and pleasure.

Such are the verbal traditions handed down to them from their ancestors. They are regarded as sacred and considered authentic. Whoever dared to believe differently would be ostracised. These natives also believe that we live under the vault of heaven; they do not suspect the existence of the antipodes. They think the sea has its gods, and believe quite as many foolish things about them as Greece, the friend of lies, talked about Nereids and other marine gods—Glaucus, Phorcus, and the rest of them.

When the priest has finished his speech he inhales the smoke of certain herbs, puffing it in and out, pretending to thus purge and absolve the people from their sins. After this ceremony the natives return home, convinced that the inventions of this impostor not only soothe the spirits, but contribute to the health of their bodies. (Anghierra, 1912, pp. 262–267; Swanton, 1922, pp. 43–45.)

Besides the few notes bearing on mythology contained in the above quotation, the following material from Lawson gives practically all the information we possess:

As I told you before, the priests make their orations at every feast, or other great meeting of the Indians. I happened to be at one of these great meetings, which was at the funeral of a Tuskeruro Indian, that was slain with lightning at a feast the day before, where I was amongst the rest. It was in July, and a very fair day, where, in the afternoon, about six or seven o'clock, as they were dealing out their victuals, there appeared a little black cloud to the northwest; so we went out from the place where we were all at victuals, and went down to the cabins where I left the Indians and went to lie in my canoe, which was convenient enough to keep me dry. The lightning came so terrible and down in long streams, that I was afraid it would have taken hold of a barrel of powder I had in my vessel, and so blown me up; but it pleased God that it did me no harm; yet the violence of the wind had blown all the water away, where I rid at anchor, so that my canoe lay dry, and some Indian women came with torches in their hands to the side of the canoe, and told me an Indian was killed with lightning. The next day, I think, he was buried, and I staid to see the ceremony, and was very tractable to help the Indians to trim their reeds and make the coffin, which pleased them very much, because I had a mind to see the interment. Before he was interred, according to their custom, they dealt every one some hot victuals, which he took and did what he would with. Then the doctor began to talk, and told the people what lightning was, and that it killed everything that dwelt upon the earth; nay, the very fishes did not escape; for it often reached the porpoises and other fish, and destroyed them; that everything strove to shun it except the mice, who, he said, were the busiest in eating their corn in the fields when it lightened the most. He added, that no wood or tree could withstand it, except the black gum, and that it would run round that tree a great many times to enter therein, but could not effect it. Now you must understand that sort of gum will not split or rive; therefore, I suppose, the story might arise from thence. At last he began to tell the most ridiculous, absurd parcel of lies about lightning that could be; as that an Indian of that nation had once got lightning in the likeness of a partridge; that no other lightning could harm him whilst he had that about him; and that after he had kept it for several years it got away from him; so that he then became as liable to be struck with lightning as any other person. There was present at the same time an Indian that had lived from his youth, chiefly in an English house; so I called to him and told him what a parcel of lies the conjurer told, not doubting that he thought so as well as I, but I found to the contrary; for he replied, that I was much mistaken, for that old man, who, I believe was upwards of an hundred years old, did never tell lies; and as for what he said, it was very true, for he knew it himself to be so. Thereupon seeing the fellow's ignorance, I talked no more about it.

Then the doctor proceeded to tell a long tale of a great rattlesnake, which, a great while ago, lived by a creek in that river, which was Neus, and that it killed abundance of Indians; but at last a bald eagle killed it and they were rid of a serpent that used to devour whole canoes full of Indians at a time.

I have been something tedious upon this subject, on purpose to show what strange, ridiculous stories these wretches are inclinable to believe. I suppose these doctors understand a little better themselves, than to give credit to any such fooleries, for I reckon them the cunningest knaves in the world. (Lawson, 1860, pp. 344–347.)

From Francisco of Chicora, Peter Martyr obtained a story of tailed men which embodies a common Southeastern mythic element, though it was recorded by the Spanish historian as if it had been related as a historical fact.

There is another country called Inzignanin, whose inhabitants declare that, according to the tradition of their ancestors, there once arrived amongst them men with tails a meter long and as thick as a man's arm. This tail was not movable like those of the quadrupeds, but formed one mass as we see is the case with fish and crocodiles, and was as hard as bone. When these men wished to sit down, they had consequently to have a seat with an open bottom; and if there was none, they had to dig a hole more than a cubit deep to hold their tails and allow them to rest. Their fingers were as long as they were broad, and their skin was rough, almost scaly. They ate nothing but raw fish, and when the fish gave out they all perished, leaving no descendants. (Anghierra, 1912, vol. 2, pp. 262–264; Swanton, 1922, p. 43.)

French writers state that the sun and moon were the principal objects of Timucua worship, and at the beginning of spring a special sacrifice, to be described presently, was made to the former (pl. 97). It is thus probable that the role of the sun was the more important, which would align Timucua religion with that prevalent elsewhere in the Southeast. The extreme reverence in which chiefs were held, amounting to a religious cult, suggests Natchez and Taensa ideology. The sea was also an object of reverence, and it is safe to assume the extensive development of spiritology which we find among primitive peoples generally. (Le Moyne, 1875, p. 13; Gatschet, 1877–1880, vol. 16, p. 637; Swanton, 1922, pp. 381–382.)

It is not clear to what extent the large quadrilateral town house of the Timucua performed the functions of a temple. There was a temple in Ocita on Tampa Bay, however, on the roof of which was a bird with gilded eyes and within "some pearls spoilt by fire and of little value" such as the Indians bored to string together as beads, and there is mention of a temple in Tocobaga on Old Tampa Bay (Robertson, 1933, p. 33; Barcia, 1723, p. 127). The descriptions of these buildings seem to suggest the temples of the lower Mississippi tribes rather than Timucua town houses of the conventional type.

In 1562 Ribault set up a stone pillar on which were the arms of the King of France, on an island near the mouth of St. Johns River, and 2 or 3 years later Laudonnière, leader of the second expedition, found that it was

crowned with crowns of bay, and, at the foot thereof, many little baskets full of mill [i.e., corn], which they call in their language tapaga tapola. Then, when they came hither, they kissed the same with great reverence, and besought us to do the like.

Le Moyne says of this:

On approaching, they found that these Indians were worshipping this stone as an idol; and the chief himself, having saluted it with signs of reverence such as his subjects were in the habit of showing to himself, kissed it. His men followed his example, and we were invited to do the same. Before the monument there lay various offerings of the fruits, and edible or medicinal roots, growing thereabouts; vessels of perfumed oils; a bow, and arrows; and it was wreathed around from top to bottom with flowers of all sorts, and boughs of the trees esteemed choicest. (Laudonnière, 1586, pp. 69–70; Le Moyne, 1875, p. 4; Swanton, 1922, p. 382.)

Of the priests or medicine men, Laudonnière states:

They have their priests, to whom they give great credit, because they are great magicians, great soothsayers, and callers upon devils. These priests serve them instead of physicians and surgeons; they carry always about with them a bag full of herbs and drugs, to cure the sick who, for the most part, are sick of the pox. (Laudonnière, 1586, p. 8; Swanton, 1922, p. 385.)

The medicine man or shaman was called in to pray over the new
corn, he performed ceremonies in order to find a lost object, he
brought on rain and tempest, he was asked to pray over a new fishweir so that many more fish would enter, and, when it thundered,
he would blow toward the sky and repeat formulae (Gatschet, 1877–
1880, vol. 16, pp. 635–638; vol. 17, pp. 500–501; vol. 18, pp. 489–491;
Swanton, 1922, pp. 383–385). Following is Le Moyne's description
of the performances of an aged shaman in order to forecast the result
of Chief Utina's expedition against the Potano:

> The sorcerer . . . made ready a place in the middle of the army, and, seeing
> the shield which D'Ottigny's page was carrying, asked to take it. On receiving
> it, he laid it on the ground, and drew around it a circle, upon which he in-
> scribed various characters and signs. Then he knelt down on the shield, and
> sat on his heels, so that no part of him touched the earth, and began to recite
> some unknown words in a low tone, and to make various gestures, as if en-
> gaged in a vehement discourse. This lasted for a quarter of an hour, when
> he began to assume an appearance so frightful that he was hardly like a human
> being; for he twisted his limbs so that the bones could be heard to snap
> out of place, and did many other unnatural things. After going through with
> all this he came back all at once to his ordinary condition, but in a very fatigued
> state, and with an air as if astonished; and then, stepping out of his circle, he
> saluted the chief, and told him the number of the enemy, and where they were
> intending to meet him. (Le Moyne, 1875, pp. 5–6; Swanton, 1922, p. 385.)

The event is said to have verified the prediction.

Pareja mentions "the ceremony of the laurel [evidently the *Ilex*]
performed to serve the Demon" (Gatschet, 1877–1880, vol. 18, p. 491;
Swanton, 1922, pp. 381–382). Reference has been made to the "chief
cult," and the following ceremony related by Le Moyne illustrates it:

> Their custom is to offer up the first-born son to the chief. When the day
> for the sacrifice is notified to the chief, he proceeds to a place set apart for
> the purpose, where there is a bench for him, on which he takes his seat. In
> the middle of the area before him is a wooden stump two feet high, and as
> many thick, before which the mother sits on her heels, with her face covered
> in her hands, lamenting the loss of her child. The principal one of her female
> relatives or friends now offers the child to the chief in worship, after which
> the women who have accompanied the mother form a circle, and dance around
> with demonstrations of joy, but without joining hands. She who holds the
> child goes and dances in the middle, singing some praises of the chief. Mean-
> while, six Indians, chosen for the purpose, take their stand apart in a certain
> place in the open area; and midway among them the sacrificing officer, who is
> decorated with a sort of magnificence, and holds a club. The ceremonies being
> through, the sacrificer takes the child, and slays it in honor of the chief, before
> them all, upon the wooden stump. The offering was on one occasion performed
> in our presence. (Le Moyne, 1875, p. 13; Swanton, 1922, p. 382.)

Elvas declares that human sacrifices were made by the Indians
about Tampa Bay:

> Since they are servants of the devil, they are accustomed to offer him souls
> and blood of their Indians or of any other people they can get. They say that

when he desires that that sacrifice be made to him, he talks with them and tells them he is thirsty and that they should offer a sacrifice to him. (Robertson, 1933, p. 42.)

Farther south among the Calusa Indians, we again find this custom. Laudonnière says, on the authority of a Spaniard who had been a captive there, that the Calusa chief had persuaded his subjects

that his sorceries and charms were the causes that made the earth bring forth her fruit; and, that he might the easier persuade them that it was so he retired himself once or twice a year to a certain house, accompanied by two or three of his most familiar friends, where he used certain enchantments; and, if any man intruded himself to go to see what they did in this place, the king immediately caused him to be put to death.

Moreover, they told me, that, every year, in the time of harvest, this savage king sacrificed one man, which was kept expressly for this purpose, and taken out of the number of the Spaniards, which, by tempest, were cast away upon the coast. (Laudonnière, 1586, p. 132; Swanton, 1922, p. 388.)

Lopez de Velasco has the following to say on this subject:

Every time that a son of the cacique dies, each neighbor sacrifices (or kills) his sons or daughters who have accompanied the dead body of the cacique's son.

When the cacique himself, or the cacicua dies, every servant of his or hers, as the case may be, is put to death.

Each year they kill a Christian captive to feed their idol, which they adore, and they say that it has to eat every year the eyes of a man, and then they all dance around the dead man's head. (Swanton, 1922, p. 389.)

We have two rather good accounts of ceremonies performed by the Indians of the southeast coast of Florida. The first took place at Hobe among the Jeaga Indians:

Night being come and the moon being up, an Indian, who performed their ceremonies, stood out, looking full at the moon, making a hideous noise, and crying out, acting like a mad man for the space of half an hour, all the Indians being silent till he had done; after which they made a fearful noise, some like the barking of a dog, wolf, and other strange sounds; after this, one got a log and set himself down, holding the stick or log upright on the ground, and several others got about him, making a hideous noise, singing to our amazement; at length their women joined the concert, and made the noise more terrible, which they continued till midnight. (Dickenson, 1803, p. 19; Swanton, 1922, p. 396.)

At Ais between the 18th and 25th of August Dickenson was witness of a ceremonial resembling in some measure the Creek busk, though these Indians were not agriculturalists:

It now being the time of the moon's entering the first quarter the Indians had a ceremonious dance, which they began about 8 o'clock in the morning. In the first place came in an old man, and took a staff about 8 feet long, having a broad arrow on the head thereof, and thence halfway painted red and white, like a barber's pole. In the middle of this staff was fixed a piece of wood, shaped like unto a thigh, leg, and foot of a man, and the lower part of it was painted black. This staff, being carried out of the cassekey's house, was set fast in the ground standing upright, which being done he brought out a basket containing six rattles, which were taken out thereof and placed at the foot of the staff. Another old man came in and set up a howling like unto a mighty dog, but beyond him for length of breath, withal making a proclamation. This being done and most of them having painted themselves, some red, some black, some with black and red, with their bellies girt up as tight as well they could girt themselves with ropes, having their sheaths of arrows at their backs and their bows in their hands, being gathered together about the staff, six of the chiefest men in esteem amongst them, especially one who is their doctor, took up the rattles and began a hideous noise, standing round the staff with their rattles and bowing to it without ceasing for about half an hour. Whilst these six were thus employed all the rest were staring and scratching, pointing upwards and downwards on this and the other side, every way looking like men frightened, or more like furies. Thus they behaved until the six had done shaking their rattles; then they all began to dance, violently stamping on the ground for the space of an hour or more without ceasing, in which time they sweat in a most excessive manner, so that by the time the dance was over, by their sweat and the violent stamping of their feet, the ground was trodden into furrows, and by morning the place where they danced was covered with maggots; thus, often repeating the manner, they continued till about 3 or 4 o'clock in the afternoon, by which time many were sick and faint. Being gathered into the cassekey's house they sat down, having some hot casseena ready, which they drank plentifully of, and gave greater quantities thereof to the sick and faint than to others; then they eat berries. On these days they eat not any food till night.

The next day, about the same time, they began their dance as the day before; also the third day they began at the usual time, when many Indians came from other towns and fell to dancing, without taking any notice one of another. This day they were stricter than the other two days, for no woman must look upon them, but if any of their women went out of their houses they went veiled with a mat. (Dickenson, 1803, pp. 52–54; Swanton, 1922, pp. 396–397.)

In the same town Dickenson observed the ceremony of the black drink:

The Indians were seated as aforesaid, the cassekey at the upper end of them, and the range of cabins was filled with men, women, and children, beholding us. At length we heard a woman or two cry, according to their manner, and that very sorrowfully, one of which I took to be the cassekey's wife; which occasioned some of us to think that something extraordinary was to be done to us; we also heard a strange sort of a noise, which was not like the noise made by a man, but we could not understand what, nor where it was; for sometimes it sounded to be in one part of the house, and sometimes in another, to which we had an ear. And indeed our ears and eyes could perceive or hear nothing but what was strange and dismal, and death seemed to surround us; but time discovered this noise to us. The occasion of it was thus:

In one part of this house, where a fire was kept, was an Indian, having a pot on the fire wherein he was making a drink of a shrub, which we understood afterwards by the Spaniards is called Casseena, boiling the said leaves, after they had parched them in a pot; then with a gourd, having a long neck, and at the top of it a small hole, which the top of one's finger could cover, and at the side of it a round hole of two inches diameter. They take the liquor out [of] the pot, and put it into a deep round bowl, which being almost filled, contains nigh three gallons; with this gourd they brew the liquor and make it froth very much; it looks of a deep brown color. In the brewing of this liquor was this noise made, which we thought strange; for the pressing of the gourd gently down into the liquor, and the air it contained being forced out of a little hole at the top, occasioned a sound, and according to the time and motion given, would be various. The drink when made cool to sup, was in a shell first carried to the cassekey, who threw part of it on the ground and the rest he drank up, and then made a long hem; and afterwards the cup passed to the rest of the cassekey's associates as aforesaid; but no other person must touch or taste of this sort of drink; of which they sat sipping, chattering, and smoking tobacco, or some other herb instead thereof, for the most part of the day.

In the evening we being laid on the place aforesaid (on mats on the floor), the Indians made a drum of a skin, covering therewith the deep bowl, in which they brewed their drink, beating thereon with a stick; and having a couple of rattles made of a small gourd, put on a stick with small stones in it, shaking it, they began to set up a most hideous howling, very irksome to us; and some time after came many of their young women, some singing, some dancing. This continued till midnight, after which they went to sleep. (Dickenson, 1803, pp. 33–36; Swanton, 1922, pp. 394–395.)

Plate 98 is Le Moyne's representation of the black drink ceremony among the Timucua.

Dickenson was likewise witness of the reception of a visiting ambassador from the Ais by the chief of the Santa Lucia Indians. The latter was dressed and painted for the occasion. The chief of the visitors sat beside the local chief and the rest mixed. Later, presents were exchanged and finally they smoked, talked, and drank casseena during the remainder of the visit (Dickenson, 1803, pp. 36–37; Swanton, 1922, p. 395).

Pareja's catechism reveals a number of native omens, taboos, and beliefs of various sorts, though some few of these may have been unwarranted assumptions of Old World customs and ideas. When an owl of a certain species hooted, it was thought to be talking and it was appealed to for help. If this owl, or another known as the "red owl" (*mochuelo*), hooted, they said, "Do not interrupt it or it will do you harm." Its cry was thought to be a portent, usually of something harmful. If a person uttered a cry when woodpeckers were making a noise it was thought he would have nosebleed. If one heard the cry of a fawn he must put herbs into his nostrils to keep from sneezing, and, if he did sneeze nonetheless, he must go home and bathe in an infusion of herbs or he would die. When one jay chattered to another it was a sign that some visitor was coming. In winter the small partridge (*la gallina pequeña*) must not be eaten. When a snake was encountered, either on a country trail or in the house, it was believed to portend misfortune. When the fire crackled, war was about to break out, and war was also forecast from lightning. Belching either portended death or signified that there would be much food.

As might have been anticipated, much credence was given to dreams. Tremblings or twitchings of certain parts of the body indicated that a visitor was coming. If one's eyes trembled, it portended weeping. If his mouth twitched, it was a sign that something bad was going to happen to the individual, or that people were talking about him, or that a feast was to take place.

The first acorns, and apparently the first fruits, gathered were not eaten, nor was the first ripe corn or the corn in a field struck by lightning. The first fish caught in a weir was not eaten but laid down beside it, so that a great quantity of fish would come into it with the next tide. It was thought that if the first fish caught in such a weir were thrown into hot water, no other fish would be caught. After eating bear meat one drank from a different shell from that ordinarily used, so that he would not fall sick. After a man had lost his wife, a woman her husband, or either a relative, the survivors would not eat corn which had been sowed by the deceased or corn from the land the deceased was wont to sow. They would give it to someone else or have it destroyed. After attending a burial, a person bathed and abstained for some time from eating fish. Before tilling a field an ancient ceremony was recited to the shaman (or perhaps under his leadership). Prayer was offered—that is, a formula was repeated—over the first corn, and when the corncrib was opened a formula was recited over the first flour. A ceremony accompanied with formulae was performed with laurel when chestnuts (?) and palmetto berries were gathered; wild fruits were not eaten until formulae had been repeated over them, but perhaps this applied only to the first fruits of the season. Apparently corn from a newly broken field was not eaten, but it is hard to imagine that this law was absolute. Unless prayers had been offered to the "spirit" by a doctor no one was allowed to approach the corncrib or open it. Some ceremony is mentioned as having taken place early in the season, in which six old men ate a pot of "fritters."

There were many hunting taboos. When a hunting party was preparing to set out, the chief had formulae repeated over tobacco, and when the hunting ground was reached, all of the arrows were laid together and the medicine man repeated other formulae over them. It was usual to give the medicine man the first deer that was killed. Formulae were also recited before they went to fish in a lake, and afterward the shaman prayed over the fish that had been caught and was given half. The first fish caught, however, was, after the usual formulae, placed in the storehouse. Pareja also mentions a kind of hunting ceremony performed by kicking with the feet, probably some form of sympathetic magic, and it appears that not a great deal of flesh was eaten immediately after the hunt for fear that no more animals would be killed. It was also thought that no more game would be killed if the lungs and liver of an animal were thrown into cold water in preparation for cooking. If a hunter pierced an animal with an arrow without killing it, he repeated a formula over his next arrow, believing that it was then sure to in-flict a mortal wound. If the grease of partridges or other small game which had been caught with a snare or lasso was spilled, it was thought that the snare would catch nothing more. Formulae were uttered to enable hunters to find turtles. Bones of animals caught in a snare or trap were not thrown away but hung up or placed on the roof of the house. If this ceremony were omitted, it was thought that the animals would not enter the snare or trap again. When they went to hunt deer and took the antlers of another deer with which to stalk the animals, they repeated formulae over them. If a man went to a fishweir immediately after having had intercourse with his wife, it was thought that no more fish would enter it.

A gambler rubbed his hands with certain herbs in order that he might be fortunate in play. A runner is also said to have taken an herb to make him win, and this seems to have been in the form of a drink. (Pareja, 1613, pp. 123–133; Gatschet, 1877–1880, vol. 16, pp. 635–638; vol. 17, pp. 500–501; vol. 18, pp. 489–491; Swanton, 1922, pp. 383–385.)

We have far too little satisfactory knowledge regarding the re-ligion of the early Cherokee. Timberlake is probably right in saying that they believed in one superior being, very likely one of the same character as the celestial deity of the Creeks and Choctaw and closely associated with the sun (Timberlake, Williams ed., 1927, p. 87.) Ac-cording to Mooney's informants, however, the sun was feminine, as ap-pears to have been the belief of the Yuchi and Shawnee. The moon, however, was a male, sun's brother (Mooney, 1900, p. 252 et seq.). The cosmogonic myth recorded by Mooney represents the animals as living together in the sky world and the earth as drawn from beneath a primeval ocean by the little Water-beetle, after the pattern of the well-known earth-diver story. The sky vault is of solid rock and the earth an island suspended in a sea of water by cords at the 4 cardinal points which will sometime break and submerge all the present land. The Appalachian mountains were made by the wings of the Buzzard flying over when the land was still soft; the sun was raised to its present convenient height in several successive moves by the conjurers. There is another world beneath this with a different climate, as is proved by the temperature of springs. There were a great many minor spirits, and the connection of some of these with disease has kept knowledge of them alive down to the present time. Olbrechts lists upward of 70, the greater part animal beings, the rest various sorts of human or manlike spirits, including giants, pygmies, and Two Men together, the Enemy, Fire, Flint, Little Flint, Little Fog, Little Frost, Ghost, Important Thing (some sort of monster), Old One, Pain, Speaker, Spirits, Sun, Big Whirlwind, Little Whirlwind (Mooney, 1900, pp. 239–240; 1932, pp. 42–50). They believed in survival after death and, according to Timberlake, in a different fate hereafter, depending upon actions in this life, though Olbrechts could not find a trace of this and the exact native attitude on this point is probably lost (Timberlake, Williams ed., 1927, p. 87; Mooney, 1932, p. 142). Ceremonies were performed in the town houses, and we are sometimes told that they formerly kept a perpetual fire in the town house at Echota, but these houses were not so much like temples as the communal edifices we find in some other parts of the section. Numer-. ous places in the Cherokee country were held in awe as the abodes of supernatural beings but we hear little of offerings made to them (French ms.; Mooney, 1900, pp. 404–419, 395–396, 501–503).

Individuals dealing with the occult and those treating diseases cannot be separated clearly. They included several classes, the curers proper, the priests, who performed rites at running water over persons desiring not only relief from sickness and protection against it but success in the ball game, in love, and in hunting, and who aspired to long life; prognosticators of future events or diviners; midwives; and those who practiced witchcraft. Their influence extended to all departments of the tribal and individual life. Women could perform these functions as well as men though there were not so many of them. Treatment consisted in administering an infusion of certain plants internally or externally, blowing on the affected part, sprinkling with medicine, exposure of the patient to vapors from the medicine, the sweat bath, massage, vomiting into the river, symbolic means, scratching, sucking and burying the disease, circumambulation of the sick man, accompanied by various food and other taboos and regulations. The administration of most remedies was accompanied by the repetition of set formulae of which a great mnay have been recorded (Mooney, 1932, pp. 83–88).

Our earliest note regarding the operations of rain makers and doctors is from Charles Hicks, a prominent mixed-blood chief who says:

They have a similar plan of choosing one or two men to represent the clans in what is called making rain.

In making rain, seven men or women are chosen to represent the clan, who keep a fast during the time the conjurer is about to obtain rain, and when the rain comes he sacrifices the tongue of a deer that is procured for that purpose. The conjurer himself observes a strict fast with frequent bathings during the time he is making rain. On such occasions the conjurer speaks a language different from the present language of the nation, and which few understand. They who design to follow the practices are taught by those who understand it. . . .

The doctors among the Cherokee suppose that cures are to be made in 7 nights of the different disorders which the human body is subject to. During these cures the doctors are remarkably strict to keep out of the house where the patient lies such persons as have handled a dead body, women, &c. for it is held among the

Cherokees that these persons are impure until bathing in the water of the seventh night in the morning. Some changes have of late taken place—instead of seven, four nights are now deemed sufficient. (Hicks *in* Raleigh Register.)

Payne refers to six Cherokee festivals the second of which is the one generally denominated the "green corn dance" (Bartram, 1909, p. 74). This corresponded to the busk of the Creeks but unfortunately we have but few descriptions of it and those very meagre. Timberlake was told that it was

performed in a very solemn manner, in a large square before the town-house door: the motion here is very slow, and the song in which they offer thanks to God for the corn he has sent them, far from unpleasing. (Timberlake, Williams ed., 1927, pp. 88–89.)

This trifling notice may be supplemented by a longer account by Charles Lanman, which owes its length unfortunately to flowery language rather than the demands of the subject. However, it is interesting and begins as far back as the ceremonies concerned with planting. Lanman obtained his information from Mr. Preston Starritt of Tennessee.

The beautiful valley to which we have journeyed is entirely surrounded with mountains, about five miles square, watered by a charming stream, and inhabited by two thousand aborigines, who are divided into seven clans, and located in seven villages. The ruling men of the tribe have signified to their people that the period for planting corn has arrived, and that they must gather themselves together for the purpose of submitting to the annual ceremonies of purification. For doing this they have a double object: they would, in the first place, expunge from their bodies every vestige of all the colds and diseases with which they may have been afflicted during the past winter; and, in the second place, they would propitiate the Great Spirit, so as to secure his blessing upon the crops which they are about to deposit in the ground. The moon being now at its full and a fitting location having been selected, the chiefs and magicians congregate together for the purpose of submitting to the annual ceremonies of purification. made to keep out all evil spirits and enemies, and the medicine men then proceed to walk in single file, and with measured steps, completely around the spot which they would render sacred, and which is generally half a mile in diameter, marking their route by plucking a single leaf from every tree or bush which they may happen to pass, all these leaves being carefully deposited in a pouch carried for the purpose. In the meantime, the brotherhood of chiefs have not been unemployed, for while the most aged individual of all has been making a collection of roots, the remainder have built a rude dam, and thereby formed a pond or pool of water on the creek which invariably waters the sacred enclosure. The entire population of the valley are now summoned to the outskirts of the sacred enclosure, and a general invitation extended to all to approach and join the chiefs and magicians in the rite they are about to perform; it being understood, however, that no man, under penalty of death, shall venture to participate, who has left a single wrong unrevenged, or committed any unmanly deed, and no woman who has given birth to a child since the preceding full moon. In the center of the sacred ground, and in the vicinity of the pool, a large fire is now made, around which the multitude are congregated. The night is clear and the moon and stars are flooding the earth with light.

An earthen pot is now placed upon the fire, the roots gathered by the old chief, numbering seven varieties, are placed therein, also the leaves plucked by the magicians, when the pot is filled with water by seven virgins, who are promoted to this honor by the appointment of the senior chief. After the contents of the pot have been thoroughly boiled, and a most bitter but medicinal beverage been made, all the persons present are called upon to take seven sips of the bitter liquid, and then directed to bathe no less than seven times in the neighboring pool, the waters of which have been rendered sacred by the incantations of the priests. All these things being done, the multitude assembles around the fire once more, and, to the music of a strange wild singing, they dance until the break of day, and then disperse to their several homes. The friendship of the Great Spirit has now been secured, and therefore, as opportunity offers, the Indians proceed to loosen their ground, as best they may, and then plant their corn. This labor is performed chiefly by the women, and the planted fields are considered as under their especial charge. Though planted in the greatest disorder, they keep their cornfields entirely free of weeds, and the soil immediately around the corn in a loose condition. At every full moon they are commonly apprehensive that some calamity may befall their crop, and, by way of keeping the Great Spirit on their side, the women have a custom of disrobing themselves, at the dead hour of night, and of walking entirely around the field of corn.

And now that the sunshine and showers of summer are performing their ministry of good in bringing the corn to its wonted perfection, it may be well to make the reader acquainted with the following facts: As the Indians purify themselves and perform their religious rites only when the moon is at its full, so do they refrain from plucking a single ear of corn until they have partaken of their annual harvest or green corn feast. This feast occurs on the night of the full moon nearest to the period when the corn becomes ripe; and by a time-honored law of the nation, no man, woman, or child is ever permitted, under penalty of death, to pluck a single roasting-ear. So rigidly enforced is this law that many Cherokees are known to have lost their lives for disobeying it, while many families have suffered the pangs of hunger for many days, even while their fields were filled with corn, merely because the harvest moon had not yet arrived, and they had not partaken of their annual feast. If a full moon should occur only one week after the corn had become suitable to pluck, the Indians will not touch a single ear until the next moon, even if it should then be so hard as to require pounding before becoming suitable for food. During the ripening period the cornfields are watched with jealous care, and the first stalk that throws out its silken plume is designated by a distinguishing mark. In assigning reasons for this peculiar care, the Indians allege that until the harvest feast has taken place the corn is exclusively the property of the Great Spirit, and that they are only its appointed guardians; and they also maintain that, when the corn is plucked before the appointed moon has arrived, the field which has thus been trespassed upon is sure to be prostrated by a storm or be afflicted with the rot; and therefore it is that they are always greatly alarmed when they discover that a cornfield has been touched, as they say, by the Evil One.

But the harvest moon is now near at hand, and the chiefs and medicine men have summoned the people of the several villages to prepare themselves for the autumnal festival. Another spot of ground is selected, and the same sanctifying ceremony is performed that was performed in the previous spring. The most expert hunter in each village has been commissioned to obtain game, and while he is engaged in the hunt the people of his village are securing the blessing of the Great Spirit by drinking, with many mystic ceremonies, the liquid made from seven of the most bitter roots to be found among the mountains. Of all the game which may be obtained by the hunters, not a single animal is to be served up at the feast whose bones have been broken or mutilated; nor shall a rejected animal be brought within the magic circle, but shall be given to those of the tribe who, by some misdeed, have rendered themselves unworthy to partake of the feast. The hunters are always compelled to return from the chase at the sunset hour, and long before they come in sight of their villages they invariably give a shrill whistle, as a signal of good luck, whereupon the villagers make ready to receive them with a wild song of welcome and rejoicing.

The pall of night has once more settled upon the earth, the moon is in its glory, the watch-fire has been lighted within the magic circle, and the inhabitants of the valley are again assembled together in one great multitude. From all the cornfields in the valley the magicians have collected the marked ears of corn, and deposited them in the kettles with the various kind of game which may have been slaughtered, from the bear, the deer, and the turkey, to the opossum, the squirrel, and the quail. The entire night is devoted to eating, and the feast comes not to an end until all the food has been dispatched, when, in answer to an appropriate signal from the medicine man, the bones which have been stripped of their flesh are collected together and pounded to a kind of powder, and scattered through the air. The seven days following this feast are devoted to dancing and carousing, and at the termination of this period the inhabitants of the valley retire to their various villages, and proceed to gather in their crops of the sweet maize or Indian corn. (Lanman, 1856, vol. 2, pp. 424–428.)

A valuable early epitome of Cherokee ceremonies is furnished by Charles Hicks, a literate chief who wrote down the following narrative in the year 1818:

Before eating the green corn when in the milk, the people collect in the different towns and villages at night, and when the — ("this word is not understood in Mr. Hick's original") comes, the conjurer takes some of the grains of seven ears of corn and feeds the fire with them, i. e., burns them. After this each family is allowed to cook and eat their roasting-ears, but not before they drink a tea of wild horehound. In like manner they observe the same custom before eating the bean when it fills in the hull.

The green corn dance, so called, has been highly esteemed formerly. This is held when the corn is getting hard and lasts four days, and when the national council sits—a quantity of venison being procured to supply the dance. It is said that a person was formerly chosen to speak to the people on each day in a language that is partly lost—at least there is very little of it known now. At such times as the above, a piece of land is laid off and persons appointed to occupy it— no others being allowed to use it while the feast continues.

There is a custom, which still prevails, of making a new fire every year, generally in the month of March. The fire is made by drilling in a dried grape vine, which begins in the morning after an all night dance. Seven persons are appointed to perform this with the conjurer. After the fire is made, each family in the town comes and procures the new fire, putting out all the old fires in their houses.

The physic dance was very much in use formerly, but partly neglected now. This belongs to the women in particular, except seven men who are chosen, one out of each clan, to carry the water to boil the physic, and when boiled, to carry it to the people, for old and young to drink. But they never drink of it until the singer has proclaimed, with his song, on the top of the Town House, "*Hayan wah, Yautheaunu*" (repeating the same several times) and [they have] painted all the posts of the house white with clay, and danced two of the nights in seven, and in the morning after the last night bathed themselves in the water . . . .

The Eagle-tail dance is still in use among the Cherokees. The design of this dance is to stimulate in the minds of the young growing people the spirit of war. The old warriors rehearsing in the dance the dangers they have passed through in attacking their enemies, the distance they have travelled, the time they have been out, &c. &c. Some victuals are usually set apart for the boys to eat at day break, and when the boys have eaten they go out of the town house and are met in the entry by the young men, who have a battle with mud collected for the purpose.

It is also customary to give Eagle feathers as pledges of friendship in making peace among red people. (Hicks *in* Raleigh Register.)

Olbrechts says that "the importance the Cherokee ascribe to dreams as causes of disease is quite remarkable," and this is a characteristic which they share with their relatives the Iroquois and other related tribes. Anciently dreams were regarded mainly as the causes of disease, but in later times there has been more of a tendency to consider them as omens of coming disease or of other future happenings. Omens were drawn from the howling of dogs and foxes, the hooting of the night owl, the sight of a shooting star and so on, and there was the usual efflorescence of taboos. Epidemics such as smallpox were usually attributed, correctly enough, to the white man (Mooney, 1932, pp. 35–39).

Cosmogonic myths have already been touched upon. In addition to the ones noted may be mentioned myths to account for differentiation between diurnal and nocturnal beasts; gift of fire by the Thunders and placing of same in the bottom of a hollow sycamore tree until some was obtained by Water Spider after the other animals had failed; origin of game and corn from an ancient couple, Kanati (The Lucky Hunter) and Selu (Corn); origin of sin; liberation of animals from underground cave; invention of diseases by animals in order to cope with mankind, and help furnished by the plants in supplying medicines; determination of the Sun to destroy mankind, diversion of her determination by having Rattlesnake kill her daughter, attempted recovery of the latter from the land of the dead but ultimate failure resulting in irreversibility of death; rescue of tobacco from the geese, journey to the sunrise and discovery of the nature of the sky and sun; origin of spots on the moon; nature of thunder and stars; origin of the Pleiades and the pine tree; origin of the Milky Way; origin of strawberries; origin of fish and frogs, and the deluge. In addition to these legends, Mooney has recorded for us a number of quadruped, bird, snake, fish, and insect myths, of which the most striking are those regarding supernatural serpents, and there are various wonder stories and miscellaneous myths and legends (Mooney, 1900, pp. 239–427).

The Creeks believed that the earth was flat and square and that the sky was a solid vault which rose and fell at intervals. Meteors of the more impressive kind were thought to be snakes or lions, and the Milky Way was called the spirits' road. Eclipses were supposed to be caused by a great toad which was trying to swallow the sun or moon. The moon was supposed to be inhabited by a man and a dog; the sun was connected with the supreme being. The rainbow was believed to be a big serpent and was called "the cutter off of the rain." Upon the vault of heaven lived the sky deity and the souls of the happy. Bad spirits were thought to reside in the west. Underneath was another inhabited world similar to ours, some said a succession of worlds.

The Creek supreme deity was known as Hisagita-imisi, "the preserver of breath," or Ibofånga, "the one sitting above," who bore a rather close relation to the sun but was not quite equivalent to it. His representative on earth was the busk fire, and the fire spirit seems to have been in some measure his messenger. There were two spirits connected very closely with the busk, called Yaholå and Hayū'ya. The latter appears in Hawkins' version of the migration legend split into four spirits which are evidently identical with the four cardinal points and probably the winds which blow from them. Thunder, including lightning as well, plays an important part in the myths as a being in human form, but Adair seems to identify him with Hisagita-imisi. In one of the Tuggle myths Wind appears as a single being with many children. Animals, plants, and, indeed, most created and some artificial things possessed magic powers and were the abode of spirits in human form. There were also many monsters possessed of human mentality. In early times the Indians would not willingly kill a wolf or a rattlesnake. Besides their solitary state, animals might live in towns, and we have, in particular, several stories of visits to snake towns, usually those belonging to water serpents. The mammalian and reptilian organisms living in water were often mentioned under the term "masters of waters," and they were supposed to be able to bring on or withhold rain. The Tie-snake was a very powerful water serpent capable of carrying off a cow or horse. According to one tale, it originated from a transformed human being. The sharp-breasted snake was supposed to be responsible for many of the marks made by lightning, the horned snake was a favorite assistant of heroes, its horns furnishing a powerful hunting or war medicine, and it shared with the celestial Thunder Being the power of producing lightning. A very short snake was in the habit of flying heavenward from its den under ground and appears to have been connected with the whirlwind. There are many stories regarding a monster lizard that used to live in hollow trees after the manner of a bear. The eagle and a small hawk were very highly esteemed. The hoot owl and a small red-headed woodpecker were able to foresee events and indicate them by their cries or their mere presence. Dogs often appear in myths as helpers.

Like all other Indians of the Southeast so far as our information goes, the Creeks had profound respect for a race of dwarfs or fairies which were able to endow human beings with supernatural power. They also believed in giants. The mythology had a place for long-eared animals like mules, bearlike creatures with huge tusks, pointed-eared animals, speckled cowlike creatures, the chief deer, water-king deer, and various kinds of cannibals. Some of the malevolent ones were in the habit of trailing people by means of rollers similar to chunk stone. The most talked of charm was a quartzlike stone called sabīa said to have been borne in the flowers of certain plants. Various roots and fruits were also used as charms, such as the "physic-nut, or Indian olive" of Bartram carried by deer hunters, who supposed that it had "the power of charming or drawing that creature to them; from whence, with the traders, it has obtained the name of the physic-nut, which means, with them, charming, conjuring or fascinating" (Bartram, 1940, p. 59); also the thigh bone of the highland terrapin, strings of bison hair, the horn of the horned snake, as already mentioned, and bones of the panther. A medicine plant of special power was the hitci-pâkpâgi, "old men's tobacco." The use of these was accompanied by magical songs and incantations similar to the ones employed in curing diseases. In this connection should be mentioned the medicine "ark" taken along with a war party, and the town or tribal palladium of the Tukabahchee, consisting of a number of copper and brass plates of relatively modern, probably Spanish, introduction.

Ghosts of those slain in war were believed to haunt the dwellings of the living until their deaths had been avenged. Then they went west, and the good at least ascended to the sky, while malevolent spirits remained in the west, the witchcraft quarter. The road to the land of the dead was supposed to be beset with several different perils, including a lake, serpents, a battlefield, and a great eagle.

Shamans belonged to several distinct classes. One class, called "Knowers," was able to prophesy future events and diagnose diseases. Twins were likely to become efficient Knowers. The priests or doctors were graduates of certain schools presided over by old practitioners who took them off by themselves, made them sweat, fast, and take medicines, and instructed them in the mysteries of the art. One of these men was always chosen as war leader, and the medicine maker or high priest of the town was from this class. Elevation to this office depended also in many cases upon clan affiliations. There were also controllers of the weather, controllers of floods in streams, and dew makers. Witches and wizards were implicitly believed in and witchcraft was no doubt practiced consciously, the methods in general being similar to those found in other parts of the world. A wizard was supposed to be filled with lizards, and possibly other animals, which forced him to commit murder periodically, but it was possible to restore a wizard to his right mind by making him throw the lizards up. Insignia were worn by doctors indicative of their attainments, as a buzzard feather by one who could heal gunshot wounds, a fox skin by one who could treat snake bite, an owl feather if he could trail an enemy in the dark, and so on.

Dreams had a powerful influence over the dreamer but not as great apparently as among the Cherokee. Sneezing indicated that something good was being said about the person. Locations might be lucky or unlucky. Before eating, bits of food were thrown into the fire, and there were numerous other taboos connected with eating and hunting.

Dances partook of both a social and a ceremonial character. Most of them were named after animals and with each was connected a certain number of songs. An infusion of the *Ilex vomitoria* was used at the beginning of all serious councils and in most of the sacred ceremonies, and it was brewed in accordance with a certain ritual with appropriate songs. The great ceremonial of the year, the busk or "green corn dance," occurred usually in July or August and in any case when the first ears of the flour corn became fit to eat. It was sometimes preceded by three minor feasts or "stomp dances," a month apart. It corresponded to the new year, and was regarded as involving a moral as well as an economic regeneration, typified by the extinction and relighting of the fires, a general pardon of all crimes except murder, and preparation of medicines to preserve the general health throughout the year to come. Although war dances and certain war ceremonies were connected with it, the military arm was represented in its defensive aspects, discord was avoided, and an atmosphere of tranquillity made to prevail everywhere. Most of the ceremonies were of 4 days' duration but some extended to 8, in which case 4 days were devoted to rites connected with corn and 4 to rites connected with animal food. There was in each section, a day of assembly, a day of feasting, a day of fasting, and a day for breaking up. The warriors took medicine four times on the day of fasting, new titles were bestowed upon those who had distinguished themselves, the young were lectured and admonished by the clan heads, and the adults listened to long addresses by the best available speakers. There were also ball games during the day and dances at night around a fire in the center of the Square Ground. It was believed that this ceremony had been bestowed by the supreme deity for the renewal and perpetuation of the health of his people. At Tukabahchee a special ceremony was gone through in connection with the copper and brass plates owned in that town.

A number of illustrations of Creek Square Grounds are shown in plates 99–104, two of Tukabahchee, one of Nuyaka, one of Pakan Tallahassee, two of Eufaula, two of Alabama, three of Chiaha Seminole, including one of the principal town officers in the year 1912, and one of Mikasuki. (See also pls. 39, fig. 2; 40, fig. 2; 59, fig. 1.)

Anciently there was a long myth, varying somewhat in the different towns, which detailed the origin of the Creek Nation and its various sacred ceremonies. There were also myths which told of the origin of corn, of the doings of a hero called Orphan, the widely distributed story of the twin heroes—one of natural, the other of supernatural origin—stories of Thunder, stories of monster lizards, and of cannibals, the friendly dogs who aided their master, the man who turned into a snake, and numerous tales of the trickster Rabbit which are mostly importatations from the Old World (Swanton, 1928 a, pp. 477–636).

Chickasaw religion was very similar to the religion of the Creeks. There was a supreme being living in the sky world and connected with both sky and sun, and manifested on earth in fire, especially fires in the sacred grounds. There were also numerous servant spirits. Among the minor supernatural beings were giants called ło^{n}fa who were wont to carry off women and sometimes flayed men. There were pygmies like those of Creek mythology. There were also beings which seem to personify the frost, the horned snakes, and tie snakes. Reverence for rattlesnakes was very great and an Indian would never kill one. The screech owl was associated with witchcraft. Charms or personal medicines were common, portions of deer killed in the woods were sacrificed and sometimes the entire animal, and bits of food were thrown into the fire during meals. If we may trust Adair, certain food taboos were very strictly observed, and sympathetic magic was widespread.

After death, souls were thought to travel west and the good ones climbed to the sky world to live with the supreme being, but the malevolent spirits remained in the western quarter, the quarter from which witchcraft emanated. If a man had been killed by enemies, however, his spirit haunted the eaves of the house until his death had been avenged. There is mention of a final destruction of the world by fire.

There were numerous dances for both social and religious purposes, and when there was an abundance of food, the people frequently enjoyed a succession of social feasts and dances accompanied by games and a general merrymaking. Most tribes held these in the fall but Adair tells of Chickasaw fetes as if in spring. He speaks as though the Chickasaw had a busk in his time. This was probably true at least of those Chickasaw who had settled among the Upper Creeks, and

Speck indicates a vestigial observance of the kind, but it evidently dropped out of use later, the principal ritual known to them then being the Pishofa ceremony held mainly to restore a sick person to health. It was naturally enough regimented by the shaman, and everything connected with it was directed to rehabilitation of the patient through suggestion. The ceremony of the black drink also seems to have been known to them. Adair was the beneficiary of a ceremony to keep off witches.

At least some of the shamans or doctors enjoyed official positions, and Adair speaks as if there were a head priest over the entire nation. They treated the sick by perambulations, by appeals to various animals, and by sympathetic magic. The Chickasaw had rain makers like the Creeks and an ineradicable belief in witches and wizards (Swanton, 1928 c, pp. 247–263).

Even comparatively early missionaries lament that the Choctaw were relatively indifferent to religion, but there is evident, nevertheless, the sky deity concept and its association with the sun along with numerous subordinate beings, among which we may recognize the ever-present pygmies, a spirit combining the characteristics of man and deer, white spirits living in water pools, a malevolent spirit able to read men's thoughts, a "Long Black Being," humanlike but with small eyes and long pointed ears, and something which looks like a personification of the will-o'-the-wisp. The horned owl appears as a sinister character apparently associated with witchcraft. The cry of the screech owl portended sudden death, the sapsucker brought news of all kinds, and domestic fowl were supposed to give friendly warning of approaching trouble.

The world was believed to be flat, and the vault of heaven a solid shell upon which lived other beings, undoubtedly including the sky god. In the beginning the earth was flat and marshy, and while it was still in that condition a being in human form descended from above and caused the sacred hill of Nanih Waiya to arise, out of which he then brought the red people. After that, hills were formed and the earth dried, and later men came into possession of corn. Their social and political institutions were revealed to them at Nanih Waiya. An earlier form of the legend brings the Choctaw to Nanih Waiya from the west. We have a number of versions of the flood myth, most of which show traces of white contamination. Solar eclipses were attributed to a black squirrel or black squirrels endeavoring to swallow the sun. Thunder and Lightning were represented to Bushnell as two great birds. There are several stories of the origin of corn, which was of immense consequence in the economy of this tribe.

The attitude toward charms, sacrifices, and dreams was evidently identical with what has been noted in connection with the Creeks and

Chickasaw. According to Wright, a man was believed to have two souls. The shilombish, or outside shadow, became a ghost after his death and frequently assumed the form and imitated the cries of a fox or owl. The shilup, or inside shadow, went to the land of souls after death where those who had committed murder were segregated and consigned to a kind of hell. It was on account of the approaching journey of the shilup to the land of souls that the body of the deceased was provided with food and clothing and various implements. There seems to have been the same delay of the soul (shilup) in taking up its journey to the west until its death had been avenged that we have found elsewhere.

There was a marked paucity in ceremonies of a religious nature as might have been anticipated from the character of Choctaw culture. Mention is made of a "green corn dance," lasting 5 days, and there can be no reasonable doubt that such a ceremony existed but we have only fragmentary notes regarding it. Some say that the Choctaw formerly had Pishofa dances, but others affirm that, if there were any at all, they were borrowed from the Chickasaw. They had numerous dances of a social or semisocial character and at some of these they wore masks. Catlin was very much struck by the eagle dance and has left us a painting of it. To what extent religious rites and religious emotions entered into these it is no longer possible to say.

So far as can be made out, the Choctaw had two classes of medicine men, those who used occult means and arrogated to themselves the gift of prophecy, and mere physic makers. The former, however, performed in part the functions of the latter. From the meager notices vouchsafed to us, it would appear that medicine men of the first class went through ordeals in order to reach their station somewhat like those which prospective Creek priests underwent. They claimed to be able to foretell events and to see what was taking place at a distance, and many of the Frenchmen believed in them. Here again we find a distinct class of rain makers from whom the fair-weather makers were distinguished, and there was the same belief in witchcraft. We also hear of an herb used in producing rain. As among the Creeks, twins were thought to have peculiar powers and here again they were beneficent rather than the reverse (Swanton 1931 a, pp. 194–241).

Before passing on, reference may be made to certain interesting sacred objects discovered in Mobile Bay when the French founded Louisiana. The chances are that they have been lost, but possibly they may yet turn up in France. On March 4, 1702, soon after the first fort had been started in Mobile Bay, at Twenty-seven Mile Bluff, Iberville sent his brother Bienville "to visit many abandoned settlements of the savages," in the islands in the neighborhood. Iberville says that his brother made a savage show him the place where their gods are, of which all the nations in the neighborhood tell so many stories, and where the Mobilians come to offer sacrifices. They pretend that one can not touch them without dying immediately; that they are descended from heaven. It was necessary to give a gun to the savage who showed the place to them. He approached them only stealthily and to within ten paces. They found them by searching on a little rise in the canes, near an ancient destroyed village in one of these islands. They brought them out. They are five figures: of a man, a woman, a child, a bear, and an owl, made in plaster so as to look like the savages of this country. For my part I think it was some Spaniard who, at the time of De Soto, made in plaster the figures of these savages. It appeared that that had been done a long time ago. We have them at the establishment; the savages, who see them there, are surprised at our hardihood and that we do not die. I am bringing them to France although they are not much of a curiosity. (Margry, 1875–1886, vol. 4, pp. 512–513; Swanton, 1922, p. 161.)

Its state religion was the most important factor in the life of the Natchez nation. While their cult included, and in fact depended upon, the supposition of a great body of minor beings, called characteristically servant spirits, there was a single supreme deity, living in the sky world, and closely connected with the sun, if not identical with it. At some period in the remote past the son of this deity had descended to earth, brought civilization to the Natchez Indians, given them their laws and social and ceremonial usages, and finally retired into a natural or artificial stone ever afterward preserved in the Natchez temple, leaving the government of his people to his descendants, the Sun caste or clan. In this temple a perpetual fire was maintained and preserved by certain guardians, any remissness on whose part was severely punished. There was also preserved here the figure of a rattlesnake and a number of small carved images. The southern third of the temple was set off from the rest and was probably that which contained the sacred stone. It is evident that, in spite of its exceptional sanctity and peculiar accessories, this building was similar to the ossuaries found elsewhere in the Southeast as far as Virginia, and it is not strange to read that it contained a raised platform on which were hampers enclosing the bones of leading members of the Sun caste. Immediately after the funeral ceremonies for the principal Suns, we know that their bodies were buried in or close to the temple, but it is pretty certain that they were exhumed later, the bones separated from the flesh, and placed in the hampers as above indicated. We are told that the great chief and his wife came to this temple every evening and every morning "to worship their idols." Here the first fruits of the harvest are said to have been brought annually. The firewood was hickory with the bark removed except that twigs of a tree which seems to have been the hackberry were added to it. It was piled about a honeylocust. It was natural that lightning should be regarded with great reverence, and that the destruction of the temple by a lightning bolt should be regarded as a sign of divine wrath. When this happened to the temple of the Taensa, whose customs were almost identical with those of the Natchez, five women threw their infants into the flames to placate the deity. One who had been struck by lightning and had recovered was thought able to cure any disease. We have only a slender knowledge of the other religious beliefs and customs of the Natchez tribe. We are told that they threw bits of bread to the four cardinal points before eating, that they fasted, and had legends regarding a deluge and regarding the way in which the first fire had been obtained. It is probable that the development of the state cult had reduced in some measure the importance of private manipulators of the supernatural, but they existed. We are told that they obtained their power by isolation in a cabin, fasting, invocations to the spirits, a constant noise made with a gourd rattle, and bodily contortions. There were also weather controllers, who made it fair or brought on rain through their incantations accompanied by symbolic acts. Belief in personal immortality is evident both from the direct statements of early writers and from the mortuary rites, and two of our informants state that the good and the evil suffered different fates, though the good appear to have been those who observed the national customs and laws, and the bad those who violated them (Swanton, 1911, pp. 158–180). Du Pratz has attempted to give us an idea of the common Natchez dance without too much success (pl. 105).

The Taensa temple differed in some interesting particulars from that of the Natchez but there was little distinction in the cult taken as a whole, so far as we can discover (Swanton, 1911, pp. 259–269). Most of the other tribes along the lower Mississippi had temples, but they were generally smaller and the cults connected with them were evidently more attenuated. In the time of De Soto it appears that the Natchez culture, or cultures similar to it, were more widely distributed. A splendid picture of the Acolapissa temple has been preserved to us by De Batz, a French architect or engineer, who informs us that ceremonies were performed before certain images kept within (Bushnell, 1927, pp. 3–4, pl. 1 [pl. 62 herein]). The Tunica temple in their old homes on the Yazoo was on a mound like that of the Natchez and was visited by a war party, just before setting out and immediately after their return, but the Tunica performed fewer ceremonies about it than did the Natchez or Taensa around their own. We know that earthen figures were kept in the temple, however, and La Harpe says "their household gods are a frog and a figure of a woman which they worship, thinking that they represent the sun" (Margry, 1875–1886, vol. 6, p. 247; Swanton, 1911, p. 318; see Haas, 1942). The association of the sun and frog reminds us of the big frog which the Cherokee believed was trying to swallow the solar orb when an eclipse occurred. Gravier states that:

they acknowledge nine gods—the sun, thunder, fire, the god of the east, south, north, and west, of heaven and of earth. In each cabin there is a great post which supports it, at the foot of which there are two or three little earthen pots near the fire, out of which they take a little ashes to put in these pots, from I know not what superstition. (Shea, 1861, pp. 133–134; Swanton, 1911, pp. 318–319.)

Elsewhere we find the sun, fire, and heaven at least represented by a single deity. The principal Tunica myth preserved is the story of Thunder, which is shared with a number of other tribes. There is also a rather elaborate flood myth (Swanton, 1911, pp. 319–324).

The Chitimacha Indians shared the common Southeastern belief in a sky god, though there is evidence that, like the corresponding deity of the Yuchi and Cherokee, it was originally feminine. Information obtained by the writer would seem to indicate that this god was also the trickster, an unusual combination in the section. Each youth underwent solitary confinement in some house until he obtained a guardian spirit and this is also affirmed of each girl. Thunder is said to have been made by the supreme being, Kutnahīn. There were numerous stories regarding the animals in which they appear as having dealings with human beings. A kind of wild canary, tcintc, was able to talk with men and women and to foretell the weather. There was a spirit called New Spirit which passed from east to west in the spring and returned in the fall, and a monster called Long-nose Spirit which destroyed human beings and was later identified with the elephant. There was a belief in four trees of peculiar sanctity, one at the mouth of the Mississippi, one somewhere in the east, one at the entrance of Vermilion Bay, and one at a town called Hipinimsh on Grand Lake. In the summer a great ceremony was held in the dance houses and this seems to have corresponded to the Creek busk. In the Chitimacha creation legend we find a version of the Earth Diver story in which Crawfish finally succeeds in obtaining earth for the future continents. The sky deity taught them the use of the bow and arrow, how to make fire, and the religious observances. Animals took part in their councils and each family came to be associated with a certain animal species. The moon and sun were supposed to be man and wife, the wife more powerful because she had taken medicines and baths more regularly. At the time of the flood mankind was saved inside of an earthen pot at the bottom of the ocean. Fire was obtained from an old blind man in whose custody it had been placed. Knowledge of doctoring, fishing, and of the use of corn was brought to earth by three men who got these things from the sky god. The soul was said to survive the death of the body and be reborn through some woman (Swanton, 1911, pp. 352–360).

According to the fragment of Atakapa religious belief which has come down to us, they came out of the sea and were given their first rules of conduct by a man sent down by "God," and men are differentiated after death in accordance with their lives. There was also belief in a deluge (Swanton, 1911, p. 363).

The Spanish missionaries, Casañas, Espinosa, and Hidalgo, report that the Caddo believed there was a supreme deity whom they called Ayo-Caddi-Aymay, and they had an elaborate temple cult and a long cosmic legend, a version of the "Thrown Away" story. The missionary reports regarding this cult have been given in Bureau of American Ethnology Bulletin 132 (Swanton, 1942, pp. 210–234).

MEDICAL PRACTICES

Medical practices are very closely bound up with shamanism and priestcraft. The best treatment of the subject by far, as developed in any Southeastern tribe, is by Mooney and Olbrechts in Bulletin 99 of the Bureau of American Ethnology, a specific discussion of the Swimmer Manuscript on Cherokee Sacred Formulas and Medicinal Prescriptions. Here the causes of disease in accordance with native belief are given as natural causes and supernatural causes, the latter embracing diseases caused by spirits of the sun, fire, moon, river, Thunder and his two sons, purple man, blue man, black man, the little people, animal spirits (of which a long list is given), human and animal ghosts, witches, and man killers; also diseases due to the machinations of a human agent, diseases traceable to a woman's menstrual condition, dreams (and possibly omens, though they may not have causal significance), and neglected taboos, to which may be added diseases attributable to the white people (Mooney, 1932, pp. 14–39). In both Cherokee and Creek mythology we find emphasis laid upon animals as disease bringers and upon plants as healers. In fact, the greater number of remedies were of vegetable origin, an infusion being made and taken internally, hot or cold, or applied externally. Certain objects were often added on account of their supposed magical properties. The medicine was often blown into by the doctor, and this was usual among the Creeks and widely practiced throughout the Southeast, a tube being ordinarily employed, after which the patient was sprayed or exposed to the vapors—most pronouncedly in the sweat bath—massaged, made to vomit into the river, scratched, the affected part sucked, and the disease buried, or the patient was circumambulated, probably at a former period to the accompaniment of a rattle. Prescriptions as to diet and various taboos governing the behavior were inculcated. Most important of all to the success of the treatment was the repetition of the proper magical formulae. Surgery was resorted to to a very limited extent.

One sort of treatment which undoubtedly played a powerful part in early Cherokee medicine, as we know it did in the medical practice of other Indian tribes, is the appeal to the imagination, and this is scarcely touched upon by Mooney and Olbrechts. It was probably responsible for more cures than all other methods together. Most of the doctors are, and probably always were, drawn from the male sex, but there were true women doctors and naturally enough all of the midwives were women. Apart from priests and midwives, Cherokee practitioners are divided by Olbrechts into curers, diviners or conjurers, and wizards and witches. Knowledge of the healing art was transmitted by the instruction of novices, and some member of a doctor's family was most likely to become one, but this seems to have been a natural outgrowth of the conditions and not due to any definite regulation (Mooney, 1932, pp. 14–39).

We learn from Hariot that the Algonquian doctors of North Carolina used suction in curing disease and that they believed that sickness could be caused by missiles sent by witches (Hariot, 1893, p. 42). Strachey has these paragraphs on Powhatan doctoring:

Concerning a greene wound cawsed eyther by the stroake of an axe, or sword, or such sharpe thinge, they have present remedy for, of the juyce of certayne hearbes; howbeyt a compound wound (as the surgeons call it) where, beside the opening and cutting of the flesh, any rupture is, or bone broken, such as our small shotte make upon them, they knowe not easily how to cure, and therefore languish in the misery of the payne thereof. Old ulcers likewise, and putrified hurts are seldome seene cured amongst them: howbeit, to scarrefye a swelling, or make incisyon, they have a kind of instrument of some splinted stone.

Every spring they make themselves sick with drincking the juyce of a roote which they call wighsacan and water, wherof they take soe great a quantity, that yt purgeth them in a very violent manner, so that in three or four daies after they scarce recover their former health. Sometymes they are sore trobled with dropseyes, swelling, aches, and such like deceases, by reason of their uncleanenes and fowle feeding; for cure whereof they buyld a stove in the forme of a dove howse, with matts soe close, that a fewe coals therein, covered with a pott, will make the patient sweat extreamely.

For swelling, also, they use small pieces of touch wood in the forme of cloves, which, pricking on the grief, they burne close to the flesh, and from thence drawe the corruption with their mouthe. They have many professed phisitians, who, with their charmes and rattles, with an infernall rowt of words and accions, will seeme to suck their inward grief from their navells, or their affected places; but concerning our chirugians they are generally so conceipted of them, that they believe that their plaisters will heale any hurt. (Strachey, 1849, pp. 108–109.)

Spelman had a more intimate knowledge of the Potomac Indians:

When any be sicke among them, ther preests cums unto the partye whom he layeth on the ground uppon a matt, And hauing a boule of water, sett between him and the sicke partye; and a Rattle by it, The preest kneelinge by the sick mans side dipps his hand in the boule, which takinge vp full of watter, he supps into his mouth, spowting it out againe, vppon his oune armes, and brest, then takes he the Rattle, and with one hand takes that, and with the other he beates his brest, makinge a great noyes, which hauinge dunn he easilye Riseth (as loith to wake

the sicke bodye, first with one legge, then with the other, And beinge now gott
vp, he leaysuerly goeth about yᵉ sicke man shakinge his Rattle uery softly ouer
his bodye: and with his hand he stroketh yᵉ greaued parts of the sicke, then doth
he besprinkell him with water mumblinge certayne words ouer him, and so for
that time leaue him.

But if he be wounded after thes cermonys dunn unto him he with a litle flint
stone gasheth the wound makinge it to runn and bleede which he settinge his
mouth unto it suckes out, and then aplies a certayne roote betten to powter unto
yᵉ Sore.   (Smith, John, Arber ed., 1884, pp. cix–cx.)

Beverley devotes an entire chapter to "the diseases and cures of the
Indians" of Virginia, the substance of which is as follows:

The *Indians* are not subject to many Diseases, and such as they have, generally
come from excessive Heats, and sudden Colds, which they as suddenly get away
by Sweating. But if the Humour happen to fix, and make a pain in any particular
Joynt, or Limb, their general cure then is by burning, if it be in any part that
will bear it; their method of doing this, is by little Sticks of Lightwood, the Coal
of which will burn like a hot Iron; the sharp point of this they run into the Flesh,
and having made a Sore, keep it running till the Humour be drawn off: Or else
they take Punck, (which is a sort of a soft Touchwood, cut out of the knots of
Oak or Hiccory Trees, but the Hiccory affords the best,) this they shape like a Cone,
(as the *Japoneses* do their *Moxa* for the Gout) and apply the Basis of it to the
place affected. Then they set fire to it, letting it burn out upon the part, which
makes a running Sore effectually.

They use Smoaking frequently and Scarrifying, which, like the *Mexicans*, they
perform with a Rattle-Snakes Tooth. They seldom cut deeper than the *Epidermis*,
by which means they give passage to those sharp waterish Humours, that lye
between the two Skins, and cause Inflamations. Sometimes they make use of
Reeds for Cauterizeing, which they heat over the Fire, till they are ready to
flame, and then apply them upon a piece of thin wet Leather to the place aggriev'd
which makes the Heat more pierceing.

Their Priests are always Physicians, and by the method of their Education in
the Priesthood, are made very knowing in the hidden qualities of Plants, and
other Natural things, which they count a part of their Religion to conceal from
every body, but from those that are to succeed them in their holy Function. They
tell us, thaie God will be angry with them, if they should discover that part of
their knowledge; so they suffer only the Rattle Snake Root to be known, and such
other Antidotes, as must be immediately apply'd; because their Doctors can't
be always at hand to remedy those sudden misfortunes, which generally happen
in their Hunting or Travelling.

They call their Physick *Wisoccan*,* not from the name of any particular Root
or Plant, but as it signifies Medicine in general. . . .

The Physick of the *Indians*, consists of the most part, in the Roots and Barks
of Trees, they very rarely using the Leaves either of Herbs or Trees; what they
give inwardly, they infuse in Water, and what they apply outwardly, they stamp
or bruise, adding Water to it, if it has not moisture enough of itself; with the
thin of this they bathe the part affected, then lay on the thick, after the manner
of a Pultis, and commonly dress round, leaving the sore place bare.

They take great delight in Sweating, and therefore in every Town they
have a Sweating-House, and a Doctor is paid by the Publick to attend it. They

---

* Newport's party was shown "the herbe called in their tongue *wisacan,* which they
say heales poysoned woundes. It is lyvewort or bloudwort" (Smith, John, Arber
ed., 1884, pp. clxviii).

commonly use this to refresh themselves, after they have been fatigu'd with Hunting, Travel, or the like, or else when they are troubl'd with Agues, Aches, or Pains in their Limbs.   Their method is thus, the Doctor takes three or four large Stones, which after having heated red hot, he places 'em in the middle of the Stove, laying on them some of the inner Bark of Oak beaten in a Mortar, to keep them from burning.   This being done, they creep in six or eight at a time, or as many as the place will hold, and then close up the mouth of the Stove, which is usually made like an oven, in some Bank near the Water side.   In the mean while, the Doctor, to raise a Steam, after they have been stewing a little while, pours cold Water on the Stones, and now and then sprinkles the Men to keep them from fainting.   After they have sweat as long as they can well endure it, they sally out, and (tho it be in the depth of Winter) fortwith plunge themselves over Head and Ears in cold Water, which instantly closes up the Pores, and preserves them from taking cold.   The heat being thus suddenly driven from the extream parts to the Heart, makes them a little feeble for the present, but their Spirits rally again, and they instantly recover their Strength, and find their Joynts as supple and vigorous as if they never had travell'd, or been indispos'd.   So that I may say as *Bellonius* does in his Observations on the *Turkish* Bagnio's, All the Crudities contracted in their Bodies are by this means evaporated and carry'd off.   (Beverley, 1705, bk. 3, pp. 49–51.)

Lawson gives practically all that we know regarding the medical practices of the Siouan tribes, along with material on those of the Tuscarora Indians, which seem to have differed little.   His rather naive account is as follows:

You must know that the doctors or conjurers, to gain a greater credit among these people, tell them that all distempers are the effects of evil spirits, or the bad spirit, which has struck them with this or that malady, therefore none of these physicians undertakes any distemper but that he comes to an exorcism to effect the cure, and acquaints the sick party's friends, that he must converse with the good spirit, to know whether the patient will recover or not, if so, then he will drive out the bad spirit and the patient will become well.   Now the general way of their behavior in curing the sick, a great deal of which I have seen, and shall give some account thereof, in as brief a manner as possible, is, when an Indian is sick, if they think there is much danger of life, and that he is a great man or hath good friends, the doctor is sent for.   As soon as the doctor comes into the cabin, the sick person is set on a mat or skin stark naked, lying on his back and all uncovered, except some small trifle that covers their nakedness when ripe, otherwise, in very young children, there is nothing about them.   In this manner the patient lies, when the conjurer appears, and the king of that nation comes to attend him with a rattle made of a gourd, with peas in it.   This the king delivers into the doctor's hand, whilst another brings a bowl of water, and sets it down. Then the doctor begins, and utters some few words very softly; afterwards he smells of the patient's navel and belly, and sometimes scarifies him a little with a flint or an instrument made of rattle snake's teeth for that purpose; then he sucks the patient and gets out a mouthful of blood and serum, but serum chiefly, which, perhaps, may be a better method in many cases than to take away great quantities of blood, as is commonly practiced, which he spits in the bowl of water.   Then he begins to mutter, and talk apace, and at last to cut capers and clap his hands on his breech and sides, till he gets into a sweat, so that a stranger would think he was running mad, now and then sucking the patient, and so, at times, keeps sucking, till he has got a great quantity of very ill colored matter out of the belly, arms, breast, forehead, temples, neck, and most parts, still continuing his grimaces, and antic postures, which are not to be matched in Bedlam. At last you will see the doctor all over of a dripping sweat, and scarce able to utter one word, having quite spent himself; then he will cease for a while, and so begin again till he comes in the same pitch of raving and seeming madness, as before, all this time the sick body never so much as moves, although, doubtless, the lancing and sucking must be a great punishment to them, but they certainly are the patientist and most steady people under any burden that I ever saw in my life. At last, the conjurer makes an end, and tells the patient's friends, whether the person will live or die; and then one that waits at this ceremony, takes the blood away, which remains in a lump, in the middle of the water, and buries it in the ground, in a place unknown to any one, but he that inters it. Now, I believe a great deal of imposture in these fellows; yet I never knew their judgment fail, though I have seen them give their opinion after this manner, several times. (Lawson, 1860, pp. 347–349.)

Lawson then goes on to narrate how an Indian conjurer was able to detect a thief, ostensibly by occult processes (see pp. 753–754), and continues:

One of the Tuskeruro kings had brought in a slave to the same governor (Seth Southwell, Gov. of North Carolina), to whom he had sold him; and before he returned fell sick at the governor's house; upon which the doctor that belonged to this king's nation was sent for, being a man that was held to be the greatest conjurer amongst them. It was three days before he could arrive, and he appeared, when he came, to be a very little man, and so old, that his hair was as white as ever was seen. When he approached the sick king, he ordered a bowl of water to be brought him and three chunks of wood, which was immediately done. Then he took the water and set it by him, and spurted a little on him, and with the three pieces of wood he made a place to stand on, whereby he was raised higher; he being a very low statured man; then he took a string of ronoak, which is the same as a string of small beads; this he held by one end between his fingers; the other end touched the king's stomach, as he stood on the logs. Then he began to talk, and, at length, the bystanders thought really that they heard somebody talk to him, but saw no more than what first came in. At last, this string of beads, which hung thus perpendicular, turned up as an eel would do, and without any motion of his, they came all up, in a lump, under his hand, and hung so for a considerable time, he never closing his hand, and at length returned to their pristine length and shape, at which the spectators were much frightened. Then he told the company that he would recover, and that his distemper would remove into his leg, all which happened to be exactly as the Indian doctor had told. These are matters of fact, and, I can, at this day, prove the truth thereof by several substantial evidences that are men of reputation, there being more than a dozen people present when this was performed; most of whom are now alive. . . .

The cures I have seen performed by the Indians, are too many to repeat here; so I shall only mention some few, and their method. They cure scald heads infallibly, and never miss. Their chief remedy, as I have seen them make use of, is, the oil of acorns, but from which sort of oak I am not certain. They cure burns beyond credit. I have seen a man burnt in such a manner, when drunk, by falling into a fire, that I did not think he could recover; yet they cured him in ten days so that he went about. I knew another blown up with powder, that was cured to admiration. I never saw an Indian have an ulcer, or foul wound in my life; neither is there any such thing to be found amongst them. They cure the pox by a berry that salivates as mercury does; yet they use sweating and decoctions very much with it, as they do almost on every occasion; and when they are thoroughly heated, they leap into the river. The pox is frequent in some of these nations; amongst which I knew one woman die of it; and they could not, or would not, cure her. We had a planter in Carolina who had got an ulcer in his leg, which had troubled him a great many years; at last he applied himself to one of these Indian conjurers, who was a Pampticough Indian, and was not to give the value of fifteen shillings for the cure. Now, I am not positive whether he washed the ulcer with any thing before he used what I am now going to speak of, which was nothing but the rotten, doated grains of indian corn, beaten to powder and the soft down growing on a turkey's rump. This dried the ulcer up immediately, and no other fontanel was made to discharge the matter, he remaining a healthful man till the time he had the misfortune to be drowned, which was many years after. Another instance, not of my own knowledge, but I had it confirmed by several dwellers in Maryland, where it was done, was, of an honest planter that had been possessed with a strange, lingering distemper, not usual amongst them, under which he emaciated and grew every month worse than another, it having held him several years, in which time he had made trial of several doctors, as they call them, which, I suppose, were ship surgeons. In the beginning of this distemper, the patient was very well to pass, and was possessed of several slaves, which the doctors purged all away, and the poor man was so far from mending that he grew worse and worse every day. But it happened that one day as his wife and he were commiserating his miserable condition, and that he could not expect to recover, but looked for death very speedily, and condoling the misery he should leave his wife and family in, since all his negroes were gone. At that time, I say, it happened that an Indian was in the same room, who had frequented the house for many years, and so was become as one of the family, and would sometimes be at this planter's house and at other times amongst the Indians.

This savage, hearing what they talked of, and having a great love for the sick man, made this reply to what he had heard: Brother, you have been a long time sick, and I know you have given away your slaves to your English doctors. What made you do so, and now become poor? They do not know how to cure you; for it is an Indian distemper, which your people know not the nature of. If it had been an English disease, probably they could have cured you; and had you come to me at first I would have cured you for a small matter, without taking away your servants that made corn for you and your family to eat; and yet, if you will give me a blanket to keep me warm, and some powder and shot to kill deer withal, I will do my best to make you well still. The man was low in courage and pocket too, and made the Indian this reply: Jack, my distemper is past cure, and if our English doctors cannot cure it I am sure the Indians cannot. But his wife accosted her husband in very mild terms, and told him, he did not know but God might be pleased to give a blessing to that Indian's undertaking more than he had done to the English; and further added, if you die I cannot be much more miserable, by giving this small matter to the Indian; so I pray you, my dear, take my advice, and try him—to which, by her persuasions, he consented. After the bargain was concluded, the Indian went into the woods and brought in both herbs and roots, of which he made a decoction, and gave it the man to drink, and bade him go to bed, saying, it should not be long before he came again, which the patient performed as he had ordered; and the potion he had administered made him sweat after the most violent manner that could be, whereby he smelled very offensively both to himself, and they that were about him; but in the evening, towards night, Jack came, with a great rattle snake in his hand alive, which frightened the people almost out of their senses; and he told his patient that he must take that to bed with him; at which the man was in a great consternation, and told the Indian he was resolved to let no snake come into his bed, for he might as well die of the distemper he had, as be killed with the bite of that serpent. To which the Indian replied, he could not bite him now nor do him any harm, for he had taken out his poison teeth, and shewed him that they were gone. At last, with much persuasion, he admitted the snake's company, which the Indian put about his middle, and ordered no body to take him away on any account, which was strictly observed, although the snake girded him as hard for a great while, as if he had been drawn in by a belt which one pulled at with all his strength. At last the snake's twitches grew weaker and weaker, till, by degrees, he felt him not; and opening the bed he was found dead, and the man thought himself better. The Indian came in the morning, and seeing the snake dead, told the man that his distemper was dead along with that snake, which proved so as he said, for the man speedily recovered his health and became perfectly well.

They cure the spleen, which they are much addicted to, by burning with a reed. They lay the patient on his back, so put a hollow cane into the fire, where they burn the end thereof till it is very hot, and on fire at the end: Then they lay a piece of thin leather on the patient's belly, between the pit of the stomach and the navel, so press the hot reed on the leather, which burns the patient so that you may ever after see the impression of the reed where it was laid on, which mark never goes off so long as he lives. This is used for the belly-ach sometimes . . . . They make use of no minerals in their physic, and not much of animals; but chiefly rely on vegetables. They have several remedies for the tooth-ache, which often drive away the pain: but if they fail, they have recourse to punching out the tooth with a small cane set against the same on a bit of leather. Then they strike the reed and so drive out the tooth; and howsoever it may seem to the Europeans, I prefer it before the common way of drawing teeth by those instruments that endanger the jaw, and a flux of blood often follows which this method of punch never is attended withal: neither is it half the pain. The spontaneous plants of America the savages are well acquainted withal, and a flux of blood never follows any of their operations. They are wholly strangers to amputation, and for what natural issues of blood happen immoderately, they are not to seek for a certain and speedy cure. Tears, rozins, and gums, I have not discovered that they make much use of; and as for purging and emetics, so much in fashion with us, they never apply themselves to, unless in drinking vast quantities of their yaupon or tea, and vomiting it up again as clear as they drink it. This is a custom amongst all those that can procure that plant, in which manner they take it every other morning or oftener, by which method they keep their stomachs clean without pricking the coats, and straining nature, as every purge is an enemy to. Besides the great diuretic quality of their tea carries off a great deal that perhaps might prejudice their health by agues and fevers, which all watery countries are addicted to; for which reason I believe it is that the Indians are not so much addicted to that distemper as we are, they preventing its seizing upon them by this plant alone. Moreover, I have remarked, that it is only those places bordering on the ocean and great rivers, that this distemper is frequent in, and only on and near the same places this evergreen is to be found, and none up towards the mountains, where these agues seldom or never appear. Nature having provided suitable remedies in all countries, proper for the maladies that are common thereto. The savages of Carolina have this tea in veneration above all the plants they are acquainted withal, and tell you the discovery thereof was by an infirm Indian, that labored under the burden of many rugged distempers, and could not be cured by all their doctors: so one day he fell asleep, and dreamed that if he took a decoction of the tree that grew at his head, he would certainly be cured. Upon which he awoke, and saw the yaupon or cassena tree, which was not there when he fell asleep. He followed the direction of his dream and became perfectly well in a short time. Now, I suppose no man has so little sense as to believe this fable, yet it lets us see what they intend thereby, and that it has, doubtless, worked feats enough to gain it such an esteem amongst these savages who are too well versed in vegetables to be brought to a continual use of any one of them, upon a mere conceit of fancy, without some apparent benefit they found thereby . . . The bark of the root of the sassafras tree I have observed is much used by them. They generally torrefy it in the embers, so strip off the bark from the root, beating it to a consistence fit to spread, so lay it on the grieved part, which both cleanses a fowl ulcer, and after scarrification being applied to a contusion or swelling, draws forth the pain and reduces the part to its pristine state of health, as I have often seen effected. Fats and unguents never appear in their chirurgery when the skin is once broken. The fats of animals are used by them to render their limbs pliable, and when wearied, to relieve the joints, and this not often, because they approve of the sweating house in such cases, above all things . . . .

They are never troubled with the scurvey, dropsy, nor stone. The phthisic, ashma, and diabetes, they are wholly strangers to. Neither do I remember I ever saw one paralytic amongst them. The gout, I cannot be certain whether they know what it is, or not. Indeed, I never saw any nodes or swellings, which attend the gout in Europe; yet they have a sort of rheumatism or burning of the limbs, which tortures them grievously, at which time their legs are so hot, that they employ the young people continually to pour water down them. I never saw but one or two thus afflicted. The struma is not uncommon amongst these savages, and another distemper, which is, in some respects, like the pox, but is not attended with no(!) gonorrhæa. This not seldom bereaves them of their nose. I have seen three or four of them rendered most miserable spectacles by this distemper. Yet, when they have been so negligent, as to let it run on so far without curbing of it; at last, they make shift to patch themselves up, and live for many years after; and such men commonly turn doctors. I have known two or three of these no nose doctors in great esteem amongst these savages. The juice of the tulip tree is used as a proper remedy for this distemper. What knowledge they have in anatomy, I cannot tell, neither did I ever see them employ themselves therein, unless as I told you before, when they make skeletons of their kings and great men's bones. . . . The small pox has been fatal to them, they do not often escape, when they are seized with that distemper, which is a contrary fever to what they ever know. Most certain, it has never visited America, before the discovery thereof by the christians. Their running into the water, in the extremity of this disease, strikes it in, and kills all that use it. Now they are become a little wiser; but formerly it destroyed whole towns, without leaving one Indian alive in the village. The plague was never known amongst them, that I could learn by what enquiry I have made. These savages use scarrification almost in all distempers. Their chief instruments for that operation is the teeth of rattlesnakes, which they poison withal. They take them out of the snake's head, and suck out the poison with their mouths, and so keep them for use, and spit out the venom, which is green, and are never damaged thereby. The small pox and rum, have made such a destruction amongst them that, on good grounds, I do believe, there is not the sixth savage living within two hundred miles of all our settlements, as there were fifty years ago. (Lawson, 1860, pp. 347-363.)[40]

Elsewhere he has something to say about the use of certain vegetable products as medicine. Bark taken from the root of the elm (apparently the common elm) was beaten, whilst green, to a pulp, and then dried in the chimney where it turned of a reddish color.

This [he says] they use as a sovereign remedy to heal a cut or green wound, or any thing that is not corrupted. Pelletory grows on the sand banks and islands. It is used to cure the toothache by putting a piece of bark in the mouth, which being very hot draws a rhume from the mouth, and causes much spittle. The Indians use it to make their composition, which they give to their young men and boys when they are husquenawed. (Lawson, 1860, p. 167.)[41]

The following note by the same writer may be added though it may be said to involve a cure of mediocrity rather than disease:

Enquiring of them if they never got any of the Bezoar stone, and giving them a description how it was found, the Indians told me, they had great plenty of it, and asked me, what use I could make of it? I answered them, that the white men used it in physic, and that I would buy some of them, if they would get it against I came that way again. Thereupon, one of them pulled out a leather-pouch, wherein was some of it in powder; he was a notable hunter, and affirmed to me, that that powder blown into the eyes, strengthened the sight and brain exceedingly, that being the most common use they made of it. (Lawson, 1860, p. 85.)

The naturalist Catesby was, as might have been anticipated, less impressed by the esoteric elements in Indian medical practices, and in general his treatment of the subject is valuable on account of his training and background. His remarks are of general application though he seems to have been best acquainted with the tribes visited by Lawson and with the Chickasaw.

The *Indians* have healthful constitutions, and are little acquainted with those diseases which are incident to *Europeans*, as gout, dropsies, stone, asthma, phthisic, calentures, paralytic, apoplexies, small-pox, measles, &c. Although some of them arrive to a great age, yet in general they are not a long liv'd people, which in some measure may be imputed to their great negligence of their health by drunkenness, heats and colds, irregular diet and lodging, and infinite other disorders and hardships (that would kill an *European*) which they daily use. To this happy constitution of body is owing their great use of physic, and their superficial knowledge therein, as proportionable. No malady is taken in hand without an exorcism to effect the cure; by such necromantic delusions, especially if the patient recovers, these crafty doctors, or conjurers (which are both in one) raise their own credit; insinuating the influence they have with the good spirit to expunge the evil one out of the body of the patient, which was the only cause of their sickness. There are three remedies that are much used by all the *Indians* of the northern continent of *America:* these are bagnio's or sweating houses, scarrification, and the use of *Casena* or *Yapon.* The first is used in intermiting

---

[40] The casseena is discussed again on pp. 153-154 of Lawson's work, also the sassafras.
[41] He describes the actions gone through by a Tuscarora medicine man (p. 104).

fevers, colds, and other disorders of the body: these bagnio's are usually placed on the banks of a river, and are of stone, and some of clay; they are in form and size of a large oven, into which they roll large stones heated very hot; the patient then creeps in, and is closely shut up; in this warm situation he makes lamentable groans, but after about an hour's confinement, out from his oven he comes, all reeking with torrents of sweat, and plunges into the river. However absurd this violent practice may seem to the learned, it may reasonably be supposed that in so long a series of years they have used this method, and still continue so to do, they find the benefit of it.

Amongst the benefits which they receive by this sweating, they say it cures fevers, dissipates pains in the limbs contracted by colds, and rheumatic disorders, creates fresh spirits and agility, enabling them the better to hunt.

When the *Indians* were first infected by the *Europeans* with the small-pox, fatal experience taught them that it was a different kind of fever from what they had been ever used to, and not to be treated by this rough method of running into the water in the extremity of the disease, which struck in and destroy'd whole towns before they could be convinced of their error. Scarrification is used in many distempers, particularly after excessive travel: they cut the calves of their legs in many gashes, from which oftentimes is discharg'd a quantity of coagulated blood, which gives them present ease, and they say, stops and prevents approaching disorders. The instrument for this operation is one of the deadly fangs of a rattlesnake, first cleansed from its venom by boiling it in water.

Something on the use of *Ilex vomitoria* follows, and he concludes with a few remarks on native surgery:

Indians are wholly ignorant in Anatomy, and their knowledge in Surgery very superficial; amputation and phlebotomy they are strangers to; yet they know many good vulnerary and other plants of virtue, which they apply with good success: the cure of ulcers and dangerous wounds is facilitated by severe abstinence, which they endure with a resolution and patience peculiar to themselves. They knew not the small-pox in north *America*, till it was introduced by the Europeans. (Catesby, 1731–43, vol. 2, p. xv.)

The monk San Miguel gives an interesting, because early, account of the Yaupon and the ceremonies connected with it. His observations were made among the Guale Indians about the present St. Simons Island. After describing a small figure or "idol" in the head chief's house not far from the door, he says:

Near the feet of the idol was a large jar with a wide mouth (tinaja de boca ancha), full of a drink which they call cacina, and around the big jar and the idol was a great number of jars (ollas) of two makes (asumbres), also full of cacina: an Indian would take each of these in his hands and give them reverently to those who had taken part in the game, who were seated on the long bed, and each one took his and drank it: whereupon their bellies became like kettle drums and as they drank their bellies grew and swelled up: they continued thus for a while, and we thought to see the end of that fiesta, when we saw each one of them opening his mouth with much calmness, throw out a great stream of water as clear as when he had drunk it, and others on their knees on the ground, scattering the water thus made in every direction: all who do this are leading men: this was the end of that solemn ceremony.

Cacina is the name they give to a little shrub of the shape and form of the myrtle, and in order to make the tea they drink out of it which they call cacina, they parch the leaf in a deep earthen pan, and when it is well parched they pour water over it, and while it is still boiling they draw it off and drink it hot, and again pour water over it: its odor is like that of lye: these Indians and the Spaniards drink it in the morning and they say that it is of benefit against the stone, and that because it makes him urinate no Indian has that disease: I drank it several times in the house where I stayed in St. Augustine, and it produces the effect they claim and does not have a bad taste, but it cannot be used as a dainty like chocolate: this (cacina) is the common drink of Spaniards and Indians, and there is no remembrance that they used sassafras except in sickness.

I was told afterwards that they mixed sea water with the cacina with which the Indians regaled us so as to be able to vomit it out, and they do not eat that day until they have vomited it: but I do not hold this as absolutely assured, because afterwards I saw an old Christianized chief named Don Felipe, a name adopted by him from that of the king, who always vomited after he had taken it without having had any sea water, and so it may be that the vomiting is only by the grave men among them and not by others. (Garcia, 1902, pp. 196–197.)

In Florida we find the customary relations between priest, prophet, and medicine man:

They have their priests, to whom they give great credit, because they are great magicians, great soothsayers, and callers upon devils. These priests serve them instead of physicians and surgeons; they carry always about with them a bag full of herbs and drugs, to cure the sick who, for the most part, are sick of the pox. (Laudonnière, 1586, p. 8; Swanton, 1922, p. 385.)

Ribault mentions, among the presents which his people received from the Indians, "roots like rinbabe (rhubarb), which they hold in great estimation, and make use of for medicine" (French, 1875, p. 177; Swanton, 1922, p. 386). And Le Moyne thus describes their method of treating disease:

Their way of curing diseases is as follows: They put up a bench or platform of sufficient length and breadth for the patient . . . and lay the sick person upon it with his face up or down, according to the nature of his complaint; and, cutting into the skin of the forehead with a sharp shell, they suck out blood with their mouths, and spit it into an earthen vessel or a gourd bottle. Women who are suckling boys, or who are with child, come and drink this blood, particularly if it is that of a strong young man; as it is expected to make their milk better, and to render the children who have the benefit of it bolder and more energetic. For those who are laid on their faces they prepare fumigations by throwing certain seeds on hot coals; the smoke being made to pass through the nose and mouth into all parts of the body, and thus to act as an emetic, or to overcome and expel the cause of the disease. They have a certain plant, whose name has escaped me, which the Brazilians call *petum* (*petun*), and the Spaniards *tapaco*. The leaves of this, carefully dried, they place in the wider part of a pipe; and setting them on fire, and putting the other end in their mouths, they inhale the smoke so strongly, that it comes out at their mouths and noses, and operates powerfully to expel the humors. In particular they are extremely subject to the venereal disease, for curing which they have remedies of their own, supplied by nature [pl. 106]. (Le Moyne, 1875, pp. 8–9; Swanton, 1922, pp. 385–386.)

An account of the different orders of shamans and medicine men among the Creeks has already been given. It was noted that there is a distinction between the Knowers or Diagnosticians and the Fasters or Doctors proper, and something has been said about the training of the latter and their insignia. In 1912 there was a famous Knower called Yahola living at a station named after him a few miles out of Muskogee, Oklahoma. His abode (pl. 107, fig. 1) was surrounded by bare spots connected in intricate patterns which he is said to have made to represent the several Creek Square Grounds. Formerly, these practitioners ran around the patient shaking a rattle, invoking various supernatural beings and making use of objects of symbolic significance. This was largely to ascertain the nature of the disease after which the doctor would give directions to steam the patient, or to give him a medicine consisting of an infusion of roots, bark, or other substances, usually drawn from the vegetable kingdom. Plate 107, figure 2, shows the frame of a sweat house at the Chiaha Seminole Square Ground. This type, however, may have been due to influences from the west. There might be one or many ingredients used. After they had been assembled, the doctor usually blew into the compound through a cane tube and chanted certain formulae needed to give efficacy to the whole. While he was doing this, he generally faced the east but the direction might vary, depending on the prescription, and sometimes he faced all four cardinal points in succession, commonly ending, however, with the east. The head of the sick man was ordinarily laid to the east, and bark, roots, and other materials were taken from the east side of a tree or other object. Blood-letting and sucking, either with the mouth or by means of a cow horn, was a common method of treatment. Bandages and splints were employed and the sick were carried about on litters, as Le Moyne states was the Timucua custom. When a warrior had been wounded, he was placed in a hut by himself, his diet was carefully regulated, and in particular he was guarded from all contact with women. Swan states that, when a doctor was unsuccessful, he often attributed his failures to the cats and dogs about the house which were then killed promptly or sent out of the neighborhood. Not infrequently a doctor who lost his patient was himself killed. Doctors sometimes engaged in supernatural combats with each other. It was claimed by some that a doctor's power consisted in certain creatures who constituted his strength so long as he could control them, but when he lost his power over them he died and they ran away from him in the forms of animals of various kinds like lizards and snakes. According to the Alabama and Koasati, it was the presence of lizards which caused a man to possess the powers of a wizard. Before entering upon official duties medicine men, at least sometimes, had to undergo certain special fasts and ceremonies. As in the case of the Cherokee, most sicknesses were supposed to come from animals, real or mythical, and a story collected by Dr. Speck represents each animal as creating a disease and specifying the remedy for it. While the practices of the several medicine men were genetically similar, there were numerous specific differences, and some specialized on certain kinds of disease or certain types of remedy. Among the various diseases may be enumerated diseases from the deer, bear, bison, rabbit, raccoon, squirrel, dog, wolf, rat or mouse, lion (?), wildcat, panther, mole, opossum, beaver, otter, muskrat, eagle, buzzard, "many-snakes," "gatherers-in-the-waters," snake, turtle, terrapin, alligator, perch, "periwinkle," slug, millipede, ant, "mastodon" (?), various mythic creatures, rainbow, thunder, sun, fire, diseases caused by women, etc. (Swanton, 1928, pp. 614–670; Speck, 1907 b, pp. 121–133; 1909, pp. 132–137).

There appears to have been little difference between Creek medical practice in general and the practice of the Chickasaw, but the Pishofa ceremony was either peculiar to the latter or particularly prominent among them. This was undertaken for the express purpose of restoring some sick person to health, and it was under the charge of a doctor who prescribed the details. It may be described as a collective drive upon the imagination of the patient, and no doubt was highly beneficial in certain cases.[42] The Chickasaw doctors as priests have been treated elsewhere, and their procedure in restoring wounded warriors has also been covered in discussing Creek practice. Adair extols the efficacy of their treatment of snake bite, and mentions among their remedies button snakeroot, a yellow-flowered water lily, and ginseng, to which the black drink might be added. Among diseases recognized by the Chickasaw may be enumerated diseases caused by the snake, dog, deer, red snake, little people, wolf, bear, skunk, big hog, red squirrel, squirrel, heat, beaver, otter, mole, eagle, owl, ground rattlesnake, blue snake, burning ghost, screech owl, to which we may add the disease mentioned by Adair as "the cattle distemper" (Swanton, 1928 c, pp. 263–272).

Our earliest mention of medical practice among the Choctaw speaks mainly of the custom of cupping:

When there is a sick person among them they have the doctor come to the place where he is, who, after having conjured or demanded of their Spirit if the sick person will get well, bleeds him with a piece of flint. Eight or ten incisions are made in the skin in the space of the size of a crown (*écu*), as when one cups, over which they place one end of a pierced horn and suck it until the horn is full of blood. As these jugglers sometimes wish to hide their ignorance they say that someone has thrown a spell over them (the patients) and then they adroitly put some bison wool or a little piece of wood into the bottom of the horn, and after having sucked the sick man and poured out the blood

---

[42] Cf. W. B. Parker quoted in Foreman, 1934, pp. 142–143.

which is in the horn, they show this wood or bison wool to the parents of the sick man, which they make them believe is a charm; then this juggler passes as a very wise man. (Swanton, 1918, pp. 61–62; 1931 a, p. 228.)

Bossu's account is almost as old:

When a Chacta is sick, he gives all that he has to be treated, but if the sick man dies, his relatives attribute his death to the doctor and not to the condition of the patient. Consequently they kill the doctor if they feel so inclined, but this happens seldom because there is always a back door. Besides, these doctors are acquainted with many plants good to cure the maladies to which one is exposed in this country. They can heal with certainty the bites of rattlesnakes and other poisonous creatures.

When savages have been wounded by a bullet or arrows, the jugglers or doctors begin by sucking the patient's wound and spitting out the blood, which is called in France *guérir du secrêt*. In their dressings they do not make use of lint of pledgets, but of a powdered root which they blow into the wound to make it suppurate and another which makes it dry up and close. They clear the wounds of gangrene (*cangrêne*) by bathing them in a decoction of certain roots with which they are acquainted. (Swanton, 1931 a, p. 229; Bossu, 1768, vol. 2, pp. 96–98.)

Coming down into the nineteenth century, we have a very good résumé of native Choctaw practice from Folsom, himself a Choctaw. After remarking that females as well as males practiced medicine, in equal numbers he maintains, he says:

The doctors made use of herbs and roots in various forms, applied and given in different modes—for emetics, cathartics, sweat, wounds, and sores; they also made use of cold baths, scarification, cupping and blistered by means of burning punk, and practiced suction to draw out pain; some used enchantment, while others practiced by magic, pretending to have learned the art of healing . . . by special revelation, communicated to them in some retired and unfrequented forest. It was in this way, also, it is said, that the war-prophets were raised up to lead the people to battle. At a high price and much expense the doctors of both sexes learned the mode and manner of the use of herbs and roots . . . They have, among other things, an effectual remedy for the bite of the rattle-snake, or of any other venomous reptile, the bite of which they consider very easy of cure. (Cushman, 1899, pp. 367–368; Swanton, 1931 a, p. 226.)

Cushman speaks of sweat bathing as the last resort of the doctor and states that it was astonishingly effective in "intermittent fevers." We are also told that the doctor danced, sang, beat upon a drum, and uttered formulae, calling at times upon the four quarters of the earth (Cushman, 1899, pp. 258–260; Swanton, 1931 a, pp. 230–231). Dances resembling the Pishofa dances seem to have been held at times.

Although Cushman overvalued native medical knowledge, the two following paragraphs by him are inserted as giving an idea of some of the native remedies and the effect of the influx of diseases introduced by the whites:

In cases of bowel affections they use persimmons dried by the heat of the sun and mixed with a light kind of bread. In case of sores, they applied a poultice of pounded ground ivy for a few days, then carefully washing the afflicted part with the resin of the copal-tree which proved very efficacious; to produce a copious perspiration, a hot decoction of the China root swallowed, had the desired effect. They possessed an antidote for the bite and sting of snakes and insects, in the root of a plant called rattlesnake's master, having a pungent yet not unpleasant odor. The root of the plant was chewed, and also a poultice made of it was applied to the wound, which at once checked the poison and the patient was well in a few days. The medical properties of the sassafras, sarsaparilla, and other medicinal plants, were known to them. They possessed many valuable secrets to cure dropsy, rheumatism, and many other diseases, which, no doubt, will ever remain a secret with them, proving that their powers of observation, investigation and discrimination, are not, by any means, to be regarded as contemptible; while their belief, that the Great Spirit has provided a remedy in plants for all diseases to which poor humanity seems an heir, and never refuses to make it known to those who seek the knowledge of it by proper supplications, is praiseworthy in them to say the least of it. (Cushman, 1899, pp. 228–229; Swanton, 1931 a, p. 234.)

He has the following to say of the mortality among Indians owing to white contact:

The greatest mortality among them was generally confined to the younger children; while longevity was a prominent characteristic among the adults. After the age of six or eight years the mortality of disease among them was less than among the white children of the present day after that age. But after those baneful diseases, scarlet fever, measles, mumps, whooping-cough, diseases unknown to them before, had been introduced among them, the fatality among the children was distressing, frequently destroying the greater number of children in a village or neighborhood:—being wholly ignorant as they were of the proper mode of treatment was a great cause of the fearful fatality. Mental or nervous diseases were unknown to the ancient Choctaws; and idiocy and deformity were seldom seen. But of all the "diseases" introduced among them by the whites, the most pernicious and fatal in all its features, bearings, and consequences, to the Choctaw people, was, is, and ever will be, Okahumma (red water or whiskey); which, when once formed into habit, seemed to grow to a species of insanity equal even to that so often exhibited among the whites. (Cushman, 1899, p. 230; Swanton, 1931 a, pp. 234-235.)

Du Pratz supplies us with a unique account of the regimentation of a sick person among the Natchez:

When the natives are sick they eat no fish and very little meat, and they even abstain from that entirely if the nature of the malady demands it. Then they take only hominy or meal cooked in meat broth. If the sick person is worse they have a small quantity of coarse meal cooked in the same rich broth, and give of this broth [itself] only to one who is doing well.

As soon as a man is indisposed his wife sleeps with another woman on the bed which touches that of the sick person at the foot or at the head. The husband of this neighbor finds another place in which to lie down. In this way the wife is in a position to help her husband without inconveniencing him in any manner. (Du Pratz, 1758, vol. 3, pp. 12-13; Swanton, 1911, p. 80.)

We might look for greater separation between priests and medicine men in this tribe, but it was probably prevented by the absorption of priestly functions by the civil leaders included in the Sun caste. The author of the Luxembourg Memoir tells us how supernatural powers, including the healing of diseases, were attained:

In order to attain these sublime functions a savage shuts himself into his cabin alone for nine days without eating, with water only; everyone is forbidden to disturb him. There, holding in his hand a kind of gourd filled with shells, with which he makes a continual noise, he invokes the Spirit, prays Him to speak to him and to receive him as a doctor and magician, and that with cries, howls, contortions and terrible shakings of the body, until he gets himself out of breath and foams in a frightful manner. This training being completed at the end of nine days, he comes out of his cabin triumphant and boasts of having been in conversation with the Spirit and of having received from Him the gift of healing maladies, driving away storms, and changing the weather. From that time they are recognized as doctors and are very much respected; people have recourse to them in sickness and to obtain favorable weather; but it is always necessary to carry presents. It sometimes happens that having received them, if the sick person is not cured or the weather does not change, the doctor is killed as an imposter; a fact which causes the most skillful among them only to receive presents when they see an appearance of cure or of change in the weather. (Swanton, 1911, pp. 178-179.)

Le Petit's description of their method of practice, while unsympathetic, is perhaps the best we have:

All their art consists in different juggleries; that is to say, that they dance and sing night and day about the sick man and smoke without ceasing, swallowing the smoke of the tobacco. These jugglers eat scarcely anything during all the time that they are engaged in the cure of the sick, but their chants and their dances are accompanied by contortions so violent that, although they are entirely naked and should naturally suffer from cold, yet they are always foaming at the mouth. They have a little basket in which they keep what they call their spirits; that is to say, small roots of different kinds, heads of owls, small parcels of the hair of fallow deer, some teeth of animals, some small stones or pebbles, and other similar trifles.

It appears that to restore health to the sick, they invoke without ceasing that which they have in their basket. Some of them have there a certain root which by its smell can put serpents to sleep and render them senseless. After having rubbed their hands and body with this root, they take hold of those reptiles without fearing their bite, which is mortal. Sometimes they cut with a flint, the part affected with the malady, and then suck out all the blood they can draw from it, and in returning it immediately into a dish, they at the same time spit out a little piece of wood, or straw, or leather, which they have concealed under the tongue. Drawing it to the attention of the relatives of the sick man, "There," say they, "is the cause of the sickness." These medicine men are always paid in advance. If the sick man recovers their gain is very considerable, but if he should die they are sure to have their heads cut off by the relatives or friends of the deceased. This invariably takes place, and even the relatives of the medicine man find nothing at all of which to complain, and do not testify any concern. (Thwaites, 1897–1901, vol. 68, pp. 150–157; Swanton, 1911, pp. 179–180.)

The cupping horn was also used. According to Du Pratz:

The *alexis* never use lancets to draw blood, but when they have a sick person who they think needs to be bled they take a splinter of flint with which they make many incisions in the flesh of the sick person in the place where he feels the pain. After that they suck the blood, either with the mouth or with the end of a bison horn, which they have sawed off and of which they have made a kind of cone (*cornet*) which they apply to the place. This is what they call a bleeding. (Dumont, 1753, vol. 1, pp. 172–173; Swanton, 1911, pp. 80–81.)

Du Pratz and other Louisiana writers express high regard for the efficacy of Indian treatments, but the recovery of men living in the manner of the ancient Natchez is less to be wondered at now that we understand how much nature will bear and do by herself. Du Pratz states that he sent to France more than 300 simples obtained from the natives "with their numbers, and a memorandum which detailed their qualities and taught the manner of using them" (Du Pratz, 1758, vol. 1, pp. 211–212; Swanton, 1911, pp. 83–84). He himself extols the virtues of the sweet gum, a vine he calls "the barbed creeper," the China root, the maidenhair fern, the ground ivy, and some other native productions (Du Pratz, 1758, vol. 2, pp. 28–29, 55–58, 60–62; Swanton, 1911, pp. 84–85). The Natchez also used the sweat bath, and I am sure all physicians will be glad to learn the following simple remedy for insanity, an Indian secret revealed to us by Dumont de Montigny:

To what I have already said [on the subject of the native doctors] I will add here something about their method of curing lunatics, those who have lost their senses on account of some fear or by some other accident. It is this which the savages call "no longer having a soul (*esprit*)." For there are insane in Louisiana as well as in Europe, and it is there that one can say truly that all the insane are not in the Petites-Maisons, because such establishments are entirely unknown among these barbarians. Here is the method followed by the Alexis in treating this sickness.

These savage doctors use on these occasions neither baths, nor bleedings, nor any of the remedies which are in use among ourselves for such maladies. They merely take lettuce seed (*graine de laitue*) and nuts with their shells on, in equal measure, and having placed all in a mortar, or more correctly in an Indian crusher, they crush them and pound them until they form a kind of opiate (or paste?), two or three drahms of which they make their sick people take morning and evening. With this single remedy they cure them completely. (Dumont, 1753, vol. 2, pp. 278–279.)

The writer obtained the names of a considerable number of plants used as medicines from a Natchez informant in the Cherokee country south of Fort Gibson. It was still believed that animals caused diseases. When a man becomes sick at the stomach and vomited it was thought that a dead person was eating out of the same dish with him. Doctors would blow into pots of medicine and sing appropriate songs for each, facing the east as they did so. Sometimes they addressed the four points of the compass in which case they began with the north and ended with the east as with the Creeks. They always got bark, roots, or limbs from the east side of a tree or bush because that was the good luck quarter and stood for strength while the west meant weakness and death (Swanton, 1928, pp. 666–670). The little that we know regarding the medical practices of other lower Mississippi tribes discloses nothing differing in any manner from the corresponding customs of the Natchez. For a general study of medicinal plants in this area, consult Lydia Averrill Taylor (1940).

For Caddo medical practices, see Bureau of American Ethnology Bulletin 132 (Swanton, 1942, pp. 219–226).

CONCLUSION

The material assembled in the present bulletin seems to support the thesis that human culture in a natural physiographic area tends to remain constant, or evolve at the same rate, that units of alien population entering it tend to become absorbed by the culture they find, while units separating from it tend to abandon much of the culture they took with them. This is true when the cultures of the peoples concerned do not vary too widely, and it does not mean that culture is absolutely dependent on environment, or that past history has no bearing on present condition. Diverse origins of units in any natural area are marked by lags in the movement toward conformity which are of different rates in different series of cultural features. Upon the whole this lag is least pronounced in items of material culture and such intangibles as are not clothed with peculiar social or religious value, greater in factors of social and ceremonial organization, still greater in linguistic differences, and ordinarily greatest of all in physical characteristics. Where, as in the Southeastern province, physical characteristics are not sufficiently marked to be the occasion for emotional attitudes a steady mixture of these features with all the rest is likely to take place so that no accurate classification involving all of them is possible. Some tribes may be placed definitely in one or another category but in certain cases it cannot be done. Language, on the other hand, gives us a clear-cut categorization and is upon the whole the most useful single criterion for this purpose. Our principal difficulty here is that there has been a tendency to indicate linguistic stocks or families as if they were all of equal weight and as if the differences between them were equal, but, as has been shown by Professor Sapir and his pupils, whether they are actually related or not, North American stocks may be ranged in about half a dozen main structural groups and the stocks themselves do not differ by equal increments. In the eastern part of North America, for instance, the great Algonquian stock to the north and east seems to diverge fundamentally from all the rest. A secondary distinction is to be drawn between the Caddoan and Iroquoian peoples on one side and the Muskhogean-Siouans on the other, including in the latter probably the other small stocks of the Southeast.

Algonquian people had penetrated the area under consideration along the eastern seaboard so as to include Chesapeake Bay and the Sound region of North Carolina. At a much later period a central Algonquian tribe, the Shawnee, settled upon Cumberland River and still later gave off branches to the southward which added significant elements to the histories of Alabama, Georgia, and South Carolina. One small division of the Illinois Confederation, the Michigamea, reached northeastern Arkansas before the coming of the whites, but their history is really part of that of the upper Mississippi Valley and they require scant notice here.

Iroquoians were represented by four tribes, or confederations of tribes, in the area under consideration. One of these, the Tuscarora, with which the Coree and Neusiok were perhaps affiliated, were settled upon the Roanoke, Neuse, Tar, and Pamlico Rivers; on the Meherrin River was a small related tribe of that name; and beyond them the Nottoway, also on a river which perpetuates their name. After the Tuscarora War of 1711–13 that tribe and its immediate allies moved north and united with the Five Nations of the Iroquois. More significant in the history of the Southeast were the Cherokee, who spoke a language diverging considerably from other Iroquoian tongues. They occupied the region of the southern Appalachians to which they had perhaps descended at a rather recent period from homes farther north.

The Caddoan stock was represented by a group of tribes bearing the general name Caddo, living in and near the point where the States of Louisiana, Texas, Arkansas, and Oklahoma come together.

The Siouan peoples were represented in four different areas. Two of these were occupied by single tribes, and a third by 20 tribes or more which covered most of the Piedmont region of Virginia and North and South Carolina besides the Coastal Plain of South Carolina between Cape Fear River and Bull Bay. It also extended over most of West Virginia and an indefinite distance westward. These tribes formed two distinct dialectic groups: a northern, in Virginia and to the westward; and a southern, in the Carolinas. One of the two isolated tribes, the Biloxi, was about the bay which has received its name and on Pascagoula River, while the other was along the lower course of the Yazoo in the present State of Mississippi. This last, the Ofo, however, descended from the Ohio River region at a very late period, and it is believed that the appearance of the Biloxi near the Gulf of Mexico was also late. At the mouth of Arkansas River was a Siouan tribe, the Quapaw, connected with the great western division of this family.

The Muskhogean stock is the stock of the Southeast par excellence. It occupied the central section, the very heart of the Gulf region from the Mississippi River to the Savannah and from the Tennessee to the Gulf excepting for minor areas already indicated. As originally defined by Powell, it embraced two powerful peoples, the Choctaw in the southwest and the Creek Confederation in the east and center, each speaking a distinct language and possessed of a distinct cultural life. Intermediate were the Chickasaw which spoke the language of the former but shared numerous cultural features with the latter. The Apalachee seem to have been related by language to the Choctaw, but little is known of their cultural pattern. There were several smaller tribes which shared the culture either of the Choctaw or the Creeks. On the Mississippi, however, was a group, represented most conspicuously by the Natchez, which spoke a widely divergent Muskhogean tongue and had a correspondingly divergent culture. In the opposite direction we find a similar condition in northern Florida, where the Timucua tribes also had divergent Muskhogean languages, or a divergent language, and corresponding customs. The connections of the inhabitants of southern Florida are unknown but they are believed to have been more directly with the Choctaw and Apalachee. A near neighbor of the Natchez on the Mississippi was the Tunica group, including five tribes; westward of the mouth of the Mississippi, the Chitimacha group of three tribes; and, extending beyond them to the neighborhood of Galveston, the Atakapa, with certain connected tribes in the interior of Texas beyond the Trinity. Westward of the Atakapa again were other small linguistic groups, the Karankawa, Tonkawa, Coahuilteco, and Tamaulipeco, constituting either widely divergent languages of one stock or several small independent families. Little has been preserved of these languages and their past history and affiliations are highly problematical, yet it is not impossible that they were connected with the Siouan-Muskhogean languages as part of a larger whole extending to California, where they are supposed to have been represented by the great Hokan family. This is the theory of Sapir and there is considerable to support it. In any case, the Tunica, the Chitimacha, the Atakapa, and their allies are believed to have belonged to one stock which is in close structural agreement with the Muskhogean and Siouan languages. From the Atakapa, inclusive, westward the tribes actually fall outside of the cultural area of the Southeast.

COMMON CULTURAL CHARACTERS

In the discussion which follows I shall deal principally with the Algonquians of the Northeast, the Siouans of the Northeast interior, the Creeks, Timucua, Choctaw, Chickasaw, Cherokee, Natchez, Tunica, Chitimacha, and Caddo, material from the remaining tribes being very fragmentary. It must be pointed out at the beginning that some features peculiar to certain areas may be traced directly to physiographic differences. Thus, the lives of the Cherokee were affected considerably by their location in the southern Appalachians and those of the coastal Algonquians and Calusa, for instance, by adjustment to a littoral existence. The difference in life zones also reacted upon the cultures of the people, the Cherokee and some of the Virginia Siouans including within their territory the only fragments of the Boreal region and the Transitional zone of the Austral region to be found in the Southeast, and the southern Florida Indians falling into the Tropical zone. The uniformity in culture which the Southeast as a whole exhibits undoubtedly is connected with the fact that the greater part of it is in one zone, the Lower Austral, and most of the remainder in the closely related Upper Austral. Differences observable among the Cherokee and in southern Florida are undoubtedly attributable in some measure to environment. Those Cherokee cultural elements which show divergencies from the Southeastern area as a whole and resemblances with Iroquois features may, of course, be set down as holdovers from former stock association. If, as seems probable, the tribes of southern Florida were related to the Apalachee and Choctaw, the peculiarities of their culture may fairly be attributed to the influence exerted by the natural area in which they had settled. On the other hand, when we find tribes scattered through the same natural area from the Atlantic to Texas exhibiting variations, we know that some factor other than present environment has been at work. Such general cultural variations are reinforced in many cases by physical or linguistic differences, but in other cases these are weak or absent and we have to fall back on an inherent tendency of the human mind to vary independently of any variation in the external world.

To begin with, certain cultural characteristics are found practically throughout the area in question. So far as we are aware the natural environment was exploited in about the same manner and to the same extent everywhere. Corn, beans, pumpkins and squashes, and a species of tobacco were raised by all of the tribes from Virginia to Louisiana. The only exceptions seems to have been the tribes of southern Florida and the marginal tribes of the southwest, including the Atakapa and Tonkawa. These last seemed not to have adjusted themselves to horticultural life partly on account of the sudden drop in rainfall in their territories and partly because of the greater attractions of fishing on the coast and bison hunting in the interior. We know that southern Florida was suited to corn culture because the Seminole who occupied it at a later period and still live there raised the crop. We must suppose the abstinence of the earlier peoples was due in part to the greater attractions of fishing and partly to the extent to which they resorted to the flour of the Zamia. If the truth were known, however, I think we should find that the corn complex did not reach central Florida until a comparatively late date. Recent studies of varieties of corn have demonstrated a marked difference between those of the West Indies and those of North America, the implication being that the cultivation of this plant was introduced from Mexico. Sunflowers were apparently cultivated by most of the horticultural tribes. From Virginia to Louisiana the methods employed in clearing the ground and in caring for the crops were very similar.

The stalking of deer is described from all parts of the area in much the same terms. Surrounds may have been used oftener by the northern tribes, as if the custom had emanated from that quarter, but it was not of much use in this region, since bison were scattered in relatively small bands and it was not as necessary in hunting deer. If the devices used in hunting small animals and birds differed regionally, our data are not sufficient to prove it. Fishing customs were variable, but mainly because conditions varied. Fishing on the sea coast was naturally carried on in a different manner from fishing on inland streams, and the same regional demands were, so far as we can see, met in the same way. Thus fishweirs of similar pattern seem to have been employed indifferently by the Algonquian, Muskhogean, and Floridian peoples, and probably by the Siouans also, though we do not happen to have a description of this industry from the Siouan tribes of the coast. In the interior, fish poisoning is reported from the more important interior tribes of different stocks, the only omission where we might have expected it being among the Caddo. Tribes like the Natchez along rivers having a continuous flow all the year round would be less likely to resort to the practice. Similarly, inland fish traps would naturally be used in regions where the rivers had a fairly rapid current, and the principal area answering to that description is the southern Appalachians and the territories immediately adjoining. Here, however, we find the same indifference to stock affiliation in the use of the device. It occurs in the country of the Algonquians, Siouans, and Iroquoians, and at least close to that of the Muskhogeans. All of the tribes had dogs, and so far as we know they were of the same breeds. The treatment of animal and vegetable foods seems to have been practically the same everywhere. House types varied but with certain limits, and all consisted of a framework of poles covered with withes, wattle, grass, or palmetto, and nearly everywhere we find the same sort of bed, a raised shelf inside along the wall. Smoke holes were usual but not invariable accompaniments of houses, and there was usually but one door, which faced the east or south. Stockades reinforced with towers are reported from Virginia to the Mississippi and were probably known to the Caddo though we seem to have no description from Caddo territory. The breechclout, women's skirt, and untailored shirts, cloaks, and blankets are reported from practically all sections, and the clothing, or unclothing, of children was about the same. A simple type of textile woven from the inner bark of trees or a kind of grass seems to have been known in all sections except probably by the wandering Texas bands, who fall properly outside of the Southeastern province. The same sorts of material were used for cords and threads. Feather garments were known throughout the region. Shell beads and pearls were made or extracted in all sections and were highly valued. A certain amount of copper had been introduced from the north and it was known to nearly all the tribes. All references to porcupine quill work in the historic period represent importations from the north, and are without diagnostic significance. Necklaces, ear ornaments, bracelets, arm and leg bands, the use of paint and tattoo marks were found throughout, and it is only in the special types of decorations that we come upon diagnostic traits. There is little or nothing in historical records regarding flint working, ground stone implements, pipes, chunkey stones, or pottery by which we may classify tribes or tribal groups. This work must fall on the archeologists. References to wooden stools have come to us from all parts of the area except perhaps the northeastern sections. However, they represent West Indian contact and are of little classificatory value. Everywhere we have reports of the employment of dishes of wood and horn, wooden mortars, chests, and cradles, but the records are not sufficient to establish regional types. Almost the same may be said of reed and shell knives, clubs, bows and arrows, and perhaps also of blowguns and shields, but we shall see presently that the introduction of bows and arrows along the Gulf may have been late. Dugout canoes and rafts were employed everywhere, but we also find bark canoes utilized in the interior of the country and without distinction as between tribes. Chiefs were borne about on litters except perhaps in the extreme northeast and west. Basketry and mats were universally employed. The artistic development again seems to have been rather uniform. Drums, rattles, and flutes or flageolets are reported from all quarters.

Superficially the social life of the southeastern Indians was much the same. Unless forced into stockades by war, the towns consisted of neighborhoods of single houses or groups of houses extending through the woods, sometimes for several miles, though with a center for social gatherings and ceremonial observances. Descent was usually reckoned in the female line, and if there were exogamous subdivisions, they were transmitted in the same way. There were, however, many tribal variations which we will take up presently. In so far as we are acquainted with them, the terms of relationship and names followed similar patterns. This similarity extended to other social usages, but the burial customs, which are of exceptional importance to the archeologist, show certain marked regional differences. Finally, the background of the religious beliefs of these tribes and their medical practices were also similar, but the religious attitude seems to have varied considerably from one tribe to another and the ceremonial patterns were often markedly distinct.

CULTURAL DIFFERENCES

So much for the resemblances. Now let us consider the more important divergencies from the norm. The head types, which we know, of course, from the investigations of modern students, not from early authorities, leave us in considerable uncertainty. There was a brachycephalic element particularly in evidence along the Mississippi and one or two seemingly earlier dolichocephalic elements widely extended and increasing in prominence toward the Atlantic coast.

All early writers describe the Indians as tall, particularly the Cherokee, but there was a short female type among the Creeks. Du Pratz observed a single dwarf in the Natchez nation and says that he measured four and a half feet. Lawson saw one hump-backed Indian and one blind man. Garcilaso reported a tribe containing many blind men. The head hair is described as long, deep black, and lustrous but the body hair scanty and usually removed carefully. Nevertheless De Soto met one chief in southern Georgia with a beard, Blande and his companions reported that the Indians on Roanoke River wore beards, and Lawson noted that the Keyauwee had mustaches.

Early writers sought to find differing psychical characteristics in the several tribes but are not very consistent or convincing. Undoubtedly these apparent differences were due to the tribal mores as, for instance, when the Creeks, a warlike and aggressive people, are accused of an overbearing disposition, and a corresponding mildness is attributed to the Choctaw.

Language was evidently a powerful unifying factor, but it may be doubted whether related but mutually unintelligible tongues tended to keep the cultural patterns of two tribes similar any more than wholly unrelated tongues. If they show closer resemblances, the fact may be explained by the more recent contact of the peoples concerned, not by the mere fact of related speech.

Turning to the economic cycle, we seem to find that the winter hunt was common to all of the tribes except possibly some of those of south Florida and Louisiana, but the coast Indians spent much of their summer by their fishweirs or in fishing operations generally, while the inland tribes depended more on food gathering and minor hunting operations. They spent part of this time alike enjoying the produce of their fields, and the Natchez spring fast seems to have been broken very early by the maturing of the "little corn." Month names among the Algonquian tribes, Siouan tribes, and those along the Mississippi seem to have been taken mainly from food plants, while the names used by the interior tribes, Creeks, Yuchi, and Choctaw, refer more often to the weather.

In the matter of alimentation the Southeast was practically a unit except perhaps for southern Florida and, of course, the wandering tribes of the west, which are practically beyond it. Elsewhere the seacoast also brought about certain differences, in a measure among the Chitimacha but more particularly among the Algonquian tribes of the northeast. It is in the latter region that we begin to hear of caches in the ground, granaries elsewhere being elevated on posts.

There were two principal types of houses which overlapped throughout the center of the region, while one extended farther west and the other farther east. The first of these was represented typically by the the winter house of the Chickasaw, Choctaw, and Cherokee and included the winter ceremonial house of the Creeks and some of the Siouan tribes. This was circular and consisted of a framework of poles built around two or three series of posts, the framework being covered with wattle and plastered with mud, over which was grass or mats. The Natchez and some of their neighbors made a similar house but perfectly square. Westward among most of the Caddo and farther into the Plains, the wattle gave place entirely to grass. In Florida most of the private houses and some of the town houses were circular but without the clay covering and were thatched with palmetto. Northeast this type even reached the Algonquian country and is represented by the temple of the town of Pomeioc. The rectangular or summer house was found among the Chickasaw and Choctaw, and was the common house pattern of the Creeks. Some of the town houses of the Timucua Indians and the Guale people were built upon this plan, and it is related to the open arbor of the modern Seminole. A similar open arbor is said to have been employed in summer by the Siouans. It was the common summer house of the Cherokee and was probably related to the long type found in the Algonquian country, though here it seems to have merged into the oval and circular dwelling which we usually call wigwam. The Quapaw appear to have had oval structures after the patterns of wigwams. The Chesapeake houses were further distinguished by the presence of two doors. Usually there was but one door and that facing east or south. Such refinements of civilization as wash basins presented to guests after eating and towels seem to have been confined to Virginia. The ceremonial washing of guests existed in the Sound country of North Carolina and among the Caddo. A wooden head rest in lieu of a pillow is reported from Florida, but in only one instance.

As material for textiles, palmetto displaced mulberry bark in southern Florida, and "silk grass" seems to have been utilized in Virginia more than any other material, but these variations may have been due to the environment. The feather mantles to which reference has already been made ordinarily consisted of turkey feathers, but Dumont speaks of swan feathers among the Natchez, and Bartram says that the Creeks employed feathers of the flamingo. Material for the costume was usually of deerskin, but in southern Florida breechclouts were made of palmetto leaves. Judging by the De Soto narratives, the Creek Indians must have worn leggings in advance of the other tribes. Bartram says that the Indian women did not wear these but Beverley, copying Michel, represents a Virginia Siouan woman accoutered in this manner. Garments woven of native textiles were ordinarily worn by women, but there is one reference in the De Soto narratives to usage of such a garment by men, and the ancients seen by La Salle's followers in the house of the Taensa chief wore long garments made of mulberry bark. In Florida and southeastern Georgia women made their garments out of tree moss. Lawson notes that Carolina women used such garments when they were in mourning. The Choctaw prepared a fabric from bison hair and "fibre from a very strong herb" but it does not appear that this was exclusively their product. Whatever the significance may be, it is a fact that Hariot, Smith, and Strachey do not describe the moccasins and White's drawings do not show them. The illustrations in Beverley's work showing Indians with moccasins are all from Michel and probably illustrate the costumes of Siouans. Lawson speaks of them and they were certainly used by all of the tribes. However, it is a fact that moccasins were generally discarded except when Indians were on a journey. Lawson also tells us that, besides fur and feathers, Siouan women used blankets woven of opossum hair.

If we had a detailed description of male methods of wearing the hair throughout the Southeast it would probably give us an additional means of classification of considerable value, for the hints that are dropped are interesting enough. We learn, for instance, that the Creeks shaved their heads on the sides leaving a roach from front to back along the top of the head and a fringe of hair along the forehead. The usage of the Chickasaw, Cherokee, and Yuchi was the same, and it is interesting to find that medicine men among the Algonquians treated their hair similarly. On the other hand, the Choctaw allowed the hair on their heads to grow long and were known as "Long Hairs" from that circumstance. In later times we are told specifically that the nothern Choctaw, influenced by the Chickasaw, had altered this custom. From one reference in Le Moyne it seems that the custom of roaching had entered Florida. Since the Timucua used their hair as a temporary quiver for arrows, however, it is evident that it was less drastically treated than by the Creeks and their neighbors. It was assumed that the Pensacola tribe, "Hair People," was so named because of the same custom as that which obtained among their neighbors, the Choctaw. Some of the Mississippi tribes seem to have roached their hair, or at least shaved it very short, while others wore it long and some of them cut it on one side like the Virginia Indians. This last treatment was originally intended to avoid the danger of entangling the hair with the bowstring. Some of the Caddo had the same custom.

While shell beads were used everywhere, they were resorted to most in the northeast among the Algonquian and Siouan peoples, where they had probably become a medium of barter in the prehistoric period. Shell gorgets, judging by the archeological remains along with the historic notices, were used principally in a belt extending from the Sound region of North Carolina to the country of the Caddo, from whose territory many excellent specimens have been recovered. As noted above, the references to decorative work with porcupine quills probably apply to northern Indians visiting the southern country temporarily or to objects obtained in trade. Remains of this animal are not reported farther south than Tennessee, and there they must have died out at a remote period. Objects of this kind were, therefore, intrusive, as was nearly all the gold which came in Spanish vessels wrecked on the Florida coast. Palmetto-leaf hats were sometimes worn by girls in Florida, and other unique objects in this region were earrings made of fish bladders dyed red. Cherokee, Creek, and Chickasaw dandies cut slits around the rims of their ears and wound copper wire through the openings, thereby expanding the ears enormously. Spike-shaped ear ornaments are reported in historic times mainly along the lower Mississippi but anciently the custom seems to have extended farther east. The Creeks, Alabama, Chickasaw, Cherokee, Bayogoula, Caddo, and Chitimacha wore nose ornaments and so did a few Virginia Indians but they were ordinarily absent elsewhere and certainly so in Florida. The eastern Indians generally employed a kind of hair dye made from the puccoon root along with bear grease, but it is not reported from the lower Mississippi. Algonquian and Siouan women are said to have made no use of paint while only Creek women of a particular class employed it, but it was resorted to constantly by the Indian women in Florida, along the lower Mississippi, and among the Caddo. Only on the lower Mississippi do we hear of Indian women blackening their teeth. The Buzzard Men of the Choctaw and presumably Chitimacha, and all of the Indians of Florida let their fingernails grow long; those of North Carolina at least did not. Frontal head deformation was common on the lower course of the Mississippi, among the Choctaw, Chickasaw, Waxhaw, and probably the Catawba, and was resorted to by some Caddo as late as the time of De Soto. There seems to be no record of the chunkey game in Virginia among the Virginia Siouans or in Florida, but the omission means little. In historic times labrets are reported only on the Texas coast, but they were found at Key Marco by Cushing. Wooden stools were also found at Key Marco and they are reported in historic times from the Mobile, Chickasaw, and Natchez tribes. Stone mortars seem to have been used in making flour in the central section of the Southeast in prehistoric times, but the tribes found in occupancy all used mortars of wood. If Strachey is correct in stating that these were made by the women, that would register as a Virginia peculiarity. The kunti mortars were made by excavating hollows in the sides of fallen trees, and I was told by a Choctaw that this was the only way any were made before axes were introduced, but this is certainly erroneous. In Virginia and the Carolinas in very early times there was in use a club with flints fixed into the side making something like a sword. The black locust was the principal wood used for bows east of the Mississippi and the Osage orange the principal one west of it. In 1541 the Tula, a Caddo tribe, were using lances, though they seem to have been unknown to the Indians farther east. At the same time we learn that spear throwers had survived at the mouth of the Mississippi, and Cushing found an abundance of them at Key Marco, though these may or may not have been of ancient date. In 1528, however, Narvaez and his companions were attacked near Pensacola by Indians with "darts" which may have been thrown from atlatls, since they had no bows and arrows. Here also is almost the only reference to a sling in the Southeast. The northeastern Algonquians had shields made of bark; elsewhere they were of cane or bison hide. Dugouts were used on the coast and the larger rivers, and bark canoes inland, utility evidently determining distribution. The litters in which chiefs and other persons of eminence were borne about in most of these tribes seem to have given way to the shoulders of willing or appointed subjects among the Caddo and to have been absent in Virginia. In the last-mentioned region mats were usually made of rushes, elsewhere of cane. Similarly with baskets, the eastern Algonquians and Siouans made their baskets mainly of rushes, silk grass, and a kind of root, while the tribes west of them made them of canes. Palmetto baskets were made in Florida, and by the Alabama Indians if cane failed them. Some of the Creeks used hickory splints, and the modern Natchez resorted to roots of the buck bush. Wooden images were found upon sacred edifices from western Florida to the Mississippi. The Creeks had them in their Square Grounds. Towards the northeast, wooden images were used inside of the sacred buildings or were set up in fields. Wind instruments seem to have been somewhat more in evidence in the eastern part of the section than the western.

In the Algonquian region some evidences of the old family hunting territories apparently survived. Autocracy was highly developed in the Algonquian and Siouan sections, and occasionally elsewhere, as by Tascalusa and by self-made men, but in Florida, among the Natchez and their allies, and among the Chitimacha, leadership was determined largely by descent. This was to some extent true also of the Creeks, of the Chickasaw less so, while the Choctaw were among the most democratic of all Southeastern people. The Caddo operated under a theocracy. Totemic clans were most highly developed among the Creeks, Timucua, and Cherokee, and had extended to the Chickasaw and eastern Caddo. Castes had developed or were in process of developing among the Chitimacha, Natchez, and Timucua, and had extended their influence to the Chickasaw, Creeks, and western Caddo. Moieties were particularly prominent among the Choctaw and Chickasaw but also important among the Creeks. In the northeast and southwest we find female descent with few or no divisions. The marginal Shawnee and Quapaw had totemic divisions with male descent. The Yuchi combined both systems. The terms of relationship resembled the Crow type most closely, but those of the Shawnee and Quapaw were of the Omaha type and the Caddo of the Mackenzie type. Timucua terms of relationship featured prominently the fact of the status of the individual through whom the relationship came, whether living or dead. In cases of adultery the eastern Siouans punished only the man, the Chickasaw only the woman, the Creeks both.

Burial customs differed considerably and they are of particular importance to the archeologist as well as the ethnologist. Bodies of chiefs among the Virginia Algonquians were deprived of the softer parts, sand was filled in inside the skin around the bones, and then they were laid upon scaffolds at one end of the sacred ossuary of the tribe, which also contained images of the gods. Spelman, speaking probably of the Potomac tribe, says that the bodies were left in ossuaries until the flesh fell away, when the bones were wrapped in a mat and taken to the abandoned house of the deceased, where they remained until the house fell to ruins. Common people were buried "in graves like ours" and thus apparently at full length. Among the eastern Siouans the corpse was wrapped in mats and laid in a long grave covered with bark laid over a ridge pole, the whole being covered in turn with earth. After the flesh had rotted away, the bones were taken up, cleaned, placed in proper relation to one another, wrapped in a clean white deerskin and laid in the quiozogon or ossuary. The mounds made for dead Santee and Tuscarora Indians were thus merely vaults over the bodies. A reburial custom was reported among the South Carolina Siouans by Peter Martyr on the authority of a native informant. A Timucua chief was buried in the earth, a mound raised above, around which arrows were stuck, and his drinking shell was placed on top. Afterward his house and property were burned. The Tocobaga Indians separated the bones from the flesh and buried the former ceremonially. The Tekesta also separated the bones and placed them in a grave box. The Cherokee buried in the earth either at full length or flexed. The Creeks and Chickasaw flexed the bodies of their dead and buried them under the floors of their houses, but Choctaw usage was more elaborate. They placed their dead first on scaffolds, and, after some time had elapsed, a functionary known as a Buzzard Man cleaned the bones, burned or buried the flesh, and returned the bones to the family of the deceased enclosed in a hamper. At intervals the people of each Choctaw canton assembled to carry the accumulated hampers of bones to a specified spot, where they were buried and a mound raised over them. In the early part of the nineteenth century the missionaries induced them to give up this custom for burial in the earth. Bodies of Biloxi and Pascagoula chiefs were dried and placed with those of their predecessors around the insides of their temples. Natchez commoners seem to have been buried much like the Creeks, in the earth; the chiefs were laid in the ground in or near the temple and their bones exumed later to be placed in hampers inside of that edifice. The customs of the Bayogoula, Houma, and Chitimacha were probably like those of the Choctaw. The Tunica seem to have buried their dead in the earth. Among the Natchez as well as in Florida it was customary to burn the house of the deceased. For the Caddo, see Bulletin 132 (Swanton, 1942).

In the Algonquian and eastern Siouan areas poisoning seems to have been a popular method of disposing of enemies. It is rarely mentioned elsewhere. Among the Algonquians of the northeast we also learn of the use of tribal marks tattooed on the shoulder. The religion of the same people centered around quadrangular temples in which were kept images of their deities in a special apartment at one end. In their territory we also hear of altar stones, some near the temples, some scattered about their country. The bodies of their chiefs and principal men were laid on a staging at one end of the temple. The eastern Siouans had similar buildings but we are not well informed regarding their internal arrangement. The Natchez temple was also quadrangular with a partition at one side but with the accompaniment of a perpetually burning fire and a special corps of guardians. The Caddo cult was similar to that of the Natchez but their temples were circular.

As a peculiar element in Southeastern myths we may mention tailed men who appear in stories from the eastern Siouans, the Cherokee, and the Alabama.

Human sacrifices were offered by the Natchez and their allies and by the Indians of Florida.

CULTURAL SUBAREAS

I reiterate an earlier statement that the cultures of all of the tribes of this area were basically the same. When we attempt to distinguish cultural subareas we find constant difficulty in placing our boundaries. In spite of this and in spite of the fact that a discussion of these will involve considerable repetition, I will venture to undertake it.

Upon th ewhole, classification based on language is found to justify itself when other cultural features are examined, and to justify itself to some extent, but much less, when we consider physical characteristics. The culture of the area presents itself in its most typical forms among the tribes from northern Florida and the Savannah River to and including most of the lower valley of the Mississippi and the Red. The Indians of southern Florida were probably set apart from these rather by their environment than by any more deeply seated differences. The Cherokee, Chitimacha, and Caddo owed some of their peculiarities to the same cause and others to difference in origin and early associations. The most distinct subarea of all was that occupied by the Algonquian tribes of the Chesapeake and the coast of North Carolina, which shares so much with the peoples farther north on that coast that its position is questionable. Nevertheless, it is not open to doubt that these tribes were subjected to strong influences from the tribes below, though their immediate neighbors, the Siouan peoples, did not themselves attain to a very elevated position in the cultural scale and Speck, our leading authority on the Catawba, is of the opinion that their culture was relatively low. This seems to be confirmed, also, by the lack of any striking antiquities, particularly mounds, in their old country. When you cross the Savannah River going east, you pass almost immediately out of the mound country except in the former territory of the Cherokee.

These Siouan Indians were rather sharply divided on linguistic grounds into a northern branch which anciently occupied the Piedmont and mountain areas of Virginia and extended over much, and probably all, of West Virginia, and a southern branch in central North Carolina and the northern part of South Carolina. It is believed that the culture of these two branches differed considerably, but our information regarding them, particularly regarding the Virginia Siouans, is so meager that it is possible to enumerate few cultural differences except speech on which this opinion is based. Lawson implies, although not certainly, that the Virginia Siouans lacked community ceremonial buildings such as the southern tribes had, and Lederer's description of four exogamous divisions may perhaps have applied merely to the northern group, but both points are very uncertain. So many of the industries and customs of these Siouans are like those found either north or south of their territories that we get the impression of groups which had borrowed rather than originated. Let us now enumerate some of the cultural peculiarities found among the Algonquians and Siouans. These are of a decidedly miscellaneous character extending all the way from the fundamental to the trivial, but we have to remember that we are seriously cramped in our sources of information.

We find that the Algonquians spent much of the summer season by their fishweirs, and that the names of their months were derived largely from the names of food plants and animals. Here for the first time we hear of caches in the ground instead of on posts. The type of dwelling was ordinarily of the conical or oval wigwam pattern, but some buildings, particularly those for sacred purposes, were long. The temple in the town of Pomeioc was, however, rounded, and its shape may be attributed to southern influences. The longer houses were provided with two doors quite unlike Southeastern houses in general. A refinement of culture appears in the houses of the chiefs where basins and towels were presented to distinguished guests at meals. The ceremonial washing which Barlowe noted in North Carolina was probably another instance of the same thing. In textiles "silk grass" seems to have been used more than mulberry bark. Leggings were put on only in preparing to travel through underbrush, and, as above noted, we have only bare mention of moccasins by Smith or Strachey and they are absent from the costumes of men and women shown in White's drawings. They appear merely in Beverley's reproductions of Michel's sketches of Siouan Indians. However, knowing that all of these Indians were in the habit of leaving their moccasins off when they were about their houses, and how universally they were employed, not much reliance should be placed on this circumstance. They shaved their heads on the right side for the utilitarian purpose of keeping it away from the bowstring. The medicine men, however, cut their hair in the Creek fashion. We are specifically informed that these Indians did not allow their fingernails to grow long like the Florida Indians. They employed a type of flat bead to which the name roanoke was given, but this was probably the common name for bead and seems to have been bestowed also upon the marginella shells with which they decorated their clothing. This apparently accompanied a considerable expansion in trade, which was also reflected in the penal laws. Murder and adultery could here be compounded for money, whereas farther south the death penalty or severe floggings were meted out. This is the only country in which shell gorgets are known to have been made, though there is every reason to suppose that the industry was widely spread. Only a few wore nasal ornaments. Along with the use of bear grease on their hair they combined that of the puccoon root, which gave it a reddish tinge. The women made no use of paint. There was no marked head deformation. There is no record of the chunkey game in this area. A curious fact, if it may be relied upon, is Strachey's assertion that the women, among their other industries, made mortars. They made use of a swordlike club with flint edges, and bark shields. There is no mention of litters for carrying about leading men. Mats were usually made of rushes, and baskets of rushes, silk grass, and a kind of root. The literature seems to supply evidence that traces of the old hunting territories of the Algonquians had survived. Autocracies based on individual ability were rather characteristic of the section. Succession of chiefs was traced through the female line, but there were no clans. They had ossuaries or temples in which were placed the bodies of their chiefs, but these were treated somewhat differently from the custom prevailing farther south, and the scaffold on which they were laid seems to have occupied one end of the ossuary instead of the circuit of the walls. The viscera were removed from the skin, the bones replaced in order and sand filled in between. The Potomac Indians placed the bodies of their chiefs in ossuaries until the flesh fell away, and then wrapped the bones in a mat and put them in the chief's house, which they allowed to fall to ruin. The common people were buried at full length in the earth. Poison was often used in getting rid of personal enemies. The tribal mark is said to have been tattooed on one shoulder. Carved images of the deity were kept in each temple in a small apartment cut off from the rest of the building. They had altar stones near the temples and also scattered through the country at which offerings were made. Female chiefs seem to have been fairly common. A chief met strangers at the head of his warriors and blowing on a flute. In the case of Powhatan, at least, a fixed tribute was exacted from the subject chiefs. At puberty boys and girls were both subjected to a severe ceremonial lashing at a rite called the huskanaw. Divorce is said to have been considered disgraceful and was unusual.

Some of the eastern Siouan tribes seem to have been unusually hairy or unusually remiss in removing hair from their bodies, since Blande and his companions found the Indians on Roanoke River wearing beards and Lawson tells us that the Keyauwee preserved their mustaches. Like the Algonquians they named their months largely from food animals and plants. Trading was developed to a considerable extent, the Eno Indians even raising surplus crops for purposes of trade. The town house of the Waxhaw was circular and this was probably typical of the southern Siouan tribes in general. Open arbors were used in summer. As has been noted, Michel represents a northern Siouan woman wearing leggings, and this may have been customary with them. When in mourning the southern Siouan women wore garments of tree moss. Roanoke beads were considerably utilized; no nose ornaments are mentioned. The puccoon root was rarely used to dye the hair, but instead another kind of root not as yet identified. Paint was not employed by the women, but the Waxhaw and some of the other southern Siouans were addicted to temporal skull deformation. They used the same kind of flint-edged club or sword as their Algonquian neighbors, and their baskets were made of the same materials, rushes, silk-grass, and roots. In some of these tribes the power of the chief was very highly developed, and we hear of powerful chieftainesses. There is no evidence of totemic divisions except the one reference by Lederer and it is not certainly known to which tribe, or tribes, he refers, or that the names he gives were actually totemic. In cases of adultery the male offender alone was punished. Bodies of the chiefs were buried, apparently at full length, and bark was laid over them, resting on a kind of ridge pole, the whole being finally covered with earth. Later the bones were exhumed, cleaned, wrapped in deerskins, and laid in the tribal ossuary. Bodies of commoners were simply left in the ground. Like the Algonquians, they made use of poison to get rid of personal enemies. Their sacred buildings were, however, circular, unlike most of those of their northern neighbors. One of the oldest references to mythologic tailed men is reported from their country. The huskanaw also existed among them. War titles are said to have been taken from the names of wild animals and fishes. A widow was not obliged to undergo ceremonial mourning for her deceased husband and was permitted to remarry at once. Divorce was easy. Enemies were killed to accompany the souls of the dead. During mourning the hair was unbound but not cut off. The Waxhaw and probably other tribes had the custom of the spiral fire maintained during councils. The ceremonial use of tobacco seems not to have been as pronounced as farther west. There was a class of adult slaves recruited from war captives and prevented from escape by mutilation of the feet. The harvest festival was relatively unimportant, but at certain of their ceremonies there was a considerable use of wooden images.

As has been pointed out, north and south Florida belonged to somewhat different ecological areas and the people were also linguistically somewhat diverse. The inhabitants of southern Florida moved from the seacoast seasonally less than those of the north. Human sacrifices were offered in both parts of the peninsula, and the Tocobaga of the west coast and Tekesta of the southeast coast separated the bones of their dead chiefs from the flesh and reburied them. Judging by the remains at Key Marco, the southern Floridians formerly used atlatls and wooden stools and wore labrets. All of these Indians, of course, lived largely upon fish. Their houses were thatched with palmetto and most of them seem to have been circular, but others were rectangular and some of the town houses were very long. Wooden head rests are reported instead of pillows, and palmetto replaced mulberry bark for use in textiles and in the manufacture of breechclouts and baskets. Women's garments were largely of tree moss. The hair was generally worn long. Palmetto leaf hats were worn by girls. The Timucua had ear ornaments made of fish bladders dyed red, but nose ornaments are not reported. The fingernails were left untrimmed like those of the Buzzard Men among the Choctaw. The chunkey game is not recorded from this area. The power of the chief seems to have been absolute and to have been regulated largely by descent, and there seems to have been a caste system or a strong tendency toward it. In the north were totemic clans, the status, living or dead, of a person through whom relationship came having a great deal to do in determining the term employed. A north Florida chief was buried under a mound upon which his drinking cup was placed and the whole surrounded by a circle of arrows. His house was then burned along with his principal possessions. Leggings seem to have been uncommon but leg ornaments more common than farther north. A rude lodge took the place of the summer house. Mourning was strictly enjoined on widows.

The Creeks were one of the typical central Muskhogean tribes, speaking one of the two most important Muskogean tongues. The month names in their language refer largely to the weather rather than food animals or plants. Their common house patterns for both summer and winter were rectangular, but the winter ceremonial

house was circular.   They seem to have used leggings more often than
the surrounding tribes.   Women's garments were partly of skins and
partly of textiles, except on the Georgia coast where tree moss was
often employed.   They shaved their heads along the sides leaving a
roach at the top and a fringe of hairs along the forehead.   Some
porcupine-quill work was found among them but this was evidently
imported.   The male dandies enlarged their ears by twisting copper
wire around the rim of the ear, and nose ornaments were worn.   Only
prostitutes among the women painted their faces.   The heads were
not intentionally deformed.   Wooden images were used in the square
grounds.   Leadership depended in some measure on clan status.
Totemic clans were highly developed and moieties existed but they
did not govern marriage as rigidly as among some other tribes.   In
cases of adultery both of the guilty parties were punished.   Bodies
of the dead were flexed and buried under the house floors.   The hair
was reddened by means of the same root as that used by the eastern
Siouans.   Certain plants were substituted for salt.   The war titles
conferred consisted for the most part of certain distinct types formed
of two words (except where the diminutive suffix was employed), the
second being usually hadjo, fiksiko, imathla, tastanagi, yahola, or
miko.   Strict mourning was imposed upon widows and widowers,
particularly on the former.   The "spiral fire" was used during councils.   In stories of the incorporated Alabama tribe recurs the legend
of the mythic tailed men.   The calumet ceremony had reached them
but only at a very late period.

The Choctaw were another typical Muskhogean tribe but with a
somewhat distinct set of characters.   They had broader heads and
faces than the Creeks and were credited with a more pacific disposition.   Their month names were, however, similar in type to those
used by the Creeks.   They depended upon agriculture for their food
more than any of the other southern tribes, and raised enough corn
to employ part in trade with their neighbors.   They had the circular,
clayed-up winter house and an oblong, or rather oval, summer house
with two smoke holes.   The Choctaw men anciently allowed their hair
to grow long, and the bone-pickers or "Buzzard Men" kept their fingernails untrimmed.   They were addicted to the custom of frontal head
deformation.   Wooden stools seem to have been known to them as
well as to their neighbors.   The tribe was democratic and the chiefs'
powers limited.   There were no totemic clans but moieties were highly
developed.   The mortuary process was a long one, the body of the
deceased being first placed upon a scaffold, the flesh subsequently
removed from its bones and the latter placed in a hamper and kept
in the dwelling of the dead man's relatives until a considerable number of baskets of bones had been accumulated in this way, when all of

those in the neighborhood were carried to a mound on some appointed occasion and buried. The woman was severely punished in cases of adultery, and a class of prostitutes existed formed in part from these. The war titles were usually of a particular pattern ending in the word "killer." Strict observance of mourning ceremonies was imposed upon women.

The Chickasaw language varied little from that of the Choctaw, but their physical type is reported to have become different owing to the captives adopted into the tribe, and many of their customs approached those of the Creeks. Their winter houses, private and ceremonial, were circular like those of the Choctaw. They roached their head hair like the Creeks, wound copper wire in their ears in the same manner, and used nose ornaments. They were addicted to frontal head deformation like the Choctaw, and they made the same kind of wooden stools. Leadership seems to have depended partly on birth but also partly on accomplishment. Moieties were well developed and a caste system seems to have been in process of developing. Their fundamental units were local groups like those of the Choctaw but they had totemic clans, probably adopted from the Creeks. In cases of adultery they punished only the woman, but their burials were under the house floors, as in the case of the Creeks. Personal war names were after the Choctaw pattern. In other words, there is little one can detect that is not related to something among the Creeks or Choctaw.

The Cherokee differed somewhat in physical type and fundamentally in language from the tribes just considered. The private and town winter houses were circular, the summer houses quadrangular. They shaved their heads like the Creeks and many of them wound copper wire in their ears after the same fashion. They also wore nose ornaments. There were seven totemic clans and a seven system permeated their ceremonialism. They buried their dead in the earth, and sometimes under stone piles. Stories of tailed men were recorded among them by Mooney. Dreams were noted with especial care and lustrations were constantly employed.

The Yuchi are observed to differ somewhat in physical type from the Creeks among whom they live, but most of their customs are now the same. In early times they roached their heads like the Creeks and the Cherokee. Their social system was similar to that of the Creeks except that they had a dichotomous division into two societies, chiefs and warriors, membership in which was transmitted through the male line.

The Natchez were one of the tribes which practiced temporal head deformation. They depended upon their crops much more than most other tribes except the Choctaw. They took the names of their months largely from those of food plants or food animals, and constructed a peculiar square type of house. Part roached their hair and part let it grow long, at least on one side like the Virginia Algonquians. Women used paint as well as the men and in addition blackened their teeth. They manufactured wooden stools and carried about their chiefs and leading men on litters. Government was a theocracy embodying a caste system transmitted after a peculiar pattern. Commoners seem to have been buried in the earth somewhat after the Chickasaw and Creek manner, but bodies of chiefs and nobles were buried in or near the temple, the bones being later exhumed and placed in hampers in that building. The Natchez temple was quadrangular in pattern with a partition at the southern end containing the tribal palladium, and a perpetual fire in the larger room was tended by a special group of functionaries. On the roof of the temple were three wooden birds. The burial of a chief or noble was accompanied by a number of human sacrifices, some voluntarily undertaken. Spike-shaped ear ornaments were worn by the women. They obtained salt in trade from tribes farther west. Besides corn they reaped a certain grain which they sowed on sand banks in the Mississippi River. In historic times they had acquired the calumet ceremony.

The Chitimacha depended largely on a fish diet and also used the flesh of alligators. They roached the hair of their heads, and practiced frontal head deformation. They used nose ornaments and they had a class of undertakers like the "Buzzard Men" of the Choctaw who allowed their fingernails to grow long in the same manner. They made considerable use in their dietary of the seeds of water lilies. They were fine basket makers. There was a true caste system, and leadership was dependent on descent. They are said to have used poison to destroy their enemies. The division of labor between the sexes is said to have been particularly favorable to the women. Their burial customs were like those of the Choctaw. This tribe or one nearly related to it seems to have preserved the use of the atlatl into the historic period. They had acquired the calumet ceremony before the French arrived in their country.

The customs of the Tunica seem to have resembled those of other lower Mississippi tribes. According to one authority, work in the fields fell mainly upon males. Persimmons were especially abundant in their country, and were put up in large quantities by them. They had temples but not as elaborate ceremonies connected with them as the Natchez. So far as we know, they buried their dead in the earth and did not exhume the bodies for reburial. They were particularly addicted to tattooing and the women blackened their teeth. They were skilled in dressing skins and making pottery, and were much engaged in the boiling down and selling of salt.

All of the western and most of the eastern Caddo lived in grass houses like those of the Wichita, but a few of those on Red River had houses with wattle walls. They wore their hair in a manner reminding Europèans of the Turks, and occasionally reddened it with certain kinds of duck feathers. They indulged less in tattooing than the tribes along the Mississippi. They were noted for their pottery and engaged much in boiling down and selling salt. They also traded in the wood of the Osage orange, the favorite bowwood west of the Mississippi. They did excellent work in ornamenting shell gorgets. Visitors were greeted with wailing and bathed ceremonially. In 1541 some of them seem to have practiced frontal skull deformation, but this was given up before the French and Spaniards entered their country. At that early period they also used lances in battle. Warriors assembled in a special house to go through certain ceremonies before setting out to war, and when the day came this was burned down. The calumet ceremony had reached the eastern Caddo by 1687 but not the western bands. Chiefs had great power but the Hasinai Confederation, at least, seems to have been a theocracy. Chiefs were borne directly on the shoulders of their subjects instead of in litters. The eastern Caddo apparently had a well-developed totemic clan system similar to that of the Creeks, but in the west although a totemic system existed it was much modified and the relations between the clans suggest caste differences. Their terms of relationship class them as of the Mackenzie type in this particular. The corpses of leading men were treated with elaborate rites and sometimes they were cremated. They had circular temples with priestly guardians and ceremonies connected with them similar to those of the Natchez. The cult seems to have been solar, or rather celestial, and the stars constitute a conspicuous element in their myths.

A word or two might be said regarding the marginal Quapaw and Shawnee tribes. Quapaw houses were rectangular or rather oval, apparently a wigwam pattern with mats used as covering instead of bark. They were without temples. Their social organization included numerous gentes with patrilineal descent and probably moieties and other features like the Dhegiha Siouans.

Shawnee houses were similar to those of other central Algonquians. In their settlement among the Creeks on Tallapoosa River they had a town house said to be rectangular but perhaps oval. Their original social organization was gentile and they had many totemic divisions with male descent. Shamanism was highly developed, the reputation of this tribe in such matters being very widely spread.

Toward the west the cultural province of the Southeast ended sharply with the Caddo and Chitimacha tribes. The Tonkawa, Atakapa, Bidai, and Karankawa and the tribes beyond them extending into northeastern Mexico and on the coast to Panuco, lived mainly by food gathering and hunting, and had a culture so low that I have elsewhere spoken of the region as a kind of ethnological "sink." From the researches of Collins it seems that the higher culture once extended farther toward the west, at least along the coast, but the boundary in the early period of white contact is very abrupt and very marked. Toward the north the Southeastern cultural area also appears to have shrunken, the earthworks and other signs of cultural advance in the Ohio and upper Mississippi valleys testifying to a former marked extension in that direction. In historic times the boundary was nearly identical with the northern boundaries of the Chickasaw, Creeks, and Cherokee. Westward of the Mississippi one Siouan tribe, the Quapaw, had penetrated as far south as the mouth of Arkansas River and taken on some aspects of Southeastern culture. The southernmost of the central group of Algonquian tribes, the Shawnee, also penetrated the region, though most of their penetration took place after white contact. From this contact, however, they seem to have acquired certain Southeastern characteristics. Toward the northeast the boundary of this culture area is by no means as distinct. Representatives of three stocks, Iroquoian, Siouan, and Algonquian, lay close together here and in immediate contact with the more typical Southeastern tribes but they did not take on Southeastern culture in full measure. The Cherokee, although it is probable that they arrived in their historic territories at a very late time, acquired more of the culture they found there than the Algonquians or Siouans. In their case and in that of the Tuscarora, however, who lay farther east, we may suspect that they had been in contact with the southern tribes from a very early epoch, though their southern location was probably late. The Algonquian tribes of the North Carolina and Virginia coasts, while showing the effects of southern contact, retain more features derived from their connection with the Algonquian tribes to the north but along with them new characters which suggest the appearance of an entirely independent culture area, one showing some traits reminiscent of the north Pacific coast. The Siouan tribes to the west and south of them exhibit, in the few items of information we have, a lower type of culture than even the Algonquians, though the paucity of our information here forbids dogmatism. Such a conclusion is, at least, in line with Speck's findings among the Catawba and it is supported by the paucity of archeological remains that may be attributed to them. If these Siouans were to be treated as marginal peoples and the tidewater Algonquians as a nascent and distinct cultural province, we should be about as correct in our diagnosis as when we include them in the great province of the Southeast. There are also some grounds for excluding from the typical section of the Southeast the tribes of southern Florida, but the differences here seem attributable rather to a difference in the life province, that is, the environment, and the origin of these people is probably traceable to the north. Somewhat similar differences for an analogous reason seem to have existed among the Chitimacha and their allies about the mouth of the Mississippi.

Our Southeastern province proper, therefore, includes the tribes of Florida, the Creek Confederation with its absorbed tribes, the Chickasaw, the Choctaw, the Natchez, the Tunica, the Chitimacha, and the Caddo and the smaller tribes affiliated with them. There were also two Siouan tribes, the Biloxi and Ofo, but it is believed that they entered the country at a very late date. All that we know of them, however, aligns them with the other tribes of the Southeast.

Between all of these tribes or tribal groups last enumerated there were minor differences. As has just been intimated, the people of northern and southern Florida did not possess throughout the same cultural characters, and each was unlike, in many characters, the tribes farther north and west. The Creeks and Choctaw, although clearly related by language, showed striking contrasts in other particulars, the one being aggressive, having taken in many formerly independent groups, having totemic clans as well as rather weakly developed moieties, and complicated social and ceremonial systems, while the latter were relatively peaceful, given to agricultural pursuits, without totemic divisions but with strongly marked moieties, weak social and ceremonial structures, and giving way rapidly to the new ideas introduced by the whites. The Chickasaw had borrowed almost everything from the Creeks or Choctaw. The Natchez and their allies with their theocratic system, theocratic aristocracy, and complicated temple rituals were differentiated from both. The Caddo seem to have resembled the Natchez in their rituals but differed in their social organization. The Tunica must have represented something distinct from and probably more primitive than both. Finally, the Chitimacha combined a pure caste system with funeral rites reminiscent of the Choctaw. The points in which these several groups differed were mainly linguistic, or connected with the social organization or ceremonial life. Differences in material culture are often found associated with differences in environment, or with importations from some specific quarter. Had the information been preserved, we should doubtless be able to trace even matters concerning the material culture of the people to psychological differences or prejudices, and the weighting to be allowed to the several sets of factors must be determined by a study of some better preserved cultural province.

It is not my purpose to intrude upon the field that properly belongs to the archeologist, but I would merely add that the remains seem to point to the Mississippi Valley and the Gulf coast as the territories which gave birth to the culture which later overspread the Southeast.

CENTRAL INTRUSION

As I pointed out in the Forty-second Annual Report (Swanton, 1928 b), there are evidences that at least some Creeks were rather late intruders from the northwest and had wedged apart certain usages which had formerly extended over the area more evenly. Among these I mentioned frontal head deformation, which was found among the eastern Siouans and western tribes but not among the Creeks, and ossuaries and reburial customs similarly divided by the Creeks. It should be added, however, that we seem to have evidence of the use of ossuaries by some eastern Creeks in 1540. A third difference appears in the manner of dressing the hair by males. It was shaved at the sides of the head by the central tribes, but allowed to grow long by the Choctaw and some of the tribes of Virginia, Carolina, Florida, and the Mississippi Valley. We read of ceremonial bathing of strangers in North Carolina and again among the Caddo. On the other hand, the wearing of nasal ornaments, though limited or entirely wanting among the eastern tribes, was in vogue from the Creeks westward and had barely entered Virginia. The Creeks may have been responsible for the severe treatment of adulterers, which reached a maximum among them and appears to have died out east and west. This is rendered all the more likely by Hawkins' remark that the Abihka Creeks were responsible for the laws governing it. These same Indians may have been the late Muskogee arrivals which introduced the other changes just commentated upon, including also perhaps the use of rectangular hot houses. Nevertheless, we know that the Abihka Indians were in the Upper Creek country as early as the time of De Luna, 1560.

COMPARISON OF THE SOUTHEAST WITH CORRESPONDING AREAS IN OTHER PARTS OF THE WORLD

In the classification of J. Russell Smith, Professor of Economic Geography at Columbia University, the Gulf region finds its climatic counterparts in northeastern China, and small areas in southeastern South America, southeastern Africa, and southeastern Australia. He characterizes the type as follows:

Warm temperate, eastern margin or China type of climate is found in areas in the same latitude as those having the Mediterranean type, but on the eastern side of continents. These areas have abundant summer rains, thus providing vegetation with heat and moisture at the same time. Of the six areas which have this climate the Asiatic, peopled by the Chinese, the Japanese and the Koreans, supports greater populations than any other. Southeastern United States, with about 700,000 square miles of this type of climate, is one of the great potential food reserves of the world. The South American, the African and the Australian areas are much smaller, not so well supplied with rain and attached to large tropical land areas from which locusts, boll weevils and other pests come to ravish and destroy the crops. (*Article on* Climate *in* Encyclopaedia of the Social Sciences.)

A study of the areas in question, however, seems to indicate that insect pests were a minor element in keeping population down. In Australia the aborigines lived upon foods supplied spontaneously by nature and seem to have been better off than any others on the continent, except perhaps those immediately north and south. The corresponding part of Africa was populated chiefly by Zulus who cultivated the land but, under the influence of the cattle area to the north, considered their herds of more importance. The South American territory of this type, like the last two, was in immediate contact with the summer rain belt to the north, but here the highlands were held, not by pastoral people, but by hunters and fishers (the Gê tribes), who also occupied portions of the territory in question, and at a period not remote had extended over considerably more. Agriculture had worked in along the La Plata and the Brazilian coast and involved the cultivation of corn after the general American manner but in addition the raising of manioc and some other plants. The extension of agriculture in this region seems to have been stimulated in large measure by the northward and eastward spread of the Tupi from a home in or near Paraguay. The superiority of the farming tribes to the hunters is attested by all writers, and, as exhibited by a tribe like the Caingua, it seems to have brought about conditions like those introduced by the analogous corn culture in North America, greater ease in living conditions, a less migratory existence, and the stimulation of intertribal trade. However, we do not find the higher development of civilization shown by our mound-building tribes, and it may be suspected that this was due to a relatively recent introduction of agriculture. The densest population and apparently the highest culture was among the Tupi tribes of the Brazilian coast, especially about the present Rio de Janeiro. If insect pests from contiguous tropical land areas were a significant item in keeping population down, one wonders why the effects were not apparent in China. Perhaps it is to be partly explained by the chains of mountains along the southern boundary of the republic. Whatever drawbacks existed, they were more than counterbalanced by intensive cultivation, and the use of domestic animals and fertilizer. Our own Southeast was cut off from the corresponding monsoon region of America in a much more complete manner by the Gulf of Mexico and Strait of Florida in the east and desert country farther west. Nevertheless, there is evidence that cultural elements from the south invaded this region from time to time, as we have had occasion to see. The differences exhibited between the manner in which mankind had exploited these several regions seem to have been due rather to the human cultural contribution than natural advantages, although the relative size of the areas and environing conditions played a limited part. Thus the China area, in conjunction with the monsoon region south of it, supported the largest population on the globe both relatively and actually. The corresponding parts of Australia were the most populous portions of that continent from purely natural causes. The same was probably true in Africa but this was owing to the concentration of population in the monsoon region rather than in the relatively insignificant warm temperate area. In the New World the contrary condition is found. The heaviest population absolutely and relatively was on the Pacific side of the continent in both North and South America. But it is also true that the secondary concentrations of population were on the eastern coasts of America and that they also covered the same two climatic zones, reckoning the West Indies with the Gulf region and the Brazilian coast with the Uruguay-Rio Grande do Sul territory. Although it is without particular geographical significance, it is interesting to note that in every continent of both the Old and the New World the largest population is on the main mountain axis or between that and the nearest ocean: on the Pacific coast of Australia, the coasts of the Pacific and Indian Oceans in Asia, on the coast of the Indian Ocean and the axis itself in Africa, and on the axis and the Pacific coast in America.

Similarity in climatic conditions has not, therefore, brought about similarity in culture. This being the case, it might seem at first sight as if the differences might be due to inequality in racial endowment on the part of the inhabitants of the several regions, and the idea derives some color from the fact that the area showing the highest culture is occupied by representatives of the Mongolian race, and the area showing the lowest by people generally placed low in the mental scale. The status of the inhabitants of the other three does not, however, bear this out, because the Zulus of southeast Africa are superior if anything to the Indians of southern Brazil, Uruguay, and Paraguay, and if we place our Gulf Indians above them, on the ground of their former culture as exemplified in the mounds, we shall be forced into the illogical position of placing the Bantu in between two groups of American Indians.

We shall arrive at a much more satisfactory solution of the cultural question if we take into consideration historical and broader environmental factors. Roughly, for our present purposes, we may trace the higher cultures of the world to two central regions, one in the Old World extending from Egypt to northwestern China, taking in the skirts of the Plateau of Iran and northwestern India; the other a long, narrow territory in the New World from southern Mexico to

Bolivia. Again, all evidence indicates that man came into existence in the Old World and probably not far from the cultural center above described, while the New World is a relatively late colony. Culture in the Old World in the section indicated thus had a longer period in which to mature and time to reach a higher level. It is not surprising to find that it did so. It is also not surprising to find that the higher cultures tend to appear near these two centers if environmental conditions permit. In the present instance eastern Asia is close to the center of Old World culture, closer than any other of the climatic regions we have been comparing and it is not surprising, therefore, that its culture is the highest of all. Southeast Africa is much farther away but was in time penetrated by the developed agricultural and pastoral life originating probably in Asia. Southeast Australia, on the other hand, is far removed from the higher Old World cultures and, what is even more important, is separated from them by stretches of sea and the more important obstruction of desert land in the northwestern part of the continent. In America, the Gulf region and southeastern South America are about equally removed from the New World apical center, but the jungles of the southern continent present more of an obstacle to the distribution of the attainments of the central area than did the few hundred miles of clear, if semi-arid, land at the northwestern corner of the Gulf of Mexico. Moreover, there were relatively few natural interferences to coastal trade in the latter while South American civilization was practically prohibited from reaching any part of the eastern shores of that continent by sea. If corn originated in southern Mexico as many believe, the fact furnishes an additional reason for the greater maturity of Gulf culture. Although Australia is nearer the higher center of culture in the Old World and in so far has had superior advantages to the New World areas, these were more than counterbalanced by the inaccessability of the continent and the inhospitable nature of the territory over which that culture would have had to spread. On comparing the two New World areas with the one in south Africa, we find no such striking difference in level. Seemingly, the fact that Bantus were able to tap a more highly developed cultural center which communicated to them a knowledge of both farming and cattle raising, was counterbalanced somewhat by their greater distance from the center. This was particularly true as compared with the opportunities of our Gulf region, which upon the whole should, I believe, be rated somewhat higher. In giving this relative allocation, no judgment is involved of the capacities of the people themselves. The analysis of the situation we have given rather tends to discount any such conclusions regarding them. Had the Australians instead of the Chinese, been so placed as to be able to avail themselves of accomplishments of Asiatic culture, there is no certainty that they would not have gone as far, and had the Chinese been subjected to the environmental handicaps of the Australians, they might not have advanced beyond the Australian level.

All of the areas compared have this in common, that they lie outside of the greater central sources of civilization, which it may be remarked parenthetically are not in the same climatic zones in the Old and New Worlds. The area with which we are chiefly concerned was dependent, as we have seen, on the New World civilizational center to the south of it. Although the specific traits which it exhibits seem to be peculiar to it, the great underlying cultural factors belong clearly, as Kroeber maintains, to the civilizations of Mexico, Central America, and Peru. Southeastern culture is an outlier of the culture there. It is a suburb of the American capital region. Yet the peoples within it present enough variety in language, culture, and even physical type, and their movements, demonstrated and inferred, enough of a sample of the workings of the mass mind to furnish the student a fair picture of the greatnesses and vagaries of the great humanity of which they and we form a part.

Here we lay aside the pen—or rather the typewriter. Though students of culture still have work to do here, the future study of the Southeastern Indians rests mainly with the archeologists.

SOURCE MATERIALS

Our knowledge of the history and ethnology of these tribes varies greatly. Of some we know little more than the names; of others we have a few notes by one or two early explorers and missionaries; of still others we have at least one fairly good description; and of a very few, such as the Creeks, Choctaw, Chickasaw, Cherokee, and Natchez, we have several fairly detailed sources of information, but it must be said emphatically that our records are imperfect in some particulars in every case. I will review rapidly our principal sources of information regarding the more important of these peoples.

Material on the tribes of the Creek Confederation taken as a whole is fairly extensive, but we have few details regarding the differences between the constituent members of it which must once have been marked. It included all of those given under the heads Muskogee, Hitchiti group, and Alabama group, and at various times parts of the Guale Indians and Yamasee, Cusabo, Natchez, Tawasa, Yuchi, and Shawnee, and all of the Osochi, which were probably of Timucuan origin. The adherence of the Natchez, Yuchi, and Shawnee was comparatively recent. They were once large, independent tribes— the Shawnee always remaining such—and we have considerable bodies of material regarding them. The Seminole, including the Mikasuki, on the other hand, represent a late separatist movement, and there is available a somewhat independent set of authorities dealing with them.

Our principal sources of information for the rest of the Creek Confederacy are the works of William Bartram, Benjamin Hawkins, Le Clerc Milfort, Bernard Romans, Caleb Swan, George Stiggins, James Adair, Ethan Allen Hitchcock, Albert S. Gatschet, Frank G. Speck, and my own notes.

For the Seminole and Mikasuki we rely upon James Adair, William Bartram, Benjamin Hawkins, Clay MacCauley, Alanson Skinner, A. S. Gatschet, Alexander Spoehr, and some recent work by Minnie Moore Wilson and Frances Densmore, to which I have added a few notes drawn from the western Seminole.

Practically everything regarding the Apalachee must be taken from the Spanish records beginning with those of the Narvaez and De Soto expeditions, and but little remains outside of their history and one short text in their language.

A small body of material which applies to the Alabama in distinction from the rest of the Creeks may be derived from Bossu, Hawkins, Schoolcraft, Gatschet, and some of my own notes.

Adair and Stiggins give us a little information regarding the peculiarities of the Koasati, and there are a few notes from Hawkins, Gatschet, and myself.

The Tuskegee have been made the subject of a special report by Frank G. Speck.

In a recent publication (Swanton, 1931) I have assembled all of the more readily available source material on the Choctaw except that bearing on their material culture. Among the original sources must be mentioned an anonymous French document preserved in the Newberry Library, Chicago, of the Choctaw section of which I published a translation some years back, and I have reproduced the original in the appendix to the Bureau of American Ethnology Bulletin just cited (Swanton, 1931). To these must be added Adair, M. Bossu, George Catlin, J. F. H. Claiborne, H. B. Cushman, Le Clerc Milfort, Bernard Romans, A. S. Gatschet, Henry S. Halbert, John Edwards, D. I. Bushnell, Jr., and the reports of some of the early French explorers, notably De Lusser and Régis du Roullet.

Chickasaw material is not so extensive, but here we have one great advantage in that it was the tribe which James Adair knew best, and his material regarding the Chickasaw is basal to everything in the Southeast inside and outside of that tribe. To this may be added many names of the Choctaw authorities already mentioned, such as the anonymous French memoir, Claiborne, Cushman, and particularly Romans, a paper printed in Schoolcraft's Indian Tribes, and recent notes by Speck.

We learn most about the Houma from the narratives of Iberville and Gravier; most about the Pascagoula, Mobile, and Tohome from the Pénicaut narrative in the Margry documents; most of the Acolapissa from Pénicaut and Charlevoix; and most of the Bayogoula and Mugulasha from the journals of Iberville's two ships. Our knowledge of the Napochi is almost confined to material drawn from the narratives of the De Luna expedition edited by Priestly and the Historia of Padilla. To our material on the Acolapissa must be added the De Batz sketches of their temple made available by Mr. Bushnell.

Our very meager knowledge of the Cusabo is furnished mainly by the French Huguenots, the narratives of Hilton and Sandford, Alexander Hewat's Historical Account of the Rise and Progress of the Colonies of South Carolina and Georgia, and materials from manuscript sources, now made partially available by Milling (1940) in Red Carolinians. We must also turn to the same French narratives for the greater part of our information regarding the Timucua except on the items of language and social organization, which the Franciscan missionary Pareja furnishes us. To this we must add the information contained in a report by Bishop Calderón of Cuba, under whose spiritual charge were the Florida settlements, and some recently published Franciscan documents. Fontaneda's Memoir is our chief source for the Calusa Indians of southwest Florida and Jonathan Dickenson for those of the east coast, though they are a century and a half apart.

Turning now to the Natchez, we find that the two most extensive treatments were by Le Page du Pratz and Dumont de Montigny, but there are several other fairly considerable bodies of information, including an anonymous French narrative published at Luxemburg in 1752, letters by the missionaries Gravier, Le Petit, and Charlevoix, and a description by Pénicaut. The most that we know of the customs and usages of the Taensa is in the documents detailing La Salle's descent of the Mississippi to the Gulf in 1682, Iberville's visit in 1700, and those of the missionaries La Source, De Montigny, and Le Petit.

Early data regarding Tunican peoples is scanty. Most that we have on the Tunica proper comes from the missionaries La Source and Gravier and the explorer De la Harpe. To this Dr. Gatschet and I have added some data on the language and the myths and a small body of ethnological information, and a very complete grammar of the language by Dr. Mary R. Haas has now appeared. Regarding the Koroa, Yazoo, and Tiou we have nothing except some incidental notes in the journals of La Salle's companions and two or three items in the Mémoires of Dumont de Montigny, Le Page du Pratz, and Diron d'Artaguette.

A few items regarding the customs and beliefs of the Chitimacha Indians were recorded by, or for, Martin Duralde early in the nineteenth century and sent to William Dunbar, by whom they were transmitted to the American Philosophical Society in Philadelphia. A considerable body of material has since been collected by Dr. A. S. Gatschet, some by myself, and much fuller material, as yet unpublished, by Dr. Morris Swadesh. For the Atakapa we are dependent on the Duralde letter and a few notes in the manuscripts of early French and American travelers and explorers. There are some notes on the western Atakapa in the Spanish archives, but they are decidedly scanty. For the language, see Gatschet and Swanton (1932).

Spaniards and English made contacts with several bands of Yuchi at different periods and the accounts supplied by them are most interesting, but the amount of ethnologic material is very small. Noteworthy among these are Bartram's and Hawkins' descriptions of the Yuchi towns among the Lower Creeks. Gatschet also collected some materials regarding this peculiar tribe, but the outstanding work on Yuchi ethnology has been done in modern times by Speck. An excellent body of texts in the Yuchi language has been collected and published by Günter Wagner, and I have done considerable in Bureau of American Ethnology Bulletin 73 (Swanton, 1922) to unravel the somewhat involved early history of these people.

The Catawba Indians were once so prominent in colonial history that it is surprising that no definite attempt was ever made in the earlier period to prepare a description of them, yet it happens that the first notes on any tribe in the Southeast which may pretend to the term extensive come from a related people. This is the material obtained by Peter Martyr d'Anghierra from the Indian Francisco of Chicora, probably a member of the Shakori tribe. The next important narrative in time is that of John Lawson, who traversed the country of the Siouan Indians of the two Carolinas and the Tuscarora in 1700–01, and third we may place the narrative of John Lederer, which antedates Lawson's material by about 30 years. Catesby copies considerably from Lawson but adds items from his own experience. Brickell copies to the extent of plagiarism. We are also obliged to rely considerably on Lawson and Lederer for our knowledge of the Tutelo and other Virginia Siouans. More recently, notes have been taken down from the survivors of these tribes by Hale, Sapir, Frachtenberg, and Speck. The greater part of the manuscript and early printed material regarding them was published by Mooney in The Siouan Tribes of the East, a work which is still an authority on the subject. Recent Bureau of American Ethnology Bulletins by Bushnell provide an identification of the sites of the Manahoac and Monacan towns and supply some notes regarding them. Mooney's work has been supplemented most effectively now by the Red Carolinians of Dr. Milling. Nearly all of the later original work among both the Catawba and Tutelo has been done by Speck.

Dumont de Montigny gives us an interesting description of the manner in which the Biloxi and Pascagoula disposed of their dead, and in the closing decade of the last century J. O. Dorsey collected some details regarding the social organization of the former. Little remains of the Ofo except their remarakable history and a brief vocabularly (Dorsey and Swanton, 1912).

There is no extended treatment of the marginal tribe of Quapaw, and we must rely upon the writings of early travelers such as Marquette, the chroniclers of La Salle, Le Sueur, La Harpe, on Father Poisson the Jesuit, some notes by Dumont de Montigny, and later material from Thomas Nuttall. J. O. Dorsey published some notes on their social organization.

For the Cherokee the standard work is Mooney's Myths of the Cherokee, which, including its notes, covers a very much wider field than the title indicates. Mooney also published a smaller report on The Sacred Formulas of the Cherokees, and collected a much greater body of formulas, some of which have been published under the editorship of Dr. Frans Olbrechts (Mooney and Olbrechts, 1932), who added much new material. In the Newberry Library, Chicago, is a considerable body of unpublished notes by John Howard Payne. Besides Mooney, the later history of the tribe has been treated at length by Dr. Grant Foreman and Dr. Chapman J. Milling. Considering the importance of the tribe, ethnological information regarding it is decidedly meager. The best of the published sources is William Bartram, to whose name we must add those of Timberlake, Adair, Haywood, and Hicks. Studies of Cherokee social organization have been made recently by Eggan, Gilbert, and Bloom, and an extensive paper by Gilbert was published by the Bureau of American Ethnology in 1943. (See Gilbert, 1943.)

The writings of Lawson and De Graffenried give our fullest notes regarding the Tuscarora and their allies, and in modern times they have been especially studied by J. N. B. Hewitt, himself of Tuscarora descent.

When we turn to the North Carolina Algonquians, our main reliance is the writings of the Raleigh colonists, particularly Thomas Hariot's First Plantation of Virginia, illustrated with John White's drawings, while for the Powhatan Indians we must rely on the works of John Smith, and William Strachey's Historie of Travaile into Virginia Britannia, to which Robert Beverley's History of Virginia adds important items, though it is in part compiled from the works of Smith and Hariot. Although mainly devoted to Maryland, Raphael Semmes' Captains and Marines of Early Maryland throws much light on Indian life south of the Potomac. Along with Smith's narrative must be placed the relations of Newport and Spelman, and work in this field is now being pursued energetically by Dr. Maurice A. Mook.

There is as yet no single good work on the Shawnee. Henry Harvey's History of the Shawnee Indians, published in 1855, is useful; Mooney has many notes on them in his various writings; and The Wilderness Trail, by Charles A. Hanna, is important for the movements of the Shawnee bands. In Bureau of American Ethnology Bulletin 73 I have brought together considerable material bearing on the movements of those Shawnee who went south (Swanton, 1922). More recently Drs. Charles F. and Erminie W. Voegelin have added greatly to our knowledge of the Shawnee language and along with it their history and institutions. The appearance of Shawnese Traditions, by C. C. Trowbridge, edited by Vernon Kinietz and Erminie W. Voegelin, has been of special service to students of this ubiquitous people. In the present paper our interest in this tribe and the Quapaw is purely marginal.

The most important sources of information regarding the Caddo are the narrative of Henri Joutel, La Salle's companion during the Texas misadventure, and the reports of the Spanish Franciscan missionaries Casañas de Jesus Maria, Francisco Hidalgo, and Isidro Felis de Espinosa. The Historia, and particularly the Memorias, of Juan A. de Morfi are also important, but he derives his material mainly from Hidalgo and Espinosa. Items regarding this tribe were collected by Prof. H. E. Bolton and incorporated into articles contributed to the Handbook of American Indians, especially part 2, and printed in his own works. Reference may also be made to the concluding chapters of M. R. Harrington's monograph entitled "Certain Caddo Sites in Arkansas," and to a sketch of these people by Mrs. Lee C. Harby in the Annual Report of the American Historical Association for the year 1894, pages 63–92. A collection of Caddo Myths was made by Dr. G. A. Dorsey some years ago and printed by the Carnegie Institution, and in 1941 Dr. Parsons added some "Notes on the Caddo." Most of the essential parts of this material I brought together in Bulletin 132 of the Bureau of American Ethnology (Swanton, 1942).

The later history of the Five Civilized Tribes has been completely covered by Foreman and Debo. For my few notes on the physical characteristics of the Indians of this section, I have relied mainly upon the writings of Boas, Hrdlička, Collins, and Krogman.

BIBLIOGRAPHY

ADAIR, JAMES
1775. The history of the American Indians. London. (New ed., edited by Samuel Cole Williams under the auspices of the Nat. Soc. Colonial Dames Amer., in Tenn. The Watauga Press, Johnson City, Tenn., 1930.)

ALVORD, CLARENCE W., and BIDGOOD, LEE
1912. First explorations of the Trans-Allegheny Region by the Virginians, 1650–1674. Cleveland.

AMERICAN STATE PAPERS
> 1832, 1834. Documents, legislative and executive, of the Congress of the United States. Class II, Indian Affairs, vols. 1–2.
> 1832–1861. Documents of the Congress of the United States in relation to the Public Lands. Class VIII, Public Lands, vols. 1–8.

ANGHIERRA, PETER MARTYR DE
> 1912. De orbe novo. Trans. by F. A. MacNutt. 2 vols. New York.

ANONYMOUS
> 1752. Mémoire sur La Louisiane ou Le Mississippi. Luxembourg.

ARBER, EDWARD, ED. *See* SMITH, JOHN, 1884.

ARCHER, GABRIEL
> 1884. A relayton of the discovery, &c. 21 May–22 June 1607. *In* Smith, John, Works, Arber ed., pp. xl–lv. Also attributed to Christopher Newport.

ARROWPOINTS
> 1925–1936. Mimeographed monthly of the Ala. Anthrop. Soc. Montgomery, Ala.

ARTHUR, GABRIEL, JOURNEYS OF. *See* ALVORD, CLARENCE W., and BIDGOOD, LEE, 1912, pp. 207–226.

BANDELIER, AD. F. *See* NUÑEZ CABEZA DE VACA, ALVAR.

BARCIA CARBALLIDO Y ZUÑIGA, ANDRÉS G.
> 1723. Ensayo cronológico para la historia general de la Florida, 1512–1722, por Gabriel de Cardenas Z. Cano (pseud.). Madrid.

BARNWELL, COL. JOHN
> 1908. The Tuscarora expedition. Letters of Colonel John Barnwell. South Carolina Hist. and Geneal. Mag., vol. 9, No. 1, pp. 28–58.

BARTRAM, WILLIAM
> 1792. Travels through North and South Carolina, Georgia, East and West Florida, the Cherokee country, the extensive territories of the Muscogulges or Creek Confederacy, and the country of the Chactaws. London. (Note: Other editions of op. cit. are Philadelphia, 1791, and New York, 1940.)
> 1909. Observations on the Creek and Cherokee Indians. 1879. With prefatory and supplementary notes by E. G. Squier. Report. Complete. Trans. Amer. Ethnol. Soc., vol. 3, pt. 1, pp. 1–81. (Facsimile reprint of 1853 ed.)
> 1943. Travels in Georgia and Florida, 1773–74. A report to Dr. John Fothergill. Annotated by Francis Harper. Trans. Amer. Phil. Soc., n. s., vol. 33, pt. 2.

BASSETT, JOHN SPENCER
> 1901. The writings of "Colonel William Byrd of Westover in Virginia Esqr." New York.

BATTS, THOMAS, JOURNAL OF. *See* ALVORD, CLARENCE W., and BIDGOOD, LEE; and BUSHNELL, DAVID I., JR., 1907 a.

BEALS, RALPH L.
> 1932. The comparative ethnology of northern Mexico before 1750. Ibero-Americana: 2. Univ. Calif.

BEAURAIN, LE SIEUR
> 1831. Journal historique de l'établissement des Français a La Louisiane. Nouvelle-Orléans and Paris. (Printed as a production of Bernard de la Harpe.)

BECKNER, LUCIEN
> 1932. Eskippakithiki: the last Indian town in Kentucky. Filson Club. Hist. Quart., vol. 6, No. 4, pp. 355–382.

BELKNAP, JEREMY, and MORSE, JEDIDIAH
    1798. The report of a committee of the board of correspondents of the Scots
        Society for Propogating Christian Knowledge, who visited the Oneida
        and Mohekunuk Indians in 1796. Coll. Mass. Hist. Soc., ser. 1, vol. 5,
        pp. 29–30.
BÉRENGER, JEAN
    Ms. Mémoire on Louisiana. Newberry Library, Chicago.
BEVERLEY, ROBERT
    1705. The history and present state of Virginia, in four parts . . . By a
        native and inhabitant of the place. London.
BIDGOOD, LEE. See ALVORD, CLARENCE W., and BIDGOOD, LEE.
BIEDMA, LUIS HERNANDEZ DE. See BOURNE, EDWARD GAYLORD, EDITOR.
BIENVILLE, JEAN BAPTISTE LE MOYNE, SIEUR DE
    Ms. Memoir. Copy obtained from the Newberry Library, Chicago. Printed
        in Miss. Provincial Archives, ed. Rowland, Dunbar, and Sanders,
        Albert Godfrey, vol. 3, Jackson, Miss., 1932. In Découvertes et
        établissements, du Français dans l'Ouest et dans le Sud de l'Amérique
        septentrionale, ed. Margry, Pierre, vol. 4, pp. 432–444. Paris, 1880.
BLANDE, EDWARD, EXPLORATIONS OF. See ALVORD, CLARENCE W., and BIDGOOD, LEE,
    pp. 109–130.
BLOOM, LEONARD
    1939. The Cherokee clan: a study in acculturation. Amer. Anthrop., n. s.,
        vol. 41, No. 2, pp. 266–268.
BLUDWORTH, G. T.
    1937. How the Alabamas came southward. Publ. Tex. Folk-Lore Soc., No. 13,
        pp. 298–299.
BOAS, FRANZ
    1895. Zur Anthropologie der Nord-Amerikanischen Indianer. Gesellschaft
        für Anthropologie, Ethnol. u. Urgeschichte, vol. 27, pp. 366–411. Berlin.
BOLTON, HERBERT EUGENE
    1908. The native tribes about the East Texas missions. Quart. Tex. State
        Hist. Assoc., vol. 11, No. 4, pp. 249–276.
    1914. Athanase de Mézières and the Louisiana-Texas frontier, 1768–1780.
        Documents published for the first time from the original Spanish and
        French manuscripts, chiefly in the archives of Mexico and Spain;
        translated into English; edited and annotated, by Herbert Eugene
        Bolton. 2 vols. Cleveland.
    1915. Texas in the middle eighteenth century. Studies in Spanish colonial
        history and administration. Univ. Calif. Publ. Hist., vol. 3.
    1925. Arredondo's historical proof of Spain's title to Georgia. A contribu-
        tion to the history of one of the Spanish borderlands. Edited by
        Herbert E. Bolton. Univ. Calif. Press, Berkeley; and Cambridge
        Univ. Press, London.
BOSSU, JEAN BERNARD
    1768. Nouveaux voyages aux Indes Occidentales . . . 2 vols. Paris.
BOURNE, EDWARD GAYLORD, EDITOR
    1904. Narratives of the career of Hernando De Soto. 2 vols. Trail Makers
        (series). New York. (Note: Reprints of op. cit. are in Great
        American explorers, David Nutt, London, 1905; and American ex-
        plorers, Allerton Book Co., New York, 1922.)

BOYD, MARK F.
 1934. A topographical memoir on east and west Florida with itineraries of
   General Jackson's army, 1818. By Capt. Hugh Young, Corps of Topographical Engineers, U. S. A. With an introduction and annotations
   by Mark F. Boyd and Gerald M. Ponton. Florida Hist. Soc. Quart.,
   vol. 13, No. 1, pp. 16–50, and No. 2, pp. 82–104.
 1937. Marcos Delgado from Apalache to the Upper Creek country in 1686.
   Fla. Hist. Soc. Quart., vol. 16, No. 1, pp. 1–32.
BOYD, WILLIAM K.
 1929. William Byrd's histories of the dividing line between Virginia and
   North Carolina. With introduction and notes by William K. Boyd.
   Raleigh, N. C.
BRANNON, PETER A.
 1909. Aboriginal remains in the middle Chattahoochee Valley of Alabama
   and Georgia. Amer. Anthrop., n. s., vol. 11, pp. 186–198.
 1920. Handbook of the Alabama Anthropological Society, 1920. Publ. Ala.
   State Dept. Archives and History. Historical and Patriotic Ser.
   Montgomery, Ala.
 1935. The Southern Indian trade. Montgomery, Ala. *See also* Arrowpoints.
BRICKELL, JOHN
 1737. The natural history of North-Carolina. With an account of the trade,
   manners, and customs of the Christian and Indian inhabitants.
   Dublin. (An almost complete replica of Lawson.)
BRINTON, DANIEL G.
 1859. Notes on the Floridian peninsula, its literary history, Indian tribes
   and antiquities. Philadelphia.
BURRAGE, HENRY S., EDITOR
 1906. Early English and French voyages, 1534–1608. *In* Original narratives
   of early American history. New York.
BUSHNELL, DAVID I., JR.
 1906. The Sloane collection in the British Museum. Amer. Anthrop., n. s.,
   vol. 8, pp. 671–685.
 1907. Virginia—from early records. Amer. Anthrop., n. s., vol. 9, pp. 31–44.
 1907 a. Discoveries beyond the Appalachian mountains in September, 1671.
   Amer. Anthrop., n. s., vol. 9, pp. 45–56.
 1907 b. The Virginia Indians. Amer. Anthrop., n. s., vol. 9, p. 448.
 1908. The account of Lamhatty. Amer. Anthrop., n. s., vol. 10, pp. 568–574.
 1909. Various uses of buffalo hair by the North American Indians. Amer.
   Anthrop., n. s., vol. 11, pp. 401–425.
 1909 a. The Choctaw of Bayou Lacomb, St. Tammany Parish, Louisiana.
   Bur. Amer. Ethnol. Bull. 48.
 1910. Myths of the Louisiana Choctaw. Amer. Anthrop., n. s., vol. 12, pp.
   526–535.
 1913. Notes on the Indians of Maryland, 1705–1706. Amer. Anthrop., n. s.,
   vol. 15, pp. 535–536.
 1919. Native villages and village sites east of the Mississippi. Bur. Amer.
   Ethnol. Bull. 69.
 1920. Native cemeteries and forms of burial east of the Mississippi. Bur.
   Amer. Ethnol. Bull. 71.
 1922. Some new ethnologic data from Louisiana. Journ. Washington Acad.
   Sci., vol. 12, No. 13, pp. 303–307.
 1927. Drawings of A. DeBatz in Louisiana, 1732-1735. Smithsonian Misc.
   Coll., vol. 80, No. 5.

BUSHNELL, DAVID I., JR.—Continued.
1930. The five Monacan towns in Virginia, 1607. Smithsonian Misc. Coll., vol. 82, No. 12.
1934. Tribal migrations east of the Mississippi. Smithsonian Misc. Coll., vol. 89, No. 12.
1935. The Manahoac tribes in Virginia, 1608. Smithsonian Misc. Coll., vol. 94, No. 8.
BYINGTON, CYRUS
1915. A dictionary of the Choctaw language. Edited by H. S. Halbert and J. R. Swanton. Bur. Amer. Ethnol. Bull. 46.
BYRD, WILLIAM
1866. History of the dividing line and other tracts. 2 vols. Richmond, Va.
1917. Letter by William Byrd, May 26, 1686, to John Clinton. Va. Mag. Hist. and Biogr., vol. 25, pp. 129–130. See also Bassett, John Spencer; and Boyd, William K.
CABEZA DE VACA, ALVAR NUÑEZ. See NUÑEZ CABEZA DE VACA, ALVAR.
CALDERÓN, GABRIEL DIAZ VARA. See WENHOLD, LUCY L.
CALHOUN, ROBERT DABNEY
1934. The Taënsa Indians: the French explorers and Catholic missionaries in the Taënsas country. Louisiana Hist. Quart., vol. 17, pp. 411–435, 642–679.
CANDLER, ALLEN D. See GEORGIA, COLONIAL RECORDS OF THE STATE OF.
CARRIER, LYMAN
1923. The beginnings of agriculture in America. New York.
CARROLL, B. R.
1836. Historical collections of South Carolina; embracing many rare and valuable pamphlets, and other documents, relating to the history of that state, from its first discovery to its independence, in the year 1776. 2 vols. New York.
CASAÑAS DE JESUS MARIA, FRAY FRANCISCO
1927. Descriptions of the Tejas or Asinai Indians, 1691–1722. Translated from the Spanish by Mattie Austin Hatcher. I and II. Fray Francisco Casañas de Jesus Maria to the Viceroy of Mexico, Aug. 15, 1691. Southwestern Hist. Quart., vol. 30, pp. 206–218, 283–304. Spanish text in Bur. Amer. Ethnol. Bull. 132, pp. 241–263. See Swanton, 1942.
CASIS, LILIA M., TRANSLATOR
1899. Carta de Don Damian Manzanet á Don Carlos de Siguenza sobre el Descubrimiento de la Bahía del Espíritu Santo. Quart. Tex. State Hist. Assoc., vol. 2, No. 4, pp. 253–312.
CASTAÑEDA, CARLOS E. See MORFI, FRAY JUAN AGUSTIN DE, 1935; and SÁNCHEZ, JOSÉ MARÍA.
CATESBY, MARK
1731–1743. The natural history of Carolina, Florida, and Bahama Islands. 2 vols. London.
CATLIN, GEORGE
1844. Letters and notes on the manners, customs, and condition of the North American Indians. 2 vols. New York and London.
1913. Illustrations of the manners and customs of the North American Indians. 2 vols. Philadelphia.
CHABOT, FREDERICK M. See MORFI, FRAY JUAN AGUSTIN DE, 1932.
CHARD, THORNTON
1940. Did the first Spanish horses landed in Florida and Carolina leave progeny? Amer. Anthrop., n. s., vol. 42, No. 1, pp. 90–106.

CHARLEVOIX, PIERRE F. X. DE
  1761. Journal of a voyage to North America. 2 vols. London. (*Also in* French's Historical collections of Louisiana, 1851.)
  1866–1872. History and general description of New France. Translated by John G. Shea. Vols. 1–6. New York. (First ed. 3 vols., Paris 1744.)
CLAIBORNE, J. F. H.
  1880. Mississippi as a province, territory, and State. Vol. 1 (only volume printed). Jackson, Miss.
COLECCIÓN DE DOCUMENTOS INÉDITOS, relativos al descubrimiento, conquista y organización de las antiguas posesiones españolas de América y Oceanía. 42 vols.
  1864–1884. Madrid.
COLECCÍON DE DOCUMENTOS INÉDITOS, relativos al descubrimiento, conquista y organización de las antiguas posesiones españolas de ultramar. Vols. 1–13.
  1885–1900. Madrid.
COLLINS, HENRY B., JR.
  1941. Relationships of an early Indian cranial series from Louisiana. Journ. Washington Acad. Sci., vol. 31, No. 4, pp. 145–155.
CORRESPONDENCE ON THE SUBJECT OF THE EMIGRATION OF INDIANS.
  1834–1835. Sen. Doc. 512, 23d Congr., 1st sess. Vols. 1–5.
COX, ISAAC JOSLIN, EDITOR
  1905. The journeys of René Robert Cavelier, Sieur de La Salle. 2 vols. Trail Makers (series). New York.
COXE, DANIEL
  1928. The southern frontier, 1670–1732. Duke Univ. Press, Durham, N. C. call'd Florida, and by the French La Louisiane ... *In* Historical collections of Louisiana ... compiled with historical and biographical notes, and an introduction, by B. F. French ... Pt. 2, 2nd ed., pp. 221–276. Philadelphia. (1st ed. London, 1741.)
CRANE, VERNER W.
  1928. The southern frontier, 1670–1732. Duke Univ. Press, Durham, N. C.
CULIN, STEWART
  1907. Games of the North American Indians. 24th Ann. Rep. Bur. Amer. Ethnol., 1902–1903.
CUMMING, WILLIAM PATTERSON
  1938. Geographical misconceptions of the Southeast in the cartography of the seventeenth and eighteenth centuries. Journ. Southern Hist., vol. 4, No. 4, pp. 476–493.
  1939. The earliest permanent settlement in Carolina: Nathaniel Batts and the Comberford map. Amer. Hist. Review, vol. 45, No. 1.
CUSHING, FRANK HAMILTON
  1896. Exploration of ancient Key dwellers' remains on the Gulf coast of Florida. Proc. Amer. Philos. Soc., vol. 35, pp. 329–432.
CUSHMAN, H. B.
  1899. History of the Choctaw, Chickasaw, and Natchez Indians. Greenville, Texas.
CUSTIS, PETER. *See* FREEMAN, THOMAS, and CUSTIS, PETER.
DAVILA PADILLA, FRAY AUGUSTIN
  1625. Historia de la fundacion y discurso de la provincia de Santiago de Mexico de la Orden de Predicadores por los vidas de sus varones insignes y casos notables de Nueva España. Brussels.

DAVIS, T. FREDERICK
    1935. History of Juan Ponce de Leon's voyages to Florida. Fla. Hist. Soc. Quart., vol. 14, No. 1.
DE BATZ, A. *See* BUSHNELL, DAVID I., JR., 1927.
DEBO, ANGIE
    1932. Southern refugees of the Cherokee Nation. *In* Southwestern Hist. Quart., vol. 35, No. 4, pp. 255–266.
    1934. The rise and fall of the Choctaw Republic. Norman, Okla.
    1940. And still the waters run. Princeton.
    1941. The road to disappearance. Norman, Okla.
DE GRAFFENRIED, BARON
    1886. Narrative. Translated by M. du Four from the original MS. in the public library at Yverdon, Switzerland. Colonial Records of North Carolina, vol. 1, 1662 to 1712, pp. 905–986.
DE KERLÉREC, CHEVALIER
    1907. Rapport du Chevalier de Kerlérec, Gouverneur de la Louisiane française sur les peuplades des vallées du Mississippi et du Missouri (1758). C. R. Congr. Int. Amér., 15th sess., vol. 1, pp. 61–86. Québec.
DELANGLEZ, JEAN
    1938. The journal of Jean Cavelier, the account of a survivor of La Salle's Texas expedition, 1684–1688. Translated and annotated by Jean Delanglez. Inst. Jesuit Hist. Publ. Chicago.
DE LA VENTE
    1907. Letter by De la Vente quoted by M. l'abbé Amédée Gosselin. C. R. Congr. Int. Amér., 15th sess., vol. 1, p. 37. Québec.
DELGADO, MARCOS. EXPEDITION. *See* BOYD, MARK F.
DE LUNA, TRISTAN DE. *See* PRIESTLY, HERBERT INGRAM
DE MONTIGNY, MR. [REV. FRANCIS JOLLIET]
    1861. Letter of, *in* Early voyages up and down the Mississippi, by Cavelier, St. Cosme, Le Sueur, Gravier, and Guignas. With an introduction, notes, and an index, by John Gilmary Shea. Pp. 75–79.
DENSMORE, FRANCES
    1937. The Alabama Indians and their music. *In* Straight Texas. Publ. Tex. Folk-Lore Soc., No. 13.
    1943. A search for songs among the Chitimacha Indians in Louisiana. Anthrop. Pap. No. 19, Bur. Amer. Ethnol. Bull. 133, pp. 1–5.
    1943 a. Choctaw music. Anthrop. Pap. No. 28, Bur. Amer. Ethnol. Bull. 136, pp. 101–188.
DE SALAZAR, CERVANTES
    1914. Crónica de la Nueva España. Hispanic Soc. Amer. Madrid.
DE SIGUENZA, DON CARLOS. *See* LEONARD, IRVING A.; *and* BARCIA CARBALLIDO Y ZUÑIGA, ANDRÉS G.
DE SOTO, HERNANDO. *See* BOURNE, EDWARD GAYLORD, EDITOR; ROBERTSON, JAMES A., TRANSLATOR AND EDITOR; *and* U. S. DE SOTO EXPEDITION COMMISSION.
DE VILLIERS, LE BARON MARC
    1922. Documents concernant l'histoire des Indiens de la région orientale de la Louisiane. Journ. Soc. Amér. Paris, n. s., vol. 14, pp. 127–140. Paris.
    1923. Notes sur les Chactas d'apres les journaux de voyage de Régis du Roullet (1729–1732). Journ. Soc. Amér. Paris, n. s., vol. 15, pp. 223–250. Paris.
    1925. Extrait d'un journal de voyage en Louisiane du Pere Paul du Ru (1700). Journ. Soc. Amér. Paris, n. s., vol. 17, pp. 119–135. Paris.
DICE, LEE R. *See* SHELFORD, VICTOR E.

DICKENSON, JONATHAN
  1803. Narrative of a shipwreck in the Gulph of Florida. 6th ed., Stanford,
        N. Y.
DONALDSON, THOMAS
  1886. The George Catlin Indian gallery in the U. S. National Museum (Smith-
        sonian Institution), with memoir and statistics. Rep. U. S. Nat. Mus.
        for 1885.
DORSEY, GEORGE A.
  1905. Traditions of the Caddo. Carnegie Inst. Washington Publ. No. 41.
DORSEY, JAMES OWEN
  1897. Siouan sociology: a posthumous paper. 15th Ann. Rep. Bur. Amer.
        Ethnol., 1893–1894, pp. 205–244.
DORSEY, JAMES OWEN, and SWANTON, JOHN R.
  1912. A dictionary of the Biloxi and Ofo languages, accompanied with thirty-
        one Biloxi texts and numerous Biloxi phrases. Bur. Amer. Ethnol.
        Bull. 47.
DOUAY, FATHER ANASTASIUS, NARRATIVE. See SHEA, JOHN GILMARY, 1852, pp.
  197–224.
DUMONT DE MONTIGNY
  1753. Mémoires historiques sur la Louisiane. Edited by Le Mascrier. 2 vols.
        Paris.
DU POISSON, FATHER
  Letter of. See Thwaites, Reuben Gold, Jesuit relations . . ., vol. 67, pp.
  276–325.
DURALDE, MARTIN. See GALLATIN, ALBERT; SWANTON, JOHN R., 1911; and GAT-
  SCHET, ALBERT S., and SWANTON, JOHN R., 1932.
DU ROULLET, RÉGIS
  Journal of a visit made to the Choctaw nation in 1732. In Archives Naval
  Hydrog. Service, Paris. Copy in Ms. Div., Lib. Congr., Washington, D. C.
DU RU, PÈRE PAUL. See DE VILLIERS, LE BARON MARC.
DYER, J. O.
  1916. The early history of Galveston. Pt. 1. Galveston, Tex.
  1917. The Lake Charles Atakapas (cannibals), period of 1817–1820. Gal-
        veston, Tex.
EDWARDS, JOHN
  1932. The Choctaw Indians in the middle of the nineteenth century. Chron-
        icles of Oklahoma, vol. 10, No. 3, pp. 392–425. Oklahoma City, Okla.
EGGAN, FRED
  1937. Historical changes in the Choctaw kinship system. Amer. Anthrop.,
        n. s., vol. 39, No. 1, pp. 34–52.
ELVAS, NARRATIVE OF A GENTLEMAN OF. See ROBERTSON, JAMES A., TRANSLATOR
  AND EDITOR.
ESPINOSA, FRAY ISIDRO FELIS DE
  1927. Descriptions of the Tejas or Asinai Indians, 1691–1722. Translated
        from the Spanish by Mattie Austin Hatcher. IV, Fray Isidro Felis
        de Espinosa on the Asinai and their allies. Southwestern Hist.
        Quart., vol. 31, pp. 150–180. Spanish text in Bur. Amer. Ethnol. Bull.
        132, pp. 273–300. See Swanton, 1942.
FAIRBANKS, G. R.
  1871. History of Florida, 1512–1842. Philadelphia.
FALLAM, ROBERT, DISCOVERIES OF. See ALVORD, CLARENCE W., and BIDGOOD, LEE;
  and BUSHNELL, DAVID I., JR., 1907 a.
FENNEMAN, NEVIRO M.
  —. Physical areas of the United States.

FISKE, JOHN
1901. The discovery of America. 2 vols. Boston and New York.
FLANNERY, REGINA
1939. An analysis of coastal Algonquian culture. Catholic Univ. Amer.,
Anthrop. Ser., No. 7. Univ. Press, Washington.
FLOYD'S ARMY, LETTER FROM AN OFFICER IN. MS COPY RECEIVED FROM DR. CHARLES
C. HARROLD.
FONTAINE, REV. JAMES. See MAURY, ANN.
FONTANEDA, HERNANDO DE ESCALANTE
1854. Memoria de las cosas y costa y Indios de la Florida. In Buckingham
Smith's Letter of Hernando de Soto, and Memoir of Hernando de
Escalante Fontaneda. Washington. (Note: Other eds. of op. cit.
are Documentos Inéditos, vol. 5, pp. 532–548, Madrid, 1866; and a
French trans. in Ternaux-Compans, Voyages, vol. 20, pp. 9–42, Paris,
1841.)
FORD, JAMES A., and WILLEY, GORDON R.
1941. An interpretation of the prehistory of the eastern United States. Amer.
Anthrop., pt. 1, n. s., vol. 43, No. 3, pp. 325–363.
FORDYCE, JOHN R.
1929. Trailing De Soto. A paper presented at the Conference on Midwestern
Archaeology held at St. Louis, Mo., May 19, 1929, under the auspices
of the National Research Council and printed in the report of its
proceedings. Bull. Nat. Res. Council, No. 74. Washington.
1934. De Soto in Arkansas. Arkansas Hist. Review, vol. 1, No. 2, p. 3.
1936. The explorations of Hernando de Soto in the southern part of the
United States. Military Engineer, vol. 28, No. 157, pp. 1–7; and
No. 158, pp. 113–119.
FOREMAN, GRANT
1930. Indians and pioneers, the story of the American Southwest before 1830.
Yale Univ. Press, New Haven, Conn.
1930 a. A traveler in Indian territory. The journal of Ethan Allen Hitchcock,
later Major-General in the United States Army. Edited and
annotated by Grant Foreman. Cedar Rapids, Iowa.
1932. Indian removal: The emigration of the five civilized tribes of Indians.
Univ. Okla. Press, Norman, Okla.
1933. Advancing the frontier, 1830–1860. Univ. Okla. Press, Norman, Okla.
1934. The five civilized tribes. Univ. Okla. Press, Norman, Okla.
FRACHTENBERG, LEO J.
1913. Contributions to a Tutelo vocabulary. Amer. Anthrop., n. s., vol. 15,
pp. 477–479.
FREEMAN, THOMAS, and CUSTIS, PETER
1806. An account of the Red River in Louisiana, drawn up from the returns
of Messrs. Freeman and Custis to the War Office of the United
States, who explored the same in the year 1806.
FRENCH, B. F.
1846–1853. Historical collections of Louisiana, embracing many rare and
valuable documents relating to the natural, civil, and political
history of that State. 5 pts. New York. (Note: Later numbers are 1869, New York; and 1875, New York.)
FREIRE-MARRECO, BARBARA. See ROBBINS, WILFRED WILLIAM, et. al.
GAFFAREL, PAUL LOUIS JACQUES
1875. Histoire de la Floride française. Paris.

GALLATIN, ALBERT
   1836. A synopsis of the Indian tribes in North America.   Trans. Amer. Antiq.
         Soc., Archæologia Americana, vol. 2.   Cambridge, Mass.
GARCIA, GENARO
   1902. Dos antiguos relaciones de la Florida.   Mexico.
GARCILASO DE LA VEGA (EL INCA)
   1723. La Florida del Inca.   Historia del Adelantado, Hernando de Soto,
         Gouernador, y Capitan General del Reino de la Florida y de Otros
         Heroicos Caballeros, Españoles, e Indios.   2d ed.   Madrid.
GATSCHET, ALBERT S.
   1877–1880. The Timucua language.   (Read before the American Philosophical
         Society, April 6, 1877, April 5, 1878, Feb. 20, 1880.)   Proc. Amer.
         Philos. Soc., vol. 16, pp. 625–642; vol. 17, pp. 490–504; vol. 18,
         pp. 465–502.   Philadelphia.
   1883. The Shetimasha Indians of St. Mary's Parish, Southern Louisiana.
         Trans. Anthrop. Soc. Washington, vol. 2, pp. 148–158.
   1884, 1888. A migration legend of the Creek Indians.   Vol. 1, Brinton's Li-
         brary of Aboriginal American Literature, No. 4, Philadelphia,
         1884.   Vol. 2, Trans. Acad. Sci. St. Louis, vol. 5, Nos. 1 and 2,
         St. Louis, 1888.
GATSCHET, ALBERT S., and SWANTON, JOHN R.
   1932. A dictionary of the Atakapa language, accompanied by text material.
         Bur. Amer. Ethnol. Bull. 108.
GEIGER, REV. MAYNARD
   1937. The Franciscan conquest of Florida (1573–1618).   Catholic Univ. Amer.,
         Studies in Hispanic-American History, vol. 1.   Washington.
   1940. Biographical dictionary of the Franciscans in Spanish Florida and
         Cuba (1528–1841).   Franciscan Studies, vol. 21.   St. Anthony Guild
         Press, Paterson, N. J.
GEORGIA, COLONIAL RECORDS OF THE STATE OF
   1904–1909. Compiled and published under the authority of the Legislature by
         Allen D. Candler, Atlanta, Ga.
GEORGIA HISTORICAL SOCIETY
   1840–1878. Collections.   4 vols.   Savannah, Ga.
GERARD, W. R.
   1904. Tapehanek dialect of Virginia .   Amer. Anthrop., n. s., vol. 6, pp. 313–330.
   1907. Virginia's Indian contributions to English.   Amer. Anthrop., n. s., vol.
         9, pp. 87–112.
GILBERT, WILLIAM HARLEN, JR.
   1937. Eastern Cherokee social organization.   In Social anthrop. North Amer.
         tribes, pp. 283–338, Chicago, Ill.
   1943. The Eastern Cherokees.   Anthrop. Pap. No. 23, Bur. Amer. Ethnol. Bull.
         133, pp. 169–413.
GOSSELIN, M. L'ABBÉ AMÉDÉE.
   1907. Les sauvages du Mississippi (1698–1708) d'après le correspondance des
         missionnaires des Missions Étrangères de Québec.   C. R. Congr. Int.
         Amér., 15th sess., vol. 1, pp. 31–51.   Québec.
GOWER, CHARLOTTE D.
   1927. The northern and southern affiliations of Antillean culture.   Mem.
         Amer. Anthrop. Assoc. No. 35.   Menasha, Wis.
GRAVIER, J.   See SHEA, JOHN GILMARY, 1852, pp. 115–163; and THWAITES, REUBEN
   GOLD, JESUIT RELATIONS, 1896–1901, vol. 65, pp. 100–179.

GREEN, JOHN A.
1936. Governor Perier's expedition against the Natchez Indians. Louisiana Hist. Quart., vol. 19, No. 3, pp. 1-33.
GREGORIE, ANNE KING.
1925. Notes on Sewee Indian remains. Contr. Charleston Mus., No. 5. Charleston.
HAAS, MARY R.
1939. Natchez and Chitimacha clans and kinship terminology. Amer. Anthrop., n. s., vol. 41, No. 4, pp. 597-610.
1940. Creek inter-town relations. Amer. Anthrop., n. s., vol. 42, No. 3, pp. 479-489.
1940 a. Tunica. *Extract from* Handbook Amer. Ind. Langs. vol. 4.
1942. The Solar Deity of the Tunica. Pap. Mich. Acad. Sci., Arts and Letters, vol. 28, pp. 531-535.
HABIG, MARION A.
1934. The Franciscan Père Marquette; a critical biography of Father Zénobe Membré, O. F. M., La Salle's chaplain and missionary companion 1645(ca.)-1689, with maps and original narratives. Franciscan Studies, No. 13. New York.
HAKLUYT SOCIETY
1847-1889. Publications, vols. 1-79. London.
HALBERT, HENRY SALE
1882. Courtship and marriage among the Choctaws of Mississippi. Amer. Nat., vol. 16, pp. 222-224. Philadelphia.
1888. The Choctaw Achahpih (Chungkee) game. Amer. Antiq., vol. 10, pp. 283-284. Chicago.
1891. Pyramid and old road in Mississippi. Amer. Antiq., vol. 13, pp. 348-349. Chicago.
1894. A Choctaw migration legend. Amer. Antiq., vol. 16, pp. 215-216. Chicago.
1895. The Choctaw Robin Goodfellow. Amer. Antiq., vol. 17, p. 157. Chicago.
1899. Nanih Waiya, the sacred mound of the Choctaws. Publ. Miss. Hist. Soc., vol. 2, pp. 223-234. Oxford, Miss.
1900. Funeral customs of the Mississippi Choctaws. Publ. Miss. Hist. Soc., vol. 3, pp. 353-366. Oxford, Miss.
1901. The Choctaw creation legend. Publ. Miss. Hist. Soc., vol. 4, pp. 267-270. Oxford, Miss.
1901 a. District divisions of the Choctaw nation. Publ. Ala. Hist. Soc., Misc. Coll., vol. 1, pp. 375-385. Mongomery, Ala.
See also Byington, Cyrus.
HALE, HORATIO
1883. The Tutelo tribe and language. Proc. Amer. Philos. Soc., vol. 21, No. 114. Philadelphia.
HALL, JAMES. *See* McKENNEY, THOMAS L., and HALL, JAMES.
HAMILTON, PETER J.
1910. Colonial Mobile, an historical study largely from original sources, of the Alabama-Tombigbee basin from the discovery of Mobile Bay in 1519 until the demolition of Fort Caroline in 1820. Revised and enlarged edition. Boston and New York.
HANDBOOK OF AMERICAN INDIANS NORTH OF MEXICO. *See* HODGE, FREDERICK WEBB, EDITOR.

HANNA, CHARLES A.
1911. The wilderness trail, or the ventures and adventures of the Pennsylvania traders on the Allegheny Path with some new annals of the old West, and the records of some strong men and some bad ones. 2 vols. New York and London.
HARBY, MRS. LEE C.
1895. The Tejas: Their habits, government and superstitions. Ann. Rep. Amer. Hist. Assoc., 1894, pp. 63–82.
HARIOT [HARRIOT], THOMAS
1893. Narrative of the first English plantation of Virginia. Reprint. London. (Note: Earlier eds. of op. cit. are 1588 and 1590.)
HARPER, ROLAND M.
1937. A statistical study of the Croatans (a little known people in North and South Carolina). Rural Sociology, vol. 2, No. 4, pp. 444–457.
HARRINGTON, JOHN PEABODY. See ROBBINS, WILFRED WILLIAM.
HARRINGTON, M. R.
1908. Catawba potters and their work. Amer. Anthrop., n. s., vol. 10, No. 3, pp. 399–407.
1920. Certain Caddo sites in Arkansas. Ind. Notes and Monogr. (Misc. 10), Mus. Amer. Ind., Heye Foundation. New York.
1922. Cherokee and earlier remains on upper Tennessee River. Ind. Notes and Monogr. (Misc. 24), Mus. Amer. Ind., Heye Foundation. New York.
HARRISSE, HENRY
1892. The discovery of North America. A critical documentary and historic investigation. London and Paris.
HARVEY, HENRY
1855. History of the Shawnee Indians, from the year 1681 to 1854 inclusive. Cincinnati.
HATCHER, MATTIE AUSTIN. See CASSAÑAS; ESPINOSA; HIDALGO; PADILLA; and KRESS.
HAWKINS, BENJAMIN
1848. A sketch of the Creek country, in 1798 and 1799. Ga. Hist. Soc. Coll., vol. 3. Savannah.
1916. Letters of Benjamin Hawkins, 1796–1806. Ga. Hist. Soc. Coll., vol. 9. Savannah.
HAYWOOD, JOHN
1823. The natural and aboriginal history of Tennessee, up to the first settlements therein by the white people in the year 1768. Nashville.
HEARD, ELMA
1937. Two tales from the Alabamas. Publ. Tex. Folk-Lore Soc., No. 13, pp. 294–297.
HENNEPIN, LOUIS
1698. A new discovery of a vast country in America extending above four thousand miles between New France and New Mexico. London.
HENSHAW, H. W.
1890. Indian origin of maple sugar. Amer. Anthrop., o. s., vol. 3, pp. 341–352.
HERRERA, ANTONIO DE
1720. Historia general de los hechos de los Castellanos en las islas i tierra firme del mar oceano. 5 vols. Madrid.

HEWAT, ALEX
1779. Historical account of the rise and progress of the colonies of South Carolina and Georgia. 2 vols. London.

HEYE, GEORGE G., HODGE, F. W., and PEPPER, GEORGE H.
1918. The Nacoochee Mound in Georgia. Contr. Mus. Amer. Ind., Heye Foundation, vol. 4, No. 3. New York.

HICKS, CHARLES. See RALEIGH REGISTER.

HIDALGO, FRAY FRANCISCO
1927. Description of the Tejas or Asinai Indians, 1691-1722. Translated from the Spanish by Mattie Austin Hatcher. III, Fray Francisco Hidalgo to the Viceroy, November 20, 1710. (Extract) Fray Francisco Hidalgo to the Viceroy, November 4, 1716. Southwestern Hist. Quart., vol. 31, pp. 50-62. (For Spanish text of Hidalgo letter of Nov. 4, 1716, see Swanton, 1942, pp. 265-271.)

HILTON, WILLIAM
1897. A true relation of a voyage upon discovery of part of the coast of Florida, from the lat. of 31 deg. to 33 deg. 45 m. north lat. in the ship Adventure, William Hilton, commander . . . sailed from Spikes Bay Aug. 10, 1663. S. C. Hist. Soc. Coll., vol. 5, pp. 18-28.

HINKE, PROF. WM. J., TRANSLATOR. See MICHEL, FRANCIS LOUIS

HITCHCOCK, ETHAN ALLEN, JOURNAL. See FOREMAN, GRANT, 1930 a.

HODGE, FREDERICK WEBB, EDITOR
1907, 1910. Handbook of American Indians north of Mexico. Bur. Amer. Ethnol. Bull. 30, pts. 1 and 2. See also Heye, George G.

HODGSON, ADAM
1823. Remarks during a journey through North America in the years 1819, 1820, and 1821. New York.

HOLMES, WM. H.
1903. Aboriginal pottery of the eastern United States. 20th Ann. Rep. Bur. Amer. Ethnol., 1898-1899, pp. 1-237.
1919. Handbook of aboriginal American antiquities. Pt. 1. Bur. Amer. Ethnol. Bull. 60.

HRDLIČKA, ALEŠ
1922. The anthropology of Florida. Publ. No. 1, Fla. State Hist. Soc. DeLand, Fla.

HUTCHINS, THOMAS
1784. An historical narrative and topographical description of Louisiana and West-Florida. Philadelphia.

IBERVILLE, PIERRE LE MOYNE D'. See DE VILLIERS, LE BARON MARC; and MARGRY, PIERRE, VOL. 4.

JEFFERSON, THOMAS
1801. Notes on the State of Virginia; with a map of Virginia, Maryland, Delaware, and Pennsylvania. Philadelphia. (Note: Another ed. of op. cit. is 1825, Philadelphia.)

JESUIT RELATIONS AND ALLIED DOCUMENTS. See THWAITES, REUBEN GOLD, EDITOR.

JONES, CHARLES C.
1873. Antiquities of the southern Indians, particularly of the Georgia tribes. New York.

JONES, LYNDS. See SHELFORD, VICTOR E., EDITOR.

JOUTEL, HENRI, RELATION DE. See MARGRY, PIERRE, vol. 3, pp. 89-534.

KENNY, MICHAEL
    1934. The romance of the Floridas. New York.
KIMBER, EDWARD
    1744. A relation or journal, of a late expedition to the gates of St. Augustine,
        on Florida; conducted by the Hon. General James Oglethorpe with
        a detachment of his regiment, etc. from Georgia. By a gentleman,
        volunteer in the said expedition. London. (Note: Later ed. of op.
        cit. is 1935, Boston.)
KINIETZ, VERNON, and VOEGELIN, ERMINIE W.
    1939. Shawnee traditions: C. C. Trowbridge's account. Occasional Contr.
        Mus. Anthrop., Univ. Mich., No. 9. Ann Arbor, Mich.
KOPMAN, H. H.   See SHELFORD, VICTOR E., EDITOR.
KRESS, MARGARET KENNEY
    1931. Diary of a visit of inspection of the Texas missions made by Fray
        Gaspar José de Solís in the year 1767–68. Translated by Margaret
        Kenney Kress with introductory note by Mattie Austin Hatcher.
        Southwestern Hist. Quart., vol. 35, pp. 28–76.
KROEBER, A. L.
    1939. Cultural and natural areas of native North America. Univ. Calif.
        Publ. Amer. Archaeol., and Ethnol., vol. 38, pp. xii, 1–242.
KROGMAN, WILTON MARION
    1935. The physical anthropology of the Seminole Indians of Oklahoma, with
        an introduction by Corrado Gini. Comitato Italiano per lo studio dei
        problemi della popolazione. Ser. 3, vol. 2. Rome.
LA HARPE, BERNARD DE.   See BEAURAIN, LE SIEUR; and MARGRY, PIERRE, vol. 6,
    pp. 243–306.
LAMHATTY, ACCOUNT OF.   See BUSHNELL, DAVID I., JR., 1908.
LANMAN, CHARLES
    1856. Adventures in the wilds of the United States and British American
        provinces. 2 vols., Philadelphia.
LA SALLE, NICOLAS DE.   See MARGRY, PIERRE, vol. 1, pp. 547–570.
LA SALLE, RÉNÉ ROBERT CAVELIER, SIEUR DE
    Account of La Salle's voyage. See Shea, John Gilmary, 1861, pp. 15–42.
    See also Cox, Isaac Joslin, Editor; and Delanglez, Jean.
LA SOURCE, M. THAUMUR DE
    Letter of.   See Shea, John Gilmary, 1852, pp. 79–86.
LAUDONNIÈRE, RENÉ GOULAINE DE
    1586. L'histoire notable de la Floride située ès Indes Occidentales, con-
        tenant les trois voyages faits en icelle par certains Capitaines et
        Pilotes françois, qui y a commandé l'espace d'un an trois moys: a
        laquelle a esté adjousté un quatriesme voyage fait par le Capitaine
        Gourgues, mise en lumière par M. Basnier. Paris. (Note: Later
        ed. of op. cit. is 1853, Paris.)
LAWSON, JOHN
    1860. History of Carolina, containing the exact description and natural
        history of that country. Raleigh, N. C. (Note: Other eds. of op.
        cit. are 1714, London; and 1937, Richmond, Va.)
LE CLERCQ, CHRÉTIEN.   See SHEA, JOHN GILMARY, 1852, pp. 183–196; and COX,
    ISAAC JOSLIN, EDITOR.

LEDERER, JOHN
1912. The discoveries of John Lederer in three several marches from Virginia to the west of Carolina and other parts of this continent; begun in March, 1669, and ended September, 1670. Together with a general map of the whole territory which he traversed. Collected and translated by Sir William Talbot, Baronet. *In* Alvord, Clarence W., and Bidgood, Lee. (Note: Other eds. of op. cit. are London, 1672; and Rochester, 1902.)

LE MOYNE, JACQUES
1875. Narrative of Le Moyne, an artist who accompanied the French expedition to Florida under Laudonnière, 1564. Translated from the Latin of De Bry. Boston.

LEONARD, IRVING A., TRANSLATOR AND EDITOR
1939. Spanish approach to Pensacola, 1689–1693. Quivira Soc. Publ., vol. 9.

LE PAGE DU PRATZ, ANTOINE S.
1758. Histoire de la Louisiane. 3 vols. Paris.

LE PETIT, FATHER
Letter to d'Avaugour. *See* Thwaites, Reuben Gold, Jesuit Relations . . ., vol. 68, pp. 120–223. Cleveland.

LESSER, ALEXANDER, and WELTFISH, GENE
1932. Composition of the Caddoan linguistic stock. Smithsonian Misc. Coll., vol. 87, No. 6.

LE SUEUR, NARRATIVE. *See* MARGRY; BEAURAIN; PÉNICAUT; *and* SHEA, JOHN GILMARY, 1861, pp. 87–111.

LOWERY, WOODBURY
1901. The Spaniish settlements within the present limits of the United States, 1513–1561. New York and London.
1905. Spanish settlements within the present limits of the United States: Florida, 1564–1574. New York and London.
Mss. in Library of Congress.

MACCAULEY, CLAY
1887. The Seminole Indians of Florida. 5th Ann. Rep. Bur. Amer. Ethnol., 1883–1884, pp. 469–531.

MCKENNEY, THOMAS L., and HALL, JAMES.
1854. History of the Indian tribes of North America. 3 vols. Philadelphia.

MANGELSDORF, P. C., and REEVES, R. G.
1939. The origin of Indian corn and its relatives. Tex Exp. Station Bull. No. 574. May.

MARGRY, PIERRE
1875–1886. Découvertes et établissements des Français dans l'Ouest et dans le Sud de l'Amérique septentrionale (1614–1754). Mémoires et documents originaux recueillis et publiés par Pierre Margry. 6 vols. Paris.

MARQUETTE, FATHER JACQUES. *See* SHEA, JOHN GILMARY, 1852, pp. 3–66, 231–264; *and* STECK, FRANCIS BORGIA.

MAURY, ANN
1907. Memoirs of a Huguenot family, translated and compiled from the original autobiography of Rev. James Fontaine. By Ann Maury. Reprinted from the original edition of 1852. New York and London. (The journal of John Fontaine, son of James, is incorporated in the work.)

MEMBRÉ, FATHER ZÉNOBE. *See* SHEA, JOHN GILMARY, 1852, pp. 78–184; HABIG, MARION A.; *and* MARGRY, PIERRE, vol. 2, pp. 206–212.

MERA, H. P. *See* SCHOLES, FRANCE V.

MERENESS, NEWTON D., EDITOR
1916. Travels in the American colonies. New York.

MERRIAM, C. HART
1898. Life zones and crop zones of the United States. Bull. 10, Biol. Surv. Dept. Agri.

MÉZIÈRES, ATHANASE DE. *See* BOLTON, HERBERT EUGENE, 1914.

MICHEL, FRANCIS LOUIS
1916. Report of the journey of Francis Louis Michel from Berne, Switzerland, to Virginia, October 2, 1701—December 1, 1702. Va. Mag. Hist. and Biog., Va. Hist. Soc., vol. 24, pp. 1–43, 113–141, 275–303. Translated and edited by Prof. Wm. J. Hinke, Ph. D.

MICHELSON, TRUMAN
1912. Preliminary report on the linguistic classification of Algonquian tribes. 28th Ann. Rep. Bur. Amer. Ethnol., 1906–1907, pp. 221–290b.

MILFORT, [LE CLERC]
1802. Mémoire au coup-d'oeil rapide sur mes différens voyages et mon séjour dan la nation Crëck. Paris.

MILLING, CHAPMAN J.
1940. Red Carolinians. Univ. N. C. Press, Chapel Hill, N. C.

MOOK, MAURICE A.
1943. The anthropological position of the Indian tribes of Tidewater Virginia. William and Mary Coll. Quart. Hist. Mag., 2d ser., vol. 23, No. 1, pp. 27–40.
1943 a. A newly discovered Algonkian tribe of Carolina. Amer. Anthrop., n. s., vol. 45, No. 4, pp. 635–637.
1943 b. The ethnological significance of Tindall's map of Virginia. William and Mary Quart. Hist. Mag., 2d ser., vol. 23, No. 4, pp. 371–408.

MOONEY, JAMES
1890. Cherokee ball play. Amer. Anthrop., o. s., vol. 3, pp. 105–132.
1891. The sacred formulas of the Cherokees. 7th Ann. Rep. Bur. Ethnol., 1885–1886, pp. 301–397.
1895. The Siouan tribes of the east. Bur. Amer. Ethnol. Bull. 22.
1897. The Ghost-dance religion and the Sioux outbreak of 1890. 14th Ann. Rep. Bur. Ethnol., 1892–1893, pt. 2.
1900. Myths of the Cherokee. 19th Ann. Rep. Bur. Amer. Ethnol., 1897–1898, pt. 1.
1928. The aboriginal population of America north of Mexico. Smithsonian Misc. Coll., vol. 80, No. 7.

MOONEY, JAMES, and OLBRECHTS, FRANS M.
1932. The Swimmer manuscript: Cherokee sacred formulas and medicinal prescriptions by James Mooney; revised, completed, and edited by Frans Olbrechts. Bur. Amer. Ethnol. Bull. 99.

MOORE, CLARENCE B.
See writings on archeological work in the southern United States, published in the Journ. Acad. Nat. Sci. Phila., 2d ser., vols. 10–19, 1894–1918.

MORFI, FRAY JUAN AGUSTIN DE

1932. Excerpts from the memorias for the history of the Province of Texas, being a translation of those parts of the memorias which particularly concern the various Indians of the Province of Texas; their tribal divisions, characteristics, customs, traditions, superstitions, and all else of interest concerning them. With a prolog, appendix, and notes by Frederick M. Chabot. Privately printed.

1935. History of Texas, 1673–1779. Translated, with biographical introduction and annotations, by Carlos Eduardo Castañeda. 2 pts. Quivira Soc. Albuquerque.

MORSE, JEDIDIAH

1822. A report to the Secretary of War of the United States, on Indian affairs, comprising a narrative of a tour performed in the summer of 1820. New Haven, Conn. See also Belknap, Jeremy.

MYER, WILLIAM E.

1928. Indian trails of the Southeast. 42d Ann. Rep. Bur. Amer. Ethnol., 1924–1925, pp. 727–857.

NARRATIVES OF EARLY VIRGINIA. See TYLER, LYON GARDINER, EDITOR.

NASH ROY

1931. Report to the Commissioner of Indian Affairs concerning conditions among the Seminole Indians of Florida. Survey and report made in 1930 by Roy Nash. Sen. Doc. No. 314, 71st Congr., 3d sess.

NEEDHAM, JAMES, JOURNEYS OF. See ALVORD CLARENCE W., and BIDGOOD, LEE, pp. 207–226.

NEWPORT, CAPT., RELATION. See ARCHER, GABRIEL.

NEW YORK

1849–51. The documentary history of the State of New York; arranged under direction of the Hon. Christopher Morgan, Secretary of State, by E. B. O'Callaghan, M.D. 4 vols. Albany.

1853–1887. Documents relating to the colonial history of the State of New York, vols. 1–15. Albany.

NORTH CAROLINA

1886–1890. The colonial records of North Carolina, vols. 1–10. Raleigh, N. C.

1895–1896, 1898–1906. State records of North Carolina. Vols. 11–14. Winston, N. C. Vols. 15–26. Goldsboro.

NUÑEZ CABEZA DE VACA, ALVAR

1905. The journey of Alvar Nuñez Cabeza de Vaca . . . translated from his own narrative by Fanny Bandelier. Trail Makers (series). New York. (Also edited by F. W. Hodge in Spanish explorers in the United States in Original narratives of early American history. New York, 1907.)

NUNN, GEORGE ERMA

1924. The geographical conceptions of Columbus; a critical consideration of four problems. Amer Geogr. Soc., Res. Ser. No. 14.

OGLETHORPE'S VISIT TO CAWETA IN 1740 [1739]. See BUSHNELL, DAVID I., JR., 1908.

OLBRECHTS, FRANS M. See MOONEY, JAMES, 1932.

OVIEDO Y VALDÉZ, GONZALO FERNÁNDEZ DE (EL CAPITAN)

1851–1855. Historia general y natural de las Indias. 4 vols. Madrid.

PADILLA, JUAN ANTONIO

1919. Texas in 1820. Translated by Mattie Austin Hatcher. I, Report on the barbarous Indians of the Province of Texas. Southwestern Hist. Quart., vol. 23, No. 1, pp. 47–68.

PAINE, JOHN HOWARD
Manuscript materials on the Cherokee in Newberry Library, Chicago.
PAREJA, FRANCISCO
1612. Cathecismo, en lengva Castellana, y Timuquana. Mexico.
1613. Confessionario, en lengua Castellana, y Timuquana. Mexico.
1886. Arte de la lengva Timvqvana compvesta en 1614. Bibliothèque Ling. Amér., vol. 11, Paris.
PARSONS, ELSIE CLEWS
1941. Notes on the Caddo. Mem. Amer. Anthrop. Assoc., No. 57.
PEARCE, J. E., and JACKSON, A. I.
1912. A prehistoric rock shelter in Val Verde County, Texas. 143 pp. Univ. Texas. Bull. No. 3327, Bur. Res. and Social Sci. Study No. 6. Anthrop. Pap., vol. 1, No. 3.
PÉNICAUT, RELATION DE. LES PREMIERS POSTES DE LA LOUISIANE. See MARGRY, PIERRE, vol. 5, pp. 375–586.
PEPPER, GEORGE H. See HEYE, GEORGE G.
PERCY, GEORGE, OBSERVATIONS. See SMITH, JOHN, WORKS, ARBER ED., 1884, pp. lvii–lxxiii; Tyler ed., 1907, pp. 5–23.
PICKENS, A. L.
1943. A comparison of Cherokee and Pioneer bird-nomenclature. Southern Folklore Quart., vol. 7, No. 4, pp. 213–221.
PONTON, GERALD M. See BOYD, MARK F., 1934.
POPE, JOHN
1792. Tour through the northern and western territories of the United States. Richmond, Va.
POWELL, J. W.
1891. Indian linguistic families of America north of Mexico. 7th Ann. Rep. Bur. Amer. Ethnol., 1885–1886, pp. 1–142.
PRIESTLY, HERBERT INGRAM, EDITOR
1928. Luna papers. Publ. Fla. State Hist. Soc., No. 8. 2 vols. Deland, Fla.
RALEIGH REGISTER
1818.
Manners, customs, &c. of the Cherokee Indians, taken down by a missionary named Hoyt, copied by Calvin Jones and sent by him in a letter dated Oct. 13, 1818, to Mr. Gales, who was apparently editor of the Raleigh Register, in which journal it was printed. (This article contains statements by Shief Charles Hicks.)
READ, WILLIAM ALEXANDER
1927. Louisiana place-names of Indian origin. Univ. Bull., La. State Univ., n. s., vol. 19, No. 2.
1928. Indian place-names in Louisiana. La. Hist. Quart., July.
1931. Louisiana-French. La. State Univ. Studies, No. 5. Baton Rouge, La.
1934. Florida place-names of Indian origin and Seminole personal names. La. State Univ. Studies, No. 11. Baton Rouge, La.
1937. Indian place-names in Alabama. La. State Univ. Studies, No. 29. Baton Rouge, La.
RIBAULT, JEAN. See FRENCH, B. F
RICHARDSON, WILLIAM
1931. An account of the Presbyterian mission to the Cherokees, 1757–1759. Tenn. Hist. Mag., ser. 2, vol. 1, No. 2, pp. 125–128.

Rights, Douglas L.
  1928. A voyage down the Yadkin-Great Peedee River. Winston-Salem, N. C.
  1931. The trading path to the Indians. North Carolina Hist. Rev., vol. 8,
        No. 4, pp. 403–426. Raleigh, N. C.
Rivers, William James
  1874. A chapter in the early history of South Carolina. Charleston.
Robbins, Wilfred William; Harrington, John Peabody; and Freire-Marreco,
    Barbara
  1916. Ethnobotany of the Tewa Indians. Bur. Amer. Ethnol. Bull. 55.
Robertson, James Alexander, Editor and Translator
  1933. True relation of the hardships suffered by Governor Fernando de
        Soto and certain Portuguese gentlemen during the discovery of the
        Province of Florida, now newly set forth by a Gentleman of Elvas.
        Translated and edited by James Alexander Robertson. 2 vols. Fla.
        State Hist. Soc. De Land.
  1938. Letter written to the secular Cabildo of Santiago de Cuba by Her-
        nando de Soto. Espiritu Santo. Florida, July 9, 1539. In Fla.
        Hist. Soc. Quart., vol. 16, No. 3, pp. 174–178.
Romans, Bernard
  1775. A concise natural history of East and West Florida. Vol. 1 (vol. 2
        unpublished). New York.
Ross, Mary
  1930. With Pardo and Boyano on the fringes of the Georgia coast. Georgia
        Hist. Quart., vol. 14, No. 4, pp. 267–285.
Rouse, Irving
  1940. Some evidence concerning the origins of West Indian pottery-making.
        Amer. Anthrop., n. s., vol. 42, No. 1, pp. 49–80.
Rowland, Dunbar, and Sanders, Alfred Godfrey, editors
  1927, 1929, 1932. Mississippi Provincial Archives, French Dominion. 3 vols.
        Jackson, Miss.
Ruidiaz y Caravia, Eugenio
  1894. La Florida su conquista y colonización por Pedro Menéndez de
        Avilés. 2 vols. Madrid.
St. Cosme, J. F. Buisson, Letter of, to the Bishop [of Quebec] See Shea,
    John Gilmary, 1861, pp. 45–75.
Salley, Alexander S., Editor
  1911. Narratives of early Carolina, 1650–1708. In Original narratives of
        early American history. New York.
Sánchez, José María
  1926. A trip to Texas in 1828. Translated by Carlos E. Castañeda. South-
        western Hist. Quart., vol. 29, No. 4, pp. 249–288.
Sanders, Alfred Godfrey. See Rowland, Dunbar, and Sanders, Alfred Godfrey.
Sandford, Robert
  1897. The Port Royall discovery. Being the relation of a voyage on the
        coast of the province of Carolina formerly called Florida in the
        continent of the Northerne America from Charles River neere Cape
        Feare in the County of Clarendon and the lat: of 34: deg: to Port
        Royall in the north lat: of 32 d. begun 14th June 1666. Per-
        formed by Robert Sandford Esqr secretary and chiefe register for
        the Right Honble the Lords Proprietors of their County of Claren-
        don in the Province aforesaid. S. C. Hist. Soc. Coll., vol. 5, pp. 57–82.
Sapir, Edward
  1913. A Tutelo vocabulary. Amer. Anthrop., n. s., vol. 15, pp. 295–297.
  1920. The Hokan and Coahuiltecan languages. Int. Journ. Amer. Ling.,
        vol. 1, No. 4, pp. 280–290.

SAUER, CARL ORTWIN
1934. The distribution of aboriginal tribes and languages in northwestern Mexico. Ibero-Americana: 5. Univ. Calif.

SCAIFE, WALTER
1892. America—Its geographical history. Suppl. Baltimore.

SCHAEFFER, GEORGE E. See SPECK, FRANK, and SCHAEFFER, GEORGE E. See also SPECK, FRANK G., and HERZOG, GEORGE; introduction.

SCHOLES, FRANCE V., and MERA, H. P.
1940. Some aspects of the Jumano problem. Contr. Amer. Anthrop. and Hist. No. 34. Reprint from Carnegie Inst. Washington Publ. No. 523, pp. 265-299.

SCHOOLCRAFT, HENRY R.
1851-1857. Historical and statistical information respecting the history, condition and prospects of the Indian tribes of the United States. Collected and prepared under the direction of the Bureau of Indian Affairs. Vols. 1-6. Philadelphia.

SEMMES, RAPHAEL
1937. Captains and mariners of early Maryland. Baltimore.

SERRANO Y SANZ, MANUEL, EDITOR
1913. Documentos históricos de la Florida y la Luisiana siglos XVI al XVIII. Madrid.

SHAFTESBURY PAPERS. See COLL. SOUTH CAROLINA HIST. SOC., vol. 5, 1897.

SHEA, JOHN GILMARY
1852. Discovery and exploration of the Mississippi Valley. New York. (2d ed. Albany, 1903.)
1861. Early voyages up and down the Mississippi. Albany.
1886. Ancient Florida. Chap. 4 in Winsor, Justin, Narrative and Critical History of America, vol. 2, pp. 231-298.
See also Charlevoix, Pierre F. X. de; and De Montigny.

SHELFORD, VICTOR E., EDITOR
1926. Naturalist's guide to the Americas. Baltimore.

SHETRONE, HENRY CLYDE
1900. The mound builders. New York and London.

SIBLEY, JOHN
1832. Historical sketches of the several Indian tribes in Louisiana, south of the Arkansas river, and between the Mississippi and River Grande. (Message from the President communicating discoveries made by Captains Lewis and Clark, Washington, 1806.) In Amer. State Pap., Class II, Ind. Affairs, vol. 1. (Also in Ann. Congr., 9th Congr., 2d sess., cols. 1076-1088.)

SKINNER, ALANSON
1913. Notes on the Florida Seminole. Amer. Anthrop., n. s., vol. 15, pp. 63-77.

SMITH, BUCKINGHAM
1857. Coleccion de varios documentos para la historia de la Florida y tierras adyacentes . . . vol. 1. London.
See also Fontaneda, Hernando de Escalante.

SMITH, JOHN
1884. Works, 1608-1631. Ed. by Edward Arber. English Scholar's Library. No. 16. Birmingham.
1907. Idem. Ed. by Lyon Gardiner Tyler. In Narratives of Early Virginia, 1606-1625. New York.

SMITH, J. RUSSELL
1930–1935. *Article on* Climate. Encyclo. Social Sci. New York.
SMITHER, HARRIET
1932. The Alabama Indians of Texas. Southwestern Hist. Soc., vol. 36, No. 2, pp. 83–108.
SOLÍS, FRAY GASPAR JOSÉ DE
1931. Diary of a visit of inspection of the Texas missions made by Fray Gaspar José de Solís in the year 1767–1768. Translated by Margaret Kenney Kress with introductory note by Mattie Austin Hatcher. Southwestern Hist. Quart., vol. 35, pp. 28–76. (Original recorded in Memorias de Nueva España: Documentos para la historia eclesiastica y civil de la Provincia de Texas, vol. 27, pt. 2, pp. 248–297. Transcript Library, Univ. Tex.)
SOUTH CAROLINA HISTORICAL AND GENEALOGICAL MAGAZINE
1900–1917. Vols. 1–18.
SOUTH CAROLINA HISTORICAL SOCIETY
1857–1897. Collections. Vols. 1–5. Charleston and Richmond.
SPARK, JOHN. *See* HAKLUYT SOCIETY, PUBLICATIONS.
SPECK, FRANK G.
1907. Some outlines of aboriginal culture in the Southeastern States. Amer. Anthrop., n. s., vol. 9, pp. 287–295.
1907 a. Some comparative traits of the Maskogian languages. Amer. Anthrop., n. s., vol. 9, pp. 470–483.
1907 b. The Creek Indians of Taskigi town. Mem. Amer. Anthrop. Assoc., vol. 2, pt. 2.
1907 c. Notes on Chickasaw ethnology and folk-lore. Journ. Amer. Folk-Lore, vol. 20, pp. 50–58.
1909. Ethnology of the Yuchi Indians. Anthrop. Publ. Univ. Mus., Univ. Pa., vol. 1, No. 1. Philadelphia.
1916. Remnants of the Machapunga Indians of North Carolina. Amer. Anthrop., n. s., vol. 18, pp. 271–276.
1924. The ethnic position of the Southeastern Algonkian. Amer. Anthrop., n. s., vol. 26, pp. 184–200.
1935. Siouan tribes of the Carolinas as known from Catawba, Tutelo, and documentary sources. Amer. Anthrop., n. s., vol. 37, pt. 2, pp. 201–225.
1938. The question of matrilineal descent in the southeastern Siouan area. Amer. Anthrop., n. s., vol. 40, pp. 1–12.
1938 a. The cane blowgun in Catawba and Southeastern ethnology. Amer. Anthrop., n. s., vol. 40, No. 2, pp. 198–204.
1943. A social reconnaissance of the Creole Houma Indian trappers of the Louisiana bayous. American Indigena, vol. 3, No. 2, pp. 135–145; No. 3, pp. 211–220.
SPECK, FRANK G., and HERZOG, GEORGE
1942. The Tutelo Spirit Adoption Ceremony. With intro., The Tutelo Indians in Pennsylvania History, by Claude E. Schaeffer, Asst. State Anthrop. Pa. Hist. Comm.
SPECK, FRANK G., and SCHAEFFER, GEORGE E.
1942. Catawba kinship and social organization, with a résumé of Tutelo kinship terms. Pt. 1. Amer. Anthrop., n. s., vol. 44, pp. 555–575.

SPELMAN, HENRY. *See* SMITH, JOHN, WORKS, ARBER ED., 1884.

SPENCER, REV. JOAB

1908. The Shawnee Indians: their customs, traditions and folklore. Trans.
  Kans. State Hist. Soc., vol. 10, pp. 382–402.

SPIER, LESLIE

1924. Wichita and Caddo relationship terms. Amer. Anthrop., n. s., vol.
  26, No. 2, pp. 258–263.

1925. The distribution of kinship systems in North America. Univ. Washington Publ. Anthrop., vol. 1, No. 2, pp. 69–88. Seattle, Wash.

SPINDEN, HERBERT J.

1928. The population of ancient America. Geogr. Rev., vol. 18, No. 4, pp
  641–660.

STECK, FRANCIS BORGIA.

1928. The Jolliet-Marquette expedition, 1673. Glendale, Calif.

STIGGINS, GEORGE

A historical narration of the genealogy, traditions and downfall of the
  Ispocoga or Creek tribe of Indians writ by one of the tribe. (Ms. in
  possession of the Wisconsin Hist. Soc.)

STRACHEY, WILLIAM

1849. The historie of travaile into Virginia Britannia, expressing the cos-
  mographie and commodities of the country, together with the manners and customs of the people. Hakluyt Soc. Publ., vol. 6. London.

SURGÈRES, M. LE CHEVALIER DE, JOURNAL DE LA FRÉGATE LE MARIN.

In MARGRY, PIERRE, 1880, VOL. 4, PP. 211–289.

SWAN, CALEB

1855. Position and state of manners and arts in the Creek, or Muscogee
  nation in 1791. *In* Schoolcraft, Indian Tribes, vol. 5, pp. 251–283.
  Philadelphia.

SWANTON, JOHN R.

1911. Indian tribes of the lower Mississippi Valley and adjacent coast of
  the Gulf of Mexico. Bur. Amer. Ethnol. Bull. 43.

1917. Unclassified languages of the southeast. Int. Journ. Amer. Ling., vol.
  1, No. 1, pp. 47–49.

1918. An early account of the Choctaw Indians. Mem. Amer. Anthrop.
  Assoc., vol. 5, No. 2.

1919. A structural and lexical comparison of the Tunica, Chitimacha, and
  Atakapa languages. Bur. Amer. Ethnol. Bull. 68.

1922. Early history of the Creek Indians and their neighbors. Bur. Amer.
  Ethnol. Bull. 73.

1923. New light on the early history of the Siouan peoples. Journ. Washington Acad. Sci., vol. 13, pp. 33–43.

1928. Social organization and social usages of the Indians of the Creek
  Confederacy. 42d Ann. Rep. Bur. Amer. Ethnol., 1924–1925, pp.
  23–472.

1928. a. Religious beliefs and medical practices of the Creek Indians. 42d
  Ann. Rep. Bur. Amer. Ethnol., 1924–1925, pp. 473–672.

1928 b. Aboriginal culture of the Southeast. 42d Ann. Rep. Bur. Amer.
  Ethnol., 1924–1925, pp. 673–726.

1928 c. Social and religious beliefs and usages of the Chickasaw Indians
  44th Ann. Rep. Bur. Amer. Ethnol., 1926–1927, pp. 169–273.

SWANTON, JOHN R.—Continued.

1929. The Tawasa language. Amer. Anthrop., n. s., vol. 31, pp. 435–453.

1929 a. Myths and tales of the Southeastern Indians. Bur. Amer. Ethnol. Bull. 88.

1930. The Kaskinampo Indians and their neighbors. Amer. Anthrop., n. s., vol. 32, No. 3, pp. 405–418.

1931. The Caddo social organization and its possible historical significance. Journ. Washington Acad. Sci., vol. 21, No. 9, pp. 203–206.

1931 a. Source material for the social and ceremonial life of the Choctaw Indians. Bur. Amer. Ethnol. Bull. 103.

1932. Choctaw moieties. A note in Amer. Anthrop., n. s., vol. 34, No. 2, p. 356.

1932 a. Ethnological value of the De Soto narratives. Amer. Anthrop., n. s., vol. 34, No. 4, pp. 570–590.

1934. Newly descovered Powhatan bird names. Journ. Washington Acad. Sci., vol. 24, No. 2, pp. 96–99.

1936. Early history of the Eastern Siouan tribes. In Essays in Anthropology presented to A. L. Kroeber. Univ. Calif. Press. Berkeley, Calif.

1942. Source material on the history and ethnology of the Caddo Indians. Bur. Amer. Ethnol. Bull. 132.

See also Byington, Cyrus; Dorsey, James Owen; and Gatschet, Albert S.

TAYLOR, LYDIA AVERILL

1940. Plants used as curatives by certain Southeastern tribes. Botanical Mus. Harvard Univ., Cambridge, Mass.

THOMAS, CYRUS

1891. Catalogue of prehistoric works east of the Rocky Mountains. Bur. Amer. Ethnol. Bull. 12.

THWAITES, REUBEN GOLD, EDITOR

1896–1901. Jesuit relations and allied documents. Travels and explorations of the Jesuit missionaries in New France, 1610–1791. 73 vols. Cleveland.

TIMBERLAKE, LIEUT. HENRY

1765. The memoirs of Lieut. Henry Timberlake (who accompanied the three Cherokee Indians to England in the year 1762) containing . . . an accurate map of their Over-hill settlement . . . London.

See also Williams, Samuel Cole, 1927 and 1928.

TOOKER, W. W.

1895. Algonquian appellatives of the Siouan tribes of Virginia. Amer. Anthrop., o. s., vol. 8, pp. 376–392.

1898. The problem of the Rechahecrian Indians of Virginia. Amer. Anthrop., o. s., vol. 11, No. 9, pp. 261–270.

TONTI, HENRI DE. See MARGRY, PIERRE, 1876, vol. 1, pp. 572–616; and COX, ISAAC JOSLIN, EDITOR, 1905, vol. 1, pp. 1–65.

TUCKER, SARA JONES

1942. Indian villages of the Illinois country, vol. 2, Scientific Papers, Illinois State Mus.; pt. 1, Atlas. Springfield, Ill.

TUOMEY, M.

1858. Second biennial Report on the Geology of Alabama.

TYLER, LYON GARDINER, EDITOR

1907. Narratives of Early Virginia, 1606–1625. In Original narratives of early American history. New York.

U. S. De Soto Expedition Commission
1939. Final report of the United States De Soto Expedition Commission. House Doc. No. 71, 76th Cong., 1st sess.

Verrazzano, Giovanni da
1810. The relation of Iohn de Verrazzano a Florentine, of the land by him discouered in the name of His Maiestie. Written in Diepe the eight of Iuly, 1524. *In* Hakluyt, Richard. Collection of voyages, vol. 3, 1810, pp. 357–364.
1850. Divers voyages touching the discovery of America and the islands adjacent. Collected and published by Richard Hakluyt . . . in the year 1582. Edited, with notes and an introduction, by John Winter Jones . . . London. Works issued by the Hakluyt Society [No. 7].

Voegelin, C. F.
1941. Internal relationships of Siouan languages. Amer. Anthrop., n. s., vol. 43, No. 2, pt. 1, pp. 246–249.
See also Kinietz, Vernon, and Voegelin, C. F., 1935.

Voegelin, C. F. and E. W.
1935. Shawnee name groups. Amer. Anthrop., n. s., vol. 37, pt. 4, pp. 615–635.

Voegelin, Erminie Wheeler
1940. The place of agriculture in the subsistence economy of the Shawnee. Pap. Mich. Acad. Sci., Arts, and Letters, vol. 26, pp. 513–520.

Wagner, Günter
1931. Yuchi tales. Publ. Amer. Ethnol. Soc., vol. 13. New York.

Walker, S. T.
1880. Preliminary explorations among the Indian mounds in Southern Florida. Ann. Rep. Smithsonian Inst., for 1879., pp. 392–413.

Walker, Winslow M.
1935. A Caddo burial site at Natchitoches, Louisiana. Smithsonian Misc. Coll., vol. 94, No. 14.

Washburn, Cephas
1869. Reminiscences of the Indians. Richmond.

Watson, J. R. *See* Shelford, Victor E.

Weer, Paul
1939. Preliminary notes of the Muskhogean family. Prehis. Res. Ser., Ind. Hist. Soc., vol. 1, No. 7, pp. 241–286.

Weltfish, Gene. *See* Lesser, Alexander.

Wenhold, Lucy L.
1936. A 17th century letter of Gabriel Diaz Vara Calderón, Bishop of Cuba, describing the Indians and Indian missions of Florida. Smithsonian Misc. Coll., vol. 95, No. 16.

Whitford, A. C.
1941. Textile fibers used in eastern aboriginal North America. Anthrop. Pap. Amer. Mus. Nat. Hist., vol. 38, pt. 1. New York.

Willey, Gordon R. *See* Ford, J. A.

Williams, Samuel Cole, Editor
1927. Lieut. Henry Timberlake's memoirs, 1756–1765; with annotations, introduction, and index. Johnson City, Tenn.
1928. Early travels in the Tennessee country, 1540–1800; with introductions, annotations, and index. Johnson City, Tenn. *See* Adair, James.

Willson, Minnie Moore
1896. The Seminoles of Florida. Philadelphia. (2d ed. New York, 1910.)

Wilson, Samuel. *See* Carroll, B. R.

WINSOR, JUSTIN,, EDITOR
    1884–1889. Narrative and critical history of America. 8 vols. Boston and
        New York.
WOODWARD, THOMAS SIMPSON
    1859. Woodward's reminiscences of the Creek or Muscogee Indians, con-
        tained in letters to friends in Georgia and Alabama. Montgomery,
        Ala. Reprint 1939, Montgomery, Ala.
WYMAN, LENTHALL. *See* SHELFORD, VICTOR E.
YOUNG, CAPT. HUGH, MEMOIR. *See* BOYD, MARK F., 1934.

Abaioa, Indian town, 35.
Abbeville, Fla., 44.
Aberdeen, near Morgan's Ferry, 51.
Abihka, 81, 124, 153, 160, 184, 186, 216, 652, 823.
    country, Shawnee supposed to have settled in, 185.
        Tulsa Old Town in, 125.
    name, interpretation of, 216.
    population, 82.
    principal division of Upper Creeks, 81.
    sketch of, 81–82.
    Square Ground, near Eufaula, Okla., 81.
"Abihka-in-the-West," Abihka Square Ground, near Henryetta, Okla., 81.
Abihkutci, Abihka town, 82.
    branch of Coosa, 125.
    "Little Abihka," Abihka town, 81.
Abino, town, 193.
Abyache, 140.
Accohanoc, 175.
Accomack, implements for hunting and fishing, 582.
    weapons, 582.
Acer rubrum, use of, 606, 609.
Achese, town on Flint River, visited by De Soto, 127.
Achuse, port of, 50.
    province of, 42.
Ackia, Bienville troops defeated by Chickasaw before, 117.
Acolapissa, 29, 73, 82, 95, 99, 117, 130, 139, 140, 158, 161, 190, 195, 216, 829.
    attack on Natchitoches, 99.
    Chickasaw attack on, 77.
    fishing, 340.
    houses, 419.
    images, 619.
    name, interpretation of, 216.
    population, 83.
    shaving, 498.
    sketch of, 82–83.
    source material on, 829.
    tattooing, 536.
    temple, 613, 619, 780.
        door of, 429
        reference to sketch of by De Batz, 82
Acosta, *see* Koasati.
Acoste, *see* Koasati.
Acuera, 83, 164, 193.
    population, 83.
    sketch of, 83.
    Timucua tribe, 83.
    town of, identification with Ocale by Garcilaso, 83.

Adaes, settlement of Spaniards at, 156
Adai, Caddo tribe, 83, 98.
    population, 84.
    sketch of, 83–84.
    Spanish mission founded among, in Louisiana, 75.
    visited by De Leon Expedition, 74, 98.
    Zacatecan mission to, 75.
Adair, James, 114, 119, 121, 124, 129, 193, 250, 280, 297, 298, 305, 325, 328, 427, 428, 440, 448, 457, 716, 723, 724, 725, 777, 828, 831.
    on agricultural methods 304, 309, 310.
    on artistic development 613, 616, 617.
    on bags and purses 480.
    on bracelets, 522.
    on Cherokee pipes, 542, 546.
    on Chickasaw hunting, 265, 317, 323, 324, 330, 331.
    on chunkey stones, 547.
    on clothing, 461, 463, 464, 469, 470, 473, 524.
        worn by medicine men, 478, 479.
    on communication, means of, 733.
    on cooking, 354, 355, 356, 358, 359, 360, 362, 365, 367, 368, 372.
    on dependence of Indians on European goods, 544.
    on doors, 429.
    on ear ornaments, 513.
    on featherwork, 455.
    on finger rings, 522.
    on fire making, 423, 424.
    on fishing, 335, 336, 337, 338, 339, 341.
    on flint, use of, 544.
    on food of Chickasaw, 289, 290.
    on food preserving, 373, 374, 376.
    on games, 678, 682, 683.
    on greasing and coloring of hair and skin, 528.
    on hair dressing, 498, 500, 501, 504, 506.
    on head bands, 508, 510.
    on head deformation, 538.
    on household utensils, 555, 556, 559, 561, 562, 563, 564.
    on houses, 387, 388, 389, 420, 421.
    on implements for hunting and fishing, 573, 578, 579, 582, 583.
    on marriage, 705, 706.
    on mats and baskets, 604.
    on mnemonic devices, 611, 612.

Adair, James, on moral characteristics of Choctaw, 231, 232.
  on musical instruments, 625, 627.
  on names, 673.
  on needles and sewing, 454.
  on nose ornaments, 515.
  on number of Indian fugitives from Florida, 85, 192.
  on origin of Indians about Fort Toulouse, 22.
  on physical characteristics of Cherokee, 224, 229.
  on pottery, 553.
  on religious customs, 694.
  on salt substitutes, 303.
  on social organization, 653.
  on Southeastern Indians, 262.
  on tattooing, 534.
  on thread and textiles, 449, 451, 452, 453.
  on time, divisions of, 262.
  on tobacco, 384.
  on transportation, 594, 596, 597, 601.
  on wampum, 484.
  on war customs, 692, 694, 696, 697, 698.
  on weapons, 573, 578, 579, 583.
  reference by to towns of "Koo-a-sah-te," 27.
  "thirty men" of, 192.
Adshusheer, Eno village found by Lawson, on Eno River, N. C., 131, 183, 627, 753.
Adventure, English ship from which Capt. William Hilton visited Cusabo, 128.
Aesculus pavia, uses of, 247.
Africa, climatic province in, analogous to Southeastern United States, 7.
  natives of, 824, 825.
  southeast, relation to cultural area, 826.
Agile, Timucua town, 41.
Agricultural pursuits, 256.
Aguacaleyquen, Timucua, town visited by De Soto, 41, 202, 628.
  Indians of, *see* Utina.
Aguacay, province where salt was found by De Soto, 738.
"Agua dulce," *see* Fresh Water Indians.
Aguaquiri, town mentioned by Pardo, identification with Guaquili, 46, 67.
Aguayo, Marquis de, 156, 158, 162.
  raft constructed for, by Hasinai, 597.
Ahone, good diety of the Powhatans, 744.
Ahoya, classification of tribe, 67.
Ahoyabe, identification of, 67.
"Aia Chin," name of Guale mission, 136.
Ais, 84, 134, 141.
  country, Menendez, march to, 134.
  member of Muskhogean linguistic family, 239.
  musical instruments, 625.

Ais, population, 85.
  religious beliefs and usages of, 763.
  sketch of, 84–85.
  social customs, 649.
  tribe on Indian River, Fla., 84.
  See also Eyish.
Ajoica, 168.
Akawentcaka, band of Tuscarora, 199.
Akokisa, 85, 130, 172, 216.
  associated with Deadose and Patiri in mission of San Ildefonso, 96.
  Bidai allied with, according to Belle Isle, 96.
  name given by Spaniards to Atakapa Indians in Texas, 85, 93.
    interpretation of in Atakapa language, 216.
  population, 85.
  sketch of, 85–86.
  Spanish mission established among, 75.
  See also Arkokisa.
Akoroa, name used by Marquette for Koroa, 147.
Alabama, 22, 27, 28, 86, 97, 146, 152, 166, 170, 171, 189, 191, 196, 339, 343, 345, 808, 810, 827, 828.
  body paint, 529, 530.
  burial customs, 724.
  clans and gentes, 657.
  clothing, 470, 473.
  conspicuous part taken in Creek War by, 191.
  cooking, 369.
  divided and part moved to Louisiana, 191.
  domestic animals, 345.
  doors, construction, 429.
  ear ornaments, 513, 514.
  few descended from Biloxi, 97.
  finger rings, 522.
  fire making, 427.
  flint, use of, 543, 544.
  games, 678, 686.
  group, migration of, 27–28.
  hair dressing, 500, 506.
  head band, 510.
  household utensils, 567, 560.
  houses, modern, 395.
  hunting migrations, 263.
  implements for hunting and fishing, 575, 579, 583, 586.
  mats and baskets, 606.
  metals, use of 495, 496.
  migration legends, western origin indicated by, 22.
  migrations, 32.
  musical instruments, 624.
  name, interpretation of, in Alabama language, 216.
  necklaces, 517, 518, 520.
  nose ornaments, 515.
  population, 88.
  pottery, 551.
  probably affiliated with Muklasa, 152.
  religious customs, 695.

Alabama, sketch of, 86–88.
  smoke-holes and windows, 427.
  source material on, 828.
  Square Ground, 776.
    use of flags at, 431.
  united with Koasati in Texas, 145,
    146.
  weapons, 575, 579, 583, 586.
  woman, origin legend obtained from
    by Swanton, 23.
Alabama River, 31, 39, 49, 60, 87, 96.
  at Durand's Bend, Dallas County,
    site of "Talisi province" en-
    countered by De Soto, 125.
  junction of Tombigbee River and,
    Mobile and Tohome located
    below, 151.
  site of Mobile town called Atha-
    hachi, home of chief Tascalusa,
    150.
  stockaded towns located on, 433,
    434.
  Tawasa established near Fort Tou-
    louse, on upper, 191.
Alabama, State of, 1, 13, 14, 29, 48, 80.
Alachua, description of capital of
  (Cuscowilla), 396.
Alachua County, Fla., home of Potano,
  when visited by De Soto. 41, 173.
Alachua plains, Fla., home of Oconee
  when visited by Bartram, 165.
Alachua prairie, Fla., Oconee established
  on, 181.
Alafia River, crossed by De Soto, 41.
Albany, treaty made by northern and
  southern Indians at, 178.
  treaty with Iroquois, made by
    Powhatans at, 175.
Albemarle Sound, N. C., 76.
  home of Keyauwee, 145.
  home of Weapemeoc, 18, 206.
  Machapunga located between Pam-
    lico and, 148.
Algonquian origin stories, linguistic support of, 31.
Algonquian Shawnee, cultural level of,
  10.
Algonquian stock, 10, 27, 799, 800, 803,
  806, 808, 809, 810, 812, 820, 821.
  population, 12.
  (See table 1, facing p. 10.)
  tribe, 137, 242, 493.
  tribes of North Carolina, absence
    of origin traditions from, 24.
Algonquians, 15, 32, 163, 170, 238, 242,
  257, 296, 463, 662, 665, 743, 801, 802,
  813, 814, 831.
  activities, 259.
  altars, 549, 814.
  beds, 422.
  burial customs, 719, 810, 814.
  clans and gentes, 655, 656, 657, 814.
  clothing, 457, 814.
  communication, means of, 735.
  crime and punishment, 730, 814.
  eating habits, 257.
  fire making, 422.
  games, 674, 685, 814.

Algonquians, hair dressing, 501, 814.
  of priests, 501, 808, 814.
  head bands, 508.
  head deformation not practiced by,
    541, 814.
  household utensils, 556, 814.
  huskanaw practiced by, 712, 815.
  implements for hunting and fish-
    ing, 567.
  marriage customs, 701, 703, 815.
  migrations, 32.
  pottery, 554, 814.
  religious beliefs and usages, 745,
    814.
  smoke-holes and windows, 427.
  social organization, 641, 814.
  source material on, 831.
  war customs, 687.
  weapons, 567.
  wigwams, 413, 416, 420.
"Alibamons," 146.
Alibamo tribe, 52, 53.
  fort of, 52, 53.
  See also Alabama.
Alleghanian Faunal Area, 19.
Allegheny, Pierre Chartier settled at,
  184, 185.
Allen Parish, La., 145, 146.
Alligator, noted chief, ancestry of, 64.
Alligator Creek, 43.
Alligator Mounds, La., 54.
Allston, Washington, artist, 154.
Alonzo, sole survivor of first white
  settlement in Virginia, 70, 71.
Alosa alabama, use as food, 266.
Alosa alosa, 266.
Alosa finta, 266.
"Altamaca," see Altamaha.
Altamaha, division of Yamasee, 189,
  208, 209.
  encountered by De Soto, 43.
  location, 44.
  province visited by De Soto, 208.
Altamaha River, 125, 132, 269.
  See also Talaxe.
"Altapaha," see Altamaha.
Aluete, Cusabo chief, flight of "vassals"
  of, to St. Simons Island, 128.
Alvord, Clarence W., and Bidgood, Lee,
  302, 303, 325, 347, 351, 682.
  on beards, 498.
  on body paint, 530.
  on bracelets, 521.
  on canes of corn, use of, 368.
  on communication, means of, 735.
  on food preserving, 380.
  on forts, 437.
  on hair dressing, 499, 503.
  on houses, 411, 413.
  on implements for hunting and
    fishing, 588.
  on mnemonic devices, 610.
  on social organization, 647.
  on towns, 636.
  on trade, 739, 740.
  on transportation, 594, 596,
  on wampum, 484.
  on weapons, 588.

Amacano, 88, 119.
  possibly Yamasee, 208.
  sketch of, 88.
Amacapiras, see Macapiras.
Amacarisse mission, 209, 210.
Amadas, Philip, 75.
Amadas and Barlowe, entertained by wife of Granganimeo, 742.
Amaye, province of, 57.
Amelanchier canadensis, use of, 279.
Amelia Island, probable site of Santa Maria mission, 209.
"Amercario," town on Savannah River, 209.
American rule, hostilities between Choctaw and Creeks ended by, 122.
Aminoya, Indian village, 58, 188, 434, 651.
Amonate, see Pocahontas.
Anacape, Fla., 133.
Anadarko, 89, 99, 158.
  chief of, 599.
  identification with Nondacao, 57.
  population, 89.
  sketch of, 89.
  See also Caddo.
Añasco, Juan de, 40, 42, 44, 45, 52.
"Andasses or Iroquois," mentioned in French document, 163.
Andrada, Captain of Spanish troops cut off by Potano, 174.
Angelico (*Ligusticum actaeifolium*), use of, 271, 276, 526.
Angelina County, Tex., later home of Biloxi, 97.
Angelina River, Tex., 89.
  Cherokee members of Bowl's band settled along, 113.
  settlement of Nacogdoche on, 89, 156.
Anghierra, Perter Martyr de, 36, 346, 409, 647, 722, 811, 830.
  on artistic development, 615, 616.
  on head deformation, 539, 540.
  on methods used to increase size of chiefs, 540.
  on religious beliefs and usages, 754, 755, 758, 759, 760, 761.
  on social organization, 647, 648.
  on threads and textiles, 450.
Anglo-Saxons, history of relations of with Indians, 75–81.
Anilco, battle of, with De Soto army, 56.
Anilco, province of, 55, 56.
Anilco, town, 58, 434, 651.
Anilco River, Ark., 53.
Animal kingdom, uses of, 249–253.
Animals, domestication of, 344–351.
Animal symbolism for places or qualities, 735.
Annual economic cycle, 255–265.
Antiquity of man in Gulf region as based on archeology, 33.
Antoine Creek, Ark., 55.
Antonico, Fla., 133.

Apache, 130.
  Nabedache and Bidai, expedition against, 96.
  Nabedache expedition against, 86.
Apafalaya, name used by Ranjel for Choctaw, 121.
Apafalaya, province of, 51.
Apafalaya River, 51.
Apalachee, 11, 13, 16, 19, 20, 28, 29, 34, 37, 38, 55, 73, 77, 89, 119, 143, 165, 168, 170, 188, 189, 191, 194, 210, 213, 216, 348, 801, 802, 828.
  arrow points, materials used for, 34.
  attack on Yuchi by, 213.
  broken up by English and Creek expedition, 63.
  country, 88, 127, 150, 195, 208, 210, 333.
  destruction of, 194.
  encountered by De Soto, 41, 42.
  forts or stockades, 433, 434.
  implements for hunting and fishing, 580, 581.
  members of Muskhogean linguistic family, 238.
  migrations 15, 32, 63.
  missionary work begun among, 62.
  moved with Taensa to Bayou Boeuf, La., 188.
  name, interpretation of, 216.
  population, 91.
  province of, 89.
  revolt, 1647, results of, 90.
  sketch of, 89–91.
  social organization, 654.
  source material on, 828.
  Spanish post at town of, 62.
  towns of, 56, 633.
  transportation, means of, 598.
  weapons, 580, 581.
Apalachee Bay, Fla., 5.
"Apalache ó Sachile," name used on Spanish map, 169.
Apalachicola, 26, 28, 77, 107, 116, 138, 165, 181, 210, 213, 216.
  movements of due to tribal war, 63.
  name, interpretation of in Muskhogean dialects, 216.
  population, 92.
  sketch of, 91–92.
Apalachicola Fort, 92.
Apalachicola Nation, towns constituting, 92.
Apalachicola River, 13, 19, 29, 32, 89, 92, 107, 125, 169, 179, 180, 189, 190.
  site of Tamathli town, 189.
Apalachicola village, establishment of stockade in, by Spaniards, 1689, 63.
Apalachocoli, 194.
Apalo, Timucua word for "fort," 174, 433.
Apica, see Abihka.
Apios tuberosa, use as food, 270, 286, 292, 296, 362.
Apocynum cannabinum, uses of, 247.
Appalachian highlands, southern, 14.
Appalachian Mountains, 5, 12, 20, 46.

Appalachian Plateau, 4, 14.
Appalachian region, occupied by Cherokee, 800, 802.
  extent of Yuchi remaining in, 215.
  possible source of stone for Florida Indians' arrow points, 541.
Appalachian Valley, 4, 14, 68.
Appamatuke, land subject to Powhatan, 643.
Appomattox River, pearl fishery located at mouth of, 489.
Aquixo, branch of the Tunica encountered by De Soto, 52, 54.
  location, 54.
  province of, 53.
  stockaded towns in, 433.
Aracuchi, a town of Cataba-speaking Siouans, 67.
Aranama, 256.
  Spanish Mission established among, 75.
Aransas Pass, 59.
Arawakan invasion, reference to, 33.
"Archichepa," name used by Calderón, 144.
Archi-magus, name used by Adair for Chickasaw medicine men, 478.
Argentina, 7.
Arikara, Dakota tribe, 241.
  chunkey game played by, 548.
Arkadelphia, Ark., 55.
  home of Cahinnio, 100.
Arkansas, State of, 1, 2, 13, 24, 25, 27, 32, 74.
  first Christian ceremony conducted in, 52.
Arkansas Indians, flint obtained from, 542.
  houses, 416, 417.
  See also Quapaw.
Arkansas Post, Quapaw reported on Arkansas River above, 176.
Arkansas River, 13, 29, 31, 53, 71, 72.
  Natchez band settled near Abihka on, 160.
  Osochi settled near city of Muskogee on north side of, 169.
  Quapaw town located on, 176, 800.
  site of Uzitiuhi, Quapaw village, 166, 800.
Arkansas Valley, 4.
Arkokisa, 240.
  See also Akokisa.
Armor, 588–589.
Army, De Soto's, description of, 40.
Arratobo, town subject to San Juan del Puerto, 179.
Arrohateck, land subject to Powhatan, 643.
Arrow points, Avoyel connection with, 94.
Arroyo San Pedro, site of Nabedache village, 154.
Arthur, Gabriel, 77, 152, 206, 208, 213, 325, 347, 504.
  accompanied Yuchi against Spaniards, 213.

Arthur, Gabriel, on towns, 636.
  on transportation, means of, 594.
  only white to visit Moneton, 152.
  taken on hunting expedition by the Indians, 351, 596.
Artistic development, 613–624.
Arundinaria macrosperma, use of, 585.
Asao, (St. Simons Island) chief of, 617.
  games played at, 683.
  greetings to chief of by Indians, 723.
Asaquah, Indian chief, 163.
Ascension Parish, La., home of Houma, 139.
Asclepias pulchra, uses of, 247.
Asclepias syriaca, uses of, 247.
Asclepias tuberosa, uses of, 247.
Ashley Barony, name of land ceded by Coosa, 129.
Ashley River, Coosa tribe located on upper course of, 124, 128.
Asia, climatic province in, analogous to Southeastern United States, 7.
Asia, eastern, relation to cultural area, 826.
Asiatic culture, effect on other cultural areas, 827.
Asilanabi, branch of Okchai, 167, 173.
Asile, town of the Yustaga, 216.
Asimina triloba, uses of, 248.
"Asumpción del Puerto," mission founded by Bishop Calderón, 208.
  renamed San Luis, 209.
Atakapa, 11, 17, 30, 85, 120, 140, 169, 198, 216, 240, 737, 801, 802, 820, 830.
  flint obtained by, 542.
  flood story of, 23.
  located in Texas, called Akokisa by the Spaniards, 85.
  migrations, 32.
  name, interpretation of, in Choctaw, 216.
  names used by, 674.
  population, 94.
  religious beliefs and usages, 781, 782.
  sketch of, 93–94.
  trade, 737.
Atakapan group, 172.
Atakullakulla, "Little Carpenter," Cherokee chief, 229.
Atasi, 153.
  artistic development, 616.
  Muskogee town of, 94, 139, 147, 197.
  population, 94.
Atcik-hata, see Hitchiti, 138, 217.
Atcina Hatchee (Cedar Creek), 144.
Atcina-ulga, perhaps branch of Coosa, 125.
Athahachi, Mobile town, 49.
  visited by Spaniards, 150.
Atlantic coast, sea salt from, used by Southeastern Indians, 243.
Atlatls, attack on Spanish by Indians using, 59.
  Indian name for throwing stick, 584.

Atoka, Okla., later home of Biloxi, 97.

Atriplex hastata, halberd-leaved orache, 270, 306.

Attacapan linguistic family, 240.
   name of Atakapa applied to by French, 93.

Attacapan stock, 240.

Attoyac River, Eyeish living on, 132.
   settlement of Nacogdoche on, 156.

Aucilla, *see* Agile.

Aucilla River, Fla., 41, 89.
   Mission of San Francisco de Oconi located west of, 165.

Augusta, Ga., 12, 13, 26, 30, 45, 65, 73, 137, 153.
   near site of Cofitachequi, 137.

Augustin, Domingo, Jesuit missionary, 135.

Auke Thome, *see* Catoma Creek.

Aulédly, Apalachicola town, 92.

Australia, aborigines of, compared with Indians, 824, 825.
   climatic province in, analogous to Southeastern United States, 7.
   southeast, relation to cultural area, 826.

Australians, effect of environment on culture of, 827.

Austroriparian Faunal Area, Indian tribes occupying, 20.

Autauga, Tawasa Town, 87, 88.

Aute, Indian town in Autauga Co., Ala., 37, 191.

"Aux Alibamons," *see* Fort Toulouse.

Ávila, Pedro Árias de, governor of Panama and father-in-law of Hernando de Soto, 39, 40.

Aviles, Menendez de, *see* Menendez de Áviles.

Avoyel, 13, 19, 737.
   early occupants of Marksville Prairie, Red River, 198, 655.
   members of Muskhogean linguistic family, 239.
   name, interpretation of in Natchez language, 216.
   population, 94.
   quarries located in country of, 542.
   sketch of, 94–95.
   traders of flint, 543.
   traditional offshoot of Natchez, 23.

Awnings, sunshades, and flags, 430–432.

Axacan, meaning and pronunciation of word, 71.
   province of, 70, 71.

Axacan Bay, *see* Santa Maria de Axacan Bay.

Axes, 544–545.

Ayala, Torres de, expedition of, 326.

Ayanabe, French supported by, 121.

Ayaocuto, chief of, led rebellion against whites, 202.

Ayaocuto, town rebuilt by Capt. Juan Fernandez de Florencia, 202.

Ayays, point at which De Soto crossed the Ouachita, 55, 58.

Ayish Creek, named after Eyeish, 132.

Ayllon colony, on South Carolina coast, 135.

Ayllon documents, reference to, 66, 67.

Ayllon, Lucas Vasquez de, 36, 37, 45.
   horses brought by, 346.
   on head deformation 539, 540.

Ayllon settlement, near Cusabo, 128.

Aymay, *see* Hymahi.
   See also Guiomaez.

Ayo-Caddi-Aymay, name of Caddo chief god, 782.

Ayubale, 165.

Bacciferous sp., use of, 288, 289.

Bacon, Nathaniel, 164, 175.
   Occaneechi attacked and defeated by, 164.
   Powhatans attacked and massacred by, 175.

Bags and purses, 479–480.

Bahama Channel, 71.

Bahama Islands, 33.
   raided for slaves, 101.

Baker County, Ga., 43.

Balboa, Vasco Nuñez de, 35.

Ballast Point, near Tampa, Fla., stone obtained from, 541.

Bantu, tribe living in Africa, 825, 826.

Barbadoes, colonists from, 103.

Barcia Carballido y Zuñiga, Andres G., 90.

Barlowe, Arthur, 75, 437, 472, 662, 742, 813.
   on artistic development, 614.
   on ear ornaments, 510.
   on hair dressing, 498, 501.
   on head bands, 509.
   on household utensils, 556.
   on implements for hunting and fishing, 567, 572.
   on pottery, 554.
   on social organization, 646.
   on transportation, means of, 592, 594, 595.
   on war customs, 687.
   on weapons, 567, 572.

Barnard, Timothy, father of Timpoochee Barnard, 214.

Barnard, Timpoochee, chief of Yuchi, 154, 214.
   aided whites in Creek War, 214.

Barnwell, Col. John, 66, 129, 183, 186, 199, 207, 209.
   joined by Cusabo in Tuscarora expedition, 129.
   joined by Sewee in Tuscarora expedition, 183.
   joined by Winyaw in Tuscarora expedition, 207.
   joined by Yamasee in Tuscarora expedition, 209.
   leader of colonists in first campaign against Tuscarora, 199.
   on forts, 438.
   on identity of Sissipahaw, 183.
   on towns, 631.

Barra of San Pedro, Spanish mission established near, 187.

Barreda, Fray Rodrigo de la, driven from mission by Chatot, 107.
Barricade, erected by Indians, against Spaniards, 86.
Barroto, Enríquez, Pensacola visited by expedition under, 172.
Barton, B. S., 286.
Bartram, William, 138, 147, 154, 165, 182, 215, 271, 297, 298, 303, 320, 326, 345, 422, 428, 431, 738, 769, 807, 828, 830, 831.
    Alabama Indians found on Mississippi by, 87.
    description of Council house of Creeks, 379, 392, 393 (fig.).
    description of Seminole town of Cuscowilla, 396.
    on artistic development, 616.
    on beads, 485.
    on bracelets, 522.
    on clothing, 457, 458, 461, 463, 464, 470, 472, 473, 474, 475.
        worn by medicine men, 478.
    on cooking, 361, 366, 370.
    on ear ornaments, 512, 513.
    on featherwork, 455.
    on fishing, 338, 582.
    on food preserving, 379.
    on food used by Cherokee, 284, 286, 287.
    on games, 676, 677, 678, 683.
    on greasing and coloring of hair and skin, 527, 528, 530.
    on hair dressing, 499.
    on head bands, 509.
    on head deformation, 539.
    on horses of Florida Indians, 348.
    on household utensils, 561.
    on houses of Creeks, 390, 394, 402, 403, 404 (fig.).
    on implements for hunting and fishing, 575, 582.
    on marriage customs, 704.
    on mats and baskets, 606.
    on metal mines at Chisca, 490.
    on moral characteristics of Cherokee, and Muscogulges, 231.
    on movements of Apalachicola, 92.
    on musical instruments, 625, 627, 629.
    on necklaces, 518, 520.
    on ornamentation, 490.
    on physical characteristics of Cherokee, Creeks, Muscogulges, Seminole, Chickasaw, Choctaw, 223, 224.
    on pottery, 551.
    on religious beliefs and usages, 774.
    on tattooing, 533.
    on towns, 634, 635, 636.
    on transportation, means of 594, 597, 598.
Bassett, John Spencer, ed. Wm. Byrd's notes, 276, 305, 325, 346.
    on clothing, 470.
    on cooking, 371.
    on fire making, 423.

Bassett, John Spencer, on fishing, 336.
    on fort built by Indians, 439.
    on hair dressing, 499, 505.
    on household utensils, 556.
    on hunting habits, 319, 332.
    on implements for hunting and fishing, 573.
    on musical instruments, 625.
    on necklaces, 517.
    on religious beliefs and usages, 749–751, 752.
    on skin dressing, 444.
    on thread and textiles, 449, 452.
    on trade among the Indians, 741, 742.
    on weapons, 573.
    on woodcraft, 311.
Fatodendron arboretum, use of, 279.
Battle of Horseshoe Bend, final battle of Creek War, 112, 114.
Battle of Mabila, between De Soto army and Indians of Tascalusa, 50, 150.
Battle of the Two Lakes, 41, 42.
Batts, Thomas, 76, 152, 157, 178, 200, 302.
    visit to Saponi on Otter River, 178.
Batz, A. de, reference to sketch of Louisiana Indians by, 94.
Bay of Achuse (Pensacola), soldiers under Tristan de Luna, sent to Nanipacana, from, 151.
"Bay of Chuse," early Spanish name for Mobile Bay or Pensacola, 47.
Bayogoula, 73, 139, 140, 177, 188, 195, 216, 327, 808, 829.
    amalgamation of with Acolapissa and Houma, 82.
    attacked and almost destroyed by Taensa, 188.
    attacked and almost destroyed Mugulasha, 177, 195.
    bracelets, 522.
    burial customs, 729, 811.
    clothing, 462, 472, 473, 476.
    ear ornaments, 514.
    fort built of canes, 439.
    hair dressing, 501, 507.
    houses, 419.
    images of animal figures in temple, 618.
    name, interpretation of, in Choctaw or Chickasaw, 216.
    nose ornaments, 515.
    population, 83, 95.
    site, long occupancy of, 29.
    sketch of, 95.
    smoke holes and windows, 427.
    source material on, 829.
    temple architecture, 430, 618.
    towns, 638, 639.
Bayou Boeuf, La., 97.
    Choctaw settled near Biloxi and Pascagoula on, 196.
    site of Chatot settlement, 108, 171.
    Taensa moved with Apalachee to, 188.

Bayou Castine, La., 82.

Bayou d'Arro, La., 91, 188.

Bayou de la Coeur, Pascagoula territory located between Bayou Philippe and, 171.

Bayou Goula, La., 95.
below Baton Rouge, visited by Iberville, 327.

Bayou Jean de Jean, La., 91, 188.

Bayou Lafourche, La., 30.
home of Chitimacha, 119, 120.
home of Houma, 140.
site of Chawasha village, 108.
site of Washa tribe, 204.
Taensa granted permission to settle on Mississippi at entrance of, 188.

Bayou La Teche, La., home of Chitimacha, 119, 120.

Bayou Philippe, Pascagoula territory located between Bayou de la Coeur and, 171.

Bayou Rapides, 87, 97.

Bayou St. Jean, near New Orleans, home of Houma, 139.

Bayou Sara, 191.

Bayou Teche, La, 30, 93.

Bayou Treache, on Red River, assigned to Quapaw, 176.

Bazares, Guido de, 59.

Beads, use of by Indians, 481–488, 517, 518, 523.

Beans, hyacinth (*Dolichos* sp.), use of as food, 285, 286, 288.

Beans, kidney (*Phaseolus* sp.), use of, 288.

Beans, use of, 269.

Bear, hunting of, 321–324.

Bear, uses of, 249, 277, 295, 297, 439, 440, 449, 527.

Bear Creek, 96.
site of defeat of Shawnee by Chickasaw, 185.

Bear Fort, a town of the Alabama, 87.

Bear River Indians, 148.

Beards, worn by some Indians, 498.
and mustaches, worn by Keyauwee males, 144, 498.

Beaufort, S. C., 45, 61.
location of earliest Huguenot colony, 128.

Beaurain, Le Sieur, 130, 162.

Bedias Creek, Tex., 96.

Beds, description of, 422.

Belknap, Jeremy, member of committee of Scots Society for Propagating Christian Knowledge, 236.
on moral characteristics of Oneida and Mahican Indians, 236.

Bellefonte Island, 48.

Belle Isle, Bidai mentioned in narrative of, 96.
estimate of Akokisa population by, 86.

Belts, ornamentation on, 523–525, 611, 612.

Benjamin Paul, Chitimacha chief, information on Chitimacha supplied by, 121.

Bennetts Creek, N. C., site of Chowanoc reservation, 124.

Benoist, Chicksaw defeat of force under, 118.

Benton, Ark., 54.

Beranger, Jean, Akokisa vocabulary recorded by, 85, 94.

Berkeley, 175, 336.

Beverley, Robert, 277, 304, 235, 328, 423, 427, 428, 432, 462, 709, 813, 831.
on agricultural habits, 307.
on altars, of, 549.
on artistic development, 614, 615.
on axes, 545.
on bags and purses, 479.
on bracelets and arm bands, 521.
on clothing, 459, 460, 463, 464, 473, 475, 525.
worn by medicine men, 478.
on coloring of manufactured articles, 609.
on cooking, 351, 352, 353, 356, 360, 364, 367, 368, 370.
on corn, 274.
on divisions of time by Indians of Virginia, 257.
on ear ornaments, 511.
on fire making, 426.
on fishing, 333, 334.
on foods, 275, 276.
on forts, 438.
on games, 685.
on greasing and coloring of hair and skin, 526, 527, 529, 530.
on hair dressing, 502.
on head bands, 509.
on household utensils, 556, 562.
on houses, 415.
on hunting, 317, 318.
on implements for hunting and fishing, 564, 573, 577, 582.
on mats and baskets, 603.
on medical practices, 784, 785.
on mnemonic devices, 610.
on money or wampum, 482.
on musical instruments, 625, 627.
on necklaces, 516, 517, 519.
on ornaments, 481, 482.
on quarries, 542.
on religious beliefs and usages, 744, 745, 746, 747, 748.
on salt substitutes, 276, 303.
on social organization, 645, 646.
on stone, use of, 543.
on tobacco, 383.
on transportation, means of, 592, 593, 595, 596.
on war customs, 687.
on weapons, 564, 573, 577, 582.

Bible, printed in syllabary invented by Sequoya, Cherokee chief, 113.

Bibliography, Southeastern tribes, 832–855.

Bidai, 58, 93, 130, 172, 216, 240, 820.
  Deadose separated from, 130.
  name, interpretation of, 216.
  one of the tribes served by the Mission of San Ildefonso, 86.
  population of, 96.
  possible merging of Akokisa with, 86.
  sketch of, 96.
Biedma, Luis Hernandez de, 132, 155, 216, 347, 367, 408, 430, 433, 435, 440.
  Alabama province named by, 86.
  "Black Water" province mentioned by, 25.
  on Casqui, 27.
  on Moscoso route, 57.
  on musical instruments, 624.
  on ornamentation, pearls, etc, 488.
  on pottery, 549.
  on report of stockaded fort, 52.
  on transportation, 593.
Bienville, Jean Baptiste Le Moyne, Sieur de, 13, 16, 72, 77, 85, 99, 103, 106, 107, 108, 109, 117, 118, 120, 130, 147, 151, 159, 162, 168, 169, 173, 176, 191, 204, 211.
  Acolapissa visited by, 82.
  alliance with Yatasi made by, 211.
  all nations along Mississippi induced to declare war against Chitimacha by, 120.
  Biloxi visited by, 96.
  Chawasha moved to Mississippi by, 109.
  estimate by of Apalachee losses in war with English, 90.
  of Avoyel population, 94.
  of Bayogoula population, 95.
  exploring party sent westward by, 93.
  fort in Mobile Bay constructed by, 151.
  Fort Toulouse established by, 87.
  joint attack on Chickasaw defeated under command of, 117.
  memoirs, 103, 106, 176.
  number of Acolapissa warriors according to, 83.
  peace with Chitimacha made by, 120.
  Pensacola reported on Pearl River by, 173.
  report on Adai population, 84.
  ship under Captain Bond, turned back by, 108.
  tribe of cannibals reached by, 93.
  uprising among Natchez put down by, 159.
  visit to Doustioni, 130.
    to Natchitoches, 99.
  Washita village visited by, 204.
Big Black River, 195.
Big Canoe Creek, Ala., site of town Tasqui, 200.
Big Cypress band, see Mikasuki, 150, 182.

Big Eufaula, Eufaula settlement on Tallapoosa River, 131.
Big Lake, Ark., Michigamea found by Marquette on, 149.
Big Sandy River, 200.
Big Sawokli, Sawokli town, 180.
Big Shoal, see Tcahki thlako.
Big Thicket, Tex., 96.
Big Tohome, band of Tohome tribe, 196.
Big Town, see Tálwa láko.
Big Tulsa, town opposite Tukabahchee, 125.
Big Uchee Creek, 26.
  Yuchi settled near mouth of, 214.
Billiout, Baptiste, member of Houma tribe, 140.
Biloxi, 31, 73, 80, 85, 95, 97, 98, 103, 104, 171, 196, 216, 241, 800, 822, 831.
  burial customs of, 727, 811.
  classified with Tutelo by Voegelin, 11.
  construction of fort of, 437.
  interpretation of name, 216.
  later settlement in Angelina County, Tex., 97.
  Pascagoula, and Caddo, emigration to Oklahoma, 97.
  Pascagoula and Moctobi, combined population, 98.
  population, 98.
  settlement in Texas, 97.
  Siouan tribe, 98.
  sketch of, 96–98.
  source material on, 831.
  terms of relationship, 669.
Biloxi Bay, Tex., 72, 96, 103, 151, 800.
Biloxi Bayou, named for Biloxi, 97, 171.
Birds, uses of, 251, 253, 441, 573, 574.
Birth, see Customs relating to birth, education, and the division of labor between the sexes.
Bishop of Cuba, see Calderón.
Bison, hunting of, 324–328.
  uses of, 249, 297, 326, 327, 439, 449.
Black lead, used by Southeastern Indians, 243.
"Blackmoors teeth," see Marginella sp., 485.
Black Pawnee, see Caddo, 229.
Black River, S. C., trading post established at, 207.
  Waccamaw moved south of, 203.
Black Warrior River, Ala., 14, 25, 50, 51, 60.
  site of settlement of Napochi tribe, 157.
"Black Water," meaning of Choctaw name Okelousa, 167.
Black Water Creek, Ala., 26.
Blande, Edward, 149, 157, 163, 164, 183, 199, 805, 815.
  discovered Nahyssan southeast of Petersburg, N. C., 157.
  Meherrin visited by party of, 149.
  Nottoway visited by, 163, 183.

Bloodroot (*Sanguinaria canadensis*), use of, 606.
Bloom, Leonard, 831.
Blount, *see* Blunt, Tom.
Blowguns, 585–586.
"Bluemouths," use of name for some Indians, 516.
Blue Ridge, 4, 14.
Blue Ridge Mts., Va., Moneton "old-fields," found west of, 152.
Bluff Culture, discovery of in Ozarks, 14, 33.
Blunt, Tom, chief of Tuscarora, 199.
Boas, Franz, 220, 832.
Boats, Spaniards build seven to descend Mississippi, 58.
Bobadilla, Isabel de, wife of De Soto, 40.
Bocootawwonaukes, Indian tribe who worked copper mines, 493.
Body paint, 528–532.
Boehmeria cylindrica, uses of, 247.
Bolivia, boundary of cultural area, 826.
Bollaert, 146.
Bolton, Herbert Eugene, 420, 640, 832.
    location of San Ildefonso Mission identified by, 96.
Bond, English Captain, 77.
    Chawasha and Washa attack on ship under, 108.
    expedition turned back at English Turn, under command of, 108.
Bonfouca, Choctaw town, 638.
Bossu, Jean Bernard, 680, 697, 705, 715, 828.
    on hair dressing, 500.
    on household utensils, 561, 563.
    on hunting migrations of Alabama Indians, 263.
    on implements for hunting and fishing, 585.
    on medical practices of Indians, 795.
    on weapons, 585.
"Bosten or Boatswain," Seminole Chief, house of, 396, 397 (fig.).
Botetourt County, Va., 23, 24.
Boukfouka, Choctaw town, 637.
Bouquet, Colonel, 119, 161.
Bourbons, progress of France under, 71.
Bourne, Edward Gaylord, 268, 281, 297, 299, 300, 302, 325, 333, 346, 347, 365, 367, 373, 374, 376, 378, 406, 408, 426, 430, 431, 433, 434, 439, 440, 442, 448, 451, 459, 462, 469, 485, 652.
    on coloring of manufactured articles, 608, 609.
    on hair dressing, 498.
    on head bands, 508.
    on household utensils, 560.
    on implements for hunting and fishing, 576, 580, 583, 587, 588.
    on musical instruments, 624, 628.
    on ornamentation, 488, 522.
    on pottery, 549.
    on Temple of Talomeco, 588, 602.
    on transportation, means of, 593, 598, 602.

Bourne, Edward Gaylord, on weapons, 566, 576, 580, 583, 587, 588.
Bowl, Chief, Cherokee crossed Mississippi River under, 112.
    band joined by Tahchee, 114.
    killed and his Cherokee followers driven out by Texas Government, 113.
Bows and arrows, 571–582.
Boyano, Lieutenant, 65.
    fort constructed by, 115, 205.
    Fort San Juan left in charge of, 109.
    Yuchi forts stormed by, 213, 437.
Bracelets and arm bands, 531–522.
Brame, J. Y., on location of Chiaha, 68.
    on location of Talicpacana, Moculixa, and Zabusta villages (Choctaw names), 50.
Brannon, Peter A., on quarry worked by Indians, 542.
Brantz, Lewis, 328.
Brazil, 7.
    inhabitants of, 825.
Brazos and Colorado Rivers, settlement of Eyeish between, 132.
Brazos River, tract of land secured by United States for use of Caddo, 99.
Breeds, *see* Cherokee, 224.
Brevoortia patronus, use as food, 266.
Brickell, John, 830.
Bridges, 601–602.
Brier Creek, crossed by De Soto, 44.
    settlement of Yuchi near, 214.
Brinton, Daniel G., identification of mythological creek Caloose-hutche with Black Warrior River suggested by, 25.
British forts on Mississippi, Galvez expedition against, 93.
British slave traders, raid against Chawasha in interest of, 109.
Broad River, S. C., 61, 205.
    home of Cusabo, 128.
    lands about ceded by Coosa, 129.
"Broken Arrow," Coweta town near Fort Mitchell, 127.
Brown, murdered by Indians, 163.
Brown, Thomas, trader of Congarees, 205.
Buckerville, Ark., 55.
Buck, Lucy, short vocabulary of Tutelo words collected from, 201.
Buffalo, *see* Bison.
Bullard, Ga., 44.
Bull's Bay, S. C., 182.
Bull's Island, Bull's Bay, S. C., Charleston colonists met Sewee on, 182.
Burial customs, 718–729.
Burns Island, 48, 68, 115.
    See also Chiaha province.
Burrage, Henry S., ed. narratives containing material, 325, 370, 382, 432, 440, 663.
    on agricultural habits of Virginia Indians, 258, 280.
    on artistic development, 614.
    on clothing, 472.

Burrage, Henry S., on copper mine operated by Nottoways, 491, 492.
  on ear ornaments, 510.
  on fort built by the Indians, 437.
  on hair dressing, 498, 500, 501.
  on head bands, 509.
  on household utensils, 556.
  on implements for hunting and fishing, 567, 572, 589.
  on pottery, 554.
  on religious beliefs, 742.
  on skin dressing, 442.
  on social organization, 646.
  on transportation, means of, 592, 594, 595.
  on war customs, 687.
  on weapons, 567, 572, 589.
Burrells Ford, 47.
Bushnell, David I., Jr., 157, 178, 198, 336, 369, 462, 470, 681, 736, 828, 829, 830.
  on artistic development, 613.
  on hair dressing, 505, 506.
  on head bands, 509.
  on household utensils, 558, 560.
  on housing methods of the Choctaw, 401, 402, 412, 413, 428.
  on implements for hunting and fishing, 585.
  on mats and baskets, 604.
  on musical instruments, 625.
  on pottery, 551.
  on quarries, 543.
  on skin dressing, 446.
  on thread and textiles, 449.
  on towns, 634.
  on use of copper, 493.
  on weapons, 585.
  sketch of Acolapissa temple by De Batz recovered by, 82.
  testimony of Lamhatty, an Indian, preserved by, 92.
Busk, name of Creek ceremony, 763.
"Buzzard Roost", see Chatakague.
Byington, Cyrus, on cooking methods, 358.
  on implements for hunting and fishing, 588.
  on weapons, 588.
Byrd, William, 149, 163, 164, 176, 305, 311, 319, 325, 332, 336, 345, 423, 444, 452.
  on clothing, 470, 502.
  on hair dressing, 499.
  on household utensils, 556.
  on implements for hunting, and fishing, 573.
  on musical instruments, 625.
  on religious beliefs and usages, 749, 750, 751, 752.
  on weapons, 573.
  visit to Nottoway, 163, 412, 439, 741.
Cabeza de Vaca, Alvar Nuñez, 39, 74, 172, 450, 736.
  on appearance of Indians who kept two members of Narvaez expedition, 38.

Cabeza de Vaca, Alvar Nuñez, on clothing, 459, 460.
  on implements for hunting and fishing, 582, 587.
  on Indian robe of "martin-ermine skin," 38.
  on labrets, 515, 516.
  on location of Han, 85.
  on musical instruments, 628.
  on towns, 633.
  on transportation, means of, 589.
  on weapons, 582, 587.
Cabot, John, voyage of, 34.
Cabrera, Governor, 121.
Cacores, see Shakori.
Caddo, 11, 14, 19, 21, 24, 27, 33, 57, 58, 75, 84, 89, 98, 99, 100, 132, 142, 156, 157, 216, 292, 301, 310, 396, 662, 665, 666, 729, 799, 800, 801, 803, 804, 806, 807, 808, 809, 810, 811, 812, 819, 820, 822, 832.
  Adai a tribe of, 83.
  Alabama band living near, 87.
  and Muskogee names, resemblances between, 31.
  beds, 422.
  body paint, 531.
  burial customs, 820.
  caste system, 662, 820.
  ceding of lands to United States by, 99, 142.
  clans and gentes, 654, 655, 657, 820.
  clothing, 439, 469, 475, 476.
  confederation, composed of horticultural tribes, 17.
  country, 72.
    Quapaw removed to, on Red River, 176.
  derivation of clan organizations with female descent, 32.
  domestic animals, use of, 345.
  doors turned toward east, 428.
  faithful to Federal Government during Civil War, 99.
  food, 292, 355.
  found by De Soto in Ouachita Province, 14.
  games, 548, 684, 686.
  greasing and coloring of hair and skin, 528, 820.
  hair dressing, 501, 507, 820.
  head deformation abandoned, 537, 820.
    former practice of, 540, 820.
  household utensils, 556, 558, 559, 560, 561.
  houses, 419, 421, 819.
  hunting, 312, 317, 324, 328.
  included in Southeastern cultural province, 10.
    (See table 1, facing p. 10.)
  language, reference to, 57.
  linguistic division, 141.
  marriage customs, 708, 709.
  medicine men of Bidai esteemed by, 96.
  mental and moral characteristics, 237.

Caddo, migrations, 31, 32.
   musical instruments, 629.
   name, interpretation of, 216.
   ornamentation, 486.
   physical characteristics, 229.
   population, 99, 100.
   pottery, 549, 820.
      distribution of, 31.
   relationship, terms of, 670.
   religious beliefs and usages, 782, 812, 820.
   settlement in Texas, 13, 97, 99, 142.
   sketch of, 98–100.
   smoke-holes and windows lacking, 427.
   social customs, 723, 820, 823.
   social organization 651, 820.
   storehouses, 381.
   tattooing, 536, 820.
   territory, withdrawal of missions from, 99, 158, 162.
   towns of, 640.
   transportation, means of, 599, 820.
   tribes, 136, 141, 161, 186, 241.
      territory of entered by Moscoso, 57.
   visited by Henry de Tonti, 99.
   war customs, 701.
Caddoan stock, 10, 98, 141, 799, 800.
   location, 32.
   population, 12.
   (See table 1, facing p. 10.)
Caddo Gap, Ark., 55.
   residence of Caddo, 98.
Caddo Jake, Caddo brave, speaker of Natchitoches dialect, 161.
Caddo River, 55.
Cafaqui, Indian town, 44.
Cahinnio, 100.
   calumet rite practiced by, 599.
   identification with Caddo, 98.
   population, 100.
   sketch of, 100.
   trade with, 738.
   visited by companions of La Salle, 100.
Cahoque, see Coça.
Caimulga Creek, site of Chickasaw town, 117.
Caingua, native tribe of South America, 824.
Cakeres, god of the Powhatan Indians, 743.
Calahuchi, Apalachee town, 89.
Calcasieu Parish, La., see Allen and Jefferson Parishes, 145.
Calcasieu River, La., 93.
   Pakana reported by Sibley on, 170.
Calderón, Pedro, Bishop of Cuba, 40, 42, 108, 137, 144, 146, 151, 173, 174, 179, 180, 194, 197, 208, 281, 326, 380, 829.
   Florida missions visited by, 62.
   mission founded by, 208.
   on agricultural methods, 309.
   on Chacta province, 121.
   on clothing, 471.

Calderón, Pedro, Bishop of Cuba, on council house, 407.
   on hunting, 319.
   on Mobile settlement, 151.
   on moral characteristics of Florida Indians, 233.
Calion, 55.
"Caloose Creek," probably Okalusa or Okeloosa Creek, 167.
Caloose-hutche, meaning of name, 25.
   name of creek in Muskogee origin myth, 25.
   possible identification with Black Warrior River, 25.
   possible identification with Black Water Creek, Ala., 26.
Calos, expedition from St. Augustine to town of, 102.
Calpista, Indian village, 54.
"Caluça," name possibly applied to Mississippi Indians in general, 167.
   See Okelousa.
Calumet, name for "peace pipe," 547, 699.
Calusa, 12, 16, 20, 36, 59, 101, 102, 148, 173, 191, 192, 195, 216, 282, 802, 829.
   bracelets, 521.
   burial customs, 722.
   called Choctaw by some early writers, 102.
   clothing, 457, 471.
   continuance on west coast of Florida till end of Seminole War, 102.
   country, landing by Cordova in, 101.
      landing by Miruelo in, 101.
      landing by Ponce de Leon in, 101.
      Menendez' visit to, 101, 192.
      reconnaissance by Spaniards, 102.
      withdrawal of Guale to, 136.
   departure from San Antonio, 101.
   Fontaneda's captivity among, reference to, 90.
   gold acquired from shipwrecked European vessels by, 35, 101.
   headdress, 504.
   home of, on Florida Peninsula, 101.
   identification with tribe found by Ponce de Leon in Florida, 34.
   members of Muskhogean linguistic stock, 239.
   Menendez, visit to Tocobaga with chief of, 195.
   movements, 64.
   name, interpretation of, 216.
   necklaces, 518.
   Ponce de Leon killed by, 101.
   population, 102.
   religious beliefs and usages among, 763.
   said by Romans to have gone to Cuba, 192.
   shell beads, 485.
   sketch of, 101–102.

Calusa, source material on, 829.
  territory, fertility of, 20.
  treatment of prisoners by, 101.
  tribe of southwestern Florida, a littoral community, 18–19.
  village, erection in fort by Francisco de Reynoso, 101.
"Calusa Province," 173.
Camden, 55.
Campti, La., site of French settlement, 142.
Canada, 71, 72, 73.
Canadian River, one Biloxi living there among Creeks, 97.
  temporary home of Koasati, 145.
Canadian Zone, 19.
Canary Islands, 40.
Canasauga, 31.
Canasoga, Indian village, 47, 48.
  derivation of word, 70.
Canche, see Cauchi.
Canço, Governor Mendez de, meeting between Ais chief and, 84, 85.
  Tekesta country traversed by, 192.
Cane, importance to Indians, 244.
  rafts constructed by De Soto army, 50.
Caney Creek, Tex., possible home of Patiri, 172.
Canna indica, use of, 289.
Canna sp., use of as food, 288, 289.
Cannasauga stream, 47.
Cannibalism, resorted to by Spaniards at Santa Lucia, Fla., 134.
Cannibals, tribe of reached by Bienville party, probably Atakapa, 93.
  tribe of reported by Penicaut, 85.
Canoe Creek, 49.
  Indian name for, 69.
Canoes and rafts, 589–598.
  See Transportation.
Canos, name given by Pardo to Cofitachequi, 64.
Cantino, Alberto, 34.
Caoque, see Coça.
Capachequi, Indian province of, 42, 43, 89.
  name used by De Soto, 102.
  probably related to Hitchiti, 89.
Capaha, see Pacaha, 490.
Caparaz, 102, 119.
  Amacano associated with, 88.
  connection with doctrina named San Luis, 102, 119.
  possible connection with Capachequi, 102.
Capasi, chief of Apalachee, litter used to carry, 598.
Cape Canaveral, corn field north of, 255.
Cape Cod, 5.
Cape Colony, 7.
Cape Fear, 40.
Cape Fear Indians, 103, 172, 217, 278.
  name, interpretation of, 217.
  population, 103.
  possible connection with Waccamaw, 103.

Cape Fear Indians, sketch of, 103.
Cape Fear River, 15.
Cape Hatteras, N. C., home of Hatteras tribe, 137.
Cape Lookout, 5.
Capinans, 103.
  Biloxi town, 31.
  name, resemblance of to Capitanesses, 103.
  sketch of, 103–104.
Capitanesses, name used for Indians, on Carte Figurative, 103.
  See Capinans.
Capuaca, town subject to Mission of Nombre de Dios, 179.
Carabay, town subject to San Juan del Puerto, 179.
Cariaria, see Rhus coriaria, 385.
Carolana, name given by Coxe to Louisiana, 77.
Carolina Indians, armor, 588, 589.
  clothing, 472.
  eastern, origin belief of, 24.
  hair dressing, 503.
  musical instruments, 626.
  necklaces, 516, 517.
  physical characteristics, 228.
Carolinas, 73, 77.
  English of, 73.
  Indians remaining in after the removal, 80.
  Siouans of, 15.
Carolinian Faunal Area, Indian tribes occupying, 19.
Carrier, Lyman, 270.
Carroll, B. R., on hunting, 313.
Carrosa, identification with Okalusa, 65.
Carr Shoals, point where De Soto crossed Oconee River, 44.
Cartaret County, N. C., home of Neusiok tribe, 162.
Cartaya, Spanish ensign, 173.
Cartogechaye Creek, 47.
Casañas de Jesus Maria, Fray Francisco, 57, 832.
  Anadarko mentioned by, 89.
  missions in Texas founded by, 74.
  value of report of on Hasinai Indians, 74.
Casapullas Indians, towns of depopulated, 129.
Cascangui, see Icafui, 141.
Casiste, town on Alabama River, passed by Spaniards, 49, 127, 143.
Casqui, affinities with Koasati, 27.
  country of, 54.
  encountered by De Soto, 27, 52, 53, 54, 628.
  linguistic evidence of belonging to Muskhogean stock, 27.
  towns of, reference to, 433.
  See also Kaskinampo.
Casquin, see Casqui.
  See also Kaskinampo.
Casquinampo, see Kaskinampo.
Cassatees, see Koasati.

Cassen, George, executed by Powhatan Indians, 644.
Cassine vomitoria, use as drink by Cherokee, 284.
"Cassine yapon," *see Cassine vomitoria*.
Castacha, town supporting the French, 122, 637.
Castanea sp., 288.
Castes, 661–663.
Castilla del Oro, Spanish name for region about Gulf of Darien, 35.
Castillo, Diego del, borders of Hasinai country reached by, 74.
Catahoula Lake, La., associated with salt manufacture, 302.
Catalte, province of, 56,
    location, 57.
Catastomidae, use of, 267.
Catataugh, brother of Powhatan, 644.
Catawba, 11, 19, 20, 21, 24, 30, 60, 64, 66, 67, 77, 104, 105, 111, 129, 131, 145, 149, 160, 172, 178, 183, 186, 203, 205, 206, 207, 208, 217, 242, 278, 665, 809, 812, 821, 830.
    absorption by Indian and white population, 105.
    aid to English colonists against Tuscarora, 104.
    blowgun, 586.
    country, reached by Lederer, 76.
    displacement by Cherokee in prehistoric era, 14.
    "Flat Head," name used for, 539.
    games, 548.
    head deformation perhaps practiced by, 539, 540.
    household utensils, 564.
    joined by Shakori and Eno, 183.
    killed by Natchez and Wateree, 205.
    language, loss of, 105.
    location, 32.
    members of Church of Jesus Christ of Latter Day Saints, 105.
    name, suggested derivation of, 217.
    occupancy of South Carolina by, 64.
    origin legend, 23.
    population, 105.
    pottery, 554, 555.
    probably joined by Sewee, 183.
    relations with colonists, 104.
    retreat to Virginia, 104.
    service in Revolution against British and Cherokee, 104.
    settlement near Sculleyville, Okla., 105.
    Siouan towns, 67.
    sketch of, 104–105.
    smallpox attacks, 104.
    source material on, 830.
    Sugeree related to and ultimately united with, 186.
    temporary residence in Haywood County, N. C., 105.
    treaty with State of South Carolina, 104.

Catawba River, site of Iswa tribe, 104.
Catesby, Mark, 441, 450, 458, 830.
    on agricultural activities of Algonquians, 259, 260, 307, 308.
    on axes, 545.
    on birth customs, 712, 713.
    on clothing, 460, 463, 470.
    on coloring of manufactured articles, 609.
    on communication, means of, 734.
    on cooking, 352, 353, 356, 364, 369, 370, 371.
    on crime and punishment, 731.
    on ear ornaments, 511.
    on food preserving, 374, 376.
    on gorgets, 519.
    on greasing and coloring of hair and skin, 527.
    on hair dressing, 499, 503.
    on household utensils, 562, 563.
    on houses, 411, 412, 421.
    on hunting, 314, 318, 319.
    on implements for hunting and fishing, 568, 573, 578.
    on mats and baskets, 602, 604.
    on medical practices, 790, 791.
    on moral characteristics, 235, 236.
    on physical characteristics of Carolina Indians, 228.
    on skin dressing, 444.
    on stone pipes, 546.
    on tattooing, 533.
    on thread and textiles, 453.
    on trade, 738, 739, 741.
    on transportation, means of, 592.
    on war customs, 690, 691.
    on weapons, 568, 573, 578.
    on woodcraft, 310, 311.
"Catfish" (*Ictalurus caerulescens*), use as food, 267.
    blue (*Ictalurus furcatus*), use as food, 266.
    mud (*Leptops olivaris*), use as food, 266.
Catherine Creek, N. C., site of Chowanoc reservation, 124.
Catlin, George, 154, 182, 186, 679, 680, 828.
Catoma Creek, affluent of Alabama River, Montgomery Co., 196.
Cauchi, Indian town, 65, 66, 110.
    Siouan name for Canasoga, 68.
"Caux," Belle Isle's name for Akokisa, 85.
Caxa, town on Alabama River, entered by De Soto, 150.
Caxiti, name used by De Luna, for Kasihta, 143.
Cayas Province, 54.
    salt found in, by De Soto, 737.
Cayomulgi, Shawnee town, 185.
Cayuga, country of, Saponi settled in, 178, 179.
    Saponi and Tutelo formally adopted by, 178.
Cayuga Inlet, Tutelo settled in town of Coreorgonel on, 201.

Cayuga Lake, 201.
Cedarglades, Ark., 55.
Céloron, Canadian commander of force against Chickasaw, 117.
Cenis, term used by La Salle, 162.
    See also Hasinai.
Census, English, of Indian population, 1715, 77, 91.
Central America, 35.
    possible migrations from to Gulf Area, 33.
    relation to cultural area, 827.
Central intrusion, 823.
Ceremonials, *see* Religious beliefs and usages.
Chacaiauchia, Nacogdoche chief, 156.
Chacta, name used by Bishop Calderón for Choctaw, 121, 795.
Chactoos, name used by Sibley for Chatot, 108.
Chaguate Province, La., *see* Chaguete Province.
Chaguete Province, La., salt found in, by De Soto, 738.
Chakchiuma, 19, 29, 51, 105, 106, 107, 123, 139, 140, 141, 147, 190, 195, 217.
    allied with French in Natchez War, 106.
    burial customs, 729.
    Ibitoupa apparently united with, 140.
    incorporation with Chickasaw and Choctaw, 106.
    involvement in war between Choctaw and Chickasaw, 106.
    name, interpretation of in Choctaw and Chickasaw, 217.
    population, 107.
    relations with French, 106.
    sketch of, 105–106.
    town stockaded, 433.
Chalahume, Indian town, 66, 69, 70.
Chalaque, province of, meaning of name, 46.
    tribal identity of population discussed, 46.
Chamaerops sp., 285, 286.
Chanky, town supporting the French, 122.
Chapman, Dr. J. Milling, 21.
Charenton, on Bayou Teche, home of few survivors of Chitimacha, 120.
Charles City County, Va., home of Powhatan band, 130.
Charleston, S. C., 12, 16, 32, 62.
    home of Cusabo, 128.
    visit of Pedee to, 172.
    settlement of, 77.
Charleston Harbor, site of South Carolina colony settlement, 129.
Charlevoix, Father Pierre F. K. de, 159, 161, 166, 195, 212, 261, 417, 829.
    on artistic development, 617, 618.
    on Chawasha, 109.
    on house of Acolapissa Chief, 82.
    on population, 83.
    on towns, 639, 640.
    on war customs, 700.

Charlotte Harbor, 35.
Chartier, Martin, Frenchman who lived in Pennsylvania with Piqua band of Shawnee, 184.
    instigator of Shawnee removal from Pennsylvania, 185.
Chartier, Pierre, son of Martin Chartier, settled at Allegheny, 184.
Chartier's band of Shawnee, 15.
Chartier's town, located on Allegheny River, below Kishiminetas River, 184.
Chasee, town of Yamasee, 209.
Chatakague, Shawnee settlement in Talladega country, 185.
Chatot, 63, 73, 107, 108, 171, 197, 213.
    and Apalachicola, attacked by Creeks, 107.
    departure from Spanish Florida, 108
    establishment of missions among, 107.
    Fray Rodrigo de la Barreda driven out by, 107.
    location of, 29.
    migration to French territory, 108.
    population, 108.
    probable merging with Choctaw in Oklahoma, 108.
    removal to lands on Dog River, 108.
    sketch of, 107–108.
Chattahoochee River, 14, 63, 78, 92, 118, 127, 131, 137, 138, 143, 146, 153, 165, 168, 169, 180, 184, 189, 200, 210, 211, 213, 214.
    branch of Sawokli living with Lower Creeks below falls of, 180.
    Chiaha withdrawal with Creeks to, 116.
    former home of Coweta, 127.
    identification with river mentioned in Chekilli origin myth, 26.
    Kasihta village on, burned by Spanish expedition, 143.
    Oconee settled among Lower Creeks on, 165.
    probable location of Oconee, before removal to Oconee River, 165.
    site of Kolomi settlement, 146.
    temporary home of Tuskegee, 200.
    Yuchi settled on, 213, 214.
Chattahoochee towns, former home of Eufaula, 132, 636.
Chattahoochee Valley, 11.
Chattanooga, Tenn., 48, 68.
    Tuskegee band located near, 200.
Chattooga Ridge, S. C., Cheraw first visited by De Soto near, 109.
Chattooga River, 47.
Chatuache, mission, northward from Santa Elena, 128.
Chaunis Temoatan, copper mines located at, 491, 492.
Chauvignerie, 149, 199.
Chawasha, 73, 108, 109, 117, 168, 169, 204, 217, 240.
    allied to Chitimacha, 108.
    and Washa, met by M. de Nouaille, 109.

Chawasha, attacked by Natchez, Chickasaw, and Yazoo, 108.
   disappearance of tribe, 109.
   moved by Bienville to right bank of Mississippi, 109.
   name, interpretation of, 217.
   population, 109.
   sketch of, 108–109.
   social organization, 651.
   supposed massacre by black slaves, 109.
   tribal attacks on, 77.
"Chearhaw," see Upper Creeks, 115.
"Chehaw," see Upper Creeks, 115.
Chehaw River, S. C., between Edisto and Combahee, 115.
Chehawhaw Creek, 28.
   named for Chiaha, 115.
Chekika, Calusa chief, killed by Colonel Harney, 102.
Chekilli, Kashita chief, 25, 26.
   migration legend told to Oglethorpe by, 167, 733.
Chépart, commandant, cause of Natchez uprising, 159.
Cheraw, 67, 109, 110, 131, 145, 172, 183, 186, 203, 205, 206, 208, 411, 739.
   first visited by Spaniards under De Soto, 109.
   fort built by Pardo in country of (Joara), 65.
      See also Joara and Kuala.
   Siouan tribe, 109.
   sketch of, 109–110.
   visited by Spaniards under Juan Pardo, 109.
Cherokee, 11, 19, 21, 28, 30, 66, 68, 70, 77, 104, 105, 110–114, 115, 117, 121, 135, 145, 160, 164, 165, 200, 203, 213, 215, 217, 223, 241, 296, 335, 336, 662, 665, 800, 801, 802, 805, 806, 808, 810, 812, 813, 818, 821, 827, 831.
   beds, 422.
   birth customs, 713, 714.
   bracelets and arm bands, 522.
   burial customs, 723, 724, 811, 818.
   clans and gentes, 654, 656, 657, 818.
   clothing, 439, 457, 460, 464, 472.
   cooking, 356, 367.
   country, 13.
      Nottoway flight to, for protection against whites, 163.
      Oconee located on Seneca Creek, Oconee Co., S. C., in, 165.
      penetrated by British under Colonel Chicken, 111.
   crime and punishment, 731.
   crossing of Mississippi River under Chief Bowl, 112.
   defeat by Chickasaw, 112, 118.
   defeat by forces under Colonel Grant, 112.
   destruction of Fort Loudon by, 112.
   discovery of gold near Dahlonega, Ga., and effect on, 113.
   discussion of, incomplete, 1.

Cherokee, domestic animals, 351.
   doors, 428.
   ear ornaments, 512, 513, 818.
   education of children, 713, 714.
   extension down Tennessee River, 111.
   fire making, 424.
   first mission established among, by Moravians, 112.
   flags, 431.
   food, 284, 297, 298.
   form of government modeled after United States adopted by, 113.
   friendship with English in Revolution, 78.
   games, 548, 675, 676, 679, 683, 686.
   grant of land by Mexican Government to, repudiated by U. S. Government, 113.
   greasing and coloring of hair and skin, 527, 528.
   hair dressing, 499, 500, 505, 818.
   head deformation not practiced by, 541.
   household utensils, 562.
   houses, 402, 403, 421, 818.
   implements for hunting and fishing 569, 573, 578, 583, 585, 586.
   included in Southeastern cultural province (see table 1, facing p. 10).
   internal dissensions among, 113.
   Iroquoian language spoken by, 241
   Kituhwa, old name for, 23.
   largest tribe of Southwest, 14.
   location, 14.
   mats and baskets, 604, 607.
   medical practices, 782, 783, 793, 794.
   members of Iroquoian family, 110.
   metals use of, 495.
   moral characteristics, 231, 233.
   movements, 14, 15, 31.
   musical instruments, 625, 629.
   name, interpretation of, in Muskogee, 217.
   names used by, 672.
   necklaces, 518, 520.
   nose ornaments, 515, 818.
   not inhabitants of province of Chalaque, 46.
   number remaining after the Indian removal, 80.
   ornamentation, 490.
   part taken in Moore's expedition against Tuscarora, 111.
   part taken in Revolutionary War, 112.
   part taken in Yamasee War, 111.
   physical characteristics, 223, 224, 233, 818.
   pipes, 542, 546, 547, 555.
   population, 11, 114.
   pottery, 553.
   protection asked against Catawba, Shawnee, and Congaree by, 111.

Cherokee, reference to Mooney's history of, 21.
relationship, terms of, 667, 668, 670.
relations with colonists, 112.
religious beliefs and usages, 767, 768, 769, 770–772, 818.
remnants of, given reservation in western North Carolina, 113.
removal by Federal Government to west, by force, cause of great suffering, 80, 113.
removal to Spanish territory of Texas, 112, 113.
sketch of, 110–115.
smallpox epidemic, 111.
smoke-holes and windows, 427.
social organization, 653.
source material, 831.
tattooing, 533.
threads and textiles, 449.
tobacco, 384.
town house, 402, 403.
towns of, 636.
tradition, early home of Eufaula mentioned in, 131.
transportation, means of, 593, 594, 595, 596.
treaty made with South Carolina, 111.
value of Appalachian quarries to, 20.
visit to English court, 111, 112.
visited by Henry Timberlake, 112.
wampum, 484.
war customs, 690, 691, 692.
war with English, 1759–61, 80.
weapons, 569, 573, 578, 583, 585, 586.
Cherokee Killer, see Cherokeeleechee.
Cherokeeleechee (Cherokee Killer), Apalachicola chief, 92.
Cherokee Nation, few Natchez members of, 160.
final termination of, 113.
Cherokee Phoenix, weekly paper printed in Cherokee and English, 113.
Chesapeake Bay, 76.
entered by Spaniards, 70.
Spanish name for, 70.
tribes, war customs of, 688, 689.
Chesapeake Indians, remained unconquered, 646.
Chestowee, see Tsistuyi.
Chests, wooden, 560–562.
Chiaha, 29, 70, 115, 138, 150, 168, 169, 181, 217, 268.
living with Creeks on Ocmulgee River, 115.
location, 28.
name, interpretation of, 217.
pearl fishery at, 489.
population, 116.
"province," see Burns Island.
sketch of, 115–116.
Square Ground, 776.
stockaded towns found at, 433.

Chiaha, town of, 48, 65, 66, 69.
Spanish force moved by Lt. Boyano to, 109, 110, 115.
tribe associated with Creek Confederation, 115.
Chiaha Indian, chief of Lower Creeks, 506, 516.
Chiala, 93.
Chickahamania River, Powhatan established himself on, 643.
Chickahominy, 175.
tribe, ruled by priests, 646.
Chickasaw, 11, 13, 16, 17, 19, 25, 30, 51, 55, 60, 77, 78, 82, 86, 105, 106, 107, 108, 111, 112, 122, 139, 148, 149, 158, 160, 161, 163, 167, 185, 188, 190, 194, 198, 211, 212, 217, 224, 238, 262, 280, 297, 299, 384, 437, 665, 736, 801, 806, 808, 809, 810, 818, 821, 822, 827, 828.
artistic developement, 617.
attack by French forces on, 117.
attack on Acolapissa, 79.
attack on De Soto expedition, 116, 549, 628.
attack on Yatasi, 211.
attacks against French continued after treaty, 117.
axes, 544.
body paint, 528, 531.
bracelets, 522.
burial customs, 724, 811, 818.
canoes, 576.
caste system, 662, 818.
clans and gentes, 654, 655, 657, 818.
clothing, 439, 440, 441, 453, 461, 464, 473, 524.
worn by medicine men, 478, 479, 519.
communications opened by Colonel Welch with, 117.
cooking, 354, 372.
council house, later Court House of Johnston Co., Okla., 118.
country, Natchez forced to leave, 81.
crime and punishment, 732, 818.
defeat of force under Benoist and Reggio by, 118.
defeat of Shawnee on Bear Creek by, 185.
displacement by Cherokee in eastern Tennessee in prehistoric era, 15.
doors turned toward east, 428, 430.
ear ornaments, 513, 818.
farming, 309, 310.
featherwork, 455.
fire making, 423.
fishing, 336, 337.
flint, use of, 543.
games, 548, 675, 678, 679, 680, 682, 683, 684.
hair dressing, 499, 500, 506, 808, 818.
head bands, 508.

Chickasaw, head deformation practiced, 540, 818.
 horses, 348, 349, 741.
 household utensils, 559, 561, 818.
 houses, 387, 388, 400, 420, 421, 818.
 hunting, 265, 315, 316, 331.
 Iroquois war party destroyed by, 117.
 lands confiscated by South Carolina, 118.
 marriage customs, 705, 706, 707.
 mats and baskets, 604.
 medical practices, 794.
 members of Muskhogean linguistic family, 238, 818.
 metals, use of, 495.
 moieties, 663, 664, 818.
 musical instruments, 624, 625, 627, 628, 629.
 name, interpretation of, 217.
 names used by, 672, 673, 674, 818.
 nose ornaments, 515, 818.
 official relations with United States Government begun, 118.
 Old Fields, site of defeat of Cherokee by, 112, 118.
 original home in State of Miss., 116.
 peace treaty with, obtained by armed force under Céloron, 117.
 population, 118, 119.
 pottery, 553.
 relationship, terms of, 666, 667, 668, 669, 670.
 religious beliefs and usages, 776, 777.
 removal to southern part of Indian Territory, 118.
 responsible for disturbance along lower Mississippi, 117.
 sketch of, 116–119.
 smallpox attack, 117.
 smoke-holes and windows, 427.
 social customs relating to women, 715, 716, 818.
 social organization, 653, 818.
 source material on, 828.
 stockades, 433.
 tattooing, 533, 534.
 territory, fertility of, 20.
 thread and textiles, 453.
 town in which De Soto passed winter of 1541, 27.
 towns, 637.
 trade, 741.
 transportation, means of, 589, 598, 601.
 village, 81.
 wampum, 484.
 war customs, 693, 696.
 war with French, 73.
 weapons, 583.
 weaving, 453.
Chickasawhay, French supported by, 121.
Chicken, Colonel, 114.
 British penetration into Cherokee country under, 111.

Chicopa Creek, Miss., 140.
Chicora, Francisco of, list made by, 206, 208.
Chicora, identification with Shakori, 66.
Chief of Coça, Chiaha said to be subject to, 115.
Chihaque, see Chiaha.
Chillicothe, name of town, 184.
 Shawnee band of Indians, 184.
"Chilokee," word defined, 46.
Chilucan, 119, 217.
 meaning of term, 119, 217.
 probable remnants of old Timucua population of Cumberland Island, 119.
 probably related to Florida groups, 119.
China, 7.
 effect of climate on, 824, 825.
 northwestern, boundary of cultural area, 825.
China brier, see Smilax sp.
Chine, 119, 217.
 Amacano associated with, 88.
 name, interpretation of, 217.
 population, 119.
Chine, a chief, mission named after, 107.
Chinese, cultural advancement, 827.
Chinisca, town subject to San Juan del Puerto, 179.
Chipola, mission established near middle course of, 107.
Chiquito, 194.
Chiquola, mentioned by Laudonnière, 143.
Chisca, mines located at, 490, 492.
 name used by De Soto for Yuchi, 212, 213, 490, 492.
 province of, 48.
 town of, destroyed by Boyano, 65.
Chisi, town visited by De Soto, on Flint River, 43, 127.
 See also Ichisi.
Chitimacha, 12, 17, 30, 73, 108, 119–121, 159, 189, 217, 240, 283, 292, 296, 332, 334, 336, 665, 737, 801, 806, 808, 809, 810, 812, 819, 822, 829.
 bracelets, 522.
 burial customs, 729, 811, 819.
 castes, 661, 819.
 Charenton on Bayou Teche, home of last survivors of, 120.
 clans and gentes, 654, 657, 819.
 culture, 18.
 ear ornaments, 514.
 finger rings, 522.
 fire making, 425.
 flint obtained by, 542.
 games, 684, 686.
 gorgets, 520.
 group included in Southeastern cultural province, 10.
  (See table 1, facing p. 10.)
 hair dressing, 501, 507, 819.
 head deformation practiced by, 540, 819.
 household utensils, 559, 819.

Chitimacha, implements for hunting and fishing, 579, 585.
   mats and baskets, 603, 608, 819.
      colors used on, 610.
   migrations, 32.
   murder of St. Cosme and three other Frenchmen by, 72, 120, 159.
   musical instruments, 627, 629.
   name, interpretation of, 217.
   names used by, 674.
   nose ornaments, 515.
   origin legend, 23.
   ornaments, 524.
   population, 121.
   relationship, terms of, 669.
   religious beliefs and usages, 781.
   St. Denis expedition against, 95, 97.
   sketch of, 119–121.
   smoke-holes and windows, 427.
   social organization, 650, 651.
   source material on, 829, 830.
   temple, 619.
   trade, 738.
   transportation, means of, 596.
   treachery of Taensa to, 120.
   war, 73.
   weapons, 579, 585.
Chitimachan stock, 240, 801.
Choctaw, 11, 16, 17, 19, 21, 25, 30, 33, 38, 60, 73, 78, 80, 94, 97, 106, 107, 108, 117, 118, 145, 147, 148, 151, 160, 171, 173, 196, 212, 224, 225, 238, 262, 280, 296, 299, 437, 665, 696, 801, 802, 805, 806, 808, 809, 810, 817, 822, 827, 828.
   agriculture, 264, 817.
   allies of French against Natchez, 160.
   artistic development, 613.
   bags and pouches, 480.
   beads, 487.
   birth customs, 716.
   bows made of hickory, 245, 578.
   burial customs, 725, 726, 811, 817.
   buzzard men and women, 537, 561, 726, 809, 811, 817.
   caste system, 662.
   clans and gentes, 655, 817.
   clothing, 450, 471.
   communication, means of, 734.
   crime and punishment, 732, 733, 818.
   district, archeological evidence of population movement found in, 16.
   doors, 428, 430.
   dyes, 487, 609.
   early name for Calusa, 102.
   education of children, 716, 717.
   featherwork, 455.
   fingernails, 537, 817.
   "Flat Head," name for, 539.
   food, 288, 289, 297, 299.
   games, 548, 675, 678, 679, 680, 681, 682, 683, 684, 685, 686.
   hair dressing, 500, 504, 507, 808, 817, 823.

Choctaw, head deformation practiced by, 538, 539, 540, 817.
   hickory, use of for bows, 245, 578.
   hostility between Creeks and, 78.
      ended by American control of Mississippi, 122.
   household utensils, 559, 560, 564, 817.
   houses, 401, 402, 421, 817.
   hunting, 315, 316.
   implements for hunting and fishing, 565, 578, 585.
   incorporation into State of Oklahoma, 122.
   labor, division between sexes, 717.
   language, 28, 95.
      village names in, 50.
   last Council House of, at Tuskahoma, Okla., 123.
   location, 32.
   "Long Hairs," ancient name for, 51.
   loyal to French in war with Chickasaw, 73.
   marriage customs, 706, 707.
   mats and baskets, 604, 606, 607.
   medical practices among, 794, 795.
   members of Muskhogean linguistic family, 238, 817.
   metals, use of, 495.
   mnemonic devices, 612.
   moieties, 663, 664.
   moral characteristics, 231, 232.
   musical instruments, 625, 626, 627, 629.
   names used by, 672, 673, 674, 818.
   Nation, Okla., 105, 196.
      home of Catawba, 105.
   never at war with United States, as a tribe, 122.
   number remaining after Indian removal, 80.
   Paⁿs falaya, ancient name for, 51.
   physical characteristics, 225, 817.
   pipes, 546.
   population, 123.
   relationship, terms of, 666, 667, 668, 670.
   religious beliefs and usages, 777–779.
   shields, 588.
   sketch of, 121–123.
   skin dressing, 446, 447.
   smoke-holes and windows, 527, 817.
   social customs relating to women, 716, 817.
   social organization, 653, 817.
   source material, 828.
   tattooing, 534.
   territory, fertility of, 20.
   threads and textiles, 449, 450, 454.
   tobacco, 384, 385.
   towns, 637, 638.
   transportation, means of, 589, 601.
   treaty signed with United States, 122.
   tribes of lower Mississippi, migration of, 28–29.

Choctaw, war customs, 696, 697, 698.
weapons, 565, 578, 585, 588.
Choctawhatchee River, Fla., 107, 125, 146, 180, 191.
home of Koasati, 146.
named for Chatot, 107.
named for Sawokli, 180.
Cholupaha, Timucuan town, 41.
Chorakae, see Cherokee, 111.
Chosha, see Taensa, 189.
Choula, 123, 140, 141, 217.
name, interpretation of, 217.
population, 123.
probably a band of Ibitoupa, 123.
sketch of, 123.
Chowan County, N. C., last home of Chowanoc, 124.
Chowan River, N. C., home of Chowanoc, 124.
Meherrin killed by Catawba on east side of, 149.
Chowanoc, 124, 217.
name, interpretation of, 217.
population, 124.
sketch of, 124.
supposed to be extinct, 124.
Chowockeleehatchee, branch of Tulsa, 125.
"Chowokolohatches," Eufaula settlement, 131.
"Choye," 211.
Christ Church Parish, north of Cooper River, 103.
Christian ceremony, first conducted in Arkansas, 52.
"Christian Towns," see Timucua towns, 133.
Chrysobalanus icaco, use of, 282.
Chuaquin, town rebuilt by Capt. Juan de Fernandez de Florencia, 202.
Chubbehatchee Creek, 49.
Hothliwahali, Upper Creek town, located on mouth of, 139.
Chukochartie, see Red House Hammock.
Chunkey, a game played by Indians, 682–684.
stones, 547–548.
Church of Jesus Christ of Latter Day Saints, Catawba members of, 105.
Cinnebar, use of, 243.
Civil War, effect on Cherokee, 113.
Claiborne, Ala., 49.
Claiborne, J. F. H., 328, 673, 704, 706, 726, 828.
Clam (Venus mercenaria), use of, 481.
Clans, Seminole, 225.
Clans and gentes, 654–661.
association with linguistic groups, 661.
table of distribution, 658–660.
Clark County, Ky., 15.
Clarke County, Ala., 50.
Clarksville, Va., site of Occaneechi settlement near, 164.
Classification, linguistic and political, of Southeastern tribes, 10.
(See table 1, facing p. 10.)

Clay, use of, 243.
Climate of the Southeast, 5–7.
Climatic provinces in other countries analogous to Southeastern U. S., 7.
Clothing, children's, 475–477, 804.
materials, 439–442, 804.
medicine men's, 477–479.
men's, 456–469.
women's, 469–477.
Clubs, 566–570.
See Implements for hunting, fishing, and war.
Coahuila, linguistic family, geographical extent of, 74.
province of, 74.
Coahuiltecan, 240.
stock, source of information on, 39.
tribes, missions among, 75.
Coahuilteco, 30, 801.
Coaque, see Coco.
Coast and inland Indian tribes, organization contrasted, 19.
Coastal Plain, 4, 15, 16.
subdivisions of, 4–5.
Coça, 60.
Chief of, 651.
Chiaha said to be subject to, 115.
cushion used by, 432.
head band of feathers worn by, 508.
litter used to carry, 598.
musical instruments used by followers of, 628.
Indian town of, 13, 56.
language, identification of as Creek, 60.
province of, 48, 60, 61.
See also Coosa.
Cocapoy, Cusabo town destroyed by Spaniards, 129.
Cocapoy, inhabitants of severely handled by Spaniards, 128.
Coccoloba uvifera, use of, 282.
Cocculus carolinus, uses of, 247, 343, 487.
Cofa, place where Spaniards left their only piece of ordinance, 138.
Coffins, wooden, 561.
Cofitachequi, abandoned settlement near, visited by De Soto, 115, 268, 440, 451, 652.
bracelets worn at, 521, 522.
classified as Muskogee center, 67.
clothing worn at, 455, 459, 462.
coloring of articles used at, 608.
Coweta possibly Indians of, 127.
implements for hunting and fishing, used in, 564, 569, 571.
Lady (or chieftainess) of, 45, 46, 47, 651.
escape from Spaniards by, 47.
forced to accompany De Soto expedition, 46.
litter used to carry, 598, 599.
necklace worn by, 516.
pearls carried by, 560.
presents brought to Spaniards by, 45.

Cofitachequi, mentioned in De Soto narratives, 143, 432, 448, 488, 560, 738.
  metals used at, 490.
  near site of Augusta, Ga., visited by bulk of De Soto's army, 137.
  pearl fishery located at, 489.
  skin dressing, 442.
  temple, 619.
  trade, 739.
  tribe later called Creeks, 442.
  visited by Henry Woodward, 143.
  visited by Juan Pardo, 143.
  weapons used in, 564, 569, 571, 587, 589.
  Yupaha capitol, 44, 45, 64, 65, 67.
Colapissas, see Acolapissa.
"Cold Meal," parched corn taken on hunting expeditions, 261, 699.
Coles Creek culture, 33.
Coligoa, see Coligua.
Coligua, Indian town, 54, 147.
  province of, 55.
Colima province, salt found at, by De Soto, 737.
Collins, Henry B., Jr., 220, 821, 832.
Colomokee Creek, Clay Co., Ga., 146.
Colomokee mounds, 14.
Colonial documents, Meherrin mentioned in, 163.
Colonists, American, in territories east of Mississippi; hostility of Indians to, 79.
  in territories west of Mississippi, conditions favorable for, 79.
Colony, French, first, founded in South Carolina, 61.
  history of, 61.
Colony, French, second, destroyed by Spaniards under Menendez, 62.
  founded by Laudonnière on St. Johns River, 62.
Colony, Huguenot, in Florida, 74.
Colony, Spanish, founded by De Luna, history of, 60–61.
Colorado River, removal of Akokisa to, 86.
Coloring of manufactured articles, 608–610.
Columbia, Ia., 55.
Columbia, S. C., 57.
  fort called "the Congarees" established nearly opposite, 124.
Columbus, Christopher, 23.
Columbus, falls at, mentioned in Chekilli origin myth, 26.
Comanches, trade with, 737.
Combahee River, 115, 124, 129.
  land granted to Kiawa south of, 129.
Combs, 564.
  See Household utensils.
Commerce Landing, Tenn., 53.
Communication, means of, 733–736.
Communities, aboriginal Indian, types described, 17–19.

Comparison of Southeast with corresponding areas in other parts of the world, 823–827.
Concubines, male, 732.
  occupations of, 713.
Conemaugh River, see Kiskiminetas River.
Conestoga, 149, 163, 164, 175.
  sought refuge with Occaneechi, 164.
Confederacies, Indian, 19.
"Conestogo, in Pensilvania," 177.
Congaree, 111, 124, 144, 178, 217, 278, 346.
  and Santee, sent as slaves to West Indies, 124, 178.
  games, 685.
  household utensils, 557.
  incorporation with Catawba, and loss of identity, 124.
  name, interpretation of in Catawba language, 217.
  pipes, 545.
  population, 124.
  ruled by a "queen," 124.
  sketch of, 124.
  towns, 632.
  war of South Carolina colonists against Santee and, 124, 178.
Congaree River, S. C., home of Congaree, 124.
Conjurers, practices of, 786–790.
Connamox, name used by Lawson for Coree or Coranine, 126.
Connetstageh, see Conestoga, 163.
Connewawtenty of Connetstageh, 163.
Conoy, 201.
Convolvulus sp., use as food, 285, 286, 288.
Cook, Zach, a Tukabahchee Indian, 343, 345.
  on pottery, 552.
Cooper River, site of Christ Church Parish, north of, 103.
Cooper, Seminole chief, arrangement of hair, 506.
Coosa, 26, 67, 69, 70, 77, 116, 121, 124–126, 128, 129, 134, 153, 217.
  apparently one of original tribes of Muskogee, 124.
  branches of, 125.
  French supported by, 121.
  lands ceded by S. C. tribe, 129.
  members of Muskhogean linguistic family, 239.
  name interpretation of, 217.
  population, 126.
  sketch of, 124–126.
  still found in northern Alabama by English traders in 17th century, 125.
  town of, 634.
  two tribes called by name of, 124.
  war with Napochies, 116, 125, 347.
  See also Coça.
Coosa County, Alabama, home of Pakana, 170.

"Coosada Old Town," name used on Vignoles map of Florida, 146.
"Coosa of Chickasaw Camp," 126.
Coosa Old Town, 200.
Coosa River, 22, 25, 26, 28, 31, 32, 46, 48, 72, 87, 145, 153, 166, 170, 184, 191, 197, 200, 214.
Old Coosa town located on, 125, 128.
Coosa River Muskogee, 67.
Coosa Valley, 11.
occupied by Cherokee by permission of Creeks, 112.
Coosaw, see Coosa.
Coosawattee, valley of the, occupied by Cherokee, 112.
Coosawhatchie River, 64, 124, 128.
Copper, use of, 71, 243, 490–494, 510, 522.
in province of Chisca, 48.
Coranine, see Coree.
Córdova, Francisco Hernandez de, attacked by Indians in Florida, 35.
landing in Calusa country, 101.
Cords, threads, and textiles, 448–454.
Coree, 15, 126, 800.
and Machapunga, assigned land on Mattamuskeet Lake, Hyde Co., N. C., 126, 148.
apparently extinct, 126.
of Point Lookout destroyed by Machapunga, 690.
popuation, 126.
sketch of, 126.
town of, 631.
tribe occupying peninsula near mouth of Neuse River, N. C., 126.
Coreorgonel, town destroyed by Sullivan, 201.
located on Cayuga Lake, 201.
Corn, guinea (Panicum sp.), use of, 288.
Corn (Zea sp.), 268, 269, 274, 281, 288, 289, 296, 373.
cooking, 351–359.
planting, 306, 307, 308.
Coronado, Francesco de, explorations of, 74.
Corpus Christi Pass, 59.
Cosapuya, interpretation of name, 217.
See Cusabo.
Cossa, Indian town, 66.
"Costa Indians," see Ais.
Coste, Koasati town mentioned by De Soto's chroniclers 27.
See also Koasati, 145, 268.
Costehe, see Coste.
See Koasati, 145.
town of, 69.
Costehe Indians, identification as Coste, 48.
and as Koasati, 65, 68.
Cotton Gin Port, Tex., 51.
Council Hill, settlement of Osochi located at, 169.
Court House of Johnston County, at Tishomingo, Okla., formerly last Chickasaw Council House, 118.

"Cousah Old Fields," location, 125.
Coushatta, La., named for Koasati, 145.
Coussana, see Inkillis Tamaha.
Cow Creek Indians, see Muskogee, 182.
Cowatoe, 111.
Cowe, Cherokee town, 675.
Coweta, 26, 126, 127, 131, 143, 153, 180, 185, 197.
Chattahoochee River, former home of, 127.
chief of, sometimes called "Emperor of the Creeks," 127.
clothing, 470.
Franciscan friars ordered out of country by, 62, 92.
Fray Juan Ocon ordered away from mission by, 180.
household utensils, 558, 604.
images, 616.
member of Creek Confederation, 126.
moieties, 664.
moved to Ocmulgee to be near English, 127.
Muskogee tribe among Lower Creeks, 126.
originally part of Kasihta, 126.
population, 127.
possibly visited by De Soto, 127.
pottery, 551.
removal to Arkansas River near town of Coweta, 127.
return to Chattahoochee after Yamasee War, 127.
sketch of, 126–127.
town of, burned by Spaniards under Matheos, 63.
towns of, 633.
Coxe, Daniel, 108, 115, 166, 180.
claims of upheld by ship under Captain Bond, 108.
Louisiana claimed by, 77.
name Chehawhaw extended by to Tallapoosa River, 28.
name Samboukia applied by to town of Sawokli, 28.
pearl fisheries mentioned by, 489.
Coz, Captain Martinez de, soldiers under, destroyed by Tocobaga, 195.
Coza, identification as Coosa, 65.
Cozao, classification of tribe, 67.
Crabapples (Malus sp.), use of, 272.
Cradles, 562–563, 713, 716, 717.
Crane Creek, 46.
Crane, Verner W., on hair dressing, 505.
Craven County, N. C., home of Neusiok tribe, 162.
Craven, Governor, Yamasee defeated by English under, 209.
Crawfish, red, symbol of Houma, 29.
Cree language, resemblances to in Powhatan dialect, 24, 31.
Creek and English expedition, 1704, 63.
Creek census, 186.
Creek Confederation, 19, 20, 27, 121, 126, 128, 137, 138, 153, 217, 239, 801, 822, 827, 828.

Creek Confed., Chiaha member of, 115.
  Coweta member of, 126.
  founded at Ocmulgee Old Fields, 138.
  population, 154.
  source material on, 827, 828.
  traditional origin of, 92.
  See also under separate tribes, and especially Muskogee.
Creek country, 13.
  Chickasaw town established in, 117.
  Koasati settled in, 145.
  Muskogee representatives in northern section of, 125, 143.
  Square Ground reestablished in, by Okmulgee, 168.
  Tukabahchee Square Ground established in, in Okla., 197.
  Tuskegee settled in, west of Mississippi, 2u0.
Creek language, reference to, 70.
  spoken by Coça Indians, 60.
Creek months, names of, 262.
Creek Nation, 22, 146, 152, 153, 168, 169, 170, 210, 214, 215, 242.
  moieties among, 664.
Creek reserve, Kealedji settled in southeastern part of, 144.
Creek Sam, Natchez brave, oldest speaker of Natchez tongue, 160.
Creek War, 79, 122, 133, 147, 152, 173, 181, 182, 191, 197, 207, 214.
  Coweta sided with whites during, 127.
  no part taken in by Abihka, 81.
  part taken in by the Alabama, 87.
  part taken by Cherokee in, 112.
  part taken by Coosa tribes in, 125.
Creeks, 1, 11, 16, 19, 26, 27, 28, 29, 30, 43, 77, 91, 107, 111, 112, 115, 116, 118, 121, 122, 135, 139, 145, 150, 152, 154, 160, 161, 167, 170, 197, 210, 238, 262, 297, 665, 736, 801, 805, 806, 807, 809, 810, 816, 821, 822, 823, 827.
  Abihka a name used in migration legends of, 81.
  anklets of terrapin shells worn by women of, during dances, 523.
  artistic development, 616, 617.
  attack on Chatot and Apalachicola, 107.
  bags or purses, 480.
  bead substitute, 486.
  beds, 422.
  birth customs, 714.
  bracelets and arm bands, 522.
  burial customs, 724, 725, 811, 817.
  caste system, 662.
  ceremonial dances, 264, 456.
  children, treatment of, 715.
  clans and gentes, 654, 656, 657.
  clothing, 439, 457, 461, 463, 464, 471, 472, 475, 476, 817.
    worn by medicine men, 478.
  coloring for manufactured articles, 609.
  communication, means of, 733, 734.

Creeks, crime and punishment, 731, 732, 817.
  defeat by Chickasaw, 118.
  dietary, 285.
  domestic animals, 345, 348, 349.
  doors, 428.
  ear ornaments, 512, 513, 817.
  featherwork, 455.
  finger rings, 522.
  fire making, 423, 424, 817.
  flags, 431.
  flint, use of, 543.
  games, 548, 675, 677, 678, 679, 680, 681, 682, 683, 684, 685, 686.
  greasing and coloring of hair and skin, 527, 528, 530, 817.
  hair dressing, 499, 501, 505, 506, 808, 817.
  head deformation not practiced by, 541, 817.
  home customs, 714, 716, 718.
  household utensils, 556.
  houses, 390, 391 (fig.), 392, 394, 395, 421, 817.
  hunting, 331.
  illuminating, 426.
  images, 616, 617, 817.
  implements for hunting and fishing, 575, 578, 586, 587, 694.
  marriage customs, 703, 704, 705, 706, 707, 817.
  mats and baskets, 604, 605.
  medical practices, 794.
  meeting of Washington with, 146, 154.
  members of Muskhogean linguistic family, 238, 816.
  metal, use of, 495.
  mnemonic devices, 611, 612.
  moral characteristics, 230.
  movements, 63.
  musical instruments, 625, 627.
  names used by, 672, 673, 674.
  necklaces, 518, 520.
  nose ornaments, 515.
  oak logs for sacred fires, 245.
  ornamentation, 490.
  permission granted Cherokee to remain in Tennessee Valley by, 112.
  physical characteristics, 222, 223, 224, 225.
  pipes, 547, 817.
  political trading, 78.
  pottery making, 551, 553.
  relationship, terms of, 666, 667, 668, 669, 670.
  relations with Choctaw improved by U. S. control of Mississippi, 122.
  religious beliefs and usages, 772, 773, 774.
  skin dressing, 445, 446.
  smoke-holes and windows, 427.
  sufferings in Indian removal, 80.
  tattooing, 533.
  threads and textiles, 449, 454.
  towns, 633, 634.

Creeks, transportation, means of, 594.
 Upper, see Upper Creeks.
 wampum, 484.
 war customs, 690, 693, 694, 695,
  696.
 weapons, 575, 578, 586, 587, 694.
 withdrawal from Tennessee Valley,
  112.
Crenay, Baron de, 144.
Crime and punishment, 730–733.
Croatan Indians, Raleigh's colonists
 supposed to have taken refuge with,
 76, 137.
Croatans, 145, 172, 178, 183.
Crosses, erected by De Soto, 43, 44, 52.
Crouetchitou, Indian village, 637.
Crow system of relationship, 666, 670.
Crowley's Ridge, Miss., 53.
Cuba, Island of, 33, 34, 36, 61.
 De Soto made governor of, 40.
 movement of Florida Indians to, 64.
 removal of Guacata to, 134.
 removal of Jeaga to, 141.
Cuban Indians, settled in Calusa
 country, 239.
Cucurbita citrullus, use of, 635.
Cucurbita lagenaria, use of, 275.
Cucurbita sp., use of, 286, 293, 296.
Cucurbita verrucosa, use of, 635.
Cuera, Don Martin de, defeat of by
 Apalachee, 90.
Culin, Stewart, on games, 548, 686.
Cullasaja Creek, 47.
Cultural areas, 825, 826.
Cultural characters, common, 801–805.
Cultural differences, 805–812.
Cultural subareas, 812–823.
Cumberland Island, Ga., 119, 132, 141,
 187, 209, 215.
 named San Pedro by Spaniards, 187.
 occupied by Yamasee, 187.
 populated by old Timucua, 119,
  187, 215.
Cumberland River, 31.
 home of Shawnee in 17th century,
  184.
Cumberland, temporary home of Kaskinampo, 143.
Cumberland Valley, Shawnee expelled
 from, 111, 117.
Cuming, Sir Alexander, mission to
 Cherokee lead by, 111.
Cupressus disticha, use of, 594.
Curtis, Robert John, painting of Osceola
 by, 182.
Cusabo, 28, 67, 115, 124, 126, 128–129,
 178, 217, 280, 404, 827, 829.
 arrows, 572.
 assisted South Carolina colonists
  against Santee and Congaree,
  178.
 attacked by Westo, 129.
 Barnwell's Tuscarora expedition
  joined by, 129.
 games, 682.
 group of tribes, in southern Carolina, 128.

Cusabo, joined Sewee to help South
 Carolina colonists repel Spaniards,
 183.
 name, interpretation of, 217.
 Palawana Island granted to, 129.
 population, 129.
 possible union with Catawba, 129.
 province, Indians of, reference to
  description of by Ribault Expedition, 61.
 sketch of, 128–129.
 source material on, 829.
 town destroyed, 30.
 towns, 632.
 visited by Capt. Robert Sandford,
  128.
 visited by Capt. William Hilton of
  English ship Adventure, 128.
Cuscowilla, capitol of Alachua tribe, description, 396.
Cushing, Frank Hamilton, on artistic
 development of the Key Marco people,
 620–623.
 on beads, 485.
 on ear ornaments, 511, 512.
 on fishing, 337, 338, 339, 340.
 on mat making, 604.
 on relics found at Key Marco, 504,
  511, 516, 518, 521, 524, 556, 557,
  560, 562, 565, 566, 569, 570, 572,
  584, 589, 590, 591, 603, 619, 620–
  623, 809.
 on skin-dressing tools, 447, 448.
Cushions, use of, 432, 598.
Cushman, H. B., missionary, 673, 679,
 680, 683, 828.
 on household utensils, 563.
 on houses, 401, 408, 409.
 on hunting habits of Choctaw, 316.
 on incorporation of Chakchiuma
  with Chickasaw and Choctaw,
  106.
 on medical practices, 795, 796.
 on use of horses by Choctaw, 349,
  350.
Customs relating to birth, education,
 and the division of labor between the
 sexes, 709–718.
Cwarennoc, name used for Coree or
 Coranine on Hariot's map, 126.
Cycleptus elongatus, use as food, 267.
Cyclones, West India, 5.
Cypress (Cupressus disticha), use of, 594.
D'Abbadie, Governor of Louisiana, 189.
Dahlonega, Ga., discovery of gold near,
 and effect on Cherokee, 113.
Dancing, 748, 775.
Darien, 39, 101.
 Gulf of, 35.
D'Artaguette, Diron, 161, 829.
D'Artaguette, Pierre, attack on Chicka-
 saw by French forces under, 117.
 failure of in war with Chickasaw,
  73.
Dasemonquepeuc, Indian town in North
 Carolina, 508, 713.
 tattooing worn by women of, 532.

Datha, Indian chief, 615, 647, 755, 758.
Davenport, 156.
Davila, Father, sole survivor of Guale uprising, 135.
Dávila, Pedrárias, see Avila, Pedro Árias de.
Davila, see Padilla, Davila.
Davion, Tunica missionary, 72, 106, 159, 188, 198.
Davis, T. Frederick, on identity of Indians contacted by Ponce de Leon, 34.
    on location of Ponce de Leon's settlement in Florida, 36.
    on voyages of Ponce de Leon, 35.
Daycao River, 58.
Deadose, 130, 172, 240.
    associated with Akokisa and Patiri in mission of San Ildefonso, 96.
    one of tribes served by Mission of San Ildefonso, 86.
    possible extermination by epidemic, 130.
    raid by Nabedache against Apache joined by, 130.
    separated from Bidai Indians, 130.
    settled for a time at San Xavier Mission, 130.
    sketch of, 130.
    tribe living between Trinity and Navasota Rivers, Tex., 130.
Deasonville culture, 33.
De Batz, A., French draftsman, 122, 198, 419, 429, 613, 829.
    reference to sketch of Acolapissa temple by, 82.
Debo, Angie, 832.
De Crenay map, 133, 142, 173, 189, 190, 196, 207.
    Biloxi site shown on, 96.
Deer, great importance of, 249, 295, 297, 439, 448, 449, 457.
    hunting methods for, 312–321, 803.
De Gourgues, Timucua chief·Saturiwa visited by, 555.
De Graffenried, Baron, 631, 831.
    on religious beliefs and usages, 755.
De Kerlérec, Chevalier, 98, 109, 121, 139, 140, 151, 166, 171, 197, 198, 204.
    on Chawasha village near New Orleans, 109.
De la Vente, missionary, 118, 123.
    on morals, 237.
Delaware, 100, 113.
    westward origin indicated by tradition, 24.
De Leon, Alonzo, expedition across Caddo country, 98.
De Leon, Juan Ponce, 35.
    discovery of Florida by, 34.
    hostile reception by Indians, 35.
    settlement in Florida established by, 36.
    visited Nabedache, 155.
Delgado, Marcos, 28, 121.
    visit to Upper Creeks by, 63.
De Luna, see Luna, Tristan de.

De Mézières, Athanase, 155, 211.
De Montigny, see Dumont de Montigny.
Demopolis, Ala., 50.
Densmore, Frances, songs from Florida Seminole obtained by, 102, 828.
De Richebourg, 161.
De Soto, Hernando, 39, 64, 67, 69, 81, 83, 102, 108, 110, 115, 116, 121, 125, 127, 137, 138, 139, 141, 143, 145, 147, 150, 151, 154, 155, 156, 158, 164, 167, 169, 173, 174, 176, 188, 189, 190, 193, 200, 202, 204, 208, 212, 213, 267, 297, 300, 301, 312, 324, 333, 343, 351, 373, 376, 381, 433, 459, 462, 472, 587, 807.
    Altamaha, visited by, 208.
    Apalachee province reached by, 89.
    attacked by Chickasaw, 52, 116, 549, 624.
    battle of Two Lakes, 41.
    battle with Tula Indians, 55.
    birthplace, 39.
    Brier Creek crossed by, 44.
    burial, 56.
    Chawasha probably encountered by, 108.
    Cheraw first visited by Spaniards under, 109.
    death, 56.
    discovery of Chickasaw in Miss., 116.
    encounter with Eyeish, 132.
    encounter with Tula in southwestern Ark., 98, 100.
    entered Mobile territory in Ala., 150, 430.
    entry into Havana, 40.
    erection of crosses, 43.
    extent of territory for conquest granted to, 40.
    expedition against Chakchiuma, 105.
    first Christian ceremony in Ark., conducted under, 52.
    first friendly Indians encountered, 43.
    Florida taken possession of by, 40.
    Georgia reached by, 44.
    governorship of Cuba given to, 40.
    horses brought by, 346.
    landed in territory of Oçita near Tampa Bay, Fla., 151, 165, 613.
    location of Indian tribes encountered, 14, 17, 21, 22, 26, 28, 29, 30.
    march begun, 40.
    Mississippi River reached by, 52.
    Moscoso successor to, 158.
    Muskogean interpreter with, 67.
    Okalusa heard of by Spaniards under, 167.
    on food used by natives, 265.
    passage of the Savannah, 45.
    pearls given by "Lady of Cofitachequi" to, 45.
    period following, 59–81.
    port of embarkation, 40.
    possibly attacked by Washa, 204.

De Soto, Hernando, Potano first encountered by, 173.
  rise of Tascalusa's Indians at Mobile against, 50.
  snow reported by, 55.
  Timucua encountered by, 40–42, 193.
  trade in copper mentioned by, 492, 737.
  tribes encountered by:
    Altamaha, 43.
    Apalachee, 41, 42.
    Aquixo, 52.
    Casqui, 52, 54.
    Chisi (Ichisi), 43.
    Guachoya, 56.
    Quizquiz, 52.
    Timucua, 40–42.
    Utiangue, 55.
    Yustaga, 216.
    (See also under individual names of tribes.)
  visted Ocale tribe northeast of Withlacoochee River, Fla., 164, 628.
  wife of, 40.
  Yuchi found by in eastern Tennessee, 212.
  Yustaga province traversed by, 216.
De Soto army, description of, 40.
  visit to Cofitachequi by bulk of, 137, 143.
De Soto chroniclers, 67.
  distribution of Indian popuulation revealed by, 12, 26, 31.
  no mention of Kadohadacho made by, 141.
De Soto Expedition, 39–59, 828.
De Soto map, reference to, 46.
De Soto narratives, Acuera mentioned in, 83.
De Villiers, Le Baron Marc, on towns, 637, 638.
Dickenson, Jonathan, 134, 136, 141, 255, 334, 338, 369, 404, 405, 408, 427, 457, 590, 829.
  on clothing, 471.
  on food, 281, 282.
  on hair dressing, 504.
  on religious beliefs and usages, 763, 764, 765.
  on social customs, 649.
  on transportation, means of, 595.
  reference to account of Ais by, 84.
Dioscorea villosa, uses of, 244, 270, 293, 362.
Diospyros sp., use of, 287, 288, 564.
Dirca palustris, uses of, 248.
Dishes and spoons of wood and horn, 556–558.
  See Household utensils.
Displacement of prehistoric Indians discussed, 21.
Distribution of raw materials, 253–255.
Dixon's Mills, Ga., 50.
Dolichos sp., use of as food, 285, 286, 288.

Dominican Friars, 70.
Don Felipe, Calusa chief, death of, 101.
Don Juan, Tacatacuru chief, 187.
  desire to become "mico mayor" of Guale, 187.
  succeeded by his sister's daughter, 187.
Don Luis, chief apparently of Tekesta, 192, 523.
  adornment worn by, on visit to San Miguel, 523.
Don Luis, brother of chief of Axacan province, settlement with missionaries in Virginia, 70.
  taken to Mexico by Spaniards, 70.
  treachery of, 70.
  visit to Spanish court, 70.
Doors, 428–432, 804.
Dormon, Miss Caroline, 198.
Dorosoma cepedianum, use as food, 266.
Dorsey, Dr. George A., 832.
Dorsey, Dr. James Owen, 684, 727, 831.
  on collection of Indian material at Indian Creek, La., 97, 657.
Dougherty County, Ga., 43.
Doustioni, 130, 211.
  allies of Kadohadacho, 130.
  home of near Natchitoches in northern Louisiana, 130.
  known also as Souchitiony, Dulchinois, and Oulchionis, 130.
  population, 130.
  probably lost identity in Natchitoches, 130.
  settled on Red River by St. Denis, 130.
  sketch of, 130.
  visited by Bienville and St. Denis, 130.
Drake, Sir Francis, 76.
Drake's Salt Works, 57.
Drum, black (Pogonias chromis), use as food, 267.
  freshwater (Haplodinotus grunniens), use as food, 267.
Drums, 624–626.
  See Musical instruments.
Drupi sp., use of, 288, 289.
Dublin, Ga., 44.
Duhare, province in South Carolina, 647, 721.
Dulchanchellin, chief of band of Utina met by Narvaez, 202.
Dulchinois, see Doustioni, 130.
Dumont de Montigny, missionary, 107, 109, 118, 159, 160, 188, 189, 198, 290, 236, 261, 327, 427, 430, 662, 681, 684, 727, 729, 734, 807, 829, 831.
  established among Taensa, 188.
  on artistic development, 618.
  on children, education of, 718.
  on clothing, 472, 476.
  on cooking, 357, 358, 371.
  on deer hunting by Natchez, 315, 316, 321, 322, 325, 353.
  on feather mantles, 455.
  on fire making, 425, 427.

Dumont de Montigny, on food preserving, 377, 378.
    on hair dressing, 500, 501, 507.
    on head deformation, 538.
    on houses, 416, 417, 420.
    on mats and baskets, 608.
    on medical practices of Indians, 798.
    on moth prevention, 444.
    on musical instruments, 627.
    on necklaces, 519.
    on ornamentation, 486, 490.
    on pipes, 547.
    on pottery, 550.
    on skin dressing, 443, 444.
    on supposed massacre of Chawasha, 109.
    on symbol of Houma Indians, 29.
    on tattooing, 535.
    on thread and textiles, 449.
    on tobacco, 385, 386.
    on transportation, means of, 600, 601.
Dunbar, William, 830.
Du Pratz, see Le Page du Pratz, Antoine.
Duralde, Martin, 829, 830.
    Eastern Atakapa vocabulary obtained by, 94.
Durand's Bend, Alabama River, Dallas Co., site of "Talisi province" encountered by De Soto, 49, 125.
Durham, N. C., 183.
Du Roullet, Régis, 828.
    on towns, 637.
Dutch maps, reference to, 30.
Dyer, J. O., 737.
    on quarries worked by Indians, 542.
Dyes, made by Indians, 605, 606, 607, 609.
Eakins, D. W., on mnemonic devices of the Indians, 612.
Ear ornaments, 510–514.
Early County, Ga., 43.
Ebenezer Creek, on Savannah River, home of Yuchi, 214.
Echeconnee stream, Ga., 314.
Echinochloa crusgalli, use of, 286, 291.
Echota, Cherokee town, 768.
Ecija, Spanish navigator, 177, 182, 739.
Edisto, town of, 632.
Edisto River, S. C., 115, 124.
    home of Cusabo, 128.
Education, see Customs relating to birth, education, and the division of labor between the sexes.
Edwards, John, 828.
Eggan, Fred, 831.
Egwǎ'nǐ, Cherokee word meaning river, 165.
Egypt, northeastern boundary of cultural area, 825.
"Ekun-duts-ke," name of town, 142.
Elkhatchee, western branch of Tallapoosa, site of Okchai settlement, 167.
Elton, La., 145.

Elvas, Narrative of a Gentleman of, 46, 51, 53, 121, 132, 155, 156, 158, 266, 267, 268, 299, 321, 347, 351, 428, 429, 433, 435, 440, 451, 457.
    mention of "Black Water" province by, 25.
    name of Alabama given to small village by, 86.
    on artistic development, 619.
    on body paint, 529.
    on Casqui, 27.
    on clothing, 458, 469, 473.
    on crossing of Georgia River by De Soto, 44.
    on food preserving, 378.
    on hair dressing, 506.
    on head bands, 508.
    on household utensils, 558, 560.
    on houses, 386, 387, 408.
    on hunting, 330.
    on implements for hunting and fishing, 564, 571, 576, 577, 580, 583.
    on metals, use of, 490.
    on musical instruments, 624, 628.
    on number of survivors of De Soto expedition, 59.
    on ornamentation, 488.
    on pottery, 549.
    on religious beliefs and usages, 762.
    on salt, use of, 301.
    on skin dressing, 442.
    on stockaded town, 434.
    on sunshade carried over the chief, 430, 431, 652.
    on towns, 632.
    on transportation, means of, 593, 598, 601, 602.
    on weapons, 564, 571, 576, 577, 580, 583.
    See also Robertson, James Alexander, ed.
Embalming methods, as practiced by Indians, 719, 721.
"Emperor of the Creeks," name sometimes applied to chief of Coweta, 127.
"Empire of Powhatan," see Powhatan Confederation.
Emuckfa, battle of, 114.
Emusas, see Yamasee, 210, 211.
Enciso, 35.
End-town, see Talledega.
England, Florida and French possessions east of Mississippi ceded to, 62, 64, 78.
    history of relations with Indians, 75–78.
English, aid given to Alabama in tribal war by, 87.
    assisted by Catawba against French at Fort Duquesne, 104.
    attacked by Yamasee, whom they defeated, 209.
    census of 1715, Alabama population given by, 88.
    Chickasaw supported in war with French by, 73.

English, convoy, ascending Mississippi, attack on, 166.
 early struggles between Spaniards and, 63.
 influence strong among Natchez, 159.
 Pamlico first discovered on Pamlico River, N. C., by, 170.
 relations with Indians, 75–78.
 slave hunters, attack on Acolapissa by, 82.
 traders, Coosa found by in Ala. in 17th century, 125.
 Waxhaw discovered by, in North and South Carolina, 206.
 Yamasee uprising against, 63.
English and Creek expedition, 1704, 63.
English and Indian allies, attack on by Apalachocola, 92.
English Turn, scene of encounter between French and English, 77.
Eno, 66, 130, 131, 145, 183, 186, 217, 380, 815.
 apparently united with Catawba, 131.
 found by Lawson on Eno River near Hillsboro, N. C., 131, 183.
 games, 548, 682.
 houses, 413.
 included in Tuscarora list, by Lawson, 131.
 name, interpretation of, 217.
 location, 131.
 moved to South Carolina and united with Catawba, 131.
 population, 131.
 possible identity with Weanoc or Wyanoke, 130.
 sketch of, 130–131.
 trade, 739.
Enoree River, S. C., may be clue to original habitat of Eno, 131.
Eno River, N. C., Occaneechi found by Lawson on, 164.
 Adshusheer, village on, 183.
 named for Eno, 131.
Ephippick, Apalachicola town, 92.
Equale, Fla., see Toquale.
Erie, Ala., 50.
Eryngium yuccaefolium, uses of, 248.
Esaw, see Catawba Indians, 564.
Eskippakithiki, Shawnee town on Lulbegrud Creek, Clark Co., Ky., 185.
Espinosa, Fray Isidro Felis de, 158, 674, 832.
 on musical instruments, 629.
Etanie, Seminole settlement, 194.
 located in Utina country, 202.
Etiwaw, a Cusabo tribe, allied with whites against Congaree and Santee, 124.
 See also Itwams.
Etowah River, Ga., 14.
 Eufaula on affluent of, 131.
Etowah works, 26.
Euchee Old Fields, 213.

Eufaula, 26, 131, 132, 153, 160, 181, 203, 215.
 artistic development, 617.
 early home on Euharlee Creek, Ga., 131.
  on Talladega Creek, Ala., 131.
 Muskogee tribe, 131.
 population, 132.
 removal to Oklahoma with Creeks, 132.
 sketch of, 131–132.
 Square Ground, 81, 776.
Eufaula Hatchee or Eufaula Oldtown, home of Eufaula of Talladega Creek, Ala., 26, 131, 132.
Eufaula Oldtown, see Eufaula Hatchee.
Euharlee Creek, Ga., early home of Eufaula, 26, 131.
Expedition of Hernandez de Soto, 39–59.
Eyeish, 98, 132.
 almost destroyed by smallpox, 132.
 Caddo tribe living on Ayish Creek, San Augustine Co., Tex., 132.
 first mentioned in Elvas and Biedma narratives, 132.
 identification with Hais, 57.
 on Attoyac River in 1785, 132.
 population, 132.
 relation to Caddo, 98, 132.
 settlement between the Brazos and Colorado, 132.
 sketch of, 132.
 union with other Caddo tribes, 132.
 Zacatecan mission to, 75.
Fagus sp., use of, 288.
Fallam, Robert, 76, 152, 157, 200, 302.
Farming, effect upon the growth of states, 17–18.
Featherwork, 454–456, 472.
Federal Government, relations with Cherokee, 113.
Fernandez, Benito, death of, 43.
Fernandino, Simon, 76.
Ferrara, Duke of, 34.
Ferriday, 56.
Filache, Fla., 133.
Filipina Bay, Spanish name for Mobile Bay, 60.
Finger rings, 522–523.
Fire Chief (often known as Mingo Luak), Chitimacha chief, 120.
Fire making, 422–427.
First Seminole War, 79.
Fishing, 343–344, 485, 803.
Fish Pond Indians, see Okchai, 166, 167.
Fish, uses of, 251, 253.
Fishweirs, stone, on Tampa Bay, 243, 548.
Fitch, Tobias, reference to Abihka town by, 82.
"Five Civilized Tribes," 181.
 tribes comprised in, 19.
Flageolets, 628–629.
 See Musical instruments.
"Flat Heads," name used for Catawba and Choctaw, 539.
Flint implements, 543–544.

"Flint People," name used for Avoyel Indians, 542, 543.
Flint River, 26, 63, 89, 92, 107, 127, 138, 153, 168, 169, 189, 214.
    identification with River of Capachequi, 42.
    Spaniards' Rio Grande, 43.
    probably named for flint quarries, 542.
    towns visited by De Soto probably on, 127.
Florencia, Capt. Juan Fernandez de, Apalachee commandant, Chatot uprising suppressed by, 107.
    rebuilds Timucua towns, 202.
Florida, ancient inhabitants known from Laudonnière expedition, 62.
    cession to England, 62, 78, 84.
    discovery, 34, 35.
    Governor of, 83.
        expedition sent against Oconee, by, 165.
    Guacata tribe on southeast coast, 134.
    Huguenot colony in, 74.
    Indians, arm bands, 522.
        body paint, 531.
        clothing, 457, 525.
        ear ornaments, 511.
        leg ornaments, 523.
        moral characteristics, 233.
        necklaces, 518.
        on implements for hunting and fishing, 575, 577.
        use of beads, 485.
        use of pearls, 488.
        weapons, 575, 577.
    invasion of, by Andrew Jackson, 150, 181.
    Potano Indians of, 11.
    possession of taken by De Soto, 40.
    purchased by United States, 79.
    southern, Indians of, 34.
        cultural level, 10.
    Spanish control of, 62.
    Timucua and Apalachee Indians of, 11.
    Yamasee moved to, 63.
Florida, Cape of, 37.
Florida Keys, 12, 84.
Florida Peninsula, 22, 34, 63.
    south of Tampa Bay, home or Calusa, 12, 101.
Florida, State of, 1, 5, 11, 12, 16, 18, 19, 20, 21, 29, 30, 32, 34, 35, 36, 37, 40, 52, 59, 61, 64, 70, 71, 73, 74, 78, 83, 87.
Folsom, Choctaw informant, 795.
Fontaine, Rev. James, on houses, 412, 421.
    on population of Fort Christanna, 178, 347.
    on towns, 632.
    on use of horses, 348.
Fontaneda, Hernando Escalante de, 101, 133, 134, 141, 239, 298, 347, 738, 829.
    Ais mentioned by, 84.
Fontaneda, Hernando Escalante de, chief source of information on Calusa, 59.
    life among, 90, 101.
    on clothing, 471.
    on food habits about Lake Okeechobee, 255, 256, 282.
    on story of Apalachee gold, 90.
Food, 244–253, 255, 265–295.
    cooking of, 351–372.
    discussion, 296–304.
    preparation of vegetable, 351–368.
    preservation, 372–386.
    tables of, 293, 294, 295.
        animal, 295.
        vegetable, 293, 294.
Ford, James A., on occupancy of Bayogoula site, 29.
    opinion on age of Bayogoula remains cited, 94.
Ford and Chambers, significance of archeological evidence in relation to Natchez movements collected by, 29.
Ford and Willey, cited on archeology of Gulf area, 33.
Foreman, Dr. Grant, 831, 832.
    cited on Indian movements, 79–80.
    on bags, 480.
    on burial customs, 725.
    on cooking, 354, 355, 361.
    on fire making, 424.
    on hair dressing, 506.
    on houses of Chickasaw, 400.
    on implements for hunting and fishing, 564.
    on mnemonic devices, 612.
Fort, palisaded, of Yuchi, 65.
Fort Caroline, 89.
Fort Christanna, Va., 19, 152, 164, 178, 179, 201, 632.
    Manahoac brought to, 148.
    Saponi placed by Governor Spotswood near, 178.
Fort Duquesne, Catawba aid to English at, 104.
    Cherokee and British attack on, 112.
Fort Gaines, Shawnee band moved near, 184.
Fort Loudon, destruction by Cherokee, 78, 112.
Fort Louis, 87.
    first French establishment in Mobile Bay, 72.
Fort Mitchell, settlement of Coweta above, 127.
Fort Moore, Chickasaw settlement established near, 117.
Fort Moultrie, aided by Catawba, 104.
Fort Necessity, 57.
"Fort Noo-he-roo-ka," fort captured by Moore in Tuscacora War, 438, 439.
    See also Hancock, King, fort built by.
Fort Rosalie, on Mississippi, named after Duchess of Pontchartrain, 72, 159.
    rebuilt on Mississippi, 166, 195.

Fort St. Peter, Miss., established near Yazoo town, 211.
  massacre of garrison by Koroa and Yazoo, 147.
Fort San Juan, built by Capt. Juan Pardo, 65, 109.
  destroyed by Cheraw, 110.
Fort Toulouse, at junction of Coosa and Tallapoosa Rivers, 22, 72, 170, 171.
  established by French, 78.
  Pakana settled near, 170.
  Pawokti settled near, 171.
  Shawnee refusal to join English and Creeks in attack on, 185.
  Tawasa located near, 191.
Foucault, French missionary, murdered by Yazoo, 211.
  avenged by Koroa Chiefs, 147.
Four Hole Swamp, S. C., home of Natchez band, 160.
"Fowl Town," see Tutalosi.
Fox, Indian tribe, 518.
  clans and gentes, 656.
  language, affinity with Shawnee, 31.
Frachtenberg, Dr. Leo J., 201, 830.
Fragaria sp., 637.
France, colonization efforts of, 71.
  progress under the Bourbons, 71.
Franciscan missions, in northern Florida, success of, 62.
  in Texas, 83.
Franciscan monks, sent to Apalachicola, 92.
Franciscans, missions to Guale taken over by, 135.
  See also Missionaries.
Francisco de los Tejas, first Franciscan mission in Texas, 83.
Francisco of Chicora, Indian brave, 37, 182, 183, 647, 830.
  account of Indians obtained from, by Peter Martyr, 36.
  brought home by Ayllon expedition, 183.
Franklin, N. C., 17.
Franquelin, map of, 165.
Frederica, Ga., Christian Gottlieb Priber, imprisoned and died in, 111.
Fredericksburg township, claimed by Wateree, 205.
French, B. F., 462, 504, 533.
French, allies of Chakchiuma in Natchez War, 106.
  allies of Utina in raid on Potano, 173, 202.
  attack on Chickasaw, 117.
  attack with Choctaw on Natchez, 160.
  census, 170, 173, 191, 200.
  Chickasaw war with, 73.
  colony, history of first established in South Carolina, 61.
    second, destroyed by Spanish under Menendez, 62.
    established on St. Johns River by Laudonnière, 61.

French, defeat by Chickasaw, 74.
  destruction of Mission of San Miguel de Linares by, 83.
  displaced by Spaniards, 173, 202.
  estimate of Alabama population, 88.
  first fort constructed on Mississippi by, 161.
  Indian population conditions at time of contact with, 13.
  Indian tribes found on Georgia-South Carolina coast by, 26.
  Kadohadacho on Red River, Ark., reached, 141.
  Natchitoches discovered by, under Tonti, 161.
  Ofo settled on Red River as allies of, 166.
  on ear ornaments, 511.
  settlement near old Caddo town, 142.
    removed to Campti, La., 142.
  supported by four of the Sixtowns, 121.
  Tohome discovered by, 196.
  under Ribault and Laudonnière, Tacatacuru visited by, 187.
French and Indian War, part taken by Cherokee in, 112.
Fresh Water ("Agua Dulce") Indians 133, 193, 194.
  population, 133.
  sketch of, 133.
Fresh Water province, 174, 202.
Fresh Water Timucua, reached by Ponce de Leon, 193.
Friar Point, Miss., 53, 54.
Fulton, Colonel, one of purchasers of Biloxi and Pascagoula lands, 97.
Fus-hatchee, 125, 134, 142, 147, 153, 217.
  Creek town, on south side of Tallapoosa River, 125, 133, 142, 147, 181. 191.
  joined by Kan-hatki, 142, 181.
  name, interpretation of in Muskogee tongue, 217.
  population, 134.
  sketch of, 133–134.
  Tawasa with, 191.
Gaffarel, Paul Louis Jacques, 281, 371, 407.
  on arrows, 579.
  on clothing, 471.
  on hair dressing, 504.
  on tattooing, 534.
  on use of beads, 485.
Gallatin, Albert, 140, 161.
Gallegos, Baltasar de, Chief Constable, De Soto Expedition, 40, 46, 51, 83.
  promoted to Master of the Camp, 52.
Galphin, George, on location of Indian town of Cofitachequi, 45.
Galveston Bay, Tex., 85, 93.
Galveston Harbor, 59.
Galveston Island, 39, 74, 85.

Galvez, Governor, Atakapa enlisted in expedition of against English by, 93, 94.
Games, 674–686.
Garay, Francisco de, Governor of Jamaica, 35.
Garcia, Genaro, 222, 281, 303, 329, 338, 351, 358, 367, 422, 429, 441, 442.
  on artistic development, 617.
  on beads, 485.
  on body paint, 532.
  on clothing, 457, 471.
  on cooking, 357.
  on fingernails, length of, 537.
  on games, 683.
  on hair dressing, 504.
  on household utensils, 558.
  on houses, 405.
  on leg ornaments, 523.
  on medical practices, 792.
  on necklaces, 518.
  on skin dressing, 442.
  on social customs, 713, 723.
  on transportation, means of, 590, 594.
Garcilaso de la Vega (El Inca), 126, 138, 150, 155, 246, 268, 270, 286, 321, 333, 373, 406, 428, 431, 433, 434, 435, 440, 448, 451, 457, 458, 633, 737, 738, 805.
  identification of Acuera with Ocale, 83.
  name of Alabama given to a province by, 86.
  on artistic development, 614, 619.
  on bison, 324, 325.
  on clothing, 469, 472.
  on coloring of manufactured articles, 609.
  on De Soto's crossing of Georgia River, 44.
  on fire making, 426.
  on fishing, 334, 548.
  on flint, use of, 544.
  on hair dressing, 498, 501, 503.
  on head bands, 508.
  on head deformation, 537.
  on household utensils, 555, 561.
  on implements for hunting and fishing, 566, 567, 571, 576, 577, 580, 581, 583, 584, 587.
  on mats and baskets, 602, 603.
  on metals, use of, 490, 738.
  on necklaces, 516.
  on ornamentation, 488.
  on palisades, 434, 435.
  on pearl gathering, 488.
  on musical instruments, 624, 628.
  on salt, 301.
    substitutes for, 303.
  on sunshade or flag carried by followers of Tascalusa, 431.
  on Temple of Talomeco, 45, 566–567.
  on town of Mabila, 434.
  on towns, 634.
  on transportation, means of 593, 595, 598, 601.

Garcilaso de la Vega on weapons, 566, 567, 571, 576, 577, 580, 581, 583, 584 587.
Garcitas Creek, site of La Salle settlement, 71.
Gates, Sir Thomas, deputy governor of Virginia, 493.
Gatschet, Dr. Albert S., 97, 120, 152, 156, 198, 217, 218, 219, 292, 499, 734, 761, 762, 767, 828, 829, 830.
  Apalachee families on North Canadian Rivers noted by, 91.
  Atakapa vocabulary collected by, 92.
  Hitchiti stories recorded by, 22.
  on artistic development, 619.
  on bracelets, 522.
  on branch towns of Abihka, 81:
  on burial customs, 729.
  on ear ornaments, 514.
  on finger rings, 522.
  on gorgets, 520.
  on greasing and coloring of hair and skin, 528.
  on hairdressing, 501, 507.
  on nose ornaments, 515.
  on ornamentation, 524.
  report on Biloxi on Indian Creek, near Lecompte, La., 97.
Gaytan, Juan, 50.
Gê tribes, natives of South America, 824.
Geography of the Southeast, life zones in area, 1–10.
Georgia, State of, 1, 13, 14, 16, 19, 21, 26, 28, 48, 61, 70, 73, 153.
  census, 191.
  Colonial Records, 119.
  founded by English, 78.
  reached by De Soto, 44.
Gerard, W. R., 31.
  on food, 271.
Gholsonville, Va., 149, 178.
Gilbert, William Harlen, Jr., 831.
Gill, Dr. Theodore, on fish used as food, 267.
Gleditsia meliloba, use of, 287.
Glen, Governor, interview with Indians, 163.
  letter on Wateree, 205.
  Pedee asked to join Catawba by, 172.
Glover, Charlesworth, 215.
Gold, discovery near Dahlonega, Ga., and effect on Cherokee, 113.
  beads, Central American designs on, 35.
  extent of use of among Indians, 35, 494.
  report of, received by De Soto, 42.
  reported to French among Apalachee, 90.
  sources of, 35, 59.
Goliad, 75.
Gomez, Estevan, 37.
"Good Humor," *see* Stimafutchki.
Gordillo, Francisco, early explorations by, 36.

Gordon, Governor of Pennsylvania, Pierre Chartier reprimanded by, 185.
Gorgets, 518, 519, 520.
  See also Necklaces, 519.
Gourgues, Dominique de, 62.
  assisted by Saturiwa in his punitive expedition, 179.
Government modeled after United States adopted by Cherokee, 113.
Governor of Florida, punitive expedition against Guale uprising undertaken by, 135.
Grand Lake, La., 12, 17, 30.
  home of Chitimacha, 119.
Grand River reservation, Ont., Tuscarora allied with Great Britain in Revolution, located on, 199.
Granganimeo, North Carolina coast noble, 510, 646.
  hair, manner of dressing, 501.
  wife of, Amadas and Barlowe entertained by, 742.
    clothes worn by, 472.
    ear ornaments worn by, 510.
    head band worn by, 509.
Grant, Colonel, Cherokee defeat by forces under, 112.
Grass, cockspur (*Echinochloa crusgalli*), use of, 286, 291.
Gravier, J., Jesuit missionary, 72, 77, 140, 159, 166, 177, 198, 212, 327, 417, 462, 684, 829.
  on agricultural methods, 261.
  on artistic development, 617.
  on food preserving, 380, 381.
  on greasing and coloring of hair and skin, 528.
  on hair dressing, 501.
  on pottery, 550.
  on religious beliefs, 780, 781.
  on staining of teeth, 536.
  on towns, 639.
  visit to Bayogoula, 95.
Greasing and coloring of hair and skin, 526–528.
Great Britain, cession of Florida to, 62, 64, 78, 84, 91.
  conditions in Southeastern U. S., at close of second war with, 79.
  some Tuscarora allied with in Revolutionary War, 199.
Great Houmas, settlement of Houma, 139.
Great Lakes, 32, 71.
Great River people, 33.
"Great Sun of the Natchez," title of chief, 246, 555, 599, 600, 601, 612, 700, 728.
Great Sun, town of Natchez visited by Iberville, 159.
Greenleaf Mountains, site of Square Ground of Natchez, 160.
"Green Leaf," *see* Asilanabi.
Green Peach War, 169, 207.
  Wiwohka responsible for, 207.
Greenville, 50.

Gregg, Alexander, on origin of Catawba Indians, 23.
Grenada Road, 106.
Grenville, Sir Charles, 76.
Grierson, Robert, Scotch trader, resided at Hilibi, 137.
Grigra, 134, 217.
  name, interpretation of, 217.
  Natchez Nation, joined by, 134.
  population, 134.
  sketch of, 134.
  Tunica spoken by, 240.
Gris, *see* Grigra.
Groundnuts (*Apios tuberosa*), use of, 292, 296, 362.
Grovehill, Ala., 50.
Guacata, 84, 134, 192.
  east coast Indians accompanied to Cuba by, 134.
  kind treatment of Menendez' men by, 134.
  location, 134.
  members of Muskhogean linguistic family, 239.
  population unknown, 134.
  sketch of, 134.
  uprising against Spaniards, 134.
  See also Ais.
Guachoya, town on Mississippi River, where De Soto died, 56, 58, 158, 188, 434, 651.
Guacuca River, identification of as Ochlockonee River, 42.
Gualdape, name used for Ayllon colony on South Carolina coast, 135.
Gualdape River, identity of discussed, 37.
  possibly name for Savannah River, 135.
Guale, Indians of, 30, 133, 135, 141, 187, 194, 202, 210, 211, 217, 222, 351, 806, 827.
  attacked by Yuchi, Creeks, and Cherokee, in English interest, 63, 135.
  body paint, 532.
  bracelets, 521.
  clothing, 457.
  doors, material of, 429.
  fingernails and toenails, length of, 537.
  hair dressing, 504.
  household utensils, 558.
  houses, 405, 421.
  incorporation with Yamasee and final disappearance, 136.
  leg ornaments, 523.
  mats and baskets, 603.
  medical practices, 791, 792.
  moved to Florida by Spaniards, 63.
  name given by Spaniards to "province" on coast of Georgia, 18, 26, 37, 135.
    interpretation of, 217.
  physical characteristics, 222.
  population, 136.
  sketch of, 135–136.

Guale, pronounced Wali in English, 135.
repulsed by Tacatacuru after destruction of missions, 187.
smoke-holes and windows, 427.
transfer to Santa Maria, San Juan, and Santa Cruz, 136.
uprising of suppressed, 135.
visited by Menendez, 64.
wars between Indians of Cusabo province and, 128.
withdrawal to Calusa country, 136.
Guale, town in southern part of province of, 132, 135.
Guancane, *see* Nacanish.
Guaquili, town of, 46, 67.
Guasco, Hasinai tribe visited by Spaniards, 136, 741.
encountered by Moscoso, 57.
Guasili, town near Murphy, N. C., perhaps occupied by Cherokee, 110.
identification with Hiwassee, 31, 47, with Tocar, 68.
reached by De Soto, 47.
Guatari, 110, 205.
classification, 67.
identification of with, Wateree 65, 205.
visit of Pardo to, 65.
Guatari River, 66.
Guatariatiqui, council held by Juan Pardo at, 65, 205.
Guaycaya, *see* Waccamaw.
Gueza, identification of, 67, 206.
Guiomaez, identification of Indian town of, 67.
See also Hymahi.
Gulf Indians, clothing, 462.
Gulf of Mexico, *see* Mexico, Gulf of.
Gulf peoples, source of external modifying forces, 33.
Gulf region, American, relation to cultural area, 826.
length of human occupation based on archeological evidence, 33.
Gunter's Landing, 28.
Guzman, Juan de, death of, 59.
Haas, Dr. Mary R., 829.
Haig, murdered by Indians, 163.
Haigler, Catawba chief, killed, 104.
Hainai, 99, 100, 136, 137, 155, 162.
Caddo tribe belonging to Hasinai Confederation, 136.
population, 137.
removal from Texas to north side of Red River, 136.
reported last in 1878, 137.
sketch of, 136–137.
Hair, long, worn by Choctaw, 121, 808.
manner of dressing, 498–507, 805.
"Hair People," name used for Pensacola tribe, 808.
Hais, Indian tribe encountered by Moscoso, 57.
See also Eyeish.
Ha-ish, *see* Eyeish.
Haiti, 33.
Hakluyt Society, papers of, 407, 460, 471, 494, 519, 529, 531, 534, 543, 546, 571, 577.
Halbert, Henry Hale, 679, 680, 683, 727, 828.
on burial chests, 561.
on burial customs, 727.
on incorporation of Chakchiuma with Chickasaw and Choctaw, 106.
Hale, Horatio, 201, 258, 830.
Hamilton, Peter J., 35.
Han, identification of, 85.
Hanahaskies, *see* Nahyssan.
Hanathaskies, *see* Nahyssan.
Hancock, King, fort built by, 438.
Hanna, Charles A., 832.
Hanna, Okla., site of Okchai Square Ground, 167.
site of Square Ground of Hilibi, 137.
Haplodinotus grunniens, 267.
Haplodinotus sp. "pexe pereo" identified as, 267.
Harby, Mrs. Lee C., 832.
Harney, Colonel, conflicts with, 102.
Hariot, Thomas, 126, 305, 325, 335, 783, 831.
on agricultural methods of the Algonquians, 258, 305, 306.
on artistic development, 614, 615.
on axes, 545.
on bags or purses, 479.
on bear hunting, 321.
on body paint, 529.
on bracelets, 521.
on burial customs, 719.
on clothing, 441, 458, 459, 469, 475.
worn by medicine men, 477.
on coloring of articles, 609.
on communication, means of, 735.
on cooking methods, 353, 356, 358, 359, 360, 361, 362, 363, 364, 365, 366.
on deer hunting, 312, 313.
on dietary of the Algonquian tribes, 268, 269, 270, 271, 272, 273, 276, 277, 298, 303.
on ear ornaments, 510.
on fishing methods, 337.
on forts built by Indians, 438.
on hair dressing, 498, 501.
on head bands, 508, 509.
on houses, 413, 414.
on implements for hunting and fishing, 567, 572, 577, 582, 588.
on leg ornaments, 523.
on metals, use of, 491, 492, 495.
on musical instruments, 626.
on necklaces, 516, 519.
on pottery making, 554.
on religious beliefs and customs, 742, 743.
on salt and salt substitutes, 303.
on social organization, 646.
on tattooing, 532.
on tobacco, 382, 383.
on towns of Indians, 630, 631.

Hariot, Thomas, on transportation, means of, 591.
  on treatment of fingernails and toe-nails, 537.
  on weapons, 567, 572, 577, 582, 588.
Harrington, John P., 420.
Harrington, M. R., 555, 832.
Harrisse, Henry, on identification of Florida on Cantino map, 34.
  on place of Verrazano's landing, 37.
Hartford, Captain, 111.
Harvey, Henry, 832.
Hashuk-humma, Illinois troops defeated by Chickasaw at, 117.
Hasinai Confederation, 57, 58, 89, 98, 136, 154, 155, 156, 162, 419, 420, 588, 820.
  Anadarko a tribe of, 89.
  Casañas report on, 74.
  composed of horticultural tribes, 17.
  musical instruments, 629.
  transportation, means of, 597.
  tribes visited by Moscoso connected with, 57.
Hat, see Head bands, 508.
Hatcheetcaba, Kealedji town, 144, 207.
Hatcheetcaba, Sawokli town, 180, 181, 207.
Hatcher, Mattie Austin, 428.
Hatchet Creek, Ala., 49.
  Okchai tribe, branch of, on 167.
  Pakana's first known home on, 170.
  Wakokai located on, 203.
Hathagálgi, "Whites," Creek division, 664.
Hathawekela, most prominent band in history of Gulf tribes, 184.
  reported in Pennsylvania, 184.
  Shawnee band, 184.
Hatteras Indians, 70.
  Algonquian tribe reported as living about Cape Hatteras, N. C., 137.
  Lawson on, 76.
  population, 137.
  possible identity with Croatan Indians, 137.
  sketch of, 137.
  traces of white blood shown by, 137.
Havana, Cuba, 42, 61, 70.
  De Soto's entry into, 40.
  encounter between Acuera Indians and expedition from, 83.
  movement of Calusa to, 84.
  transference of Spanish garrison from San Antonio, to 101.
Haw, see Sissipahaw.
Hawkins, Benjamin, 116, 118, 126, 127, 132, 133, 137, 138, 142, 143, 144, 150, 161, 167, 168, 169, 171, 173, 181, 189, 191, 197, 200, 203, 214, 215, 217, 300, 371, 823, 828, 830.
  description of Alabama towns by, 87.
  identification of White town of Lower Creeks by, 92.
  on Abihka Indians, 81.
  on housing methods of the Indians, 3890

Hawkins, Benjamin, on hunting practices of Alabama Indians, 263, 264.
  on implements for hunting, fishing or war, 587.
  on marriage customs of the Indians, 704.
  on method of sugar making among the Cherokee, 367.
  on towns, 633, 634.
  on use of honey by the Creeks, 300.
  on war customs of the Indians, 695.
Hawkins, Sir John, 62, 193, 207, 285, 325.
  expedition of, 75.
  French colony in Florida visited by, 62.
Hawkinsville, Ga., 44.
Haw Old Fields, N. C., 186.
Haw River, N. C., principal settlement of Sissipahaw near, 186.
Hayaga, English pronunciation of Jaega, 141.
Haynoke, name used by Governor Yardley for Eno, 130.
Haywood County, N. C., temporary home of Catawba, 105.
Haywood, John, 335, 831.
Head bands, nearest approach to a hat, 508–510.
Head deformation, 537–541.
Helena, Ark., 27.
Helianthus giganteus, use of, 269, 288, 305, 306.
Henryetta, Okla., 81.
Henry IV, King of France, 71.
Henshaw, H. W., 285.
Herrera, Antonio de, 35.
Hewat, Alexander, 829.
Hewitt, J. N. B., 199, 219, 657, 831.
Hibiscus esculentus, use of, 289.
Hicachirico, town subject to San Juan del Puerto, 179.
Hichita Station, home of Hitchiti, 138.
"Hickory Ground," see Otciapofa.
Hickory, uses of, 245.
Hicks, Charles, Cherokee chief, 653, 654, 831.
  on Cherokee festivals, 771–772.
  on crime and punishment, 731.
  on operations of rain makers and doctors, 768, 769.
Hidalgo, Francisco, missionary, 832.
Hidatsa, chunkey game played by, 548.
Highlands, N. C., 47.
High Log, Yuchi town, 214.
High Point, N. C., site of home of Keyauwee, 144.
Hihaje, Hitchiti village, 138.
"Hilapi," town listed by Bishop Calde-rón, 137.
Hilibi, 137, 138, 153, 203, 217.
  identification of with town of Ilapi, 46.
  interpretation of name, 217.
  Muskogee town and subtribe in Creek Confederation, 137.
  population, 137.
  sketch of, 137–138.

Hillabeehatchee, Ga., probably named for Hilibi, 137.
Hillsboro Bay, Fla., settlement of Mococo found at, 151.
Hillsboro, N. C., Eno village found near site of, 131.
Hillsboro River, 41.
Hilton, Capt. William, 829.
visited Cusabo from English Ship *Adventure*, 128.
Hispaniola, 37, 61.
History of Southeastern Indians, De Soto period, 39–59.
from period of first white contact to De Soto expedition, 33–39.
post-De Soto period, 59–81.
Hitchcock, Ethan Allen, 828.
on houses, 389, 400.
Hitchiti, 29, 43, 115, 127, 128, 131, 138, 168, 169, 180, 181, 208, 217, 657, 827.
Capachequi Indians probably related to, 89.
encountered by De Soto, 44.
group, 28.
household utensils used by, 560.
indication of western origin 22.
interpretation of name, 217.
migrations of, 32.
language, 16, 28, 29.
affinity with Alabama and Koasati, 28.
spoken by Apalachicola, 92.
sketch of, 138.
-speaking Indians, 135, 150, 153, 182, 217.
Hiwassee, Indian town, identification of as Guasili, 31.
meaning of name, 31.
Hiwassee River, 47, 48.
site of Tsistuyi, 213.
Hobai, word for war chief, 694.
Hobe, hair-dressing worn by, when met by Dickenson, 504.
name used by Dickenson for Jeaga, 141, 763.
Hobo-hithli Yahola, powerful man in Creek Nation, 653.
Hodge, Frederick Webb, 274, 517.
on the Yamasee, 595.
Hodgson, Adam, missionary, 123, 395.
on towns, 633.
Hogs, domestic fowl, and cattle, 351.
Hokan family group, 801.
Holmes, William H., on quarries worked by Indians, 542, 543.
Homochitto, 195.
Honduras, 33.
Honey, use by natives, 268, 281.
Hoopah Ullah, name of Choctaw settlement, 734.
Horruque, *see* Surruque.
Horse Cave, 47.
Horsechestnut, scarlet flowering (*Pavia* sp.), use of by Indians, 314.
Horses, fate of De Soto's, 58.
use by Indians, 345–351.
Horseshoe Bend, assistance of Cherokee to U. S. in battle of, 80.

Horticulture, 304–310.
Hostaqua, *see* Yustaga.
Hotalgi-huyana, town founded by Osochi and Chiaha, 116, 169.
Hothli-taiga, branch of Coosa, 125.
Hothliwahali, final removal to Oklahoma, 139.
identification with Ulibahali, 49.
interpretation of name, Muskogee language, 217.
location, 139.
population, 139.
Upper Creek town, 139, 153, 217.
Hot Springs, Ark., 24, 29.
aboriginal novaculite working near, 14.
Houma, 17, 30, 73, 105, 139, 140, 167, 168, 177, 198, 217, 829.
allies of Quinipissa against Bayogoula, 177.
amalgamation with Acolapissa and Bayogoula, 82.
artistic development of, 617.
branch, probably, of Chakchiuma (q. v.), 139.
burial customs of, 729, 811.
clothing of, 462, 473, 476.
coloring for articles used by, 610.
destroyed partly, by "an abdominal flux.", 139.
games played by, 684.
hair dressing, 507.
head deformation, 538, 540.
hostility to Bayogoula, 95.
houses, 418.
implements for hunting and fishing, 585.
intermarriage with Atakapa, 140.
interpretation of name, 217.
joined by Okalousa against village of the Tangipahoa Indians, 167.
missions started by Jesuits for, 139.
musical instruments used by, 625.
ornamentation on belts, etc., 524.
population, 83, 140.
red crawfish symbol of, 29.
removal to Bayou St. Jean near New Orleans, and then to Ascension Parish, 139.
sketch of, 139–140.
smoke-holes and windows lacking, 427.
source material on, 829.
temple of, 617.
towns of, 639.
tribe located on Mississippi River opposite mouth of Red River, 139, 198.
Tunica uprising against, 139, 198.
weapons, 585.
Household utensils, 555–564.
Houses, 386–420, 803, 806.
Houston, Gen. Sam, friendly attitude towards Cherokee of, 113.
Hrdlička, Aleš, 219, 220, 832.
Huckleberry, tree (*Batodendron arboretum*), use of by natives, 279.

Hudson, Peter, Choctaw informer, 353.
  on cooking methods of the Indians, 353, 354, 355.
Hughes, English trader, killed by Tohome Indian, 196.
Huguenot colony, 128, 152, 179, 202.
  close to Beaufort, location of the earliest, 128.
  St. Johns River, site of second, 128, 179.
  second, destroyed by Menendez, 74, 128.
  settlement on James River for a while, 152.
  Utina assisted by, against Potano, 202.
Huguenots, in second French expedition to Florida, 61.
Hunter, George, map of, 177.
  on Salude settlement in Pennsylvania, 177.
Hunting, 310–332, 766–767.
  bear, 321–324.
  bison, 324–328.
  deer, 312–321.
  other animals, 328–332.
Huskanaw, custom practiced by Indians, 712.
Huspaw, town of Yamasee, 209.
Hutchins, Capt. Thomas, 97, 119, 120, 121, 123, 140, 166.
Hydrastis canadensis, uses of, 248.
Hymahi, Indian town, 45.
  See also Aymay *and* Guiomaez.
Ibaha, Ibaja, Timucua name for Guale, 135.
  See also Iguaja *and* Yupaha.
Ibarra, Governor, 135, 187.
  comments on church at San Pedro, 187.
  visited Guale on Florida coast, 135.
Iberville, Pierre le Moyne d', 29, 83, 98, 99, 103, 106, 109, 116, 118, 119, 123, 139, 148, 151, 157, 159, 160, 161, 166, 171, 177, 188, 189, 190, 195, 196, 197, 198, 204, 219, 430, 437, 439, 462, 473, 829.
  Avoyel warriors met by, 94.
  Bayogoula visited by, 95.
  Biloxi first tribe encountered by, 96.
  Biloxi town found abandoned by, 96.
  colony at Biloxi, Bayogoula alliance with, 95.
  established himself on Biloxi Bay, 151.
  first permanent French settlement in Louisiana established by, 72.
  founder of Louisiana, renewed alliance with Houma, 139.
  old Indian village sites reported by, 13.
  on Caddo, 99.
  on clothing, 476, 524.
  on coloring of manufactured articles, 610.

Iberville, Pierre le Moyne d', on hair dressing, 501.
  on staining of teeth, 536.
  on towns, 638, 639.
  visited Quinipissa, second time, 177.
  visited Taensa, and described tribe, 188.
  Washa tribe on way up Mississippi, met by, 204.
Ibetap okla, members of Choctaw nation, 141.
Ibi, *see* Yui.
Ibitachuco, Apalachee town, 37, 41.
  description of town of, 633.
Ibitoupa, 19, 123, 140, 141, 194, 195, 217.
  interpretation of name, Choctaw language, 217.
  possible relation to Ibetap okla, members of Choctaw nation, 141.
  population, 141.
  probable union with Chakchiuma, 140.
  sketch of, 140–141.
  small tribe on Yazoo River, Miss., 140.
Icafui, 141, 193, 194.
  a Timucua province or tribe, 141.
Icasqui of Biedma, *see* Casqui.
Ichisi, town visited by De Soto, on Flint River, 127.
  clothing worn by women of, 451.
  See also Chisi.
Ictalurus caerulescens, use as food, 267.
Ictalurus furcatus, use as food, 266.
Idabell, Okla., home of Thliotombi, a very old Choctaw, 123.
"Idol Kiwasa," illustrated by White, 523.
Iguaja, 135, 136.
  See also Ibaha.
Ilapi, Indian town, 45.
  town mentioned by Ranjel as being near Cofitachequi, 137.
  See possibly Hilibi.
Ilex sp., 762.
  vomitoria, used for War drink, 699, 738, 739, 775, 791.
Illinois Confederation, 150, 800.
Illinois country, 73.
Illinois Indians, 147, 149.
Illinois post, 117.
Illinois, State of, 30, 31.
Implements, for hunting, fishing and war, 564–589.
  serving transportation, 589–602.
Imukfa, branch of Coosa, 125.
Inamahari, name of a Siouan idol, 758.
Inca Empire, 39.
India, northwestern, included in cultural area, 825.
Indian confederacies, 19.
  infants, color of skin, 224.
  moral characteristics, 235, 236, 237.

Indian population, coast, 12.
    interior, 12.
    of Louisiana, 1930, 83.
    of Southeast in post-removal period, 80.
    prehistoric movements.of, 21–23.
    (See also map 10, p. 22.)
    traditions of, 22.
    removal, ultimate fate of tribes affected by, 79–81.
Indian Creek, La., home of few Biloxi, 97.
Indian Lake, see Lake Prien.
Indian Office, U. S., 119, 146, 176.
Indian River, Fla., 84.
    site of Ais town, 134.
Indians, Cuban, settled in Calusa country, 239.
    of Georgia coast, organization of, 18.
    of southern Florida, effect of white contact on, 64.
    movements of, 64.
    southern, physical characteristics, 223.
    west of Chitimacha and Caddo, cultural level of, 10.
Indian States, semiautonomous, gradual extinction of, 80.
Indian Territory, 118, 153, 176.
    northeastern part ceded to Quapaw by United States, 176.
    removal of Chickasaw to southern part of, 118.
    Southeastern Indians collected in eastern part of, 80.
Infants, Indian, color of skin of, 224.
Iniahica, Apalachee town, 41, 42, 89.
Inkillis Tamaha (Coussana or Toussana), 122.
Interior Low Plateaus, 4, 5.
Intuchculgau, Yuchi settlement on, Ga., 214.
Ipisagi, branch of Coosa, 125.
Ipomoea batata, use as food, 285.
Ipomoea pondurata, use as food, 270, 285, 286.
Iran, Plateau of, included in cultural area, 825.
Iron, meteoric, used by Southeastern Indians, 244.
Iroquoian family, 110.
    language, spoken by Cherokee, 241.
    population, 12.
    stock, 10, 163, 799, 800, 803, 821. (*See* table 1, facing p. 10.)
    tribe(s), 15, 32, 163, 241, 242, 656.
    clans and gentes among the, 656, 657.
    location of, 32.
    visited by expedition, 76.
Iroquois, 24, 31, 104, 117, 152, 163, 164, 166, 200. 201, 664, 665, 736, 802.
    derivation of clan organizations with female descent, 32.
    language affinity to Caddo, 31.

Iroquois, occupations of women, 711.
    See Nottoway.
Iroquois Confederation, 692.
"Isla de Mocama," Yamasee mission, 209.
Island of Lacasine, see Island of Woods.
Island of Woods, principal Atakapa village, 93.
Ispokogi, ceremonial name for Tukabahchee, 185.
Issa, 66.
    See also Iswa *and* Ysa.
Istanane, possible identification of as Biloxi, 96.
Isthmus of Panama, see Panama, Isthmus of.
Iswa, band of Catawbas, 104, 217.
    interpretation of name, 217.
    66, 67.
    See also Ysa.
Itaba, Indian town, 49.
Itwans, 129.
    See also Etiwaw.
Iviahica, see Iniahica.
Ivitachuco, Apalachee village, 89.
Ivy, poison (*Rhus radicans*), use of by Indians, 606.
Jachene atchoukina, native village, 637.
Jachou, Yazoo village, 637.
Jackson, Gen. Andrew, assisted by Cherokee in Creek War, 80.
    callous to Indians, 80.
    home of Mikasuki in Florida burned by, 150.
    invasion of Florida and burning of Seminole town, 79, 181.
James River, Va., home of Monacan on, 152.
    home of Powhatan band, 130.
    Manahoac settled near falls of, 148.
Jamestown, Va., first permanent settlement of English at, 76.
    founded among Powhatan Indians, 175.
Jeaga, 141.
    members of Muskhogean linguistic family, 239.
    population, 141.
    probably united with Florida east coast tribes and removed to Cuba, 141.
    religious beliefs and usages, 763.
    sketch of, 141.
    small tribe, first mentioned by Fontaneda, 141.
Jefferson County, Florida, original home of Mikasuki located in, 150.
Jefferson Parish, La., 145, 146.
Jefferson, Thomas, 140, 175, 198.
Jeffreys' Atlas, 177.
Jesuit missionaries, 70, 135, 175.
Jesup, Gen. Thomas S., bad faith toward Indians, 80.
    capture and imprisonment of Osceola by, 181.
Jewfish (*Promicrops itaiara*), use as food, 267.

Joara, 65, 66, 69.
  See also Cheraw *and* Xuala.
Johns Pass, 37.
Johnson, Sir William, 201.
Johnson, William Ely, Tunica inform-
  ant, 198.
Jolliet, Louis, 71.
Jones' Bluff, 73.
Jones, Charles C., 738.
  on Indian quarries, 541, 542.
  on transportation, means of, 589.
Jonesville, La., possible site of Indian
  village of Anilco, 56.
Jopassus, brother of chief Powhatan,
  749.
Jordan River, 37.
Jororo, town occupied by Tocobaga and
  Pohoy, 195.
Joutel, Henri, historian of La Salle ex-
  pedition, 98, 100, 130, 132, 154, 158,
  416, 832.
  Anadarko mentioned by, 89.
  on food preserving, 381.
  on hair dressing, 501, 507, 528.
  on household utensils, 556, 559.
  on houses, 419, 420.
  on pipes, 547.
  on tattooing, 536.
  on towns, 640.
  on transportation among Caddo,
    599.
Juada, *see* Cheraw *and* Xuala.
Juglans cinerea, use of, 364.
Jumano, *see* Shuman.
Jumper, from the Upper Creek towns,
  brains with Osceola of Seminole up-
    rising, 181, 506.
  ancestry of, 64.
Junco, Juan de, Indian interpreter, 202.
Juniata River, temporary home of
  Tuscarora, 199.
Jupiter Inlet, Fla., Dickenson shipwrecked near, 84.
  home of Jeaga, 141.
Kadohadacho, 98, 100, 130, 141, 142,
  157, 158, 161, 211, 217.
  associated with Nasoni, Nanatsoho,
    and part of Natchitoches, on
    Red River, Ark., 141, 157.
  clans and gentes, 655.
  legend of flood told by, 142.
  migration down Red River, 24.
  name, interpretation of, 217.
  population, *see* Caddo, 142.
  sketch of, 141–142.
  slaughtered by Osages, and driven
    to Sodo Creek, west of Red
    River, 142.
  temporary union with Quapaw, 142.
Kadohadacho Confederacy, 100, 141.
Kafitalaya, town supporting the French,
  122.
Kanawha River, W. Va., Moneton
  found living on, 152.
Kan-hatki (White Ground), Creek town,
  87, 125, 133, 142, 147, 153, 181, 217.
  joined with Seminole, 133, 181.

Kan-hatki, name, interpertation of, in
  Muskogee tongue, 217.
  population, 142.
  sketch of, 142.
Kansas, southeastern part of, ceded to
  Quapaw by U. S., 176.
Kantak, Choctaw plant, *see Smilax* sp.
Kan-tcati (Red Ground), Abihka town,
  81, 82, 87.
  Indians of, 87.
Kappa, Indian town, on Miss. River
  640, 641.
Karankawa, 17, 30, 801, 820.
  easternmost tribe of, 39.
  flint obtained from Atakapa by,
    542, 737.
  possible merging of Akokisa with,
    86.
  Spanish mission established among
    75.
Karankawan stock, 240.
  source of information on, 39.
Kasha, *see* Caxa.
Kasihta, 26, 49, 92, 118, 126, 127, 138,
  143, 153, 154, 180, 197, 214.
  artistic development, 617.
  part of Muskogee element among
    Lower Creeks, 143.
  population, 143.
  sketch of, 143.
  town burned by Spanish under
    Matheos, 63.
  towns, 633, 664.
Kaskaskia, joined by Michigamea in
  Ill., 149.
Kaskinampo, 27, 143, 144, 145, 163, 217.
  combined with Koasati, 144, 145.
  found near site of Helena, Ark., 143.
  identification of Casqui with, 53.
  mentioned by De Soto as Casqui or
    Casquin, 143.
  name, interpretation of, 217.
  population, 144.
  prehistoric location, 15.
  sketch of, 143–144.
  See also Casqui.
Kateraras, favorite town of Tuscarora
  chief, 199, 739.
Kayomalgi (Mulberry Place), Abihka
  town, 81.
Kealedji, 144, 153, 218.
  name, interpretation of in Musko-
    gee tongue, 218.
  population, 144.
  settled in southeastern part of
    Creek reserve, 144.
  sketch of, 144.
  town of, 139, 197.
  town of Atasi associated with, 94.
Kecoughtan, Indian village, 709.
Kegquouhtan, description of Indian
  town of, 630.
  (Same as Kecoughtan.)
Kellogg, Remington, 282.
  on whale hunting in Florida, 329.
Kentucky River, 23.

Kentucky, State of, 2.
  Green River people in, 33.
Keowa, 111.
Keowee, 163.
Keowee River, S. C., possibly connected with name Keyauwee, 145.
Kerlérec, Governor, see De Kerlérec.
Ketenuaka, band of Tuscarora, 199.
Kewasowok, Indian word for gods, 742.
Key, John, of Costango, last man who spoke Tutelo language fluently, 201, 663, 664.
Keyauwee, 110, 131, 144, 145, 164, 178, 183, 186, 200, 201, 208.
  beards and mustaches, 144, 498, 805, 815.
  body paint, 530.
  clans and gentes, 654.
  population, 145.
  ruled by a Congaree through marriage with chieftainess, 144.
  sketch of, 144–145.
Key Marco, Fla., description of Indian relics found at, 408, 409, 504, 511, 512, 516, 518, 521, 524, 556, 557, 560, 562, 565, 569, 584, 589, 590, 591, 603, 619, 620–623, 809.
Kiamichi River, Okla., home of Biloxi. 97.
Kiamulgatown, Abihka town, 82.
  mentioned in Creek census, 186.
Kiawa, 115, 129.
Kichai, 241.
Kickapoo, clans and gentes, 656.
  language, affinity with Shawnee, 31.
Killip, E. P., 270, 288.
Kimber, Edward, 439, 457, 694.
  on clothing, 461, 463, 464.
  on war customs, 694, 695.
Kinchafoonee River, 43.
  home of Yuchi located on, 214.
Kinder, La., 145.
Kinemo, see Skunnemoke.
King Gilbert and Coosaboys, part taken by in Barnwell's expedition against St. Augustine, 129.
"King Johnny," chief of joint settlement of Pedee and Cape Fear tribes, 172.
Kinietz, Vernon, editor, 832.
Kiskiminetas River, 185.
Kispogogi, Shawnee band of Indians, 184.
Kispokotha, later name for Shawnee band, 185.
  Tecumseh member of, 185.
Kitcopataki, branch of Hilibi, 137, 138.
Kituhwa, old name for Cherokee, 23.
Kiwasa, Indian God, 614.
Knives, 564–566.
Knox Creek, 46.
Koasati, 27, 28, 53, 68, 69, 70, 80, 88, 125, 144, 145, 146, 152, 214, 665, 828.
  joined by Alabama on Tombigbee River, 87.
  mats and baskets, 605.
  nose ornaments, 515.

Koasati, on island in Tennessee River, 145.
  part of tribe moved to Tex., 145.
  pestilence among, 145.
  united with Alabama, 145.
  population, 146.
  sketch of, 145–146.
  source material, 828.
  Square Ground, 617.
  terms of relationship, 666, 668.
  town identified with Coste, 27.
  united with Kaskinampo, 145.
Koe-chito, town supporting the French, 122.
Ko-i-ha-tco, Seminole brave, 226.
Kolomi, 146, 147, 153, 181, 218.
  apparently united with Fushatchee, Kanhatki, and Atasi, 147.
  Muskogee town or tribe, 146.
  name, interpretation of in Muskogee language, 218.
  population, 147.
  sketch of, 146–147.
  town burned by Spaniards under Matheos, 63.
  ultimate fate unknown, 147.
  Upper Creek Town, description of, 393, 634.
Kolomi Miko, Chief at Suwannee Oldtown, 147.
Koosah town, old Creek town, 594.
Koroa, 13, 19, 55, 106, 147, 148, 166, 194, 195, 198, 199, 211, 301, 829.
  allies of Natchez, 73.
  attacked by Chakchiuma and Choctaw, in the French interest, 147.
  attacked by Chickasaw, 106.
    Quapaw, 147.
  clothing, 462.
  last heard of in attack on Tunica Indians, 148.
  murderer of Foucault, French missionary, slain by chiefs of, 147, 198.
  murder of Missionary P. Seuel and massacre of garrison of Fort St. Peter by, 147.
  participated in Natchez uprising, 166.
  pearls purchased by La Salle from, 489.
  population, 148.
  severely treated by Quapaw and Illinois, 147.
  sketch of, 147–148.
  smoke-holes and windows lacking, 427.
  source material on, 829.
  trade with, 738.
  towns, 640.
  Tunica spoken by, 240.
Kowaliga Creek, affluent of Tallapoosa, home of Okchai, 166.
  home of the Kealedji, 144.
Kroeber, Alfred L., 11.

Krogman, Wilton Marion, 220, 221, 832.
　on physical characteristics of Seminole of Okla., 220, 221.
Kulumi, see Kolomi.
Kunti, red, see Smilax sp.
Kunti, white, (kunti hátki), see Zamia integrifolia.
Labor, see Customs relating to birth, education, and the division of labor between the sexes.
Labrets, 515–516.
Lacame, see Nacanish.
Lacane, Indian tribe encountered by Moscoso, 57.
　See Nacanish.
La Clair, Fusilier de, purchase of Atakapa land by, 93.
Lacrosse, game adapted from the Indians, 674.
"Lady of Cofitachequi," see Cofitachequi, Lady of.
La Encarnacion a la Santa Cruz de Sabacola, see Santa Cruz de Sabacola el Menor, 179.
Lafourche Parish, home of Houma, 140.
La Harpe, Bernard de, 85, 98, 106, 109, 121, 123, 130, 140, 141, 148, 155, 158, 166, 167, 189, 198, 204, 212, 831.
　Anadarko visited by, 89.
　Avoyel mentioned by, 94.
　estimate of Akokisa population, 86.
　number of Acolapissa warriors according to, 83.
　on images, 618, 780.
　on location of Biloxi, 97.
　visited Kadohadacho on Red River, above mouth of Little River, Ark., 141.
La Incarnacion, Sawokli mission, 107.
Lake Bistineau, 57.
Lake Charles, 93, 94.
Lake City, Fla., 41.
Lake Macdon, 83.
Lake Okeechobee, 16, 64.
　food habits about, 255.
Lake Pontchartrain, La., 82, 97.
　removal of Natchitoches from Red River to 130, 161.
　Tangipahoa located on affluent of, 190.
Lake Prien, formerly Indian Lake, 93.
Lake St. Joseph, La., 13, 31, 72, 95.
　site of Taensa villages, visited by La Salle, 166, 188.
Lake Salvador, 204.
La Loire, accompanied to Mobile by Taensa, 188.
　See also Ursins, M. de la Loire des.
Lameco, see Chiaha.
Lamhatty, Indian informant on expeditions against Apalachicola, 92.
　account of, 171, 180.
　map of, 736.
Lampblack, used by Southeastern Indians, 243.
Lances, spears, and javelins, 582–585.

"Land of San Luis," Apalachee town, 107.
Lane, Ralph, first colony on Roanoke Island established under, 76.
Langley, Jackson, Koasati informant, 146.
　on pottery, 553.
Language, influence of, 238–242, 805.
Lanman, Charles, on Cherokee festivals, 769–771.
L'Anse des Chactas, on Mobile Bay, temporary home of Chatot, 108.
Laportea canadensis, uses of, 247.
"La Purificación de Tama, called Yamases," 208.
Large-mouthed black bass (Micropterus salmoides), use as food, 266.
Larkin's Landing, Koasati settlement, 145.
Las Alas, 65.
La Salle, Réné Robert Cavalier, Sieur de, 29, 30, 71, 95, 98, 105, 139, 141, 147, 154, 159, 162, 166, 176, 188, 190, 300, 807, 829, 831.
　assassination of by his followers, 71, 98, 141.
　fate of Huguenot colony in France founded by, 74.
　first mention of Kadohadacho by companions of, 141.
　journey of, down Miss., 105, 139, 166, 640.
　Natchez town on Miss. visited by, 159.
　on pearls, 489.
　on towns, 640.
　quest of Miss. River by, 98, 596.
　Taensa visited by, at Lake St. Joseph, La., 188.
　Tiou probably the Indians called Koroa by, 195.
　treaty of peace made withTaensa, 188.
La Source, M. Thaumur, missionary, 72, 188, 198, 829.
　missionary, Taensa visited by, 188.
　on images, 618.
　on towns, 639.
Lathyrus myrtifolius, 269.
Lathyrus venosus, 269.
Laudonnière, Réné Goulaine de, 133, 143, 151, 168, 187, 193, 216, 281, 297, 300, 334, 346, 448, 454, 648, 682.
　main source of knowledge of ancient inhabitants of Florida, 62.
　on agricultural methods, 308.
　on body paint, 531.
　on burial customs, 721.
　on cooking, 358.
　on honey, 268.
　on household utensils, 555, 556.
　on implements for hunting and fishing, 572, 577.
　on mats and baskets, 603, 604.
　on medical practices, 792.
　on pottery, 551.

Laudonnière, on religious beliefs and usages, 761, 763.
　on seasonal habits of Timucua, 260.
　on stone, 541.
　on tattooing, 533.
　on weapons, 572, 577.
　second French expedition to Florida under, 61.
　Tacatacuru visited by French under, 187.
Lavaca Bay, 71.
Lawson, John, 104, 124, 126, 131, 144, 145, 164, 177, 178, 183, 186, 199, 200, 205, 206, 207, 208, 243, 297, 298, 325, 335, 336, 337, 338, 426, 427, 429, 441, 448, 456, 457, 654, 709, 711, 739, 805, 807, 813, 815, 830, 831.
　Congaree found by, on small affluent of Santee River, 124.
　death, during Tuscarora War, 199.
　found Eno and Shakori in one village, Adshusheer, on Eno River, 183.
　hospitably received by Waxhaw, 206.
　Little Watteree, visited by, 65.
　on agricultural methods, 305.
　on artistic development of the Indians, 615.
　on bags or purses, 479.
　on bracelets, 521.
　on burial customs, 719, 720, 721.
　on Catawba, 104.
　on clothing, 460, 464, 470, 472, 473, 475.
　　worn by medicine men, 478.
　on communication, means of, 736.
　on cooking 351, 356, 358, 360, 364, 365, 366, 367, 368, 369, 370, 371.
　on crime and punishment, 731.
　on dirt eating by children, 280.
　on domestic animals, 345, 346, 347.
　on ear ornaments, 511.
　on fate of Roanoke colonists, 76.
　on featherwork, 456.
　on fire making, 423.
　on fishing, 339, 344.
　on food, 277, 278, 279, 280, 304.
　on food preserving 373, 374, 379.
　on games, 674, 682, 685, 686.
　on glass as substitute for flint, 543.
　on greasing and coloring of hair and skin, 526, 530.
　on hair dressing, 498, 499, 503.
　on head deformation, 539.
　on home customs, 711.
　on household utensils, 557, 562, 564.
　on houses, 410, 411, 412, 413, 421.
　on hunting, 313, 314, 318, 329, 330, 331.
　on huskanaw, 712.
　on implements for hunting and fishing, 565, 573, 577, 578, 582.
　on marriage customs, 703.
　on mats and baskets, 602, 603.
　on medical practices, 785, 786–790.
　on mnemonic devices, 611.

Lawson, John, on moral characteristics, 234, 235.
　on musical instruments, 625, 627, 628.
　on names, 671.
　on necklaces, 517, 519.
　on origin belief of Carolina Indians, 24.
　on physical characteristics of North Carolina Indians, 226, 227.
　on pottery, 554.
　on religious beliefs and usages, 752, 753, 756, 757, 759, 760.
　on salt trade, 302, 303.
　on seasonal activities of Siouan tribes, 259.
　on skin dressing, 444.
　on social customs, 756, 757.
　on social organization, 646, 647.
　on thread and textiles, 449, 450.
　on tobacco, 384.
　on towns, 632.
　on trade, 740.
　on transportation, means of, 592, 594, 595.
　on wampum, 482, 483, 485.
　on war customs, 689, 690.
　on weapons, 565, 573, 578, 582.
　on whaling, 329.
　on woodcraft, 311, 312.
　Santee on Santee River, visited by, 177.
　Siouan country visited by, 77.
League of the Iroquois, Tutelo adopted into, 201.
Le Blanc, M., plantation established in interest of, 211.
Le Challeux, on bows, 579.
　on shell beads, 485.
　on tattooing, 534.
Lecompte, La., later home of Biloxi, 97.
Lederer, John, 104, 110, 111, 131, 148, 157, 164, 178, 183, 199, 205, 206, 280, 302, 411, 448, 682, 813, 815, 830.
　Cheraw tribe reported on Yadkin River by, 110.
　Manahoac found on Mohawk Creek by, 148.
　on body paint, 530.
　on bracelets, 521.
　on communication, means of, 735.
　on ear ornaments, 510.
　on houses of Eno, 413.
　on mnemonic devices, 610.
　on social organization, 647.
　on trade, 739.
　Saponi on Otter River visited by, 178.
　Siouan tribes visited by, 76.
　　on origin of, 24.
　Tuscarora at "Katearas" visited by, 199.
　"Ushery" visited by, 104.
　Wateree found on upper Yadkin by, 205.
Legends, migration and origin, of Southeastern Indians, 22–25.

Leg ornaments, 523.

Le Moyne, Jacques, 133, 168, 179, 187, 193, 216, 281, 305, 334, 407, 433, 456, 458, 460, 682, 738, 761, 808.
  description of Timucua fort, 436.
  on agricultural methods, 260, 308, 309.
  on axes, 545.
  on body paint, 531.
  on bracelets, 521.
  on clothing, 473, 523.
  on ear ornaments, 511.
  on fingernails and toenails, length of, 536, 589.
  on food-preserving methods, 376, 377, 380.
  on hair-dressing methods, 499, 504.
  on head bands, 508, 510.
  on household utensils, 556.
  on implements for hunting and fishing, 576, 579, 589.
  on leg ornaments, 523.
  on marriage customs, 599, 705.
  on mats and baskets, 604.
  on medical practices, 792.
  on metals, 491, 495.
  on musical instruments, 628, 629.
  on necklaces, 518, 520.
  on ornamentation, 524.
  on pottery, 551.
  on punishments, 648.
  on religious beliefs and usages, 762.
  on scalping, 504.
  on tattooing, 534.
  on Timucua hunting, 313, 331, 332.
  on tobacco, 382.
  on towns, 632.
  on transportation, means of, 599.
  on weapons, 576, 579, 589.

Leon, Capt. Alonso de, expedition to Texas under, 74.
  founder of Mission of San Francisco de los Tejas, 83.

Leon, Ponce de, 101, 133, 193.
  country of Fresh Water Timucua reached by, 193.
  killed by Calusa, 101.
  landing in Calusa country, 101.

Leonard, Irving A., 441.
  on buffalo, 326.
  on thread and textiles, 450.

Le Page Du Pratz, Antoine S., 107, 108, 120, 148, 149, 161, 166, 168, 171, 189, 190, 196, 197, 212, 217, 247, 248, 269, 305, 310, 327, 346, 349, 351, 430, 440, 443, 448, 662, 681, 684, 733, 736, 829.
  Avoyel mentioned by, 94.
  located Okalousa on Miss. River above Pointe Coupée, 167.
  on agricultural methods of Natchez, 310.
  on artistic development, 613, 618.
  on attack of Chawasha and Washa on Captain Bond's ship, 108.
  on axes, 545.
  on bison hunting, 328.

Le Page Du Pratz, Antoine S., on bracelets, 522.
  on ceremonies at peace negotiations with Chitimacha, 120.
  on clothing, 461, 463, 464, 465, 472, 473, 474, 476.
  on coloring for manufactured articles, 610.
  on cooking, 353, 357, 358, 359, 360, 362, 363, 368, 369.
  on doors of sacred buildings, 429.
  on ear ornaments, 514.
  on enumeration of months by Natchez, 260, 261.
  on feather mantles, 455.
  on fire making, 425.
  on food, 290, 291, 299.
    preserving, 374, 376, 381.
  on fort, construction of, 436, 437.
  on games, 686.
    deer-hunting game, 319, 320.
  on hair dressing, 500, 507.
  on head band, 509.
  on head deformation, 538.
  on household utensils, 555, 559, 561, 563.
  on houses, 418, 419.
  on hunting, 315, 316, 322, 323, 327, 330, 332.
  on illumination, 426.
  on implements for hunting and fishing, 565, 575, 576, 579, 588.
  on marriage customs, 708.
  on mats and baskets, 603, 608.
  on medical practices, 796, 797, 798.
  on mnemonic devices used by St. Denis, 612, 613.
  on moral characteristics, 237.
  on musical instruments, 627.
  on names, 674.
  on origin legend of Natchez, 22, 23.
  on ornamentation, 486, 489, 490.
  on physical characteristics of Natchez, 228, 229.
  on pottery, 549, 550.
  on salt making, 301, 302.
  on social organization, 650.
  on tattooing, 535, 536.
  on thread and textiles, 449, 450, 453.
  on tobacco, 385, 386.
  on transportation, means of, 593, 594, 595, 597, 599, 600.
  on war customs, 701.
  on weapons, 565, 568, 575, 579, 588.

Le Petit, Father, Jesuit missionary, 148, 159, 161, 212, 261, 708, 829.
  on medical practices, 797.
  on war customs, 700.

Leptops olivaris, use as food, 266.

Les Allemands, post where M. de Nouaille met Chawasha and Washa, 109, 204.

Le Sueur Narrative, 831.

Levantine with De Soto, death of, 60.

Lewis, Jackson, Creek informant, 323, 335, 342, 344.
  on blowguns, 586.

Lewis Jackson, Creek informant, on dyes, 605.
    on food preserving, 374, 375.
    on houses, 392.
    on mats and baskets, 605.
    on pottery, 551, 552.
    on skin dressing, 446.
    on threads and textiles, 448, 452, 454.
Lewis, T. M. N., 213.
Lexington Plain, 5, 15.
Liberty, Tex., 86.
Life zones, causes of location of various groups, 20.
    in Southeastern territory, 7–10.
    position of tribes relative to, 19.
Ligusticum actaeifolium, use of, 271.
Ligusticum canadense, 362.
Lily, pond (*Nelumbo lutea*), use of, 292, 296.
Limoges, Father de, successor to Father du Rut, in mission to Houma, 139.
Linden, Ga., 50.
Lines Creek, 51.
Lipan, Spanish mission established among, 75.
Liquidambar styraciflua, use of, 385.
Lisbon, 34.
Lithospermum vulgare, uses of, 248.
Littafutchee, Creek name of Canoe Creek, 69.
Litters, 598–601.
Little Abihka, *see* Abihkutci.
Little Barataria Bayou, La., 140.
Little Chiaha, name of Chiaha village, 116.
Little Eufaula, Eufaula settlement on Tallapoosa River, 131.
Little Hitchiti, on Flint River, 138.
Little Houmas, settlement of Houma, 139.
Little Missouri River, 55.
Little Okchai, *see* Okchaiutci, 166.
Little River, Kadohadacho settlement on Red River above mouth of, 141.
Little Rock, Ark., possible home of Koroa, 54, 147.
Little Sawokli, Sawokli town, 180, 181.
Little Tennessee River, N. C., home of Tuskegee band, 47, 200.
Little Tohome, band of Tohome tribe, 196.
Little Tulsa, *see* Otciapofa, 125.
Little Uchee Creek, Yuchi located about mouth of, 213.
Little Wateree, visit of Lawson to, 65. *See* Wateree Chickanee, 205.
Livingston, Tex., 86.
Liwahali, *see* Hothliwahali.
Lobillo, Juan Rodriguez, 45.
Locations of tribes, *see* Sketches of Southeastern tribes and their population, 81–216.
Locust, honey (*S. triacanthus*), use of, 285, 287, 297.
    water, 287.

Logansport, La., Anadarko encountered by Moscoso near, 89.
"Long Hair," name used by Adair for Choctaw, 121, 504, 808.
Long Island, 48.
López, Fray Baltazar, stationed at San Pedro, 187, 202.
"Lost Colony of Roanoke," 76.
Louisiana, 1, 12, 13, 19, 24, 29, 73, 78, 86, 89, 91.
    Alabama remaining in, 87.
    cession of, to U. S., 99.
    founded by Iberville, 72, 96, 139.
    given to Spain by treaty of 1762, 74.
    home of Doustioni in NW. part of, 130.
    Indian population of, 1930, 83.
    Indians little affected by political changes, 75.
    named Carolana by Coxe, 77.
    ownership by France, Spain, and U. S. mentioned, 75.
    Spanish mission among Adai founded in, 75.
    Tchefuncte culture of, 33.
    tribes settling in after the removal, 80.
Louisiana Indians, reference to De Batz' sketch of, 94.
Louisiana tribes, reference to Iberville's estimate of, 95.
Louvigny map, reference to, 28.
Lower Austral Zone, 20.
Lower Creek country, Oconee moved to, 181.
Lower Creeks, 29, 46, 64, 67, 78, 90, 107, 126, 143, 165, 180, 185, 189, 210, 215, 830.
    branch of Sawokli living among, 180.
    called Apalachicola by Spaniards, 92.
    Coweta, one of Muskogee tribes among, 126.
    head bands, 509.
    Kasihta tribes part of Muskogee element among, 143.
    movement to Ocmulgee River due to Spanish occupation of their country, 63.
    plunder of San Carlos de los Chacatos, by, 107.
    source material on, 830.
    sympathetic to whites in Creek War, 69, 79.
    unsuccessful visit of Franciscan friars to, 62.
    White town of, 92.
Lower Eufaula, Eufaula settlement on Chattahoochee River, 131, 132, 180.
"Lower-Quarter," town of one-eyed people among N. C. Indians, 227.
Lower Yamasee, 208, 209.
Lowery, Woodbury, 35.
    on identification of Florida on Cantino map, 34

Lowery, Woodbury, on identity of Indians contacted by Ponce de Leon, 34, 36.
Lumber River, Indians of, 186, 206.
Luna, Tristan de, 60, 61, 81, 125, 126, 139, 143, 151, 157, 172, 196, 829.
 expedition to Upper Creeks, 59–61, 491.
 Hothliwahali visited by Spanish major under, 139.
 Nanipacana, Mobile town, reached by soldiers sent by, 151.
 soldiers led into province of Coosa by officer under, 125, 126, 157.
 troops under, joined Coosa against Napochi, 157.
"Lun-ham-ga town in the Abecas," 82.
Lutchapoga, branch of Tulsa, 125.
Lyon's Bluff, captured in struggle between Chakchiuma, Chickasaw, and Choctaw, 106.
Mabila, description by Garcilaso, 434, 435.
 fortified Indian town, 13, 50.
 ruins of, 121, 427, 433.
 site of battle between Spaniards and Mobile, 50, 150, 431.
Macapiras, 148, 195, 196.
 apparently destroyed in a pestilence, 148.
 exact connection unknown, 148.
 placed in Mission near St. Augustine, 195, 196.
 tribe living near the Calusa, 148.
Macarisqui, see Amacarisse mission, 209.
Macariz, see Nombre de Dios, 210.
Macaya, see Maiaca.
MacCauley, Clay, 283, 330, 339, 828.
 on agricultural methods of Seminole, 305.
 on artistic development, 624.
 on bracelets and arm bands, 522.
 on clothing, 467, 468, 474, 475, 476, 477, 525.
 on cooking, 357, 361, 362.
 on ear ornaments, 514.
 on finger rings, 523.
 on fire making, 425, 427.
 on foods used by the Seminoles, 283, 284.
 on hair dressing, 500, 506.
 on household utensils, 558, 559, 560, 563.
 on housing, 397, 398, 422.
 on hunting among the Seminole, 314, 331.
 on implements for hunting and fishing, 574, 578.
 on mats and baskets, 605.
 on moral characteristics of Seminoles, 234.
 on necklaces, 517, 520, 521.
 on ornamentation on clothing, 525.
 on physical characteristics of Seminoles, 225, 226, 234.
 on thread and textiles, 452.
 on weapons, 574, 578.

McGillivray, Alexander, resident of Little Tulsa, 125, 732.
Machaba, Yustaga settlement, 216.
Machapunga, 126, 148, 218.
 and Coree assigned land on Mattamuskeet Lake, Hyde County, N. C., 126, 148.
 Coree destroyed by, 126.
 gradual disappearance of, 148.
 interpretation of name, Algonquian tongue, 218.
 population, 148.
 sketch of, 148.
 tribe living between Albemarle and Pamlico Sounds, N. C., 148.
 war customs of, 690.
Machicomuck, Indian word for Temple, 742.
McIntosh, William, Coweta head man, killed by party of warriors, 127, 154, 653.
McKee Island, site of Tali town, 48.
McKenny, Thomas L., and Hall, James, 182, 530.
Mackenzie type of terms of relationship, 820.
Macocquer, see Pumpkins.
Macon, Ga., 14.
 Ocmulgee Old Fields on present site of, 138.
Macon trail, 47.
McQueen, James, Tulsa Indians moved to Tallapoosa from Talladega county, by, 125.
"Maharineck," see Meherrin.
"Mahehoualaima," see Tangibao, 190.
"Maheouala," see Tangibao.
Mahican, moral characteristics, 236.
Maiaca, Fla., 133.
Maiajuaca, Fla., 133.
Maldonado, Francisco, commander of fleet of De Soto, 42, 50, 150, 196, 440, 459.
Malus sp., use of, 272.
Manahoac, 19, 148, 149, 157, 179, 201, 218, 830.
 attacked by whites and Powhatan Indians, 148.
 disappearance from history, 149.
 interpretation of name, 218.
 population, 149.
 settled near falls of James River, Va., 148, 157.
 tribe living in Piedmont country, on Rappahannock River, Va., 148.
 union with Saponi and Occaneechi under name of Saponi, 149, 164.
Manchac, Taensa had village at, 188.
Manchac River, 87.
Mandan, chunkey game played by, 548.
Mangoac, see Nottoway.
Manks Nessoneicks, see Nahyssan.
Manteo, Indian taken to England, 1595, 76.
Many Waters, Timucua town, 41.

Maple, red or soft (*Acer rubrum*), use of, 606.

Marbury, 127, 144, 170, 173, 186, 200, 215.

Maréchal-d'-Estées, French vessel, officers from killed by Akokisa, 85.

Marginella sp., uses of, 252, 259, 484, 485, 741.

Margry, Pierre, 292, 327, 360, 381, 451, 462, 579, 709, 737, 738, 829.
    on artistic development, 613, 618, 619.
    on clothing, 473, 476.
    on coloring for manufactured articles, 610.
    on construction of fort, 437, 439.
    on ear ornaments, 514.
    on hair dressing, 507.
    on head deformation, 538.
    on housing, 416, 419, 420.
    on mats and baskets, 603.
    on musical instruments, 625, 627.
    on nose ornaments, 515.
    on ornamentation on belts, etc, 524.
    on religious beliefs and usages, 779.
    on social customs, 649, 650.
    on staining of teeth, 536.
    on towns, 638, 639, 640, 641.
    on transportation among the Caddo, 599.
    on use of pearls, 489, 516.

Marksville, La., location of Avoyel, 94, 95, 97.
    last home of Ofo, 166.

Marksville culture, 33.

Marksville Prairie, Tunica settled on land bought from Avoyel, at, 198.

Marquette, Father Jacques, 71, 147, 149, 166, 176, 416, 831.

Marriage customs, 701–709.

"Marten-ermine," Indian robe of, 38.

Martin, Capt. Herman, borders of Hasinai country reached by, 74.

Martyr, Peter, *see* Anghierra, Peter Martyr de.

Mascarasi, *see* Amacarisse mission.

Massanet, Father Damian, 74.
    companion of De Leon, on expedition across Caddo country, 98.
    Mission of San Francisco de las Tejas, founded by, 83.
    Texas mission in Nabedache village, founded by, 155.

"Massawomeckes," Indian tribe, shields carried by, 588.

Massinacack, Va., Monacan settlement, 152.

Matacumbe Island, Indian of, 192.

Matagorda Bay, 74.

Match coat, name used for outer coat, 460.

Mateczungua, Siouan idol, 759.

Materials used in building, 421, 422.

Matheos, Antonio, 62, 121.

Mathews, Maurice, 111.

Mathicómuck, Indian word for temple, 614.

Matienzo, Juan Ortez de, 36.

Mats and baskets, 602–608.

Mattamuskeet Lake, Hyde County, N. C., Coree and Machapunga assigned land on, 126, 148.

Mattamuskeet, N. C. village of Machapunga tribe, 148.

Mattapanient, land subject to Powhatan, 643.

Mattapony, 175.

Mauilla, *see* Mabila.

Maury, Ann, 348.
    on towns, 632.

Mavila, *see* Mabila.

"May apple," *see* Maypop.

Maypop (*Passiflora incarnata*), use as food, 285, 286.

Meats, preservation of, 372–377.
    treatment of, 368–372.

Medical practices, 782–799.

Medicine men, clothing of, 477–479.

Megalops cyprinoides, use as food, 267.

Meherrin, 15, 31, 149, 163, 164, 241, 800.
    found by Virginia colonists on the Meherrin River, 149.
    fugitive Conestoga among, 163, 164.
    Iroquoian tribe in Virginia, 241.
    population, 149.
    probable union with Saponi on Roanoke River, 149.
    sketch of, 149.

Meherrin River, N. C., 124, 148, 149, 183, 201, 800.

Meigs County, Tenn., Yuchi tribe located in, 212.

Meillac, type of West Indian pottery. origin of, 33.

Melden, *see* Orache.

Melette post office, Tukabahchee Square Ground established near, in Oklahoma, 197.

Melons (*Cucurbita citrullus*), use by Indians, 635.

Melton's Bend, 50.

Membré, Father Zénobe, on social customs, 649, 650.

Memphis, Tenn., 53.

Men, arm bands worn by, 522
    bags and purses, 479–480
    body paint, 529, 531
    clothing, 456–469, 525, 807.
    ear ornaments, 510–514.
    hair dressing, 501–507, 526, 807.
    head bands, 508–510.
    head deformation, 539.
    home customs, 711.
    moral characteristics, 229, 230, 231, 232, 234, 235, 236, 237.
    necklaces, 517, 518, 519, 520, 521.
    occupations, 710, 711, 715, 716, 717, 718.
    physical characteristics, 223, 224, 225, 226, 227, 228, 229, 233, 234.
    tattooing, 533, 535, 536.

Menard mound group, reference to, 54.

Menendez de Aviles, Pedro, Lieutenant Governor of Florida, 45, 71, 101, 128, 134, 187, 192, 195, 196.
  Ais visited by, 84.
  Atlantic coast explored by, 192.
  departure from San Antonio, followed by killing of Calusa chief, 101, 192.
  destruction of second Hugenot colony by, 62, 128, 134.
  effort to form settlement in Virginia, 70.
  fort of San Felipe built by, 64.
  marriage to sister of Calusa chief, 101.
  return to Havana from Ais country by, 134.
  Tacatacuru visited by, 187.
  Tekesta braves taken on visit to Spain by, 192.
  visit to Calusa country, 101, 192.
  visit to Fort San Antonio, 101.
  visit to Tocobaga, accompanied by chief of Calusa, 195.
Menhaden (*Brevoortia patronus*), use as food, 266.
"Menheyricks," see Meherrin.
Menstrual periods, customs practiced at, 713, 714, 715, 716.
Mequachake, Shawnee band of Indians, 184.
Mera, see Sholes and Mera.
Mereness, Newton D., 326.
Mermentou River, 93.
Merriam, C. Hart, on fauna and flora of Southeast, 9–10.
Messianic story, among the Indians, 751.
Metalwork, 490–498.
Meteoric iron, use of, 494.
Mexican Government, grant of land to Cherokee by, repudiated by U. S. Government, 113.
Mexico, 18, 22, 23, 35, 58, 59, 64, 70, 71, 74, 101, 142.
  possible migrations from, to Gulf region, 33.
  southern part, boundary of cultural area, 825, 826, 827.
Mexico City, 59, 74.
Mexico, Gulf of, 5, 13, 22, 31, 34, 35, 38, 39, 172, 243, 826.
  home of Pensacola, 172.
  relation to cultural area, 826.
  sea salt from, 243.
Mexico, Republic of, 75.
Mézières, Athanese de, Adai reported extinct by, 83.
Miami, clans and gentes, 656.
Michel, Francis Louis, Swiss traveler, 152, 462, 464, 813, 815.
  on hair dressing, 499, 503.
  on head bands, 509.
  on mats and baskets, 603.
  on necklaces, 517.
  on nose ornaments, 514.
  on pottery, 554.
  on stone pipes, 545.

Michel, Francis Louis, Swiss traveler,
  on trade, 740.
  on wampum, 483.
Michelson, Truman, 31.
Michigamea, 149, 218, 800.
  driven from Arkansas by Quapaw or Chickasaw, 149.
  found by Marquette on Big Lake, Ark., 149.
  identity apparently lost by, 149.
  interpretation of name, Algonquian tongue, 218.
  joined Kaskaskia in territory of present Illinois, 149.
  members of Illinois Confederation, 800.
  original home on headwaters of Sangamon River, Illinois, 149.
  population, 149.
  sketch of, 149–150.
Mico Chlucco, the Long Warrior, King. of the Seminoles, 509.
Micropterus salmoides, use of as food, 266
Middle Mississippi area, 32.
Mikasuki, 116, 150, 181, 182, 189, 214, 218, 226, 827.
  name, interpretation of, 218.
  part taken in Seminole War by, 150.
  population, 150.
  prominent Seminole tribe, 150, 181, 182.
  sketch of, 150.
  source materials on, 828.
  Square Ground of, 776.
  probably branch of Chiaha, 116, 150.
  town of the, burned by Andrew Jackson, 150.
Mikonopi, titular chief of Seminole and chief of Oconee, 181, 182.
Milfort, Le Clerc, 696, 736, 828.
  on household utensils, 561.
  on mnemonic devices, 611, 612.
Miller and Fulton, lands sold by Pascagoula to, 171.
  Taensa sale of land to, 91.
Miller County, Ga., 43.
Miller's Bluff, La., 57.
Miller, William, one of purchasers of Biloxi and Pascagoula lands, 97.
Milling, Chapman J., 163, 177, 829, 830, 831.
  cited on Indian removal, 79–80.
  on identity of Indians who killed Haig and Brown, 163.
  on purpose of British census of Carolina Indians, 77.
Mineral kingdom, how drawn upon by Southeastern Indians, 242.
Minet, map of, 165.
Mingo Luak (Fire Chief), Chitimacha chief, 120.
Minko lusa, "Black Chief," Chakchiuma chief, 105.
Miruelo, Diego, 35.
  landing in Calusa country, 101.
  Timucua coast skirted by, 193.
Missionaries, Franciscan Spanish, 16.

Mission of Nombre de Dios, 209, 210.
Chilucan in, 119.
served Saturiwa, 179, 194.
Mission of Nombre de Dios de Amacarisse, *see* Mission of Nombre de Dios.
Mission of Nuestra Señora de Guadalupe, 155, 156, 179.
Mission of Señora de la Candelaria de la Tama, 189.
Mission of Nuestra Señora de la Luz, abandonment of, 86.
establishment of, 86.
Mission of Nuestra Señora de la Purísima Concepción, mission among Hainai, later withdrawn to San Antonio River, 136.
Mission of Nuestra Señora de los Dolores de los Ais, established and abandoned twice among Eyeish, 132.
Mission of San Buenaventura, Chilucan and Mocama in, 119.
Mission of San Francisco de los Neches, *see* Mission of San Francisco de los Texas.
Mission of San Francisco de los Texas, rebuilt on Neches River, 155, 156, 162.
Mission of San Francisco de Oconi, located west of Aucilla River, 165.
Mission of San Francisco Solano, 75.
Mission of San Francisco Xavier de Nájera, 75.
Mission of San Ildefonso, established in Texas, 86, 96, 130, 172.
Mission of San José de Aguayo, 75.
Mission of San José de los Nazones, 89.
location, 158.
Mission of San Juan Capistrano, 89.
Mission of San Juan de Guacara, 168, 202.
Mission of San Matheo, probably in Yustaga territory, 216.
Mission of San Pedro Mocama, established by the Franciscans on San Pedro Id, Ga., 187.
Mission of Santa Catalina, 168, 202.
Mission of Santa Cruz de Tarihica, 168, 202.
Missions, Spanish, in Texas, brief history of, 74–75.
(*For missions, see also under individual names.*)
Mississippi River, 2, 4, 5, 11, 12, 13, 19, 20, 21, 23, 26, 27, 29, 39, 56, 57, 58, 59, 63, 73, 74, 77, 93, 95, 97, 98, 112, 120, 133, 139, 140, 141, 147, 153, 158, 159, 161, 166, 167, 171, 198.
Acolapissa removed to, 82.
Alabama found by Bartram on, 87.
crossed by Cherokee, 112.
crossed by De Soto, 53.
exploration of by the French, 71, 72.
fort constructed by St. Denis on, 82, 161.
French possessions west of, ceded to Spain, 78.

Mississippi River, Houma located on, opposite mouth of Red River, 139, 198.
identification of with river in Muskogee myth, 25.
Mobile reported on island near mouth of, 151.
mouth discovered by Pineda, 35.
Natchez visited by La Salle on, 159.
Ofo found by Marquette, on east bank of, 166.
Okelousa lived west of, in early part of 18th century, 167.
Quapaw reported on, near junction with Arkansas, 176.
quest of by La Salle, 98.
use of pearls by Indians on, 489.
war against Chitimacha declared by all nations along, 120.
Mississippi, State of, 1, 13, 86.
entry into Union as State, 122.
migrations of Choctaw tribes of, 28–29.
original home of Chickasaw, 11, 116.
Mississippi Valley, 21.
Mnemonic devices, 610–613.
Mobile, 22, 35, 39, 49, 60, 64, 70, 72, 73, 87, 90, 91, 150, 151, 172, 190, 191, 196, 197, 210, 218, 809, 829.
apparently merged with Choctaw, 151.
French post near, 63.
French post ceded to England by treaty of 1763, 74.
games, 682.
name, interpretation of, 218.
population, 151.
protected from Tohome by French, 196.
reported at war with Pensacola Indians, 151, 172.
settled with Tohome, 151, 196.
sketch of, 150–151.
social organization, 654.
source material on, 829.
tribes gathered around French post near, 73.
Mobile and Tohome, war against the Alabama, 87.
Mobile Bay, Ala. 13, 42, 47, 60, 72, 87, 96.
Alonzo Alvarez de Pineda, first visited, 35, 150.
fort constructed by Bienville in, 151, 196.
Mobile River, discovery by Pineda, 13, 35.
Mobile settled at mouth of, 151, 191, 196.
Mocama, 119, 209.
Mocoço, 151, 193.
province or tribe, found by De Soto at inner end of Hillsboro Bay, Fla., 151.
Moctobi, 103.
possible synonym for Biloxi, 103.

Moçulixa, Indian village, 50.
Mohawk Creek, Va., Manahoac found
　by Lederer on, 148.
Moieties, 663–665.
Moloa, Fla., 133.
Monacan, 19, 30, 152, 201, 218, 462,
　509, 830.
　　country, Monasukapanough located
　　　by John Smith in, 178.
　　hair dressing, 499.
　　name, interpretation of, 218.
　　population, 152.
　　probably settled among Iroquois,
　　　152.
　　tribe or confederation on James
　　　River, Va., 152.
Monacantown, Indians of, necklaces,
　517.
　　nose ornaments, 514.
　　pottery, 554.
　　stone pipes, 545.
　　trade, 740.
Monahassanaugh, see Nahyssan.
Monasukapanough, see Saponi.
Monclova, founding of, 74.
Moneton, 152, 218.
　　found on Kanawha River, W. Va.,
　　　152.
　　may have joined Tutelo, 152.
　　name, interpretation of, 218.
　　population, 152.
　　sketch of, 152.
Mongolian races, comparison with In-
　dians, 825.
Monk's Corner, Berkeley Co., S. C.,
　home of Sewee, 183.
Montgomery, Ala., 27, 49.
　　home of Tawasa when discovered
　　　by De Soto, 190.
Montgomery, Col., force under destroyed
　by Cherokee, 112.
Montgomery, Tex., 96.
Mook, Maurice A., 831.
Mooney, James, 21, 24, 84, 91, 94, 95,
　98, 107, 109, 114, 119, 123, 124, 131,
　140, 149, 151, 152, 161, 169, 174, 175,
　176, 189, 190, 193, 194, 195, 196, 199,
　201, 202, 205, 206, 207, 208, 211, 215,
　216, 285, 296, 657, 664, 675, 676, 692,
　714, 723, 724, 767, 768, 772, 782, 783,
　818, 830, 831, 832.
　　and Olbrechts, 672, 783.
　　estimate of Indian population north
　　　of Mexico, 11, 12.
　　on derivation of the name Xuala,
　　　46.
　　on identification of town of Tanas-
　　　qui, 68.
　　on identification of Usi, 66.
　　on physical characteristics, 229.
　　on transportation, means of, 597.
Moore, Clarence B., archeological sites
　at mouth of Apalachicola reported by,
　13.
Moore, Col. James, 111, 143, 439.
　　Apalachee disrupted by force under,
　　　90.

Moore, Col. James, expedition of, out-
　fitted on the Ocmulgee River, 143.
　　　part taken by Cherokee in, 111.
　　leader of Creek and English expedi-
　　　tion, 1704, 63.
　　leader of second South Carolina
　　　expedition against Tuscarora,
　　　199.
Moravians, first mission among Chero-
　kee, established by 112.
Morfí, Fray Juan Agustín de, 155, 156,
　172, 345, 674, 832.
　　on clothing, 476.
　　on glue, 575.
　　on mental and moral characteristics
　　　of Caddo, 237.
　　on transportation, means of, 597.
　　on weapons, 575.
Morgan's Ferry, 51.
Morse, Jedidiah, 98, 108, 119, 146, 168,
　171, 190, 198.
　　estimate of Alabama population in
　　　Texas, 88.
　　estimate of Apalachee in Louisiana,
　　　91.
　　estimate of number of Biloxi
　　　moving to Texas, 97.
　　member of committee of Scots
　　　Society for Propagating Chris-
　　　tian Knowledge, 236.
Mortars, wooden, 558–560.
Morus rubra, use of, 287.
Moscoso, Luis de, 57, 58.
　　Anadarko encountered by, 89.
　　demotion of, 52.
　　horses brought by, 346.
　　Master of the Camp in De Soto's
　　　army, 41.
　　Spaniards under, 155, 158, 186.
　　successor to De Soto, 56, 158.
Mose, mission to which Yamasee moved,
　210.
Mosholatubbee, Choctaw chief, during
　emigration period of tribe, 122.
Mosopelea, see Ofo.
Motacilla sp., Indian belief in regard to,
　697.
Mounds, Indian, on Pine Island, 43.
Moundville, 14, 158.
Moundville people, possible occupants
　of Ranjel's Oka Lusa province, 25.
Mount Pleasant, 92.
Movements of Indian populations, effect
　of Spanish contact, 13–14.
Mowhemcho, Va., Monacan town, 152.
Moyano, see Boyano.
Muckalee River, 43.
Mucoço, see Mocoço, 151.
Mugulasha, attacked and almost de-
　stroyed by Bayogoula, 95, 177.
　　Bayogoula living in town with, 94.
　　source material on, 829.
　　See also Quinipissa.
Muklasa, 152, 153, 218.
　　name, interpretation of in Ala-
　　　bama tongue, 218.
　　population, 153.

Muklasa, probably branch of the Alabama, 88.
  sketch of, 152–153.
  town affiliated with Alabama Indians or the Koasati, 152.
Mulberry, red (*Morus rubra*), use as food, 287.
"Mulberry Place," *see* Cayomulgi.
Muscle Shoals, Tennessee River, Yuchi located above, 30, 212.
Muscogulges, moral characteristics, 231.
  physical characteristics, 223, 224.
Musical instruments, 624–629.
Muskhogean bands, games 548.
Muskhogeans, 68, 177, 682, 817.
  clans and gentes, 656, 657, 817.
  social customs, 723, 817.
Muskhogean-Siouan stock, 799, 801.
Muskhogean stock, 10, 27, 238, 239.
  displacement by Cherokee in eastern Tennessee in prehistoric times, 14, 15.
  historical works on, 21.
  legends of, 22.
  (See table 1, facing, p. 10.)
Muskhogean tribes included in Southeastern cultural province, 10.
  (See table 1, facing p. 10.)
Muskogee, 16, 26, 28, 29, 33, 42, 43, 88, 92, 110, 124, 125, 127, 128, 131, 132, 135, 143, 146, 153, 154, 166, 167, 181, 182, 215, 218, 226, 404, 827.
  ancestors of, legend related by Chekilli, 167.
  and Caddo names, reference to resemblances between, 31.
  artistic development, 616.
  clothing, 468, 817.
  crime and punishment, 817.
  derivation of clan organizations with female descent, 32.
  hair dressing, 506, 817.
  known as Ichisi to Hitchiti, 43.
  language, 46, 68.
  migration legends indicate western origin, 22, 27.
  migrations, 22, 25–27, 32.
  name, interpretation of, 218.
  population, 154.
  Province of Cofitachequi belonged to, 46.
  relationship, terms of, 667, 668.
  sketch of, 153, 154.
  weaving, 453.
Muskogee Confederation, *see* Creek Confederation.
Muskrat, Indian robes probably made of skins of, 38.
Muspa, name applied to Calusa, 64.
Myer, William E., 335.
Nabahydache, *see* Nabedache.
Nabedache, 99, 130, 154, 155, 156, 162, 218.
  attacked by epidemic, 155.
  name, interpretation of, in Caddo tongue, 218.

Nabedache, population, 155.
  raid against Apache joined by Bidai, 96.
  joined by Deadose, 86, 130.
  sketch of, 154–155.
  Spanish mission founded among, 74, 99.
  tribe, member of Hasinai Confederation, 99.
  village, mission San Francisco de los Texas, founded at, 155.
Nabochi, *see* Napochi.
Naçacahoz, Indian tribe visited by Moscoso, 57.
  see Nacogdoche.
Nacachau, 155, 162.
  population, 155.
  probably absorbed in Neche tribe, 155.
  sketch of, 155.
Nacanish, Caddo tribe, 155, 156, 619.
  encountered by Spaniards under Moscoso in La. or Tex., 155.
  population unknown, 155.
  "Province of Guacane," identified with, 619.
  reported on Naconicho Bayou by French and Spanish, 155.
  sketch of, 155.
Nacao, *see* Naconicho Bayou.
Nacodoches, *see* Nacogdoche.
Nacogdoche, 155, 156, 158, 162.
  found on Angelina River, 156.
  population, 156.
  sketch of, 156.
  success of Spanish mission among, 75.
  united with Caddo, 156.
Nacogdoches, city of, 58, 89.
Nacogdochitos, *see* Nacogdoche.
Naconicho Bayou, reported settlement of Nacanish at, 155.
Nacono, 155, 156, 162.
  apparently joined Caddo, 156.
  population, 156.
  settlement of, on Neches River, 155.
  sketch of, 156.
  tribe of Hasinai Confederation, 156.
Nacotchtank, tribe visited by Henry Fleet, 596.
Nadako, *see* Anadarko.
Naguatex, tribe encountered by Moscoso on Red River near site of Shreveport, 57, 154.
  identified as Namidish, 57, 599.
  meaning of name, 154.
Nahyssan, 157.
  attacked by whites and Powhatan Indians, 157.
  joined with Saponi, 157.
  Siouan tribe discovered on the James River, Va., 157.
  sketch of, 157.
Names, 671–674.
  tribal, interpretation of, 216–219.

Namidish, Caddo tribe called "place of salt" people, 301.
  chief of, visited strangers on foot, 599.
  identification with Naguatex, 57, 599.
  trade with, 738.
Nanatsoho, 141, 157.
  allied with Kadohadatcho, Natchitoches, and Nasoni, 157.
  population unknown, 157.
  sketch of, 157.
  tribe of Caddo Indians, 157.
Naniaba, 151, 197.
Nanih Waiya hill, "hill of origins," (Choctaw), 122.
Nanipacana, "Hill Top," Mobile town, reached by De Luna expedition, 60, 61, 151.
Nansemond, 175.
Nanticoke, 201.
  means of transportation, 596.
  origin indicated as westward by tradition, 24.
Napetaca, Timucua village visited by De Soto, 41, 202.
  Indians of, see Utina.
Napissa, 116, 158.
  reported by Iberville united with Chickasaw, 158.
Napochi, 126, 157, 158, 218, 829.
  at war with Coosa, and defeated by Spaniards and Coosa, 157.
  linguistic evidence of relation to Choctaw and Mobile, 60.
  name, interpretation of, 218.
  one of tribes nearest to prehistoric settlement at Moundville, 158.
  population unknown, 158.
  probably Napissa mentioned by Iberville, 116.
  sketch of, 157–158.
  source material on, 829.
  tribe on Black Warrior River, Ala. 157.
Naquiscoça, Indian tribe visited by Moscoso, 57.
  see Nacogdoche.
Narvaez, Panfilo de, 40, 41, 52, 59.
  Apalachee encountered by, 89.
Narvaez Expedition, 37–39, 150, 172, 193, 196, 201, 346, 458, 460, 504, 582, 584, 587, 589, 619, 628, 633, 828.
  death of two members, 49.
  survivors of, 74.
  two members abducted by Indians, 38.
Nashitosh, see Natchitoches.
Nashville Basin, 5, 15.
Naskobo, town supporting the French, 122.
Nasoni, 141, 142, 157, 158.
  identification with Nisohone, 57.
  population, 158.
  settlement located SW. of Shreveport, 158.
  sketch of, 158.

Natao, see Adai.
Natasi, 158, 211.
  Caddo tribe on Red River, 158.
Natchez, 11, 13, 17, 19, 20, 21, 23, 29, 33, 54, 77, 99, 108, 129, 147, 148, 158–161, 172, 188, 194, 195, 203, 212, 291, 297, 298, 299, 338, 665, 801, 803, 805, 806, 807, 809, 810, 818, 822, 827, 829.
  advanced culture of, 22.
  agricultural methods, 310, 818.
  attack on Natchitoches, 99, 161.
  axes, 544, 545.
  band of, settled near Abihka on Arkansas River, 160.
  birth customs, 717.
  burial customs, 728, 811, 819.
  castes, 661, 819.
  clans and gentes, 655, 657.
  clothing, 439, 440, 448, 449, 457, 461, 463, 464, 465, 474.
  coloring for manufactured articles, 610.
  crime and punishment, 733.
  division of labor between men and women, 717.
  divisions of Muskhogean stock, 10. (See table 1, facing p. 10.)
  doors, 428, 430.
  ear ornaments, 514, 819.
  education of children, 717.
  enumeration of months, 260, 261, 262, 269, 818.
  feather mantles, 455.
  First Fruits Ceremony, 681.
  first mission established among, 72.
  food preserving, 374, 377.
  fortified on Sicily Island, 212.
  French trading post established among, to counteract English influence, 159.
  games, 681, 682, 684.
    deer-hunting game, 319, 320.
  hair dressing, 500, 507, 819.
  head deformation practiced by, 537, 540, 818.
  Great Sun, title of chief, 246, 555, 599, 600, 601, 612, 650, 700, 728.
    head band of feathers worn by, 509.
    house of Great Sun, 82.
  household utensils, 559, 561, 563, 819.
  houses, 418, 419, 421, 819.
  hunting, 315, 316, 319, 321.
  illumination, 426.
  images, 618, 819.
  implements for hunting and fishing, 575, 576, 579, 583.
  joined by Tiou, 195.
  language lost to most members and tribe about extinct, 160.
  location, 29.
  marriage customs, 707, 708.
  mats and baskets, 603, 607.
  medical practices, 796, 798.

Natchez, members of Muskhogean linguistic family, 239, 819.
migrations, 32.
mnemonic devices, 611, 612.
moieties, 664.
murder of Frenchmen by, resulted in short war, 159.
names, 673, 819.
necklaces, 519, 520.
origin legend, 22, 23.
ornamentation, 490.
Palawana Island granted to, 129, 160.
pearls, 489, 516.
physical characteristics, 228, 229.
pipes, 547, 819.
population, 160.
pottery, 549, 550, 553, 554.
rebellion, 1729, 73.
religious beliefs and usages, 779, 780, 812, 819.
sketch of, 158–161.
skin dressing, 443,.
smoke holes and windows, lacking, 427.
social organization, 650, 654.
source material on, 829.
staining of teeth, 536, 819.
tattooing, 535.
temple, 613.
territory, fertility of, 20.
thread and textiles, 449, 450.
towns, 638.
trade with, 738.
transportation for the "Great Sun" by, 599, 600, 601, 819.
uprising put down by Bienville, 159.
See Natchez War.
visited by De Montigny and Davion, missionaries, 159, 188.
visited by Iberville, at town of the Great Sun, 159.
vocabularies collected by early ethnologists, 160.
war customs, 698, 699, 700, 701.
weapons, 575, 576, 579, 583.
welcomed by Abihka, 81.
Natchez Bluff, 20.
Natchez, City of, 23, 30.
trading house established at, 72.
Natchez Nation, joined by Grigra, 134.
Natchez War, 30, 72, 78, 106, 107, 109, 117, 134, 147, 166, 198, 212.
Natchitoches, 83, 85, 98, 99, 130, 141, 155, 157, 158, 160, 161, 162, 188, 204, 211, 218.
accompanied Caddo tribes to Texas and Oklahoma, 161.
attacked by Acolapissa, 82, 99.
defeat of Natchez by, 161.
discovered by French under Tonti, 161, 188.
fishing, 340.
loyalty to whites in Natchez rebellion, 73.
name, interpretation of, 218.

Natchitoches, pleasant relations with St. Denis maintained by, 161.
population, 162.
removal from Red River to Lake Pontchartrain by St. Denis, 130, 161.
settled by St. Denis beside Acolapissa, 82.
sketch of, 161–162.
tattooing, 536.
trade with, 738.
"upper" town allied with Kadohadacho, 161.
visit of Bienville to, 72, 99, 161.
Natchitoches, town on Red River, founded by French, 72, 85.
Naufawpi Creek, 26.
Nautaugue, see Nottoway.
Navasota River, Tex., Deadose tribe living near, 130.
Nawatesh, see Naguatex.
Nawphawpe Creek, see Naufawpi.
Nazadachotzi, see Nacogdoche.
Nechaui, 155, 162.
Nacono settled on Neches River, opposite, 155, 162.
population unknown, 162.
tribe of Hasinai Confederacy, 162.
Neche, 155, 156, 162.
almost destroyed by Yojuane Indians, 162.
Hasinai tribe on Neches River, 162.
mission of San Francisco de los Neches established near, 162.
population, 162.
sketch of, 162.
village, mission reestablished near, 155, 162.
visited by La Salle, 162.
Neches River, Tex., 57, 96.
Biloxi Bayou a branch of, 171.
Cherokee members of Bowl's band settled along, 113.
establishment of mission in vicinity of, 99, 162.
Nabedache village near Arroyo San Pedro, west of, 154.
Nacachau village on east side of, 155.
Nacono settled on, opposite the Nechaui, 155, 156, 162.
settlement of Koasati on, 145, 146.
site of Neche village near Nacogdoche on, 162.
Neckband, see Necklaces.
Necklaces, 516–521.
Necoes, village, 103.
Needham, James, 77, 208.
Negro, death of, with De Soto, 60.
member of Narvaez expedition, 38, 39.
slaves, marriage of with Ais women, 84.
Neighbours, Robert S., agent of Caddo Indians, 99.
Nelumbo lutea, use of, 289, 292, 296.
Neumann, 221.

Neuse River, N. C., 126, 131, 162, 199, 207.
  home of Eno near headwaters of, 131.
  peninsula occupied by Coree or Coranine near mouth of, 126, 800.
  site of Neusiok village, 162.
  Woccon located near Goldsboro, on, 207.
Neusiok, 15, 162, 800.
  population, 162.
  probably joined Tuscarora, 162.
  tribe on south side of Neuse River, N. C., 162.
New Netherlands, 200.
New Orleans, 73, 82, 86, 94, 95, 97.
  founding of, 72.
  tribes gathered around, 73.
Newport, Captain, Monacan towns visited by, 152.
  on pearls worn by Indian chief, 488.
  relation of, 831.
New River, 48.
New South Wales, 7.
New Tamathli, see Tcawokli.
New Windsor, S. C., Apalachee settled near, by Moore, 90.
New Yamacraw, Yamasee moved to, 210.
Nicholas Ford, 47.
Nicotiana rustica, uses of, 244, 383, 384, 386.
Nikonha, Tutelo brave, last survivor, 201.
Niojo, town subject to San Juan del Puerto, 179.
Nisione, see Nasoni.
Nissohone, Indian tribe encountered by Moscoso, 57, 158.
  see Nasoni.
Nitahauritz, see Bear Fort.
Nita holihta, see Bear Fort.
Nitiwaga Nation, 163.
Nittaweega, see Nottoway.
Nombre de Dios, mission of, 119, 179, 194, 209, 210.
Nondacao, see Anadarko.
Nondaco, Indian tribe encountered by Moscoso, 57.
Nondo, see Angelico.
Non-Muskogees, 181, 662.
Norsemen, reference to voyages of, 33.
North Augusta, S. C., 90.
North Canadian River, Apalachee families on, 91.
North Carolina Indians, body paint, 529.
  clothing, 475.
  coloring of manufactured articles, 609.
  hair dressing, 498, 501.
  images, 614.
  physical characteristics, 226, 227, 228.
  ornamentation, 488.
  towns, 630, 631.
  transportation, means of, 595.

North Carolina, State of, 1, 2, 18, 19, 30, 36, 37, 66, 70, 76.
  Algonquian tribes of, 24.
  coast explored by first Raleigh expedition, 75.
  culture pattern of tidewater tribes, 10.
  refusal to accept Catawba, 105.
  reservation for Cherokee established in western, 113.
  Tuscarora of Piedmont escarpment of, 11.
Northwest origin of eastern Siouans indicated by legends, 23.
Nose ornaments, 514–515.
Notowega, see Nottoway.
"Nottaway and Schockoores oldfields," mentioned by Blande, 183.
Nottoway, 15, 31, 141, 163, 164, 183, 218, 241.
  arrows, 573.
  bracelets, 521.
  Cherokee, apparently joined by, 164.
  copper, 491, 492.
  fled to Cherokee country after murdering whites, 163.
  fort, 439.
  found on Nottoway River, 163.
  Iroquoian tribe in Virginia, 241, 800.
  mentioned in Raleigh narratives under name of Mangoac, 163.
  musical instruments, 625.
  name, interpretation of, in Algonquian tongue, 163, 218.
  necklaces, 517.
  population, 164.
  ruled by a "queen," 163.
  sketch of, 163–164.
  visited by Edward Blande and company, 163.
  visited by William Byrd, 163, 412, 439, 741.
Nottoway River, N. C., 15, 124, 163, 183, 800.
Nouaille, M. de, 109, 139, 204.
  meeting with Chawasha and Washa near "Les Allemands," 109.
  on amalgamation of Bayogoula and Houma with Acolapissa, 82.
  report on Houma, 139.
Novaculite, aboriginal workings in, about Hot Springs, Ark., 14.
Nuestra Señora de Guadalupe, mission of, 155, 156, 179.
Nuestra Señora de la Candelaria de la Tama, mission near the Apalachee, 189.
Nuestra Señora de la Luz, mission of, 86.
Nuestra Señora de la Purísima Concepción, mission for Hainai, later withdrawn to San Antonio River, 136.
Nuestra Señora de los Dolores de los Ais, mission for Eyeish Indians, founded and abandoned, 132.
Nuevo Leon, 74.

Nunn, George Erma, on early Portuguese expedition, 34.
Nuttall, Thomas, 831.
Nuyaka, see Tukpafka, 125.
    Square Ground, 776.
Oak, uses of, 245.
    live (Quercus virginiana), use of, 273, 279.
Ocala, Fla., 164.
Ocale, Timucua town, 4, 164, 193.
    population unknown, 164.
    probably related to Acuera, 83, 164.
    visited by De Soto, in Florida, 164.
Occaneechi, 131, 145, 149, 164, 178, 183, 200, 201, 218.
    accompanied other tribes to north, taking name of Saponi, 164.
    attacked and defeated by Nathaniel Bacon, 164.
    body color, 530.
    Conestoga driven out by, 164.
    Conestoga sought refuge with, 164.
    found by Lawson on Eno River, near Hillsboro, N. C., 164, 183.
    located at Fort Christanna with the Tutelo, Manahoac, and other tribes, 164.
    Manahoac united with Saponi and, 149, 164.
    name, interpretation of, 218.
    population, 164.
    sketch of, 164.
    trade, 739, 740.
    trail, 76.
    tribe located on Roanoke River, Va., 164.
    See also Saponi and Tutelo.
Ochesee Creek, interpretation of name, 217.
Ochesee, name of Muskogee in Hitchiti language, 217.
Ochlockonee River, 42.
Oçita, 151, 164, 165, 173, 193.
    De Soto landing in territory of, 40, 151, 165.
    probably identical with province called Pohoy (q. v.), 165, 193.
    temple of, 761.
    town of seized by Spaniards, 164.
    tribe near Tampa Bay, Fla., discovered by De Soto, 165.
Ocklawaha River, Fla., 64.
    Acuera located on, 83.
Ocmulgee Old Fields, home of Hitchiti, 138.
Ocmulgee River, 14, 44, 115, 127, 138, 143, 144, 153, 189, 200, 208, 213, 217, 297.
    home of Chiaha, 115.
    home of Ocute, as related by De Soto, 138.
    home of Sawokli before Yamasee War, 180.
    Kasihta drawn to join other Creek towns on, 143.
    settlement of Lower Creeks on, 63.

Ocmulgee River, temporary home of Coweta, to be near English traders, 127.
    temporary home of Tuskegee, 200.
Oconee, 138, 165, 181, 189, 197.
    Mikonopi, chief of, 181.
    nucleus of Seminole Nation, 165, 181.
    population, 165.
    sketch of, 165.
    southern branch absorbed by Apalachee, 165.
    visited by Bartram in Alachua plains, Fla., 165.
Oconee mission, located among Apalachee, 165.
    located on Georgia coast, 165.
Oconee River, Ga., 44.
    location of northern branch of Oconee, 165, 181.
Oconee Town of Cherokee, located near Walhalla, Oconee Co.,S. C., 165.
Ocon, Fray Juan, visit to Sawokli, 180.
Ocotoque, Yamasee town, 209.
Ocute, De Soto's name for Hitchiti, 44, 138, 297.
Ofo, 31, 73, 94, 106, 148, 165, 166, 198, 199, 212, 218, 241, 800, 822, 831.
    attacked by Chickasaw, 106.
    classified with Tutelo by Voegelin, 11.
    death of last survivor, 166.
    found by Hutchins on west side of Miss., 166.
    found by Marquette on east bank of Miss., 166.
    movement to Tunica, as allies of French, 166.
    name, interpretation of, 218.
    part in attack on English convoy on Miss., 166.
    population, 166.
    related to Biloxi, 104.
    settled among Taensa on Lake St. Joseph, 166.
    sketch of, 165–166.
    source material on, 831.
    two divisions of, 165.
    vocabulary obtained from last survivor, 166.
    See also Tunica.
Ofogoula, 31.
    See Ofo.
Ofulo, see Yfulo.
Ogden, Ark., 24.
Ogeechee River, 44.
    home of Yuchi, 214.
Oglethorpe, Governor, 153, 167, 210, 326, 361, 505, 506.
    landed on Savannah with first Georgia colonists, 210.
    legend of Muskogee origin told by Kasihta chief Chekilli to, 25.
    on clothing, 470.
    on household utensils, 558.
    on mats and baskets, 604.
    on pottery, 551.
    on towns, 633, 634.

Ohio River, 2, 21, 31.
  called by Illinois "River of the
    Arkansas," 31.
  earliest known home of Shawnee,
    184.
  northern boundary of Chickasaw
    established by Treaty of Hope-
    well at, 118.
  traditional home of Quapaw, above
    mouth of Wabash, 176.
Ohio, State of, 30, 31.
Ohio Valley, 2, 13, 96.
Oka holo, town supporting the French,
  122.
Oka Lusa, a province described by
  Ranjel, 26.
Okalusa, 25, 65.
  French supported by, 121.
Okalusa Creek, 167.
Okawaigi, Sawokli town, 180, 181.
Okchai, 88, 147, 153, 166, 167, 173, 207,
  218.
  joined by Wiwohka, 207.
  Muskogee town and tribe on west
    side of Coosa River, 166.
  name, interpretation of, 218.
  part joined Seminole in Florida,
    167.
  population, 167.
  settled on Kowaliga Creek, until
    removal to Okla., 166.
  sketch of, 166–167.
  See also Asilanabi.
Okchaiutci, Indians of, 88.
  population, 88.
  town of, formed of Alabama Indi-
    ans, 166.
    movements of Alabama of, 87.
    origin of name, 88.
Oke, Indian God, 615, 743.
Okeloosa Creek, *see* Okalusa Creek.
Okelousa, 109, 167, 168, 169, 204, 218.
  allies of Houma against Tangipa-
    hoa, 167.
  located by Du Pratz above Pointe
    Coupée on Miss. River, 168.
  name, interpretation of, in Choc-
    taw and Chickasaw tongues, 218.
  population, 168.
  probably united with Houma, 168.
  sketch of, 167–168.
  tribe living west of the Miss., 167.
Oketee, Yamasee town, 209.
  See also Ocotoque.
Okeus, Indian God, 744.
  See also Oke.
Okfuskee, 81, 125, 131, 153, 197.
  Eufaula settled on Tallapoosa River
    below, 131.
  group descended from Coosa, 125,
    153.
Okiti-yakani, Sawokli town, 138, 180,
  181.
Oklahoma, State of, 88, 91, 93, 122, 132,
  138, 153, 170, 180, 198, 214.
  Choctaw citizens of, 122.
  Creeks citizens of, 153.

Oklahoma, State of, Eufaula went with
  Creeks to, 132.
  formerly Indian Territory, 80.
  Hitchiti moved with Seminole to,
    138.
  home of Chickasaw Nation, 198.
  Pakana settled with Creek Nation
    in, 170.
  Pascagoula accompanied the Biloxi
    to, 171.
  Quapaw citizens of, 176.
  Yuchi moved to, with Creeks, 214.
Oklawaha River, Fla., Yamasee retired
  to, 210.
Okmulgee, 116, 138, 154, 168, 169, 180,
  218.
  branch of Hitchiti, located on
    Chattahoochee, 168.
  located east of Flint River, 168.
  name, interpretation of, in Hitchiti
    tongue, 218.
  population, 168.
  Sawokli moved to Okla. and settled
    near, 180.
  sketch of, 168.
Okmulgee, Okla., Apalachicola settled
  near, 92.
  council house of tribe located at,
    154.
Okra (*Hibiscus esculentus*), use of, 289.
Oktahasasi, village of Hilibi, 137, 138.
Olbrechts, Dr. Frans, 831.
  on Indian beliefs, 772.
  See Mooney and Olbrechts.
Old Biloxi, site of first permanent French
  settlement in La., 72.
Old Coosa town, on Coosa River, 125.
"Old Creek Place," *see* Coosawatee,
  valley of the.
"Oldfields," of Moneton, found west of
  Blue Ridge Mts., Va., 152.
Old Mikasuki, Jefferson Co., Fla., first
  settlement of Mikasuki, 150.
Old Spring Hill, Ga., 50.
Old Tamathli, town on Chattahoochee
  River, 180, 181, 189, 190.
Old Tampa Bay, Fla., site of Tocobaga,
  195.
Oldtown Creek, Brunswick Co., site of
  Cape Fear Indian colony, 103.
Oldtown Lake, 54.
Olibahali, *see* Hothliwahali.
Olitifar, 69.
Olive, a south Texas tribe, 74.
Olivella sp., uses of, 252, 485.
Olmos, Father, missionary work in
  South Tex. by, 74.
Olustee Creek, 41.
Omaha system of relationship, 669.
Omens, meaning of, 765, 766, 772.
Omusee Creek, 210.
Onatheaqua, 168, 193.
  name for Timucuans on Le Moyne
    map, 168.
  population, 168.
  sketch of, 168.
  Timucua tribe, 168.

Oneida, 199.
 moral characteristics, 236.
Oni Talimon, 122.
Ony, *see* Oni Talimon.
Ooe-ása (probably Wiha asha, "home
 of emigrants"), Chickasaw town established in Creek country, 117.
Opaya Mataha, grand chief of Chickasaw, 653.
Opechancanough, brother of Powhatan,
 644.
 bodyguard of, 689.
 mats and baskets used by followers
 of, 603.
 Powhatan uprisings under, 175.
 Smith taken prisoner by, 689.
Opelousa, 87, 93, 94, 109, 145, 168, 169,
 218, 240, 737.
 located near site of Opelousas City,
 169.
 name, in interpretation of Choctaw
 or Chickasaw tongues, 218.
 population, 169.
 probably joined Atakapa, 169.
 sketch of, 168–169.
Opelousas City, 87, 169.
Opiłłako, *see* Pilthlako.
Opilthlucco, branch of Flint River,
 home of Yuchi located on, 214.
Opitchapan, brother of Powahtan, 644.
Opossum, uses of, 449, 450.
Opothleyoholo, Creek chief, 154.
Oquechiton, discussion of linguistic
 affiliation of word, 60.
 native name for Black Warrior
 River, 60.
Orache, halberd-leaved (*Atriplex hastata*),
 use of, 270, 306.
Orange Co., N. C., Occaneechi occupied
 a village near Hillsboro in, 164.
Orapaks, habitation of Powhatan on
 Chickahamania River, 643, 644.
Origin myth of Muskogee, 25.
Origin of Southeastern tribes, discussion
 of, 22.
Orista, province of, 18.
Ornamentation, 481–541.
 differences between ornaments worn
 by men and women. 541.
Orobio y Basterra, Capt., estimate of
 Akokisa population by, 86.
Orontium aquaticum, use of, 271, 272.
Ortiz, Juan, interpreter for De Soto,
 40, 151, 693.
 death of, 55.
Osage-orange (*Toxylon pomiferum*), use
 of, 578, 579.
Osage reservation, 176.
Osages, 142, 466, 518, 547.
Osceola, belongings of, 468.
 brains of Seminole uprising, 181,
 182.
 capture and imprisonment of, 80,
 181.
Osochi, 29, 116, 138, 168, 169, 216, 239,
 547, 827.
 located between Chattahoochee and
 Flint Rivers, 169.

Osochi, moved to west bank of Chattahoochee and settled above Chiaha 169.
 part settled at Council Hill to be
 near the Hitchiti, 169.
 population, 169.
 removed to Okla., and settled on
 Arkansas River, near city of
 Muskogee, 169.
 sketch of, 169.
Ospo, Guale mission station, 135.
Ossachile, *see* Osochi.
Ostenaco, Cherokee chief, 692.
Otariyatiqui, classification of, 67.
Otciapofa, or "Hickory Ground," name
 of town on Coosa River, 125, 144, 153.
 clans and gentes, 656.
Otci'si, Hitchiti word applied to Mus-
 kogee, 127.
Otoa, *see* Tamathli.
Otsoté, Indian village, 640, 641.
Otter River, Campbell Co., Va., home
 of Saponi, 178.
Ouacha, French form of Washa, 204.
Ouachita, *see* Washita.
Ouachita Mountains, 14.
Ouachita Plateau, 4, 14.
Ouachita Province, Indian population
 found by De Soto in, 14.
Ouachita River, Ark. and La., 13, 29, 55,
 56.
 Avoyel on, 95.
 early home of Tunica, 197, 198.
 identification with River of Cayas
 or Anilco, 54.
 named for Washita tribe, 204.
Ouadé, Huguenot name for Guale set-
 tlement, 135.
Ougapa, Indian town on Miss., 641.
Oulchionis, *see* Doustioni.
Oustack, name used by Lederer for
 Yuchi, 213.
 See also Westo.
Outasite, *see* Ostenaco.
Oviedo y Valdez, Gonzalo Fernandez
 de (el Capitan), on houses, 405, 406,
 421.
Ozark Plateau, 4, 14.
Ozarks, Bluff Dwellers of the, 33.
 discovery of Bluff Culture in the, 14
Pacaha, town in Arkansas, with moat
 and stockade, 433, 435.
 shields found at, 588.
Pacaha, tribe met by De Soto, 53, 54,
 176, 212, 490, 589, 737.
Padgeeligau, on Flint River, home of
 Yuchi, 214.
Padilla, Fray Augustin, 60.
Padilla, Davila, 829.
 on horses, 347.
Padilla, Juan Antonio, estimate of
 Anadarko population by, 89.
 on poisoned arrows, 576.
 on towns, 634.
Pafallaya, meaning and derivation of
 name, 51.
 name used by Elvas for province,
 51, 121.

Pagellus acarne, 266.
Pagonias chromis, 267.
Paint, made by Southeastern Indians, 243.
Pakan Tallahassee Indians, mentioned by the Spanish, 170.
Pakan Tallahassee, Square Ground of, 776.
Pakana, 91, 153, 170, 189, 218.
  first known on Hatchet Creek, Coosa Co., Ala., 170.
  name, interpretation of in Muskogee tongue, 218.
  population, 170.
  sketch of, 170.
  supposed to have united with Alabama in Tex., 170.
Palachocolas, *see* Parachocolas Fort.
Palawana Island, granted to Cusabo, 129.
  granted to Natchez, 129, 160
Paliaca, town subject to Mission of Nombre de Dios, 179.
Palisema, province of, 54, 55.
Palmetto, blue (*Rhapidophyllum hystrix*) use as food, 285, 287, 296.
Palm, needle (*Rhapidophyllum hystrix*), use as food, 285, 287.
Pamaunche, King, Indian chief, 610.
Pamaunke, land subject to Powhatan, 643.
Pamaunke River, 643.
Pamlico, 170.
  allies of Tuscarora, 170.
    bad treatment by Tuscarora, 170.
  first discovered by English, 170.
  first reported on Pamlico River, N. C., 170.
  population, 170.
  sketch of, 170.
  smallpox among, 170.
  vocabulary preserved, 170.
Pamlico River, N. C., 170, 199, 800.
  home of Pamlico Indians, 170.
Pamlico Sound, N. C., 15.
  Machapunga lived between Albemarle Sound and, 148.
Pamunkey, 175.
Pamunkey chief, pearls worn by, 488.
Panama, Isthmus of, 33, 35.
Panicum maximum, uses of, 244, 288, 293.
Panicum sp., use of as food, 285, 286, 288.
Pan-Indian movements, reference to, 81.
Paⁿs-falaya, meaning "Long Hair," name for Choctaw, 51, 121.
Panuco, Mexico, 35, 37, 59, 74.
Parachocolas Fort, 92.
Paraguay, inhabitants of, 825.
  original home of Tupi, 824.
Pardo, Juan, Spanish captain, 28, 30, 45, 46, 67, 69, 104, 109, 110, 115, 125, 126, 145, 151, 183, 186, 200, 205, 213, 647.
  Cofitachequi visited by, 143.
  destruction of fort established by, 205.

Pardo, Juan, expedition of, 64–66.
  fort at Chattooga Ridge built by, 109.
  Koasati among tribes who opposed, 145.
  narratives on location of town of Ilapi, 45.
  on route of De Soto after leaving Cofitachequi, 46.
Pareja, Father, 165, 281, 382, 499, 648, 657, 661, 762, 765, 766, 767, 829.
Parker, Wm. B., 142, 400.
Pascagoula, 73, 80, 97, 103, 151, 170, 171, 196, 197, 218, 327, 829, 831.
  accompanied the Biloxi to Okla., 171.
  agricultural methods, 310.
  burial customs, 727, 811.
  crossed Miss. and settled on Red River, 171.
  food preserving, 377, 378.
  lands sold to Miller and Fulton by, 171.
  moved to Gulf Coast, according to Du Pratz, 171.
  musical instruments, 625, 627.
  name, interpretation of in Choctaw and Chickasaw tongues, 218.
  permitted to locate at confluence of the Rigolet du Bon Dieu and Red River, 171.
  population, 171.
  pottery, 550, 551.
  probably died out, 171.
  removed to lands granted them by Choctaw, on Bayou Boeuf, 171.
  settlement in Texas, 97.
  sketch of, 170–171.
  source material on, 829, 831.
  territory between Bayou de la Coeur and Bayou Philippe granted to, 171.
  visited by Bienville on Pascagoula River, 170.
  visited by Iberville on Pascagoula River, 171.
  See also Biloxi.
Pascagoula River, 96, 97, 103, 151, 170, 196, 800.
  Biloxi fort on, 437.
  site of Pascagoula village, 103, 151, 170.
Pasquotank, tribe of Weapemeoc confederation, 206.
Passionflower (*Passiflora incarnata*), use as food, 274, 285, 286, 289, 294, 297.
Patapsco River, Md., home of part of Shawnee, 184.
Patiri, 130, 172, 240.
  associated with Akokisa and Deadose in Mission of San Ildefonso, 86, 96.
  final history unknown, 172.
  population unknown, 172.
  sketch of, 172.
  tribe in central Tex. west of Trinity River, 172.
Patofa, Indian town, 44.

Patomecke tribes, war customs of, 688.
Paul, Benjamin, Chitimacha chief, 657, 686.
Pavia sp., use of, 314.
Pawcorance, word for altar stone, 745, 746.
Pawnee, 241, 665.
Pawokti, 22, 28, 87, 88, 171.
  associated with Tawasa, 171.
  moved to Mobile with Tawasa, 171.
  moved to upper Alabama when Fort Toulouse was established, 171.
  population unknown, 171.
  sketch of, 171.
  town or tribe first mentioned on Lamhatty map, 171.
  See also Alabama *and* Tawasa.
Payankatank, people of, attacked by warriors of Powhatan, 644, 645.
Payne, John Howard (mss.), 831.
Paynes Landing, treaty with Florida Indians negotiated at, 181.
Peaches, apparently obtained from Spaniards, 279.
Peachtree Creek, 47, 68.
  identification of town site at mouth of, with Guasili, 47.
Pea Creek Yuchi, 213, 214.
  disappearance of, 214.
  established near Tukabahchee, 214.
Peak, *see* Wampum.
Pearl River, Miss., 82, 97.
  location of pearl fishery of Natchez, 489, 738.
  Pensacola reported by Bienville on, 173.
Pearls, effect of Spaniards' loss of at battle of Mabila, 50.
  in ossuaries of Cofitachequi and Talimeco, 45.
  necklace of, presented to De Soto by "Lady of Cofitachequi," 45.
  taken by Spaniards, 46.
  use of by Indians, 488–489, 510, 516, 560, 567, 571, 583, 619.
Peas, use of, 269.
  marsh (*Lathyrus myrtifolius*), use of, 269.
Pedee, 103, 172, 203, 207, 218.
  Cape Fear Indians formed settlement under "King Johnny" with, 172.
  flight to South after killing Catawba, 172.
  name, interpretation of, 218.
  population, 172.
  sketch of, 172.
  tribe on Pee Dee River, S. C., 172, 203.
Pee Dee River, S. C., 19, 66, 67.
  home of Winyaw tribe, 207.
  Keyauwee settled with Cheraw on, 145.
  Pedee found on, when Charleston, S. C., was founded, 172.
  Waccamaw located on lower, 203.

Pedrárias Dávila, *see* Ávila, Pedro Árias de.
Pedro, Indian captured by De Soto, 42, 44.
Peltandra virginica, use of, 271, 272. 276, 296, 363.
Pénicaut, French traveler, 106, 120, 130, 147, 159, 211, 327, 829.
  on agricultural methods of Pascagoula 310.
  on artistic development, 618, 619.
  on clothing, 473, 476.
  on expedition of St. Denis against Chitimacha, 120.
  on fishing, 340.
  on hair dressing, 498.
  on images, 619.
  on musical instruments, 625, 627.
  on pearls, 489, 516.
  on pottery, 550, 551.
  on tattooing, 536.
  tribe of cannibals reported by, 85.
Pennsylvania, State of, 31.
Pensacola, 39, 42, 63, 73, 90, 91, 107, 151, 172, 173, 210, 218.
  apparently, united with Choctaw, 173.
  Gulf of Mexico home of, 172.
  name, interpretation of in Choctaw tongue, 218.
  population, 173.
  reported at war with Mobile, 151, 172.
  reported by Bienville in village on Pearl River, 173.
  sketch of, 172–173.
  Spaniards encountered, 172.
  visited by expedition under Barroto, 172.
Pensacola Bay, Fla., 38, 47, 60.
  port used by De Soto, 42.
  survey of by Spaniards, 96, 156 196.
Pensacola district, archeological evidence of population movement found in, 16.
Peoria, 150.
Percy, George, on body paint, 529.
  on cooking, 355.
  on date of Biloxi settlement near New Orleans, 97.
  on ear ornaments, 510.
  on hair dressing, 499, 502.
  on implements for hunting and fishing, 568, 572, 577, 581.
  on musical instruments, 629.
  on tattooing, 532.
  on tobacco, 383.
  on transportation, means of, 593.
  on war customs, 687.
  on weapons, 568, 572, 577, 581.
Perico, *see* Pedro.
Perquiman, tribe of Weapemeoc confederation, 206.
Perrier, Governor, 109, 147, 160, 161, 204.
  advance of against Natchez, 147, 160.

Perrier, Governor, Chawasha town destroyed by slaves by permission of, 109.
　　Natchez sent to West Indies as slaves by, 160.
Perrine, Doctor, botanist, killed by Calusa, 102.
Perryman family, 154.
　　played part in Creek Nation, 168.
Persimmon (*Diospyros* sp.), use as food, 272, 287, 288, 292, 363, 373, 564.
Peru, 59, 101.
　　De Soto's part in conquest of, 39.
　　relation to cultural area, 827.
Petersburg, Va., site of village of Nahyssan, 157.
Phaseolus sp, use as food, 285, 286, 288.
Philadelphia, Miss., home of Choctaw John Wesley, 123.
Philip II, King of Spain, plan to establish colonies in America, 59, 70.
Physical and mental characteristics, 219–238.
Piache, see Piachi.
Piachi, hostility of inhabitants to Spaniards, 49.
　　Mobile town visited by Spaniards, 150.
　　Tascalusa's capital town, 39, 49.
Picolata, site of San Diego de Salamototo, 179.
Piedmont country, 31.
　　clothing worn, 470.
　　ear ornaments in, 511.
　　greasing and coloring of hair and skin, 527.
　　implements of arrowwood used in, 573.
　　home of Manahoac tribe, 148.
　　musical instruments, 627.
　　names used in, 671.
Piedmont Plateau, tribes occupying, 15.
Piedmont Province, 14.
Pierrette, Rosa, last survivor of Ofo tribe, 166.
Pigeon, passenger, places named for, 298, 299.
Pilthlako, 173, 218.
　　name, interpretation of in Creek tongue, 218.
　　population, 173.
　　possibly removed to Florida after Creek War, 173.
　　sketch of, 173.
　　town or tribe reported on De Crenay map, 173.
Pineda, Alonzo Alvarez de, 16, 21, 36, 52, 150, 193, 196.
　　Florida expedition of, 35.
　　Mobile Bay first visited by, 13, 150.
　　Timucua coast skirted by, 193.
Pine Island, Ga., reference to Indian mounds on, 43.
Pine Island, Tenn., 27.
　　home of Kaskinampo, 144.
　　probable home of Koasati, 145.
　　site of Indian town of Coste, 48.

Pintahae, name of Indian town on Staunton River, 157.
Pinzon, Martin Alonzo, 33.
Pipisco, Indian chief, clothes worn by wife of, 472.
　　entourage of wife of, 645.
　　head band of beads worn by wife of, 509.
Piqua, name of town, 184.
Piqua, Shawnee band of Indians, 184, 185.
Pirogues, constructed by De Soto's army, 51.
Piscataways, means of transportation, 596.
Pischenoa, meaning of word, 95.
　　tribe encountered by Tonti, 95.
Pishofa ceremony, to restore persons to health, 777, 778, 794.
Pizarro, Francisco, Peruvian expedition of, 39.
Planta solis, use as food, 269, 306.
Plants, medicinal, use of, 798.
Plaquemine, northern limits of Chitimacha, 120.
Pleasant Porter, played part in Creek Nation, 168.
Plums (*Drupi* sp.), use of, 289, 373.
Plums, coco (*Chrysobalanus icaco*), use of, 282.
Pocahontas, daughter of Powhatan, 175, 671.
Pocasabo, town of Yamasee, 209.
Pochahuntas, see Pocahontas.
Pocone, see Puccoon.
Pocotaligo, head of Upper Yamasee, 209.
Pocoughtronack, hair dressing, 504.
　　name used by Smith for Bocootawwonauke, 493, 504.
　　possibly Potawatomi, 504.
Poetan, see Powhatan.
Pogonias chromis, 267.
Pohoy, 148, 165, 173, 193, 195.
　　attack on Christian Indians, 195.
　　epidemic among, 173, 195.
　　placed in Santa Fe Mission, 173, 195.
　　population, 173.
　　sketch of, 173.
　　tribe or province on Tampa Bay, 173.
　　visited by Spanish expedition under Cartaya, 173.
　　See Oçita.
Point au Chien, La., 140.
Point Coupée, Ofo found on Miss. above, 166.
　　Okelousa located west and above, 168.
Point Lookout, 15.
Pojoi, see Pohoy.
"Pojoy River," mentioned by Calderón, 173.
Polk County, Tex., present location of Alabama Indians, 87.
Polonza, Bay of, Spanish name for Pensacola Bay, 60.

Polyodon spatula, use as food, 266, 267.
Pomeioc, tattooing worn by women of, 532.
temple in town of, 742, 806, 813.
Pomo, Indian tribe, 665.
Pomolobus chrysochloris, 267.
Ponca, brought to live with Quapaw and later removed to own reservation, 176.
Ponce, Hernan, partnership of De Soto with, 39.
Ponce de Leon, Juan, *see* De Leon, Juan Ponce.
Ponpon, home of Yuchi according to Hawkins, 214.
Pontchartrain, Duchess of, Fort Rosalie named after, 72, 159.
Pooy, *see* Pohoy.
Pope, John, on fire making, 424.
on tattooing, 533.
Pope Alexander VI, lands granted to Spain by, 1493, 34.
Population, Indian, 82, 83, 84, 86, 87, 88, 91, 92, 94, 95, 96, 98, 99, 100, 102, 103, 105, 107, 108, 109, 114, 116, 118, 119, 121, 123, 124, 126, 127, 129, 130, 131, 132, 133, 134, 136, 137, 138, 139, 140, 141, 142, 143, 144, 145, 146, 147, 148, 149, 150, 151, 152, 153, 154, 155, 156, 157, 158, 160, 161, 162, 164, 165, 166, 167, 168, 169, 170, 171, 172, 173, 174, 175, 176, 177, 178, 179, 180, 182, 183, 186, 187, 189, 190, 191, 193, 194, 195, 196, 197, 198, 199, 200, 201, 202, 203, 204, 205, 206, 207, 208, 210, 211, 212, 215, 641.
centers, abandoned in prehistoric era, 14.
conditions at time of French contact, 13.
distribution according to De Soto chroniclers, 12.
effect of Spanish contact on, 21.
estimate by Mooney, 11, 12.
in prehistoric and historic eras compared, 21.
Indian traditions on movements of, 22.
of Southeastern areas, 11–14.
prehistoric movements, 13–14.
relation of to natural areas, 14–21.
summarized, 32–33.
(See map 10, facing p. 22.)
Porcupine-quill work, 489, 490.
Port Royal, Huguenot colony, 135.
Port Royal River, French name for Broad River, 61.
Porter, Gen. Peter B., 119, 146, 176.
"Posoye," *see* Pohoy.
Post-De Soto period, 59–81.
Potano, 11, 16, 19, 41, 173, 174, 179, 193, 194, 762.
apparently scattered to other tribes, 174.
cut off Spanish soldiers under Captain Andrada, 174.

Potano, defeated by Spanish and driven from their town, 174.
French colonists assisted by Utina in raid on, 173, 202.
population, 174.
powerful Timucuan tribe, encountered by De Soto in Alachua Co., Fla., 173.
sketch of, 173–174.
visited St. Augustine, 174.
Potato, marsh (*Apios tuberosa*), use as food, 270.
sweet (*Convolvulus* sp.), use of, 288.
(*Ipomoea batata*), use as food, 285.
(*Ipomoea pondurata*), use as food, 270, 285, 286.
Potawatomi, 493.
clans and gentes, 656.
Potaya, town subject to San Juan del Puerto, 179.
"Potcas hatchee," *see* Hatchet Creek.
Poteskeet, tribe of Weapemeoc confederation, 206.
Potomac Indians, 175, 184, 730, 743, 811, 814.
marriage customs, 701, 702.
medical practices, 783, 784.
religious beliefs and usages, 743, 749.
Potomac River, 15.
Pots, material of, 243.
Potter, Rev. Elam, 119.
Pottery, 549–555.
Poúhka, *see* Pawokti.
Powell, J. W., 93, 193, 238, 240, 801.
Powhatan, chief of tribe bearing his name, 175, 493, 641, 642, 643, 644, 815.
body guard of, 689.
cushion used by described, 432.
destruction of other Virginia tribes by, 687.
pearls sent to Smith by, 488.
punishments inflicted by, 644, 730.
treasure house of, 615.
wives of, 702.
Powhatan, Indians, 11, 15, 18, 76, 111, 130, 148, 157, 175, 176, 218, 221, 299, 831.
beards worn by priests, 498.
birth customs, 709, 710.
body paint, 529.
burial customs, 718, 719.
ceremonial houses, 415, 416.
clothing worn by priests, 477.
confederation of tribes in tidewater Virginia, 175.
crime and punishment, 730.
defeated in attack with whites on Nahyssan, 157.
dialect, Cree resemblances in, 24, 31.
division of seasons by, 257.
doors, 428.
ear ornaments, 510.
food, preservation of, 377, 379, 380.

Powhatan, Indians, games, 675.
　George Cassen executed by, 644.
　hair dressing, 499, 501, 502.
　　of priests, 501.
　head bands, 509.
　　worn by priests, 509.
　home manners, 711.
　household utensils, 556.
　houses, 415.
　involved in slave rising under Nat
　　Turner, 175.
　Jamestown founded among, 175.
　marriage customs, 701, 702.
　massacre of by whites under Na-
　　thanial Bacon, 175.
　medical practices, 783.
　musical instruments, 624, 625.
　name, interpretation of, 218.
　names used by, 671.
　physical characteristics, 222.
　population, 175.
　relations with chief, 641, 642.
　religious beliefs and usages, 743,
　　744, 745, 747.
　sketch of, 175–176.
　smoke-holes and windows, 427.
　soap and towels, 432.
　source material on, 831.
　stone pipes, 545.
　temple of, 614, 744.
　threads and textiles, 448.
　towns, 629, 630.
　trade, 740.
　transportation, means of, 602.
　treatment of women, 710.
　treaty with Iroquois made at
　　Albany, 175.
　war customs, 687.
Prairie Creek, 50.
Prehistoric movements, see Population,
　Indian, prehistoric movements of.
Prehistory of Gulf Region based on
　archeological finds, 33.
Priber, Christian Gottlieb, resident of
　Cherokee country, 111.
Priestly, Herbert Ingram, editor, 682,
　829.
Prieto, Father Martin, Apalachee visited
　by, 90.
　founded 3 missions in Potano coun-
　　try, 174, 202.
Presidio of Nuestra Señora del Pilar de
　los Adaes, 83.
Promicrops itaiara, 267.
Province of Chalaque, see Chalaque.
"Province of Guacane," see Nacanish.
Puccoon, use of, 526, 527.
Pueblos, 74.
Pumpkins (macocquer), use of, 305, 306.
Purcell, 119.
Purses, bags and, 479–480.
Pusale, beach of, 173.
Pushmataha, Choctaw chief, 653.
　uprising against U. S. prevented by,
　　122.

Quapaw, 11, 19, 31, 53, 71, 106, 142, 147,
　149, 166, 176, 195, 212, 218, 241, 292,
　299, 301, 665, 666, 800, 806, 810, 820,
　821, 831, 832.
　assigned land on Bayou Treache, on
　　Red River, 176.
　attack on Yazoo and Koroa, 212.
　beds, 422.
　citizens of Okla., 176.
　clans and gentes, 654, 657, 820.
　country, Virginia explorers reach,
　　77.
　destruction of Tiou by, 195, 212.
　discussion of, incomplete, 1.
　doors, 430.
　head deformation not practiced,
　　541.
　household utensils, 556.
　houses, 416, 417, 820.
　joined Ponca on reservation, 176.
　moieties, 665, 820.
　name, interpretation of in Siouan
　　dialect, 218.
　pipes, 546.
　population, 176.
　relationship, terms of, 669.
　removal to Caddo country on Red
　　River, 176.
　removal to Kansas and Indian Ter-
　　ritory, 176.
　reported by Marquette on Miss.
　　near junction with Arkansas, 176.
　reported by Sibley on Arkansas
　　River, above Arkansas Post, 176.
　sketch of, 176.
　smoke holes and windows lacking,
　　427.
　source material on, 831.
　temporary union with Kadoha-
　　dacho, 142.
　territory ceded to U. S., 176.
　towns, 13, 71, 72, 640.
　trade, 737, 738.
　traditional home on Ohio River,
　　176.
　transportation, means of, 594.
　unsuccessful attack upon Chakchi-
　　uma, 106.
Quarries, Southern Appalachian, 20.
　worked by Indians, 541, 542.
Queensland, 7.
Quercus virginiana, use of, 273, 279.
Quereteran Fathers, missions under,
　transferred, 75.
　mission of San Francisco de los
　　Neches established by, 162.
　　withdrawal from Caddo terri-
　　　tory, 99.
Quexos, Pedro de, early explorations by,
　36, 37.
Quexuga, Siouan idol, 759.
Quigualtam, Indian tribe, 56.
Quigualtam, Natchez chief, 159.
Quigualtam province, attack by Indians
　of, on Moscoso's army, 59.
Quigualtanqui, province of, 13.
Quigualtanqui, see Quigualtam.

Quiguate, Indian town, 54, 651.
Quinahaqui, classification of, as Catawba-Siouan town, 67.
Quinipissa, 29, 152, 158, 176, 177, 190, 218.
    found by La Salle at mouth of Miss., 176, 190.
    name, interpretation of, in Choctaw and Chickasaw tongues, 218.
    population, 177.
    See Bayogoula.
    sketch of, 176–177.
    supposed to have united with Mugulasha, 177.
    treacherous attack on La Salle, 177.
    visited by Iberville for second time, 177.
Quinipissa River, 95.
Quioccosan, Indian word meaning temple, 744.
Quioquascacke, name of God of the Potomacs, 743.
Quiozogon, Siouan word for temple, 753.
Quipana, Indian village, 55.
Quirotoqui, *see* Quinahaqui.
Quiyoughcohanock, Indian village, 709.
Quizquiz, possible branch of Tunica encountered by De Soto, 52.
Quizquiz, province of, location, 54.
Rabun Gap, 47.
Raccoon Creek, 48.
Racuchi, *see* Aracuchi.
Radcliffe, Dr. Lewis, on fish, 266.
Rafts, constructed of cane by De Soto army, 50.
Raleigh, Sir Walter, attempts at colonization by, 75–76.
Raleigh colonists, 18.
    Nottoway first mentioned by, 163.
    refuge with Croatan, 137.
    Weapemeoc found in North Carolina by, 206.
Ramon, Capt. Domingo, 155, 162.
    founder of Texas Mission, San Francisco de los Texas, 155.
    garrison stationed at Mission of San Francisco de los Neches by, 162.
Ramsey, J. G. M., 123.
Ranjel, Rodrigo 46, 48, 121, 137, 281, 299, 346, 347, 365, 406, 430, 432, 433, 440, 462.
    name of Alabama given to small village by, 86.
    on Casqui, 27.
    on clothing, 469.
    on coloring of manufactured articles 608.
    on De Soto's route, 48.
    on fighting qualities of Tula Indians, 55.
    on head bands, 508.
    on household utensils, 560.
    on implements for hunting and fishing, 580, 583, 587.
    on mats and baskets, 602.
    on musical instruments, 624, 628.

Ranjel, Rodrigo, on point where De Soto crossed the Little Tennessee, 47.
    on province of Caluça, 25.
    on skin dressing, 442.
    on stockaded town on Alabama River, 434.
    on sunshade carried over the chief, 430, 652.
    on thread and textiles, 451.
    on transportation, means of, 598, 601, 602.
    on weapons, 580, 583, 587.
    on wet spring experienced by De Soto expedition, 44.
Rapahanna, chief of, ear ornaments worn by, 510.
    necklace worn by, 516.
Rapides, La., 94.
Rappahannock, 175.
Rappahannock chief, body paint worn by, 529.
    hair dressing of, 502.
Rappahannock River, Va., Manahoac lived on upper waters of, 148.
Rasps, 629.
Rassawek, Va., Monacan settlement, 152.
Rattles, 626–628.
Raw materials, distribution of, 253–255.
    utilized by Southeastern Indians, 242, 255.
Reatkin, *see* Yadkin.
Rechahecrians, 111.
Red Crawfish people, branch of Chakchiuma on Yazoo River, 29.
Red-earth, *see* Kan-tcati.
Red Ground, *see* Kan-tcati.
"Red House," *see* Tcuko tcati.
Red House Hammock, Ga., 26.
Red ocher, use of to make paint, 243.
Red River, 21, 24, 29, 30, 72, 84, 94.
    Alabama Indians on, 87.
    Apalachee settlement on, 91.
    Biloxi located on by Hutchins, 97.
    Houma opposite mouth of, 139, 198.
    identification of with river in Muskogee myths, 25.
    Kadohadacho located above bend of, 141, 142.
    Koasati on, 145, 146.
    land granted Choctaw along, 122.
    later home of Cahinnio, 100
    Nabedache living near Shreveport on, 154.
    Natasi tribe site, 158.
    Ofo settled near mouth of, as allies of French, 166.
    Pakana settled with Taensa and Apalachee on, 170.
    point at which crossed by Moscoso, 57.
    Quapaw removed to Caddo country on, 176.
    removal of Hainai from Texas to north side of, 137.
    removal of Natchitoches by St. Denis from, 130, 161.

Red River, Taensa located on, 188.
    Upper Nasoni located south of, 158.
    Yatasi on, as reported by Tonti, 211.
Red Shoes, Chitimacha chief, head of tribe on Bayou La Teche, 120.
Reggio, Chickasaw defeat of force under, 118.
Registe Dardin and wife, survivors of Chitimacha, 121.
Reincarnation, belief in, 746, 781.
Relationship, terms of, 665–670.
Religious beliefs and usages, 742–782.
Removal of Indians, 79–80.
Reptiles, as food, 281, 369.
    uses of, 252.
Revolutionary War, part taken by Cherokee in, 112.
Reynoso, Francisco de, sent to Calusa village to erect fort, 101.
Rhapidophyllum hystrix, use as food, 285.
Rhus coriaria, use of, 385.
Rhus glabra, use of, 385, 527.
Rhus radicans, use of, 606.
Rhus sp., use of, 610.
Rhus truphydon, uses of, 245, 606, 609.
Ribault, Jean, 128, 133, 187, 193, 281, 335, 458.
    founder of first Huguenot colony, 61, 128.
    monument erected by, in South Carolina, taken to Cuba by Rojas, 61.
    on body paint, 531.
    on ear ornaments, 511.
    on hair dressing, 503.
    on housing, 406, 407, 408.
    on mats and baskets, 604.
    on medical practices, 792.
    on metal, 491.
    on necklaces, 518.
    on tattooing, 533.
    on transportation, means of, 594.
    Tacatacuru visited by French under, 187.
Richardson, William, Presbyterian missionary, on the town house of the Cherokee, 402, 403.
Rickohokan, 111.
Ridge, Major, head of removal party against Cherokee, 114.
Rights, Douglas L., on body paint, 530.
Rigolet de Bon Dieu, 97.
    Pascagoula located on confluence of Red River and, 171.
Rinconada de Carlos, mission from, 102.
Rio de las Palmas, province of, 37,40.
Rio Grande, Spanish name for Flint River in Florida, 43.
    Spanish name for the Mississippi, 55.
Ritanoe, copper mines located at, 492.
Rivanna River, Va., Monacan settled near mouth of, 152.
    site of Saponi when located by John Smith, 178.
"River Coroas," 147.

River of Anilco, *see* River of Cayas.
River of Capachequi (Flint River), 42.
River of Casqui, 54.
River of Cayas, 53, 54.
"River of Chicaça," Miss. (Tombigbee River), 51.
River of the Arkansas, 31.
"River of the Chiaha," *see* Tallapoosa River.
"River of the Cussatees," sometimes used for the Tennessee River, 27, 145.
River of the Deer, 41.
"River of the Tioux," *see* Big Black River.
River of the Tutelo, *see* Big Sandy River.
Rivers, William James, 205.
Roanoke, gorget worn by women of, 519.
    name given to bead money, 482, 483,
Roanoke Indians, hair dressing, 498, 805.
    tattooing, 532.
Roanoke Island, N. C., frequented by Hatteras tribe, 137.
    Raleigh's attempts to establish a colony on, 76.
    where Raleigh colonists landed, 18.
Roanoke River, 149, 164, 178, 199, 200, 800.
    Meherrin joined Tuscarora on, 149.
    Occaneechi located on island in, 164.
    Otter River, northern tributary of, 178.
Robeline, La., 83.
Robertson, James Alexander, ed., 321, 330, 344, 345, 346, 347, 351, 376, 407, 428, 431, 433, 434, 435, 440, 451, 455, 457, 458, 462, 464, 469, 761.
    on artistic development, 613, 619.
    on body paint, 529.
    on coloring of manufactured articles, 608, 609.
    on cushions, use of by lady of Cofitachequi, 432.
    on fish eaten, 266, 333.
    on flint implements, 543.
    on food preserving, 378.
    on hair dressing, 506.
    on head band, 508.
    on honey, 268.
    on household utensils, 558, 560.
    on houses, 387, 408.
    on implements for hunting and fishing, 564, 571, 580, 583, 588.
    on musical instruments, 624, 628.
    on ornamentation, 488.
    on pottery, 549.
    on religious beliefs and usages, 763.
    on salt, 301.
    on skin dressing, 442.
    on sunshade carried before the chiefs about Tascalusa, 430, 652.
    on Temple of Talomeco, 566.
    on towns, 632.
    on trade, 741.

Robertson, James Alexander, ed., on transportation, means of, 590, [593, 597, 598, 599, 602.
   on weapons, 564, 571, 580, 583, 588.
   See also Elvas, Narrative of a Gentleman of.
Rock Landing, site of Oconee settlement on Oconee River, 165.
Rockdale, Milam County, Tex., 86, 96.
   San Ildefonso Mission near site of, 130.
Rocky Mountains, 5.
Roenoke, *see* Wampum.
Rogel, Jesuit missionary, companion of Mendendez in visit to Fort San Antonio, 101.
   departure from San Antonio to Havana, 101.
   missionary work attempted by, 128.
Rojas, Don Hernando de Manrique de, remains of first French settlement in South Carolina destroyed by, 61.
Roman Catholic faith, attempt to "reduce" Ais to, 84.
Romans, Bernard, 118, 119, 123, 131, 181, 192, 193, 288, 299, 325, 379, 400, 679, 680, 681, 683, 715, 725, 828.
   on coloring of manufactured articles 609.
   on communications, means of, 734.
   on cooking, 353, 356, 358, 362, 370, 371, 372.
   on deer hunting among the Chickasaw, 315.
   on departure of Calusa from east coast of Florida, 84, 102, 154, 192, 193.
   on dietary of the Creeks, 285.
   on Eufaula Indians in Florida, 131.
   on featherwork, 455.
   on food of Choctaws, 288.
   on games, 685.
   on head deformation, 539.
   on horses used by Creeks, 349.
   on household utensils, 561, 564.
   on hunting, 330.
   on implements for hunting and fishing, 585, 588.
   on marriage customs, 706.
   on musical instruments, 627, 629.
   on social organization, 653.
   on tobacco, use of, by Choctaw, 384, 385.
   on towns, 637.
   on war customs, 697, 698.
   on weapons, 585, 588.
Rome, Italy, 34.
Ross, John, Cherokee chief, 113, 114, 195.
   intertribal Indian council called by, 81.
Ross, Mary, on identity of Indian town of Guiomaez, 67.
Rouillet, Regis de, 151.
Rouse, Irving, on origin of Meillac pottery, 33.

Roussin, Sieur, Tiou sold land to, 195.
Ruidiaz y Caravia, Eugenio, 65, 437, 634.
Ruiz, Pedro, missionary at San Pedro, 187, 647.
Rusk County, Tex., 89.
Rut, Father du, Jesuit priest, started mission in Houma village, 139.
Sabacola el Grande, 179.
"Sabacola," name used in journal of Capt. Tapia, 180.
   Spanish pronunciation of Sawokli, 179.
Sabal palmetto, uses of, 246.
Sabine River, 89, 93, 156.
   band of Alabama located on, 87.
   last recorded home of Chatot on, 108.
   settlement of Koasati on, 145.
Sabougla Creek, origin of name, 28.
"Sabougla," tribe on Yazoo River, in State of Miss., 180.
Sacchuma, name used by De Soto for Chakchiuma, 105.
   See Chakchiuma.
Saddles, 601.
Sadkeche, town of Yamasee, 209.
Safety Harbor, Fla., site of main Tocobaga town, 195.
Sagittaria sp., use of, 292, 293, 297.
St. Andrews Bay district, archeological evidence of population movement found in, 16.
St. Andrews Sound, Ga., to Savannah River, site of Guale "province," 135.
St. Augustine, Fla., 63, 84, 85, 90, 102, 129, 133, 135, 173, 184, 193, 202, 211.
   Apalachee in missions around, 91.
   founding of, 62, 133, 193.
   Macapiras brought to a mission near, 148.
   site of Timucua towns, 133, 179.
   Timucua chiefs brought to, 202.
   visited by Potano, 174.
St. Catherines, concession near Natchez towns, 159.
St. Catherines Island, 144.
   church built at, 135.
   present name of Guale Island, 135.
St. Cosme, J. F., missionary, 72, 73, 159, 188, 189.
   killed by Chitimacha, 72, 108, 120, 159.
   on morals, 236, 237.
   work among Natchez, 159.
St. Denis, French commander, 99, 120, 130, 155, 160, 161, 211.
   alliance made with Yatasi, 211.
   Avoyel mentioned by, 94.
   Bayogoula assistance in expedition against Chitimacha under, 95.
   defeat of Natchez near Natchitoches by, 160.
   establishment of post among Natchitoches by, 99.
   expedition against Chitimacha lead by, 120.

St. Denis, French commander, killing of Spaniards in eastern Tex., prevented by, 155.
   Natchitoches settled beside Acolapissa by, 82.
   relations with Biloxi, 97.
   rescue of Simars de Belle-Isle from Akokisa by, 85.
   support given him by Indians, 72.
   visit to Doustioni, 130.
St. Francis River, 53, 54.
St. Johns, Fla., site of Timucua towns, 133, 179, 193, 201.
St. Johns parish, home of Cape Fear Indians, 103.
St. Johns River, 5, 12, 16, 32, 61, 90.
   discovery of, 36.
   French colonists located on, 173.
   site of Santa Cruz, near mouth of, 136.
   site of second Huguenot colony, 128, 134, 179.
St. John the Baptist, a river so named in N. or S. Carolina, 36.
St. Lawrence River, 71.
St. Lucie River, Fla., 84, 134.
St. Lucie Sound, Fla., 134.
St. Marks, Fla., 63, 180, 210.
St. Simons, church built at, 135.
   "vassals" of Aluete, Cusabo chief, fled to, 128.
St. Stephens parish, home of Cape Fear tribes, 103.
Sakapadai, probably branch of Wakokai tribe, 203, 204.
Salas, Gaspar de, Ocute village visited by, 138.
   Yamasee visited by, 208.
Salazar, Governor of Florida, 108, 136, 174, 180, 194, 208, 210.
   estimate of Apalachee population by, 91.
Salle, Nicolas de la, on towns, 638.
Salley, Alexander S., editor, on fire making, 422.
Salt, and salt substitutes, use of, 268, 270, 274, 300, 301, 303, 304.
Salt, obtained by De Soto's army, 55, 57.
Salt Creek, 55.
Salt Province, 54.
Saltkechers, home of Yuchi located at, by Hawkins, 214.
Saluda, 177, 184.
   population unknown, 177.
   probably a band of Shawnee Indians on way from Augusta to Pa., 177, 184.
   sketch of, 177.
Saluda Pass, 20.
Saluda River, 46.
Salude, see Saluda.
Samboukia, name given by Coxe to town of Sawokli, 28.
   See Sabougla.
Sam, Creek, see Creek Sam.
Sam, Watt, Natchez informant to Dr. Swanton, 628.

San Agustin de Ahumada, province of, establishment and destruction of, 86.
San Agustin de Urica, 202.
San Antonio, Tex., 23, 75, 89.
   fort visited by Menendez, 101.
   mission of Cosapuya nation, 129.
"San Antonio de Enacape," 133, 194, 209.
San Antonio de la Tama, town destroyed by Creeks, 210.
San Antonio River, 17.
   Mission of Nuestra Señora de la Purísima Concepción, removed to, 136.
San Augustine, Tex., 57.
San Augustine County, Tex., home of Eyeish, 132.
San Buenaventura, mission in Potano country, 174, 195, 196.
   mission occupied by Chilucan and Mocama, 119.
San Carlos de los Chacatos, mission named after Chatot, plundered by Lower Creeks, 107, 108.
Sandbanks, only settlement of Hatteras, 137.
San Diego de Laca, mission of, 179.
San Diego de Salamototo, mission of, served Saturiwa, 179.
Sand Mountain, 49.
Sandusky, migration of Shawnee from, to Abihka country, 185.
San Felipe de Athuluteca, mission on Cumberland I., 209.
San Felipe, fort of, 64.
Sanford, Capt. Robert, 829.
   on towns, 632.
   visit to Cusabo by, 128.
San Francisco de Chuaquin, 202.
San Francisco de los Neches, see San Francisco de los Texas.
San Francisco de los Texas, mission founded in the Nabedache village, 83, 155, 156, 162.
San Francisco de Oconi, mission west of Aucilla River, 165.
San Francisco, mission in Potano country, 174.
San Francisco Solano, Spanish mission, 75.
San Francisco Xavier de Nájera, Spanish mission, 75.
San Gabriel, 96.
San Gabriel River, 86.
   probable site of San Ildefonso Mission, 130.
Sangamon River, Ill., Michigamea around the headwaters of, 149.
Sanguinaria canadensis, uses of, 248, 606.
Sanguinaria gallium, use of, 609.
Sanguinaria sp., use as skin color by Carolina Indians, 228.
San Ildefonso de Chamini, mission of, 202.

San Ildefonso Mission, established in Texas, 86.
 founded for Bidai, Deadose, and Patiri, and abandoned by Indians, 96.
 home of Deadose, Akokisa, and Patiri Indians, 130, 172.
San José de Aguayo, Spanish mission, 75.
San José de los Nazones, established for Anadarko and Nasoni, 89.
 mission on Shawnee Creek, 158.
 transferred and renamed, 89.
San Juan Capistrano, Spanish mission, founded, 89.
San Juan de Guacara, mission for the Timucuans, 168, 202.
San Juan del Puerto, Spanish mission serving Saturiwa, 179, 194.
San Juan Island, transferral of Guale to, 136.
San Julian, Fla., 133.
San Lorenzo de Vitachuco, mission, 208.
San Lucar, Spain, De Soto's port of debarkation, 40.
San Luis, Acuera mission, 83.
San Luis, Apalachee mission, 88, 90, 179, 209.
San Luís de Candelaria, mission near San Lorenzo de Vitachuco, 208.
San Luis, doctrina near seacoast, 102, 109.
San Luis, town of, 90.
San Marcos, Yustaga settlement, 91, 216.
San Martin de Ayaocuto, see San Martin de Timucua.
San Martin de Timucua, probably same as San Martin de Ayaocuto, 202.
San Matheo, town subject to San Juan del Puerto, 179.
 mission of, 216.
San Miguel, Andreas de, Spanish monk, 222, 281, 303, 338, 351, 422, 427, 429, 442.
 on artistic development, 617.
 on beads, 485.
 on body paint, 532.
 on bracelets, 521.
 on clothing, 457, 471.
 on cooking, 353, 356.
 on games, 682, 683.
 on hair dressing, 504.
 on household utensils 558.
 on houses, 405, 421.
 on leg ornaments, 523.
 on medical practices, 791, 792.
 on physical characteristics of Guale Indians about St. Simons I., Ga., 222.
 on social customs, 723.
 on transportation, means of, 590, 594.
 on whaling practices in Florida, 329.
San Miguel, mission in Potano country, 174.

San Miguel de Linares, mission established among Adai, destruction of, 83.
San Nicolas de Tolentino, mission for Chatot, 107, 108.
San Pablo, town subject to San Juan del Puerto, 179.
San Pedro de los Chines, mission named after Chatot chief, 107, 119.
 apparently abandoned, 187.
San Pedro Island, Spaniards' name for Cumberland Island, 187, 216.
 request of Guale to be transferred to, 136.
San Pedro Mocama, mission established by Franciscans on San Pedro Island, 187.
San Pedro Tacatacuru, Cumberland Island, Icafui visited by missionary at, 141, 194.
 Fra Baltasar López, missionary, stationed at, 202.
"San Salvador de Mayaca," 133, 209.
San Sebastian, Fla., 133.
Santa Ana, chief of, imprisoned by De Soto, 174.
 mission in Potano country, 174.
Santa Catalina, mission for the Timucuans, 168, 202.
Santa Cruz, Christianized Sawokli withdrew with missionaries to, 180.
 transfer of Guale to, 136.
Santa Cruz de Cachipile, 202.
Santa Cruz de Sabacola el Menor, mission established by Bishop Calderón, 179.
Santa Cruz de Tarihica, mission for Timucuans, 168, 202.
Santa Elena, 45, 59, 61, 65, 66, 67, 70, 632.
 Capt. Juan Pardo at, 109, 115, 205.
 established in Florida by Menendez, 64, 128.
 fort built by Boyano in Chiaha, 65.
Santa Fe de Toloco, Mission of, 174.
 Pohoy placed in, 173.
Santa Fe River, Fla., 41, 193, 201.
 home of Timucua tribe, 193.
Santa Lucia, Fla., founded by followers of Menendez, 134.
 Spaniards took refuge with Guacata at, 192.
 Spanish mission established among Acuera, 83.
 Spanish mission founded among Guacata, 84.
Santa Maria, mission probably on Amelia Island, 209.
Santa Maria de Axacan Bay, Spanish name for Chesapeake Bay, 70.
Santa Maria de los Angeles de Arapaja, mission of, 202.
Santa Maria de Sena, on island of Napoyca, under San Pedro mission, 187.
Santa Maria Island, transfer of Guale to, 136.

Santee, 124, 177, 178, 183, 207, 218, 302.
    burial customs, 721, 811.
    clothing worn by medicine men,
        478.
    featherwork, 456.
    food, 278.
    found by English on Santee River,
        S. C., 177.
    hunting, 314.
    name, interpretation of, 218.
    population, 178.
    probably united with Catawba, 178.
    sent as slaves with Congaree to
        West Indies, 124, 178.
    sketch of, 177–178.
    social organization, 647.
    storehouses, 379.
    towns, 632.
    united with Congaree against South
        Carolina colonists, 124, 178.
    visited by Lawson on Santee River,
        177.
Santee River, S. C., 66.
    Charleston colonists met Sewee on,
        183.
    Congaree found on small affluent
        of, 124.
    identified with Guatari River, 37.
    possible identification with Jordan
        River, 37.
    site of Catawba villages, 104.
Santi, Apalachee woman mentioned by
    Gatschet, 91.
Santiago de Cuba, de Soto's landing at,
    40.
Santisima Nombre de Maria, second
    mission founded in Nabedache vil-
    lage, 155.
Santo Domingo, Island of, 35, 36, 37.
Santo Domingo, on island of Napoyca,
    under San Pedro mission, 187.
San Xavier, Mission of, 86.
    Bidai settled near, 96.
    home of Deadose, 130.
San Xavier River, 96.
Saogahatchee, branch of Tulsa, 125.
Sapatchitou, Indian village, 638.
Sapelo, church planned at, 135.
Sapir, Dr. Edward, 801, 830.
    Tutelo vocabulary collected by,
        201.
Sapona Town, settlement of Saponi
    near Roanoke River, 178, 753.
Saponi, 30, 131, 145, 149, 152, 157, 164,
    178, 179, 183, 200, 201, 278.
    adopted with Tutelo by Cayuga,
        178.
    fire making, 423.
    found by Lawson on Yadkin River,
        178.
    joined Nahyssan below junction of
        Staunton and Dan Rivers, 157,
        178.
    Manahoac united with Occaneechi
        and Saponi under name of, 149,
        164, 201.

Saponi, moved north with Tutelo to
    Shamokin, Pa., 178, 201.
    placed by Governor Spotswood near
        Fort Christanna, Va., 178.
    population, 178, 179.
    presumably   incorporated   with
        Tutelo, 178.
    remnant with Cayuga on Seneca
        River, Seneca Co., N. Y., 178.
    removed to Otter River, Campbell
        Co., Va., 178.
    sketch of, 178–179.
    small band in Person Co., N. C.,
        178.
    united with Occaneechi, and crossed
        Roanoke River, 178.
    visited by Lawson on Yadkin River,
        near Salisbury, N. C., 178.
    See also Meherrin and Tutelo.
Saquechuma, name used by De Soto for
    Chakchiuma, 105.
Sára, see Cheraw.
Saraw, see Cheraw.
Sargus rondeletti, 266.
"Sasquesahanocks," shields carried by,
    588.
Satapo, Indian town, 65, 68, 70.
    classification, 68.
Satuache, see Chatuache.
Saturiwa, 179, 193, 194, 693.
    assisted de Gourgues in punitive
        expedition, 179.
    musical instruments, 628.
    population, 179.
    relations with Spanish missions,
        179.
    sketch of, 179.
    Timucua tribe near mouth of St.
        Johns River, 179.
    visited by De Gourgues, 555.
    war customs, 693.
Saturiwa, Indian chief, 693.
Sauapa, see Sauxpa and Sissipahaw.
Sauer, Carl Ortwin, 241.
Sauk, 518, 564.
    clans and gentes, 654.
    language, affinity with Shawnee, 31.
Sauvolle, 177.
    on location of Biloxi, 96.
Sauxpa, discussion of synonyms for, 66,
    67.
    See Sissipahaw.
Savannah Indians, 163, 184, 224.
    settled on Chattahoochee near Fort
        Gaines, 184.
Savannah River, 15, 30, 44, 46, 67, 90,
    91, 92.
    Apalachee settled on, 63.
    boundary of Guale "province," 135.
    Cusabo tribes located on, 128.
    part of Apalachicola settled on, 63.
    passage of by De Soto, 45.
    possible identification with River
        of Gualdape, 37.
    Shawnee moved to, 184, 186.
    Yuchi driven from by Shawnee, 213.

Sawanogi, 142.
Sawokli, 22, 131, 138, 150, 179, 181, 189, 218.
  branch of among Lower Creeks, 180.
  driven from home by Indians and English, 180.
  gave up Square Ground to join Hitchiti, 180.
  name, interpretation of, in Hitchiti tongue, 218.
  population, 180, 181.
  settled in Okla. near Okmulgee, 180.
  sketch of, 179–181.
  town called Samboukia by Coxe, 28.
  town on Yazoo River shown on Louvigny map, 28.
Sawokli mission, 107, 180.
Saxapahaw, on Haw River, N. C., principal settlement of Sissipahaw, 186.
Sayre, Pa., home of part of Saponi, 178.
Scaife, Walter, on identification of Florida river discovered by Pineda, 35.
Schaeffer, George E., 655.
Schermerhorn, 119, 123, 146.
Schneider, Martin, Moravian missionary on houses of Cherokee, 403.
  on townhouse of Cherokee, 403.
  on towns, 636, 637.
Schockoores, see Shakori.
Scholes, France V., and Mera, H. P., 241.
Schoolcraft, Henry R., 98, 119, 142, 828.
  on origin of Caddo, 24.
  on origin of Catawba, 23.
Schuller, Rudolph, on early Portuguese expedition, 34.
Scratchers, 564.
Scuppernong (Vitis rotundifolia), use of, 288.
Seagrapes (Coccoloba uvifera), use of, 282.
Secotan, images in, 614.
  necklaces worn by girls of, 516.
  temple in, 742.
  town of, 631, 743.
  "wreathes" worn by women of, 508.
Segura, Father Juan Bautista, Jesuit missionary, 70.
  visited Tekesta with brother of chief, 192.
Seminole, 19, 30, 64, 92, 132, 133, 138, 147, 150, 181, 182, 190, 194, 215, 218, 220, 221, 225, 226, 283, 802, 806, 827, 828.
  agricultural methods, 305.
  arm bands, 522.
  artistic development, 624.
  beds, 422.
  body paint, 528.
  bows and arrows, 574, 578.
  clans, 225, 226.
  clothing, 467, 468, 474, 475, 477, 525.
  cooking, 354, 369.
  ear ornaments, 514.
  finger rings, 523.
  fire making, 425, 427.

Seminole, food, 283, 284, 297.
  games, 675.
  hair dressing, 500.
  head bands, 509.
  horses, 348.
  household utensils, 559, 560, 563.
  houses, 395, 396, 397 (fig.), 398, 399, 421, 422.
  hunting, 331.
  language identified as Creek, 181, 182.
  mats and baskets, 605.
  members of Muskhogean linguistic family, 238.
  metals, 495.
  Mico Chlucco (the Long Warrior), King of the, 509.
  moral characteristics, 234.
  musical instruments, 625, 629.
  name, interpretation of, in Muskogee tongue, 218.
  necklaces, 517, 520.
  number remaining in Southeast after Indian removal, 80.
  ornamentation, 487.
  physical characteristics, 220, 221, 225, 226, 234.
  population, 182.
  removal to Seminole Co., Okla., 80, 182.
  resistance to treaty of removal, 80.
  sketch of, 181–182.
  skin dressing, 447.
  songs, 102.
  source materials on, 828.
  territory, ceremonial ground maintained by Hitchiti in, 138.
  towns, 634, 635.
  tribes joining in Florida, 87.
  visited by Frances Densmore, 102.
  weapons, 574, 578.
Seminole Nation, 142, 150, 165, 182, 189, 210.
  in Okla., Kan-hatki population moved to, 142.
Seminole War, 64, 79, 80, 102, 150, 181, 182.
Semmes, Raphael, 831.
  on transportation, means of, 596.
Seneca country, Tuscarora located on reservation in, 199.
Seneca Creek, Oconee Co., S. C., location of northern branch of Oconee, 165.
Seneca Indians, 163.
Seneca River, Seneca Co., N. Y., home of remnant of Saponi, 178.
Sequoya, Cherokee Chief, settled in Arkansas, 113.
  phonetic symbols adapted by, 735.
Seretee, see Santee.
Serrano y Sanz, Manuel, 269, 302, 437.
Serropé, see Surruque.
Sesostrie Yauchicant, see Young, Sam.
Settico, Cherokee town, 431.
Seuel, P., missionary, murdered by Koroa and Yazoo, 147.

Seville, Spain, 40.
Sewee, 182, 183, 219, 318.
  joined Barnwell in Tuscarora expedition, 183.
  located in South Carolina, 182.
  met by Charleston colonists on Bull's I., 182.
  name, interpretation of in Catawba language, 219.
  population, 183.
    causes of reduction, 183.
  probably joined Catawba, 183.
  sketch of, 182–183.
  with Cusabo helped colonists repel Spaniards, 183.
Sewee Bay, 15.
  See Bull's Bay, S. C.
Sexes, see Customs relating to birth, education, and the division of labor between the sexes.
Shabonee, Peter, see Chartier, Pierre.
Shad (Alosa alabama), use as food, 266.
  (Alosa alosa), 266.
  (Alosa finta), 266.
  gizzard (Dorosoma cepedianum,) use as food, 266.
Shakori, 66, 145, 178, 183, 186, 200, 201, 219, 740, 830.
  earliest home in South Carolina, 183.
  moved to North Carolina between Meherrin and Nottoway Rivers, 183.
  name, interpretation of, 219.
  population, 183.
  reported neighbors of Eno, 183.
  sketch of, 183.
  united with Catawba, 183.
  See Sugeree.
Shamans, medicine men of Indians, 774, 793.
Shamokin, Pa., Saponi located with Tutelo near, 178, 201.
Shawano, 225.
Shawnee, 11, 13, 19, 81, 92, 104, 111, 113, 117, 163, 177, 184, 186, 213, 214, 219, 242, 302, 666, 669, 800, 810, 820, 821, 827, 832.
  bands, list of, 183.
  clans and gentes, 654, 656.
  driven from Cumberland Valley by Chickasaw and Cherokee, 117.
    discussion of incomplete, 1.
  ear ornaments, 513.
  English colony rescued by, 77.
  head deformation not practiced by, 541.
  language, linguistic affinities of, 31.
  led by Chartier to Clark Co., Ky., 15, 185.
  moved from Pennsylvania because of reprimand to Chartier, 185.
  moved to Savannah River, 184.
  name, interpretation of in Algonquian dialect, 219.
  nose ornaments, 515.

Shawnee, on Ohio River, in early historic times, 184.
  origin in north indicated by migration legends, 24.
  Piqua band of among Abihka, 184.
  population in Southeast, 186.
  prehistoric location, 15.
  Saluda probably band of, 177, 184.
  settled near Patapsco River, Md., 184.
  settlement on Tallapoosa River, 185.
  sketch of, 184–186.
  source material, 832.
  town, Kan-hatki mistakenly called a, 142.
  unsuccessful attack on Chickasaw, 185.
  Westo driven from Savannah River by, 184.
  Yuchi driven from Savannah River by, 213.
Shawnee Creek, Tex., 89.
  mission of San José de los Nazones, located on, 158.
Shaws Point, Fla., landing place of De Soto's army, 40.
Shea, John Gilmary, 262, 327, 381, 417, 462, 501, 507, 684.
  on artistic development, 618.
  on greasing and coloring of hair and skin, 528.
  on pottery, 550.
  on religious beliefs and usages, 781.
  on towns, 639.
Shell Bay, Apalachee fort near, 42.
Shell-midden people of Tennessee River, 33.
Shells, uses of, 252, 253, 550, 591.
Shields, 587–588.
Sholes and Mera, 241.
Shooting Creek, 47.
Short Arrow, see Skunnemoke.
Shoshi, see Sewee.
Shreveport, La., 57.
  accompanied by Yuchi to Tallapoosa River, 214.
Shuman, 241.
Sibley, John, 86, 88, 89, 91, 94, 98, 108, 132, 136, 137, 140, 142, 146, 155, 162, 169, 170, 171, 188, 189, 198, 204, 211.
  Adai vocabulary preserved by, 84.
  Avoyel women on Ouachita reported by, 94.
  location of Alabama Indian band reported by, 87.
  location of chief Akokisa town according to, 86.
  on Chatot on Bayou Boeuf, under name of "Chactoos," 108.
  on Kadohadacho flood legend, 142.
  on Kadohadacho migration, 24.
  report on Adai settlement by, 83.
Sicily Island, site of fort of Natchez, 160, 212.
Sigüenza y Góngora, Don Carlos de, explorations of, 326.

Silver, method of working, 496, 497.
  use of, 494–498.
Silver Bluff, on Ogeechee, home of Yuchi, 214.
  site of Indian town of Ilapi, authority for identification of, 45.
Silver Springs, Fla., 41.
Simahi, Apalachee woman mentioned by Gatschet, 91.
Simars de Belle-Isle, captive of Akokisa, 85.
Singing, 747.
Sinica, Cherokee town, 636.
Siouan dialectic groups, origin of, 32.
Siouan language, 241.
Siouan peoples, regions occupied by 800, 821.
  visited by Needham and Arthur, 77.
Siouan Quapaw, cultural level, 10.
Siouan settlement, first, 67.
Siouan stock, 10.
  historical works on, 21.
  population, 12.
  (See table 1, facing p. 10.)
Siouans, 157, 175, 177, 241, 242, 318, 655, 800, 801, 803, 806, 808, 809, 810, 812, 813, 815, 830.
  birth customs, 711.
  bracelets, 521.
  burial customs, 719, 720, 811.
  clans and gentes, 655, 656, 657, 703.
  clothing, 472, 815.
  crime and punishment, 731, 815.
  featherwork, 456.
  fingernails and toenails, treatment of, 537.
  games, 548, 685, 686.
  hair dressing, 499, 503, 815.
  head bands, 508.
  head deformation not practiced by, 541.
  household utensils, 562, 815.
  houses, 410, 411, 413, 815.
  huskanaw practiced by, 712, 815.
  marriage customs, 703.
  medical practices, 785, 786–790.
  musical instruments, 628.
  nose ornaments, 514.
  pottery, 554.
  religious beliefs and usages, 749, 750, 785, 815, 816.
  slavery practiced by, 816.
  smoke-holes and windows, 427.
  social organization, 646.
  source material on, 830.
  trade, 739, 815.
  transportation, means of, 592.
  visited by Lawson, 77.
Siouan tribes, 19, 20.
  Biloxi a member of, 96.
  cultural level, 10.
  eastern, migration legends indicate origin in northwest, 23.
  Lederer's visit to, 76.
  location, 15.
  migrations, 30–31.

Siouan tribes, movement of, 67.
  of coast of the Carolinas, 36.
  seasonal activities, 259, 806.
Sissipahaw, 67, 183, 186.
  apparently branch of Shakori, 183, 186.
  population, 186.
  probably united with Keyauwee, Shakori, Eno, Cheraw, and Catawba, 186.
  Sauxpa synonym for, 66.
  sketch of, 186.
  synonym of Shakori, 66.
  tribe first located near the Santee, 186.
Sixtown Indians, 121.
Skaruren, band of Tuscarora, 199.
  See Tuscarora.
Skenne-mok, see Skunnemoke.
Sketches of Southeastern tribes and their population, 81–216.
Skin dressing, 442–448.
Skinner, Alanson, 284, 828.
  on agricultural methods, 305.
  on clothing, 468, 469, 475, 477.
  on cooking, 359, 369.
  on hair dressing, 506.
  on houses, 398, 399.
  on ornamentation, 487.
  on silver, 497, 498.
  on skin dressing, 447.
  on towns, 635.
Skogari, town on north branch of Susquehanna in Columbia Co., Pa., 201.
Skunnemoke (Short Arrow), Atakapa Indian, land sold by, 93.
Slave hunters, English, attack on Acolapissa by, 82.
Slings, 587.
Smallpox, attack among Chickasaw, 117.
  destructive to Catawba, 104.
  destructive to Eyeish, 132.
  epidemic among Cherokee, 111.
  nearly destroyed Pamlico, 170.
  Sewee much reduced by, 183.
Smilax pseudochina, use of, 287.
Smilax sp., use of, 271, 288, 289, 292, 293, 296, 360, 361.
Smith, Buckingham, 65, 609.
  on fish, 267, 268.
  on identification of Sauxpa, 66.
Smith, J. Russell, 823.
  on climate, 823–824.
Smith, John, 157, 178, 278, 305, 325, 330, 335, 336, 338, 339, 427, 441, 442, 710, 813, 831.
  captured by Opechancanough, 689.
  discovered Nahyssan on James River, Va., 157.
  discovered tribe called Monasukapanough in Monacan country, 178.
  on agricultural methods, 304, 307.
  on artistic development, 614, 615.
  on axes, 545.

Smith, John, on burial customs, 718, 719:
  on clothing, 469.
  on coloring of manufactured articles
    609.
  on cooking, 351, 352, 355, 364, 366,
    372.
  on crime˘and˘punishment, 730.
  on division of year into seasons by
    Powhatan Indians, 257.
  on ear ornaments, 511.
  on eating habits of Algonquian
    tribes, 257, 258, 277.
  on featherwork, 456.
  on fire making, 423.
  on flint, 544.
  on food preserving, 377.
  on foods, 274, 275, 276, 277.
  on forts, 438.
  on games, 675.
  on greasing and coloring of hair and
    skin, 526.
  on hair dressing, 502.
    of priests, 502.
  on head bands, 509.
  on home manners, 711.
  on household utensils, 556, 558.
  on houses, 414.
  on hunting, 313, 314, 317.
  on implements for hunting and
    fishing, 564, 568, 572, 576, 577,
    579, 581, 582, 588.
  on marriage customs, 701, 702.
  on mats and baskets, 603.
  on medical practices, 784.
  on metals, 493.
  on mnemonic devices, 610, 611.
  on musical instruments, 624, 625,
    626, 627, 629.
  on names, 671.
  on pearl fishery at mouth of Appa-
    mattox River, Va., 489.
  on pearl necklace, 516.
  on pearls, 489.
  on religious beliefs and usages, 743,
    745, 747.
  on soap and towels, use of, by
    Powhatan, 432.
  on social organization, 642, 643,
    644, 645.
  on tattooing, 532.
  on threads and textiles, 448.
  on tobacco, 383.
  on towns, 630.
  on trade, 740.
  on transportation, means of, 592,
    596, 602.
  on war customs, 689.
  on weapons, 564, 568, 572, 577, 579,
    581, 582, 588.
Smoke-holes and windows, 427–428, 803.
Snow, reported by De Soto chroniclers,
  55.
Soacatino, 57, 186.
  Caddo tribe visited by Spaniards
    under Moscoso, 186.
Social organization, 641–674.
Societal and ceremonial life, 629–799.

Socsósky, Apalachicola town, 92.
Sodo Creek, west of Red River, home of
  Kadohadacho, 142.
Solameco, see Chiaha.
Solís, Fray Gaspar José de; 292.
  on clothing, 476.
  on hunting, 312.
Soloy, town subject to Mission of
  Nombre de Dios, 179.
Sonoran Fauna Areas, Upper and Lower,
  tribes occupying, 20.
Sorghum drummondii, use of, 286, 288.
Souchitiony, see Doustioni.
Souel, Father, murdered by Yazoo in
  Natchez War, 212.
Source material, 827–832.
Sources, historical, 21.
South America, climatic province in,
  analogous to Southeastern United
  States, 7.
  natives of, 824, 825.
  southeastern, relation to cultural
    area, 826.
South American ethnological province,
  the part of North America reached
  by Columbus included in, 33.
South American Indians, reference to,
  33.
South Carolina colonists, aided by
  Cusabo and Sewee in repelling Span-
  iards, 183.
  war against Congaree and Santee,
    waged by, 124.
  war with Coosa and Stono waged
    by, 129.
  with allied Indians, attacked and
    defeated Tuscarora, 199.
South Carolina colony, settlement in
  Charleston Harbor, 129, 184.
South Carolina, State of, 1, 2, 14, 16, 18,
  19, 30, 36, 45, 61, 62, 64, 66, 67, 70, 92.
  archives of, relate relations with
    Waxhaw and Catawba, 206.
  Ayllon colony on coast of, 135, 183.
  British census of Indians in, 77.
  Chickasaw lands confiscated by,
    118.
  documents of, relating to Cape Fear
    Indians, 103.
  earliest home of Shakori, 183.
  location of reservation for Catawba,
    105.
  Piedmont region, Catawba of, 11.
  province founded by English, 177.
  ravaged by "Notowega," 164.
  removal of Yamasee to, 136.
  treaty with Catawba, 104.
  treaty with Cherokee, 111.
South Florida tribes, population of, 12.
Southeast Indians, history from period
  of first white contact to De Soto
  expedition, 33–39.
  history of, 33–81.
  history of De Soto period, 39–59.
  history of post-De Soto period,
    59–81.
  raw materials utilized by, 242.

Southeastern area, climate of, 5–7.
  considered as archeological province, 2.
  considered as ethnological province, 1.
  fauna and flora of, Merriam on, 9–10.
  Indian population of, 11–14.
    See Population.
  life zones of, position of tribes relative to, 8, 9, 20.
  significance of geographical difference in, 2.
  tribes composing cultural province of, 10, 19, 21–33.
    sketches of and their population, 81–216.
    (See table 1, facing p. 10.)
"Southern Hopewell" culture, 33.
Spain, 35, 59.
  French possessions west of Miss., ceded to, 78.
  loss of territory in North America, 78.
  reference to land granted to by Pope Alexander VI, 34.
Spaniards, 101, 122, 127, 130, 134, 136, 138, 143, 150, 155, 156, 157, 158, 164, 192, 202.
  and English, early struggle between, 63.
  Calusa discovered in Florida by, 16.
  Casiste town on Alabama River passed by, 127, 143.
  cross set up in main square of Ocute village by, 138.
  Cumberland Island named San Pedro by, 187.
  driven out by Tekesta, took refuge with Guacata at Santa Lucia, 192.
  driven to cannibalism by number of refugees from colony of Tekesta, 134.
  gold heard of from Indian Pedro, 42.
  Guasco visited by, 136.
  Indians of Gulf of Mexico encountered by, 172.
  killing of, in eastern Tex., prevented by St. Denis, 155.
  northward advance of resisted by Eno, 130.
  Oçita town seized as headquarters, 164.
  Okelousa heard of by, 167.
  post of Pensacola established by, 172.
  removal from Calusa country to Havana, 101.
  repelled by South Carolina colonists aided by Cusabo and Sewee, 183.
  Soacatino visited by, 186.
  Surruque attacked by, 187.
  Tascalusa, Mobile chief, visited by, 150.
Spaniards, Tawasa first mentioned by, 190.
  Tekesta found by, in Florida, 191.
  tribes found on Georgia-South Carolina coast by, 16.
  trouble between Choctaw and Creeks fomented by, 122.
  united with Coosa against Napochi, 157.
  uprising of Guacata against, 134.
  war with Ais, 84.
Spanish census, 189, 190, 194.
Spanish Cortes, secularization of Texas missions by, 75.
Spanish expedition, Kasihta village burned by, 143.
  Pohoy visited by, 173.
Spanish Jesuits, unsuccessful in establishing a mission among Powhatan, 175.
Spanish mutineers, well received by Tekesta, 192.
Spanish post, located at St. Augustine, Fla., 184.
Spanish troops, cut off by Indians, 128.
Spark, John, on body paint, 529, 531.
  on bows of Florida Indians, 577.
  on metals, 491.
  on skin dressing, 442, 444, 445.
  on tattooing, 534.
  on tobacco, 382.
  on wooden pillow, use of by Indians, in Florida, 432.
Spears, attack on Spaniards by Indians using, 59.
Speck, Frank G., 140, 215, 217, 218, 219, 225, 342, 345, 464, 662, 716, 794, 812, 821, 828, 830.
  on artistic development, 623.
  on bags and purses, 480.
  on body paint, 530, 531.
  on clothing, 465, 466, 467, 474, 525.
  on cooking, 354, 357, 366, 370.
  on divisions of time among the Yuchi, 263.
  on featherwork, 456.
  on finger rings, 523.
  on fire making, 424, 425.
  on fishing, 335, 338, 340, 341, 342.
  on food preserving, 378.
  on hair dressing, 505.
  on household utensils, 557, 558, 559.
  on houses, 399, 400.
  on hunting, 314, 316, 317, 331.
  on implements for hunting and fishing, 573, 574, 578, 579, 582. 586.
  on mats and baskets, 605.
  on moieties, 663, 664.
  on necklaces, 517, 518.
  on ornamentation, 487.
  on ornaments, 465.
  on physical characteristics of Creeks and Yuchi, 225.
  on pottery, 553.
  on silver working, 497.
  on thread and textiles, 450.

Speck, Frank G., on weapons, 573, 574, 578, 579, 582, 586.
on Yuchi sewing, 454.
Spelman, Henry, 274, 276, 305, 831.
on agricultural methods, 304, 306, 307.
on burial customs, 719.
on crime and punishment, 730.
on games, 675.
on hair dressing, 498, 501.
on home manners, 711.
on houses, 414.
on hunting, 318, 320.
on marriage customs, 701, 702.
on medical practices, 783, 784.
on names, 671.
on religious beliefs and usages, 743, 747.
on social organization, 642.
on tomahawks, primitive type, 568, 588.
on war customs, 688.
Spier, Leslie, 666, 669.
on the Crow system of relationship, 666.
Spinden, Herbert J., 11.
Spiritu Santo harbor, Mobile reported by Calderón on island near, 151.
Spoehr, Alexander, 828.
Spokogi, ceremonial name for Tukabahchee, 185.
Spoonbill (*Polyodon spatula*), use as food 266, 267.
Spotswood, Governor, 131, 178, 201.
removal of Eno with Cheraw and Keyauwee to frontiers of North Carolina proposed by, 131.
Saponi removed to Fort Christanna, Va., by, 178.
Sprague, Andrew, Tutelo vocabulary collected from, 201.
Spring Gardens, 30.
Square Ground, Atasi Indians, 616.
established by Tukabahchee in southeastern part of Creek territory in Okla., 197.
given up by Sawokli to join Hitchiti, 180.
known as Thliwahali ground, 133.
Lower Eufaula, long given up, 132.
maintained by Chiaha among Seminole, 116.
Hilibi near Hanna, Okla., 137.
Mikasuki in the Seminole Nation, 150.
Natchez in Greenleaf Mt., 160.
Okchai in Okla., 167.
Pakana in Okla., 170.
Tukabahchee at Yeager near Holdenville, 197.
Yuchi in Okla., 214.
reestablished by Okchai near Hanna, Okla., 167.
Okmulgee in northeast of Creek territory, 168.
Square Grounds, Creek ones illustrated, 776.

Squash (*Cucurbita verrucosa*), use of, 635.
Squirrel King, Chickasaw chief, 73, 117, 118.
Stanley, John Mix, painting of intertribal Indian council by, 81.
Starkville, 106.
Starritt, Preston, information on Cherokee festivals obtained from, 769–771.
Staunton River, site of Indian town, 157.
Steatite, use of, 243.
Stegaraki, branch of Mannahoac, 219.
interpretation of name, 219.
See Stuckanox.
Stekoa Creek, 47.
Stephen's Bluff, 51.
Stewart County, Ga., site of Kolomi settlement, 146.
Stiggins, George, Tawasa chronicler, 191, 828.
estimate of Alabama population by, 88.
on marriage customs, 704, 705.
on moral characteristics among Creeks, 230.
on possession of brass drum by Abihka, 81.
on war club, 568, 569.
Stimafutchki, or "Good Humor," Koasati chief, 146.
Stockade, establishment of, by Spanish in Apalachicola village, 1689, 63.
Stockaded town, probably Tocar, 65.
Stockades, 433–439, 804.
Stokes Ferry, 41.
Stone, sources of raw material, 541–543.
pipes, 545–547.
uses of, 243, 541–549.
Stone People, see Avoyel.
Stono, fought with Coosa against South Carolina colonists, 129.
Stools, wooden, 555–556.
Strachey, William, 218, 278, 299, 304, 305, 317, 325, 330, 335, 346, 427, 428, 430, 440, 441, 442, 448, 456, 813, 831.
on age of Powhatan Indians' settlement in North Carolina, 24.
on agricultural methods, 307.
on artistic development, 614, 615.
on birth customs and treatment of young, 709, 710.
on burial customs, 719.
on clothing, 459, 462, 469, 470, 472, 473, 475.
worn by medicine men, 477, 478.
on cooking, 351, 352, 355, 356, 360, 363, 370, 371, 372.
on copper mines at Ritanoe, 492, 493.
on crime and punishment, 730.
on ear ornaments, 510, 511.
on fate of Roanoke colonists, 76.
on fishing, 336, 338, 339.
on food, 274, 275, 276.
on food preserving, 377, 379, 380.
on games, 674, 675, 685.

Strachey, William, on greasing and coloring of hair and skin, 526, 529.
  on hair dressing, 499, 502, 526.
  on head bands, 509.
  on household utensils, 556.
  on houses, 414, 415, 416.
  on hunting methods of Virginia Indians, 258, 313.
  on implements, hunting and fishing, 564, 568, 572, 573, 579, 581, 582, 588.
  on marriage customs, 702.
  on medical practices, 783.
  on mental characteristics of Virginia Indians, 229.
  on musical instruments, 625, 627, 629.
  on names, 671.
  on necklaces, 516, 520.
  on occupations of men and women, 710, 711.
  on physical characteristics of Powhatan Indians, 222, 229.
  on pottery, 554.
  on religious beliefs and usages, 743, 744, 746, 748, 749.
  on soap and towels, 432.
  on social organization, 641, 642, 645.
  on tattooing, 532.
  on thread and textiles, 450.
  on tobacco, 383.
  on towns, 629, 630.
  on trade, 740.
  on transportation, means of, 592, 593.
  on war customs, 687, 688.
  on weapons, 564, 568, 572, 573, 579, 581, 582, 588.
Strawberry, wood (*Fragaris* sp.), 637.
Stuart, John, 119.
Stuckanox, 201.
Subtile, French vessel, fate of Indian captives on, 85–86.
Succatabee, Chickasaw chief, successor of Squirrel King, 118.
Suckers (*Catastomidae*), use of, 267.
Sugar Creek, Mecklenburg Co., N. C., and York Co., S. C., home of Sugeree tribe, 186.
"Sugar Town," name of Catawba settlement, 186.
Sugeree, 186, 219.
  name, interpretation of in Catawba language, 219.
  population, 186.
  possible branch of Shakori, 186.
  related to Catawba, with whom they united, 186.
  sketch of, 186.
  tribe on Sugar Creek, Mecklenburg Co., N. C., and York Co., S. C. 186.
Sukaispoga, branch of Coosa, 125.
Sullivan, Coreorgonel destroyed by, 201.

Sumac (*Rhus coriaria*), use of, 385.
  low (*Rhus truphydon*), use of, 606.
  smooth (*Rhus glabra*), use of, 385. 527.
Sumulga Hatchee River, Fla., home of Yamasee, 210.
Sun caste, rules of, among the Natchez, 662.
Sunepáh, Apalachicola town, 92.
Sunflower (*Helianthus giganteus*), "planta solis," use as food, 269, 288, 305, 306.
Sunflower Landing, Miss., point at which De Soto crossed the Miss., 53.
Surreche, *see* Surruque.
Surruque, 187.
  attacked by Spaniards, 187.
  final history unknown, 187.
  not located on Lake Okeechobee, 187.
  population, 187.
  small tribe about Cape Canaveral, Fla., 187.
Susquehanna Indians, 31, 148, 149, 157, 163.
  apparently joined Meherrin, 149.
  attacks on Manahoac by, 148, 157.
  clubs, 568.
Susquehanna River, home of Tutelo, 200.
  temporary home of Tuscarora, 199.
Suwannee Oldtown, 147.
Suwannee River, Fla., 37, 181, 201.
  called River of the Deer, 41.
  location of Seminole town burned by Andrew Jackson, 181.
  pearl fishery located at, 489.
Swadesh, Dr. Morris, 121, 830.
Swan, Caleb, Government agent, 142, 222, 262, 288, 390, 422, 427, 828.
  on clothing, 471, 475.
  on household utensils, 556, 564.
  on houses, 394.
  on mats and baskets, 604.
  on mental chracteristics, 229, 230.
  on physical characteristics, 222, 223, 230.
  on pipes 542, 547.
  on pottery, 551.
  on skin dressing, 445.
  on thread and textiles, 452.
  on transportation, means of, 598.
Swannanoa, Gap, named for Cheraw 110.
Swanton, John R., 132, 162, 229, 241, 242, 280, 282, 289, 291, 292, 297, 298, 299, 301, 315, 330, 334, 371, 381, 428, 430, 431, 436, 437, 439, 441, 448, 449, 458, 459, 461, 463, 828, 830, 831, 832.
  on agricultural methods, 309.
  on artistic development, 613, 616, 618, 619.
  on bags and purses, 480.
  on body paint, 529, 531.
  on burial customs, 722, 725 727, 728, 729.
  on clans and gentes, 655, 657.

Swanton, John R., on clothing, 471, 475.
on ear ornaments, 514.
on caste systems, 662.
on coloring for manufactured articles, 610.
on crime and punishment, 731, 732, 733.
on fire making, 425, 427.
on flint, 543.
on food preserving, 374, 376, 377.
on games, 678, 680, 681, 682, 683, 684, 685, 686.
on hair dressing, 500, 503, 504, 507, 527, 528.
on head deformation, 538, 540.
on horses, 349.
on household utensils, 555, 556, 559, 560, 561.
on houses, 400, 401, 417, 419, 420.
on implements for hunting and fishing, 563, 565, 568, 569, 571, 572, 576, 577, 579, 582, 583, 588.
on marriage customs, 705, 706, 707, 708.
on mats and baskets, 603, 604, 607, 608.
list of kinds, 607.
on medical practices, 792, 794, 795, 796, 797, 798.
on migrations, 264.
on mnemonic devices, 611.
on moieties, 663, 664.
on musical instruments, 625, 626, 627, 629.
on names, 672, 673, 674.
on necklaces, 519, 520.
on nose ornaments, 515.
on ornamentation, 524.
on pipes, 546, 547.
on pottery, 550, 551.
on religious beliefs and usages, 754, 761, 762, 763, 764, 765, 767, 776, 777, 778, 779, 780, 781.
on skin dressing, 447.
on social customs, 713, 715, 716, 717, 718.
on social organization, 647, 648, 649, 650, 651.
on tattooing, 516, 533, 534, 535.
on thread and textiles, 450.
on tobacco, 382.
on towns, 632, 633, 634, 638, 639, 640.
on transportation, means of, 589, 594, 595, 596, 597, 599, 600, 601.
on war customs, 693, 694, 695, 696, 697, 698, 700, 701.
on weapons, 589, 594, 595, 596, 597, 600, 601.
on whale hunting in Florida, 329.
Sweat baths, description of, 784, 785, 791.
Sweat-lodges, stone, 243.
Sweetgum (Liquidambar sp.), use of, 385.
Sylacauga, see Chatakague.

Syllabary, submitted by Sequoya, Cherokee Chief, 113.
Symbols, Indian, 29.
Tacatacuru, 187, 193, 194, 215, 219.
interpretation of name, 219.
population, 187.
Timucua name for tribe on Cumberland Island, Ga., 187.
uprising of Guale suppressed by, 187.
visited by French under Ribault and Laudonnière, 187.
Taensa, 13, 19, 31, 72, 73, 91, 120, 159, 166, 170, 188, 189, 191, 204, 301, 655, 829.
abandonment of old villages for fear of Yazoo and Chickasaw, 188.
accompanied La Loire to Mobile, 188.
artistic development of, 618.
assigned to village of Tawasa, 188, 191.
Bayogoula driven out by, 95.
clothing of, 458, 461.
doors, position of, 428, 430.
head deformation, 540.
housing, 418.
mats used by chief of, 603.
members of Muskhogean linguistic family, 239.
movements, 188, 189.
population, 189.
religious beliefs and usages, 780.
sketch of, 188–189.
smoke holes and windows lacking, 427.
social organization, 649, 650.
source material on, 829.
temple, 613, 618.
towns of, 638.
trade with, 738.
use of pearls by, 489.
villages of, 72, 73, 99, 161, 166.
visited by La Salle at Lake St. Joseph, La., 188.
visited by missionaries, 188.
Taensa Bayou, at head of Grand Lake, home of Taensa, 189.
Tagaya, identification of, 67.
Taguanate, Indian town, 58.
Tahchee, 113, 114.
Tahlequah, intertribal Indian council held at, 81.
Taitt, 127, 144, 146, 170, 200.
Tala, town supporting French, 122.
Talasi, see Tanasqui.
Talaxe (Talashe), name used for Altamaha River, and town in province of Guale, 125, 132, 269.
Tali, town of, 26, 48, 59.
Talicpacana, Indian town, 50.
Taliepataua, see Talicpacana.
Talimeco, temple of, 45.
town on Savannah River, 45, 46, 602.

Talimuchasy, Indian town, 49.
  meaning of the word,49.
Talisi, Indian town, 49.
"Talisi province," Alabama River, encountered by De Soto 125, 433.
Taliwa, 112.
Talladega country, Shawnee settled in, 185.
  Chiaha move to, 28.
  Tulsa Indians moved to Tallapoosa from, 125.
Talladega County, Ala., 81.
Talladega Creek, 25, 26, 125, 131.
  home of Eufaula at early date on, 131.
Talladega Creeks, sympathetic to whites in Creek War, 79.
Talladega, (End Town) Abihka town, 81, 82.
Talladega Shawnee, departure from Creek Nation, 185.
Talladega Square Ground, 81.
Tallahassee, City of, 16, 41, 179.
Tallahatchie River, 116.
Tallapoosa River, 22, 26, 27, 28, 30, 32, 49, 60, 72, 87, 125, 131, 132, 133, 137, 139, 142, 145, 146, 152, 153, 166, 167, 170, 184, 191, 197, 200, 214.
  Coosa moved down upon, 125.
  Eufaula settled below Okfuskee on, 131, 132.
  Koasati settlement on junction of Coosa and, 145.
  Kolomi settlement on, 146, 634.
  Muklasa town on lower course of, 152.
  Shawnee settlement near junction with Coosa River, 184, 185, 214.
  site of Hilibi settlement, on affluent of, 137.
  site of home of Kealedji, 144.
  site of town of Fus-hatchee, 133, 142, 191.
  site of Upper Creek town called Hothliwahali, 139.
  sometimes called "River of the Chiaha," 115.
  stockaded towns located on, 433.
  sympathetic to whites in Creek War, 79.
  Tulsa Indians moved from Talladega country by James McQueen, to, 125.
Tallapoosa Valley, 11.
Tallapoosa Yuchi, 214.
Tallassehatchee Creek, 25, 125.
Talmutcasi, see Tukabahchee Tallahassee.
Talomeco, Temple of, description of, 566, 567, 571, 583, 587, 588, 602, 614.
Talwa ahassi, "Old town," see Tanasqui.
Tàlwa łako (Big town), Apalachicola town, 92.
Taly, Indian tribe, 212.
Tama, mission, 209, 210.
  province visited by Gaspar de Salas, and some missionaries, 208.

Tama, see Tamathli, 189.
Tamahita, 146.
Tamahita, town of, 636.
Tamahitan, hair dressing, 505.
  possibly Yuchi, 505.
Tamali, see Tamathli.
Tamaroa, 159.
Tamathli, 138, 181, 189, 190.
  located on Apalachicola River, 189.
  part of Seminole nation, 189.
  population, 190.
  probably swallowed up in Mikasuki band of Seminole, 189.
  sketch of, 189–190.
Tamaulipas, State of, Mexico, 17.
Tamaulipeco, 801.
"Tamaxle nuevo," Lower Creek town, 189.
Tampa Bay, Fla., 12, 13, 16, 26, 37, 42, 101, 165, 173, 181.
  fishweirs of rough stone constructed on, 243.
  Oçita located near entrance to, 165.
  south of, home of Calusa, 101.
Tanasi, see Tanasqui.
Tanasqui, classification of, 70.
  identification of by Mooney, 68.
  town on Tennessee River, occupied by Cherokee, 65, 68, 111.
"Tangibao," town on the Mississippi, partly burned, 190.
Tangipahoa, 82, 83, 167, 190, 219.
  interpretation of name, Choctaw tongue, 219.
  population, 190.
  probably related to Acolapissa, 190.
  remnants probably united with Acolapissa, 190.
  sketch of, 190.
  tribe located on affluent of Lake Pontchartrain, 190.
Tanico, encampment of De Soto at, 98.
  province of, 54, 55.
  salt made at, 549.
Tapia, Capt. Francisco Milan, journal of, 180.
Taposa, 19, 107, 190, 195.
  earliest mention by Iberville, 190.
  population, 190.
  sketch of, 190.
  tribe on upper Yazoo River, 190.
  See Chakchiuma.
Tappahannock, 175.
Tar River, N. C. 131, 199.
  home of Eno near headwaters of, 131.
  Tuscarora located on, 800.
Tarpon (Megalops cyprinoides), 267.
Tascalusa, chief of the Mobile, 49, 50, 69, 70, 651, 652, 810.
  clothing of, 459.
  feather mantle worn by, 455, 459.
  head band worn by, 508.
  musical instruments used by followers of, 628.
  relations with Spaniards, 50, 150.

Tascalusa, chief of the Mobile, stool used by, 555.
    sunshade carried over, 430, 431, 608, 652.
    visited by Spaniards, 150, 430, 432.
Tascalusa, town of, 66.
Taskigi Creeks, fishing, 342.
    implements for hunting and fishing, 574, 578, 586.
    mats and baskets made by, 605.
    pottery, 553.
    weapons, 574, 578, 586.
Tasqui, Ala., town seen by De Soto, 28, 48, 49, 66, 69, 200, 631.
    discovered by Juan Pardo, 28, 66, 69, 200.
Tassanak Okla., Mobilian name of Avoyel, 94.
Tattooed Serpent, name of Natchez chief, 650, 728.
Tattooing, 532–536.
Tawakoni, 100.
Tawasa, 28, 63, 73, 88, 134, 147, 171, 188, 190, 191, 193, 239, 827.
    finally joined the Alabama Indians, 87, 191.
    located near Mobile by Bienville, 191.
    moved to district between Coosa and the Tallapoosa Rivers, 191.
    part moved to Louisiana with Alabama Indians, 191.
    population, 191.
    removed from Mobile River to make way for Taensa, 191.
    settled with French at Mobile, 191.
    sketch of, 190–191.
    tribe first mentioned by De Soto, living on site of Montgomery, Ala., 190.
    uprooted by attacks of northern Indians, 171, 191.
Tawasa, town of, 22, 87, 88.
Taylor, Nancy, one of last speakers of Natchez tongue, 160.
Tcahki thlåko (Big Shoal), Abihka town, 81.
Tcahki thlåko, branch of Coosa, 125.
Tcatoksofka, branch of Coosa, 125, 207.
Tcawokli, Sawokli town on Chattahoochee River, 180, 190.
Tchefuncte, prehistoric culture of Louisiana, 33.
Tchula, modern town named after Choula, 123.
Tcilokogalgi, "People of different speech," division of Creek Nation, 664.
Tcuko tcati or "Red House," Eufaula settlement in Florida, 131, 181.
Tcuthlåko-nini, branch of Coosa, 125.
Tecumseh, endeavor of to draw Choctaw into war with Creeks against United States, 122.
    Kispokotha chief, 185.
Teeth, staining of, 536.

Teguanate, Indian town, 651.
Tejas, name used for Caddo, 98.
Tekesta, 85, 134, 191, 192, 193, 282, 816.
    burial customs of, 649, 722, 811, 816.
    captives held by Calusa, sent home by Menendez, 192.
    converted by Menendez, 192.
    disappearance as a separate tribe, 192.
    joined with Calusa in killing Spaniards, 192.
    members of Muskhogean linguistic family, 239.
    necklaces worn by, 518.
    population, 193.
    peace made with Spaniards by, 192.
    sketch of, 191–193.
    Spaniards joined by refugees from colony of, 134.
    tribe found by Spaniards on coast of Florida, 191.
    trouble with missionaries, caused by the soldiers, 192.
    See also Ais.
Telfair County, Fla., 44.
Tellico blockhouse, conference between colonists and Cherokee held at, 112.
Tellico Creek, Tuskegee settlement near mouth of, 200.
Temple in Talimeco, description of by Garcilaso, reference to, 45.
    pearls in, 45.
    reference to sketch of by De Batz, 82.
Temples, 566, 567, 571, 583, 587, 588, 602, 614, 615, 617, 618, 631, 632, 638, 639, 742, 744, 746, 753, 761, 779, 780.
Tennessee, 2, 30, 68.
    shell-midden people of, 33.
    Yuchi found by De Soto in eastern, 212.
Tennessee River, 20, 26, 27, 28, 30, 31, 32, 46, 47, 48, 68, 69, 143, 145, 153, 163, 200, 212, 215.
    Kaskinampo moved from Cumberland to, 143.
    Koasati living on island in, 145.
    Tuskegee bands living on, 200.
Tennessee Valley, 47.
    occupied by Cherokee, 112.
Tensas River, Perrier advanced against Natchez on, 147.
    home of Taensa till removed to Red River, 188.
Tenskwatawa, Shawnee prophet, 186.
Teodoro, Doroteo, a Greek with Narvaez expedition, 38, 39.
Tequesta, see Tekesta.
Terra Ceia Island, 40.
    apparent site of Oçita town seized by Spaniards, 165.
Terrebonne Parish, La., 83.
    home of Houma, 140.
Tessuntee River, 47.
Tewa, trade among, 737.

Texas, State of, 1, 12, 23, 24, 56, 59, 74, 89.
  admission as State, 75.
  Atakapa Indians in, called Akokisa, 85, 93.
  brief history of missions in, 74–75.
  cultural level of tribes of, 10.
  estimate of Alabama Indians in, 88.
  independence established, 75.
  location of Alabama who settled in, 87.
  part of Republic of Mexico, 75.
    removal of Caddo to, 142.
  peoples of eastern extension of, 30.
  Presidio of Nuestra Señora de Pilar de los Adaes, capital of, for 50 years, 83.
  tribes of, 18, 80.
    See Hasinai.
  Yatasi moved from Louisiana to, 211.
Texas or Tejas, name used for Caddo, 98.
  De Leon's expedition to, 74.
  See Caddo, 237.
"The Congarees," fort opposite Columbia, S. C., established by, 124.
Thlapthláko, branch town of Hothliwahali, 139.
Thlathlogalga, see Okchai, 167.
Thlikatcka, or "Broken Arrow," noted Coweta town near Fort Mitchell, 127.
Thliotombi, Choctaw brave, 123.
Thliwahali, 133, 134, 147.
  See Hothliwahali,.
Thomas, Cyrus, on quarries worked by Indians, 542, 543.
Thomasville, Ga., 50.
Thome Creek, see Catoma Creek.
Thompson, Charlie, Alabama Chief, on food preserving, 375.
  on mats and baskets, 606.
    Indian names for types of, 606.
  on pottery, 552.
Thurston, Captain, 111.
Thwaites, Reuben Gold, editor, 416, 418, 473, 476, 507, 536, 618, 639, 650, 684, 700, 797.
Tidewater tribes of Virginia and North Carolina, cultural pattern of, 10.
Tillandsia usneoides, uses of, 247.
Timbalier Islands, 59.
Timberlake, Lt. Henry, 112, 224, 298, 326, 328, 336, 349, 351, 767, 768, 831.
  Cherokee visited by, 112.
  on bracelets and arm bands, 522.
  on burial customs, 723.
  on clothing, 459, 460, 461, 463, 464.
  on cooking, 356.
  on ear ornaments worn by the Indians, 513.
  on education of children, 714.
  on fishing, 335.
  on flags, 431.
  on food of the Cherokee country, 284.
  on games, 683.

Timberlake, Lt. Henry, on hair dressing, 499, 500, 505.
  on housing methods of the Cherokee, 402, 403, 404 (fig.).
  on implements for hunting and fishing, 569, 573, 578, 583, 585.
  on moral characteristics of Cherokees, 233.
  on musical instruments, 625.
  on names, 672.
  on necklaces, 518.
  on nose ornaments, 515.
  on ornamentation, 490.
  on physical characteristics of the Cherokee, 224, 233.
  on pipes, 546.
  on pottery, 553.
  on religious beliefs and usages, 769.
  on tobacco, 384.
  on transportation, means of, 593, 594, 595, 596.
  on war customs, 691, 692.
  on weapons, 569, 573, 578, 583, 585.
Timucua, 11, 29, 37, 40, 41, 135, 136, 141, 154, 168, 169, 173, 174, 179, 187, 193, 194, 202, 215, 216, 239, 255, 281, 348, 665, 801, 806, 808, 810, 816, 829.
  Acuera a branch of, 83.
  agricultural habits, 260, 308, 309.
  burial customs, 722, 811.
  chiefs, brought to St. Augustine by Juan de Junco, 202.
  clans and gentes among the, 654, 657.
  clothing, 457, 458, 471, 473, 524.
  crime and punishment among the, 731.
  dialect, spoken by Tawasa, 28.
  division of Muskogean stock, 10.
    (See table 1, facing p. 10.)
  domestic customs, 713.
  doors, use, 428.
  ear ornaments, 511.
  encountered by De Soto, 40–42.
  evidence regarding western origin, 23.
  feather work, 456.
  food preserving, 380.
  forts or stockades of, 433.
  Franciscans gain control of, 62.
  games, 682.
  granaries, made of stone, 243, 380.
  greasing and coloring of hair and skin. 527.
  hair dressing, 503, 808.
  historical works on, 21.
  household utensils, 556.
  housing, 408.
  hunting, 319, 331, 332.
  implements for hunting and fishing, 579, 583, 589.
  located north of Santa Fe River, Fla., 193.
  marriage customs, 705, 709.
  mats and baskets, 604.
  medical practices, 793.
  migrations, 32, 63.

Timucua, musical instruments, 628.
  names, 672, 673.
  necklaces, 518, 519, 520.
  notes of Hawkins' narrative, 75.
  population, 194.
  population of Cumberland Island,
    Ga., 119, 187.
  "rebels" fled to Apalachicola River,
    169.
  relationship terms, 666, 667, 668,
    669.
  religious beliefs and usages, 761,
    765.
  removed to Tomoka River, Volusia
    County, Fla., 194.
  settlement of Yamasee with, 63.
  smoke holes and windows, 427.
  social customs, 723.
  social organization, 648, 654.
  source material, 829.
  tattooing, 533.
  tongue, linguistic relationship of,
    22.
  towns, on lagoons south of St.
    Augustine, Fla., 133, 194.
  treatment of fingernails and toe-
    nails by, 536, 537.
  war customs, 692, 693, 695.
  weapons, 579, 583, 589.
  See also Utina, 201.
Timucua coast, skirted by various explorers, 193.
Timucua group, disappearance of, 133,
  194.
  includes all tribes of linguistic
    family of Timucua, 193.
  much reduced by pestilence, 193.
  sketch of, 193–194.
Timucua rebellion, 1656, Apalachee involved in, 90.
  reference to, 83.
Timucuan, 193, 239, 827.
Timuquanan, Powell's name for Timucuan, 193, 239.
Tin-fai-yai-kaix, son of Ko-i-ha-tco, 226.
Tiou, 19, 95, 107, 147, 194, 195, 640, 829.
  apparently joined the Natchez
    tribe, 195.
  completely destroyed by Quapaw,
    195.
  land sold to Sieur Roussin by, 195.
  moved near Natchez, under pres-
    sure from the Chickasaw, 194,
    195.
  population, 195.
  sent by Natchez to rouse Tunica
    against French, 195.
  settlement on Mississippi near Fort
    Adams, 194.
  sketch of, 194–195.
  source material on, 829.
  tribe on Yazoo River, 194.
  Tunica spoken by, 240.
Tippo Bayou, apparently named after
  Ibitoupa, 140.
Tlascaltec, settled about Presidio of
  San Augustin de Ahumada, 86.

Toa, Indian village, 43.
  affiliations discussed, 43.
  See Tamathli, 189.
Toalli, see Tamathli.
Toasi, see Tawasa.
Tobacco (Nicotiana rustica), use of, 244,
  381–386.
Tobacco-pipe clay, used by Southeastern
  Indians, 243.
Tobar, Nuño de, 43.
Tocal (ques), 110.
Tocal, see Tocar.
Tocar, 110.
  classification of, 67.
  Siouan name for Guasili, stockaded
    Indian town, 65.
Tocare, see Tocar.
Tocax, 110.
  See Tocar.
Toccogulegau on Kintchofoonee Creek,
  home of Yuchi, 214.
Tockwogh fort, described by Smith, 438.
Tocobaga, 148, 193, 195, 196.
  attack with Pohoy on Christian
    Indians, 195.
  burial customs 722, 811, 816.
  effect of pestilence on, 195.
  population, 196.
  sketch of, 195–196.
  soldiers under Captain Martinez de
    Coz, destroyed by, 195.
  temple at, on Tampa Bay, 761.
  tribe or "province" located at head
    of Old Tampa Bay, 195.
  visited by Menendez, with Chief of
    Calusa, 195.
Tocoy, Fla., 133.
Tohome, 35, 73, 151, 190, 196, 197, 219,
  829.
  cordial relations established by
    Iberville with, 196.
  fusion with Choctaw Nation, 196.
  Hughes, English Trader, killed by,
    196.
  interpretation of name, 219.
  moved just above Mobile, 196.
  population, 197.
  prevented from attacking Mobile
    by French, 196.
  protected by French from Alabama
    Indians, 196.
  settled with Mobile on Mobile
    River, 151.
  sketch of, 196–197.
  source material on, 829.
  trade with, 738.
  tribe discovered by French on
    Tombigbee River, 196.
  visited by French, 196.
    by brother of Iberville, 196.
  See also Mobile.
Tohtogagi, branch of Coosa, 125.
Tolameco, Creek word for "Chief
  Town," 115.
Toloco, town rebuilt by Capt. Juan
  Fernandez de Florencia, 202.

Tomahitans, 115, 213.
  See Yuchi, 213.
Tomatly, town of Upper Yamasee, 189, 209.
Tomatola, Cherokee County, N. C., 189.
Tombigbee River, 26, 50, 72, 73, 116, 145, 151, 196, 214, 738.
  called by Spaniards the "River of Chicaça," 51.
  settlement of Alabama and Koasati on, 87.
Tome River, identification with Tombigbee River, 196.
Tomochichi, Muskogee chief, 153, 210.
  visited England with his followers, 210.
Tomoka River, Volusia County, Fla., home of Timucua when last known, 63, 194.
Tomotley Ford on Little Tennessee River, Monroe Co., Tennessee, 190.
"Tompacuas," possibly name for Tocobaga, 195.
Tonahowi, nephew of Tomochichi, 153.
Tongigua, village on Mississippi moved over and settled with Toriman at junction with Arkansas, 176, 640, 641.
Tonikan stock, 240.
Tonkawa, 17, 30, 58, 801, 802, 820.
  Spanish mission established among, 75.
Tonkawan stock, 240.
  source of information on, 39.
Tonti, Henri de, 71, 72, 99, 105, 118, 139, 141, 147, 160, 161, 177, 188, 189, 194, 211.
  alliance made with Houma by, 139.
  attack on, by Chakchiuma, 105.
  peace made with Quinipissa by, 177.
  Taensa villages made headquarters of, 188, 461.
  visit of, to Caddo, 99.
  visit of, to Kadohadacho on Red River, Ark., 141.
Tooan Tuh or Dustu ("Spring Frog"), Cherokee Chief, prominent among Cherokee auxiliaries in Jackson's army, 114.
Tooker, W. W., 218.
Tooptatmeer, Woccon town in North Carolina, 207.
Toquale, Fla., 133.
Toriman, Tongigua village joined with, on Mississippi at junction with Arkansas, 176, 640.
Torres, Pedro de, 143.
Totero, 164.
  housing, 412.
Totopotamoi or Totopotomoy, Powhatan chief, 157.
  Pamunkey chief, joined Virginians in attack on Siouan tribes, 175.
Toucha Creek, near Bayou Sara, 191.
Tour, M. de la, plantation established by, 211.
Tourima, Indian town, 641.
  See also Toriman.
Toussana. *see* Inkillis Tamaha.

Towels and soap, use of, 432, 433, 644, 645.
Towns, 629–641, 645.
Towns Hill, 46, 47.
Toxawa, 111.
Toxodendron radicans, use of, 609.
Toxylon pomiferum, used by Indians, 578.
Trade, 736–742.
Traders, English and French, 27.
Traditions of Southeastern tribes on population movements, 22.
Trails, Macon, 47.
  Occaneechi, 76.
  war, from Virginia, 48.
Transitional Zone, Indian tribes occupying, 19.
Transportation, implements serving, 589–602.
Trascaluza, *see* Tascalusa.
Treaty of Dancing Rabbit Creek, signed between the United States and Choctaw, 122.
Treaty of Hopewell, establishment of northern boundary of Chickasaw by, 118.
Treaty of New Echota, removal of Cherokee to west provided by, 113.
Tribal names, interpretation of, 216–219.
Tribes occupying interior of Southeastern area, 19.
Trinity Bay, Tex., 85, 93.
Trinity River, Tex., 58, 85, 86, 93.
  Cherokee members of Bowl's band settled among, 113.
  Deadose tribe living near, 130.
  identification of with Daycao River, 58.
  Patiri lived west of, 172.
  settlement of Koasati on, 145, 146.
  settlement of Nacanish on, 155.
  site of Spanish settlement, 156.
Tropical Zone of southern Florida, Indian tribes occupying, 20.
Trowbridge, C. C., 832.
Trumbull, 154.
Tsala Apopka Lake, 41.
Tsistuyi, town on Hiwassee River, 213.
Tuasi, Indian town, 49.
  See also Tawasa, 190, 433.
Tubby, Simpson, Choctaw informant, 343, 344.
Tuckahoe (*Orontium aquaticum*), use by natives, 271, 276.
Tucuro, town, 193.
Tukabahchee, 125, 144, 153, 185, 197, 214, 219, 242, 384.
  American flag presented to, 431.
  artistic development of, 617.
  close association between Kispokotha and, 185.
  early settlement in Alabama, 197.
  housing, 389, 400 (fig.).
  interpretation of name, Creek tongue, 219.
  mentioned in Spanish letters, 197.

Tukabahchee, migration of, 27.
  plates, tradition about, 185.
  population, 197.
  refusal of, to join Tecumseh, 185.
  religious beliefs and usages, 774.
  retired to Lower Creeks to live with Coweta, 185, 197.
  sketch of, 197.
  square ground of, 617, 776.
  town of Atasi associated with, 94.
Tukabahchee Oldtown, 27.
Tukabahchee Tallahassee or Talmutcasi, branch of Coosa, 125, 197.
  tribe or town supposed to have immigrated from the north, 197.
Tukpafka, branch of Wakokai tribe, 203, 204.
Tukpafka (later called Nuyaka), branch of Coosa, 125, 203.
Tula, 98, 100, 809.
  Caddo tribe, 55.
  encounter by De Soto, 100.
  implements for hunting, fishing and war used by, 583.
  location of, 55.
  name for Caddo, used by De Soto, 98, 100.
  province of, 55.
Tulafina, town of Yamasee, 209.
Tulsa, 125, 153, 154.
  branches of, 125.
  moved to Tallapoosa from Talladega country by James McQueen, 125.
Tulsa Old Town, in Abihka country, 125.
Tulsa people, earliest reference to, 125.
Tunica, 12, 13, 14, 17, 20, 27, 29, 30, 31, 33, 94, 95, 97, 106, 139, 148, 166, 194, 195, 197–199, 211, 212, 219, 291, 301, 380, 665, 801, 819, 822, 829.
  absence of origin legends among, 23.
  Aquixo a branch of, 54.
  attacked by Yazoo, 212.
  Avoyel settled with, 94.
  burial customs of, 729, 811, 819.
  clans and gentes among the, 656.
  clothing of, 462, 472, 473, 476.
  greasing and coloring of hair and skin by, 528.
  hair dressing, 501, 507.
  head deformation, 540.
  household utensils, 556, 557, 564.
  images used by, 617.
  inclusion in Southeastern cultural province, 10.
  interpretation of name, 219.
  language spoken by, 240.
    Sam Young, Tunica chief, last speaker of, 198.
  loyalty to whites in Natchez rebellion, 73.
  migrations of, 32.
  mission established among, by Davion, 72.
  months, names of, not preserved, 262.

Tunica, moved from Mississippi to Marksville Prairie on Red River, 198.
  Pacaha a branch of, 53.
  population, 198.
  possible location in Ouachita Province, 14.
  pottery, 550, 819.
  relationship, terms, 669.
  religious beliefs and usages, 781, 819.
  removal from Yazoo River, 198.
  settled among Houma, near Red River, 139, 198.
  sided with French during Natchez uprising, 198.
  sketch of, 197–199.
  smoke holes and windows lacking, 427.
  social organization, 650.
  source material, 829.
  tattooing worn by, 819.
  towns, of, 639.
  trade with, 738, 819.
  tribe located on Yazoo River, near its mouth, 197.
  unsuccessfully urged by Tiou to fight French, 195.
  uprising against Houma, 198.
Tunica Oldfields, location, 29, 54.
Tunican stock, 10.
  (See table 1, facing p. 10.)
  historical works on, 21.
  population, 12.
Tunica group, 239, 801.
Tunica temple, 618, 780.
Tunsa, see Antonico.
Tuomey, M., on quarries, 542.
Tupelo, 51.
Tupi, spread of tribe in South America, 824.
Turkey, most useful bird, 251, 298, 574.
Turner, Nat, leader of slave uprising, involving Powhatans, 175.
Tuscarood, see Tuscarora, 199.
Tuscarora, 15, 19, 24, 31, 111, 131, 149, 162, 170, 183, 199, 219, 241, 297, 410, 800, 821, 830, 831.
  allies of Great Britain in Revolutionary War given lands in Grand River Reservation, Ontario, 199.
  bracelets, 521.
  burial customs, 719, 720, 721, 760, 811.
  clans and gentes, 654, 657.
  discussion of incomplete, 1.
  dominant tribe of eastern North Carolina, 241.
  ear ornaments, 510.
  forts, 438.
  games, 685.
  hair dressing, 499, 503.
  household utensils, 557.
  housing, 412.
  huskanaw practiced by, 712.
  interpretation of name, 219.
  medical practices, 786–790.

Tuscarora, neutrals in Tuscarora War, remained in North Carolina under Chief Tom Blunt, 199.
  population, 199.
  religious belief, 751, 755, 757, 759, 760.
  removed to New York after Tuscarora War, 199.
  reservation in Seneca country, N. Y., finally given to, 199.
  sketch of, 200.
  source material, 830, 831.
  towns of, 631.
  trade among, 739, 740.
  tribe or confederation, 199.
  under treaty with English, attacked the Pamlico and made them slaves, 170.
  visited by Lawson, whom they killed during Tuscarora War, 199.
  visited by Lederer at "Katearas," 199.
Tuscarora Expedition, 631.
  Cusabo Indians joined Barnwell in, 129.
  joined by Winyaw tribe, 207.
  Sewee joined Barnwell in, 183.
Tuscarora War, 148, 162, 199, 438, 800.
  result of, 77.
Tuskahoma, Okla., last Council House of Choctaw at, 123.
Tuskegee, 49, 111, 125, 200, 219, 828.
  band of, on Tennessee River, just below Chattanooga, 200.
  finally settled in Creek territories, west of Mississippi, 200.
  interpretation of name, 219.
  migration of, 28.
  one band united with Cherokee, on Little Tennessee River, 200.
  population, 200.
  portion settled beyond Beggs close to Yuchi, 200.
  sketch of, 200.
  source material on, 828.
  third band located on Tuskegee Creek, 200.
  town of, burned by Spaniards under Matheos, 63.
Tuskegee Creek, N. C., site of band of Tuskegee, 200.
Tutalosi or "Fowl Town," on Flint River, 138.
Tutelo, 30, 31, 131, 145, 148, 149, 152, 157, 164, 178, 179, 183, 200, 201, 219, 278, 665, 830.
  apparently practically extinct, 201.
  clans and gentes among the, 655, 657.
  classification of with Biloxi and Ofo by Voegelin, 27.
  crossed the Roanoke with the Saponi, Occaneechi, Keyauwee, and Shakori, 200, 201.
  formally adopted into League of the Iroquois, 201.

Tutelo, interpretation of name unknown, 219.
  living on island in Roanoke River, near Staunton and Dan, 200.
  name applied by Iroquois to Siouan tribes of Virginia, 200.
  part of tribe located near Buffalo, N. Y., 201.
  population, 201.
  Saponi apparently incorporated with, 178.
  sketch of, 200–201.
  source material, 830.
  tribe located near Salem, Va., visited by Batts and Fallam, 200.
  vocabulary collected by several people, 201.
    from old woman named Lucy Buck, 201.
  with Saponi moved northward and settled at Shamokin, Pa., 201.
Tut'hayi, Apalachee women mentioned by Gatschet, 91.
Twenty-seven Mile Bluff, Ala., 72.
  site of fort erected by Bienville, 151.
Typha latifolia, uses of, 247.
Uçachile, Timucua town, 41.
  tribe, *see* Osochi.
Uchean stock, 10.
  (See table 1, facing p. 10.)
  historical works on, 21.
  population, 12.
Uchee, physical characteristics, 224.
Uchee Billy, Yuchi chief, in Florida, 30, 214.
Uchee Creek, near Augusta, Ga., 213.
  site of Coweta town called Wetumka, 127.
Ucita, *see* Oçita.
Ufera, *see* Yufera.
Uitachuco, *see* Ivitachuco.
Ulibahali, 49.
  name in De Soto narratives for Hothliwahali, 139.
Ullibahali, *see* Ulibahali.
United States Census, 146, 199, 200.
United States Department of Indian Affairs, 123, 137, 182.
United States Government, Choctaw as a tribe never at war with, 122.
  official relations with Chickasaw begun by, 118.
  sales of Indian lands to Miller and Fulton confirmed by, 97.
United States Indian Office, *see* Indian Office, U. S.
Upper Austral Zone, 19.
Upper Creeks, 5, 22, 30, 64, 70, 73, 77, 115, 139, 160, 181, 210, 213, 214, 215.
  Abihka a division of, 81.
  called Alabama by French, 92.
  pipes, 542, 547.
  pottery, 551.
  visit of Delago to, 63.
Upper Creek towns, Osceola from, and brains of Seminole uprising, 181.

Upper Nasoni, located near Red River, 158.
Upper Yamasee, 189, 209.
Uriutina, Timucua village visited by De Soto, 41, 202.
    Indians of, *see* Utina.
Urriparacoxi, inland tribe, 40, 41.
Ursins, M. de la Loire des, 188.
Urtica gracilis, use of, 247.
Uruguay, 7.
    inhabitants of, 825.
Uscamacu, classification of tribe, 67.
Ushery, trade among, 739.
    visit by Lederer to, 104.
Usi, 67, 104.
    discussion of synonyms for, 66.
    synonym for Xoxi, 67.
Ustaqua, *see* Yustaga.
Utamussack, great temple of, 744, 745, 746.
    clothing worn by priests, 477.
Utiaca, town, 193.
Utiangue, palisaded town visited by Spaniards, 55, 433.
    town where Juan Ortiz died, 40.
Utina, 16, 17, 168, 173, 174, 179, 193, 194, 201, 202, 219.
    assisted by French colonists in raid on Potano, 173, 202.
    disappearance of, 202.
    Indians of towns of Aguacaleyquen, Uriutina, and Napetaca identified as, 202.
    name, interpretation of, in Timucua tongue, 219.
    population, 202.
    sketch of, 201–202.
    tribe or confederation, located between Santa Fe and Suwannee Rivers, 201.
    visited by Father Prieto, 202.
    war customs, 693.
    See also Timucua.
Utina, Indian chief, 762.
Uto-Aztecan family, 241.
Uzitiuhi, Quapaw village on Arkansas River, 166.
Vandera, Juan de, 65, 68, 69.
    history of Juan Pardo's expedition written by, 186, 206.
Vaudreuil, Governor of Louisiana, letter written by, 185.
Vegetable foods, preparation of, 351–368.
Vegetable kingdom, use of 244–248, 442.
Velasco, Don Luis de, Viceroy of Mexico, 59, 70.
Velasco, Lopez de, 282.
    on burial customs, 649.
    on religious beliefs and usages, 763.
    on social customs, 649.
    on whaling in Florida, 329.
Velásquez, captain in Villafañe's expedition, 70.
Venus mercenaria, use of, 481.
Vera, Fray Francisco Gutierrez de, missionary, visit to Sawokli, 180.

Vera Cruz, town subject to San Juan del Puerto, 179.
Vermilion Bayou, La., 93.
Verrazzano, Giovanni da, 193.
    explorations of Atlantic coast by, 37.
    Timucua coast skirted by, 193.
Verret, Bob, leading man among Houma, 140.
Vespucci, Amerigo, alleged expedition of, discussed, 34.
Vicksburg, 20.
Victoria Cove, 47.
Vignoles' map of Florida, 146.
Villafañe, Angel de, 61, 70.
Villareal, Francisco de, missionary left with Tekesta by Menendez, 192.
Virginia, 2, 15, 18.
    colony, 175.
    explorers from, 77.
    Indians remaining in after the removal, 80.
    Piedmont region of, 31.
    Powhatan Indians of, 11.
    Siouans of, 15.
    Spanish period in history of, 70–71.
    tidewater tribes of, culture pattern of, 10.
    war trail from, 48.
Virginia Indians, 149, 201, 830.
    agricultural methods, 258.
    arrows, 572.
    artistic development, 615.
    clothes, 472, 473, 525.
    coloring for manufactured articles, 609.
    divisions of time by, 257.
    fire making, 423.
    flint, 543.
    hair dressing, 502, 503.
    household utensils, 562.
    houses, 415.
    hunting, 258.
    images, 614, 615.
    mats and baskets, 604.
    medical practices, 784, 785.
    mental characteristics, 229.
    musical instruments, 626.
    ornamentation, 488.
    social organization, 643.
    source material on, 830.
    tattooing, 532.
    towns, 630.
    transportation, means of, 592.
    wampum, 482.
    war customs, 688, 689.
Vitis rotundifolia, use of, 288.
Vitis vinifera, ftn., 287.
Vivier, Father, 176.
Voegelin, Drs. Charles F. and Erminie W., 832.
    on dialectic classification of Biloxi and Ofo, 11.
Volcine Chiki, Tunica chief, 198.
Wabash River, 23, 176, 185.
Wacata, *see* Guacata.

Waccamaw, 103, 203, 207.
  hostile to colonists during Yamasee War, 203.
  located on Lower Pee Dee River, 203.
  moved south of Black River, 203.
  population, 203.
  sketch of, 203.
  some killed by Cherokee and Natchez, 203.
  tribe established in South Carolina, 203.
  See also Woccon.
Waccamaw River, 67.
Waco, 100.
Wagner, Gunter, 242,830.
"Wahali," Muskogee word for "the south," 135.
Wahunsonacock, *see* Powhatan.
Wainoakes, trade relations with English, 740.
Wakerobin, Virginia (*Peltandra virginica*), use of, 271, 272, 276, 296, 363.
Wakokai, 153, 203, 204, 219.
  Muskogee settlement on Hatchet Creek, 203.
  population, 204.
  removed to southwestern part of Creek territory, 203.
  sketch of, 203–204.
Walam Olum, 734.
Walhalla, Oconee Co., S. C., site of Oconee northern branch, 165.
Walker County, Ala., 26.
Walker, S. T., on blue flint outcrop at Trouble Creek, Fla., 541.
Walker, Winslow M., on relics found at Caddo burial site, 537.
Wampum, 481, 482.
Wanchese, an Indian brought to England, 1585, 76.
Wappo, California tribe, 665.
War, 686–701.
War trail from Virginia, 48.
War Woman Creek, 47.
Wars, between tribes, British instigation of, 77.
Washa, 73, 108, 168, 169, 204, 219, 240.
  De Soto's Spaniards possibly fought by, 204.
  moved to the Mississippi, above New Orleans, 204.
  name, interpretation of, 219.
  population, 204.
  scattered in French families, 204.
  sketch of, 204.
  tribe on Bayou Lafourche, 204.
  See also Chawasha.
Washington, George, visit of Creeks to, 146, 154.
Washita, 204, 301.
  destroyed by Taensa, 204.
  population, 204.
  settled near Natchitoches, 204.
  sketch of, 204.
  small Caddo tribe located on Ouachita River, 204.
  trade, 738.

Washita River, refuge of Caddo, to escape massacre, 99.
Wassador, Indian word for all metals, 491.
Watcina, Creek word for Virginians, 77.
Wat Coosa, chief, Cape Fear Indians, 103.
Wateree, 205, 219.
  first reported by Juan Pardo, 205.
  guns obtained from Cheraw, for use in Yamasee War, 205.
  identification with Guatari, 65, 205.
  land bought by Thomas Brown from, 205.
  name, interpretation of, 219.
  part taken in Yamasee War, 205.
  population, 205.
  probably joined Catawba, 205.
  ruled by two chieftainesses, 205.
  settled on Wateree River, below Camden, 205.
  sketch of, 205.
  social organization, 647.
"Wateree Chickanee," possibly the Guatariatiqui, 205.
  See also Little Wateree.
Wateree Jack, relations with South Carolina colony, 205.
Wateree River, S. C., 124, 205.
  home of Wateree tribe, 205.
Waterproof, La., 56.
Watt Sam, Natchez brave, son of Creek Sam, 160.
Waxhaw, 67, 206, 345, 809, 816.
  accompanied Yamasee to Florida, 206.
  beds, 422.
  doors, 430.
  festivities, 757, 758.
  found by English in North and South Carolina, 206.
  head deformation practiced by, 539, 540, 815.
  houses, 411, 413, 815.
  Lawson hospitably received by, 206.
  musical instruments, 625, 627.
  population, 206.
  refuge taken with Cheraw after attack by Catawba, 206.
  Sauxpa synonym for, 66.
  sketch of, 206.
Weanoc, possibly identical with Eno, 130.
Weapemeoc, 18, 206, 212.
  found by Raleigh colonists in northeastern North Carolina, 206.
  population, 206.
  sketch of, 206.
Weesock, possibly name for Waxhaw, 206.
Welch, Colonel, communications with Chickasaw opened by, 117.
Weleetka, Okla., Alabama Square Grounds near, 88.
Weroance, or werowance, word meaning chief, 516, 641, 644.
  definition of term, 642.

Weróans, *see* Weroance.

Werowance Eyanoco, copper mines belonging to, 492.

Werowocomoco, settlement of Powhatan, 175, 643, 645.

Wesley, John, home of, 123.

West Abeka, town supporting the French, 122.

West Indian cyclones, 5.

    pottery, origin of Meillac type of, 33.

West Indies, 22, 33, 35, 74.

    possible migration from to Gulf region, 33.

West Virginia, mountains of, 5.

Western plains, 5.

Westlake, Ga., 44.

Westo, 129, 184, 213, 214, 215, 588, 589.

    Cusabo attacked by, 129.

    driven from Savannah River by Shawnee, 184.

    town, located near Augusta, Ga., 184, 437, 635.

    town, on Savannah River, visited by Woodward, 111, 117, 184.

    war with, 77.

Wetumka, branch village of the Alabama, 88.

Wetumka, Coweta village, on Uchee Creek, near Fort Mitchell, 127.

Wetumpka, Ala., town near Koasati settlement, 87, 146.

Wetumpka Creek, identification with mythological "Owatuka-river," 26.

White, John, leader of colonists on Roanoke Island, 76.

    drawings of, 831.

White Earth, concession established near Natchez town, 159.

White Ground, *see* Kan-hatki.

White River, identification with River of Casqui, 54.

White Spring, 43.

White town of Lower Creeks, 92.

Whitford, Carl, 246, 247, 248.

Whittaker, Alexander, on quarries worked by Indians, 542.

Whooping Creek, 26.

Wichita, 100, 214, 421.

    visited by Coronado, 74.

Wicocomoco, 175.

Wiha asha, *see* Ooe-ása.

WI hīli, or "Sweet Water," town mentioned by Hawkins, 197.

Wild plants, uses of, 244.

Williams, S. C., 328, 403, 404, 637.

Williams Island, 48.

Williamsburg Co., 103.

Willinawaw, Cherokee chief, 692.

Wills Creek, 49.

Wilson, George, Chickasaw chief, 118.

Wilson, Minnie Moore, 828.

Wilson, Samuel, 313.

Wimbee River, 67.

Winding Stair Trail, 47.

Windsor, Bertie Co., N. C., Saponi settlement near, 178.

Wingina, Nelson Co., Va., supposed site of village of Nahyssan tribe, 157.

Winnebago, 219.

Winston County, Ala., 26.

Winyaw, 203, 206, 207.

    allied with whites against Waccamaw, 207.

    apparently joined Catawba, 207.

    on Winyaw Bay and Pee Dee River, S. C., 207.

    population, 207.

    sketch of, 206–207.

    trading post established on Black River for, 207.

Winyaw Bay, S. C., home of Winyaw, 207.

Wiogufki, branch of Wakokai tribe, 203, 204.

    busk ground of Wakokai tribe, 203.

Wisacky, name used by Lederer for Waxhaw, 206.

Wisconsin, State of, 2.

Withlacoochee River, Fla., 37, 41.

    site of Ocale village, 164, 601, 628.

Wiwohka, 144, 153, 207, 219.

    called responsible for Creek War, 207.

    joined Okchai tribe, 207.

    name, interpretation in Creek tongue, 219.

    noted on De Crenay map, 207.

    old Creek town or tribe, 207.

    population, 207.

    sketch of, 207.

Woccon, 203, 207, 208.

    allies of Tuscarora against whites, 207.

    population, 208.

    probably joined Catawba, 207.

    reported by Lawson on Neuse River, N. C., 207.

    sketch of, 207–208.

    vocabulary preserved, 208.

Wolf, Mose, Chickasaw chief, 118.

Women, body paint, 530.

    bracelets, 521.

    clothing, 469–477, 524, 525, 807.

    ear ornaments, 513, 514.

    games, 685, 686.

    hair dressing, 498–501, 711.

    head deformation not practiced on, 541.

    home customs, 711, 714.

    moral characteristics, 230, 231, 232.

    necklaces, 517, 520.

    occupations, 710, 711, 713, 715, 716, 717, 718.

    physical characteristics, 223, 224, 226, 227.

    pipes, 545.

    pottery, 549, 550, 553, 554.

    punishments, 732, 733.

    rattles worn during dances by Creeks, 627.

    social customs at births and menstrual periods, 713, 714, 715, 716, 717.

Women, tattooing, 532, 534, 535, 536.
  the teeth, staining of, 536, 809.
  treatment of, 710.
Wood, Abraham, on Cheraw settlement, 110, 208.
  whites sent to visit Yuchi on Tennessee River by, 213.
Wood, articles made of, 555–556, 558–562.
Woodcraft, 310–312.
Woods, used in building houses, 421, 422.
Woodville, Tex., 87.
Woodward, Henry, 62, 117, 143, 184, 213.
  Chickasaw mentioned by, 117.
  earliest account of Cherokee in narrative by, 111.
  on towns, 635.
  visited Cofitachequi from Charleston, S. C., 143.
  Yuchi visited by, 213, 437.
Woodward, Thomas Simpson, 111.
  on removal of Tulsa Indians to the Tallapoosa from Talladega country by James McQueen, 125.
Wright, Allen, Choctaw chief, claimed descent from a Koroa, 148.
Wyanoke, possible identification with Eno, 130.
Wyanoke Creek, named after Wyanoke Indians, 131.
Wyatt, Governor, Powhatan uprising defeated by, 175.
Xacatin, see Soacatino.
Xalaque, see Chalaque, Province of.
Xeres de los Caballeros, Province of Estremadura, Spain, 39.
Xoara, 205.
Xoxi, see Sewee.
  Usi synonym for, 67.
Xuala, 31, 48, 64, 67.
  location, 46.
  reached by De Soto, 46.
  See also Cheraw.
Xualla, see Cheraw, 109.
Yadkin, 208.
  population unknown, 208.
  relationship unknown, 208.
  sketch of, 208.
  tribe located on Yadkin River, 208.
Yadkin River, Cheraw reported on by Lederer, 110.
  home of Yadkin tribe, 208.
  near Salisbury, N. C., home of Saponi, 178.
  Tutelo located near headwaters of, 200.
  Wateree reported on, by Lederer, 205.
Yakna-Chitto, "Big Country," treachery of Taensa to, 120.
  associated with Chitimacha, 120.
Yalobusha River, 28, 140, 180.
  home of Ibitoupa on Yazoo River beyond the mouth of, 140.

Yamacraw, 153, 209, 210.
  after death of Tomochichi, moved to New Yamacraw, 210.
Yamasee, 19, 28, 43, 73, 107, 115, 133, 136, 187, 189, 206, 208–211, 827.
  Amacano possibly part of, 88.
  attacks on supported by English, 63.
  band under Tomochichi joined Creek Nation, 210.
  English influence on in Florida, 77.
  exterminated by Muscogulges, ftn., 231.
  fled to Florida after Yamasee uprising, 209.
  headed insurrection aginst English, 209.
  joined Barnwell in Tuscarora expedition, 209.
  joined Seminole Nation, 210.
  members of Muskhogean linguistic family, 239.
  movements of, 63, 64.
  once subordinate to Hitchiti, 208
  part of settled in Apalachee country, 208, 210.
  population, 210, 211.
  retired to Oklawaha River, Fla., 210.
  sketch of, 208–211.
  social organization, 654.
  transportation, means of, 595.
  uprising, effect on English, 87.
  withdrawal to frontiers of South Carolina, 209.
"Yamasee stroke," method of paddling, 595.
Yamasee War, 77, 78, 103, 104, 111, 127, 129, 138, 143, 153, 165, 168, 180, 183, 184, 203, 205, 214.
  effect on Apalachicola, 92.
  reference to, 90, 93.
Yamiscaron, province named by Francisco of Chicora, 208.
  See Yamasee.
Yardley, Governor, 130, 131, 183.
Yatasi, 158, 211.
  alliance made with Bienville, 211.
  alliance made with St. Denis, 211.
  Caddo tribe reported by Tonti on Red River, 211.
  hard pressed by Chickasaw, 211.
  moved from Louisiana to Texas with other Caddo tribes, 211.
  population, 211.
  sketch of, 211.
"Yattken," see Yadkin.
Yaupon, ceremonies connected with, 791.
Yazoo, 13, 77, 106, 108, 117, 123, 147, 148, 160, 166, 188, 194, 198, 199, 211, 212, 736, 829.
  accessory to murder of Foucault, 211.
  allies of Natchez, 73.
  burial customs, 729.
  doors, 430.

Yazoo, found by Tonti on Yazoo River, Miss., 211.
  houses, 416, 417.
  joined hostile Indians in Natchez War, 212.
  murdered Father Souel in Natchez War, 212.
  participated in Natchez uprising, 166.
  population, 212.
  sketch of, 211–212.
  smoke-holes and windows lacking, 427.
  source material on, 829.
  took part in attack on Tunica, 212.
  towns, 637.
  trade, 738.
  Tunica spoken by, 240.
  warned by Chakchiuma against Chickasaw, 106.
  with Koroa and Tiou, attacked by Quapaw, 212.
  See also Tunica.
Yazoo River, Miss., 19, 28, 29, 31, 72, 73, 104, 123, 140, 147, 166, 180, 190, 194.
  earliest home of Tiou tribe, 194, 195.
  home of Biloxi and Ofo, 104, 166, 800.
  home of Ibitoupa, 140.
  home of Taposa, 190.
  home of Yazoo Indians, 211.
Yazoo and Yalobusha Rivers, junction of, home of Chakchiuma, 106.
Ybaha, *see* Guale Indians.
"Yca Potano," Potano town, 174.
Yeager, Tukabahchee Square Ground maintained at, 197.
Yenyohol, listed by Francisco of Chicora, 206.
Yeopim, 206, 212.
  lands sold by chief of, 206.
  See also Weapemeoc.
Yesan, *see* Nahyssan.
Yfulo, town possibly of Eufaula in province of Guale, 132.
Yoa, town of Yamasee, 209.
Yojuane, 162.
  French supported by, 121.
  Neche almost destroyed by, 162.
Youghtanud, land subject to Powhatan 643.
Young, Capt. Hugh, 116, 132, 138, 150, 168, 190, 210, 215.
Young, Sam, last speaker of Tunica language, 198.
Ysa, Indian town, 64.
  possible identification with Iswa, 104.
  See also Issa *and* Iswa.
Ysicas, 213.
Yucatan, 34, 35.
Yucca arkansana, uses of, 247.
Yuchean stock, *see* Uchean stock.

Yuchi, 13, 20, 30, 48, 63, 77, 92, 111, 115, 135, 146, 154, 197, 200, 206, 212–215, 219, 239, 242, 325, 665, 806, 808, 810, 827, 830.
  attacked by Apalachee, 213.
  bags and purses, 480.
  body paint, 530, 531.
  clans and gentes, 657, 818.
  clothing, 464, 465, 466, 467, 474, 525.
  cooking, 354, 366, 370.
  displacement of in eastern Tennessee in prehistoric era by Cherokee, 14, 15.
  divisions of time, 263.
  driven from the Savannah by Shawnee, 213.
  established on Savannah River, 214.
  featherwork, 456.
  finger rings, 522.
  fire making, 424, 425.
  fishing, 335, 338, 340, 341.
  fortifications, 437.
  found by De Soto in eastern Tennessee, 212.
  found by Hawkins on Tallapoosa River, 214.
  games, 677.
  hair dressing, 505, 808, 818.
  household utensils, 557, 559.
  houses, 394.
  hunting, 316, 320, 331.
  identification with Chisca, 65.
  implements for hunting and fishing, 573, 574, 578, 582, 586.
  language, reference to, 70.
  led by Timpoochee Barnard, aided whites in Creek War, 214.
  mats and baskets, 605.
  metals, 490, 497.
  migrations, 30.
  moieties, 664, 818.
  moved to Spring Garden, Volusia County, Fla. under chief Uchee Billy, 214.
  name, interpretation of, 219.
  necklaces, 517, 518.
  origin, belief of, 23.
  ornamentation, 487.
  ornaments, 505.
  part of remained with Cherokee in Appalachian region, 215.
  physical characteristics, 225, 818.
  population, 215.
  removed to Chattahoochee River, near Apalachicola, 213, 214.
  removed to Oklahoma with Creeks, 214.
  retired to Ocmulgee, 213.
  settled in Florida, 213, 242.
  settled near Augusta, Ga., 213.
  sewing, 454.
  sketch of, 212–215.
  skin dressing, 444, 445.
  small party moved to Florida, 214.

Yuchi, social system, 818.
  source material on, 830.
  relationship, terms of, 666, 669.
  thread and textiles, 450.
  towns, 636.
  transportation, means of, 594, 596.
  Tuskegee settled near, beyond Beggs, 200.
  visited by whites sent by Abraham Wood, on Tennessee River, 213.
  weapons, 573, 574, 578, 582, 586.
Yufala, see Eufaula.
Yufera, 132, 193, 215, 219.
  name, interpretation of, 219.
  population unknown, 215.
  relations uncertain, 215.
  sketch of, 215.
  town between Altamaha and Cumberland Island, 132, 215.
Yui, 193, 194, 215.
  fortunes uncertain, 215.
  population, 215.
  sketch of, 215.

Yui, Timucua tribe in southeastern Georgia near Cumberland I., 215.
Yupaha, province of, 42, 44, 135.
  See also Sbaha and Sguaja.
Yupwauremau, Woccon town, in North Carolina, 207.
Yustaga, 193, 216.
  apparently joined rest of Timucua, 216.
  hostile to Apalachee, 216.
  in northwestern Florida, 216.
  population, 216.
  province visited by De Soto, 216.
  sketch of, 216.
Zabusta, Indian village, 50.
Zacatecan Fathers, missions withdrawn from Caddo Territory by, 99.
Zacatecan missions, Tex., 75.
Zamia integrifolia, use of, 271, 283, 297, 361, 803.
Zautoouys, Indian town, 641.
Zea sp., use of, 285, 286, 288, 353.
Zulus, natives of Africa, 824, 825.

O

NCFA

INTERTRIBAL INDIAN COUNCIL CALLED BY JOHN ROSS AT TAHLEQUAH, CHEROKEE NATION, IN JUNE 1843.

(After Stanley.)

2. WIFE AND CHILDREN OF CHARLIE THOMPSON.

1. CHARLIE THOMPSON IN 1910, LATER CHIEF OF THE ALABAMA INDIANS, NOW DECEASED.

Peabody Museum, Harvard University

DRAWING BY A. DE BATZ SHOWING INDIANS OF SEVERAL NATIONS—ILLINOIS. ATAKAPA. FOXES.

1. HOME OF ARMOJEAN REON, ONE OF THE LAST SPEAKERS OF THE ATAKAPA LANGUAGE.

2. HOME OF THE CATAWBA CHIEF, SAM BLUE.

1. A GROUP OF CATAWBA GIRLS, 1918.

2. LADIES' RELIEF SOCIETY OF THE CHURCH OF JESUS CHRIST OF LATTER DAY
SAINTS, CATAWBA RESERVATION.

1. Old Catawba House, 1918.

2. Old Catawba House, 1918.

HOUSE OF WORSHIP OF THE CHURCH OF JESUS CHRIST OF LATTER DAY SAINTS ON THE CATAWBA RESERVATION.

CHEROKEE INDIANS SENT TO ENGLAND IN 1730 WITH SIR ALEXANDER CUMING.

(Courtesy of the British Museum.)

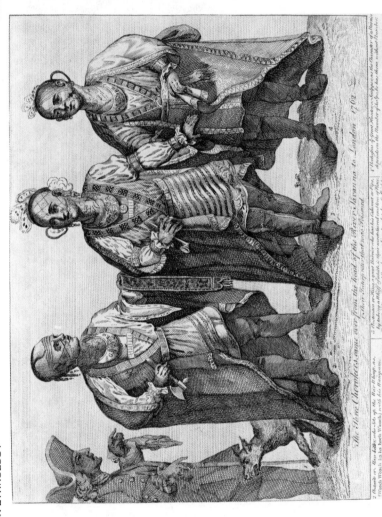

THREE CHEROKEE CHIEFS SENT TO ENGLAND IN 1762.
(Courtesy of the British Museum.)

1. AUSTENACO, THE GREAT WARRIOR.
(After a drawing by Sir Joshua Reynolds,
reproduced in the Royal Magazine.)

2. THE CHEROKEE CHIEF CUNNE SHOTE, IN 1762. Courtesy of D. I. Bushnell, Jr.
(After Parsons.

2. JOHN ROSS.
(After McKenney and Hall.)

1. SEQUOYA.
(After McKenney and Hall.)

2. TAHCHEE (CHEROKEE PRONUNCIATION OF HIS ENGLISH
NAME "DUTCH").

(After McKenney and Hall.)

Tahchee was among the first of the tribe to move to Arkansas and
was only 5 years old at the time. He was afterward prominent
in wars with the Osage, being engaged during his life in more

1. MAJOR RIDGE.

(After McKenney and Hall.)

Charactiristick Chicasaw Head

2. A CHICKASAW WARRIOR.
(After Romans.)

1. TOOAN TUH (CHEROKEE: DÚSTÚ, "SPRING FROG").
(After McKenney and Hall.)

Tooan Tuh was a great ball player and warrior. He served under Jackson in the battle at the Horseshoe Bend. He was among the first Cherokee to move beyond the Arkansas, and was active in wars with the Osage.

1. George Wilson, a Chickasaw Indian.

2. Home of a Chickasaw Indian Named Mose Wolf, at Steedman, Okla.

THE LAST CHICKASAW COUNCIL HOUSE, AT TISHOMINGO, OKLA.

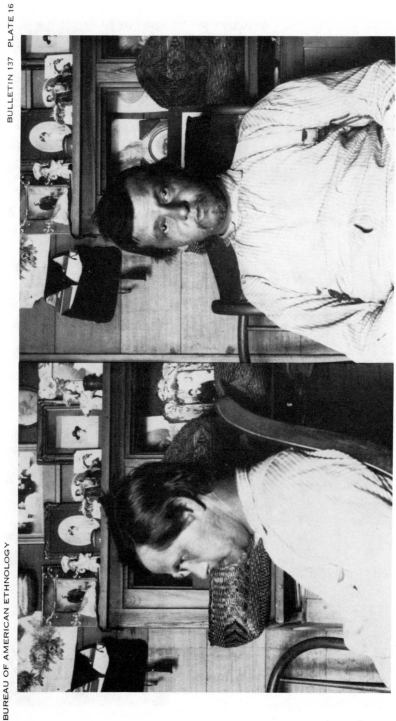

BENJAMIN PAUL, LAST CHIEF OF THE CHITIMACHA INDIANS AND ONE OF THE LAST SPEAKERS OF THE CHITIMACHA LANGUAGE.

REGISTE DARDIN AND WIFE, CHITIMACHA INDIANS, CHARENTON, LA.

1. The Sacred Hill of Nanih Waiya, in the Old Choctaw Nation.

2. View From the Top of Nanih Waiya Hill, Looking East.

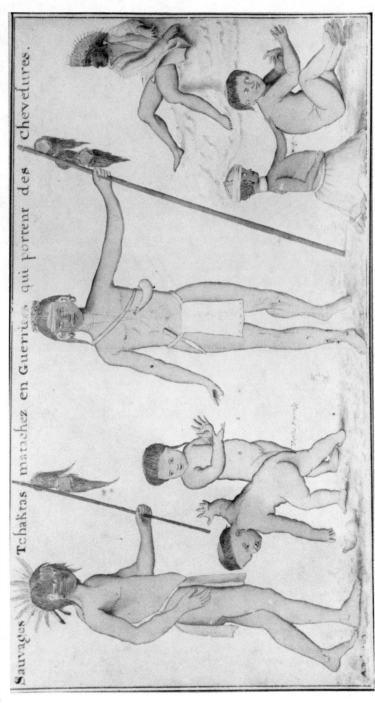

Sauvages Tchaktas matachez en Guerriers qui portent des chevelures.

CHOCTAW INDIANS, FROM THE SKETCH BY DE BATZ.

Peabody Museum, Harvard University

2. MO-SHO-LA-TUB-BEE, ANOTHER FAMOUS CHOCTAW CHIEF.
(After Catlin.)

1. PUSHMATAHA, THE GREAT CHOCTAW CHIEF.
(After McKenney and Hall.)

1. HOME OF A CHOCTAW INDIAN NAMED JOHN WESLEY, NEAR PHILADELPHIA, MISS

2. JOHN WESLEY AND FAMILY.

1. THLIOTOMBI, AN OLD CHOCTAW INDIAN LIVING NEAR IDABELL, OKLA., AND HIS FAMILY

2. THE OLD CHOCTAW COUNCIL HOUSE AT TUSKAHOMA, OKLA.

1. BOB VERRET AND BAPTISTE BILLIOUT, HOUMA INDIANS, TERREBONNE PARISH, LA., 1907.

2. HOUMA INDIANS ON LOWER BAYOU LAFOURCHE, LA., 1907.

1. HOUMA INDIANS ON LOWER BAYOU LAFOURCHE, LA., 1907.

2. HOUMA INDIANS ON LITTLE BARATARIA BAYOU, LA., 1907.

1. OLD HOUMA WOMAN, POINT AU CHIEN, LA.

2. OLD HOUMA HOUSE, AT POINT AU CHIEN, LA., 1907.

STIMAFUTCHI, OR "GOOD HUMOR" OF THE COOSADES (KOASATI) CREEKS.
(Sketch by Trumbull in 1790.)

2. MOTHER OF JACKSON LANGLEY. KINDER, LA.

1. JACKSON LANGLEY, KOASATI CHIEF LIVING
NEAR KINDER, LA.

KOASATI INDIAN SCHOOL NEAR KINDER, LA.

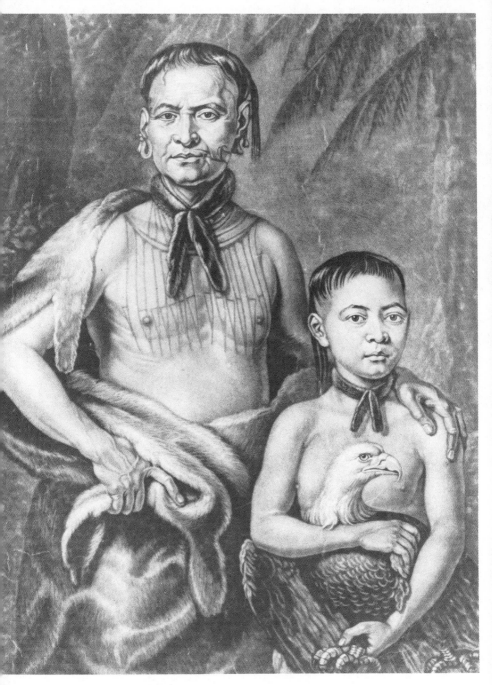

OMO CHACHI MICO (TOMOCHICHI), OR KING OF YAMACRAW, AND HIS NEPHEW, TONAHOWI.
(From painting by Verelst.   Courtesy of the British Museum.)

TOMOCHICHI MEETING OGLETHORPE IN ENGLAND.
Painting by William Verelst; Courtesy, The Henry Francis du Pont Winterthur Museum

2. MICO CHLUCCO (MICO THLAKKO), THE LONG WARRIOR, OR
KING OF THE SEMINOLES.
(After William Bartram.)

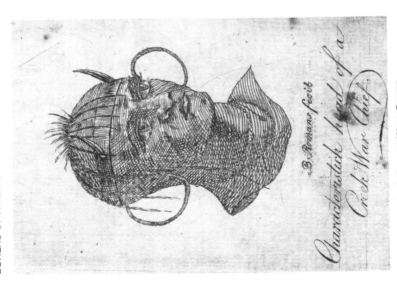

B. Romans fecit

Characteristick head of a
Creek War Chief

1. A CREEK WAR CHIEF.
(After Romans.)

2. HOPOTHLE MÍCO (HOP-HITHLI MIKO), OR THE TALASEE KING OF THE CREEKS.
(After a sketch by Trumbull, 1790.)

1. TUSKATCHE MÍCO (PROPERLY FUS-HATCHEE MIKO), OR THE BIRDTAIL KING OF THE CUSITAHS (KASIHTA).
(After a sketch by Trumbull, 1790.)

2. "HYSAC, OR THE WOMAN'S MAN," A CREEK INDIAN.
(After a sketch by Trumbull, 1790.)

1. "JOHN—A CREEK".
(After a sketch by Trumbull, 1790.)

2. OPOTHLEYOHOLO (HOPO-HITHLI YOHOLO), THE GREAT WAR SPEAKER AND LEADER OF THE CREEK INDIANS. (After McKenney and Hall.)

NCFA

1. BEN PERRYMAN, A PROMINENT CREEK INDIAN. (After a painting by Catlin.)

Painting attributed to Washington Allston;
Alabama Department of Archives and History

2. WILLIAM MCINTOSH. CHIEF OF THE COWETA
INDIANS AND THE LOWER CREEKS.

1. WILLIAM MCINTOSH. CHIEF OF THE COWETA INDIANS
AND THE LOWER CREEKS.
(After McKenney and Hall.)

2. YOHOLOMICCO, A CREEK INDIAN.
(After McKenney and Hall.)

1. TIMPOOCHEE BARNARD. CHIEF OF THE YUCHI INDIANS
AMONG THE LOWER CREEKS.
(After McKenney and Hall.)

2. MENAWA, A CREEK INDIAN.
(After McKenney and Hall.)

1. TUSTENNUGGEE EMATHLA, OR JIM BOY, A LEADER
OF THE THLAPTHLAKO CREEK INDIANS
(After McKenney and Hall.)

OLD CREEK COUNCIL HOUSE, OKMULGEE, OKLA.
(Courtesy of the Creek Indian Memorial Association.)

LAST CREEK COUNCIL HOUSE, OKMULGEE, OKLA., AS IT APPEARED IN 1920.
(Courtesy of the Creek Indian Memorial Association.)

1 CREEK SAM, A NATCHEZ INDIAN, AT HIS HOME NEAR BRAGGS, OKLA.   CREEK SAM WAS THE FATHER OF WATT SAM.

2. WATT SAM, PRINCIPAL NATCHEZ INFORMANT OF THE WRITER AND OF DR. HAAS IN THE DOORWAY OF HIS HOME, 1908.

1. NANCY TAYLOR, ONE OF THE LAST SPEAKERS OF THE NATCHEZ TONGUE, 1908.

2. SQUARE GROUND IN THE GREENLEAF MOUNTAINS, OKLA., WHERE WATT SAM OFFICIATED AS THE MEDICINE MAKER.

1. ROSA PIERRETTE, LAST SPEAKER OF THE OFO LANGUAGE, MARKSVILLE, LA.
(Print kindly supplied by Miss Caroline Dormon, Saline, La.)

2. BALL POST AND GROUND CONNECTED WITH THE SQUARE GROUND SHOWN ON
PLATE 39, FIGURE 2.

National Portrait Gallery
Smithsonian Institution

THE BOOTON PORTRAIT OF POCAHONTAS.

Peabody Museum, Harvard University

THE TIMUCUA CHIEF SATURIWA.

2. THE SEMINOLE CHIEF TOKOS IMATHLA
("TUKOSEEMATHLA").
(After McKenney and Hall.)

1. THE SEMINOLE HEAD CHIEF, MIKONOPI.
(After McKenney and Hall.)

Charleston Museum

OSCEOLA, FROM THE PAINTING IN THE CHARLESTON MUSEUM BY ROBERT JOHN
CURTIS.

2. OSCEOLA. FROM THE PAINTING BY KING.
(After McKenney and Hall.)

1. OSCEOLA.
(From painting by Catlin.)

NCFA

2. THE SEMINOLE CHIEF AHOLOCHI ("YE-HOW-LO-GEE"), OR CLOUD.

NCFA

1. THE SEMINOLE CHIEF HENIHA IMATHLA ("EA-MAT-LA"), OR KING PHILIP.

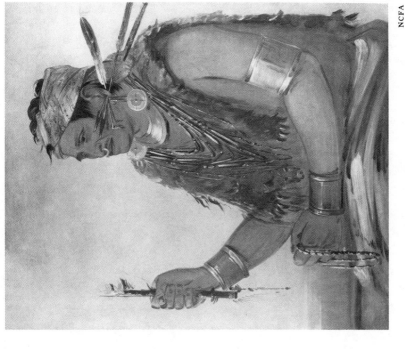

NCFA

2. TENSKWATAWA ("TEN-SQUAT-A-WAY"), THE SHAWNEE PROPHET. (After Catlin.)

1. THE SEMINOLE CHIEF HOLAHTA MIKO ("OLACTOMICCO"), OR BILLY BOWLEGS. (After McKenney and Hall.)

BUFFALO TAMER, CHIEF OF THE TUNICA INDIANS IN 1732, AND THE WIFE AND CHILD
OF THE CHIEF HE SUCCEEDED, WHO WAS KILLED BY THE NATCHEZ IN JUNE 1731.
From the sketch by De Batz in the collection of the late D. I. Bushnell, Jr.

2. VOLCINE CHIKI, CHIEF OF THE TUNICA INDIANS IN 1910.

1. WILLIAM ELY JOHNSON, DR. A. S. GATSCHET'S TUNICA
INFORMANT, TAKEN AT MARKSVILLE, LA., ABOUT 1910.

SAM YOUNG, OR SESOSTRIE YAUCHICANT, LAST SPEAKER OF THE TUNICA LANGUAGE.

From a print by Miss Caroline Dormon, Saline, La.

TIMUCUA INDIANS SOWING THEIR FIELDS.

(After Le Moyne.)

"THEIR MANNER OF FISHYNGE IN VIRGINIA."
(After White.)

TIMUCUA INDIANS COOKING.

(After Le Moyne.)

Le Moyne explains that in preparation for a feast, cooks were chosen especially for the purpose and these, strangely enough, were males, the choice evidently indicating that the feast was of a ceremonial nature.

1. "THEIR SEETHEYNGE OF THEIR MEATE IN EARTHEN POTTES."
(After White.)

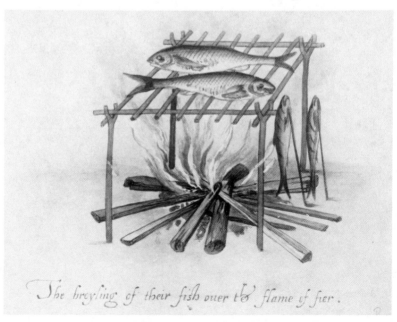

The breyling of their fish ouer the flame of fier.

2. "THE BROWYLLINGE OF THEIR FISHE OVER THE FLAME."
(After White.)

THE TIMUCUA INDIANS DRYING FOOD.
(After Le Moyne.)

STOREHOUSE OF THE TIMUCUA INDIANS.
(After Le Moyne.)

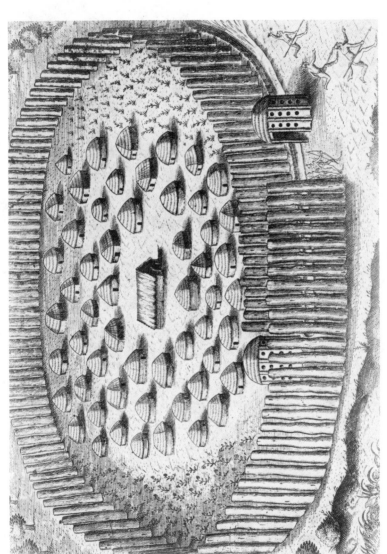

A STOCKADED TOWN OF THE TIMUCUA INDIANS.
(After Le Moyne.)

CREEK HOUSE OF THE LATER PATTERN.
From drawing by Tidball reproduced in Swan's Report.

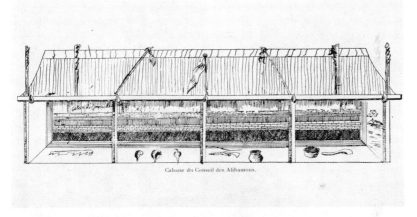

Cabane du Conseil des Alibamons.

1. SQUARE GROUND CABIN OF THE ALABAMA INDIANS ("CABANE DU CONSEIL DES ALIBAMONS") IN THE EIGHTEENTH CENTURY.
From a sketch in the French archives reproduced by Du Terrage.

2. NORTHERN SEMINOLE HOUSE.
(After MacCauley.)

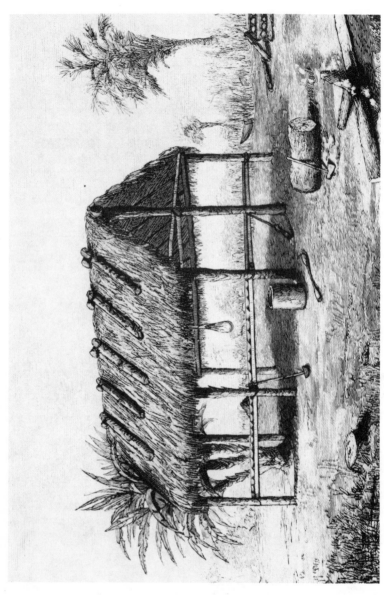

SEMINOLE HOUSE.
(After MacCauley.)

CHOCTAW PALMETTO HOUSE.
(After Bushnell.)

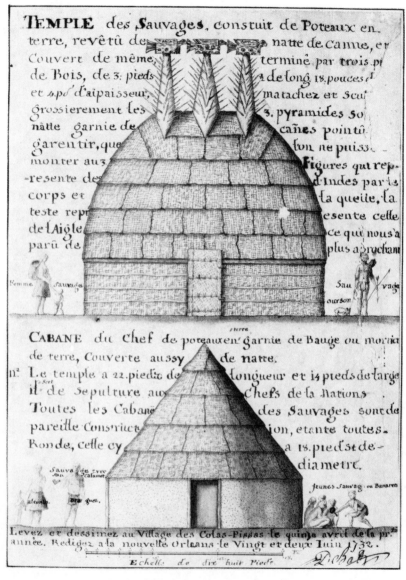

ACOLAPISSA TEMPLE AND CABIN OF THE CHIEF.
From the sketch by De Batz in the collection of the late D. I. Bushnell, Jr.

THE NATCHEZ TEMPLE, SHOWN IN CONNECTION WITH THE FUNERAL CEREMONIES
OF THE TATTOOED-SERPENT.
(After Du Pratz.)

"A WEROAN OR GREAT LORDE OF VIRGINIA."
(After White.)

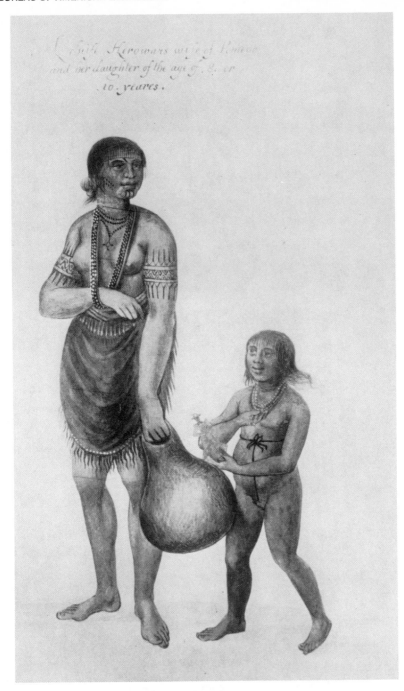

"A Cheiff Ladye of Pomeiooc."
(After White.)

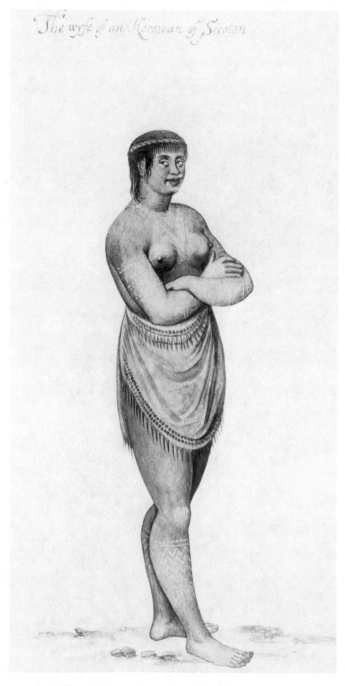

The wyfe of an Herowan of Secotan

"ONE OF THE CHEIFF LADYES OF SECOTA."
(After White.)

"A YOUNG GENTILL WOEMAN DOUGHTER OF SECOTA."
(After White.)

"A Cheiff Lorde of Roanoac."
(After White.)

Naturels en Été

1. NATIVE IN SUMMER, LOUISIANA.
(After Du Pratz.)

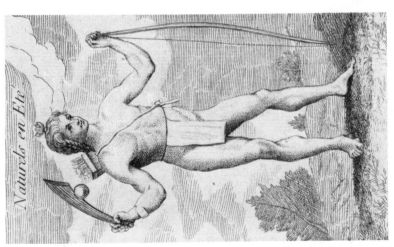

Femme & Fille

2. A WOMAN AND HER DAUGHTER,
LOUISIANA.
(After Du Pratz.)

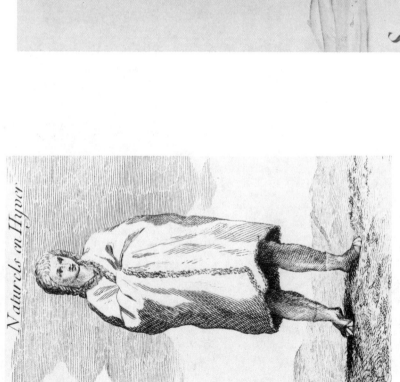

Naturels en Hyver.

Sauvage en habit d'hiver.

1. NATIVE IN WINTER.
(After Du Pratz.)

Peabody Museum, Harvard University

1. AN ALABAMA WOMAN DRESSING A SKIN, POLK COUNTY, TEX.

2. ALABAMA GOURD BOTTLE, POLK COUNTY, TEX.

2. ALABAMA MORTAR AND PESTLE, POLK COUNTY.

1. ALABAMA GARTER AND HAIR ORNAMENT, POLK
COUNTY, TEX.

2. CADDO MORTAR AND PESTLE. NEAR ANADARKO. OKLA.

1. HITCHITI WOMAN POUNDING CORN. NEAR SYLVIAN. OKLA.

"THE MANNER OF MAKINGE THEIR BOATES."
(After White.)

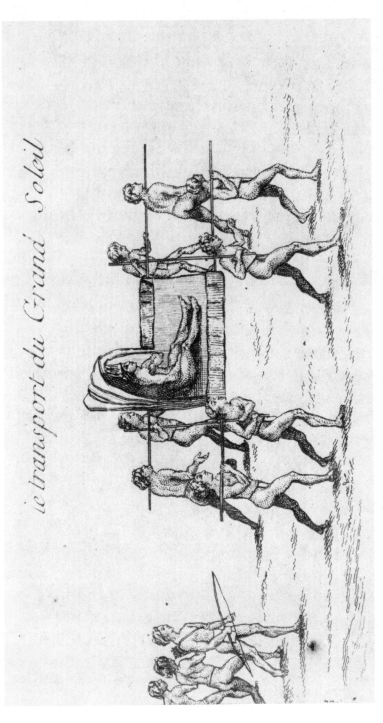

le transport du Grand Soleil

CONVEYANCE OF THE GREAT SUN OF THE NATCHEZ
(After Du Pratz.)

2. BALL STICKS AND RATTLE USED BY WATT SAM, A NATCHEZ INDIAN LIVING NEAR BRAGGS, OKLA.

1. CHITIMACHA MAT (NOW IN MUSEUM OF THE AMERICAN INDIAN), FROM A PHOTOGRAPH TAKEN AT CHARENTON, LA., IN 1907.

"THE TOWNE OF POMEIOOC."
(After White.)

In his description quoted on page 631, Hariot's *A* is the oval house with a pointed roof to the back on the right side, and *B* is the longest house on the left, open at the end and on the side. The pond marked *C* in Hariot's reproduction is beyond the stockade back of the temple.

"THE TOWNE OF SECOTA."
(After White.)

In Hariot's reproduction, the text accompanying which is given on page 631: *A* designates the building on the lower left-hand corner; *B* is the plot about the fire just back of *A; C* is in the lower right-hand corner; *D* (not given in text) is the feasting place in the center; *E* is in the middle, back of the houses; *F* is in the right-hand corner; *G* is field of ripe corn; *H* is field of newly planted corn to show spacing of plants; *I* is a field of pumpkins in a narrow belt detween *D* and *H; K* is fireplace between houses where religious ceremonies took place; *L* is at the middle upper margin in the middle.

Peabody Museum, Harvard University
THE VILLAGE OF SAM JONES, OR ARPEIKA, A HITCHITI SEMINOLE CHIEF IN FLORIDA.
(After Eastman.)

A CHOCTAW BALL PLAYER.
(After Catlin.)

TIMUCUA GAMES.
(After Le Moyne.)

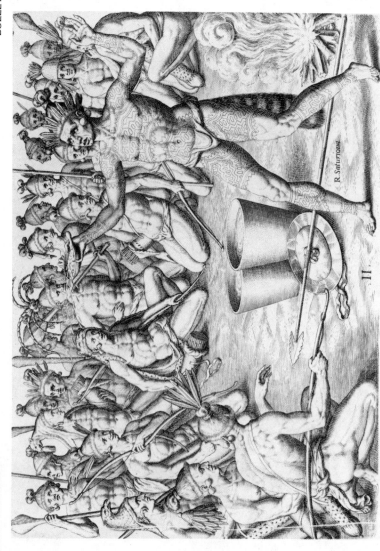

CEREMONY PERFORMED BY THE TIMUCUA CHIEF SATURIWA BEFORE GOING TO WAR.
(After Le Moyne.)

Plan du Fort.

Prisonier au Cadre.

PLAN OF A FORT AND A PRISONER IN THE FRAME PREPARED FOR EXECUTION.

(After Du Pratz.)

PROCESSION OF THE PEACE CALUMET.
(After Du Pratz.)

BRINGING A WIFE TO A TIMUCUA CHIEF.
(After Le Moyne.)

The Tombe of their Cherounes or cheife personages their flesh clen taken of from the bones saue the skynn and heare of theire heads w'ch flesh is dried and enfolded in matts laide at theire feete their bones alse being made dry or couered w'th deare skynns not alterinc their forme or proportion. With theire Kywash, which is an Image of wood keeping the deade.

"THE TOMBE OF THEIR WEROWANS OR CHEIFF LORDES."
(After White.)

BURIAL OF A TIMUCUA CHIEF.
(After Le Moyne.)

CREEK GRAVES IN OKLAHOMA

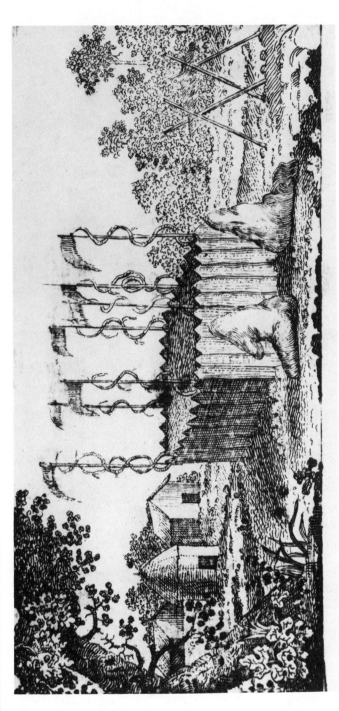

A CHOCTAW BURIAL PLACE.
(After Romans.)

TWO PICTOGRAPHS.
(After Romans.)

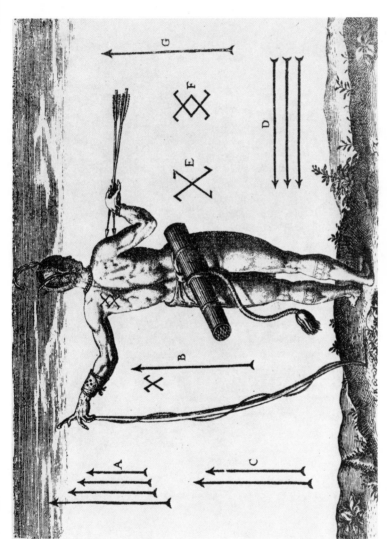

"THE MARCKES OF SUNDRYE OF THE CHEIF MENE OF VIRGINIA."
(After White.)

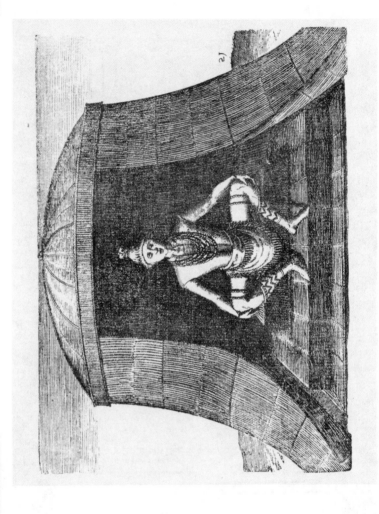

"THE IDOL KIWASA," IN AN ALGONQUIAN TRIBE OF NORTH CAROLINA.
(After White.)

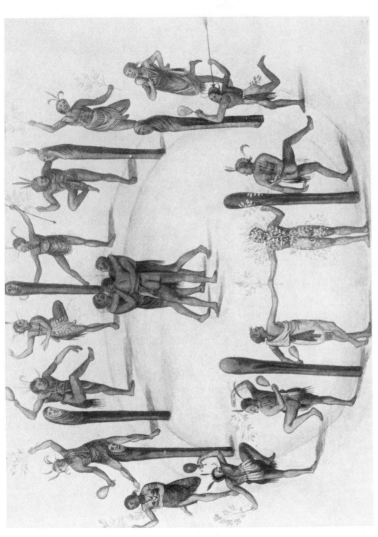

"THEIR DANSES WHICH THEY USE ATT THEIR HYGHE FEASTES."
(After White.)

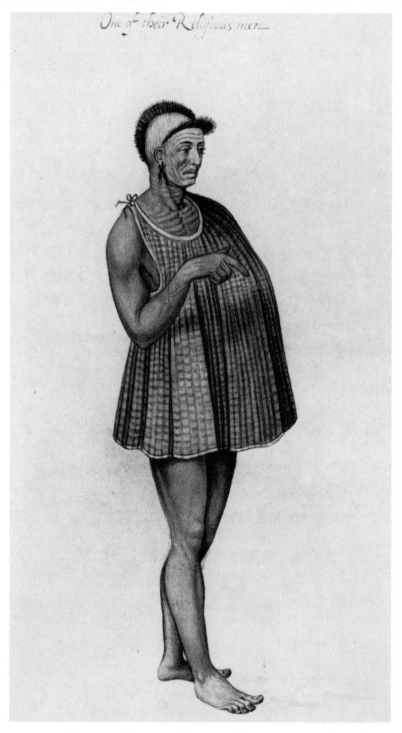

One of their Religious men

"ONE OF THE RELIGEOUS MEN IN THE TOWN OF SECOTA."
(After White.)

"THE CONIUERER."
(After White.)

"THEIR MANNER OF PRAINGE WITH RATTELS ABOWT THE FYER."
(After White.)

TIMUCUA SACRIFICE TO THE SUN.
(After Le Moyne.)

TIMUCUA INDIANS TAKING THE BLACK DRINK.
(After Le Moyne.)

1.

2.

TWO VIEWS OF THE TUKABAHCHEE SQUARE GROUND IN 1912.

1. The Nuyaka Square Ground in 1912.

2. The Pakan Tallahassee Square Ground in 1912.

1. PART OF THE EUFAULA SQUARE GROUND IN 1912.

2. RECEPTACLE FOR THE CEREMONIAL POTS AND OTHER ARTICLES IN THE EUFAULA SQUARE GROUND, 1912.

1. THE ALABAMA SQUARE GROUND WEST OF HANNA, OKLA., IN 1912.

2. RECEPTACLE FOR THE CEREMONIAL POTS AND OTHER ARTICLES IN THE
ALABAMA SQUARE GROUND, 1912.

1.

2.

TWO VIEWS OF THE SQUARE GROUND OF THE CHIAHA SEMINOLE, SEMINOLE
COUNTY, OKLA., 1912.

1. LEADERS OF THE CHIAHA SEMINOLE SQUARE GROUND, SEMINOLE COUNTY, OKLA., IN 1912.

2. THE MIKASUKI SQUARE GROUND, SEMINOLE COUNTY, OKLA., 1912.

GENERAL DANCE OF THE NATCHEZ INDIANS.
(After Du Pratz.)

TREATMENT OF THE SICK BY TIMUCUA INDIANS.
(After Le Moyne.)

1. HOME OF THE "KNOWER" YAHOLA, NEAR MUSKOGEE, OKLA., 1912.

2. SWEAT LODGE FRAME AT CHIAHA SEMINOLE SQUARE GROUND, SEMINOLE COUNTY, OKLA., 1912.

CLASSICS
OF
SMITHSONIAN
ANTHROPOLOGY

This series of reprints makes available in inexpensive form some of the many distinguished publications in anthropology issued over the years by the Smithsonian Institution.

Some of these publications first appeared as long as a century or more ago. Yet most are still of great historical importance; many contain unique primary data that must form the basis for all future studies of vanished ways of life; and some are fundamental theoretical studies that will continue to be part of the basic tool-kit of all anthropologists for many years to come.

The original publications appeared in several different series sponsored at various times by a number of divisions of the Institution. They ranged in size from brief articles and reports to mammoth multi-volume studies and compilations. Despite their importance, hardly any of them are still in print or have been reprinted; they must be sought in large libraries or bought from second-hand booksellers at premium prices.

The *Classics in Smithsonian Anthropology* series is sponsored by the Department of Anthropology of the Smithsonian to increase the accessibility of a select number of the more significant of these studies. Suggestions for publications to be reprinted may be sent to the Smithsonian Institution Press, Washington, D.C. 20560.

Issued to date:

CALENDAR HISTORY OF THE KIOWA INDIANS, by James Mooney (1898)–197

THE INDIANS OF THE SOUTHEASTERN UNITED STATES, by John R. Swanton (1946)

ISBN 0–87474–895–X